CODE OF FEDERAL REGULATIONS

D0558119

Title 24

Housing and Urban Development

Parts 200 to 499

Revised as of April 1, 2019

Containing a codification of documents
of general applicability and future effect

As of April 1, 2019

Published by the Office of the Federal Register
National Archives and Records Administration
as a Special Edition of the Federal Register

U.S. GOVERNMENT OFFICIAL EDITION NOTICE

Legal Status and Use of Seals and Logos

The seal of the National Archives and Records Administration (NARA) authenticates the Code of Federal Regulations (CFR) as the official codification of Federal regulations established under the Federal Register Act. Under the provisions of 44 U.S.C. 1507, the contents of the CFR, a special edition of the Federal Register, shall be judicially noticed. The CFR is prima facie evidence of the original documents published in the Federal Register (44 U.S.C. 1510).

It is prohibited to use NARA's official seal and the stylized Code of Federal Regulations logo on any republication of this material without the express, written permission of the Archivist of the United States or the Archivist's designee. Any person using NARA's official seals and logos in a manner inconsistent with the provisions of 36 CFR part 1200 is subject to the penalties specified in 18 U.S.C. 506, 701, and 1017.

Use of ISBN Prefix

This is the Official U.S. Government edition of this publication and is herein identified to certify its authenticity. Use of the 0–16 ISBN prefix is for U.S. Government Publishing Office Official Editions only. The Superintendent of Documents of the U.S. Government Publishing Office requests that any reprinted edition clearly be labeled as a copy of the authentic work with a new ISBN.

 U.S. GOVERNMENT PUBLISHING OFFICE

U.S. Superintendent of Documents • Washington, DC 20402–0001

http://bookstore.gpo.gov

Phone: toll-free (866) 512-1800; DC area (202) 512-1800

Table of Contents

Cite this Code: **CFR**

*To cite the regulations in
this volume use title,
part and section num-
ber. Thus, 24 CFR 200.1
refers to title 24, part
200, section 1.*

Explanation

The Code of Federal Regulations is a codification of the general and permanent rules published in the Federal Register by the Executive departments and agencies of the Federal Government. The Code is divided into 50 titles which represent broad areas subject to Federal regulation. Each title is divided into chapters which usually bear the name of the issuing agency. Each chapter is further subdivided into parts covering specific regulatory areas.

Each volume of the Code is revised at least once each calendar year and issued on a quarterly basis approximately as follows:

Title 1 through Title 16...as of January 1
Title 17 through Title 27 ....as of April 1
Title 28 through Title 41 ....as of July 1
Title 42 through Title 50...as of October 1

The appropriate revision date is printed on the cover of each volume.

LEGAL STATUS

The contents of the Federal Register are required to be judicially noticed (44 U.S.C. 1507). The Code of Federal Regulations is prima facie evidence of the text of the original documents (44 U.S.C. 1510).

HOW TO USE THE CODE OF FEDERAL REGULATIONS

The Code of Federal Regulations is kept up to date by the individual issues of the Federal Register. These two publications must be used together to determine the latest version of any given rule.

To determine whether a Code volume has been amended since its revision date (in this case, April 1, 2019), consult the "List of CFR Sections Affected (LSA)," which is issued monthly, and the "Cumulative List of Parts Affected," which appears in the Reader Aids section of the daily Federal Register. These two lists will identify the Federal Register page number of the latest amendment of any given rule.

EFFECTIVE AND EXPIRATION DATES

Each volume of the Code contains amendments published in the Federal Register since the last revision of that volume of the Code. Source citations for the regulations are referred to by volume number and page number of the Federal Register and date of publication. Publication dates and effective dates are usually not the same and care must be exercised by the user in determining the actual effective date. In instances where the effective date is beyond the cut-off date for the Code a note has been inserted to reflect the future effective date. In those instances where a regulation published in the Federal Register states a date certain for expiration, an appropriate note will be inserted following the text.

OMB CONTROL NUMBERS

The Paperwork Reduction Act of 1980 (Pub. L. 96–511) requires Federal agencies to display an OMB control number with their information collection request.

Many agencies have begun publishing numerous OMB control numbers as amendments to existing regulations in the CFR. These OMB numbers are placed as close as possible to the applicable recordkeeping or reporting requirements.

PAST PROVISIONS OF THE CODE

Provisions of the Code that are no longer in force and effect as of the revision date stated on the cover of each volume are not carried. Code users may find the text of provisions in effect on any given date in the past by using the appropriate List of CFR Sections Affected (LSA). For the convenience of the reader, a "List of CFR Sections Affected" is published at the end of each CFR volume. For changes to the Code prior to the LSA listings at the end of the volume, consult previous annual editions of the LSA. For changes to the Code prior to 2001, consult the List of CFR Sections Affected compilations, published for 1949-1963, 1964-1972, 1973-1985, and 1986-2000.

"[RESERVED]" TERMINOLOGY

The term "[Reserved]" is used as a place holder within the Code of Federal Regulations. An agency may add regulatory information at a "[Reserved]" location at any time. Occasionally "[Reserved]" is used editorially to indicate that a portion of the CFR was left vacant and not accidentally dropped due to a printing or computer error.

INCORPORATION BY REFERENCE

What is incorporation by reference? Incorporation by reference was established by statute and allows Federal agencies to meet the requirement to publish regulations in the Federal Register by referring to materials already published elsewhere. For an incorporation to be valid, the Director of the Federal Register must approve it. The legal effect of incorporation by reference is that the material is treated as if it were published in full in the Federal Register (5 U.S.C. 552(a)). This material, like any other properly issued regulation, has the force of law.

What is a proper incorporation by reference? The Director of the Federal Register will approve an incorporation by reference only when the requirements of 1 CFR part 51 are met. Some of the elements on which approval is based are:

(a) The incorporation will substantially reduce the volume of material published in the Federal Register.

(b) The matter incorporated is in fact available to the extent necessary to afford fairness and uniformity in the administrative process.

(c) The incorporating document is drafted and submitted for publication in accordance with 1 CFR part 51.

What if the material incorporated by reference cannot be found? If you have any problem locating or obtaining a copy of material listed as an approved incorporation by reference, please contact the agency that issued the regulation containing that incorporation. If, after contacting the agency, you find the material is not available, please notify the Director of the Federal Register, National Archives and Records Administration, 8601 Adelphi Road, College Park, MD 20740-6001, or call 202-741-6010.

CFR INDEXES AND TABULAR GUIDES

A subject index to the Code of Federal Regulations is contained in a separate volume, revised annually as of January 1, entitled CFR INDEX AND FINDING AIDS. This volume contains the Parallel Table of Authorities and Rules. A list of CFR titles, chapters, subchapters, and parts and an alphabetical list of agencies publishing in the CFR are also included in this volume.

An index to the text of "Title 3—The President" is carried within that volume.

The Federal Register Index is issued monthly in cumulative form. This index is based on a consolidation of the "Contents" entries in the daily Federal Register.

A List of CFR Sections Affected (LSA) is published monthly, keyed to the revision dates of the 50 CFR titles.

REPUBLICATION OF MATERIAL

There are no restrictions on the republication of material appearing in the Code of Federal Regulations.

INQUIRIES

For a legal interpretation or explanation of any regulation in this volume, contact the issuing agency. The issuing agency's name appears at the top of odd-numbered pages.

For inquiries concerning CFR reference assistance, call 202–741–6000 or write to the Director, Office of the Federal Register, National Archives and Records Administration, 8601 Adelphi Road, College Park, MD 20740-6001 or e-mail *fedreg.info@nara.gov*.

SALES

The Government Publishing Office (GPO) processes all sales and distribution of the CFR. For payment by credit card, call toll-free, 866-512-1800, or DC area, 202-512-1800, M-F 8 a.m. to 4 p.m. e.s.t. or fax your order to 202-512-2104, 24 hours a day. For payment by check, write to: US Government Publishing Office – New Orders, P.O. Box 979050, St. Louis, MO 63197-9000.

ELECTRONIC SERVICES

The full text of the Code of Federal Regulations, the LSA (List of CFR Sections Affected), The United States Government Manual, the Federal Register, Public Laws, Public Papers of the Presidents of the United States, Compilation of Presidential Documents and the Privacy Act Compilation are available in electronic format via *www.govinfo.gov*. For more information, contact the GPO Customer Contact Center, U.S. Government Publishing Office. Phone 202-512-1800, or 866-512-1800 (toll-free). E-mail, *ContactCenter@gpo.gov*.

The Office of the Federal Register also offers a free service on the National Archives and Records Administration's (NARA) World Wide Web site for public law numbers, Federal Register finding aids, and related information. Connect to NARA's web site at *www.archives.gov/federal-register*.

The e-CFR is a regularly updated, unofficial editorial compilation of CFR material and Federal Register amendments, produced by the Office of the Federal Register and the Government Publishing Office. It is available at *www.ecfr.gov*.

OLIVER A. POTTS,
Director,
Office of the Federal Register
April 1, 2019.

THIS TITLE

Title 24—HOUSING AND URBAN DEVELOPMENT is composed of five volumes. The first four volumes containing parts 0–199, parts 200–499, parts 500–699, parts 700–1699, represent the regulations of the Department of Housing and Urban Development. The fifth volume, containing part 1700 to end, continues with regulations of the Department of Housing and Urban Development and also includes regulations of the Board of Directors of the Hope for Homeowners Program, and the Neighborhood Reinvestment Corporation. The contents of these volumes represent all current regulations codified under this title of the CFR as of April 1, 2019.

For this volume, Gabrielle E. Burns was Chief Editor. The Code of Federal Regulations publication program is under the direction of John Hyrum Martinez, assisted by Stephen J. Frattini.

Title 24—Housing and Urban Development

(This book contains parts 200 to 499)

Subtitle B—Regulations Relating to Housing and Urban Development (Continued)

CHAPTER II—OFFICE OF ASSISTANT SECRETARY FOR HOUSING—FEDERAL HOUSING COMMISSIONER, DEPARTMENT OF HOUSING AND URBAN DEVELOPMENT

EDITORIAL NOTE: Nomenclature changes to chapter II appear at 59 FR 14090, Mar. 25, 1994.

SUBCHAPTER A—GENERAL

SUBCHAPTER B—MORTGAGE AND LOAN INSURANCE PROGRAMS UNDER NATIONAL HOUSING ACT AND OTHER AUTHORITIES

SUBCHAPTER C—PLANNING ASSISTANCE TO HOUSING SPONSORS [RESERVED]

SUBCHAPTER D—PUBLICLY FINANCED HOUSING PROGRAMS [RESERVED]

SUBCHAPTERS E–H [RESERVED]

SUBCHAPTER I—HUD-OWNED PROPERTIES

SUBCHAPTER A—GENERAL

PART 200—INTRODUCTION TO FHA PROGRAMS

7

AUTHORITY: 12 U.S.C. 1702–1715z–21; 42 U.S.C. 3535(d).

SOURCE: 36 FR 24467, Dec. 22, 1971, unless otherwise noted.

EDITORIAL NOTE: Nomenclature changes to part 200 appear at 69 FR 18803, Apr. 9, 2004.

§ 200.1 Purpose.

This part sets forth requirements that are applicable to several of the programs of the Federal Housing Administration, an organizational unit within the Department of Housing and Urban Development. Program requirements applicable to FHA programs and other HUD programs also can be found in 24 CFR part 5. The specific program regulations should be consulted to determine which requirements in this part 200 or 24 CFR part 5 are applicable.

[61 FR 14398, Apr. 1, 1996]

Subpart A—Requirements for Application, Commitment, and Endorsement Generally Applicable to Multifamily and Health Care Facility Mortgage Insurance Programs; and Continuing Eligibility Requirements for Existing Projects

SOURCE: 61 FR 14399, Apr. 1, 1996, unless otherwise noted.

§ 200.3 Definitions.

(a) The definitions "department", "elderly person", "family", "HUD", and "Secretary", as used in this subpart A, shall have the meanings given these terms in 24 CFR part 5.

(b) The terms *"first mortgage"*, *"hospital"*, *"maturity date"*, *"mortgage"*, *"mortgagee"*, and *"state"*, as used in this subpart A shall have the meaning given in the section of the National Housing Act (12 U.S.C. 1701), as amended, under which the project mortgage is insured.

(c) As used in this subpart A:

Act means the National Housing Act, (12 U.S.C. 1701) as amended.

Commissioner means the Federal Housing Commissioner.

FHA means the Federal Housing Administration.

Insured mortgage means a mortgage which has been insured by the endorsement of the credit instrument by the Commissioner, or the Commissioner's duly authorized representative.

Project means a property consisting of site, improvements and, where permitted, equipment meeting the provisions of the applicable section of the Act, other applicable statutes and regulations, and terms, conditions and standards established by the Commissioner.

[61 FR 14399, Apr. 1, 1996, as amended at 77 FR 5675, Feb. 3, 2012]

ELIGIBLE MORTGAGOR

§ 200.5 Eligible mortgagor.

(a) Except as provided in paragraph (b) of this section, the mortgagor:

(1) Shall be a single asset mortgagor entity acceptable to the Commissioner, as limited by the applicable section of the Act, and shall possess the powers necessary and incidental to operating the project, except that the Commissioner may approve a non-single asset mortgagor entity under such circumstances, terms and conditions determined and specified as acceptable to the Commissioner; and

(2) Shall not be a natural person or tenant in common.

(b)(1) For multifamily project mortgages for which HUD issued a firm commitment for mortgage insurance before September 1, 2011, and for multifamily project mortgages insured under section 232 of the Act (12 U.S.C. 1715w), the mortgagor shall be a natural person or entity acceptable to the Commissioner, as limited by the applicable section of the Act, and shall possess the powers necessary and incidental to operating the project.

(2) For multifamily project mortgages for which HUD issued a firm commitment for mortgage insurance

on or after September 1, 2011, the regulations of paragraph (a) of this section shall apply, unless the mortgagor demonstrates to the satisfaction of the Commissioner that financial hardship to the mortgagor would result from application of the regulations in paragraph (a) of this section due to the reasonable expectations of the mortgagor that the transaction would close under the regulations in effect prior to September 1, 2011, in which case, the regulations of paragraph (b)(1) shall apply.

[76 FR 24369, May 2, 2011]

§200.6 Employer identification and social security numbers.

The requirements set forth in 24 CFR part 5, regarding the disclosure and verification of social security numbers and employer identification numbers by applicants and participants in assisted mortgage and loan insurance and related programs, apply to these programs.

ELIGIBLE MORTGAGEE

§200.10 Lender requirements.

The requirements set forth in part 202 of this chapter regarding approval, recertification, withdrawal of approval, approval for servicing, report requirements and conditions for supervised mortgagees, nonsupervised mortgagees, investing mortgagees, and governmental and similar institutions, apply to these programs.

[62 FR 20081, Apr. 24, 1997]

§200.11 Audit requirements for State and local governments as mortgagees.

Requirements set forth in 2 CFR part 200, subpart F, apply to State and local governments (as defined at 2 CFR 200.90 and 200.64, respectively) that receive mortgage insurance as mortgagees.

[80 FR 75936, Dec. 7, 2015]

ELIGIBLE MORTGAGE

§200.15 Maximum mortgage.

Mortgages must not exceed either the statutory dollar amount or loan ratio limitations established by the section of the Act under which the mortgage is insured, except that the

Commissioner may increase the dollar amount limitations:

(a) By not to exceed 170 percent, in any geographical area, in which the Commissioner finds that cost levels so require; and

(b) By not to exceed 170 percent, or 215 percent in high-cost areas, where the Commissioner determines it necessary on a project-by-project basis.

[73 FR 17239, Mar. 31, 2008]

§200.16 Project mortgage adjustments and reductions.

The principal amount computed in accordance with the applicable section of the Act for the insured mortgage shall be subject to additional adjustments and reductions in accordance with terms and conditions established by the Commissioner.

§200.17 Mortgage coverage.

The mortgage shall cover the entire property included in the project.

§200.18 Minimum loan prohibition.

A mortgagee may not require that the mortgage exceed a minimum amount established by the mortgagee, as a condition of providing a loan secured by a mortgage insured under this part.

MISCELLANEOUS PROJECT MORTGAGE INSURANCE

§200.20 Refinancing insured mortgages.

An existing mortgage insured under the Act, or an existing mortgage held by the Secretary that is subject to a mortgage restructuring and rental assistance sufficiency plan under the Multifamily Assisted Housing Reform and Affordability Act, 42 U.S.C. 1437f note (MAHRA), may be refinanced pursuant to section 223(a)(7) of the Act and such terms and conditions as may be established by the Commissioner. The term of such refinancing in connection with the implementation of an approved restructuring plan under section 401, subpart C of this title, may be up to, but not more than, 30 years.

[72 FR 66037, Nov. 26, 2007]

§ 200.21 Reinsurance of Commissioner held mortgages.

Any mortgage assigned to the Commissioner in connection with payment under a contract of mortgage insurance, or executed in connection with a sale by the Commissioner of any property acquired under any section or title of the Act, may be insured pursuant to provisions of section 223(c) of the Act and such terms and conditions established by the Commissioner.

§ 200.22 Operating loss loans.

An insured loan to cover the operating losses of a project with an existing Commissioner insured mortgage may be made in accordance with provisions of section 223(d) of the Act and such terms and conditions established by the Commissioner.

§ 200.23 Projects in declining neighborhoods.

A Mortgage financing the repair, rehabilitation or construction of a project located in an older declining urban area shall be eligible for insurance pursuant to provisions of section 223(e) of the Act and such terms and conditions established by the Commissioner.

§ 200.24 Existing projects.

A mortgage financing the purchase or refinance of an existing rental housing project or refinance of the existing debt of an existing cooperative project under section 207 of the Act, or for refinancing the existing debt of an existing nursing home, intermediate care facility, assisted living facility, or board and care home, or any combination thereof, under section 232 of the Act, may be insured pursuant to provisions of section 223(f) of the Act and such terms and conditions established by HUD.

[79 FR 42189, July 21, 2014]

§ 200.25 Supplemental loans.

A loan, advance of credit or purchase of an obligation representing a loan or advance of credit made for the purpose of financing improvements or additions to a project covered by a mortgage insured under any section of the Act or Commissioner-held mortgage, or equip-ment for a nursing home, intermediate care facility, board and care home, assisted living facility, or group practices facility, may be insured pursuant to the provisions of section 241 of the Act and such terms and conditions established by HUD.

[72 FR 67545, Nov. 28, 2007]

MISCELLANEOUS CROSS CUTTING
REGULATIONS

§ 200.30 Nondiscrimination and equal opportunity.

The requirements set forth in 24 CFR part 5, and subparts I, J, and M of this part pertaining to nondiscrimination and equal opportunity, apply to these programs.

§ 200.31 Debarment and suspension.

The requirements set forth in 2 CFR part 2424 apply to these programs.

[72 FR 73494, Dec. 27, 2007]

§ 200.32 Participation and compliance requirements.

The requirements set forth in 24 CFR part 200, subpart H, apply to these programs.

§ 200.33 Labor standards

(a) The requirements set forth in 29 CFR parts 1, 3 and 5 for compliance with labor standards laws apply to projects under these programs to the extent that labor standards apply as provided in section 212 of the Act, provided that:

(1) The labor standards provisions do not apply to projects insured under sections 207 or 232 pursuant to section 223(f) of the Act; and

(2) Supplemental loans under section 241 of the Act are subject to the provisions of section 212 applicable to the section or title pursuant to which the mortgage covering the project is insured or pursuant to which the original mortgage was insured.

(b) The requirements set forth in 24 CFR part 70 apply to those programs with respect to which there is a statutory provision allowing HUD waiver of Davis-Bacon prevailing wage rates for volunteers.

(c) Project commitments, contracts and agreements, as determined by the

Commissioner, and construction contracts and subcontracts, shall include terms, conditions and standards for compliance with applicable requirements set forth in 29 CFR parts 1, 3 and 5 and section 212 of the Act.

(d) No advance under a loan or mortgage that is subject to the requirements of section 212 shall be eligible for insurance unless there is filed with the application for the advance a certificate as required by the Commissioner certifying that the laborers and mechanics employed in construction of the project have been paid not less than the wage rates required under section 212.

§ 200.34 Property and mortgage assessment.

The requirements set forth in 24 CFR part 200, subpart E, regarding the mortgagor's responsibility for making those investigations, analysis and inspections it deems necessary for protecting its interests in the property apply to these programs.

§ 200.35 Appraisal standards—nondiscrimination requirements.

(a) *Nondiscrimination in the selection of appraiser.* In the selection of an appraiser, there shall be no discrimination on the basis of race, color, religion, national origin, sex, age, or disability.

(b) *Nondiscrimination in appraisal determination.* The certification required by the Uniform Standards of Professional Appraisal Practice must include a statement that the racial/ethnic composition of the neighborhood surrounding the property in no way affected the appraisal determination.

§ 200.36 Financial reporting requirements.

The mortgagor must comply with the financial reporting requirements in 24 CFR part 5, subpart H.

[63 FR 46592, Sept. 1, 1998]

§ 200.37 Preventing crime in federally assisted housing.

See part 5, subparts I and J of this title, for provisions concerning preventing crime in federally assisted housing, including programs administered under section 236 and under sections 221(d)(3) and 221(d)(5) of the National Housing Act.

[66 FR 28797, May 24, 2001]

§ 200.38 Protections for victims of domestic violence.

(a) The requirements for protection for victims of domestic violence, dating violence, sexual assault, or stalking in 24 CFR part 5, subpart L (Protection for Victims of Domestic Violence, Dating Violence, Sexual Assault, or Stalking) apply to programs administered under section 236 and under sections 221(d)(3) and (d)(5) of the National Housing Act, as follows:

(1) Multifamily rental housing under section 221(d)(3) of the National Housing Act (12 U.S.C. 17151(d)) with a below-market interest rate (BMIR) pursuant to section 221(d)(5), with implementing regulations at 24 CFR part 221. The Section 221(d)(3) BMIR program insured and subsidized mortgage loans to facilitate new construction or substantial rehabilitation of multifamily rental cooperative housing for low- and moderate-income families. The program is no longer active, but Section 221(d)(3) BMIR properties that remain in existence are covered by VAWA. Coverage of section 221(d)(3) and (d)(5) BMIR housing does not include section 221(d)(3) and (d)(5) BMIR projects that refinance under section 223(a)(7) or 223(f) of the National Housing Act where the interest rate is no longer determined under section 221(d)(5).

(2) Multifamily rental housing under section 236 of the National Housing Act (12 U.S.C. 1715z–1), with implementing regulations at 24 CFR part 236. Coverage of the section 236 program includes not only those projects with FHA-insured project mortgages under section 236(j), but also non-FHA-insured projects that receive interest reduction payments ("IRP") under section 236(b) and formerly insured section 236 projects that continue to receive interest reduction payments through a "decoupled" IRP contract under section 236(e)(2). Coverage also includes projects that receive rental assistance payments authorized under section 236(f)(2).

(b) For the programs administered under paragraph (a) of this section,

13

"covered housing provider" as such term is used in 24 CFR part 5, subpart L, refers to the mortgagor, or owner, as applicable.

[81 FR 80805, Nov. 16, 2016]

FEES AND CHARGES

§ 200.40   HUD fees.

The following fees apply to mortgages to be insured under this part.

(a) *Application fee—SAMA letter (for new construction).* An application fee of $1 per thousand dollars of the requested mortgage shall accompany the application for a SAMA letter. An additional fee of $1 per thousand dollars of the requested mortgage amount shall be charged for the review of plans and specifications.

(b) *Application fee—feasibility letter (for substantial rehabilitation).* An application fee of $3 per thousand dollars of the requested mortgage amount shall accompany the application for a feasibility letter.

(c) *Application fee—conditional commitment.* For a mortgage being insured under section 223(f) of the Act (12 U.S.C. 1715n), an application-commitment fee of $3 per thousand dollars of the requested mortgage amount shall accompany an application for conditional commitment.

(d)(1) *Application fee—firm commitment: General.* An application for firm commitment shall be accompanied by an application-commitment fee in an amount determined by the Secretary, which when added to any prior fees received in connection with the same application, shall not exceed $5.00 per thousand dollars of the requested mortgage amount to be insured. The payment of an application-commitment fee shall not be required in connection with an insured mortgage involving the sale by the government of housing or property acquired, held, or contracted pursuant to the Atomic Energy Community Act of 1955 (42 U.S.C. 2301 *et seq.*).

(2) *Application fee—Section 232 Programs.* For purposes of mortgages insured under HUD's regulations in 24 CFR part 232, subpart C, an application for firm commitment shall be accompanied by an application fee in an amount determined by the Secretary, which shall not exceed $5.00 per thousand dollars of the requested mortgage amount to be insured.

(e) *Inspection fee—(1) In general.* The firm commitment may provide for the payment of an inspection fee in an amount not to exceed $5 per thousand dollars of the commitment. If an inspection fee is required, it shall be paid as follows:

(i) If the case involves insurance of advances, at the time of initial endorsement; or

(ii) If the case involves insurance upon completion, before the date construction is begun.

(2) *Existing projects.* For a mortgage being insured under section 223(f) of the Act, if the application provides for the completion of repairs, replacements and/or improvements (repairs), the Commissioner will charge an inspection fee equal to one percent (1%) of the cost of the repairs. However, where the Commissioner determines the cost of repairs is minimal, the Commissioner may establish a minimum inspection fee that exceeds one percent of the cost of repairs and can periodically increase or decrease this minimum fee.

(f) *Fees on increases—in general.* This section applies to all applications except applications involving hospitals, which are covered in 24 CFR part 242.

(1) *Increase in firm commitment before endorsement.* An application, filed before initial endorsement (or before endorsement in a case involving insurance upon completion), for an increase in the amount of an outstanding firm commitment, shall be accompanied by a combined additional application and commitment fee. This combined additional fee shall be in an amount that will aggregate $5 per thousand dollars of the amount of the requested increase. If an inspection fee was required in the original commitment, an additional inspection fee shall be paid in an amount computed at the same dollar rate per thousand dollars of the amount of increase in commitment as was used for the inspection fee required in the original commitment. When insurance of advances is involved, the additional inspection fee shall be paid at the time of initial endorsement. When insurance upon completion is involved,

the additional inspection fee shall be paid before the date construction is begun; or, if construction has begun, it shall be paid with the application for increase.

(2) *Increase in mortgage between initial and final endorsement.* Upon the filing of an application between initial and final endorsement, for an increase in the amount of the mortgage, either by amendment or by substitution of a new mortgage, a combined additional application and commitment fee shall accompany the application. This combined additional fee shall be in an amount that will aggregate $5 per thousand dollars of the amount of the increase requested. If an inspection fee was required in the original commitment, an additional inspection fee shall accompany the application in an amount not to exceed the $5 per thousand dollars of the amount of the increase requested.

(3) *Loan to cover operating losses.* In connection with a loan to cover operating losses (see Sec. 200.22), a combined application and commitment fee of $5 per thousand dollars of the amount of the loan applied for shall be submitted with the application for a firm commitment. No inspection fee shall be required.

(g) *Reopening of expired commitments.* An expired commitment may be reopened if a request for reopening is received by the Commissioner within 90 days of the expiration of the commitment. The reopening request shall be accompanied by a fee of 50 cents per thousand dollars of the amount of the expired commitment. If the reopening request is not received by the Commissioner within the required 90-day period, a new application, accompanied by the required application and commitment fee, must be submitted.

(h) *Transfer fee.* Upon application for the approval of a transfer of physical assets or the substitution of mortgagors, a transfer fee of 50 cents per thousand dollars shall be paid on the original face amount of the mortgage in all cases, except that a transfer fee shall not be paid where both parties to the transfer transaction are nonprofit purchasers, or when the transfer of physical assets or the substitution of mortgagors occurs contemporaneously with the restructuring of a mortgage pursuant to a restructuring plan under part 401, subpart C of this title.

(i) *Refund of fees.* If the amount of the commitment issued or increase in mortgage granted is less than the amount applied for, the Commissioner shall refund the excess amount of the application and commitment fees submitted by the applicant. If an application is rejected before it is assigned for processing, or in such other instances as the Commissioner may determine, the entire application and commitment fee or any portion thereof may be returned to the applicant. Commitment, inspection and reopening fees may be refunded, in whole or in part, if it is determined by the Commissioner that there is a lack of need for the housing or that the construction or financing of the project has been prevented because of condemnation proceedings or other legal action taken by a governmental body or public agency, or in such other instances as the Commissioner may determine. A transfer fee may be refunded only in such instances as the Commissioner may determine.

(j) *Fees not required.* (1) The payment of an application, commitment, inspection, or reopening fee shall not be required in connection with the insurance of a mortgage involving the sale by the Secretary of any property acquired under any section or title of the Act.

(2) The payment of an application or commitment fee shall not be required in connection with the insurance of a mortgage used to facilitate a restructuring plan under part 401, subpart C of this title.

[61 FR 14414, Apr. 1, 1996, as amended at 72 FR 66037, Nov. 26, 2007; 72 FR 67545, Nov. 28, 2007; 80 FR 48027, Aug. 11, 2015]

§200.41 Maximum mortgagee fees and charges.

(a) Mortgagee fees and charges included in the mortgage must be for actual required services provided to the mortgagor by the mortgagee, and shall not exceed common market rates for such services as determined by the Commissioner.

(b) Mortgagee charges for prepayment of the mortgage and late mortgage payments shall not exceed that determined appropriate by the Commissioner.

COMMITMENT APPLICATIONS

§ 200.45   Processing of applications.

(a) *Preapplication conference.* Except for mortgages insured under section 241(f) or 242 of the Act, the local HUD Office will determine whether participation in such a conference is required as a condition to submission of an initial application for either a site appraisal and market analysis (SAMA) letter (for new construction), a feasibility letter (for substantial rehabilitation), or for a firm commitment. The project sponsor may elect (after the preapplication conference if required) to submit an application for a SAMA or a feasibility letter (as appropriate), or for a firm commitment for insurance depending upon the completeness of the drawings, specifications and other required exhibits. An application for a SAMA or feasibility letter may be submitted by the project sponsor. An application for a firm commitment for insurance must be submitted by both the project sponsor and an approved mortgagee. Applications shall be submitted to the local HUD Office on HUD-approved forms. No application will be considered unless accompanied by all exhibits required by the form and program handbooks. At the option of the local HUD Office, the SAMA/Feasibility letter stage of processing can be combined with the firm commitment stage of processing.

(b) *Firm commitment requirement.* An application for a firm commitment must be made by an approved mortgagee for any project for which a mortgagor seeks mortgage insurance under the Act.

(c) *Staged applications.* Staged applications leading to an application for firm commitment shall be made as determined appropriate by the Commissioner, and in accordance with such terms and conditions established by the Commissioner. The intermediate stages to firm commitment may include a site appraisal and market analysis (SAMA) letter stage or a feasibility letter stage and a conditional commitment. The conditional commitment stage applies only to mortgages

to be insured pursuant to section 223(f) of the Act.

(d) *Effect of SAMA letter, feasibility letter, and firm commitment*—(1) *SAMA letter.* (i) The issuance of a SAMA letter indicates completion of the site appraisal and market analysis stage to determine initial acceptability of the site and recognition of a specific market need. The SAMA letter is not a commitment to insure a mortgage for the proposed project and does not bind the Commissioner to issue a firm commitment to insure. The SAMA letter precedes the later submission of acceptable plans and specifications for the proposed project and is limited to advising the applicant as to the following determinations of the Commissioner, which shall not be changed to the detriment of an applicant, if the application for a firm commitment is received before expiration of the SAMA letter:

(A) The land value fully improved (with off-site improvements installed);

(B) The acceptability of the proposed project site, the proposed composition, number and size of the units and the market for the number of proposed units. Where the application is not acceptable as submitted, but can be made acceptable by a change in the number, size, or composition of the units, the SAMA letter may establish the specific lesser number of units which would be acceptable and any acceptable alternative plan for the composition and size of units; and

(C) The acceptability of the unit rents proposed. Where rent levels are unacceptable, the SAMA letter may establish specific rents which are acceptable.

(ii) After receiving a SAMA letter, the sponsor shall submit design drawings and specifications in a timeframe prescribed by the Commissioner. The Commissioner will review and comment on design development and the drawings and specifications. The comments will be provided to the sponsor for use in preparing a firm commitment application.

(2) *Feasibility letter.* The issuance of a feasibility letter indicates approval of the preliminary work write-up and outline specifications and completion of

technical processing involving the estimated rehabilitation cost of the project, the "as is" value of the site, the detailed estimates of operating expenses and taxes, the specific unit rents, the vacancy allowance, and the estimated mortgage amount. The issuance of a feasibility letter is not a commitment to insure a mortgage for the proposed project and does not bind the Commissioner to issue a firm commitment to insure. Determinations found in a feasibility letter are not to be binding upon the Department and may be changed in whole or in part at any later point in time. The letter may even be unilaterally terminated by the Commissioner if found necessary.

(3) *Conditional commitment.* The issuance of a Section 223(f) conditional commitment indicates completion of technical processing involving the estimated value of the property, the detailed estimates of rents, operating expenses and taxes and an estimated mortgage amount.

(e) *Term of SAMA letter, feasibility letter, and conditional commitment.* A SAMA letter, a feasibility letter, and a conditional commitment shall be effective for whatever term is specified in the respective letter or commitment.

(f) *Rejection of an application.* A significant deviation in an application from the Commissioner's terms or conditions in an earlier stage application commitment or agreement shall be grounds for rejection. The fees paid to such date shall be considered as having been earned notwithstanding such rejection.

(Approved by the Office of Management and Budget under control number 2502–0029)

[61 FR 14415, Apr. 1, 1996]

§200.46 Commitment issuance.

Upon approval of an application for insurance, a commitment shall be issued by the Commissioner setting forth the terms and conditions upon which the mortgage will be insured. The commitment term and any extension or reopening of an expired commitment shall be in accordance with standards established by the Commissioner.

§200.47 Firm commitments.

A valid firm commitment must be in effect at the time the mortgage instrument is endorsed.

(a) *Insurance upon completion.* The commitment shall provide the terms and conditions for the insurance of the mortgage:

(1) After completion of construction or substantial rehabilitation of the project; or

(2) Upon completion of required work, except as deferred by the Commissioner in accordance with terms, conditions and standards established by the Commissioner, for an existing project without substantial rehabilitation.

(b) *Insured advances.* The commitment shall provide for insurance of the mortgage as provided in paragraph (a) of this section, and for the insurance of mortgage money advanced in accordance with terms and conditions established by the Commissioner during: construction; substantial rehabilitation; or other work acceptable to the Commissioner.

REQUIREMENTS INCIDENT TO INSURED
ADVANCES

§200.50 Building loan agreement.

The mortgagor and mortgagee must execute a building loan agreement approved by the Commissioner, that sets forth the terms and conditions under which progress payments may be advanced during construction, before initial endorsement of the mortgage for insurance.

§200.51 Mortgagee certificate.

The mortgagee shall certify to the Commissioner that it will conform with terms and conditions established by the Commissioner for the mortgagee's control of project funds, and other incidental requirements established by the Commissioner.

§200.52 Construction contract.

The form of contract between the mortgagor and builder shall be as prescribed by the Commissioner in accordance with terms and conditions established by the Commissioner.

§ 200.53   Initial operating funds.

The mortgagor shall deposit cash with the mortgagee, or in a depository satisfactory to the mortgagee and under control of the mortgagee, in accordance with terms, conditions and standards established by the Commissioner for:

(a) Accruals for taxes, ground rates, mortgage insurance premiums, and property insurance premiums, during the course of construction;

(b) Meeting the cost of equipping and renting the project subsequent to its completion in whole or part; and

(c) Allocation by the mortgagee for assessments required by the terms of the mortgage in an amount acceptable to the Commissioner.

§ 200.54   Project completion funding.

(a) Except as provided in paragraph (d) of this section, the mortgagor shall deposit with the mortgagee cash deemed by the Commissioner to be sufficient, when added to the proceeds of the insured mortgage, to assure completion of the project and to pay the initial service charge, carrying charges, and legal and organizational expenses incident to the construction of the project. The Commissioner may accept a lesser cash deposit or an alternative to a cash deposit in accordance with terms and conditions established by the Commissioner, where the required funding is to be provided by a grant or loan from a Federal, State, or local government agency or instrumentality.

(b) An agreement acceptable to the Commissioner shall require that funds provided by the mortgagor under requirements of this section must be disbursed in full for project work, material, and incidental charges and expenses before disbursement of any mortgage proceeds, except:

(c) Low-income housing tax credit syndication proceeds, historic tax-credit syndication proceeds, New Markets Tax Credits proceeds, or funds provided by a grant or loan from a Federal, State, or local governmental agency or instrumentality under requirements of this section need not be fully disbursed before the disbursement of mortgage proceeds, where approved by the Commissioner in accordance with terms, conditions, and standards established by the Commissioner;

(d) In the case of a mortgage insured under any provision of this title executed in connection with the purchase, construction, rehabilitation, or refinancing of a multifamily tax credit project, the Commissioner may not require:

(1) The escrowing of equity provided by Low-Income Housing Tax Credits for the project pursuant to Title 26, section 42 of the Internal Revenue Code of 1986;

(2) The escrowing of equity provided by historic rehabilitation tax credits, New Markets Tax Credits, or any other form of security, such as a letter of credit.

[75 FR 51915, Aug. 23, 2010]

§ 200.55   Financing fees and charges.

Fees and charges approved by the Commissioner in excess of the initial service charge shall be deposited with the mortgagee in cash before initial endorsement, except as otherwise preapproved by the Commissioner.

§ 200.56   Assurance of completion for on-site improvements.

The mortgagor shall furnish assurance of completion of the project in the form and amount provided by terms, conditions and standards established by the Commissioner.

GENERAL REQUIREMENTS

§ 200.60   Assurance of completion for offsite facilities.

An assurance of completion for offsite utilities, streets, and other facilities required for a buildable site shall be provided in an amount and form acceptable to the Commissioner, except where a municipality or other public body has, in a manner acceptable to the Commissioner, agreed to install such improvements without cost to the mortgagor.

§ 200.61   Title.

(a) Marketable title to the project must be vested in the mortgagor as of the date the mortgage is filed for record.

(b) Title evidence for the Commissioner's examination shall include a lender's title insurance policy, which title policy provides survey coverage based on a survey acceptable to the title company and the Commissioner; or as the Commissioner may otherwise require, in accordance with terms, conditions and standards established by the Commissioner.

(c) Endorsement of the credit instrument for insurance shall evidence the acceptability of title evidence.

§ 200.62 Certifications.

Any agreement, undertaking, statement or certification required by the Commissioner shall specifically state that it has been made, presented, and delivered for the purpose of influencing an official action of the FHA, and of the Commissioner, and may be relied upon by the Commissioner as a true statement of the facts contained therein.

§ 200.63 Required deposits and letters of credit.

(a) *Deposits.* Where the Commissioner requires the mortgagor to make a deposit of cash or securities, such deposit shall be with the mortgagee or a depository acceptable to the mortgagee. The deposit shall be held by the mortgagee in a special account or by the depository under an appropriate agreement approved by the Commissioner.

(b) *Letter of credit.* Where the use of a letter of credit is acceptable to the Commissioner in lieu of a deposit of cash or securities, the letter of credit shall be issued to the mortgagee by a banking institution and shall be unconditional and irrevocable:

(1) The mortgagee of record may not be the issuer of any letter of credit without the prior written consent of the Commissioner.

(2) The mortgagee shall be responsible to the Commissioner for collection under the letter of credit. In the event a demand for payment thereunder is not immediately met, the mortgagee shall immediately provide a cash deposit equivalent to the undrawn balance of the letter of credit.

PROPERTY REQUIREMENTS

§ 200.70 Location and fee interest.

The property must be held by an eligible mortgagor, and must conform with requirements pertaining to property location and fee or lease interests of the section of the Act under which the mortgage is insured.

§ 200.71 Liens.

The project must be free and clear of all liens other than the insured mortgage, except that the property may be subject to an inferior lien as provided by terms and conditions established by the Commissioner for an inferior lien:

(a) Made or held by a Federal, State or local government instrumentality;

(b) Required in connection with: an operating loss loan insured pursuant to a section 223(d) of the Act; a supplemental loan insured pursuant to section 241 of the Act; or a mortgage to purchase or refinance an existing project pursuant to section 223(f) of the Act; or

(c) As otherwise provided by the Commissioner.

§ 200.72 Zoning, deed and building restrictions.

The project when completed shall not violate any material zoning or deed restrictions applicable to the project site, and shall comply with all applicable building and other governmental codes, ordinances, regulations and requirements.

§ 200.73 Property development.

(a) The property shall be suitable and principally designed for the intended use, as provided by the applicable section of the Act under which the mortgage is insured, and have long-term marketability. Design, construction, substantial rehabilitation and repairs shall be in accordance with standards established by the Commissioner.

(b) A project may include such commercial and community facilities as the Commissioner deems acceptable.

(c) The improvements shall constitute a single project. Not less than five rental dwelling units or personal care units, 20 medical care beds, or 50 manufactured home pads, shall be on one site, except that such limitations do not apply to group practice facilities.

§ 200.74 Minimum property standards.

The requirements set forth in subpart S of this part apply to these programs, except for hospitals insured under section 242 of the Act and group practice facilities insured under title XI of the Act.

§ 200.75 Environmental quality determinations and standards.

Requirements set forth in 24 CFR part 50, Protection and Enhancement of Environmental Quality, 24 CFR part 51, Environmental Criteria and Standards, 24 CFR part 55, Implementation of Executive Order 11988, Flood Plain Management, and as otherwise required by the Commissioner apply to these programs.

§ 200.76 Smoke detectors.

Smoke detectors and alarm devices must be installed in accordance with standards and criteria acceptable to the Commissioner for the protection of occupants in any dwelling or facility bedroom or other primary sleeping area.

§ 200.77 Lead-based paint poisoning prevention.

Requirements set forth in 24 CFR part 35 apply to these programs.

§ 200.78 Energy conservation.

Construction, mechanical equipment, and energy and metering selections shall provide cost effective energy conservation in accordance with standards established by the Commissioner.

MORTGAGE PROVISIONS

§ 200.80 Mortgage form.

The mortgage shall be:

(a) Executed on a form approved by the Commissioner for use in the jurisdiction in which the property securing the mortgage is situated, which form shall not be changed without the prior written approval of the Commissioner.

(b) Executed by an eligible mortgagor.

(c) A first lien on the property securing the mortgage, which property conforms with the property standards prescribed by the Commissioner.

§ 200.81 Disbursement of mortgage proceeds.

The mortgagee shall be obligated, as a part of the mortgage transaction, to disburse the principal amount of the mortgage to the:

(a) Mortgagor or mortgagor's account;

(b) Mortgagor's creditors for the mortgagor's account, subject to the mortgagor's consent.

§ 200.82 Maturity.

The mortgage shall have a maturity satisfactory to the Commissioner, and shall contain complete amortization or sinking-fund provisions satisfactory to the Commissioner.

(a) The maximum mortgage term may not exceed the lesser of:

(1) Any limits included under the applicable section of the Act.

(2) Thirty-five years for existing projects, except that the mortgage term may be up to 40 years under terms and conditions established by the Commissioner, and 40 years for proposed construction and substantial rehabilitation projects.

(3) Seventy-five percent of the estimated remaining economic life of the physical improvements.

(b) The minimum mortgage term shall not be less than 10 years.

§ 200.83 Interest rate.

(a) The mortgage shall bear interest at the rate agreed upon by the mortgagee and the mortgagor.

(b) Interest shall be payable in monthly installments on the principal amount of the mortgage outstanding on the due date of each installment.

(c) The amount of any increase approved by the Commissioner in the mortgage amount between initial and final endorsement in excess of the amount that the Commissioner had committed to insure at initial endorsement shall bear interest at the rate agreed upon by the mortgagee and the mortgagor.

§ 200.84 Payment requirements.

The mortgage shall provide for:

(a) A single aggregate payment each month for all payments to be made by the mortgagor to the mortgagee.

(b) The mortgagor to pay to the mortgagee:

(1) Interest and principal on the first day of each month in accordance with an amortization plan agreed upon by the mortgagor, the mortgagee and the Commissioner.

(i) Date of first payment to interest shall be the endorsement date or, where there are insured advances, the initial endorsement date.

(ii) Date of first payment to principal. The Commissioner shall estimate the time necessary to complete the project and shall establish the date of the first payment to principal so that the lapse of time between completion of the project and commencement of amortization will not be longer than necessary to obtain sustaining occupancy.

(2) An amount on each interest payment date sufficient to accumulate in the hands of the mortgagee one payment period prior to its due date, the next annual mortgage insurance premium payable by the mortgagee to the Commissioner. Such payments shall continue only so long as the contract of insurance shall remain in effect.

(3) Equal monthly payments as will amortize the ground rents, if any, and the estimated amount of all taxes, water charges, special assessments, and fire and other hazard insurance premiums, within a period ending one month prior to the dates on which the same become delinquent.

(4) The mortgage shall further provide:

(i) That such payments shall be held by the mortgagee, for the purpose of paying such items before they become delinquent.

(ii) For adjustments in case such estimated amounts shall prove to be more, or less, than the actual amounts so paid therefor by the mortgagor.

(c) The mortgagee to apply each mortgagor payment received to the following items in the order set forth:

(1) Premium charges under the contract of mortgage insurance.

(2) Ground rents, taxes, special assessments, and fire and other hazard insurance premiums.

(3) Interest on the mortgage.

(4) Amortization of the principal of the mortgage.

§ 200.85 Covenant against liens.

(a) The mortgage shall contain a covenant against the creation by the mortgagor of liens against the property superior or inferior to the lien of the mortgage except for such inferior lien as may be approved by the Commissioner in accordance with provisions of § 200.71; and

(b) A covenant against repayment of a Commissioner approved inferior lien from mortgage proceeds other than surplus cash or residual receipts, except in the case of an inferior lien created by an operating loss loan insured pursuant to section 223(d) of the Act, or a supplemental loan insured pursuant to section 241 of the Act.

§ 200.86 Covenant for fire and other hazard insurance.

The mortgage shall contain a covenant binding the mortgagor to maintain fire and extended coverage insurance on the property in accordance with terms and conditions established by the Commissioner.

§ 200.87 Mortgage prepayment.

(a) *Prepayment privilege.* Except as provided in paragraph (c) of this section or otherwise established by the Commissioner, the mortgage shall contain a provision permitting the mortgagor to prepay the mortgage in whole or in part upon any interest payment date, after giving the mortgagee 30 days' notice in writing in advance of its intention to so prepay.

(b) *Prepayment charge.* The mortgage may contain a provision for such charge, in the event of prepayment of principal, as may be agreed upon between the mortgagor and the mortgagee, subject to the following:

(1) The mortgagor shall be permitted to prepay up to 15 percent of the original principal amount of the mortgage in any one calendar year without any such charge.

(2) Any reduction in the original principal amount of the mortgage resulting from the certification of cost which the Commissioner may require

shall not be construed as a prepayment of the mortgage.

(c) *Prepayment of bond-financed or GNMA securitized mortgages.* Where the mortgage is given to secure GNMA mortgage-backed securities or a loan made by a lender that has obtained the funds for the loan by the issuance and sale of bonds or bond anticipation notes, or both, the mortgage may contain a prepayment restriction and prepayment penalty charge acceptable to the Commissioner as to term, amount, and conditions.

(d) *HUD override of prepayment restrictions.* In the event of a default, the Commissioner may override any lockout, prepayment penalty or combination thereof in order to facilitate a partial or full refinancing of the mortgaged property and avoid a claim.

§ 200.88   Late charge.

(a) The mortgage may provide for the collection by the mortgagee of a late charge in accordance with terms, conditions, and standards of the Commissioner for each dollar of each payment to interest or principal:

(1) More than 10 days in arrears to cover the expense involved in handling delinquent payments;

(2) For multifamily project mortgages for which HUD issued a firm commitment for mortgage insurance before September 1, 2011, and for multifamily project mortgages insured under section 232 of the Act (12 U.S.C. 1715w), more than 15 days in arrears to cover the expense involved in handling delinquent payments.

(b) Late charges shall be separately charged to and collected from the mortgagor and shall not be deducted from any aggregate monthly payment.

[76 FR 24369, May 2, 2011]

COST CERTIFICATION

§ 200.95   Certification of cost requirements.

(a) Before initial endorsement of the mortgage for insurance, the mortgagor, the mortgagee, and the Commissioner shall enter into an agreement in form and content satisfactory to the Commissioner for the purpose of precluding any excess of mortgage proceeds over statutory limitations. Under this agreement, the mortgagor shall disclose its relationship with the builder, including any collateral agreement, and shall agree:

(1) To enter into a construction contract, the terms of which shall depend on whether or not there exists an identity of interest between the mortgagor and the builder.

(2) To execute a Certificate of Actual Costs, upon completion of all physical improvements on the mortgaged property.

(3) To apply in reduction of the outstanding balance of the principal of the mortgage any excess of mortgage proceeds over statutory limitations based on actual cost.

(b) The provisions of paragraph (a) of this section relating to disclosure and the requirement for a construction contract shall not apply where the mortgagor is the general contractor.

§ 200.96   Certificates of actual cost.

(a) The mortgagor's certificate of actual cost, in a form prescribed by the Commissioner, shall be submitted upon completion of the physical improvements to the satisfaction of the Commissioner and before final endorsement, except that in the case of an existing project that does not require substantial rehabilitation and where the commitment provides for completion of specified repairs after endorsement, a supplemental certificate of actual cost will be submitted covering the completed costs of any such repairs. The certificate shall show the actual cost to the mortgagor, after deduction of any kickbacks, rebates, trade discounts, or other similar payments to the mortgagor, or to any of its officers, directors, stockholders, partners or other entity member ownership, of construction and other costs, as prescribed by the Commissioner.

(b) The Certificate of Actual Cost shall be verified by an independent Certified Public Accountant or independent public accountant in a manner acceptable to the Commissioner.

(c) Upon the Commissioner's approval of the mortgagor's certification of actual cost such certification shall be final and incontestable except for fraud or material misrepresentation on the part of the mortgagor.

§ 200.97 Adjustments resulting from cost certification.

(a) *Fee simple site.* Upon receipt of the mortgagor's certification of actual cost there shall be added to the total amount thereof the Commissioner's estimate of the fair market value of any land included in the mortgage security and owned by the mortgagor in fee, such value being prior to the construction of the improvements.

(b) *Leasehold site.* In the event the land is held under a leasehold or other interest less than a fee, the cost, if any, of acquiring the leasehold or other interest is considered an allowable expense which may be added to actual cost provided that in no event shall such amount be in excess of the fair market value of such leasehold or other interest exclusive of proposed improvements.

(c) *Adjustment.* If the amount calculated in accordance with paragraphs (a) or (b) of this section exceeds the statutory dollar amount limits or loan ratio limits permitted by the section of Act under which the mortgage is to be insured, or program loan ratio limits established by the Commissioner in the absence of statutory limits, the amount must be reduced to the applicable limits before final endorsement.

ENDORSEMENT

§ 200.100 Insurance endorsement.

The credit instrument shall be initially and finally endorsed simultaneously for insurance pursuant to a commitment to insure upon completion. Where the advances of construction funds are to be insured pursuant to a commitment for insured advances, initial endorsement of the credit instrument shall occur before any mortgage proceeds are insured and the time of final endorsement shall be as set forth in paragraph (b) of this section.

(a) *Initial endorsement.* The Commissioner shall indicate the insurance of the mortgage by endorsing the original credit instrument and identifying the section of the Act and the regulations under which the mortgage is insured and the date of insurance.

(b) *Final endorsement.* When all advances of mortgage proceeds have been made and all the terms and conditions of the commitment have been met to the Commissioner's satisfaction the Commissioner shall indicate on the original credit instrument the total of all advances approved for insurance and again endorse such instrument.

(c) *Contract rights and obligations.* The Commissioner and the mortgagee or lender shall be bound from the date of initial endorsement, whether the initial and final endorsement occur simultaneously or are split, by the provisions of the Contract Rights and Obligations set forth in the respective regulations for each section of the Act, as follows: Section 207 of the Act (24 CFR part 207); Section 213 of the Act (24 CFR part 213); Section 220 of the Act (24 CFR part 220); Section 221 of the Act (24 CFR part 221); Section 231 of the Act (24 CFR part 231); Section 232 of the Act (24 CFR part 232); Section 234 of the Act (24 CFR part 234); Section 241 of the Act (24 CFR part 241); Section 242 of the Act (24 CFR part 242); title XI of the Act (24 CFR part 244).

§ 200.101 Mortgagor lien certificate.

The mortgagor shall certify at the final endorsement of the mortgage for insurance as to each of the following:

(a) That the mortgage is the first lien upon and covers the entire project, including any equipment financed with mortgage proceeds.

(b) That the property upon which the improvements have been made or constructed and the equipment financed with mortgage proceeds are free and clear of all liens other than the insured mortgage and such other liens as may be approved by the Commissioner.

(c) That the certificate sets forth all unpaid obligations in connection with the mortgage transaction, the purchase of the mortgaged property, the construction or rehabilitation of the project or the purchase of the equipment financed with mortgage proceeds.

REGULATION OF MORTGAGORS

§ 200.105 Mortgagor supervision.

(a) As long as the Commissioner is the insurer or holder of the mortgage, the Commissioner shall regulate the mortgagor by means of a regulatory agreement providing terms, conditions and standards established by the Commissioner, or by such other means as the Commissioner may prescribe.

(b) The Commissioner may delegate to the mortgagee or other party the Commissioner's authority, in whole or in part, in accordance with the terms, conditions and standards established by the Commissioner in any executed Regulatory Agreement or other instrument granting the Commissioner supervision of the mortgagor.

[61 FR 14399, Apr. 1, 1996, as amended at 65 FR 61074, Oct. 13, 2000]

§ 200.106 Projects with limited distribution mortgagors and program assistance.

(a) *Regulation as limited distribution mortgagors.* In addition to regulation under § 200.105, limited distribution mortgagors for projects receiving "assistance within the jurisdiction of the Department" (as defined in § 4.3 of this title) may be regulated by the Commissioner as to additional matters, by regulation or otherwise, including as to the amount of the permissible distribution to the mortgagor.

(b) *Increased distributions.* The Commissioner may permit increased distributions of surplus cash, in excess of the amounts the Commissioner otherwise permits for limited distribution mortgagors, to a limited distribution mortgagor who participates in a HUD-approved initiative or program to preserve housing stock with below-market rents as affordable housing. The increased distribution will be limited to a maximum amount based on market rents and calculated according to HUD instructions. Funds that the mortgagor is authorized to retain under section 236(g)(2) of the National Housing Act are not considered distributions to the mortgagor.

(c) *Pre-emption.* Any State or local law or regulation that restricts distributions to an amount lower than permitted by the Commissioner under authority of this section is preempted to the extent provided in section 524(f) of the Multifamily Assisted Housing Reform and Affordability Act of 1997.

[65 FR 61074, Oct. 13, 2000]

Subpart B—Electronic Submission of Required Data for Mortgage Defaults and Mortgage Insurance Claims for Insured Multifamily Mortgages

SOURCE: 64 FR 4769, Jan. 29, 1999, unless otherwise noted.

§ 200.120 Purpose and applicability.

(a) *Purpose.* The purpose of this subpart B is to require mortgagees of all multifamily projects whose mortgages are insured or coinsured by HUD to submit electronically information regarding mortgage delinquencies, defaults, reinstatements, elections to assign, and withdrawals of assignment elections, and related information, as that information is required by 24 CFR part 207 and Form HUD–92426 (which is available at the Department of Housing and Urban Development, HUD Customer Service Center, 451 7th Street, SW, Room B–100, Washington, DC 20410; telephone (800) 767–7468).

(b) *Applicability.* This subpart applies to all HUD multifamily mortgage insurance and coinsurance programs.

§ 200.121 Requirements and effectiveness.

(a) Multifamily mortgagees, which are required by 24 CFR part 207 to report mortgage delinquencies, defaults, reinstatements, assignment elections, withdrawals of assignment elections, and related information, must submit this information electronically, over the Internet, in accordance with the following schedule of effectiveness:

(1) Mortgagees having 70 or more insured mortgage loans must comply with this section by no later than March 1, 1999;

(2) Mortgagees having from 26 to 69 insured mortgage loans must comply with this section by no later than January 1, 2000;

(3) Mortgagees having from 11 to 25 insured mortgage loans must comply with this section by no later than January 1, 2001;

(4) Mortgagees having 10 or fewer insured mortgage loans must comply with this section by no later than January 1, 2002.

(b) *Exception.* On or after January 1, 2002, mortgagees that hold or service fewer than 10 multifamily mortgages may continue to report mortgage delinquencies, defaults, reinstatements, assignment elections, withdrawals of assignment elections, and related information in writing on Form HUD–92426 only with specific HUD approval. HUD will grant such approval, upon application by the mortgagee, for reasons of hardship due to insufficient financial resources to purchase the required hardware and Internet access.

(c) HUD will not accept reports of information regarding defaults, reinstatements, assignment elections, and related information in a manner that is not in accordance with this section. Failure on the part of mortgagees to report this information as required by 24 CFR part 207 and this section may result in HUD's application of the sanctions and surcharges specified in 24 CFR part 207.

Subparts C–D [Reserved]

Subpart E—Mortgage Insurance Procedures and Processing

APPLICATION FOR INSURANCE

§ 200.145 **Property and mortgage assessment.**

(a) The mortgagor is responsible for making those investigations, analyses and inspections it deems necessary for protecting its interests in the property.

(b) Any appraisals, inspections, environmental assessments, and technical or financial evaluations conducted by or for the Commissioner are performed to determine the maximum insurable mortgage, and to protect the Commissioner and the FHA insurance funds. Such appraisals, inspections, assessments and evaluations neither create nor imply a duty or obligation from HUD to the mortgagor, or to any other party, and are not to be regarded as a warranty by HUD to the mortgagor, or any other party, of the value or condition of the property.

(c) For all new construction as well as structural repairs and/or renovations of existing properties, to the extent that an inspection is required to determine if construction quality of a one- to four-unit property is acceptable as security for an FHA-insured loan, the following requirements apply:

(1)(i) In areas where local jurisdictions provide building code enforcement and the requisite documentation, the lender shall provide a copy of:

(A) The building permit, or its equivalent, and a copy of the certificate of occupancy, or its equivalent; or

(B) A satisfactory inspection notice for work completed, or its equivalent.

(ii) The documentation provided under paragraph (c)(1)(i) of this section shall be considered satisfactory evidence of completion of the work.

(2) In jurisdictions that do not provide building code enforcement and requisite documentation, three inspections are required for new construction. For existing construction, only one inspection and certification of work completed for structural repairs and renovations is required. For both new and existing construction, the lender shall, in order to ensure compliance with FHA requirements:

(i) Select a Residential Combination Inspector (or its successor designation) or a Combination Inspector (or its successor designation) certified by the International Code Council (or its successor organization) who is licensed or certified as a home inspector in accordance with the applicable State and local requirements governing the licensing or certification of those jurisdictions that license or certify such inspectors in the respective jurisdiction. The lender shall provide a certification from such inspector that the new construction and/or structural repair or renovation work is completed satisfactorily and in compliance with any applicable building code.

(ii) In the absence of such Residential Combination Inspector and Combination Inspector, the lender shall obtain an inspection performed by a third party, who is a registered architect, a professional engineer, or a trades person or contractor, and who has met the licensing and bonding requirements of the State in which the property is located. The lender shall provide a certification from such inspector that the inspector is licensed and bonded under applicable State law, and that the new construction and/or structural repair or renovation work is completed satisfactorily and in compliance with any applicable building code.

[61 FR 14404, Apr. 1, 1996, as amended at 83 FR 31042, July 3, 2018]

CLAIMS FOR LOSSES

§ 200.153 Presentation of claim.

In the event the insured lender is entitled under the contract of mortgage insurance to receive a claim settlement, the mortgagee presents a claim for insurance benefits in accordance with the Secretary's instructions.

[61 FR 14404, Apr. 1, 1996]

§ 200.156 Settlement of claims.

Upon the Secretary's approval of a claim, the claim will be settled by issuance of cash, debentures or both, and, in certain cases, by issuance of a certificate of claim. However, in the event a final claim is in a negative amount, the claim will be settled by the mortgagee's payment of cash or surrender of debentures at par plus accrued interest to the Secretary.

[61 FR 14404, Apr. 1, 1996]

§ 200.157 Provisions and characteristics of debentures.

(a) *Series and fund.* Debentures are issued in appropriate series and are the obligation of and issued in the name of the particular mortgage insurance fund under which the mortgage is insured.

(b) *Registration and denominations.* Debentures in certificated form are issued in denominations of $50, $100, $500, $1,000 and $10,000 with the name of the owner inscribed on the face of the certificate. Debentures in book entry form are issued in a minimum amount of one dollar and in increments of one cent with the name of the owner recorded in an account master record on the books of the Treasury.

(c) *Rate of interest and interchangeability.* Debentures carry a rate of interest prescribed by the Commissioner but not in excess of an annual rate determined by the Secretary of the Treasury in accordance with prescribed statutory formula involving yields or prices of outstanding marketable obligations of the United States. Debentures in certificated form of the same series bearing the same interest rate and having the same maturity date shall be freely interchangeable between the various authorized denominations and may be exchanged for similar debentures in book entry form. Debentures in book entry form cannot be exchanged for debentures in certificated form.

(d) *Negotiability and Redemption.* Debentures in certificated form are negotiable and, if in book entry form, are transferable in the manner described in applicable Treasury regulations. Debentures are fully guaranteed as to principal and interest by the United States. Debentures are redeemable on call issued by the Commissioner.

(e) *Payment of principal and interest.* Principal and interest on debentures shall be payable when due at the Department of the Treasury, Washington, DC, or any Government agency or agencies in the United States which the Secretary of the Treasury may from time to time designate for that purpose. The principal and interest shall be payable to the owner whose name shall be inscribed on the debenture in certificated form, to the owner designated as assignee as shown by executed assignments for maturing or called certificated debentures, or to the owner whose name shall be recorded in the account master record of the book entry debentures.

(f) *Transfer and use*—(1) *In general.* Debentures in certificated form are negotiable and, if in book entry form, are transferable in the manner described in applicable Treasury regulations. They may be used by approved mortgagees in lieu of cash for payment of FHA mortgage insurance premiums.

(2) *Mutual Mortgage Insurance Fund debentures.* Debentures of the Mutual Mortgage Insurance Fund may be used to pay mortgage insurance premiums on mortgages insured under sections 203(b), 203(h), and 203(i), of the National Housing Act.

(3) *Cooperative Management Housing Insurance Fund debentures.* Debentures which are the obligation of the Cooperative Management Housing Insurance Fund may be used to pay premiums on mortgages and loans which are insured under that Fund. Where the insurance of a mortgage or loan is transferred

from the General Insurance Fund to the Cooperative Management Housing Insurance Fund, or where a mortgage or loan is endorsed for insurance pursuant to a commitment transferred to the Cooperative Management Housing Insurance Fund, debentures issued in connection with such mortgage or loan may be used to pay insurance premiums of either the Cooperative Management Housing Insurance Fund or the General Insurance Fund.

(4) *General Insurance Fund and debentures of other funds.* Debentures of the General Insurance Fund and those debentures issued as obligations of mortgage insurance funds and accounts in existence prior to the enactment of the Housing and Urban Development Act of 1965 (other than the Mutual Mortgage Insurance Fund) which are transferred by the 1965 Act to the General Insurance Fund may be used to pay mortgage insurance premiums only on the following mortgages and loans:

(i) Those which are the obligation of the General Insurance Fund.

(ii) Those transferred from the General Insurance Fund to the Cooperative Management Housing Insurance Fund.

(iii) Those endorsed for insurance pursuant to commitments transferred to the Cooperative Management Housing Insurance Fund.

[36 FR 24467, Dec. 22, 1971, as amended at 59 FR 49815, Sept. 30, 1994]

§ 200.158 Applicability of Treasury regulations to debenture transactions.

The Department of the Treasury acts as fiscal agent for the Commissioner in connection with transactions and operations relating to debentures. Treasury's General Regulations Governing U.S. Securities (31 CFR part 306) and its Supplemental Regulations Governing Federal Housing Administration Debentures (31 CFR part 337) have been and are adopted as revised and amended, to the extent applicable, as the regulations of the Commissioner governing the issuance of, transactions in and redemption of debentures, including the payment of interest thereon with the following exceptions:

(a) *Payment of final interest on maturing or called debentures.* If the notice of maturity or call for redemption shall so provide, the final installment of in-terest payable on any debentures at maturity or earlier redemption date may be paid with the principal in accordance with the assignments on the debentures instead of by separate check drawn to the order of the registered payee and forwarded to him at his address of record.

(b) *Closing of transfer books.* If the call for redemption shall so provide, the books maintained by the Treasury Department may be closed against transfers and denominational exchanges in debentures for three full months preceding any interest payment date with respect to any debentures called for redemption on such interest payment date.

[36 FR 24467, Dec. 22, 1971, as amended at 59 FR 49815, Sept. 30, 1994]

§ 200.159 Relief on account of lost, stolen, destroyed, mutilated or defaced debentures.

The statutes of the United States and the regulations of the Treasury Department governing relief on account of the loss, theft, destruction, mutilation or defacement of United States securities, so far as applicable and as necessarily modified to relate to debentures, are adopted as the regulations of the Commissioner for the issuance of substitute debentures or the payment of lost, stolen, destroyed, mutilated or defaced debentures.

§ 200.160 Redemption of debentures prior to maturity.

Debentures shall, at the option of the Commissioner and with the approval of the Secretary of the Treasury, be redeemable at par plus accrued interest on any semiannual interest payment date on 3 months' notice of redemption given in such manner as the Commissioner shall prescribe. The debenture interest on the debentures called for redemption shall cease on the semiannual interest payment date designated in the call notice. The Commissioner may include with the notice of redemption an offer to purchase the debentures at par plus accrued interest at any time during the period between the notice of redemption and the redemption date. If the debentures are purchased by the Commissioner after such call and prior to the named redemption date, the debenture interest shall cease on the date of purchase.

§ 200.161 Administration of debenture transactions.

The Secretary of the Treasury or the Acting Secretary of the Treasury is authorized and empowered, on behalf of the Commissioner, to administer the regulations governing any transactions and operations in debentures, to do all things necessary to conduct such transactions and operations, and to delegate such authority at his discretion to other officers, employees, and agents of the U.S. Treasury Department. At his discretion the Secretary, the Under Secretary, or any Assistant Secretary of the Treasury acting by direction of the Secretary, is authorized to waive any such regulation on behalf of the Commissioner in any particular case where a similar regulation of the Treasury Department with respect to United States bonds or interest thereon would be waived.

§ 200.162 Certificates of claim.

The certificate of claim issued to the mortgagee at the time debentures are issued constitutes an agreement by the FHA that after the FHA has recovered its investment in a particular property any excess over and above such investment is available for payment on the certificate of claim. Certificates of claim bear interest at the rate of 3 percent per annum.

Subpart F—Placement and Removal Procedures for Participation in FHA Programs

SECTION 203(k) REHABILITATION LOAN CONSULTANTS

§ 200.190 HUD list of qualified 203(k) consultants.

(a) *Qualified consultant list.* HUD maintains a list of qualified consultants for use in the rehabilitation loan insurance program authorized by section 203(k) of the National Housing Act (12 U.S.C. 1709(k)) (referred to as the "203(k) Program").

(b) *Consultant functions.* Only a consultant included on the list may be selected by the lender to conduct any consultant function under the 203(k) Program (see § 203.50(l) of this title).

(c) *Disclaimer.* The inclusion of a consultant on the list means only that the consultant has met the qualifications and conditions prescribed by the Secretary for placement on the list of consultants qualified for the 203(k) Program. The inclusion of a consultant on the list does not create or imply a warranty or endorsement by HUD of the consultant, nor does it represent a warranty of any work performed by the consultant.

[67 FR 52380, Aug. 9, 2002]

§ 200.191 Placement of 203(k) consultant.

(a) *Application.* To be considered for placement on the list, a consultant must apply to HUD using an application (or materials) in a form prescribed by HUD.

(b) *Eligibility.* To be eligible for placement on the list:

(1) The consultant must demonstrate to HUD that it either:

(i) Has at least three years' experience as a remodeling contractor, general contractor or home inspector; or

(ii) Is a state-licensed architect or state-licensed engineer;

(2) If located in a state that requires the licensing of home inspectors, the consultant must submit proof of such licensing;

(3) The consultant must submit a narrative description of the consultant's ability to perform home inspections, prepare architectural drawings, use proper methods of cost estimating and complete draw inspections.

(4) The consultant must certify that it has read and fully understands the requirements of the HUD handbook on the 203(k) Program (4240.4) and all HUD Mortgagee Letters and other instructions relating to the 203(k) Program.

(5) The consultant must not be listed on:

(i) The General Services Administration's Suspension and Debarment List;

(ii) HUD's Limited Denial of Participation List; or

(iii) HUD's Credit Alert Interactive Voice Response System.

(6) The consultant must have passed a comprehensive examination on the

203(k) Program, if HUD has developed such an exam.

(c) *Delayed effective date of examination requirement for consultants currently on the list.* Consultants who are included on the list on the date when the requirement for the examination described in paragraph (b)(6) of this section becomes effective have until 6 months following this date to pass the comprehensive exam. Failure to pass the examination by the deadline date constitutes cause for removal under § 200.192.

[67 FR 52380, Aug. 9, 2002]

§ 200.192 Removal of 203(k) consultant.

(a) *Cause for removal.* HUD may remove a consultant from the list for any cause that HUD determines to be detrimental to HUD or its programs. Cause for removal includes, but is not limited to:

(1) Poor performance on a HUD quality control field review;

(2) Failure to comply with applicable regulations or other written instructions or standards issued by HUD;

(3) Failure to comply with applicable Civil Rights requirements;

(4) Being debarred or suspended, or subject to a limited denial of participation;

(5) Misrepresentation or fraudulent statements;

(6) Failure to retain standing as a state licensed architect or state-licensed engineer (unless the consultant can demonstrate the required three years experience as a home inspector or remodeling contractor);

(7) Failure to retain standing as a state licensed home inspector, if the consultant is located in a sate that requires such licensing; or

(8) Failure to respond within a reasonable time to HUD inquiries or requests for documentation.

(b) *Procedure for removal.* A consultant that is debarred or suspended, or subject to a limited denial of participation will be *automatically* removed from the list. In all other cases, the following procedure for removal will be followed:

(1) HUD will give the consultant written notice of the proposed removal. The notice will state the reasons for, and the duration of, the proposed removal.

(2) The consultant will have 20 days from the date of the notice (or longer, if provided in the notice) to submit a written response appealing the proposed removal and to request a conference. A request for a conference must be in writing and must be submitted along with the written response.

(3) A HUD official will review the appeal and send a response either affirming, modifying, or canceling the removal. The HUD official will not be someone who was involved in HUD's initial removal decision. HUD will respond with a decision within 30 days of receiving the appeal or, if the consultant has requested a conference, within 30 days after the completion of the conference. HUD may extend the 30-day period by providing written notice to the consultant.

(4) If the consultant does not submit a timely written response, the removal will be effective 20 days after the date of HUD's initial removal notice (or after a longer period provided in the notice). If a written response is submitted, and the removal decision is affirmed or modified, the removal will be effective on the date of HUD's notice affirming or modifying the initial removal decision.

(c) *Placement on the list after removal.* A consultant that has been removed from the list may apply for placement on the list (in accordance with § 200.191) after the period of the consultant's removal from the list has expired. An application will be rejected if the period for the consultant's removal from the list has not expired.

(d) *Other action.* Nothing in this section prohibits HUD from taking such other action against a consultant, as provided in 2 CFR part 2424, or from seeking any other remedy against a consultant, available to HUD by statute or otherwise.

[67 FR 52380, Aug. 9, 2002, as amended at 72 FR 73494, Dec. 27, 2007]

§ 200.193 Responsibilities of 203(k) consultants on the list.

All consultants included on the list are responsible for:

(a) Obtaining and reading the HUD handbook on the 203(k) Program (4240.4) and any updates to the handbook.

(b) Complying with the HUD handbook on the 203(k) Program (4240.4), and any updates to the handbook, when performing any consultant function under the 203(k) Program.

(c) Obtaining and reading all Mortgagee Letters and other instructions issued by HUD relating to the 203(k) Program.

(d) Complying with all Mortgagee Letters and other instructions issued by HUD relating to the 203(k) Program, when undertaking any consultant function under the 203(k) Program.

(e) Complying with HUD's request for documentation relating to any 203(k) project on which the consultant has worked.

(f) Complying with HUD's monitoring requirements relating to the 203(k) Program.

[67 FR 52381, Aug. 9, 2002]

NONPROFIT ORGANIZATION

§ 200.194 Placement of nonprofit organization on Nonprofit Organization Roster.

(a) *Nonprofit Organization Roster.* HUD maintains a roster of nonprofit organizations that are qualified to participate in certain specified FHA activities. In order to be recognized as a nonprofit organization for purposes of single family regulations in this chapter, an organization must:

(1) Be included in the Roster; and

(2) Comply with any requirements stated in a specific applicable provision of the single family regulations in this chapter.

(b) *Application.* To be included in the Roster, a nonprofit organization must apply to HUD using an application (or materials) in a form prescribed by HUD (which may require an affordable housing program narrative for the activities the nonprofit organization proposes to carry out). The nonprofit organization must specify in its application the FHA activities it proposes to carry out.

(c) *HUD response to application.* HUD's review of the application will result in one of the following:

(1) Approval of the nonprofit organization to participate in all, or some, of the FHA activities specified in its application and the addition of the nonprofit organization to the Roster.

(2) Rejection due to deficiencies in the application. HUD will provide the nonprofit organization with a period to correct these deficiencies.

(3) Rejection due to the nonprofit organization's failure to submit a program that complies with applicable single family regulations in this chapter, Mortgagee Letters, or other standards or instructions issued by HUD.

(d) *Reapplication after two years.* The placement of a nonprofit organization on the Roster expires after two years. The nonprofit organization must reapply for placement on the Roster, in accordance with paragraph (b) of this section, before expiration of the two-year period.

[67 FR 39239, June 6, 2002]

§ 200.195 Removal of nonprofit organization from Nonprofit Organization Roster.

(a) *Cause for removal.* HUD may remove a nonprofit organization from the FHA Nonprofit Organization Roster established under § 200.194. Removal may be for any cause that HUD determines to be detrimental to FHA or any of its programs, including but not limited to:

(1) Failure to comply with applicable single family regulations in this chapter, Mortgagee Letters or other written instructions or standards issued by HUD;

(2) Failure to comply with applicable Civil Rights requirements;

(3) Holding a significant number of FHA-insured mortgages that are in default, foreclosure, or claim status (in determining the number considered "significant," HUD may compare the number of insured mortgages held by the nonprofit organization against the similar holdings of other nonprofit organizations);

(4) Being debarred or suspended, subject to a limited denial of participation, or otherwise sanctioned by HUD;

(5) Failure to further all objectives described in the affordable housing program narrative;

(6) Misrepresentation or fraudulent statements; or

30

(7) Failure to respond within a reasonable time to HUD inquiries, including recertification requests or other requests for further documentation.

(b) *Procedure for removal.* A nonprofit organization that is debarred or suspended or subject to a limited denial of participation will be automatically removed from the FHA Nonprofit Organization Roster. In all other cases, the following procedure for removal applies:

(1) HUD will give the nonprofit organization written notice of the proposed removal. The notice will include the reasons for the proposed removal and the duration of the proposed removal.

(2) The nonprofit organization will have 20 days from the date of the notice (or longer, if provided in the notice) to submit a written response appealing the proposed removal and to request a conference. A request for a conference must be in writing and must be submitted along with the written response.

(3) A HUD official will review the appeal and provide an informal conference if requested. The HUD official will send a response either affirming, modifying, or canceling the removal. The HUD official will not be someone who was involved in HUD's initial removal decision. HUD will respond with a decision within 30 days of receiving the response, or, if the nonprofit organization has requested a conference, within 30 days after the completion of the conference. HUD may extend the 30-day period by providing written notice to the nonprofit organization.

(4) If the nonprofit organization does not submit a timely written response, the removal will be effective 20 days after the date of HUD's initial removal notice (or after a longer period provided in the notice). If a written response is submitted, and the initial removal decision is affirmed or modified, the removal will be effective on the date of HUD's notice affirming or modifying the initial removal decision.

(c) *Placement on the Roster after removal.* A nonprofit organization that has been removed from the FHA Nonprofit Organization Roster may apply for placement on the Roster (in accordance with §200.194) after the nonprofit organization's removal from the Roster has expired. An application will be rejected if the period for the nonprofit organization's removal from the Roster has not expired.

(d) *Other action.* Nothing in this section prohibits HUD from taking such other action against a nonprofit organization, as provided in 2 CFR part 2424, or from seeking any other remedy against a nonprofit organization, available to HUD by statute or otherwise.

[67 FR 39239, June 6, 2002, as amended at 72 FR 73494, Dec. 27, 2007]

Subpart G—Appraiser Roster

Source: 64 FR 72869, Dec. 28, 1999, unless otherwise noted.

§200.200 What is the Appraiser Roster?

(a) *Appraiser Roster.* HUD maintains a list of appraisers. A mortgagee must select only an appraiser from this list for the appraisal of a property that is to be the security for an FHA-insured single family mortgage.

(b) *Disclaimer.* Since an appraisal is performed to determine the maximum insurable mortgage and to also protect the FHA insurance funds, the inclusion of an appraiser on the Appraiser Roster does not create or imply a warranty or endorsement to a prospective homebuyer or to any other organization or individual by HUD of the listed appraiser nor does it represent a warranty of any appraisal performed by the listed appraiser. The inclusion of an appraiser on the Appraiser Roster means only that a listed appraiser has met the qualifications and conditions, prescribed by the Secretary, for inclusion on the Appraiser Roster.

§200.202 How do I apply for placement on the Appraiser Roster?

(a) Application. To apply for placement on the Appraiser Roster, you must submit an application to HUD.

(b) Eligibility. To be eligible for placement on the Appraiser Roster:

(1) You must be a state-certified appraiser with credentials that complied with the applicable certification criteria established by the Appraiser Qualification Board (AQB) of the Appraisal Foundation and in effect at the

time the certification was awarded by the issuing jurisdiction; and

(2) You must not be listed on:

(i) The General Services Administration's Suspension and Debarment List;

(ii) HUD's Limited Denial of Participation List; or

(iii) HUD's Credit Alert Verification Reporting System.

[73 FR 1432, Jan. 8, 2008, as amended at 76 FR 72308, Nov. 23, 2011]

§ 200.204 What actions may HUD take against unsatisfactory appraisers on the Appraiser Roster?

An unsatisfactory appraiser may be subject to removal, education requirements, or other actions, as follows:

(a) *Removal from the Appraiser Roster.* HUD officials, as designated by the Secretary, may at any time remove a listed appraiser from the Appraiser Roster for cause, in accordance with paragraphs (a)(1) through (a)(3) of this section. The provisions of paragraphs (a)(1) through (a)(3) of this section do not apply to removal actions taken under any section in 2 CFR part 2424 or to any other remedy against an appraiser, available to HUD by statute or otherwise.

(1) *Cause for removal.* Cause for removal includes, but is not limited to:

(i) Significant deficiencies in appraisals, including non-compliance with Civil Rights requirements regarding appraisals;

(ii) Losing standing as a state-certified appraiser due to disciplinary action in any state in which the appraiser is certified;

(iii) Prosecution for committing, attempting to commit, or conspiring to commit fraud, misrepresentation, or any other offense that may reflect on the appraiser's character or integrity;

(iv) Failure to perform appraisal functions in accordance with instructions and standards issued by HUD;

(v) Failure to comply with any agreement made between the appraiser and HUD or with any certification made by the appraiser;

(vi) Being issued a final debarment, suspension, or limited denial of participation;

(vii) Failure to maintain eligibility requirements for placement on the Appraiser Roster as set forth under this subpart or any other instructions or standards issued by HUD; or,

(viii) Failure to comply with HUD-imposed education requirements under paragraph (d) of this section within the specified period for complying with such education requirements.

(2) *Procedure for removal.* If you are a listed appraiser and HUD decides to remove you for cause from the Appraiser Roster, the following procedure applies to you unless you have been issued a final debarment, suspension, or limited denial of participation, in which case you are subject to paragraph (a)(3) of this section:

(i) You will be given written notice of your proposed removal. The notice will include the reasons for your proposed removal and the duration of your proposed removal.

(ii) You will have 20 days from the date of your notice of proposed removal to submit a written response appealing the proposed removal and to request a conference. A request for a conference must be in writing and must be submitted along with a written response.

(iii) Within 30 days of receiving your written response, or if you have requested a conference, within 30 days after the completion of your conference, a HUD official, designated by the Secretary, will review your appeal and will send you a final decision either affirming, modifying, or canceling your removal from the Appraiser Roster. HUD may extend this time upon giving you notice. The HUD official designated by the Secretary to review your appeal will not be someone involved in HUD's initial removal decision nor will it be someone who reports to a person involved in that initial decision.

(iv) If you do not submit a written response, your removal will be effective 20 days after the date of HUD's initial removal notice. If you submit a written response, and the removal decision is affirmed or modified, your removal or modification will be effective on the date of HUD's notice affirming or modifying the initial removal decision.

(3) *Automatic removal for issuance of final debarment, suspension, or limited denial of participation.* If you are a listed appraiser and you have been issued a final debarment, a suspension, or a

limited denial of participation, the provisions of paragraph (a)(2) of this section do not apply to you, and you will be automatically removed from the Appraiser Roster.

(b) *Reinstatement.* If an appraiser who has been removed from the Roster wants to be reinstated on the Roster, the appraiser must follow the procedures and requirements contained in this subpart for placement on the Roster. Before an appraiser is eligible to reapply for placement on the Roster, the appraiser shall comply with the terms of any applicable remedial training education requirements, and the time period for the appraiser's removal from the Roster shall have expired.

(c) *Automatic suspension from Appraiser Roster*—(1) *Appraisers subject to state disciplinary action.* An appraiser whose state certification in any state has been revoked, suspended, or surrendered as a result of a state disciplinary action is automatically suspended from the Appraiser Roster and prohibited from conducting FHA appraisals in any state until HUD receives evidence demonstrating that the state-imposed sanction has been lifted.

(2) *Expirations not due to state disciplinary action.* An appraiser whose certification in a state has expired is automatically suspended from the Appraiser Roster in that state and may not conduct FHA appraisals in that state until HUD receives evidence that demonstrates renewal, but may continue to perform FHA appraisals in other states in which the appraiser is certified.

(d) *Education requirements.* Where there is evidence that an appraiser is deficient in FHA appraisal requirements, HUD may require an appraiser to undergo professional training.

(e) *Other action.* Nothing in this section prohibits HUD from taking any other action against an appraiser, as provided under 2 CFR part 2424, or from seeking any other remedy against an appraiser, available to HUD by statute or otherwise.

[65 FR 17977, Apr. 5, 2000, as amended at 68 FR 26950, May 16, 2003; 72 FR 73494, Dec. 27, 2007; 73 FR 1432, Jan. 8, 2008; 76 FR 72308, Nov. 23, 2011]

§ 200.206 What are my responsibilities as an appraiser listed on the Appraiser Roster?

All appraisers listed on the Appraiser Roster are responsible for:

(a) Obtaining and reading the HUD Appraiser Handbook (4150.2) and any updates to the Handbook;

(b) Complying with the HUD Appraiser Handbook (4150.2), and any updates to the Handbook, when performing all appraisals of properties for HUD single family mortgage insurance purposes; and

(c) Complying with all other instructions and standards issued by HUD when performing all appraisals of properties for HUD single family mortgage insurance purposes.

Subpart H—Participation and Compliance Requirements

SOURCE: 81 FR 71263, Oct. 14, 2016, unless otherwise noted.

§ 200.210 Policy.

(a) *Regulations.* It is HUD's policy that, in accordance with the intent of the National Housing Act (12 U.S.C. 1701 *et seq.*), and with other applicable federal statutes, participants in HUD's housing and healthcare programs be responsible individuals and organizations who will honor their legal, financial and contractual obligations. Accordingly, as provided in this subpart, HUD will review the prior participation of Controlling Participants, as defined in §200.212 and §200.216, as a prerequisite to participation in HUD's multifamily housing and healthcare programs listed in §200.214.

(b) *Processing Guide.* The regulations in this subpart are supplemented by the Processing Guide for Previous Participation Reviews of Prospective Multifamily Housing and Healthcare Programs' Participants (Guide), which is found on HUD's Web site at *www.hud.gov.* This Guide elaborates on the basic procedures involved in the previous participation review process. For any significant changes made to this Guide, HUD will provide advance notice and the opportunity to comment, providing a comment period of no less than 30 days.

§ 200.212 Definitions.

As used in this subpart:

Commissioner means the Assistant Secretary for Housing-Federal Housing Commissioner, or the Commissioner's delegates and designees.

Controlling Participant means an individual or entity serving in a capacity for a Covered Project that makes the individual or entity subject to Previous Participation review under this subpart, as further described in § 200.216.

Covered Project means a project in which the participation of a Controlling Participant is conditioned on Previous Participation review under this subpart, as further described in § 200.214.

Previous Participation means a Controlling Participant's previous participation in Covered Projects, and, if applicable, other federal, state and local housing programs, in accordance with the definition of Risk.

Risk. In order to determine whether a Controlling Participant's participation in a project would constitute an unacceptable risk, the Commissioner must determine whether the Controlling Participant could be expected to participate in the Covered Project in a manner consistent with furthering the Department's purposes. The Commissioner's review of Previous Participation shall consider compliance with applicable statutes, regulations and program requirements. The Commissioner must consider the Controlling Participant's previous financial and operational performance in Covered Projects that may indicate a financial or operating risk in approving the Controlling Participant's participation in the subject Triggering Event. At the Commissioner's discretion, as necessary to determine financial or operating risk and to the extent the Commissioner determines such information to be reliably available, the Commissioner may consider the Controlling Participant's participation and performance in any federal, state or local government program. The Commissioner may exclude any Previous Participation the Commissioner determines to be of limited value, unreliable or irrelevant in evaluating risk and/or any Previous Participation in which the Controlling Participant did not exercise, actually or constructively, control. Any information collection in connection with review of Previous Participation must follow all applicable requirements for information collection.

Triggering Event means an occurrence in connection with a Covered Project that subjects a Controlling Participant to Previous Participation review under this subpart, as further described in § 200.218.

§ 200.214 Covered Projects.

The following types of multifamily and healthcare projects are Covered Projects subject to the requirements of this subpart, provided however that single family projects are excluded from the definition of Covered Projects:

(a) *FHA insured projects.* A project financed or which is proposed to be financed with a mortgage insured under the National Housing Act, a project subject to a mortgage held by the Secretary under the National Housing Act, or a project acquired by the Secretary under the National Housing Act.

(b) *Housing for the elderly or persons with disabilities.* Housing for the elderly financed or to be financed with direct loans or capital advances under section 202 of the Housing Act of 1959, as amended; and housing for persons with disabilities under section 811 of the Cranston-Gonzalez National Affordable Housing Act.

(c) *Risk Share projects.* A project that is insured under section 542(b) or 542(c) of the Housing and Community Development Act of 1992(12 U.S.C. 17107 note).

(d) *Projects subject to continuing HUD requirements.* A project that is subject to a use agreement or any other affordability restrictions pursuant to a program administered by HUD's Office of Housing.

(e) *Subsidized Projects.* Any project in which 20 percent or more of the units now receive or will receive a subsidy in the form of:

(1) Interest reduction payments under section 236 of the National Housing Act (12 U.S.C. 1715z–1);

(2) Rental Assistance Payments under section 236 of the National Housing Act (12 U.S.C. 1715z–1);

(3) Rent Supplement payments under section 101 of the Housing and Urban Development Act of 1965 (12 U.S.C. 1701s); or

(4) Project-based housing assistance payment contracts under section 8 of the United States Housing Act of 1937 (42 U.S.C. 1437f) administered by HUD's Office of Housing.

§ 200.216 Controlling Participants.

(a) *Definition.* Controlling Participants are those entities and individuals (i) serving as a Specified Capacity with respect to a Covered Project and (ii) the entities and individuals in control of the Specified Capacities. Each of the following capacities for a Covered Project is a "Specified Capacity:"

(1) An owner of a Covered Project;

(2) A borrower of a loan financing a Covered Project;

(3) A management agent;

(4) An operator (in connection with healthcare projects insured under the following section of the National Housing Act: Section 232 (12 U.S.C. 1715w) and section 242 (12 U.S.C. 1715z–7));

(5) A master tenant (in connection with any multifamily housing project insured under the National Housing Act (12 U.S.C. 1701 *et seq.*) and in connection with certain healthcare projects insured under sections 232 or section 242 of the National Housing Act);

(6) A general contractor; and

(7) In connection with a hospital project insured under section 242 of the National Housing Act (12 U.S.C. 1715z–7), a construction manager;

(b) *Control of entities.* To the extent any Specified Capacity listed in paragraph (a) of this section is an entity, any individual(s) or entities determined by HUD to control the financial or operational decisions of such Specified Capacity shall also be considered Controlling Participants. Without limiting the foregoing and unless otherwise determined by HUD, the following individuals or entities shall be considered Controlling Participants:

(1) Individuals or entities with the ability to direct the day-to-day operations of a Specified Capacity or a Covered Project;

(2) Individuals or entities that own at least 25 percent of an entity that is a Specified Capacity;

(3) Individuals or entities with the ability to direct the entity to enter into agreements relating to the Triggering Event that necessitates review of Previous Participation, including without limitation individuals or entities that own at least 25 percent of entities determined to control an entity that is a Specified Capacity; and

(4) In connection with a hospital project insured under section 242 of the National Housing Act (12 U.S.C. 1715z–7), members of a hospital Board of Directors (or similar body) and executive management (such as the Chief Executive Officer and Chief Financial Officer) that HUD determines to have control over the finances or operation of a Covered Project.

(c) *Exclusions from definition.* The following individuals or entities are not Controlling Participants for purposes of this subpart:

(1) Passive investors and investor entities with limited liability in Covered Projects benefiting from tax credits, including but not limited to low-income housing tax credits pursuant to section 42 of title 26 of the United States Code, whether such investors are syndicators, direct investors or investors in such syndicators and/or investors;

(2) Individuals or entities that do not exercise financial or operational control over the Covered Project, a Specified Capacity or another Controlling Participant;

(3) Unless determined by HUD to exercise day-to-day control over the operations or finances of a Specified Capacity or Covered Project, board members of a non-profit corporation who are not officers or otherwise part of the executive management teams of the non-profit;

(4) Mortgagees acting in their capacity as such; and

(5) Public housing agencies (PHAs).

§ 200.218 Triggering Events.

(a) Each of the following is a Triggering Event that may subject a Controlling Participant to Previous Participation review under § 200.220:

35

(1) An application for FHA mortgage insurance;

(2) An application for funds provided by HUD pursuant to a program administered by HUD's Office of Housing, such as but not limited to supplemental loans;

(3) A request to change any Controlling Participant for which HUD consent is required with respect to a Covered Project; or

(4) A request for consent to an assignment of a housing assistance payment contract under section 8 of the United States Housing Act of 1937 or of another contract pursuant to which a Controlling Participant will receive funds in connection with a Covered Project.

(b) The Commissioner may also require a review of a potential owner's Previous Participation in connection with a loan sale or other form of property disposition, including foreclosure sale. Notwithstanding anything contained in the regulations in this subpart to the contrary, any such review shall be in accordance with the terms, conditions, provisions and other requirements set forth by the Commissioner in connection with such loan sale or property disposition which may differ, in whole or in part, from the regulations in this subpart.

§ 200.220 Previous Participation review.

(a) *Scope of review.* (1) Upon the occurrence of a Triggering Event, as provided in § 200.218, the Commissioner shall review the Previous Participation of the relevant Controlling Participants in considering whether to approve the participation of the Controlling Participants in connection with the Triggering Event in accordance with the definition of Risk in § 200.212.

(2) The Commissioner will not review Previous Participation for interests acquired by inheritance or by court decree.

(3) In connection with the submittal of an application for any Triggering Event, applicants shall identify the Controlling Participants and, to the extent requested by HUD, make available to HUD the Controlling Participant's Previous Participation in Covered Projects.

(b) *Results of review.* (1) Based upon the review under paragraph (a) of this section, the Commissioner will approve, disapprove, limit, or otherwise condition the continued participation of the Controlling Participant in the Triggering Event, in accordance with paragraphs (c) and (d) of this section.

(2) The Commissioner shall provide notice of the determination to the Controlling Participant including the reasons for disapproval or limitation. The Commissioner may provide notice of the determination to other parties as well, such the FHA-approved lender in the transaction.

(c) *Basis for disapproval.* (1) The Commissioner must disapprove a Controlling Participant if the Commissioner determines that the Controlling Participant is suspended, debarred or subject to other restriction pursuant to 2 CFR part 180 or 2 CFR part 2424;

(2) The Commissioner may disapprove a Controlling Participant if the Commissioner determines:

(i) The Controlling Participant is materially restricted, including voluntarily, from doing business with HUD (other than the restrictions listed in paragraph (c)(1) of this section) or any other governmental department or agency if the Commissioner determines that such restriction demonstrates a significant risk to proceeding with the Triggering Event; or

(ii) The Controlling Participant's record of Previous Participation reveals significant risk to proceeding with the Triggering Event.

(d) *Alternatives to disapproval.* In lieu of disapproval, the Commissioner may:

(1) Condition or limit the Controlling Participant's participation;

(2) Temporarily withhold issuing a determination in order to gather more necessary information; or

(3) Require the Controlling Participant to remedy or mitigate outstanding violations of HUD requirements to the Commissioner's satisfaction in order to participate in the Triggering Event.

§ 200.222 Request for reconsideration.

(a) Where participation in a Triggering Event has been disapproved, otherwise limited or conditioned because of Previous Participation review, the Controlling Participant may request reconsideration of such determination by a review committee or reviewing officer as established by the Commissioner. Reconsideration decisions shall not be rendered by the same individual who rendered the initial review.

(b) The Controlling Participant shall submit requests for such reconsideration in writing within 30 days of receipt of the Commissioner's notice of the determination under §200.220.

(c) The review committee or reviewing officer shall schedule a review of such requests for reconsideration. The Controlling Participant shall be provided written notification of such a review; such notice shall provide at least 7 business days advanced notice of the reconsideration. The Controlling Participant shall be provided the opportunity to submit such supporting materials as the Controlling Participant desires or as the review committee or reviewing officer requests.

(d) Before making its decision, the review committee or reviewing officer will analyze the reasons for the decision(s) for which reconsideration is being requested, as well as the documents and arguments presented by the Controlling Participant. The review committee or reviewing officer may affirm, modify, or reverse the initial decision. Upon making its decision, the review committee or reviewing officer will provide written notice of its determination to the Controlling Participant setting forth the reasons for the determination(s).

Subpart I—Nondiscrimination and Fair Housing

§200.300 Nondiscrimination and fair housing policy.

Federal Housing Administration programs shall be administered in accordance with:

(a) The nondiscrimination and fair housing requirements set forth in 24 CFR part 5, including the prohibition on inquiries regarding sexual orientation or gender identity set forth in 24 CFR 5.105(a)(2); and

(b) The affirmative fair housing marketing requirements in 24 CFR part 200, subpart M and 24 CFR part 108.

[77 FR 5675, Feb. 3, 2012]

Subpart J—Equal Employment Opportunity

§200.400 Purpose.

The purpose of this subpart is to assist in achieving the aims of part III of Executive Order 11246 and the relevant regulations of the Secretary of Labor and the Secretary of Housing and Urban Development.

§200.405 Notice to public.

Participants in insurance programs under the National Housing Act shall be informed, as early as possible upon indicating their interest in any such program, of the established policy of nondiscrimination in employment in construction, repair or rehabilitation work financed with assistance under the Act.

§200.410 Definition of term "applicant".

(a) In any mortgage or loan insurance transaction under this chapter where the Commissioner will control the mortgagor either through the ownership of corporate stock or under the provisions of a regulatory agreement, the term *applicant* as used in §200.415 shall mean the mortgagor.

(b) In any transaction other than one specified in paragraph (a) of this section, the term *applicant* as used in §200.415 shall mean the developer, or the builder, dealer or contractor performing the construction, repair or rehabilitation work for the property owner.

§200.415 Agreement of applicant.

An applicant, prior to the Commissioner's issuance of any commitment or other loan approval, shall agree (in a form prescribed by the Commissioner) that there shall be no discrimination against anyone who is employed in carrying out work receiving assistance pursuant to this chapter, or against an applicant for such employment, because of race, color, religion, sex, handicap, age, or national origin.

[58 FR 41000, July 30, 1993]

§ 200.420 Equal opportunity clause to be included in contracts and subcontracts.

(a) The equal opportunity clause prescribed by the Commissioner pursuant to the regulations of the Secretary of Labor (41 CFR chapter 60) shall be included in each nonexempt contract and subcontract for work receiving FHA assistance.

(b) Subcontracts less than $50,000 may incorporate by reference the equal opportunity clause.

(c) The equal opportunity clause shall be deemed to be a part of each nonexempt contract or subcontract whether or not it is physically incorporated in such contract.

§ 200.425 Exemptions.

(a) *Transactions of $10,000 or under.* Contracts and subcontracts not exceeding $10,000 are exempt from the requirements of the equal opportunity clause. No contractor or subcontractor shall procure supplies or services in less than usual quantities to avoid applicability of the equal opportunity clause.

(b) *Contracts and subcontracts for indefinite quantities.* Contracts and subcontracts for indefinite quantities are exempt from the requirements of the equal opportunity clause if the amount to be ordered in a single year under any such contract will not exceed $10,000.

(c) *Work outside the United States.* Contracts and subcontracts with regard to work performed outside the United States by employees who were not recruited within the United States are exempt from the requirements of the equal opportunity clause.

(d) *Others.* Other exemptions set forth in the regulations of the Secretary of Labor at 41 CFR 60–1.5 apply to transactions under this subpart.

§ 200.430 Sanctions.

Failure or refusal to comply and give satisfactory assurances of future compliance with the requirements of this subpart shall be proper basis for applying sanctions. The sanctions shall be applied in accordance with the provisions of Executive Order 11246 and the relevant regulations of the Secretary of Labor.

Subparts K–L [Reserved]

Subpart M—Affirmative Fair Housing Marketing Regulations

SOURCE: 37 FR 75, Jan. 5, 1972, unless otherwise noted.

§ 200.600 Purpose.

The purpose of this subpart is to set forth the Department's equal opportunity regulations for affirmative fair housing marketing under FHA subsidized and unsubsidized housing programs.

§ 200.605 Authority.

The regulations in this subpart are issued pursuant to the authority to issue regulations granted to the Secretary by section 7(d) of the Department of Housing and Urban Development Act of 1965, 42 U.S.C. 3535(d), and implement the functions, powers, and duties imposed on the Secretary by Executive Order 11063, 27 FR 11527, and title VIII of the Civil Rights Act of 1968, as amended, 42 U.S.C. 3608.

[40 FR 20080, May 8, 1975]

§ 200.610 Policy.

It is the policy of the Department to administer its FHA housing programs affirmatively, as to achieve a condition in which individuals of similar income levels in the same housing market area have a like range of housing choices available to them regardless of their race, color, religion, sex, handicap, familial status or national origin. Each applicant for participation in FHA subsidized and unsubsidized housing programs shall pursue affirmative fair housing marketing policies in soliciting buyers and tenants, in determining their eligibility, and in concluding sales and rental transactions.

[40 FR 20080, May 8, 1975, as amended at 58 FR 41337, Aug. 3, 1993]

§200.615 Applicability.

The affirmative fair housing marketing requirements, as set forth in paragraphs (a) through (f) of §200.620, shall apply to all applicants for participation in FHA subsidized and unsubsidized housing programs whose application is hereafter approved for development or rehabilitation of:

(a) Multifamily projects and manufactured home parks of five or more lots, units or spaces, and initial submissions by a lender for an application for mortgage insurance on a single family property, where the property is located in a subdivision and the builder or developer intends to sell five or more properties in the subdivision; or

(b) Dwelling units, when the applicant's participation in FHA housing programs had exceeded or would thereby exceed development of five or more such dwelling units during the year preceding the application, except that there shall not be included in a determination of the number of dwelling units developed by an applicant those in which a single family dwelling is constructed or rehabilitated for occupancy by a mortgagor on property owned by the mortgagor and in which the applicant had no interest prior to entering into the contract for construction or rehabilitation.

[37 FR 75, Jan. 5, 1972, as amended at 50 FR 9268, Mar. 7, 1985; 58 FR 41337, Aug. 3, 1993]

§200.620 Requirements.

With respect to all FHA subsidized or unsubsidized programs in which the applicant hereafter participates (except for housing for which a conditional commitment has been issued prior to the effective date of these regulations), the applicant shall meet the following requirements or, if he contracts marketing responsibility to another party, be responsible for that party's carrying out the requirements:

(a) Carry out an affirmative program to attract buyers or tenants, regardless of sex, handicap or familial status, of all minority and majority groups to the housing for initial sale or rental. An affirmative marketing program shall be in effect for each multifamily project throughout the life of the mortgage. Such a program shall typically involve publicizing to minority persons the availability of housing opportunities regardless of race, color, religion, sex, handicap or familial status or national origin, through the type of media customarily utilized by the applicant, including minority publications or other minority outlets which are available in the housing market area. All advertising shall include either the Department-approved Equal Housing Opportunity logo or slogan or statement and all advertising depicting persons shall depict persons of majority and minority groups, including both sexes.

(b) Maintain a nondiscriminatory hiring policy in recruiting from both minority and majority groups, including both sexes and the handicapped, for staff engaged in the sale or rental of properties.

(c) Instruct all employees and agents in writing and orally in the policy of nondiscrimination and fair housing.

(d) Specifically solicit eligible buyers or tenants reported to the applicant by the Area or Insuring Office.

(e) Prominently display in all offices in which sale or rental activity pertaining to the project or subdivision takes place the Department-approved Fair Housing Poster and include in any printed material used in connection with sales or rentals, the Department-approved Equal Housing Opportunity logo or slogan or statement.

(f) Post in a conspicuous position on all FHA project sites a sign displaying prominently either the Department-approved Equal Housing Opportunity logo or slogan or statement.

[37 FR 75, Jan. 5, 1972, as amended at 40 FR 20080, May 8, 1975; 40 FR 53008, Nov. 14, 1975; 58 FR 41337, Aug. 3, 1993]

§200.625 Affirmative fair housing marketing plan.

Each applicant for participation in FHA housing programs to which these regulations apply shall provide on a form to be supplied by the Department information indicating his affirmative fair housing marketing plan to comply with the requirements set forth in §200.620. This form, once approved by HUD, will be available for public inspection at the sales or rental offices of the applicant.

§ 200.630 Notice of housing opportunities.

The Director of each Field Office shall prepare monthly a list of all projects covered by this subpart, and of all initial submissions by lenders for single family mortgage insurance where the property is located in a subdivision and the builder or developer intends to sell five or more properties in the subdivision, on which commitments have been issued during the preceding 30 days. The Director shall maintain a roster of interested organizations and individuals (including public agencies responsible for providing relocation assistance and local housing authorities) who have expressed a wish to receive the monthly list, and shall provide the list to these organizations and individuals.

[58 FR 41337, Aug. 3, 1993]

§ 200.635 Compliance.

Applicants failing to comply with the requirements of this subpart will make themselves liable to sanctions authorized by regulations, rules or policies governing the program pursuant to which the application was made, including but not limited to denial of further participation in departmental programs and referral to the Department of Justice for suit by the United States for injunctive or other appropriate relief. The Department will enforce compliance through the procedures outlined in 24 CFR part 108.

[37 FR 75, Jan. 5, 1972, as amended at 58 FR 41337, Aug. 3, 1993]

§ 200.640 Effect on other requirements.

The requirement for compliance with this part is in addition to, and not in substitution for, any other requirements imposed by or under Executive Order 11063 or the Fair Housing Act.

[58 FR 41337, Aug. 3, 1993]

APPENDIX TO SUBPART M OF PART 200— EQUAL HOUSING OPPORTUNITY INSIGNIA

The Equal Housing Opportunity insignia are as follows:

Equal Housing Opportunity logo:

EQUAL HOUSING OPPORTUNITY

Equal Housing Opportunity statement: "We are pledged to the letter and spirit of U.S. policy for the achievement of equal housing opportunity throughout the Nation. We encourage and support an affirmative advertising and marketing program in which there are no barriers to obtaining housing because of race, color, religion, sex, or national origin."

Equal Housing Opportunity slogan: "Equal Housing Opportunity."

[37 FR 75, Jan. 5, 1972, as amended at 40 FR 20080, May 8, 1975]

Subpart N [Reserved]

Subpart O—Lead-Based Paint Poisoning Prevention

SOURCE: 64 FR 50224, Sept. 15, 1999, unless otherwise noted.

§ 200.800 Lead-based paint.

The Lead-Based Paint Poisoning Prevention Act (42 U.S.C. 4821–4846), the Residential Lead-Based Paint Hazard Reduction Act of 1992 (42 U.S.C. 4851–4856), and implementing regulations at part 35, subparts A, B, F, G, I, and R of this title, apply to activities under these programs, except for single family mortgage insurance and guarantee programs. Sections 200.805 and 200.810 apply to single family mortgage insurance and guarantee programs administered by HUD.

§200.805 Definitions.

Applicable surface. All intact and non-intact interior and exterior painted surfaces of a residential structure.

Defective paint surface. Paint on applicable surfaces that is cracking, scaling, chipping, peeling or loose.

Lead-based paint surface. A paint surface, whether or not defective, identified as having a lead content greater than or equal to 1 mg/cm².

§200.810 Single family insurance and coinsurance.

(a) *General.* (1) The requirements of this section apply to any one-to four-family dwelling which was constructed before 1978 and is the subject of an application for mortgage insurance under section 203(b) or other sections of the National Housing Act relating to the insurance or coinsurance of mortgages on one-to-four-family dwellings. Such other sections include:

(i) Section 244 (coinsurance);

(ii) Section 213 (cooperative housing insurance);

(iii) Section 220 (rehabilitation and neighborhood conservation housing insurance);

(iv) Section 221 (housing for moderate income and displaced families);

(v) Section 222 (mortgagor insurance for servicemen);

(vi) Section 809 (armed services housing for civilian employees);

(vii) Section 810 (armed services housing in impacted areas);

(viii) Section 234 (mortgage insurance for condominiums);

(ix) Section 235 (mortgage assistance payments for home ownership and project rehabilitation);

(x) Section 237 (special mortgage insurance for low and moderate income families); and

(xi) Section 240 (mortgage insurance on loans for purchase of fee simple title from lessors).

(2) [Reserved]

(3) Applications for insurance in connection with a refinancing transaction where an appraisal is not required under the applicable procedures established by the Commissioner are excluded from the coverage of this section. Any housing assisted under the programs set out in this section for which no new activity is applied for or required is not covered by this section.

(b) *Appraisal.* The appraiser shall, when appraising a dwelling constructed prior to 1978, inspect the dwelling for defective paint surfaces.

(c) *Treatment of defective paint surfaces.* For defective paint surfaces, treatment shall be provided to defective areas. Treatment of hazards shall consist of covering or removing defective paint surfaces. Covering may be accomplished by such means as adding a layer of wallboard to the wall surface. Depending on the wall condition, wallcoverings which are permanently attached may be used. Covering or replacing trim surfaces is also permitted. Paint removal may be accomplished by such methods as scraping, heat treatment (infra-red or coil type heat guns) or chemicals. Machine sanding and use of propane or gasoline torches (open-flame methods) are not permitted. Washing and repainting without thorough removal or covering does not constitute adequate treatment. In the case of defective paint spots, scraping and repainting the defective area is considered adequate treatment. Treatment of a defective paint surface is not required if such a surface is found to not be a lead-based paint surface by a lead-based paint inspector certified pursuant to procedures of the U.S. Environmental Protection Agency at 40 CFR part 745.

(d) *Home equity conversion mortgage insurance.* The requirements of this section, as modified by the following sentence, apply to a dwelling which is the subject of an application for mortgage insurance under section 255 of the National Housing Act (home equity conversion insurance) unless the mortgagor provides the certification described in §206.45(d) of this title. The defective paint surface may be treated after the mortgage is endorsed for insurance, provided that the defective paint surface is treated as expeditiously as possible in accordance with the repair work provisions contained in §206.47 of this title.

[64 FR 50224, Sept. 15, 1999, as amended at 69 FR 34275, June 21, 2004]

Subpart P—Physical Condition of Multifamily Properties

SOURCE: 65 FR 77240, Dec. 8, 2000, unless otherwise noted.

§ 200.850 Purpose.

The purpose of this subpart is to establish the physical conditions standards and physical inspection requirements that are applicable to certain multifamily housing properties.

§ 200.853 Applicability.

This subpart applies to:

(a) Housing assisted by HUD under the following programs:

(1) All Section 8 project-based assistance. "Project-based assistance" means Section 8 assistance that is attached to the structure (see 24 CFR 982.1(b)(1) regarding the distinction between "project-based" and "tenant-based" assistance);

(2) Section 202 Program of Supportive Housing for the Elderly (Capital Advances);

(3) Section 811 Program of Supportive Housing for Persons with Disabilities (Capital Advances); and

(4) Section 202 loan program for projects for the elderly and handicapped (including 202/8 projects and 202/162 projects).

(b) Housing with mortgages insured or held by HUD, or housing that is receiving insurance from HUD, under the following authorities:

(1) Section 207 of the National Housing Act (NHA) (12 U.S.C. 1701 *et seq.*) (Rental Housing Insurance);

(2) Section 213 of the NHA (Cooperative Housing Insurance);

(3) Section 220 of the NHA (Rehabilitation and Neighborhood Conservation Housing Insurance);

(4) Section 221(d)(3) of the NHA (Market Interest Rate (MIR) Program);

(5) Section 221(d)(3) and (5) of the NHA (Below Market Interest Rate (BMIR) Program);

(6) Section 221(d)(4) of the NHA (Housing for Moderate Income and Displaced Families);

(7) Section 231 of the NHA (Housing for Elderly Persons);

(8) Section 232 of the NHA (Mortgage Insurance for Nursing Homes, Intermediate Care Facilities, Assisted Living Facilities, Board and Care Homes);

(9) Section 234(d) of the NHA (Rental) (Mortgage Insurance for Condominiums);

(10) Section 236 of the NHA (Rental and Cooperative Housing for Lower Income Families);

(11) Section 241 of the NHA (Supplemental Loans for Multifamily Projects). (Where, however, the primary mortgage of a Section 241 property is insured or assisted by HUD under a program covered in this part, the coverage by two HUD programs does not trigger two inspections); and

(12) Section 542(c) of the Housing and Community Development Act of 1992 (12 U.S.C. 1707 note) (Housing Finance Agency Risk Sharing Program).

§ 200.855 Physical condition standards and physical inspection requirements.

(a) *Applicable standards and requirements.* The physical condition standards and physical inspection requirements in 24 CFR part 5, subpart G, are applicable to the properties assisted or insured that are listed in § 200.853.

(b) *Entity responsible for inspection of property.* The regulations that govern the programs listed in § 200.853, or regulatory agreements or contracts, identify the entity responsible for conducting the physical inspection of the property which is HUD, the lender or the owner. For properties with more than one HUD insured loan, only the first mortgage lender is required to conduct the physical inspection. The second mortgage lender will be provided a copy of the physical inspection report by the first mortgage lender.

(c) *Timing of inspections.* (1) For a property subject to an annual inspection under this subpart, the inspection shall be conducted no earlier than 9 months and no later than 15 months from the date of the last required inspection. In no event, however, shall the physical inspection be conducted after the end of the calendar year following the one year anniversary date of the last required inspection.

(2) For a property subject to an inspection every two years under this subpart, the inspection shall be conducted no earlier than 21 months and

no later than 27 months from the date of the last required inspection. In no event, however, shall the physical inspection be conducted after the end of the calendar year following the two year anniversary date of the last required inspection.

(3) For a property subject to an inspection every three years under this subpart, the inspection shall be conducted no earlier than 33 months and no later than 39 months from the date of the last required inspection. In no event, however, shall the physical inspection be conducted after the end of the calendar year following the three year anniversary date of the last required inspection.

(4) For a newly endorsed multifamily property, the first inspection required under this subpart will be conducted no earlier than 21 months but not later than 27 months from the date of final endorsement. In no event, however, shall the inspection be conducted after the end of the calendar year following the two year anniversary date of final endorsement.

(5)(i) For assisted-living facilities, board and care facilities, and intermediate care facilities, the initial inspection required under this subpart will be conducted within the same time restrictions set forth in paragraph (c)(4) of this section, and any further inspections will be conducted at a frequency determined consistent with §200.857, except that HUD may exempt such facilities from physical inspections under this part if HUD determines that the State or local government has a reliable and adequate inspection system in place, with the results of the inspection being readily and timely available to HUD; and

(ii) For any other Section 232 facilities, the inspection will be conducted only when and if HUD determines, on the basis of information received, such as through a complaint, site inspection, or referral by a State agency, on a case-by-case basis, that inspection of a particular facility is needed to assure protection of the residents or the adequate preservation of the project.

[65 FR 77240, Dec. 8, 2000, as amended at 77 FR 55135, Sept. 7, 2012]

§200.857 Administrative process for scoring and ranking the physical condition of multifamily housing properties.

(a) *Scoring and ranking of the physical condition of multifamily housing properties.* (1) HUD's Real Estate Assessment Center (REAC) will score and rank the physical condition of certain multifamily housing insured properties listed in §200.853 in accordance with the procedures described in this section. The physical condition inspection of the property, upon which REAC bases its score and ranking, is conducted by the responsible entity in accordance with §200.855.

(2) Depending upon the results of its physical condition inspection, a multifamily housing property will be assigned one of three designations—standard 1 performing, standard 2 performing and standard 3 performing—in accordance with the ranking process described in paragraph (b) of this section.

(b) *Methodology for Ranking.* (1) Multifamily housing properties will be ranked in accordance with the methodology provided in this paragraph (b). Multifamily housing properties are scored on the basis of a 100 point scale. Because scores may include fractions, a score that includes a fraction below one half point will be rounded to the next lower full point and a score that includes a fraction of one half point or higher will be rounded to the next higher full point (*e.g.*, 89.4 will be rounded to 89, 89.5 will be rounded to 90).

(i) *Standard 1 Performing Property.* If a property receives a score of 90 points or higher on its physical condition inspection, the property will be designated a standard 1 performing property. Properties designated as standard 1 performing properties will be required to undergo a physical inspection once every three (3) years.

(ii) *Standard 2 Performing Property.* If a property receives a score of 80 points or higher but less than 90 on its physical condition inspection, the property will be designated a standard 2 performing property. Properties designated as standard 2 performing properties will be required to undergo a physical inspection once every two (2) years.

(iii) *Standard 3 Performing Property.* If a property receives a score of less than 80 points, the property will be designated a standard 3 performing property. Properties designated as standard 3 performing properties will continue to undergo an annual physical inspection as currently required under covered HUD programs.

(2) Owners of multifamily housing properties scoring in a standard 1 or standard 2 range which have been cited by the REAC as having a Exigent Health and Safety (EHS) deficiency(s) must resolve the deficiency(s), as required by paragraph (c)(2) of this section, to be classified as standard 1 and standard 2 properties.

(3) Regardless of the performance designation assigned to an owner's property, an owner is obligated to maintain its property in accordance with HUD's uniform physical condition standards as required by 24 CFR part 5, subpart G, the Regulatory Agreement and/or the Housing Assistance Payment (HAP) Contract. Good management principles require an owner to conduct routine inspections of its projects, develop improvement plans, and again, maintain its property to meet the standard of decent, safe, sanitary and in good repair.

(c) *Owner's review of physical inspection report and identification of objectively verifiable and material error.* (1) Upon completion of a physical inspection of a multifamily housing property, the REAC will provide the owner or owner's representative, on the date of the physical inspection, notice of any items classified as EHS deficiencies. REAC also will provide the owner with the entire physical inspection report (electronically through the internet or by mail approximately 10 working days from the date of the report), which provides the physical inspection results and other information relevant to the inspection, including any items classified as EHS deficiencies and already provided to the owner, on the date of the inspection (EHS deficiencies are relayed by the inspector on the date of the inspection).

(2) The owner must carefully review the physical inspection report, particu-

larly those items classified as EHS. The owner is also responsible for conducting its own survey of the total project based on the REAC's physical inspection findings. The owner must mitigate all EHS items immediately, and the owner must file a written report with the applicable Multifamily Hub Director within 3 business days of the date of the inspection, which is the date the owner was provided with the EHS notice. The report filed by the owner must provide a certification and reasonable evidence that the EHS items have been resolved.

(3) If, following review of the physical inspection results and score, the owner reasonably believes that an objectively verifiable and material error (or errors) occurred in the inspection, which, if corrected, will result in a significant improvement in the property's overall score ("significant improvement" is defined in paragraph (d)(4) of this section), the owner may submit a written request for a technical review. The technical review request must be received in writing no later than 30 calendar days (as established by the postmark, if applicable) from the date the physical inspection results are transmitted to the owner by REAC, whether the results and score are transmitted to the owner via the Internet or by hard copy via certified mail.

(d) *Technical review of physical inspection results.* A request for a technical review of physical inspection results must be submitted in writing to REAC and must be received by REAC no later than the 30th calendar day, as applicable under paragraph (c)(3) of this section, following submission of the physical inspection report to the owner, as provided in paragraph (c)(1) of this section.

(1) *Request for technical review.* The request must be accompanied by the owner's reasonable evidence that an objectively verifiable and material error (or errors) occurred which if corrected will result in a significant improvement in the overall score of the owner's property. A technical review of physical inspection results will not be conducted based on conditions that were corrected subsequent to the inspection. Upon receipt of this request from the owner, the REAC will review

the physical inspection and the owner's evidence. If the REAC's review determines that an objectively verifiable and material error (or errors) has been documented and that it is likely to result in a significant improvement in the property's overall score, the REAC will take one or a combination of the following actions: undertake a new inspection; correct the original inspection; or issue a new physical condition score.

(2) *Burden of proof that error occurred rests with owner.* The burden of proof rests with the owner to demonstrate that an objectively verifiable and material error (or errors) occurred in the REAC's inspection through submission of evidence, which if corrected will result in a significant improvement in the property's overall score. To support its request for a technical review of the physical inspection results, the owner may submit photographic evidence, written material from an objective source such as a local fire marshal or building code official, or other similar evidence.

(3) *Material errors.* An objectively verifiable material error must be present to allow for a technical review of physical inspection results. Material errors are those that exhibit specific characteristics and meet specific thresholds. The three types of material errors are as follows.

(i) *Building data error.* A building data error occurs if the inspection includes the wrong building or a building that was not owned by the property, including common or site areas that were not a part of the property. Incorrect building data that does not affect the score, such as the address, building name, year built, etc., would not be considered material, but is of great interest to HUD and will be corrected upon notice to the REAC.

(ii) *Unit count error.* A unit count error occurs if the total number of units considered in scoring is incorrect. Since scoring uses total units, the REAC will examine instances where the participant can provide evidence that the total units used is incorrect.

(iii) *A non-existent deficiency error.* A non-existent deficiency error occurs if the inspection cites a deficiency that does not exist.

(4) *Significant improvement.* Significant improvement refers to the correction of a material error, asserted by the owner, which causes the score for the owner's property to cross an administratively significant threshold (for example, the property would be redesignated from standard 3 performing to standard 2 performing or from standard 2 performing to standard 1 performing), or to result in an increase of 10 points or more.

(5) *Determining whether material error occurred and what action is warranted.* Upon receipt of the owner's request for technical review of a property's physical inspection results, the REAC will evaluate the owner's property file and the evidence provided by the owner that an objectively verifiable and material error occurred which, if corrected, would result in a significant improvement in the property's overall score. If the REAC's evaluation determines that an objectively verifiable and material error (or errors) has been reasonably documented by the owner and if corrected would result in a significant improvement in the property's overall score, then the REAC shall take one or a combination of the following actions:

(i) Undertake a new inspection;

(ii) Correct the inspection report; or

(iii) Issue a new physical condition score.

(6) *Responsibility for the cost of a new inspection.* If a new inspection is undertaken by the REAC and the new inspection score results in a significant improvement in the property's overall score, then HUD shall bear the expense of the new inspection. If no significant improvement occurs, then the owner must bear the expense of the new inspection. The inspection cost of a new inspection, if paid by the owner, is not a valid project operating expense. The new inspection score will be considered the final score.

(e) *Adjustment of physical condition score based on considerations other than technical review and reinspection.* (1) Under certain circumstances, HUD may find it appropriate to review the results of a physical inspection which are anomalous or have an incorrect result due to facts and circumstances affecting the inspected property which

45

are not reflected in the inspection or reflected inappropriately in the inspection. These circumstances include, but are not necessarily limited to, inconsistencies between local code requirements and the HUD physical inspection protocol; conditions which are permitted by variance or license or which are preexisting physical features nonconformities and are inconsistent with the HUD physical condition protocol; or cases where the owner has been scored for elements (*e.g.*, roads, sidewalks, mail boxes, resident owned appliances, etc.) that it does not own and is not responsible for maintaining.

(2) To seek a score adjustment on the basis of these circumstances as provided in paragraph (e) of this section, the owner must submit a request for an adjustment to REAC with appropriate proof of the circumstances that resulted in the incorrect physical conditions results. This process may result in a reinspection and/or rescoring of the inspection after review and approval of the owner's submission of appropriate proof of the anomalous or inappropriate application.

(3) An owner may submit the request for this adjustment to REAC either prior to or after the physical inspection has been concluded. If the owner submits a request for adjustment after the physical inspection has been concluded, the owner must submit its request to REAC within 45 days following the submission of the physical inspection report, as provided in paragraph (c)(1) of this section. HUD may, but is not required to review a request made after this period has expired.

(4) This adjustment process, provided in this paragraph (g), may result in a reinspection and/or rescoring of the inspection after review and approval of the owner's submission of appropriate proof of the anomalous or inappropriate application.

(f) *Issuance of final score and publication of score.* (1) The physical condition score of the property is the final score if the owner files no request for technical review, as provided in paragraph (c) of this section, or for other adjustment of the physical condition score, as provided in paragraph (e) of this section. If the owner files a request for technical review or score adjustments

in accordance with paragraphs (c) and (e) of this section, the final physical condition score is the score issued by HUD after any adjustments are determined necessary and made by HUD at the conclusion of these processes.

(2) HUD will make public the final scores of the owners through posting on HUD's internet site, or through FEDERAL REGISTER publication or other appropriate means.

(g) *Owner's responsibility to notify residents of inspection; and availability of documents to residents*—(1) *Notification to residents.* An owner must notify its residents of any planned physical inspections of their units or the housing development generally.

(2) *Availability of documents for review.* Once the technical review and database adjustment periods have expired, as provided in paragraphs (d) and (e) of this section, respectively, the owner must make its physical inspection report and all related documents available to its residents during regular business hours upon reasonable request for review and copying. Related documents include the owner's survey plan, plan of correction, certification and related correspondence.

(i) Once the owner's final physical condition score is issued and published, the owner must make any additional information, such as the results of any reinspection, appeal requests, available for review and copying by its residents upon reasonable request during regular business hours.

(ii) The owner must maintain the documents related to the physical inspection of the property, as described in this paragraph (g)(2), available for review by residents for a period of 60 days from the date of submission to the owner of the physical condition score for the property in which the residents reside.

(3) The owner must post a notice to the residents in the owner's management office and on any bulletin boards in all common areas that advises residents of the availability of the materials described in paragraphs (g)(2) of this section. The notice should include the name, address and telephone number of the HUD Project Manager.

(4) Residents are encouraged to comment on this information provided by

the owners and submit any comments directly to the applicable Field Office. Should residents discover the owner provided HUD with a false certification during the review they are encouraged to notify the Hub or Program Center where appropriate inquiry and action will be taken.

(h) *Administrative review of properties.* The file of a multifamily property that receives a score of 30 points or less on its physical condition inspection will be referred to HUD's Departmental Enforcement Center (DEC) for evaluation. The files of any of the multifamily housing properties may be submitted to the DEC or to the appropriate HUD Multifamily Hub Director (MFD) for evaluation, or both, at the discretion of the Office of Housing.

(1) *Notification to owner of submission of property file to the MFD and DEC.* The Department will provide for notification to the owner that the file on the owner's property is being submitted to the MFD and/or the DEC for evaluation. The notification will be provided at the time the REAC issues the physical inspection report to the owner or at such other time as a referral occurs.

(2) *30–Day period for owner to provide the DEC with supporting and relevant information and documentation.* The owner has 30 calendar days, from the date of the REAC notification to the owner, to provide comments, proposals, or any other information to the DEC which will assist the MFD and DEC in conducting a comprehensive evaluation of the property. A proposal provided by an owner may include the owner's plan to correct deficiencies (corrective action plan). During the 30-day response time available to the owner, the DEC may encourage the owner to submit a corrective action plan. The corrective action plan, if timely submitted during the 30-day period (whether on the owner's initiative or at the request of the DEC), may serve as additional information for the DEC to consider in determining appropriate action to take at the conclusion of the evaluation period. If not submitted during the 30-day response time, a corrective action plan may be required of the owner at the conclusion of the DEC's evaluation of the property.

(3) *Evaluation of the property.* During the evaluation period, the DEC will perform an analysis of the multifamily housing property, which may include input from tenants, HUD multifamily officials, elected officials, and others as may be appropriate. Although the MFD will assist with the evaluation, for insured mortgages, the DEC will have primary responsibility for the conclusion of the evaluation of the property after taking into consideration the input of interested parties as described in this paragraph (h)(2). The DEC's evaluation may include a site visit to the owner's property.

(4) *Continuing responsibilities of HUD Multifamily Program Offices and Mortgagee.* During the period of DEC evaluation, HUD's multifamily program offices continue to be responsible for routine asset management tasks on properties and all servicing actions (*e.g.,* rent increase decisions, releases from reserve account approvals). In addition, during this period of evaluation, the mortgagee shall continue to carry out its duties and responsibilities with respect to the mortgage.

(i) *Enforcement action.* If, at the conclusion of the evaluation period, the DEC determines that enforcement action is appropriate, the DEC will provide notification to the owner of the DEC's decision to formally accept the property for enforcement purposes.

(1) *DEC Owner Compliance Plan.* (i) After notification to the owner of the DEC's decision, the DEC will produce a proposed action plan (DEC Compliance Plan), the purpose of which is to improve the physical condition of the owner's property, and correct any other known violations by the owner of its legal obligations. The DEC Compliance Plan will describe:

(A) The actions that will be required of the owner to correct, mitigate or eliminate identified property deficiencies, problems, hazards, and/or correct any other known violations by the owner;

(B) The period of time within which these actions must be completed; and

(C) The compliance responsibilities of the owner.

(ii) The DEC Compliance Plan will be submitted to the MFD for review and concurrence. If the MFD does not concur, the DEC Compliance Plan will be submitted to the Deputy Assistant Secretary for Housing and the Deputy Director of the DEC for review and concurrence. If the DEC Compliance Plan remains unapproved, a final decision on the plan will be made by HUD's Deputy Secretary in consultation with the General Counsel, the Assistant Secretary for Housing, and the Director of the DEC.

(iii) Following submission of the DEC Compliance Plan to the owner, the owner will be provided a period of 30 calendar days to review and accept the DEC Compliance Plan. If the owner agrees to comply with the DEC Compliance Plan, the plan will be forwarded to the appropriate Multifamily Office for implementation and monitoring of completion of the plan's requirements.

(2) *Counter compliance plan proposal by owner.* The owner may submit an acceptable counter proposal to the DEC Compliance Plan. An owner's counter proposal to a DEC Compliance Plan must be submitted no later than the 30th day following submission of the DEC Compliance Plan to the owner. The DEC, in coordination with the MFD, may enter into discussions with the owner to achieve agreement to a revised DEC Compliance Plan. If the owner and the DEC agree on a revised DEC Compliance Plan, the revised plan will be forwarded to the appropriate Multifamily Office for implementation and monitoring of completion of the plan's requirements.

(3) *Non-cooperation and Non-compliance by owner.* If at the conclusion of the 30th calendar day following submission of the DEC Compliance Plan to the owner, the DEC receives no response from the owner, or the owner refuses to accept the DEC Compliance Plan, or to present a counter compliance plan proposal, or if the owner accepts the DEC Compliance Plan or revised DEC Compliance Plan, but refuses to take the actions required of the owner in the plan, the DEC may take appropriate enforcement action.

(4) *No limitation on existing enforcement authority.* The administrative process provided in this section does not prohibit the Office of Housing, the DEC, or HUD generally, to take whatever action may be necessary when necessary (notwithstanding the commencement of this process), as authorized under existing statutes, regulations, contracts or other documents, to protect HUD's financial interests in multifamily properties and to protect the residents of these properties.

(j) *Limitations on material alteration of physical inspection software.* HUD will not materially alter the physical inspection requirements in a manner which would materially increase the cost of performing the inspection.

[65 FR 77240, Dec. 8, 2000, as amended at 72 FR 54517, Sept. 25, 2007]

Subpart R [Reserved]

Subpart S—Minimum Property Standards

§ 200.925 Applicability of minimum property standards.

All housing constructed under HUD mortgage insurance and low-rent public housing programs shall meet or exceed HUD Minimum Property Standards, except that this requirement shall be applicable to manufactured homes eligible for insurance pursuant to § 203.43f of this chapter only to the extent provided therein. The Minimum Property Standards may be waived to the same extent as the other regulatory requirements for eligibility for insurance under the specific mortgage insurance program involved.

[58 FR 60248, Nov. 15, 1993]

§ 200.925a Multifamily and care-type minimum property standards.

(a) *Construction standards.* Multifamily or care-type properties shall comply with the minimum property standards contained in the handbook identified in § 200.929(b)(2). In addition, each such property shall, for the Department's purposes, comply with:

(1) The applicable State of local building code, if the property is located within a jurisdiction which has a building code accepted by the Secretary under § 200.925a(d); or

(2)(i) The applicable State or local building code, and

(ii) Those portions of the codes identified in § 200.295c which are designated by the HUD Field Office serving the jurisdiction in which the property is to be located, if the property is located in a jurisdiction which has a building code partially accepted by the Secretary; or

(3) The appropriate codes, as identified in §200.925c(c), if the property is not located within a jurisdiction which has a building code accepted by the Secretary.

(b) *Conflicting standards.* The minimum property standards contained in the handbook identified in §200.929(b)(2) do not preempt state or local standards, nor do they alter or affect a builder's obligation to comply with any state or local requirements. However, a property shall be eligible for benefits only if it complies with all applicable minimum property standards, including referenced standards.

(c) *Standard for evaluating local building codes.* The Secretary shall compare the portions of a local or State building code applicable to residential or institutional occupancy, as appropriate, submitted under §200.925a(d) to the list of construction related areas contained in §200.925b.

(1) A State or local code will be accepted if it regulates each area on the list.

(2) A State or local building code will be partially accepted if it regulates most of the areas on the list. However, no code may be partially accepted if it fails to regulate the subarea for seismic design (see §200.925b(c)(5)), or if it fails to regulate subareas in more than one of the following major areas listed in §200.925b: fire safety, light and ventilation, structural loads and seismic design, foundation systems, materials standards, construction components, glass, mechanical, plumbing, electrical, and elevators.

(3) For purposes of this paragraph, a state or local code regulates an area if it establishes a standard concerning that area. However, for earthquake loads (see §200.925b(c)(5)), ASCE 7–88 is mandatory.

(d) *Review process and acceptance*—(1) *Jurisdictions without previously accepted building codes.* The following submission requirements apply to developers and other interested parties in jurisdictions without building codes, jurisdic-

tions with building codes which have never been submitted for acceptance, and jurisdictions with building codes which have been submitted for acceptance and neither accepted nor partially accepted by the Secretary.

(i) Developers or other interested parties must comply with one of the following by the time of application for insurance or other benefits:

(A) The developer or other interested party may choose to comply with the appropriate codes as identified in §200.925c. If the developer or other interested party so chooses, then the multifamily or care-type property shall be constructed in accordance with one of the model codes designated in paragraph (c)(1), (2) or (3) of §200.925c and with any other code or codes identified in the same paragraph. In such instances, the developer or other interested party shall notify the Department of the code or group of codes with which it intends to comply by the time of application for insurance or other benefits; or

(B) The developer or other interested party may choose to comply with the State or local building code, if such code is acceptable to the Secretary. To obtain the Secretary's acceptance, the developer or other interested party shall submit the material specified in paragraph (d)(1)(ii) of this section to the HUD Field Office serving the jurisdiction in which the property is to be constructed. Such material may be submitted at any time; provided, however, that it must be submitted no later than the time of application for mortgage insurance or other benefits.

(ii) If, under paragraph (d)(1)(i)(B) of this section, the developer or other interested party chooses to comply with the State or local building code as prescribed in paragraph (a)(1) of this section, it shall submit the following material to the HUD field Office serving the jurisdiction in which the property is to be constructed:

(A) A copy of the jurisdiction's building code, including all applicable service codes, appendices and referenced standards; and

(B) A copy of the statute, ordinance, regulation, or order establishing the code, if such statute, ordinance, regulation or order is not contained in the building code itself.

However, the developer or other interested party need not submit any document already on file in the Field Office.

(2) *Jurisdictions with previously accepted or partially accepted building codes.* The following submission requirements apply to developers and other interested parties in any jurisdiction with a building code which has been accepted or partially accepted by the Secretary:

(i) At the time of application for mortgage insurance or other benefits, the developer or other interested party shall submit to the HUD Field Office serving the jurisdiction in which the property is to be constructed.

(A) A certificate stating that, since its acceptance by the Secretary, the jurisdiction's building code has not been changed; or

(B)(*1*) A copy of all changes to the jurisdiction's building code, including all applicable service codes and appendices, which have been made since the date of the code's acceptance by the Secretary. However, the developer or other interested party need not submit any part already in the possession of the Field Office; and

(*2*) A copy of the statute, ordinance regulation, or order making such changes in the code.

(3) *Notification of decision.* The Secretary shall review the material submitted under paragraphs (d) (1)(ii) and (2)(i). Following that review, the Secretary shall issue a written notice (except in the case of a previously accepted code which hasn't been changed) to the submitting party stating whether the State or local building code has been accepted, partially accepted, or whether the Secretary's previous acceptance or partial acceptance has been continued; the basis for the Secretary's decision; and a notification of the submitting party's right to present its views concerning the denial of acceptance if the code is neither accepted nor partially accepted. The Secretary may, in his discretion, permit either an oral or written presentation of views.

(i) If a developer or other interested party is notified that a State or local building code has not been accepted,

then the multifamily or care-type properties eligible for HUD benefits in that jurisdiction shall be constructed in accordance with the appropriate codes indicated in § 200.925c(c). In such instances, the developer or other interested party shall notify the HUD Field Office of the code or codes with which it chooses to comply, in accordance with § 200.925a(d)(1)(i)(A).

(ii) If a developer or other interested party is notified that a State or local building code has been partially accepted, then the multifamily or care-type properties eligible for HUD benefits in that jurisdiction shall be constructed in accordance with the applicable State or local building code, plus those additional requirements identified in the written notice issued by the Secretary under § 200.925a(d)(3). The written notice shall identify, in accordance with appendix J of the Handbook identified in § 200.929(b)(2), those portions of the codes listed at § 200.925c(a) with which the property must comply.

(iii) Each Regional Office will maintain a current list of jurisdictions with accepted building codes and a current list of jurisdictions with partially accepted building codes. The lists will state the most recent date of each code's acceptance or partial acceptance and will be available to any interested party upon request. In addition, the list of jurisdictions whose codes have been partially accepted shall identify those portions of the codes listed at § 200.925c(a) with which the property must comply.

(Approved by the Office of Management and Budget under control number 2502–0321)

[49 FR 18695, May 1, 1984, as amended at 51 FR 28699, Aug. 11, 1986; 58 FR 60248, Nov. 15, 1993; 59 FR 36695, July 19, 1994]

§ 200.925b Residential and institutional building code comparison items.

HUD will review each local code submitted under this chapter to determine whether it regulates all of the following areas and subareas:

(a) *Fire safety.* (1) Construction types permitted;

(2) Allowable height and area;

(3) Fire separations;

(4) Fire resistance requirements;

(5) Means of egress (number and distance);

(6) Individual unit smoke detectors;

(7) Building alarm systems;

(8) Highrise criteria;

(b) *Light and ventilation.* (1) Habitable rooms;

(2) Bath and toilet rooms.

(c) *Structural loads and seismic design.* (1) Design live loads;

(2) Design dead loads;

(3) Snow loads;

(4) Wind loads.

(5) Earthquake loads (in localities identified by ASCE 7–88 (formerly ANSI A58.1–82) as being in seismic zones 1, 2, 3, or 4, and Guam).

(6) Special loads, i.e., soil pressure, railings, interior walls etc.

(d) *Foundation systems.* (1) Soil tests;

(2) Foundation depths;

(3) Footings;

(4) Foundation materials criteria;

(5) Piles, i.e., materials, allowable stresses, design;

(6) Excavation;

(e) *Materials standards.*

(f) *Construction components.* (1) Steel;

(2) Masonry;

(3) Concrete;

(4) Gypsum;

(5) Lumber;

(6) Roof construction and covering;

(7) Chimneys and fireplaces.

(g) *Glass.* (1) Thickness/area requirements;

(2) Safety glazing.

(h) *Mechanical.* (1) Heating, cooling and ventilation systems;

(2) Boilers and pressure vessels;

(3) Gas, liquid and solid fuel piping and equipment;

(4) Chimneys and vents;

(5) Ventilation (air changes).

(i) *Plumbing.* (1) Materials standards;

(2) Sizing and installing drainage systems;

(3) Vents and venting;

(4) Traps;

(5) Cleanouts;

(6) Plumbing fixtures;

(7) Water supply and distribution;

(8) Storm drain systems.

(j) *Electrical.* (1) Wiring design and protection;

(2) Wiring methods and materials;

(3) Equipment for general use;

(4) Special equipment;

(5) Special conditions;

(6) Communication systems.

(k) *Elevators.* (1) Reference ASME/ ANSI Standard A 17.1–1987; and the ASME/ANSI A17.1b–1989 Addenda.

(2) Acceptance tests and periodic tests.

[49 FR 18696, May 1, 1984, as amended at 51 FR 28699, Aug. 11, 1986; 58 FR 60248, Nov. 15, 1993; 59 FR 36695, July 19, 1994]

§200.925c Model codes.

(a) *Incorporation by reference.* The following publications are incorporated by reference under 5 U.S.C. 552(a) and 1 CFR part 51. The incorporation by reference of these publications has been approved by the Director of the Federal Register. The locations where copies of these publications are available are set forth below.

(1) *Model Building Codes*—(i) *The BOCA National Building Code, 1993 Edition, The BOCA National Plumbing Code, 1993 Edition, and the BOCA National Mechanical Code, 1993 Edition,* excluding Chapter I, Administration, for the Building, Plumbing and Mechanical Codes and the references to fire retardant treated wood and a distance of 4 feet (1219 mm) from the wall in exception number 1 of paragraph 705.6 and 707.5.2 number 2 (Chapter 7) of the Building Code, but including the Appendices of the Code. Available from Building Officials and Code Administrators International, Inc., 4051 West Flossmoor Road, Country Club Hills, Illinois 60478.

(ii) *Standard Building Code, 1991 Edition, including 1992/1993 revisions. Standard Plumbing Code, 1991 Edition, Standard Mechanical Code, 1991 Edition, including 1992 revisions, and Standard Gas Code, 1991 Edition,* including the 1992 revisions, but excluding Chapter I—Administration from each standard code and the phrase "or fire retardant treated wood" in reference note (a) of table 600 (Chapter 6) of the Standard Building Code, but including Appendices A, C, E, J, K, M, and R. Available from the Southern Building Code Congress International, Inc., 900 Montclair Road, Birmingham, Alabama 35213.

(iii) *Uniform Building Code, 1991 Edition,* including the 1993 Accumulative Supplement, but excluding Part I—Administrative, and the reference to fire retardant treated plywood in section

2504(c)3 and to fire retardant treated wood in 1–HR type III and V construction referenced in paragraph 4203.2., but including the Appendix of the Code. *Uniform Plumbing Code, 1991 Edition, including the 1992 Code Changes* but excluding Part I—Administration, but including the Appendices of the Code. *Uniform Mechanical Code, 1991 Edition,* including the 1993 Accumulative Supplement but excluding Part I—Administrative, but including the Appendices of the Code. All available from the International Conference of Building Officials, 5360 South Workman Mill Road, Whittier, California 90601.

(2) *National Electrical Code,* NFPA 70, 1993 Edition, including appendices. Available from the National Fire Protection Association, Batterymarch Park, Quincy, Massachusetts 02269.

(3) *National Standard Plumbing Code,* 1993 Edition. Available from the National Association of Plumbing-Heating-Cooling Contractors, P.O. Box 6808, Falls Church, Virginia 22046.

(b) *Model Code Compliance Requirements.* (1) When a multifamily or care-type property is to comply with one of the model building codes set forth in paragraph (a)(1) of this section, the following requirements of those model codes shall not apply to those properties:

(i) Those provisions of the model codes that do not pertain to residential or institutional buildings;

(ii) Those provisions of the model codes that establish energy requirements for multifamily or care-type structures; and

(iii) Those provisions of the model codes that require or allow the issuance of permits of any sort.

(2) Where the model codes set forth in paragraph (a)(1) of this section designate a building, fire, mechanical, plumbing or other official, the Secretary's designee in the HUD Field Office serving the jurisdiction in which the property is to be constructed shall act as such official.

(c) *Designation of Model Codes.* When a multifamily or care-type property is to comply with a model code, it shall comply with one of the model codes designated in paragraphs (c)(1), (2), or (3) of this section, and with any other code or codes identified in the same

paragraph. However, seismic design is a mandatory requirement. In addition, the property shall comply with all of the standards that are incorporated into the code or codes by reference. By the time of application for insurance or other benefits, the developer or other interested party shall notify the Department of the code or group of codes to which the developer intends to comply.

(1) *The BOCA National Building Code, The BOCA National Plumbing and The BOCA National Mechanical Code,* 1993 Editions.

(2) *Standard Building Code, Standard Plumbing Code, Standard Mechanical Code and Standard Gas Code,* 1991 Editions, including the revisions specified in paragraph (a)(1)(ii) of this section, and the *National Electrical Code,* 1993 Edition.

(3) *Uniform Building Code, Uniform Plumbing Code and Uniform Mechanical Code,* 1991 Editions, including the 1993 Accumulative Supplements to the Building and Mechanical Codes, and the 1992 Code Changes to the *Uniform Plumbing Code,* and the *National Electrical Code,* NFPA 70, 1993 Edition.

(4) *The National Electrical Code,* NFPA 70, 1993 Edition.

[49 FR 18696, May 1, 1984, as amended at 51 FR 28699, Aug. 11, 1986; 58 FR 60248, Nov. 15, 1993; 59 FR 36695, July 19, 1994]

§ 200.926 Minimum property standards for one and two family dwellings.

(a) *Construction standards—*(1) *Applicable structures.* The standards identified or contained in this section, and in §§ 200.926a–200.926e, apply to single family detached homes, duplexes, three-unit homes, and to living units in a structure where the units are located side-by-side in town house fashion. Section 200.926d(c)(4) also applies to four-unit homes.

(2) *Applicability of standards to new construction.* The standards referenced in paragraph (a)(1) of this section are applicable to structures which are:

(i) Approved for insurance or other benefits prior to the start of construction, including approval under the Direct Endorsement process described in § 203.5 of this chapter, or under the Lender Insurance process described in § 203.6 of this chapter;

(ii) Approved for insurance or other benefits based upon participation in an insured warranty program; or

(iii) Insured as new construction based upon a Certificate of Reasonable Value issued by the Department of Veterans Affairs.

(b) *Conflicting standards.* The requirements contained in §200.926d do not preempt local or State standards, nor do they alter or affect a builder's obligation to comply with any local or State requirements. However, a property shall be eligible for benefits only if it complies with the requirements of this subpart, including any referenced standards. When any of the requirements identified in §200.926c are in conflict with a partially accepted local or state code, the conflict will be resolved by the HUD Field Office servicing the jurisdiction in which the property is to be located.

(c) *Standard for evaluating local or state building codes.* The Secretary shall compare a local building code submitted under paragraph (d) of this section or a State code to the list of construction related areas contained in §200.926a.

(1) A local or State code will be accepted if it regulates each area and subarea on the list.

(2) A State or local building code will be partially accepted if it regulates most of the areas on the list. However, no code may be partially accepted if it fails to regulate the subarea for seismic design (see §200.926a(c)(5)), or if it fails to regulate subareas in more than one of the following major areas listed in §200.926a: fire safety, light and ventilation, structural loads and seismic design, foundation systems, materials standards, construction components, glass, mechanical, plumbing, and electrical.

(3) For purposes of this paragraph, a local or State code regulates an area or subarea if it establishes a standard concerning that area or subarea. However, for earthquake loads (see §200.926a(c)(5)), ASCE 7–88 is mandatory.

(d) *Code selection.* Any materials required to be submitted under this section must be submitted by the time the lender or other interested party applies

for mortgage insurance or other benefits.

(1) *Jurisdictions without previously accepted building codes.* The following submission requirements apply to lenders and other interested parties in jurisdictions without building codes, jurisdictions with building codes which have never been submitted for acceptance, and jurisdictions with building codes which previously have been submitted for acceptance and have not been accepted or partially accepted by the Secretary.

(i) In jurisdictions without local building codes:

(A) If the State building code is acceptable, the lender or other interested party must comply with the State building code and the requirements of §200.926d;

(B) If the State building code is partially acceptable, the lender or other interested party must comply with:

(1) The acceptable portions of the partially acceptable code; and

(2) Those portions of the CABO One and Two Family Dwelling Code designated by the HUD Field Office in accordance with §200.926c; and

(3) The requirements of §200.926d.

(C) If there is no State building code or if the State building code is unacceptable, the lender or other interested party must comply with:

(1) The CABO One and Two Family Dwelling Code as identified in §200.926b(a); and

(2) The requirements of §200.926d.

(ii) In jurisdictions with local building codes which have never been submitted for review, lenders or other interested parties must:

(A) Comply with the requirements of paragraph (d)(1)(i) (A), (B) or (C) of this section, as appropriate;

(B) Request the Secretary's acceptance of the local building code in accordance with paragraph (d)(1)(iv) of this section.

(1) If the Secretary determines that the local building code is unacceptable, then the lender or other interested party must comply with the requirements of paragraph (d)(1)(i) (A), (B) or (C) of this section as appropriate.

(2) If the Secretary determines that the local code is partially acceptable,

then the lender or other interested party must comply with:

(*i*) The acceptable portions of the partially acceptable local code; and

(*ii*) Those portions of the CABO One and Two Family Dwelling Code designated by the HUD Field Office in accordance with § 200.926c; and

(*iii*) The requirements of § 200.926d.

(*3*) If the Secretary determines that the local code is acceptable, then the lender or other interested party must comply with the local building code and the requirements of § 200.926d.

(iii) In jurisdictions with local building codes which previously have been submitted for review and which have been found unacceptable by the Secretary:

(A) If the local code has not been changed since the date the code or changes thereto were submitted to the Secretary, the lender or other interested party must comply with the requirements of paragraph (d)(1)(i) (A), (B) or (C) of this section, as appropriate; or

(B) If the local code has been changed since the date when the code or changes thereto were submitted to the Secretary, the lender or other interested party must submit a copy of all changes to the local building code, including all applicable service codes and appendices and a copy of the statute, ordinance, regulation or order making such changes in the code, which have been made since the date when the code or other changes thereto were last submitted to the Secretary. However, the lender or other interested party need not submit any part already in the possession of the HUD Field Office. Based upon the Secretary's determination concerning the acceptability of the local code as changed, the lender or other interested party must comply with the requirements of paragraph (d)(1)(ii)(B) (*1*), (*2*) or (*3*) of this section, as appropriate.

(iv) In order to obtain the Department's approval of a local code, the lender or other interested party must submit the following material to the HUD Field Office serving the jurisdiction in which the property is to be constructed:

(A) A copy of the jurisdiction's local building code, including all applicable service codes and appendices; and

(B) A copy of the statute, ordinance, regulation, or order establishing the code, if such statute, ordinance, regulation or order is not contained in the building code itself.

However, the lender or other interested party need not submit any document already on file in the HUD Field Office.

(2) *Jurisdictions with previously accepted or partially accepted building codes.* The following submission requirements apply to lenders or other interested parties in any jurisdiction with a building code which has been accepted or partially accepted by the Secretary:

(i) The lender or other interested party shall submit to the HUD Field Office serving the jurisdiction in which the property is to be constructed:

(A) A certificate stating that, since the date when the code or any changes thereto were last submitted to the Secretary, the jurisdiction's local building code has not been changed; or

(B)(*1*) A copy of all changes to the jurisdiction's building code, including all applicable service codes and appendices, which have been made since the date when the code or other changes thereto were last submitted to the Secretary. However, the lender or other interested party need not submit any part already in the possession of the HUD Field Office; and

(*2*) A copy of the statute, ordinance, regulation, or order making such changes in the code.

(ii) If, based upon changes to the local building code, the Secretary determines that it is unacceptable, the lender or other interested party must comply with the requirements of paragraph (d)(1) (i)(A), (B) or (C) of this section, as appropriate.

(iii) If the local building code was previously found by the Secretary to be partially acceptable and there have been no changes to it or if the local building code was previously found by the Secretary to be partially acceptable and if, based upon changes to it, the Secretary determines that it is still partially acceptable or if the local building code was previously found by the Secretary to be acceptable and if, based upon changes to it, the Secretary determines that it is partially acceptable, then the lender or other interested party must comply with paragraphs (d)(1)(ii)(B)(2) (*i*), (*ii*) and (*iii*) of this section.

(iv) If the local building code was previously found by the Secretary to be partially acceptable and if, based upon changes to it, the Secretary determines that it is acceptable, or if the local building code was previously found by the Secretary to be acceptable and there have been no changes to the code, or if the local building code was previously found by the Secretary to be acceptable and if, based upon changes to it, the Secretary determines that it is still acceptable, then the lender or other interested party must comply with the local building code and the requirements of §200.926d.

(3) *Notification of decision.* (i) Fire retardant treated plywood, where approved by a State or local building code, shall not be permitted for use in roof construction unless a HUD technical suitability bulletin has been issued by the Department for that product.

(ii) The Secretary shall review the material submitted under §200.926(d). Following that review, the Secretary shall issue a written notice (except where there is a previously accepted or partially accepted code which has not been changed) to the submitting party stating whether the local building code is acceptable, partially acceptable, or not acceptable. Where the local building code is not acceptable, the notice shall also state whether the State code is acceptable, partially acceptable or not acceptable. The notice shall also contain the basis for the Secretary's decision and a notification of the submitting party's right to present its views concerning the denial of acceptance if the code is neither accepted nor partially accepted. The Secretary may, in his or her discretion, permit either an oral or written presentation of views.

(4) *Department's responsibilities.* (i) Each Regional and Field Office will maintain a current list of jurisdictions with accepted local or State building codes, a current list of jurisdictions with partially accepted local or State building codes and a current list of jurisdictions with local or State building codes which have not been accepted. For local codes, the lists will state the most recent date when the code or changes thereto were submitted to the Secretary. The lists, which shall be prepared by the Field Offices and submitted to the Regional Offices, will be available to any interested party upon request. In addition, the list of jurisdictions whose codes have been partially accepted shall identify in accordance with §200.926c those portions of the codes listed at §200.926b(a) with which the property must comply.

(ii) The Department is responsible for obtaining copies of the State codes and any changes thereto.

(Approved by the Office of Management and Budget under control number 2502–0474)

[50 FR 39592, Sept. 27, 1985, as amended at 57 FR 27927, June 23, 1992; 57 FR 58340, Dec. 9, 1992; 58 FR 13536, Mar. 12, 1993; 58 FR 41337, Aug. 3, 1993; 58 FR 60249, Nov. 15, 1993; 59 FR 36695, July 19, 1994; 62 FR 30225, June 2, 1997; 64 FR 56110, Oct. 15, 1999]

§200.926a Residential building code comparison items.

HUD will review each local and State code submitted under this subpart to determine whether it regulates all of the following areas and subareas:

(a) *Fire Safety.* (1) Allowable height;

(2) Fire separations;

(3) Fire resistance requirements;

(4) Egress doors and windows;

(5) Unit smoke detectors;

(6) Flame spread.

(b) *Light and ventilation.* (1) Habitable rooms;

(2) Bath and toilet rooms.

(c) *Structural loads and seismic design.* (1) Design live loads;

(2) Design dead loads;

(3) Snow loads (for jurisdictions with snow loading conditions identified in Section 7 of ASCE–7–88 (formerly ANSI A58.1–82);

(4) Wind loads;

(5) Earthquake loads (for jurisdictions in seismic zones 3 or 4, as identified in Section 9 of ASCE–7–88 (formerly ANSI A58.1–82)).

(d) *Foundation systems.* (1) Foundation depths;

(2) Footings;

(3) Foundation materials criteria.

(e) *Materials standards.* (1) Materials standards.

(f) *Construction components.* (1) Steel;
(2) Masonry;
(3) Concrete;
(4) Lumber;
(5) Roof construction and covering;
(6) Chimneys and fireplaces.

(g) *Glass.* (1) Thickness/area requirements;
(2) Safety glazing.

(h) *Mechanical.* (1) Heating, cooling and ventilation systems;
(2) Gas, liquid and solid fuel piping and equipment;
(3) Chimneys and vents;
(4) Ventilation (air changes).

(i) *Plumbing.* (1) Materials standards;
(2) Sizing and installing drainage systems;
(3) Vents and venting;
(4) Traps;
(5) Cleanouts;
(6) Plumbing fixtures;
(7) Water supply and distribution;
(8) Sewage disposal systems.

(j) *Electrical.* (1) Branch circuits;
(2) Services;
(3) Grounding;
(4) Wiring methods;
(5) Cable;
(6) Conduit;
(7) Outlets, switches and junction boxes;
(8) Panelboards.

[50 FR 39594, Sept. 27, 1985, as amended at 59 FR 36695, July 19, 1994]

§ 200.926b   Model codes.

(a) *Incorporation by reference.* The following model code publications are incorporated by reference in accordance with 5 U.S.C. 552(a) and 1 CFR part 51. The incorporation by reference of these publications has been approved by the Director of the Federal Register. The locations where copies of these publications are available are set forth below.

(1) *CABO One and Two Family Dwelling Code,* 1992 Edition, including the 1993 amendments, but excluding Chapter I—Administrative, and the phrase "or approved fire retardant wood" contained in the exception of paragraph R–218.2.2(2), but including the Appendices A, B, D, and E of the Code. (Available from the Council of American Building Officials, Suite 708, 5203 Leesburg Pike, Falls Church, VA 22041.)

(2) *Electrical Code for One and Two Family Dwellings,* NFPA 70A, 1990 Edition, including Tables and Examples. Available from the National Fire Protection Association, Batterymarch Park, Quincy, MA 02269.

(b) *Model code compliance requirements.* (1) When a one or two family dwelling is to comply with the model codes set forth in § 200.926b(a), the following requirements of those model codes shall not apply to those properties:

(i) Those provisions of the model codes that establish energy requirements for one and two family dwellings; and

(ii) Those provisions of the model codes that require or allow the issuance of permits of any sort.

(2) Where the model codes set forth in paragraph (a) of this section designate a building, fire, mechanical, plumbing or other official, the Secretary's designee in the HUD Field Office serving the jurisdiction in which the dwelling is to be constructed shall act as such official.

(c) *Designation of Model Codes.* When a one or two family dwelling or townhouse is to comply with portions of the model code or the entire model code, the dwelling shall comply with the CABO One and Two Family Dwelling Code 1992 Edition, including the 1993 amendments, or portion thereof as modified by § 200.926e of this part and designated by the HUD Field Office serving a jurisdiction in which a property is located. In addition, the property shall comply with all of the standards which are referenced for any designated portions of the model code, and with the Electrical Code for One and Two Family Dwellings, NFPA 70A/1990.

[50 FR 39594, Sept. 27, 1985, as amended at 58 FR 60249, Nov. 15, 1993]

§ 200.926c   Model code provisions for use in partially accepted code jurisdictions.

If a lender or other interested party is notified that a State or local building code has been partially accepted, then the properties eligible for HUD benefits in that jurisdiction shall be constructed in accordance with the applicable State or local building code, plus those additional requirements identified below. Depending upon the major area identified in §200.926a which is not adequately regulated by the State or local code, the HUD Field Office will designate, in accordance with the schedule below, those portions of one of the model codes with which the property must comply.

SCHEDULE FOR MODEL CODE SUPPLEMENTS TO LOCAL OR STATE CODES

Deficient major items from §200.926a as determined by field office review	Portions of the CABO One and Two Family Dwelling Code, 1992 Edition, including the 1993 amendments, with which a property must comply
(a) Fire safety	Chapters 2, 9; Section R–402.
(b) Light and ventilation	Chapter 2; Section R–309.
(c) Structural loads and seismic design.	Chapter 2.
(d) Foundation systems	Chapter 3.
(e) Materials standards	Chapter 26.
(f) Construction components	Part III.
(g) Glass	Chapter 2.
(h) Mechanical	Part IV.
(i) Plumbing	Part V.
(j) Electrical	Electrical code for 1- and 2-family dwellings (NFPA 70A–1990).

[50 FR 39594, Sept. 27, 1985, as amended at 58 FR 60249, Nov. 15, 1993; 59 FR 36695, July 19, 1994]

§200.926d Construction requirements.

(a) *Application*—(1) *General.* These standards cover the agency requirements for accessibility to physically handicapped people, variations to standards, real estate entity, trespass and utilities, site conditions, access, site design, streets, dedication of utilities, drainage and flood hazard exposure, special construction and product acceptance, thermal requirements, and water supply systems.

(2) *Requirements for accessibility to physically handicapped people.* The HUD Field Office will advise project sponsors as to the extent accessibility will be required for new construction of one- and two-family dwellings on a project-by-project basis.

(i) *Technical standards.* See HUD Handbook, 4910.1, Sections 100–1.3b and 100–1.3c.

(3) *Variations to standards*—(i) *New materials and technologies.* See paragraph (d) of this section. Alternatives, nonconventional or innovative methods and materials shall be equivalent to these standards in the areas of structural soundness, durability, economy of maintenance or operation and usability.

(ii) *Variation procedures.* Variations from the requirements of any standard with which the Department requires compliance shall be made in the following ways:

(A) For a particular design or construction method to be used on a single case or project, the decision is the responsibility of the Field Office. Headquarters concurrence is not required.

(B) Where a variation is intended to be on a repetitive basis, a recommendation for a Local Acceptable Standard, substantiating data, and background information shall be submitted by the Field Office to the Director, Office of Manufactured Housing and Regulatory Functions.

(iii) Variances which require individual analysis and decision in each instance are not considered as repetitive variances even though one particular standard is repeatedly the subject of variation. Such variances are covered by paragraph (a)(3)(ii)(A) of this section.

(b) *General acceptability criteria*—(1) *Real estate entity.* The property shall comprise a single plot except that a primary plot with a secondary plot for an appurtenant garage or for other use contributing to the marketability of the property will be acceptable provided the two plots are in such proximity as to comprise a readily marketable real estate entity.

(2) *Service and facilities*—(i) *Trespass.* Each living unit shall be one that can be used and maintained individually without trespass upon adjoining properties, except when the windowless wall of a detached dwelling is located on a side lot line. A detached dwelling may be located on a side lot line if:

(A) legal provision is made for permanent access for the maintenance of the exterior portion of the lot line wall, and

(B) the minimum distances from the dwelling to the dwellings on the abutting properties are not less than the sum of the side yard distances computed as appropriate for the type of opposing walls. (minimum distance 10 ft).

(ii) *Utilities.* Utility services shall be independent for each living unit, except that common services such as water, sewer, gas and electricity may be provided for living units under a single mortgage or ownership. Separate utility service shut-off for each unit shall be provided. For living units under separate ownership, common utility services may be provided from the main to the building line when protected by an easement or convenant and maintenance agreement acceptable to HUD, but shall not pass over, under or through any other living unit. Individual utilities serving a living unit may not pass over, under or through another living unit under the same mortgage unless provision is made for repair and maintenance of utilities without trespass or when protected by an easement or covenant providing permanent access for maintenance and repair of the utilities. Building drain cleanouts shall be accessible from the exterior where a single drain line within the building serves more than one unit.

(3) *Site conditions.* (i) The property shall be free of those foreseeable hazards and adverse conditions which may affect the health and safety of occupants or the structural soundness of the improvements, or which may impair the customary use and enjoyment of the property. The hazards include toxic chemicals, radioactive materials, other pollution, hazardous activities, potential damage from soil or other differential ground movements, ground water, inadequate surface drainage, flood, erosion, or other hazards located on or off site. The site must meet the standards set forth in 24 CFR part 51, and HUD Handbook 4910.1, section 606 for termite and decay protection.

(ii) When special conditions exist or arise during construction which were unforeseen and which necessitate precautionary or hazard mitigation measures, the HUD Field Office shall require corrective work to mitigate potential adverse effects from the special conditions as necessary. Special conditions include rock formations, unstable soils or slopes, high ground water levels, springs, or other conditions which may adversely affect a property. It shall be the builder's responsibility to ensure

proper design, construction and satisfactory performance where these conditions are present.

(4) *Access.* (i) Each property shall be provided with vehicular or pedestrian access by a public or private street. Private streets shall be protected by permanent easement.

(ii) Each living unit shall have a means of access such that it is unnecessary to pass through any other living unit.

(iii) The rear yard shall be accessible without passing through any other living unit.

(iv) For a townhouse type dwelling, access to the rear yard may be by means of alley, easement, passage through the dwelling, or other means acceptable to the HUD Field Office.

(c) *Site design—*(1) *General.* (i) A site design shall be provided which includes an arrangement of all site facilities necessary to create a safe, functional, healthful, durable and energy efficient living environment.

(ii) With the exception of paragraph (c)(4) of this section, these site design standards apply only in communities that have not adopted criteria for site development applicable to one and two family dwellings.

(iii) Single family detached houses situated on individual lots located on existing streets with utilities need not comply with the requirements of paragraphs (c)(2) and (c)(3) of this section.

(2) *Streets.* (i) Existing or proposed streets on the site shall connect to private or public streets and shall provide all-weather access to all buildings for essential and emergency use, including access needed for deliveries, service, maintenance and fire equipment.

(ii) Streets shall be designed for dedication for public use and maintenance or, when approved by the HUD Field Office, may be retained as private streets where protected by permanent easements.

(3) *Dedication.* Utilities shall be located to permit dedication to the local government or appropriate public body.

(4) *Drainage and flood hazard exposure—*(i) *Residential structures with basements located in FEMA-designated areas of special flood hazard.* The elevation of the lowest floor in structures with basements shall be at or above the base

flood level (100-year flood level) required for new construction or substantial improvement of residential structures under regulations for the National Flood Insurance Program (NFIP) (see 44 CFR 60.3 through 60.6), except where variances from this standard are granted by communities under the procedures of the Federal Emergency Management Agency (FEMA) at 44 CFR 60.6(a) or exceptions from this NFIP standard for basements are approved by FEMA in accordance with procedures at 44 CFR 60.6(c).

(ii) *Residential structures without basements located in FEMA-designated areas of special flood hazard.* The elevation of the lowest floor in structures without basements shall be at or above the FEMA-designated base flood elevation (100-year flood level).

(iii) *Residential structures located in FEMA-designated "coastal high hazard areas".* (A) Basements or any permanent enclosure of space below the lowest floor of a structure are prohibited.

(B) Where FEMA has determined the base flood level without establishing stillwater elevations, the bottom of the lowest structural member of the lowest floor (excluding pilings and columns) and its horizontal supports shall be at or above the base flood level.

(iv)(A) In all cases in which a Direct Endorsement (DE) mortgagee or a Lender Insurance (LI) mortgagee seek to insure a mortgage on a newly constructed one-to four-family dwelling (including a newly erected manufactured home) that was processed by the DE or LI mortgagee, the DE or LI mortgagee must determine whether the property improvements (dwelling and related structures/equipment essential to the value of the property and subject to flood damage) are located in a 100-year floodplain, as designated on maps of the Federal Emergency Management Agency. If so, the DE mortgagee, before submitting the application for insurance to HUD, or the LI mortgagee, before submitting all the required data regarding the mortgage to HUD, must obtain:

(*1*) A final Letter of Map Amendment (LOMA);

(*2*) A final Letter of Map Revision (LOMR); or

(*3*) A signed Elevation Certificate documenting that the lowest floor (including basement) of the property improvements is built at or above the 100-year flood elevation in compliance with National Flood Insurance program criteria 44 CFR 60.3 through 60.6.

(B) Under the DE program, these mortgages are not eligible for insurance unless the DE mortgagee submits the LOMA, LOMR, or Elevation Certificate to HUD with the mortgagee's request for endorsement.

(v) *Streets.* Streets must be usable during runoff equivalent to a 10-year return frequency. Where drainage outfall is inadequate to prevent runoff equivalent to a 10-year return frequency from ponding over 6 inches deep, streets must be made passable for commonly used emergency vehicles during runoff equivalent to a 25-year return frequency, except where an alternative access street not subject to such ponding is available.

(vi) *Crawl spaces.* Crawl spaces must not pond water or be subject to prolonged dampness.

(d) *Special construction and product acceptance—(1) Structural features of factory produced (modular or panelized) housing or components.*

(i) For factory fabricated systems or components, HUD Handbook 4950.1, "Technical Suitability of Products Program Technical and Processing Procedures" shall apply.

(ii) The requirements of this part shall apply to structural features, consisting of factory fabricated systems or components assembled either at the factory or at the construction site, if the total construction is covered by these standards and can be inspected on-site for determination of compliance.

(2) *Non-structural or non-standard features.* These features include methods of construction, systems, sub-systems, components, materials and processes which are not covered by these requirements. *See* HUD Handbook 4950.1 for procedures to be followed in order to obtain acceptance of non-structural components or materials. *See* HUD Handbook 4910.1, appendix F for a list of Use of Materials Bulletins. Products and methods shall conform to the appropriate Use of Materials Bulletin.

(3) *Standard Features.* These features include methods of construction, systems, sub-systems, components, materials and processes which are covered by national society or industry standards. For a list of standards and practices to which compliance is required, see HUD Handbook 4910.1, Appendix C and Appendices E and F, available from HUD, 451 Seventh Street, SW., Attention: Mailroom B–133, Washington, DC 20410.

(e) *Energy efficiency.* All detached one- and two-family dwellings and one-family townhouses not more than three stories in height shall comply with the CABO Model Energy Code, 1992 Edition, Residential Buildings, except for Sections 101.3.1, 101.3.2, 104, and 105, but Section 101.3.2.2, Historic Buildings, shall remain, and including the Appendix, and HUD intermediate MPS Supplement 4930.2 Solar Heating and Domestic Hot Water Systems, 1989 edition.

(f) *Water supply systems*—(1) *General.* (i) Each living unit shall be provided with a continuing and sufficient supply of safe water under adequate pressure and of appropriate quality for all household uses. Newly constructed residential property for which a building permit has been applied for on or after June 19, 1988 from the competent authority with jurisdiction in this matter shall have lead-free water piping. For purposes of these standards, water piping is "lead free" if it uses solders and flux containing not more than 0.2 percent lead and pipes and pipe fittings containing not more than 8.0 percent lead. This system shall not impair the function or durability of the plumbing system or attachments.

(ii) The chemical and bacteriological standards of the local health authority shall apply. In the absence of such standards, those of the appropriate State agency shall apply. A water analysis may be required by either the health authority or the HUD Field Office.

(iii) Whenever feasible, connection shall be made to a public water system. When a public system is not available, connection shall be made to a community system which complies with HUD Handbook 4940.2, if feasible.

(2) *Individual water systems.* (i) The system should be capable of delivering a flow of 5 gpm over at least a 4 hour period.

(ii) The chemical and bacteriological standards of the local health authority shall apply. In the absence of such standards, those of the appropriate State agency shall apply. A water analysis may be required by either the health authority or the HUD Field Office.

(iii) After installation, the system shall be disinfected in accordance with the recommendations or requirements of the local health authority. In the absence of a health authority, system cleaning and disinfection shall conform to the current EPA Manual of Individual Water Supply Systems.

(iv) Bacteriological or chemical examination of a water sample collected by a representative of the local or state health authority shall be made when required by that authority or the HUD Field Office.

(3) *Location of wells.* (i) A well located within the foundation walls of a dwelling is not acceptable except in arctic or subarctic regions.

(ii) Water which comes from any soil formation which may be polluted, contaminated, fissured, creviced or less than 20 ft. below the natural ground surface is not acceptable, unless acceptable to the local health authority.

(iii) Individual water supply systems are not acceptable for individual lots in areas where chemical soil poisoning has been or is practiced if the overburden of soil between the ground surface and the water bearing strata is coarse grained sand, gravel, or porous rock, or is creviced in a manner which will permit the recharge water to carry the toxicants into the zone of saturation.

(iv) The following table shall be used in establishing the minimum acceptable distances between wells and sources of pollution located on either the same or adjoining lots. These distances may be increased by either the health authority having jurisdiction or the HUD Field Office.

DISTANCE FROM SOURCE OF POLLUTION

Source of pollution	Minimum horizontal distance (feet)
Property Line	10
Septic Tank	50
Absorption Field	[1]100
Seepage Pit	[1]100
Absorption Bed	[1]100
Sewer Lines w/Permanent Watertight Joints	10
Other Sewer Lines	50
Chemically Poisoned Soil	[3]25
Dry Well	50
Other	([2])

[1] This clearance may be increased or decreased depending upon soil and rock penetrated by the well and aquifer conditions. The clearance may be increased in creviced limestone and permeable strata of gravel and sand. The clearance may be reduced to 50 ft. only where the ground surface is effectively separated from the water bearing formation by an extensive, continuous and impervious strata of clay, hardpan, or rock. The well shall be constructed so as to prevent the entrance of surface water and contaminants.

[2] The recommendations or requirements of the local health authority shall apply.

[3] This clearance may be reduced to 15 feet only where the ground surface is effectively separated from the water bearing formation by an extensive, continuous and impervious strata of clay, hardpan, or rock.

(4) *Well construction.* (i) The well shall be constructed so as to allow the pump to be easily placed and to function properly.

(ii)(A) All drilled wells shall be provided with a sound, durable and watertight casing capable of sustaining the loads imposed.

(B) The casing shall extend from a point several feet below the water level at drawdown or from an impervious strata above the water level to 12 in. above either the ground surface or the pump room floor. The casing shall be sealed at the upper opening to a depth of at least 15 feet.

(iii) Bored wells shall be lined with concrete, vitrified clay or equivalent materials.

(iv) The space between the casing or liner and the wall of the well hole shall be sealed with cement grout.

(v) The well casing shall not be used to convey water except under positive pressure. A separate drop pipe shall be used for the suction line.

(vi) When sand or silt is encountered in the water-bearing formation, the well shall either be compacted and gravel packed, or a removable strainer or screen shall be installed.

(vii) The surface of the ground above and around the well shall be compacted and graded to drain surface water away from the well.

(viii) Openings in the casing, cap, or concrete cover for the entrance of pipes, pumps or manholes shall be watertight.

(ix) If a breather is provided, it shall extend above the highest level to which surface water may rise. The breather shall be watertight, and the open end shall be screened and positioned to prevent entry of dust, insects and foreign objects.

(5) *Pump and equipment.* (i) Pumps shall be capable of delivering the volume of water required under normal operating pressure within the living unit. Pump capacity shall not exceed the output of the well.

(ii) Pumps and equipment shall be mounted to be free of objectionable noises, vibrations, flooding, pollution, and freezing.

(iii) Suction lines shall terminate below maximum drawdown of the water level in the well.

(iv) Horizontal segments of suction line shall be placed below the frost line in a sealed casing pipe or in at least 4 in. of concrete. The distance from suction line to sources of pollution shall be not less than shown in the table at paragraph (f)(3)(iv) of this section.

(6) *Storage tanks.* (i) A pressure tank having a minimum capacity of 42 gallons shall be provided. However, prepressured tanks and other pressurizing devices are acceptable provided that delivery between pump cycles equals or exceeds that of a 42 gallon tank.

(ii) Tanks shall be equipped with a clean-out plug at the lowest point, and a suitable pressure relief valve.

(Approved by the Office of Management and Budget under control number 2502–0474)

[50 FR 39594, Sept. 27, 1985, as amended at 53 FR 11271, Apr. 6, 1988; 56 FR 5350, Feb. 11, 1991; 57 FR 9609, Mar. 19, 1992; 57 FR 27927, June 23, 1992; 58 FR 41337, Aug. 3, 1993; 58 FR 60249, Nov. 15, 1993; 59 FR 19112, Apr. 21, 1994; 62 FR 30225, June 2, 1997; 64 FR 56110, Oct. 15, 1999]

§ 200.926e Supplemental information for use with the CABO One and Two Family Dwelling Code.

The following shall be used in Table No. R–202, Climatic and Geographic Design Criteria of the CABO One and Two Family Dwelling Code.

(a) *Roof live loads.*

Roof slope 3 in 12 or less: 20 psf
Roof slope over 3 in 12: 15 psf
Roof used as deck: 40 psf

(b) *Roof snow load.* The roof snow load shall be in accordance with section 7 of ASCE 7–88.

(c) *Wind pressures.* The minimum Design Wind Pressures (net pressures) set forth below apply to areas designated as experiencing basic wind speeds up to and including 80 mph, as shown in ASCE 7–88, Figure 1, Basic Wind Speed Map. These pressures also apply to buildings not over 30 ft. in height above finish grade, assuming exposure C or defined in ASCE 7–88.

(1) *Minimum design wind pressure criteria.* (i) Buildings (for overturning racking or sliding); p = 20 psf.

(ii) Chimneys, p = 30 psf.

(iii) Exterior walls, p = 15 psf inward or outward. Local pressure at corners of walls shall be not less than p = 30 psf outward. These local pressures shall not be included with the design pressure when computing overall loads. The pressures shall be applied perpendicularly outward on strips of width equal to 10 percent of the least width of building.

(iv) Partitions, p = 10 psf.

(v) Windows, p = 20 psf inward or outward.

(vi) Roof, p = 20 psf inward or outward.

Roofs with slopes greater than 6 in 12 shall be designed to withstand pressures acting inward normal to the surface, equal to the design wind pressure for exterior walls. Overhanging eaves, cornices, and ridges, 40 psf upward normal to roof surface. These local pressures shall not be included with the design pressure when computing overall loads. The pressures shall be applied perpendicularly outward on strips of width equal to 10 percent of the least width of building. Net uplift on horizontal projection of roof shall not be less than 12 psf.

(2) *Severe wind design pressures.* If the construction is higher than 30 ft., or if it is located in an area experiencing wind speeds greater than 80 mph, higher design wind pressures than shown above are required. Use Section 6 of ASCE 7–88 for higher criteria and for determining where wind speeds greater than 80 mph occur. Pressures are assumed to act horizontally on the gross area of the vertical projection of the structure except as noted for roof design.

(d) Seismic conditions shall be in accordance with Section 9 of ASCE 7–88.

(e) *Subject to damage from: weathering.* A jurisdiction's weathering region shall be as established by the map in ASTM C 62–83.

(f) *Subject to damage from: frost line depth.* Exterior wall footings or foundation walls including those of accessory buildings shall extend a minimum of 6 in. below the finished grade and, where applicable, the prevailing frost line.

(g) *Subject to damage from: termites.* "Yes" shall be used in locations designated as Regions I, II or III. "No" shall be used in locations designated as Region IV. The map for Termite Infestation Probability in appendix A of CABO, One and Two Family Dwelling Code shall be used to determine the jurisdiction's region.

(h) *Subject to damage from: decay.* "Yes" shall be used in locations designated as moderate to severe and slight to moderate. "No" shall be used in locations designated as none to slight. The Decay Probability map in appendix A of CABO, One and Two Family Dwelling Code shall be used to determine the jurisdiction's decay designation.

(Approved by the Office of Management and Budget under control number 2502–0338)

[50 FR 39599, Sept. 27, 1985, as amended at 59 FR 36695, July 19, 1994]

§ 200.927 Incorporation by reference of minimum property standards.

The Minimum Property Standards as contained in the handbooks identified in § 200.929(b) are incorporated by reference into this section as though set forth in full in accordance with 5 U.S.C. 552(a) and 1 CFR part 51.

[50 FR 39592, Sept. 29, 1985]

§ 200.929 Description and identification of minimum property standards.

(a) *Description.* The Minimum Property Standards describe physical standards for housing. They are intended to provide a sound basis for determining the acceptability of housing built under the HUD mortgage insurance and low-rent public housing programs. The Minimum Property Standards refer to material standards developed by industry and accepted by HUD. In addition, under Section 521 of the National Housing Act, HUD adopts its own technical suitability standards for materials and products for which there are no industry standards acceptable to HUD. These standards are contained in Use of Materials Bulletins that apply to products and methods and Materials Releases that apply to specific materials. Use of Materials Bulletins and Materials Releases are addenda to the Minimum Property Standards. Unless otherwise stated, the current edition, issue, or version of each of these documents, as available from its source, is applicable to this subpart S. A list of the Use of Materials Bulletins, Materials Releases, and MPS Appendix listing the applicable referenced Standards may be obtained from the Construction Standards Division, Office of Manufactured Housing and Construction Standards, room 6170 Department of Housing and Urban Development, 451 7th Street, SW, Washington, DC 20410.

(b) *Identification.* The Minimum Property Standards have been published as described below:

(1) MPS for One and Two Family Dwellings. *See* §§200.926, 200.926 (a) through (e).

(2) MPS for Housing 4910.1, 1994 edition. This volume applies to buildings and sites designed and used for normal multifamily occupancy, including both unsubsidized and subsidized insured housing, and to care-type housing insured under the National Housing Act. It also includes, in Appendix K, a reprint of the MPS for One and Two Family Dwellings identified in paragraph (b)(1) of this section.

[39 FR 26895, July 24, 1974, as amended at 42 FR 33890, July 1, 1977; 47 FR 29524, July 7, 1982; 47 FR 35761, Aug. 17, 1982; 49 FR 18695, May 1, 1984; 50 FR 39592, Sept. 29, 1985; 51 FR 28699, Aug. 11, 1986; 58 FR 60250, Nov. 15, 1993; 63 FR 5423, Feb. 2, 1998]

§200.929a **Fair Housing Accessibility Guidelines.**

Builders and developers may use the Department's Fair Housing Accessibility Guideline when designing or constructing covered multifamily dwelling units in order to comply with the Fair Housing Act. The Guidelines may be found in the 24 CFR Chapter I, Subchapter A, Appendix II, titled Fair Housing Accessibility Guidelines—Design Guidelines for Accessible/Adaptable Dwellings.

[58 FR 60250, Nov. 15, 1993]

§200.931 **Statement of availability.**

(a) Updated copies of the Minimum Property Standards and Use of Materials Bulletins are available for public examination in the Office of Consumer and Regulatory Affairs, Department of Housing and Urban Development, room 9156, 451 Seventh St. SW., Washington, D.C. 20410–8000. In addition, copies of volumes 1, 2, and 3 of the Minimum Property Standards may be purchased from the U.S. Government Printing Office, Washington, D.C. 20402.

(b) Publications approved by the Director of the Federal Register for incorporation by reference in accordance with 5 U.S.C. 552(a) and 1 CFR part 51 are available for inspection at the National Archives and Records Administration (NARA). For information on the availability of this material at NARA, call 202–741–6030, or go to: *http://www.archives.gov/federal_register/code_of_federal_regulations/ibr_locations.html.*

[63 FR 5423, Feb. 2, 1998]

§200.933 **Changes in minimum property standards.**

Changes in the Minimum Property Standards will generally be made every three years. Changes will be made in accordance with HUD policy for the adoption of rules and regulations set forth in part 10 of this title. Notice of such changes will be published in the FEDERAL REGISTER. As the changes are made, they will be incorporated into the volumes of the Minimum Property Standards to which they apply. The volumes available for public examination and for purchase will contain all changes up to the date of examination or purchase. An official, historic file of such changes will be available in the office of the Rules Docket Clerk in the HUD Central Office in Washington, DC, and in each HUD Regional, Area, and Insuring Office. A similar copy of the standards will also be maintained in the Office of the Federal Register, Washington, DC.

[39 FR 26895, July 24, 1974, as amended at 58 FR 60250, Nov. 15, 1993]

§ 200.934 User fee system for the technical suitability of products program.

(a) *General*. This section establishes fee requirements for the issuance of Structural Engineering Bulletins (SEBs), Mechanical Engineering Bulletins (MEBs), Truss Connector Bulletins (TCBs), Area Letters of Acceptance (ALAs), Materials Releases (MRs), and review of program administrator applications submitted pursuant to § 200.935 of this title.

(b) *Filing address—(1) Applications containing payment*. When applications for or correspondence concerning SEBs, MEBs, TCBs, MRs, or program administrator approval contain payment, such applications or correspondence shall be sent to the following address:

U.S. Department of Housing and Urban Development, Technical Suitability of Product Fees, P.O. Box 954199, St. Louis, MO. 63195–4199.

(2) *Other correspondence*. All other correspondence concerning SEBs, MEBs, TCBs, MRs, and program administrator acceptance shall be sent to the following address:

Manufactured Housing and Construction Standards Division, Department of Housing and Urban Development, 451 Seventh Street, SW., Attn: Mail Room B–133, Washington, DC 20410.

(3) *Application for ALAs*. Applications for or correspondence concerning ALAs shall be submitted to the Housing Division of the field office having jurisdiction over the area in which the production facility of the system is located, except that applications containing payment shall be addressed to the attention of the Collection Officer for deposit to Account No. 86–09–0300.

(c) *Fees*. Applicants for renewal and applicants for acceptance as program

administrators under § 200.935 of this title shall include the entire processing fee with the application. All other applicants shall submit one half of the required processing fee with each application. The applicant shall pay the balance when the draft issuance is returned to HUD with the applicant's concurrence signature. The Department will not prepare a final document for printing and distribution until it has received the full processing fee. From time to time, as may be necessary, the Department will establish and amend the fee schedule by publication of a Notice in the FEDERAL REGISTER.

(d) *Initial application and review—(1) Content of applications*. Each application shall include only one item. All applications will be promptly processed on receipt by the Department.

(i) With respect to Mechanical Engineering Bulletins (MEBs), Structural Engineering Bulletins (SEBs), Truss Connector Bulletins (TCBs), and Area Letters of Acceptance (ALAs), each structural design shall constitute a different item.

(ii) With respect to Materials Releases (MRs), each product or system shall constitute a different item.

(2) *Revisions*. A recipient of a technical suitability document issued by the Department may apply for revision of that document at any time. The revision may be in the form of an amendment of or supplement to the document, for which the recipient will be charged the applicable revision fee. However, where the Department determines that a proposed revision constitutes a different item, the schedule of fees for initial applications shall apply.

(3) *Renewals*. Each issuance shall be valid for a period of three years from the date of initial issuance or most recent renewal, whichever is later. An applicant shall submit an application for renewal with the entire required fee three months before the expiration of the three-year period. Failure to submit a timely renewal application along with the required fee shall constitute a basis for cancellation of the issuance.

(4) *Initial and revision applications requiring further study or additional data*. In its discretion, the Department may

request an applicant to submit additional data or to conduct further study to supplement or clarify an initial application or an application for revision of a previously issued technical suitability document. If the applicant fails to comply with the Department's request within ninety days of the date of that request or within such longer time as may be specified by the Secretary, the Department will return the application to the applicant. The Department will not refund any fees paid toward an application returned under this paragraph. The application will be considered further only if it is resubmitted along with payment of the full fee as required by these regulations.

(5) *Ineligible applications.* If the Secretary determines that an application or request will not be considered because it is not eligible for issuance of a technical suitability document, the Department will promptly return the application or request, refund any fees paid, and explain why the application or request is ineligible.

(6) *Cancellation of a technical suitability document.* If the Department determines that (i) the conditions under which a technical suitability document was issued have so changed as to affect the production of, or to compromise the integrity of, the material, product, or system approved thereby, or (ii) that the producer has changed its organizational form without notifying HUD, or (iii) that the producer is not complying with the responsibilities it assumed as a condition of HUD's acceptance of its material, product or system, the Department will notify the producer or manufacturer that the technical suitability document may be cancelled. However, before cancelling a technical suitability document, the Department will give the manufacturer reasonable notice in writing of the specific reasons therefore and an opportunity to present its views on why the technical suitability document should not be cancelled. No refund of fees will be made on a cancelled document.

(e) *Identification.* (1) Applications for issuance of a MEB, SEB, TCB, or MR submitted to HUD Headquarters will be identified with a case number. The applicant will be notified of the case number when receipt of the application

is acknowledged. Thereafter, the case number will be used on all correspondence relating to the application. When a final draft of a new document is prepared for publication and distribution, a bulletin or release number will be assigned to the new issuance.

(2) In the case of an application for an ALA submitted to a field office, the application will be processed in accordance with the identification and processing procedures established by the responsible field office. The field office will notify the applicant of receipt of the application and inform the applicant of the procedures that will be followed with respect to the issuance of an ALA.

(Information collection requirements in paragraphs (b), (c), (d)(1), (2), (3) and (4) were approved by the Office of Management and Budget under control number 2502-0313)

[49 FR 31856, Aug. 9, 1984, as amended at 58 FR 60250, Nov. 15, 1993]

§ **200.935 Administrator qualifications and procedures for HUD building products certification programs.**

(a) *General.* This section establishes administrator qualifications and procedures for the HUD Building Products Certification Programs under section 521 of the National Housing Act and the HUD Minimum Property Standards. Under these programs organizations acceptable to HUD validate manufacturers' certifications that certain building products or materials meet applicable standards. HUD may decide to implement a certification program for a particular building product or material for a variety of reasons, such as when deemed necessary by HUD to facilitate the introduction of new and innovative products or materials; or in response to reports of fraud or misrepresentation by manufacturers in advertising that their product or materials comply with a standard.

(b) *Definitions*—(1) *Certification program ("program").* The procedure under which accepted administrators validate manufacturers' certifications that particular building products or materials meet applicable HUD standards. A separate program is used to validate certifications for each particular product or material for which HUD requires certifications.

(2) *Program administrator ("administrator").* An organization which conducts the program validating the manufacturer's certification that a particular building product or material meets applicable HUD standards.

(c) *Administrator qualifications and application procedures*—(1) *Qualifications.* Each program administrator shall be capable of conducting a certification program with respect to organization, staff and facilities, and have a reputation for adhering to high ethical standards. To be considered acceptable for conducting a certification program, each administrator shall:

(i) Be a technically qualified organization with past experience in the administration of certification programs. The certification program(s) shall be under the supervision of a qualified professional with six years of experience in interpreting testing standards, test methods, evaluating test reports and quality control programs. Each administrator is responsible for staffing the program with qualified professional personnel with experience in interpreting testing standards, test methods, evaluating test reports and quality control programs. The staff shall be adequate to service all aspects of the program.

(ii) Have field inspectors trained to make selections of materials for testing from manufacturer's stock or from distributors' establishments and to conduct product compliance inspections. Such inspectors must be trained and experienced in evaluating manufacturer's quality control records to ascertain with a reasonable degree of assurance that continuing production remains in compliance with the applicable standard set forth in the Use of Materials (UM) Bulletin. When inspectors are used to evaluate laboratory operations, they shall be qualified and under the supervision of the administrator. They shall be knowledgeable in such areas as test methods, quality control, testing techniques, and instrument calibration.

(iii) Have facilities and capabilities for communications with manufacturers, laboratories, and HUD, including publication of a directory of certified products and a list of accredited laboratories, if required by the program.

(iv) Have adequate policies and practices for preserving information entrusted to its care. HUD reserves the right to review all technical records related to the program for the purpose of monitoring.

(v) Have a copy of all applicable standards, test methods and related information necessary to carry out the program.

(vi) Have a registered or pending certification mark at the United States Patent Office and be willing to license, on a uniform basis, the use of that mark by manufacturers as a validation of the manufacturer's certification that the product complies with the applicable standard.

(2) *Applications procedures.* Any organization desiring HUD acceptance as a qualified administrator to conduct a certification program shall make application in writing to the Director, Office of Architecture and Engineering Standards. The application shall state the particular certification program for which acceptance is requested and include information indicating compliance with each of the qualification requirements by number and subsection. Attached to the application shall be:

(i) A list of certification programs in which the organization is participating or has participated and the types of participation (sponsor, administrator, testing laboratory, etc.).

(ii) A procedural guide used in one of these programs.

(iii) A directory or listing used in one of these programs.

(iv) A reproduction or facsimile of the organization's registered or pending mark.

(v) A proposed procedural guide for the particular certification program. HUD certification program procedures described in paragraph (d) of this section shall be followed.

(3) *Acceptance.* HUD shall review each submission and notify the applicant whether or not they are accepted or rejected. HUD shall be notified immediately of any change(s) in the administrator's submission regarding program procedures and/or major personnel associated with the program. HUD reserves the right to suspend or debar an administrator in accordance with 2 CFR part 2424.

(d) *HUD building products certification procedures*—(1) *Certification program development.* Certification program development by an administrator shall be based upon the procedures and standards for the specific building product described in a Use of Materials Bulletin or a Materials Release.

(2) *License agreement.* Each administrator shall have a written license agreement with each participating manufacturer binding each to the provisions of the specific program and authorizing the manufacturer to use the administrator's mark, seal, or label on its products. The administrator shall have the right to terminate any agreement prior to an expiration date, for example, if there has been a breach of the requirement of the certification program by the manufacturer.

(3) *Laboratory approval.* The administrator shall review laboratories that apply for participation in this program on the basis of the procedures described in paragraph (e) of this section. A list of approved laboratories shall be maintained by the administrator. When the certification program allows the use of the administrator's testing laboratories, the laboratories shall be reviewed by a qualified party acceptable to HUD. As accreditation procedures are made available through the National Voluntary Laboratory Accreditation Program (NVLAP) for specifc products, HUD may require such accreditation.

(4) *Initial testing and quality control review*—(i) *Initial testing.* Each participating manufacturer shall submit to the appropriate administrator, the product(s) specification and statement(s) that the product complies with the applicable standard. The administrator shall select samples of the product(s), or when HUD specifies as acceptable, a prototype. The particular method of sample selection shall be determined by HUD for each specific product certification program. Other methods of initial sample selection may be used if deemed necessary. If a failure occurs on the initial tests, additional sampling and testing may be done at the manufacturer's request. The administrator's validation of the manufacturer's declaration of certifi-

cation shall be withheld until a finding of compliance is achieved.

(ii) *Quality assurance system review.* (A) Each administrator shall examine a participating manufacturer's facilities and quality assurance system procedures to determine that they are adequate to assure continuing production of the product that complies with the applicable standard. These quality assurance system procedures shall be documented in the administrator's and the manufacturer's files. If a manufacturer's quality assurance system is not satisfactory to the administrator, validation of the manufacturer's declaration of certification shall be withheld. The following American Society for Quality Control (ASQC) standards, which are incorporated by reference, may be used as guidelines in any quality assurance review:

(*1*) ASQC Q9000–1–1994 Quality Management and Quality Assurance Standards Guidelines for Selection and Use;

(*2*) ASQC Q9001–1994 Quality Systems—Model for Quality Assurance in Design, Development, Production, Installation, and Servicing;

(*3*) ASQC Q9002–1994 Quality Systems—Model for Quality Assurance in Production, Installation, and Servicing;

(*4*) ASQC Q9003–1994 Quality Systems—Model for Quality Assurance in Final Inspection and Test;

(*5*) ASQC Q9004–1–1994 Quality Management and Quality System Elements-Guidelines.

(B) These standards have been approved by the Director of the Federal Register for incorporation by reference in accordance with 5 U.S.C. 552(a) and 1 CFR part 51. They are available from the American Society for Quality Control (ASQC), 611 East Wisconsin Avenue, Milwaukee, WI 53202.

(5) *Notice of validation.* When initial testing, quality control review, and evaluation of other technical data are satisfactory to the administrator, a Notice of Validation or Certification shall be issued to the manufacturer. This allows the use of the administrator's registered mark on the product label.

(6) *Labeling.* Each administrator shall issue to the manufacturer labels, tags, marks containing the administrator's

validation mark, and the manufacturer's certification of compliance with the applicable standard. The registered administrator's (validator's) mark shall be on the label. A sponsor's (association, testing agencies, society or others) mark may be used in addition to the administrator's mark. The manufacturer's certification of compliance to the standard may be coded. Additional information such as type, grade, class, etc., may also be coded. When coding is used, the code shall be described in the directory or listing.

(7) *Directory or listing.* When required by the program, the administrator shall publish a directory or listing for all certified products. The directory shall list the items described in paragraph (d)(6) of this section. The directly shall also carry a complete list of approved laboratories and shall be updated to reflect additions or deletions of certified products and laboratories. Directories or listings shall be published periodically as described in the specific program. Each administrator shall make a complimentary distribution of the directory or listing to the HUD Field Offices and other government agencies designated by HUD. A subscription fee may be charged to others requesting copies.

(8) *Periodic tests and quality control inspections.* Samples of the certified product or prototype shall be selected periodically from the plant, warehouse inventory or sales points. The samples shall be sent to an administrator-approved laboratory and tested in accordance with the applicable standard. The frequency of testing shall be described in the specific building product program. The administrator shall periodically visit the manufacturer's facility to assure that the initially accepted quality control procedures are being followed.

(9) *Product decertification.* If a failure should occur in any test, the laboratory shall notify the administrator and the manufacturer. The manufacturer shall notify the administrator if a retest if requested. If a retest is not requested, validation shall be withdrawn. If the manufacturer requests a retest, the administrator shall select new samples and submit them to the same or another laboratory at the manufacturer's expense, for retest of only the test requirement(s) in which the failure(s) occurred. If the specified number of specimens pass the retest, the product can continue to be validated and listed. If the designated number of specimens described in the UM Bulletin fail, the administrator shall decertify the product. The manufacturer may request that a new selection be made of the product after corredction or modifications and be subjected to the initial acceptance testing procedure or to a program of retesting established by the administrator. The administrator may decertify the product on the basis of inadequate quality control by the manufacturer. The administrator shall notify the manufacturer, HUD headquarters and the HUD Field Offices of any decertification within 7 days. When the product is decertified the magnufacturer shall remove labels, tags or marks from all production and inventory in his/her control determined to be in noncompliance.

(10) *Challenge response.* Any person or organization may submit a sample of a manufacturer's certified product to the administrator in substantiation of a claim of noncompliance. Submission shall be made to the administrator that validated the manufacturer's product. The administrator shall notify the manufacturer that its product has been challenged and shall make arrangements to obtain test samples of the challenged product. An estimate of the cost of the special sample selection and testing shall be made to the complainant. The complainant shall pay the estimated cost of the investigation in advance of any testing of the challenged product, unless HUD believes the complaint to be in the public's interest. HUD may conduct its own investigation when deemed necessary based upon a complaint or a product failure. The administrator shall submit the sample of the challenged product to an approved laboratory of the administrator's choice with the request to test compliance of only the challenged requirement(s). If the samples tested prove that the product failed to meet the standard, the product shall be decertified immediately. The manufacturer whose product is decertified shall reimburse the administrator for all

costs of the investigation and the administrator shall refund the complainant's advance payment. If the tests prove that the product does comply with the standard, the complainant shall be notified that the tests do not support the complaint and that the advance fee has been used for the cost of testing and investigating the claim.

(11) *Maintainance of the program.* Each administrator shall maintain the program in conformance with administrative letters issued by HUD for the purpose of clarifying procedures and interpreting the applicable standard. These letters may also be used to revise and amend the procedures used in specific programs. Significant changes in any program shall be published in the FEDERAL REGISTER.

(e) *Laboratory qualifications.* The following laboratory qualifications apply to all testing laboratories participating in the program including manufacturer's laboratories and the administrator's own laboratories when designated in the specific program.

(1) *Organization and personnel.* Laboratories wishing to participate in a certification program shall apply to the administrator and shall furnish the following information:

(i) Name of laboratory, address, telephone number, name and title of official to be contacted for this program.

(ii) Name and qualifications of person assigned by the laboratory to supervise testing under a specific certification program.

(iii) Name and qualifications of engineers and other key personnel who shall conduct the testing.

(iv) Brief review of training program for personnel associated with program to assure the operational efficiency and uniformity of the testing and quality control procedures.

Each laboratory shall notify the administrator of any change in its submission regarding procedures and/or major personnel associated with the program.

(2) *Equipment and facilities.* Each laboratory shall:

(i) Describe the test instruments and testing facilities to be used in making the test(s) required by the applicable standard. Information shall include: Item of equipment, manufacturer, type or model, serial number, range, precision, frequency of calibration and dates of calibration.

(ii) Provide photographs of the listed equipment.

(iii) Provide a description of the applicable standards and calibration equipment being used and the calibration procedures followed, including National Bureau of Standards traceability, when applicable. List outside organizations providing calibration services, if used.

(iv) Demonstrate that measurements can be made with existing equipment and repeated precision within the limits established by the applicable standards. Administrator may periodically require laboratories to conduct collaborative testing on standard reference materials.

(v) Provide evidence, when regulated temperatures and humidity are required, that charts are maintained from a continuous recorder registering both wet and dry bulb temperature or relative humidity. The charts are to be properly dated, retained and available for inspection.

(vi) Provide a list of standards, test methods and other information necessary to carry out the program.

(3) *Testing methodology.* (i) Describe concisely the procedures for conducting the tests required and the specific equipment to be used.

(ii) Attach a sample test report showing representative test results and accompanied by test data forms for each test required. When approved for program participation, testing laboratories may be required by administrator to report test results on standard summary report forms.

(4) *Subcontractors.* If a testing laboratory plans to subcontract any of its testing to other laboratories, only approved laboratories acceptable to the administrator shall be used.

(5) *Laboratory quality control.* The laboratory shall develop operating quality control procedures acceptable to the administrator. The procedures of the American Council of Independent Laboratories[1] may be used as a guideline.

[1] Copies are available from the American Council of Independent Laboratories, Inc., 1725 "K" Street, NW., Washington, DC 20006.

(6) *Approval of laboratories.* Administrators shall develop detailed laboratory approval requirements and conduct periodic inspections to assure each test laboratory's capability. Laboratory approval may be granted for 2 years. Reapproval of the laboratory shall be necessary every 2 years. When a program allows the use of an administrator's own laboratories, these laboratories shall be reviewed by a qualified third party acceptable to HUD. Documentation of acceptance for administrator laboratories shall be maintained by the administrator and HUD. Administrator laboratories shall be subject to reapproval every two years.

(7) *Withdrawal of approval.* Laboratory approval shall be withdrawn or temporarily suspended if it is determined that the laboratory is not complying with the approved requirements. Causes for suspension include, but are not limited to, the following:

(i) Incompetence.

(ii) Failure to test in accordance with the test methods described in the standard.

(iii) Issuance of test reports which fail to comply with the requirements described in the specific product certification program.

(iv) Falsification of the information reported.

(v) A statement implying validation of the product using a test report which constitutes only part of the total standard.

(vi) Deceptively utilizing references in advertising or other promotional activities.

(vii) Submission of incomplete or inadequate information and documentation called for herein.

[44 FR 54656, Sept. 20, 1979, as amended at 63 FR 5423, Feb. 2, 1998; 72 FR 73494, Dec. 27, 2007]

§ 200.936 Supplementary specific procedural requirements under HUD building products certification program for solid fuel type room heaters and fireplace stoves.

(a) *Applicable standards.* Solid fuel type room heaters and fireplace stoves certified under the HUD Building Products Certification Program shall be designed, assembled and tested in conformance with the following standards, which are incorporated by reference:

(1) ANSI/UL 737 (1978), for fireplace stoves;

(2) ANSI/UL 1482 (1979), for solid fuel type room heaters with coal amendments.

(b) *Labelling.* (1) Under the procedures set forth in paragraph (d)(6) of § 200.935, concerning labelling of a product, the administrator's validation mark and the manufacturer's certification of compliance with the applicable standards are required to be on the certification label issued by the administrator to the manufacturer. In the case of solid fuel type room heaters and fireplace stoves, the following additional information must be included on the certification label:

(i) The manufacturer's statement of conformance to the HUD Building Products Certification Program;

(ii) The manufacturer's name and the identity and location of manufacturing plant;

(iii) The specification designation and manufacturer series or model number; and

(iv) The type of fuel to be used.

(2) The certification label must be permanently affixed to the heater or stove and be readily visible after the heater or stove is installed.

(c) *Periodic tests and quality control inspections.* Under the procedures set forth in paragraph (d)(8) of § 200.935, concerning periodic tests and quality control inspections, the frequency of testing for a product must be described in the specific building product certification program. In the case of solid fuel type room heaters and fireplace stoves, testing and inspection shall be conducted as follows:

(1) Once every four years, beginning with the initial administrator visit, a sample of each certified product shall be selected by the administrator for testing for compliance with the applicable standards in a laboratory which has been accredited under the National Voluntary Laboratory Accreditation Program.

(2) The administrator shall visit the manufacturer's facility two times a

year to assure that the initially accepted quality control procedures are being followed.

[48 FR 1955, Jan. 17, 1983]

§ 200.937 **Supplementary specific procedural requirements under HUD building product standards and certification program for plastic bathtub units, plastic shower receptors and stalls, plastic lavatories, plastic water closet bowls and tanks.**

(a) *Applicable standards.* (1) Plastic bathtub units, plastic shower receptors and stalls, plastic lavatories, and plastic water closet bowls and tanks shall be designed, assembled and tested in compliance with the following standards, which are incorporated by reference:

ANSI Z124.1—(1980) Plastic Bathtub Units
ANSI Z124.2—(1980) Plastic Shower Receptors and Stalls
ANSI Z124.3—(1980) Plastic Lavatories
ANSI Z124.4—(1983) Plastic Water Closet Bowls and Tanks

(2) These standards have been approved by the Director of the Federal Register for incorporation by reference. They are available from the American National Standards Institute, Inc., 11 West 42nd Street, New York, NY 10036. The standards are also available for inspection at the National Archives and Records Administration (NARA). For information on the availability of this material at NARA, call 202–741–6030, or go to: *http:// www.archives.gov/federal_register/ code_of_federal_regulations/ ibr_locations.html.*

(b) *Labeling.* (1) Under the procedures set forth in paragraph (d)(6) of § 200.935, concerning labeling of a product, the administrator's validation mark and the manufacturer's certification of compliance with the applicable standards are required to be on the certification label issued by the administrator to the manufacturer. In the case of plastic bathtub units, plastic shower receptors and stalls, plastic lavatories, and plastic water closet bowls and tanks, the following additional information shall be included on the certification label:

(i) Manufacturer's statement of conformance to UM 73a;

(ii) Manufacturer's name and code identifying the plant location.

(2) The certification label shall be affixed to each plastic bathroom fixture.

(c) *Periodic tests and quality control inspections.* Under the procedures set forth in paragraph (d)(8) of § 200.935, concerning periodic tests and quality control inspections, the frequency of testing for a product shall be described in the specific building product certification program. In the case of plastic bathroom fixtures, testing and inspection shall be conducted as follows:

(1) At least every six months, the administrator shall visit the manufacturer's facility to select a sample of each certified plastic bathtub unit, plastic shower receptor and stall, plastic water closet bowl and tank for testing in an approved laboratory, in accordance with applicable standards.

(2) At least every twelve months, the administrator shall visit the manufacturer's facility to select a sample of each certified plastic lavatory for testing in accordance with applicable standards.

(3) The administrator shall also review quality control procedures at each visit to determine that they continue to be followed.

[49 FR 378, Jan. 4, 1984, as amended at 59 FR 36695, July 19, 1994]

§ 200.940 **Supplementary specific requirements under the HUD building product standards and certification program for sealed insulating glass units.**

(a) *Applicable standards.* (1) All sealed insulating glass units shall be designed, manufactured, and tested in compliance with the American Society for Testing and Materials standard: ASTM E–774–92 Standard Specification for Sealed Insulating Glass Units.

(2) This standard has been approved by the Director of the Federal Register for incorporation by reference. The standard is available from the American Society for Testing and Materials, 1916 Race Street, Philadelphia, PA 19103. This standard is also available for inspection at the National Archives and Records Administration (NARA). For information on the availability of this material at NARA, call 202–741– 6030, or go to: *http://www.archives.gov/*

federal_register/
code_of_federal_regulations/
ibr_locations.html.

(b) *Labeling.* Under the procedures set forth in § 200.935(d)(6) concerning labeling of a product, the administrator's validation mark and the manufacturer's certification of compliance with the applicable standards are issued by the administrator to the manufacturer. Each sealed insulating glass unit shall be marked as conforming to UM 82a. The label shall be located on each sealed insulating unit so that it is available for inspection. The label shall include the manufacturer's name and plant location.

(c) *Periodic tests and quality assurance inspections.* Under the procedures set forth in § 200.935(d)(8) concerning periodic tests and quality assurance inspections, the frequency of testing for a product shall be described in the specific building product certification program. In the case of sealed insulating glass units, testing and inspection shall be conducted as follows:

(1) At least once a year, the administrator shall visit the manufacturer's facility to select a sample, of the maximum size commercially available, for testing in a laboratory approved by the administrator.

(2) The administrator shall also review the quality assurance procedures twice a year to assure that they are being followed by the manufacturer.

[58 FR 67674, Dec. 22, 1993]

§ 200.942 Supplementary specific procedural requirements under HUD building product standards and certification program for carpet and carpet with attached cushion.

(a) *Applicable standards.* (1) Carpet and carpet with attached cushion certified for this program shall be designed, manufactured and tested in accordance with the following standards:

(i) AATCC 20A–81—Fiber Analysis: Quantitative;

(ii) AATCC 16E–82—Colorfastness to Light: Water-Cooled Xenon-Arc Lamp, Continuous Light;

(iii) AATCC 8–85—Colorfastness to Crocking: AATCC Crockmeter Method;

(iv) AATCC 24–85—Insect, Resistance to Textiles to;

(v) ASTM D1335–67 (Reapproved 1972)—Standard Test Method for Tuft Bind of Pile Floor Coverings;

(vi) ASTM D3676–78 (Reapproved 1983)—Standard Specification for Rubber Cellular Cushion Used for Carpet or Rug Underlay;

(vii) ASTM E648–78—Standard Test Method for Critical Radiant Flux of Floor-Covering Systems Using a Radiant Heat Energy Source;

(viii) ASTM D2646–79—Standard Methods of Testing Backing Fabrics;

(ix) ASTM D3936–80—Standard Test Method for Delamination Strength of Secondary Backing of Pile Floor Coverings;

(x) ASTM D297–81—Standard Methods for Rubber Products—Chemical Analysis;

(xi) ASTM D418–82—Standard Methods of Testing Pile Yarn Floor Covering Construction; and

(xii) National Bureau of Standards DOC FF 1–70. (ASTM D2859–76)—Standard Test Method for Flammability of Finished Textile Floor Covering Materials.

(2) These standards have been approved by the Director of the Federal Register for incorporation by reference. They are available from the (i) American Association of Textile Chemists and Colorists (AATCC), P.O. Box 12215, Research Triangle Park, NC 27709;

(ii) American Society for Testing and Materials (ASTM), 1916 Race Street, Philadelphia, PA 19103; and

(iii) U.S. Department of Commerce, National Bureau of Standards, Washington, DC 20234.

The standards are also available for inspection at the National Archives and Records Administration (NARA). For information on the availability of this material at NARA, call 202–741–6030, or go to: http://www.archives.gov/federal_register/code_of_federal_regulations/ibr_locations.html.

(b) *Labeling.* (1) Under the procedures set forth in § 202.935(d)(6), concerning labeling of a product, the administrator's validation mark and the manufacturer's certification of compliance with the applied standard is required to be on the certification label issued by the administrator to the manufacturer. In the case of carpet and carpet with attached cushion, the following additional information shall be included on the certification label, mark or stamp:

(i) Manufacturer's name or code identifying the manufacturing plant location; and

(ii) Manufacturer's statement of compliance with UM 44d.

(2) The certification mark shall be applied to each carpet at intervals of at least every six feet, not less than one foot from the edge.

(c) *Periodic tests and quality control inspections.* (1) Five samples of carpet and carpet with attached cushion shall be tested annually by the administrator or by an administrator-approved laboratory. Three samples of each certified quality shall be taken from the plant annually. Of these, two shall be interim samples (taken every six months) and one an annual sample. In addition, two samples of each certified quality shall be taken annually from sources other than the manufacturer, *i.e.*, brought in the market place from distributors or stores, not from the factory. The administrator shall select samples for testing, and testing shall be conducted, in accordance with the applicable standards in a laboratory accredited by the National Voluntary Laboratory Accreditation Program (NVLAP) of the National Bureau of Standards, U.S. Department of Commerce.

(2) The administrator shall visit the manufacturer's facility at least once every six months to assure that the initially accepted quality control procedures continue to be followed.

[51 FR 17928, May 16, 1986]

§ 200.943 **Supplementary specific requirements under the HUD building product standards and certification program for the grademarking of lumber.**

(a) *Applicable standard.* (1) In accordance with UM 38j, lumber shall be grademarked in compliance with the U.S. Department of Commerce Voluntary Product Standard PS 20–94 American Softwood Lumber Standard.

(2) This standard has been approved by the Director of the Federal Register for incorporation by reference in accordance with 5 U.S.C. 552(a) and 1 CFR part 51. It is available from the U.S. Department of Commerce, NIST, Office of Voluntary Product Standards, Gaithersburg, MD 20899.

(b) *Labeling.* Under the procedures set forth in § 200.935(d)(6) concerning labeling of a product, the administrator's validation mark and the manufacturer's certification of compliance with the applicable standard are required on the certification label issued by the administrator to the manufacturer. However, in the case of grademarking of lumber, the following information shall be included on the certification label or mark:

(1) The registered symbol which identifies the grading agency;

(2) Species or species combination;

(3) Grade;

(4) Identification of the applicable grading rules when not indicated by the species identification or agency symbol;

(5) Mill or grader;

(6) For members which are less than 5 inches in nominal thickness, indication that the lumber was green or dry at the time of dressing;

(7) Indication that the lumber was finger jointed; and

(8) The certification mark shall be affixed to each piece of lumber.

(c) *Periodic tests and quality assurance.* Periodic tests and quality assurance inspections shall be carried out by the American Lumber Standard Committee as defined in PS 20–94.

[63 FR 5423, Feb. 2, 1998]

§ 200.944 **Supplementary specific requirements under the HUD building product standards and certification program for plywood and other performance rated wood-based structural-use panels.**

(a)(1) All plywood made to specifications of Voluntary Product Standard, PS 1–83, "Construction and Industrial Plywood" (published by the U.S. Department of Commerce, National Bureau of Standards (May 1984)) and grade marked as PS 1–83 shall conform to the requirements of PS 1–83, except that all veneers may be D-grade. A copy of PS

1–83 may be obtained from the U.S. Department of Commerce, National Institute for Standards and Technology, Office of Product Standards, Gaithersburg, MD 20899.

(2) All plywood panels not meeting the veneer grade requirements of PS 1–83, and all performance rated composite and nonveneer structural-use panels shall comply with the requirements described in the APA PRP–108, "Performance Standards and Policies for Structural-Use panels" (published by the American Plywood Association, June 1988). However, in ASTM D–3043–87, "Standard Methods of Testing Structural Panels in Flexure" (published by the American Society for Testing and Materials, August 28, 1987), Method B may be used in lieu of Method C for measuring the mechanical properties of the panel, provided that the test specimen has a width of at least 12 inches. The impact load shall be 150 ft. lbs. for single-layer floor panels excluding any floor finishes. Copies of the APA Standard may be obtained from the American Plywood Association, P.O. Box 11700, Tacoma, WA 98411–0770. Copies of the ASTM Standard may be obtained from the American Society of Testing and Materials, 1916 Race Street, Philadelphia, PA 19103.

(3) Structural-use panels shall be installed in accordance with the manufacturer's installation instructions and Form No. E30K, "APA Design/Construction Guide-Residential and Commercial" (published by the American Plywood Association, January 1989).

(4) These standards have been approved by the Director of the Federal Register for incorporation by reference in accordance with 5 U.S.C. 552(a) and 1 CFR part 51. Copies of the standards are available for inspection at the National Archives and Records Administration (NARA). For information on the availability of this material at NARA, call 202–741–6030, or go to: *http://www.archives.gov/federal_register/code_of_federal_regulations/ibr_locations.html*.

(b) *Labeling.* Under the procedures set forth in § 200.935(d)(6) concerning labeling of a product, the administrator's validation mark and the manufacturer's certification of compliance with the applicable standards are required to be on the certification label issued by the administrator to the manufacturer. Panels that conform to the Performance Standards and Policy for Structural-Use Panels shall be marked as conforming to UM 40c. All panels complying with APA PRP–108 shall be marked with a label formatted in the manner similar to the trademark examples shown in APA PRP–108. All panels will be marked with the mill number. The certification mark shall be stamped on each panel and be located so that it is available for inspection.

(c) *Periodic tests and qualify control inspections.* Under the procedures set forth in § 200.935(d)(8) concerning periodic tests and quality control inspections, the frequency of testing for a product shall be described in the specific building product certification program. In the case of plywood and wood-based structural-use panels, testing and inspection shall be conducted as follows:

(1) Testing shall be done in an Administrator's laboratory or an Administrator-approved laboratory every three months. All plywood qualified for conformance with PS 1–83 shall be tested in accordance with PS 1–83.

(2) All thickness and lay-ups of structural-use panels in production made in conformance with the Performance Standards shall be tested in accordance with procedures set forth in APA PRP–108 Performance Standards and Policies for Structural-Use Panels (published by the American Plywood Association Standard June 1988).

(3) The Administrator shall examine each manufacturer's quality control procedures to assure they are the same as or equivalent to those set forth under the Quality Assurance Policy section 4.2.3 of the publication referenced in paragraph (2) above or PS 1–83 section 3.8.6.6, Reexamination.

(4) The Administrator shall inspect the manufacturer's procedures at the plant at least every three months to assure that the initially accepted quality control procedures are being followed.

[55 FR 38785, Sept. 20, 1990]

§200.945 Supplementary specific requirements under the HUD building product standards and certification program for carpet.

(a) *Applicable standards.* (1) All carpet shall be designed, manufactured, and tested in compliance with the following standards from the American Society for Testing and Materials and the American Association of Textile Chemists and Colorists:

(i) ASTM D418–92—Standard Test Methods for Tuft and Yarn Length of Uncoated Floor Coverings;

(ii) ASTM D1335–67—(Reapproved 1972) Standard Test Method for Tuft Bind of Pile Floor Coverings;

(iii) ASTM D 2646–87—Standard Test Methods for Backing Fabrics;

(iv) ASTM D 3936–80—Standard Test Method for Delamination Strength of Secondary Backing of Pile Floor Coverings;

(v) AATCC Test Method 16e–82—Colorfastness to Light: Water-Cooled Xenon-Arc Lamp, Continuous Light;

(vi) AATCC Test Method 165–86—Colorfastness to Crocking: Carpets—AATCC Crock Meter Method;

(vii) ASTM D 3676–78—(Reapproved 1989) Standard Specification for Rubber Cellular Cushion Used for Carpet or Rug Underlay;

(viii) ASTM D 3574–91—Standard Test Methods for Flexible Cellular Materials—Slab, Bonded and Molded Urethane Foams.

(2) These standards have been approved by the Director of the Federal Register for incorporation by reference. The standards are available from the American Society for Testing and Materials, 1916 Race Street, Philadelphia, PA 19103 and the American Association of Textile Chemists and Colorists, P.O. Box 12215, Research Triangle Park, NC 27709. These standards are also available for inspection at the National Archives and Records Administration (NARA). For information on the availability of this material at NARA, call 202–741–6030, or go to: *http:// www.archives.gov/federal_register/ code_of_federal_regulations/ ibr_locations.html.*

(b) *Labeling.* Under the procedures set forth in §200.935(d)(6) concerning labeling of a product, the administrator's validation mark and the manufacturer's certification of compliance with UM 44d are required to be on the certification label issued by the Administrator to the manufacturer. The label shall be placed on each carpet every six feet not less than one foot from the edge.

(c) *Periodic tests and quality assurance inspection.* Under the procedure set forth in §200.935(d)(8), testing and inspection shall be conducted as follows:

(1) Every six months, three samples and one annual field sample of carpet shall be submitted to the Administrator for testing in a laboratory accredited by the National Voluntary Laboratory Accreditation Program of the U.S. Department of Commerce.

(2) The administrator also shall review the quality assurance procedures every six months to assure that they are being followed by the manufacturer.

[58 FR 67674, Dec. 22, 1993]

§200.946 Building product standards and certification program for exterior finish and insulation systems, use of Materials Bulletin UM 101.

(a) *Applicable standards:* (1) All Exterior Finish and Insulation Systems shall be designed, manufactured, and tested in compliance with the following standards:

(i) ASCE 7–93, American Society of Civil Engineers—Minimum Design Loads for Buildings and Other Structures.

(ii) ASTM C 150–94 Standard Specification for Portland Cement.

(iii) ASTM C 920–87 Standard Specification for Elastomeric Joint Sealants.

(iv) ASTM C–1186–91 Standard Specification for Flat Non-Asbestos Fiber-Cement Sheets.

(v) ASTM D 579–90 Standard Specification for Greige Woven Glass Fabrics.

(vi) ASTM D 3273–86—(Reapproved 1991) Standard Test Method for Resistance to Growth of Mold on the Surface of Interior Coatings in an Environmental Chamber.

(vii) ASTM E 330–90 Standard Test Method for Structural Performance of Exterior Windows, Curtain Walls, and Doors by Uniform Static Air Pressure Difference.

(viii) ASTM E 695–79 (Reapproved 1991), Standard Method of Measuring Relative Resistance of Wall, Floor, and Roof Construction to Impact Loading.

(ix) ASTM G 26–93 Standard Practice for Operating Light-Exposure Apparatus (Xenon-Arc Type) With and Without Water for Exposure of Nonmetallic Materials.

(x) Council of American Building Officials, Model Energy Code, 1993 Edition.

(xi) EIMA Test Method 101.01–95 (modified ASTM C67–91) Standard Test Method for Freeze/Thaw Resistance of Exterior Insulation and Finish Systems (EIFS), Class PB.

(xii) EIMA Test Method 101.02–95 (modified ASTM E331–91)—Standard Test Method for Resistance to Water Penetration of Exterior Insulation and Finish Systems (EIFS), Class PB.

(xiii) EIMA Test Method 101.03–95 (modified ASTM C297–91)—Standard Test Method for Determining the Tensile Adhesion Strength of an Exterior Insulation and Finish System (EIFS), Class PB.

(xiv) EIMA Test Method 105.01–95—Standard Test Method for Alkali Resistance of Glass Fiber Reinforcing Mesh for Use in Exterior Insulation and Finish Systems (EIFS), Class PB.

(xv) European Agreement Union Technical Committee—June 88—UEAtc Directives for the Assessment of External Insulation System for Walls (Expanded Polystyrene Insulation Faced with a Thin Rendering) Section 3.3.3.3.

(2) These standards have been approved by the Director of the Federal Register for incorporation by reference in accordance with 5 U.S.C. 552(a) and 1 CFR part 51. They are available from:

(i) American Society Civil Engineers (ASCE) 345 East 47th Street, New York, NY 10017.

(ii) American Society for Testing and Materials (ASTM), 1916 Race Street, Philadelphia, Pennsylvania 19103;

(iii) Council of American Building Officials, 5203 Leesburg Pike, Falls Church, Virginia 22041;

(iv) EAUTC Centre Scientifique ET Technique Du Batiment (CSTB), 84 Avenue Jesu Jaures, B.P. 02–77421 Marne-LA-Valee Cedex 2, Paris, France.

(v) Exterior Insulation Manufacturers Association (EIMA), 2759 State Road 580, Suite 112, Clearwater, Florida 34621–3350.

(3) The standards are available also for inspection at the Office of Manufactured Housing and Regulatory Functions, Standards and Products Branch, Department of Housing and Urban Development, room 3214, L'Enfant Plaza, 490E, Mail Room B–133, Washington, DC 20410–8000, and at the National Archives and Records Administration (NARA). For information on the availability of this material at NARA, call 202–741–6030, or go to: *http:// www.archives.gov/federal_register/ code_of_federal_regulations/ ibr_locations.html.*

(b) *Labeling.* Under the procedures as set forth in § 200.935(d)(6), concerning labeling of a product, the administrator's validation mark and the manufacturer's certification of compliance with the applied standard is required to be on the certification label issued by the administrator to the manufacturers. In the case of exterior wall insulation and finish systems, the certification label containing the administrator's mark shall be permanently affixed on the package or container of base and finish coating materials. Further, additional information shall be included on the certification label or mark:

(1) Manufacturer's name.

(2) Manufacturer's statement of conformance with UM 101.

(c) The Administrator shall visit the manufacturer's or sponsor's facility every 6 months, to assure that the initially accepted quality assurance procedures are being followed. At least every four years, the Administrator also shall have the exterior wall insulation and finish systems tested in an approved laboratory to assure that the original performance is maintained.

(d) The administrator's (or administration-accepted inspection agency) inspection of EFIS system installation of 5000 sq. ft. or more, shall be made during and upon completion of the construction. Reports of the inspection shall be made to the owner. These reports shall state:

(1) The coverage of the finish coat per square foot for a given volume of finish.

(2) The minimum thickness of the base and finish coatings.

(3) The fiberglass mesh is installed properly around joints and insulation. All penetrations, including windows, flashing, etc., are sealed; and there is a caulk and sealant continuity evaluation; and

(4) There is a caulk and sealant continuity evaluation with special concerns on maintenance.

(e) The manufacturer shall warrant their exterior wall insulation and finish system, including any caulks and sealants, for twenty years against faulty performance. The warranty shall include correction of delamination, chipping, denting, peeling, blistering, flaking, bulging, unsightly discoloration, or other serious deterioration of the system such as the intrusion of water through the wall or structural failure of the system's surface materials. Should any of these defects occur, the manufacturer shall make a pro-rata allowance for replacement or pay the owner the amount of the allowance. The manufacturer shall not be liable for damages or defects resulting from misuse, natural catastrophes, or other causes beyond the control of the manufacturer. The contractor shall provide a statement to the owner that the product has been installed in compliance with HUD requirements and that the manufacturer's warranty does not relieve the builder, in any way, of responsibility under the terms of the Builder's Warranty required by the National Housing Act, or under any other housing program.

[60 FR 47841, Sept. 14, 1995]

§ 200.947 Building product standards and certification program for polystyrene foam insulation board.

(a) *Applicable standards.* (1) All polystyrene foam insulation board shall be designed, manufactured, and tested in compliance with the American Society for Testing and Materials (ASTM) standard C–578–92, Standard Specification for Rigid, Cellular Polystyrene Thermal Insulation.

(2) This standard has been approved by the Director of the Federal Register for incorporation by reference. The standard is available from the American Society for Testing and Materials, 1916 Race Street, Philadelphia, PA 19103. This standard is also available

for inspection at the National Archives and Records Administration (NARA). For information on the availability of this material at NARA, call 202–741–6030, or go to: *http://www.archives.gov/federal_register/code_of_federal_regulations/ibr_locations.html.*

(b) *Labeling.* Under the procedures set forth in § 200.935(d)(6) concerning labeling of a product, the administrator's certification of compliance with the applicable standards and the type of board are required to be on the certification label issued by the administrator to the manufacturer.

(c) *Periodic tests and quality assurance inspection.* Under the procedure set forth in § 200.935(d)(8), testing and inspection shall be conducted as follows:

(1) At least every six months, the administrator shall visit the manufacturer's facility to select a sample of each certified polystyrene foam insulation board for testing by a laboratory approved by the administrator.

(2) The administrator also shall review the quality assurance procedures every six months to assure that they are being followed by the manufacturer.

[58 FR 67675, Dec. 22, 1993]

§ 200.948 Building product standards and certification program for carpet cushion.

(a) *Applicable standards.* (1) All carpet cushion shall be designed, manufactured, and tested in compliance with the following standards from the American Society for Testing and Materials:

(i) ASTM D 1667–76—(Reapproved 1990) Standard Specification for Flexible Cellular Materials—Vinyl Chloride Polymers and Copolymers (Closed-Cell Foam);

(ii) ASTM D2646–87—Standard Test Methods for Backing Fabrics;

(iii) ASTM D629–88—Standard Test Methods for Quantitative Analysis of Textiles;

(iv) ASTM D3574–91—Standard Test Methods for Flexible Cellular Materials—Slab, Bonded, and Molded Urethane Foams;

(v) ASTM D3676–78—Standard Specification for Rubber Cellular Cushion Used for Carpet or Rug Underlay.

(2) These standards have been approved by the Director of the Federal Register for incorporation by reference. The standards are available from the American Society for Testing Materials, 1916 Race Street, Philadelphia, PA 19103. These standards are also available for inspection at the National Archives and Records Administration (NARA). For information on the availability of this material at NARA, call 202–741–6030, or go to: *http:// www.archives.gov/federal_register/ code_of_federal_regulations/ ibr_locations.html.*

(b) *Labeling.* Under the procedures set forth in § 200.935(d)(6) concerning labeling of a product, the administrator's validation mark, the manufacturer's certification of compliance with the applicable standards, and the type and class all are required to be on the certification label issued by the administrator to the manufacturer.

(c) *Periodic tests and quality assurance inspection.* Under the procedure set forth in § 200.935(d)(8), testing and inspection shall be conducted as follows:

(1) At least every six months, the administrator shall visit the manufacturer's facility to select a sample of each certified carpet cushion for testing by a laboratory approved by the administrator.

(2) The administrator also shall review the quality assurance procedures every six months to assure that they are being followed by the manufacturer.

[58 FR 67675, Dec. 22, 1993]

§ 200.949 Building product standards and certification program for exterior insulated steel door systems.

(a) *Applicable standards.* (1) All Exterior Insulated Steel Door Systems shall be designed, manufactured, and tested in compliance with the following standards from the American Society for Testing and Materials and Insulated Steel Door Systems Institute:

(i) ASTM A591/A591M–89—Standard Specification for Steel Sheet, Electrolytic-Zinc Coated, for Light Coating Mass Applications;

(ii) ISDSI–100–90—Door Size Dimensional Standard and Assembly Tolerances for Insulated Steel Door Systems;

(iii) ISDSI–101–83—(Reapproved 1989) Air Infiltration Performance Standard for Insulated Steel Door Systems;

(iv) ISDSI–102–84—Installation Standard for Insulated Steel Door Systems;

(v) ISDSI–104–86—Water Penetration Performance Standard for Insulated Steel Door Systems;

(vi) ISDSI–105–80—Test Procedure and Acceptance Criteria for Physical Endurance for Steel Doors and Hardware Reinforcings;

(vii) ISDSI–106–80—Test Procedure and Acceptance Criteria for Prime Painted Steel Surfaces for Steel Doors and Frames;

(viii) ISDSI–107–80—Thermal Performance Standard for Insulated Steel Door Systems;

(ix) ASTM F476–84—(Reapproved 1991) Standard Test Methods for Security of Swinging Door Assemblies.

(2) These standards have been approved by the Director of the Federal Register for incorporation by reference. These standards are available from the American Society for Testing and Materials, 1916 Race Street, Philadelphia, PA 19103 or the Insulated Steel Door Institute, 712 Lakewood Center North, 14600 Detroit Avenue, Cleveland, OH 44107. These standards are also available for inspection at the National Archives and Records Administration (NARA). For information on the availability of this material at NARA, call 202–741–6030, or go to: *http:// www.archives.gov/federal_register/ code_of_federal_regulations/ ibr_locations.html.*

(b) *Labeling.* Under the procedures set forth in § 200.935(d)(6) concerning labeling of a product, the administrator's certification of compliance with the applicable standards is required to be on the certification label issued by the administrator to the manufacturer.

(c) *Periodic tests and quality assurance inspection.* Under the procedure set forth in § 200.935(d)(8), testing and inspection shall be conducted as follows:

(1) At least every four years, the administrator shall visit the manufacturer's facility to select a sample of each certified exterior insulated steel door system for testing by an approved laboratory in accordance with the applicable standard.

(2) The administrator also shall review the quality assurance procedures every year to assure that they are being followed by the manufacturer.

[58 FR 67675, Dec. 22, 1993]

§200.950 Building product standards and certification program for solar water heating system.

(a) *Applicable standards.* (1) All solar water heating systems shall be designed, manufactured, and tested in compliance with Solar Rating and Certification Corporation (SRCC) Document OG–300–93, Operating Guidelines and Minimum Standards for Certifying Solar Water Heating Systems: An Optional SWH System Certification and Rating Program. Section 10 of the SRCC standard has been omitted because it was considered proprietary, since it describes an administrative program specifically carried out by SRCC.

(2) This standard has been approved by the Director of the Federal Register for incorporation by reference. The standard is available from the Solar Rating and Certification Corporation, 777 North Capitol Street, NE., suite 805, Washington, DC 20002. This standard is also available for inspection at the National Archives and Records Administration (NARA). For information on the availability of this material at NARA, call 202–741–6030, or go to: *http://www.archives.gov/federal_register/code_of_federal_regulations/ibr_locations.html.*

(b) *Labeling.* Under the procedures set forth in §200.935(d)(6) concerning labeling of a product, the administrator's validation mark and the manufacturer's certification of compliance with the applicable standards are required to be on the certification label issued by the administrator to the manufacturer. Each solar water heating system shall be marked as conforming to UM 100. The label shall include the manufacturer's name and plant location.

(c) *Periodic tests and quality assurance inspection.* Under the procedure set forth in §200.935(d)(8), testing and inspection shall be conducted as follows:

(1) The Administrator shall visit the manufacturer's factory every two years to assure that the initially accepted quality assurance procedures are being followed.

(2) At least every four years, the administrator shall visit the manufacturer's facility to select a sample of each certified solar water heating system for testing by a laboratory approved by the administrator.

(d) *Warranty.* The manufacturer shall provide, at no cost, a full five-year warranty against defects in material or workmanship, on the absorber plate, cooling passages, and the collector (excluding any glass), running from the date of installation of the solar water heating system. The warranty also shall include the full costs of field inspection, parts, and labor required to remedy the defects, and will include the cost of replacement at the site if required. This warranty is not required to cover defects resulting from exposure to harmful materials, fire, flood, lightning, hurricane, tornado, hailstorms, earthquakes, or other acts of God, vandalism, explosions, harmful chemicals or other fluids, fumes or vapors. This exclusion will apply to the operation of the collector under excessive pressures or excessive flow rates, misuse, abuse, negligence, accidents, alterations, falling objects or other causes beyond the control of the manufacturer. Following the initial five years, the manufacturer shall provide a limited no-cost five-year warranty for collector parts on a prorata allowance basis.

[58 FR 67676, Dec. 22, 1993]

§200.952 Supplementary specific requirements under the HUD building product standards and certification program for particleboard interior stair treads.

(a) *Applicable standards.* (1) All interior particleboard stair treads shall be designed, manufactured, and tested in compliance with ANSI A208.1–1993 Particleboard, Grade M–3.

(2) This standard has been approved by the Director of the Federal Register for incorporation by reference in accordance with 5 U.S.C. 552(a) and 1 CFR part 51, and is available from the American National Standards Institute, Inc., 11 West 42nd Street, New York, NY 10036.

(b) *Labeling.* Under the procedures set forth in § 200.935(d)(6) concerning labeling of a product, the administrator's validation mark and the manufacturer's certification of compliance with the applicable standard are required to be on the certification label issued by the administrator to the manufacturer. Each interior particleboard stair tread shall include the manufacturer's statement of conformance to UM 70b, a statement that this product is for interior use only, and the manufacturer's name and plant location.

(c) *Periodic tests and quality assurance.* Under the procedures set forth in § 200.935(d)(8) concerning periodic tests and quality assurance inspections, the frequency of testing for a product shall be described in the specific building product certification program. In the case of interior particleboard stair treads, testing and inspection shall be conducted as follows:

(1) At least once every three months, the administrator shall visit the manufacturer's facility to select a sample for testing in a laboratory approved by the administrator.

(2) The administrator shall also review the quality assurance procedures twice a year to assure that they are being followed by the manufacturer.

[63 FR 5424, Feb. 2, 1998]

§ 200.954 **Supplementary specific requirements under the HUD building product standard and certification program for construction adhesives for wood floor systems.**

(a) *Applicable standards.* (1) All construction adhesives for field glued wood floor systems shall be designed, manufactured, and tested in compliance with the following American Society for Testing and Materials (ASTM) standard: D 3498–93 Standard Specification for Adhesives for Field-Gluing Plywood to Lumber Framing for Floor Systems except that the mold and bacteria resistance tests shall not be included.

(2) This standard has been approved by the Director of the Federal Register for incorporation by reference in accordance with 5 U.S.C. 552(a) and 1 CFR part 51, and is available from the American Society for Testing & Materials Inc., 100 Barr Harbor Drive, West Conshohocken, PA. 19428.

(b) *Labeling.* Under the procedures set forth in § 200.935(d)(6) concerning labeling of a product, the administrator's validation mark and the manufacturer's certification of compliance with the applicable standard are required to be on the certification label issued by the administrator to the manufacturer. Each container shall be marked as being in compliance with UM 60a. The label shall also include the manufacturer's name, plant location, and shelf life.

(c) *Periodic tests and quality assurance.* Under the procedures set forth in § 200.935(d)(8) concerning periodic tests and quality assurance inspections, the frequency of testing for a product shall be described in the specific building product certification program. In the case of construction adhesives for field glued wood floor systems, testing and inspection shall be conducted as follows:

(1) At least every six months, the administrator shall visit the manufacturer's facility to select a sample for testing in a laboratory approved by the administrator.

(2) The administrator shall also review the quality assurance procedures twice a year to assure that they are being followed by the manufacturer.

[63 FR 5424, Feb. 2, 1998]

§ 200.955 **Supplementary specific requirements under the HUD building product standard and certification program for fenestration products (windows and doors).**

(a) *Applicable standards.* (1) All windows and doors shall be designed, manufactured, and tested in compliance with American Architectural Manufacturers Association (AAMA) standard, AAMA/NWWDA 101/I.S.2–97 Voluntary Specifications for Aluminum, Vinyl (PVC) and Wood Windows and Glass Doors.

(2) This standard has been approved by the Director of the Federal Register for incorporation by reference in accordance with 5 U.S.C. 552(a) and 1 CFR part 51, and is available from the American Architectural Manufacturers Association, 1827 Walden Office Square, Suite 104, Schaumburg, IL 60173.

(b) *Labeling.* Under the procedures set forth in §200.935(d)(6) concerning labeling of a product, the administrator's validation mark and the manufacturer's certification of compliance with the applicable standards are required to be on the certification label issued by the administrator to the manufacturer. Each window or glass door shall include the manufacturer's name, plant location, and statement of compliance with UM 111.

(c) *Periodic tests and quality assurance inspections.* Under the procedures set forth in §200.935(d)(8) concerning periodic tests and quality assurance inspections, the frequency of testing for a product shall be described in the specific building product certification program. In the case of windows and glass doors, testing and inspection shall be conducted as follows:

(1) At least once every four years, the administrator shall visit the manufacturer's facility to select a commercial sample for testing in a laboratory approved by the administrator.

(2) The administrator shall also review the quality assurance procedures twice a year to assure that they are being followed by the manufacturer.

[63 FR 5424, Feb. 2, 1998]

Subpart T—Social Security Numbers and Employer Identification Numbers; Assistance Applicants and Participants

§200.1001 Cross-reference.

The provisions in subpart B of part 5 of this title apply to Social Security Numbers and Employer Identification Numbers for assistance applicants and participants.

[61 FR 11118, Mar. 18, 1996]

Subpart U—Social Security Numbers and Employer Identification Numbers; Applicants in Unassisted Programs

§200.1101 Cross-reference.

The provisions in subpart B of part 5 of this title apply to Social Security Numbers and Employer Identification Numbers for applicants in unassisted programs.

[61 FR 11118, Mar. 18, 1996]

Subpart V—Income Information; Assistance Applicants and Participants

§200.1201 Cross-reference.

The provisions in subpart B of part 5 of this title apply to income information for assistance applicants and participants.

[61 FR 11118, Mar. 18, 1996]

Subpart W—Administrative Matters

§200.1301 Expiring programs—Savings clause.

(a) No new loan assistance, additional participation, or new loans are being insured under the programs listed in this section. Existing loan assistance, ongoing participation, or insured loans under the programs shall continue to be governed by regulations in effect as described in this section.

(b) Any existing loan assistance, ongoing participation, or insured loans under the programs listed in this paragraph will continue to be governed by the regulations in effect as they existed immediately before October 11, 1995 (24 CFR parts 205, 209, 224–228, 240, 277, 278, 1994 edition):

(1) Part 205, Mortgage Insurance for Land Development (Title X of the National Housing Act, repealed by section 133(a) of the Department of Housing and Urban Development Reform Act of 1989 (Public Law 101–235, approved December 15, 1989).

(2) Part 209, Individual Homes; War Housing Mortgage Insurance (12 U.S.C. 1736–1743).

(3) Part 224, Armed Services Housing-Military Personnel (12 U.S.C. 1736–1746a).

(4) Part 225, Military Housing Insurance (12 U.S.C. 1748b).

(5) Part 226, Armed Services Housing-Civilian Employees (12 U.S.C. 1748h–1).

(6) Part 227, Armed Services Housing-Impacted Areas (12 U.S.C. 1478h–2).

(7) Part 228, Individual Residences; National Defense Housing Mortgage Insurance (12 U.S.C. 1750 as amended by 42 U.S.C. 1591c).

(8) Part 240, Mortgage Insurance on Loans for Fee Title Purchase (12 U.S.C. 1715z-5).

(9) Part 277, Loans for Housing for the Elderly or Handicapped (12 U.S.C. 1701q).

(10) Part 278, Mandatory Meals Program in Multifamily Rental or Cooperative Projects for the Elderly or Handicapped (12 U.S.C. 1701q).

(c) Any existing loan assistance, ongoing participation, or insured loans under the programs listed in this paragraph will continue to be governed by the regulations in effect as they existed immediately before May 11, 1996 (24 CFR parts 215, 222, and 237, 1995 edition):

(1) Part 215, Rent Supplement Payments Program (12 U.S.C. 1715f).

(2) Part 222, Service Person's Mortgage Insurance Program (12 U.S.C. 1715m).

(3) Part 237, Special Mortgage Insurance for Low and Moderate Income Families (12 U.S.C. 1715z-2).

(d) Any existing loan assistance, ongoing participation, or insured loans under the program listed in this paragraph will continue to be governed by the regulations in effect as they existed immediately before December 26, 1996 (24 CFR part 233, 1995 edition):

(1) Part 233, Experimental Housing Mortgage Insurance Program (12 U.S.C. 1715x).

(2) [Reserved]

(e) Any existing loan assistance, ongoing participation, or insured loans under the program listed in this paragraph will continue to be governed by the regulations in effect as they existed immediately before August 15, 2014 (24 CFR part 257):

(1) Part 257, HOPE for Homeowners Program (12 U.S.C. 1701z-22).

(2) [Reserved]

(f) No new emergency mortgage assistance, emergency mortgage relief loans, advances of credit or emergency mortgage relief payments, or any other type of assistance permitted under the Emergency Housing Act of 1975, title I of the Emergency Homeowners' Relief Act (12 U.S.C. 2701), as amended by section 1496 of the Dodd-Frank Wall Street Reform and Consumer Protection Act (Pub. L. 111-203) is being provided under the programs listed below.

Any existing emergency assistance, emergency mortgage relief loans, advances of credit or emergency mortgage relief payments under these programs will continue to be governed by the regulations in effect as they existed immediately before September 8, 2014 (24 CFR part 2700):

(1) Part 2700, Emergency Homeowners' Loan Program (12 U.S.C. 2701 *et seq.*)

(2) [Reserved]

(g) Any existing loan assistance (including recapture of loan assistance), ongoing participation, or insured loans under the program listed in this paragraph will continue to be governed by the regulations in effect as they existed immediately before May 4, 2015 (24 CFR part 235, 2014 Edition):

(1) Part 235, Mortgage Insurance and Assistance Payments for Home Ownership and Project Rehabilitation (12 U.S.C. 1715z).

(2) [Reserved]

(h) Any existing loan assistance (including recapture of loan assistance), ongoing participation, or insured loans under the program listed in this paragraph will continue to be governed by the regulations in effect as they existed immediately before February 10, 2016 (24 CFR part 280, 2015 Edition):

(1) Part 280, Mortgage Insurance and Assistance Payments for Home Ownership and Project Rehabilitation (12 U.S.C. 17151).

(2) [Reserved]

[79 FR 41423, July 16, 2014, as amended at 79 FR 46182, Aug. 7, 2014; 80 FR 18096, Apr. 3, 2015; 81 FR 1121, Jan. 11, 2016]

§ 200.1303 Annual income exclusions for the Rent Supplement Program.

(a) The exclusions to annual income described in 24 CFR 5.609(c) apply to those rent supplement contracts governed by the regulations at 24 CFR part 215 in effect immediately before May 1, 1996 (contained in the April 1, 1995 edition of 24 CFR, parts 200 to 219), in lieu of the annual income exclusions described in 24 CFR 215.21(c) (contained in the April 1, 1995 edition of 24 CFR, parts 200 to 219).

(b) The mandatory deductions described in 24 CFR 5.611(a) also apply to the rent supplement contracts described in paragraph (a) of this section in lieu of the deductions provided in the definition of "adjusted income" in 24 CFR 215.1 (as contained in the April 1, 1995 edition of 24 CFR, parts 200 to 219).

(c) The definition of "persons with disabilities" in paragraph (c) of this section replaces the terms "disabled person" and "handicapped person" used in the regulations in 24 CFR part 215, subpart A (as contained in the April 1, 1995 edition of 24 CFR, parts 200 to 219). *Person with disabilities*, as used in this part, has the same meaning as provided in 24 CFR 891.305.

[66 FR 6224, Jan. 19, 2001]

Subpart Y—Multifamily Accelerated Processing (MAP): MAP Lender Quality Assurance Enforcement

SOURCE: 70 FR 43242, July 26, 2005, unless otherwise noted.

§ 200.1500 Sanctions against a MAP lender.

(a) In addition to any other legal remedy available to HUD, HUD may take the following actions with respect to a MAP lender:

(1) Warning letter;

(2) Probation;

(3) Suspension;

(4) Termination;

(5) Limited Denial of Participation (LDP);

(6) Referral to the Mortgagee Review Board; and

(7) Referral to the Office of Inspector General.

(b) The actions listed in paragraphs (a)(1) through (a)(4) of this section are carried out in accordance with the requirements of this subpart. An LDP is a sanction applied in accordance with subpart J of 2 CFR part 2424 to participants in loan transactions other than FHA-insured lenders. The Mortgagee Review Board procedures are found at 24 CFR part 25.

[70 FR 43242, July 26, 2005, as amended at 72 FR 73494, Dec. 27, 2007]

§ 200.1505 Warning letter.

(a) *In general.* HUD may issue a warning letter, which specifies problems or violations identified by HUD, to a MAP lender.

(b) *Effect of warning letter.* The warning letter:

(1) Does not suspend a lender's MAP privileges;

(2) May impose a higher level of review of the lender's underwriting by HUD;

(3) May direct the taking of a corrective action; and

(4) May require a meeting in a designated HUD office with the principal owners or officers, or both, of the MAP lender to discuss the specified problems and violations, and possible corrective actions.

(c) *Relationship to other sanctions.* The issuance of a warning letter is not subject to the MAP Lender Review Board procedures in accordance with § 200.1535, and is not a prerequisite to the probation, or suspension, or termination of MAP privileges.

§ 200.1510 Probation.

(a) *In general.* Only the MAP Lender Review Board (or Board) may place a lender on probation, in accordance with the procedures of § 200.1535.

(b) *Effect of probation.* (1) Probation is intended to be corrective in nature and not punitive. As a result, release from probation is conditioned upon the lender meeting a specific requirement or requirements, such as replacement of a staff member. A lender's failure to take prompt corrective action after being placed on probation may be the basis for a recommendation of either suspension or termination. Any such recommendation shall, when possible, go to a MAP Lender Review Board composed of the same members who issued the original probation.

(2) During the probation period, a MAP lender:

(i) Shall be removed from the MAP-Approved Lender list posted on HUD's website;

(ii) May not submit, and HUD may not accept, materials after the close of business of the date of the probation letter for a new application under MAP for multifamily mortgage insurance from HUD; and

(iii) May continue to process any existing application for multifamily mortgage insurance submitted to a

Multifamily Hub or Program Center before the date of the probation letter.

(3) The MAP Lender Review Board may impose a higher level of review of the lender's underwriting by HUD;

(4) Probation is nationwide in effect.

(c) *Duration of probation.* (1) Probation continues until all specific corrective actions required by the MAP Lender Review Board (for example, exclusion of a specific staff member from work on MAP loans) are taken by the MAP lender. When all corrective actions have been taken, the MAP lender shall notify the Board. Once the Board is satisfied that the corrective actions have occurred, the probation period shall end.

(2) A false statement that corrective action has been taken constitutes a false certification and may constitute a violation of 18 US.C. 1001.

(3) When probation is lifted, the lender's name shall be promptly reinstated on the MAP-Approved Lender list posted on HUD's Web site.

§ 200.1515 Suspension of MAP privileges.

(a) *In general.* Only the MAP Lender Review Board may suspend a lender's eligibility for MAP, in accordance with the procedures of § 200.1535.

(b) *Effect of suspension.* (1) A suspension may impose any conditions that may be imposed by probation.

(2) During the suspension period a MAP lender:

(i) Shall be removed from the MAP-approved lender list posted on HUD's Web site;

(ii) May not submit, and the HUD field office may not accept, materials after the close of business of the date of the suspension letter for a new application for multifamily mortgage insurance from HUD; and

(iii) May continue to process any existing application for multifamily mortgage insurance submitted to a Multifamily Hub or Program Center before the date of the suspension letter.

(3) The MAP Lender Review Board may impose a higher level of review of the lender's underwriting by HUD;

(4) Suspension is nationwide in effect.

(c) *Duration of suspension.* (1) Suspension may not exceed 12 months, except

where conditions are imposed. If both a time period and conditions are imposed, a suspension shall terminate only when:

(i) The time period of the suspension has expired;

(ii) The MAP lender has submitted a certification of compliance with those conditions to the Board; and

(iii) The Board has notified the MAP lender it has received the certification of compliance and is satisfied that the corrective actions have occurred.

(2) When suspension is lifted, the lender's name shall be promptly reinstated on the MAP-Approved Lender list posted on HUD's Web site.

§ 200.1520 Termination of MAP privileges.

(a) *In general.* Except as provided in paragraph (b) of this section, only the MAP Lender Review Board may terminate a lender's MAP privileges, in accordance with the procedures of § 200.1535.

(b) *Administrative termination.* HUD will notify a lender of immediate termination of MAP privileges when either of the following circumstances is present:

(1) Failure by the MAP lender to maintain its status as an FHA-approved lender; or

(2) Failure by the MAP lender to maintain a minimum level of MAP lender activity, as evidenced by failure to submit either a pre-application package or firm commitment application at least once every 12 months.

(c) *Effect of termination.* (1) The terminated lender shall be removed from the MAP-Approved Lender list on HUD's Web site.

(2) A terminated lender may not submit, and the HUD field office may not accept, materials after the close of business of the date of the termination letter for new multifamily mortgage insurance from HUD.

(3) Any MAP pre-application or MAP application in process may no longer be processed under MAP by the terminated lender. The lender will either:

(i) Immediately transfer the transaction to the traditional application processing (TAP) procedure. HUD will completely reprocess all stages of the transaction; or

(ii) Immediately transfer the project to a new MAP lender. The new MAP lender must completely reprocess all stages of the transaction. At no time can the new MAP lender assign the pre-application, the firm application, the mortgage insurance commitment, or the insured construction loan back to the original MAP lender.

(4) HUD will not endorse any MAP loan processed by the terminated lender unless a firm commitment was issued before the date of termination.

(i) Firm commitments involving new construction or substantial rehabilitation must be immediately transferred to a new MAP lender. At no time can the new MAP lender assign the firm mortgage insurance commitment, or the insured construction loan, back to the original MAP lender.

(ii) Firm commitments issued for Section 223(f) projects may be transferred before final endorsement to any approved FHA lender or kept in the lender's portfolio.

(iii) For those construction loans that have been initially endorsed, the MAP lender will lose its MAP privileges for construction loan administration. HUD will assume all the construction loan administration duties it normally performs for TAP processing.

(iv) The original lender may service a transferred loan once it is finally endorsed.

(5) Termination is nationwide in effect.

(6) When a MAP lender loses its MAP lender status as a result of termination, the lender's status to process transactions using TAP is unaffected, provided that the lender has maintained its status as an FHA-approved multifamily lender.

(d) *Reinstatement.* An application for reinstatement of MAP authority may not be made until at least 12 months after the date of termination. The requirements for reinstatement shall be the same as for initial qualification, and the applicant must show that the problems that led to termination have been resolved.

§ 200.1525 Settlement agreements.

(a) HUD staff, as authorized, may negotiate a settlement agreement with a MAP lender before or after the issuance of a warning letter or referral to the MAP Lender Review Board. Once a matter has been referred to the MAP Lender Review Board, only the Board may approve a settlement agreement.

(b) Settlement agreements may provide for:

(1) Cessation of any violation;

(2) Correction or mitigation of the effects of any violation;

(3) Removal of lender staff from positions involving origination, underwriting, and/or construction loan administration;

(4) Actions to collect sums of money wrongfully or incorrectly paid by the MAP lender to a third party;

(5) Implementation or revision of a quality control plan or other corrective measure acceptable to HUD; and

(6) Modification of the duration or provisions of any administrative sanction deemed to be appropriate by HUD.

(c) A MAP lender's compliance with a settlement agreement is evidenced by the lender certifying its compliance with the conditions of the agreement, and HUD's determination that the lender is in compliance with the conditions of the agreement.

(d) Failure by a MAP lender to comply with a settlement agreement may result in a probation, or suspension, or termination of MAP privileges, or referral to the Mortgagee Review Board.

§ 200.1530 Bases for sanctioning a MAP lender.

It is HUD policy that approved MAP lenders are expected to comply at all times with HUD's underwriting and construction loan administration requirements and not to take any action that presents a risk to HUD's insurance funds. A MAP lender's improper underwriting and construction loan administration activities may lead to a warning letter or other sanction from HUD. Examples of such activities include, but are not limited to, the following:

(a) *Minor offenses that may be the basis for a warning letter include:*

(1) Failure to provide required exhibits or the submission of incomplete or inaccurate exhibits. Although the MAP lender will be permitted to correct minor errors or provide additional information, substantial inaccuracies or

lack of significant information will result in a return of the application and retention of any fee collected;

(2) Repeated failure to complete processing to firm commitment unrelated to an underwriting analysis that demonstrates that the process should not proceed to firm commitment;

(3) Preparation of an underwriting summary that is not supported by the appropriate documentation and analysis;

(4) Failure to notify the HUD processing office promptly of changes in the mortgage loan application for a firm commitment submitted, such as changes in rents, numbers of units, or gross project area;

(5) Failure to meet MAP closing requirements or construction loan administration requirements;

(6) Business practices that do not conform to those generally accepted by prudent lenders or that show irresponsibility; and

(7) Failure to cooperate with a Lender Qualifications and Monitoring Division review by HUD.

(b) *Serious offenses that might be a basis for a warning letter or probation, suspension, or termination include:*

(1) Receipt of multiple warning letters over any one-year period. In determining which sanction to pursue as a result of prior warning letters, HUD will consider the facts and circumstances surrounding those warning letters and the corrective actions, if any, undertaken by the lender;

(2) Fraud or material misrepresentation in the lender's participation in FHA multifamily programs;

(3) Lender collusion with, or influence upon, third party contractors to modify reports affecting the contractor's independent evaluation;

(4) A violation of MAP procedures by a third party contractor, which the MAP lender knew, or should have known, was occurring and which, if performed by the MAP lender itself, would constitute a ground for a sanction under this chapter;

(5) Evidence that a lender's inadequate or inaccurate underwriting was a cause for assignment of an FHA-insured mortgage and claim for insurance benefits to HUD;

(6) Identity-of-interest violations as defined by Chapter 2 of the MAP Guide;

(7) Payment by, or receipt of a payment by, a MAP lender of any kickback or other consideration, directly or indirectly, which would affect the lender's independent evaluation, or represent a conflict of interest, in connection with any FHA-insured mortgage transaction;

(8) Failure to comply with any agreement, certification, undertaking, or condition of approval listed in a MAP lender's application for approval;

(9) Noncompliance with any requirement or directive of the MAP Lender Review Board;

(10) Violation of the requirements of any contract with HUD, or violation of the requirements in any statute or regulation;

(11) Submission of false information, or a false certification, to HUD in connection with any MAP mortgage transaction;

(12) Failure of a MAP lender to respond in a timely manner to inquiries from the MAP Lender Review Board in accordance with this subpart;

(13) Indictment or conviction of a MAP lender or any of its officers, directors, principals, or employees for an offense that reflects on the responsibility, integrity, or ability of the lender to participate in the MAP initiative;

(14) Employing or retaining an officer, partner, director, or principal at the time when the person was suspended, debarred, ineligible, or subject to an LDP under 2 CFR part 2424, or otherwise prohibited from participation in HUD programs, when the MAP lender knew or should have known of the prohibition;

(15) Employing or retaining an employee who is not an officer, partner, director, or principal, and who is or will be working on HUD-FHA program matters, at a time when that person was suspended, debarred, ineligible, or subject to an LDP under 2 CFR part 2424, or otherwise prohibited from participation in HUD programs, when the MAP lender knew or should have known of the prohibition;

(16) Failure to cooperate with an audit or investigation by the HUD Office of Inspector General or an inquiry

by HUD into the conduct of the MAP lender's FHA-insured loans; and

(17) Failure to fund MAP mortgage loans or any misuse of mortgage loan proceeds.

[70 FR 43242, July 26, 2005, as amended at 72 FR 73494, Dec. 27, 2007]

§200.1535 MAP Lender Review Board.

(a) *Authority*—(1) *Sanctions.* The MAP Lender Review Board (or Board) is authorized to impose appropriate sanctions on a MAP lender after:

(i) Conducting an impartial review of all information and documentation submitted to the Board; and

(ii) Making factual determinations that there has been a violation of MAP requirements.

(2) *Settlement agreements.* The Board is authorized to approve settlement agreements in accordance with §200.1525 of any matter pending before the Board.

(3) *Extensions.* The Board is authorized to extend, on its own initiative or for good cause at the written request of a MAP lender, any time limit otherwise applicable under this section. Notice of any such extension shall be timely provided to a MAP lender.

(b) *Notice of violation.* Before the Board reviews a matter for consideration of a sanction, the Board's Chairman will issue written notice of violation to the MAP lender's contact person as listed on the Multifamily MAP Web site. The notice is sent by overnight delivery and must be signed for by an employee of the MAP lender upon receipt. The notice:

(1) Informs the lender that the Board is considering a specific violation;

(2) States the specific facts alleged concerning the violation, with citation to the HUD requirements that have been violated;

(3) Includes as attachments copies of all documents evidencing the violation and upon which the Board will rely in reaching a decision;

(4) Provides the lender with the opportunity to request in writing, within 15 business days after the date of the issuance of the notice, to:

(i) Meet for an informal conference with the Board in person or by video conference using HUD facilities at Headquarters or one of HUD's field offices; and

(ii) Present written evidence and any other relevant information at the conference;

(5) Requires a written response to be submitted to the Board by a date specified within the notice;

(6) Provides the street address, email address, or facsimile (FAX) number for purposes of receiving the lender's request for an informal conference and written response; and

(7) Is made part of the administrative record of the Board's decision of the matter.

(c) *Response to notice.* (1) The MAP lender's written response required by the notice of violation may not exceed 15 double-spaced typewritten pages and must include an executive summary, a statement of the facts, an argument, and a conclusion. The response and supporting documentation must be submitted in triplicate.

(2) Failure to respond by the dates specified within the notice may result in a determination by the Board without conducting an informal conference with the MAP lender and without consideration of any written response submitted by the MAP lender.

(d) *Informal conference.* (1) The Board will schedule an informal conference and notify the lender of the time and place of the conference, if one is requested.

(2) At the conference, the Board will meet with the lender or its designees and HUD staff to review documentary evidence and presentations by both sides.

(3) Oral statements made at the informal meeting will not be considered as part of the administrative record of the Board's determination, except:

(i) The Board may note for the record and consider voluntary admissions, made by the lender or a representative of the lender, of any element of the violation charged;

(ii) Statements substantiated by any additional documents or evidence submitted in accordance with paragraphs (e)(1) or (e)(3) of this section; and

(iii) Transcripts prepared and submitted in accordance with paragraph (e)(2) of this section.

(e) *Post-conference submissions.* (1) Any additional documents, evidence, or written arguments relevant to the notice of violation and the informal conference that the lender or HUD staff wish to present to the Board, must be presented within five business days after date of the informal conference.

(2) No transcript of the informal conference will be made, unless the lender elects to have a transcript made by a certified court reporter at its own expense. If the lender elects to have a transcript made, the lender must provide three copies of the transcript to HUD within five business days after the date of the informal conference. The transcript will not become a part of the administrative record of the Board's decision unless it is submitted within the required five-day period frame.

(3) Following the receipt of any post-conference submissions, the Board may request or permit additional documents or evidence to be submitted within a period set by the Board for inclusion in the administrative record.

(f) *Board action.* (1) The Board will confer to consider the evidence included in the administrative record and make a final decision concerning the matter. Any record of confidential communications between and among Board members at this stage of the proceedings is privileged from disclosure and will not be regarded as a part of the administrative record of any matter.

(2) In determining what action is appropriate concerning the matter, the Board considers, among other factors:

(i) The seriousness and the extent of the violation;

(ii) Any history of prior offenses;

(iii) Deterrence of future violations;

(iv) Any inappropriate benefits received by the MAP lender;

(v) Potential inappropriate benefit to other persons; and

(vi) Any mitigating factors.

(3) Board decisions will be determined by majority vote.

(g) *Notice of action.* (1) The Board will issue its final decision within 10 business days after the date of the informal conference or the expiration of any period allowed for the submission of documents and evidence, whichever is later.

(2) The Board will notify the MAP lender of its final decision by overnight delivery of a written notice of the final decision to the MAP lender's contact person as listed on the Multifamily MAP Web site. The Board will also notify HUD field offices of its final decision.

(3) The final decision finds that a violation either does, or does not, exist. If a violation is found to exist, the final decision:

(i) States the violation and any factual findings of the Board;

(ii) States the nature and duration of the sanction;

(iii) Informs the MAP lender of its right to an appeal conference and identifies the appeals official to be contacted; and

(iv) May add to or modify the violation as stated in the initial notice of violation.

§ 200.1540   Imminent harm notice of action.

The Board may issue an imminent harm notice of action to terminate a MAP lender, or to place a MAP lender on probation or suspension without advance notice to the MAP lender in those instances where the Board determines there exists a need to protect the financial interest of HUD from imminent harm. In all such instances, the Board shall notify the lender of the Board's decision promptly and give the reasons for the decision in accordance with § 200.1535(g)(2) and (3). The lender shall have the right to submit materials to the Board and to appear before the Board to seek prompt reconsideration of the Board's decision in accordance with the procedures of § 200.1535.

§ 200.1545   Appeals of MAP Lender Review Board decisions.

(a) *Request for appeal.* Whenever the Board imposes a sanction of probation, suspension, or termination against a MAP lender, the lender may request, in writing, an appeal conference before the appeals official. The MAP lender must deliver the written request for an appeal to the appeals official within 10 business days after the date noted on the notice of action or the right to an appeal is deemed waived. Participation in the appeal process under this section is not a prerequisite to filing an action for judicial review under the Administrative Procedure Act.

(b) *Appeals Official.* The appeals official must be an individual who has not been previously involved with the proceedings or settlement discussions at issue.

(c) *Notice of action in effect.* The notice of action issued by the Board remains in effect while the appeal is pending.

(d) *Scheduling of appeal.* (1) Upon receipt of the request for an appeal, the appeals official will promptly notify the MAP lender of the time and place of the appeal conference. The appeal conference will be held within 10 business days after receipt of the MAP lender's appeal request, except as provided in paragraph (d)(2) of this section.

(2) A MAP lender may request, and the appeals official may agree, to have an appeal conference held more than 10, but not more than 30 business days after the date of the lender's request for an appeal.

(e) *Scope of appeal.* The appeals official may consider information included in the administrative record and any new information presented at the appeal conference that is substantiated in accordance with paragraph (f) of this section. In addition, the appeals official may consider voluntary admissions by the lender or a representative of the lender of any element of the violation charged.

(f) *Additional documents*—(1) *Transcript.* No transcript of the appeal conference will be made, unless the MAP lender elects to have a transcript made by a certified court reporter at its own expense. If the lender elects to have a transcript made, it must provide three copies of the transcript to the appeals official within five business days after the date of the appeal conference.

(2) *Other documents.* Any additional, relevant documents or written arguments that the MAP lender wishes to present to the appeals official must be presented within five business days after the date of the appeal conference.

(g) *Determination of appeal.* Within 10 business days after the date of the ap-

peal conference or the expiration of the period allowed for the submission of documents and written arguments, whichever is later, the appeals official will make a written determination to confirm, modify, or overturn the Board's decision and notice of action. If the appeals official overturns the Board's decision, the lender shall immediately return to an active status as a MAP lender and the written determination to overturn will be posted on HUD's MAP Web site.

APPENDIX A TO PART 200—STANDARDS INCORPORATED BY REFERENCE IN THE MINIMUM PROPERTY STANDARDS FOR HOUSING (HUD HANDBOOK 4910.1)

The following publications are incorporated by reference in the HUD Minimum Property Standards (MPS) in 24 CFR part 200. The MPS are available for public inspection and can be obtained for appropriate use at 490 L'Enfant Plaza East, Suite 3214, or at each HUD Regional, Area, and Service Office. Copies are available for inspection at the National Archives and Records Administration (NARA). For information on the availability of this material at NARA, call 202–741–6030, or go to: *http://www.archives.gov/ federal_register/code_of_federal_regulations/ ibr_locations.html.* The individual standards referenced in the MPS are available at the address contained in the following table. They are also available for public inspection at the HUD, Manufactured Housing and Construction Standards Division, Suite 3214, 490 L'Enfant Plaza East, Washington, DC 20024.

Air Conditioning Contractors of America 1513 16th Street, NW., Washington, DC 20036, (202) 483–9370.

Load Calculation for Residential Winter and Summer Air Conditioning, Manual J 1986

Aluminum Association, 900 19th Street, NW., Washington, DC 20006, Telephone (202) 862–5100.

AA-ASM 35–80 Specifications for Aluminum Sheet Metal Work in Building Construction

American Architectural Manufacturers Association, 1540 East Dundee Road, Paletine, IL 60067, Telephone (708) 202–1350.

AAMA–800–92 Voluntary Specifications and Test Methods for Sealants

AAMA–1503.1–88 Voluntary Test Method for Thermal Transmittance and Condensation Resistance of Windows, Doors and Glazed Wall Sections

AAMA 1504–88 Voluntary Standards for Thermal Performance of Windows, Doors and Glazed Wall Sections

American Concrete Institute, P. O. Box 19150, Redford Station, Detroit, Michigan 48219, Telephone (313) 532–2600.

ACI 211.1–89 Standard Practice for Selecting Proportions for Normal, Heavyweight and Mass Concrete

ACI 211.2–91 Standard Practice for Selecting Proportions for Structural Lightweight Concrete

ACI 213R–87 Guide for Structural Lightweight Aggregate Concrete

ACI 301–89 Specifications for Structural Concrete for Buildings

ACI 302.1R–80 Guide for Concrete Floor and Slab Construction

ACI 304R–89 Guide for Measuring, Mixing, Transporting and Placing Concrete

ACI 305R–77 Hot Weather Concreting (Revised 1989)

ACI 306R–78 Cold Weather Concreting (Revised 1988)

ACI 311.4R–80 Guide for Concrete Inspection (Revised 1988)

ACI 315–80 Guide for Detailing of Concrete Reinforcement

ACI 318–89 Building Code Requirements for Reinforced Structural Plain Concrete (Revised 1992)

ACI 322–72 Structural Plain Concrete

ACI 347–78 Recommended Practice for Concrete Formwork (Reapproved 1984)

ACI 504R–77 Guide to Joint Sealants for Concrete Structures

ACI 506–90 Recommended Practice for Shotcreting

ACI 515.1R–79 A Guide to the Use of Waterproofing, Dampproofing, Protective and Decorative Barrier Systems for Concrete (Revised 1985)

ACI 533.1R–69 Quality Standards and Tests for Precast Concrete Wall Panels

ACI 533.2R–69 Selection and Use of Materials for Precast Concrete Wall Panels

ACI 533.3R–70 Fabrication, Handling and Erection of Precast Concrete Wall Panels

American Forest & Paper Association, (formerly National Forest Products Association), 1250 Connecticut Ave., NW., Washington, DC 20036. National Design Specification for Wood Construction—1991.

American National Standards Institute, 11 West 42nd Street, New York, NY 10036, Telephone (212) 642–4900.

ANSI A108.1A–92 Specifications for Installation of Ceramic Tile, in the Wet Set Method with Portland Cement Mortar

ANSI A137.1–1988 Specifications for Ceramic Tile

ANSI/BHMA A156.2–1989 Standard for Bored and Preassembled Locks and Latches

ANSI/NKCA A161.1–1985 Recommended Performance and Construction Standards for Kitchen and Vanity Cabinets (Approved March 18, 1986)

ANSI A208.1–1989 Wood Particleboard

ANSI/AAMA 101–1988 Voluntary Specifications for Aluminum Prime Windows and Sliding Glass Doors

ANSI/AAMA 1002.10–1983 Voluntary Specifications for Aluminum Insulating Storm Products for Windows and Sliding Glass Doors

ANSI/AAMA 1102.7–1989 Voluntary Specifications for Aluminum Storm Doors

ANSI/AAMA 1402–1986 Standard Specifications for Aluminum Siding, Soffit and Fascia (ANSI Approved 1989)

ANSI/ACI 214–77 Recommended Practice for Evaluation of Strength Test Results of Concrete (Reapproved 1983)

ANSI/AHA A135.4–1982 Basic Hardboard (Reaffirmed 1988)

ANSI/AHA A135.6–1990 Hardboard Siding

ANSI/AHA A194.1–1985 Cellulosic Fiber Board

ANSI/APA 1–1984 Mosaic-Parquet Hardboard Slat Flooring

ANSI/NSPI–1–91 Standard for Public Swimming Pools

ANSI Z34.1–1987 American National Standard for Certification, Third-Party Certification Program

ANSI Z124.5–1989 American National Standard for Plastic Toilet Seats (Water Closet Seats)

American Society of Civil Engineers, 345 East 47th Street, New York, NY 10017.

ASCE 7–88 Minimum Design Loads for Buildings and Other Structures (Formerly ANSI A58.1)

American Society of Mechanical Engineers, 345 E 47th Street, New York, NY 10017.

ASME/ANSI A17.1–87 Safety Code for Elevators and Escalators Including the A17.1b-89 Addenda

ASME A 112.18.1M89 Plumbing Fixture Fittings

American Society for Testing and Materials, 1916 Race Street, Philadelphia, PA 19103, Telephone (215) 299–5400.

ASTM C 12–91 Standard Practice for Installing Vitrified Clay Pipe Lines

ASTM C 208–72 Insulating Board (Cellulosic Fiber), Structural and Decorative (Reapproved 1982)

ASTM C 209–84 Standard Methods of Testing Insulating Board (Cellulosic Fiber), Structural and Decorative

ASTM C 216–91c Standard Specification for Facing Brick (Solid Masonry Units Made from Clay or Shale)

ASTM C 220–91 Standard Specification for Flat Asbestos-Cement Sheets

ASTM C 221–91 Standard Specification for Corrugated Asbestos-Cement Sheets

ASTM C 223–91 Standard Specification for Asbestos-Cement Siding

ASTM C 509–91 Standard Specification for Elastomeric Cellular Preformed Gasket and Sealing Material

ASTM C 516–80 Standard Specification for Vermiculite Loose Fill Thermal Insulation (Reapproved 1985)

ASTM C 549–81 Standard Specification for Perlite Loose Fill Insulation (Reapproved 1986)

ASTM C 578–92 Standard Specification for Rigid, Cellular Polystyrene Thermal Insulation

ASTM C 640–83 Standard Specification for Insulation Board, Thermal (Cork)

ASTM C 726–88 Standard Specification for Mineral Fiber and Roof Insulation Board

ASTM C 739–91 Standard Specification for Cellulosic Fiber (Wood-Based) Loose-Fill Thermal Insulation

ASTM C 754–88 Standard Specification for Installation of Steel Framing Members to Receive Screw-Attached Gypsum

ASTM C 834–91 Standard Specification for Latex Sealants

ASTM C 841–90 Standard Specification for Installation of Interior Lathing and Furring

ASTM C 842–85 Standard Specification for Application of Interior Gypsum Plaster (Reapproved 1990)

ASTM C 843–92 Standard Specification for Application of Gypsum Veneer Plaster

ASTM C 844–85 Standard Specification for Application of Gypsum Base to Receive Gypsum Veneer Plaster

ASTM C 846–76 Standard Practice for Application of Structural Insulating Board (Fiberboard) Sheathing (Reapproved 1982)

ASTM C 864–90 Standard Specification for Dense Elastomeric Compression Seal Gaskets, Setting Blocks and Spacers.

ASTM C 926–90 Standard Specification for Application of Portland Cement-Based Plaster

ASTM C 1036–91 Standard Specification for Flat Glass

ASTM D 1037–89 Standard Test Methods for Evaluating the Properties of Wood-Base Fiber and Particle Panel Materials

ASTM C 1048–91 Standard Specification for Heat-Treated Flat Glass-Kind HS, Kind FT Coated and Uncoated Glass

ASTM D 1557–91 Test Method for Laboratory Compaction Characteristics of Soil Using the Modified Method (56,000 ft-lbf/ft$_3$ (2,700 kN-m/m$_3$))

ASTM D 2316–75 Standard Recommended Practice for Installing Bituminized Fiber Drain and Sewer Pipe (Reapproved 1984)

ASTM D 2321–89 Standard Practice for Underground Installation of Thermoplastic Pipe for Sewers and Other Gravity-Flow Applications

ASTM D 3656–89 Standard Specifications for Insect Screening and Louver Cloth Woven From Vinyl-Coated Glass Yarns

ASTM D 3679–92 Standard Specification for Rigid Poly (Vinyl Chloride) (PVC) Siding

ASTM E 72–80 Standard Methods of Conducting Strength Tests of Panels for Building Construction

ASTM E 283–91 Standard Test Method for Determining the Rate of Air Leakage Through Exterior Windows, Curtain Walls, and Doors Under Specified Pressure Differences Across the Spectrum

ASTM E 330–90 Standard Test Method for Structural Performance of Exterior Windows, Curtain Walls, and Doors by Uniform Static Air Pressure Difference

ASTM E 331–86 Standard Test Method for Water Penetration of Exterior Windows, Curtain Walls, and Doors by Uniform Static Air Pressure Difference

ASTM E 380–91a Standard Practices for Use of the International Systems of Units (SI) (the Modernized Metric System)

American Society of Heating, Refrigerating and Air Conditioning Engineers, 1791 Tullie Circle, NE, Atlanta, GA 30329. ASHRAE Handbook—Fundamentals—1989. ASHRAE Cooling and Heating Load Calculation Manual—GRP 158 1979. ASHRAE Handbook—Equipment—1988. ASHRAE Handbook—HVAC Systems and Applications—1987.

American Welding Society, 550 NW Le Jeune Road, P. O. Box 351040, Miami, FL 33126, Telephone (305) 443–9353. ANSI/AWS D1.1–90 Structural Welding Code—Steel. ANSI/AWS D1.4–79 Structural Welding Code-Reinforcing Steel.

The Asphalt Institute, Asphalt Institute Building, College Park, MD 20740 Telephone (301) 277–4258.

MSI–1–81 Thickness Design—Asphalt Pavements for Highways and Streets

Asphalt Roofing Manufacturers Association, 6288 Montrose Road, Rockville, MD 20852, Telephone (301) 231–9050. Residential Asphalt Roofing Manual—1988.

Carpet and Rug Institute, 310 Holiday Avenue, Box 2048, Dalton, GA 30722–0048, Telephone (404) 278–3176. How to Specify Commercial Carpet Installation, 1984.

Council of American Building Officials, Suite 708, 5203 Leesburg Pike, Falls Church, VA 22041, Telephone (703) 931–4533. CABO One and Two Family Dwelling Code 1992 edition with Errata Package and 1993 Amendments. CABO Model Energy Code 1992 edition CABO/ANSI A117.1–92 Accessible and Usable Buildings and Facilities.

Department of Agriculture, Publications Division, 14th and Independence Avenue, SW., Washington, DC 20050, Telephone (202) 447–3957.

Agriculture Handbook No. 73, Wood Frame House Construction

Home and Garden Bulletin No. 64. Subterranean Termites—Their Prevention and Control in Buildings, October 1983

Home and Garden Bulletin No. 73, Wood Decay in Houses, How to Prevent and Control It, May 1986

Department of Commerce, National Institute of Standards and Technology, Gaithersburg, Maryland 20899, Telephone (301) 975–4025. PS 1–83 Product Standard for Construction and Industrial Plywood with Typical APA Trademarks. PS 2–92 Performance Standard for Wood-Based Structural-Use Panels.

Commercial Standards:

CS 138–55 Insect Wire Screening

CS 242–62 1 ¾'' Steel Doors & Frames

Department of Defense, Naval Publication and Forms Center, 5801 Taber Road, Philadelphia, PA 19120, Telephone (215) 697–2179.

Federal Specifications:

L-S–125B Screening, Insect, Non-metallic Febuary 3, 1972

L-F–001641 Floor Covering Translucent or Transparent Vinyl Surface with Backing—1971 and Amendment 2—September 24, 1982

L-F–00450A Flooring, Vinyl Plastic (GSAFSS)—1970 and Amendment 1, August 5, 1975

L-F–475A Floor Covering Vinyl, Surface Tile and Roll, with Backing including Amendment 2—February 9, 1971

HH-I–521F Insulation Blankets, Thermal (Mineral Fiber—for Ambient Temperatures—1980)

HH-I–526C Insulation Board, Thermal (Mineral Fiber)—1968

HH-I–529B Insulation Board, Thermal (Mineral Aggregate)—1971

HH-I–530B Insulation Board, Thermal, Unfaced, Polyurethane or Polyisocyanurate and Interim I—1982

HH-I–551E Insulation Block and Boards, Thermal (Cellular Glass) Fiber, for Ambient Temperatures, 1974

HH-I–558B Insulation Blocks, Boards, Blankets, Felts Sleeving (Pipe and Tube Covering), and Pipe Fitting Covering, Thermal (Mineral Fiber, Insulation Type) and Amendment 3—1976

HH-I–574B Insulation, Thermal (Perlite) and Interim Amendment—1976

HH-I–585C Insulation, Thermal (Vermiculite) and Interim Amendment 1—1976

HH-I–1030B Insulation, Thermal (Mineral Fiber, for Pneumatic or Poured Application)—1980

HH-I–1252B Insulation, Thermal Reflective, (Aluminum Foil) and Interim Amendment 1—1976

HH-I–1972 Insulation Board, Thermal, Faced, Gen; 1, 2, 3, Polyurethane and Polyisocyanurate and 4, 5 & 6 Amendments—1985

LLL-I–535B Insulation Board, Thermal, Cellulosic Fiber, 1977

SS-S–346C Siding (Shingles, Clapboards, and Sheets) 1968

SS-T–312B Tile, Floor: Asphalt, Rubber, Vinyl-Composition and Interim Amendment—1979

Department of Housing and Urban Development, 451 Seventh Street, SW., Mail Room B–133, Washington, DC 20410, Telephone (202) 755–7440.

Handbooks:

4940.2–1973 Minimum Design Standards for Community Water Supply Systems

4940.3–1992 Minimum Design Standards for Community Sewerage Systems (Rev. 1–92)

4950.1–1988 Technical Suitability of Products Program, Technical and Processing Procedures (Rev. 2 which includes revisions and changes through October 24, 1991)

4930.2–1989 HUD Intermediate MPS Supplement, Solar Heating & Domestic Hot Water Systems

Use of Materials Bulletins:

25d Power Driven, Mechanically Driven and Manually Driven Fasteners—9/5/73

38h Grademarking of Lumber—7/31/79

44c HUD/FHA Standard for Carpet and Carpet Certification Program—2/22/78 (Plus Addendum 1 & 2)

48 Labels of Independent Programs for Certifying Pressure-Treated Lumber and Plywood (Plus 5 Supplements—11/15/67)

52a Quality Certification and Labeling for Wood Flush Doors—10/7/75)

58a Acrylic Plastic Sheets for Glazing—9/2/75

60 Field Glued Plywood & Wood Frame Structural Floor Systems—12/9/70

62a Factory-Applied Laminated Roofing Systems Based on Chlorosulfonated Polyethylene (CPSE)—11/16/72

65 Controlled Density Cellular Concrete Floor Fill—10/11/73

67 Polycarbonate Plastic Sheets for Glazing—9/3/75

70a Particleboard Interior Stair Treads and Certification Program—5/19/82

71 Polystyrene Foam Insulation Sheathing Board—1/10/77

72 HUD Standard for Carpet Cushion—2/6/80

76 Chlorinated Poly (Vinyl Chloride) CPVC and Polybutylene (PB) Hot and Cold Water Distribution—4/25/78

77a Cast Iron Sanitary Drainage System with Hubless Pipe and Fittings—3/28/80

78 Polyethylene (PE), Acrylonitrile-Butadiene-Styrene (ABS), Poly Vinyl Chloride (PVC) and Polybutylene (PB) Plastic Piping for Domestic Cold Water Service—4/25/78

79a Acrylonitrile-Butadiene-Styrene (ABS) and Poly (Vinyl Chloride) (PVC) Plastic Drain, Waste and Vent Pipe and Fittings—3/7/82

80 Spray Applied Cellulosic Thermal Insulation—10/31/79

101 HUD Building Product Standards and Certification Program for Exterior Wall

Insulation and Finish Systems, July 26, 1993

Environmental Protection Agency, Office of Drinking Water, 401 M Street, SW., Washington, DC 20460, Telephone (202) 382–5533.

EPA 570/9–82–004 Manual of Individual Water Supply (NTIS–PB 85242279) Systems (October 1982)

Flat Glass Marketing Association, White Lakes Professional, Building 3310 Harrison Street, Topeka, KS 66611, Telephone (913) 266–7013. FGMA Glazing Manual—1986. FGMA Sealant Manual—1990.

Hardwood Plywood Manufacturers Association, P.O. Box 2789, 1825 Michael Faraday Drive, Reston, VA 22090, Telephone (703) 435–2900. ANSI/HPMA LHF–1987 Laminated Hardwood Flooring.

Insect Screening Weavers Assn., 2000 Maple Hill Street, P.O. Box 309, Yorktown Heights, NY 10598. IWS–089 Insect Wire Screening (Wire Fabric).

National Academy of Sciences, 2101 Constitution Avenue, NW., Washington, DC 20418. Publication 1571 Criteria for Selection and Design of Residential Slabs-on-Ground, Report #33, Building Research Advisory Board (BRAB), 1968.

National Association of Home Builders, Research Center, 400 Prince Georges Boulevard, Upper Marlboro, MD 20772, Telephone (301) 249–4000. Insulation Manual, Homes and Apartments—1979.

National Association of Plumbing-Heating-Cooling Contractors, P.O. Box 6808, Falls Church, VA 22046, Telephone (703) 237–8100. National Standard Plumbing Code—1993.

National Fire Protection Association, Batterymarch Park, Quincy, MA 02269, Telephone 1–800–344–3555.

ANSI/NFPA 58–89 Standard for the Storage and Handling of Liquefied Petroleum Gases

NFPA 54–88 National Fuel Gas Code (ANSI Z223.1–1988) NFPA 70–93 National Electrical Code

National Institute of Building Sciences, 1201 L Street, NW., Washington, DC 20005. Metric Guide for Federal Construction—1992.

National Oak Flooring Manufacturers Association, 22 North Front Street, Memphis, TN 38103. Official Grading Rules, Oak, Beech, Birch, Hard Maple, Pecan (OFGR/Vol. 1, No. 1/1986 and the 1989 Addendum). Hardwood Flooring Finishing/Refinishing Manual, 1986. Hardwood Flooring Installation Manual, 1986.

National Roofing Contractors Association, One O'Hare Centre, 6250 River Road, Rosemont, IL 60018, Telephone (708) 318–6722. NRCA Roofing and Waterproofing Manual, 1989.

National Terrazzo and Mosaic Association, 3166 Des Plaines Avenue, Suite 132, Des Plaines, IL 60018, Telephone (708) 635–7744. NTMA Specifications, Details and Technical Data, "Terrazzo Ideas & Design Guide", 1990.

National Wood Window and Door Association, 205 West Touhy Avenue, Park Ridge, IL 60018, Telephone (708) 299–5200.

ANSI/NWWDA IS 1–87 Industry Standard for Wood Flush Doors

ANSI/NWWDA IS 2–87 Industry Standard for Wood Windows

NWWDA IS 3–88 Industry Standard for Wood Sliding Patio Doors

ANSI/NWWDA IS 6–86 Industry Standard for Wood Stile and Rail Doors

Post-tensioning Institute, 301 West Osborn, Suite 3500, Phoenix, AZ 85013, Telephone (602) 870–7540. Design and Construction of Post-tensioned Slabs-on-Ground—1980.

Prestressed Concrete Institute, 175 West Jackson Boulevard, Suite 1859, Chicago, IL 60604, Telephone (312) 786–0353.

PCI MNL 116 Manual for Quality Control for Plants and Production for Precast Prestressed Concrete Products—1985 PCI MNL 117 Manual for Quality Control for Plants and Production of Architectural Precast Concrete Products—1977

Resilient Floor Covering Institute, 966 Hungerford Drive, Suite 12–B, Rockville, MD 20850, Telephone (301) 340–8580. Recommended Installation Specifications for Vinyl Composition, Solid Vinyl and Asphalt Tile Floorings, 1987.

Safety Glazing Certification Council, c/o ETL Testing Laboratories, Industrial Park, Route 11, Cortland, New York 13045, Telephone (607) 753–6711. Certified Products Directory—1990.

Southern California Association of Cabinet Manufacturers, 1933 South Broadway, L. 39, Los Angeles, CA 90007, Telephone (213) 749–4355. Certified Construction Standards and Specifications, Guide for Uniform Cabinet Specifications—1973 (Revised 1985).

Steel Door Institute, 30200 Detroit Road, Cleveland, OH 44145, Telephone (216) 899–0010. ANSI/SDI A123.1–82 Nomenclature for Steel Doors and Steel Door Frames.

Tile Council of America, Inc., Box 326, Princeton, NJ 08542–0326, Telephone (609) 921–7050. Handbook for Ceramic Tile Installation—1993.

Underwriters Laboratories, 333 Pfingsten Road, Northbrook, IL 60062, Telephone (708) 272–8800. Electrical Appliance and Utilization Equipment Directory, 1992.

Water Quality Association, 4151 Naperville Road, Lisle, IL 60532. Telephone (708) 396–1600.

WQA S–100 Household Commericial and Portable Exchange Water Softeners—1985

WQA S–200 Household and Commercial Water Filters—1988

WQA S–300 Point-of-Use, Low Pressure Reverse Osmosis Drinking Water Systems—1984

WQA S–400 Point-of-Use Distillation Drinking Water Systems—1986

Wood Moulding and Millwork Producers, P.O. Box 25278, Portland, OR 97225, Telephone (503) 292–9288.

WM 3–79 Exterior Wood Door Frames

[58 FR 60250, Nov. 15, 1993]

SUBCHAPTER B—MORTGAGE AND LOAN INSURANCE PROGRAMS UNDER NATIONAL HOUSING ACT AND OTHER AUTHORITIES

PART 201—TITLE I PROPERTY IMPROVEMENT AND MANUFACTURED HOME LOANS

AUTHORITY: 12 U.S.C. 1703; 15 U.S.C. 1639c; 42 U.S.C. 3535(d).

SOURCE: 50 FR 43523, Oct. 25, 1985, unless otherwise noted.

Subpart A—General

§ 201.1 Purpose.

These regulations implement the provisions of section 2 of title I of the National Housing Act (12 U.S.C. 1703). They contain the requirements under which an approved financial institution may obtain insurance on loans made for the alteration, repair or improvement of property, for the purchase of a manufactured home and/or the lot on which to place such home, for the purchase and installation of fire safety equipment in existing health care facilities, and for the preservation of historic structures. The insurance granted by the Secretary of Housing and Urban Development shall be available only for loans involving property located within a State, as that term is defined in § 201.2. The insurance can cover up to 10 percent of the amount of all insured Title I loans in the financial institution's portfolio, as reflected in the total amount of insurance coverage contained at any time in an insurance coverage reserve account established by the Secretary, less amounts for insurance claims paid. As limited by the amount of insurance coverage in such a reserve account, the insurance can cover up to 90 percent of the loss of any individual loan.

[50 FR 43523, Oct. 25, 1985, as amended at 61 FR 19795, May 2, 1996]

§ 201.2 Definitions.

As used in the regulations in this part the term:

Act means the National Housing Act, 12 U.S.C. 1703.

Actuarial method means the method of allocating payments made on a loan between the outstanding balance of the principal amount borrowed and the interest due on a loan obligation, under which a payment is applied first to the accrued interest, and any remainder is subtracted from, or any deficiency is added to, the unpaid balance of the obligation.

Borrower means one who applies for and receives a loan insured under this part. The term may also include any co-maker or co-signer or any assumptor who is obligated for the repayment of a loan obligation insured under this part.

Combination loan means a loan made for the purchase or refinancing in a single transaction of a manufactured home and a manufactured home lot, and may also include a garage, patio, carport, or other comparable appurtenance.

Dealer means, in the case of property improvement loans, a seller, contractor, or supplier of goods or services. In the case of manufactured home loans, *dealer* means one who engages in the business of manufactured home retail sales.

Dealer loan means a loan where a dealer, having a direct or indirect financial interest in the transaction between the borrower and the lender, assists the borrower in preparing the credit application or otherwise assists the borrower in obtaining the loan from the lender. In the case of a property improvement loan, the lender may disburse the loan proceeds solely to the borrower, or jointly to the borrower

and the dealer or other parties to the transaction. In the case of a manufactured home loan, the lender may disburse the loan proceeds solely to the dealer or the borrower, or jointly to the borrower and the dealer or other parties to the transaction.

Debtor means the borrower, any co-maker or co-signer, and any assumptor who is liable for the repayment of a defaulted loan obligation insured under this part.

Default means a failure by the borrower to make any payment due under the note, when such failure continues for a period of 30 days. For the purpose of these regulations, the "date of default" shall be considered as 30 days after the first failure to make an installment payment on the note which is not covered by subsequent payments, when applied to the overdue installments in the order in which they became due.

Direct loan means a loan for which a borrower makes application directly to a lender without any assistance from a dealer. The credit application, signed by the borrower, may be filled out by the borrower or by a person acting at the direction of the borrower who does not have a financial interest in the loan transaction. The lender may disburse the loan proceeds solely to the borrower or jointly to the borrower and other parties to the transaction. If a dealer takes legal action required by State law in order for the lender to obtain a valid and enforceable lien against the property, such action by the dealer will not convert an otherwise direct loan to a dealer loan.

Discount points means a fee charged by the lender, separate from interest but part of the total finance charges on the loan, that is part of the lender's total yield on the loan needed to maintain a competitive position with other types of investments. One discount point equals one percent of the principal amount of the loan. As discount points on the loan increase, the interest rate can be expected to decrease in a fairly consistent relationship.

Existing structure means a dwelling, including a manufactured home, that was completed and occupied at least 90 days prior to an application for a Title I loan, or a nonresidential structure that was a completed building with a distinctive functional use prior to an application for a Title I loan. However, these occupancy and completion requirements shall not apply to:

(1) Loans having a principal obligation of $1000 or less; or

(2) Residential structures which have been damaged by conditions determined by the President to warrant relief under the provisions of title 42, chapter 68, of the United States Code.

Fire safety equipment loan means a loan made to finance the purchase and installation of any device or construction feature which is recognized in the latest edition of the Department of Housing and Urban Development's Minimum Property Standards for Care Type Housing (HUD Handbook 4920.1) or the Fire Safety Code of the National Fire Protection Association, and which is designed to reduce the risk of death, personal injury, or property damage resulting from a fire in a health care facility.

Furniture means movable articles of personal property relating to a home or dwelling, such as beds, chairs, sofas, lamps, tables, rugs, etc.; however, furniture does not include:

(1) Items built into the home or dwelling such as wall-to-wall carpeting or heating or cooling equipment; or

(2) Large appliances such as refrigerators, ovens, ranges, dishwashers, clothes washers or clothes dryers.

Health care facility means a proprietary facility or facility of a private nonprofit corporation or association, licensed or regulated by the State or by the municipality or other political subdivision in which the facility is located, and operated as one or more of the following:

(1) A nursing home for the accommodation of convalescents or other persons who are not acutely ill and not in need of hospital care, but who require skilled nursing care and related medical services performed under the general direction of persons licensed by the law of the State where the facility is located to provide such care or services;

(2) An intermediate health care facility for the accommodation of persons who, because of incapacitating infirmities, require minimum but contin-

uous care, but not continuous medical care or nursing services;

(3) An extended health care facility for inpatient care for convalescents or chronic disease patients who require skilled nursing care and related medical services; or

(4) Other comparable health care facility.

Historic preservation loan means a loan to finance the preservation (restoration or rehabilitation) of an historic residential structure which is listed on the National Register of Historic Places or which is certified by the Secretary of the Interior as conforming with National Register criteria.

Lender means a financial institution that:

(1) Holds a valid Title I contract of insurance and is approved by the Secretary under 24 CFR part 202 to originate, purchase, hold, service, and/or sell loans insured under this part; or

(2) Is under suspension or holds a Title I contract of insurance that has been terminated, but that remains responsible for servicing or selling Title I loans that it holds and is authorized to file insurance claims on such loans.

Loan means a disbursement of proceeds (funds) or an advance of credit to or for the benefit of a borrower who promises to repay the principal amount of such disbursement or advance, plus interest, if any, at a stated annual rate over time, with the borrower's obligation evidenced by the borrower's execution of a note. *Loan* also means a purchase by a lender of a note evidencing such obligation, or a refinancing of an existing obligation with or without an additional disbursement of proceeds or advance of credit.

Manufacturer's invoice means a document issued by a manufacturer and provided with a manufactured home to a retail dealer which separately details the wholesale (base) prices at the factory for specific models or series of manufactured homes and itemized options (large appliances, built-in items and equipment), plus actual itemized charges for freight from the factory to the dealer's lot or the homesite (including any rental of wheels and axles) and for any sales taxes to be paid by the dealer. The invoice may recite such prices and charges on an itemized basis or by stating an aggregate price or charge, as appropriate, for each category. The manufacturer shall certify on the invoice, or on a supplement which is attached to and made a part of the invoice, as follows:

The undersigned certifies under applicable criminal and civil penalties for fraud and misrepresentation that: (1) The wholesale (base) prices for the manufactured home and itemized options, the charges for freight and dealer-paid sales taxes, and all other statements in this invoice are true and accurate; (2) all such prices reflect the actual dealer costs at the factory, as quoted in the applicable current manufacturer's wholesale (base) price list; (3) except for any payments of volume incentives or special benefits related to this transaction, all such prices and charges exclude any costs of trade association fees or charges, discounts, bonuses, refunds, rebates, prizes, loan discount points or other financing charges, or anything else of more than nominal value which will inure to the benefit of the dealer and/or home purchaser at any date; and (4) the manufacturer has not made and will not make any payments to or for the benefit of the dealer and/ or home purchaser that are not disclosed on this invoice or invoice supplement.

Manufactured home means a transportable structure, comprised of one or more modules, each built on a permanent chassis, with or without a permanent foundation, designed for occupancy as a principal residence by a single family. A new manufactured home shall comply with the minimum property standards prescribed by the Secretary to assure its livability and durability that are published as the Manufactured Home Construction and Safety Standards implementing the National Manufactured Housing Construction and Safety Standards Act of 1974, 42 U.S.C. 5401–5426, at 24 CFR part 3280. To qualify for a manufactured home loan insured under this part, an existing manufactured home must have been constructed in accordance with standards published at 24 CFR part 3280 and must meet standards similar to the minimum property standards applicable to existing homes insured under title II of the Act, as prescribed by the Secretary.

Manufactured home improvement loan means a loan made to finance the alteration, repair or improvement of an existing manufactured home which is classified as personalty by the State or locality in which the property is located. The proceeds of a manufactured home improvement loan may also be used for improvements to the homesite, as long as the borrower is the owner of the home and the underlying real estate.

Manufactured home loan means a loan for the purchase or refinancing of a manufactured home and/or the lot on which to place such home. Unless otherwise indicated, the term includes manufactured home purchase loans, manufactured home lot loans, and combination loans.

Manufactured home lot loan means a loan for the purchase or refinancing of a portion of land acceptable to the Secretary as a manufactured home lot. A manufactured home lot may consist of platted or unplatted land, a lot in a recorded or unrecorded subdivision or in an improved area of such subdivision, or a lot in a planned unit development. A manufactured home lot may also consist of an interest in a manufactured home condominium project (including any interest in the common areas) or a share in a cooperative association which owns and operates a manufactured home park.

Manufactured home purchase loan means a loan for the purchase or refinancing of a manufactured home exclusive of any lot or site, and may also include a garage, patio, carport, or other comparable appurtenance.

Multifamily property improvement loan means a loan to finance the alteration, repair, improvement, or conversion of an existing structure used or to be used as an apartment house or a dwelling for two or more families. The multifamily structure may not be owned by a corporation, partnership, or trust, unless the prior approval of the Secretary is obtained for an exception to this requirement.

Nonresidential property improvement loan means a loan made to finance the construction of a new exclusively nonresidential structure or the alteration, repair or improvement of an existing structure that is nonresidential. Such a structure may be temporarily used for residential purposes while the borrower constructs a new dwelling to replace a dwelling previously occupied by the borrower that was destroyed or damaged by conditions determined by the President to warrant relief under the provisions of title 42, chapter 68, of the U.S.C., provided that the credit application is filed within one year from the date of such a determination.

Note means the written instrument evidencing the borrower's signature to a promise to repay the principal indebtedness and to pay any interest due on a loan, whether the instrument is separate from or included within another document, and unless otherwise specified means also any security instrument with respect to that loan obligation.

Owner means a person, including a borrower, who has title in whole or in part to the property which is the subject of a loan transaction.

Principal residence means a home where the borrower expects to live at least nine months of the year.

Property improvement loan means a loan made to finance actions or items that substantially protect or improve the basic livability or utility of a property. Unless otherwise indicated, the term includes single family, multifamily and nonresidential property improvement loans; manufactured home improvement loans where the home is classified as personalty; historic preservation loans; and fire safety equipment loans in existing health care facilities.

Rehabilitation means the process of returning an historic residential structure to a state of utility, through repair or alteration, which makes possible an efficient contemporary use. In rehabilitation, those portions of the property important in illustrating historic, architectural and cultural values are preserved or restored.

Restoration means the process of accurately recovering the form and details of an historic residential structure as it appeared at a particular period of time by removing later work and by replacing missing original work.

Security instrument means a properly recorded chattel mortgage, real estate mortgage or deed of trust, or conditional sales contract.

Single family property improvement loan means a loan to finance alterations, repairs and improvements to or

in connection with an existing structure used or to be used as a single family residence, including an existing one-family manufactured home that qualifies as real property in that the home is placed on a permanent foundation, the home and lot are classified as realty by the State or locality in which the property is located, and any loans on the property are secured by mortgages or deeds of trust covering the home and lot.

Solar energy system means any addition, alteration or improvement to an existing structure for single family or multifamily residential use which is designed to utilize wind or solar energy to reduce the energy requirements of that structure from other energy sources, and which complies with standards prescribed by the Secretary.

Special benefits means benefits other than volume incentives for dealers which a home manufacturer funds from general corporate revenues by charging them against corporate overhead and profit without changing the wholesale (base) price of a manufactured home (or series of homes), as reflected in the manufacturer's published wholesale (base) price list, and which are limited to payments by the manufacturer directly to:

(1) A financial institution to *buy down* or reduce the interest rate, discount points, or other fees or charges related to a lending agreement for a dealer's manufactured home inventory or *floor plan* financing needs; or

(2) One or more advertising media for all or part of the costs of advertising the manufacturer's homes, one or more dealer's services, and related manufactured home materials and products in such media.

State means any State of the United States, Puerto Rico, the District of Columbia, Guam, American Samoa, the Commonwealth of the Northern Mariana Islands, or the United States Virgin Islands.

Volume incentives means specified dollar benefits to dealers under a published marketing and promotional plan, payable by a home manufacturer in cash or in kind in amounts or levels relating to the volume of sales of manufactured homes to dealers, other than benefits of a nominal value of less than $10 per home, which:

(1) The manufacturer funds from general corporate revenues by including them in the prices quoted in the manufacturer's wholesale (base) price list and charging them against corporate overhead and profit;

(2) Whether or not available on an optional basis, do not increase or decrease the wholesale (base) prices for the sale of a specific home or options or the charges for freight and dealer-paid sales taxes as detailed in the manufacturer's invoice, for a specific sale to a retail dealer;

(3) The manufacturer provides without creating a special product line where the cost of the benefits is the only substantive difference between the special product line and other essentially similar homes;

(4) Whether or not also of benefit to the ultimate purchaser, do not increase or decrease the retail price of the home;

(5) Are available to any dealer in a particular market area doing business with the manufacturer;

(6) The manufacturer provides only for volume sales of manufactured homes to dealers over a specified period of time;

(7) The plan provides in escalating and different amounts or levels related to either the number of homes (or modules) sold or the dollar value of such sales to a dealer, or some combination of such elements, in a specified period of time;

(8) Are structured so that only some of the dealer participants are expected to be paid the maximum benefits under the program, with substantial numbers of participants expected to receive less than the maximum amount or level of benefits; and

(9) Accrue for volume sales to a dealer over a specified period of time which is at least quarterly in length, and are paid not more frequently than quarterly.

Wholesale (base) price list means the price list or lists, as periodically amended, which are published and distributed by a home manufacturer to all retail dealers in a given marketing area, quoting the actual wholesale (base) prices at the factory for specific models or series of manufactured homes and itemized options offered for sale to such dealers during a specified period of time. The wholesale (base) prices may include the manufacturer's projected costs of providing volume incentives and special benefits related to sales to dealers during the period. All such wholesale (base) prices shall exclude any costs of trade association fees or charges, discounts, bonuses, refunds, rebates, prizes, loan discount points or other financing charges, or anything else of more than nominal value which will inure to the benefit of a dealer and/or home purchaser at any date. Each price list and amendment shall be retained by the manufacturer for a minimum period of six years from the date of publication so as to be available to HUD and other Federal agencies upon request.

[50 FR 43523, Oct. 25, 1985, as amended at 54 FR 36263, Aug. 31, 1989; 56 FR 52428, Oct. 18, 1991; 57 FR 6480, Feb. 25, 1992; 57 FR 45246, Sept. 30, 1992; 60 FR 13836, Mar. 14, 1995; 61 FR 5206, Feb. 9, 1996; 61 FR 19795, May 2, 1996; 66 FR 56419, Nov. 7, 2001; 77 FR 51468, Aug. 24, 2012]

§ 201.3 Applicability of the regulations.

The regulations in this part may be amended by the Secretary at any time. Such amendment shall not adversely affect the insurance privileges of a lender on any loan that has been made or for which a loan application has been approved before the effective date of the amendment.

[61 FR 19796, May 2, 1996]

§ 201.4 Rules of construction.

As used in this part, and unless the context indicates otherwise, words in the singular include the plural, and words in the plural include the singular.

[56 FR 52429, Oct. 18, 1991]

§ 201.5 Waivers.

Waiver of lender's noncompliance. The Secretary may waive a lender's noncompliance with any provision of this part, subject to statutory limitations, when it is determined that enforcement of the regulations would impose an injustice upon a lender which has substantially complied with the regulations in good faith and refunded or credited any excess charge made, and when such waiver does not involve an increase in the Secretary's obligation beyond that which would have been involved if the lender was in full compliance with the regulations.

[56 FR 52429, Oct. 18, 1991, as amended at 61 FR 5206, Feb. 9, 1996]

§201.6 Disclosure and verification of Social Security and Employer Identification Numbers.

To be eligible for loan insurance under this part, the borrower must meet the requirements for the disclosure and verification of Social Security and Employer Identification Numbers, as provided by part 200, subpart U, of this chapter.

(Approved by the Office of Management and Budget under control number 2502–0059)

[54 FR 39692, Sept. 27, 1989, as amended at 55 FR 420, Jan. 5, 1990]

§201.7 Qualified mortgage.

(a) *Qualified mortgage.* A mortgage insured under section 2 of title I of the National Housing Act (12 U.S.C. 1703), except for mortgage transactions exempted under §203.19(c)(2), is a safe harbor qualified mortgage that meets the ability to repay requirements in 15 U.S.C. 1639c(a).

(b) *Effect of indemnification on qualified mortgage status.* An indemnification demand or resolution of a demand that relates to whether the loan satisfied relevant eligibility and underwriting requirements at the time of consummation may result from facts that could allow a change to qualified mortgage status, but the existence of an indemnification does not per se remove qualified mortgage status.

[78 FR 75237, Dec. 11, 2013]

Subpart B—Loan and Note Provisions

§201.10 Loan amounts.

(a) *Property improvement loans.* (1) The total principal obligation for a property improvement loan shall not exceed the actual cost of the project plus any applicable fees and charges author-ized at §201.25(b), up to the following maximum loan amounts:

(i) Single family property improvement loans—$25,000, except that a loan for a manufactured home that qualifies as real property shall be limited to $17,500.

(ii) Multifamily property improvement loans—$60,000 or an average of $12,000 per dwelling unit, whichever is less.

(iii) Nonresidential property improvement loans—$25,000.

(iv) Manufactured home improvement loans—$7,500.

(v) Historic preservation loans—the lesser of $15,000 per dwelling unit in a residential structure or $45,000 per residential structure.

(vi) Fire safety equipment loans—$50,000.

(2) No property improvement loan shall be approved where the total outstanding balance of all title I property improvement loans on the same property exceeds the maximum loan amount prescribed for that type of loan. If more than one type of property improvement loan is involved, the total outstanding balance of such loans on a particular property shall not exceed the maximum loan amount prescribed for the larger type of loan.

(b) *Manufactured home purchase loans.* (1) The total principal obligation for a loan to purchase a new manufactured home shall not exceed the sum of the following itemized amounts, up to a maximum of $48,600:

(i) 130 percent of the sum of the wholesale (base) prices of the home and any itemized options and the charge for freight, as detailed in the manufacturer's invoice;

(ii) The charge for any sales taxes to be paid by the dealer, as detailed in the manufacturer's invoice;

(iii) The actual dealer's cost of transportation to the homesite, set-up and anchoring, including the rental of wheels and axles (if not included in the freight charges);

(iv) The actual dealer's cost of skirting;

(v) The actual dealer's cost of a garage, carport, patio or other comparable appurtenance to the manufactured home, as approved by the Secretary;

(vi) The actual dealer's cost of purchasing and installing a central air conditioning system or heat pump, if not installed by the manufacturer; and

(vii) Any applicable charges authorized at § 201.25(b).

(2) The total principal obligation for a loan to purchase an existing manufactured home shall not exceed the lesser of the following amounts, up to a maximum of $48,600:

(i) 95 percent of the appraised value of the home as equipped and furnished (as determined by a HUD-approved appraisal) and 95 percent of any itemized amounts allowed under paragraphs (b)(1)(iii) through (vii) of this section, if incurred; or

(ii) 95 percent of the purchase price of the home.

(3) The purchase price of a manufactured home financed with a manufactured home purchase loan shall include the retail cost to the borrower of all items set forth in the purchase contract, including any applicable charges authorized under § 201.25(b).

(c) *Manufactured home lot loans.* The total principal obligation for a loan to purchase and, if necessary, develop a lot suitable for a manufactured home, including on-site water and utility connections, sanitary facilities, site improvements and landscaping, shall not exceed 95 percent of either the appraised value of the developed lot (as determined by a HUD-approved appraisal) or the total of the purchase price and development costs, whichever is less, up to a maximum of $16,200.

(d) *Combination loans.* (1) The total principal obligation for a loan to purchase a new manufactured home and a lot on which to place the home shall not exceed the sum of the following itemized amounts, up to a maximum of $64,800:

(i) 130 percent of the sum of the wholesale (base) prices of the home and any itemized options and the charge for freight, as detailed in the manufacturer's invoice;

(ii) The charge for any sales taxes to be paid by the dealer, as detailed in the manufacturer's invoice;

(iii) The actual dealer's cost of transportation to the homesite, set-up and anchoring, including the rental of wheels and axles (if not included in the freight charge);

(iv) The actual dealer's cost of purchasing and installing a central air conditioning system or heat pump, if not installed by the manufacturer;

(v) The appraised value of the developed manufactured home lot (as determined by a HUD-approved appraisal, including on-site water and utility connections, sanitary facilities, site improvements and landscaping) or the purchase price, whichever is less;

(vi) The actual dealer's cost of appurtenances to the home such as a permanent foundation, garage, carport or patio; and

(vii) Any applicable charges authorized at § 201.25(b).

(2) The total principal obligation for a loan to purchase an existing manufactured home and lot shall not exceed the lesser of the following amounts, up to a maximum of $64,800:

(i) 95 percent of the total appraised value of the home, the lot, and any appurtenances (as determined by a HUD-approved appraisal), plus 95 percent of any applicable charges authorized at § 201.25(b); or

(ii) 95 percent of the purchase price of the home, the lot, and any appurtenances.

(3) The purchase price of a manufactured home and a lot financed with a combination loan shall include the retail cost to the borrower of all items set forth in the purchase contract or contracts, including any applicable charges authorized under § 201.25(b).

(e) *Manufactured home loan limits in high-cost areas.* (1) The maximum loan amounts otherwise applicable under paragraphs (b), (c) and (d) of this section may be increased by an amount not to exceed 40 percent where the manufactured home and/or lot is purchased and located in Alaska, Guam or Hawaii.

(2) The maximum loan amounts otherwise applicable under paragraphs (c) and (d) of this section may be increased for any geographical area except Alaska, Guam or Hawaii to the extent deemed necessary by the Secretary; however, any increased loan amount may not exceed the lesser of (i) 185 percent of the dollar amounts specified in paragraphs (c) and (d) of this section;

or (ii) the dollar amounts specified in paragraphs (c) and (d) of this section, as increased by the same percentage by which 95 percent of the median 1-family house price in the area (as determined by the Secretary for purposes of §203.18) exceeds $67,500.

(f) *Loan refinancing.* (1) The total principal obligation of a loan made to refinance a borrower's existing insured property improvement loan shall not exceed the maximum loan amount permitted under this section for the particular type of loan, provided that any amount in excess of the cost to the borrower of prepaying the existing loan shall be made available only to finance additional property improvements meeting the requirements of this part.

(2) The total principal obligation of a loan made to refinance a borrower's existing insured manufactured home loan shall not exceed the lesser of the cost to the borrower of prepaying the existing loan or the maximum loan amount permitted under this section for the particular type of loan.

(3) The total principal obligation of a loan made to refinance a borrower's existing uninsured manufactured home loan shall not exceed the cost to the borrower of prepaying the existing loan or the appraised value of the property (as determined by a HUD-approved appraisal), whichever is less, up to the maximum loan amount permitted under this section for the particular type of loan.

(4) When a borrower's existing manufactured home lot is being refinanced in connection with the purchase of a manufactured home, the total principal obligation of the combination loan shall be determined in accordance with paragraph (d)(1) or (d)(2) of this section.

(5) When a borrower's existing manufactured home is being refinanced in connection with the purchase of a manufactured home lot, the total principal obligation of the combination loan shall not exceed the lesser of the following amounts, up to a maximum of $64,800:

(i) The cost to the borrower of prepaying any existing loan on the home, plus the purchase price of the lot; or

(ii) The appraised value of the home and lot (as determined by a HUD-approved appraisal).

(g) *Minimum loan amount.* A lender may not require, as a condition of providing a loan insured under this part, that the principal amount of the loan exceed a minimum amount established by the lender.

[50 FR 43523, Oct. 25, 1985, as amended at 52 FR 33406, Sept. 3, 1987; 53 FR 8880, Mar. 18, 1988; 54 FR 10537, Mar. 14, 1989; 54 FR 36264, Aug. 31, 1989; 56 FR 52429, Oct. 18, 1991; 57 FR 45246, Sept. 30, 1992; 58 FR 41001, July 30, 1993; 59 FR 9084, Feb. 25, 1994; 61 FR 19796, May 2, 1996; 62 FR 20082, Apr. 24, 1997]

§201.11 Loan maturities.

(a) *Property improvement loans.* The term of a property improvement loan shall be not less than six months and not more than 20 years and 32 days from the date of the loan, except that:

(1) The maximum term for a single family property improvement loan on a manufactured home that qualifies as real property shall not exceed 15 years and 32 days from the date of the loan;

(2) The maximum term for a manufactured home improvement loan shall not exceed 12 years and 32 days from the date of the loan; and

(3) The maximum term for an historic preservation loan shall not exceed 15 years and 32 days from the date of the loan.

(b) *Manufactured home loans.* The term of a manufactured home loan shall be not less than six months and not more than 20 years and 32 days from the date of the loan, except that:

(1) The maximum term for a manufactured home lot loan shall not exceed 15 years and 32 days from the date of the loan; and

(2) The maximum term for a multi-module manufactured home and lot in combination shall not exceed 25 years and 32 days from the date of the loan.

(c) *Loan refinancing.* A loan to be refinanced under this part may be refinanced for an extended period.

(1) The term of a loan to refinance a borrower's existing insured property improvement or manufactured home loan shall not exceed the maximum term permitted under paragraph (a) or (b) of this section for the particular type of loan. In addition, the total time

period from the date of the original loan to the final maturity of the refinanced loan shall not exceed:

(i) In the case of a property improvement loan, the maximum term permitted under paragraph (a) of this section plus 9 years and 11 months; and

(ii) In the case of manufactured home loan, the maximum term permitted under paragraph (b) of this section plus 4 years and 11 months.

(2) The term of a loan made to refinance a borrower's existing uninsured manufactured home loan shall not exceed the maximum term permitted under paragraph (b) of this section for the particular type of loan.

(3) When a borrower's existing manufactured home lot is being refinanced in connection with the purchase of a manufactured home, the term of the combination loan shall not exceed the maximum term permitted under paragraph (b) of this section for the particular type of loan.

(4) When a borrower's existing manufactured home is being refinanced in connection with the purchase of a manufactured home lot, the term of the combination loan shall not exceed the maximum term permitted under paragraph (b) of this section for the particular type of loan.

[50 FR 43523, Oct. 25, 1985, as amended at 52 FR 33406, Sept. 3, 1987; 54 FR 10537, Mar. 14, 1989; 56 FR 52430, Oct. 18, 1991; 57 FR 45246, Sept. 30, 1992; 61 FR 19796, May 2, 1996]

§ 201.12 Requirements for the note.

The note shall bear the genuine signature of each borrower and of any co-maker or co-signer, be valid and enforceable against the borrower and any co-maker or co-signer, and be complete and regular on its face. The borrower and any co-maker or co-signer shall execute the note for the full amount of the loan obligation. Although the note may be executed by the borrower on an earlier date, the date of the loan shall be the date that the loan proceeds are disbursed by the lender. Such date shall be entered on the note when disbursement occurs. The note shall separately recite the principal amount and any interest at an agreed annual rate that comprises the borrower's payment obligation. The lender shall assure that the note and all other documents evidencing the loan transaction are in compliance with applicable Federal, State, and local laws. If the note is executed on behalf of a corporation, partnership, or trust by an authorized representative, it shall create a binding obligation on such entity.

[61 FR 19797, May 2, 1996]

§ 201.13 Interest and discount points.

The interest rate for any loan shall be negotiated and agreed to by the borrower and the lender, and such interest rate shall be fixed for the full term of the loan and recited in the note. Interest on the loan shall accrue from the date of the loan, and shall be calculated on a simple interest basis. The lender and the borrower may negotiate the amount of discount points, if any, to be paid by the borrower as part of the borrower's initial payment. The lender shall not require or allow any party other than the borrower to pay any discount points or other financing charges in connection with the loan transaction.

[61 FR 19797, May 2, 1996]

§ 201.14 Payments on the loan.

The note normally shall provide for equal installment payments due weekly, biweekly, semi-monthly or monthly. The note may provide for either or both of the first and final payments to vary in amount but not to exceed 1½ times the regular installment. Where the borrower has an irregular flow of income, the note may be payable at quarterly or semi-annual intervals corresponding with the borrower's flow of income. The first scheduled payment after the borrower's initial payment shall be due no later than two months from the date of the loan. Multiple payment schedules may not be used in connection with any loan.

§ 201.15 Late charges to borrowers.

(a) *Imposition of late charge.* The note may provide for imposition of a late charge unless precluded by State law. The late charge may be imposed only for installments of principal and interest which are in arrears for the greater of 15 calendar days or the number of days required by applicable State law before such a charge may be imposed.

Late charges must be billed to the borrower or reflected in the payment coupon, and evidence of any late charges that have been paid must be in the loan file if an insurance claim is made.

(b) *Amount of late charge.* The late charge shall not exceed the lesser of five percent of each installment of principal and interest, up to a maximum of $10 per installment for any property improvement loan and $15 per installment for any manufactured home loan, or the maximum amount permitted by applicable State law.

(c) *Method of payment.* Payment of any late charge cannot be deducted from the monthly payment for principal and interest, but must be an additional charge to the borrower.

(d) *Daily interest in lieu of late charges.* In lieu of late charges, the note may provide for interest to accrue on installments in arrears on a daily basis at the interest rate in the note.

[54 FR 36264, Aug. 31, 1989]

§201.16 Default provision.

The loan note shall contain a provision for acceleration of maturity, at the option of the holder, upon a default by the borrower.

§201.17 Prepayment provision.

The note shall contain a provision permitting full or partial prepayment of the loan without penalty, except that the borrower may be assessed reasonable and customary charges for recording a release of the lender's security interest in the property, if permitted by State law.

[61 FR 19797, May 2, 1996]

§201.18 Modification agreement or repayment plan.

(a) *Modification agreement or repayment plan.* A written but unrecorded modification agreement acceptable to the lender and executed by the borrower may be used in lieu of refinancing of a delinquent or defaulted loan to reduce or increase the monthly payment, but not to increase the term or the interest rate, so as to assure that the delinquent or defaulted loan is brought current before or by the end of the loan term. A modification agreement may also be used in lieu of refinancing in connection with a loan that is current to effect a reduction in the interest rate, and in the monthly payment, for the remainder of the loan term. When a modification agreement is used, no insurance reporting is required under §201.30.

(b) *Repayment plan.* The lender may elect to negotiate an informal repayment plan with the borrower to enable a temporary delinquency to be cured within a short period of time. The lender may document the terms of the repayment plan by sending a letter to the borrower reciting the terms of their agreement. When a repayment plan is used, no insurance reporting is required under §201.30.

[52 FR 33406, Sept. 3, 1987, as amended at 54 FR 10537, Mar. 14, 1989]

§201.19 Refinanced and assumed loans.

(a) *Conditions on refinancing.* (1) An existing insured property improvement loan or manufactured home loan may be refinanced without an advance of funds only under the following conditions:

(i) A loan that is in default may not be refinanced for an amount greater than the original principal balance of the loan;

(ii) The refinancing of a loan for the original borrower shall be subject to all of the requirements of this part, except §§201.20(b) and (c), 201.21(b) through (e), 201.22, 201.23, and 201.26;

(iii) If there are co-makers or co-signers on the original note, the lender shall require the same co-makers or co-signers on the refinanced note, unless the lender obtains the Secretary's approval to release a co-maker or co-signer from liability under the note in accordance with §201.24(e); and

(iv) A loan that was assumed in accordance with paragraph (c) of this section may be refinanced, subject to all of the requirements of this part except §§201.20(b) and (c), 201.21(b) through (e), 201.22, 201.23, and 201.26, as long as the original borrower and any intervening assumptors were released from liability for repayment of the loan at the time the loan was assumed. A lender may not refinance a previously assumed loan under any other circumstances, unless the requirements of

§ 201.22 are also met and the Secretary has approved a release of the original borrower and any intervening assumptors in accordance with § 201.24(e).

(2) An existing insured property improvement loan may be refinanced with an advance of funds for additional improvements only under the following conditions:

(i) The existing insured loan must not be in default; and

(ii) The refinancing shall be subject to all of the requirements of this part applicable to the particular type of loan and to the additional improvements being financed.

(3) An existing uninsured manufactured home loan may be refinanced only for the original borrower and only under the following conditions:

(i) The existing uninsured loan must not be in default;

(ii) Refinancing of an existing uninsured manufactured home purchase loan or combination loan shall be subject to all the requirements of this part applicable to the particular type of loan except §§ 201.23 and 201.26(b)(4);

(iii) Refinancing of an existing uninsured manufactured home lot loan in connection with the purchase of a manufactured home shall be subject to all of the requirements of this part; and

(iv) Refinancing of an existing uninsured manufactured home purchase loan in connection with the purchase of a manufactured home lot shall be subject to all of the requirements of this part except § 201.26(b)(4).

(b) *Note and security requirements for refinanced loans.* (1) Refinancing of a loan requires the execution of a new note and cancellation of the old note.

(2) Refinancing of a loan that was secured when originated, regardless of the principal balance of the note at the time of refinancing, is required to be secured.

(3) Refinancing of a loan that was not secured when originated is not required to be secured if no additional funds are advanced.

(4) When a refinanced loan is secured, the lender shall obtain and record a new security instrument in accordance with § 201.24 and shall release the original lien, unless State law permits a renewal and extension of the original lien.

(5) Copies of all documents pertaining to the original loan must be retained in the loan file for the refinanced loan.

(c) *Assumed loans.* (1) At the option of the lender, an existing insured property improvement loan or manufactured home loan may be assumed, subject to the following conditions:

(i) A determination by the lender that the assumptor is eligible under § 201.20(a) or 201.21(a) and meets the requirements of § 201.22; and

(ii) The execution of an assumption agreement that is satisfactory to the lender and is signed by the assumptor and the original borrower or previous assumptor at the time of assumption.

(2) The lender shall not permit an assumption under any circumstances other than those contained in this section, and shall include appropriate provisions in any note or security agreement to enforce this requirement.

(3) Prior to the execution of the assumption agreement, the lender shall provide the assumptor with a written notice, to be signed by the assumptor and retained in the loan file, that:

(i) States that the loan being assumed is insured by HUD, and describes the actions the Secretary may take to recover the debt if the assumptor defaults on the loan and an insurance claim is paid; and

(ii) Constitutes the assumptor's agreement to pay penalties and administrative costs imposed by HUD as authorized by 31 U.S.C. 3717.

(4) If the other requirements of paragraph (c) of this section are met, the lender at its option may release the original borrower and any intervening assumptors from liability for the repayment of a loan obligation insured under this part. The prior approval of the Secretary under § 201.24(e) is not required. The lender shall retain documentation of the release in the loan file.

[52 FR 33406, Sept. 3, 1987, as amended at 56 FR 52430, Oct. 18, 1991]

Subpart C—Eligibility and Disbursement Requirements

§ 201.20 Property improvement loan eligibility.

(a) *Borrower eligibility*. (1) To be eligible for a property improvement loan (other than a manufactured home improvement loan), the borrower shall have at least a one-half interest in one of the following:

(i) Fee simple title to the real property;

(ii) Lease of the real property for a fixed term which expires not less than six calendar months after the final maturity of the loan; or

(iii) A properly recorded land installment contract for the purchase of the real property.

(2) To be eligible for a manufactured home improvement loan, the borrower shall have at least a one-half interest in the manufactured home, and the home must be the principal residence of the borrower.

(b) *Eligible use of the loan proceeds*. (1) The loan proceeds shall be used only for the purposes disclosed in the loan application. If the borrower plans to use a dealer or contractor to carry out the improvement work, the lender shall obtain a copy of a proposal or contract that describes in detail the work to be performed and the estimated or actual cost. If the borrower plans to carry out the improvement work without the services of a dealer or contractor, the borrower shall be required to furnish a detailed written description of the work to be performed, the materials to be furnished, and their estimated cost.

(2) The loan proceeds shall be used only to finance property improvements that substantially protect or improve the basic livability or utility of the property. The Secretary will establish a list of items and activities that may not be financed with the proceeds of any property improvement loan. If a lender has any doubt as to the eligibility of any item or activity, it shall request a specific ruling by the Secretary before making a loan.

(3) The loan proceeds shall only be used to finance property improvements that are started after loan approval, unless:

(i) The prior approval of the Secretary is obtained for an exception to this requirement; or

(ii) The property is located in a major disaster area declared by the President, and the lender determines that emergency action is needed to repair damage resulting from the disaster.

(c) *Special pre-application requirements*. (1) Where the proceeds are to be used for an historic preservation loan, the proposed improvements shall be reviewed and approved by the State Historic Preservation Officer (or other person authorized by the Secretary of the Interior to make such reviews) prior to making application for a loan. The purpose of the review is to determine that (i) the structure is an historic residential structure listed on the National Register of Historic Places or certified by the Secretary of the Interior as conforming with National Register criteria, and (ii) the proposed improvements comply with criteria set by the Secretary of the Interior for the preservation of historic structures.

(2) Where the proceeds are to be used for a fire safety equipment loan, the proposed improvements shall be reviewed and approved by the State or local agency having primary jurisdiction over the fire safety requirements of health care facilities prior to making application for a loan.

[50 FR 43523, Oct. 25, 1985, as amended at 56 FR 52430, Oct. 18, 1991; 61 FR 19797, May 2, 1996; 62 FR 65181, Dec. 10, 1997]

§ 201.21 Manufactured home loan eligibility.

(a) *Borrower eligibility*. To be eligible for a manufactured home loan (whether a manufactured home purchase loan, a manufactured home lot loan, or a combination loan), the borrower must become the owner of the particular property which is to be financed with such a loan. Where the loan involves a manufactured home which is classified as realty, ownership of the home must be in fee simple. Where the loan involves a manufactured home lot, ownership of the lot must be in fee simple, except where the lot consists of a share in a cooperative association which owns and operates a manufactured home park.

(b) *Eligible use of loan proceeds.* (1) The loan proceeds may be used for the purchase or refinancing of a manufactured home, a suitably developed lot on which to place a manufactured home already owned by the borrower, or a manufactured home and a suitably developed lot for the home in combination. The loan proceeds may also be used to refinance an existing manufactured home already owned by the borrower in connection with the purchase of a manufactured home lot, or to refinance a lot already owned by the borrower in connection with the purchase of a manufactured home. Where the proceeds are for a manufactured home purchase loan or combination loan, the home must be the borrower's principal residence. Where the proceeds are for a manufactured home lot loan, the borrower's manufactured home must be placed on the lot and occupied as the borrower's principal residence within six months after the date of the loan.

(2) A manufactured home financed with an insured loan under this part may be either:

(i) A new home, which is one that is purchased by the borrower within 18 months after the date of manufacture and has not been previously occupied; or

(ii) An existing home, which is one that does not meet the criteria for a new home. In order to be eligible for financing with an insured loan under this part, the manufactured home, its warranty and the site on which the home is placed must meet the requirements of paragraphs (c) through (e) of this section.

(3) The proceeds of a loan to purchase a new manufactured home or a new manufactured home and lot shall not be used to purchase furniture or wheels and axles, and the cost of these items shall not be included in the total principal obligation calculated under § 201.10 (b)(1) or (d)(1).

(4) The proceeds of a manufactured home purchase loan may be used for the purchase, construction or installation of a garage, carport, patio or other comparable appurtenance to the manufactured home, as stated in the retail purchase contract and as approved by the Secretary. The proceeds of a combination loan may be used for the purchase, construction or installation of a permanent foundation, garage, carport, patio or other comparable appurtenance to the manufactured home.

(5) The Secretary will establish a list of items and activities that may not be financed with the proceeds of any manufactured home loan. If a lender has any doubt as to the eligibility of any item or activity, it shall request a specific ruling by the Secretary before making a loan.

(c) *Construction, transportation and installation requirements.* (1) The manufactured home shall be certified by the manufacturer under applicable criminal and civil penalties for fraud and misrepresentation to have been constructed in compliance with the National Manufactured Housing Construction and Safety Standards Act of 1974, 42 U.S.C. 5401–5426, so as to conform to all applicable Federal construction and safety standards, as evidenced by a label or tag affixed to the manufactured home in accordance with 24 CFR 3280.8.

(2) During any period of transportation from the factory to the borrower's homesite, the structural integrity of the manufactured home shall be maintained so that it will be livable and durable.

(3) The installation or erection of the manufactured home on the homesite shall comply with the manufacturer's requirements for anchoring, support, stability and maintenance. Any permanent foundation shall be constructed in accordance with the current edition of HUD's Permanent Foundations Guide for Manufactured Housing (HUD Handbook 4930.3).

(4) For any manufactured home purchase loan or combination loan involving a sale of the manufactured home by a dealer, the dealer shall inspect the manufactured home, as installed or erected on the homesite, for structural damage or other defects resulting from the transportation and installation of the home. The dealer shall also test the performance of the home's plumbing, mechanical and electrical systems to assure that they are fully operational.

(d) *Manufacturer's warranty requirements.* (1) To induce the Secretary to insure a title I loan under this part for the purchase of a new manufactured home and to induce a borrower to purchase such a home, the home manufacturer shall furnish the borrower with a written warranty, duly executed by an authorized representative of the manufacturer on a HUD-approved form. The warranty shall be provided without cost to the borrower. The effective date of the warranty shall be the date of delivery of the manufactured home to the borrower, regardless of when the warranty was executed by the manufacturer or was delivered to the borrower.

(2) The warranty shall obligate the home manufacturer to take appropriate action to correct any nonconformity with the standards prescribed in paragraph (c)(1) of this section or any defects in materials or workmanship which become evident within one year after the date of delivery. This warranty shall be in addition to, and not in derogation of, all other rights and privileges which the borrower may have under any other law or instrument during such period or thereafter. A copy of the warranty shall be retained in the lender's loan file.

(3) Prior to making a loan involving a new manufactured home, the lender shall investigate whether the home manufacturer is substantially complying with its warranty obligations on other homes financed by the lender under any program. If the lender knows, because of consumer complaints, dealer comments or other information concerning the manufacturer received in the course of business, that consumers have complained about warranty performance, the lender shall ascertain whether such complaints have been resolved. The lender's findings shall be documented in the loan file. Such documentation may reference information or materials contained in other files of the lender, provided that the file contains a written certification signed by a responsible loan officer under applicable criminal and civil penalties for fraud and misrepresentation that the lender's findings are supported by such other information or materials.

(4) If the lender concludes under paragraph (d)(3) of this section that a manufacturer may not be honoring its warranties, the lender shall immediately notify the Secretary in writing, with documentation of the facts and circumstances.

(e) *Manufactured homesite standards.* (1) To assure the suitability of the homesite, the manufactured home shall be placed on a leased site in a manufactured home park or on an individual manufactured home lot or other site owned or leased by the borrower that meets the following standards. A manufactured home may be placed on a site within Indian trust or otherwise restricted lands if the borrower owns or leases the site, or if the borrower obtains written permission acceptable to the Secretary from the trustee or the tribal authority who controls the use of the site.

(2) The manufactured homesite shall be served by adequate public or community water and sewerage systems, unless appropriate local officials certify that either or both such systems are unavailable to provide an adequate level of service to the manufactured homesite. If either or both such systems are not available, the manufactured homesite shall comply with local or State minimum lot area requirements for the provision of onsite water supply and/or sewage disposal.

(3) When the manufactured home is to be placed on a leased site in a manufactured home park, the lender shall obtain certifications from the appropriate State or local government officials that the park complies with minimum standards relating to vehicular access, water supply, sewage disposal, utility connections, and other aspects of park development. Where minimum State and local standards for park development are not established or enforced, the lender shall obtain a certification from a registered civil engineer that the park meets minimum standards for park development prescribed by the Secretary.

(4) When the manufactured home is to be placed on an individual manufactured home lot or other site owned or leased by the borrower (or on an Indian land site under paragraph (e)(1) of this section), the lender shall obtain certifications from the appropriate local government officials that:

(i) The site complies with local zoning ordinances and regulations, if any;

(ii) Adequate vehicular access from a public right-of-way is available to the site;

(iii) Adequate water supply and sewage disposal facilities are available to or on the site; and

(iv) Any other minimum local standards and requirements for site suitability are met. Where minimum local standards for water supply and sewage disposal are not established or enforced, the lender shall obtain a certification from a registered civil engineer that the site meets minimum standards for water supply and sewage disposal prescribed by the Secretary.

(Approved by the Office of Management and Budget under control number 2502–0328)

[50 FR 43523, Oct. 25, 1985; 51 FR 1496, Jan. 14, 1986, as amended at 54 FR 36264, Aug. 31, 1989; 56 FR 52431, Oct. 18, 1991; 61 FR 19797, May 2, 1996]

§ 201.22 Credit requirements for borrowers.

(a) *Credit application and review.* (1) Before making a loan insured under this part, the lender shall exercise prudence and diligence to determine whether the borrower and any co-maker or co-signer is solvent and an acceptable credit risk, with a reasonable ability to make payments on the loan obligation. All documentation supporting this determination and relating to the lender's review of the credit of the borrower and of any co-maker or co-signer shall be retained in the loan file.

(2) The lender shall obtain a separate dated credit application on a HUD-approved form, executed by the borrower and any co-maker or co-signer under applicable criminal and civil penalties for fraud and misrepresentation, for each loan made. The lender shall verify that the borrower's Social Security Number is valid, through such documentation as may be prescribed by the Secretary.

(3) The lender shall conduct a credit investigation based on the credit application, and shall obtain written verification of or otherwise document the current employment and current income of the borrower and any co-maker or co-signer. If the borrower or any co-maker or co-signer has changed employment within the past two years,

the lender shall obtain written verification of or otherwise document the person's prior employment and prior income during the two-year period. If the borrower or any co-maker or co-signer was self-employed during any period of the previous two years, the lender shall obtain documentation of the person's income during such period of self-employment.

(4) The lender shall also determine the total amount of the borrower's existing and proposed title I loans to ensure that the loan amounts in § 201.10 are not exceeded.

(5) As part of its credit investigation, the lender shall obtain a consumer credit report stating the credit accounts and payment history of the borrower and of any co-maker or co-signer. Subject to state or local law, the lender shall check with the inquirers concerning all credit inquiries reported within the previous 90 days to determine whether the borrower or the co-maker or co-signer has incurred debts not listed on the credit application. If a consumer credit report is not available or is incomplete, the loan file shall contain other documentation of the lender's diligent investigation of the credit of the borrower or of the co-maker or co-signer.

(6) If the consumer credit report does not contain the necessary information, the lender shall obtain written verification that the borrower is not over 30 days delinquent on any senior mortgages or deeds of trust on the property being improved with a property improvement loan.

(7) The lender shall verify, in such manner as the Secretary may prescribe, whether the borrower is in default or a claim has been paid in connection with any loan obligation owed to or insured or guaranteed by the Federal Government.

(8) For any loan with a total principal balance in excess of $5,000, the lender shall obtain written verification of the source of all funds of the borrower required for the borrower's initial payment, if such payment will be in excess of five percent of the loan.

(9) Before making a final determination on the creditworthiness of the borrower, the lender shall conduct a face-to-face or telephone interview with the

110

borrower and any co-maker or co-sign-er to resolve any discrepancies in the information on the credit application and to assure that the information is accurate and complete.

(10) After a thorough credit inves-tigation and in the absence of informa-tion to the contrary, the lender may rely upon all statements of fact made by the borrower or any co-maker or co-signer in a credit application.

(b) *Income requirements.* (1) For any Title I loan, the credit application and review must establish that the bor-rower's income will be adequate to meet the periodic payments required by the loan, as well as the borrower's other housing expenses and recurring charges. For a borrower's income to be considered adequate, housing expenses and total fixed expenses generally may not exceed maximum percentages of ef-fective gross income established by the Secretary. If these expense-to-income ratios are exceeded, the borrower's in-come may be considered adequate only if the lender determines and documents in the loan file the existence of com-pensating factors concerning the bor-rower's creditworthiness that support approval of the loan.

(2) In determining whether the bor-rower's income is adequate, the fol-lowing definitions are applicable:

(i) *Effective gross income* is defined as continuing income from all sources that is reasonably expected to be avail-able during the first two years of the loan obligation, without any deduction for income taxes or other items.

(ii) *Total fixed expenses* is the sum of the borrower's housing expenses and other recurring charges.

(iii) *Housing expenses* includes all payments for principal, interest, loan or mortgage insurance charges, ground rent or leasehold charges, real estate taxes, hazard insurance, and home-owners association or condominium fees, but does not include utility costs.

(iv) *Other recurring charges* include all payments on automobile loans, fur-niture loans, student loans, install-ment loans, revolving charge accounts, alimony or child support, and any other debt for which the obligation is expected to continue for six months or more.

(c) *Evidence of delinquency, default or misrepresentation.* Except with the prior approval of the Secretary the lender shall not approve a loan if the lender has knowledge of any of the following circumstances:

(1) The borrower is past due more than 30 days as to the payment of prin-cipal or interest under the original terms of a loan obligation owed to or insured or guaranteed by the Federal Government, unless the debt has since been discharged or satisfied; or

(2) The borrower has previously made material misstatements of fact on ap-plications for loans or other assistance.

(Approved by the Office of Management and Budget under control number 2502–0328)

[50 FR 43523, Oct. 25, 1985, as amended at 51 FR 32060, Sept. 9, 1986; 54 FR 10537, Mar. 14, 1989; 56 FR 52431, Oct. 18, 1991; 57 FR 6480, Feb. 25, 1992; 61 FR 19797, May 2, 1996]

§ 201.23 Borrower's initial payment.

(a) *General requirement.* The borrower shall be responsible for the payment in cash of any costs that will not be paid, or are not eligible to be paid, from the proceeds of the loan. Such costs pay-able by the borrower may include any required downpayment, any discount points to be paid by the borrower to the lender, any other fees and charges that may not be financed, and any other costs in excess of the loan amount. No part of such costs payable by the borrower may be loaned, ad-vanced, or paid to or for the benefit of the borrower by the dealer, the manu-facturer, or any other party to the loan transaction. If the borrower obtains all or any part of such costs through a gift or a loan from some other source, the borrower must disclose the source of such gift or loan on the credit applica-tion. Any such loan must be secured by property or collateral owned by the borrower independently of the property securing repayment of the Title I loan, unless the prior approval of the Sec-retary is obtained for an exception to this requirement. The lender shall con-sider any such loan obligation in per-forming the credit investigation. Docu-mentation of any initial payment shall be retained by the lender in the loan file.

(b) *Manufactured home purchase loans.* In the case of a manufactured home purchase loan, the borrower shall make a minimum cash downpayment of at least five percent of the purchase price of the home. The borrower's equity in an existing manufactured home and any movable appurtenances may be traded-in on a new home and accepted in lieu of full or partial cash downpayment, but without any cash payment to the borrower. The existing manufactured home being traded-in shall be clearly identified, and the borrower's equity in the home shall be based upon the retail value of the home and appurtenances (as determined by a HUD-approved appraisal), less the total of all loans outstanding on the home and appurtenances.

(c) *Manufactured home lot loans.* In the case of a manufactured home lot loan, the borrower shall make a minimum cash downpayment of at least five percent of the total of the purchase price and development costs for the lot.

(d) *Combination loans.* In the case of a combination loan, the borrower shall make a minimum cash downpayment of at least five percent of the purchase price of the manufactured home and lot. If the borrower already owns a manufactured home or a lot on which a manufactured home is to be placed, the borrower's equity in such home or lot may be accepted in lieu of full or partial cash downpayment on a combination loan, but without any cash payment to the borrower.

[61 FR 19798, May 2, 1996]

§ 201.24 Security requirements.

(a) *Property improvement loans*—(1) *Property improvement loans in excess of $7,500.* (i) Any property improvement loan in excess of $7,500 shall be secured by a recorded lien on the improved property. The lien shall be evidenced by a mortgage or deed of trust, executed by the borrower and all other owners in fee simple.

(ii) If the borrower is a lessee, the borrower and all owners in fee simple must execute the mortgage or deed of trust. If the borrower is purchasing the property under a land installment contract, the borrower, all owners in fee simple, and all intervening contract sellers must execute the mortgage or deed of trust.

(iii) The lien need not be a first lien on the property; however, the lien securing the Title I loan must hold no less than the second lien position. This requirement shall not apply where the first and second mortgages were made at the same time or the second mortgage was provided by a state or local government agency in conjunction with a downpayment assistance program.

(2) *Property improvement loans of $7,500 or less.* Any property improvement loan for $7,500 or less (other than a manufactured home improvement loan) shall be similarly secured if, including any such additional loans, the total amount of all Title I loans on the improved property is more than $7,500.

(3) *Manufactured home improvement loans.* Manufactured home improvement loans need not be secured.

(b) *Manufactured home loans.* Any manufactured home loan shall be secured by a recorded lien on the home (or lot or home and lot, as appropriate), its furnishings, equipment, accessories, and appurtenances. The lien shall be a first lien, superior to any other lien on that property, and shall be evidenced by a properly recorded financing statement, a properly recorded security instrument executed by the borrower and any other owner of the property, or another acceptable instrument, such as a certificate of title issued by the State and containing a recitation of the lender's lien interest in the manufactured home.

(c) *Recording and perfection of security.* The lender shall assure that the legal description of the property as recited in the security instrument is accurate, and that the security instrument creates a valid and enforceable lien on the property in the jurisdiction in which the property is located. The security instrument shall be recorded and perfected in the manner specified by applicable State law in the State where the property is located.

(d) *Substitution or subordination of security.* The Secretary may approve substitution or subordination of security where the security value will not be impaired or reduced.

(e) *Release of liability or lien.* The lender shall not release the borrower or any co-maker or co-signer from any liability under a note or from any lien securing a loan insured under this part without the prior approval of the Secretary.

[50 FR 43523, Oct. 25, 1985, as amended at 51 FR 32060, Sept. 9, 1986; 54 FR 36265, Aug. 31, 1989; 61 FR 19798, May 2, 1996; 66 FR 56419, Nov. 7, 2001]

§ 201.25 **Charges to borrower to obtain loan.**

(a) *Fees and charges that may be financed in a property improvement loan.* The Secretary will establish a list of fees and charges that may be included in a property improvement loan. Such fees and charges shall have been incurred in connection with the origination of the loan, and their inclusion shall not increase the total principal obligation beyond the maximum loan amounts in § 201.10.

(b) *Fees and charges that may be financed in a manufactured home loan.* The Secretary will establish a list of fees and charges that may be included in a manufactured home loan. Such fees and charges shall have been incurred in connection with the origination of the loan, and their inclusion shall not increase the total principal obligation beyond the maximum loan amounts in § 201.10.

(c) *Fees and charges that may not be financed.* The Secretary will establish a list of fees and charges incurred by the lender that may be collected from the borrower in the initial payment, but may not be included in the loan amount or otherwise financed or advanced by the dealer, the manufacturer, or any other party to the loan transaction.

(d) *Fees and charges that may not be paid.* Neither the lender nor the borrower may pay a referral fee to any dealer, home manufacturer, contractor, supplier, real estate broker, loan broker, or any other party in connection with the origination of a loan insured under this part.

[61 FR 19798, May 2, 1996]

§ 201.26 **Conditions for loan disbursement.**

(a) *Property improvement loans.* The lender shall comply with the following applicable requirements before disbursing the proceeds of a property improvement loan.

(1) The lender shall ensure that the following conditions are met:

(i) The borrower is eligible for a property improvement loan in accordance with § 201.20(a) (1) or (2); and

(ii) The interest of the borrower in the property is valid, through such title or other evidence as are generally acceptable to prudent lending institutions and leading attorneys in the community in which the property is situated.

(2) The proposed use of the loan proceeds shall be documented in accordance with the requirements of § 201.20(b)(1).

(3) Where the proceeds are to be used for an historic preservation loan, the lender shall ensure that the proposed improvements have been approved by the State Historic Preservation Officer in accordance with § 201.20(c).

(4) Where the proceeds are to be used for a fire safety equipment loan, the lender shall ensure that the proposed improvements have been approved by the State or local agency having jurisdiction over the fire safety requirements of health care facilities in accordance with § 201.20(c).

(5) In the case of a dealer loan, the lender shall obtain a completion certificate, on a HUD-approved form and signed by the borrower and the dealer under applicable criminal and civil penalties for fraud and misrepresentation, certifying that

(i) the improvements are eligible and have been completed in general accordance with the contract or cost estimate furnished to the lender, and

(ii) The borrower has not obtained the benefit of and will not receive any cash payment, rebate, cash bonus, sales commission, or anything of more than nominal value from the dealer as an inducement for the consummation of the transaction.

(6) In the case of a dealer loan made on or after December 7, 2001, the lender may disburse the loan proceeds solely to the borrower, or jointly to the borrower and the dealer or other parties to the transaction.

113

(7) In the case of a dealer loan, the lender must conduct a telephone interview with the borrower before the disbursement of the loan proceeds. The lender, at minimum, must obtain an oral affirmation from the borrower to release funds to the dealer. The lender shall document the borrower's oral affirmation.

(8) For any property improvement loan, the lender shall provide the borrower with a written notice, to be signed by the borrower and retained in the loan file, that:

(i) States that the loan will be insured by HUD and describes the actions the Secretary may take to recover the debt if the borrower defaults on the loan and an insurance claim is paid;

(ii) Constitutes the borrower's agreement to pay penalties and administrative costs imposed by HUD as authorized by 31 U.S.C. 3717; and

(iii) In the case of a direct loan, constitutes an acknowledgement of the borrower's postdisbursement obligation to furnish a completion certificate and to permit an on-site inspection by the lender or its agent in accordance with §§ 201.40(b) and (c).

(9) The lender shall assure that the loan file is complete and contains the note, security instrument, and copies of all other documents relating to the property improvement loan transaction.

(b) *Manufactured home loans.* The lender shall comply with the following applicable requirements before disbursing the proceeds of a manufactured home loan.

(1) The lender shall ensure that the borrower is eligible for a manufactured home loan in accordance with § 201.21(a).

(2) The lender shall assure that the loan file is complete, and shall obtain the following documents for retention in the loan file:

(i) A signed copy of the purchase contract between the borrower and the dealer or seller;

(ii) A copy of the manufacturer's invoice, where the loan involves the purchase of a new manufactured home;

(iii) Copies of itemized statements of other costs, fees and charges, whether paid by the borrower or financed with the loan proceeds; and

(iv) The note and security instrument and copies of all other documents relating to the loan transaction.

(v) The note, security instrument and copies of all other documents relating to the loan transaction.

(3) The lender shall obtain certifications from the borrower under applicable criminal and civil penalties for fraud and misrepresentation that:

(i) The manufactured home being financed with a manufactured home purchase loan or combination loan will be occupied as the borrower's principal residence;

(ii) Where the proceeds are for a manufactured home lot loan, the borrower's manufactured home will be placed on the lot and will be occupied as the borrower's principal residence within six months after the date of the loan;

(iii) The initial payment required under § 201.23 was made, and no part of the initial payment was borrowed from or otherwise advanced or paid to or for the benefit of the borrower by the dealer or seller, the manufacturer, or any other party to the transaction, and if any part of the initial payment was obtained through a gift or loan, the source of the gift or loan and the security for any such loan was disclosed on the credit application;

(iv) While any portion of the loan obligation on a manufactured home purchase loan is unpaid, the manufactured home may be moved only to a new site in compliance with § 201.21 (c) and (e), and only with the lender's prior approval;

(v) While any portion of the loan obligation on a combination loan is unpaid, the manufactured home will not be moved to a new site;

(vi) The borrower has paid the remaining unpaid balance on any other manufactured home loan secured by a different property, unless the prior approval of the Secretary is obtained for an exception to this requirement; and

(vii) The borrower has not obtained the benefit of and will not receive any cash payment, rebate, cash bonus, or anything of more than nominal value from the manufacturer or dealer as an inducement for the consummation of the transaction.

(4) For any manufactured home purchase loan or combination loan involving the sale of a manufactured home by a dealer, the lender shall obtain a placement certificate, on a HUD-approved form and signed by the dealer under applicable criminal and civil penalties for fraud and misrepresentation, certifying that:

(i) The manufactured homesite meets the requirements of §201.21(e);

(ii) The structural integrity of the manufactured home was maintained during the process of transporting the home to the borrower's homesite;

(iii) The manufactured home has been installed or erected on the homesite in accordance with the manufacturer's requirements for anchoring, support, stability and maintenance;

(iv) If the manufactured home is placed on a permanent foundation, such foundation has been constructed in accordance with the requirements of §201.21(c)(3);

(v) The dealer has performed the inspection and tests required under §201.21(c)(4) and has determined that the manufactured home has sustained no structural damage or other defects resulting from its transportation or installation, and all plumbing, mechanical and electrical systems are fully operational;

(vi) Any initial payment required under §201.23 was made by the borrower, and no part of the initial payment was loaned, advanced, or paid to or for the benefit of the borrower by the manufacturer, dealer, or any other party to the loan transaction; and

(vii) The borrower has not obtained the benefit of and will not receive any cash payment, rebate, cash bonus, or anything of more than nominal value from the manufacturer or dealer as an inducement for the consummation of the transaction.

(5) The lender shall obtain and file the certifications by local officials or a civil engineer which are required under §201.21(e) to document the suitability of the manufactured homesite.

(6) For any direct manufactured home purchase loan or combination loan involving the relocation of the manufactured home to a new homesite owned or leased by the borrower, the lender (or an agent of the lender that is not a manufactured home dealer) shall conduct a site-of-placement inspection to verify that:

(i) States that the loan will be insured by HUD and describes the actions the Secretary may take to recover the debt if the borrower defaults on the loan and an insurance claim is paid;

(ii) The manufactured home and any itemized options and appurtenances included in the purchase price of the home or to be financed with the loan proceeds have been delivered and installed; and

(iii) The manufactured home has been properly erected or installed on the homesite without any apparent structural damage or other serious defects resulting from its transportation or installation, and all plumbing, mechanical and electrical systems are fully operational.

(7) The lender shall provide the borrower with a written notice, to be signed by the borrower and retained in the loan file, that:

(i) States that the loan will be insured by the HUD and describes the actions the Secretary may take to recover the debt if the borrower defaults on the loan and an insurance claim is paid; and

(ii) Constitutes the borrower's agreement to pay penalties and administrative costs imposed by HUD as authorized by 31 U.S.C. 3717.

(8) Where a manufactured home purchase loan involves a manufactured home which is to be located on Indian trust or otherwise restricted lands, the lender shall obtain written permission from the trustee or the tribal authority who controls the site for the lender to repossess the home in the event of default by the borrower and acceleration of the loan.

(Approved by the Office of Management and Budget under control number 2502–0328)

[50 FR 43523, Oct. 25, 1985, as amended at 51 FR 32060, Sept. 9, 1986; 54 FR 36265, Aug. 31, 1989; 56 FR 52432, Oct. 18, 1991, 57 FR 6480, Feb. 25, 1992; 61 FR 19798, May 2, 1996; 62 FR 65181, Dec. 10, 1997; 66 FR 56420, Nov. 7, 2001]

§201.27 Requirements for dealer loans.

(a) *Dealer approval and supervision.* (1) The lender shall approve only those dealers which, on the basis of experience and information, the lender considers to be reliable, financially responsible, and qualified to satisfactorily perform their contractual obligations to borrowers and to comply with the requirements of this part. However, in no case shall the lender approve a dealer that is unable to meet the following minimum qualifications:

(i) *Net worth.* All property improvement and manufactured home dealers shall have and maintain a net worth of not less than $32,000 and $63,000, respectively. The required net worth must be maintained in assets acceptable to the Secretary.

(ii) *Business experience.* All property improvement loan and manufactured home dealers must have demonstrated business experience as a property improvement contractor or supplier, or in manufactured home retail sales, as applicable.

(2) The lender's approval of a dealer shall be documented on a HUD-approved form, signed and dated by the dealer and the lender under applicable criminal and civil penalties for fraud and misrepresentation, and containing information supplied by the dealer on its trade name, places of business, type of ownership, type of business, and names and employment history of the owners, principals, officers, and salespersons. The dealer shall furnish a current financial statement prepared by someone who is independent of the dealer and is qualified by education and experience to prepare such statements, together with such other documentation as the lender deems necessary to support its approval of the dealer. The lender shall obtain a commercial credit report on the dealer and consumer credit reports on the owners, principals, and officers of the dealership.

(3) The lender shall require each dealer to apply annually for reapproval. The dealer shall furnish the same documentation as is required under paragraph (a)(2) of this section to support its application for reapproval. In no case shall the lender reapprove a dealer that is unable to meet the minimum net worth requirements in paragraph (a)(1) of this section.

(4) The lender shall supervise and monitor each approved dealer's activities with respect to loans insured under this part. The lender shall visit each approved dealer's places of business at least once in every six months to review its Title I performance and compliance. The lender shall maintain a file on each approved dealer which contains the executed dealer approval form and supporting documentation required under paragraph (a)(2) of this section, together with information on the lender's experience with Title I loans involving the dealer. Each dealer file shall contain information about borrower defaults on Title I loans over time, records of completion or site-of-placement inspections conducted by the lender or its agent, copies of letters concerning borrower complaints and their resolution, and records of the lender's periodic review visits to the dealer's premises. The lender may also require that the dealer furnish records on individual loan transactions, if needed to enable the lender to review the dealer's Title I performance and compliance.

(5) If a dealer does not satisfactorily perform its contractual obligations to borrowers, does not comply with Title I program requirements, or is unresponsive to the lender's supervision and monitoring requirements, the lender shall terminate the dealer's approval and immediately notify the Secretary with written documentation of the facts. A dealer whose approval is terminated under these circumstances shall not be reapproved without prior written approval from the Secretary. The lender may in its discretion terminate the approval of a dealer for other reasons at any time.

(6) The lender shall require each approved (or reapproved) dealer to provide written notification of any material change in its trade name(s), place(s) of business, type of ownership, type of business, or principal individuals who control or manage the business. The dealer shall furnish such notification to the lender within 30 days after the date of any material change.

(7) As a condition of manufactured home dealer approval (or reapproval), the lender may require a manufactured home dealer to execute a written

agreement that, if requested by the lender, the dealer will resell any manufactured home repossessed by the lender under a title I insured manufactured home purchase loan approved by the lender as a dealer loan involving that dealer.

(b) *Provision for full or partial recourse.* In the case of a dealer-originated manufactured home purchase loan or combination loan, the lender and the dealer may agree to a provision in the loan documents for partial or full recourse against the dealer, to reduce or eliminate the lender's loss in the event of foreclosure or repossession. Such recourse provision shall specify that, for a default occurring within a period of not more than three years from the date of the loan, the dealer shall reimburse the lender for a fixed percentage of the unpaid amount of the loan obligation, after deducting the proceeds from the sale of the property and any amounts received or retained by the lender after the date of default. However, the extent of the dealer's liability may not exceed 100 percent of the unpaid amount of the loan obligation prior to such deductions. When a claim is filed, the lender shall notify the Secretary if the loan was subject to a recourse agreement and whether the recourse agreement has been honored. If without the lender's approval a dealer has failed to honor its recourse obligation, the lender shall notify the Secretary and shall assign the recourse obligation to the Secretary in filing an insurance claim.

(Approved by the Office of Management and Budget under control number 2502–0328)

[50 FR 43523, Oct. 25, 1985, as amended at 56 FR 52433, Oct. 18, 1991; 61 FR 19799, May 2, 1996; 66 FR 56420, Nov. 7, 2001]

§201.28 Flood and hazard insurance, and Coastal Barriers properties.

(a) *Flood insurance.* No property improvement loan or manufactured home loan shall be eligible for insurance under this part if the property securing repayment of the loan is located in a special flood hazard area identified by the Federal Emergency Management Agency (FEMA), unless flood insurance on the property is obtained by the borrower in compliance with section 102 of the Flood Disaster Protection Act of 1973 (42 U.S.C. 4012a). Such insurance shall be obtained at any time during the term of the loan that the lender determines that the secured property is located in a special flood hazard area identified by FEMA, and shall be maintained by the borrower for the remaining term of the loan, or until the lender determines that the property is no longer in a special flood hazard area, or until the property is repossessed or foreclosed upon by the lender. The amount of such insurance shall be at least equal to the unpaid balance of the Title I loan, and the lender shall be named as the loss payee for flood insurance benefits.

(b) *Hazard insurance.* No manufactured home purchase loan or combination loan shall be eligible for insurance under this part unless hazard insurance on the manufactured home is obtained by the borrower and the lender is named as a loss payee of insurance benefits. Such insurance shall be maintained by the borrower for the full term of the loan or until the property is repossessed or foreclosed by the lender, and in an amount at least equal to the unpaid balance of the loan, except that the amount of insurance coverage shall be not less that the actual cash value of the home where State law precludes a higher amount. If the borrower fails to maintain such insurance, the lender shall obtain it at the borrower's expense. If the home is not insured against hazards and sustains damage which would normally be covered by such insurance during the borrower's ownership, the appraised value of the home for claim purposes will be adjusted in accordance with §201.51(b)(3). Upon acquiring title to the property through repossession or foreclosure, the lender shall maintain hazard insurance upon the property in the amount prescribed above until its disposition and sale.

(c) *Coastal barriers properties.* No title I insurance shall be made available under this part for any property improvement loan or manufactured home loan except pursuant to a loan application approved before October 18, 1982, with respect to any property within the Coastal Barriers Resources System established by the Coastal Barriers Resources Act (16 U.S.C. 3501).

[50 FR 43523, Oct. 25, 1985, as amended at 51 FR 32060, Sept. 9, 1986; 53 FR 10537, Mar. 14, 1989; 54 FR 36265, Aug. 31, 1989; 61 FR 19799, May 2, 1996]

§ 201.29 Ineligible participants.

No loan may be insured under this part where the lender has been advised in writing by HUD or otherwise knows that any participant in the transaction as a dealer, home manufacturer, contractor, supplier, or broker, or as its agent or representative, has been suspended or debarred, or has otherwise been determined by HUD to be ineligible to participate in the title I program.

Subpart D—Insurance of Loans

§ 201.30 Reporting of loans for insurance.

(a) *Date of reports.* The lender shall transmit a loan report on each loan reported for insurance within 31 days from the date of the loan's origination or purchase from a dealer or another lender. The loan report must be submitted on the form prescribed by the Secretary, and must contain the data prescribed by HUD. Any loan refinanced under this part shall similarly be reported on the prescribed form within 31 days from the date of refinancing. When a loan insured under this part is transferred to another lender without recourse, guaranty, guarantee, or repurchase agreement, a report on the prescribed form shall be transmitted to the Secretary within 31 days from the date of the transfer. No transfer of loan report is required when a loan insured under this part is transferred with recourse or under a guaranty, guarantee, or repurchase agreement.

(b) *Late reports.* The Secretary may accept a late report on a loan where the lender certifies that the obligation is not in default.

(c) *Electronic loan reporting.* With the prior approval of the Secretary, the lender may use electronic transmission to report loans for insurance in accordance with paragraph (a) of this section.

(Approved by the Office of Management and Budget under control number 2502–0328)

[50 FR 43523, Oct. 25, 1985, as amended at 56 FR 52434, Oct. 18, 1991; 66 FR 56420, Nov. 7, 2001]

§ 201.31 Insurance charge.

(a) *Insurance charge.* For each eligible property improvement loan and manufactured home loan reported and acknowledged for insurance, the lender shall pay to the Secretary an insurance charge equal to 1.00 percent of the loan amount, multiplied by the number of years of the loan term. The insurance charge shall be paid in the manner prescribed in paragraph (b) of this section; however, no charge shall be made for a period of 14 days or less, and a charge for a full month shall be made for a period of more than 14 days. There shall be no abatement or refund of an insurance charge except as provided in paragraph (e) of this section.

(b) *Payment of insurance charge.* (1) For any loan having a maturity of 25 months or less, payment of the entire insurance charge prescribed in paragraph (a) of this section is due on the 25th calendar day after the date the Secretary acknowledges the loan report.

(2)(i) For any loan having a maturity in excess of 25 months, payment of the insurance charge shall be made in annual installments, with the first installment due on the 25th calendar day after the date the Secretary acknowledges the loan report, and the second and successive installments due on the 25th calendar day after the date of billing by the Secretary.

(ii) For any loan having a maturity in excess of 25 months, payment shall be made in annual installments of 1.00 percent of the loan amount until the insurance charge is paid.

(3) All insurance charges are considered earned when paid.

(4) The Secretary may require that loan insurance charges be remitted electronically. Instructions implementing this requirement shall be communicated to all affected lenders.

(c) *Penalty charge and interest.* Insurance charges not received from the lender by the due date specified in paragraph (b) of this section shall be assessed a penalty charge of four percent of the amount of the payment. Insurance charges received from the lender more than 30 days after the due date specified in paragraph (b) of this section shall also be assessed daily interest at the current United States Treasury value of funds rate, as published periodically in the FEDERAL REGISTER. However, no penalty charge or daily interest shall be assessed if the Secretary fails to acknowledge receipt of the loan report or fails to issue a proper billing to the lender for the insurance charges.

(d) *Adjustment on notes transferred.* Where there is a transfer of loan obligations between lenders and the insurance charges on such obligations have already been paid, any adjustment of such charges shall be made by the lenders involved. Any unpaid installments of the insurance charge shall be paid by the purchasing lender.

(e) *Refund or abatement of insurance charges.* A lender shall be entitled to a refund or abatement of insurance charges only in the following instances:

(1) Where the loan obligation has been refinanced, the unearned portion of the charge on the original obligation shall be credited to the charge on the refinanced loan.

(2) Where the loan obligation is prepaid in full or an insurance claim is filed, charges falling due after such prepayment or claim shall be abated.

(3) When a loan (or portion thereof) is found to be ineligible for insurance, charges paid on the ineligible portion shall be refunded, except where the Secretary determines that there was fraud or misrepresentation by the lender in the loan transaction. Such refund shall be made only if a claim is denied by the Secretary or the ineligibility is reported by the lender promptly upon discovery and confirmed by the Secretary. In no event shall a charge be refunded on the basis of loan ineligibility where the application for refund is made after the loan is paid in full. If a loan or claim has been denied and is subsequently resubmitted, the refunded amount of the insurance charge plus any accrued insurance charge shall be repaid.

(f) *Lender passing insurance charge on to borrower.* The insurance charge may be passed on to the borrower, provided that such charge is fully disclosed to the borrower.

[50 FR 43523, Oct. 25, 1985, as amended at 54 FR 36265, Aug. 31, 1989; 60 FR 13855, Mar. 14, 1995; 66 FR 56420, Nov. 7, 2001]

§ 201.32 Insurance coverage reserve account.

(a) *Establishment.* The Secretary shall establish an insurance coverage reserve account for each lender. The amount of insurance coverage in each reserve account shall equal 10 percent of the amount disbursed, advanced, or expended by the lender in originating or purchasing eligible loans registered for insurance under this part, less the amount of all insurance claims approved for payment in connection with losses on such loans.

(b) *Transfer of insured loans.* The lender shall not sell, assign or otherwise transfer any insured loan or loan reported for insurance to a transferee lender not approved to originate and purchase title I loans under a valid title I contract of insurance. Nothing contained herein shall be construed to prevent the pledging of such a loan as collateral security under a trust agreement, or otherwise, in connection with a bona fide loan transaction.

(c) *Transfer of insurance coverage.* Not more than $5,000 in insurance coverage shall be transferred to or from a lender's reserve account during any fiscal year (October 1 through September 30) without the prior approval of the Secretary. Except in cases involving the sale, assignment or transfer of loans sold with recourse or under a guaranty, guarantee or repurchase agreement, the Secretary shall transfer insurance coverage to or from a lender's reserve account to accompany the loan transfers reported by lenders under § 201.30.

(1) In all cases involving the sale, assignment or transfer of loans sold without recourse, guaranty, guarantee, or repurchase agreement, the Secretary shall transfer insurance coverage to the reserve account established for the transferee lender in an amount equal to 10 percent of the actual purchase

price or the net unpaid principal balance, whichever is lesser, but not to exceed the amount of insurance coverage in the transferor lender's reserve account prior to the transfer. Insurance coverage shall be added to the existing amount of insurance coverage in the transferee lender's reserve account. The Secretary may transfer insurance coverage with earmarking when a determination is made that it is in the Secretary's interest to do so.

(2) In cases involving the transfer of loans sold with recourse or under a guaranty, guarantee or repurchase agreement, no insurance coverage will be transferred and no reports will be required.

(3) An existing insured property improvement loan or manufactured home loan may not be refinanced by a lender different from the originating or purchasing lender of record, unless the loan has been sold, assigned, or transferred to the new lender under paragraph (c) of this section and the Secretary has transferred insurance coverage for the loan under the applicable requirements of this paragraph.

(d) *Recovery shall not affect insurance coverage reserve account.* Amounts which may be recovered by the Secretary after payment of an insurance claim shall not be added to the amount of insurance coverage remaining in a lender's reserve account.

[50 FR 43523, Oct. 25, 1985, as amended at 52 FR 33407, Sept. 3, 1987; 54 FR 10537, Mar. 14, 1989; 56 FR 52434, Oct. 18, 1991; 61 FR 19799, May 2, 1996]

Subpart E—Loan Administration

§ 201.40 Post-disbursement loan requirements.

(a) *Discovery of misstatements of fact.* If, after a loan has been made, the lender discovers any material misstatement of fact or that the loan proceeds have been misused by the borrower, dealer or any other party, it shall promptly report this to the Secretary. In such case, the insurance of the loan shall not be affected unless such material misstatement of fact or misuse of loan proceeds was caused by or was knowingly sanctioned by the lender or its employees (see § 201.31(e)(3)), provided that the validity of any lien on the property has not been impaired.

(b) *Requirements on property improvement loans.* (1) After receiving the proceeds of a direct property improvement loan, and after the work is completed to the borrower's satisfaction, the borrower shall submit a completion certificate to the lender, on a HUD-approved form and signed by the borrower under applicable criminal and civil penalties for fraud and misrepresentation, certifying that:

(i) The improvements have been completed,

(ii) the amount borrowed has been spent on improvements eligible under § 201.20(b) and in accordance with the contract or cost estimate furnished to the lender prior to disbursement of the loan proceeds, and

(iii) The borrower has not obtained the benefit of and will not receive any cash payment, rebate, cash bonus, sales commission, or anything of more than nominal value from any contractor or supplier as an inducement for the consummation of the loan transaction.

(2) The borrower shall submit the completion certificate promptly upon the work's completion, but not later than six months after the disbursement of the loan proceeds, with one six-month extension if necessary. If the borrower fails to submit the completion certificate within these time limits, an on-site inspection shall be conducted in accordance with paragraph (c) of this section.

(3) The borrower is not required to submit a completion certificate when the property improvement loan is made by or on behalf of a State or local government agency or a nonprofit organization, the loan proceeds are held in an escrow account pending completion of the improvements, and the loan proceeds are disbursed from the escrow account in stages, with the written approval of the borrower and based upon the percentage of work completed.

(c) *Inspection requirement on property improvement loans.* The lender or its agent shall conduct an on-site inspection on any property improvement loan where the principal obligation is $7,500 or more, and on any direct property improvement loan where the borrower fails to submit a completion certificate as required under paragraph (b) of this section. On a dealer loan, the inspection shall be completed within 60 days after the date of disbursement. On a direct loan, the inspection shall be completed within 60 days after receipt of the completion certificate, or as soon as the lender determines that the borrower is unwilling to cooperate in submitting the completion certificate. The purpose of the inspection is to verify the eligibility of the improvements and whether the work has been completed. If the borrower will not cooperate in permitting an on-site inspection, the lender shall report this fact to the Secretary.

(d) *Inspection requirement on dealer manufactured home loans.* For any manufactured home purchase loan or combination loan involving the sale of a manufactured home by a dealer, the lender (or an agent of the lender that is not a manufactured home dealer) shall conduct a site-of-placement inspection within 60 days after the date of disbursement to verify that:

(1) The terms and conditions of the purchase contract have been met;

(2) The manufactured home and any itemized options and appurtenances included in the purchase price of the home or financed with the loan proceeds have been delivered and installed; and

(3) The placement certificate executed by the borrower and the dealer is in order.

(Approved by the Office of Management and Budget under control number 2502–0328)

[50 FR 43523, Oct. 25, 1985, as amended at 56 FR 52434, Oct. 18, 1991; 61 FR 19799, May 2, 1996]

§201.41 Loan servicing.

(a) *Generally.* The lender shall service loans in accordance with accepted practices of prudent lending institutions. It shall have adequate facilities for contacting the borrower in the event of default, and shall otherwise exercise diligence in collecting the amount due. The lender shall remain responsible to the Secretary for proper collection efforts, even though actual loan servicing and collection may be performed by an agent of the lender. The lender shall have an organized means of identifying, on a periodic basis, the payment status of delinquent loans to enable collection personnel to initiate and follow-up on collection activities, and shall document its records to reflect its collection activities on delinquent loans.

(b) *Partial payments.* The lender shall accept any partial payment (inclusive of late charges) under an executed modification agreement or an acceptable repayment plan, and either apply it to the borrower's account or hold it in a trust account pending disposition. When partial payments held for disposition aggregate a full monthly installment, they shall be applied to the borrower's account, thus advancing the date of the oldest unpaid installment. If a partial payment is received more than 60 days after the date of default and was not submitted under a repayment plan or a modification agreement, the partial payment may be returned to the borrower, with a letter of explanation.

§201.42 Bankruptcy, insolvency or death of borrower.

(a) *Bankruptcy or insolvency.* The lender shall file a proof of claim with the court having jurisdiction when the lender has timely information that a borrower is involved in bankruptcy or insolvency proceedings, except that a proof of claim need not be filed if the court notifies the lender that the borrower has no assets and a proof of claim should not be filed. The notice of bankruptcy and a copy of the proof of claim (or the notice from the court that a proof of claim is not required) shall be retained in the loan file.

(b) *Death of a borrower.* The lender shall file a proof of claim with the court having jurisdiction when the lender has timely information that a borrower is deceased, unless the lender determines that there will not be a probate proceeding. A copy of the proof of claim (or documentation as to why a proof of claim was not filed) shall be retained in the loan file.

(c) *Responsibility of the lender after insurance claim is filed.* After the Secretary pays an insurance claim, the Secretary will notify the bankruptcy or probate court, as appropriate, that the loan has been assigned to the

121

United States and will request substitution as the party to whom the claim is owed. Until the insurance claim is paid, the lender shall take all steps necessary to protect the interests of the holder of the note in any bankruptcy or probate proceeding.

[54 FR 36266, Aug. 31, 1989]

§ 201.43 Administrative reports and examinations.

The Secretary may call upon a lender for any reports deemed necessary in connection with the regulations in this part and may inspect the loan files, records, books and accounts of the lender as they pertain to the loans reported for insurance.

Subpart F—Default Under the Loan Obligation

§ 201.50 Lender efforts to cure the default.

(a) *Personal contact with the borrower before acceleration and foreclosure or repossession.* The lender shall undertake foreclosure or repossession of the property securing a Title I loan that is in default only after the lender has serviced the loan in a timely manner and with diligence in accordance with the requirements of this part, and has taken all reasonable and prudent measures to induce the borrower to bring the loan account current. Before taking action to accelerate the maturity of the loan, the lender or its agent shall contact the borrower and any co-maker or co-signer, either in a face-to-face meeting or by telephone, to discuss the reasons for the default and to seek its cure. If the borrower and the co-makers or co-signers cannot be located, will not discuss the default, or will not agree to its cure, the lender may proceed to take action under paragraph (b) of this section. The lender shall document the results of its efforts to contact the borrower and any co-maker or co-signer, and shall place in the loan file a copy of any modification agreement or repayment plan that has been offered.

(b) *Notice of default and acceleration.* Unless the borrower cures the default or agrees to a modification agreement or repayment plan, the lender shall provide the borrower with written notice that the loan is in default and that the loan maturity is to be accelerated. In addition to complying with applicable State or local notice requirements, the notice shall be sent by certified mail and shall contain:

(1) A description of the obligation or security interest held by the lender;

(2) A statement of the nature of the default and of the amount due to the lender as unpaid principal and earned interest on the note as of the date 30 days from the date of the notice;

(3) A ·demand upon the borrower either to cure the default (by bringing the loan current or by refinancing the loan) or to agree to a modification agreement or a repayment plan, by not later than the date 30 days from the date of the notice;

(4) A statement that if the borrower fails either to cure the default or to agree to a modification agreement or a repayment plan by the date 30 days from the date of the notice, then, as of the date 30 days from the date of the notice, the maturity of the loan is accelerated and full payment of all amounts due under the loan is required;

(5) A statement that if the default persists the lender will report the default to an appropriate credit reporting agency; and

(6) Any other requirements prescribed by the Secretary.

(c) *Reinstatement of the loan.* The lender may rescind the acceleration of maturity after full payment is due and reinstate the loan only if the borrower brings the loan current, executes a modification agreement, or agrees to an acceptable repayment plan.

(d) *Notice to credit reporting agency.* If the loan maturity is accelerated and the loan is not reinstated, the lender shall report the default to an appropriate credit reporting agency.

(Approved by the Office of Management and Budget under control number 2502–0328)

[50 FR 43523, Oct. 25, 1985, as amended at 52 FR 33407, Sept. 3, 1987; 56 FR 52434, Oct. 18, 1991; 57 FR 6480, Feb. 25, 1992]

§201.51 Proceeding against the loan security.

(a) *Property improvement loans.* (1) After acceleration of maturity on a secured property improvement loan, the lender may either proceed against the loan security under its title I security instrument or make claim under its contract of insurance. If the lender proceeds against the loan security, it may submit an insurance claim only if it complies with the requirements of paragraph (a)(2) of this section.

(2) The lender may proceed against the secured property under its Title I security instrument and later submit a claim under its contract of insurance only with the prior approval of the Secretary. The Secretary's decision will be based upon all relevant factors, including but not limited to the appraised value and the amount of all outstanding loan obligations on the property, the estimated costs of foreclosure and disposition, and the anticipated time to dispose of the property. In proceeding against the secured property, the lender shall comply with all applicable State and local laws, and shall take all actions necessary to preserve its rights, if any, to obtain a valid and enforceable deficiency judgment against the borrower.

(3) After acceleration of maturity on a defaulted unsecured property improvement loan, the lender may submit a claim under its contract of insurance.

(b) *Manufactured home loans.* (1) After acceleration of maturity on a defaulted manufactured home loan, the lender shall proceed against the loan security by foreclosure or repossession, as appropriate, in compliance with all applicable State and local laws, and shall acquire good, marketable title to the property securing the loan. The lender shall also take all actions necessary under State and local law to preserve its rights, if any, to obtain a valid and enforceable deficiency judgment against the borrower.

(2) Prior to foreclosure or repossession, the lender or its agent shall make a visual inspection of the property and prepare a report on its condition for placement in the loan file. If the lender determines that the property has been abandoned, the lender shall take such steps as are permitted under State or local law to repossess or foreclose upon the property, without waiting for the notice period under §201.50(b) to run.

(3) The lender shall obtain a HUD-approved appraisal of the property as soon after repossession as possible, or earlier with the permission of the borrower. This appraisal shall be performed on the homesite, unless the site owner requires that the home be removed before the appraisal can be performed, and it should reflect the retail value of comparable manufactured homes in similar condition and in the same geographic area where the repossession occurred. When the manufactured home is without hazard insurance and has sustained, at any time prior to the sale or disposition of the home, damage which would normally be covered by such insurance, the lender shall report this situation in submitting an insurance claim, and the appraised value shall be based upon the retail value of comparable homes in good condition and in the same geographic area, without any deduction for such damage.

(Approved by the Office of Management and Budget under control number 2502–0328)

[50 FR 43523, Oct. 25, 1985, as amended at 54 FR 10537, Mar. 14, 1989; 54 FR 36266, Aug. 31, 1989; 56 FR 52435, Oct. 18, 1991]

§201.52 Acquisition by voluntary conveyance or surrender.

The lender may accept a voluntary conveyance of title to or ownership of the property securing a manufactured home loan which is in default, provided that (a) the lender accepts the conveyance in full satisfaction of the borrower's obligation, and (b) no claim is submitted under its contract of insurance. The lender may accept voluntary surrender of the property without satisfaction of the borrower's obligation, provided that if the lender intends thereafter to submit a claim under its contract of insurance, the lender shall acquire title to or ownership of the property and then dispose of and sell the property in compliance with State and local law, so as to assure that it can assign a valid and enforceable obligation, including any deficiency against the borrower, to the Secretary when submitting its claim. If the lender accepts a voluntary conveyance of title or a voluntary surrender of the property, the notice of default and acceleration under § 201.50(b) shall not be required.

[50 FR 43523, Oct. 25, 1985, as amended at 61 FR 19799, May 2, 1996]

§ 201.53 Disposition of manufactured home loan property.

Where the lender obtains title to property securing a manufactured home loan by repossession or foreclosure, the property shall be sold for the best price obtainable before making an insurance claim. In the case of a combination loan, the manufactured home and lot shall be sold in a single transaction and the manufactured home may not be removed from the lot, unless the prior approval of the Secretary is obtained for a different procedure. The best price obtainable shall be the greater of:

(a) The actual sales price of the property, after deducting the cost of repairs, furnishings, and equipment needed to make the property marketable, and after deducting the cost of transportation, set-up, and anchoring if the manufactured home is moved to a new homesite; or

(b) The appraised value of the property before repairs (as determined by a HUD-approved appraisal obtained in accordance with § 201.51(b)(3)).

[50 FR 43523, Oct. 25, 1985, as amended at 61 FR 19799, May 2, 1996]

§ 201.54 Insurance claim procedure.

(a) *Claim application.* A claim for reimbursement for loss on any eligible loan shall be made on a HUD-approved form, executed by a duly qualified officer of the lender under applicable criminal and civil penalties for fraud and misrepresentation. The insurance claim shall be fully documented and itemized, and shall be accompanied by all documents and materials required by the Secretary for claim review. The claim submission shall contain original copies of all notes, security instruments, assumption agreements, releases of liability for repayment of the loan, judgments obtained by the lender against the borrower, and any related documents and forms, except where State or local law requires their reten-

tion by the lender or a governmental body such as a court. As appropriate, the claim application shall be supported by the following:

(1) Documentation of the lender's efforts to effect recourse against any dealer in accordance with any recourse agreement under § 201.27(b) between the lender and the dealer and contained in the loan documents;

(2) Certification under applicable criminal and civil penalties for fraud and misrepresentation that the lender has complied with all applicable State and local laws in carrying out any foreclosure or repossession, including copies of all notices served upon the borrower or published in connection with such foreclosure or repossession; and

(3) Where a borrower has declared bankruptcy or insolvency or is deceased, copies of the documentation required to be retained in the loan file under § 201.42.

(b) *Maximum claim period.* (1) An insurance claim shall be filed not later than the following dates:

(i) For property improvement loans—nine months after the date of default.

(ii) For manufactured home loans—three months after the date of sale of the property securing the loan, but not to exceed 18 months after the date of default.

(2) The Secretary may extend the claim filing period in a particular case, but only if the lender shows clear evidence that the delay in claim filing was in the interest of the Secretary or was caused by one of the following:

(i) Litigation related to the loan;

(ii) Management control of the lender or the Title I loan portfolio was assumed by a Federal or State agency; or

(iii) The borrower had experienced a loss of income or other financial difficulties directly attributable to a major disaster declared by the President, and additional time was needed to provide forbearance on a property improvement loan.

(3) If a borrower is a "person in military service" as that term is defined in the Soldiers' and Sailors' Civil Relief Act of 1940 and is in default on a loan insured under this part, any period of military service after the date of default shall be excluded in computing

the maximum time period for filing an insurance claim.

(c) *Resubmitted and supplemental claims.* (1) Any insurance claim which is resubmitted with an appeal of a claim denial or a request for a waiver of the regulations in accordance with §201.5(b) shall be filed within six months after the date of the claim denial.

(2) Any supplemental insurance claim shall be filed within six months after the date of payment on the initial claim. A reprocessing fee, in an amount prescribed by the Secretary, will be charged for any supplemental claim.

(d) *Assignment of lender's rights to the United States.* Upon the filing of the insurance claim, the lender shall assign its entire interest in the loan note (or in a judgment in lieu of the note), in any security held, and in any claim filed in probate, bankruptcy or insolvency proceedings, to the United States of America. The assignment shall be made in the form provided in paragraph (f) of this section, provided that if this form is not valid or generally acceptable in the jurisdiction involved, a form which is valid and generally acceptable in the jurisdiction where the judgment or security was taken shall be used. If the security interest has been assigned to the United States, the assignment shall be recorded in that jurisdiction prior to filing the insurance claim, unless the Secretary determines that recordation by the lender in that jurisdiction is impractical.

(e) *Valid and enforceable obligation when assigned.* The loan obligation evidenced by the note must be both valid and enforceable against the debtor at the time the note is assigned to the United States of America. If the Secretary has reason to believe that the obligation may not be either valid or enforceable against the borrower, the Secretary may either deny the claim and reassign the loan note to the lender, or require the lender to repurchase the paid claim and accept reassignment of the note. The lender will be notified of the reasons for the claim denial or repurchase. If the lender subsequently obtains a valid and enforceable judgment against the borrower for the unpaid balance of the loan, the lender

may resubmit the claim with an assignment of the judgment.

(f) *Form of assignment.* A lender shall use the following form of assignment, or one generally acceptable in the jurisdiction involved, properly dated, to assign the lender's entire interest in a loan note, judgment, real estate mortgage, deed of trust, conditional sales contract, chattel mortgage, mechanic's lien, or any security, in making an insurance claim:

All right, title, and interest of the undersigned is hereby assigned (without warranty, except that the loan qualifies for insurance) to the United States of America (HUD).

(Financial Institution) _____
By: _____
Title: _____
Date: _____

If the assignment does not appear on the note or other instrument that is assigned, it shall be duly executed on an allonge which is attached to such note or other instrument.

(g) *Denial of insurance claim.* The Secretary may deny a claim for insurance in whole or in part based upon a violation of these regulations, unless a waiver of compliance with the regulations is granted under §201.5.

(h) *Incontestability of insurance claim payment.* Any insurance claim payment on a title I loan shall be final and incontestable after two years from the date the claim was certified for payment by the Secretary, in the absence of fraud or misrepresentation on the part of the lender, unless a demand for repurchase of the loan obligation is made on behalf of the United States prior to the expiration of the two-year period.

(Approved by the Office of Management and Budget under control number 2502–0328)

[50 FR 43523, Oct. 25, 1985; 51 FR 5068, Feb. 11, 1986, as amended at 51 FR 32060, Sept. 9, 1986; 56 FR 52435, Oct. 18, 1991; 57 FR 6480, Feb. 25, 1992; 61 FR 19800, May 2, 1996]

§201.55 Calculation of insurance claim payment.

The lender will be reimbursed in an amount not to exceed 90 percent of its loss on any eligible loan up to the amount of insurance coverage in the lender's insurance coverage reserve account established by the Secretary under §201.32, if the insurance claim is made in accordance with the requirements of this part. The amount of the insurance claim payment shall be computed as follows:

(a) *Property improvement loans.* For property improvement loans, the insurance claim payment shall be 90 percent of the following amounts:

(1) The unpaid amount of the loan obligation (net unpaid principal and the uncollected interest earned to the date of default, calculated according to the terms of the note executed for any loan application that is approved prior to the effective date of these regulations, and calculated according to the actuarial method for all loans for which loan applications are approved on or after the effective date of these regulations). Where the lender has proceeded against the secured property under § 201.51(a)(2), the unpaid amount of the loan obligation shall be reduced by the proceeds received from the property's sale or disposition, after deducting the following:

(i) The balances due on any obligations senior to the Title I loan obligation; and

(ii) Customary and reasonable expenses for foreclosure and disposition, as determined by the Secretary.

(2) Interest on the unpaid amount of the loan obligation from the date of default to the date of the claim's initial submission for payment plus 15 calendar days, calculated at the rate of seven percent per annum. However, interest shall not be paid for any period greater than nine months from the date of default.

(3) The amount of uncollected court costs, including fees paid for issuing, serving, and filing a summons.

(4) The amount of attorney's fees on an hourly or other basis for time actually expended and billed, not to exceed $500.

(5) The amount of expenses for recording the assignment of the security to the United States.

(b) *Manufactured home loans.* For manufactured home loans, the insurance claim payment shall be 90 percent of the sum of the following amounts:

(1) The unpaid amount of the loan obligation (net unpaid principal and the uncollected interest earned to the date of default, calculated according to the

actuarial method), after deducting the following amounts:

(i) The best price obtainable for the property after lawful repossession or foreclosure, as determined in accordance with § 201.53;

(ii) All amounts to which the lender is entitled after the date of default from any source relating to the property, including but not limited to such items as rent, other income, recourse recovery against the dealer, hazard insurance benefits, secured interest protection insurance benefits, and rebates on prepaid insurance premiums; and

(iii) Amounts retained by the lender after the date of default, including amounts held or deposited to the account of the borrower or to which the lender is entitled under the loan transaction, and which have not been applied in reduction of the borrower's indebtedness.

(2) Interest on the unpaid amount of the loan obligation from the date of default to the date of the claim's initial submission for payment plus 15 calendar days, calculated at the rate of seven percent per annum. However, interest shall not be paid for any period greater than nine months from the date of default.

(3) For manufactured home purchase loans, the amount of costs paid to a dealer or other third party to repossess and preserve the manufactured home and other property securing repayment of the loan (including the costs of site inspection, property appraisal, hazard insurance premiums, personal property taxes, and site rental, as appropriate), plus actual costs not to exceed $1,000 per module for removing and transporting the home to a dealer's lot or other off-site location.

(4) The amount of a sales commission paid to a dealer, real estate agent or other third party for the resale of the repossessed or foreclosed manufactured home and/or lot. Where the home is resold on-site, the commission shall not exceed 10 percent of the sales price. Where the home is resold off-site, the commission shall not exceed seven percent of the sales price.

(5) For manufactured home lot loans, and for combination loans where both the foreclosed manufactured home and

lot are classified as realty, the amount of:

(i) State or local real estate taxes, ground rents, and municipal water and sewer fees or liens, prorated to the date of disposition of the property;

(ii) Special assessments which are noted on the loan application or which become liens after the insurance is issued, prorated to the date of disposition of the property;

(iii) Premiums for hazard insurance on the manufactured home, prorated to the date of disposition of the property; and

(iv) Transfer taxes imposed upon any deeds or other instruments by which the property was acquired by the lender.

(6) The amount of uncollected court costs, including fees paid for issuing, serving, and filing a summons.

(7) The amount of attorney's fees on an hourly or other basis for time actually expended and billed, not to exceed $1,000.

(8) The amount of expenses for recording the assignment of the security to the United States, and for costs of repossession or foreclosure other than attorney's fees and those incurred under paragraph (b)(3), but not to exceed costs which are customary and reasonable in the jurisdiction where the repossession or foreclosure takes place, as determined by the Secretary.

[50 FR 43523, Oct. 25, 1985, as amended at 54 FR 10537, Mar. 14, 1989; 54 FR 36266, Aug. 31, 1989; 56 FR 52435, Oct. 18, 1991; 57 FR 30395, July 9, 1992; 61 FR 19800, May 2, 1996]

Subpart G—Debts Owed to the United States Under Title I

SOURCE: 58 FR 47379, Sept. 9, 1993, unless otherwise noted.

§201.60 General.

(a) *Applicability.* The provisions in this subpart apply to the collection of debts owed to the United States arising out of the Title I program. These debts include, but are not limited to:

(1) Amounts owed on loans assigned to the United States by insured lenders as the result of defaults by borrowers;

(2) Unpaid insurance charges owed by lenders; and

(3) Unpaid obligations of lenders arising from repurchase demands.

(b) *Departmental debt collection regulations.* Except as modified by this subpart, collection of debts arising out of the Title I program is subject to the Department's debt collection regulations in subpart C of 24 CFR part 17.

§201.61 Claims against debtors—principal amount of debt.

(a) *Liability.* A debtor is liable to the Secretary for the principal amount of the debt, as described in paragraphs (b), (c), or (d) of this section, as appropriate.

(b) *Property improvement notes.* In the case of an assigned note for a property improvement loan, the principal amount of the debt is the unpaid amount of the loan obligation, as defined in §201.55(a)(1) of this part, plus amounts described in §§201.55(a) (3), (4), (5).

(c) *Manufactured home notes.* In the case of an assigned note for a manufactured home loan, the principal amount of the debt is the unpaid amount of the loan obligation, as defined in §201.55(b)(1) of this part, plus amounts described in §§201.55(b) (3) through (8).

(d) *Assigned judgments.* In the case of a judgment obtained by the lender on a property improvement loan or a manufactured home loan and assigned to the Secretary, the principal amount of the debt is the amount of the judgment.

§201.62 Claims against debtors—interest, penalties, and administrative costs.

(a) *Interest.* In addition to the principal amount of the debt, the debtor is liable for the payment of interest. Interest accrues on the principal amount of the debt as of the date of default, as defined in §201.2(h) of this part, as follows:

(1) In the case of a debt based upon the assignment of a defaulted note, interest is assessed at the lesser of the rate specified in the note or the United States Treasury's current value of funds rate in effect on the date the Title I insurance claim was paid.

(2) In the case of a debt based upon the assignment of a judgment, interest is assessed at the lesser of the rate specified in the judgment or the United

127

States Treasury's current value of funds rate in effect on the date the Title I insurance claim was paid.

(b) *Penalties and administrative costs.* The Secretary shall assess reasonable administrative costs and penalties as authorized in 31 U.S.C. 3717, unless there is no provision in the note providing for such charges and the debtor has not otherwise consented to liability for such charges.

§ 201.63   Claims against lenders.

Claims against lenders for money owed to the Department, including unpaid insurance charges and unpaid repurchase demands, shall be collected in accordance with 24 CFR part 17, subpart C.

PART 202—APPROVAL OF LENDING INSTITUTIONS AND MORTGAGEES

Subpart A—General Requirements

AUTHORITY: 12 U.S.C. 1703, 1709 and 1715b; 42 U.S.C. 3535(d).

SOURCE: 62 FR 20082, Apr. 24, 1997, unless otherwise noted.

Subpart A—General Requirements

§ 202.1   Purpose.

This part establishes minimum standards and requirements for approval by the Secretary of lenders and mortgagees to participate in the Title I and Title II programs.

§ 202.2   Definitions.

Act means the National Housing Act (12 U.S.C. 1702 *et seq.*).

Claim means a single family insured mortgage for which the Secretary pays an insurance claim within 24 months after the mortgage is insured.

Default means a single family insured mortgage in default for 90 or more days within 24 months after the mortgage is insured.

Lender or *Title I lender* means a financial institution that:

(a) Holds a valid Title I Contract of Insurance and is approved by the Secretary under this part as a supervised lender under § 202.6, a nonsupervised lender under § 202.7, an investing lender under § 202.9, or a governmental or similar institution under § 202.10; or

(b) Is under suspension or held a Title I contract that has been terminated but remains responsible for servicing or selling Title I loans that it holds and is authorized to file insurance claims on such loans.

Loan or *Title I loan* means a loan authorized for insurance under Title I of the Act.

Mortgage, Title II mortgage or insured mortgage means a mortgage or loan insured under Title II or Title XI of the Act.

Mortgagee or *Title II mortgagee* means a mortgage lender that is approved to participate in the Title II programs as a supervised mortgagee under § 202.6, a nonsupervised mortgagee under § 202.7, an investing mortgagee under § 202.9, or a governmental or similar institution under 202.10.

Multifamily mortgagee means a mortgagee approved to participate only in multifamily Title II programs, except that for purposes of § 202.8(b)(1) the term also means a mortgagee approved to participate in both single family and multifamily Title II programs.

Normal rate means the rate of defaults and claims on insured mortgages for the geographic area served by a HUD field office, or other area designated by the Secretary, in which a mortgagee originates mortgages.

Origination approval agreement means the Secretary's agreement that a mortgagee is approved to originate single family insured mortgages.

Title I program(s) means an insurance program or programs authorized by Title I of the Act.

Title II program(s) means an insurance program or programs authorized by Title II or Title XI of the Act.

[62 FR 20082, Apr. 24, 1997, as amended at 62 FR 65181, Dec. 10, 1997; 75 FR 20731, Apr. 20, 2010]

§202.3 Approval status for lenders and mortgagees.

(a) *Initial approval.* A lender or mortgagee may be approved for participation in the Title I or Title II programs upon filing a request for approval on a form prescribed by the Secretary and signed by the applicant. The approval form shall be accompanied by such documentation as may be prescribed by the Secretary.

(1) Approval is signified by:

(i) The Secretary's agreement that the lender or mortgagee is considered approved under the Title I or Title II programs, except as otherwise ordered by the Mortgagee Review Board or an officer or subdivision of the Department to which the Mortgagee Review Board has delegated its power, unless the lender or mortgagee voluntarily relinquishes its approval;

(ii) Consent by the lender or mortgagee to comply at all times with the general approval requirements of §202.5, and with additional requirements governing the particular class of lender or mortgagee for which it was approved as described under subpart B at §§202.6 through 202.10; and

(iii) Under the Title I program, the issuance of a Contract of Insurance constitutes an agreement between the Secretary and the lender and which governs participation in the Title I program.

(2) Limitations on approval:

(i) Separate approval as lender or mortgagee is required for participation in the Title I or Title II programs, respectively. Application must be made, and approval will be granted, on the basis of one or both categories of programs, as is appropriate.

(ii) Separate approval as mortgagee is required for the Single Family Mortgage Insurance Programs and for the Multifamily Mortgage Insurance Programs. Application must be made, and approval will be granted, on the basis of either or both categories, as is appropriate.

(iii) In addition to the requirements for approval as a Title II mortgagee, the Secretary may from time to time issue eligibility requirements for participation in specific programs, such as the Direct Endorsement program.

(iv) A Title II mortgagee may be approved to operate either on a nationwide basis or on a geographically restricted basis in only those areas designated by the Secretary.

(v) A Title I lender may originate loans or purchase advances of credit only within a geographic lending area approved by the Secretary. Expansion of this lending area shall be subject to a determination by the Secretary that the lender is able to originate loans in compliance with part 201 of this chapter within such expanded area.

(3) *Authorized agents.* A mortgagee approved under §§202.6, 202.7, or 202.10 as a nonsupervised mortgagee, supervised mortgagee, or governmental or similar institution approved as a Direct Endorsement mortgagee under 24 CFR 203.3 may, with the approval of the Secretary, designate a nonsupervised or supervised mortgagee with Direct Endorsement approval under 24 CFR 203.3 as authorized agent for the purpose of underwriting loans. The application for mortgage insurance may be submitted in the name of the FHA-approved mortgagee or its designated authorized agent under this paragraph.

(b) *Recertification.* On each anniversary of the approval of a lender or mortgagee, the Secretary will determine whether recertification, i.e., continued approval, is appropriate. The Secretary will review the yearly verification report required by §202.5(m) and other pertinent documents, ascertain that all application and annual fees have been paid, and request any further information needed to decide upon recertification.

(c) *Termination*—(1) *Termination of the Title I Contract of Insurance*—(i) *Notice.*

A Contract of Insurance may be terminated in accordance with its terms by the Secretary or by the Secretary's designee upon giving the lender at least 5 days prior written notice.

(ii) *Informal meeting.* If requested, and before expiration of the 5-day notice period, a lender shall be entitled to an informal meeting with the Department official taking action to terminate the Contract of Insurance.

(iii) *Effect of termination.* Termination of a Contract of Insurance shall not affect:

(A) The Department's obligation to provide insurance coverage with respect to eligible loans originated before the termination, unless there was fraud or misrepresentation;

(B) A lender's obligation to continue to pay insurance charges or premiums and meet all other obligations, including servicing, associated with eligible loans originated before termination; or

(C) A lender's right to apply for and be granted a new Title I Contract of Insurance, provided that the requirements for approval under this part are met.

(2) *Credit Watch Termination.* (i) *Scope and frequency of review.* The Secretary will review, on an ongoing basis, the number of defaults and claims on mortgages originated, underwritten, or both, by each mortgagee in the geographic area served by a HUD field office. HUD will make this rate information available to mortgagees and the public through electronic means and will issue instructions for accessing this information through a Mortgagee Letter. For this purpose, and for all purposes under paragraph (c) of this section, a mortgage is considered to be originated in the same federal fiscal year in which its amortization commences. The Secretary may also review the insured mortgage performance of a mortgagee's branch offices individually and may terminate the authority of the branch or the authority of the mortgagee's overall operation.

(ii) *Credit Watch Status.* Mortgagees are responsible for monitoring their default and claim rate performance. A mortgagee is considered to be on Credit Watch Status if, at any time, the mortgagee has a rate of defaults and claims on insured mortgages originated, underwritten, or both, in an area which exceeds 150 percent of the normal rate and its origination approval agreement has not been terminated.

(iii) *Notice of termination.* (A) *Notice of termination of origination approval agreement.* The Secretary may notify a mortgagee that its origination approval agreement will terminate 60 days after notice is given, if the mortgagee had a rate of defaults and claims on insured mortgages originated in an area which exceeded 200 percent of the normal rate and exceeded the national default and claim rate for insured mortgages.

(B) *Notice of termination of direct endorsement approval.* The Secretary may notify a mortgagee that its direct endorsement approval under 24 CFR part 203 will terminate 60 days after notice is given, if the mortgagee had a rate of defaults and claims on insured mortgages underwritten in an area which exceeded 200 percent of the normal rate and exceeded the national default and claim rate for insured mortgages. The termination of a mortgagee's direct endorsement approval pursuant to this section is separate and apart from the termination of a mortgagee's direct endorsement approval under 24 CFR part 203.

(C) *No need for prior action by Mortgagee Review Board.* The termination notices described in paragraphs (c)(2)(ii)(A) and (B) of this section may be given without prior action by the Mortgagee Review Board.

(D) *Underserved areas.* Before the Secretary sends the termination notice, the Secretary shall review the Census tract concentrations of the defaults and claims. If the Secretary determines that the excessive rate is the result of mortgage lending in underserved areas, as defined in 24 CFR 81.2, the Secretary may determine not to terminate the mortgagee's origination approval agreement and/or direct endorsement approval.

(iv) *Request for informal conference.* Prior to termination the mortgagee may submit a written request for an informal conference with the Deputy Assistant Secretary for Single Family Housing or that official's designee. HUD must receive the written request no later than 30 calendar days after the date of the proposed termination notice. Unless HUD grants an extension, the informal conference must be held no later than 60 calendar days after the date of the proposed termination notice. After considering relevant reasons and factors beyond the mortgagee's control that contributed to the excessive default and claim rates, the Deputy Assistant Secretary for Single Family Housing or designee may withdraw the termination notice.

(v) *Limitation on the establishment of new branches.* Upon receipt of a proposed termination notice of its origination approval agreement, the mortgagee shall not establish a new branch or new branches for the origination of FHA-insured mortgages in the area or areas that are covered by the proposed termination notice. As of January 18, 2005, a mortgagee that is in receipt of a notice of proposed termination may not establish any new branch in the location or locations cited in the proposed termination notice until either:

(A) The proposed termination notice is withdrawn or

(B) The Secretary reinstates the mortgagee's origination approval agreement, in accordance with paragraph (e) of this section.

(vi) *Effects of termination.* (A) *Termination of origination approval agreement.* If a mortgagee's origination approval agreement is terminated, it may not originate single family insured mortgages unless the origination approval agreement is reinstated by the Secretary in accordance with paragraph (e) of this section, notwithstanding any other provision of this part except §202.3(c)(2)(vii)(A).

(B) *Termination of direct endorsement approval.* If a mortgagee's direct endorsement approval is terminated, it may not underwrite single family insured mortgages for the area(s) identified in the termination notice, unless the direct endorsement approval is reinstated by the Secretary in accordance with paragraph (e) of this section, notwithstanding any other provision of this part except §202.3(c)(2)(vii)(A).

(vii) *Rights and obligations in the event of termination.* Termination of the origination approval agreement and/or direct endorsement approval shall not affect:

(A) The eligibility of the mortgage for insurance, absent fraud or misrepresentation, if the mortgagor and all terms and conditions of the mortgage had been approved before the termination by the Direct Endorsement or Lender Insurance mortgagee or were covered by a firm commitment issued by the Secretary; however, no other mortgages originated or underwritten after the date of termination by the mortgagee shall be insured unless the mortgagee's origination approval agreement and/or direct endorsement approval is reinstated by the Secretary;

(B) The right of a mortgagee whose direct endorsement approval has been terminated to transfer cases to another mortgagee with direct endorsement approval for the area covered by the termination.

(C) A mortgagee's obligation to continue to pay insurance premiums and meet all other obligations, including servicing, associated with insured mortgages;

(D) A mortgagee's right to apply for reinstatement of the origination approval agreement and/or direct endorsement approval in accordance with paragraph (e) of this section; or

(E) A mortgagee's right to purchase insured mortgages or to service its own portfolio or the portfolios of other mortgagees with which it has a servicing contract.

(d) *Withdrawal and suspension of approval.* Lender or mortgagee approval may be suspended or withdrawn by the Mortgagee Review Board as provided in part 25 of this title.

(e) *Reinstatement*—(1) *General.* A mortgagee whose origination approval agreement and/or direct endorsement approval has been terminated under paragraph (c) of this section may apply for reinstatement if:

(i) The origination approval agreement and/or direct endorsement approval for the affected branch or branches has been terminated for at least six months; and

(ii) The mortgagee continues to be an approved mortgagee meeting the general standards of §202.5 and the specific requirements of §§202.6, 202.7, 202.8 or 202.10, and 202.12.

131

(2) *Application for reinstatement.* The mortgagee's application for reinstatement must:

(i) Be in a format prescribed by the Secretary and signed by the mortgagee;

(ii) Be accompanied by an independent analysis of the terminated office's operations and identifying the underlying cause of the mortgagee's unacceptable default and claim rate. The independent analysis must be prepared by an independent Certified Public Accountant (CPA) qualified to perform audits under the government auditing standards issued by the General Accounting Office; and

(iii) Be accompanied by a corrective action plan addressing each of the issues identified in the independent analysis described in paragraph (e)(2)(ii) of this section, along with evidence demonstrating that the mortgagee has implemented the corrective action plan.

(3) *HUD action on reinstatement application.* The Secretary will grant the mortgagee's application for reinstatement if the mortgagee's application is complete and the Secretary determines that the underlying causes for the termination have been satisfactorily remedied.

[62 FR 20082, Apr. 24, 1997, as amended at 62 FR 30225, June 2, 1997; 62 FR 65181, Dec. 10, 1997; 69 FR 75807, Dec. 17, 2004; 75 FR 20731, Apr. 20, 2010; 78 FR 57060, Sept. 17, 2013]

§ 202.4 Request for determination of compliance.

Pursuant to section 539(a) of the Act, any person may file a request that the Secretary determine whether a lender or mortgagee is in compliance with § 202.12(a) or with provisions of this chapter implementing sections 223(a)(7) and 535 of the Act such as §§ 201.10(g), 203.18d and 203.43(c)(5) of this chapter (only section 535 applies to lenders). The request for determination shall be made to the following address: Department of Housing and Urban Development, Office of Lender Activities and Program Compliance, 451 Seventh Street SW., Washington, DC, 20410. The Secretary shall inform the requestor of the disposition of the request. The Secretary shall publish in the FEDERAL REGISTER the disposition of any case referred by the Secretary to the Mortgagee Review Board.

§ 202.5 General approval standards.

To be approved for participation in the Title I or Title II programs, and to maintain approval, a lender or mortgagee shall meet and continue to meet the general requirements of paragraphs (a) through (n) of this section (except as provided in § 202.10(b)) and the requirements for one of the eligible classes of lenders or mortgagees in §§ 202.6 through 202.10.

(a) *Business form.* (1) The lender or mortgagee shall be a corporation or other chartered institution, a permanent organization having succession, or a partnership. A partnership must meet the requirements of paragraphs (a)(1)(i) through (iv) of this section.

(i) Each general partner must be a corporation or other chartered institution consisting of two or more persons.

(ii) One general partner must be designated as the managing general partner. The managing general partner shall comply with the requirements of paragraphs (b), (c), and (f) of this section. The managing general partner must have as its principal activity the management of one or more partnerships, all of which are mortgage lenders or property improvement or manufactured home lenders, and must have exclusive authority to deal directly with the Secretary on behalf of each partnership. Newly admitted partners must agree to the management of the partnership by the designated managing general partner. If the managing general partner withdraws or is removed from the partnership for any reason, a new managing general partner shall be substituted, and the Secretary shall be immediately notified of the substitution.

(iii) The partnership agreement shall specify that the partnership shall exist for the minimum term of years required by the Secretary. All insured mortgages and Title I loans held by the partnership shall be transferred to a lender or mortgagee approved under this part prior to the termination of the partnership. The partnership shall be specifically authorized to continue its existence if a partner withdraws.

(iv) The Secretary must be notified immediately of any amendments to the partnership agreement that would affect the partnership's actions under the Title I or Title II programs.

(2) *Use of business name.* The lender or mortgagee must use its HUD-registered business name in all advertisements and promotional materials related to FHA programs. HUD-registered business names include any alias or "doing business as" (DBA) on file with FHA. The lender or mortgagee must keep copies of all print and electronic advertisements and promotional materials for a period of 2 years from the date that the materials are circulated or used to advertise.

(3) *Non-FHA-approved entities.* A lender or mortgagee that accepts a loan application from a non-FHA-approved entity must confirm that the entity's legal name and Tax ID number are included in the FHA loan origination system record for the subject loan. The loan to be insured by FHA must be underwritten by the FHA-approved lender or mortgagee.

(b) *Employees.* The lender or mortgagee shall employ competent personnel trained to perform their assigned responsibilities in consumer or mortgage lending, including origination, servicing, and collection activities, and shall maintain adequate staff and facilities to originate and service mortgages or Title I loans, in accordance with applicable regulations, to the extent the mortgagee or lender engages in such activities.

(c) *Officers.* All employees who will sign applications for mortgage insurance on behalf of the mortgagee or report loans for insurance shall be corporate officers or shall otherwise be authorized to bind the lender or mortgagee in the origination transaction. The lender or mortgagee shall ensure that an authorized person reports all originations, purchases, and sales of Title I loans or Title II mortgages to the Secretary for the purpose of obtaining or transferring insurance coverage.

(d) *Escrows.* The lender or mortgagee shall not use escrow funds for any purpose other than that for which they were received. It shall segregate escrow commitment deposits, work comple-

tion deposits, and all periodic payments received under loans or insured mortgages on account of ground rents, taxes, assessments, and insurance charges or premiums, and shall deposit such funds with one or more financial institutions in a special account or accounts that are fully insured by the Federal Deposit Insurance Corporation or the National Credit Union Administration, except as otherwise provided in writing by the Secretary.

(e) *Servicing.* A lender shall service or arrange for servicing of the loan in accordance with the requirements of 24 CFR part 201. A mortgagee shall service or arrange for servicing of the mortgage in accordance with the servicing responsibilities contained in subpart C of 24 CFR part 203 and in 24 CFR part 207, with all other applicable regulations contained in this title, and with such additional conditions and requirements as the Secretary may impose.

(f) *Business changes.* The lender or mortgagee shall provide prompt notification to the Secretary, in such form as prescribed by the Secretary, of:

(1) All changes in its legal structure, including, but not limited to, mergers, terminations, name, location, control of ownership, and character of business; and

(2) Any officer, partner, director, principal, manager, supervisor, loan processor, loan underwriter, loan originator, of the lender or mortgagee, or the lender or mortgagee itself, that is subject to one or more of the sanctions in paragraph (j) of this section.

(g) *Financial statements.* The lender or mortgagee shall:

(1) Furnish to the Secretary a copy of its audited financial statements within 90 days of its fiscal year end, except as provided in § 202.6(c);

(2) Furnish such other information as the Secretary may request; and

(3) Submit to an examination of that portion of its records that relates to its Title I and/or Title II program activities.

(h) *Quality control plan.* The lender or mortgagee shall implement a written quality control plan, acceptable to the Secretary, that assures compliance with the regulations and other issuances of the Secretary regarding loan or mortgage origination and servicing.

(i) *Fees*. The lender or mortgagee, unless approved under § 202.10, shall pay an application fee and annual fees, including additional fees for each branch office authorized to originate Title I loans or submit applications for mortgage insurance, at such times and in such amounts as the Secretary may require. The Secretary may identify additional classes or groups of lenders or mortgagees that may be exempt from one or more of these fees.

(j) *Ineligibility*. For a lender or mortgagee to be eligible for FHA approval, neither the lender or mortgagee, nor any officer, partner, director, principal, manager, supervisor, loan processor, loan underwriter, or loan originator of the lender or mortgagee shall:

(1) Be suspended, debarred, under a limited denial of participation (LDP), or otherwise restricted under 2 CFR part 2424 or 24 CFR part 25, or under similar procedures of any other federal agency;

(2) Be indicted for, or have been convicted of, an offense that reflects adversely upon the integrity, competency, or fitness to meet the responsibilities of the lender or mortgagee to participate in the Title I or Title II programs;

(3) Be subject to unresolved findings as a result of HUD or other governmental audit, investigation, or review;

(4) Be engaged in business practices that do not conform to generally accepted practices of prudent mortgagees or that demonstrate irresponsibility;

(5) Be convicted of, or have pled guilty or *nolo contendere* to, a felony related to participation in the real estate or mortgage loan industry:

(i) During the 7-year period preceding the date of the application for licensing and registration; or

(ii) At any time preceding such date of application, if such felony involved an act of fraud, dishonesty, or a breach of trust or money laundering;

(6) Be in violation of provisions of the Secure and Fair Enforcement (SAFE) Mortgage Licensing Act of 2008 (12 U.S.C. 5101 *et seq*.) or any applicable provision of state law; or

(7) Be in violation of any other requirement established by the Secretary.

(k) *Branch offices*. A lender may, upon approval by the Secretary, maintain branch offices for the origination of Title I or Title II loans. A branch office of a mortgagee must be registered with the Department in order to originate mortgages or submit applications for mortgage insurance. The lender or mortgagee shall remain fully responsible to the Secretary for the actions of its branch offices.

(l) *Conflict of interest and responsibility*. A mortgagee may not pay anything of value, directly or indirectly, in connection with any insured mortgage transaction or transactions to any person or entity if such person or entity has received any other consideration from the mortgagor, seller, builder, or any other person for services related to such transactions or related to the purchase or sale of the mortgaged property, except that consideration, approved by the Secretary, may be paid for services actually performed. The mortgagee shall not pay a referral fee to any person or organization.

(m) *Reports*. Each lender and mortgagee must submit an annual certification on a form prescribed by the Secretary. Upon application for approval and with each annual recertification, each lender and mortgagee must submit a certification that it has not been refused a license and has not been sanctioned by any state or states in which it will originate insured mortgages or Title I loans. In addition, each mortgagee shall file the following:

(1) An audited or unaudited financial statement, within 30 days of the end of each fiscal quarter in which the mortgagee experiences an operating loss of 20 percent of its net worth, and until the mortgagee demonstrates an operating profit for 2 consecutive quarters or until the next recertification, whichever is the longer period; and

(2) A statement of net worth within 30 days of the commencement of voluntary or involuntary bankruptcy, conservatorship, receivership, or any transfer of control to a federal or state supervisory agency.

(n) *Net worth*—(1) *Applicability*. The requirements of this section apply to approved supervised and nonsupervised lenders and mortgagees under §202.6 and §202.7, and approved investing lenders and mortgagees under §202.9. For ease of reference, these institutions are referred to as "approved lenders and mortgagees" for purposes of this section. The requirements of this section also apply to applicants for FHA approval under §§202.6, 202.7, and 202.9. For ease of reference, these entities are referred to as "applicants" for purposes of this section.

(2) *Phased-in net worth requirements for 2010 and 2011*—(i) *Applicants.* Effective on May 20, 2010, applicants shall comply with the net worth requirements set forth in paragraph (n)(2)(iii) of this section.

(ii) *Approved mortgagees.* Effective on May 20, 2011, each approved lender or mortgagee with FHA approval as of May 20, 2010 shall comply with the net worth requirements set forth in paragraphs (n)(2)(iii) or (n)(2)(iv) of this section, as applicable.

(iii) *Net worth requirements for non-small businesses.* Each approved lender or mortgagee that exceeds the size standard for its industry classification established by the Small Business Administration at 13 CFR 121.201 Sector 52 (Finance and Insurance), Subsector 522 (Credit Intermediation and Related Activities) shall have a required minimum net worth of not less than $1,000,000. No less than 20 percent of the approved lender or mortgagee's required minimum net worth must be liquid assets consisting of cash or its equivalent acceptable to the Secretary.

(iv) *Net worth requirements for small businesses.* Each approved lender or mortgagee that meets the size standard for its industry classification established by the Small Business Administration at 13 CFR 121.201 Sector 52 (Finance and Insurance), Subsector 522 (Credit Intermediation and Related Activities) shall have a required minimum net worth of not less than $500,000. No less than 20 percent of the approved lender or mortgagee's required minimum net worth must be liquid assets consisting of cash or its equivalent acceptable to the Secretary. If, based on the audited financial statement or other financial report that is required to be prepared at the end of

its fiscal year and provided to HUD at the commencement of the new fiscal year, an approved lender or mortgagee no longer meets the Small Business Administration size standard for its industry classification, the approved lender or mortgagee shall meet the net worth requirements set forth in paragraph (n)(2)(iii) of this section for a non-small business approved lender or mortgagee by the last day of the fiscal year in which the audited financial statement or other financial report, as applicable, was submitted.

(3) *Net worth requirements for 2013 and subsequent years.* Effective May 20, 2013:

(i) Irrespective of size, each applicant and each approved lender or mortgagee, for participation solely under the FHA single family programs, shall have a net worth of not less than $1 million, plus an additional net worth of one percent of the total volume in excess of $25 million of FHA single family insured mortgages originated, underwritten, purchased, or serviced during the prior fiscal year, up to a maximum required net worth of $2.5 million. No less than 20 percent of the applicant's or approved lender or mortgagee's required net worth must be liquid assets consisting of cash or its equivalent acceptable to the Secretary.

(ii) *Multifamily net worth requirements.* Irrespective of size, each applicant for approval and each approved lender or mortgagee for participation solely under the FHA multifamily programs shall have a minimum net worth of not less than $1 million. For those multifamily approved lenders or mortgagees that also engage in mortgage servicing, an additional net worth of one percent of the total volume in excess of $25 million of FHA multifamily mortgages originated, purchased, or serviced during the prior fiscal year, up to a maximum required net worth of $2.5 million, is required. For multifamily approved lenders or mortgagees that do not perform mortgage servicing, an additional net worth of one half of one percent of the total volume in excess of $25 million of FHA multifamily mortgages originated during the prior fiscal year, up to a maximum required net worth of $2.5 million, is required. No less than 20 percent of the applicant's or approved lender's or mortgagee's required net worth must be liquid assets consisting of cash or its equivalent acceptable to the Secretary.

(iii) *Dual participation net worth requirements.* Irrespective of size, each applicant for approval and each approved lender or mortgagee that is a participant in both FHA single-family and multifamily programs must meet the net worth requirements as set forth in paragraph (n)(3)(i) of this section.

[75 FR 20732, Apr. 20, 2010; 75 FR 23582, May 4, 2010; 77 FR 51468, Aug. 24, 2012; 78 FR 57060, Sept. 17, 2013]

Subpart B—Classes of Lenders and Mortgagees

§ 202.6   Supervised lenders and mortgagees.

(a) *Definition.* A supervised lender or mortgagee is a financial institution that is a member of the Federal Reserve System or an institution whose accounts are insured by the Federal Deposit Insurance Corporation or the National Credit Union Administration. A supervised mortgagee may submit applications for mortgage insurance. A supervised lender or mortgagee may originate, purchase, hold, service or sell loans or insured mortgages, respectively.

(b) *Additional requirements.* In addition to the general approval requirements in § 202.5, a supervised lender or mortgagee shall meet the following requirements:

(1) *Net worth.* The net worth requirements appear in § 202.5(n).

(2) *Notification.* A lender or mortgagee shall promptly notify the Secretary in the event of termination of its supervision by its supervising agency.

(3) *Fidelity bond.* A Title II mortgagee shall have fidelity bond coverage and errors and omissions insurance acceptable to the Secretary and in an amount required by the Secretary, or have alternative insurance coverage, approved by the Secretary, that assures the faithful performance of the responsibilities of the mortgagee.

(4) *Audit report.* Except as provided in paragraph (c) of this section, a lender or mortgagee must:

(i) Comply with the financial reporting requirements in 24 CFR part 5, subpart H. Audit reports shall be based on audits performed by a certified public accountant, or by an independent public accountant licensed by a regulatory authority of a State or other political subdivision of the United States on or before December 31, 1970, and shall include:

(A) Financial statements in a form acceptable to the Secretary, including a balance sheet and a statement of operations and retained earnings, a statement of cash flows, an analysis of the lender's or mortgagee's net worth adjusted to reflect only assets acceptable to the Secretary, and an analysis of escrow funds; and

(B) Such other financial information as the Secretary may require to determine the accuracy and validity of the audit report.

(ii) Submit a report on compliance tests prescribed by the Secretary.

(c) *Financial statement requirements for small supervised lenders and mortgagees—* (1) *Definitions.* For the purposes of this section, the following definitions apply:

(i) *Federal banking agency* means the Board of Governors of the Federal Reserve System; the Federal Deposit Insurance Corporation; and the National Credit Union Administration; or any successor agency thereof.

(ii) *Small supervised lender or mortgagee* means a supervised lender or mortgagee possessing consolidated assets below the threshold for required audited financial reporting as established by the federal banking agency that is responsible for the oversight of that supervised lender or mortgagee.

(2) *Financial statement requirements.* Small supervised lenders and mortgagees shall not be subject to the requirement to submit a copy of an audited financial statement under § 202.5(g) and the audit report requirements under paragraph (b)(4) of this section. Small supervised lenders and mortgagees are required, within 90 days of their fiscal year end, to furnish to the Secretary the unaudited financial regulatory report—a consolidated or fourth quarter Report of Condition and Income (Federal Financial Institutions Examination Council forms 031 and 041, also

known as the "Call Report"), a consolidated or fourth quarter Thrift Financial Report, or a consolidated or fourth quarter NCUA Call Report (NCUA Form 5300 or 5310), or such other financial regulatory report as may be required—that aligns with the small supervised lender's or mortgagee's fiscal year end and that the small supervised lender or mortgagee is required to submit to their respective federal banking agency.

(3) *Requirement for audited financial statement and other information based on determination of heightened risk to the FHA insurance fund.* If the Secretary determines that a small supervised lender or mortgagee poses a heightened risk to the FHA insurance fund, the lender or mortgagee must provide, upon request, additional financial documentation, up to and including an audited financial statement, and other information as the Secretary determines necessary. The Secretary may determine that a small supervised lender or mortgagee poses a heightened risk to the FHA insurance fund based upon, but not limited to, one or more of the following factors:

(i) Failing to provide required financial submissions under §202.6(c)(2) within the required 90-day period following the lender's or mortgagee's fiscal year end;

(ii) Maintaining insufficient adjusted net worth or unrestricted liquid assets as required by §202.5(n);

(iii) Reporting opening cash and equity balances that do not agree with the prior year's reported cash and equity balances;

(iv) Experiencing an operating loss of 20 percent or greater of the lender's or mortgagee's net worth for the annual reporting period as governed by §202.5(m)(1);

(v) Experiencing an increase in loan volume over the prior 12-month period, determined by the Secretary to be significant;

(vi) Undertaking significant changes to business operations, such as a merger or acquisition; and

(vii) Other factors that the Secretary considers appropriate in indicating a heightened risk to the FHA insurance fund.

[75 FR 20734, Apr. 20, 2010, as amended by 78 FR 57060, Sept. 17, 2013]

§202.7 Nonsupervised lenders and mortgagees.

(a) *Definition.* A nonsupervised lender or mortgagee is a lending institution which has as its principal activity the lending or investing of funds in real estate mortgages, consumer installment notes, or similar advances of credit, or the purchase of consumer installment contracts, and which is not approved under any other section of this part. A nonsupervised mortgagee may submit applications for mortgage insurance. A nonsupervised lender or mortgagee may originate, purchase, hold, service or sell insured loans or mortgages, respectively.

(b) *Additional requirements.* In addition to the general approval requirements in §202.5, a nonsupervised lender or mortgagee shall meet the following requirements:

(1) *Net worth and liquid assets.* The net worth and liquidity requirements appear in §202.5(n).

(2) *Credit source*—(i) *Title I.* A lender shall have and maintain a reliable warehouse line of credit or other funding program acceptable to the Secretary of not less than $500,000 for use in originating or purchasing Title I loans.

(ii) *Title II.* Except for multifamily mortgagees, a mortgagee shall have a warehouse line of credit or other mortgage funding program acceptable to the Secretary which is adequate to fund the mortgagee's average 60 day origination operations, but in no event shall the warehouse line of credit or funding program be less than $1,000,000.

(3) *Audit report.* (i) A lender or mortgagee must comply with the financial reporting requirements in 24 CFR part 5, subpart H. Audit reports shall be based on audits performed by a certified public accountant, or by an independent public accountant licensed by a regulatory authority of a State or other political subdivision of the United States on or before December 31, 1970, and shall include:

(A) A financial statement in a form acceptable to the Secretary, including

137

a balance sheet and a statement of operations and retained earnings, a statement of cash flows, an analysis of the mortgagee's net worth adjusted to reflect only assets acceptable to the Secretary, and an analysis of escrow funds; and

(B) Such other financial information as the Secretary may require to determine the accuracy and validity of the audit report.

(ii) A mortgagee must submit a report on compliance tests prescribed by the Secretary.

(4) *Fidelity bond.* A Title II mortgagee shall have fidelity bond coverage and errors and omissions insurance acceptable to the Secretary and in an amount required by the Secretary, or alternative insurance coverage approved by the Secretary, that assures the faithful performance of the responsibilities of the mortgagee.

[62 FR 20082, Apr. 24, 1997, as amended at 62 FR 65182, Dec. 10, 1997; 63 FR 9742, Feb. 26, 1998; 63 FR 44361, Aug. 18, 1998; 67 FR 53451, Aug. 15, 2002; 77 FR 51468, Aug. 24, 2012]

§ 202.8 Sponsored third-party originators.

(a) *Definitions—Sponsor.* (1) With respect to Title I programs, a sponsor is a lender that holds a valid Title I Contract of Insurance and meets the net worth requirement for the class of lender to which it belongs.

(2) With respect to Title II programs, a sponsor is a mortgagee that holds a valid origination approval agreement, is approved to participate in the Direct Endorsement program, and meets the net worth requirement for the class of mortgagee to which it belongs.

(3) Each sponsor shall be responsible to the Secretary for the actions of its sponsored third-party originators or mortgagees in originating loans or mortgages, unless applicable law or regulation requires specific knowledge on the part of the party to be held responsible. If specific knowledge is required, the Secretary will presume that a sponsor has knowledge of the actions of its sponsored third-party originators or mortgagees in originating loans or mortgages and the sponsor is responsible for those actions unless it can rebut the presumption with affirmative evidence.

Sponsored third-party originator. A sponsored third-party originator may hold a Title I Contract of Insurance or Title II Origination Approval Agreement if it is an FHA-approved lender or mortgagee. If the sponsored third-party originator is not an FHA-approved lender or mortgagee, then the sponsored third-party originator may not hold a Title I Contract of Insurance or Title II Origination Approval Agreement. A sponsored third-party originator is authorized to originate Title I direct loans or Title II mortgage loans for sale or transfer to a sponsor or sponsors, as defined in this section, that holds a valid Title I Contract of Insurance or Title II Origination Approval Agreement and is not under suspension, subject to the sponsor determining that the third-party originator has met the eligibility criteria of paragraph (b) of this section.

(b) *Eligibility to originate loans to be insured by FHA.* A sponsored third-party originator may originate loans to be insured by FHA, provided that:

(1) The sponsored third-party originator is working with and through an FHA-approved lender or mortgagee; and

(2) The sponsored third-party originator or an officer, partner, director, principal, manager, supervisor, loan processor, or loan originator of the sponsored third-party originator has not been subject to the sanctions or administrative actions listed in § 202.5(j), as determined and verified by the FHA-approved lender or mortgagee.

[75 FR 20734, Apr. 20, 2010, as amended at 77 FR 51468, Aug. 24, 2012]

§ 202.9 Investing lenders and mortgagees.

(a) *Definition.* An investing lender or mortgagee is an organization that is not approved under any other section of this part. An investing lender or mortgagee may purchase, hold or sell Title I loans or Title II mortgages, respectively, but may not originate Title I loans or Title II mortgages in its own name or submit applications for the insurance of mortgages. An investing lender or mortgagee may not service Title I loans or Title II mortgages without prior approval of the Secretary.

(b) *Additional requirements.* In addition to the general approval requirements in §202.5, an investing lender or mortgagee shall meet the following requirements:

(1) *Funding arrangements.* An investing lender or mortgagee shall have, or have made arrangements for, funds sufficient to support a projected investment of at least $1,000,000 in property improvement, manufactured home or real estate loans or mortgages.

(2) *Officers and staff.* In lieu of the staffing and facilities requirements in §202.5(b), an investing lender or mortgagee shall have officers or employees who are capable of managing its activities in purchasing, holding, and selling Title I loans or Title II mortgages.

(3) *Fidelity bond.* An investing mortgagee shall maintain fidelity bond coverage and errors and omissions insurance acceptable to the Secretary and in an amount required by the Secretary, or alternative insurance coverage approved by the Secretary, that assures the faithful performance of the responsibilities of the mortgagee.

[62 FR 20082, Apr. 24, 1997, as amended at 63 FR 9742, Feb. 26, 1998; 75 FR 20734, Apr. 20, 2010]

§202.10 Governmental institutions, Government-sponsored enterprises, public housing agencies and State housing agencies.

(a) *Definition.* A Federal, State or municipal governmental agency, a Federal Reserve Bank, a Federal Home Loan Bank, the Federal Home Loan Mortgage Corporation, or the Federal National Mortgage Association may be an approved lender or mortgagee. A mortgagee approved under this section may submit applications for Title II mortgage insurance. A lender or mortgagee approved under this section may originate, purchase, service or sell Title I loans and insured mortgages, respectively. A mortgagee or lender approved under this section is not required to meet a net worth requirement. A mortgagee shall maintain fidelity bond coverage and errors and omissions insurance acceptable to the Secretary and in an amount required by the Secretary, or alternative insurance coverage approved by the Secretary, that assures the faithful per-

formance of the responsibilities of the mortgagee. There are no additional requirements beyond the general approval requirements in §202.5 or as provided under paragraph (b) of this section.

(b) *Public housing agencies and State housing agencies.* Under such terms and conditions as the Secretary may prescribe and notwithstanding the general requirements of §202.5 or the requirements of paragraph (a) of this section, a public housing agency or its instrumentality or a State housing agency may be approved as a mortgagee for the purpose of originating and holding multifamily mortgages funded by issuance of tax exempt obligations by the agency.

(c) *Audit requirements.* The insuring of loans and mortgages under the Act constitutes "Federal financial assistance" (as defined in 2 CFR 200.40) for purposes of audit requirements set out in 2 CFR part 200, subpart F. Non-Federal entities (as defined in 2 CFR 200.69) that receive insurance as lenders and mortgagees shall conduct audits in accordance with 2 CFR part 200, subpart F.

[62 FR 20082, Apr. 24, 1997, as amended at 80 FR 75936, Dec. 7, 2015]

Subpart C—Title I and Title II Specific Requirements

§202.11 Title I.

(a) *Types of administrative action.* In addition to termination of the Contract of Insurance, certain sanctions may be imposed under the Title I program. The administrative actions that may be applied are set forth in 24 CFR part 25. Civil money penalties may be imposed against Title I lenders and mortgagees pursuant to 24 CFR part 30.

(b) *Grounds for action.* Administrative actions shall be based upon both the grounds set forth in 24 CFR part 25 and as follows:

(1) Failure to properly supervise and monitor dealers under the provisions of part 201 of this title;

(2) Exhaustion of the general insurance reserve established under part 201 of this title;

(3) Maintenance of a Title I claims/loan ratio representing an unacceptable risk to the Department; or

(4) Transfer of a Title I loan to a party that does not have a valid Title I Contract of Insurance.

[75 FR 20734, Apr. 20, 2010]

§ 202.12   Title II.

(a) *Tiered pricing*—(1) *General requirements*—(i) *Prohibition against excess variation.* The customary lending practices of a mortgagee for its single family insured mortgages shall not provide for a variation in mortgage charge rates that exceed 2 percentage points. A variation is determined as provided in paragraph (a)(6) of this section.

(ii) *Customary lending practices.* The customary lending practices of a mortgagee include all single family insured mortgages originated by the mortgagee, including mortgages that were originated by the mortgagee's sponsored third-party originator(s).

(iii) *Basis for permissible variations.* Any variations in the mortgage charge rate up to two percentage points under the mortgagee's customary lending practices must be based on actual variations in fees or cost to the mortgagee to make the mortgage loan, which shall be determined after accounting for the value of servicing rights generated by making the loan and other income to the mortgagee related to the loan. Fees or costs must be fully documented for each specific loan.

(2) *Area.* For purposes of this section, an area is:

(i) An area used by HUD for purposes of § 203.18(a) of this chapter to determine the median 1-family house price for an area; or

(ii) The area served by a HUD field office but excluding any area included in paragraph (a)(2)(i) of this section.

(3) *Mortgage charges.* Mortgage charges include any charges under the mortgagee's control and not collected for the benefit of third parties. Examples are interest, discount points and origination fees.

(4) *Interest rate.* Whenever a mortgagee offers a particular interest rate for a mortgage type in an area, it may not restrict the availability of the rate in the area on the basis of the principal amount of the mortgage. A mortgagee may not direct mortgage applicants to any specific interest rate category on the basis of mortgage size.

(5) *Mortgage charge rate.* The mortgage charge rate is defined as the amount of mortgage charges for a mortgage expressed as a percentage of the initial principal amount of the mortgage.

(6) *Determining excess variations.* Variation in mortgage charge rates for a mortgage type is determined by comparing all mortgage charge rates offered by the mortgagee within an area for the mortgage type for a designated day or other time period, including mortgage charge rates for all actual mortgage applications.

(7) *Mortgage type.* A mortgage type for purposes of paragraph (a)(6) of this section will include those mortgages that are closely parallel in important characteristics affecting pricing and charges, such as level of risk or processing expenses. The Secretary may develop standards and definitions regarding mortgage types.

(8) *Recordkeeping.* Mortgagees are required to maintain records on pricing information, satisfactory to the Secretary, that would allow for reasonable inspection by HUD for a period of at least 2 years. Additionally, many mortgagees are required to maintain racial, ethnic, and gender data under the regulations implementing the Home Mortgage Disclosure Act (12 U.S.C. 2801–2810).

(b) *Servicing.* Any mortgagee that services mortgages must be approved by the Secretary under § 202.6, § 202.7 or § 202.10, or be specifically approved for servicing under § 202.9(a).

(c) *Report and corrective plan requirements.* If a mortgagee approved for participation in Title II programs is notified by the Secretary that it had a rate of defaults and claims on HUD-insured mortgages during the preceding year, or during recent years, which was higher than the normal rate, it shall submit a report, within 60 days, containing an explanation for the above-normal rate of defaults and claims, and, if required by the Secretary, a plan for corrective action with regard to mortgages in default and its mortgage processing system in general.

[62 FR 20082, Apr. 24, 1997, as amended at 75 FR 20734, Apr. 20, 2010; 77 FR 51469, Aug. 24, 2012]

PART 203—SINGLE FAMILY MORTGAGE INSURANCE

Subpart A—Eligibility Requirements and Underwriting Procedures

AUTHORITY: 12 U.S.C. 1709, 1710, 1715b, 1715z–
16, 1715u, 1717z–21, and 1735d; 15 U.S.C. 1639c;
42 U.S.C. 3535(d).

SOURCE: 36 FR 24508, Dec. 22, 1971, unless
otherwise noted.

Subpart A—Eligibility Requirements and Underwriting Procedures

DIRECT ENDORSEMENT, LENDER
INSURANCE, AND COMMITMENTS

§ 203.1 Underwriting procedures.

The three underwriting procedures
for single family mortgages are:

(a) *Direct Endorsement.* This procedure, which is described in § 203.5, is
available for mortgagees that are eligible under § 203.3.

(b) *Lender insurance.* This procedure, which is described in §203.6, is available for mortgagees that are eligible for the Direct Endorsement program under §203.5, and that are also approved according to §203.4.

(c) *Issuing of commitments through HUD offices.* Processing through HUD offices as described in §203.7, with issuance of commitments, is available only for mortgages that are not eligible for Direct Endorsement processing under §203.5(b) or to the extent required in §203.3(b)(4), §203.3(d)(1), or as determined by the Secretary.

[62 FR 30225, June 2, 1997]

§203.3 Approval of mortgagees for Direct Endorsement.

(a) *Direct Endorsement approval.* To be approved for the Direct Endorsement program set forth in §203.5, a mortgagee must be an approved mortgagee meeting the requirements of §§202.13, 202.14 or 202.17 and this section.

(b) *Special requirements.* The mortgagee must establish that it meets the following qualifications.

(1) The mortgagee has five years of experience in the origination of single family mortgages. The Secretary will approve a mortgagee with less than five years experience in the origination of single family mortgages if a principal officer has had a minimum of five years of managerial experience in the origination of single family mortgages.

(2) The mortgagee has on its permanent staff an underwriter that is authorized by the mortgagee to bind the mortgagee on matters involving the origination of mortgages through the Direct Endorsement procedure and that is registered with the Secretary and such registration is maintained with the Secretary. The technical staff may be employees of the mortgagee or may be hired on a fee basis from a roster maintained by the Secretary. The mortgagee shall use appraisers permitted by §203.5(e).

(3) [Reserved]

(4) The mortgagee must submit initially 15 mortgages processed in accordance with §§203.5 and 203.255. Separate approval is required to originate mortgages under part 206 of this chapter through the Direct Endorsement program unless at least 50 mortgages

closed by the mortgagee have been insured under part 206 of this chapter prior to September 15, 1995. Other mortgagees who have not closed at least 50 mortgages under part 206 of this chapter must submit five (5) Home Equity Conversion Mortgages, processed in accordance with §§203.3 and 203.255. The documents required by §203.255 will be reviewed by the Secretary and, if acceptable, commitments will be issued prior to endorsement of the mortgages for insurance. If the underwriting and processing of these 15 mortgages (or the 5 Home Equity Conversion Mortgages) is satisfactory, then the mortgagee may be approved to close subsequent mortgages and submit them directly for endorsement for insurance in accordance with the process set forth in §203.255. Unsatisfactory performance by the mortgagee at this stage constitutes grounds for denial of participation in the program, or for continued pre-endorsement review of a mortgagee's submissions. If participation in the program is denied, such denial is effective immediately and may be appealed in accordance with the procedures set forth in paragraph (d)(2) of this section. Unsatisfactory performance solely with respect to mortgages under 24 CFR part 206 may, at the option of the Secretary, be grounds for denial of participation or for continued pre-endorsement review for 24 CFR part 206 mortgages without affecting the mortgagee's processing of mortgages under other parts.

(5) The mortgagee shall promptly notify those HUD offices which have granted approval under this section of any changes that affect qualifications under this section.

(c) [Reserved]

(d) *Mortgagee sanctions.* Depending upon the nature and extent of the noncompliance with the requirements applicable to the Direct Endorsement process, as determined by the Secretary, the Secretary may take any of the following actions:

(1) *Probation.* The Secretary may place a mortgagee on Direct Endorsement probation for a specified period of time for the purpose of evaluating the mortgagee's compliance with the requirements of the Direct Endorsement procedure. Such probation is distinct

from probation imposed by the Mortgagee Review Board under part 25 of this chapter. During the probation period specified by this section, the mortgagee may continue to process Direct Endorsement mortgages, subject to conditions required by the Secretary. The Secretary may require the mortgagee to:

(i) Process mortgages in accordance with paragraph (b)(4) of this section;

(ii) Submit to additional training;

(iii) Make changes in the quality control plan required by § 202.5(h) of this chapter; and

(iv) Take other actions, which may include, but are not limited to, periodic reporting to the Secretary, and submission to the Secretary of internal audits.

(2) *Termination of Direct Endorsement approval.* (i) A mortgagee's approval to participate in the Direct Endorsement program may be terminated in a particular jurisdiction by the local HUD office or on a nationwide basis by HUD Central Office. The HUD office instituting the termination action shall provide the mortgagee with written notice of the grounds for the action and of the right to an informal hearing before the office initiating the termination action. Such hearing shall be expeditiously arranged, and the mortgagee may be represented by counsel. Any termination instituted under this section is distinct from withdrawal of mortgagee approval by the Mortgagee Review Board under part 25 of this title.

(ii) After consideration of the materials presented, the decision maker shall advise the mortgagee in writing whether the termination is rescinded, modified or affirmed.

(iii) The mortgagee may appeal such decision to the Deputy Assistant Secretary for Single Family Housing or his or her designee. A decision by the Deputy Assistant Secretary or designee shall constitute final agency action.

(iv) Termination of an origination approval agreement under part 202 of this chapter for a mortgagee or one or more branch offices automatically terminates Direct Endorsement approval for the mortgagee or the branch office

or offices without any further requirement to comply with this paragraph.

(Approved by the Office of Management and Budget under control number 2502-0005)

[57 FR 58345, Dec. 9, 1992, as amended at 60 FR 42758, Aug. 16, 1995; 61 FR 2651, Jan. 26, 1996; 62 FR 20088, Apr. 24, 1997; 62 FR 65182, Dec. 10, 1997]

§ 203.4 Approval of mortgagees for Lender Insurance.

Each mortgagee that chooses to participate in the Lender Insurance program must use the Lender Insurance process to insure all of the mortgages that it underwrites, unless the mortgages are ineligible for the Direct Endorsement program as provided in § 203.5(b), or unless HUD determines that the mortgages are ineligible for the Lender Insurance program.

(a) *Direct Endorsement approval.* To be approved for the Lender Insurance program described in § 203.6, a mortgagee must be unconditionally approved for the Direct Endorsement program as provided in § 203.3.

(b) *Performance: Claim and default rate.* (1) In addition to being unconditionally approved for the Direct Endorsement program, a mortgagee must have had an acceptable claim and default rate (as described in paragraph (b)(3) of this section) for at least 2 years prior to its application for participation in the Lender Insurance program, and must maintain such a claim and default rate in order to retain Lender Insurance approval.

(2) HUD may approve a mortgagee that is otherwise eligible for Lender Insurance approval, but has an acceptable claim and default record of less than 2 years, if:

(i) The mortgagee is an entity created by a merger, acquisition, or reorganization completed less than 2 years prior to the date of the mortgagee's application for Lender Insurance approval;

(ii) One or more of the entities participating in the merger, acquisition, or reorganization had Lender Insurance approval at the time of the merger, acquisition, or reorganization;

(iii) All of the lending institutions participating in the merger, acquisition, or reorganization that had Lender Insurance approval at the time of the merger, acquisition, or reorganization had an acceptable claim and default record for the 2 years preceding the mortgagee's application for Lender Insurance approval; and

(iv) The claim and default record of the mortgagee derived by aggregating the claims and defaults of the entities participating in the merger, acquisition, or reorganization, for the 2-year period prior to the mortgagee's application for Lender Insurance approval, constitutes an acceptable rate of claims and defaults, as defined by this section.

(3) A mortgagee has an acceptable claim and default rate if its rate of claims and defaults is at or below 150 percent of the average rate for insured mortgages in the state(s) in which the mortgagee operates.

(c) *Reviews.* HUD will monitor a mortgagee's eligibility to participate in the Lender Insurance program on an ongoing basis.

(d) *Termination of approval.* (1) HUD may immediately terminate the mortgagee's approval to participate in the Lender Insurance program, in accordance with section 256(d) of the National Housing Act (12 U.S.C. 1715z–21(d)), if the mortgagee:

(i) Violates any of the requirements and procedures established by the Secretary for mortgagees approved to participate in HUD's Lender Insurance program, Direct Endorsement program, or the Title II Single Family mortgage insurance program; or

(ii) If HUD determines that other good cause exists.

(2) Such termination will be effective upon receipt of HUD's notice advising of the termination. Within 30 days after receiving HUD's notice of termination, a mortgagee may request an informal conference with the Deputy Assistant Secretary for Single Family Housing or designee. The conference will be conducted within 30 days after HUD receives a timely request for the conference. After the conference, the Deputy Assistant Secretary (or designee) may decide to affirm the termination action or to reinstate the mortgagee's Lender Insurance program approval. The decision will be communicated to the mortgagee in writing, will be deemed a final agency action,

and, pursuant to section 256(d) of the National Housing Act (12 U.S.C. 1715z–21(d)), is not subject to judicial review.

(3) Lender Insurance authority is automatically terminated for a mortgagee whose nationwide Direct Endorsement approval under § 203.3(d)(2) is terminated, without imposing any further requirement on the mortgagee to comply with this paragraph.

(4) Any termination instituted under this section is distinct from withdrawal of mortgagee approval by the Mortgagee Review Board under 24 CFR part 25.

(e) *Reinstatement.* A mortgagee whose Lender Insurance authority is terminated under this section may apply for reinstatement if the Lender Insurance authority for the mortgagee has been terminated for at least 6 months. In addition to addressing the criteria for Lender Insurance approval specified in paragraphs (a) and (b) of this section, the application for reinstatement must be accompanied by a corrective action plan addressing the issues resulting in the termination of the mortgagee's Lender Insurance authority, along with evidence that the mortgagee has implemented the corrective action plan. HUD may grant the mortgagee's application for reinstatement if the mortgagee's application is complete and HUD determines that the underlying causes for the termination have been satisfactorily remedied.

[62 FR 30226, June 2, 1997, as amended at 62 FR 65182, Dec. 10, 1997; 77 FR 3604, Jan. 25, 2012]

§ 203.5 Direct Endorsement process.

(a) *General.* Under the Direct Endorsement program, the Secretary does not review applications for mortgage insurance before the mortgage is executed or issue conditional or firm commitments, except to the extent required by § 203.3(b)(4), § 203.3(d)(1), or as determined by the Secretary. Under this program, the mortgagee determines that the proposed mortgage is eligible for insurance under the applicable program regulations, and submits the required documents to the Secretary in accordance with the procedures set forth in § 203.255. This subpart provides that certain functions shall be performed by the Secretary (or Commissioner), but the Secretary may specify that a Direct Endorsement mortgagee shall perform such an action without specific involvement or approval by the Secretary, subject to statutory limitations. In each case, the Direct Endorsement mortgagee's performance is subject to pre-endorsement and post-endorsement review by the Secretary under § 203.255 (c) and (e).

(b) *Eligible programs.* (1) All single family mortgages authorized for insurance under the National Housing Act must be originated through the Direct Endorsement program, except the following:

(i) Mortgages underwritten for insurance by mortgagees that have applied for participation in, and have been approved for, the Lender Insurance program;

(ii) Mortgages authorized under sections 203(n), 203(p), 213(d), 221(h), 221(i), 225, 233, 237, 809, or 810 of the National Housing Act, or any other insurance programs announced by FEDERAL REGISTER notice; or

(iii) As provided in § 203.1.

(2) The provision contained in § 221.55 of this chapter regarding deferred sales to displaced families is not available in the Direct Endorsement program.

(c) *Underwriter due diligence.* A Direct Endorsement mortgagee shall exercise the same level of care which it would exercise in obtaining and verifying information for a loan in which the mortgagee would be entirely dependent on the property as security to protect its investment. Mortgagee procedures that evidence such due diligence shall be incorporated as part of the quality control plan required under § 202.5(h) of this chapter. The Secretary shall publish guidelines for Direct Endorsement underwriting procedures in a handbook, which shall be provided to all mortgagees approved for the Direct Endorsement procedure. Compliance with these guidelines is deemed to be the minimum standard of due diligence in underwriting mortgages.

(d) *Mortgagor's income.* The mortgagee shall evaluate the mortgagor's credit characteristics, adequacy and stability of income to meet the periodic payments under the mortgage and all other obligations, and the adequacy of the mortgagor's available assets to close the transaction, and render an underwriting decision in accordance with applicable regulations, policies and procedures.

(e) *Appraisal.* (1) A mortgagee shall have the property appraised in accordance with such standards and requirements as the Secretary may prescribe. A mortgagee must select an appraiser whose name is on the FHA Appraiser Roster, in accordance with 24 CFR part 200, subpart G.

(2) The mortgagee shall not discriminate on the basis of race, color, religion, national origin, sex, age, or disability in the selection of an appraiser.

(3) A mortgagee and an appraiser must ensure that an appraisal and related documentation satisfy FHA appraisal requirements, and both bear responsibility for the quality of the appraisal in satisfying such requirements. A Direct Endorsement Mortgagee that submits, or causes to be submitted, an appraisal or related documentation that does not satisfy FHA requirements is subject to administrative sanction by the Mortgagee Review Board pursuant to parts 25 and 30 of this title.

[57 FR 58346, Dec. 9, 1992; 58 FR 13537, Mar. 12, 1993, as amended at 59 FR 50463, Oct. 3, 1994; 60 FR 42759, Aug. 16, 1995; 61 FR 36263, July 9, 1996; 62 FR 20088, Apr. 24, 1997; 62 FR 30226, June 2, 1997; 69 FR 43509, July 20, 2004; 77 FR 51469, Aug. 24, 2012]

§ 203.6 Lender Insurance process.

Under the Lender Insurance program, a mortgagee approved for the program conducts its own pre-insurance review, insures the mortgage, and agrees to indemnify HUD in accordance with § 203.255(f).

[62 FR 30226, June 2, 1997]

§ 203.7 Commitment process.

For single family mortgage programs that are not eligible for Direct Endorsement processing under § 203.5, or for Lender Insurance processing under § 203.6, the mortgagee must submit an application for mortgage insurance in a form prescribed by the Secretary prior to making the mortgage loan. If:

(a) A mortgage for a specified property has been accepted for insurance through issuance of a conditional commitment by the Secretary or a certificate of reasonable value by the Department of Veterans Affairs, and

(b) A specified mortgagor and all other proposed terms and conditions of the mortgage meet the eligibility requirements for insurance as determined by the Secretary, the Secretary shall approve the application for insurance by issuing a firm commitment setting forth the terms and conditions of insurance.

[57 FR 58346, Dec. 9, 1992; 58 FR 13537, Mar. 12, 1993, as amended at 62 FR 30226, June 2, 1997]

MISCELLANEOUS REGULATIONS

§203.9 Disclosure regarding interest due upon mortgage prepayment.

Each mortgagee with respect to a mortgage under this part shall at or before closing with respect to any such mortgage, provide the mortgagor with written notice in a form prescribed by the Commissioner describing any requirements the mortgagor must fulfill upon prepayment of the principal amount of the mortgage to prevent the accrual of any interest on the principal amount after the date of such prepayment. This paragraph shall apply to any mortgage executed after August 22, 1991, and before January 21, 2015.

[56 FR 18947, Apr. 24, 1991, as amended at 79 FR 50837, Aug. 26, 2014]

§203.10 Informed consumer choice for prospective FHA mortgagors.

(a) *Mortgagee to provide disclosure notice.* A mortgagee must provide a prospective FHA mortgagor with an informed consumer choice disclosure notice if, in the mortgagees's judgment, the prospective FHA mortgagor may qualify for similar conventional mortgage products offered by the mortgagee. The mortgagee should base this judgment on the mortgagee's initial assessment of the prospective FHA mortgagor's eligibility for a conventional mortgage product. If a mortgagee is unsure about a prospective FHA mortgagor's eligibility for a conventional mortgage product, the mortgagee should provide the prospective FHA mortgagor with an informed consumer choice disclosure notice.

(b) *Informed consumer choice disclosure notice*—(1) *Contents of notice.* The informed consumer choice disclosure notice must:

(i) Provide a one page generic analysis comparing the mortgage costs of an FHA-insured mortgage with the mortgage costs of similar conventional mortgage products offered by the mortgagee that the prospective FHA mortgagor may qualify for;

(ii) Provide information about when the requirement to pay FHA mortgage insurance premiums terminates; and

(iii) Meet the requirements of section 203(b)(2) of the National Housing Act (12 U.S.C. 1709(b)(2)).

(2) *Format of disclosure notice.* The informed consumer choice disclosure notice must be provided in a format prescribed by the Commissioner. HUD has prepared a model informed consumer choice disclosure notice that represents this format and that meets the requirements of section 203(b)(2) of the National Housing Act (12 U.S.C. 1709(b)(2)). The model informed consumer choice disclosure notice contains the minimum elements of an informed consumer choice disclosure notice. These elements must be included in a mortgagee's informed consumer choice disclosure notice. A mortgagee, however, may include additional elements in an informed consumer choice disclosure notice to better reflect the mortgagee's products or to provide information that the mortgagee believes is meaningful and helpful to the mortgagee's customers.

(3) *Availability of model disclosure notice.* HUD's model informed consumer choice disclosure notice is made available to FHA-approved mortgagees through Mortgagee Letter and is available to the public through the internet at HUD's web site at *http://www.hud.gov* or by contacting: Home Mortgage Insurance Division, Office of Insured Single Family Housing, U.S. Department of Housing and Urban Development, 451 Seventh Street, SW, Washington, DC 20410–8000; telephone (202) 708–2700 (this is not a toll-free number), or the nearest HUD Homeownership Center (Atlanta, GA (888) 696–4687; Denver, CO (800) 543–9378; Philadelphia, PA (800) 440–8647; or Santa Ana, CA (888) 827–

5605). Hearing- or speech-impaired individuals may access these numbers via TTY by calling the toll-free Federal Information Relay Service at (800) 877–8339.

(c) *Timing.* When required under paragraph (a) of this section, a mortgagee must provide an informed consumer choice disclosure notice to a prospective FHA mortgagor not later than three business days after the mortgagee receives the prospective FHA mortgagor's application.

(d) *Revision of notice.* A mortgagee should revise its informed consumer choice disclosure notice periodically to reflect prevailing market conditions. To ensure that the informed consumer choice disclosure notice reflects prevailing market conditions, a mortgagee must revise its informed consumer choice disclosure notice at least once annually.

(e) *Applicability.* This section applies to any application for mortgage insurance authorized under section 203(b) of the National Housing Act (12 U.S.C. 1709) that the mortgagee receives on or after September 2, 1999.

(f) *Definitions.* As used in this section:

Application means the submission of financial information in anticipation of a credit decision.

Conventional mortgage means conventional mortgage as used in section 305(a)(2) of the Federal Home Loan Mortgage Corporation Act (12 U.S.C. 1454(a)(2)) or section 302(b)(2) of the Federal National Mortgage Association Charter Act (12 U.S.C. 1717(b)(2)), as applicable.

Mortgagee means mortgagee as defined in § 202.2 of this chapter.

Prospective FHA mortgagor means a person who submits an application to a mortgagee to obtain mortgage insurance authorized under section 203(b) of the National Housing Act (12 U.S.C. 1709).

[64 FR 29765, June 2, 1999, as amended at 64 FR 34984, June 30, 1999]

§ 203.12 Mortgage insurance on proposed or new construction.

(a) *Applicability.* This section applies to an application for insurance of a mortgage on a one-to four-family dwelling, unless the mortgage will be secured by a dwelling that:

(1) Was completed more than one year before the date of the application for insurance or, under the Direct Endorsement Program, was completed more than one year before the date of the appraisal; or

(2) Is being sold to a second or subsequent purchaser.

(b) *Procedures.* (1) Applications for insurance to which this section applies will be processed in accordance with procedures prescribed by the Secretary. These procedures may only provide for endorsement for insurance of a mortgage covering a dwelling that is:

(i) Approved under the Direct Endorsement Program or the Lender Insurance Program; or

(ii) Located in a subdivision approved by the Rural Housing Service.

(2) The mortgagee must submit a signed Builder's Certification of Plans, Specifications and Site (Builder's Certification). The Builder's Certification must be in a form prescribed by the Secretary and must cover:

(i) Flood hazards;

(ii) Noise;

(iii) Explosive and flammable materials storage hazards;

(iv) Runway clear zones/clear zones;

(v) Toxic waste hazards;

(vi) Other foreseeable hazards or adverse conditions (i.e., rock formations, unstable soils or slopes, high ground water levels, inadequate surface drainage, springs, etc.) that may affect the health and safety of the occupants or the structural soundness of the improvements. The Builder's Certification must be provided to the appraiser for reference before the performance of an appraisal on the property.

(3) If a builder (or developer) intends to sell five or more properties in a subdivision, an Affirmative Fair Housing Marketing Plan (AFHMP) that meets the requirements of 24 CFR part 200, subpart M must be submitted and approved by HUD no later than the date of the first application for mortgage insurance in that subdivision. Thereafter, applications for insurance on other properties sold by the same builder (or developer) in the same subdivision may make reference to the existing previously approved AFHMP.

[64 FR 56110, Oct. 15, 1999]

§203.14 Builders' warranty.

Applications relating to proposed construction must be accompanied by an agreement in form satisfactory to the Secretary, executed by the seller or builder or such other person as the Secretary may require, and agreeing that in the event of any sale or conveyance of the dwelling, within a period of one year beginning with the date of initial occupancy, the seller, builder, or such other person will at the time of such sale or conveyance deliver to the purchaser or owner of such property a warranty in form satisfactory to the Secretary warranting that the dwelling is constructed in substantial conformity with the plans and specifications (including amendments thereof or changes and variations therein which have been approved in writing by the Secretary) on which the Secretary has based on the valuation of the dwelling. Such agreement must provide that upon the sale or conveyance of the dwelling and delivery of the warranty, the seller, builder or such other person will promptly furnish the Secretary with a conformed copy of the warranty establishing by the purchaser's receipt thereon that the original warranty has been delivered to the purchaser in accordance with this section.

[57 FR 58346, Dec. 9, 1992]

§203.15 Certification of appraisal amount.

An application with respect to insurance of mortgages must be accompanied by an agreement satisfactory to the Commissioner, executed by the seller, builder or such other person as may be required by the Commissioner, whereby the person agrees that before any sale of the dwelling, the person will deliver to the purchaser of the property a written statement, in a form satisfactory to the Commissioner, setting forth the amount of the appraised value of the property as determined by the Commissioner.

[58 FR 41001, July 30, 1993]

§203.16 Certificate and contract regarding use of dwelling for transient or hotel purposes.

Every application filed with respect to insurance of mortgages on a two-,

three-, or four-family dwelling, or a single-family dwelling which is one of a group of 5 or more single-family dwellings held by the same mortgagor, must be accompanied by a contract in form satisfactory to the Commissioner, signed by the proposed mortgagor covenanting and agreeing that so long as the proposed mortgage is insured by the Commissioner the mortgagor will not rent the housing or any part thereof covered by the mortgage for transient or hotel purposes, together with the mortgagor's certification under oath that the housing or any part thereof covered by the proposed mortgage will not be rented for transient or hotel purposes. For the purpose of this subchapter rental for transient or hotel purposes shall mean (a) rental for any period less than 30 days or (b) any rental if the occupants of the housing accommodations are provided customary hotel services such as room service for food and beverages, maid service, furnishing and laundering of linen, and bellboy service.

§203.16a Mortgagor and mortgagee requirement for maintaining flood insurance coverage.

(a) If the mortgage is to cover property improvements (dwelling and related structures/equipment essential to the value of the property and subject to flood damage) that:

(1) Are located in an area designated by the Federal Emergency Management Agency (FEMA) as a floodplain area having special flood hazards, or

(2) Are otherwise determined by the Commissioner to be subject to a flood hazard, and if flood insurance under the National Flood Insurance Program (NFIP) is available with respect to these property improvements, the mortgagor and mortgagee shall be obligated, by a special condition to be included in the mortgage commitment, to obtain and to maintain NFIP flood insurance coverage on the property improvements during such time as the mortgage is insured.

(b) No mortgage may be insured that covers property improvements located in an area that has been identified by FEMA as an area having special flood hazards, unless the community in

151

which the area is situated is participating in the National Flood Insurance Program and such insurance is obtained by the mortgagor. Such requirement for flood insurance shall be effective one year after the date of notification by FEMA to the chief executive officer of a flood prone community that such community has been identified as having special flood hazards.

(c) The flood insurance must be maintained during such time as the mortgage is insured in an amount at least equal to either the outstanding balance of the mortgage, less estimated land costs, or the maximum amount of the NFIP insurance available with respect to the property improvements, whichever is less.

[64 FR 56111, Oct. 15, 1999]

ELIGIBLE MORTGAGES

§ 203.17 Mortgage provisions.

(a) *Mortgage form.* (1) The term *mortgage* as used in this part, except § 203.43c, means a first lien as is commonly given to secure advances on, or the unpaid purchase price of, real estate under the laws of the jurisdiction where the property is located, and may refer both to a security instrument creating a lien, whether called a *mortgage*, *deed of trust*, *security deed* or another term used in a particular jurisdiction, as well as the credit instrument, or note, secured thereby.

(2)(i) The mortgage shall be in a form meeting the requirements of the Commissioner. The Commissioner may prescribe complete mortgage instruments. For each case in which the Commissioner does not prescribe complete mortgage instruments, the Commissioner

(A) Shall require specific language in the mortgage which shall be uniform for every mortgage, and

(B) May also prescribe the language or substance of additional provisions for all mortgages as well as the language or substance of additional provisions for use only in particular jurisdictions or for particular programs.

(ii) Each mortgage shall also contian any provisions necessary to create a valid and enforceable secured debt under the laws of the jurisdiction in which the property is located.

(b) *Mortgage multiples.* A mortgage shall involve a principal obligation in a multiple of $1.

(c) *Payments.* The mortgage shall:

(1) Come due on the first of the month.

(2) Contain complete amortization provisions satisfactory to the Secretary and an amortization period not in excess of the term of the mortgage.

(3) Provide for payments to principal and interest to begin not later than the first day of the month following 60 days from the date the mortgage is executed (or the date a construction mortgage is converted to a permanent mortgage, if applicable).

(d) *Maturity.* The mortgage shall have a term of not more than 30 years from the date of the beginning of amortization.

(e) *Property Standards.* The mortgage must be a first lien upon the property that conforms with property standards prescribed by the Commissioner.

(f) *Disbursement.* The entire principal amount of the mortgage must have been disbursed to the mortgagor or to his or her creditors for his or her account and with his or her consent.

[36 FR 24508, Dec. 22, 1971, as amended at 45 FR 29278, May 2, 1980; 48 FR 28804, June 23, 1983; 49 FR 21319, May 21, 1984; 53 FR 34281, Sept. 6, 1988; 54 FR 39525, Sept. 27, 1989; 57 FR 58347, Dec. 9, 1992; 61 FR 36263, July 9, 1996]

§ 203.18 Maximum mortgage amounts.

(a) *Mortgagors of principal or secondary residences.* The principal amount of the mortgage must not exceed the lesser of the following amounts that apply:

(1) The dollar amount limitation that applies for the area under section 203(b)(2)(A) of the National Housing Act including any increase in the dollar limitation under § 203.29, as announced in accordance with § 203.18(h);

(2)(i) The amount based on appraised value that is permitted by section 203(b)(10) of the National Housing Act, if that provision is in effect and applies to the mortgage; or

(ii) If section 203(b)(10) is not in effect or otherwise does not apply to the mortgage, the lesser of the amounts based on appraised value that are permitted by section 203(b)(2)(B) of the National Housing Act and paragraph (g) of this section;

(3) An amount equal to 85 percent of the appraised value if the mortgage covers a dwelling that is to be occupied as a secondary residence (as defined in paragraph (f)(2) of this section).

(b) *Veteran qualifications.* The special veteran terms provided in section 203(b)(2) of the National Housing Act shall apply only if the mortgagor submits one of the following certifications:

(1) A certification issued by the Secretary of Defense establishing that the veteran performed extra hazardous service while serving in the armed forces for a period of less than 90 days; or

(2) A Certificate of Eligibility from the Department of Veterans Affairs establishing that the person served 90 days or more on active duty in the armed forces (U.S. Army, Navy, Marine Corps, Air Force, Coast Guard, the Army Reserve, the Naval Reserve, the Marine Corps Reserve, the Air Force Reserve, the Coast Guard Reserve, the National Guard of the United States, or the Air National Guard of the United States); that he or she enlisted before September 8, 1980; and that he or she was discharged or released under conditions other than dishonorable (a copy of the veteran's discharge papers or Form DD–214 shall be submitted with the certificate); or

(3) A Certificate of Eligibility from the Department of Veterans Affairs establishing that the person:

(i)(A) Originally enlisted in a regular component of the armed forces after September 7, 1980; or entered on active duty after October 16, 1981, and he or she had not previously completed a period of active duty of at least 24 months or been discharged or released from active duty under 10 U.S.C. 1171; and

(B) Has completed, since enlistment or entering on active duty, either:

(1) Twenty-four months of continuous active duty, or the full period for which he or she was called or ordered to active duty, whichever is shorter; or

(2) Any other period of active duty if he or she was discharged or released

from duty under 10 U.S.C. 1171 or 1173; was discharged or released from duty for disability incurred or aggravated in the line of duty; or has a disability which the Department of Veterans Affairs has determined to be compensable under 38 U.S.C. chap. 11; and

(ii) Was discharged or released under conditions other than dishonorable (a copy of the veteran's discharge papers or Form DD–214 shall be submitted with the certification).

(c) *Eligible non-occupant mortgagors.* A mortgage may be executed by an eligible non-occupant mortgagor (as that term is defined in paragraph (f)(3) of this section) for up to an amount authorized for the appropriate loan type in paragraph (a) of this section except where a lesser amount is expressly provided for in this part.

(d) *Outlying area properties.* A mortgage covering a single family residence located in an area in which the Commissioner finds that it is not practicable to obtain conformity with many of the requirements essential to the insurance of mortgages in built-up, urban areas; or a mortgage covering a single family dwelling that is to be used as a farm home on a plot of land that is two and one-half or more acres in size and adjacent to an all-weather public road, may not exceed:

(1) In the case of a mortgagor who is to occupy the dwelling as a principal residence (as defined in paragraph (f)(1) of this section):

(i) 75 percent of the dollar limitation under (a)(1).

(ii) 97 percent of the appraised value of the property as of the date the mortgage is accepted for insurance, if:

(A) The Commissioner approved the dwelling for insurance before the beginning of construction; or

(B) Construction was completed more than one year before the date of the application for insurance; or

(C) The Secretary of Veterans Affairs approved the dwelling for guaranty, insurance, or direct loan before the beginning of construction.

(iii) If the property does not meet the requirements of paragraph (d)(1)(ii) of this section, 90 percent of the appraised value of the property as of the date the mortgage is accepted for insurance.

(2) In the case of a mortgagor who is to occupy the dwelling as a secondary residence (as defined in paragraph (f)(2) of this section):

(i) The amount permitted in paragraph (d)(1)(i) of this section, or

(ii) 85 percent of the appraised value of the property as of the date the mortgage is accepted for insurance.

(e) *Disaster victims.* A mortgage covering a single family dwelling, in an amount not in excess of the maximum dollar limitation specified in paragraph (a)(1) of this section (unless a higher maximum mortgage amount is authorized under § 203.29), and not in excess of the lesser of 100 percent of the appraised value of the property or the cost of acquisition as of the date the mortgage is accepted for insurance, shall be eligible for insurance if:

(1) The mortgage is executed by a mortgagor who is to occupy the dwelling as a principal residence (as defined in paragraph (f)(1) of this section);

(2) The mortgagor establishes that the home which he or she previously occupied as owner or tenant was destroyed or damaged to such an extent that reconstruction or replacement is required as a result of a flood, fire, hurricane, earthquake, storm, riot or civil disorder or other catastrophe which the President has determined to be a major disaster; and

(3) The application for insurance is filed within one year from the date of such presidential determination, or within such additional period of time as the period of federal assistance with respect to such disaster may be extended.

(f) *Definitions.* As used in this section:

(1) *Principal residence* means the dwelling where the mortgagor maintains (or will maintain) his or her permanent place of abode, and typically spends (or will spend) the majority of the calendar year. A person may have only one principal residence at any one time.

(2) Secondary residence means a dwelling: (i) Where the mortgagor maintains or will maintain a part-time place of abode and typically spends (or will spend) less than a majority of the calendar year; (ii) which is not a vacation home; and (iii) which the Commissioner has determined to be eligible for insurance in order to avoid undue hardship to the mortgagor. A person may have only one secondary residence at a time.

(3) *Eligible non-occupant mortgagor* means a mortgagor (or co-mortgagor, as appropriate) who is not to occupy the dwelling as a principal residence or a secondary residence and who is—

(i) A public entity, as provided in section 214 or 247 of the National Housing Act, or any other State or local government or agency thereof;

(ii) A private nonprofit or public entity, as provided in section 221(h) or 235(j) of the National Housing Act, or other private nonprofit organization that is exempt from taxation under section 501(c)(3) of the Internal Revenue Code of 1986 and intends to sell or lease the mortgaged property to low or moderate income persons, as determined by the Secretary;

(iii) An Indian tribe, as provided in section 248 of the National Housing Act;

(iv) A serviceperson who is unable to meet the occupancy requirement because of his or her duty assignment, as provided in section 216 of the National Housing Act or subsection (b)(4) or (f) of section 222 of the National Housing Act;

(v) A mortgagor or co-mortgagor under subsection 203(k) of the National Housing Act; or

(vi) A mortgagor who, pursuant to § 203.43(c) of this part, is refinancing an existing mortgage insured under the National Housing Act for not more than the outstanding balance of the existing mortgage, if the amount of the monthly payment due under the refinancing mortgage is less than the amount due under the existing mortgage for the month in which the refinancing mortgage is executed.

(4) *Appraised value* means the sum of:

(i) The lesser of sales price (with any adjustments required by the Secretary) or the amount set forth in the written statement required under § 203.15; and

(ii) Borrower-paid closing costs allowed under § 203.27(a)(1)–(3), except that closing costs do not apply if section 203(b)(10) of the National Housing Act is in effect and neither sales price nor closing costs apply for purposes of paragraph (g) of this section.

(5) *Undue hardship* means that affordable housing which meets the needs of the mortgagor is not available for lease, or within reasonable commuting distance from the mortgagor's home to his or her work place.

(6) *Vacation home* means a dwelling that is used primarily for recreational purposes and enjoyment, and that is not a primary or secondary residence.

(g) *Maximum principal obligation.* Except for mortgages meeting the requirements of §203.18(b), §203.18(e) or §203.50(f), and notwithstanding any other provision of this section, a mortgage may not involve a principal obligation in excess of 98.75 percent of the appraised value of the property (97.75 percent, in the case of a mortgage with an appraised value in excess of $50,000), plus the amount of the mortgage insurance premium paid at the time the mortgage is insured.

(h) *Notice of maximum mortgage amount.* A maximum mortgage amount based on the 1-family median house price for an area under paragraph (a)(1) of this section may be made effective by:

(1) Providing direct notice to affected mortgagees through an administrative issuance; or

(2) Publishing a notice in the FEDERAL REGISTER.

(i) *Energy efficient mortgages.* The principal amount of energy efficient mortgages may exceed the maximum amounts determined under paragraph (a)(1) of this section under conditions prescribed by the Secretary in accordance with section 106 of the Energy Policy Act of 1992.

[36 FR 24508, Dec. 22, 1971]

EDITORIAL NOTE: For FEDERAL REGISTER citations affecting §203.18, see the List of CFR Sections Affected, which appears in the Finding Aids section of the printed volume and at *www.govinfo.gov.*

§203.18a Solar energy system.

(a) The dollar limitation provided in §203.18(a) may be increased by up to 20 percent if such an increase is necessary to account for the increased cost of the residence due to the installation of a solar energy system.

(b) *Solar energy system* is defined as any addition, alteration, or improvement to an existing or new structure which is designed to utilize wind energy or solar energy either of the active type based on mechanically forced energy transfer or of the passive type based on convective, conductive, or radiant energy transfer or some combination of these types to reduce the energy requirements of that structure from other energy sources and which is in conformity with such criteria and standards as shall be prescribed by the Secretary in consultation with the Secretary of Energy.

[45 FR 51770, Aug. 5, 1980]

§203.18b Increased mortgage amount.

(a) If any party believes that a mortgage limit established by the Secretary under §203.18(a)(1) does not accurately reflect the median house prices in an area, the party may submit documentation in support of an alternative mortgage limit. For purposes of this section, an area (1) must be at least the size of a county, whether or not the area is located within a metropolitan statistical area, as established by the Office of Management and Budget; and (2) may be an area for which the mortgage limits established under §203.18(b)(1) apply.

(b)(1) The documentation referred to in paragraph (a) of this section must consist of sufficient housing sales price data for the entire geographic area for which the request is made to justify an alternative mortgage limit. The documentation should include a listing of actual sales prices in the area for all or nearly all new and existing 1-family homes and condominiums, over a period of time varies with sales volume, as follows:

(i) For 500 or more sales per month, a one-month reporting period;

(ii) For 250 through 499 sales per month, a two-month reporting period.

(iii) For less than 250 sales per month, a three-month reporting period.

The listing should contain a brief address for each property, its county location, its sale price, the month and year of its sale, and whether it is new or existing. In areas where the ratio of existing sales to new sales is three-to-one or greater, an increase in the mortgage limit may be based on 95 percent of the average of the new and the existing median sales prices. In these areas, the documentation referred to in this paragraph may also include separate median sales prices for both the new and existing homes.

(2) Requests for an increased mortgage limit based upon documentation of median house prices for the area should be sent to the appropriate HUD field office.

(c) In the case of an area where the Commissioner determines that the median one-family house price does not reasonably reflect the sales prices of newly constructed homes because of an existing stock whose value is static or declining, the Commissioner may give greater weight to the sales prices of new homes in determining median house price in such area. Without limiting the discretion of the Commissioner in fashioning appropriate methods of implementing the foregoing authority in particular circumstances based upon a demonstration of good cause satisfactory to the Commissioner, in areas where evidence satisfactory to the Commissioner indicates that existing home sales outnumber new home sales by three-to-one or better, the *median sales price* will be calculated as the greater of (1) the average of the median sales price for new and existing homes, and (2) the composite median price of all sales.

(Approved by the Office of Management and Budget under control number 2502–0302)

[45 FR 76377, Nov. 18, 1980, as amended at 47 FR 917, Jan. 7, 1982; 49 FR 12697, Mar. 30, 1984; 49 FR 14338, Apr. 11, 1984; 53 FR 8880, Mar. 18, 1988; 56 FR 18947, Apr. 24, 1991; 58 FR 41002, July 30, 1993; 59 FR 13882, Mar. 24, 1994; 60 FR 16033, Mar. 28, 1995]

§ 203.18c One-time or up-front mortgage insurance premium excluded from limitations on maximum mortgage amounts.

After determining any maximum insurable mortgage amount under the provisions of this subpart, the maximum insurable amount of any mortgage may be increased by the amount of any one-time or up-front mortgage insurance premium that will be financed as part of the mortgage.

[57 FR 15211, Apr. 24, 1992]

§ 203.18d Minimum principal loan amount.

A mortgagee may not require, as a condition of providing a loan secured by a mortgage insured under this part, that the principal amount of the mortgage exceed a minimum amount established by the mortgagee.

[53 FR 8880, Mar. 18, 1988]

§ 203.19 Qualified mortgage.

(a) *Definitions.* As used in this section:

(1) *Average prime offer rate* means an annual percentage rate that is derived from average interest rates, points, and other loan pricing terms currently offered to mortgagors by a representative sample of mortgagees for mortgage transactions that have low-risk pricing characteristics as published by the Consumer Financial Protection Bureau (CFPB) from time to time in accordance with the CFPB's regulations at 12 CFR 1026.35, pertaining to prohibited acts or practices in connection with higher-priced mortgage loans.

(2) *Annual percentage rate* is the measure of the cost of credit, expressed as a yearly rate, that relates the amount and timing of value received by the mortgagor to the amount and timing of payments made and is the rate required to be disclosed by the mortgagee under 12 CFR 1026.18, pertaining to disclosure of finance charges for mortgages.

(3) *Points and fees* has the meaning given to "points and fees" in 12 CFR 1026.32(b)(1) as of January 10, 2014. Any changes made by the CFPB to the points and fees definition may be adopted by HUD through publication of a notice and after providing FHA-approved mortgagees with time, as may be determined necessary, to implement.

(b) *Qualified mortgage.* (1) *Limit.* For a single family mortgage to be insured under title II of the National Housing Act (12 U.S.C. 1701 *et seq.*), except for mortgages for manufactured housing and mortgages under paragraph (c) of this section, the total points and fees payable in connection with a loan used to secure a dwelling shall not exceed the CFPB's limit on points and fees for qualified mortgage in its regulations at

12 CFR 1026.43(e)(3) as of January 10, 2014. Any changes made by the CFPB to the limit on points and fees may be adopted by HUD through publication of a notice and after providing FHA-approved mortgagees with time, as may be determined necessary, to implement.

(2) *Rebuttable presumption qualified mortgage.* (i) A single family mortgage insured under title II of the National Housing Act (12 U.S.C. 1701 *et seq.*), except for mortgages for manufactured housing and mortgages under paragraph (c) of this section, that has an annual percentage rate that exceeds the average prime offer rate for a comparable mortgage, as of the date the interest rate is set, by more than the combined annual mortgage insurance premium and 1.15 percentage points for a first-lien mortgage is a rebuttable presumption qualified mortgage that is presumed to comply with the ability to repay requirements in 15 U.S.C. 1639c(a).

(ii) To rebut the presumption of compliance, it must be proven that the mortgage exceeded the points and fees limit in paragraph (b)(1) of this section or that, despite the mortgage having been endorsed for insurance under the National Housing Act, the mortgagee did not make a reasonable and good-faith determination of the mortgagor's repayment ability at the time of consummation, by failing to evaluate the mortgagor's income, credit, and assets in accordance with HUD underwriting requirements.

(3) *Safe harbor qualified mortgage.* (i) A mortgage for manufactured housing that is insured under Title II of the National Housing Act (12 U.S.C. 1701 *et seq.*) is a safe harbor qualified mortgage that meets the ability to repay requirements in 15 U.S.C. 1639c(a); and

(ii) A single family mortgage insured under title II of the National Housing Act (12 U.S.C. 1701 *et seq.*), except for mortgages under paragraph (c) of this section, that has an annual percentage rate that does not exceed the average prime offer rate for a comparable mortgage, as of the date the interest rate is set, by more than the combined annual mortgage insurance premium and 1.15 percentage points for a first-lien mortgage is a safe harbor qualified mort-

gage that meets the ability to repay requirements in 15 U.S.C. 1639c(a).

(4) *Effect of indemnification on qualified mortgage status.* An indemnification demand or resolution of a demand that relates to whether the loan satisfied relevant eligibility and underwriting requirements at the time of consummation may result from facts that could allow a change to qualified mortgage status, but the existence of an indemnification does not per se remove qualified mortgage status.

(c) *Exempted transactions.* The following transactions are exempted from the requirements in paragraph (b) of this section:

(1) Home Equity Conversion Mortgages under section 255 of the National Housing Act (12 U.S.C. 1715z–20); and

(2) Mortgage transactions exempted by the CFPB in its regulations at 12 CFR 1026.43(a)(3) as of January 10, 2014. Any changes made by CFPB to the list of exempted transactions may be adopted by HUD through publication of a notice and after providing FHA-approved mortgagees with time, as may be determined necessary, to implement.

(d) *Ability to make adjustments to this section by notice.* The FHA Commissioner may make adjustments to this section, including the calculations of fees or the list of transactions excluded from compliance with the requirements of this section as the Commissioner determines necessary for purposes of meeting FHA's mission, after solicitation and consideration of public comments.

[78 FR 75237, Dec. 11, 2013]

§ 203.20 **Agreed interest rate.**

(a) The mortgage shall bear interest at the rate agreed upon by the mortgagee and the mortgagor.

(b) Interest shall be payable in monthly installments on the principal amount of the mortgage outstanding on the due date of each installment.

[36 FR 24508, Dec. 22, 1971, as amended at 49 FR 19457, May 8, 1984]

§ 203.21 **Amortization provisions.**

The mortgage must contain complete amortization provisions satisfactory to the Commissioner, requiring monthly payments by the mortgagor not in excess of his reasonable ability to pay as determined by the Commissioner. The sum of the principal and interest payments in each month shall be substantially the same.

§ 203.22 **Payment of insurance premiums or charges; prepayment privilege.**

(a) *Payment of periodic insurance premiums or charges.* Except with respect to mortgages for which a one-time mortgage insurance premium is paid pursuant to § 203.280, the mortgage may provide for monthly payments by the mortgagor to the mortgagee of an amount equal to one-twelfth of the annual mortgage insurance premium payable by the mortgagee to the Commissioner. Such payments continue only so long as the contract of insurance shall remain in effect or for such shorter period as mortgage insurance premiums are payable by the mortgagee to the Commissioner.

(b) *Prepayment privilege.* The mortgage shall contain a provision permitting the mortgagor to prepay the mortgage in whole or in part at any time and in any amount. The mortgage shall not provide for the payment of any charge on account of such prepayment.

[36 FR 24508, Dec. 22, 1971, as amended at 37 FR 8661, Apr. 29, 1972; 48 FR 28804, June 23, 1983; 50 FR 25914, June 24, 1985; 61 FR 36263, July 9, 1996; 79 FR 50837, Aug. 26, 2014]

§ 203.23 **Mortgagor's payments to include other charges.**

(a) The mortgage shall provide for such equal monthly payments by the mortgagor to the mortgagee as will amortize:

(1) The ground rents, if any;

(2) The estimated amount of all taxes;

(3) Special assessments, if any;

(4) Flood insurance premiums, if flood insurance is required by the Commissioner; and

(5) Fire and other hazard insurance premiums, if any. The mortgage shall further provide that such payments shall be held by the mortgagee in a manner satisfactory to the Commissioner for the purpose of paying such ground rents, taxes, assessments, and insurance premiums before the same become delinquent, for the benefit and account of the mortgagor. The mortgage must also make provisions for adjustments in case the estimated amount of such taxes, assessments, and insurance premiums shall prove to be more, or less, than the actual amount thereof so paid by the mortgagor. Such payments shall be held in an escrow subject to § 203.550.

(b) The mortgagor shall not be required to pay premiums for fire or other hazard insurance which protects only the interests of the mortgagee, or for life or disability income insurance, or fees charged for obtaining information necessary for the payment of property taxes. The foregoing does not apply to charges made or penalties exacted by the taxing authority, except that a penalty assessed or interest charged by a taxing authority for failure to timely pay taxes or assessments shall not be charged by the mortgagee to the mortgagor if the mortgagee had sufficient funds in escrow for the account of the mortgagor to pay such taxes or assessments prior to the date on which penalty or interest charges are imposed.

(c) Mortgages involving a principal obligation not in excess of $9,000 may contain a provision requiring the mortgagor to pay to the mortgagee an annual service charge at such rate as may be agreed upon between the mortgagee and the mortgagor, but in no case shall such service charge exceed one-half of one percent per annum. Any such service charge shall be payable in monthly installments on the principal then outstanding. The provisions of this paragraph shall not apply to mortgages endorsed for insurance pursuant to applications received by the Commissioner on or after July 17, 1961.

[36 FR 24508, Dec. 22, 1971, as amended at 37 FR 25231, Nov. 29, 1972; 41 FR 47934, Nov. 10, 1976; 59 FR 53901, Oct. 26, 1994]

§ 203.24 **Application of payments.**

(a) All monthly payments to be made by the mortgagor to the mortgagee shall be added together and the aggregate amount thereof shall be paid by the mortgagor each month in a single payment. The mortgagee shall apply the same to the following items in the order set forth:

(1) Premium charges under the contract of insurance (other than a one-time or up-front mortgage insurance premium paid in accordance with §§203.280, 203.284 and 203.285), charges for ground rents, taxes, special assessments, flood insurance premiums, if required, and fire and other hazard insurance premiums;

(2) Interest on the mortgage;

(3) Amortization of the principal of the mortgage; and

(4) Late charges, if permitted under the terms of the mortgage and subject to such conditions as the Commissioner may prescribe.

(b) Any deficiency in the amount of any such aggregate monthly payment shall, unless made good by the mortgagor prior to, or on, the due date of the next such payment, constitute an event of default under the mortgage.

[36 FR 24508, Dec. 22, 1971, as amended at 37 FR 25231, Nov. 29, 1972; 50 FR 25914, June 24, 1985; 61 FR 36263, July 9, 1996]

§203.25 Late charge.

The mortgage may provide for the collection by the mortgagee of a late charge, not to exceed four per cent of the amount of each payment more than 15 days in arrears, to cover servicing and other costs attributable to the receipt of payments from mortgagors after the date upon which payment is due.

[41 FR 49734, Nov. 10, 1976]

§203.26 Mortgagor's payments when mortgage is executed.

(a) The mortgagor must pay to the mortgagee, upon execution of the mortgage, a sum that will be sufficient to pay the ground rents, if any, the estimated taxes, special assessments, flood insurance premiums, if required, and fire and other hazard insurance premiums for the period beginning on the last date on which each such charge would have been paid under the normal lending practices of the lender and local custom (if each such date constitutes prudent lending practice), and ending on the due date of the first full installment payment under the mortgage, plus an amount sufficient to pay the mortgage insurance premium from the date of closing the loan to the

date of the first monthly payment under the mortgage or, where applicable, the one-time mortgage insurance premium payable pursuant to §203.280.

(b) The mortgagee may also collect from the mortgagor a sum not exceeding one-sixth of the estimated total amount of such taxes, special assessments, insurance premiums and other charges to be paid during the ensuing 12-month period.

[41 FR 49734, Nov. 10, 1976, as amended at 48 FR 28804, June 23, 1983]

§203.27 Charges, fees or discounts.

(a) The mortgagee may collect from the mortgagor the following charges, fees or discounts:

(1) [Reserved]

(2) A charge to compensate the mortgagee for expenses incurred in originating and closing the loan, *provided* that the Commissioner may establish limitations on the amount of any such charge.

(3) Reasonable and customary amounts, but not more than the amount actually paid by the mortgagee, for any of the following items:

(i) Recording fees and recording taxes or other charges incident to recordation;

(ii) Credit Report;

(iii) Survey, if required by mortgagee or mortgagor;

(iv) Title examination; title insurance, if any;

(v) Fees paid to an appraiser or inspector approved by the Commissioner for the appraisal and inspection, if required, of the property. Notwithstanding any limitations in this paragraph (a)(3) if the mortgagee is permitted by applicable regulations to use the services of staff appraisers and inspectors for processing mortgages, and does so, the mortgagee may collect from the mortgagor the reasonable and customary amounts for such appraisals and inspections.

(vi) Such other reasonable and customary charges as may be authorized by the Commissioner.

(4) Reasonable and customary charges in the nature of discounts.

(5) Interest from the date of closing or the date on which the mortgagee disburses the mortgage proceeds to the

account of the mortgagor or the mortgagor's creditors, whichever is later, to the date of the beginning of amortization.

(b)–(c) [Reserved]

(d) Before the insurance of any mortgage, the mortgagee shall furnish to the Secretary a signed statement in a form satisfactory to the Secretary listing any charge, fee or discount collected by the mortgagee from the mortgagor. All charges, fees or discounts are subject to review by the Secretary both before and after endorsement under § 203.255.

(e) Nothing in this section will be construed as prohibiting the mortgagor from dealing through a broker who does not represent the mortgagee, if he prefers to do so, and paying such compensation as is satisfactory to the mortgagor in order to obtain mortgage financing.

[36 FR 24508, Dec. 22, 1971, as amended at 43 FR 19846, May 9, 1978; 45 FR 30602, May 8, 1980; 45 FR 33966, May 21, 1980; 47 FR 29525, July 7, 1982; 48 FR 11940, Mar. 22, 1983; 48 FR 28804, June 23, 1983; 49 FR 19457, May 8, 1984; 57 FR 58347, Dec. 9, 1992; 58 FR 13537, Mar. 12, 1993; 73 FR 68239, Nov. 17, 2008]

§ 203.28 Economic soundness of projects.

The mortgage must be executed with respect to a project which, in the opinion of the Commissioner, is economically sound, except that this section shall not apply in each of the following instances:

(a) To a mortgage of the character described in § 203.18(d) and with respect to such a mortgage, the Commissioner shall determine that the mortgage is an acceptable risk giving consideration to the need for providing adequate housing for families of low and moderate income, particularly in suburban and outlying areas or small communities.

(b) To a mortgage of the character described in § 203.18 (e).

(c) To a mortgage of the character described in § 203.43a.

(d) To a mortgage in a federally impacted area described in § 203.43e.

(e) To a rehabilitation loan of the character described in § 203.50.

[36 FR 24508, Dec. 22, 1971, as amended at 42 FR 57434, Nov. 2, 1977; 45 FR 33966, May 21, 1980; 53 FR 8880, Mar. 18, 1988]

§ 203.29 Eligible mortgages in Alaska, Guam, Hawaii, or the Virgin Islands.

(a) *When is an increased mortgage limit permitted for these areas?* For Alaska, Guam, Hawaii or the Virgin Islands, the Commissioner may increase the maximum mortgage amount permitted by section 203(b)(2)(A) of the National Housing Act when authorized by section 214 of that Act, through the procedures described in § 203.18(h).

(b) If a party believes that the otherwise applicable mortgage limit needs to be increased to reflect the extent to which high costs make it infeasible to construct dwellings without sacrificing sound standards of construction, design or livability, the party may submit documentation in support of an alternative mortgage limit. This documentation should include actual or estimated costs of such items as design, construction, materials, and labor. In addition, actual sales prices of new homes may be submitted, together with any other documentation requested by the Commissioner. Requests for alternative mortgage limits, together with supporting documentation should be sent to the appropriate HUD field office. The field office will forward the request and supporting material, with the field office's recommendation, to the Commissioner for determination.

(c) If the Alaska Housing Authority, or the Government of Guam, Hawaii or the Virgin Islands or any agency or instrumentality of those entities, is the mortgagor or the mortgagee, or the mortgagor is regulated or restricted as to rents or sales, charges, capital structure, rate of return, and methods of operation to such an extent and in such manner as the Commissioner determines advisable to provide reasonable rental and sales prices and a reasonable return on the investment, any mortgage otherwise eligible for insurance under this subpart may be insured:

(1) In any case where the Alaska Housing Authority, or the government of Guam, Hawaii, the Virgin Islands, or any agency or instrumentality of those entities, is the mortgagor, without regard to any requirement that the mortgagor occupy the dwelling as a principal residence or a secondary residence (as these terms are defined in §203.18(f)), or meet loan-to-value or comparable limitations based on the failure of the mortgagor to meet this occupancy requirement;

(2) Without regard to any requirement that the mortgagor has paid on account of the property a prescribed percentage of the appraised value of the property; or

(3) Without regard to any requirement that the mortgagor certify that the mortgaged property is free and clear of all liens other than the mortgage offered for insurance and that there will not be any unpaid obligations contracted in connection with the mortgage transaction or the purchase of the mortgaged property.

(d) The provisions of §203.28 requiring economic soundness shall not be applicable to mortgages covering property located in Alaska, in Guam, in Hawaii, or in the Virgin Islands, but the Commissioner shall find that the property or project is an acceptable risk, giving consideration to the acute housing shortage in Alaska, Guam, Hawaii, or the Virgin Islands.

(Approved by the Office of Management and Budget under control number 2502–0302)

[36 FR 24508, Dec. 22, 1971, as amended at 49 FR 14338, Apr. 11, 1984; 55 FR 34804, Aug. 24, 1990; 56 FR 18948, Apr. 24, 1991; 64 FR 14569, Mar. 25, 1999]

§203.30 Certificate of nondiscrimination by the mortgagor.

The mortgagor shall certify to the Commissioner as to each of the following points:

(a) That neither he, nor anyone authorized to act for him, will refuse to sell or rent, after the making of a bonafide offer, or refuse to negotiate for the sale or rental of, or otherwise make unavailable or deny the dwelling or property covered by the mortgage to any person because of race, color, religion, national origin, familial status (except as provided by law), or handicap.

(b) That any restrictive covenant on such property relating to race, color, religion, or national origin is recognized as being illegal and void and is hereby specifically disclaimed.

(c) That civil action for preventative relief may be brought by the Attorney General in any appropriate U.S. District Court against any person responsible for a violation of this certification.

(d) That buildings having four (4) or more units, which were built for first occupancy after March 13, 1991, were constructed in compliance with the Fair Housing Act new construction requirements in 24 CFR 100.205.

[36 FR 24508, Dec. 22, 1971, as amended at 57 FR 58347, Dec. 9, 1992; 61 FR 36264, July 9, 1996]

§203.31 Mortgagor of a principal residence in military service cases.

(a) A mortgage that is otherwise eligible for insurance under any of the provisions of this part may be insured without regard to any requirement contained in this part that the mortgagor occupy the dwelling as a principal residence (as defined in §203.18(f)(1)) at the time of insurance, or that the mortgagor meet loan-to-value or comparable limitations based on the failure of the mortgagor to meet an occupancy requirement, if:

(1) The Commissioner is satisfied that the inability of the mortgagor to meet the occupancy requirement is by reason of his or her entry into military service after the filing of an application for insurance; and

(2) The mortgagor expresses an intent (in such form as the Commissioner may prescribe), to meet the occupancy requirement upon his or her discharge from the service.

(b) A serviceperson will also be considered to meet the occupancy requirement referred to in paragraph (a) of this section for mortgage insurance purposes, if the following conditions are satisfied:

(1) The serviceperson and his or her family expect to meet the occupancy requirement referred to in paragraph (a) of this section for two or more years. The Commissioner may shorten

this period to one year, if (i) the serviceperson's family will occupy the property for at least one year and (ii) the serviceperson is assigned to a combat zone or other hazardous duty area where the family cannot accompany him or her; and

(2) The property is located in an area in which the prospects of resale are reasonable.

(Approved by the Office of Management and Budget under control number 2502–0059)

[55 FR 34804, Aug. 24, 1990]

ELIGIBLE MORTGAGORS

§ 203.32 Mortgage lien.

(a) Except as otherwise provided in this section, a mortgagor must establish that, after the mortgage offered for insurance has been recorded, the mortgaged property will be free and clear of all liens other than such mortgage, and that there will not be outstanding any other unpaid obligations contracted in connection with the mortgage transaction or the purchase of the mortgaged property, except obligations that are secured by property or collateral owned by the mortgagor independently of the mortgaged property.

(b) With prior approval of the Secretary, the mortgaged property may be subject to a secondary mortgage or loan made or insured, or other secondary lien held, by a Federal, State, or local government agency or instrumentality, or an entity designated in the homeownership plan submitted by an applicant for an implementation grant under the Homeownership and Opportunity for People Everywhere (HOPE) program, or an eligible nonprofit organization as defined in § 203.41(a)(5) of this part, provided that the required monthly payments under the insured mortgage and the secondary mortgage or lien shall not exceed the mortgagor's reasonable ability to pay as determined by the Secretary.

(c) With the prior approval of the Secretary, the mortgaged property may be subject to a second mortgage held by a mortgagee not described in paragraph (b) of this section. Unless the mortgage is for the purpose described in paragraph (d) of this section,

it shall meet the following requirements:

(1) The required monthly payments under the insured mortgage and the second mortgage shall not exceed the mortgagor's reasonable ability to pay, as determined by the Commissioner;

(2) Periodic payments, if any, shall be collected monthly and be substantially the same;

(3) The sum of the principal amount of the insured mortgage and the second mortgage shall not exceed the loan-to-value limitation applicable to the insured mortgage, and shall not exceed the maximum mortgage limit for the area;

(4) The repayment terms shall not provide for a balloon payment before ten years, or for such other term as the Commissioner may approve, except that the mortgage may become due and payable on sale or refinancing of the secured property covered by the insured mortgage; and

(5) The mortgage shall contain a provision permitting the mortgagor to prepay the mortgage in whole or in part at any time, and shall not provide for the payment of any charge on account of such prepayment.

(d)(1) With the prior approval of the Commissioner, the mortgaged property may be subject to a junior (second or third) mortgage securing the repayment of funds advanced to reduce the mortgagor's monthly payments on the insured mortgage following the date it is insured, if the junior mortgage meets the following requirements:

(i) The junior mortgage shall not provide for any payment of principal or interest until the property securing the junior mortgage is sold or the insured mortgage is refinanced, at which time the junior mortgage shall become due and payable;

(ii) The total amount of repayments under the junior mortgage shall not exceed the least of:

(A) One-half of the mortgagor's equity interest in the property at the time of sale or refinancing;

(B) Three times the amount of funds advanced to effect the interest rate buy-down; or

(C) The sum of the original loan amount plus the total accrued interest on the junior mortgage at the time of repayment; and

(iii) The junior mortgage shall contain a provision permitting the mortgagor to prepay the mortgage in whole or in part at any time, and shall not provide for the payment of any charge on account of such prepayment. Any full or partial prepayment will not be recoverable by the mortgagor if, by application of paragraph (d)(1)(ii) on sale or refinancing of the property, a lesser amount than the amount prepaid would have been due.

(2) The sum of the principal amount of the insured mortgage, any second mortgage made under paragraph (b) or (c) of this section, and the mortgage securing the repayment of funds advanced to reduce the borrower's monthly payments (whether a second or third mortgage) may exceed the loan-to-value limitation applicable to the insured mortgage, but such sum may not exceed the maximum mortgage limit for the area.

[45 FR 19223, Mar. 25, 1980, as amended at 50 FR 20906, May 21, 1985; 56 FR 4477, Feb. 4, 1991; 58 FR 42647, Aug. 11, 1993]

§203.33 Relationship of income to mortgage payments.

(a) Adequacy of mortgagor's gross income. A mortgagor must establish, to the satisfaction of the Secretary, that his or her gross income is and will be adequate to meet (1) the periodic payments required by the mortgage submitted for insurance and (2) other long-term obligations.

(b) Determinations of adequacy of mortgagor income under this section shall be made in a uniform manner without regard to race, color, religion, sex, national origin, familial status, handicap, marital status, actual or perceived sexual orientation, gender identity, source of income of the mortgagor, or location of the property.

[37 FR 16390, Aug. 12, 1972, as amended at 54 FR 38649, Sept. 20, 1989; 59 FR 59648, Nov. 18, 1994; 77 FR 5675, Feb. 3, 2012]

§203.34 Credit standing.

A mortgagor must have a general credit standing satisfactory to the Commissioner.

§203.35 Disclosure and verification of Social Security and Employer Identification Numbers.

To be eligible for mortgage insurance under this part, the mortgagor must meet the requirements for the disclosure and verification of Social Security and Employer Identification Numbers, as provided by part 200, subpart U, of this chapter.

(Approved by the Office of Management and Budget under control numbers 2502–0059, 2502–0159, and 2502–0268)

[54 FR 39693, Sept. 27, 1989]

§203.36 [Reserved]

ELIGIBLE PROPERTIES

§203.37 Nature of title to realty.

A mortgage, to be eligible for insurance, must be on real estate held in fee simple, or on leasehold under a lease for not less than 99 years which is renewable, or under a lease having a period of not less than 10 years to run beyond the maturity date of the mortgage.

[49 FR 21319, May 21, 1984]

§203.37a Sale of property.

(a) Sale by owner of record—(1) Owner of record requirement. To be eligible for a mortgage insured by FHA, the property must be purchased from the owner of record and the transaction may not involve any sale or assignment of the sales contract.

(2) Supporting documentation. The mortgagee shall obtain documentation verifying that the seller is the owner of record and must submit this documentation to HUD as part of the application for mortgage insurance, in accordance with §203.255(b)(12). This documentation may include, but is not limited to, a property sales history report, a copy of the recorded deed from the seller, or other documentation (such as a copy of a property tax bill, title commitment, or binder) demonstrating the seller's ownership.

(b) Time restrictions on re-sales—(1) General. The eligibility of a property for a mortgage insured by FHA is dependent on the time that has elapsed between the date the seller acquired the property (based upon the date of settlement) and the date of execution of the sales contract that will result in the FHA mortgage insurance (the re-sale date). The mortgagee shall obtain documentation verifying compliance with the time restrictions described in this paragraph and must submit this documentation to HUD as part of the application for mortgage insurance, in accordance with § 203.255(b).

(2) *Re-sales occurring 90 days or less following acquisition.* If the re-sale date is 90 days or less following the date of acquisition by the seller, the property is not eligible for a mortgage to be insured by FHA.

(3) *Re-sales occurring between 91 days and 180 days following acquisition.* (i) If the re-sale date is between 91 days and 180 days following acquisition by the seller, the property is generally eligible for a mortgage insured by FHA.

(ii) However, HUD will require that the mortgagee obtain additional documentation if the re-sale price is 100 percent over the purchase price. Such documentation must include an appraisal from another appraiser. The mortgagee may also document its loan file to support the increased value by establishing that the increased value results from the rehabilitation of the property.

(iii) HUD may revise the level at which additional documentation is required under § 203.37a(b)(3) at 50 to 150 percent over the original purchase price. HUD will revise this level by FEDERAL REGISTER notice with a 30 day delayed effective date.

(4) *Authority to address property flipping for re-sales occurring between 91 days and 12 months following acquisition.* (i) If the re-sale date is more than 90 days after the date of acquisition by the seller, but before the end of the twelfth month after the date of acquisition, the property is eligible for a mortgage to be insured by FHA.

(ii) However, HUD may require that the lender provide additional documentation to support the re-sale value of the property if the re-sale price is 5 percent or greater than the lowest sales price of the property during the preceding 12 months (as evidenced by the contract of sale). At HUD's discretion, such documentation must include, but is not limited to, an appraisal from another appraiser. HUD

may exclude re-sales of less than a specific dollar amount from the additional value documentation requirements.

(iii) If the additional value documentation supports a value of the property that is more than 5 percent lower than the value supported by the first appraisal, the lower value will be used to calculate the maximum mortgage amount under § 203.18. Otherwise, the value supported by the first appraisal will be used to calculate the maximum mortgage amount.

(iv) HUD will announce its determination to require additional value documentation through issuance of a FEDERAL REGISTER notice. The requirement for additional value documentation may be established either on a nationwide or regional basis. Further, the FEDERAL REGISTER notice will specify the percentage increase in the re-sale price that will trigger the need for additional documentation, and will specify the acceptable types of documentation. The FEDERAL REGISTER notice may also exclude re-sales of less than a specific dollar amount from the additional value documentation requirements. Any such FEDERAL REGISTER notice, and any subsequent revisions, will be issued at least thirty days before taking effect.

(v) The level at which additional documentation is required under § 203.37a(b)(4) shall supersede that under § 203.37a(b)(3).

(5) *Re-sales occurring more than 12 months following acquisition.* If the re-sale date is more than 12 months following the date of acquisition by the seller, the property is eligible for a mortgage insured by FHA.

(c) *Exceptions to the time restrictions on sales.* The time restrictions on sales described in paragraph (b) of this section do not apply to:

(1) Sales by HUD of Real Estate-Owned (REO) properties under 24 CFR part 291 and of single family assets in revitalization areas pursuant to section 204 of the National Housing Act (12 U.S.C. 1710);

(2) Sales by another agency of the United States Government of REO single family properties pursuant to programs operated by these agencies;

(3) Sales of properties by nonprofit organizations approved to purchase

HUD REO single family properties at a discount with resale restrictions;

(4) Sales of properties that were acquired by the sellers by inheritance;

(5) Sales of properties purchased by an employer or relocation agency in connection with the relocation of an employee;

(6) Sales of properties by state- and federally-chartered financial institutions and government-sponsored enterprises (GSEs);

(7) Sales of properties by local and state government agencies; and

(8) Only upon announcement by HUD through issuance of a notice, sales of properties located in areas designated by the President as federal disaster areas. The notice will specify how long the exception will be in effect.

(d) *Sanctions and indemnification.* Failure of a mortgagee to comply with the requirements of this section may result in HUD requesting indemnification of the mortgage loan, or seeking other appropriate remedies under 24 CFR part 25.

[68 FR 23375, May 1, 2003, as amended at 69 FR 77116, Dec. 23, 2004; 71 FR 33142, June 7, 2006]

§203.38   Location of dwelling.

At the time a mortgage is insured there must be located on the mortgaged property one or more dwellings designed principally for residential use for not more than four families.

[61 FR 36264, July 9, 1996]

§203.39   Standards for buildings.

The buildings on the mortgaged property must conform with the standards prescribed by the Commissioner.

§203.40   Location of property.

The mortgaged property shall be located within the United States, Puerto Rico, Guam, the Virgin Islands, the Commonwealth of the Northern Mariana Islands, and American Samoa. The mortgaged property, if otherwise acceptable to the Commissioner, may be located in any community where the housing standards meet the requirements of the Commissioner.

[49 FR 12697, Mar. 30, 1984, as amended at 61 FR 36264, July 9, 1996]

§203.41   Free assumability; exceptions.

(a) *Definitions.* As used in this section:

(1) *Low- or moderate-income housing* means housing which is designed to be affordable, taking into account available financing, to individuals or families whose household income does not exceed 115 percent of the median income for the area, as determined by the Secretary with adjustments for smaller and larger families. The Secretary may approve a higher percentage up to 140 percent.

(2) *Eligible governmental or nonprofit program* means a program operated pursuant to a program established by Federal law, operated by a State or local government, or operated by an eligible nonprofit organization, if the program is designed to assist the purchase of low-or moderate-income housing including rental housing.

(3) *Legal restrictions on conveyance* means any provision in any legal instrument, law or regulation applicable to the mortgagor or the mortgaged property, including but not limited to a lease, deed, sales contract, declaration of covenants, declaration of condominium, option, right of first refusal, will, or trust agreement, that attempts to cause a conveyance (including a lease) made by the mortgagor to:

(i) Be void or voidable by a third party;

(ii) Be the basis of contractual liability of the mortgagor for breach of an agreement not to convey, including rights of first refusal, pre-emptive rights or options related to mortgagor efforts to convey;

(iii) Terminate or subject to termination all or a part of the interest held by the mortgagor in the mortgaged property if a conveyance is attempted;

(iv) Be subject to the consent of a third party;

(v) Be subject to limits on the amount of sales proceeds retainable by the seller; or

(vi) Be grounds for acceleration of the insured mortgage or increase in the interest rate.

(4) *Tax-exempt bond financing* means financing which is funded in whole or in part by the proceeds of qualified mortgage bonds described in section 143 of the Internal Revenue code of 1986, or

any successor section, on which the interest is exempt from Federal income tax. The term does not include financing by qualified veterans' mortgage bonds as defined in section 143(b) of the Code.

(5) *Eligible nonprofit organization* means an organization of the type described in section 501(c)(3) of the Internal Revenue Code of 1986 as an organization exempt under section 501(a) of the Code, which has:

(i) Two years experience as a provider of low- or moderate-income housing;

(ii) A voluntary board; and

(iii) No part of its net earnings inuring to the benefit of any member, founder, contributor or individual.

(b) *Policy of free assumability with no restrictions.* A mortgage shall not be eligible for insurance if the mortgaged property is subject to legal restrictions on conveyance, except as permitted by this part.

(c) *Exception for eligible governmental or nonprofit programs.* Legal restrictions on conveyance are acceptable if:

(1) The restrictions are part of an eligible governmental or nonprofit program and are permitted by paragraph (d) of this section; and

(2) The restrictions will automatically terminate if title to the mortgaged property is transferred by foreclosure or deed-in-lieu of foreclosure, or if the mortgage is assigned to the Secretary.

(d) *Exception for eligible governmental or nonprofit programs—specific policies.* For purposes of paragraph (c) of this section, restrictions of the following types are permitted for eligible governmental or nonprofit programs, provided that a violation of legal restrictions on conveyance may not be grounds for acceleration of the insured mortgaged or for an increase in the interest rate, or for voiding a conveyance of the mortgagor's interest in the property, terminating the mortgagor's interest in the property, or subjecting the mortgagor to contractual liability other than requiring repayment (at a reasonable rate of interest) of assistance provided to make the property affordable as low- or moderate-income housing:

(1) Except as otherwise provided in the HOME Investment Partnerships (HOME) and the Homeownership and Opportunity for People Everywhere (HOPE) programs, the mortgagor may be prohibited from selling the property at a price greater than the price permitted under the program, or the mortgagor may be required to pay a portion of the sales proceeds to a governmental body or an eligible nonprofit organization, as long as the mortgagor is not prohibited from recovering:

(i) The sum of the mortgagor's original purchase price, the mortgagor's reasonable costs of sale, the reasonable costs of improvements made by the mortgagor, and any negative amortization on a graduated payment mortgage insured under § 203.45 of this part; and

(ii) A reasonable share, as determined by the Secretary, of the appreciation in value which shall be the sales price reduced by the sum determined under paragraph (d)(1)(i) of this section.

(2) Legal restrictions on conveyance may extend beyond the term of the mortgage, subject to paragraph (c)(2) of this section and any limitations applicable in the jurisdiction.

(3) Except as otherwise required by the HOME and HOPE programs, rights under an option to purchase, preemptive rights to purchase or rights of first refusal shall only be held by a governmental body or eligible nonprofit organization, or another individual or organization approved by the Secretary, and shall be exercised by them (or an assignee who will purchase and occupy the property) only within a reasonable time after the event permitting exercise of the rights occurs, not to exceed a period of time determined by the Secretary. The Secretary may approve another individual or organization under the preceding sentence even if the restriction is not part of an eligible governmental or nonprofit program.

(4) In addition to the restrictions stated in paragraph (d)(3) of this section, the purchase price under an option may not be less than the sum of the mortgagor's original purchase price, the mortgagor's reasonable costs of sale, the reasonable costs of improvements made by seller, and a reasonable share, as determined by the Secretary, of the appreciation in value.

(5) The mortgagor may be required to continue to be an owner-occupant.

(6) The mortgagor may be limited in his or her ability to choose a purchaser for the property, but only to the extent necessary to ensure that the property is preserved as low- or moderate-income housing.

(7) The mortgagor for a rehabilitation loan insured under §203.50 of this part may hold title subject to a condition subsequent, provided that the holder of the right of entry for condition broken also executes the mortgage, and that the right is exercisable only for failure by the mortgagor to complete the rehabilitation or occupy the property as agreed by the mortgagor.

(8) Property may be subject to a legal restriction on conveyance to the extent approved in writing by an authorized representative of the Secretary prior to September 10, 1993.

(e) *Exception for tax-exempt bond financing.* A mortgage may be funded through tax-exempt bond financing and may include a due-on-sale provision in a form approved by the Secretary which permits the mortgagee to accelerate a mortgage that no longer meets Federal requirements for tax-exempt bond financing or for other reasons acceptable to the Secretary. Except as provided in this paragraph (e), a mortgage funded through tax-exempt bond financing shall comply with all form requirements prescribed under §203.17(a) of this part and shall contain no other provisions designed to enforce compliance with Federal or State requirements for tax-exempt bond financing. Other legal restrictions on conveyance are permitted as provided in other paragraphs of this section.

(f) *Exception for protective covenants excluding non-elderly.* Mortgaged property may be subject to protective covenants which prohibit or restrict occupancy by, or transfer to, persons who are not elderly if:

(1) The restrictions do not have an undue effect on marketability; and

(2) The restrictions do not constitute illegal discrimination and are consistent with the Fair Housing Act and all other applicable nondiscrimination laws.

(g) *Exceptions for specific jurisdictions.* Notwithstanding the provisions of paragraph (b) of this section, mort-gages insured on certain Indian land or Hawaiian home lands under sections 247 and 248 of the National Housing Act and §§203.43h and 203.43i of this part, or on property in the Northern Mariana Islands or American Samoa, shall not be ineligible for insurance under this section solely because applicable law does not permit free alienability of title to all persons.

[58 FR 42648, Aug. 11, 1993; 59 FR 15112, Mar. 31, 1994]

§203.42 Rental properties.

(a) A mortgage on property upon which there is a dwelling to be rented by the mortgagor shall not be eligible for insurance if the property is a part of, or adjacent or contiguous to, a project, or group of similar rental properties, in which the mortgagor has a financial interest in eight or more dwelling units.

(b) Paragraph (a) of this section shall not apply where:

(1) A mortgage qualifies as a rehabilitation loan under §203.50 of this part;

(2) The mortgage is to be used for the rehabilitation of property located in a specific area or neighborhood that has been targeted by a State or local government for redevelopment, in accordance with a specific program that involves substantial public or private commitments in support of neighborhood improvement or redevelopment; and

(3) The State or local government has approved, and has submitted to the Commissioner a plan describing the program of neighborhood redevelopment and revitalization, including the geographic area targeted for redevelopment, and the nature and proportion of public or private commitments that have been made in support of the redevelopment program.

(c) No two-, three-, or four-family dwelling, and no single-family dwelling, if it is part of a group of five or more single-family dwellings held by the same mortgagor, or any part or unit thereof, shall be rented or offered for rent for transient or hotel purposes, as defined in §203.16, so long as the dwelling is subject to any insured mortgage.

[56 FR 27692, June 17, 1991, as amended at 61 FR 36264, July 9, 1996]

§ 203.43 Eligibility of miscellaneous type mortgages.

(a) A mortgage which meets the requirements of this subpart, except as modified by this section, shall be eligible for insurance under this subpart subject to compliance with the additional requirements of this section.

(b) The mortgage may be accepted for insurance if:

(1) Executed in connection with the sale by the Government, or any agency or official thereof, of any housing acquired or constructed under Public Law 849, Seventy-sixth Congress, as amended; Public Law 781, Seventy-sixth Congress, as amended; or Public Law 9, 73 or 353, Seventy-seventh Congress, as amended (including any property acquired, held or constructed in connection with such housing or to serve the inhabitants thereof); or

(2) Executed in connection with the sale by the Public Housing Administration, or by any public housing agency with the approval of the said Administration, or any housing (including any property acquired, held or constructed in connection with such housing or to serve the inhabitants thereof) owned or financially assisted pursuant to the provisions of Public Law 671, Seventy-sixth Congress; or

(3) Executed in connection with the sale by the Government, or any agency or official thereof, or any of the so-called Greenbelt towns, or parts thereof, including projects, or parts thereof, known as Greenhills, OH; Greenbelt, MD; and Greendale, WI, developed under the Emergency Relief Appropriation Act of 1935; or of any of the village properties or employee's housing under the jurisdiction of the Tennessee Valley Authority; or of any housing under the jurisdiction of the Department of the Interior located within the town area of Coulee Dam, WA, acquired by the United States for the construction, operation, and maintenance of Grand Coulee Dam and its appurtenant works or of any permanent housing under the jurisdiction of the Department of the Interior constructed under the Boulder Canyon Project Act of December 21, 1928, as amended and supplemented, located within the Boulder City municipal area; or

(4) Executed in connection with the sale by the Government, or any agency or official thereof, of any housing (including any property acquired, held, or constructed in connection therewith or to serve the inhabitants thereof) pursuant to the Atomic Energy Community Act of 1955, as amended: *Provided*, That such insurance shall be issued without regard to any preferences or priorities except those prescribed by the National Housing Act or the Atomic Energy Community Act of 1955, as amended; or

(5) Executed in connection with the sale by a State or municipality, or an agency, instrumentality, or political subdivision of either, of a project consisting of any permanent housing (including any property acquired, held or constructed in connection therewith or to serve the inhabitants thereof), constructed by or on behalf of such State, municipality, agency, instrumentality or political subdivision, for the occupancy of veterans (persons who have served in the active military or naval service of the United States at any time on or after September 16, 1940, and prior to July 26, 1947, or on or after June 27, 1950, and prior to February 1, 1955) their families and others: *Provided*, That the principal obligation of a mortgage referred to in this paragraph shall not exceed 90 percent of the appraised value of the mortgaged property; or

(6) Executed in connection with the first resale, within two years from the date of its acquisition from the Government, of any portion of a project or property of the character described in paragraphs (b) (1), (2), (3), and (4) of this section.

(c) The Commissioner may insure under this part, without regard to any limitation upon eligibility contained in the other provisions of this subpart, any mortgage given to refinance an existing mortgage insured under the National Housing Act. The refinancing mortgage must meet the following special requirements:

(1)(i) Except as provided by paragraph (c)(1)(ii) of this section, the refinancing mortgage must be in an amount that does not exceed the least of (A) the original principal amount of the existing mortgage; (B) the sum of the outstanding principal balance of the existing mortgage, plus loan closing charges approved by the Commissioner; or (C) in the case of an eligible non-occupant mortgagor (as defined in §203.18(f)), the outstanding balance of the existing mortgage.

(ii) In the case of graduated payment mortgages insured under section 203 of the Act pursuant to section 245 (a) or (b) of the Act (§203.45 or §203.46 [as in effect immediately before its removal at 52 FR 32754, published August 28, 1987]), the refinancing mortgage must have a principal amount that does not exceed the outstanding balance of the existing mortgage.

(iii) If a one-time mortgage insurance premium (MIP) was financed as part of the existing mortgage referred to in paragraphs (c)(1) (i) and (ii) of this section, the amount of the premium refund to which the mortgagor is entitled must be deducted in determining the original principal amount and the unpaid principal balance of the existing mortgage under paragraph (c)(1)(i) of this section and the outstanding balance of the existing mortgage under paragraph (c)(1)(ii) of this section. However, the maximum amount of the refinancing mortgage computed in accordance with this paragraph (c)(1) may be increased by the amount of the one-time MIP (if any) associated with the refinancing mortgage;

(2) It must have a term which does not exceed the unexpired term of the existing mortgage, except that in any case where the Commissioner determines that an extension of the term of the mortgage will inure to the benefit of the applicable insurance fund, taking into consideration the outstanding insurance liability under the existing insured mortgage, the term may be extended to the lesser of (i) 30 years or (ii) the unexpired term of the existing mortgage, plus 12 years;

(3) The mortgage must result in a reduction in regular monthly payments by the mortgagor, except:

(i) When a fixed rate mortgage is given to refinance an adjustable rate mortgage held by a mortgagor who is to occupy the dwelling as a principal residence or secondary residence, as these terms are defined in §203.18(f); or

(ii) When refinancing a mortgage for a shorter term will result in an increase in the mortgagor's regular monthly payments of no more than $50. In the case of a graduated payment mortgage, the reduction in regular monthly payments means a reduction from the payment due under the existing mortgage for the month in which the refinancing mortgage is executed.

(4) It must be made by a mortgagor whose record of payment on the existing mortgage meets standards established by the Commissioner; and

(5) The mortgagee may not require a minimum principal amount to be outstanding on the loan secured by the existing mortgage.

(d)–(f) [Reserved]

(g) The provisions of §203.28 shall not apply to mortgages insured under this section.

(h) The provisions of §203.38 shall not apply to mortgages of the character described in paragraph (b) of this section and at the time any such mortgage is insured there must be located on the mortgaged property a dwelling unit designed principally for residential use for not more than eight families.

(i)–(j) [Reserved]

(k) The Commissioner may insure under this part, without regard to any limitation upon eligibility contained in this subpart, any mortgage assigned to the Commissioner in connection with payment under a contract of mortgage insurance, or executed in connection with a sale by the Commissioner of any property acquired in the settlement of an insurance claim under any section or title of the National Housing Act.

[36 FR 24508, Dec. 22, 1971, as amended at 45 FR 30602, May 8, 1980; 47 FR 29525, July 7, 1982; 52 FR 4139, Feb. 10, 1987; 52 FR 37287, Oct. 6, 1987; 52 FR 44861, Nov. 23, 1987; 53 FR 8880, Mar. 18, 1988; 55 FR 34805, Aug. 24, 1990; 55 FR 38033, Sept. 14, 1990; 61 FR 36264, July 9, 1996]

§203.43a Eligibility of mortgages covering housing in certain neighborhoods.

(a) A mortgage financing the repair, rehabilitation, construction, or purchase of property located in an older declining urban area shall be eligible

169

for insurance under this subpart subject to compliance with the additional requirements of this section.

(b) The mortgage shall meet all of the requirements of this subpart, except such requirements as are judged to be not applicable on the basis of the following determinations to be made by the Commissioner:

(1) That the conditions of the area in which the property is located prevent the application of certain eligibility requirements of this subpart.

(2) That the area is reasonably viable, and there is a need in the area for adequate housing for families of low and moderate income.

(3) That the mortgage to be insured is an acceptable risk.

(c) Mortgages complying with the requirements of this section shall be insured under this subpart pursuant to section 223(e) of the National Housing Act. Such mortgages shall be insured under and be the obligation of the Special Risk Insurance Fund.

(d) For restrictions against approving mortgage insurance for a certain category of newly legalized alien, see 24 CFR part 49.

[36 FR 24508, Dec. 22, 1971, as amended at 55 FR 18493, May 2, 1990]

§ 203.43b [Reserved]

§ 203.43c Eligibility of mortgages involving a dwelling unit in a cooperative housing development.

A mortgage involving a dwelling unit in a cooperative housing development which meets the requirements of this subpart, except as modified by this section, shall be eligible for insurance under section 203(n) of the National Housing Act.

(a) The provisions of §§ 203.16a, 203.17, 203.18, 203.18a, 203.23, 203.24, 203.26, 203.37, 203.38, 203.43h, 203.43i, 203.43j, 203.44, 203.49, and 203.50 of this part do not apply to mortgages insured under section 203(n) of the National Housing Act.

(b) As used in connection with the insurance of mortgages under this section and § 203.437 of this part: (1) The term *mortgage* shall mean a first lien given to secure a loan made to finance the unpaid purchase price of a Corporate Certificate together with the

applicable Occupancy Certificate of a cooperative ownership housing corporation in which the permanent occupancy of the dwelling units is restricted to members of such corporation, and may refer both to a security instrument creating a lien, whether called a *mortgage, deed of trust, security deed* or another term used in a particular jurisdiction, as well as the credit instrument, or note, secured thereby.

(2) *Corporation* shall mean an organization which holds title to a cooperative housing development which is covered by a blanket mortgage or mortgages insured by FHA under the National Housing Act.

(3) *Corporate Certificate* shall mean such stock certificates, membership certificates, or other instruments which the laws of the jurisdictions in which the cooperative housing development is located require to evidence ownership of a specified interest in the corporation.

(4) *Occupancy Certificate* shall mean a written instrument provided by the corporation to each holder of a Corporate Certificate which grants an exclusive right of possession of a specific dwelling unit in the cooperative housing development.

(5) References in this subpart to a dwelling, residence or property which is sold, conveyed, covered by a mortgage or subject to a lien shall be construed to mean the Corporate Certificate together with the Occupancy Certificate, except that where such references when interpreted in light of section 203(n) of the National Housing Act clearly indicate the intent to be the dwelling unit, such reference shall mean the dwelling unit identified in the Occupancy Certificate.

(c) The organizational documents of the cooperative corporation must provide that: (1) Either the Secretary or a mortgagee under a mortgage insured under this section shall be a member of the cooperative corporation for so long as either owns a Corporate Certificate;

(2) A mortgage insured under this section shall be a first lien upon the property covered by the mortgage;

(3) The Secretary may exercise the voting rights which are attributable to

each Corporate Certificate owned by the Secretary;

(4) The Secretary may designate as her proxy an agent for the purpose of exercising the voting rights of the Secretary which are attributable to the corporate Certificate or Certificates owned by the Secretary;

(5) The Secretary may cease making monthly payments attributable to any dwelling unit for which the Secretary owns a Corporate Certificate six months after the Secretary notifies the corporation to sell the Corporate Certificate or upon default by the corporation on the blanket mortgage covering the dwelling unit;

(6) The Secretary or a mortgagee shall not be obligated to make payments to the corporation for any amounts unpaid by a mortgagor under a mortgage insured under this section prior to the date the Secretary or the mortgagee becomes the owner of the Corporate Certificate.

(d) The corporation shall have entered into an agreement with the Secretary and the mortgagee which: (1) Requires that the corporation shall furnish the Secretary with the most recent annual financial report certified to have been based on generally accepted accounting principles and the most recent monthly or quarterly financial report;

(2) Waives any option or right of first refusal the corporation may have to purchase any Corporate Certificate covered by a mortgage insured under section 203(n) of the National Housing Act, unless the corporation pays the full amount due under such mortgage or pays the full amount of the Secretary's investment if the Secretary is the owner of the Corporate Certificate, whichever is greater.

(3) Except with the approval of the Secretary, waives all authority the corporation may have to approve or reject the buyer of a Corporate Certificate owned by the Secretary or the buyer of a Corporate Certificate covered by a mortgage insured under Section 203(n) of the National Housing Act.

(4) Requires the corporation on notice by the Secretary to act as her agent for a fee to be determined by the Secretary for the limited purposes of:

(i) Selling all Corporate Certificates of the corporation owned by the Secretary;

(ii) Renting and collecting rents on any dwelling unit for which the Secretary owns the Corporate Certificate.

(5) Provides that the Secretary shall not be obligated to make payments to the corporation for outstanding debts of the mortgagor;

(6) Requires the corporation to furnish to a mortgagee or to the Secretary, on request:

(i) A statement, certified by the officer charged with maintenance of the Corporate Certificate Transfer Book, that such book currently shows that the mortgagee or the Secretary is the owner of any Corporate Certificate transferred to the mortgagee or the Secretary; and

(ii) The Occupancy Certificate in the name of the mortgagee or the Secretary.

(7) Requires the corporation to notify the mortgagee, whose name and address has been provided, of any default in corporation fee payments by the mortgagor within 15 days of such default;

(8) Requires the mortgagee to notify the corporation of any default in mortgage payments by the mortgagor within 15 days of such default;

(9) Requires the corporation upon notice by the Secretary or the mortgagee, when the Secretary or the mortgagee is the owner of the Corporate Certificate, and for a fee to be determined by the Secretary to evict any person or persons from a dwelling unit identified in the Occupancy Certificate.

(10) Contains such other provisions as the Secretary may require.

(e) The mortgagee shall obtain such security and other undertakings as may be required to establish a first lien on the Corporate Certificate and the Occupancy Certificate under the laws of the State where the Cooperative Housing Development is located.

(f) The mortgage involves a one-family dwelling unit in a cooperative housing development which is covered by a blanket mortgage or mortgages insured under the National Housing Act.

(g) The mortgage shall not exceed the balance remaining after subtracting, from the amount determined under

§§ 203.18(a), 203.18(g) and 203.18a of this part, an amount equal to the portion of the unpaid balance of the blanket mortgage covering the cooperative development which is attributable to the dwelling unit the mortgagor is entitled to occupy as of the date the mortgage is accepted for insurance.

(h) The mortgage shall be executed upon a form conforming to the applicable provisions of this part and shall:

(1) Involve a principal obligation in multiples of $50.

(2) Come due on the first of the month.

(3) Contain complete amortization provisions satisfactory to the Secretary and an amortization period not in excess of the term of the mortgage.

(4) Be for a term not to exceed 30 years or the remaining term of the blanket mortgage covering the cooperative development or three-quarters of the remaining economic life of the building improvements, whichever is less.

(5) Provide for payments to principal and interest to begin not later than the first day of the month following 60 days from the date the mortgagee's certificate on the commitment was executed.

(6) Contain a provision stating that the failure of the mortgagor to pay the mortgagor's share of the common expenses or assessments and charges imposed by the corporation as provided in the instruments establishing the cooperative shall be considered a default.

(i) The entire principal amount of the mortgage must have been disbursed to the mortgagor or to his creditors for his account and with his consent.

(j) The mortgage must be executed by a mortgagor who intends to be an occupant of the unit.

(k) The mortgagee shall collect from the mortgagor upon the execution of the mortgage: (1) A sum that will be sufficient to pay the mortgage insurance premium for the period beginning on the date of the closing of the loan and ending on the date of the first monthly payment under the mortgage or (2), where applicable, the one-time mortgage insurance premium payable pursuant to § 203.280.

(l) The mortgagee shall upon application for a mortgage insurance commitment provide true copies of the following organizational documents of the cooperative corporation for examination and approval by the appropriate HUD Field Office:

(1) Certificate of Incorporation;

(2) Regulatory Agreement;

(3) By-Laws as amended;

(4) The financial statements required in paragraph (d)(1) of this section;

(5) Proposed Occupancy Certificate;

(6) Proposed Corporate Certificate;

Provided that one or more of the requirements of this paragraph may be waived by the Secretary if the documents have been approved by the Secretary and the mortgagee submits with the application a statement certified by an officer of the cooperative corporation that no changes have been made in the documents since such approval.

[42 FR 40431, Aug. 10, 1977, as amended at 45 FR 29278, May 2, 1980; 45 FR 76377, Nov. 18, 1980; 48 FR 12085, Mar. 23, 1983; 48 FR 28804, June 23, 1983; 49 FR 23584, June 6, 1984; 52 FR 48201, Dec. 21, 1987; 53 FR 8881, Mar. 18, 1988; 53 FR 9869, Mar. 28, 1988; 53 FR 34282, Sept. 6, 1988; 56 FR 24631, May 30, 1991; 58 FR 41002, July 30, 1993]

§ 203.43d Eligibility of mortgages in certain communities.

Notwithstanding any other requirements of this subpart, a mortgage covering a one- to four-family dwelling occupied by the mortgagor as a principal residence (as defined in § 203.18(f)(1)) is eligible for insurance if the following requirements are met:

(a) The property is located in a community where the Secretary determines that:

(1) Temporary adverse economic conditions exist throughout the community as a direct and primary result of outstanding claims to ownership of land in the community by an American Indian tribe, band, or Nation;

(2) Such ownership claims are reasonably likely to be settled, by court action or otherwise;

(3) As a direct result of the community's temporarily impaired economic condition, owners of homes in the community occupied as principal residences (as defined in § 203.18(f)(1)) have been involuntarily unemployed or underemployed and have, thus, incurred substantial reductions in income that

significantly impair their ability to continue timely payment of their mortgages;

(4) As a result, widespread mortgage foreclosures and distress sales of homes are likely in the community; and

(5) Fifty or more individuals were joined as parties defendant or were members of a defendant class prior to December 31, 1976 in litigation involving claims to ownership of land in the community by an American Indian tribe, band or Nation.

(b) The mortgagor, as a direct result of the community's temporarily impaired economic condition, has been involuntarily unemployed or underemployed and has thus incurred a substantial reduction in income which significantly impairs the owners ability to continue timely payment of the mortgage.

(c) The mortgagee certifies that the security instrument has been recorded and is a good and valid first lien on the property except for the claims specified in paragraph (a)(1) of this section.

(d) The mortgagee agrees upon insurance of the mortgage to assign such mortgage to the Secretary within 30 days from the date of the issuance of the insurance certificate and if such assignment does not take place, the contract of insurance is terminated and becomes null and void.

(e) Any individual, organization, institution or governmental agency shall be considered a mortgagee for the purposes of this section.

(f) Mortgages complying with the requirements of this section shall be insured under this subpart pursuant to section 203(o) of the National Housing Act. Such mortgages shall be insured under and be the obligation of the Special Risk Insurance Fund.

(g) The mortgage was executed and filed for record on or before October 12, 1977.

[42 FR 57434, Nov. 2, 1977, as amended at 55 FR 34805, Aug. 24, 1990]

§203.43e [Reserved]

§203.43f Eligibility of mortgages covering manufactured homes.

A mortgage covering a one-family manufactured home (as defined in 24 CFR 3280.2(a)(16)) that meets the requirements of this subpart, except as modified by this section, shall be eligible for insurance pursuant to this subpart.

(a) The manufactured home, when erected on site, shall have floor space area of not less than four hundred square feet and shall have been constructed in conformance with the National Manufactured Home Construction and Safety Standards as evidenced by a certification label affixed thereto in accordance with 24 CFR 3280.8.

(b) The mortgage shall cover the manufactured home and site, shall constitute a mortgage on a property classified and taxed as real estate, and shall have a term of not more than 30 years from the date of the beginning of amortization.

(c) In the case of a manufactured home which has not been permanently erected on a site for more than one year prior to the date of the application for mortgage insurance:

(i) The manufactured home shall be erected on a site-built permanent foundation that meets or exceeds applicable requirements of the Minimum Property Standards for One- and Two-Family Dwellings, 4900.1 (see 24 CFR 200.929(b)(1)) (MPS) and shall be permanently attached thereto by anchoring devices adequate for all loads identified in the MPS. The towing hitch or running gear, which includes axles, brakes, wheels and other parts of the chassis that operate only during transportation, shall have been removed. The finished grade level beneath the manufactured home shall be at or above the 100-year return frequency flood elevation. The site, site improvements, and all other features of the mortgaged property not addressed by the Manufactured Home Construction and Safety Standards shall meet or exceed applicable requirements of the MPS.

(ii) The space beneath the manufactured home shall be enclosed by continuous foundation-type construction designed to resist all forces to which it is subject without transmitting forces to the building superstructure. The enclosure shall be adequately secured to the perimeter of the manufactured home and be constructed of materials that conform to MPS requirements for foundations.

(iii) The manufactured home shall have an overall coefficient of heat transmission ("U_o" value) calculated in accordance with the procedures of NFPA 501 BM–1976 ("Mobile Home Heating, Cooling Load Calculations") that does not exceed the following for all locations within the following climatic zones:

Zone I .... .145
Zone II .... .099
Zone III [1] .... .087

NFPA 501 BM–1976 is incorporated by reference and is issued by and available from the National Fire Protection Association, Batterymarch Park, Quincy, MA 02269.

(iv) The manufactured home shall be braced and stiffened before it leaves the factory to resist racking and potential damage during transportation.

(v) The conditions of § 203.18(a)(2) (i) and (ii) of this subpart shall not apply to construction of the manufactured home but shall be applicable to improvement of the site, including construction of the site-built foundation.

(vi) Section 203.14 of this subpart is modified to the extent provided in this paragraph. Applications relating to insurance of mortgages under this paragraph (c) must be accompanied by an agreement in form satisfactory to the Commissioner executed by the seller or builder or such other person as the Commissioner may require agreeing that in the event of any sale or conveyance of the dwelling within a period of one year beginning with the date of initial occupancy, the seller, builder, or such other person will at the time of such sale or conveyance deliver to the purchaser or owner of such property the manufacturer's warranty on a form prescribed by the Commissioner, which shall provide that the manufacturer's warranty is in addition to and not in derogation of all other rights and remedies the purchaser or owner may have, and a warranty in form satisfactory to the Commissioner warranting that the manufactured home, the foundation, positioning and anchoring of the manufactured home to its permanent foun-

dation, and all site improvements are constructed in substantial conformity with the plans and specifications (including amendments thereof or changes and variations therein which have been approved in writing by the Commissioner) on which the Commissioner has based his valuation of the dwelling. The warranty shall also include provisions that the manufactured home sustained no hidden damage during transportation, and if the manufactured home is a double-wide, that the sections were properly joined and sealed. Such agreement must provide that upon the sale or conveyance of the dwelling and delivery of the warranty, the seller, builder or such other person will promptly furnish the Commissioner with a conformed copy of the warranty establishing by the purchaser's receipt thereon that the original warranty has been delivered to the purchaser in accordance with this section.

(d) In the case of a manufactured home which has been permanently erected on a site for more than one year prior to the dae of the application for mortgage insurance:

(i) The manufactured home shall be permanently anchored to and supported by permanent footings and shall have permanently installed utilities that are protected from freezing. The space beneath the manufactured home shall be a properly enclosed crawl space.

(ii) The site, site improvements, and all other features of the mortgaged property not addressed by the Manufactured Home Construction and Safety Standards shall meet or exceed applicable requirements of the Requirements for Existing Housing—One to Four Family Living Units (Handbook 4905.1). The finished grade level beneath the manufactured home shall be at or above the 100-year return frequency flood elevation.

(iii) The manufactured home shall have been occupied only at the location subject to the mortgage sought to be insured.

[1] Zone III includes Alaska, Montana, Wyoming, North and South Dakota, Minnesota, Wisconsin, Michigan, Maine, New Hampshire, and Vermont.

[48 FR 7735, Feb. 24, 1983, as amended at 61 FR 36264, July 9, 1996]

§203.43g Eligibility of mortgages in certain communities.

(a) A mortgage which meets the requirements of this subpart shall be eligible for insurance without regard to the limitation in this part relating to marketability of title under the following conditions:

(1) The mortgagor is to occupy the dwelling as a principal residence (as defined in §203.18(f)(1)).

(2) The defect or potential defect in title is a direct and primary result of outstanding claims to ownership of land in the community by an American Indian tribe, band, group or Nation.

(3) Fifty or more individual owners were joined as parties defendant or were members of a defendant class before April 1, 1980 in litigation involving claims to ownership of land in the community in which the property is located by an American Indian tribe, band, group or Nation pursuant to a dispute involving the Articles of Confederation, the Trade and Intercourse Act of 1790 or any similar State or Federal law.

(4) Such ownership claims are reasonably likely to be settled by court action or otherwise.

(5) Temporary adverse economic conditions exist throughout the community as a direct and primary result of such claims.

(b) Mortgages complying with the requirements of this subpart as modified by this section shall be the obligation of the Special Risk Insurance Fund.

[49 FR 21319, May 21, 1984, as amended at 55 FR 34805, Aug. 24, 1990]

§203.43h Eligibility of mortgages on Indian land insured pursuant to section 248 of the National Housing Act.

A mortgage covering a one- to four-family residence located on Indian land shall be eligible for insurance pursuant to section 248 of the National Housing Act (12 U.S.C. 1715z–13), notwithstanding otherwise applicable requirements related to marketability of title, if the mortgage meets the requirements of this subpart as modified by this section and is made by an Indian Tribe or on a leasehold estate, by an Indian who will occupy it as a principal residence. Mortgage insurance on cooperative shares is not authorized under this section.

(a) *Exemptions.* (1) The provisions of subparts I, J, and M of part 200, and §203.30, shall not apply to approval of mortgagors for mortgages insured under this section if the Indian tribe to which the prospective mortgagor belongs is subject to the Indian Civil Rights Act.

(2) In the case of an Indian tribe which is not subject to the Indian Civil Rights Act, the authorities cited in paragraph (a)(1) of this section shall apply, but any preference in the tribe's approval of the sale or assumption of a lease and mortgage under this section in favor of an eligible Indian over a non-Indian shall not be considered to be a violation of subpart I, J or M.

(b) *Eviction procedures.* Before HUD will insure a mortgage on Indian land, the tribe having jurisdiction over such property must certify to the HUD Field Office that it has adopted and will enforce procedures for eviction of defaulted mortgagors where the insured mortgage has been foreclosed.

(c) *Approval of lease and mortgage.* The lease must be on a form prescribed by HUD.

The mortgage must be on a form which meets the requirements of §203.17(a)(2). Before HUD will insure any mortgage under this section, the mortgagee must demonstrate that the Bureau of Indian Affairs, U.S. Department of Interior, has approved both the lease and mortgage.

(d) *Construction advances.* The Commissioner may issue a commitment for the insurance of advances made during construction and a Direct Endorsement mortgagee may request insurance of a mortgage that will involve the insurance of advances made during construction. The Commissioner will insure advances made by the mortgagee during construction if all of the following conditions are satisfied:

(1) The mortgage shall be a first lien on the leasehold;

(2) The mortgagor and the mortgagee execute a building loan agreement, approved by the Commissioner, setting forth the terms and conditions under which advances will be made;

(3) The advances are made only as provided in the commitment or the approval by the Direct Endorsement underwriter;

(4) The principal amount of the mortgage is held by the mortgagee in an interest bearing account, trust, or escrow for the benefit of the mortgagor, pending advancement to the mortgagor or to his or her creditors as provided in the loan agreement;

(5) The mortgage shall bear interest on the amount advanced to the mortgagor or to his or her creditors and on the amount held in an account or trust for the benefit of the mortgagor; and

(6) The Secretary had determined that no feasible financing alternative is available.

(e) *Assumption or sale of leasehold.* The form of lease must contain a provision requiring tribal consent before any assumption of an existing lease, except where title to the leasehold interest is obtained by the Secretary through foreclosure of the insured mortgage. A mortgagee other than the Secretary must obtain tribal consent before obtaining title through a foreclosure sale. Tribal consent must be obtained on any subsequent transfer from the purchaser, including the Secretary, at foreclosure sale. The lease may not be terminated by the lessor without HUD's approval while the mortgage is insured or held by the Secretary.

(f) *First lien.* The first lien requirement under this part is implemented where the mortgage is filed in the State recording system and is a first lien under that system, even though the leasehold interest securing the mortgage is located on Indian land and filed with Bureau of Indian Affairs, U.S. Department of the Interior. Any tribal government whose courts have jurisdiction to hear foreclosures must also:

(1) Enact a law satisfactory to the Commissioner providing for the satisfaction of FHA-insured and Secretary-held mortgages before other obligations (other than tribal leasehold taxes against the property assessed after the property is mortgaged) are satisfied; or

(2) Enact a law providing that State law shall determine the priority of liens against the property.

(g) *Definitions.* As used in this section and elsewhere in this part, the term:

(1) *Indian* means and individual member of any Indian tribe and that member's family.

(2) *Indian land* means trust or otherwise restricted land (i) as defined by the Secretary of the Interior, over which an Indian tribe is recognized by the United States as having governmental jurisdiction; (ii) held in trust for the benefit of any Indian tribe or individual or held by any Indian tribe or individual subject to a restriction by the United States against alienation; or (iii) acquired by Alaska natives under the Alaska Native Claims Settlement Act or any other land acquired by Alaska natives pursuant to statute by virtue of their unique status as Alaska natives.

(3) *Indian tribe* means any Indian or Alaska native tribe, band, nation, or other organized group or community of Indians or Alaskan natives recognized as eligible for the services provided to Indians or Alaska natives by the Secretary of the Interior because of its status as such an entity, or that is an eligible recipient under chapter 67 of title 31, United States Code. For purposes of engaging in section 248 insured mortgage transactions under this section, an Indian tribe may act through its duly authorized representative.

(Approved by the Office of Management and Budget under control number 2502–0340)

[51 FR 21871, June 16, 1986, as amended at 53 FR 34282, Sept. 6, 1988; 57 FR 58347, Dec. 9, 1992; 61 FR 36264, July 9, 1996]

§ 203.43i Eligibility of mortgages on Hawaiian Home Lands insured pursuant to section 247 of the National Housing Act.

(a) *Eligibility.* A mortgage on a homestead lease granted by the Department of Hawaiian Home Lands covering a one- to four-family residence located on Hawaiian home lands is eligible for insurance pursuant to section 247 of the National Housing Act (12 U.S.C. 1715z–12) if the mortgagor is a native Hawaiian who will occupy it as a principal residence, and if the mortgage meets the requirements of this subpart as modified by this section. Mortgage insurance on cooperative shares under § 203.43c on homes in federally impacted areas under §203.43e is not authorized under this section.

(b) *Exemptions from other regulations.* The provisions of subparts I, J, and M of part 200, and §203.30, to the extent that these provisions would otherwise prohibit preferences in favor of Native Hawaiians in the leasing, sale or other disposition of Hawaiian home lands, do not apply to mortgages insured pursuant to section 247 of the National Housing Act. The first lien requirement contained in §203.17 also does not apply to mortgages insured pursuant to section 247 of the National Housing Act.

(c) *Definitions.* (1) *Department of Hawaiian Home Lands* (DHHL) is a Department of the State of Hawaii responsible for management of Hawaiian home lands for the benefit of native Hawaiians.

(2) Hawaiian home lands means all lands given the status of Hawaiian home lands under section 204 of the Hawaiian Homes Commission Act of 1920 (42 Stat. 110), or under the corresponding provision of the Constitution of the State of Hawaii adopted under section 4 of the Act entitled "An Act to provide for the admission of the State of Hawaii into the Union," approved March 18, 1959 (73 Stat. 5).

(3) Native Hawaiian means any descendant of not less than one-half part of the blood of the races inhabiting the Hawaiian islands before January 1, 1778, or, in the case of an individual who is awarded an interest in a lease of Hawaiian home lands through transfer or succession, such lower percentage as may be established for such transfer or succession under section 208 or 209 of the Hawaiian Homes Commission Act of 1920 (42 Stat.111), or under the corresponding provision of the Constitution of the State of Hawaii adopted under section 4 of the Act entitled "An Act to provide for the admission of the State of Hawaii into the Union," approved March 18, 1959 (73 Stat. 5).

(d) *Conditions for insurance.* Mortgages will be eligible for insurance under this section, according to the procedures in §§203.5, 203.6, or 203.7 (as applicable), only where the Department of Hawaiian Home Lands:

(1) Will be a comortgagor;

(2) Guarantees or reimburse the Secretary for any mortgage insurance

claim paid in connection with a property on Hawaiian home lands; or

(3) Offers other security acceptable to the Secretary.

(e) *Acceptable security.* Any agreement by the Secretary to accept alternative security under paragraph (d)(3) of this section must contain provisions designed to ensure that the insurance of mortgages under this section has a neutral impact on the appropriate insurance funds. These provisions may require the Department of Hawaiian Home Lands to make an initial deposit of funds with HUD and to maintain additional funds in reserve for subsequent deposits with HUD. The initial and subsequent deposits shall be used to pay obligations incurred by HUD in connection with the insurance of mortgages under this section and any associated costs, including refunds of insurance premiums to mortgagors. If the Department of Hawaiian Home Lands agrees to make deposits in amounts acceptable to HUD, then the Secretary may agree to use a portion of the premiums received for insurance of mortgages under this section solely for payment of such obligations and associated costs.

(f) *Recordation.* The mortgagee must certify that the mortgage has been recorded with the Department of Hawaiian Home Lands.

(g) *Construction advances.* Advances made by the mortgagee during construction are eligible for insurance, according to the procedures in §§203.5, 203.6, or 203.7 (as applicable), if the Secretary determines that no feasible financing alternative is available and if:

(1) The mortgagor and the mortgagee execute a building loan agreement, approved by the Secretary, setting forth the terms and conditions under which advances will be made;

(2) The advances are made only as provided in the commitment or the approval by the Direct Endorsement or Lender Insurance underwriter;

(3) The principal amount of the mortgage is held by the mortgagee in an interest bearing account, trust, or escrow for the benefit of the mortgagor, pending advancement to the mortgagor or to his or her creditors as provided in the loan agreement; and

177

(4) The mortgage bears interest on the amount advanced to the mortgagor or to his or her creditors and on the amount held in an account or trust for the benefit of the mortgagor.

(h) *Form of lease.* The form of lease must be approved by both HUD and the Department of Hawaiian Home Lands (DHHL). The lease may not be terminated by DHHL without the approval of the Secretary while the mortgage is insured or held by the Secretary.

(i) *Eligibility of mortgagor.* In addition to the eligibility requirements contained in this subpart, possession of a lease of Hawaiian home lands issued under section 207(a) of the Hawaiian Homes Commission Act of 1920 (42 Stat.110) that has been certified by the Department of Hawaiian Home Lands as being valid, current, and not in default, shall be sufficient to certify eligibility to receive a mortgage to be insured under this section.

(Approved by the Office of Management and Budget under control number 2502–0358)

[52 FR 8067, Mar. 16, 1987, and 52 FR 28470, July 30, 1987, as amended at 53 FR 8881, Mar. 18, 1988; 53 FR 34282, Sept. 6, 1988; 57 FR 58347, Dec. 9, 1992; 61 FR 36264, July 9, 1996; 62 FR 30226, June 2, 1997; 69 FR 33525, June 15, 2004]

§ 203.43j Eligibility of mortgages on Allegany Reservation of Seneca Nation of Indians.

A mortgage on a leasehold estate covering a one- to four-family residence located on the Allegany Reservation of the Seneca Nation of Indians in the State of New York is eligible for insurance if the mortgage meets the requirements of this subpart as modified by this section.

(a) *Title.* This section applies only to a mortgage which:

(1) Does not meet the requirements of § 203.37;

(2) Is on a leasehold under a lease with a termination date in February 1991, which provides for renewal in accordance with the Act of February 19, 1875 (18 Stat. 330) and the Act of September 30, 1890 (26 Stat. 558).

A mortgage may not be on a leasehold created by a lease which is executed after the effective date of this section as a renewal or replacement of a lease described in paragraph (a)(2) of this section. A mortgage may not be secured by any other right of occupancy created in lieu of a leasehold after the effective date of this section by agreement of the Seneca Nation, court order, law or any other means.

(b) *Provisions of mortgage.* The Secretary will prescribe special mortgage provisions in the form of a mortgage rider in order better to secure the mortgagee, including:

(1) Authorization for the mortgagee to exercise the option of lease renewal if the mortgagor fails to do so, and to recover from the mortgagor authorized expenses incurred to obtain lease renewal; and

(2) Making a mortgagor failure to take steps necessary for less renewal an event of default under the mortgage.

(c) *Secretary agreement with mortgagor.* The mortgagor must enter into an agreement with the Secretary and such other parties as the Secretary may require regarding actions to be taken to obtain either a renewal of the lease or a new lease.

(d) *Certification.* The borrower must certify that it has received disclosures, in a form prescribed by the Secretary, explaining the status of the lease and the consequences of nonrenewal. The disclosure shall include a discussion of the fact that a mortgagor who does not obtain a lease renewal and loses the right of occupancy will remain liable for the outstanding balance of the mortgage.

(e) *Purchase for principal residence.* The mortgagor must be a purchaser who intends to occupy the property as a principal residence (as defined in § 203.18(f)(1)), or a current owner-occupant refinancing a mortgage which is now due or which will become due before the lease termination date in February 1991.

(f) *Relationship of income to housing expense.* For purposes of § 203.33(a), the total prospective housing expense shall include the Secretary's estimate of future lease payments during the term of the mortgage rather than lease payments in effect at the time of application.

(g) *Suspension of commitments.* The Secretary may suspend the issuance of commitments to insure mortgages under this section, for the entire period during which commitments could otherwise be issued for insurance under this section (i.e., through February 18, 1991) or for such lesser period as the Secretary may specify, by providing thirty days notice of suspension in the FEDERAL REGISTER. Regardless of its duration, a suspension to be imposed prior to February 19, 1990, will be based on a determination by the Secretary that, for mortgages insured during a specified period, the rate of monetary defaults (as measured by 90 day delinquencies) for mortgages insured under this section exceeds the rate of such monetary defaults for all insured mortgages on one- to four-family properties in the State of New York. A suspension to be imposed after February 18, 1990, will be based on a consideration by the Secretary of the probable costs to the Special Risk Insurance Fund of further commitments to insure under this section, as measured by such factors as the current and projected rate and amount of claims payments, together with other significant current and projected costs as determined by the Secretary, including a review of the actual and projected monetary default rate (as measured by 90 day delinquencies) and the actual and projected rate of lease renewal through negotiation and arbitration.

[52 FR 48201, Dec. 21, 1987, and 53 FR 9869, Mar. 28, 1988, as amended at 54 FR 32970, Aug. 11, 1989; 55 FR 34805, Aug. 24, 1990]

§203.44 Eligibility of advances.

Mortgagees may not make open-end advances under section 225 of the National Housing Act (12 U.S.C. 1715p) in connection with the mortgages insured under this chapter.

[61 FR 36264, July 9, 1996]

§203.45 Eligibility of graduated payment mortgages.

A mortgage containing provisions for varying rates of amortization corresponding to anticipated variations in family income shall be eligible for insurance under this subpart subject to compliance with the additional requirements of this section.

(a) The mortgage may provide that any interest which accrues and which is unpaid pursuant to a financing plan approved by the Secretary, shall be added to the principal obligation of the mortgage.

(b) The mortgage shall bear interest at the rate agreed upon by the mortgagee and the mortgagor.

(c) The mortgage amount shall not exceed the lesser of:

(1) The limits prescribed by §§203.18, 203.18a, and 203.29; or,

(2) An amount which, when added to all accrued mortgage interest which will be unpaid under a financing plan approved by the Secretary, shall not exceed 97 percent of the appraised value of the property covered by the mortgage as of the date the mortgage is accepted for insurance. However, if the mortgagor is a veteran, the mortgage amount, when added to all accrued mortgage interest which will be unpaid under a financing plan approved by the Secretary, shall not exceed the applicable limits prescribed for veterans in §203.18(a).

(d) The mortgage must contain complete amortization provisions satisfactory to the Secretary requiring monthly payments by the mortgagor not in excess of his reasonable ability to pay as determined by the Secretary. The sum of the payments to principal and/or interest may increase annually for a period of five years at a rate of 2½ percent, 5 percent or 7½ percent or for a period of ten years at a rate of 2 percent or 3 percent. Any required increase in payments shall occur on the anniversary date of the beginning of amortization. On the termination of the period of annual increases of payments, the sum of the payments to principal and interest in each month shall be substantially the same.

(e) The mortgagee shall fully explain to the mortgagor the nature of the obligation undertaken and the mortgagor shall certify that he or she fully understands the obligation.

(f) Sections 203.21 and 203.44 shall not apply to this section.

(g) This section applies only to mortgagors who are to occupy the dwelling as a principal residence (as defined in §203.18(f)(1)). It does not apply to a mortgage that meets the requirements of §§203.18(a)(4), 203.18 (c) through (e), 203.43, 203.43a, 203.43j, or 203.49.

(h) Mortgages complying with the requirements of this section shall be insured under this subpart pursuant to section 245 of the National Housing Act.

[41 FR 42949, Sept. 29, 1976, as amended at 45 FR 33966, May 21, 1980; 45 FR 56341, Aug. 24, 1980; 49 FR 19453, 19458, May 8, 1984; 49 FR 23584, June 6, 1984; 52 FR 48201, Dec. 21, 1987; 53 FR 8881, Mar. 18, 1988; 53 FR 9869, Mar. 28, 1988; 55 FR 34805, Aug. 24, 1990; 58 FR 41003, July 30, 1993]

§ 203.47 Eligibility of growing equity mortgages.

A mortgage containing provisions for accelerated amortization corresponding to anticipated variations in family income shall be eligible for insurance under this subpart, subject to compliance with the additional requirements of this section.

(a) The mortgage must contain complete amortization provisions, satisfactory to the Secretary, requiring monthly payments by the mortgagor not in excess of the mortgagor's reasonable ability to pay, as determined by the Secretary.

(b) The mortgage must contain a provision setting forth the payments required for principal and interest in each year of the mortgage.

(c) The monthly payments for principal and interest for the initial year, or such other initial period as the commissioner may approve, shall be determined on the basis of a 30-year level payment amortization schedule. Subsequent monthly payments for principal and interest may increase annually, biennially or at such other interval that is greater than one year, as the Commissioner may approve. The subsequent periodic increases may be up to five percent above the payments for principal and interest for the previous period.

(d) No later than at the time that a loan application is offered to a prospective mortgagor, the mortgagee shall explain fully to the mortgagor the nature of the obligation undertaken and the mortgagor shall certify that he or she fully understands the obligation.

(e) The mortgage amount shall not exceed the limits prescribed by § 203.18, 203.18a, or 203.29.

(f) Sections 203.21 and 203.44 shall not apply to this section.

(g) This section shall not apply to a mortgage which meets the requirements of § 203.43, § 203.43a, or § 203.49.

(h) Mortgages complying with the requirements of this section shall be insured under this subpart pursuant to section 245(a) of the National Housing Act.

[49 FR 19453, May 8, 1984, as amended at 49 FR 23584, June 6, 1984; 53 FR 8881, Mar. 18, 1988; 58 FR 41003, July 30, 1993]

§ 203.49 Eligibility of adjustable rate mortgages.

A mortgage containing the provisions for periodic adjustments by the mortgagee in the effective rate of interest charged shall be eligible for insurance under this subpart subject to compliance with the additional requirements of this section. This section shall apply only to mortgage loans described under sections 203(b), 203(h) and 203(k) of the National Housing Act.

(a) *Types of mortgages insurable.* The types of adjustable rate mortgages that are insurable are those for which the interest rate may be adjusted annually by the mortgagee, beginning after one, three, five, seven, or ten years from the date of the mortgagor's first debt service payment.

(b) *Interest-rate index.* Changes in the interest rate charged on an adjustable rate mortgage must correspond either to changes in the one-year London Interbank Offered Rate (LIBOR) or to changes in the weekly average yield on U.S. Treasury securities, adjusted to a constant maturity of one year. Except as otherwise provided in this section, each change in the mortgage interest rate must correspond to the upward and downward change in the index.

(c) *Amortization provisions.* The mortgage must contain amortization provisions satisfactory to the Secretary, allowing for periodic adjustments in the rate of interest charged corresponding to changes in the interest rate index.

(d) *Frequency of interest rate changes.* (1) The interest rate adjustments must occur annually, calculated from the date of the mortgagor's first debt service payment, except that, for these types of mortgages, the first adjustment shall be no sooner or later than the following:

(i) One-year adjustable rate mortgages—no sooner than 12 months or later than 18 months;

(ii) Three-year adjustable rate mortgages—no sooner than 36 months or later than 42 months;

(iii) Five-year adjustable rate mortgages—no sooner than 60 months or later than 66 months;

(iv) Seven-year adjustable rate mortgages—no sooner than 84 months or later than 90 months; and

(v) Ten-year adjustable rate mortgages—no sooner than 120 months or later than 126 months.

(2) To set the new interest rate, the mortgagee will determine the change between the initial (*i.e.*, base) index figure and the current index figure, or will add a specific margin to the current index figure. The initial index figure shall be the most recent figure available before the date of mortgage loan origination. The current index figure shall be the most recent index figure available 30 days before the date of each interest rate adjustment, except that for forward mortgages originated on or after January 10, 2015, 30 days shall mean 45 days.

(e) *Method of rate changes.* Interest rate changes may only be implemented through adjustments to the mortgagor's monthly payments.

(f) *Magnitude of changes.* The adjustable rate mortgage initial contract interest rate shall be agreed upon by the mortgagee and the mortgagor. The first adjustment to the contract interest rate shall take place in accordance with the schedule set forth under paragraph (d) of this section. Thereafter, for all adjustable rate mortgages, the adjustment shall be made annually and shall occur on the anniversary date of the first adjustment, subject to the following conditions and limitations:

(1) For one- and three-year adjustable rate mortgages, no single adjustment to the interest rate shall result in a change in either direction of more than one percentage point from the interest rate in effect for the period immediately preceding that adjustment. Index changes in excess of one percentage point may not be carried over for

inclusion in an adjustment for a subsequent year. Adjustments in the effective rate of interest over the entire term of the mortgage may not result in a change in either direction of more than five percentage points from the initial contract interest rate.

(2) For five-, seven-, and ten-year adjustable rate mortgages, no single adjustment to the interest rate shall result in a change in either direction of more than two percentage points from the interest rate in effect for the period immediately preceding that adjustment. Index changes in excess of two percentage points may not be carried over for inclusion in an adjustment in a subsequent year. Adjustments in the effective rate of interest over the entire term of the mortgage may not result in a change in either direction of more than six percentage points from the initial contract rate.

(3) At each adjustment date, changes in the index interest rate, whether increases or decreases, must be translated into the adjusted mortgage interest rate, except that the mortgage may provide for minimum interest rate change limitations and for minimum increments of interest rate changes.

(g) *Pre-Loan Disclosure.* The mortgagee is required to make available to the mortgagor, at the time of loan application, a written explanation of the features of an adjustable rate mortgage consistent with the disclosure requirements applicable to variable rate mortgages secured by a principal dwelling under the Truth in Lending Act, 15 U.S.C. 1601 *et seq.*

(h) *Disclosures.* The mortgagee of an adjustable rate mortgage shall provide mortgagors with the disclosures in the timing, content, and format required by the regulations implementing the Truth in Lending Act (15 U.S.C. 1601 *et seq.*) at 12 CFR 1026.20(c) and (d).

(i) *Cross-reference.* Sections 203.21 (level payment amortization provisions) and 203.44 (open-end advances) do not apply to this section. This section does not apply to a mortgage that meets the requirements of §§203.18(a)(4) (mortgagors of secondary residences), 203.18(c) (eligible non-occupant mortgagors), 203.18(d) (outlying area properties), 203.43 (miscellaneous type mortgages), 203.43c (mortgages involving a dwelling unit in a cooperative housing development), 203.43d (mortgages in certain communities), 203.43e (mortgages covering houses in federally impacted areas), 203.45 (graduated payment mortgages), or 203.47 (growing equity mortgages).

(j) *Aggregate amount of mortgages insured.* The aggregate number of adjustable rate mortgages insured pursuant to this section and 24 CFR part 234 in any fiscal year may not exceed 30 percent of the aggregate number of mortgages and loans insured by the Secretary under Title II of the National Housing Act during the preceding fiscal year.

(k) *Insurance authority.* Mortgages complying with the requirements ofthis section shall be insured under this subpart pursuant to section 251 of the National Housing Act.

[49 FR 23584, June 6, 1984, as amended at 53 FR 8881, Mar. 18, 1988; 54 FR 111, Jan. 4, 1989; 55 FR 34805, Aug. 24, 1990; 61 FR 36264, July 9, 1996; 69 FR 11501, Mar. 10, 2004; 70 FR 16082, Mar. 29, 2005; 72 FR 40050, July 20, 2007; 79 FR 50840, Aug. 26, 2014]

§ 203.50 Eligibility of rehabilitation loans.

A rehabilitation loan which meets the requirements of this subpart, except as modified by this section, shall be eligible for insurance under section 203(k) of the National Housing Act.

(a) For the purpose of this section:

(1) The term *rehabilitation loan* means a loan, advance of credit, or purchase of an obligation representing a loan or advancement of credit, made for the purpose of financing:

(i) The rehabilitation of an existing one-to-four unit structure which will be used primarily for residential purposes;

(ii) The rehabilitation of such a structure and refinancing of the outstanding indebtedness on such structure and the real property on which the structure is located; or

(iii) The rehabilitation of such a structure and the purchase of the structure and the real property on which it is located; and

(2) The term *rehabilitation* means the improvement (including improvements designed to meet cost-effective energy conservation standards prescribed by the Secretary and improvements for accessibility to the handicapped) or repair of a structure, or facilities in connection with a structure, and may include the provision of such sanitary or other facilities as are required by applicable codes, a community development plan, or a statewide property insurance plan to be provided by the owner or tenant of the project.

(b) The provisions of § 203.18 (except as otherwise provided in paragraphs (f) (1) and (2) of this section) and § 203.43c shall not apply to loans insured under this section.

(c) The loan shall cover a dwelling which was completed more than one year preceding the date of the application for mortgage insurance and which was approved for mortgage insurance prior to the beginning of rehabilitation.

(d)(1) The buildings on the mortgaged property must, upon completion of rehabilitation, conform with standards prescribed by the Secretary.

(2) Improvements or repairs made under this section must be designed to meet cost-effective energy conservation standards prescribed by the Secretary.

(e) The loan transaction shall be an acceptable risk as determined by the Commissioner.

(f) The loan may not exceed an amount which, when added to any outstanding indebtedness of the borrower that is secured by the property, creates an outstanding indebtedness in excess of the lesser of:

(1)(i) The limits prescribed in § 203.18(a)(1) (in the case of a dwelling to be occupied as a principal residence, as defined in § 203.18(f)(1));

(ii) The limits prescribed in § 203.18(a)(1) and (3) (in the case of a dwelling to be occupied as a secondary residence, as defined in § 203.18(f)(2));

(iii) 85 percent of the limits prescribed in § 203.18(c), or such higher limit, not to exceed the limits set forth in § 203.18(a)(1), as Commissioner may prescribe (in the case of an eligible non-occupant mortgagor as defined in § 203.18(f)(3));

(iv) The limits prescribed in § 203.18a, based upon the sum of the estimated cost of rehabilitation and the Commissioner's estimate of the value of the property before rehabilitation; or

(2) The limits prescribed in the authorities listed in this paragraph (f), based upon 110 percent of the Commissioner's estimate of the value of the property after rehabilitation.

(g) The loan limitation prescribed by paragraph (f)(2) of this section shall not be applicable where a unit of local government demonstrates to the satisfaction of the Commissioner that:

(1) The property is located within an area which is subject to a community sponsored program of concentrated redevelopment or revitalization, and,

(2) The loan limitation prescribed by paragraph (f)(2) of this section, prevents the utilization of the program to accomplish rehabilitation in the subject area, and,

(3) The interests of the mortgagor and the Commissioner are adequately protected.

(h) Insurance may be available for advances made during rehabilitation or upon completion of rehabilitation, according to the procedures in §203.5, 203.6, or 203.7 (as applicable).

(i) Rehabilitation loans which do not involve the insurance of advances, the refinancing of outstanding indebtedness or the purchase of the property need not be a first lien on the property but shall not be junior to any lien other than a first mortgage. The provisions of §§203.15, 203.19, 203.23, 203.24, 203.26, and 203.43j shall not be applicable to such loans.

(j) The Commissioner may insure advances made by the mortgagee during rehabilitation if the following conditions are satisfied:

(1) The mortgage shall be a first lien on the property.

(2) The mortgagor and the mortgagee shall execute a rehabilitation loan agreement, approved by the Commissioner, setting forth the terms and conditions under which advances will be made.

(3) The advances shall be made as provided in the reliabilitation loan agreement.

(4) The principal amount of the mortgage shall be held by the mortgagee in an interest bearing account, trust, or escrow for the benefit of the mortgagor

pending advancement to the mortgagor or his creditors as provided in the rehabilitation loan agreement.

(5) The loan shall bear interest at the rate prescribed in §203.20 on the amount advanced to the mortgagor or its creditors, and the amount held in an account or trust for the benefit of the mortgagor.

(6) If paragraph (k) of this section applies, the rehabilitation loan agreement shall restrict advancement to the mortgagor, or to creditors other than the mortgagee, so that any loan proceeds in excess of the 85 percent set forth in paragraph (f)(1)(iii) of this section shall not be advanced until the property is sold to a purchaser described in paragraph (k)(2) of this section.

(k) In the case of a dwelling (1) to be occupied neither as a principal residence nor as a secondary residence and (2) where the loan is approved for a limit higher than the 85 percent set forth in paragraph (f)(1)(iii) of this section, the eligible non-occupant mortgagor (as defined in §203.18(f)(3)) shall certify to the Commissioner that:

(1) The mortgagor will not rent (except for a rental term of not less than 30 days and not more than 60 days), sell (except where the insured mortgage is paid in full as an incident of the sale), or occupy the property before a due date approved by the Commissioner, except with the prior written approval of the Commissioner;

(2) The mortgagor agrees that, if the property is not sold before a due date approved by the Commissioner to a purchaser, acceptable to the Commissioner, who will occupy the property, assume personal liability, and agree to pay the mortgage indebtedness, any amount held in escrow, trust, or special account under paragraph (j) of this section will be applied in reduction of the outstanding principal amount of the mortgage as of the due date approved by the Commissioner;

(3) The mortgagee agrees that any portion of the fund held in escrow, trust, or special account, not applied to the mortgage in accordance with the provisions of this paragraph (k), shall

be deducted from the amount of the insurance benefits to which the mortgagee would otherwise be entitled if a claim for insurance benefits is filed.

(1) *Rehabilitation loan consultants.* HUD maintains a list of qualified consultants, in accordance with §§ 200.190 through 200.193 of this title. When the borrower elects to use the services of a consultant, the lender must select a consultant on the list to perform one or more of the following tasks:

(1) Conduct a preliminary feasibility analysis before or after the submission of a sales contract;

(2) Prepare the cost estimate, work write-up, and architectural exhibits required for the rehabilitation of the property;

(3) Conduct a plan review; and

(4) Conduct the draw inspections for the release of funds during the construction phase of the project.

(m) With regard to loans under this section executed on or after December 27, 2005, the Commissioner shall charge an up-front and annual MIP in accordance with 24 CFR 203.284 or 203.285, whichever is applicable.

[45 FR 33966, May 21, 1980, as amended at 45 FR 76378, Nov. 18, 1980; 50 FR 19926, May 13, 1985; 52 FR 48201, Dec. 21, 1987; 53 FR 8881, Mar. 18, 1988; 53 FR 9869, Mar. 28, 1988; 55 FR 34806, Aug. 24, 1990; 57 FR 58347, Dec. 9, 1992; 58 FR 41003, July 30, 1993; 59 FR 13882, Mar. 24, 1994; 62 FR 30226, June 2, 1997; 67 FR 52381, Aug. 9, 2002; 70 FR 37156, June 28, 2005; 83 FR 64272, Dec. 14, 2018]

§ 203.51 Applicability.

The provisions of §§ 203.18 (a), (c), (d), (e)(1), and (f); § 203.29(c); § 203.31; § 203.43(c); 203.43(k); § 203.43c(g); § 203.43d(a), § 203.43g(a)(1); § 203.43j(e); § 203.45(g); § 203.49(h); § 203.50(f); and § 203.50(k) of this subpart apply to mortgages insured:

(1) Pursuant to a conditional commitment or master conditional commitment issued on or after September 24, 1990; or

(2) In accordance with the Direct Endorsement program, if the underwriter of the mortgagee signs the appraisal report or master appraisal report for the property on or after September 24, 1990; or

(3) Pursuant to a certificate of reasonable value or master certificate of reasonable value issued by the Department of Veterans Affairs on or after September 24, 1990.

[55 FR 34806, Aug. 24, 1990, as amended at 57 FR 58347, Dec. 9, 1992; 61 FR 36453, July 10, 1996]

§ 203.52 Acceptance of individual residential water purification equipment.

If a property otherwise eligible for insurance under this part does not have access to a continuing supply of safe and potable water without the use of a water purification system, the requirements of this section must be complied with as a condition to acceptance of the mortgage for insurance. The mortgagee must provide appropriate documentation with the submission for insurance endorsement to address each of the requirements of this section.

(a) *Equipment.* Water purification equipment must be approved by a nationally recognized testing laboratory acceptable to the local or state health authority.

(b) *Certification by local (or state) health authority.* A local (or state) health authority certification must be submitted to HUD which certifies that:

(1) A point-of-entry or point-of-use water purification system is currently in operation on the property. If the system in operation employs point-of-use equipment, the purification system must be employed on each water supply source (faucet) serving the property. Where point-of-entry systems are used, separate water supply systems carrying untreated water for flushing toilets may be constructed.

(2) The system is sufficient to assure an uninterrupted supply of safe and potable water adequate to meet household needs.

(3) The water supply, when treated by the equipment, meets the requirements of the local (or state) health authority, and has been determined to meet local or state quality standards for drinking water. If neither state nor local standards are applicable, then quality shall be determined in accordance with standards set by the Environmental Protection Agency (EPA) pursuant to the Safe Drinking Water Act. (EPA standards are prescribed in the National Primary Drinking Water requirements, 40 CFR parts 141 and 142.)

(4) There exists a Plan providing for the monitoring, servicing, maintenance, and replacement of the water equipment, which Plan meets the requirements of paragraph (f) of this section.

(c) *Mortgagor notice and certification.* (1) The prospective mortgagor must have received written notification, before the mortgagor signed a sales contract, that the property has a hazardous water supply that requires treatment in order to remain safe and acceptable for human consumption. The notification to the mortgagor must identify specific contaminants in the water supply serving the property, and the related health hazard arising from the presence of those contaminants.

(2) The mortgagor must have received, with the notification described in paragraph (c)(1) of this section, a written good faith estimate of the maintenance and replacement costs of the equipment necessary to assure continuing safe drinking water.

(3) A copy of the notification statement (including cost estimates), dated before the date of the sales contract, and signed by the prospective mortgagor to acknowledge its receipt, must accompany the submission for insurance endorsement. If a sales contract is signed in advance of the disclosure required by this paragraph, another sales contract must be executed after the information is provided to the prospective mortgagor and he or she has acknowledged receipt of the disclosure.

(4) The prospective mortgagor must sign a certification, substantially in the form set out in this paragraph (c)(4), at the time the application for mortgage credit approval is signed. This certification must be submitted to HUD:

Mortgagor's Certificate. I hereby acknowledge and understand that the home I am purchasing has a water purification system which I am responsible for maintaining.

I undertstand that the individual water supply is unsafe for consumption unless the system is operating properly. I am aware that if I do not properly maintain the system, the water supply will not be purified or treated properly, thereby rendering the water supply unsafe for consumption.

I also understand that the Department of Housing and Urban Development does not warrant the condition of the property, will not give me any money for repairs to the water purification system, and has relied upon the local (or state) health authority to assure that the water supply, when processed by properly maintained equipment, is acceptable for human use and consumption.

_____

[Mortgagor's signature and date]

(d) *Service contract.* Before mortgage closing, the mortgagor must enter into a service contract with an organization or individual specifically approved by the local (or state) health authority to carry out the provisions of the required Plan for servicing, maintenance, repair and replacement of the water purification equipment. A copy of the signed service contract must be provided to HUD.

(e) *Escrow for maintenance and replacement.* The mortgagee must establish and maintain an escrow account which provides for the accumulation of funds paid with the mortgagor's monthly mortgage payment adequate to assure proper servicing, maintenance, repair and replacement of the water purification equipment. The amount to be collected and escrowed by the mortgagee shall be based upon information provided by the manufacturer for the maintenance and replacement of the water purification equipment and for other charges anticipated by the service contractor. The initial monthly escrow amount shall be stated in the Plan. Disbursements from the account will be limited to costs associated with the normal servicing, maintenance, repair or replacement of the water purification equipment. Disbursements may only be made to the service contractor or its successor, to equipment suppliers, to the local (or state) health authority for the performance of testing or other required services, or to another entity approved by the health authority. So long as water purification remains necessary and the mortgage is insured by HUD, the mortgagee must maintain the escrow account.

(f) *Approved Plan.* A Plan, in the form of a contract entered into by the mortgagor and mortgagee and approved by the local (or state) health authority, must set out conditions that must be met by the parties as a condition to insurance of the mortgage by HUD. To be approved by the health authority:

(1) The Plan must set forth the respective responsibilities to be assumed by the mortgagor and the mortgagee, as well as the other entities who will implement the Plan, i.e., the health authority and the service contractor. In particular:

(i) The Plan must set out the responsibilities of the health authority for monitoring and enforcing performance of the service contractor, including any successor contractor that the health authority may later have occasion to name. By its approval of the Plan, the health authority documents its acceptance of these responsibilities, and the Plan should so indicate;

(ii) The Plan must provide for the monitoring of the operation of the water purification equipment, as well as for servicing (including disinfecting), and for repairing and replacing the system, as frequently as necessary, taking into consideration the system's design, anticipated use, and the type and level of contaminants present. Installation, servicing, repair and replacement of the water purification system must be performed by an individual or organization approved for the purpose by the local (or state) health authority and identified in the Plan. In meeting the requirements of paragraph (f)(1)(ii) of this section, the Plan may incorporate by reference specific terms and conditions of the service contract required under paragraph (d) of this section.

(iii) Under the Plan, responsibility for monitoring the performance of the service contractor and for assuring that the water purification system is properly serviced, repaired, and replaced rests with the local (or state) health authority that has given its approval to the Plan. The Plan must confer on the health authority all powers necessary to effect compliance by the service contractor. The health authority's powers shall include the authority to notify the mortgagor of any noncompliance by the service contractor. The plan must provide that, upon any notification of noncompliance received from the health authority, the mortgagor shall have the right to discharge the service contractor for cause and to appoint a successor organization or individual as service contractor; and

(iv) The Plan must provide for the mortgagor to make periodic escrow payments necessary for the servicing, maintenance, repair and replacement of the water purification system, and for the mortgagee to disburse funds from the escrow account as required, to the appropriate party or parties.

(2) The Plan must provide that if the dwelling served by the water purification system is refinanced, or is sold or otherwise transferred with a HUD-insured mortgage, the Plan will:

(i) Continue in full force and effect;

(ii) Impose an obligation on the mortgagor to notify any subsequent purchaser or transferee of the necessity for the water purification system and for its proper maintenance, and of the obligation to make escrow payments; and

(iii) Require the mortgagor to furnish the purchaser with a copy of the Plan, before any sales contract is signed.

(g) *Periodic analysis.* Any Plan developed in accordance with this section must provide that an analysis of the water supply shall be obtained from the local (or state) health authority no less frequently than annually, but more frequently, if determined at any time to be necessary by the health authority or by the service contractor.

(Approved by the Office of Management and Budget under control number 2502–0474)

[57 FR 9609, Mar. 19, 1992; 57 FR 27927, June 23, 1992]

EFFECTIVE DATE

§ 203.249   Effect of amendments.

The regulations in this subpart may be amended by the Secretary at any time and from time to time, in whole or in part, but such amendment will not adversely affect the interests of a mortgagee under the contract of insurance on any mortgage or loan already insured, and will not adversely affect the interest of a mortgagee on any mortgage or loan to be insured for which either the Direct Endorsement or Lender Insurance mortgagee has approved the mortgagor and all terms and conditions of the mortgage or loan, or the Secretary has issued a firm commitment. In addition, such amendment will not adversely affect the eligibility of specific property if such property is covered by a conditional commitment issued by the Secretary, a certificate of reasonable value issued by the Secretary of Veterans Affairs, or an appraisal report approved by a Direct Endorsement or Lender Insurance underwriter.

[62 FR 30226, June 2, 1997]

Subpart B—Contract Rights and Obligations

DEFINITIONS

§ 203.251 Definitions.

As used in this subpart, the following terms shall have the meaning indicated:

(a) *Commissioner* means the Federal Housing Commissioner or his authorized representative.

(b) *Act* means the National Housing Act, as amended.

(c) *FHA* means the Federal Housing Administration.

(d) *Mortgage* is defined at §203.17(a)(1).

(e) *Mortgagor* means the original borrower under a mortgage and his heirs, executors, administrators and assigns.

(f) *Mortgagee* means the original lender under a mortgage and its successors and such of its assigns as are approved by the Commissioner.

(g)–(h) [Reserved]

(i) *Insured mortgage* means a mortgage which has been insured as evidenced by the issuance of a Mortgage Insurance Certificate or by the endorsement of the credit instrument for insurance by the Commissioner.

(j) *Contract of Insurance* means the agreement evidenced by the issuance of a Mortgage Insurance Certificate or by the endorsement of the Commissioner upon the credit instrument given in connection with an insured mortgage, incorporating by reference the regulations in this subpart and the applicable provisions of the Act.

(k) *MIP* means the mortgage insurance premium paid by the mortgagee to the Commissioner in consideration of the contract of insurance.

(l)–(m) [Reserved]

(n) *Open-end advance* means an insured advance made by an approved mortgagee in connection with a previously insured mortgage, pursuant to an open-end provision in the mortgage.

(o) *Open-end insurance charge* means the charge paid by the mortgagee to the Commissioner in consideration of the insurance of an open-end advance.

(p) *Beginning of amortization* means the date one month prior to the date of the first monthly payment to principal and interest.

(q) *Maturity* means the date on which the mortgage indebtedness would be extinguished if paid in accordance with periodic payments provided for in the mortgage.

(r) *Debentures* means registered, transferable securities in certificated or book entry form which are valid and binding obligations, issued in the name of the Mutual Mortgage Insurance Fund in accordance with the provisions of this part; such debentures are the primary liability of the Mutual Mortgage Insurance Fund and are unconditionally guaranteed as to principal and interest by the United States.

(s) *State* includes the several States, Puerto Rico, the District of Columbia, Guam, the Commonwealth of the Northern Mariana Islands, American Samoa, and the Virgin Islands.

(t) *TOTAL* is an acronym that stands for "Technology Open to Approved Lenders." TOTAL is a mortgage scorecard based on a mathematical equation that is to be used within an automated underwriting system (AUS). TOTAL is a tool to assist the mortgagee in managing its workflow and expediting the endorsement process, and is not a substitute for the mortgagee's reasonable consideration of risk and credit worthiness. Direct Endorsement mortgagees using TOTAL remain solely responsible for the underwriting decision.

[36 FR 24508, Dec. 22, 1971, as amended at 37 FR 8661, Apr. 29, 1972; 41 FR 49734, Nov. 10, 1976; 49 FR 12697, Mar. 30, 1984; 53 FR 34282, Sept. 6, 1988; 59 FR 49815, Sept. 30, 1994; 61 FR 36265, July 9, 1996; 68 FR 65826, Nov. 21, 2003]

ENDORSEMENT AND CONTRACT OF
INSURANCE

§ 203.255 Insurance of mortgage.

(a) *Mortgages with firm commitments.*
For applications for insurance involving mortgages not eligible to be originated under the Direct Endorsement program under § 203.5, or under the Lender Insurance program under § 203.6, the Secretary will either endorse the mortgage for insurance by issuing a Mortgage Insurance Certificate, provided that the mortgagee is in compliance with the firm commitment, or will electronically acknowledge that the mortgage has been insured.

(b) *Endorsement with Direct Endorsement processing.* For applications for insurance involving mortgages originated under the Direct Endorsement program under § 203.5, the mortgagee shall submit to the Secretary, within 60 days after the date of closing of the loan or such additional time as permitted by the Secretary, properly completed documentation and certifications as listed in this paragraph (b):

(1) Property appraisal upon a form meeting the requirements of the Secretary (including, if required, any additional documentation supporting the appraised value of the property under § 203.37a), or a HUD conditional commitment (for proposed construction only), or a Department of Veterans Affairs certificate of reasonable value, and all accompanying documents required by the Secretary;

(2) An application for insurance of the mortgage in a form prescribed by the Secretary;

(3) A certified copy of the mortgage and note executed upon forms which meet the requirements of the Secretary;

(4) A warranty of completion, on a form prescribed by the Secretary, for proposed construction cases;

(5) An underwriter certification, on a form prescribed by the Secretary, stating that the underwriter has personally reviewed the appraisal report and credit application (including the analysis performed on the worksheets) and that the proposed mortgage complies with HUD underwriting requirements, and incorporates each of the underwriter certification items that apply to the mortgage submitted for endorsement, as set forth in the applicable handbook or similar publication that is distributed to all Direct Endorsement mortgagees, except that where the TOTAL Mortgage Scorecard is used by the mortgagee, and the TOTAL Mortgage Scorecard has determined that the application represents an acceptable risk under terms and conditions agreed to by the FHA, a Direct Endorsement underwriter shall not be required to certify that the underwriter has personally reviewed the credit application (including the analysis performed on any worksheets). The following requirements are also applicable to the use of the TOTAL Mortgage Scorecard:

(i) Mortgagees and vendors must certify to compliance with these requirements:

(A) *Permissible users.* Only automatic underwriting systems (AUSs) developed, operated, owned, or used by FHA-approved Direct Endorsement mortgagees, Fannie Mae, or Freddie Mac, may access TOTAL, and only FHA-approved mortgagees will be able to obtain risk-assessments using TOTAL;

(B) *Limitation on use.* Results from TOTAL must not be used as the basis for rejecting any mortgage applicant. Mortgagees must provide full manual underwriting for mortgage applicants when TOTAL returns a "refer" risk score.

(C) *Vendor and mortgagee requirements.* Both mortgagees and vendors must:

(1) Use TOTAL to process FHA and other loan products specified by the FHA Commissioner only and for no other purpose;

(2) Implement quality control procedures for TOTAL usage and provide, at FHA's request, reports and loan samples that enable FHA to evaluate program operation;

(3) Not use TOTAL to direct mortgagors into other non-FHA product offerings (this requirement does not relieve a mortgagee from its obligations under § 203.10 concerning informed consumer choice for prospective FHA mortgagors);

(4) Not disassemble, decompile, reverse engineer, derive or otherwise reproduce any part of the source code or algorithm in TOTAL;

(5) Not provide feedback messages that conflict with the Equal Credit Opportunity Act; and

(6) Comply with any additional HUD/FHA requirements or procedures that are applicable to the Scorecard and may be issued through handbooks, mortgagee letters, TOTAL User Guides, or TOTAL Developers Guide following appropriate advance notification, where applicable.

(ii) *Loss of privilege to use TOTAL.* Mortgagees and AUS vendors found to violate the requirements applicable to the use of TOTAL may have their access to TOTAL and all associated privileges terminated upon appropriate notice in accordance with the following procedure:

(A) *Notice.* HUD will provide a mortgagee or vendor with a 30-day notice of a violation and loss of privilege. The notice will state the nature of the violation, the effective date of the loss of the privilege, and the duration of the loss of the privilege. The notice will become effective on the date provided in the notice, unless the mortgagee or vendor appeals the violation and loss of privilege in accordance with paragraph (b)(5)(ii)(B) of this section.

(B) *Appeal.* A party receiving a notice of violation may appeal to the Deputy Assistant Secretary for Single Family Housing (DAS-SFH), or his or her designee, before the effective date of the notice by providing evidence to refute the violation. The loss of privilege is stayed until the DAS-SFH, or designee, notifies the party that the loss of privilege has been affirmed, rescinded, or modified.

(6) Where applicable, a certificate under oath and contract regarding use of the dwelling for transient or hotel purposes;

(7) Where applicable, a certificate of intent to occupy by military personnel;

(8) Where a mortgage for an existing property is to be insured under section 221(d)(2) of the National Housing Act, a letter from the appropriate local government official that the property meets applicable code requirements;

(9) Where an individual water or sewer system is being used, an approval letter from the local health authority indicating approval of the system in accordance with §200.926d(f) of this chapter;

(10) For proposed construction if the mortgage (excluding financed mortgage insurance premium) exceeds a 90 percent loan to value ratio, evidence that the mortgagee qualifies for a higher ratio loan under one of the applicable provisions in the appropriate regulations;

(11) A mortgage certification on a form prescribed by the Secretary, stating that the authorized representative of the mortgagee who is making the certification has personally reviewed the mortgage documents and the application for insurance endorsement, and certifying that the mortgage complies with the requirements of paragraph (b) of this section. The certification shall incorporate each of the mortgagee certification items that apply to the mortgage loan submitted for endorsement, as set forth in the applicable handbook or similar publication that is distributed to all Direct Endorsement mortgagees;

(12) For a Home Equity Conversion Mortgage under part 206 of this chapter, the additional documents required by §206.15 of this chapter; and

(13) The documentation required under §203.37a providing that:

(i) The seller is the owner of record; and

(ii) That more than 90 days elapsed between the date the seller acquired the property (based upon the date of settlement) and the date of execution of the sales contract that will result in the FHA mortgage insurance.

(14) Such other documents as the Secretary may require.

(c) *Pre-endorsement review for Direct Endorsement.* Upon submission by an approved mortgagee of the documents required by paragraph (b) of this section, the Secretary will review the documents and determine that:

(1) The mortgage is executed on a form which meets the requirements of the Secretary;

(2) The mortgage maturity meets the requirements of the applicable program;

(3) The stated mortgage amount does not exceed the maximum mortgage amount for the area as most recently

announced by the Secretary, except for mortgages under 24 CFR part 206;

(4) All documents required by paragraph (b) of this section are submitted;

(5) All necessary certifications are made in accordance with paragraph (b) of this section;

(6) There is no mortgage insurance premium, late charge or interest due to the Secretary; and

(7) The mortgage was not in default when submitted for insurance or, if submitted for insurance more than 60 days after closing whether the mortgage shows an acceptable payment history.

In addition, the Secretary is authorized to determine if there is any information indicating that any certification or required document is false, misleading, or constitutes fraud or misrepresentation on the part of any party, or that the mortgage fails to meet a statutory or regulatory requirement. If, following this review, the mortgage is determined to be eligible, the Secretary will endorse the mortgage for insurance by issuance of a Mortgage Insurance Certificate. If the mortgage is determined to be ineligible, the Secretary will inform the mortgagee in writing of this determination, and include the reasons for the determination and any corrective actions that may be taken.

(d) *Submission by mortgagee other than originating mortgagee.* If the originating mortgagee assigns the mortgage to another approved mortgagee before pre-endorsement review under paragraph (c) of this section, the assignee may submit the required documents for pre-endorsement review in the name of the originating mortgagee. All certifications must be executed by the originating mortgagee (or its underwriter, if appropriate). The purchasing mortgagee may pay any required mortgage insurance premium, late charge and interest.

(e) *Post-Endorsement review for Direct Endorsement.* Following endorsement for insurance, the Secretary may review all documents required by paragraph (b) of this section. If, following this review, the Secretary determines that the mortgage does not satisfy the requirements of the Direct Endorsement program, the Secretary may place the mortgagee on Direct Endorsement probation, or terminate the authority of the mortgagee to participate in the Direct Endorsement program pursuant to § 203.3(d), or refer the matter to the Mortgagee Review Board for action pursuant to part 25 of this title.

(f) *Lender insurance*—(1)*Pre-insurance review.* For applications for insurance involving mortgages originated under the Lender Insurance program under § 203.6, the mortgagee is responsible for performing a pre-insurance review that would otherwise be performed by HUD under § 203.255(c) on the documents that would otherwise be submitted to HUD under § 203.255(b). The mortgagee's staff that performs the pre-insurance review must not be the same staff that originated the mortgage or underwrote the mortgage for insurance.

(2) *Recordkeeping.* Mortgagees must maintain records, including origination files, in a manner and for a time period to be prescribed by the Assistant Secretary for Housing—Federal Housing Commissioner, and must make them available to authorized HUD staff upon request.

(3) *Insuring the mortgage.* If, following this review, the mortgage is determined to be eligible, the mortgagee will electronically submit all required data to HUD regarding the mortgage. HUD's electronic system will acknowledge that the mortgage has been insured. HUD's electronic system may also issue a notice to the mortgagee that the mortgage has been selected for post-insurance technical review, and that the HUD case binder must be sent to the identified HUD office.

(g) *Indemnification*—(1)*General.* By insuring the mortgage, a Lender Insurance mortgagee agrees to indemnify HUD, in accordance with this paragraph.

(2) *Definition of origination.* For purposes of indemnification under this paragraph, the term "origination" means the process of creating a mortgage, starting with the taking of the initial application, continuing with the processing and underwriting, and ending with the mortgagee endorsing the mortgage note for FHA insurance.

(3) *Serious and material violation.* The mortgagee shall indemnify HUD for an FHA insurance claim paid within 5

years of mortgage insurance endorsement, if the mortgagee knew or should have known of a serious and material violation of FHA origination requirements, such that the mortgage loan should not have been approved and endorsed by the mortgagee and irrespective of whether the violation caused the mortgage default. Such a serious and material violation of FHA requirements in the origination of the mortgage may occur if the mortgagee failed to, among other actions:

(i) Verify the creditworthiness, income, and/or employment of the mortgagor in accordance with FHA requirements;

(ii) Verify the assets brought by the mortgagor for payment of the required down payment and/or closing costs in accordance with FHA requirements; or

(iii) Address property deficiencies identified in the appraisal affecting the health and safety of the occupants or the structural integrity of the property in accordance with FHA requirements, or

(iv) Ensure that the appraisal of the property serving as security for the mortgage loan satisfies FHA appraisal requirements, in accordance with §203.5(e).

(4) *Fraud or misrepresentation.* The mortgagee shall indemnify HUD for an insurance claim if the mortgagee knew or should have known that fraud or misrepresentation was involved in connection with the origination of the mortgage, regardless of whether the fraud or misrepresentation caused the mortgage default and regardless of when an insurance claim is filed.

(5) *Demand for indemnification.* The demand for indemnification will be made by either the Secretary or the Mortgagee Review Board. Under indemnification, the Lender Insurance mortgagee agrees to either abstain from filing an insurance claim, or reimburse FHA if a subsequent holder of the mortgage files an insurance claim and FHA suffers a financial loss.

[57 FR 58348, Dec. 9, 1992; 58 FR 13537, Mar. 12, 1993, as amended at 60 FR 42759, Aug. 16, 1995; 61 FR 36265, July 9, 1996; 62 FR 30227, June 2, 1997; 63 FR 29507, May 29, 1998; 68 FR 23376, May 1, 2003; 68 FR 65827, Nov. 21, 2003; 69 FR 5, Jan. 2, 2004; 77 FR 3605, Jan. 25, 2012; 77 FR 51469, Aug. 24, 2012]

§203.256 Insurance of open-end advance.

Insurance on an open-end advance will be evidenced by delivery of a certificate stating the amount of the advance, the date of insurance, and the regulations under which the advance is insured.

§203.257 Creation of the contract.

The mortgage shall be an insured mortgage from the date of the issuance of a Mortgage Insurance Certificate, from the date of the endorsement of the credit instrument, or from the date of HUD's electronic acknowledgement to the mortgagee that the mortgage is insured, as applicable. The Commissioner and the mortgagee are thereafter bound by the regulations in this subpart with the same force and to the same extent as if a separate contract had been executed relating to the insured mortgage, including the provisions of the regulations in this subpart and of the Act.

[62 FR 30227, June 2, 1997]

§203.258 Substitute mortgagors.

(a) *Selling mortgagor.* Except as provided in paragraph (d) of this section, the mortgagee may effect the release of a mortgagor from personal liability on the mortgage note, only if it obtains the Commissioner's approval of a substitute mortgagor, as provided by this section.

(b) *Purchasing mortgagor.* (1) The Commissioner may approve a substitute mortgagor with respect to any mortgage insured under §203.43h or §203.43i only if the mortgagor is to occupy the dwelling as a principal residence (as defined in §203.18(f)(1)).

(2) The Commissioner may approve a substitute mortgagor with respect to any mortgage insured under this part (except a mortgage referred to in paragraph (b)(1) of this section), only if the substitute mortgagor is to occupy the dwelling as a principal residence or as a secondary residence (as these terms are defined in §203.18(f)) or if the substitute mortgagor is an eligible non-occupant mortgagor (as defined in §203.18(f)).

(3) With respect to any mortgage covering a dwelling to be occupied as a

secondary residence, the loan to value ratio may not exceed 85 percent of the greater of:

(i) The appraised value of the property at the time the mortgage is accepted for insurance; or

(ii) The appraised value of the property at the time approval of a substitute mortgagor is requested.

(c) *Applicability-current mortgages.* Paragraph (b) of this section applies to the Commissioner's approval of a substitute mortgagor only if the mortgage executed by the original mortgagor was insured:

(1) Pursuant to a conditional commitment or master conditional commitment issued on or after December 15, 1989; or

(2) In accordance with the Direct Endorsement program, where the underwriter of the mortgagee signed the appraisal report or master appraisal report for the property on or after December 15, 1989;

(3) Pursuant to a certificate of reasonable value or master certificate of reasonable value issued by the Department of Veterans Affairs on or after December 15, 1989.

(d) *Applicability—earlier mortgages.* If the mortgage was insured:

(1) Pursuant to a conditional commitment or master conditional commitment issued on or after February 5, 1988, but before December 15, 1989; or

(2) In accordance with the Direct Endorsement program, where the approved underwriter of the mortgagee signed the appraisal report or master appraisal report for the property on or after February 5, 1988, but before December 15, 1989, or

(3) Pursuant to a certificate of reasonable value or master certificate of reasonable value issued by the Department of Veterans Affairs on or after February 5, 1988, but before December 15, 1989, the Commissioner may approve a substitute mortgagor with respect to the mortgage only if the substitute mortgagor is to occupy the dwelling as a principal residence or a secondary residence (as these terms are defined in §203.18(f)), or is an eligible non-occupant mortgagor (as defined in the following sentence), or if the mortgage has a principal balance that is not more than 75 percent of the greater of

(i) the appraised value of the property at the time the mortgage is accepted for insurance, or (ii) the appraised value of the property at the time approval of a substitute mortgagor is requested. For purposes of this paragraph (d), the term *eligible non-occupant mortgagor* has the meaning given in §203.18(f), except that paragraph (d)(3)(ii)(A) and (B) of this section apply in place of §203.18(f)(3) (i) and (ii).

(A) A public entity, as provided in section 214 or 247 of the National Housing Act; and

(B) A private nonprofit or public entity, as provided in section 221(h) or 235(j) of the National Housing Act.

If neither paragraph (b) nor the preceding portion of this paragraph (d) applies, the Commissioner may approve a substitute mortgagor without regard to whether the mortgagor is to occupy the dwelling.

(e) *Direct endorsement.* Mortgagees approved for participation in the Direct Endorsement program under §203.3 may, subject to limitations established by the Commissioner, themselves approve an appropriate substitute mortgagor under this section for mortgages which they own or service, and need not obtain further specific approval from the Commissioner.

(f) *Definition.* As used in this section, the term *substitute mortgagor* includes:

(1) Persons who, upon the release by a mortgagee of a previous mortgagor from personal liability on the mortgage note, assume this liability and agree to pay the mortgage debt; and

(2) Persons who purchase without assuming liability on the mortgage note or purchase where no release is given by the mortgagee to the previous mortgagor.

[55 FR 34806, Aug. 24, 1990, as amended at 57 FR 58349, Dec. 9, 1992; 58 FR 13537, Mar. 12, 1993; 61 FR 36453, July 10, 1996]

MORTGAGE INSURANCE PREMIUMS—IN GENERAL

§ 203.259   Method of payment of MIP.

The payment of any MIP under this subpart shall be made to the Commissioner by the mortgagee either in cash or debentures at par plus accrued interest.

[48 FR 28805, June 23, 1983]

§203.259a Scope.

(a) The Commissioner shall charge a one-time MIP pursuant to §203.280 for mortgages that:

(1) Are insured pursuant to §203.43(c) (if the mortgage to be refinanced was executed prior to July 1, 1991 and the new mortgage is executed on or after April 24, 1992); or insured pursuant to §203.43i; or

(2)(i) Are obligations of the Mutual Mortgage Insurance Fund under this part (except insured open-end advances as provided by §203.270);

(ii) Are insured pursuant to: (A) An application for a conditional commitment received on or after September 1, 1983; or

(B) An application for mortgage insurance endorsement under the single family Direct Endorsement program as provided in §203.255, where the property appraisal report is signed by the mortgagee's underwriter on or after September 1, 1983; and

(iii) Are executed before July 1, 1991.

(b) Except as provided in §203.284(h) or §203.285(d), the Commissioner shall charge an up-front MIP pursuant to §203.284 or §203.285 for mortgages executed on or after July 1, 1991 that are obligations of the Mutual Mortgage Insurance Fund. In the cases that the Commissioner deems appropriate, the Commissioner may require, by means of instructions communicated to all affected mortgages, that up-front MIP be remitted electronically.

(c) The periodic MIP provision of §§203.260 through 203.268 shall not apply to mortgages referred to in paragraph (a) of this section, nor shall they apply to mortgages to which the provision of §203.284 or §203.285 apply.

[57 FR 15211, Apr. 24, 1992, as amended at 57 FR 46983, Oct. 14, 1992; 58 FR 12902, Mar. 8, 1993; 58 FR 41003, July 30, 1993; 59 FR 13882, Mar. 24, 1994; 60 FR 34138, June 30, 1995; 61 FR 36453, July 10, 1996]

MORTGAGE INSURANCE PREMIUMS—
PERIODIC PAYMENT

§203.260 Amount of mortgage insurance premium (periodic MIP).

The mortgagee shall pay to the Commissioner an initial MIP in an amount equal to one-half of one percent of the average outstanding principal obligation of the mortgage for the first year of amortization. After payment of the initial MIP, the mortgagee shall pay to the Commissioner an amount equal to one-half of one percent of the average outstanding principal obligation of the mortgage for the 12-month period preceding each subsequent anniversary date of the beginning of amortization.

[48 FR 28805, June 23, 1983]

§203.261 Calculation of periodic MIP.

The amount of any periodic MIP shall be calculated in accordance with the original amortization provisions of the mortgage, without taking into account delinquent payments, prepayments, agreements to postpone payments, or agreements to recast the mortgage.

[48 FR 28805, June 23, 1983]

§203.262 Due date of periodic MIP.

The full initial and each annual MIP shall be due and payable to the Commissioner no later than the 10th day after the amortization anniversary date.

[61 FR 37801, July 19, 1996]

§203.264 Payment of periodic MIP.

The mortgagee shall pay each MIP in twelve equal monthly installments. Each monthly installment shall be due and payable to the Commissioner no later than the tenth day of each month, beginning in the month in which the mortgagor is required to make the first monthly mortgage payment. This will be effective for amortization beginning on or after September 1, 1996.

[61 FR 42787, Aug. 19, 1996]

§ 203.265 Mortgagee's late charge and interest.

(a) Periodic MIP which are received by the Commissioner after the payment dates prescribed by §§ 203.262 and 203.264 shall include a late charge of four percent of the amount paid.

(b) In addition to the late charge provided in paragraph (a) of this section, the mortgagee shall pay interest on any periodic MIP which are remitted to the Commissioner more than 20 days after the payment dates prescribed in § 203.264. Such interest rate shall be paid at a rate set in conformity with the Treasury Financial Manual.

[48 FR 28805, June 23, 1983, as amended at 61 FR 36265, July 9, 1996; 61 FR 37801, July 19, 1996]

§ 203.266 Period covered by periodic MIP.

The initial MIP shall cover the period beginning with the date of the issuance of a Mortgage Insurance Certificate and ending on the next anniversary of the beginning of amortization. Subsequent premium payments shall cover the twelve-month period preceding each subsequent anniversary date.

[48 FR 28805, June 23, 1983]

§ 203.267 Duration of periodic MIP.

The mortgagee shall pay the MIP to the Commissioner until the deed to the Commissioner is filed for record or the contract of insurance is terminated.

[48 FR 28805, June 23, 1983]

§ 203.268 Pro rata payment of periodic MIP.

(a) If the insurance contract is terminated before the due date of the initial MIP, the mortgagee shall pay a portion of the MIP prorated from the beginning of amortization, as defined in § 203.251, to the date of termination.

(b) If the insurance contract is terminated after the due date of the initial MIP, the mortgagee shall pay a portion of the current annual MIP prorated from the due date of the last annual MIP to the date of termination.

(c) A pro rata MIP shall not be due or payable where the mortgagee notifies the Commissioner that foreclosure or other action to acquire the property has been completed and that the property will not be conveyed to the Commissioner in exchange for insurance benefits. Any MIP due and paid after the institution of foreclosure or the date the property was otherwise acquired by the mortgagee will be refunded to the mortgagee upon receipt by the Commissioner of the notice from the mortgagee that the property will not be conveyed to the Commissioner.

[48 FR 28805, June 23, 1983, as amended at 61 FR 37801, July 19, 1996]

§ 203.269 Method of payment of periodic MIP.

In cases that the Commissioner deems appropriate, the Commissioner may require, by means of instructions communicated to all affected mortgagees, that periodic MIP be remitted electronically.

[60 FR 34138, June 30, 1995]

OPEN-END INSURANCE CHARGES—ALL MORTGAGES

§ 203.270 Open-end insurance charges.

(a) *Required charge.* In the case of an insured open-end advance the mortgagee shall pay to the Commissioner an open-end insurance charge.

(b) *Payment of charge for mortgages with periodic MIP.* The amount of any insured open-end advance shall be added to the average outstanding principal obligation of the mortgage for the purpose of determining the amount of periodic MIP as provided in §§ 203.260 through 203.268, except that the initial additional charge shall be prorated to cover the period beginning with the first day of the month following the issuance of a certificate evidencing the insurance of the open-end advance and ending on the due date of the next MIP.

(c) *Payment of charge for mortgages with one-time or up-front MIP.* In the case of a mortgage with a one-time or up-front MIP pursuant to § 203.280, § 203.284, or § 203.285 of this part, the insurance charge shall be in an amount equal to ½ percent per annum of the outstanding principal obligation of the open-end advance. Sections 203.260 through 203.268 shall apply to the open-end charge on a mortgage with a one-time or up-front MIP, except that all references to amortization dates shall refer to amortization dates of the open-end advance, references to MIP shall refer to the open-end insurance charge, and references to outstanding principal obligation of the mortgage shall refer to outstanding principal obligation of the open-end advance.

(d) *Method of payment—all mortgages.* The payment of any open-end insurance charge under this subpart shall be made to the Commissioner by the mortgagee either in cash or debentures issued by the Mutual Mortgage Insurance Fund at par plus accrued interest.

[48 FR 28806, June 23, 1983, as amended at 56 FR 24624, May 30, 1991; 57 FR 15211, Apr. 24, 1992; 57 FR 46983, Oct. 14, 1992; 58 FR 41003, July 30, 1993]

MORTGAGE INSURANCE PREMIUMS—ONE-TIME PAYMENT

§203.280 One-time or Up-front MIP.

For mortgages for which a one-time or up-front MIP is to be charged in accordance with §§203.259a, 203.284, or 203.285, the mortgagee shall, as a condition to the endorsement of the mortgage for insurance, pay to the Commissioner for the account of the mortgagor, in a manner prescribed by the Commissioner, a premium representing the total obligation for the insuring of the mortgage by the Commissioner or the up-front portion of the total obligation, as applicable, within 10 calendar days after the date of loan closing or within 10 calendar days after the date of disbursement of the mortgage proceeds, whichever is later.

[70 FR 19669, Apr. 13, 2005]

§203.281 Calculation of one-time MIP.

(a) The applicable premium percentage determined under paragraph (b) of this section assumes, for purposes of calculation, that the entire amount of the one-time MIP is added to the loan amount. The amount of the one-time MIP shall be determined by multiplying the loan amount otherwise insurable under this part by the applicable premium percentage, subject to adjustment for the portion of the MIP, if any, that is not to be included in the insured mortgage.

(b)(1) The Commissioner shall determine the applicable premium percentage in accordance with sound financial and actuarial practice.

(2) Application of the premium percentage determined under paragraph (b)(1) of this section shall not result in a MIP in excess of an amount equivalent to 1 per centum per annum of the amount of the principal obligation of the mortgage outstanding at any time, without taking into account delinquent payments or prepayments.

(c) The applicable premium percentage will be published by notice at least annually in the FEDERAL REGISTER.

[48 FR 28806, June 23, 1983, as amended at 61 FR 36265, July 9, 1996]

§203.282 Mortgagee's late charge and interest.

(a) Payment of a one-time or up-front MIP is late if not received by HUD within 10 calendar days after the date of loan closing or within 10 calendar days after the date of disbursement of the mortgage proceeds, whichever is later. Late payments shall include a late charge of four percent of the amount of the MIP.

(b) If payment of the MIP is not received by HUD within 30 days after the date of loan closing or within 30 calendar days after the date of disbursement of the mortgage proceeds, whichever is later, the mortgagee will be charged additional late fees until payment is received at an interest rate set in conformity with the Treasury Fiscal Requirements Manual.

[70 FR 19669, Apr. 13, 2005]

§203.283 Refund of one-time MIP.

(a) The Commissioner shall provide for the refund to the mortgagor of a portion of the unearned MIP paid pursuant to §203.280 if the contract of insurance covering the mortgage is terminated:

(1) By coveyance to one other than the Commissioner and a claim for the insurance benefits is not presented for payment (§203.315),

(2) By prepayment of the mortgage (§203.316), or

(3) By voluntary agreement with the approval of the Commissioner (§203.317).

(b) The Commissioner shall determine the amount of the premium refund by multiplying the amount the premium paid at the time the mortgage was insured by the applicable premium refund percentage for mortgages insured in the year the mortgage was endorsed for insurance. The Commissioner shall determine the applicable premium refund percentage for each year in an equitable manner and in accordance with sound financial and actuarial practice, taking into account: (1) Projected salaries and expenses, (2) prospective losses generated by insurance claims, and (3) expected future payments of premium refunds.

[48 FR 28806, June 23, 1983, as amended at 52 FR 1327, Jan. 13, 1987]

CALCULATION OF MORTGAGE INSURANCE PREMIUM ON OR AFTER JULY 1, 1991

§ 203.284 Calculation of up-front and annual MIP on or after July 1, 1991.

Except for insured mortgages with a term of 15 or fewer years executed on or after December 26, 1992, (see § 203.285 of this part), up-front and annual MIP will be calculated in accordance with this section.

(a) *Permanent provisions.* Any mortgage executed on or after October 1, 1994, that is an obligation of the Mutual Mortgage Insurance Fund, as well as any mortgage executed after December 27, 2005, which is insured under sections 203(k) or 234(c) of the National Housing Act (12 U.S.C. 1709(k) and 12 U.S.C. 1715y(c)) shall be subject to the following requirements:

(1) *Up-Front.* The Commissioner shall establish and collect a single premium payment in an amount not exceeding 2.25 percent of the amount of the original insured principal obligation of the mortgage.

(2) *Annual.* In addition to the premium under paragraph (a)(1) of this section, the Commissioner shall establish and collect annual premium payments in an amount not exceeding .50 percent of the remaining insured principal balance (excluding the portion of the remaining balance attributable to the premium collected under paragraph (a)(1) of this section) for the following periods:

(i) For any mortgage involving an original principal obligation (excluding any premium collected under paragraph (a)(1) of this section) that is less than 90 percent of the appraised value of the property (as of the date of the mortgage is accepted for insurance), for the first 11 years of the mortgage term.

(ii) For any mortgage involving an original principal obligation (excluding any premium collected under paragraph (a)(1) of this section) that is greater than or equal to 90 percent of the appraised value of the property (as of the date the mortgage is accepted for insurance), for the lesser of the mortgage term or the first 30 years of the mortgage term; except that, for any mortgage involving an original principal obligation (excluding any premium collected under paragraph (a)(1) of this section) that is greater than 95 percent of the appraised value, the annual premium collected during the period determined under this clause shall be in an amount not exceeding 0.55 percent of the remaining insured principal balance (excluding the portion of the remaining balance attributable to the premium collected under paragraph (a)(1) of this section).

(b) *Transition provisions; savings provision.* Mortgages that are obligations of the Mutual Mortgage Insurance Fund and that were insured during Fiscal Years 1991–1994, are governed by 24 CFR 203.284(b) as in effect on April 1, 2003, (see 24 CFR parts 200–499 revised as of April 1, 2003).

(c) *Refunds.* With respect to any mortgage subject to premiums under this section, the Commissioner shall refund all of the unearned premium charges paid on a mortgage upon termination of insurance by voluntary agreement or upon payment in full of the principal obligation of the mortgage before the maturity date.

(d)–(e) [Reserved]

(f) *Applicability of other sections.* The provisions of §§ 203.261, 203.262, 203.264, 203.265, 203.266, 203.267, 203.268, 203.269, 203.280, and 203.282 are applicable to mortgages subject to premiums under this section.

(g) *Definition.* As used in this section the term *remaining insured principal balance* means the average outstanding principal obligation of the mortgage for the first year of amortization, or for a 12-month period preceding a subsequent anniversary date of the beginning of amortization.

(h) *Exception for streamline refinance.* This section shall not apply to any mortgage insured pursuant to §203.43(c) if the mortgage to be refinanced was executed before July 1, 1991 and the new mortgage is executed on or after April 24, 1992. This exception does not have the effect of exempting streamline refinancing mortgages from the requirement that a one-time MIP be paid in accordance with §203.259a(a).

[57 FR 15211, Apr. 24, 1992, as amended at 57 FR 46983, Oct. 14, 1992; 58 FR 41003, July 30, 1993; 60 FR 34138, June 30, 1995; 61 FR 36265, July 9, 1996; 61 FR 37801, July 19, 1996; 70 FR 37156, June 28, 2005]

§ 203.285 Fifteen-year mortgages: Calculation of up-front and annual MIP on or after December 26, 1992.

(a) *Up-front.* Any mortgage for a term of 15 or fewer years executed on or after December 26, 1992, that is an obligation of the Mutual Mortgage Insurance Fund, and any mortgage executed on or after December 27, 2005, to be insured under sections 203(k) and 234(c) of the National Housing Act, shall be subject to a single up-front premium payment established and collected by the Commissioner in an amount not exceeding 2.0 percent of the amount of the original insured principal obligation of the mortgage. Upon termination of insurance by voluntary agreement, or upon payment in full of the principal obligation of the mortgage before the maturity date, the Commissioner shall refund all of the unearned premium charges paid on the mortgage pursuant to this paragraph (a).

(b) *Annual.* In addition to the premium under paragraph (a) of this section, the Commissioner shall establish and collect annual premium payments in amounts not exceeding the following percentages of the remaining insured principal balance (excluding the portion of the remaining balance attributable to the premium collected under paragraph (a) of this section) for the following periods:

(1) For any mortgage involving an original principal obligation (excluding any premium collected under paragraph (a) of this section) that is less than 90 percent of the appraised value of the property (as of the date the mortgage is accepted for insurance), no annual premium will be charged.

(2) For any mortgage involving an original principal obligation (excluding any premium collected under paragraph (a) of this section) that is greater than or equal to 90 percent of such value, but less than or equal to 95 percent of such value, an annual premium not exceeding .25 percent shall be collected for the first four years of the mortgage term.

(3) For any mortgage involving an original principal obligation (excluding any premium collected under paragraph (a) of this section) that is greater than 95 percent of such value, an annual premium not exceeding .25 percent shall be collected for the first eight years of the mortgage term.

(c) *Applicability of certain provisions.* The provisions of §§203.261, 203.262, 203.264, 203.265, 203.266, 203.267, 203.268, 203.269, 203.280, 203.282, 203.284(c), and 203.284(g) are applicable to mortgages subject to premiums under this section.

(d) *Exception for streamline refinance.* This section shall not apply to any mortgage insured pursuant to §203.43(c) if the mortgage to be refinanced was executed before July 1, 1991 and the new mortgage is executed on or after December 26, 1992.

[58 FR 41004, July 30, 1993, as amended at 60 FR 34138, June 30, 1995; 61 FR 37801, July 19, 1996; 70 FR 37156, June 28, 2005]

ADJUSTED MORTGAGE INSURANCE PREMIUM

§ 203.288 Discontinuance of adjusted premium charge.

Notwithstanding any provision in the mortgage instrument, there shall be no adjusted mortgage insurance premium due the Commissioner on account of the prepayment of any mortgage on or after May 1, 1972.

[37 FR 8662, Apr. 29, 1972]

VOLUNTARY TERMINATION

§ 203.295 Voluntary termination.

Upon request by the mortgagor and mortgagee the Commissioner may terminate the insurance contract on any mortgage under this part covering a 1-to-4 family residence. The mortgagee shall cancel the insurance endorsement on the mortgage insurance certificate or note upon receipt of notice from the Commissioner that the contract of insurance is terminated. Notwithstanding any provision in a mortgage instrument, there shall be no voluntary termination charge due the Commissioner on account of the voluntary termination of any mortgage insurance contract where the request for termination is received by the Commissioner on or after May 1, 1972.

[37 FR 8662, Apr. 29, 1972]

TERMINATION OF INSURANCE CONTRACT

§ 203.315 Termination by conveyance to other than Commissioner.

(a) For those mortgages to which the provisions of § 203.368 apply, the contract of insurance shall be terminated under the following circumstances:

(1) The mortgagee notifies the Commissioner that it will not convey title to the Commissioner and will not file a claim for the insurance benefits when:

(i) The mortgagee either acquires the property by any means, or

(ii) Acquires the property and gives such notice during the redemption period; or

(2) The mortgagee notifies the Commissioner that it will not file a claim for the insurance benefits when:

(i) The property is bid in and acquired at foreclosure by a party other than the mortgagee, or

(ii) After foreclosure of the mortgaged property by the mortgagee the property is redeemed.

(b) For those mortgages to which the provisions as set forth in § 203.368 do not apply, the contract of insurance shall be terminated under the following circumstances:

(1) The mortgagee acquires the mortgaged property but does not convey it to the Commissioner;

(2) The property is bid in and acquired at a foreclosure sale by a party other than the mortgagee;

(3) After foreclosure the property is redeemed;

(4) After foreclosure and during the redemption period the mortgagee gives notice that it will not tender the property to the Commissioner.

[52 FR 1327, Jan. 13, 1987]

§ 203.316 Termination by prepayment of mortgage.

The contract of insurance shall be terminated if the mortgage is paid in full prior to its maturity.

§ 203.317 Termination by voluntary agreement.

The contract of insurance shall be terminated if the mortgagor and mortgagee jointly request termination.

§ 203.318 Notice of termination by mortgagee.

No contract of insurance shall be terminated until the mortgagee has given written notice thereof to the Commissioner within 15 calendar days from the occurrence of one of the approved methods of termination set forth in this subpart.

[45 FR 31716, May 14, 1980]

§ 203.319 Pro rata payment of premiums and charges.

No contract of insurance shall be terminated until the mortgagee has paid to the Commissioner the pro rata portion of the current annual MIP or open-end insurance charge as set forth in this subpart.

[37 FR 8662, Apr. 29, 1972]

§ 203.320 Notice and date of termination by Commissioner.

The Commissioner shall notify the mortgagee that the contract of insurance has been terminated and the effective termination date. The termination date shall be the last day of the month in which one of the following events has occurred:

(a)(1) For those mortgages to which the provisions of § 203.368 apply, the date foreclosure proceedings were instituted by the mortgagee, or the property was otherwise acquired by the

198

mortgagee or a party other than the mortgagee (including the mortgagor or other party as redemptor) if the mortgagee notifies the Commissioner that title will not be conveyed to the Commissioner and a claim for the insurance benefits will not be presented for payment.

(2) For those mortgages to which the provisions of §203.368 do not apply, the date foreclosure proceedings were instituted, or the property was otherwise acquired by the mortgagee, if the mortgagee notifies the Commissioner that title will not be conveyed to the Commissioner.

(b) The date the mortgage was prepaid in full.

(c) The date a voluntary termination request is received by the Commissioner.

[36 FR 24508, Dec. 22, 1971, as amended at 52 FR 1327, Jan. 13, 1987]

§203.321 Effect of termination.

Upon termination of the contract of insurance, the obligation to pay any subsequent periodic MIP or open-end insurance charge shall cease and all rights of the mortgagor and mortgagee shall be terminated, except as otherwise provided in this part.

[48 FR 28807, June 23, 1983]

DEFAULT UNDER MORTGAGE

§203.330 Definition of delinquency and requirement for notice of delinquency to HUD.

(a) A mortgage account is delinquent any time a payment is due and not paid.

(b) Once each month on a day prescribed by HUD, the mortgagee shall report to HUD all mortgages insured under this part that were delinquent on the last day of the month, or that were reported as delinquent the previous month. The report shall be made in a manner prescribed by HUD.

[71 FR 16234, Mar. 31, 2006]

§203.331 Definition of default, date of default, and requirement of notice of default to HUD.

(a) *Default.* If the mortgagor fails to make any payment or to perform any other obligation under the mortgage,

and such failure continues for a period of 30 days, the mortgage shall be considered in default for the purposes of this subpart.

(b) *Date of default.* For the purposes of this subpart, the date of default shall be considered as 30 days after:

(1) The first uncorrected failure to perform any obligation under the mortgage; or

(2) The first failure to make a monthly payment that subsequent payments by the mortgagor are insufficient to cover when applied to the overdue monthly payments in the order in which they became due.

(c) *Notice of default.* Once each month, on a day prescribed by HUD, the mortgagee shall report to HUD all mortgages that were in default on the last day of the month, or that were reported as in default the previous month. The report shall be made in a manner prescribed by HUD.

(d) *Number of days in month.* For the purposes of this section, each month shall be considered to have 30 days.

[71 FR 16234, Mar. 31, 2006]

§203.332 [Reserved]

§203.333 Reinstatement of defaulted mortgage.

If after default and prior to the completion of foreclosure proceedings the mortgagor shall cure the default, the insurance shall continue as if a default had not occurred, provided the mortgagor pays to the mortgagee such expenses as the mortgagee has incurred in connection with the foreclosure proceedings and the mortgagee gives written notice of reinstatement to the Commissioner.

CONTINUATION OF INSURANCE

§203.340 Special forbearance.

(a) If the conditions of §203.614 are met and special forbearance relief is granted pursuant to that section, the contract of insurance shall continue in force except as otherwise provided in this subpart.

(b) The contract of insurance shall continue in force, except as otherwise provided in this subpart, when the conditions of this section which were effective prior to January 1, 1977, have been met and special forbearance relief is granted pursuant thereto prior to January 1, 1977.

[41 FR 49735, Nov. 10, 1976]

§ 203.341 Partial claim.

If the conditions of § 203.371 are met and a partial claim is paid pursuant to that section, the contract of insurance shall continue in force, except as otherwise provided in this subpart.

[62 FR 60129, Nov. 6, 1997]

§ 203.342 Mortgage modification.

If a mortgage is recast pursuant to § 203.616, the principal amount of the mortgage, as modified, shall be considered to be the "original principal balance of the mortgage" as that term is used in § 203.401.

[62 FR 60129, Nov. 6, 1997]

§ 203.343 Partial release, addition or substitution of security.

(a) Except as provided in § 203.389(n), a mortgagee shall not release the security or any part thereof, while the mortgage is insured, without the prior consent of the Commissioner.

(b) A mortgagee may, with the prior consent of the Commissioner, accept an addition to, or substitution of, security for the purpose of removing the dwelling to a new lot under the following conditions:

(1) The mortgagee obtains a good and valid first lien on the property to which the dwelling is removed.

(2) All damages to the structure are repaired without cost to HUD.

(3) The property to which the dwelling is removed is in an area known to be reasonably free from natural hazards or, if in a flood zone, the mortgagor will insure or reinsure under the Federal Flood Insurance Program.

(c) A mortgagee may, without the prior consent of the Commissioner, accept an addition to, or substitution of, security for the purpose of removing the dwelling to a new lot under the following conditions.

(1) The dwelling has survived an earthquake or other disaster with little damage, but continued location on the property might be hazardous.

(2) The conditions stated in paragraph (b) of this section exist.

(3) Immediately following the emergency removal the mortgagee notifies the Commissioner of the reasons for removal.

[41 FR 49735, Nov. 10, 1976]

FORBEARANCE RELIEF FOR MILITARY PERSONNEL

§ 203.345 Postponement of principal payments—mortgagors in military service.

In addition to the special forbearance relief afforded by §§ 203.340 through 203.342, if the mortgagor is a person in the military service (as defined in the Soldiers' and Sailors' Civil Relief Act of 1940), the mortgagee may, by written agreement with the mortgagor, postpone for the period of military service and three months thereafter any part of the monthly payment which represents amortization of principal. The agreement shall contain a provision for the resumption of monthly payments after such period in amounts which will completely amortize the mortgage debt within the maturity as provided in the original mortgage. The agreement shall in no way affect the amount of the annual MIP which will continue to be calculated in accordance with original amortization provisions of the mortgage.

§ 203.346 Postponement of foreclosure—mortgagors in military service.

If at any time during default the mortgagor is a "Person in military service," as such term is defined in the Soldiers' and Sailors' Civil Relief Act of 1940, the period during which the mortgagor is in such service shall be excluded in computing the period within which the mortgagee shall commence foreclosure or acquire the property by other means as provided in § 203.355 of this subpart. No postponement or delay in the prosecution of foreclosure proceedings during the period the mortgagor is in such military service shall be construed as failure on the part of the mortgagee to exercise reasonable diligence in prosecuting such proceedings to completion as required by this subpart.

[36 FR 24508, Dec. 22, 1971, as amended at 61 FR 36265, July 9, 1996]

ASSIGNMENT OF MORTGAGE

§203.350 Assignment of mortgage.

(a) *Assignment of modified mortgages pursuant to section 230, National Housing Act.* HUD may accept an assignment of any mortgage covering a one-to-four family residence if the following requirements are met:

(1) The mortgage was in default;

(2) The mortgagee has modified the mortgage under §203.616 to cure the default and to provide for mortgage payments within the reasonable ability of the mortgagor to pay, at an interest rate not exceeding current market interest rates; and

(3) Such other conditions that HUD may prescribe, which may include the requirement that the mortgagee continue to be responsible for servicing the mortgage.

(b) *Assignments pursuant to section 248, National Housing Act.* Notwithstanding the provisions of paragraph (a), the Commissioner shall, upon application by the mortgagee, approve the assignment to the Commissioner of any mortgage insured pursuant to section 248 of the National Housing Act (see §203.43h) where the mortgagor has been in default for more than 90 days. The mortgagee may not request the Commissioner to accept an assignment until the mortgagee has submitted documents to the Commissioner showing that the requirements of §203.604 have been met. HUD shall then notify the mortgagee of its approval of the mortgagee's actions under §203.604 and that the mortgagee may assign the mortgage to the Secretary, or HUD will specify what further action the mortgagee must take to meet the requirements of §203.604.

(c) *Assignment of mortgages insured pursuant to section 247, National Housing Act.* Notwithstanding the provisions of paragraph (a) of this section, the Secretary will, upon application by the mortgagee, agree to accept an assignment of any mortgage insured pursuant to section 247 of the National Housing Act (§203.43i of this part) where the mortgagor has been in default for more than 180 days, provided that the requirements of §203.665 are satisfied.

(d) *Assignment of mortgages authorized by section 203(q), National Housing Act.* Notwithstanding the provisions of paragraph (a) of this section, the Secretary will, upon application by the mortgagee, agree to accept assignment of any mortgage authorized by section 203(q) of the National Housing Act (§203.43j of this part) if

(1) The mortgagor has been in default for more than 90 days for failure to make a monthly payment,

(2) The requirements of §203.666 are satisfied, and

(3) The date of default occurs before the mortgagor and the lessor execute a lease renewal or a new lease with a term of not less than five years beyond the maturity date of the mortgage, or with a term established by an arbitration award.

If the default is non-monetary, the date of default occurs prior to an action described in paragraph (d)(3) of this section, the requirements of §203.666 are satisfied, and the mortgagor has been in default for more than 30 days, the Secretary may in his or her discretion, upon application by the mortgagee, agree to accept an assignment of the mortgage. If the leasehold estate has terminated before the mortgage has been assigned, or title to the property conveyed, to the Secretary, and the mortgage is in default for any reason for more than 30 days, the Secretary will, upon application by the mortgagee, agree to accept an assignment of the mortgage.

(e) *Filing assignment for record.* Within 30 days of the Secretary's written agreement to accept assignment of a defaulted mortgage, or within such additional time as the Secretary authorizes in writing, the mortgagee must file the assignment for record.

(Information collection requirements in paragraph (b) were approved by the Office of Management and Budget under control number 2502–0169)

[51 FR 21872, June 16, 1986, as amended at 52 FR 48202, Dec. 21, 1987; 53 FR 9869, Mar. 28, 1988; 53 FR 13404, Apr. 25, 1988; 55 FR 282, Jan. 4, 1980; 61 FR 35018, July 3, 1996]

§203.351 Application for insurance benefits and fiscal data.

On the date the assignment of the mortgage is filed for record, the mortgagee shall forward to the Commissioner the prescribed application for insurance benefits and fiscal data pertaining to the mortgage transaction, together with the receipts covering all disbursements, as required by the fiscal data form. In addition, the following requirements shall be met:

(a) *Items to be included with application.* The following items shall be forwarded to the Commissioner with the application:

(1) *Credit and security instrument.* The original credit and security instruments assigned without recourse or warranty, except that no act or omission of the mortgagee shall have impaired the validity and priority of the mortgage.

(2) *Recorded assignment instrument.* The original of the recorded assignment of mortgage. If the original of the assignment is not available, a copy shall be furnished and the original forwarded as soon as possible.

(3) *Hazard insurance.* All hazard insurance policies held in connection with the mortgaged property, together with a copy of the mortgagee's notification to the carrier authorizing the amendment of the loss payable clause substituting the Commissioner as the mortgagee.

(4) *Rights and interests.* An assignment of all rights and interests arising under the mortgage, and all claims of the mortgagee against the mortgagor or others arising out of the mortgage transaction.

(5) *Property.* All property of the mortgagor held by the mortgagee or to which it is entitled (other than the cash items which are to be retained by the mortgagee).

(6) *Records and accounts.* All records, ledger cards, documents, books, papers and accounts relating to the mortgage transaction.

(7) *Additional information.* Any additional information or data which the Commissioner may require.

(8) *Title evidence.* All title evidence held by the mortgagee. It need not be extended to include the recordation of the assignment. If a mortgagee's title policy is furnished, the Commissioner shall be a named insured under such policy.

(b) *Items to be retained by mortgagee.* The mortgagee shall retain all cash amounts held or deposited for the account of the mortgagor or to which it is entitled under the mortgage transaction that have not been applied in reduction of the principal mortgage indebtedness.

(c) Title evidence for mortgages insured under § 203.43d as set forth in § 203.385 shall accompany the application for insurance benefits.

[36 FR 24508, Dec. 22, 1971, as amended at 37 FR 7693, Apr. 10, 1972; 42 FR 57435, Nov. 2, 1977]

§ 203.353 Certification by mortgagee.

At the time of assignment of the mortgage, the mortgagee shall certify to the Commissioner that:

(a) *Priority of mortgage to liens.* The mortgage is prior to all mechanics' and materialmen's liens filed of record, regardless of when such liens attach, and prior to all liens and encumbrances, or defects which may arise except such liens or other matters as may have been approved by the Commissioner;

(b) *Amount due.* The amount stated in the instrument of assignment is actually due and owing under the mortgage;

(c) *Offsets or counterclaims.* There are no offsets or counterclaims thereto and the mortgagee has a good right to assign.

CLAIM PROCEDURE

§ 203.355 Acquisition of property.

(a) *In general.* Upon default of a mortgage, except as provided in paragraphs (b) through (i) of this section, the mortgagee shall take one of the following actions within nine months from the date of default, or within any additional time approved by the Secretary or authorized by §§ 203.345 or 203.346. For mortgages where the date of default is on or after February 1, 1998, the mortgagee shall take one or a combination of the following actions within six months of the date of default or within such additional time approved by HUD or authorized by §§ 203.345 or 203.346:

(1) Obtain a deed-in-lieu of foreclosure (see §§ 203.357, 203.389 and 203.402(f) of this part) with title being taken in the name of the mortgagee or the Secretary;

(2) Commence foreclosure;

(3) Enter into a special forbearance agreement under §203.614;

(4) Complete a modification of the mortgage under §203.616;

(5) Complete a refinance of the mortgage under §203.43(c);

(6) Complete an assumption under §203.512;

(7) File a partial claim under §203.371; or

(8) Initiate a pre-foreclosure sale under §203.370.

(b) *Vacant or abandoned property.* With respect to defaulted mortgages on vacant or abandoned property, if the mortgagee discovers, or should have discovered, that the property is vacant or abandoned, the mortgagee must commence foreclosure within the later of 120 days after the date the property became vacant, or 60 days after the date the property is discovered, or should have been discovered, to be vacant or abandoned; but no later than the number of months from the date of default as provided in paragraph (a) of this section. The mortgagee must not delay foreclosure on vacant or abandoned property because of the requirements of §203.606.

(c) *Prohibition of foreclosure within time limits.* If the laws of the State in which the mortgaged property is located, or Federal bankruptcy law:

(1) Do not permit the commencement of foreclosure within the time limits described in paragraphs (a), (b), (g), (h) and (i) of this section, the mortgagee must commence foreclosure within 90 days after the expiration of the time during which foreclosure is prohibited; or

(2) Require the prosecution of a foreclosure to be discontinued, the mortgagee must recommence the foreclosure within 90 days after the expiration of the time during which foreclosure is prohibited.

(d) *Property located on Indian land.* Upon default of a mortgage on property located on Indian land insured pursuant to section 248 of the National Housing Act (see §203.43h of this part), the mortgagee must comply with §§203.350(b) and 204.664 of this part.

(e) *Property located on Hawaiian home lands.* Upon default of a mortgage on property located on Hawaiian home lands insured pursuant to section 247 of the National Housing Act (sec §203.43i of this part), the mortgagee must comply with §§203.350(c) and 203.665 of this part.

(f) *Property located on the Allegany Reservation of the Seneca Nation of Indians.* Upon default of a mortgage on property located on the Allegany Reservation of the Seneca Nation of Indians authorized by section 203(q) of the National Housing Act (see §203.43j of this part), the mortgagee must comply with §§203.350(d) and 203.666 of this part, unless the mortgagor and the lessor have executed a lease renewal or a new lease either with a term of not less than five years beyond the maturity date of the mortgage, or with a term established by arbitration award. If a lease renewal or new lease has been executed, the mortgagee must comply with paragraph (a) of this section.

(g) *Pre-foreclosure sale procedure.* Within 90 days of the end of a mortgagor's participation in the pre-foreclosure sale procedure, *or* within the time limit described in paragraph (a) of this section, whichever is later, if no closing of an approved pre-foreclosure sale has occurred, the mortgagee must obtain a deed in lieu of foreclosure, with title being taken in the name of the mortgagee or the Secretary, or undertake one of the actions listed at §203.355(a). The end-of-participation date is defined as:

(1) Four months after the date of commencement of participation, if there is no signed Contract of Sale at that time, unless extended by the Commissioner;

(2) Six months after the date of commencement of participation, if there is a signed contract but settlement has not occurred by that date, unless extended by the Commissioner;

(3) The date the mortgagee is notified of the mortgagor's withdrawal from the Pre-foreclosure Sale procedure; or

(4) The date of the letter sent by the mortgagee to the mortgagor prior to the expiration of the customary participation period, terminating the mortgagor's opportunity to participate in the Pre-foreclosure Sale procedure.

(h) *Special forbearance.* If the mortgagor fails to meet the requirements of a special forbearance under §203.614 and the failure continues for 60 days, the mortgagee must undertake one of the actions listed at § 203.355(a) within the time limit described in paragraph (a) of this section or 90 days after the mortgagor's failure to meet the special forbearance requirements, whichever is later.

(i) *Modification under § 203.616, refinance under § 203.43(c), or assumption under § 203.512.* Provided that the mortgagee has established the mortgagor's eligibility within the time frame provided in § 203.355(a), if a mortgagee enters into a loss mitigation relief measure (*i.e.,* modification under § 203.616, refinance under § 203.43(c), or assumption under § 203.512) and it fails, the six-month period provided in § 203.355(a) is extended by an additional 90 days to allow the mortgagee to try another loss mitigation tool or go to foreclosure.

[57 FR 47970, Oct. 20, 1992, as amended at 59 FR 50143, Sept. 30, 1994; 60 FR 57678, Nov. 16, 1995; 61 FR 35018, July 3, 1996; 62 FR 60129, Nov. 6, 1997]

§ 203.356 Notice of foreclosure and pre-foreclosure sale; reasonable diligence requirements.

(a) *Notice of foreclosure and pre-foreclosure sale.* The mortgagee must give notice to the Secretary, in a format prescribed by the Secretary, within 30 days after the institution of foreclosure proceedings. The mortgagee must give notice to the Secretary, in a format prescribed by the Secretary, within the time-frame prescribed by the Secretary, of the acceptance of any mortgagor into the pre-foreclosure sale procedure.

(b) *Reasonable diligence.* The mortgagee must exercise reasonable diligence in prosecuting the foreclosure proceedings to completion and in acquiring title to and possession of the property. A time frame that is determined by the Secretary to constitute "reasonable diligence" for each State is made available to mortgagees.

[61 FR 36265, July 9, 1996]

§ 203.357 Deed in lieu of foreclosure.

(a) *Mortgagors owning one property.* In lieu of instituting or completing a foreclosure, the mortgagee may acquire property from one other than a corporate mortgagor by voluntary conveyance from the mortgagor who certifies that he does not own any other property subject to a mortgage insured or held by FHA. Conveyance of the property by deed in lieu of foreclosure is approved subject to the following requirements:

(1) The mortgage is in default at the time the deed is executed and delivered;

(2) The credit instrument is cancelled and surrendered to the mortgagor;

(3) The mortgage is satisfied of record as a part of the consideration for such conveyance;

(4) The deed from the mortgagor contains a covenant which warrants against the acts of the grantor and all claiming by, through, or under him and conveys good marketable title;

(5) The mortgagee transfers to the Commissioner good marketable title accompanied by satisfactory title evidence.

(b) *Corporate mortgagors.* A mortgagee may accept a deed in lieu of foreclosure from a corporate mortgagor in compliance with the requirements of paragraph (a) of this section, if the mortgagee obtains the prior written consent of the Commissioner.

(c) *Mortgagors owning more than one property.* The mortgagee may accept a deed in lieu of foreclosure in compliance with the provisions of paragraph (a) of this section, from an individual who owns more than one property which is subject to a mortgage insured or held by the FHA if the mortgagee obtains the prior written consent of the Commissioner.

§ 203.358 Direct conveyance of property.

In acquiring the property or conveying the property to the Commissioner the mortgagee may arrange for the deed to be made directly to the Commissioner from the mortgagor or other grantor. The mortgagee shall be responsible for determining that such conveyance will comply with all of the provisions of this part conveying good marketable title and satisfactory title evidence.

§ 203.359 Time of conveyance to the Secretary.

(a) *For mortgages insured under firm commitments issued prior to November 19, 1992 or under direct endorsement processing where the credit worksheet was signed by the mortgagee's approved underwriter prior to November 19, 1992.* After acquiring good marketable title to and possession of the property the mortgagee must transfer the property to the Secretary:

(1) Within 30 days after acquiring possession of the mortgaged property by foreclosure or other means; or

(2) Within such further time as may be necessary to complete the title examination and perfect the title.

(b) *For mortgages insured under firm commitments issued on or after November 19, 1992, or under direct endorsement processing where the credit worksheet was signed by the mortgagee's underwriter on or after November 19, 1992—(1) Conveyance by the mortgagee.* The mortgagee must acquire good marketable title and transfer the property to the Secretary within 30 days of the later of:

(i) Filing for record the foreclosure deed;

(ii) Recording date of deed in lieu of foreclosure;

(iii) Acquiring possession of the property;

(iv) Expiration of the redemption period; or

(v) Such further time as the Secretary may approve in writing.

(2) *Direct conveyance.* In cases where the mortgagee arranges for a direct conveyance of the property to the Secretary, the mortgagee must ensure that the property is transferred to the Secretary within 30 days of the reasonable diligence time frame specified in § 203.356 of this part.

[57 FR 47971, Oct. 20, 1992, as amended at 61 FR 36453, July 10, 1996]

§ 203.360 Notice of property transfer or pre-foreclosure sale and application for insurance benefits.

(a) On the date the deed is filed for record the mortgagee shall notify the Commissioner on a form prescribed by him of the filing of such conveyance and shall assign, without recourse or warranty any or all claims which the mortgagee has acquired in connection with the mortgage transaction, and as a result of the foreclosure proceedings or other means by which the mortgagee acquired or conveyed such property, except such claims as may have been released with the approval of the Commissioner.

(b) Within 30 days of the closing of an approved pre-foreclosure sale, the mortgagee shall notify the Commissioner on a form prescribed by him of the pre-foreclosure sale.

[36 FR 24508, Dec. 22, 1971, as amended at 59 FR 50144, Sept. 30, 1994]

§ 203.361 Acceptance of property by Commissioner.

Upon receipt of notice of property transfer the Commissioner shall accept title to and possession of the property as of the date of the filing for record of the deed to the Commissioner, subject to compliance with the regulations in this part.

§ 203.362 Conditions for withdrawal of application for insurance benefits.

With the consent of the Commissioner, a mortgagee may withdraw an application for insurance benefits if the mortgagee agrees that it will:

(a) Accept a reconveyance of the property under a deed which warrants against the acts of the Commissioner and all claiming by, through, or under him; and

(b) Promptly file a reconveyance for record; and

(c) Accept without continuation the title evidence which it furnished the Commissioner; and

(d) Reimburse the Commissioner for property expenditures as set forth in § 203.364.

§ 203.363 Effect of noncompliance with regulations.

(a) *For mortgages insured under firm commitments issued prior to November 19, 1992 or under direct endorsement processing where the credit worksheet was signed by the mortgagee's approved underwriter prior to November 19, 1992.* If, for any reason, the mortgagee fails to comply with the regulations in this subpart, the Secretary may hold processing of the application for insurance benefits in abeyance for a reasonable time in order to permit the mortgagee to comply, or, in the alternative, the Secretary may reconvey title to the property to the mortgagee, in which event the application for insurance benefits shall be considered as cancelled without prejudice to the rights of the mortgagee to reapply for insurance benefits at a subsequent date.

(b) *For mortgages insured under firm commitments issued on or after November 19, 1992, or under direct endorsement processing where the credit worksheet was signed by the mortgagee's underwriter on or after November 19, 1992.* If, for any reason, the mortgagee fails to comply with the regulations in this subpart, the Secretary may hold processing of the application for insurance benefits in abeyance for a reasonable time in order to permit the mortgagee to comply. In the alternative to holding processing in abeyance, the Secretary may reconvey title to the property to the mortgagee, in which event the application for insurance benefits shall be considered as cancelled and the mortgagee shall refund the insurance benefits to the Secretary as well as other funds required by § 203.364 of this part. The mortgagee may reapply for insurance benefits at a subsequent date; provided, however, that the mortgagee may not be reimbursed for any expenses incurred in connection with the property after it has been reconveyed by the Secretary, or paid any debenture interest accrued after the date of initial conveyance or after the date conveyance was required by § 203.359 of this part, whichever is earlier, and there will be deducted from the insurance benefits any reduction in the Secretary's estimate of the value of the property occurring from the time of reconveyance to the time of reapplication.

[57 FR 47971, Oct. 20, 1992, as amended at 61 FR 36453, July 10, 1996]

§ 203.364　Mortgagee's liability for property expenditures.

Where the Secretary acquires a property and thereafter it becomes necessary for the Secretary to reconvey the property to the mortgagee due to the mortgagee's noncompliance with these regulations or the application for insurance benefits is withdrawn with the consent of the Secretary, the mortgagee shall reimburse the Secretary for all expenses incurred in connection with such acquisition and reconveyance. The reimbursement shall include interest on the amount of insurance benefits refunded by the mortgagee from the date the insurance benefits were paid to the date of refund at an interest rate set in conformity with the Treasury Fiscal Requirements Manual, and the Secretary's cost of holding the property, accruing on a daily basis, from the date the deed to the Secretary was filed for record to the date of reconveyance. These costs are based on the Secretary's estimate of the taxes, maintenance and operating expenses of the property, and administrative expenses. Appropriate adjustments shall be made by the Secretary on account of any income received from the property.

[57 FR 47971, Oct. 20, 1992]

§ 203.365　Documents and information to be furnished the Secretary; claims review.

(a) *Items to be furnished the Secretary.* Within 45 days after the deed is filed for record, in the case of a conveyance claim; or, in the case of a claim arising from a pre-foreclosure sale, within 30 days after the closing of the pre-foreclosure sale, unless extended by the Commissioner, the mortgagee must forward to the Secretary:

(1) A copy of the deed to the Secretary that has been filed for record and the title evidence continued so as to include recordation of the deed; or evidence, as prescribed by the Secretary, of the closing of the pre-foreclosure sale.

(2) Fiscal data pertaining to the mortgage transaction.

(3) Any additional information or data that the Secretary may require.

(b) *Items to be retained by mortgagee.* The mortgagee must retain all cash amounts, held or deposited for the account of the mortgagor or to which it is entitled under the mortgage transaction, that have not been applied in reduction of the principal mortgage indebtedness.

(c) *Claim file to be maintained by mortgagee.* (1) The Secretary may verify the accuracy of information regarding the insurance claim either before payment of the claim or after payment by periodic reviews of the mortgagee's records. Mortgagees must reimburse the Secretary for any claim and interest overpaid because of incorrect, unsupported, or inappropriate information provided by the mortgagee, or because of failure to provide correct information.

(2) Mortgagees must maintain a claim file containing documentation supporting all information submitted for claim payment for at least three years after a claim has been paid. All claim files for claims paid during a period relating to an unresolved or ongoing claim review must be maintained until final resolution of such review. Information to be maintained in the claim file includes receipts covering all disbursements as required by the fiscal data form, ledger cards covering the mortgage transaction, and any additional information or data relevant to the mortgage transaction or insurance claim.

(3) The Secretary may review any claim file at any time during the three-year period after the claim has been paid. Denial of access to any files will be grounds for withdrawal of the mortgagee's approved lender status, debarment by the Secretary, or immediate suspension of all claim payments.

(4) Within 24 hours of a request by the Secretary, a mortgagee must make available for review, or forward to the Secretary, hard copies of identified claim files.

(d) *Statistical sampling.* HUD may use statistical sampling in selecting claims to be reviewed and in determining the amount due the Secretary because of overpayment.

[57 FR 47972, Oct. 20, 1992, as amended at 59 FR 50144, Sept. 30, 1994]

§203.366 Conveyance of marketable title.

(a) *Satisfactory conveyance of title and transfer of possession.* The mortgagee shall tender to the Commissioner a satisfactory conveyance of title and transfer of possession of the property. The deed or other instrument of conveyance shall convey good marketable title to the property, which shall be accompanied by title evidence satisfactory to the Commissioner.

(b) *Conveyance of property without good marketable title.* (1) For mortgages insured under firm commitments issued on or after November 19, 1992, or under direct endorsement processing where the credit worksheet was signed by the mortgagee's underwriter on or after November 19, 1992, if the title to the property conveyed by the mortgagee to the Secretary is not good and marketable, the mortgagee must correct any title defect within 60 days after receiving notice from the Secretary, or within such further time as the Secretary may approve in writing.

(2) If the defect is not corrected within 60 days, or such further time as the Secretary approves in writing, the mortgagee must reimburse the Secretary for HUD's costs of holding the property, accruing on a daily basis, and interest on the amount of insurance benefits paid to the mortgagee at an interest rate set in conformity with the Treasury Fiscal Requirements Manual from the date of such notice to the date the defect is corrected or until the Secretary reconveys the property to the mortgagee, as described in paragraph (b)(3) of this section. The daily holding costs to be charged a mortgagee shall include the costs specified in §203.364 of this part.

(3) If the title defect is not corrected within a reasonable time, as determined by HUD, the Secretary will, after notice, reconvey the property to the mortgagee and the mortgagee must reimburse the Secretary in accordance with §§203.363 and 203.364 of this part.

[36 FR 24508, Dec. 22, 1971, as amended at 57 FR 47972, Oct. 20, 1992; 61 FR 36453, July 10, 1996]

§203.367 Contents of deed and supporting documents.

The deed and supporting accompanying documents shall be as follows:

(a) *Deed.* A deed conveying the property to the Federal Housing Commissioner. The deed shall:

(1) Contain covenants which warrant title against acts of the grantor, and all claiming by, through, or under said grantor, if the grantor is the mortgagee or mortgagor; if the grantor is a party other than the mortgagee or mortgagor, the special warranty covenants may be limited or amended to

accord with the law of the particular jurisdiction.

(2) Recite nominal consideration, if such recital is adequate under the laws of the State in which the property is located or such other consideration as may be necessary to support the deed.

(b) *Maps or survey.* A map or diagram showing property location with reference to public streets or roads or a survey, if available. When a part of the property has been taken by condemnation proceedings or conveyance in lieu of condemnation, a map or diagram showing the part taken and the property remaining is required.

(c) *Credit documents.* The original credit and security instruments, if available or a deficiency judgment, if any, duly assigned or endorsed by the mortgagee, without recourse, to the Commissioner.

§ 203.368 Claims without conveyance procedure.

(a)(1) The requirements of this section apply to any insured mortgage subject to this subpart which was either insured pursuant to:

(i) A conditional commitment issued on or after November 30, 1983 or, as appropriate,

(ii) An application for mortgage insurance endorsement under the Single Family Direct Endorsement Program, as provided in § 203.255(b), where the property appraisal report was signed by the mortgagee's underwriter on or after November 30, 1983.

(2) The requirements of this section shall also apply to any other mortgages subject to this subpart where the mortgagee elects to provide the notice to HUD required by paragraph (d) of this section.

(b) Notwithstanding the provisions of paragraph (a) of this section, the requirements of this section do not apply if the mortgaged property has been damaged as set out in § 203.378.

(c) Nothing in this section shall affect any rights or obligations arising under the procedures set forth in subpart C of this part.

(d) After initiating proceedings to foreclose an insured mortgage within the coverage of paragraph (a)(1) of this section by judicial, statutory, or other means authorized by the mortgage instrument, the mortgagee shall furnish notice of the foreclosure to the Commissioner, containing such information as shall be prescribed by the Commissioner, together with a copy of the notice of sale, on or before the date of first publication, posting, or other notice. The mortgagee foreclosing an insured mortgage subject to this subpart and within the coverage of paragraph (a)(2) of this section may elect to become subject to this section by providing such notices to the Commissioner in accordance with the preceding sentence.

(e) Where notice of the foreclosure sale is provided pursuant to paragraph (d) of this section, the Commissioner may elect to cause the mortgaged property to be appraised and to give written notice to the mortgagee, not less than five days prior to the date of the foreclosure sale, of the Commissioner's estimate of the fair market value of the mortgaged property, less adjustments as the Commissioner may deem appropriate (which may include, without limitation, the Commissioner's estimate of holding costs and resale costs that would be incurred if title to the mortgaged property were conveyed to the Commissioner). Such amount is referred to hereafter as the "Commissioner's adjusted fair market value."

(f) If the Commissioner fails to provide notice of the Commissioner's adjusted fair market value to the mortgagee not less than five days prior to the scheduled date of foreclosure sale, this section shall have no further application and §§ 203.355 through 203.367 shall apply: *Provided,* that a mortgagee which receives the Commissioner's notice at any time prior to the foreclosure sale may waive late receipt by so notifying the Commissioner, in which case this section shall apply.

(g) If the Commissioner provides notice of the Commissioner's adjusted fair market value in accordance with paragraph (e) of this section the following shall be applicable:

(1) The mortgagee shall tender a bid at the foreclosure sale in the amount of the Commissioner's adjusted fair market value.

(2) If the mortgagee acquires title to the mortgaged property pursuant to a bid at foreclosure sale in an amount

equal to the Commissioner's adjusted fair market value, the mortgagee may elect to retain title to the property and to file a claim for the insurance benefits computed as provided in §203.401(b).

(3) If a party other than the mortgagee acquires title to the mortgaged property either pursuant to a bid at foreclosure sale or through the redemption of the property in an amount not less than the Commissioner's adjusted fair market value, the mortgagee may file a claim for the insurance benefits computed as provided in §203.401(b).

(4) If the mortgagee acquires title to the mortgaged property pursuant to a bid at foreclosure sale in an amount in excess of the Commissioner's adjusted fair market value, the mortgagee is deemed to have elected to retain title to the property and is limited to filing a claim for the insurance benefits computed as provided in §203.401(b). In the event the mortgagee can show good cause for having bid an amount in excess of the Commissioner's adjusted fair market value, the Commissioner may, at his discretion, waive the provisions of this subparagraph and allow the mortgagee to convey title to the Commissioner and file a claim for the insurance benefits computed as provided in §203.401(a). A mortgagee which has elected to follow the provisions of this section pursuant to paragraph (a)(2) of this section and bids an amount in excess of the Commissioner's adjusted fair market value shall not be subject to the provisions of this subparagraph, and may elect to retain or convey title in filing a claim for the insurance benefits.

(5) In any other case, the mortgagee may file a claim for insurance benefits only upon conveyance of title to the mortgaged property to the Commissioner.

(h) If the Commissioner provides timely notice of the Commissioner's adjusted fair market value in accordance with paragraph (e), the Commissioner may require the mortgagee to advertise the upcoming sale in addition to the standard legal notices which may be required by state law.

(i) Where a mortgagee files a claim for the insurance benefits without conveying title to the property to the

Commissioner, as authorized by this section:

(1) Sections 203.358 through 203.367 shall not be applicable.

(2) The mortgagee shall assign to the Commissioner, without recourse or warranty, any or all claims which the mortgagee has acquired in connection with the mortgage transaction and as a result of the foreclosure proceedings or other means by which the mortgagee or party other than the mortgagee acquired such property, except such claims as may have been released with the approval of the Commissioner.

(3) The mortgagee shall forward to the Commissioner:

(i) Fiscal data pertaining to the mortgage transaction;

(ii) The original credit and security instruments, if available, or a deficiency judgment, if any, duly assigned or endorsed by the mortgagee, without recourse, to the Commissioner; and

(iii) Any additional information or data which the Commissioner may require.

(4) The mortgagee shall retain all cash amounts held or deposited for the account of the mortgagor or to which the mortgagee is entitled under the mortgage transaction that have not been applied in reduction of the principal mortgage indebtedness. Cash amounts shall be itemized and deducted from the claim pursuant to §203.403. Receipts for disbursements are to be retained by the mortgagee and are to be made available upon request by the Commissioner.

(5) The mortgagee shall file its claim:

(i) Within 30 days after the mortgagee acquired good marketable title to the property; or

(ii) Within 30 days after a party other than the mortgagee acquired good marketable title to the property; or

(iii) In redemption States, within 30 days after the mortgagor or another party redeemed the property or the redemption period has expired; or

(iv) Within such other time as may be determined by the Commissioner.

(6) In any case in which the insurance benefits paid include, pursuant to §203.402(c), hazard insurance premiums paid by the mortgagee, the portion of the hazard insurance premium allocable to the period after acquisition of

title by the mortgagee or a third party shall be deducted from the mortgage insurance benefits otherwise payable.

(Approved by the Office of Management and Budget under control number 2502–0347)

[52 FR 1327, Jan. 13, 1987, as amended at 61 FR 36453, July 10, 1996]

§ 203.369   Deficiency judgments.

(a) *Mortgages insured on or after March 28, 1988.* (1) For mortgages insured pursuant to firm commitments issued on or after March 28, 1988, or pursuant to direct endorsement processing where the credit worksheet was signed by the mortgagee's underwriter on or after March 28, 1988, the Secretary may require the mortgagee diligently to pursue a deficiency judgment in connection with any foreclosure. With respect to claims filed for insurance benefits on such mortgages, any judgment obtained by the mortgagee must be assigned to the Secretary.

(2) In cases where the Secretary requires the pursuit of a deficiency judgment and provides the mortgagee with the Secretary's estimate of the fair market value of the property, less adjustments, in accordance with § 203.368(e) of this part, the mortgagee must tender a bid at the foreclosure sale in that amount, and must take all other appropriate steps in accordance with State law to obtain a deficiency judgment.

(b) *Mortgages insured before March 28, 1988.* For mortgages insured pursuant to firm commitments issued before March 28, 1988, or pursuant to direct endorsement processing where the credit worksheet was signed by the mortgagee's underwriter before March 28, 1988, the Secretary may request that the mortgage diligently pursue a deficiency judgment in connection with the foreclosure. With respect to claims filed for insurance benefits on such mortgages, any judgment obtained by the mortgagee must be assigned to the Secretary.

(c) In cases where pursuit of a deficiency judgment is requested or required under this section, the Commissioner, where the Commissioner determines it appropriate under State law requirements, may extend the otherwise applicable period of time within which a deficiency judgment (and other

claims against the mortgagor) and related credit documents must be assigned to the Commissioner under § 203.360, § 203.367 or § 203.368 of this subpart.

(d) In addition to meeting the requirements of § 203.356, in cases where the Commissioner determines it necessary because of State law requirements, the Commissioner may also require (or request, as the Commissioner may determine) the mortgagee to provide the Commissioner with notice of the mortgagee's intent to institute foreclosure proceedings a reasonable amount of time before proceedings are instituted, in order that the Commissioner may be able effectively to require or request the mortgagee, in appropriate cases, to seek a deficiency judgment.

(The information collection requirements contained in this section have been approved by the Office of Management and Budget under control number 2535–0093)

[53 FR 4387, Feb. 16, 1988, as amended at 57 FR 47972, Oct. 20, 1992; 61 FR 36453, July 10, 1996]

§ 203.370   Pre-foreclosure sales.

(a) *General.* HUD will pay FHA insurance benefits to mortgagees in cases where, in accordance with all regulations and procedures applicable to preforeclosure sales, the mortgaged property is sold by the mortgagor, after default and *prior to* foreclosure, at its current fair market value (less adjustments as the Commissioner may deem appropriate) but for less than the mortgage loan amount currently outstanding.

(b) *Notification of mortgagor.* The mortgagee shall give notice, according to prescribed procedures, of the opportunity to be considered for the pre-foreclosure sale procedure to each mortgagor in default. All notices to mortgagors must be in an accessible format, if requested, or if required by the person's known disability, as required by 24 CFR part 9.

(c) *Eligibility for the Pre-foreclosure Sale Procedure.* In order to be considered for the pre-foreclosure sale procedure, a mortgagor:

(1) Must be an owner occupant in a single family residence that is security for a mortgage insured under this part,

unless otherwise prescribed by the Secretary.

(2) Must have an account in default, for such period as determined by the Secretary, which default is the result of an adverse and unavoidable financial situation.

(3) Must have, at the time application is made to pursue a pre-foreclosure sale, a mortgaged property whose current fair market value, compared to the amount needed to discharge the mortgage, meets the criterion established by the Secretary, unless a variance is granted by the Secretary.

(4) Must have received an appropriate disclosure, as prescribed by the Secretary.

[59 FR 50144, Sept. 30, 1994, as amended at 61 FR 35018, July 3, 1996; 72 FR 56161, Oct. 2, 2007]

§ 203.371 Partial claim.

(a) *General.* Notwithstanding the conveyance, sale or assignment requirements for payment of a claim elsewhere in this part, HUD will pay partial FHA insurance benefits to mortgagees after a period of forbearance, the maximum length of which HUD will prescribe, and in accordance with this section.

(b) *Requirements.* The following conditions must be met for payment of a partial claim:

(1) The mortgagor has been delinquent for at least 4 months or such other time prescribed by HUD;

(2) The amount of the arrearage has not exceeded the equivalent of 12 monthly mortgage payments;

(3) The mortgagor is able to resume making full monthly mortgage payments;

(4) The mortgagor is not financially able to make sufficient additional payments to repay the arrearage within a time frame specified by HUD;

(5) The mortgagor is not financially qualified to support monthly mortgage payments on a modified mortgage or on a refinanced mortgage in which the total arrearage is included; and

(6) The mortgagor must have made a minimum number of monthly payments as prescribed by the Secretary on a case-by-case basis.

(c) *Repayment of the subordinate lien.* The mortgagor must execute a mortgage in favor of HUD with terms and conditions acceptable to HUD for the amount of the partial claim under § 203.414(a). HUD may require the mortgagee to be responsible for servicing the subordinate mortgage on behalf of HUD.

(d) *Application for insurance benefits.* Along with the prescribed application for partial claim insurance benefits, the mortgagee shall provide HUD with the original credit instrument no later than 60 days after execution. The mortgagee shall provide HUD with the original security instrument, required by paragraph (c) of this section, no later than 6 months following the date of execution. If the mortgagee experiences a delay from the recording authority, it may request an extension of time, in writing, from HUD. If the mortgagee does not provide the original of the note and security instrument within the prescribed deadlines, the mortgagee shall be required to reimburse the amount of the claim paid, including the incentive.

[61 FR 35018, July 3, 1996, as amended at 62 FR 60130, Nov. 6, 1997; 72 FR 56161, Oct. 2, 2007]

CONDITION OF PROPERTY

§§ 203.375–203.376 [Reserved]

§ 203.377 Inspection and preservation of properties.

The mortgagee, upon learning that a property subject to a mortgage insured under this part is vacant or abandoned, shall be responsible for the inspection of such property at least monthly, if the loan thereon is in default. When a mortgage is in default and a payment thereon is not received within 45 days of the due date, and efforts to reach the mortgagor by telephone within that period have been unsuccessful, the mortgagee shall be responsible for a visual inspection of the security property to determine whether the property is vacant. The mortgagee shall take reasonable action to protect and preserve such security property when it is determined or should have been determined to be vacant or abandoned until its conveyance to the Secretary, if such action does not constitute an illegal trespass. "Reasonable action" includes the commencement of foreclosure within the time required by § 203.355(b) of this part.

[57 FR 47972, Oct. 20, 1992]

§ 203.378 Property condition.

(a) *Condition at time of transfer.* When the property is transferred, or a mortgage is assigned to the Commissioner, the property shall be undamaged by fire, earthquake, flood, or tornado, except as set forth in this subpart.

(b) *Damage to property by waste.* The mortgagee shall not be liable for damage to the property by waste committed by the mortgagor, its heirs, successors or assigns in connection with mortgage insurance claims paid on or after July 2, 1968.

(c) *Mortgagee responsibility.* The mortgagee shall be responsible for:

(1) Damage by fire, flood, earthquake, hurricane, or tornado;

(2) Damage to or destruction of security properties on which the loans are in default and which properties are vacant or abandoned, when such damage or destruction is due to the mortgagee's failure to take reasonable action to inspect, protect and preserve such properties as required by § 203.377 of this part, as to all mortgages insured on or after January 1, 1977; and

(3) As to all mortgages insured under firm commitments issued on or after November 19, 1992, or under direct endorsement processing where the credit worksheet was signed by the mortgagee's underwriter on or after November 19, 1992, any damage of whatsoever nature that the property has sustained while in the possession of the mortgage if the property is conveyed to the Secretary without notice to and approval by the Secretary as required by § 203.379 of this part.

(d) *Limitation.* The mortgagee's responsibility for property damage shall not exceed the amount of its insurance claim as to a particular property.

[36 FR 34508, Dec. 22, 1971. Redesignated and amended at 41 FR 49735, Nov. 10, 1976; 57 FR 47973, Oct. 20, 1992; 58 FR 32057, June 8, 1993; 61 FR 36265, July 9, 1996; 61 FR 36453, July 10, 1996]

§ 203.379 Adjustment for damage or neglect.

(a) If the property has been damaged by fire, flood, earthquake, hurricane, or tornado, or, for mortgages insured on or after January 1, 1977, the property has suffered damage because of the mortgagee's failure to take action as required by § 203.377, the damage must be repaired before conveyance of the property or assignment of the mortgage to the Secretary, except under the following conditions:

(1) If the prior approval of the Secretary is obtained, there will be deducted from the insurance benefits the Secretary's estimate of the cost of repairing the damage or any insurance recovery received by the mortgagee, whichever is greater.

(2) If the property has been damaged by fire and was not covered by fire insurance at the time of the damage, or the amount of insurance coverage was inadequate to repair fully the damage, only the amount of insurance recovery received by the mortgagee, if any, will be deducted from the insurance benefits, provided the mortgagee certifies, at the time that a claim is filed for insurance benefits, that:

(i) At the time the mortgage was insured, the property was covered by fire insurance in an amount at least equal to the lesser of 100 percent of the insurable value of the improvements, or the principal loan balance of the mortgage; and

(ii) The insurer later cancelled this coverage or refused to renew it for reasons other than nonpayment of premium; and

(iii) The mortgagee made diligent though unsuccessful efforts within 30 days of any cancellation or non-renewal of hazard insurance, and at least annually thereafter, to secure other coverage or coverage under a FAIR Plan, in an amount described in paragraph (a)(2)(i) of this section, or if coverage to such an extent was unavailable at a reasonable rate, the greatest extent of coverage that was available at a reasonable rate; and

(iv) The extent of coverage obtained by the mortgagee in accordance with paragraph (a)(2)(iii) of this section was the greatest available at a reasonable rate, or if the mortgagee was unable to obtain insurance, none was available at a reasonable rate; and

(v) The mortgagee took the actions required by §203.377 of this part.

(3) The certification requirements set out in paragraph (a)(2) of this section apply to any mortgage insured by HUD on or after September 22, 1980, for which a claim has not been filed before September 30, 1986. Any mortgage insured on or after September 22, 1980, for which a claim has been filed before September 30, 1986, but the claim has not been settled before that date, will be governed by §203.379(b) (1986) Edition as it existed immediately before September 30, 1986.

(4)(i) As used in this section, *reasonable rate* means a rate that is not in excess of the rate or advisory rate set by the principal State-licensed rating organization for essential property insurance in the voluntary market, or if coverage is available under a FAIR Plan, the FAIR Plan rate.

(ii) If a State has neither a FAIR Plan nor a State-licensed rating organization for essential property insurance in the voluntary market, the mortgagee must provide to the HUD Field Office having jurisdiction, information concerning the lowest rates available from an insurer for the types of coverage involved, with a request for a determination of whether the rate is reasonable. HUD will determine the rate to be reasonable if it approximates the rate assessed for comparable insurance coverage applicable to similarly situated properties in a State that offers a FAIR Plan or maintains a State-licensed rating organization.

(b) For mortgages insured under firm commitments issued on or after November 19, 1992, or under direct endorsement processing where the credit worksheet was signed by the mortgagee's underwriter on or after November 19, 1992, the provisions of paragraph (a) of this section apply and, in addition, if the property has been damaged during the time of the mortgagee's possession by events other than fire, flood, earthquake, hurricane, or tornado, or if it was damaged notwithstanding reasonable action by the mortgagee as required by §203.377 of this part, the mortgagee must provide notice of such damage to the Secretary and may not

convey until directed to do so by the Secretary. The Secretary will either:

(1) Allow the mortgagee to convey the property damaged; or

(2) Require the mortgagee to repair the damage before conveyance, and the Secretary will reimburse the mortgagee for reasonable payments not in excess of the Secretary's estimate of the cost of repair, less any insurance recovery.

(c) In the event the damaged property is conveyed to the Secretary without prior notice or approval as provided in paragraphs (a) or (b) of this section, the Secretary may:

(1) After notice, reconvey the property to the mortgagee and the mortgagee must reimburse the Secretary in accordance with §§203.363 and 203.364 of this part, or

(2) Require the mortgagee to reimburse the Secretary for the greater of the Secretary's estimate of the cost of repair or any insurance recovery.

[57 FR 47973, Oct. 20, 1992, as amended at 61 FR 36265, July 9, 1996]

§203.380 **Certificate of property condition.**

(a) The mortgagee shall either:

(1) Certify that as of the date of the filing of deed for record, or assignment of the mortgage to the Secretary, the property was:

(i) Undamaged by fire, flood, earthquake, hurricane or tornado; and

(ii) As to mortgages insured or for which commitments to insure were issued on or after January 2, 1977, undamaged due to failure of the mortgagee to take action as required by §203.377; and

(iii) As to mortgages insured under firm commitments issued on or after November 19, 1992, or under direct endorsement processing where the credit worksheet was signed by the mortgagee's underwriter on or after November 19, 1992, undamaged while the property was in the possession of the mortgage; or

(2) Attach to its claim a copy of the Secretary's authorization to convey the property in damaged condition.

(b) In the absence of evidence to the contrary, the mortgagee's certificate or description of the damage shall be accepted by the Secretary as establishing the condition of the property, as of the date of the filing of the deed or assignment of the mortgage.

[57 FR 47973, Oct. 20, 1992, as amended at 61 FR 36265, July 9, 1996; 61 FR 36453, July 10, 1996]

§ 203.381 Occupancy of property.

The mortgagee shall certify that the property is vacant and contains no personal property as of the date of filing for record of the deed to the Secretary or that the Secretary has consented to accept the property occupied.

[45 FR 59563, Sept. 10, 1980]

§ 203.382 Cancellation of hazard insurance.

The mortgagee shall cancel any hazard insurance policy as of the date of the filing for record of the deed to the Commissioner subject to the following conditions:

(a) The amount of the return premium due the mortgagee because of such cancellation may be calculated on a "short-rate" basis and reported on fiscal data supporting the application for debentures and the amount shall be deducted from the total amount claimed.

(b) If the mortgagee's calculation of the return premium is less than the actual return, the amount of the difference between the actual refund and the calculated amount shall be remitted to the Commissioner, accompanied by the carrier's or agent's statement.

(c) If the mortgagee's calculation of the return premium is more than the actual return, the mortgagee may file with the Commissioner a claim, supported by the carrier's or agent's statement of the amount of the refund, whereupon the Commissioner shall issue a check to the mortgagee in settlement of the claim.

PROPERTY TITLE TRANSFERS AND TITLE WAIVERS

§ 203.385 Types of satisfactory title evidence.

The following types of title evidence shall be satisfactory to the Commissioner:

(a) *Fee or owner's title policy.* A fee or owner's policy of title insurance, a guaranty or guarantee of title, or a certificate of title, issued by a title company, duly authorized by law and qualified by experience to issue such instruments. If an owner's policy of title insurance is furnished, it shall show title in the Commissioner and inure to the benefit of his successors in office.

(b) *Mortgagee's policy of title insurance.* A mortgagee's policy of title insurance supplemented by an Abstract and an Attorney's Certificate of Title covering the period subsequent to the date of the mortgage, the terms of the policy shall be such that the liability of the title company will continue in favor of the Commissioner after title is conveyed to him. The policy may be drawn in favor of the mortgagee and the Federal Housing Commissioner, "as their interests may appear", with the consent of the title company endorsed thereon;

(c) *Abstract and legal opinion.* An abstract of title prepared by an abstract company or individual engaged in the business of preparing abstracts of title and accompanied by the legal opinion as to the quality of such title signed by an attorney at law experienced in examination of titles. If title evidence consists of an Abstract and an Attorney's Certificate of Title, the search shall extend for at least forty years prior to the date of the Certificate to a well recognized source of good title;

(d) *Torrens of similar certificate.* A Torrens or similar title certificate; or

(e) *Title standard of U.S. or State government.* Evidence of title conforming to the standards of a supervising branch of the Government of the United States or of any State or Territory thereof.

§ 203.386 Coverage of title evidence.

Evidence of title shall be executed as of a date to include the recordation of the deed to the Commissioner. The evidence of title shall show that according to the public records, there are not, at such date, any outstanding prior liens, including any past-due and unpaid ground rents, general taxes or special assessments.

§203.387 Acceptability of customary title evidence.

If the title and title evidence are such as to be acceptable to prudent lending institutions and leading attorneys generally in the community in which the property is situated, such title and title evidence shall be satisfactory to the Secretary and shall be considered as good and marketable. In cases of disagreement, the Secretary will make the final decision.

[57 FR 47974, Oct. 20, 1992]

§203.389 Waived title objections.

The Commissioner shall not object to title by reason of the following matters:

(a) Violations of a restriction based on race, color or creed, even where such restriction provides for a penalty of reversion or forfeiture of title or a lien for liquidated damage.

(b)(1) Aviation easements, which were approved by the Secretary at the time of the origination of the mortgage, and other customary easements for public utilities, party walls, driveways, and other purposes.

(2) Easements for public utilities along one or more of the property lines and extending not more than 10 feet therefrom and for drainage or irrigation ditches along the rear 10 feet of the property, provided the exercise of the rights thereunder do not interfere with any of the buildings or improvements located on the subject property.

(c) Easements for underground conduits which are in place and do not extend under any buildings on the subject property;

(d) Mutual easements for joint driveways constructed partly on the subject property and partly on adjoining property, provided the agreements creating such easements are of record;

(e) Encroachments on the subject property by improvements on adjoining property where such encroachments do not exceed 1 foot, provided such encroachments do not touch any buildings or interfere with the use of any improvements on the subject property;

(f) Encroachments on adjoining property by eaves and overhanging projections attached to improvements on subject property where such encroachments do not exceed 1 foot.

(g) Encroachments on adjoining property by hedges, wooden or wire fences belonging to the subject property;

(h) Encroachments on adjoining property by driveways belonging to subject property where such encroachments do not exceed 1 foot, provided there exists a clearance of at least 8 feet between the buildings on the subject property and the property line affected by the encroachment;

(i) Variations between the length of the subject property lines as shown on the application for insurance and as shown by the record or possession lines, provided such variations do not interfere with the use of any of the improvements on the subject property and do not involve a deficiency of more than 2 percent with respect to the length of the front line or more than 5 percent with respect to the length of any other line;

(j) Encroachments by garages or improvements other than those which are attached to or a portion of the main dwelling structure over easements for public utilities, provided such encroachment does not interfere with the use of the easement or the exercise of the rights of repair and maintenance in connection therewith;

(k) Violations of cost or set back restrictions which do not provide a penalty of reversion or forfeiture of title, or a lien for liquidated damages which may be superior to the lien of the insured mortgage. Violations of such restrictions which do provide for such penalties, provided such penalty rights have been duly released or subordinated to the lien of the insured mortgage, or provided a policy of title insurance is furnished expressly insuring the Commissioner against loss by reason of such penalties.

(l) Customary building and use restrictions which:

(1) Are coupled with a reversionary clause, provided there has been no violation prior to the date of the deed to the Commissioner; or

(2) Are not coupled with a reversionary clause and have not been violated to a material extent.

(m) Outstanding oil, water or mineral rights (or damage caused by the exercise of such rights) which are customarily waived by prudent leading institutions and leading attorneys in the community.

(n) The voluntary or involuntary conveyance of a part of the subject property pursuant to condemnation proceedings or in lieu of condemnation proceedings, if:

(1) The part conveyed does not exceed 10 percent by area of the property;

(2) No damage to existing structures, improvements, or unrepaired damage to sewage, water, or paving has been suffered;

(3) All of the payment received as compensation for the taking by condemnation or conveyance in lieu of condemnation has been applied to reduction of the mortgage indebtedness;

(4) The conveyance occurred subsequent to insurance of the mortgage; and

(5) There is included with the documents and information furnished the Commissioner with the application for insurance benefits, a statement by the mortgagee that the requirements of this paragraph have been met.

(o) Federal tax liens and rights of redemption arising therefrom if the following conditions are observed. If the mortgagee acquires the property by foreclosure the mortgagee shall give notice to the Internal Revenue Service (IRS) of the foreclosure action. The Commissioner will not object to an outstanding right of redemption in IRS if: (1) The Federal tax lien was perfected subsequent to the date of the mortgage lien, and (2) The mortgagee has bid an amount sufficient to make the mortgagee whole if the property is in fact redeemed by the IRS.

[36 FR 34508, Dec. 22, 1971, as amended at 41 FR 49736, Nov. 10, 1976; 72 FR 56161, Oct. 2, 2007]

§ 203.390 Waiver of title—mortgages or property formerly held by the Secretary.

(a) *Mortgages sold by the Secretary.* (1) If the Secretary sells a mortgage and such mortgage is later reassigned to him or the property covered by such mortgage is later conveyed to him, he will not object to title by reason of any lien or other adverse interest that was senior to the mortgage on the date of the original sale of such mortgage.

(2) The Secretary will accept an assignment of a mortgage previously sold by him, where the mortgagee is unable to complete foreclosure because of a defect in the mortgage instrument, a defect in the mortgage transaction, or a defect in title which existed at or prior to the time the mortgage assignment was filed for record. In such instances, the Secretary will not object to title by reason of any such defect.

(b) *Property sold by the Secretary.* (1) If a property held by the Secretary is sold by the Secretary who also insures a mortgage financing the sale, and the mortgage is later reassigned to the Secretary or the property covered by the mortgage is later conveyed to the Secretary, the Secretary will not object to title by reason of any lien or other adverse interest that was senior to the mortgage on the date the mortgage was filed for record, except where the lien or other adverse interest arose from a lien or interest that had already been recorded against the mortgagor.

(2) The Secretary will accept an assignment of a mortgage executed in connection with the sale of property by the Secretary, where the mortgagee is unable to complete foreclosure because of a defect in the mortgage instrument, a defect in the mortgage transaction, or a defect in title which existed at or prior to the time the mortgage was filed for record, except where the defect arose from a lien or interest that had already been recorded against the mortgagor on the date that the mortgage was filed for record. Except for the case of a lien or interest that had already been recorded against the mortgagor, the Secretary will not object to title by reason of any of the above defects.

[36 FR 24508, Dec. 22, 1971, as amended at 58 FR 35370, July 1, 1993; 61 FR 36265, July 9, 1996]

§ 203.391 Title objection waiver with reduced insurance benefits.

Payment of an insurance claim will not automatically be refused solely because the title evidence reveals a condition of title not taken into consideration in the original appraisal and not covered by the provisions of §203.389 of this part, or not otherwise waived in writing by the Secretary. In such instances, the Secretary may, at his or her option, approve the payment of a claim if the mortgagee agrees to accept a reduction in insurance benefits considered adequate by the Secretary to compensate for any anticipated loss to the Mutual Mortgage Insurance Fund as a result of the existence of the title condition at the time of claim.

[57 FR 47974, Oct. 20, 1992]

PAYMENT OF INSURANCE BENEFITS

§203.400 Method of payment.

(a) If the application for insurance benefits is acceptable to the Commissioner, payment of the insurance claim shall be made in cash, in debentures, or in a combination of both, as determined by the Commissioner either at, or prior to, the time of payment.

(b) An insurance claim paid on a mortgage insured under section 223(e) of the National Housing Act shall be paid in cash from the Special Risk Insurance Fund.

[80 FR 51468, Aug. 25, 2015]

§203.401 Amount of payment—conveyed and non-conveyed properties.

(a) *Conveyed properties.* Where a claim for the insurance benefits is filed in accordance with this subpart, based on the conveyance of title to the mortgaged property to the Commissioner, the amount of the insurance benefits shall be computed by adding to the original principal balance of the mortgage (as increased by the amount of open-end advances made by the mortgagee and approved by the Commissioner) which was unpaid on the date of the institution of foreclosure proceedings, on the date of the acquisition of the property otherwise after default, or on the date the property was acquired by the Commissioner under a direct conveyance by the mortgagor, the amount of all payments made by the mortgagee and allowances for items set forth in §203.402, less all applicable items set forth in §203.403.

(b) *Claims without conveyance of title.* (1) If the mortgagee acquires title to the mortgaged property pursuant to a bid amount equal to the Commissioner's adjusted fair market value and the mortgagee elects to retain title as provided in §203.368(g)(2), or if the mortgagee acquires title pursuant to a bid in excess of the Commissioner's adjusted fair market value (see §203.368(g)(4)), the amount of the insurance benefits shall be determined by deducting the amount bid at the sale from the original principal balance of the mortgage (as increased by the amount of open-end advances made by the mortgagee and approved by the Commissioner) which was unpaid on the date of institution of the foreclosure proceedings, and adding to the difference, if any, all applicable items set forth in §203.402 and subtracting therefrom all applicable items set forth in §203.403; provided however, that appropriate adjustment shall be made for any such items covered by proceeds of the foreclosure sale.

(2) If a party other than the mortgagee acquires title to the mortgaged property pursuant to a bid at foreclosure sale not less in amount than the Commissioner's adjusted fair market value, the amount of the insurance benefits shall be determined by deducting the proceeds of the foreclosure sale distributed to the mortgagee from the original principal balance of the mortgage (as increased by the amount of open-end advances made by the mortgagee and approved by the Commissioner) which was unpaid on the date of the foreclosure proceedings, and adding to the difference, if any, all applicable items set forth in §203.402 and subtracting therefrom all applicable items set forth in §203.403; provided, however, that appropriate adjustment shall be made for any such items covered by the proceeds of the foreclosure sale.

(3) If the mortgagee acquires title to the mortgaged property pursuant to a bid not less in amount than the Commissioner's adjusted fair market value, and the mortgagor or another party redeems the property, the amount of the insurance benefits shall be determined by deducting the amount paid to redeem the property and received by the mortgagee from the original principal balance of that mortgage (as increased by the amount of open-end advances made by the mortgagee and approved

by the Commissioner) which was unpaid on the date of the institution of foreclosure proceedings, and adding to the difference, if any, all applicable items set forth in § 203.402 and subtracting therefrom all applicable items set forth in § 203.403; provided however, that appropriate adjustments shall be made for any such items covered by that amount paid by the mortgagor or other party to redeem the property.

(c) *Pre-foreclosure Sales.* Where a claim for insurance benefits is filed in accordance with this subpart, based on a pre-foreclosure sale approved by or on behalf of the Secretary (under the provisions of § 203.370), the amount of insurance benefits shall be computed by adding to the original principal balance of the mortgage (as increased by the amount of open-end advances made by the mortgagee and approved by the Commissioner) which was unpaid on the date of closing of the pre-foreclosure sale, the amount of all applicable items set forth in § 203.402; provided however that appropriate adjustment shall be made for any such items covered by proceeds of the pre-foreclosure sale.

(d) *Final Payment.* (1) The mortgagee may not file for any additional payments of its mortgage insurance claim after six months from payment by the Commissioner of the final payment except for:

(i) Cases where the Commissioner requests or requires a deficiency judgment.

(ii) Other cases where the Commissioner determines it appropriate and expressly authorizes an extension of time.

(2) For the purpose of this section, the term *final payment* shall mean, in the case of claims filed for conveyed properties, the payment under subpart B of this part which is made by the Commissioner based upon the submission by the mortgagee of all required documents and information filed pursuant to § 203.365. In the case of claims filed under claims without conveyance of title, *final payment* shall mean the payment which is made by the Commissioner based upon submission by the mortgagee of all required documents and information filed pursuant to §§ 203.368 and 203.401(b). In the case of

claims filed pursuant to pre-foreclosure sales, *final payment* shall mean the payment which is made by the Commissioner based upon submission by the mortgagee of all required documents and information filed pursuant to §§ 203.370 and 203.401(d).

[52 FR 1328, Jan. 13, 1987, as amended at 56 FR 3215, Jan. 29, 1991; 59 FR 50144, Sept. 30, 1994]

§ 203.402 **Items included in payment—conveyed and non-conveyed properties.**

The insurance benefits paid in connection with foreclosed properties, whether or not conveyed to the Commissioner; and those properties conveyed to the Commissioner as a result of a deed in lieu of foreclosure; and those properties sold under an approved pre-foreclosure sale shall include the following items:

(a) Taxes, ground rents, water rates, and utility charges that are liens prior to the mortgage.

(b) Special assessments, which are noted on the application for insurance or which become liens after the insurance of the mortgage.

(c) Hazard insurance premiums on the mortgaged property not in excess of a *reasonable rate* as defined in § 203.379(a)(4).

(d) Periodic MIP or open-end insurance charges;

(e) Taxes imposed upon any deeds or other instruments by which said property was acquired by the mortgagee and transferred or conveyed to the Commissioner, or was acquired by the mortgagee and retained pursuant to § 203.368;

(f) Foreclosure costs or costs of acquiring the property otherwise (including costs of acquiring the property by the mortgagee and of conveying and evidencing title to the property to HUD, but not including any costs borne by the mortgagee to correct title defects) actually paid by the mortgagee and approved by HUD, in an amount not in excess of two-thirds of such costs or $75, whichever is the greater. For mortgages insured on or after February 1, 1998, the Secretary will reimburse a percentage of foreclosure costs or costs of acquiring the property, which percentage shall be determined in accordance with such conditions as the Secretary shall prescribe. Where the foreclosure involves a mortgage sold by the Secretary on or after August 1, 1969, or a mortgage executed in connection with the sale of property by the Secretary on or after such date, the mortgagee shall be reimbursed (in addition to the amount determined under the foregoing) for any extra costs incurred in the foreclosure as a result of a defect in the mortgage instrument, or a defect in the mortgage transaction or a defect in title which existed at or prior to the time the mortgage (or its assignment by the Secretary) was filed for record, if the mortgagee establishes to the satisfaction of the Commissioner that such extra costs are over and above those customarily incurred in the area.

(g)(1) *For mortgages insured under firm commitments issued before November 19, 1992, or under direct endorsement processing where the credit worksheet was signed by the mortgagee's underwriter before November 19, 1992*, reasonable payments made by the mortgagee, with the approval of the Secretary, for the purpose of protecting, operating, or preserving the property, or removing debris from the property.

(2) *For mortgages insured under firm commitments issued on or after November 19, 1992, or under direct endorsement processing where the credit worksheet was signed by the mortgagee's underwriter on or after November 19, 1992*, reasonable payments made by the mortgagee, with the approval of the Secretary, for the purpose of protecting, operating, or preserving the property, or removing debris from the property prior to the time of conveyance required by § 203.359 of this part.

(3) Reasonable costs for performing the inspections required by § 203.377 of this part and to determine if the property is vacant or abandoned are considered to be costs of protecting, operating or preserving the property.

(h) Any uncollected mortgage interest allowed pursuant to an approved forbearance plan;

(i) An amount which the Commissioner finds to be sufficient to compensate the mortgagee for any loss which it may have sustained on account of interest on debentures and the payment of any MIP and open-end insurance charge by reason of its having postponed the institution of foreclosure proceedings or the acquisition of the property by other means under a mortgage to which the provisions of sections 302 and 306 of the Soldiers' and Sailors' Civil Relief Act of 1940, as amended, apply during any part or all of the period of the mortgagor's military service and three months thereafter;

(j) Charges for the administration, operation, maintenance, or repair of community-owned property or the maintenance or repair of the mortgaged property, paid by the mortgagee for the purpose of discharging an obligation arising out of a covenant filed for record prior to the issuance of the mortgage; and charges for the repair or maintenance of the mortgaged property required by, and in an amount approved by, the Secretary under § 203.379 of this part.

(k)(1) Except as provided in paragraphs (k)(1)(i) and (ii) of this section, for properties conveyed to the Secretary and endorsed for insurance on or before January 23, 2004, an amount equivalent to the debenture interest that would have been earned, as of the date such payment is made, on the portion of the insurance benefits paid in cash, if such portion had been paid in debentures, and for properties conveyed to the Secretary and endorsed for insurance after January 23, 2004, debenture interest at the rate specified in § 203.405(b) from the date specified in § 203.410, as applicable, to the date of claim payment, on the portion of the insurance benefits paid in cash.

(i) When the mortgagee fails to meet any one of the applicable requirements of §§ 203.355, 203.356(b), 203.359, 203.360, 203.365, 203.606(b)(1), or 203.366 within the specified time and in a manner satisfactory to the Secretary (or within such further time as the Secretary may approve in writing), the interest allowance in such cash payment shall be computed only to the date on which the particular required action should have been taken or to which it was extended;

(ii) When the mortgagee fails to meet the requirements of § 203.356(a) within the specified time and in a manner satisfactory to the Secretary (or within such further time as the Secretary may specify in writing), the interest allowance in such cash payment shall be computed to a date set administratively by the Secretary.

(2)(i) Where a claim for insurance benefits is being paid without conveyance of title to the Commissioner in accordance with § 203.368 and was endorsed for insurance on or before January 23, 2004, an amount equivalent to the sum of:

(A) The debenture interest that would have been earned, as of the date the mortgagee or a party other than the mortgagee acquires good marketable title to the mortgaged property, on an amount equal to the amount by which an insurance claim determined in accordance with § 203.401(a) exceeds the amount of the actual claim being paid in debentures; plus

(B) The debenture interest that would have been earned from the date the mortgagee or a party other than the mortgagee acquires good marketable title to the mortgaged property to the date when payment of the claim is made, on the portion of the insurance benefits paid in cash if such portion had been paid in debentures, except that if the mortgagee fails to meet any of the applicable requirements of §§ 203.355, 203.356, and 203.368(i)(3) and (5) within the specified time and in a manner satisfactory to the Commissioner (or within such further time as the Commissioner may approve in writing), the interest allowance in such cash payment shall be computed only to the date on which the particular required action should have been taken or to which it was extended.

(ii) Where a claim for insurance benefits is being paid without conveyance of title to the Commissioner in accordance with § 203.368 and was endorsed for insurance after January 23, 2004, an amount equivalent to the sum of:

(A) Debenture interest at the rate specified in § 203.405(b) from the date specified in § 203.410, as applicable, to the date that the mortgagee or a party other than the mortgagee acquires good marketable title to the mortgaged property, on an amount equal to the amount by which an insurance

claim determined in accordance with § 203.401(a) exceeds the amount of the actual claim being paid in debentures; plus

(B) Debenture interest at the rate specified in § 203.405(b) from the date the mortgagee or a person other than the mortgagee acquires good marketable title to the mortgaged property to the date when payment of the claim is made, on the portion of the insurance benefits paid in cash, except that if the mortgagee fails to meet any of the applicable requirements of §§ 203.355, 203.356, and 203.368(i)(3) and (5) of this chapter within the specified time and in a manner satisfactory to the Commissioner (or within such further time as the Commissioner may approve in writing), the interest allowance in such cash payment shall be computed only to the date on which the particular required action should have been taken or to which it was extended.

(3)(i) Where a claim for insurance benefits is being paid following a pre-foreclosure sale, without foreclosure or conveyance to the Commissioner in accordance with § 203.370, and the mortgage was endorsed for insurance on or before January 23, 2004, an amount equivalent to the sum of:

(A) The debenture interest that would have been earned, as of the date of the closing of the pre-foreclosure sale on an amount equal to the amount by which an insurance claim determined in accordance with § 203.401(a) exceeds the amount of the actual claim being paid in debentures; plus

(B) The debenture interest that would have been earned, from the date of the closing of the pre-foreclosure sale to the date when payment of the claim is made, on the portion of the insurance benefits paid in cash, if such portion had been paid in debentures; except that if the mortgagee fails to meet any of the applicable requirements of § 203.365 within the specified time and in a manner satisfactory to the Commissioner (or within such further time as the Commissioner may approve in writing), the interest allowance in such cash payment shall be computed only to the date on which the particular required action should have been taken or to which it was extended.

(ii) Where a claim for insurance benefits is being paid following a pre-foreclosure sale, without foreclosure or conveyance to the Commissioner, in accordance with §203.370, and the mortgage was endorsed for insurance after January 23, 2004, an amount equivalent to the sum of:

(A) Debenture interest at the rate specified in §203.405(b) from the date specified in §203.410, as applicable, to the date of the closing of the pre-foreclosure sale, on an amount equal to the amount by which an insurance claim determined in accordance with §203.401(a) exceeds the amount of the actual claim being paid in debentures; plus

(B) Debenture interest at the rate specified in §203.405(b) from the date of the closing of the pre-foreclosure sale to the date when the payment of the claim is made, on the portion of the insurance benefits paid in cash, except that if the mortgagee fails to meet any of the applicable requirements of §203.365 within the specified time and in a manner satisfactory to the Commissioner (or within such further time as the Commissioner may approve in writing), the interest allowance in such cash payment shall be computed only to the date on which the particular required action should have been taken or to which it was extended.

(l) Reasonable costs of appraisal under §203.368(e) or pursuant to §203.370;

(m) Costs of additional advertising under 203.368(h);

(n) Costs of foreclosure as computed in paragraph (f) of this section where the acquiring party is one other than the mortgagee, as provided in §203.368;

(o) In any case in which the Commissioner, pursuant to §203.369, requires or requests that the mortgagee seek a deficiency judgment, an amount necessary to reimburse the mortgagee for those additional costs incurred that exceed the costs of foreclosure. In those jurisidictions that require the initiation of a judicial foreclosure action in order to obtain a deficiency judgment, a mortgagee shall receive full reimbursement for the costs of the foreclosure action, where, but for the requested deficiency judgment, judicial

foreclosure would not have been necessary.

(p) An amount approved by HUD and paid to the mortgagor as consideration for the execution of a deed in lieu of foreclosure and, if authorized by HUD, an administrative fee approved by HUD paid to the mortgagee for its role in facilitating a successful deed in lieu of foreclosure, not to be subject to the payment of debenture interest thereon.

(q) Reasonable costs incurred in evicting occupants and in removing personal property from acquired properties;

(r) Notwithstanding any other provision in this section, the mortgagee will not be reimbursed for any expenses incurred in connection with the property after a reconveyance from the Secretary to the mortgagee as provided in §203.363(b) of this part.

(s) Reasonable costs of the title search ordered by the mortgagee, in accordance with procedures prescribed by HUD, to determine the status of a mortgagor meeting all other criteria for approval to participate in the pre-foreclosure sale procedure, or to determine if a mortgagor meets the criteria for approval of the mortgagee's acceptance of a deed in lieu of foreclosure.

(t) The administrative fee as authorized by the Secretary and payable to the mortgagee for its role in facilitating a successful pre-foreclosure sale, said fee not to be subject to the payment of debenture interest thereon.

[36 FR 34508, Dec. 22, 1971, as amended at 41 FR 49736, Nov. 10, 1976; 45 FR 56801, Aug. 6, 1980; 48 FR 28806, June 23, 1983; 51 FR 28551, Aug. 8, 1986; 52 FR 1329, Feb. 13, 1987; 53 FR 4388, Feb. 16, 1988; 57 FR 47974, Oct. 20, 1992; 59 FR 50145, Sept. 30, 1994; 61 FR 35018, July 3, 1996; 61 FR 36266, July 9, 1996; 61 FR 36453, July 10, 1996; 62 FR 60130, Nov. 6, 1997; 71 FR 35993, June 22, 2006; 72 FR 56161, Oct. 2, 2007]

§203.402a Reimbursement for uncollected interest.

The mortgagee shall be entitled to receive an allowance in the insurance settlement for unpaid mortgage interest if the mortgagor fails to meet the requirements of a forbearance agreement entered into pursuant to §203.614 and this failure continues for a period of 60 days. The interest allowance shall be computed to:

(a) The earliest of the applicable following dates, except as provided in paragraph (b) of this section:

(1) The date of the initiation of foreclosure;

(2) The date of the acquisition of the property by the mortgagee by means other than foreclosure;

(3) The date the property was acquired by the Commissioner under a direct conveyance from the mortgagor;

(4) Ninety days following the date the mortgagor fails to meet the requirements of the forbearance agreement, or such other date as the Commissioner may approve in writing prior to the expiration of the 90-day period; or

(5) The date the mortgagee sends the mortgagor notice of eligibility to participate in the Pre-Foreclosure Sale procedure; or

(b) The date foreclosure is initiated or a deed in lieu is obtained, or the date such actions were required by § 203.355(c), whichever is earlier, if the commencement of foreclosure within the time limits described in § 203.355(a), (b), (g), or (h) is precluded by:

(1) The laws of the State in which the mortgaged property is located; or

(2) Federal bankruptcy law.

[60 FR 57678, Nov. 16, 1995, as amended at 61 FR 35019, July 3, 1996]

§ 203.403 Items deducted from payment—conveyed and non-conveyed properties.

There shall be deducted from the total of the added items in §§ 203.401 and 203.402 the following cash items:

(a) All amounts received by the mortgagee on account of the mortgage after the institution of foreclosure proceedings or the acquisition of the property by direct conveyance or otherwise after default.

(b) All amounts received by the mortgagee from any source relating to the property on account of rent or other income after deducting reasonable expenses incurred in handling the property.

(c) All cash retained by the mortgagee including amounts held or deposited for the account of the mortgagor or to which it is entitled under the mortgage transaction that have not been applied in reduction of the principal mortgage indebtedness.

(d) With regard to claims filed pursuant to successful pre-foreclosure sales, all amounts received by the mortgagee relating to the sale of the property.

[36 FR 24508, Dec. 22, 1971, as amended at 52 FR 1329, Jan. 13, 1987; 59 FR 50145, Sept. 30, 1994]

§ 203.404 Amount of payment—assigned mortgages.

Upon an acceptable assignment of a mortgage, the Commissioner shall pay to the mortgagee the unpaid principal balance of the loan at the time of assignment and an amount determined by:

(a) Adding the following items:

(1) Any accrued and unpaid mortgage interest.

(2) Any advances made under the mortgage and approved by the Commissioner.

(3) Reimbursement for such costs and attorney's fees as HUD finds were properly incurred in connection with the defaulted mortgage and its modification and assignment to HUD.

(4) For mortgages endorsed for insurance on or before January 23, 2004, an amount equivalent to the debenture interest that would have been earned on the portion of the insurance benefits paid in cash, as of the date such payment is made, and for mortgages endorsed for insurance after January 23, 2004, debenture interest at the rate specified in § 203.405(b), from the date specified in § 203.410 to the date of claim payment on the portion of the insurance benefits paid in cash, except that when the mortgagee fails to meet any one of the requirements of §§ 203.350(e), 203.351, and 203.353 of this chapter within the specified time and in a manner satisfactory to the Commissioner (or within such further time as the Commissioner may approve in writing), the interest allowance in such cash payment shall be computed only to the date on which the particular required action should have been taken or to which it was extended.

(5) An administrative fee to the mortgagee for modifying the mortgage.

(6) A fee for servicing the mortgage assigned to HUD, if HUD requires such servicing.

(b) Deducting all cash retained by the mortgagee, including amounts held or deposited for the account of the mortgagor or to which it is entitled under the mortgage transaction that have not been applied in reduction of the principal mortgage indebtedness.

(c) The mortgagee may not file for any additional payments of its mortgage insurance claim after six months from final payment by the Commissioner. For the purpose of this section, the term *final payment* shall mean the payment which is made by the Commissioner based upon the submission by the mortgagee of all required documents and information pursuant to §203.351 of this part.

[36 FR 24508, Dec. 22, 1971, as amended at 55 FR 283, Jan. 4, 1990; 56 FR 3215, Jan. 29, 1991; 61 FR 35019, July 3, 1996; 71 FR 35994, June 22, 2006]

§203.405 Debenture interest rate.

(a) Debentures shall bear interest from the date of issue, payable semiannually on the first day of January and the first day of July of each year at the rate in effect as of the day the commitment was issued, or as of the date the mortgage was endorsed for insurance, whichever rate is higher. For applications involving mortgages originated under the single family Direct Endorsement program, debentures shall bear interest from the date of issue, payable semiannually on the first day of January and on the first day of July of each year at the rate in effect as of the date the mortgage was endorsed for insurance;

(b) For mortgages endorsed for insurance after January 23, 2004, if an insurance claim is paid in cash, the debenture interest rate for purposes of calculating such a claim shall be the monthly average yield, for the month in which the default on the mortgage occurred, on United States Treasury Securities adjusted to a constant maturity of 10 years.

[71 FR 35994, June 22, 2006]

§203.406 Maturity of debentures.

Debentures shall mature 20 years from the date of issue.

§203.407 Registration of debentures.

Debentures shall be registered as to principal and interest.

§203.408 Form and amounts of debentures.

Debentures issued under this part shall be in such form and amounts; and shall be subject to such term and conditions; and shall include such provisions for redemption, if any, as may be prescribed by the Secretary, with the approval of the Secretary of the Treasury; and may be in book entry or certificated registered form, or such other form as the Secretary by regulation may prescribe.

[59 FR 49816, Sept. 30, 1994]

§203.409 Redemption of debentures.

Debentures shall, at the option of the Commissioner and with the approval of the Secretary of the Treasury, be redeemable at par plus accrued interest on any semiannual interest payment date on three months' notice of redemption given in such manner as the Commissioner shall prescribe. The debenture interest on the debentures called for redemption shall cease on the semiannual interest payment date designated in the call notice. The Commissioner may include with the notice of redemption an offer to purchase the debentures at par plus accrued interest at any time during the period between the notice of redemption and the redemption date. If the debentures are purchased by the Commissioner after such call and prior to the named redemption date, the debenture interest shall cease on the date of purchase.

§203.410 Issue date of debentures.

(a) *Conveyed properties, claims without conveyance, pre-foreclosure sales—* Where the property is conveyed to the Commissioner, or the mortgagee or other party acquires title to the property under the claim without conveyance procedure or the pre-foreclosure sale procedure, debenture shall be dated:

(1) If issued prior to September 2, 1964, or issued on or after such date and a certificate of claim is also issued, as of one of the dates as follows:

(i) The foreclosure proceedings were instituted;

(ii) The property was otherwise acquired by the mortgagee after default;

(iii) The property was acquired by the Commissioner, if directly conveyed

223

to the Commissioner from the mortgagor; or

(iv) The property was acquired after default by a third party under the pre-foreclosure sale procedure.

(2) If issued on or after September 2, 1964, and a certificate of claim is not issued, as of the date of default as defined in this part.

(3) As of the day after the date to which mortgage interest is computed as specified in § 203.402a, if the insurance settlement includes an allowance for uncollected interest in connection with a special forbearance.

(b) *Assigned mortgages.* Where the mortgage is assigned to the Commissioner, debentures shall be dated as of the date of the assignment.

(c) Notwithstanding paragraph (a) of this section, in connection with conveyed properties and claims without conveyance, debentures issued as reimbursement for expenditures made by a mortgagee after the date of default shall be dated as of the date the expenditure is actually made by the mortgagee.

[36 FR 24508, Dec. 22, 1971, as amended at 50 FR 3892, Jan. 29, 1985; 52 FR 1329, Jan. 13, 1987; 59 FR 50145, Sept. 30, 1994; 60 FR 57678, Nov. 16, 1995]

§ 203.411 Cash adjustment.

Any difference of less than $50 between the amount of debentures to be issued to the mortgagee and the total amount of the mortgagee's claim, as approved by the Commissioner, may be adjusted by the issuance of a check in payment thereof.

[59 FR 49816, Sept. 30, 1994]

§ 203.412 Payment for foreclosure alternative actions.

Notwithstanding the conveyance, sale, or assignment requirements for payment of a claim elsewhere in this part, HUD may pay the mortgagee, in accordance with procedures prescribed by HUD, for the following foreclosure alternative actions, in such amounts as HUD determines:

(a) Assumptions under § 203.512;

(b) Special forbearance under §§ 203.471 and 203.614;

(c) Recasting or modification of defaulted mortgages under § 203.616,

where the mortgagee is not reimbursed under § 203.405(a);

(d) Refinancing under § 203.43(c).

[61 FR 35019, July 3, 1996]

§ 203.413 [Reserved]

§ 203.414 Amount of payment—partial claims.

(a) *Claim amount.* Where a claim for partial insurance benefits is filed in accordance with § 203.371, the amount of the insurance benefits shall consist of the arrearage not to exceed an amount equivalent to 12 monthly mortgage payments, and any costs prescribed by HUD related to the default.

(b) *Servicing fee.* The claim may also include a payment for activities, such as servicing the subordinate mortgage, which HUD may require.

[61 FR 35019, July 3, 1996, as amended at 62 FR 60130, Nov. 6, 1997]

CERTIFICATE OF CLAIM

§ 203.415 Delivery of certificate of claim.

(a) If the mortgage was accepted for insurance pursuant to a commitment issued prior to September 2, 1964, the mortgagee may, by filing a written request with the application for debentures, receive in addition to the debentures and the cash adjustment check, a certificate of claim issued in accordance with section 204(e) of the Act. This certificate shall become payable (if at all) as prescribed in section 204(f) of the Act.

(b) If the mortgage was accepted for insurance pursuant to a commitment issued on or after September 2, 1964, or under the Direct Endorsement, Lender Insurance, or Coinsurance programs, no certificate of claim will be issued.

[36 FR 24508, Dec. 22, 1971, as amended at 57 FR 58349, Dec. 9, 1992; 62 FR 30227, June 2, 1997]

§ 203.416 Amount and items of certificate of claim.

The certificate shall be for an amount which the Commissioner determines to be sufficient to pay all amounts due under the mortgage and not covered by the amount of debentures and cash adjustment check. The certificate shall include a reasonable amount for necessary expenses incurred by the mortgagee in connection with the foreclosure proceedings or the acquisition of the mortgaged property otherwise and the conveyance thereof to the Commissioner, including reasonable attorneys' fees, unpaid interest, and cost of repairs to the property made by the mortgagee to remedy the waste.

§203.417 Rate of interest of certificate of claim.

Each certificate of claim shall provide that there shall accrue to the holder thereof with respect to the face amount of such certificate, an increment at the rate of 3 percent per annum.

MUTUAL MORTGAGE INSURANCE FUND AND DISTRIBUTIVE SHARES

§203.420 Nature of Mutual Mortgage Insurance Fund.

The Mutual Mortgage Insurance Fund shall consist of the General Surplus Account and the Participating Reserve Account.

§203.421 Allocation of Mutual Mortgage Insurance Fund income or loss.

For any semiannual period in which Mutual Mortgage Insurance operations shall result in a net income, or loss, the Commissioner shall allocate, after taking into account the actuarial status of the entire Mutual Mortgage Insurance Fund, such net income or such loss to the General Surplus Account and/or to the Participating Reserve Account as the Commissioner may determine to be in accord with sound actuarial and accounting practice. In determining net income or loss, the Commissioner shall take into consideration all income received from fees, premiums and earnings on investments of the fund, operating expenses and provision for losses to the fund.

[56 FR 18948, Apr. 24, 1991]

§203.422 Right and liability under Mutual Mortgage Insurance Fund.

No mortgagor or mortgagee shall have any vested right in a credit balance in either the General Surplus Account or the Participating Reserve Ac-

count. No mortgagor or mortgagee shall be subject to any liability arising under the mutuality of the Mutual Mortgage Insurance Fund.

§203.423 Distribution of distributive shares.

(a) The Commissioner may provide for the distribution to the mortgagor of a share of the participating reserve account if the contract of insurance is terminated by:

(1) Conveyance to one other than the Commissioner and a claim for the insurance benefits is not presented by the mortgage (§203.315), provided, however, in the case of a mortgage insured pursuant to an application for a conditional commitment received on or after May 19, 1988, (or, as appropriate, an application for mortgage insurance endorsement under the Single Family Direct Endorsement program, as provided in §203.255, where the property appraisal report is signed by the mortgagee's underwriter on or after May 19, 1988, no distribution shall be made if the mortgagee forecloses the mortgage or accepts a deed-in-lieu of foreclosure;

(2) Prepayment of the mortgage (§203.316); or

(3) Voluntary agreement of the mortgagor and mortgagees (§203.317).

(b) The Commissioner shall determine the amount of the distributive share by multiplying the amount of the premium or premiums paid by the applicable distributive share percentage for mortgages insured in the year the mortgage was endorsed for insurance. The Commissioner shall determine the applicable distributive share percentage in an equitable manner and in accordance with sound financial and actuarial practice, taking into account the cumulative actual financial and actuarial experiences through the end of the most recent calendar year.

[48 FR 28806, June 23, 1983, as amended at 52 FR 1329, Jan. 13, 1987; 53 FR 10530, Apr. 1, 1988; 61 FR 36453, July 10, 1996]

§203.424 Maximum amount of distributive shares.

In no event shall a distributive share of the Participating Reserve Account exceed the aggregate scheduled annual premiums of the mortgagor to the year of termination of the insurance.

§ 203.425   Finality of determination.

The determination of the Commissioner as to the amount to be paid to any mortgagor from the Mutual Mortgage Insurance Fund shall be final and conclusive.

§ 203.426   Inapplicability to housing in older declining urban areas.

The provisions of §§ 203.420 through 203.425 shall not apply to mortgages financing housing in declining urban areas meeting the requirements of § 203.43a.

§ 203.427   Statute of limitations on payment of distributive shares.

The Commissioner shall not distribute any distributive share to an eligible mortgagor under § 203.423 beginning on the date which is six years after the date the Commissioner first transmitted written notification of eligibility to the last known address of the mortgagor, unless the mortgagor has applied in accordance with procedures prescribed by the Commissioner for payment of the share within the six-year period. The Commissioner shall transfer any amounts no longer eligible for distribution under this section from the Participating Reserve Account to the General Surplus Account.

[59 FR 49816, Sept. 30, 1994]

SALE, ASSIGNMENT AND PLEDGE OF INSURED MORTGAGE

§ 203.430   Sale of interests in insured mortgages.

No mortgagee may sell or otherwise dispose of any insured mortgage, or group of insured mortgages, or any partial interest in such mortgage or mortgages by means of any agreement, arrangement or device except pursuant to this subpart.

§ 203.431   Sale of insured mortgage to approved mortgagee.

An insured mortgage may be sold to another approved mortgagee. The seller shall notify HUD of the sale within 15 calendar days, on a form prescribed by HUD and acknowledged by the buyer.

[45 FR 27929, Apr. 25, 1980]

§ 203.432   Effect of sale of insured mortgage.

When an insured mortgage is sold to another approved mortgagee, the buyer shall thereupon succeed to all the rights and become bound by all the obligations of the seller under the contract of insurance and the seller shall be released from its obligations under the contract, provided that the seller shall not be relieved of its obligation to pay mortgage insurance premiums until the notice required by § 203.431 is received by HUD.

[45 FR 27929, Apr. 25, 1980]

§ 203.433   Assignments, pledges and transfers by approved mortgagee.

(a) An assignment, pledge, or transfer of an insured mortgage or group of insured mortgages, not constituting a final sale, may be made by an approved mortgagee to another approved mortgagee provided the following requirements are met:

(1) The assignor, pledgor or transferor shall remain the mortgagee of record.

(2) The Commissioner shall have no obligation to recognize or deal with any party other than the mortgagee of record with respect to the rights, benefits and obligations of the mortgagee under the contract of insurance.

(b) An assignment or transfer of an insured mortgage or group of insured mortgages may be made by an approved mortgagee to other than an approved mortgagee provided the requirements under paragraphs (a)(1) and (2) of this section are met and the following additional requirements are met:

(1) The assignee or transferee shall be a corporation, trust or organization (including but not limited to any pension trust or profit-sharing plan) which certifies to the approved mortgagee that:

(i) It has assets of $100,000 or more; and

(ii) It has lawful authority to hold an insured mortgage or group of insured mortgages.

(2) The assignment or transfer shall be made pursuant to an agreement under which the transferor or assignor is obligated to take one of the following alternate courses of action

within 1 year from the date of the assignment or within such additional period of time as may be approved by the Commissioner:

(i) The transferor or assignor shall repurchase and accept a reassignment of such mortgage or group of mortgages.

(ii) The transferor or assignor shall obtain a sale and transfer of such mortgage or group of mortgages to an approved mortgagee.

(c) Notice to or approval of the Commissioner is not required in connection with assignments, pledges or transfers pursuant to this section.

§ 203.434 Declaration of trust.

A sale of a beneficial interest in a group of insured mortgages, where the interest to be acquired is related to all of the mortgages as an entirety, rather than an interest in a specific mortgage shall be made only pursuant to a declaration of trust, which has been approved by the Commissioner prior to any such sale.

§ 203.435 Transfers of partial interests.

A partial interest in an insured mortgage may be transferred under a participation agreement without obtaining the approval of the Commissioner, if the following conditions are met:

(a) *Principal mortgagee.* The insured mortgage shall be held by an approved mortgagee which, for the purposes of this section, shall be referred to as the *principal mortgagee.*

(b) *Interest of principal mortgagee.* The principal mortgagee shall retain and hold for its own account a financial interest in the insured mortgage.

(c) *Qualification for holding partial interest.* A partial interest in an insured mortgage shall be issued to and held only by:

(1) A mortgagee approved by the Commissioner; or

(2) A corporation, trust or organization (including, but not limited to any pension fund, pension trust, or profit-sharing plan) which certifies to the principal mortgagee that:

(i) It has assets of $100,000 or more; and

(ii) It has lawful authority to acquire a partial interest in an insured mortgage.

(d) *Participation agreement provisions.* The participation agreement shall include provisions that:

(1) The principal mortgagee shall retain title to the mortgage and remain the mortgagee of record under the contract of mortgage insurance.

(2) The Commissioner shall have no obligation to recognize or deal with anyone other than the principal mortgagee with respect to the rights, benefits and obligations of the mortgagee under the contract of insurance.

(3) The mortgage documents shall remain in the custody of the principal mortgagee.

(4) The responsibility for servicing the insured mortgages shall remain with the principal mortgagee.

GRADUATED PAYMENT MORTGAGES

§ 203.436 Claim procedure—graduated payment mortgages.

All of the provisions of this subpart are applicable to mortgages insured under the provisions of § 203.45 except as provided in this section.

(a) *Beginning of Amortization* means the date one month prior to the date of the first monthly payment to principal or interest.

(b) The phrases *unpaid principal balance of the loan* or *principal of the mortgage which was unpaid* as used in this subpart, shall be construed to refer to the outstanding mortgage amount as increased by any accrued mortgage interest which was unpaid pursuant to a financing plan approved by the Secretary.

[41 FR 42949, Sept. 29, 1976]

COOPERATIVE UNIT MORTGAGES

§ 203.437 Mortgages involving a dwelling unit in a cooperative housing development.

(a) The provisions of §§ 203.251(d), 203.366 and 203.440 through 203.495 shall not apply to mortgages insured pursuant to section 203(n) of the National Housing Act.

(b) References in this subpart to the term *deed* and *deed in lieu of foreclosure,* or the word *property* when found in the phrases *conveyance of property, acquisition of property,* or other phrases indicating transfer of property, shall be construed to mean the assignment of the Corporate Certificate and Occupancy Certificate. However, when the use of such terms, as interpreted in light of section 203(n) of the National Housing Act, clearly indicates that reference to the dwelling unit is intended, such terms shall mean the dwelling unit identified in the Occupancy Certificate.

(c) In addition to the requirements of § 203.365, the mortgagee shall forward to the Secretary within 45 days after the transfer of the Corporate Certificate:

(1) A statement certified by the officer of the corporation charged with maintenance of the Corporate Certificate Transfer Book that such book currently shows that the Secretary is the owner of the Corporate Certificate; and,

(2) The Occupancy Certificate in the name of the Secretary.

(d) The mortgagee shall tender to the Secretary good and marketable title to the Corporate Certificate and the exclusive right of permanent possession of the dwelling unit.

(e) In lieu of the types of title evidence provided in § 203.385, the Secretary will accept a legal opinion signed by an attorney at law experienced in the examination of titles that the Secretary has good and marketable title to the Corporate Certificate and the exclusive right of possession of the dwelling unit.

(f) The Secretary may accept assignment of mortgages insured under this part if it is determined by the Secretary that it is in the Department's interest to do so provided that the blanket mortgage is in default and the holder of such mortgage has announced an intention to foreclose.

[42 FR 40432, Aug. 10, 1977; 42 FR 57435, Nov. 2, 1977]

MORTGAGES ON PROPERTY LOCATED ON INDIAN LAND

§ 203.438 Mortgages on Indian land insured pursuant to section 248 of the National Housing Act.

(a) *Exemptions.* The provisions of § 203.366 shall not apply to mortgages insured pursuant to section 248 of the National Housing Act.

(b) *Claim procedure.* In addition to other actions which the mortgagee may take pursuant to this subpart in order to receive insurance benefits, a mortgagee shall be entitled to receive such benefits on a mortgage insured under § 203.43h when (1) the mortgagor is more than 90 days in default; (2) the mortgagee has submitted appropriate documentation to the Secretary in accordance with § 203.350(b); and (3) the Secretary has approved the assignment of the mortgage.

(c) *Foreclosure by HUD.* HUD may initiate foreclosure proceedings with respect to any mortgage acquired under this section in a tribal court, a court of competent jurisdiction or Federal district court. If the mortgagor remains on the property following foreclosure, HUD may seek an eviction order from the court hearing the foreclosure action.

[51 FR 21872, June 16, 1986, as amended at 61 FR 35019, July 3, 1996]

MORTGAGES ON PROPERTY LOCATED ON HAWAIIAN HOME LANDS

§ 203.439 Mortgages on Hawaiian home lands insured pursuant to section 247 of the National Housing Act.

(a) *Exemptions.* The provisions of §§ 203.351(a)(8), 203.353(a), and 203.368, do not apply to mortgages insured pursuant to section 247 of the National Housing Act.

(b) *Claim procedure.* Where the mortgage is 180 days or more in default, the mortgagee may assign the mortgage to the Secretary and file its claim for insurance benefits in accordance with the provisions of this subpart. No claim on an insured mortgage will be paid other than through assignment of the mortgage.

(c) *Notice of delinquency.* Once each month on a day prescribed by HUD, the mortgagee shall notify the Department of Hawaiian Home Lands of all mortgages insured pursuant to section 247 of the National Housing Act on leaseholds of Hawaiian home lands that are delinquent on the last day of the month, or that were reported as delinquent the previous month. The notice is in addition to the requirement in §§203.330 and 203.331.

[52 FR 8068, Mar. 16, 1987, as amended at 52 FR 9989, Mar. 27, 1987 and 52 FR 28470, July 30, 1987, and amended at 55 FR 283, Jan. 4, 1990; 71 FR 16234, Mar. 31, 2006]

MORTGAGES ON PROPERTY IN ALLEGANY
RESERVATION OF SENECA INDIANS

§203.439a **Mortgages on property in Allegany Reservation of Seneca Nation of Indians authorized by section 203(q) of the National Housing Act.**

(a) *Applicability.* This section shall apply to mortgages authorized by section 203(q) of the National Housing Act (§203.43j of this part) only when the date of default occurs before the mortgagor and the lessor execute a lease renewal or a new lease either with a term of not less than five years beyond the maturity date of the mortgage, or with a term established by an arbitration award.

(b) *Claims.* In addition to other actions which the mortgagee may take pursuant to this subpart in order to receive insurance benefits, a mortgagee shall be entitled to receive such benefits when the Secretary has agreed to accept assignment of a mortgage in accordance with §203.350(d) and the mortgagee has complied with §§203.351 and 203.353.

(c) *Exceptions.* Notwithstanding §203.366, title to a leasehold estate conveyed to the Commissioner is not required to be marketable as to the term of the lease, provided that the mortgagee has taken any actions required by the Secretary to attempt to obtain a long-term renewal of the lease. Title evidence will be required in a form satisfactory to the Commissioner (see §203.385) unless the Commissioner agrees to accept title to a leasehold estate without title evidence.

[52 FR 48202, Dec. 21, 1987, and 53 FR 9869, Mar. 28, 1988]

REHABILITATION LOANS

§203.440 **Definitions.**

All of the definitions contained in §203.50 of this subchapter shall apply to §§203.440 *et seq.* In addition the following terms shall have the meaning indicated:

(a) *Insured loan* means a loan which has been insured as evidenced by the issuance of an Insurance Certificate or by the endorsement of the note for insurance by the Commissioner.

(b) *Contract of insurance* means the agreement evidenced by the issuance of an Insurance Certificate or by the endorsement of the Commissioner upon the note given in connection with an insured loan, incorporating by reference the regulations in §§203.440 *et seq.* and the applicable provisions of the Act.

(c) *Insurance premium* means the loan insurance premium paid by the financial institution to the Commissioner in consideration of the contract of insurance.

(d) *Beginning of amortization* means the date one month prior to the date of the first monthly payment to principal and interest.

(e) *Maturity* means the date on which the loan indebtedness would be extinguished if paid in accordance with periodic payments provided for in the original note and security instrument.

(f) *Debentures* means registered, transferable securities in book entry or certificated form which are valid and binding obligations, unconditionally guaranteed as to principal and interest by the United States.

[36 FR 24508, Dec. 22, 1971, as amended at 59 FR 49816, Sept. 30, 1994]

§203.441 **Insurance of loan.**

Under compliance with the commitment, or as provided in §203.255(b) with respect to mortgages processed under the Direct Endorsement program, the Commissioner shall insure the loan evidencing the insurance by the issuance of an insurance certificate which will identify the regulations under which the loan is insured and the date of insurance.

[57 FR 58349, Dec. 9, 1992; 58 FR 13537, Mar. 12, 1993]

§ 203.442 Contract created by Insurance Certificate or by endorsement.

The loan is insured from the date of the issuance of an Insurance Certificate or from the date of the endorsement of the note. The Commissioner and the lender shall thereafter be bound by the Act and the regulations in §§ 203.440 *et seq.* with the same force and to the same extent as if a separate contract had been executed relating to the insured loan.

§ 203.443 Insurance premium.

All of the provisions of §§ 203.260 through 203.269[1] concerning mortgage insurance premiums, apply to loans insured under § 203.50.

[47 FR 30753, July 15, 1982]

§ 203.457 Voluntary termination of contract.

Upon request by the borrower and lender the Commissioner may terminate the insurance contract on the loan. The lender shall cancel the insurance endorsement on the insurance certificate or note upon receipt of notice from the Commissioner that the contract of insurance is terminated.

[37 FR 8662, Apr. 29, 1972]

§ 203.458 Termination by prepayment of loan.

The contract of insurance shall be terminated if the loan is paid in full prior to its maturity.

§ 203.459 Notice of termination by lender.

No contract of insurance shall be terminated until the lender has given written notice thereof to the Commissioner within 15 calendar days from the occurrence of one of the approved methods of termination set forth in this subpart.

[45 FR 31716, May 14, 1980]

§ 203.462 Pro rata payment of premium before termination.

No contract of insurance shall be terminated until the lender has paid to the Commissioner the pro rata portion

---

[1] Section 203.269 was removed at 48 FR 35089, Aug. 3, 1983.

of the current annual insurance premium.

§ 203.463 Notice and date of termination by Commissioner.

The Commissioner shall notify the lender that the contract of insurance has been terminated and the effective termination. The termination date shall be the last day of the month in which:

(a) The loan was prepaid; or

(b) A voluntary termination request is received by the Commissioner, or

(c) The contract of insurance is otherwise terminated with the consent of the Commissioner.

§ 203.464 Effect of termination.

Upon termination of the contract of insurance, the obligation to pay any subsequent insurance premium shall cease and all rights of the borrower and lender shall be terminated.

§ 203.466 Definition of delinquency and requirement for notice of delinquency to HUD.

(a) A mortgage account is delinquent any time a payment is due and not paid.

(b) Once each month on a day prescribed by HUD, the mortgagee shall report to HUD all mortgages insured under this part that were delinquent on the last day of the month, or that were reported as delinquent the previous month. The report shall be made in a manner prescribed by HUD.

[71 FR 16234, Mar. 31, 2006]

§ 203.467 Definition of default, date of default, and requirement of notice of default to HUD.

(a) *Default.* If the mortgagor fails to make any payment or to perform any other obligation under the mortgage, and such failure continues for a period of 30 days, the mortgage shall be considered in default for the purposes of this subpart.

(b) *Date of default.* For the purposes of this subpart, the date of default shall be considered as 30 days after:

(1) The first uncorrected failure to perform any obligation under the mortgage; or

(2) The first failure to make a monthly payment that subsequent payments

by the borrower are insufficient to cover when applied to the overdue monthly payments in the order in which they became due.

(c) *Notice of default.* Once each month, on a day prescribed by HUD, the mortgagee shall report to HUD all mortgages that were in default on the last day of the month, or that were reported as in default the previous month. The report shall be made on a form prescribed by HUD.

(d) *Number of days in month.* For the purposes of this section, each month shall be considered to have 30 days.

[71 FR 16234, Mar. 31, 2006]

§203.468 [Reserved]

§203.469 Reinstatement of defaulted loan.

If after default and prior to assignment by the lender of the loan to the Commissioner, the borrower shall pay to the lender all monthly payments in default, written notice shall be given to the Commissioner within 30 days and the insurance shall continue as if such default had not occurred.

§203.471 Special forbearance.

If the mortgagee finds that a default is due to circumstances beyond the mortgagor's control, as defined by the Secretary, the mortgagee may grant special forbearance relief to the mortgagor in accordance with the conditions prescribed by the Secretary.

[61 FR 35019, July 3, 1996]

§203.472 Relief for borrower in military service.

If the borrower is a person in military service, as defined in the Soldiers' and Sailors' Civil Relief Act of 1940, the lender may, by written agreement with the borrower, postpone for the period of military service, and 3 months thereafter, any part of the monthly payment, which represents amortization of principal. The agreement shall contain a provision for the resumption of monthly payments thereafter in amounts which will completely amortize the obligation within its original maturity. The agreement shall in no way affect the amount of the annual insurance premium which shall continue to be calculated in accordance with the original amortization provisions of the loan.

§203.473 Claim procedure.

(a) A claim for insurance benefits on a loan secured by a first mortgage shall be made, and insurance benefits shall be paid, as provided in §§203.350 through 203.414.

(b) A claim for insurance benefits on a loan secured by other than a first mortgage shall be made, and insurance benefits shall be paid, as provided in §§203.474 through 203.478. However, the lender may not, except with the approval of the Commissioner, proceed against the security and also make claim under the contract of insurance, but shall elect which method it desires to pursue.

[49 FR 21319, May 21, 1984, as amended at 61 FR 35019, July 3, 1996]

§203.474 Maximum claim period.

A claim for insurance benefits on a loan secured by other than a first mortgage shall be filed within one year from the date of default, or within such additional period of time as may be approved by the Commissioner.

[49 FR 21319, May 21, 1984]

§203.476 Claim application and items to be filed.

The claim for reimbursement on a loan secured by other than a first mortgage shall be made upon an application form prescribed by the Commissioner. The application shall be accompanied by:

(a) The fiscal data pertaining to the loan transaction as required by the fiscal data form;

(b) Receipts covering all disbursements as required by the fiscal data form;

(c) The original note and the security held, assigned to the Commissioner without recourse of warranty, except that no act or omission of the lender shall have impaired the validity and priority of such security;

(d) Any hazard insurance policies held on property serving as security for the loan, together with a copy of the lender's notification to the carrier authorizing the amendment of the loss

231

payable clause substituting the Commissioner as the holder of the security;

(e) The assignment to the Commissioner of all rights and interests arising under the loan, and all claims of the lender against the borrower or others arising out of the loan transaction;

(f) Any title evidence held by the lender;

(g) All property of the borrower held by the lender or to which it is entitled and, if the Commissioner elects to make payments in debentures, all cash held by the lender or to which it is entitled, including deposits made for the account of the borrower and which have not been applied in reduction of the principal loan indebtedness;

(h) All records, ledger cards, documents, books, papers and accounts relating to the loan transaction;

(i) Any additional information or data which the Commissioner may require.

(Approved by the Office of Management and Budget under control number 2502–0051)

[36 FR 24508, Dec. 22, 1971, as amended at 49 FR 21319, May 21, 1984; 80 FR 51468, Aug. 25, 2015]

§ 203.477 Certificate by lender when loan assigned.

At the time of the assignment of the loan, the lender shall certify to the Commissioner that:

(a) The amount stated in the instrument of assignment is actually due and owing on the loan;

(b) There are no offsets of counterclaims thereto, and the financial institution has a good right to assign.

(c) The mortgage transaction did not involve a first mortgage and the mortgage is prior to all mechanics' and materialmen's liens filed of record, regardless of when such liens attach, and prior to all liens and encumbrances other than a first mortgage, or defects which may arise except such liens or other matters as may have been approved by the Commissioner.

[36 FR 34508, Dec. 22, 1971, as amended at 45 FR 33967, May 21, 1980; 49 FR 21320, May 21, 1984]

§ 203.478 Payment of insurance benefits.

(a) *Claim computation, items included.* Upon acceptable assignment of the note and security instruments, the Commissioner shall pay the lender an amount equal to the unpaid principal balance of the loan, plus:

(1) Any accrued interest due as of the date of execution of the assignment of the loan to the Commissioner.

(2) Any advances made previously under the provisions of the loan instrument and approved by the Commissioner.

(3) Reimbursement for such reasonable collection costs, court costs and attorney's fees as may be approved by the Commissioner.

(4) Reimbursement for premiums paid on any hazard insurance policies held on the property.

(5)(i) If payment is made in cash on a mortgage endorsed for insurance on or before January 23, 2004, an amount equivalent to the debenture interest that would have been earned, as of the date insurance settlement occurs, except that where the lender fails to meet any one of the requirements of §§ 203.476 and 203.477 and such failure continues for more than 30 days (or such further time as the Commissioner may approve in writing), the debenture interest shall be computed for 30 days or the extended period;

(ii) If payment is made in cash on a mortgage endorsed for insurance after January 23, 2004, debenture interest at the rate specified in § 203.479 from the date specified in § 203.486 to the date insurance settlement occurs, except that where the lender fails to meet any one of the requirements of §§ 203.476 and 203.477 and such failure continues for more than 30 days (or such further time as the Commissioner may approve in writing), the debenture interest shall be computed for 30 days or the extended period.

(b) *Claim computation, items deducted.* If the lender is to receive cash, there shall be deducted from the total of the added items in paragraph (a) of this section any cash held by the lender or to which it is entitled including deposits made for the account of the borrower and which have not been applied in reduction of the principal loan indebtedness.

(c) *Method of payment.* Payment of an insurance claim shall be made in cash, in debentures, or in a combination of both, as determined by the Commissioner either at, or prior to, the time of payment.

(d) *Special provision—payment in debentures.* All of the provisions of §§ 203.479 through 203.487 of this subpart shall be applicable in connection with the payment in debentures of insurance benefits under this subpart.

[36 FR 24508, Dec. 22, 1971, as amended at 71 FR 35994, June 22, 2006; 80 FR 51468, Aug. 25, 2015]

§ 203.479 Debenture interest rate.

(a) Debentures shall bear interest from the date of issue, payable semiannually on the first day of January and on the first day of July every year at the rate in effect as of the date the commitment was issued, or as of the date the loan was endorsed for insurance, whichever rate is higher. The applicable rates of interest will be published twice each year as a notice in the FEDERAL REGISTER.

(b) For mortgages endorsed for insurance after January 23, 2004, if an insurance claim is paid in cash, the debenture interest rate for purposes of calculating such a claim shall be the monthly average yield, for the month in which the default on the mortgage occurred, on United States Treasury Securities adjusted to a constant maturity of 10 years.

[71 FR 35994, June 22, 2006]

§ 203.481 Maturity of debentures.

Debentures shall mature 10 years from the date of issue.

§ 203.482 Registration of debentures.

Debentures shall be registered as to principal and interest.

§ 203.483 Forms and amounts of debentures.

Debentures issued under this part shall be in such form and amounts; and shall be subject to such terms and conditions; and shall include such provisions for redemption, if any, as may be prescribed by the Secretary, with the approval of the Secretary of the Treasury; and may be in book entry or certificated registered form, or such other form as the Secretary by regulation may prescribe.

[59 FR 49816, Sept. 30, 1994]

§ 203.484 Redemption of debentures.

Debentures shall, at the option of the Commissioner and with the approval of the Secretary of the Treasury, be redeemable at par plus accrued interest on any semiannual interest payment date on 3 months' notice of redemption given in such manner as the Commissioner shall prescribe. The debenture interest on the debentures called for redemption shall cease on the semiannual interest payment date designated in the call notice. The Commissioner may include with the notice of redemption an offer to purchase the debentures at par plus accrued interest at any time during the period between the notice of redemption and the redemption date. If the debentures are purchased by the Commissioner after such call and prior to the named redemption date, the debenture interest shall cease on the date of purchase.

§ 203.486 Issue date of debentures.

The debentures shall be issued as of the date of the execution of the assignment of the loan in accordance with the requirements of § 203.476(c).

§ 203.487 Cash adjustment.

Any difference of less than $50 between the amount of debentures to be issued to the lender and the total amount of the lender's claim, as approved by the Commissioner, may be adjusted by the issuance of a check in payment thereof.

[59 FR 49816, Sept. 30, 1994]

§ 203.488 Sale of interests in insured loans.

No lender may sell or otherwise dispose of any insured loan or group of insured loans, or any partial interest in such loan or loans by means of any agreement, arrangement or device except pursuant to this subpart.

§ 203.489 Sale of insured loan to approved lender.

An insured loan may be sold to another approved lender. The seller shall

233

notify HUD of the sale within 15 calendar days, on a form prescribed by HUD and acknowledged by the buyer.

[45 FR 27929, Apr. 25, 1980]

§ 203.491 Effect of sale of insured loan.

When an insured loan is sold to another approved lender, the buyer shall thereupon succeed to all the rights and become bound by all the obligations of the seller under the contract of insurance and the seller shall be released from its obligations under the contract, provided that the seller shall not be relieved of its obligation to pay insurance premiums until the notice required by § 203.489 is received by HUD.

[45 FR 27929, Apr. 25, 1980]

§ 203.492 Assignments, pledges and transfers by approved lender.

(a) An assignment, pledge or transfer of an insured loan or group of insured loans, not constituting a final sale, may be made by an approved lender to another approved lender provided the following requirements are met:

(1) The assignor, pledgor or transferor shall remain the lender of record.

(2) The Commissioner shall have no obligation to recognize or deal with any party other than the lender of record with respect to the rights, benefits and obligations of the lender under the contract of insurance.

(b) An assignment or transfer of an insured loan or group of insured loans may be made by an approved lender to other than an approved lender provided the requirements under paragraphs (a) (1) and (2) of this section are met and the following additional requirements are met:

(1) The assignee or transferee shall be a corporation, trust or organization (including but not limited to any pension trust or profit-sharing plan) which certifies to the approved lender that:

(i) It has assets of $100,000 or more; and

(ii) It has lawful authority to hold an insured loan or group of insured loans.

(2) The assignment or transfer shall be made pursuant to an agreement under which the transferor or assignor is obligated to take one of the following alternate courses of action within one year from the date of the assignment or within such additional period of time as may be approved by the Commissioner:

(i) The transferor or assignor shall repurchase and accept a reassignment of such loan or group of loans.

(ii) The transferor or assignor shall obtain a sale and transfer of such loan or group of loans to an approved lender.

(c) Notice to or approval of the Commissioner is not required in connection with assignments, pledges or transfers pursuant to this section.

§ 203.493 Declaration of trust.

A sale of a beneficial interest in a group of insured loans, where the interest to be acquired is related to all of the loans as an entirety, rather than an interest in a specific loan, shall be made only pursuant to a declaration of trust, which has been approved by the Commissioner prior to any such sale.

§ 203.495 Transfers of partial interests.

A partial interest in an insured loan may be transferred under a participation agreement without obtaining the approval of the Commissioner, if the following conditions are met:

(a) *Principal mortgagee.* The insured loan shall be held by an approved lender which, for the purposes of this section, shall be referred to as the *principal lender*.

(b) *Interest of principal lender.* The principal lender shall retain and hold for its own account a financial interest in the insured loan.

(c) *Qualification for holding partial interest.* A partial interest in an insured loan shall be issued to and held only by:

(1) A lender approved by the Commissioner; or

(2) A corporation, trust or organization (including, but not limited to any pension fund, pension trust, or profit-sharing plan) which certifies to the principal lender that:

(i) It has assets of $100,000 or more; and

(ii) It has lawful authority to acquire a partial interest in an insured loan.

(d) *Participation agreement provisions.* The participation agreement shall include provisions that:

(1) The principal lender shall retain title to the loan and remain the lender of record under the contract of loan insurance.

(2) The Commissioner shall have no obligation to recognize or deal with anyone other than the principal lender with respect to the rights, benefits, and obligations of the lender under the contract of insurance.

(3) The loan documents shall remain in the custody of the principal lender.

(4) The responsibility for servicing the insured loans shall remain with the principal lender.

EXTENSION OF TIME

§203.496 Actions to be taken by mortgagee or lender.

With respect to any action required by the mortgagee or lender within a period of time prescribed by this subpart the Commissioner may extend such period.

AMENDMENTS

§203.499 Effect of amendments.

The regulations in this subpart may be amended by the Secretary at any time and from time to time, in whole or in part, but such amendment will not adversely affect the interests of a mortgagee under the contract of insurance on any mortgage or loan already insured, and will not adversely affect the interest of a mortgagee on any mortgage or loan to be insured for which either the Direct Endorsement or Lender Insurance mortgagee has approved the mortgagor and all terms and conditions of the mortgage or loan, or the Secretary has issued a firm commitment. In addition, such amendment will not adversely affect the eligibility of specific property if such property is covered by a conditional commitment issued by the Secretary, a certificate of reasonable value issued by the Secretary of Veterans Affairs, or an appraisal report approved by a Direct Endorsement or Lender Insurance underwriter.

[62 FR 30227, June 2, 1997]

Subpart C—Servicing Responsibilities

SOURCE: 41 FR 49736, Nov. 10, 1976, unless otherwise noted.

GENERAL REQUIREMENTS

§203.500 Mortgage servicing generally.

This subpart identifies servicing practices of lending institutions that HUD considers acceptable for mortgages insured by HUD. Failure to comply with this subpart shall not be a basis for denial of insurance benefits, but failure to comply will be cause for imposition of a civil money penalty, including a penalty under §30.35(c)(2), or withdrawal of HUD's approval of a mortgagee. It is the intent of the Department that no mortgagee shall commence foreclosure or acquire title to a property until the requirements of this subpart have been followed.

[70 FR 21578, Apr. 26, 2005]

§203.501 Loss mitigation.

Mortgagees must consider the comparative effects of their elective servicing actions, and must take those appropriate actions which can reasonably be expected to generate the smallest financial loss to the Department. Such actions include, but are not limited to, deeds in lieu of foreclosure under §203.357, pre-foreclosure sales under §203.370, partial claims under §203.414, assumptions under §203.512, special forbearance under §§203.471 and 203.614, and recasting of mortgages under §203.616. HUD may prescribe conditions and requirements for the appropriate use of these loss mitigation actions, concerning such matters as owner-occupancy, extent of previous defaults, prior use of loss mitigation, and evaluation of the mortgagor's income, credit and property.

[59 FR 50145, Sept. 30, 1994, as amended at 61 FR 35019, July 3, 1996]

§203.502 Responsibility for servicing.

(a) After January 10, 1994, servicing of insured mortgages must be performed by a mortgagee that is approved by HUD to service insured mortgages. The servicer must fully discharge the servicing responsibilities of the mortgagee as outlined in this part. The mortgagee shall remain fully responsible to the Secretary for proper servicing, and the actions of its servicer shall be considered to be the actions of the mortgagee. The servicer also shall be fully responsible to the Secretary for its actions as a servicer.

(b) Whenever servicing of any mortgage is transferred from one mortgagee or servicer to another, notice of the transfer of service shall be delivered:

(1) By the transferor mortgagee or servicer to the mortgagor. The notification shall be delivered not less than 15 days before the effective date of the transfer and shall contain the information required in § 3500.21(e)(2) of this title; and

(2) By the transferee mortgagee or servicer:

(i) *To the mortgagor.* The notification shall be delivered not less than 15 days before the effective date of the transfer and shall contain the information required in § 3500.21(e)(2) of this title; and

(ii) *To the Secretary.* This notification shall be delivered within 15 days of the transfer, in a format prescribed by the Secretary.

[36 FR 24508, Dec. 22, 1971, as amended at 57 FR 47974, Oct. 20, 1992; 57 FR 58349, Dec. 9, 1992; 59 FR 65448, Dec. 19, 1994; 61 FR 36266, July 9, 1996]

§ 203.508 **Providing information.**

(a) Mortgagees shall provide loan information to mortgagors and arrange for individual loan consultation on request. The mortgagee must establish written procedures and controls to assure prompt responses to inquiries. One or more of the following means of making information readily available to mortgagors is required:

(1) An office staffed with competent personnel located within 200 miles of the property, capable of providing timely responses to requests for information. Complete records need not be maintained in such an office if the staff is able to secure needed information and pass it on to the mortgagor.

(2) Toll-free telephone service at an office capable of providing needed information.

(b) All mortgagors must be informed of the system available for obtaining answers to loan inquiries, the office from which needed information may be obtained and reminded of the system at least annually. Toll-free telephone service need not be provided to a mortgagor other than at the office designated to serve the mortgagor nor other than from the immediate vicinity of the security property.

(c) Within thirty days after the end of each calendar year, the mortgagee shall furnish to the mortgagor a statement of the interest paid, and of the taxes disbursed from the escrow account during the preceding year. At the mortgagor's request, the mortgagee shall furnish a statement of the escrow account sufficient to enable the mortgagor to reconcile the account.

(d) Mortgagees must respond to HUD requests for information concerning individual accounts.

(e) Each servicer of a mortgage shall deliver to the mortgagor a written notice of any assignment, sale, or transfer of the servicing of the mortgage. The notice must be sent in accordance with the provisions of § 3500.21(e)(1) of this title and shall contain the information required by § 3500.21(e)(2) of this title. Servicers must respond to mortgagor inquiries pertaining to the transfer of servicing in accordance with § 3500.21(f) of this title.

(The information collection requirements contained in paragraph (c) were approved by the Office of Management and Budget under control number 2502–0235)

[41 FR 49736, Nov. 10, 1976, as amended at 48 FR 28986, June 24, 1983; 59 FR 65448, Dec. 19, 1994]

§ 203.510 **Release of personal liability.**

(a) *Procedures.* The mortgagee shall release a selling mortgagor from any personal liability for payment of the mortgage debt, if release is permitted by § 203.258 of this part, in accordance with the following procedures:

(1) The mortgagee receives a request for a creditworthiness determination for a prospective purchaser of all or part of the mortgaged property;

(2) The mortgagee or servicer performs a creditworthiness determination under § 203.512(b)(1) of this part if the mortgagee or servicer is approved

for participation in the Direct Endorsement program, or the mortgagee requests a creditworthiness determination by the Secretary;

(3) The prospective purchaser is determined to be creditworthy under the standards applicable when a release of the selling mortgagor is intended;

(4) The prospective purchaser assumes personal liability by agreeing to pay the mortgage debt; and

(5) The mortgagee provides the selling mortgagor with a release of personal liability on a form approved by the Secretary.

(b) *Release after 5 years.* (1) If a selling mortgagor is not released under the procedures described in paragraph (a) of this section, either because no request for a creditworthiness determination is submitted under paragraph (a)(1) of this section, or because there is no affirmative determination of creditworthiness under paragraph (a)(3) of this section, then the selling mortgagor is automatically released from any personal liability for payment of the mortgage debt because of section 203(r) of the National Housing Act if:

(i) The purchasing mortgagor has assumed personal liability by agreeing to pay the mortgage debt;

(ii) Five years have elapsed after the assumption; and

(iii) The purchasing mortgagor is not in default under the mortgage at the end of the five-year period.

(2) If the conditions of this paragraph (b) for a release are satisfied, the mortgagee shall provide a written release upon request to the selling mortgagor.

(3) This paragraph (b) only applies to a mortgage originated pursuant to an application by the mortgagor on or after December 1, 1986 on a form approved by the Secretary.

(c) *Mortgagee to provide notice.* A mortgagee shall inform mortgagors (including prospective mortgagors seeking information) about the procedures for release of personal liability by providing a notice approved by the Secretary when required by the Secretary.

[58 FR 42649, Aug. 11, 1993]

§ 203.512 **Free assumability; exceptions.**

(a) *Policy of free assumability with no restrictions.* A mortgagee shall not impose, agree to or enforce legal restrictions on conveyance, as defined in §203.41(a)(3) of this part, or restrictions on assumption of the insured mortgage, unless specifically permitted by this part or contained in a junior lien granted to the mortgagee after settlement on the insured mortgage.

(b) *Credit review.* If approval is required by the mortgage, the mortgagee shall not approve the sale or other transfer of all or part of the mortgaged property, or the sale or transfer of a beneficial interest in a trust owning all or part of the property, whether or not any person acquires personal liability under the mortgage in connection with the sale or other transfer, unless:

(1) At least one of the persons acquiring ownership is determined to be creditworthy under applicable standards prescribed by the Secretary;

(2) The selling mortgagor retains an ownership interest in the property; or

(3) The transfer is by devise or descent.

(c) *Investors and secondary residences.* The mortgagee shall not approve the sale of other transfer or mortgaged property to a person who cannot be approved as a substitute mortgagor as provided in §203.258 of this part because the property will not be a primary residence or a secondary residence permitted by that section.

(d) *Due-on-sale clause.* Each mortgage shall contain a due-on-sale clause permitting acceleration, in a form prescribed by the Secretary. If a sale or other transfer occurs without mortgagee approval and a prohibition in paragraphs (b) or (c) of this section applies, a mortgagee shall enforce this section by requesting approval from the Secretary to accelerate the mortgage, provided that acceleration is permitted by applicable law. The mortgagee shall accelerate if approval is granted. This paragraph applies only if the application by the mortgagor on a form approved by the Secretary is dated on or after December 1, 1986.

[58 FR 42649, Aug. 11, 1993; 59 FR 15112, Mar. 31, 1994]

PAYMENTS, CHARGES AND ACCOUNTS

§ 203.550 Escrow accounts.

(a) It is the mortgagee's responsibility to make escrow disbursements before bills become delinquent. Mortgagees must establish controls to insure that bills payable from the escrow fund or the information needed to pay such bills is obtained on a timely basis. Penalties for late payments for items payable from the escrow account must not be charged to the mortgagor unless it can be shown that the penalty was the direct result of the mortgagor's error or omission. The mortgagee shall use the procedures set forth in § 3500.17 of this title, implementing Section 10 of the Real Estate Settlement Procedures Act (12 U.S.C. 2609), to compute the amount of the escrow, the methods of collection and accounting, and the payment of the bills for which the money has been escrowed.

(b) [Reserved]

(c) In the case of escrow accounts created for purposes of § 203.52 or § 234.64 of this chapter, mortgagees may estimate escrow requirements based on the best information available as to probable payments that will be required to be made from the account on a periodic basis throughout the period during which the account is maintained.

(d) The mortgagee shall not institute foreclosure when the only default of the mortgagor occupant is a present inability to pay a substantial escrow shortage, resulting from an adjustment pursuant to this section, in a lump sum.

(e) When the contract of mortgage insurance is terminated voluntarily or because of prepayment in full, sums in the escrow account to pay the mortgage insurance premiums shall be remitted to HUD with a form approved by the Secretary for reporting the voluntary termination of prepayment. Upon prepayment in full sums held in escrow for taxes and hazard insurance shall be released to the mortgagor promptly.

(Approved by the Office of Management and Budget under control number 2502–0474)

[41 FR 49736, Nov. 10, 1976, as amended at 57 FR 9611, Mar. 19, 1992; 57 FR 27927, June 23, 1992; 59 FR 53901, Oct. 26, 1994; 60 FR 8812, Feb. 15, 1995]

§ 203.552 Fees and charges after endorsement.

(a) The mortgagee may collect reasonable and customary fees and charges from the mortgagor after insurance endorsement only as provided below. The mortgagee may collect these fees or charges from the mortgagor only to the extent that the mortgagee is not reimbursed for such fees by HUD.

(1) Late charges as set forth in § 203.25;

(2) Charges for processing or reprocessing a check returned as uncollectible; (Where bank policy permits, the mortgagee must deposit a check for collection a second time before assessing a bad check charge);

(3) Fees for processing a change of ownership of the mortgaged property;

(4) Fees and charges for arranging a substitution of liability under the mortgage in connection with the sale or transfer of the property;

(5) Charges for processing a request for credit approval of an assumptor or substitute mortgagor;

(6) Charges for substitution of a hazard insurance policy at other than the expiration of term of the existing hazard insurance policy;

(7) Charges for modification of the mortgage involving a recorded agreement for extension of term or reamortization;

(8) Fees and charges for processing a partial release of the mortgaged property;

(9) Attorney's and trustee's fees and expenses actually incurred (including the cost of appraisals pursuant to § 203.368(e) and cost of advertising pursuant to § 203.368(h)) when a case has been referred for foreclosure in accordance with the provisions of this part after a firm decision to foreclose if foreclosure is not completed because of a reinstatement of the account. (No attorney's fee may be charged for the services of the mortgagee's or servicer's staff attorney or for the services of a collection attorney other than the attorney handling the foreclosure.)

(10) The service charge provided for by § 203.23(c) and escrow charges in accordance with § 203.23(a);

(11) A trustee's fee if the security instrument in deed-of-trust states provides for payment of such a fee for execution of a satisfactory, release, or trustee's deed when the deed of trust is paid in full; and

(12) Such other reasonable and customary charges as may be authorized by the Secretary. (This shall not include:

(i) Charges for servicing activities of the mortgagee or servicer;

(ii) Fees charged by independent tax servicer organizations which contract to furnish data and information necessary for the payment of property taxes,

(iii) *Satisfaction, termination,* or *reconveyance* fees when a mortgage is paid in full (other than as provided in paragraph (a)(11) of this section), or

(iv) The fee for recordation of a satisfaction of the mortgage in states where recordation is the responsibility of the mortgagee.)

(13) Where permitted by the security instrument, attorney's fees and expenses actually incurred in the defense of any suit or legal proceeding wherein the mortgagee shall be made a party thereto by reason of the mortgage; (No attorney's fee may be charged for the services of the mortgagee's or servicer's staff attorney.)

(14) Property preservation expenses incurred pursuant to §203.377.

(b) *reasonable and customary* fees must be predicated upon the actual cost of the work performed including out-of-pocket expenses. Directors of HUD Area and Insuring Offices are authorized to establish maximum fees and charges which are reasonable and customary in their areas. Except as provided in this part, no fee or charge shall be based on a percentage of either the face amount of the mortgage or the unpaid principal balance due on the mortgage.

[41 FR 49736, Nov. 10, 1976, as amended at 52 FR 1330, Jan. 13, 1987; 61 FR 35019, July 3, 1996; 62 FR 60130, Nov. 6, 1997]

§203.554 Enforcement of late charges.

(a) A mortgagee shall not commence foreclosure when the only default on the part of the mortgagor is the failure to pay a late charge or charges (§203.25), except as provided in §203.556.

(b) A late charge attributable to a particular installment payment due under the mortgage shall not be deducted from that installment. However, if the mortgagee thereafter notifies the mortgagor of his obligation to pay a late charge, such a charge may be deducted from any subsequent payment or payments submitted by the mortgagor or on his behalf if this is not inconsistent with the terms of the mortgage. Partial payments shall be treated as provided in §203.556.

(c) A payment may be returned because of failure to include a late charge only if the mortgagee notifies the mortgagor before imposition of the charge of the amount of the monthly payment, the date when the late charge will be imposed and either the amount of the late charge or the total amount due when the late charge is included.

(d) During the 60-day period beginning on the effective date of transfer of the servicing of a mortgage, a late charge shall not be imposed on the mortgagor with respect to any payment on the loan. No payment shall be treated as late for any other purpose if the payment is received by the transferor servicer, rather than the transferee servicer that should receive the payment, before the due date (including any applicable grace period allowed under the mortgage documents) applicable to such payment.

[42 FR 15680, Mar. 23, 1977, as amended at 59 FR 65448, Dec. 19, 1994]

§203.556 Return of partial payments.

(a) For the purpose of this section, a partial payment is a payment of any amount less than the full amount due under the terms of the mortgage at the time the payment is tendered, including late charges.

(b) Except as provided in this section, the mortgagee shall accept any partial payment and either apply it to the mortgagor's account or identify it with the mortgagor's account and hold it in a trust account pending disposition. When partial payments held for disposition aggregate a full monthly installment they shall be applied to the mortgagor's account, thus advancing the date of the oldest unpaid install-ment but not the date on which the ac-count first became delinquent.

(c) If the mortgage is not in default, a partial payment may be returned to the mortgagor with a letter of expla-nation.

(d) If the mortgage is in default, a partial payment may be returned to the mortgagor with a letter of expla-nation in any of the following cir-cumstances:

(1) When payment aggregates less than 50 percent of the amount then due;

(2) The payment is less than the amount agreed to in a forbearance plan, whether or not reduced to writ-ing;

(3) The property is occupied by a ten-ant who is paying rent and the rentals are not being applied to the mortgage payments;

(4) Foreclosure has been commenced. (Foreclosure is commenced when the first action required for foreclosure under applicable law is taken.)

(e) Under the following cir-cumstances the mortgagee may return any partial payment received more than 14 days after the mortgagee has mailed to the mortgagor a statement of the full amount due, including late charges, and a notice of intention to return any payment less than such amount.

(1) Four or more monthly install-ments are due and unpaid, or

(2) A delinquency of any amount has continued for at least six months since the account first became delinquent.

[42 FR 15680, Mar. 23, 1977]

§ 203.558 Handling prepayments.

(a) *Handling prepayments for FHA-in-sured mortgages closed on or after Janu-ary 21, 2015.* With respect to FHA-in-sured mortgages closed on or after Jan-uary 21, 2015, notwithstanding the terms of the mortgage, the mortgagee shall accept a prepayment at any time and in any amount. The mortgagee shall not require 30 days' advance no-tice of prepayment, even if the mort-gage instrument purports to require such notice. Monthly interest on the debt must be calculated on the actual unpaid principal balance of the loan as of the date the prepayment is received,

and not as of the next installment due date.

(b) *Handling prepayments for FHA-in-sured mortgages closed before January 21, 2015.* (1) With respect to FHA mort-gages insured before August 2, 1985, if a prepayment is offered on other than an installment due date, the mortgagee may refuse to accept the prepayment until the first day of the month fol-lowing expiration of the 30-day notice period as provided in the mortgage, or may require payment of interest to that date, but only if the mortgagee so advises the mortgagor, in a form ap-proved by the Commissioner, in re-sponse to the mortgagor's inquiry, re-quest for payoff figures, or tender of prepayment. If the installment due date (the first day of the month) falls on a nonbusiness day, the mortgagor's notice of intention to prepay or the prepayment shall be timely if received on the next business day.

(2) With respect to FHA mortgages insured on or after August 2, 1985, but closed before January 21, 2015, the mortgagee shall not require 30 days' advance notice of prepayment, even if the mortgage instrument purports to require such notice. If the prepayment is offered on other than an installment due date, the mortgagee may refuse to accept the prepayment until the next installment due date (the first day of the month), or may require payment of interest to that date, but only if the mortgagee so advises the mortgagor, in a form approved by the Commissioner, in response to the mortgagor's inquiry, request for payoff figures, or tender of prepayment.

(3) If the mortgagee fails to meet the full disclosure requirements of para-graphs (b)(1) and (b)(2) of this section, the mortgagee may be subject to for-feiture of that portion of the interest collected for the period beyond the date that prepayment in full was re-ceived and to such other actions as are provided in part 25 of this title.

(c) *Mortgagee annual notice to mortga-gors.* Each mortgagee, with respect to a mortgage under this part, shall provide to each of its mortgagors not less fre-quently than annually a written no-tice, in a form approved by the Com-missioner, containing a statement of the amount outstanding for prepayment of the principal amount of the mortgage. With respect to FHA-insured mortgages closed before January 21, 2015, the notice shall describe any requirements the mortgagor must fulfill to prevent the accrual of any interest on the principal amount after the date of any prepayment. This paragraph shall apply to any outstanding mortgage insured on or after August 22, 1991.

[79 FR 50837, Aug. 26, 2014]

MORTGAGEE ACTION AND FORBEARANCE

§203.600 Mortgage collection action.

Subject to the requirements of this subpart, mortgagees shall take prompt action to collect amounts due from mortgagors to minimize the number of accounts in a delinquent or default status. Collection techniques must be adapted to individual differences in mortgagors and take account of the circumstances peculiar to each mortgagor.

§203.602 Delinquency notice to mortgagor.

The mortgagee shall give notice to each mortgagor in default on a form supplied by the Secretary or, if the mortgagee wishes to use its own form, on a form approved by the Secretary, no later than the end of the second month of any delinquency in payments under the mortgage. If an account is reinstated and again becomes delinquent, the delinquency notice shall be sent to the mortgagor again, except that the mortgagee is not required to send a second delinquency notice to the same mortgagor more often than once each six months. The mortgagee may issue additional or more frequent notices of delinquency at its option.

§203.604 Contact with the mortgagor.

(a) [Reserved]

(b) The mortgagee must have a face-to-face interview with the mortgagor, or make a reasonable effort to arrange such a meeting, before three full monthly installments due on the mortgage are unpaid. If default occurs in a repayment plan arranged other than during a personal interview, the mortgagee must have a face-to-face meeting with the mortgagor, or make a reasonable attempt to arrange such a meeting within 30 days after such default and at least 30 days before foreclosure is commenced, or at least 30 days before assignment is requested if the mortgage is insured on Hawaiian home land pursuant to section 247 or Indian land pursuant to section 248 or if assignment is requested under §203.350(d) for mortgages authorized by section 203(q) of the National Housing Act.

(c) A face-to-face meeting is not required if:

(1) The mortgagor does not reside in the mortgaged property,

(2) The mortgaged property is not within 200 miles of the mortgagee, its servicer, or a branch office of either,

(3) The mortgagor has clearly indicated that he will not cooperate in the interview,

(4) A repayment plan consistent with the mortgagor's circumstances is entered into to bring the mortgagor's account current thus making a meeting unnecessary, and payments thereunder are current, or

(5) A reasonable effort to arrange a meeting is unsuccessful.

(d) A reasonable effort to arrange a face-to-face meeting with the mortgagor shall consist at a minimum of one letter sent to the mortgagor certified by the Postal Service as having been dispatched. Such a reasonable effort to arrange a face-to-face meeting shall also include at least one trip to see the mortgagor at the mortgaged property, unless the mortgaged property is more than 200 miles from the mortgagee, its servicer, or a branch office of either, or it is known that the mortgagor is not residing in the mortgaged property.

(e)(1) For mortgages insured pursuant to section 248 of the National Housing Act, the provisions of paragraphs (b), (c) and (d) of this section are applicable, except that a face-to-face meeting with the mortgagor is required, and a reasonable effort to arrange such a meeting shall include at least one trip to see the mortgagor at the mortgaged property, notwithstanding that such property is more than 200 miles from the mortgagee, its servicer, or a branch office of either. In addition, the mortgagee must document that it has made at least one telephone call to the mortgagor for the purpose of trying to arrange a face-to-face interview. The mortgagee may appoint an agent to perform its responsibilities under this paragraph.

(2) The mortgagee must also:

(i) Inform the mortgagor that HUD will make information regarding the status and payment history of the mortgagor's loan available to local credit bureaus and prospective creditors;

(ii) Inform the mortgagor of other available assistance, if any;

(iii) Inform the mortgagor of the names and addresses of HUD officials to whom further communications may be addressed.

(Approved by the Office of Management and Budget under control number 2502–0340)

[41 FR 49736, Nov. 10, 1976, as amended at 51 FR 21873, June 16, 1986; 52 FR 48202, Dec. 21, 1987; 53 FR 9869, Mar. 28, 1988; 61 FR 35019, July 3, 1996; 61 FR 36266, July 9, 1996]

§ 203.605 Loss mitigation performance.

(a) *Duty to mitigate.* Before four full monthly installments due on the mortgage have become unpaid, the mortgagee shall evaluate on a monthly basis all of the loss mitigation techniques provided at § 203.501 to determine which is appropriate. Based upon such evaluations, the mortgagee shall take the appropriate loss mitigation action. Documentation must be maintained for the initial and all subsequent evaluations and resulting loss mitigation actions. Should a claim for mortgage insurance benefits later be filed, the mortgagee shall maintain this documentation in the claim review file under the requirements of § 203.365(c).

(b) *Assessment of mortgagee's loss mitigation performance.* (1) HUD will measure and advise mortgagees of their loss mitigation performance through the Tier Ranking System (TRS). Under the TRS, HUD will analyze each mortgagee's loss mitigation efforts portfolio-wide on a quarterly basis, based on 12 months of performance, by computing ratios involving loss mitigation attempts, defaults, and claims. Based on the ratios, HUD will group mortgagees in four tiers (Tiers 1, 2, 3, and 4), with Tier 1 representing the highest or best

ranking mortgagees and Tier 4 representing the lowest or least satisfactory ranking mortgagees. The precise methodology for calculating the TRS ratios and for determining the tier stratification (or cutoff points) will be provided through FEDERAL REGISTER notice. Notice of future TRS methodology or stratification changes will be published in the FEDERAL REGISTER and will provide a 30-day public comment period.

(2) Before HUD issues each quarterly TRS notice, HUD will review the number of claims paid to the mortgagee. If HUD determines that the lender's low TRS score is the result of a small number of defaults or a small number of foreclosure claims, or both, as defined by notice, HUD may determine not to designate the mortgagee as Tier 3 or Tier 4, and the mortgagee will remain unranked.

(3) Within 30 calendar days after the date of the TRS notice, a mortgagee that scored in Tier 4 may appeal its ranking to the Deputy Assistant Secretary for Single Family or the Deputy Assistant Secretary's designee and request an informal HUD conference. The only basis for appeal by the Tier 4 mortgagee is disagreement with the data used by HUD to calculate the mortgagee's ranking. If HUD determines that the mortgagee's Tier 4 ranking was based on incorrect or incomplete data, the mortgagee's performance will be recalculated and the mortgagee will receive a corrected tier ranking score.

(c) *Assessment of civil money penalty.* A mortgagee that is found to have failed to engage in loss mitigation as required under paragraph (a) of this section shall be liable for a civil money penalty as provided in § 30.35(c) of this title.

[70 FR 21578, Apr. 26, 2005]

§ 203.606 Pre-foreclosure review.

(a) Before initiating foreclosure, the mortgagee must ensure that all servicing requirements of this subpart have been met. The mortgagee may not commence foreclosure for a monetary default unless at least three full monthly installments due under the mortgage are unpaid after application of any partial payments that may have been accepted but not yet applied to the mortgage account. In addition, prior to initiating any action required by law to foreclose the mortgage, the mortgagee shall notify the mortgagor in a format prescribed by the Secretary that the mortgagor is in default and the mortgagee intends to foreclose unless the mortgagor cures the default.

(b) If the mortgagee determines that any of the following conditions has been met, the mortgagee may initiate foreclosure without the delay in foreclosure required by paragraph (a) of this section:

(1) The mortgaged property has been abandoned, or has been vacant for more than 60 days.

(2) The mortgagor, after being clearly advised of the options available for relief, has clearly stated in writing that he or she has no intention of fulfilling his or her obligation under the mortgage.

(3) The mortgaged property is not the mortgagor's principal residence and it is occupied by tenants who are paying rent, but the rental income is not being applied to the mortgage debt.

(4) The property is owned by a corporation or partnership.

[52 FR 6915, Mar. 5, 1987, as amended at 61 FR 35020, July 3, 1996]

§ 203.608 Reinstatement.

The mortgagee shall permit reinstatement of a mortgage, even after the institution of foreclosure proceedings, if the mortgagor tenders in a lump sum all amounts required to bring the account current, including foreclosure costs and reasonable attorney's fees and expenses properly associated with the foreclosure action, unless: (a) The mortgagee has accepted reinstatement after the institution of foreclosure proceedings within two years immediately preceding the commencement of the current foreclosure action, (b) reinstatement will preclude foreclosure following a subsequent default, or (c) reinstatement will adversely affect the priority of the mortgage lien.

§ 203.610 Relief for mortgagor in military service.

The mortgagee shall specifically give consideration to affording the mort-

gagor the benefit of relief authorized by §§ 203.345 and 203.346, if the mortgagor is *person in the military service* as that term is defined in the Soldiers and Sailors Civil Relief Act of 1940, as amended.

§ 203.614 Special forbearance.

If the mortgagee finds that a default is due to circumstances beyond the mortgagor's control, as defined by HUD, the mortgagee may grant special forbearance relief to the mortgagor in accordance with the conditions prescribed by HUD.

[61 FR 35020, July 3, 1996]

§ 203.616 Mortgage modification.

The mortgagee may modify a mortgage for the purpose of changing the amortization provisions by recasting the total unpaid amount due for a term not exceeding 360 months. The mortgagee must notify HUD of such modification in a format prescribed by HUD within 30 days of the execution of the modification agreement.

[62 FR 60130, Nov. 6, 1997]

MORTGAGES IN DEFAULT ON PROPERTY LOCATED ON INDIAN RESERVATIONS

§ 203.664 Processing defaulted mortgages on property located on Indian land.

Before a mortgagee requests that the Secretary accept assignment under § 203.350(b) of a mortgage insured pursuant to section 248 of the National Housing Act (§ 203.43h), the mortgagee must submit documents showing that the requirements of § 203.604 have been met.

[61 FR 35020, July 3, 1996]

MORTGAGES IN DEFAULT ON PROPERTY LOCATED ON HAWAIIAN HOME LANDS

§ 203.665 Processing defaulted mortgages on property located on Hawaiian home lands.

Before a mortgagee requests the Secretary to accept assignment under § 203.350(c) of a mortgage insured pursuant to section 247 of the National Housing Act (§ 203.43i), the mortgagee must submit documents showing that the requirements of § 203.604 have been met.

[61 FR 35020, July 3, 1996]

ASSIGNMENT AND FORBEARANCE—PROP-
ERTY IN ALLEGANY RESERVATION OF
SENECA INDIANS

**§ 203.666 Processing defaulted mort-
gages on property in Allegany Reservation of Seneca Nation of Indians.**

(a) *Applicability.* This section applies
to mortgages authorized by section
203(q) of the National Housing Act
(§ 203.43j) only if the default occurred
before the mortgagor and the lessee
execute a lease renewal or a new lease
either with a term of not less than five
years beyond the maturity date of the
mortgage, or with a term established
by an arbitration award.

(b) *Claims through assignment.* Before
a mortgagee requests the Secretary to
accept assignment under § 203.350(d) the
mortgagee must submit documents
showing that the requirements of
§ 203.604 have been met.

[53 FR 13405, Apr. 25, 1988, as amended at 61
FR 35020, July 3, 1996]

OCCUPIED CONVEYANCE

**§ 203.670 Conveyance of occupied
property.**

(a) It is HUD's policy to reduce the
inventory of acquired properties in a
manner that expands homeownership
opportunities, strengthens neighborhoods and communities, and ensures a
maximum return to the mortgage insurance fund.

(b) The Secretary will accept conveyance of an occupied property containing one to four residential units if
the Secretary finds that:

(1) An individual residing in the property suffers from a temporary, permanent, or long-term illness or injury
that would be aggravated by the process of moving from the property, and
that the individual meets the eligibility criteria in § 203.674(a);

(2) State or local law prohibits the
mortgagee from evicting a tenant residing in the property who is making
regular monthly payments to the
mortgagor, or prohibits eviction for
other similar reasons beyond the control of the mortgagee; or

(3) It is in the Secretary's interest to
accept conveyance of the property occupied under § 203.671, the property is

habitable as defined in § 203.673, and,
except for conveyances under
§ 203.671(d), each occupant who intends
to remain in the property after the
conveyance meets the eligibility criteria in § 203.674(b).

(c) HUD consents to accept good marketable title to occupied property
where 90 days have elapsed since the
mortgagee notified HUD of pending acquisition, the Department has notified
the mortgagee that it was considering
a request for continued occupancy, and
no subsequent notification from HUD
has been received by the mortgagee.

[53 FR 874, Jan. 14, 1988, as amended at 56 FR
46967, Sept. 16, 1991; 58 FR 54246, Oct. 20, 1993;
61 FR 36266, July 9, 1996]

**§ 203.671 Criteria for determining the
Secretary's interest.**

It is in the Secretary's interest to accept occupied conveyance when one or
more of the following are met:

(a) Occupancy of the property is essential to protect it from vandalism
from time of acquisition to the time of
preparation for sale.

(b) The average time in inventory for
HUD's unsold inventory in the residential area in which the property is located exceeds six months.

(c) With respect to multi-unit properties, the marketability of the property would be improved by retaining
occupancy of one or more units.

(d) The high cost of eviction or relocation expenses makes eviction impractical.

[45 FR 59563, Sept. 10, 1980, as amended at 56
FR 46967, Sept. 16, 1991; 58 FR 54246, Oct. 20,
1993]

§ 203.672 Residential areas.

(a) For the purposes of occupied conveyance considerations, a residential
area is any area which constitutes a
local economic market for the purchase and sale of residential real estate. In making determinations of residential areas, substantial weight shall
be given to delineations of such areas
commonly used by persons active in
the real estate industry in the affected
area.

(b) HUD shall establish such residential areas within six (6) months of the
publication of these regulations when
HUD's current established patterns of

dealing with the disposition of its acquired home property inventory and related recordkeeping does not coincide with paragraph (a) of this section. Under such circumstances the Secretary shall apply such established patterns in defining residential areas until the standards in paragraph (a) of this section are implemented.

[45 FR 59563, Sept. 10, 1980]

§203.673 Habitability.

(a) For purposes of §203.670, a property is habitable if it meets the requirements of this section in its present condition, or will meet these requirements with the expenditure of not more than five percent of the fair market value of the property. The cost of hazard reduction or abatement of lead-based paint hazards in the property, as required by the Lead-Based Paint Poisoning Prevention Act (42 U.S.C. 4821–4846), and the Residential Lead-Based Paint Hazard Reduction Act of 1992 (42 U.S.C. 4851–4856), and implementing regulations in part 35 of this title, is excluded from these repair cost limitations.

(b)(1) Each residential unit must contain:

(i) Heating facilities adequate for healthful and comfortable living conditions, taking into consideration the local climate;

(ii) Adequate electrical supply for lighting and for equipment used in the residential unit;

(iii) Adequate cooking facilities;

(iv) A continuing supply of hot and cold water; and

(v) Adequate sanitary facilities and a safe method of sewage disposal.

(2) The property shall be structurally sound, reasonably durable, and free from hazards that may adversely affect the health and safety of the occupants or may impair the customary use and enjoyment by the occupants. Unacceptable hazards include, but are not limited to, subsidence, erosion, flood, exposure to the elements, exposed or unsafe electrical wiring, or an accumulation of minor hazards, such as broken stairs.

(c) If repairs, including lead-based paint hazard reduction or abatement, are to be made while the property is occupied, the occupant must hold the Secretary and the Department harmless against any personal injury or property damage that may occur during the process of making repairs. If temporary relocation of the occupant is necessary during repairs, no reimbursement for relocation expenses will be provided to the occupant.

[53 FR 874, Jan. 14, 1988, as amended at 64 FR 50225, Sept. 15, 1999]

§203.674 Eligibility for continued occupancy.

(a) Occupancy because of temporary, permanent, or long-term illness or injury of an individual residing in the property will be limited to a reasonable time, to be determined by the Secretary on a case-by-case basis, and will be permitted only if all the conditions in this paragraph (a) are met:

(1) A timely request is made in accordance with §203.676, including the submittal of documents required in §203.675(b)(4).

(2) The occupant agrees to execute a month-to-month lease, at the time of acquisition of the property by the Secretary and on a form prescribed by HUD, and to pay a fair market rent as determined by the Secretary. The rental rate shall be established on the basis of rents charged for other properties in comparable condition after completion of repairs (if any).

(3) The occupant's total housing cost (rent plus utility costs to be paid by the occupant) will not exceed 38 percent of the occupant's net effective income (gross income less Federal income taxes). However, a higher percentage may be permitted if the occupant has been paying at least the required rental amount for the dwelling, or if there are other compensating factors (e.g., where the occupant is able to rely on cash savings or on contributions from family members to cover total housing costs).

(4) The occupant agrees to allow access to the property (during normal business hours and upon a minimum of two days advance notice) by HUD Field Office staff or by a HUD representative, so that the property may be inspected and any necessary repairs accomplished, or by a sales broker.

(5) The occupant discloses and verifies Social Security Numbers, as

245

provided by part 200, subpart T, of this chapter.

(b) An occupant who does not meet the illness or injury criteria in paragraph (a) of this section is eligible for continued occupancy only if all the conditions in this paragraph (b) are met:

(1) A timely request is made in accordance with § 203.676.

(2) The occupant agrees to execute a month-to-month lease, at the time of acquisition of the property by the Secretary and on a form prescribed by HUD, to pay fair market rent as determined by the Secretary, and to pay the rent for the first month in advance at the time the lease is executed. The rental rate shall be established on the basis of rents charged for other properties in comparable condition after completion of repairs (if any).

(3) The occupant will have been in occupancy at least 90 days before the date the mortgagee acquires title to the property.

(4) The occupant's total housing cost (rent plus utility costs to be paid by the occupant) will not exceed 38 percent of the occupant's net effective income (gross income less Federal income taxes). However, a higher percentage may be permitted if the occupant has been paying at least the required rental amount for the dwelling, or if there are other compensating factors (e.g., where the occupant is able to rely on cash savings or on contributions from family members to cover total housing costs).

(5) The occupant agrees to allow access to the property (during normal business hours and upon a minimum of two days advance notice) by HUD Field Office staff or by a HUD representative, so that the property may be inspected and any necessary repairs accomplished, or by a sales broker.

(6) The occupant discloses and verifies Social Security Number, as provided by part 200, subpart T, of this chapter.

(Approved by the Office of Management and Budget under control number 2502–0268)

[53 FR 874, Jan. 14, 1988, and 53 FR 8626, Mar. 16, 1988, as amended at 54 FR 39693, Sept. 27, 1989; 56 FR 46967, Sept. 16, 1991]

§ 203.675 Notice to occupants of pending acquisition.

(a) At least 60 days, but not more than 90 days, before the date on which the mortgagee reasonably expects to acquire title to the property, the mortgagee shall notify the mortgagor and each head of household who is actually occupying a unit of the property of its potential acquisition by HUD. The mortgagee shall send a copy of this notification to the appropriate HUD Field Office.

(b) The notice shall provide a brief summary of the conditions under which continued occupancy is permissible and advise them that:

(1) Potential acquisition of the property by the Secretary is pending;

(2) The Secretary requires that properties be vacant at the time of conveyance to the Secretary, unless the mortgagor or other occupant can meet the conditions for continued occupancy in § 203.670, the habitability criteria in § 203.673, and the eligibility criteria in § 203.674;

(3) An occupant may request permission to remain in occupancy in the event of acquisition of the property by the Secretary by notifying the HUD Field Office in writing, with any required documentation, within 20 days of the date of the mortgagee's notice to the occupant;

(4) If an occupant seeks to qualify for continued occupancy under the illness or injury provisions of § 203.674(a), the occupant shall provide to the HUD Field Office, at the time of the occupant's request for permission to remain in occupancy, documentation to support this claim. Documentation shall include an estimate of the time when the patient could be moved without severely aggravating the illness or injury, and a statement by a State-certified physician establishing the validity of the occupant's claim. HUD may require more than one medical opinion or may arrange an examination by a physician approved by HUD; and

(5) If an occupant fails to make a timely request, the property must be

vacated before the scheduled time of acquisition.

(Approved by the Office of Management and Budget under control number 2502–0268)

[53 FR 875, Jan. 14, 1988, and 53 FR 8626, Mar. 16, 1988, as amended at 58 FR 54246, Oct. 20, 1993]

§203.676 Request for continued occupancy.

An occupant may request permission to continue to occupy the property following conveyance to the Secretary by notifying the HUD Field Office in writing, within 20 days after the date of the mortgagee's notice of pending acquisition. Verification of illness or injury as described in §203.675(b)(4) shall be submitted within this time period if an occupant seeks to qualify for continued occupancy under the provisions of §203.674(a). The HUD Field Office will notify the mortgagee in writing that an occupied conveyance has been requested.

(Approved by the Office of Management and Budget under control number 2502–0268)

[53 FR 875, Jan. 14, 1988, and 53 FR 8626, Mar. 16, 1988, as amended at 58 FR 54246, Oct. 20, 1993]

§203.677 Decision to approve or deny a request.

(a) The HUD Field Office will provide written notification of its decision to an occupant who makes a timely request to continue to occupy the property. The decision of the HUD Field Office on this matter will be made by the Chief, Property Disposition. If the decision is to deny the request, the notice to the occupant will include a statement of the reason or reasons for the decision and of the occupant's right to appeal. The occupant may appeal HUD's decision within 20 days after the date of HUD's notice. The appeal must be addressed to the Field Office Manager and be in writing, and the occupant may provide documentation intended to refute the reasons given for HUD's decision. The occupant may also request an informal conference with a representative of the HUD Field Office Manager. A request for an informal conference must be made in writing within 10 days after the date of HUD's notice. The occupant may be rep-

resented at the conference by counsel or by other persons with pertinent expert knowledge or experience.

(b) After notification that HUD has denied a request for continued occupancy, the occupant, on his or her request, shall be permitted to review all relevant material in HUD's possession (including a copy of the inspection report if the request is denied because the property is not habitable as defined in §203.673). Only material in HUD's possession that directly pertains to conditions for continued occupancy under §§203.670, 203.673, and 203.674 may be considered material relevant for an occupant's review under this paragraph. This review shall be limited to a review of material for purposes of the informal conference or the appeal of the Department's decision. The information will only be provided after request for an informal conference or appeal has been submitted to HUD.

(c) After consideration of an appeal, the HUD Field Office will notify the applicant in writing of HUD's final decision. This final decision will be made by the HUD Field Office Manager or a representative of the Field Office Manager (other than the Chief, Property Disposition). If the decision is to deny the occupant's request, the notice to the occupant will reflect consideration of the issues raised by the occupant.

(d) If, after consideration of an appeal, the Field Office Manager denies the request for new or additional reasons, the occupant will be afforded an opportunity to request that the Field Office Manager reconsider its decision under the provisions of paragraph (c) of this section.

[53 FR 875, Jan. 14, 1988, and 53 FR 8626, Mar. 16, 1988]

§203.678 Conveyance of vacant property.

(a) HUD will require that the property be conveyed vacant if the occupant fails to request permission to continue to occupy within the time period specified in §203.676, or fails to request a conference or to appeal a decision to deny occupied conveyance within the time period specified in §203.677(a).

(b) If the mortgagee has not been notified by HUD, within 45 days of the date of the mortgagee's notification of pending acquisition, that a request for continued occupancy is under consideration, the mortgagee shall convey the property vacant, unless otherwise directed by HUD.

[53 FR 875, Jan. 14, 1988, and 53 FR 8626, Mar. 16, 1988]

§ 203.679 Continued occupancy after conveyance.

(a) Occupancy of HUD-acquired property is temporary in all cases and is subject to termination when necessary to facilitate preparing the property for sale and completing the sale.

(b) HUD will notify the occupant to vacate the property and, if necessary, will take appropriate eviction action in any of the following situations:

(1) Failure of the occupant to execute the lease required by § 203.674 (a)(2) and (b)(2), or failure to pay the rental amount required, including the initial payment at the time of execution of the lease, or to comply with the terms of the lease;

(2) Failure of the occupant to allow access to the property upon request in accordance with § 203.674 (a)(4) and (b)(5);

(3) Necessity to prepare the property for sale; or

(4) Assignment of the property by the Secretary to a different use or program.

[53 FR 876, Jan. 14, 1988, and 53 FR 8626, Mar. 16, 1988; 61 FR 36266, July 9, 1996]

§ 203.680 Approval of occupancy after conveyance.

When an occupied property is conveyed to HUD before HUD has had an opportunity to consider continued occupancy (e.g., where HUD has taken more than 90 days to make a final decision on continued occupancy in accordance with § 203.670(c)), a determination regarding continued occupancy will be made in accordance with the conditions for the initial approval of occupied conveyance. Any such determination shall be in accordance with HUD's obligations under the terms of any month-to-month lease that has been executed.

[53 FR 876, Jan. 14, 1988, and 53 FR 8626, Mar. 16, 1988]

§ 203.681 Authority of HUD Field Office Managers.

Field Office Managers shall act for the Secretary in all matters relating to assignment and occupied conveyance determinations. The decision of the Field Office Manager under § 203.677 will be final and not be subject to further administrative review.

[53 FR 876, Jan. 14, 1988, and 53 FR 8626, Mar. 16, 1988]

PART 204—COINSURANCE

AUTHORITY: 12 U.S.C. 1715z–9; 42 U.S.C. 3535(d).

§ 204.1 Termination of program.

Effective December 29, 1994, of final rule the authority to coinsure mortgages under this part is terminated, except that the Department will honor legally binding and validly issued borrower approvals issued by lenders before the termination date. This part 204, as it existed immediately before the termination date, will continue to govern the rights and obligations of coinsured lenders, mortgagors, and the Department of Housing and Urban Development with respect to loans coinsured under this part.

[59 FR 39957, Aug. 5, 1994]

PART 206—HOME EQUITY CONVERSION MORTGAGE INSURANCE

Subpart A—General

AUTHORITY: 12 U.S.C. 1715b, 1715z–20; 42 U.S.C. 3535(d)

SOURCE: 82 FR 7117, Jan. 19, 2017, unless otherwise noted.

Subpart A—General

§ 206.1 Purpose.

The purposes of the Home Equity Conversion Mortgage (HECM) Insurance program are set out in section 255(a) of the National Housing Act, Public Law 73–479, 48 Stat. 1246 (12 U.S.C. 1715z–20) ("NHA").

§ 206.3 Definitions.

As used in this part, the following terms shall have the meaning indicated.

Bona fide tenant means a tenant of the property who is not a mortgagor, borrower, a spouse or child of a mortgagor or borrower, or any other member of a mortgagor's or borrower's family.

Borrower means a mortgagor who is an original borrower under the HECM Loan Agreement and Note. The term does not include successors or assigns of a borrower.

Borrower's Advance means the funds advanced to the borrower at the closing of a fixed interest rate HECM in accordance with § 206.25.

CMT Index means the U.S. Constant Maturity Treasury Index.

Commissioner means the Federal Housing Commissioner or the Commissioner's authorized representative.

Contract of insurance means the agreement evidenced by the issuance of a Mortgage Insurance Certificate or by the endorsement of the Commissioner upon the credit instrument given in connection with an insured mortgage, incorporating by reference the regulations in subpart C of this part and the applicable provisions of the National Housing Act.

Day means calendar day, except where the term *business day* is used.

Deferral Period means the period of time following the death of the last surviving borrower during which the due and payable status of a HECM is deferred for an Eligible Non-Borrowing Spouse provided that the Qualifying Attributes and all other FHA requirements continue to be satisfied.

Eligible Non-Borrowing Spouse means a Non-Borrowing Spouse who meets all Qualifying Attributes for a Deferral Period.

Estate planning service firm means an individual or entity that is not a mortgagee approved under part 202 of this chapter or a participating agency approved under subpart B of 24 CFR part 214 and that charges a fee that is:

(1) Contingent on the prospective borrower obtaining a mortgage loan under this part, except the origination fee authorized by § 206.31 or a fee specifically authorized by the Commissioner; or

(2) For information that borrowers and Eligible and Ineligible Non-Borrowing Spouses, if applicable, must receive under § 206.41, except a fee by:

(i) A participating agency approved under subpart B of 24 CFR part 214; or

(ii) An individual or company, such as an attorney or accountant, in the *bona fide* business of generally providing tax or other legal or financial advice; or

(3) For other services that the provider of the services represents are, in whole or in part, for the purpose of improving a prospective borrower's access to mortgages covered by this part, except where the fee is for services specifically authorized by the Commissioner.

Expected average mortgage interest rate means the interest rate used to calculate the principal limit established at closing. For fixed interest rate HECMs, the expected average mortgage interest rate is the same as the fixed mortgage (Note) interest rate and is set simultaneously with the fixed interest rate. For adjustable interest rate HECMs, it is either the sum of the mortgagee's margin plus the weekly average yield for U.S. Treasury securities adjusted to a constant maturity of 10 years, or it is the sum of the mortgagee's margin plus the 10-year LIBOR swap rate, depending on which interest rate index is chosen by the borrower. The margin is determined by the mortgagee and is defined as the amount that is added to the index value to compute the expected average mortgage interest rate. The index type (CMT or LIBOR) used to calculate the expected average mortgage interest rate must be the same index type used to calculate mortgage interest rate adjustments—commingling of index types is not allowed. The mortgagee's margin is the same margin used to determine the initial interest rate and the periodic adjustments to the interest rate. Mortgagees, with the agreement of the borrower, may simultaneously lock in the expected average mortgage interest rate and the mortgagee's margin prior to the date of loan closing or simultaneously establish the expected average mortgage interest rate and the mortgagee's margin on the date of loan closing.

First 12-Month Disbursement Period means the period beginning on the day of loan closing and ending on the day before the loan closing anniversary date. When the day before the anniversary date of loan closing falls on a Federally-observed holiday, Saturday, or Sunday, the end period will be on the next business day after the Federally-observed holiday, Saturday or Sunday.

HECM means a Home Equity Conversion Mortgage.

HECM counselor means an independent third party who is currently active on FHA's HECM Counselor Roster and who is not, either directly or indirectly, associated with or compensated by, a party involved in originating, servicing, or funding the HECM, or the sale of annuities, investments, long-term care insurance, or any other type of financial or insurance product who provides statutorily required counseling to prospective borrowers who may be eligible for or interested in obtaining an FHA-insured HECM. This counseling assists elderly prospective borrowers who seek to convert equity in their homes into income that can be used to pay for home improvements, medical costs, living expenses, or other expenses.

Ineligible Non-Borrowing Spouse means a Non-Borrowing Spouse who does not meet all Qualifying Attributes for a Deferral Period.

Initial Disbursement Limit means the maximum amount of funds that can be advanced to a borrower of an adjustable interest rate HECM allowed at loan closing and during the First 12-Month Disbursement Period in accordance with §206.25.

Insured mortgage means a mortgage which has been insured as evidenced by the issuance of a Mortgage Insurance Certificate.

LIBOR means the London Interbank Offered Rate.

Loan documents mean the credit instrument, or Note, secured by the lien, and the loan agreement.

Mandatory Obligations are fees and charges incurred in connection with the origination of the HECM that are requirements for loan approval and which will be paid at closing or during the First 12-Month Disbursement Period in accordance with §206.25.

Maximum claim amount means the lesser of the appraised value of the property, as determined by the appraisal used in underwriting the loan; the sales price of the property being purchased for the sole purpose of being the principal residence; or the national mortgage limit for a one-family residence under subsections 255(g) or (m) of the National Housing Act (as adjusted where applicable under section 214 of the National Housing Act) as of the date of loan closing. The initial mortgage insurance premium must not be taken into account in the calculation of the maximum claim amount. Closing costs must not be taken into account in determining appraised value.

MIP means the mortgage insurance premium paid by the mortgagee to the Commissioner in consideration of the contract of insurance.

Mortgage means a first lien on real estate under the laws of the jurisdiction where the real estate is located. If the dwelling unit is in a condominium, the term *mortgage* means a first lien covering a fee interest or eligible leasehold interest in a one-family unit in a condominium project, together with an undivided interest in the common areas and facilities serving the project, and such restricted common areas and facilities as may be designated. The term refers to a security instrument creating a lien, whether called a *mortgage, deed of trust, security deed,* or another term used in a particular jurisdiction.

Mortgagee means original lender under a mortgage and its successors and assigns, as are approved by the Commissioner.

Mortgagor means each original mortgagor under a HECM mortgage and his heirs, executors, administrators, and assigns.

Non-Borrowing Spouse means the spouse, as defined by the law of the state in which the spouse and borrower reside or the state of celebration, of the HECM borrower at the time of closing and who is also not a borrower.

Participating agency means all housing counseling and intermediary organizations participating in HUD's Housing Counseling program, including HUD-approved agencies, and affiliates and branches of HUD-approved intermediaries, HUD-approved multi-state organizations (MSOs), and state housing finance agencies.

Principal limit means the maximum amount calculated, taking into account the age of the youngest borrower or Eligible Non-Borrowing Spouse, the expected average mortgage interest rate, and the maximum claim amount. The principal limit is calculated for the first month that a mortgage could be outstanding using factors provided by the Commissioner. It increases each month thereafter at a rate equal to one-twelfth of the mortgage interest rate in effect at that time, plus one-twelfth of the annual mortgage insurance rate. For an adjustable interest rate HECM, the principal limit increase may be made available to the borrower each month thereafter except that the availability during the First 12-Month Disbursement Period may be restricted. Although the principal limit of a fixed interest rate HECM will continue to increase at the rate provided by the Commissioner, no further funds may be made available for the borrower to draw against after closing. The principal limit may decrease because of insurance or condemnation proceeds applied to the outstanding loan balance under § 206.209(b).

Principal residence means the dwelling where the borrower and, if applicable, Non-Borrowing Spouse, maintain their permanent place of abode, and typically spend the majority of the calendar year. A person may have only one principal residence at any one time. The property shall be considered to be the principal residence of any borrower who is temporarily in a health care institution provided the borrower's residency in a health care institution does not exceed twelve consecutive months. The property shall be considered to be the principal residence of any Non-Borrowing Spouse, who is temporarily in a health care institution, as long as the property is the principal residence of his or her borrower spouse, who physically resides in the property. During a Deferral Period, the property shall continue to be considered to be the principal residence of any Non-Borrowing Spouse, who is temporarily in a health care institution, provided he or she qualified as an Eligible Non-Borrowing Spouse and physically occupied the property immediately prior to entering the health care institution and his or her residency in a health care institution does not exceed twelve consecutive months.

Property charges means, unless otherwise specified, obligations of the borrower that include property taxes, hazard insurance premiums, any applicable flood insurance premiums, ground rents, condominium fees, planned unit development fees, homeowners' association fees, and any other special assessments that may be levied by municipalities or state law.

Qualifying Attributes means the requirements which must be met by a Non-Borrowing Spouse in order to be an Eligible Non-Borrowing Spouse.

§ 206.7 Effect of amendments.

The regulations in this part may be amended by the Commissioner at any time and from time to time, in whole or in part, but amendments to subparts B and C of this part will not adversely affect the interests of a mortgagee on any mortgage to be insured for which either the Direct Endorsement mortgagee or Lender Insurance mortgagee has approved the borrower and all terms and conditions of the mortgage, or the Commissioner has made a commitment to insure. Such amendments will not adversely affect the interests of a borrower in the case of a default by a mortgagee where the Commissioner makes payments to the borrower.

§ 206.8 Preemption.

(a) *Lien priority.* The full amount secured by the mortgage shall have the same priority over any other liens on the property as if the full amount had been disbursed on the date the initial disbursement was made, regardless of the actual date of any disbursement. The amount secured by the mortgage shall include all direct payments by the mortgagee to the borrower and all other loan advances permitted by the mortgage for any purpose, including loan advances for interest, property charges, mortgage insurance premiums, required repairs, servicing charges, counseling charges, and costs of collection, regardless of when the payments or loan advances were made. The priority provided by this section shall apply notwithstanding any State constitution, law, or regulation.

(b) *Second mortgage.* If the Commissioner holds a second mortgage, it shall have a priority subordinate only to the first mortgage (and any senior liens permitted by paragraph (a) of this section).

Subpart B—Eligibility; Endorsement

§ 206.9 Eligible mortgagees.

(a) *Statutory requirements.* See sections (b)(2), (c), and 255(d)(1) of the NHA.

(b) *HUD approved mortgagees.* Any mortgagee authorized under paragraph (a) of this section and approved under part 202 of this chapter, except an investing mortgagee approved under § 202.9 of this chapter, is eligible to apply for insurance. A mortgagee approved under §§ 202.6, 202.7, 202.9 or 202.10 of this chapter may purchase, hold and sell mortgages insured under this part without additional approval.

§ 206.13 Disclosure of available HECM program options.

At the time of initial contact, the mortgagee shall inform the prospective HECM borrower, in a manner acceptable to the Commissioner, of all products, features, and options of the HECM program that FHA will insure under this part, including: fixed interest rate mortgages with the Single Lump Sum payment option; adjustable interest rate mortgages with tenure, term, and line of credit disbursement options, or a combination of these; any other FHA insurable disbursement options; and initial mortgage insurance premium options, and how those affect the availability of other mortgage and disbursement options.

§ 206.15 Insurance.

Mortgages originated under this part must be endorsed through the Direct Endorsement program under § 203.5 of this chapter, except that any references to § 203.255 in § 203.5 shall mean § 206.115. The mortgagee shall submit the information as described in § 206.115(b) for the Direct Endorsement program; the certificate of housing counseling as described in § 206.41; a copy of the title insurance commitment satisfactory to the Commissioner (or other acceptable title evidence if the Commissioner has determined not to require title insurance under § 206.45(a)); the mortgagee's election of either the assignment or shared premium option under § 206.107; and any other documentation required by the Commissioner. If the mortgagee has complied with the requirements of §§ 203.3 and 203.5, except that any reference to § 203.255 in these sections shall mean § 206.115 for purposes of this section, and other requirements of this part, and the mortgage is determined to be eligible, the Commissioner will endorse the mortgage for insurance by issuing a Mortgage Insurance Certificate.

ELIGIBLE MORTGAGES

§ 206.17 Eligible mortgages: general.

(a) [Reserved]

(b) *Interest rate and payment options.* A HECM shall provide for either fixed or adjustable interest rates in accordance with § 206.21.

(1) Fixed interest rate mortgages shall use the Single Lump Sum payment option (§ 206.19(e)).

(2) Adjustable interest rate mortgages shall initially provide for the term (§ 206.19(a)), the tenure (§ 206.19(b)), the line of credit (§ 206.19(c)), or a modified term or modified tenure (§ 206.19(d)) payment option,

subject to a later change in accordance with § 206.26.

(c) *Shared appreciation.* A mortgage may provide for shared appreciation in accordance with § 206.23.

§ 206.19   Payment options.

(a) *Term payment option.* Under the term payment option, equal monthly payments are made by the mortgagee to the borrower for a fixed term of months chosen by the borrower in accordance with this section and § 206.25(e), unless the mortgage is prepaid in full or becomes due and payable earlier under § 206.27(c).

(b) *Tenure payment option.* Under the tenure payment option, equal monthly payments are made by the mortgagee to the borrower in accordance with this section and with § 206.25(f), unless the mortgage is prepaid in full or becomes due and payable under § 206.27(c).

(c) *Line of credit payment option.* Under the line of credit payment option, payments are made by the mortgagee to the borrower at times and in amounts determined by the borrower as long as the amounts do not exceed the payment amounts permitted by § 206.25.

(d) *Modified term or modified tenure payment option.* Under the modified term or modified tenure payment options, equal monthly payments are made by the mortgagee and the mortgagee shall set aside a portion of the principal limit to be drawn down as a line of credit as long as the amounts do not exceed the payment amounts permitted by § 206.25.

(e) *Single Lump Sum payment option.* Under the Single Lump Sum payment option, the Borrower's Advance will be made by the mortgagee to the borrower in an amount that does not exceed the payment amount permitted in § 206.25. The Single Lump Sum payment option will be available only for fixed interest rate HECMs. Set asides requiring disbursements after close may be offered in accordance with paragraphs (f)(1) through (3) of this section.

(f) *Principal limit set asides*—(1) *Repair Set Aside.* When repairs required by § 206.47 will be completed after closing, the mortgagee shall set aside a portion of the principal limit equal to 150 percent of the Commissioner's estimated cost of repairs, plus the repair administration fee.

(2) *Property Charge Set Aside*—(i) *Life Expectancy Set Aside (LESA).* When required by § 206.205(b)(1) or selected by the borrower under § 206.205(b)(2)(i)(B), the mortgagee shall set aside a portion of the principal limit, consistent with the requirements of § 206.205, for payment of the following property charges: property taxes including special assessments levied by municipalities or state law, and flood and hazard insurance premiums.

(ii) *Borrower elects to have mortgagee pay property charges*—(A) *First year property charges.* When required by § 206.205(d), the mortgagee shall set aside a portion of the principal limit for payment of the following property charges that must be paid during the First 12-Month Disbursement Period: property taxes including special assessments levied by municipalities or state law, and flood and hazard insurance premiums. The mortgagee's estimate of withholding amount shall be based on the best information available as to probable payments which will be required to be made for property charges in the coming year. The mortgagee may not require the withholding of amounts in excess of the current estimated total annual requirement, unless expressly requested by the borrower. Each month's withholding for property charges shall equal one-twelfth of the annual amounts as reasonably estimated by the mortgagee.

(B) *Property charges for subsequent years.* For subsequent year property charges, the mortgagee's estimate of withholding amount shall be based on the best information available as to probable payments which will be required to be made for property charges in the coming year. If actual disbursements during the preceding year are used as the basis, the resulting estimate may deviate from those disbursements by as much as ten percent. The mortgagee may not require the withholding of amounts in excess of the current estimated total annual requirement, unless expressly requested by the borrower. Each month's withholding for property charges shall equal one-twelfth of the annual amounts as reasonably estimated by the mortgagee.

(3) *Servicing Fee Set Aside.* When servicing charges will be made as permitted by §206.207(b), the mortgagee shall set aside a portion of the principal limit sufficient to cover charges through a period equal to the payment term which would be used to calculate tenure payments under §206.25(f).

(g) *Interest accrual and repayment.* The interest charged on the outstanding loan balance shall begin to accrue from the funding date and shall be added to the outstanding loan balance monthly as provided in the mortgage. Under all payment options, repayment of the outstanding loan balance is deferred until the mortgage becomes due and payable under §206.27(c).

(h) *Disbursement limits.* (1) For all HECMs, no disbursements shall be made under any of the payment options, notwithstanding anything to the contrary in this section or in §206.25, in an amount which shall cause the outstanding loan balance after the payment to exceed any maximum mortgage amount stated in the security instruments or to otherwise exceed the amount secured by a first lien.

(2) For adjustable interest rate HECMs:

(i) No disbursements shall be made under any of the payment options during the First 12-Month Disbursement Period in excess of the Initial Disbursement Limit.

(ii) If the borrower makes a partial prepayment of the outstanding loan balance during the First 12-Month Disbursement Period, the mortgagee shall apply the funds from the partial prepayment in accordance with the Note.

(3) For fixed interest rate HECMs, if the borrower makes a partial prepayment of the outstanding loan balance any time after loan closing and before the contract of insurance is terminated, the mortgagee shall apply the funds from the partial prepayment in accordance with the Note. Any increase in the available principal limit by the amount applied towards the outstanding loan balance shall not be available for the borrower to draw against.

§206.21 **Interest rate.**

(a) *Fixed interest rate.* A fixed interest rate is agreed upon by the borrower and mortgagee.

(b) *Adjustable interest rate.* An initial expected average mortgage interest rate, which defines the mortgagee's margin, is agreed upon by the borrower and mortgagee as of the date of loan closing, or as of the date of rate lock-in, if the expected average mortgage interest rate was locked in prior to closing. The interest rate shall be adjusted in one of two ways depending on the option selected by the borrower, in accordance with paragraphs (b)(1) and (b)(2) of this section. Whenever an interest rate is adjusted, the new interest rate applies to the entire loan balance. The difference between the initial interest rate and the index figure applicable when the firm commitment is issued shall equal the margin used to determine interest rate adjustments. If the expected average mortgage interest rate is locked in prior to closing, the difference between the expected average mortgage interest rate and the value of the appropriate index at the time of rate lock-in shall equal the margin used to determine interest rate adjustments.

(1) *Annual adjustable interest rate HECMs.* A mortgagee offering an annual adjustable interest rate shall offer a mortgage with an interest rate cap structure that limits the periodic interest rate increases and decreases as follows:

(i) *Types of mortgages insurable.* The types of adjustable interest rate mortgages that are insurable are those for which the interest rate may be adjusted annually by the mortgagee, beginning after one year from the date of the closing.

(ii) *Interest rate index.* Changes in the interest rate charged on an adjustable interest rate mortgage must correspond either to changes in the one-year LIBOR or to changes in the weekly average yield on U.S. Treasury securities, adjusted to a constant maturity of one year. Except as otherwise provided in this section, each change in the mortgage interest rate must correspond to the upward and downward change in the index.

(iii) *Frequency of interest rate changes.* (A) The interest rate adjustments must occur annually, calculated from the date of the closing, except that the first adjustment shall be no sooner than 12 months or later than 18 months.

(B) To set the new interest rate, the mortgagee will determine the change between the initial (*i.e.,* base) index figure and the current index figure, or will add a specific margin to the current index figure. The initial index figure shall be the most recent figure available before the date of mortgage loan origination. The current index figure shall be the most recent index figure available 30 days before the date of each interest rate adjustment.

(iv) *Magnitude of changes.* The adjustable interest rate mortgage initial contract interest rate shall be agreed upon by the mortgagee and the borrower. The first adjustment to the contract interest rate shall take place in accordance with the schedule set forth under paragraph (b)(1)(iii) of this section. Thereafter, for all annual adjustable interest rate mortgages, the adjustment shall be made annually and shall occur on the anniversary date of the first adjustment, subject to the following conditions and limitations:

(A) For all annual adjustable interest rate HECMs, no single adjustment to the interest rate shall result in a change in either direction of more than two percentage points from the interest rate in effect for the period immediately preceding that adjustment. Index changes in excess of two percentage points may not be carried over for inclusion in an adjustment for a subsequent year. Adjustments in the effective rate of interest over the entire term of the mortgage may not result in a change in either direction of more than five percentage points from the initial contract interest rate.

(B) At each adjustment date for annual adjustable interest rate HECMs, changes in the index interest rate, whether increases or decreases, must be translated into the adjusted mortgage interest rate, except that the mortgage may provide for minimum interest rate change limitations and for minimum increments of interest rate changes.

(2) *Monthly adjustable interest rate HECMs.* If a mortgage meeting the requirements of paragraph (b)(1) of this section is offered, the mortgagee may also offer a mortgage which provides for monthly adjustments to the interest rate such that changes in the interest rate charged on an adjustable interest rate mortgage correspond either to changes in the one-year LIBOR or to changes in the weekly average yield on U.S. Treasury securities, adjusted to a constant maturity of one year (except as otherwise provided in this section, each change in the mortgage interest rate must correspond to the upward and downward change in the index), or to the one-month CMT index or one-month LIBOR index, and which sets a maximum interest rate that can be charged.

(c) *Pre-loan disclosure.* (1) At the time the mortgagee provides the borrower with a loan application, a mortgagee shall provide a borrower with a written explanation of all adjustable interest rate features of a mortgage. The explanation must include the following items:

(i) The circumstances under which the rate may increase;

(ii) Any limitations on the increase; and

(iii) The effect of an increase.

(2) Compliance with pre-loan disclosure provisions of 12 CFR part 1026 (Truth in Lending) shall constitute full compliance with paragraph (c)(1) of this section.

(d) *Post-loan disclosure.* At least 25 days before any adjustment to the interest rate may occur, the mortgagee must advise the borrower of the following:

(1) The current index amount;

(2) The date of publication of the index; and

(3) The new interest rate.

§ 206.23 Shared appreciation.

(a) *Additional interest based on net appreciated value.* Any mortgage for which the mortgagee has chosen the shared premium option (§ 206.107) may provide for shared appreciation. At the time the mortgage becomes due and payable or is paid in full, whichever occurs first, the borrower shall pay an additional amount of interest equal to a percentage of any net appreciated value of the property during the life of the mortgage. The percentage of net appreciated value to be paid to the mortgagee, referred to as the appreciation margin, shall be no more than twenty-five percent, subject to an effective interest rate cap of no more than twenty percent.

(b) *Computation of mortgagee share.* The mortgagee's share of net appreciated value is computed as follows:

(1) If the outstanding loan balance at the time the mortgagee's share of net appreciated value becomes payable is less than the appraised value of the property at the time of loan origination, the mortgagee's share is calculated by subtracting the appraised value at the time of loan origination from the adjusted sales proceeds (*i.e.,* sales proceeds less transfer costs and capital improvement costs incurred by the borrower, but excluding any liens) and multiplying by the appreciation margin.

(2) If the outstanding loan balance is greater than the appraised value at the time of loan origination but less than the adjusted proceeds, the mortgagee's share is calculated by subtracting the outstanding loan balance from the adjusted sales proceeds and multiplying by the appreciation margin.

(3) If the outstanding loan balance is greater than the adjusted sales proceeds, the net appreciated value is zero.

(4) If there has been no sale or transfer involving satisfaction of the mortgage at the time the mortgagee's share of net appreciated value becomes payable, *sales proceeds* for purposes of this section shall be the appraised value as determined in accordance with procedures approved by the Commissioner.

(c) *Effective interest rate.* To determine the effective interest rate, the amount of interest which accrued in the twelve months prior to the sale of the property or the prepayment is added to the mortgagee's share of the net appreciated value. The sum of the mortgagee's share of the net appreciated value and the interest, when divided by the sum of the outstanding loan balance at the beginning of the twelve-month period prior to sale or prepayment plus the payments to or on behalf of the borrower (but not includ-

ing interest) in the twelve months prior to the sale or prepayment, shall not exceed an effective interest rate of twenty percent.

(d) *Disclosure.* At the time the mortgagee provides the borrower with a loan application for a mortgage with shared appreciation, the mortgagee shall disclose to the borrower the principal limit, payments and interest rate which are applicable to a comparable mortgage offered by the mortgagee without shared appreciation.

§206.25 Calculation of disbursements.

(a) *Initial disbursements—*(1) *Initial Disbursement Limit—Adjustable Interest Rate HECMs:* for term, tenure, line of credit, modified term, and modified tenure payment options:

(i) The mortgagee is responsible for determining the maximum Initial Disbursement Limit.

(ii) The maximum disbursement allowed at closing and during the First 12-Month Disbursement Period is the lesser of:

(A) The greater of an amount established by the Commissioner through notice which shall not be less than 50 percent of the principal limit; or the sum of Mandatory Obligations and a percentage of the principal limit established by the Commissioner through notice which shall not be less than 10 percent; or

(B) The principal limit less the sum of the funds in the LESA for payment beyond the First 12-Month Disbursement Period and the Servicing Fee Set Aside.

(iii) The amount in the First 12-Month Disbursement Period or at any point in time may not exceed the principal limit.

(iv) Mortgagees shall monitor and track all disbursements that occur at loan closing and during the First 12-Month Disbursement Period; the total amount of disbursements shall not exceed the maximum Initial Disbursement Limit.

(v) The borrower shall notify the mortgagee at loan closing of the amount of the additional percentage of the principal limit beyond Mandatory Obligations that the borrower will draw or that will remain available to be drawn during the First 12-Month

257

Disbursement Period. The borrower may not increase or decrease this election after closing.

(2) *Borrower's Advance—Fixed Interest Rate HECMs:* for the Single Lump Sum payment option:

(i) The mortgagee is responsible for determining the maximum Borrower's Advance.

(ii) The disbursement shall only be taken at the time of closing and the maximum disbursement shall not exceed the lesser of:

(A) The greater of an amount established by the Commissioner through notice which shall not be less than 50 percent of the principal limit; or the sum of Mandatory Obligations and a percentage of the principal limit established by the Commissioner through notice which shall not be less than 10 percent; or

(B) The principal limit less the sum of the funds in the LESA for payment beyond the First 12-Month Disbursement Period and the Servicing Fee Set Aside.

(iii) The borrower shall notify the mortgagee at loan closing of the amount of the additional percentage of the principal limit beyond Mandatory Obligations that the borrower will draw. The borrower may not increase or decrease this election after closing.

(b) Mandatory Obligations for traditional and refinance transactions include:

(1) Initial MIP under § 206.105(a);

(2) Loan origination fee;

(3) HECM counseling fee;

(4) Reasonable and customary amounts, but not more than the amount actually paid by the mortgagee for any of the following items:

(i) Recording fees and recording taxes, or other charges incident to the recordation of the insured mortgage;

(ii) Credit report;

(iii) Survey, if required by the mortgagee or the borrower;

(iv) Title examination;

(v) Mortgagee's title insurance;

(vi) Fees paid to an appraiser for the initial appraisal of the property; and

(vii) Flood certifications.

(5) Repair Set Asides;

(6) Repair administration fee;

(7) Delinquent Federal debt;

(8) Amounts required to discharge any existing liens on the property;

(9) Customary fees and charges for warranties, inspections, surveys, and engineer certifications;

(10) Funds to pay contractors who performed repairs as a condition of closing, in accordance with standard FHA requirements for repairs required by the appraiser;

(11) Property tax and flood and hazard insurance payments required by the mortgagee to be paid at loan closing;

(12) Property charges not included in paragraph (b)(11) of this section and which are scheduled for payment during the First 12-Month Disbursement Period, as follows:

(i) *Adjustable Interest Rate HECMs.* (A) The total amount of property charge payments scheduled for payment from the borrower authorized option under § 206.205(d) during the First 12-Month Disbursement Period;

(B) The total amount of semi-annual disbursements scheduled to be made during the First 12-Month Disbursement Period to the borrower from a Partially-Funded LESA; or

(C) The total amount of property charges scheduled for payment during the First 12-Month Disbursement Period from a Fully-Funded LESA.

(D) Mortgagees shall use the actual insurance premium and actual tax amount; if a new tax bill has not been issued, the mortgagee must use the prior year's amount multiplied by 1.04 or an amount set by the Commissioner through notice.

(ii) *Fixed Interest Rate HECMs.* (A) The total amount of property charges scheduled for payment during the First 12-Month Disbursement Period from a Fully-Funded LESA.

(B) Mortgagees shall use the actual insurance premium and actual tax amount; if a new tax bill has not been issued, the mortgagee must use the prior year's amount multiplied by 1.04 or an amount set by the Commissioner through notice;

(13) Required pay-off of debt not secured by the property, as defined by the Commissioner through FEDERAL REGISTER notice; and

(14) Other charges as authorized by the Commissioner through notice.

(c) Mandatory Obligations for HECM for Purchase transactions include:

(1) Initial MIP under §206.105(a);

(2) Loan origination fee;

(3) HECM counseling fee:

(4) Reasonable and customary amounts, but not more than the amount actually paid by the mortgagee for any of the following items:

(i) Recording fees and recording taxes, or other charges incident to the recordation of the insured mortgage;

(ii) Credit report;

(iii) Survey, if required by the mortgagee or the borrower;

(iv) Title examination;

(v) Mortgagee's title insurance;

(vi) Fees paid to an appraiser for the initial appraisal of the property; and

(vii) Flood certifications.

(5) Delinquent Federal debt;

(6) Fees and charges for real estate purchase contracts, warranties, inspections, surveys, and engineer certifications;

(7) The amount of the principal that is advanced towards the purchase price of the subject property;

(8) Property tax and flood and hazard insurance payments required by the mortgagee to be paid at loan closing;

(9) Property charges not included in paragraph (c)(8) of this section and which are scheduled for payment during the First 12-Month Disbursement Period, as follows:

(i) *Adjustable Interest Rate HECMs.* (A) The total amount of property charge payments scheduled for payment from the borrower authorized option under §206.205(d) during the First 12-Month Disbursement Period;

(B) The total amount of semi-annual disbursements scheduled to be made during the First 12-Month Disbursement Period to the borrower from a Partially-Funded LESA; or

(C) The total amount of property charges scheduled for payment during the First 12-Month Disbursement Period from a Fully-Funded LESA.

(D) Mortgagees shall use the actual insurance premium and actual tax amount; if a new tax bill has not been issued, the mortgagee must use the prior year's amount multiplied by 1.04 or an amount set by the Commissioner through notice.

(ii) *Fixed Interest Rate HECMs.* (A) The total amount of property charges scheduled for payment during the First 12-Month Disbursement Period from a Fully-Funded LESA.

(B) Mortgagees shall use the actual insurance premium and actual tax amount; if a new tax bill has not been issued, the mortgagee must use the prior year's amount multiplied by 1.04 or an amount set by the Commissioner through notice;

(10) Required pay-off of debt not secured by the property, as defined by the Commissioner through FEDERAL REGISTER notice; and

(11) Other charges as authorized by the Commissioner through notice.

(d) *Timing of disbursements.* Mortgage proceeds may not be disbursed until after the expiration of the 3-day rescission period under 12 CFR part 1026, if applicable.

(e) *Monthly disbursements—term option.* (1) Using factors provided by the Commissioner, the mortgagee shall calculate the monthly disbursement so that the sum of paragraphs (e)(1)(i) or (e)(1)(ii) of this section added to paragraphs (e)(1)(iii), (e)(1)(iv), and (e)(1)(v) of this section shall be equal to the principal limit at the end of the payment term.

(i) An initial disbursement under paragraph (a) of this section plus any initial servicing charge set aside under §206.19(f)(3); or

(ii) The outstanding loan balance at the time of a change in payment option in accordance with §206.26, plus any remaining servicing charge set aside under §206.19(f)(3); and

(iii) The amount of the principal limit set aside in accordance with §206.19(f) which is not included in the amount set aside in paragraphs (e)(1)(i) or (e)(1)(ii) of this section;

(iv) All MIP or monthly charges due to the Commissioner in lieu of mortgage insurance premiums due through the payment term; and

(v) All interest through the remainder of the payment term. The expected average mortgage interest rate shall be used for this purpose.

(2) The mortgagee shall make all monthly disbursements through the payment term even if the outstanding loan balance exceeds the principal

limit because the actual average mortgage interest rate exceeds the expected average mortgage interest rate unless the HECM becomes due and payable under § 206.27(c). In the event of a deferral of due and payable status in accordance with § 206.27(c)(3), disbursements shall cease immediately upon the death of the borrower and no further disbursements are permissible.

(3) Mortgagees shall ensure that term monthly disbursements made to the borrower during the First 12-Month Disbursement Period do not exceed the Initial Disbursement Limit. If the sum of disbursements made during the First 12-Month Disbursement Period would exceed the Initial Disbursement Limit for that time period, the mortgagee shall decrease the monthly disbursements during the First 12-Month Disbursement Period to conform with the Initial Disbursement Limit; upon conclusion of the First 12-Month Disbursement Period, the borrower may request a payment plan recalculation.

(4) If the borrower makes a partial prepayment of the outstanding loan balance during the First 12-Month Disbursement Period, the mortgagee shall apply the funds from the partial prepayment in accordance with the Note.

(5) If the mortgagee receives repayment from insurance or condemnation proceeds after restoration or repair of the damaged property, the available principal limit and outstanding loan balance shall be reduced by the amount of such payments.

(f) *Monthly disbursements—tenure option.* (1) Monthly disbursements under the tenure payment option shall be calculated as if the number of months in the payment term equals 100 minus the lesser of the age of the youngest borrower or 95, multiplied by 12, but payments shall continue until the mortgage becomes due and payable under § 206.27(c), except that in the event that payments would exceed any maximum mortgage amount stated in the security instrument or would otherwise exceed the amount secured by the first lien, in accordance with § 206.19(h) payments will cease immediately; payments may be reinstated only in the event a new Note and mortgage are executed in accordance with § 206.27(b)(10); and in the event of a de-

ferral of due and payable status in accordance with § 206.27(c)(3) payments will cease immediately upon the death of the borrower.

(2) Mortgagees shall ensure that tenure monthly disbursements made to the borrower during the First 12-Month Disbursement Period do not exceed the Initial Disbursement Limit. If the sum of disbursements made during the First 12-Month Disbursement Period would exceed the Initial Disbursement Limit for that time period, the mortgagee shall decrease the monthly disbursements during the First 12-Month Disbursement Period to conform with the maximum Initial Disbursement Limit; upon conclusion of the First 12-Month Disbursement Period, the borrower may request a payment plan recalculation.

(3) If the borrower makes a partial prepayment of the outstanding loan balance during the First 12-Month Disbursement Period, the mortgagee shall apply the funds from the partial prepayment in accordance with the Note.

(4) If the mortgagee receives repayment from insurance or condemnation proceeds after restoration or repair of the damaged property, the available principal limit and outstanding loan balance shall be reduced by the amount of such payments.

(g) *Line of credit separately or with monthly disbursements.* If the borrower has a line of credit, separately or combined with the term or tenure payment option, the principal limit is divided into an amount set aside for servicing charges under § 206.19(f)(3), an amount equal to the line of credit (including any portion of the principal limit set aside for repairs or property charges under § 206.19(f)(1) or (2)), and the remaining amount of the principal limit (if any). The line of credit amount increases at the same rate as the total principal limit increases under § 206.3. The sum of disbursements made during the First 12-Month Disbursement Period shall not exceed the Initial Disbursement Limit. If a requested disbursement would exceed the Initial Disbursement Limit, the mortgagee may make a partial disbursement to the borrower for the amount that will not exceed the limit. Upon the conclusion of the First 12-Month Disbursement Period, the borrower may request subsequent disbursements up to the available principal limit.

(h) *Single Lump Sum payment option.* (1) Under the Single Lump Sum payment option, the Borrower's Advance shall be made by the mortgagee to the borrower in an amount that does not exceed the maximum allowable Borrower's Advance under paragraph (a)(2) of this section.

(2) If the borrower makes a partial prepayment of the outstanding loan balance any time after loan closing and before the contract of insurance is terminated, the mortgagee shall apply the funds from the partial prepayment in accordance with the Note.

(i) *Payment of MIP and interest.* At the end of each month, including the first month, interest accrued during that month shall be added to the outstanding loan balance. Where the first month is a partial month, a prorated amount of interest shall be added. Monthly MIP, which will accrue from the closing date, shall be added to the outstanding loan balance beginning with the first day of the second month after closing when paid to the Commissioner.

(j) *Mortgagee late charge.* The mortgagee shall pay a late charge to the borrower for any late disbursement. If the mortgagee does not mail or electronically transfer a scheduled monthly disbursement to the borrower on the first business day of the month or make a line of credit disbursement within 5 business days of the date the mortgagee received the request, the late charge shall be 10 percent of the entire amount that should have been paid to the borrower for that month or as a result of that request. In no event shall the total late charge exceed five hundred dollars. For each additional day that the borrower does not receive payment, the mortgagee shall pay interest at the mortgage interest rate on the late payment. Any late charge and interest shall be paid from the mortgagee's funds and shall not be added to the outstanding loan balance.

(k) *No minimum payments.* A mortgagee shall not require, as a condition of providing a loan secured by a mortgage insured under this part, that the monthly payments under the term or tenure payment option or draws under the line of credit payment option exceed a minimum amount established by the mortgagee.

§206.26   Change in payment option.

(a) *General.* The payment option may be changed as provided in this section.

(b) *Borrower request for payment plan change*—(1) *Adjustable Interest Rate HECMs.* (i) During the First 12-Month Disbursement Period, no payment plan change shall cause disbursements to exceed the Initial Disbursement Limit.

(ii) After the First 12-Month Disbursement Period, as long as the outstanding loan balance is less than the principal limit, a borrower may request a recalculation of the current payment option, a change from any payment option to another available payment option or a disbursement of any amount (not to exceed the difference between the principal limit and the sum of the outstanding loan balance and any set asides for repairs, servicing charges or property charges). A mortgage will continue to bear interest at an adjustable interest rate as agreed between the mortgagee and the borrower at loan origination. The mortgagee shall recalculate any future monthly payments in accordance with §206.25.

(iii) *Fee for change in payment.* The mortgagee may charge a fee, not to exceed an amount determined by the Commissioner, whenever there is a payment plan change or whenever payments are recalculated.

(iv) *Limitations.* The Commissioner may, through notice, establish limitations on the frequency of payment plan changes, a minimum notice period that a borrower must provide in order to make a request under paragraph (b)(1)(ii) of this section, or other limitations on payment plan change requests by the borrower.

(2) *Fixed Interest Rate HECMs.* Borrowers may not request a change in payment option.

(c) *Change due to initial repairs.* When initial repairs after closing under §206.47 are required using a Repair Set Aside, mortgagees shall comply with the following:

(1) *Adjustable Interest Rate HECMs.* (i) If repairs after closing under § 206.47 are completed without using all of the funds set aside for repairs, the mortgagee shall transfer the remaining amount to a line of credit, modified term, or modified tenure payment option and inform the borrower of the sum available to be drawn.

(ii) If repairs after closing under § 206.47 cannot be completed with the funds set aside for repairs, the mortgagee may advance additional funds to complete repairs from an existing line of credit. If a line of credit is not sufficient to make the advance or if no line of credit exists, future monthly disbursements shall be recalculated for use as a line of credit in accordance with § 206.25.

(iii) If repairs are not completed when required by the mortgage, the mortgagee shall stop monthly payments and the mortgage shall convert to the line of credit payment option. Until the repairs are completed, the mortgagee shall make no line of credit disbursements except as needed to pay for repairs required by the mortgage.

(2) *Fixed Interest Rate HECMs.* No unused set aside funds shall be made available to the borrower, except that a borrower may be reimbursed for the cost of repair materials (not including labor), in accordance with § 206.47, under conditions established by the Commissioner.

§ 206.27 Mortgage provisions.

(a) *Form.* The mortgage shall be in a form meeting the requirements of the Commissioner.

(b) *Provisions.* The terms of the mortgage shall contain an explanation of how payments will be made to the borrower, how interest will be charged, and when the mortgage will be due and payable. The mortgage shall include a provision deferring the due and payable status that occurs because of the death of the last surviving borrower for an Eligible Non-Borrowing Spouse. It shall also contain provisions designed to ensure compliance with this part and provisions on the following additional matters:

(1) Disbursements by the mortgagee under the term or tenure payment options shall be mailed to the borrower or electronically transferred to an account of the borrower on the first business day of each month beginning with the first month after closing. Disbursements under the line of credit payment option shall be mailed to the borrower or electronically transferred to an account of the borrower within five business days after the mortgagee has received a written request for disbursement by the borrower. In accordance with § 206.55, in no event may disbursements continue during a Deferral Period.

(2) The borrower shall insure all improvements on the property that serves as collateral for the HECM whether in existence at the time of origination or subsequently erected, against any hazards, casualties, and contingencies, including but not limited to fire and flood, for which the mortgagee requires insurance. Such insurance shall be maintained in the amount and for the period of time that is necessary to protect the mortgagee's investment. Whether or not the mortgagee imposes a flood insurance requirement, the borrower shall at a minimum insure all improvements on the property, whether in existence at the time of origination or subsequently erected, against loss by floods to the extent required by the Commissioner. If the mortgagee imposes insurance requirements, all insurance shall be carried with companies acceptable to the mortgagee, and the insurance policies and any renewals shall be held by the mortgagee and shall include loss payable clauses in favor of and in a form acceptable to the mortgagee.

(3) The borrower shall not participate in a real estate tax deferral program or permit any liens to be recorded against the property, unless such liens are subordinate to the insured mortgage and, if applicable, any second mortgage held by the Commissioner.

(4) A mortgage may be prepaid in full or in part in accordance with § 206.209.

(5) The borrower must keep the property in good repair.

(6) The borrower must provide for the payment of property charges in accordance with § 206.205.

(7) The payment of monthly MIP may be added to the outstanding principal balance.

(8) The borrower shall have no personal liability for payment of the outstanding loan balance. The mortgagee shall enforce the debt only through sale of the property. The mortgagee shall not be permitted to obtain a deficiency judgment against the borrower if the mortgage is foreclosed.

(9) If the mortgage is assigned to the Commissioner under §206.121(b), the borrower shall not be liable for any difference between the insurance benefits paid to the mortgagee and the outstanding loan balance including accrued interest, owed by the borrower at the time of the assignment.

(10) If State law limits the first lien status of the mortgage as originally executed and recorded to a maximum amount of debt or a maximum number of years, the borrower shall agree to execute any additional documents required by the mortgagee and approved by the Commissioner to extend the first lien status to an additional amount of debt and an additional number of years and to cause any other liens to be removed or subordinated.

(c) *Date the mortgage comes due and payable.* (1) The mortgage shall state that the outstanding loan balance will be due and payable in full if a borrower dies and the property is not the principal residence of at least one surviving borrower, except that the due and payable status shall be deferred in accordance with paragraph (c)(3) of this section if the requirements of the Deferral Period are met; or if a borrower conveys all of his or her title in the property and no other borrower retains title to the property. For purposes of the preceding sentence, a borrower retains title in the property if the borrower continues to hold title to any part of the property in fee simple, as a leasehold interest as set forth in §206.45(a), or as a life estate.

(2) The mortgage shall state that the outstanding loan balance shall be due and payable in full, upon approval of the Commissioner, if any of the following occur:

(i) The property ceases to be the principal residence of a borrower for reasons other than death and the property is not the principal residence of at least one other borrower;

(ii) For a period of longer than 12 consecutive months, a borrower fails to occupy the property because of physical or mental illness and the property is not the principal residence of at least one other borrower;

(iii) The borrower does not provide for the payment of property charges in accordance with §206.205; or

(iv) An obligation of the borrower under the mortgage is not performed.

(3) *Deferral of due and payable status.* The mortgage documents shall contain a provision deferring due and payable status, called the Deferral Period, for an Eligible Non-Borrowing Spouse until the death of the last Eligible Non-Borrowing Spouse or the requirements of the Deferral Period in §206.55 cease to be met and have not been cured as provided for in §206.57.

(d) *Second mortgage to Commissioner.* Unless otherwise provided by the Commissioner, a second mortgage to secure any payments by the Commissioner as provided in §206.121(c) must be given to the Commissioner before a Mortgage Insurance Certificate is issued for the mortgage. If the Commissioner does not require a second mortgage to be given to the Commissioner prior to the issuance of a Mortgage Insurance Certificate, the Commissioner may require a second mortgage to be given to the Commissioner at a later day in order to secure payments by the Commissioner as provided in §206.121(c).

§206.31 Allowable charges and fees.

(a) *Fees at closing.* The mortgagee may collect, either in cash at the time of closing or through an initial payment under the mortgage, the following charges and fees incurred in connection with the origination, processing, and closing of the mortgage loan:

(1) *Loan Origination Fee.* Mortgagees may charge a loan origination fee and may use such fee to pay for services performed by a sponsored third-party originator. The loan origination fee limit shall be the greater of $2,500 or two percent of the maximum claim amount of $200,000, plus one percent of any portion of the maximum claim amount that is greater than $200,000. Mortgagees may accept a lower origination fee. Mortgagees may pay fees

263

for services performed by a sponsored third-party originator and these fees may be included as part of the loan origination fee. The total amount of the loan origination fee may not exceed $6,000, except that the Commissioner may through notice adjust the maximum limit in accordance with the annual percentage increase in the Consumer Price Index of the Bureau of Labor Statistics of the Department of Labor in increments of $500 only when the percentage increase in such index, when applied to the maximum origination fee, produces dollar increases that exceed $500. The loan origination fee may be fully financed with the mortgage.

(2) *Reasonable and customary amounts.* Reasonable and customary amounts, but not more than the amount actually paid by the mortgagee, for any of the following items:

(i) Recording fees and recording taxes, or other charges incident to the recordation of the insured mortgage;

(ii) Credit report;

(iii) Survey, if required by the mortgagee or the borrower;

(iv) Title examination;

(v) Mortgagee's title insurance;

(vi) Fees paid to an appraiser for the initial appraisal of the property;

(vii) Flood certifications; and

(viii) Such other charges as may be authorized by the Commissioner.

(b) *Repair administration fee.* If the property requires repairs after closing in order to meet FHA requirements, the mortgagee may collect a fee for each occurrence as compensation for administrative duties relating to repair work pursuant to § 206.47(c) and (d), not to exceed the greater of one and one-half percent of the amount advanced for the repairs or fifty dollars. The mortgagee shall collect the repair fee by adding it to the outstanding loan balance.

§ 206.32 No outstanding unpaid obligations.

In order for a mortgage to be eligible under this part, a borrower must establish to the satisfaction of the mortgagee that after the initial payment of loan proceeds under § 206.25(a), there will be no outstanding or unpaid obligations incurred by the borrower in connection with the mortgage transaction, except for mortgage servicing charges permitted under § 206.207(b) and any future Repair Set Aside established pursuant to § 206.19(f)(1); and the initial disbursement will not be used for any payment to or on behalf of an estate planning service firm.

ELIGIBLE BORROWERS

§ 206.33 Age of borrower.

The youngest borrower shall be 62 years of age or older at the time of loan closing.

§ 206.34 Limitation on number of mortgages.

(a) Once a borrower has obtained an insured mortgage under this part, the borrower is eligible to obtain future insured HECM loan financing if the existing HECM is satisfied prior to or at the closing of the new HECM, or the borrower provides legal documentation, in a manner acceptable to the Commissioner, evidencing release of the borrower's financial obligation to satisfy the existing HECM.

(b) Current HECM borrowers that plan to sell their existing residence and use the HECM for Purchase program to obtain a new principal residence must pay off the existing FHA-insured mortgage before the HECM for Purchase mortgage can be insured.

§ 206.35 Title of property which is security for HECM.

(a) A mortgagor is not required to be a borrower; however, any borrower is required to be on title to the property which serves as collateral for the HECM, and is therefore, by definition, also a mortgagor.

(b) The mortgagor shall hold title to the entire property which is the security for the mortgage. If there are multiple mortgagors, all the mortgagors must collectively hold title to the entire property which is the security for the mortgage. If one or more mortgagors hold a life estate in the property, for purposes of this section only, the term "mortgagor" shall include each holder of a future interest in the property (remainder or reversion) who has executed the mortgage.

(c) If Non-Borrowing Spouses and non-borrowing owners of the property will continue to hold title to the property which serves as collateral for the HECM, such Non-Borrowing Spouses and non-borrowing owners must sign the mortgage as mortgagors, evidencing their commitment of the property as security for the mortgage.

(d) All Non-Borrowing Spouses and non-borrowing owners shall sign a certification that:

(1) Consents to their spouse or other borrowing owner obtaining the HECM;

(2) Acknowledges the terms and conditions of the mortgage; and

(3) Acknowledges that the property will serve as collateral for the HECM as evidenced by mortgage lien(s).

§ **206.36 Seasoning requirements for existing non-HECM liens.**

(a) The Commissioner may establish, through notice, seasoning requirements for existing non-HECM liens. Such seasoning requirements shall not prohibit the payoff of existing non-HECM liens using HECM proceeds if the liens have been in place for longer than 12 months prior to the HECM closing or if the liens have resulted in cash to the borrower in an amount of $500 or less, whether at closing or through cumulative draws prior to the date of the HECM closing.

(b) Mortgagees must provide documentation satisfactory to the Commissioner as established by notice that the seasoning requirement was met.

(c) *Home Equity Lines of Credit.* The borrower may pay off, at closing, a Home Equity Line of Credit (HELOC) that does not meet seasoning requirements from borrower funds, the HECM funds, or a combination of HECM funds and borrower funds, as long as the draw from HECM funds does not exceed the percentage approved by the Commissioner under the authority of § 206.25(a).

§ **206.37 Credit standing.**

(a) Each borrower shall have a general credit standing satisfactory to the Commissioner.

(b) *Required Financial Assessment*—(1) *Requirement for Financial Assessment prior to loan approval.* Prior to loan approval, the mortgagee shall assess the financial capacity of the borrower to comply with the terms of the mortgage and evaluate whether the HECM is a sustainable solution for the borrower, in accordance with instructions established by the Commissioner through notice. The Financial Assessment shall consider the borrower's credit history, cash flow and residual income, extenuating circumstances, and compensating factors.

(i) *Credit history.* In accordance with FHA guidelines in existence at the time of FHA Case Number assignment, mortgagees shall conduct an in-depth credit history analysis to determine if the borrower has demonstrated the willingness to meet his or her financial obligations.

(ii) *Cash flow and residual income analysis.* In accordance with FHA guidelines in existence at the time of FHA Case Number assignment, mortgagees shall conduct a cash flow and residual income analysis to determine the capacity of the borrower to meet his or her documented financial obligations with his or her documented income.

(iii) *Extenuating circumstances.* Where the borrower's credit history does not meet the criteria set by the mortgagee based on FHA guidelines in existence at the time of FHA Case Number assignment, mortgagees shall consider and document, as part of the Financial Assessment, extenuating circumstances that led to the credit issues.

(iv) *Compensating factors.* The mortgagee shall document and identify in the Financial Assessment any considered compensating factors.

(2) *Completion and approval of Financial Assessment.* The Financial Assessment shall be completed and approved by a DE Underwriter registered in HUD's system of record by the underwriting mortgagee.

(3) *Nondiscrimination.* (i) The Financial Assessment shall be conducted in a uniform manner that shall not discriminate because of race, color, religion, sex, national origin, familial status, disability, marital status, actual or perceived sexual orientation, gender identity, source of income of the borrower, location of the property, or because the applicant has in good faith

exercised any right under the Consumer Credit Protection Act (15 U.S.C. 1601 *et seq.*).

(ii) The Financial Assessment shall be conducted in compliance with all applicable laws and regulations, including but not limited to, the following:

(A) Fair Housing Act (42 U.S.C. 3601 *et seq.*);

(B) Fair Credit Reporting Act (15 U.S.C. 1681 *et seq.*);

(C) Equal Credit Opportunity Act (15 U.S.C. 1691 *et seq.*); and

(D) Regulation B (12 CFR part 1002).

§ 206.39 Principal residence.

(a) The property must be the principal residence of each borrower, and if applicable, Eligible Non-Borrowing Spouse, at closing.

(b) *HECM for Purchase.* For HECM for Purchase transactions, each borrower, and if applicable, Eligible Non-Borrowing Spouse, must occupy the property within 60 days from the date of closing.

§ 206.40 Disclosure, verification and certifications.

(a) *Disclosure and certification of Social Security and Employer Identification Numbers*—(1) *Borrower.* The borrower must meet the requirements for the disclosure and verification of Social Security and Employer Identification Numbers, as provided by part 200, subpart U, of this chapter.

(2) *Eligible Non-Borrowing Spouse.* The Eligible Non-Borrowing Spouse shall comply with the requirements for disclosure and verification of Social Security and Employer Identification Numbers by borrowers in paragraph (a)(1) of this section.

(b) *Certifications.* Each borrower and each Non-Borrowing Spouse shall provide all required certifications to HUD and the mortgagee, as required by the Commissioner.

(c) *Designation of alternate individual.* At the time of origination, the mortgagee shall request that the borrower designate an alternate individual for the purpose of communicating with the mortgagee if the mortgagee has not been able to reach the borrower. The designation of the alternate individual is at the discretion of the borrower. If the mortgagee is unable to make contact or communicate with the borrower for any reason, including death or incapacitation, the mortgagee shall communicate with the alternate individual, if one has been designated by the borrower.

§ 206.41 Counseling.

(a) *List provided.* At the time of the initial contact with the prospective borrower, the mortgagee shall give the borrower a list of the names, addresses, and telephone numbers of HECM counselors and their employing agencies, which have been approved by the Commissioner, in accordance with subpart E of this part, as qualified and able to provide the information described in paragraph (b) of this section. The borrower, any Eligible or Ineligible Non-Borrowing Spouse, and any non-borrowing owner must receive counseling.

(b) *Information to be provided.* (1) A HECM counselor must discuss with the borrower:

(i) The information required by section 255(f) of the NHA;

(ii) Whether the borrower has signed a contract or agreement with an estate planning service firm that requires, or purports to require, the borrower to pay a fee on or after closing that may exceed amounts permitted by the Commissioner or this part;

(iii) If such a contract has been signed under paragraph (b)(1)(ii) of this section, the extent to which services under the contract may not be needed or may be available at nominal or no cost from other sources, including the mortgagee; and

(iv) Any other requirements determined by the Commissioner.

(2) If the HECM borrower has an Eligible Non-Borrowing Spouse, in addition to meeting the requirements of paragraph (b)(1) of this section, a HECM counselor shall discuss with the borrower and Eligible Non-Borrowing Spouse:

(i) The requirement that the Eligible Non-Borrowing Spouse must obtain ownership of the property or other legal right to remain in the property for life, upon the death of the last surviving borrower;

(ii) A failure to obtain ownership or other legal right to remain in the property for life will result in the HECM becoming due and payable and the Eligible Non-Borrowing Spouse will not receive the benefit of the Deferral Period;

(iii) The requirement that the property must be the principal residence of the Eligible Non-Borrowing Spouse prior to and after the death of the borrowing spouse;

(iv) The requirement that the Eligible Non-Borrowing Spouse fulfills all obligations of the mortgage, including the payment of property charges and upkeep of the property; and

(v) Any other requirements determined by the Commissioner.

(3) If the HECM borrower has an Ineligible Non-Borrowing Spouse, in addition to meeting the requirements of paragraph (b)(1) of this section, a HECM counselor shall discuss with the borrower and Ineligible Non-Borrowing Spouse:

(i) The Deferral Period will not be applicable;

(ii) The HECM will become due and payable upon the death of the last surviving borrower; and

(iii) Any other requirements determined by the Commissioner.

(c) *Certificate.* The HECM counselor will provide the borrower with a certificate stating that the borrower, Non-Borrowing Spouse, and non-borrowing owner, as applicable, has received counseling. The borrower shall provide the mortgagee with a physical copy of the certificate.

§206.43 Information to borrower.

(a) *Disclosure of costs of obtaining mortgage.* The mortgagee shall ensure that the borrower has received full disclosure of all costs of obtaining the mortgage. The mortgagee shall ask the borrower about any costs or other obligations that the borrower has incurred to obtain the mortgage, as defined by the Commissioner, in addition to providing any disclosures required by law. The mortgagee shall clearly state to the borrower which charges are required to obtain the mortgage and which are not required to obtain the mortgage.

(b) *Lump sum disbursement.* (1) If the borrower requests that at least 25 percent of the principal limit amount (after deducting amounts excluded in the following sentence) be disbursed at closing to the borrower (or as otherwise permitted by §206.25), the mortgagee must make sufficient inquiry at closing to confirm that the borrower will not use any part of the amount disbursed for payments to or on behalf of an estate planning service firm, with an explanation of §206.32 as necessary or appropriate.

(2) This paragraph does not apply to any part of the principal limit used for the following:

(i) Initial MIP under §206.105(a) or fees and charges allowed under §206.31(a) paid by the mortgagee from mortgage proceeds instead of by the borrower in cash; and

(ii) Amounts set aside in accordance with §206.19(f) for repairs under §206.47, for property charges under §206.205, or for servicing charges under §206.207(b).

§206.44 Monetary investment for HECM for Purchase program.

(a) *Monetary investment.* At closing, HECM for Purchase borrowers shall provide a monetary investment that will be applied to satisfy the difference between the principal limit and the sale price for the property, plus any HECM loan-related fees that are not financed into the loan, minus the amount of the earnest deposit.

(b) *Funding sources.* To satisfy the required monetary investment, borrowers may use:

(1) Cash on hand;

(2) Cash from the sale or liquidation of the borrower's assets;

(3) HECM mortgage proceeds; or

(4) Other approved funding sources as determined by the Commissioner through notice.

(c) *Interested party contributions.* (1) The following interested party contributions are permissible:

(i) Fees required to be paid by a seller under state or local law;

(ii) Fees customarily paid by a seller in the subject property locality; and

(iii) The purchase of the Home Warranty policy by the seller.

(2) The Commissioner may define additional permissible interested party

contributions and impose requirements for permissible interested party contributions through a notice in the FEDERAL REGISTER.

ELIGIBLE PROPERTIES

§ 206.45 Eligible properties.

(a) *Title.* A mortgage must be on real estate held in fee simple; or on a leasehold that is under a lease with a duration lasting until the later of: 99 years, if such lease is renewable; or the actuarial life expectancy of the mortgagor plus a number of years specified by the Commissioner, which shall not be more than 99 years. The mortgagee shall obtain a title insurance policy satisfactory to the Commissioner. If the Commissioner determines that title insurance for reverse mortgages is not available for reasonable rates in a state, then the Commissioner may specify other acceptable forms of title evidence in lieu of title insurance.

(b) *Type of property.* The property shall include a dwelling designed principally as a residence for one family or such additional families as the Commissioner shall determine. A condominium unit designed for one-family occupancy shall also be an eligible property.

(c) *Borrower and mortgagee requirement for maintaining flood insurance coverage.* (1) During such time as the mortgage is insured, the borrower and mortgagee shall be obligated, by a special condition to be included in the mortgage commitment, to obtain and to maintain National Flood Insurance Program (NFIP) flood insurance coverage on the property improvements (dwelling and related structures/equipment essential to the value of the property and subject to flood damage) if NFIP flood insurance is available with respect to the property improvements that:

(i) Are located in an area designated by the Federal Emergency Management Agency (FEMA) as a floodplain area having special flood hazards; or

(ii) Are otherwise determined by the Commissioner to be subject to a flood hazard.

(2) No mortgage may be insured that covers property improvements located in an area that has been identified by FEMA as an area having special flood hazards, unless the community in which the area is situated is participating in the NFIP and such insurance is obtained by the borrower. Such requirement for flood insurance shall be effective one year after the date of notification by FEMA to the chief executive officer of a flood prone community that such community has been identified as having special flood hazards.

(3) The flood insurance must be maintained during such time as the mortgage is insured in an amount at least equal to the lowest of the following:

(i) 100 percent replacement cost of the insurable value of the improvements, which consists of the development or project cost less estimated land cost; or

(ii) The maximum amount of the NFIP insurance available with respect to the particular type of the property; or

(iii) The outstanding principal balance of the loan.

(d) *Lead-based paint poisoning prevention.* If the appraiser of a dwelling constructed prior to 1978 finds defective paint surfaces, 24 CFR 200.810(d) shall apply unless the borrower certifies that no child who is less than six years of age resides or is expected to reside in the dwelling, except that any reference to "mortgagor" in 24 CFR 200.810(d) shall mean "borrower" for purposes of this paragraph.

(e) *Restrictions on conveyance.* The property must be freely marketable. Conveyance of the property may only be restricted as permitted under 24 CFR 203.41 or 24 CFR 234.66 and this part, except that a right of first refusal to purchase a unit in a condominium project is permitted if the right is held by the condominium association for the project.

(f) *Location of property.* The mortgaged property shall be located within the United States, Puerto Rico, Guam, the Virgin Islands, the Commonwealth of the Northern Mariana Islands, and American Samoa. The mortgaged property, if otherwise acceptable to the Commissioner, may be located in any location where the housing standards meet the requirements of the Commissioner.

(g) *HECM for Purchase.* (1) A HECM for Purchase transaction is where title to the property is transferred to the HECM borrower and, at the time of closing, the HECM first and second liens, if applicable, will be the only liens against the property.

(2) Properties are eligible for FHA insurance under the HECM for Purchase program when construction is completed and the property is habitable, as evidenced by the issuance of a Certificate of Occupancy or its equivalent, by the local jurisdiction.

§206.47 Property standards; repair work.

(a) *Need for repairs.* Properties must meet the applicable property requirements of the Commissioner in order to be eligible. Properties that do not meet the property requirements must be repaired in order to ensure that the repaired property will serve as adequate security for the insured mortgage.

(b) *Assurance that repairs are made.* The mortgage may be closed before the repair work is completed if the Commissioner estimates that the cost of the remaining repair work will not exceed 15 percent of the maximum claim amount and the mortgage contains provisions approved by the Commissioner concerning payment for the repairs.

(c) *Reimbursement to contractor.* When repair work is completed after closing by a contractor, the mortgagee shall cause one or more inspections of the property to be made by an inspector or other qualified individual acceptable to the Commissioner in order to ensure that the repair work is satisfactory, and prior to the release of funds from the Repair Set Aside. The mortgagee shall hold back a portion of the contract price attributable to the work done before each interim release of funds, and the total of the hold backs will be released after the final inspection and approval of the release by the mortgagee. The mortgagee shall ensure that all mechanics' and materialmen's liens are released of record.

(d) *Reimbursement to borrower.* The mortgagee shall not reimburse the borrower for any labor the borrower performed. The mortgagee may reimburse the borrower for the actual cost of repair materials from the Repair Set Aside, provided that the mortgagee

causes one or more inspections of the property by an inspector or other qualified individual acceptable to the Commissioner and meets all reimbursement requirements established by the Commissioner.

(e) *HECM for Purchase.* For HECM for Purchase transactions, where major property deficiencies threaten the health and safety of the homeowner or jeopardize the soundness and security of the property, all repairs must be completed by the seller prior to closing. Appraisers shall complete the appraisal report as "Subject To" the completion of the repairs.

§206.51 Eligibility of mortgages involving a dwelling unit in a condominium.

If the mortgage involves a dwelling unit in a condominium, the project in which the unit is located shall have been committed to a plan of condominium ownership by deed, or other recorded instrument, that is acceptable to the Commissioner.

§206.52 Eligible sale of property—HECM for Purchase.

(a) *Sale by owner of record*—(1) *Owner of record requirement.* To be eligible for a mortgage insured by FHA, the property must be purchased from the owner of record and the transaction may not involve any sale or assignment of the sales contract.

(2) *Supporting documentation.* The mortgagee shall obtain documentation verifying that the seller is the owner of record and must submit this documentation to FHA as part of the application for mortgage insurance, in accordance with §§206.15 and 206.115(b)(9).

(b) *Time restrictions on re-sales*—(1) *General.* The eligibility of a property for a mortgage insured by FHA is dependent on the time that has elapsed between the date the seller acquired the property (based upon the date of settlement) and the date of execution of the sales contract that will result in the FHA mortgage insurance (the resale date). The mortgagee shall obtain documentation verifying compliance with the time restrictions described in this paragraph and must submit this documentation to FHA as part of the application for mortgage insurance, in accordance with § 206.115(b).

(2) *Re-sales occurring 90 days or less following acquisition.* If the re-sale date is 90 days or less following the date of acquisition by the seller, the property is not eligible for a mortgage to be insured by FHA.

(3) *Re-sales occurring between 91 days and 180 days following acquisition.* (i) If the re-sale date is between 91 days and 180 days following acquisition by the seller, the property is generally eligible for a mortgage insured by FHA.

(ii) However, FHA will require that the mortgagee obtain additional documentation if the re-sale price is 100 percent over the purchase price. Such documentation must include an appraisal from another appraiser. The mortgagee may also document its loan file to support the increased value by establishing that the increased value results from the rehabilitation of the property.

(iii) FHA may revise the level at which additional documentation is required under paragraph (b)(3) of this section at 50 to 150 percent over the original purchase price. FHA will revise this level by FEDERAL REGISTER notice with a 30 day delayed effective date.

(4) *Authority to address property flipping for re-sales occurring between 91 days and 12 months following acquisition.* (i) If the re-sale date is more than 90 days after the date of acquisition by the seller, but before the end of the twelfth month after the date of acquisition, the property is eligible for a mortgage to be insured by FHA.

(ii) However, FHA may require that the mortgagee provide additional documentation to support the re-sale value of the property if the re-sale price is 5 percent or greater than the lowest sales price of the property during the preceding 12 months (as evidenced by the contract of sale). At FHA's discretion, such documentation must include, but is not limited to, an appraisal from another appraiser. FHA may exclude re-sales of less than a specific dollar amount from the additional value documentation requirements.

(iii) If the additional value documentation supports a value of the property that is more than 5 percent lower than the value supported by the first appraisal, the lower value will be used to calculate the maximum claim amount. Otherwise, the value supported by the first appraisal will be used to calculate the maximum claim amount.

(iv) FHA will announce its determination to require additional value documentation through issuance of a FEDERAL REGISTER notice. The requirement for additional value documentation may be established either on a nationwide or regional basis. Further, the FEDERAL REGISTER notice will specify the percentage increase in the re-sale price that will trigger the need for additional documentation, and will specify the acceptable types of documentation. The FEDERAL REGISTER notice may also exclude re-sales of less than a specific dollar amount from the additional value documentation requirements. Any such FEDERAL REGISTER notice, and any subsequent revisions, will be issued at least thirty days before taking effect.

(v) The level at which additional documentation is required under paragraph (b)(4) of this section shall supersede that under paragraph (b)(3) of this section.

(5) *Re-sales occurring more than 12 months following acquisition.* If the re-sale date is more than 12 months following the date of acquisition by the seller, the property is eligible for a mortgage insured by FHA.

(c) *Exceptions to the time restrictions on sales.* The time restrictions on sales described in paragraph (b) of this section do not apply to:

(1) Sales by HUD of Real Estate-Owned (REO) properties under 24 CFR part 291 and of single family assets in revitalization areas pursuant to section 204 of the NHA (12 U.S.C. 1710);

(2) Sales by another agency of the United States Government of REO single family properties pursuant to programs operated by these agencies;

(3) Sales of properties by nonprofit organizations approved to purchase HUD REO single family properties at a discount with resale restrictions;

(4) Sales of properties that were acquired by the sellers by inheritance;

(5) Sales of properties purchased by an employer or relocation agency in

connection with the relocation of an employee;

(6) Sales of properties by state- and federally-chartered financial institutions and government-sponsored enterprises (GSEs);

(7) Sales of properties by local and state government agencies; and

(8) Only upon announcement by FHA through issuance of a notice, sales of properties located in areas designated by the President as federal disaster areas. The notice will specify how long the exception will be in effect.

(d) *Sanctions and indemnification.* Failure of a mortgagee to comply with the requirements of this section may result in HUD requesting indemnification of the mortgage loan, or seeking other appropriate remedies under 24 CFR part 25.

REFINANCING OF EXISTING HOME EQUITY CONVERSION MORTGAGES

§206.53 Refinancing a HECM loan.

(a) *General.* Except as otherwise provided in this section, all requirements applicable to the insurance of HECMs under this part apply to the insurance of refinanced HECMs. FHA may, upon application by a mortgagee, insure any mortgage given to refinance an existing HECM insured under this part, including loans assigned to the Commissioner as described in §206.107(a)(1) and §206.121(b).

(b) *Definition of "total cost of the refinancing".* For purposes of paragraphs (d) and (e) of this section, the term "total cost of the refinancing" means the sum of the allowable charges and fees permitted under §206.31 and the initial MIP described in §206.105(a) and paragraph (c) of this section.

(c) *Initial MIP limit.* (1) The initial MIP paid by the mortgagee pursuant to §206.105(a) shall not exceed the difference between: three percent of the increase in the maximum claim amount for the new HECM, minus the amount of the initial MIP already charged and paid by the borrower for the existing HECM that is being refinanced. No refunds will be given if the initial MIP paid on the existing HECM exceeds the initial MIP due on the new HECM.

(2) The HECM refinance authority is only applicable when the property that serves as collateral for the FHA-insured mortgage remains the same.

(3) Existing HECM borrowers refinancing an existing HECM are eligible for a MIP reduction under the conditions of this section, but existing HECM borrowers who participate in a HECM for Purchase transaction are ineligible for a reduction in the initial MIP.

(d) *Anti-churning disclosure*—(1) *Contents of anti-churning disclosure.* In addition to providing the required disclosures under §206.43, the mortgagee shall provide to the borrower its best estimate of:

(i) The total cost of the refinancing to the borrower; and

(ii) The increase in the borrower's principal limit as measured by the estimated initial principal limit on the mortgage to be insured less the current principal limit on the HECM that is being refinanced under this section.

(2) *Timing of anti-churning disclosure.* The mortgagee shall provide the anti-churning disclosure concurrently with the disclosures required under §206.43.

(e) *Waiver of counseling requirement.* The borrower and any Non-Borrowing Spouse may elect not to receive counseling under §206.41, but only if:

(1) The original HECM was assigned a Case Number on or after August 4, 2014, and the borrower and Non-Borrowing Spouse, if applicable, received counseling required under §206.41; or where the original HECM was assigned a Case Number prior to August 4, 2014, and there is no applicable Non-Borrowing Spouse.

(2) The borrower has received the anti-churning disclosure required under paragraph (d) of this section.

(3) The increase in the borrower's principal limit (as provided in the anti-churning disclosure) exceeds the total cost of the refinancing by an amount established by the Commissioner through FEDERAL REGISTER notice. FHA may periodically update this amount through publication of a notice in the FEDERAL REGISTER. Publication of any such revised amount will occur at least 30 days before the revision becomes effective.

(4) The time between the date of the closing on the original HECM and the date of the application for refinancing under this section does not exceed five years (even if less than five years have passed since a previous refinancing under this section).

DEFERRAL OF DUE AND PAYABLE STATUS

§ 206.55 Deferral of due and payable status for Eligible Non-Borrowing Spouses.

(a) *Deferral Period.* If the last surviving borrower predeceases an Eligible Non-Borrowing Spouse, and if the requirements of paragraph (d) of this section are satisfied, the due and payable status will be deferred for as long as the Eligible Non-Borrowing Spouse continues to meet the Qualifying Attributes in paragraph (c) of this section and the requirements of paragraphs (d) and (e) of this section.

(b) *End of Deferral Period.* (1) If a Deferral Period ceases or becomes unavailable because a Non-Borrowing Spouse no longer satisfies the Qualifying Attributes and has become an Ineligible Non-Borrowing Spouse, a mortgagee may not provide an opportunity to cure the default, and the HECM will become immediately due and payable as a result of the death of the last surviving borrower.

(2) If a Deferral Period ceases but the Eligible Non-Borrowing Spouse continues to meet the Qualifying Attributes, the mortgagee must provide an Eligible Non-Borrowing Spouse with 30 days to cure the default, in accordance with § 206.57.

(c) *Qualifying Attributes.* (1) In order to qualify as an Eligible Non-Borrowing Spouse, the Non-Borrowing Spouse must:

(i) Have been the spouse of a HECM borrower at the time of loan closing and remained the spouse of such HECM borrower for the duration of the HECM borrower's lifetime;

(ii) Have been properly disclosed to the mortgagee at origination and specifically named as an Eligible Non-Borrowing Spouse in the HECM mortgage and loan documents;

(iii) Have occupied, and continue to occupy, the property securing the HECM as his or her principal residence; and

(iv) Meet any other requirements as the Commissioner may prescribe by FEDERAL REGISTER notice for comment.

(2) A Non-Borrowing Spouse who meets the Qualifying Attributes in paragraph (c)(1) of this section at origination is an Eligible Non-Borrowing Spouse and may not elect to be ineligible for the Deferral Period. A Non-Borrowing Spouse that is ineligible for the Deferral Period at the time of loan origination because he or she failed to satisfy the Qualifying Attributes requirements in paragraph (c)(1) of this section is not subsequently eligible for a Deferral Period when the borrowing spouse dies or moves out of the home.

(3) An Eligible Non-Borrowing Spouse shall become an Ineligible Non-Borrowing Spouse should any of the Qualifying Attributes requirements in paragraph (c)(1) of this section cease to be met.

(d) *Additional requirements for Deferral Period.* An Eligible Non-Borrowing Spouse must satisfy and continue to satisfy the following requirements:

(1) Within 90 days from the death of the last surviving HECM borrower, establish legal ownership or other ongoing legal right to remain for life in the property securing the HECM;

(2) After the death of the last surviving borrower, ensure all other obligations of the HECM borrower(s) contained in the loan documents continue to be satisfied; and

(3) After the death of the last surviving borrower, ensure that the HECM does not become eligible to be called due and payable for any other reason.

(e) *Unaffected terms of HECM.* All applicable terms and conditions of the mortgage and loan documents, and all FHA requirements, continue to apply and must be satisfied.

(f) Nothing in this section may be construed as interrupting or interfering with the ability of the borrower's estate or heir(s) to dispose of the property if they are otherwise legally entitled to do so.

§ 206.57 Cure provision enabling reinstatement of Deferral Period.

(a) When the mortgagee is required by § 206.55(b)(2) to provide an Eligible Non-Borrowing Spouse with 30 days to cure the default, this section shall apply.

(b) If the default is cured within the 30-day timeframe, the Deferral Period shall be reinstated, unless:

(1) The mortgagee has reinstated the Deferral Period within the past two years immediately preceding the current notification to the Eligible Non-Borrowing Spouse that the mortgage is due and payable;

(2) The reinstatement of the Deferral Period will preclude foreclosure if the mortgage becomes due and payable at a later date; or

(3) The reinstatement of the Deferral Period will adversely affect the priority of the mortgage lien.

(c) If the default is not cured within the 30-day timeframe, the mortgagee shall proceed in accordance with the established timeframes to initiate foreclosure and reasonable diligence in prosecuting foreclosure.

(d) Even after a foreclosure proceeding has been initiated, the mortgagee shall permit an Eligible Non-Borrowing Spouse to cure the condition which resulted in the Deferral Period ceasing, consistent with §206.55(b)(2), and to reinstate the mortgage and Deferral Period, and the mortgage insurance shall continue in effect. The mortgagee may require the Eligible Non-Borrowing Spouse to pay any costs that the mortgagee incurred to reinstate the mortgage, including foreclosure costs and reasonable attorney's fees. Such costs may not be added to the outstanding loan balance and shall be paid from some other source of funds. The mortgagee shall reinstate the Deferral Period unless:

(1) The mortgagee has reinstated the Deferral Period within the past two years immediately preceding the latest notification to the Eligible Non-Borrowing Spouse that the mortgage is due and payable;

(2) The reinstatement of the Deferral Period will preclude foreclosure if the mortgage becomes due and payable at a later date; or

(3) The reinstatement of the Deferral Period will adversely affect the priority of the mortgage lien.

§206.59 Obligations of mortgagee.

(a) *Certifications and disclosures at closing.* At closing, the mortgagee shall obtain the appropriate certification from each borrower identified as married as well as from each identified Non-Borrowing Spouse. When a HECM borrower has identified an Ineligible Non-Borrowing Spouse, the mortgagee shall also disclose the amount of mortgage proceeds that would have been available under the HECM if he or she were an Eligible Non-Borrowing Spouse.

(b) *Divorce.* In the event of a divorce between the HECM borrower and Eligible Non-Borrowing Spouse, a mortgagee shall obtain a copy of the final divorce decree and shall not require the now Ineligible Non-Borrowing Spouse to fulfill any further requirements.

(c) *Death of borrower.* Within 30 days of being notified of the death of the borrower, the mortgagee shall:

(1) Obtain all certifications, as required by the Commissioner, from the Eligible Non-Borrowing Spouse, and continue to obtain the required certifications no less than annually thereafter for the duration of the Deferral Period; and

(2) Notify any Eligible Non-Borrowing Spouse that the due and payable status of the loan is in a Deferral Period only for the amount of time that such Eligible Non-Borrowing Spouse continues to meet all requirements established by the Commissioner.

(d) *Non-compliance with requirements.* If the Eligible Non-Borrowing Spouse ceases to meet any requirements established by the Commissioner, the mortgagee shall notify the Eligible Non-Borrowing Spouse within 30 days that the Deferral Period has ended and the HECM is immediately due and payable, unless the Deferral Period is reinstated in accordance with §206.57. The mortgagee shall obtain documentation validating the reason for the cessation of the Deferral Period and, if applicable, the reason for reinstatement of the Deferral Period.

§206.61 HECM proceeds during a Deferral Period.

(a) The HECM is not assumable. HECM proceeds may not be disbursed to any party during a Deferral Period, except as determined by the Commissioner through notice.

(b) If a Repair Set Aside was established as a condition of the HECM, funds may be disbursed from the Repair Set Aside during a Deferral Period for the sole purpose of paying the cost of those repairs that were specifically identified prior to origination as necessary to the insurance of the HECM. Repairs under this paragraph shall only be paid for using funds from the Repair Set Aside if the repairs are satisfactorily completed during the time period established in the Repair Rider or such additional time as provided by the Commissioner. Unused funds remaining beyond the established time period shall not be disbursed.

Subpart C—Contract Rights and Obligations

SALE, ASSIGNMENT AND PLEDGE

§ 206.101 Sale, assignment and pledge of insured mortgages.

(a) *Sale of interests in insured mortgages.* No mortgagee may sell or otherwise dispose of any mortgage insured under this part, or group of mortgages insured under this part, or any partial interest in such mortgage or mortgages by means of any agreement, arrangement or device except pursuant to this subpart.

(b) *Sale of insured mortgage to approved mortgagee.* A mortgage insured under this part may be sold to another approved mortgagee. The seller shall notify the Commissioner of the sale within 15 calendar days, on a form prescribed by the Commissioner and acknowledged by the buyer.

(c) *Effect of sale of insured mortgage.* When a mortgage insured under this part is sold to another approved mortgagee, the buyer shall thereupon succeed to all the rights and become bound by all the obligations of the seller under the contract of insurance and the seller shall be released from its obligations under the contract, provided that the seller shall not be relieved of its obligation to pay mortgage insurance premiums until the notice required by § 206.101(b) is received by the Commissioner.

(d) *Assignments, pledges and transfers by approved mortgagee.* (1) An assignment, pledge, or transfer of a mortgage or group of mortgages insured under this part, not constituting a final sale, may be made by an approved mortgagee to another approved mortgagee provided the following requirements are met:

(i) The assignor, pledgor or transferor shall remain the mortgagee of record.

(ii) The Commissioner shall have no obligation to recognize or deal with any party other than the mortgagee of record with respect to the rights, benefits and obligations of the mortgagee under the contract of insurance.

(2) An assignment or transfer of an insured mortgage or group of insured mortgages may be made by an approved mortgagee to other than an approved mortgagee provided the requirements under paragraphs (d)(1)(i) and (d)(1)(ii) of this section are met and the following additional requirements are met:

(i) The assignee or transferee shall be a corporation, trust or organization (including but not limited to any pension trust or profit-sharing plan) which certifies to the approved mortgagee that:

(A) It has assets of $100,000 or more; and

(B) It has lawful authority to hold an insured mortgage or group of insured mortgages.

(ii) The assignment or transfer shall be made pursuant to an agreement under which the transferor or assignor is obligated to take one of the following alternate courses of action within 1 year from the date of the assignment or within such additional period of time as may be approved by the Commissioner:

(A) The transferor or assignor shall repurchase and accept a reassignment of such mortgage or group of mortgages.

(B) The transferor or assignor shall obtain a sale and transfer of such mortgage or group of mortgages to an approved mortgagee.

(3) Notice to or approval of the Commissioner is not required in connection with assignments, pledges or transfers pursuant to this section.

(e) *Declaration of trust.* A sale of a beneficial interest in a group of mortgages insured under this part, where the interest to be acquired is related to all of the mortgages as an entirety, rather than an interest in a specific mortgage, shall be made only pursuant to a declaration of trust, which has been approved by the Commissioner prior to any such sale.

(f) *Transfers of partial interests.* A partial interest in a mortgage insured under this part may be transferred under a participation agreement without obtaining the approval of the Commissioner, if the following conditions are met:

(1) *Principal mortgagee.* The insured mortgage shall be held by an approved mortgagee which, for the purposes of this section, shall be referred to as the *principal mortgagee.*

(2) *Interest of principal mortgagee.* The principal mortgagee shall retain and hold for its own account a financial interest in the insured mortgage.

(3) *Qualification for holding partial interest.* A partial interest in an insured mortgage shall be issued to and held only by:

(i) A mortgagee approved by the Commissioner; or

(ii) A corporation, trust or organization (including, but not limited to any pension fund, pension trust, or profit-sharing plan) which certifies to the principal mortgagee that:

(A) It has assets of $100,000 or more; and

(B) It has lawful authority to acquire a partial interest in an insured mortgage.

(4) *Participation agreement provisions.* The participation agreement shall include provisions that:

(i) The principal mortgagee shall retain title to the mortgage and remain the mortgagee of record under the contract of mortgage insurance.

(ii) The Commissioner shall have no obligation to recognize or deal with anyone other than the principal mortgagee with respect to the rights, benefits and obligations of the mortgagee under the contract of insurance.

(iii) The mortgage and loan documents shall remain in the custody of the principal mortgagee.

(1v) The responsibility for servicing the insured mortgages shall remain with the principal mortgagee.

§206.102 Insurance Funds.

Loans endorsed for insurance under this part, prior to October 1, 2008, shall be obligations of the General Insurance Fund. Loans endorsed for insurance under this part, on or after October 1, 2008, shall be obligations of the MMIF.

MORTGAGE INSURANCE PREMIUMS

§206.103 Payment of MIP.

(a) The payment of any MIP due under this subpart shall be made to the Commissioner by the mortgagee in cash until an event described in paragraph (b) or (c) of this section occurs.

(b) *Payment of the mortgage.* The MIP shall no longer be remitted if the mortgage is paid in full.

(c) *Acquisition of title.* (1) If the mortgagee or a party other than the mortgagee acquires title at a foreclosure sale, or the mortgagee acquires title by a deed in lieu of foreclosure, and the mortgagee notifies the Commissioner that a claim for the payment of the insurance benefits will not be presented, the MIP shall no longer be remitted.

(2) If the mortgagee or a party other than the mortgagee acquires title at a foreclosure sale or the mortgagee acquires title by a deed in lieu of foreclosure, or where the property is sold in accordance with §206.125(c), and a claim for the payment of the insurance benefits will be presented, the MIP shall no longer be remitted as of the date of the foreclosure sale, the date the deed in lieu of foreclosure is recorded, or the date in which the sale in accordance with §206.125(c) is completed, as applicable.

§206.105 Amount of MIP.

(a) *Initial MIP.* The mortgagee shall pay to the Commissioner an initial MIP that does not exceed three percent of the maximum claim amount.

(b) *Monthly MIP.* The Commissioner may establish and collect a monthly MIP, which will accrue daily from the closing date, at a rate not to exceed 1.50 percent of the remaining insured principal balance, or up to 1.55 percent for any mortgage involving an original principal obligation that is greater than 95 percent of appraised value of the property. A mortgagee may only add the monthly MIP to the loan balance when paid to the Commissioner.

(c) *Calculation of the initial MIP.* The mortgagee shall calculate the initial MIP based on the amount of funds the borrower has elected to be made available during the First 12-Month Disbursement Period, except that the calculation shall not include any funds set aside in the Servicing Fee Set Aside, if applicable. The initial MIP calculation shall be determined based on the sum of the following amounts:

(1) For adjustable interest rate HECMs, the amount of Mandatory Obligations, the amount disbursed to the borrower at loan closing, and the amount of the available Initial Disbursement Limit not taken by the borrower at loan closing that the borrower selects to remain available during the First 12-Month Disbursement Period.

(2) For fixed interest rate HECMs, the amount of Mandatory Obligations and the amount disbursed to the borrower at loan closing.

(d) *Adjustments to initial or monthly MIP.* The Commissioner may adjust the amount of any initial or monthly MIP through notice. Such notice shall establish the effective date of any premium adjustment therein.

§ 206.107 Mortgagee election of assignment or shared premium option.

(a) *Election of option.* Before the mortgage is submitted for insurance endorsement, the mortgagee shall elect either the assignment option or the shared premium option.

(1) Under the assignment option, the mortgagee shall have the option of assigning the mortgage to the Commissioner if the outstanding loan balance is equal to or greater than 98 percent of the maximum claim amount, regardless of the deferral status, or the borrower has requested a payment which exceeds the difference between the maximum claim amount and the outstanding loan balance and:

(i) The mortgagee is current in making the required payments under the mortgage to the borrower;

(ii) The mortgagee is current in its payment of the MIP (and late charges and interest on the MIP, if any) to the Commissioner;

(iii) The mortgage is not due and payable under § 206.27(c)(1), or, if due and payable under § 206.27(c)(1), its due and payable status has been deferred pursuant to a Deferral Period;

(iv) An event described in § 206.27(c)(2) has not occurred, or the Commissioner has been so informed but has denied approval for the mortgage to be due and payable. At the mortgagee's option, the mortgagee may forgo assignment of the mortgage and file a claim under any of the circumstances described in § 206.123(a)(3)–(5); and

(v) The mortgage is a first lien of record and title to the property securing the mortgage is good and marketable. The provisions of § 206.136 pertaining to mortgagee certifications also apply.

(2) Under the shared premium option, the mortgagee may not assign a mortgage to the Commissioner unless the mortgagee fails to make payments and the Commissioner demands assignment (§ 206.123(a)(2)), but the mortgagee shall only be required to remit a reduced monthly MIP to the Commissioner. The mortgagee shall collect from the borrower the full amount of the monthly MIP provided in § 206.105(b) but shall retain a portion of the monthly MIP paid by the borrower as compensation for the default risk assumed by the mortgagee. The portion of the MIP to be retained by a mortgagee shall be determined by the Commissioner as calculated in § 206.109. For a particular mortgage, the applicable portion shall be determined as of the date of the commitment. The mortgagee retains the right to file a claim under any of the circumstances described in § 206.123(a)(2)–(5).

(b) *No election for shared appreciation.* Shared appreciation mortgages shall be insured by the Commissioner only under the shared premium option.

§ 206.109 Amount of mortgagee share of premium.

Using the factors provided by the Commissioner, the amount of the mortgagee share of the premium shall be determined for each mortgage based upon the age of the youngest borrower or Eligible Non-Borrowing Spouse and the expected average mortgage interest rate.

§206.111 Due date of MIP.

(a) *Initial MIP.* The mortgagee shall pay the initial MIP to the Commissioner within fifteen days of closing and as a condition to the endorsement of the mortgage for insurance.

(b) *Monthly MIP.* Each monthly MIP shall be due to the Commissioner on the first business day of each month except the month in which the mortgage is closed.

§206.113 Late charge and interest.

(a) *Late charge.* Initial MIP remitted to the Commissioner more than 5 days after the payment date in §206.111(a) and monthly MIP remitted to the Commissioner more than 5 days after the payment date in §206.111(b) shall include a late charge of four percent of the amount owed.

(b) *Interest.* In addition to any late charge provided in paragraph (a) of this section, the mortgagee shall pay interest on any initial MIP remitted to the Commissioner more than 20 days after closing, and interest on any monthly MIP remitted to the Commissioner more than 5 days after the payment date prescribed in §206.111(b). Such interest rate shall be paid at a rate set in conformity with the Treasury Financial Manual.

(c) *Paid by mortgagee.* Any late charge and interest owed may not be added to the outstanding loan balance and must be paid by the mortgagee.

§206.115 Insurance of mortgage.

(a) *Mortgages with firm commitments.* For applications for insurance involving mortgages not eligible to be originated under the Direct Endorsement program under §203.5 (any reference to §203.255 in §203.5 shall mean §206.115 for purposes of this section), the Commissioner will endorse the mortgage for insurance by issuing a Mortgage Insurance Certificate.

(b) *Endorsement with Direct Endorsement processing.* For applications for insurance involving mortgages originated under the Direct Endorsement program under §203.5 (any reference to §203.255 in §203.5 shall mean §206.115 for purposes of this section), the mort-

gagee shall submit to the Commissioner, within 60 days after the date of closing of the loan or such additional time as permitted by the Commissioner, properly completed documentation and certifications as listed in this paragraph (b):

(1) Property appraisal upon a form meeting the requirements of the Commissioner (including, if required, any additional documentation supporting the appraised value of the property under §206.52), and a HUD conditional commitment, or a Lender's Notice of Value issued by the Lender Appraisal Processing Program (LAPP) approved lender when the appraisal was originally completed for use in a VA application, but only if the appraiser was also on the FHA roster as of the effective date of the appraisal, and all accompanying documents required by the Commissioner;

(2) An application for insurance of the mortgage in a form prescribed by the Commissioner;

(3) A certified copy of the mortgage and loan documents executed upon forms which meet the requirements of the Commissioner;

(4) An underwriter certification, on a form prescribed by the Commissioner, stating that the underwriter has personally reviewed the appraisal report and credit application (including the analysis performed on the worksheets) and that the proposed mortgage complies with FHA underwriting requirements, and incorporates each of the underwriter certification items that apply to the mortgage submitted for endorsement, as set forth in the applicable handbook or similar publication that is distributed to all Direct Endorsement mortgagees, except that if FHA makes the TOTAL Mortgage Scorecard available to HECM mortgagees by setting out requirements applicable for the use of the TOTAL Mortgage Scorecard in a FEDERAL REGISTER notice for comment, mortgagees may follow such procedures and meet such requirements in lieu of providing the underwriter certification;

(5) Where applicable, a certificate under oath and contract regarding use of the dwelling for transient or hotel purposes;

(6) Where an individual water or sewer system is being used, an approval letter from the local health authority indicating approval of the system in accordance with § 200.926d(f);

(7) A mortgage certification on a form prescribed by the Commissioner, stating that the authorized representative of the mortgagee who is making the certification has personally reviewed the mortgage documents and the application for insurance endorsement, and certifying that the mortgage complies with the requirements of paragraph (b) of this section. The certification shall incorporate each of the mortgagee certification items that apply to the mortgage loan submitted for endorsement, as set forth in the applicable handbook or similar publication that is distributed to all Direct Endorsement mortgagees;

(8) Documents required by § 206.15;

(9) Documentation providing that the seller is the owner of record in accordance with § 206.52(a) and the time restriction requirements of § 206.52(b) are met;

(10) For HECM for Purchase transactions, a Certificate of Occupancy, or its equivalent, if required for new construction; and

(11) Such other documents as the Commissioner may require.

(c) *Pre-endorsement review for Direct Endorsement.* (1) Upon submission by an approved mortgagee of the documents required by paragraph (b) of this section, the Commissioner will review the documents and determine that:

(i) The mortgage is executed on a form which meets the requirements of the Commissioner;

(ii) The mortgage maturity meets the requirements of the applicable program;

(iii) The stated mortgage amount does not exceed 150 percent of the maximum claim amount;

(iv) All documents required by paragraph (b) of this section are submitted;

(v) All necessary certifications are made in accordance with paragraph (b) of this section;

(vi) There is no mortgage insurance premium, late charge or interest due to the Commissioner; and

(vii) The mortgage was not in default when submitted for insurance or, if submitted for insurance more than 60 days after closing, the mortgagee certifies that the borrower is current in paying all property charges or is otherwise in compliance with all the terms and conditions of the mortgage documents.

(2) The Commissioner is authorized to determine if there is any information indicating that any certification or required document is false, misleading, or constitutes fraud or misrepresentation on the part of any party, or that the mortgage fails to meet a statutory or regulatory requirement. If, following this review, the mortgage is determined to be eligible, the Commissioner will endorse the mortgage for insurance by issuance of a Mortgage Insurance Certificate. If the mortgage is determined to be ineligible, the Commissioner will inform the mortgagee in writing of this determination, and include the reasons for the determination and any corrective actions that may be taken.

(d) *Submission by mortgagee other than originating mortgagee.* If the originating mortgagee assigns the mortgage to another approved mortgagee before pre-endorsement review under paragraph (c) of this section, the assignee may submit the required documents for pre-endorsement review in the name of the originating mortgagee. All certifications must be executed by the originating mortgagee (or its underwriter, if appropriate). The purchasing mortgagee may pay any required mortgage insurance premium, late charge and interest.

(e) *Post-Endorsement review for Direct Endorsement.* Following endorsement for insurance, the Commissioner may review all documents required by paragraph (b) of this section. If, following this review, the Commissioner determines that the mortgage does not satisfy the requirements of the Direct Endorsement program, the Commissioner may place the mortgagee on Direct Endorsement probation, or terminate the authority of the mortgagee to participate in the Direct Endorsement program pursuant to § 206.15, or refer the matter to the Mortgagee Review Board for action pursuant to part 25 of this title.

(f) *Creation of the contract.* The mortgage shall be an insured mortgage from the date of the issuance of a Mortgage Insurance Certificate, from the date of the endorsement of the credit instrument, or from the date of FHA's electronic acknowledgement to the mortgagee that the mortgage is insured, as applicable. The Commissioner and the mortgagee are thereafter bound by the regulations in this subpart with the same force and to the same extent as if a separate contract had been executed relating to the insured mortgage, including the provisions of the regulations in this subpart and of the National Housing Act.

§206.116 Refunds.

No amount of the initial MIP shall be refundable except as authorized by the Commissioner.

HUD RESPONSIBILITY TO BORROWERS

§206.117 General.

The Commissioner is required by statute to take any action necessary to provide a borrower with funds to which the borrower is entitled under the mortgage and which the borrower does not receive because of the default of the mortgagee. The Commissioner may hold a second mortgage to secure repayment by the borrower under §206.27(d). Where the Commissioner does not hold a second mortgage, but makes a payment to the borrower, and such payment is not reimbursed by the mortgagee, the Commissioner shall accept assignment of the first mortgage.

§206.119 [Reserved]

§206.121 Commissioner authorized to make payments.

(a) *Investigation.* The Commissioner will investigate all complaints by a borrower concerning late payments. If the Commissioner determines that the mortgagee is unable or unwilling to make all payments required under the mortgage, including late charges, the Commissioner shall pay such payments and late charges to the borrower.

(b) *Reimbursement or assignment.* The Commissioner may demand that within 30 days from the demand, the mortgagee reimburse the Commissioner,

with interest from the date of payment by the Commissioner, or assign the insured mortgage to the Commissioner. Interest shall be paid at a rate set in conformity with the Treasury Financial Manual. If the mortgagee complies with the reimbursement demand, then the contract of insurance shall not be affected. If the mortgagee complies by assigning the mortgage for record within 30 days of the demand, then the Commissioner shall pay an insurance claim as provided in §206.129(e)(3) and assume all responsibilities of the mortgagee under the first mortgage. If the mortgagee fails to comply with the demand within 30 days, the contract of insurance will terminate as provided in §206.133(c).

(c) *Second mortgage.* If the contract of insurance is terminated as provided in §206.133(c), all payments to the borrower by the Commissioner will be secured by the second mortgage, unless otherwise provided by the Commissioner. Payments will be due and payable in the same manner as under the insured first mortgage. The liability of the borrower under the first mortgage shall be limited to payments actually made by the mortgagee to or on behalf of the borrower (including prior recoupment of the MIP remitted by the mortgagee and billed to the borrower), and shall exclude accrued interest, whether or not it has been included in the outstanding loan balance, and shared appreciation, if any. Interest will stop accruing on the first mortgage when the Commissioner begins to make payments under the second mortgage. The first mortgage will not be due and payable until the second mortgage is due and payable.

CLAIM PROCEDURE

§206.123 Claim procedures in general.

(a) *Claims.* Mortgagees may submit claims for the payment of the mortgage insurance benefits if:

(1) The conditions of §206.107(a)(1) pertaining to the optional assignment of the mortgage by the mortgagee have been met and the mortgagee assigns the mortgage to the Commissioner;

(2) The mortgagee is unable or unwilling to make the payments under the mortgage and assigns the mortgage

279

to the Commissioner pursuant to the Commissioner's demand, as provided in § 206.121(b);

(3) The borrower or other permissible party sells the property for less than the outstanding loan balance and the mortgagee releases the mortgage of record to facilitate the sale, as provided in § 206.125(c);

(4) The mortgagee acquires title to the property by foreclosure or a deed in lieu of foreclosure and sells the property as provided in § 206.125(g) for an amount which does not satisfy the outstanding loan balance or fails to sell the property as provided in § 206.127(a)(2); or

(5) The mortgagee forecloses and a bidder other than the mortgagee purchases the property for an amount that is not sufficient to satisfy the outstanding loan balance, as provided in § 206.125(e).

(b) [Reserved]

§ 206.125 Acquisition and sale of the property.

(a) *Initial action by the mortgagee.* (1) The mortgagee shall notify the Commissioner within 60 days of the mortgage becoming due and payable when the conditions stated in the mortgage, as required by § 206.27(c)(1) have occurred or when the Deferral Period ends. The mortgagee shall notify the Commissioner within 30 days when one of the conditions stated in the mortgage, as required by § 206.27(c)(2), has occurred.

(2) After notifying and receiving approval of the Commissioner when needed, the mortgagee shall notify the borrower, Eligible Non-Borrowing Spouse, borrower's estate, and borrower's heir(s), as applicable, within 30 days of the later of notifying the Commissioner or receiving approval, if needed, that the mortgage is due and payable. The mortgagee shall give the applicable party 30 days from the date of notice to engage in the following actions:

(i) Pay the outstanding loan balance, including any accrued interest, MIP, and mortgagee advances in full;

(ii) Sell the property for an amount not to be less than the amount determined by the Commissioner through notice, which shall not exceed 95 percent of the appraised value as determined under § 206.125(b), with the net proceeds of the sale to be applied towards the outstanding loan balance. Closing costs shall not exceed the greater of: 11 percent of the sales price; or a fixed dollar amount as determined by the Commissioner through FEDERAL REGISTER notice. For the purposes of this section, *sell* includes the transfer of title by operation of law;

(iii) Provide the mortgagee with a deed in lieu of foreclosure;

(iv) Correct the condition which resulted in the mortgage coming due and payable for reasons other than the death of the last surviving borrower;

(v) For an Eligible Non-Borrowing Spouse, correct the condition which resulted in an end to the Deferral Period in accordance with § 206.57; or

(vi) Such other actions as permitted by the Commissioner through notice.

(3) For a borrower, even after a foreclosure proceeding is begun, the mortgagee shall permit the borrower to correct the condition which resulted in the mortgage coming due and payable and to reinstate the mortgage, and the mortgage insurance shall continue in effect. The mortgagee may require the borrower to pay any costs that the mortgagee incurred to reinstate the borrower, including foreclosure costs and reasonable attorney's fees. Such costs shall be paid by adding them to the outstanding loan balance. The mortgagee may refuse reinstatement by the borrower if:

(i) The mortgagee has accepted reinstatement of the mortgage within the past two years immediately preceding the current notification to the borrower that the mortgage is due and payable;

(ii) Reinstatement will preclude foreclosure if the mortgage becomes due and payable at a later date; or

(iii) Reinstatement will adversely affect the priority of the mortgage lien.

(4) For an Eligible Non-Borrowing Spouse, even after a foreclosure proceeding is begun, the mortgagee shall permit the Eligible Non-Borrowing Spouse to cure the condition which resulted in the Deferral Period ceasing, in accordance with § 206.57(d).

(b) *Appraisal.* The mortgagee shall have the property appraised by an appraiser on the FHA roster, or other appraiser acceptable to, and identified by, the Commissioner through FEDERAL REGISTER notice, no later than 30 days after receipt of the request by an applicable party in connection with a potential property sale. The property shall be appraised before a foreclosure sale and have an effective appraisal date that is no more than 30 days before such sale. The appraisal shall be at the requesting party's expense unless the mortgage is due and payable. If the mortgage is due and payable, the appraisal shall be at the mortgagee's expense but the mortgagee shall have a right to be reimbursed out of the proceeds of any sale by the borrower or other permissible party. The Commissioner may, through FEDERAL REGISTER notice, identify other acceptable types of valuation for establishing the value of HECMs for the purpose of sale.

(c) *Sale by borrower or other permissible party.* Where the HECM is not due and payable, the borrower or an authorized representative of the borrower may sell the property for at least the lesser of the outstanding loan balance or the appraised value. Where the HECM is due and payable at the time the contract for sale is executed, the borrower or other party with legal right to dispose of the property may sell the property in accordance with the amount established by §206.125(a)(2)(ii). The mortgagee shall satisfy the mortgage of record (and the Commissioner will satisfy any second mortgage required by the Commissioner under §206.27(d) of record) in order to facilitate the sale, provided that there are no junior liens (except the mortgage to secure payments by the Commissioner if required under §206.27(d)) and all the net proceeds from the sale are paid to the mortgagee.

(d) *Initiation of foreclosure.* (1) The mortgagee shall commence foreclosure of the mortgage within six months of the due date defined in §206.129(d)(1), or within such additional time as may be approved by the Commissioner.

(2) If the laws of the State, city, or municipality or other political subdivision in which the mortgaged property is located or if Federal bankruptcy law does not permit the commencement of the foreclosure in accordance with §206.125(d)(1), the mortgagee shall commence foreclosure within six months after the expiration of the time during which such foreclosure is prohibited by such laws.

(3) The mortgagee shall give written notice to the Commissioner within 30 days after the initiation of foreclosure proceedings, and shall exercise reasonable diligence in prosecuting the foreclosure proceedings to completion and in acquiring title to and possession of the property. A time frame that is determined by the Commissioner to constitute "reasonable diligence" for each State is made available to mortgagees.

(4) The mortgagee shall bid at the foreclosure sale an amount at least equal to the lesser of the sum of the outstanding loan balance and any and all other incurred expenses, or the current appraised value of the property. Such a bid by any party other than the mortgagee, for the full loan balance and all associated expenses, will result in a full payoff of the loan and no claim for insurance benefits being presented to FHA.

(e) *Other bidders at foreclosure sale.* If a party other than the mortgagee is the successful bidder at the foreclosure sale, the net proceeds of the sale shall be applied to the outstanding loan balance.

(f) *Deed in lieu of foreclosure.* (1)(i) In order to avoid delays and additional expense as a result of instituting and completing a foreclosure action, the mortgagee shall accept a deed in lieu of foreclosure from the borrower or other party with legal right to dispose of the property provided it is filed for recording within 9 months of the due date and the mortgagee is able to obtain good and marketable title.

(ii) *Cash for Keys.* The Commissioner may provide a financial incentive, in an amount to be determined by the Commissioner, to be paid by the mortgagee and reimbursed through any subsequent claim where a borrower or other party with a legal right to do so deeds the property within 6 months of the due date.

(2) In exchange for the executed and delivered deed, the mortgagee shall

cancel the credit instrument and deliver it to the borrower and satisfy the mortgage of record. If applicable, the mortgagee shall request that the Commissioner cancel the credit instrument and deliver it to the borrower and satisfy the mortgage of record.

(g) *Sale of the acquired property.* (1) Upon acquisition of the property by foreclosure or deed in lieu of foreclosure, the mortgagee shall take possession of, preserve, and repair the property and shall make diligent efforts to sell the property within six months from the date the mortgagee acquired the property, or such additional time as provided by the Commissioner. The mortgagee shall sell the property for an amount not less than the appraised value (as provided under paragraph (b) of this section) unless the mortgagee does not file an application for insurance benefits or written permission is obtained from the Commissioner authorizing a sale at a lower price.

(2) Repairs shall not exceed those required by local law, or the requirements of the Commissioner or the Secretary of Veterans Affairs if the sale of the property is financed with a mortgage insured by the Commissioner or guaranteed, insured, or taken by the Secretary of Veterans Affairs. No other repairs shall be made without the specific advance approval of the Commissioner.

(3) The mortgagee shall not enter into a contract for the preservation, repair, or sale of the property with any officer, employee, or owner of ten percent or more interest in the mortgagee or with any other person or organization having an identity of interest with the mortgagee or with any relative of such officer, employee, owner, or person.

(4) The Commissioner may provide financial incentive, in an amount to be determined by the Commissioner, to be paid by the mortgagee and reimbursed through a subsequent claim when a bona fide tenant vacates the property prior to an eviction being initiated by the mortgagee.

§ 206.127 Application for insurance benefits.

(a) *Mortgagee acquires title.* (1) The mortgagee shall apply for the payment of the insurance benefits within 30 days after the sale of the property by the mortgagee or within such additional time as approved by the Commissioner. Application shall be made by notifying the Commissioner of the sale of the property, the sale price, and income and expenses incurred in connection with the acquisition, repair, and sale of the property.

(2) If the property will not be sold within six months from the foreclosure sale date where the mortgagee is the successful bidder, the mortgagee shall apply for the insurance benefit not later than 30 days after the end of the six-month period, substituting the appraised value, using a valid appraisal, for the sale price. The mortgagee may add the cost of the appraisal to the claim amount.

(b) *Party other than the mortgagee acquires title.* The mortgagee shall apply for the payment of the insurance benefits within 30 days after a party other than the mortgagee acquires title to the property. Application shall be made by notifying the Commissioner of the sale of the property and the sale price. Transferring a portfolio that includes REO properties to another entity does not constitute a "sale" under this section.

(c) *Mortgagee assigns the mortgage.* The mortgagee shall file its claim for the payment of insurance benefits within 15 days after the date the assignment of the mortgage to the Commissioner is filed for recording. The application for the payment of the insurance benefits shall include the items listed in § 206.135(a) and the certification required under § 206.136.

(d) *Contract of insurance not terminated.* Mortgagees may only file an application for insurance benefits provided the contract of insurance has not terminated.

§ 206.129 Payment of claim.

(a) *General.* If the claim for the payment of the insurance benefits is acceptable to the Commissioner, payment shall be made in cash in the amount determined under this section.

(b) *Limit on claim amount.* (1) For HECMs assigned Case Numbers prior to September 19, 2017, in no case may the claim paid under this subpart exceed the maximum claim amount. The interest allowance provided in paragraphs (d)(3)(x), (e)(2), and (f)(2)(i) of this section shall not be included in determining the limit on the claim amount.

(2) For HECMs assigned Case Numbers on or after September 19, 2017, in no case may the claim paid under this subpart exceed the maximum claim amount, as defined in §206.3. The interest allowance provided in paragraphs (d)(3)(x), (e)(2) and (f)(2)(ii) of this section shall be made in cash in the amount determined under this section and shall be included in determining the limit on the claim amount.

(c) *Shared appreciation mortgages.* The terms *loan balance* and *accrued interest* as used in this section do not include interest attributable to the mortgagee's share of the appreciated value of the property.

(d) *Amount of payment—mortgagee acquires title or is unsuccessful bidder.* This paragraph describes the amount of payment if the mortgagee acquires title by purchase, foreclosure, or deed in lieu of foreclosure, or when a party other than the mortgagee is the successful bidder at the foreclosure sale.

(1) *Due and payable date* means the date when the mortgagee notifies or should have notified the Commissioner that the mortgage is due and payable under the conditions stated in the mortgage, as required by §206.27(c)(1) or the date that the Deferral Period, as provided for in the mortgage by §206.27(c)(3), ends; or the date the Commissioner approved a due and payable request as provided for in the mortgage by §206.27(c)(2).

(2) The amount of the claim shall be computed by:

(i) Totaling the outstanding loan balance and any accrued interest and servicing fees which have not been added to the outstanding loan balance as of the due and payable date, and allowances for items set forth in paragraph (d)(3) of this section; and

(ii) Subtracting from that total the amount for which the property was sold (or the appraised value determined

under §206.127(a)(2)) and the items set forth in paragraph (d)(4) of this section.

(3) The claim shall include items listed in paragraphs (d)(3)(i) through (xiv) of this section. For HECMs with Case Numbers assigned on or after September 19, 2017, the inclusion of items listed in paragraphs (d)(3)(i), (ii), and (iii) of this section shall be limited to two-thirds of advances made by the mortgagee on such expenses.

(i) Taxes, ground rents, water rates, and utility charges that are liens prior to the mortgage;

(ii) Special assessments, which are noted on the application for insurance or which become liens after the insurance of the mortgage;

(iii) Hazard and flood insurance premiums on the mortgaged property not in excess of a *reasonable rate;*

(A) For purposes of this section, *reasonable rate* means a rate that is not in excess of the rate or advisory rate set by the principal State-licensed rating organization for essential property insurance in the voluntary market, or if coverage is available under a FAIR Plan, the FAIR Plan rate;

(B) If a State has neither a FAIR Plan nor a State-licensed rating organization for essential property insurance in the voluntary market, the mortgagee must provide to the Home Ownership Center (HOC) having jurisdiction, information concerning the lowest rates available from an insurer for the types of coverage involved, with a request for a determination of whether the rate is reasonable. FHA will determine the rate to be reasonable if it approximates the rate assessed for comparable insurance coverage applicable to similarly situated properties in a State that offers a FAIR Plan or maintains a State-licensed rating organization;

(iv) Taxes imposed upon any deeds or other instruments by which said property was acquired by the mortgagee pursuant to §206.125;

(v) Reasonable payments made by the mortgagee, with the approval of the Commissioner, for the purpose of protecting, operating, or preserving the property, or removing debris from the property;

(vi) Reasonable costs for performing property inspections required by

§ 206.140 and to determine if the property is vacant or abandoned are considered to be costs of protecting, operating or preserving the property;

(vii) Charges for the administration, operation, maintenance, or repair of community-owned property or the maintenance or repair of the mortgaged property, paid by the mortgagee for the purpose of discharging an obligation arising out of a covenant filed for record prior to the issuance of the mortgage; and charges for the repair or maintenance of the mortgaged property required by, and in an amount approved by, the Commissioner under § 206.142;

(viii) Reasonable costs of the title search ordered by the mortgagee, in accordance with procedures prescribed by FHA, to determine if the criteria for approval of the mortgagee's acceptance of a deed in lieu of foreclosure or to determine clear title to complete a pre-foreclosure sale;

(ix) Foreclosure costs or costs of acquiring the property in accordance with such conditions as the Commissioner shall prescribe;

(x) An amount equal to the interest allowance which would have been earned, from the due and payable date to the date when payment of the claim is made, if the claim had been paid in debentures, except that when the mortgagee fails to meet any one of the applicable requirements of §§ 206.125 and 206.127 of this subpart within the specified time, and in a manner satisfactory to the Commissioner (or within such further time as the Commissioner may approve in writing), the interest allowance in such cash payment shall be computed only to the date on which the particular required action should have been taken or to which it was extended.

(A) *Debenture interest rate.* The debenture interest rate provided for in § 206.146 shall be used.

(B) *Maturity of debentures.* Debentures shall mature 20 years from the date of issue.

(C) *Registration of debentures.* Debentures shall be registered as to principal and interest.

(D) *Form and amounts of debentures.* Debentures issued under this part shall be in such form and amounts; and shall be subject to such terms and conditions; and shall include such provisions for redemption, if any, as may be prescribed by the Commissioner, with the approval of the Secretary of the Treasury; and may be in book entry or certificated registered form, or such other form as the Commissioner by regulation may prescribe.

(E) *Redemption of debentures.* Debentures shall, at the option of the Commissioner and with the approval of the Secretary of the Treasury, be redeemable at par plus accrued interest on any semiannual interest payment date on three months' notice of redemption given in such manner as the Commissioner shall prescribe. The debenture interest on the debentures called for redemption shall cease on the semiannual interest payment date designated in the call notice. The Commissioner may include with the notice of redemption an offer to purchase the debentures at par plus accrued interest at any time during the period between the notice of redemption and the redemption date. If the debentures are purchased by the Commissioner after such call and prior to the named redemption date, the debenture interest shall cease on the date of purchase.

(F) *Issue date of debentures.* The issue date of debentures is determined by the due and payable date as defined in paragraph (d)(1) of this section.

(G) *Cash adjustment.* Any difference of less than $50 between the amount of debentures to be issued to the mortgagee and the total amount of the mortgagee's claim, as approved by the Commissioner, may be adjusted by the issuance of a check in payment thereof;

(xi) Any amount of incentive paid by the mortgagee in accordance with § 206.125(f)(1)(ii) or § 206.125(g)(4);

(xii) Costs of any appraisal under §§ 206.125 or 206.127, provided that the property was appraised after the mortgage became due and payable and that the mortgagee is not otherwise reimbursed for such costs;

(xiii) Reasonable payments made by the mortgagee for:

(A) Preservation and maintenance of the property;

(B) Repairs necessary to meet the objectives of the property standards required for mortgages insured by the

Commissioner, those required by local law, and such additional repairs as may be specifically approved in advance by the Commissioner; and

(C) Expenses in connection with the sale of the property including a sales commission at the rate customarily paid in the community and, if the sale to the buyer involves a mortgage insured by the Commissioner or guaranteed by the Secretary of Veterans Affairs, a discount at a rate not to exceed the maximum allowable by the Commissioner, as of the date of execution of the discounted loan. Closing costs shall not exceed the greater of: 11 percent of the sales price; or a fixed dollar amount as determined by the Commissioner through FEDERAL REGISTER notice; and

(xiv) A certification that the property is undamaged in accordance with §206.143.

(4) There shall be deducted from the amount computed in paragraph (d)(2)(i) of this section:

(i) The items listed in §206.145; and

(ii) Any adjustment for damage or neglect to the property pursuant to §§206.140, 206.141, and 206.142.

(e) *Amount of payment—assigned mortgages.* This paragraph describes the amount of payment if the mortgagee assigns a mortgage to the Commissioner under §206.107(a)(1) or §206.121(b).

(1) When a mortgagee assigns a mortgage which is eligible for assignment under §206.107(a)(1), the amount of payment shall be computed by subtracting from the outstanding loan balance on the date of assignment all cash retained by the mortgagee, including amounts held or deposited for the account of the borrower or to which it is entitled under the mortgage transaction that have not been applied in reduction of the principal mortgage indebtedness, and any adjustments for damage or neglect to the property pursuant to §§206.140, 206.141 and 206.142.

(2) The claim shall also include:

(i) Reimbursement for such costs and attorney's fees as the Commissioner finds were properly incurred in connection with the assignment of the mortgage to the Commissioner; and

(ii) An amount equivalent to the interest allowance which will have been earned from the date the mortgage was assigned to the Commissioner to the date the claim is paid, if the claim had been paid in debentures, except that if the mortgagee fails to meet any of the requirements of §206.127(c), or §206.131 if applicable, within the specified time and in a manner satisfactory to the Commissioner (or within such further time as the Commissioner may approve in writing), the interest allowance in the payment of the claim shall be computed only to the date on which the particular required action should have been taken or to which it was extended. The provisions of paragraphs (d)(3)(x)(A)-(G) of this section pertaining to debentures are applicable except that the issue date of the debentures shall be the date the mortgage was assigned to the Commissioner.

(3) When a mortgagee assigns a mortgage under §206.121(b) after demand by the Commissioner, the mortgagee will not receive the entire claim payment as contained in paragraphs (e)(1) and (2) of this section. The amount of the claim shall be computed by totaling the payments made by the mortgagee to the borrower or for the benefit of the borrower, and subtracting from the total the cash retained by the mortgagee, including amounts held or deposited for the account of the borrower or to which it is entitled under the mortgage transaction that have not been applied in reduction of the principal mortgage indebtedness, and any adjustments for damage or neglect to the property pursuant to §§206.141 and 206.142. The claim shall also be reduced by an amount determined by the Commissioner to reimburse the Commissioner for administrative expenses incurred in assuming the mortgagee's responsibility under the mortgage, which may include expenses for staff time. If more than one mortgage is assigned to the Commissioner, the administrative expenses incurred for all the mortgages assigned shall be allocated among the mortgages as determined by the Commissioner. The claim shall not include accrued interest whether or not it has been included in the loan balance.

(f) *Amount of payment-borrower sells the property.* This paragraph describes the amount of payment if the property is sold in accordance with §206.125(c) to

285

one other than the mortgagee for less than the outstanding loan balance, and the mortgagee releases the mortgage to facilitate the sale.

(1)(i) *For HECMs assigned Case Numbers prior to September 19, 2017*, the amount of the claim shall be computed by totaling the outstanding loan balance and any accrued interest and servicing fees which have not been added to the outstanding loan balance on the date the deed is recorded, and an allowance for items set forth in paragraphs (d)(3)(i)–(vii) and (d)(3)(xii) of this section, and subtracting from the total the amount for which the property was sold.

(ii) *For HECMs assigned Case Numbers on or after September 19, 2017, the following provisions apply:*

(A) *When the loan is not in due and payable status.* The amount of the claim shall be computed by totaling the outstanding loan balance and any accrued interest and servicing fees which have not been added to the outstanding loan balance on the date the deed is recorded, and an allowance for items set forth in paragraph (d)(3)(xiii)(C) of this section, and subtracting from the total the amount for which the property was sold.

(B) *When the loan is in due and payable status.* The amount of the claim shall be computed by totaling the outstanding loan balance and any accrued interest and servicing fees which have not been added to the outstanding loan balance as of the due date, the items set forth in paragraph (d)(3) of this section, and subtracting from the total the amount for which the property was sold.

(2)(i) *For HECMs assigned Case Numbers prior to September 19, 2017*, the claim shall also include an amount equivalent to the interest allowance which would have been earned from the date the deed is recorded to the date when payment of the claim is made, if the claim had been paid in debentures, and in a manner satisfactory to the Commissioner; the interest allowance in such cash payment shall be computed only to the date on which the particular action should have been taken or to which it was extended. The provisions of paragraphs (d)(3)(x)(A)-(G) of this section pertaining to debentures

apply except that the issue date of the debentures is the date the deed is recorded instead of the due date.

(ii) *For HECMs assigned Case Numbers on or after September 19, 2017, the following provisions apply:*

(A) *When the loan is not in due and payable status.* The claim shall also include an amount equivalent to the interest allowance which would have been earned from the date the deed is recorded to the date when payment of the claim is made, if the claim had been paid in debentures, and in a manner satisfactory to the Commissioner; the interest allowance in such cash payment shall be computed only to the date on which the particular action should have been taken or to which it was extended. The provisions of paragraphs (d)(3)(x)(A)-(G) of this section pertaining to debentures apply except that the issue date of the debentures shall be the date the deed is recorded.

(B) *When the loan is in due and payable status.* The claim shall also include an amount equivalent to the interest allowance which would have been earned from the due and payable date to the date when payment of the claim is made, if the claim had been paid in debentures, except that when the mortgagee fails to meet any of the applicable requirements of §§ 206.125 and 206.127 within the specified time determined by the due and payable date, as defined in paragraph (d)(1) of this section (or within such further time as the Commissioner may approve in writing), and in a manner satisfactory to the Commissioner; the interest allowance in such cash payment shall be computed only to the date on which the particular action should have been taken or to which it was extended. The provisions of paragraphs (d)(3)(x)(A)-(G) of this section pertaining to debentures apply.

CONDOMINIUMS

§ 206.131 Contract rights and obligations for mortgages on individual dwelling units in a condominium.

(a) *Additional requirements.* The requirements of this subpart shall be applicable to mortgages on individual dwelling units in a condominium, except as modified by this section.

(b) *References.* The term *property* as used in this subpart shall be construed to include the individual dwelling unit and the undivided interest in the common areas and facilities as may be designated.

(c) *Assignment of the mortgage.* If the mortgagee assigns the mortgage on the individual dwelling unit to the Commissioner, the mortgagee shall certify:

(1) To any changes in the plan of apartment ownership including the administration of the property;

(2) That as of the date the assignment is filed for record, the family unit is assessed and subject to assessment for taxes pertaining only to that unit; and

(3) To the condition of the property as of the date the assignment is filed for record. Section 234.275 of this chapter concerning the certification of condition is incorporated by reference.

(d) *Condition of the multifamily structure.* The provisions of §234.270 (a) and (b) of this chapter concerning the condition of the multifamily structure in which the property is located shall be applicable to mortgages insured under this part which are assigned to the Commissioner.

TERMINATION OF INSURANCE CONTRACT

§206.133 Termination of insurance contract.

(a) *Payment of the mortgage.* The contract of insurance shall be terminated if the mortgage is paid in full.

(b) *Acquisition of title.* (1) If the mortgagee or a party other than the mortgagee acquires title at a foreclosure sale, or the mortgagee acquires title by a deed in lieu of foreclosure, and the mortgagee notifies the Commissioner that a claim for the payment of the insurance benefits will not be presented, the contract of insurance shall be terminated.

(2) For HECMs with Case Numbers assigned on or after September 19, 2017, if the mortgagee or a party other than the mortgagee acquires title at a foreclosure sale or the mortgagee acquires title by a deed in lieu of foreclosure and a claim for the payment of the insurance benefits will be presented, the contract of insurance shall be terminated as of claim payment.

(c) *Mortgagee fails to make payments.* If the mortgagee fails to make the payments to the borrower as required under the mortgage, and does not reimburse the Commissioner or assign the mortgage to the Commissioner within 30 days from the demand by the Commissioner for reimbursement or assignment, the contract of insurance shall automatically terminate. The Commissioner may later reinstate the contract of insurance, which shall continue in force as if no termination had occurred, upon reimbursement with interest as provided in §206.121. Upon reinstatement, the mortgagee shall be liable for all MIP which would have been due if no termination had occurred, including late charge and interest as provided in §206.113.

(d) *Notice of termination.* The mortgagee shall give written notice to the Commissioner, or other notice acceptable to the Commissioner, within 15 days of the occurrence of an event under paragraphs (a) and (b) of this section. No contract of insurance shall be terminated under paragraphs (a) or (b) of this section unless such notice is given.

(e) *Voluntary termination.* The mortgagor and the mortgagee may jointly request the Commissioner to approve the voluntary termination of the mortgage insurance contract. Prior to approval, the Commissioner shall make certain that the borrower is aware of the consequences which could arise out of the voluntary termination of the contract of insurance. The mortgagee shall cancel the insurance endorsement on the Mortgage Insurance Certificate or Note upon receipt of notice from the Commissioner that the contract of insurance is terminated. Notwithstanding any provision in a mortgage instrument, there shall be no voluntary termination charge due the Commissioner on account of the voluntary termination of any mortgage insurance contract where the request for termination is received by the Commissioner.

(f) *Effect of termination.* When the insurance contract is terminated, all rights of the mortgagee shall terminate, including the right to file a claim for insurance benefits. All obligations of the Commissioner shall also cease immediately.

ADDITIONAL REQUIREMENTS

§ 206.134 Partial release, addition or substitution of security.

(a) A mortgagee shall not release the security or any part thereof, while the mortgage is insured, without the prior consent of the Commissioner.

(b) A mortgagee may, with the prior consent of the Commissioner, accept an addition to, or substitution of, security for the purpose of removing the dwelling to a new lot or replacing the dwelling with a similar or like kind on the existing lot under the following conditions:

(1) The mortgagee obtains a good and valid first lien on the property to which the dwelling is removed or the existing lot upon which the dwelling is rebuilt;

(2) All damages to the structure are repaired or all rebuilding of the structure is completed without cost to FHA; and

(3) The property to which the dwelling is removed or rebuilt is in an area known to be reasonably free from natural hazards or, if in a flood zone, the borrower will insure or reinsure under the National Flood Insurance Program.

(c) A mortgagee may, without the prior consent of the Commissioner, accept an addition to, or substitution of, security for the purpose of removing the dwelling to a new lot under the following conditions:

(1) The dwelling has survived an earthquake or other disaster with little damage, but continued location on the property might be hazardous;

(2) The conditions stated in paragraph (b) of this section exist; and

(3) Immediately following the emergency removal the mortgagee notifies the Commissioner of the reasons for removal.

§ 206.135 Application for insurance benefits and fiscal data.

(a) On the date the application for assignment is filed, the mortgagee shall submit to the Commissioner:

(1) *Credit and security instrument.* The original credit and security instruments assigned without recourse or warranty, except that no act or omission of the mortgagee shall have impaired the validity and priority of the mortgage.

(2) *Proposed assignment instrument.* A copy of the proposed assignment of mortgage.

(3) *Hazard and flood insurance.* All hazard and flood insurance (if applicable) policies held in connection with the mortgaged property, together with a copy of the mortgagee's notification to the carrier authorizing the amendment of the loss payable clause substituting the Commissioner as the mortgagee.

(4) *Rights and interests.* An assignment of all rights and interests arising under the mortgage, and all claims of the mortgagee against the borrower or others arising out of the mortgage transaction.

(5) *Property.* All property of the borrower held by the mortgagee or to which it is entitled (other than cash items which are to be retained by the mortgagee).

(6) *Records and accounts.* All records, ledger cards, documents, books, papers and accounts relating to the mortgage transaction.

(7) *Additional information.* Any additional information or data which the Commissioner may require.

(8) *Title evidence.* All title evidence held by the mortgagee. It need not be extended to include the recordation of the assignment. The title insurance policy shall be endorsed from the mortgage insurance company up to the point of assignment. At the point of assignment, the Commissioner shall be named insured under such policy.

(b) All documents required in paragraph (a) of this section must be submitted and approved before a claim for assignment may be submitted.

(c) *Recorded assignment instrument.* The original of the recorded assignment of mortgage shall be forwarded to the Commissioner as soon as received by the mortgagee, but in no case shall it be longer than 12 months after recordation. If the original of the assignment is not available, a copy shall be furnished and the original forwarded as soon as possible.

288

§ 206.136 Conditions for assignment.

(a) In order for a HECM to be eligible for assignment, the following must be met:

(1) *Priority of mortgage to liens.* The mortgage is prior to all mechanics' and materialmen's liens, regardless of when such liens attach, and prior to all liens and encumbrances, or defects which may arise based on any act or omission by the mortgagee except such liens or other matters as may have been approved by the Commissioner.

(2) *Amount due.* The amount stated in the instrument of assignment is actually due and owing under the mortgage.

(3) *Offsets or counterclaims.* There are no offsets or counterclaims thereto and the mortgagee has a good right to assign.

(b) The mortgagee shall certify that the conditions of paragraph (a) have been met.

§ 206.137 Effect of noncompliance with regulations.

If, for any reason, the mortgagee fails to comply with the regulations in this subpart, the Commissioner may hold processing of the application for insurance benefits in abeyance for a reasonable time in order to permit the mortgagee to comply. In the alternative to holding processing in abeyance, the Commissioner may reconvey title to the property or reassign the mortgage to the mortgagee, in which event the application for insurance benefits shall be considered as cancelled and the mortgagee shall refund the insurance benefits to the Commissioner as well as other funds required by §206.138. The mortgagee may reapply for insurance benefits at a subsequent date; provided, however, that the mortgagee may not be reimbursed for any expenses incurred in connection with the property after it has been reconveyed or the mortgage reassigned by the Commissioner, or paid any debenture interest accrued after the date of initial conveyance, whichever is earlier, and there will be deducted from the insurance benefits any reduction in the Commissioner's estimate of the value of the property occurring from the time of reconveyance or mortgage

reassignment to the time of reapplication.

§ 206.138 Mortgagee's liability for certain expenditures.

Where the Commissioner accepts an assignment, acquires a property after accepting an assignment of a mortgage, or otherwise pays a claim for insurance benefits and thereafter it becomes necessary for the Commissioner to either reconvey the property or reassign the mortgage to the mortgagee due to the mortgagee's noncompliance with these regulations, the mortgagee shall reimburse the Commissioner for all expenses incurred in connection with such acquisition and reconveyance or reassignment. The reimbursement shall include interest on the amount of insurance benefits refunded by the mortgagee from the date the insurance benefits were paid to the date of refund at an interest rate set in conformity with the Treasury Fiscal Requirements Manual, and the Commissioner's cost of holding the property or servicing the mortgage, accruing on a daily basis, from the date of assignment or claim payment to the date of reconveyance or reassignment. These costs are based on the Commissioner's estimate of the taxes, maintenance and operating expenses of the property, and administrative expenses. Appropriate adjustments shall be made by the Commissioner on account of any income received from the property.

§ 206.140 Inspection and preservation of properties.

The mortgagee, upon learning that a property subject to a mortgage insured under this part is vacant or abandoned, shall be responsible for the inspection of such property at least monthly, if the loan is in a due and payable status. When a mortgage is in due and payable status and efforts to reach the borrower or applicable party by telephone within that period have been unsuccessful, the mortgagee shall be responsible for a visual inspection of the security property to determine whether the property is vacant. The mortgagee shall take reasonable action to protect and preserve such security property when it is determined or should have been determined to be vacant or abandoned until assigned to the Commissioner or an application for insurance benefits is filed, if such action does not constitute an illegal trespass. "Reasonable action" includes the commencement of foreclosure within the time required by § 206.125.

§ 206.141 Property condition.

(a) *Condition at time of transfer.* When the mortgage is assigned to the Commissioner or the property is sold by the mortgagee, the property shall be undamaged by fire, earthquake, flood, or tornado, except as set forth in this subpart.

(b) *Damage to property by waste.* The mortgagee shall not be liable for damage to the property by waste committed by the borrower, its heirs, successors or assigns in connection with mortgage insurance claims.

(c) *Mortgagee responsibility.* The mortgagee shall be responsible for:

(1) Damage by fire, flood, earthquake, hurricane, or tornado; and

(2) Damage to or destruction of security properties on which the loans are in default and which properties are vacant or abandoned, when such damage or destruction is due to the mortgagee's failure to take reasonable action to inspect, protect and preserve such properties as required by § 206.140.

(d) *Limitation.* The mortgagee's responsibility for property damage shall not exceed the amount of its insurance claim as to a particular property.

§ 206.142 Adjustment for damage or neglect.

(a) Except as provided for in paragraphs (a)(1) and (a)(2) of this section: if the property has been damaged by fire, flood, earthquake, hurricane, or tornado, the damage must be repaired before assignment of the mortgage to the Commissioner; if the property has suffered damage because of the mortgagee's failure to take action as required by § 206.140, the damage must be repaired before the mortgagee sells the property.

(1) If the prior approval of the Commissioner is obtained, there will be deducted from the insurance benefits the Commissioner's estimate of the cost of repairing the damage or any insurance recovery received by the mortgagee, whichever is greater.

(2) If the property has been damaged by fire and was not covered by fire insurance at the time of the damage, or the amount of insurance coverage was inadequate to repair fully the damage, only the amount of insurance recovery received by the mortgagee, if any, will be deducted from the insurance benefits, provided the mortgagee certifies, at the time that a claim is filed for insurance benefits, that:

(i) At the time the mortgage was insured, the property was covered by fire insurance in an amount at least equal to the lesser of 100 percent of the insurable value of the improvements, or the principal loan balance of the mortgage;

(ii) The insurer later cancelled this coverage or refused to renew it for reasons other than nonpayment of premium;

(iii) The mortgagee made diligent though unsuccessful efforts within 30 days of any cancellation or non-renewal of hazard insurance, and at least annually thereafter, to secure other coverage or coverage under a FAIR Plan, in an amount described in paragraph (a)(2)(i) of this section, or if coverage to such an extent was unavailable at a reasonable rate, the greatest extent of coverage that was available at a reasonable rate;

(iv) The extent of coverage obtained by the mortgagee in accordance with paragraph (a)(2)(iii) of this section was the greatest available at a reasonable rate, or if the mortgagee was unable to obtain insurance, none was available at a reasonable rate; and

(v) The mortgagee took the actions required by § 206.140.

(b) If the property has been damaged during the time of the mortgagee's possession by events other than fire, flood, earthquake, hurricane, or tornado, or if it was damaged notwithstanding reasonable action by the mortgagee as required by § 206.140, the mortgagee must provide notice of such damage to the Commissioner and may not sell the property until directed to do so by the Commissioner. The Commissioner will either:

(1) Allow the mortgagee to sell the property damaged; or

(2) Require the mortgagee to repair the damage before sale, and the Commissioner will reimburse the mortgagee for reasonable payments not in excess of the Commissioner's estimate of the cost of repair, less any insurance recovery.

§206.143   Certificate of property condition.

(a) The mortgagee shall certify that as of the date the mortgagee sold the property in accordance with §206.125(g) or assignment of the mortgage to the Commissioner, the property was:

(1) Undamaged by fire, flood, earthquake, hurricane or tornado; and

(2) Undamaged due to failure of the mortgagee to take action as required by §206.140; and

(3) Undamaged while the property was in the possession of the mortgagee.

(b) In the absence of evidence to the contrary, the mortgagee's certificate or description of the damage shall be accepted by the Commissioner as establishing the condition of the property, as of the date of mortgagee sale or assignment of the mortgage to the Commissioner.

§206.144   Final payment.

The mortgagee may not file any supplemental claims to its mortgage insurance claim after six months from settlement by the Commissioner of the claim payment except where the Commissioner determines it appropriate and expressly authorizes an extension of time for supplemental claim filings.

§206.145   Items deducted from payment.

(a) There shall be deducted from the total of the added items in §206.129 the following cash items:

(1) All amounts received by the mortgagee on account of the mortgage after the institution of foreclosure proceedings or the acquisition of the property or otherwise after due and payable.

(2) All amounts received by the mortgagee from any source relating to the property on account of rent or other income after deducting reasonable expenses incurred in handling the property.

(3) All cash retained by the mortgagee including amounts held or deposited for the account of the borrower or to which it is entitled under the mortgage transaction that have not been applied in reduction of the outstanding loan balance.

(4) With regard to claims filed pursuant to successful short sales, all amounts received by the mortgagee relating to the sale of the property.

(b) [Reserved]

§206.146   Debenture interest rate.

(a) Debentures shall bear interest from the date of issue, payable semiannually on the first day of January and the first day of July of each year at the rate in effect as of the day the commitment was issued, or as of the date the mortgage was endorsed for insurance, whichever rate is higher. For applications involving mortgages originated under the single family Direct Endorsement program, debentures shall bear interest from the date of issue, payable semiannually on the first day of January and on the first day of July of each year at the rate in effect as of the date the mortgage was endorsed for insurance;

(b) For mortgages endorsed for insurance after January 23, 2004, if an insurance claim is paid in cash, the debenture interest rate for purposes of calculating such a claim shall be the monthly average yield, for the month in which the default on the mortgage occurred, on United States Treasury Securities adjusted to a constant maturity of 10 years.

Subpart D—Servicing Responsibilities

§206.201   Mortgage servicing generally; sanctions.

(a) *General.* This subpart identifies servicing practices that the Commissioner considers acceptable mortgage servicing practices of lending institutions servicing mortgages insured by the Commissioner. Failure to comply with this subpart shall not be a basis for denial of the insurance benefits, but a pattern of refusal or failure to comply will be cause for withdrawal of FHA mortgagee approval.

(b) *Importance of timely payments.* The paramount servicing responsibility is to make timely payments in full as required by the mortgage. Any failure of a mortgagee to make all payments required by the mortgage in a timely manner will be grounds for administrative sanctions authorized by regulations, including 2 CFR part 2424 (Debarment, Suspension, and Limited Denial of Participation), and 24 CFR part 25 (Mortgagee Review Board).

(c) *Responsibility for servicing.* (1) Servicing of insured mortgages must be performed by a mortgagee that is approved by FHA to service insured mortgages. The servicer must fully discharge the servicing responsibilities of the mortgagee as outlined in this part. The mortgagee shall remain fully responsible to the Commissioner for proper servicing, and the actions of its servicer shall be considered to be the actions of the mortgagee. The servicer also shall be fully responsible to the Commissioner for its actions as a servicer.

(2) Whenever servicing of any mortgage is transferred from one mortgagee or servicer to another, notice of the transfer of service shall be delivered:

(i) By the transferor mortgagee or servicer to the borrower. The notification shall be delivered not less than 15 days before the effective date of the transfer and shall contain the information required in 12 CFR 1024.33(b)(4); and

(ii) By the transferee mortgagee or servicer:

(A) *To the borrower.* The notification shall be delivered not less than 15 days before the effective date of the transfer and shall contain the information required in 12 CFR 1024.33(b)(4); and

(B) *To the Commissioner.* This notification shall be delivered within 15 days of the transfer, in a format prescribed by the Commissioner.

§ 206.203   Providing information.

(a) *Statements of account activity.* The mortgagee shall provide to the borrower a monthly statement regarding the activity of the mortgage for each month, as well as for the calendar year. The statement shall summarize the total principal amount which has been paid to the borrower under the mortgage during that calendar year, the MIP paid to the Commissioner and charged to the borrower, the total amount of deferred interest added to the outstanding loan balance, the total outstanding loan balance, and the current principal limit. The mortgagee shall include an accounting of all payments for property charges. The statement shall be provided to the borrower monthly until the mortgage is paid in full by the borrower. The mortgagee shall provide the borrower with a new payment plan every time it recalculates monthly payments or the payment option is changed. The statements shall be in a format acceptable to the Commissioner.

(b) [Reserved]

(c) *Servicing—Providing information.* (1) Mortgagees shall provide loan information to borrowers and arrange for individual loan consultation on request. The mortgagee must establish written procedures and controls to assure prompt responses to inquiries. One or more of the following means of making information readily available to borrowers is required:

(i) A servicing office staffed with competent personnel located within 200 miles of the property, capable of providing timely responses to requests for information. Complete records need not be maintained in such an office if the staff is able to secure needed information and pass it on to the borrower.

(ii) Toll-free telephone service at an office capable of providing needed information.

(2)(i) All borrowers must be informed of and reminded annually of the system available for obtaining answers to loan inquiries and the office from which needed information may be obtained. Toll-free telephone service need not be provided to a borrower other than at the office designated to serve the borrower nor other than from the immediate vicinity of the security property.

(ii) The mortgagee shall provide the borrower with the telephone number where the borrower may speak to employee(s) specifically designated by the mortgagee or its servicer to address inquiries concerning mortgages insured under this part. Such information shall be provided annually and whenever the servicer or the designated employee (or employee group) changes.

(3) Mortgagees must respond to FHA requests for information concerning individual accounts.

§206.205 Property charges.

(a) *General*. (1) The borrower shall be responsible for the payment of the following property charges before or on the due date: ground rents, condominium fees, planned unit development fees, and homeowners' association fees.

(2) Payment of the following property charges are obligations of the borrower and shall be made through the LESA, by the borrower, or by the mortgagee, in accordance with paragraphs (b) through (e) of this section on or before the due date: property taxes, including any special assessments levied by local or State law, hazard insurance premiums, and applicable flood insurance premiums.

(b) *Method of property charge payment*—(1) *LESA required*. For fixed or adjustable interest rate HECMs, based on the results of the Financial Assessment, the mortgagee may require the borrower to have a Fully-Funded LESA for the payment of property charges identified in paragraph (a)(2) of this section. For adjustable interest rate HECMs, based on the results of the Financial Assessment, the mortgagee may require the borrower to have a Partially-Funded LESA for the payment of property charges identified in paragraph (a)(2) of this section.

(2) *LESA not required*. (i) If, based on the results of the Financial Assessment, the mortgagee does not require the borrower to have a LESA, the borrower shall elect one of the following at closing, whereby an election of the option in paragraph (b)(2)(i)(B) or (C) of this section cannot be cancelled by the borrower:

(A) Borrower is responsible for the independent payment of all property charges;

(B) Borrower elects to have a Fully-Funded LESA for the payment of property charges identified in paragraph (a)(2) of this section; or

(C) For adjustable interest rate HECMs only, borrower elects to have the mortgagee pay property charges listed in paragraph (a)(2) of this section

which would have otherwise been required to be paid by the borrower, in accordance with paragraph (d) of this section.

(ii) Through FEDERAL REGISTER notice, the Commissioner may establish an incentive for voluntarily electing a LESA under paragraph (b)(2)(i)(B) of this section.

(c) *Life Expectancy Set Aside*—(1) *General*. (i) For a Fully-Funded LESA, the mortgagee shall:

(A) Make payments for property charges identified in paragraph (a)(2) of this section before bills become delinquent and establish controls to ensure that the information needed to pay such bills is obtained on a timely basis;

(B) Make early payments to take advantage of a discount whenever it is to the borrower's advantage;

(C) Not charge the borrower penalties for late payments for property charges unless it can be shown that the penalty was the direct result of the borrower's error or omission;

(D) Ensure that LESA funds are not held in an escrow account;

(E) Add payments for property charges to the outstanding loan balance when the mortgagee disburses funds to the taxing authority or insurance carrier; and

(F) Provide written notification to the borrower and FHA within 30 days of the mortgagee receiving notification that a property charge payment is outstanding when there are no funds or insufficient funds remaining in the LESA, and recommend that the borrower speak with a HUD-Approved Housing Counselor.

(ii) For a Partially-Funded LESA, the mortgagee shall:

(A) Ensure that LESA funds are disbursed to the borrower semi-annually;

(B) Establish controls to ensure the taxing authority, insurance carrier, or both, received the borrower's payment;

(C) Ensure the LESA funds are not held in an escrow account;

(D) Add payments disbursed to the borrower for the payment of property charges identified in paragraph (a)(2) to the outstanding loan balance when the mortgagee disburses the funds; and

(E) Provide written notification to the borrower and FHA within 30 days of the mortgagee receiving notification that a property charge payment is outstanding when there are no funds or insufficient funds remaining in the LESA, and recommend that the borrower speak with a HUD-Approved Housing Counselor.

(2) *Calculation of property charges.* (i) The projected cost of property charges that will be required over the life expectancy of the youngest borrower shall be calculated based on a formula established by the Commissioner.

(ii) The mortgagee shall not require any LESA to be funded in excess of the projected cost of property charges.

(iii) For a Fully-Funded LESA, the amount withheld from the mortgage proceeds shall equal the projected cost of property charges.

(iv) For a Partially-Funded LESA, the amount withheld from the mortgage proceeds is based on a calculation of the gap in residual income and may not exceed the projected cost of property charges.

(v) Mortgagees shall use the *HECM Financial Assessment and Property Charge Guide,* or subsequent guide issued by the Commissioner, to determine whether a LESA is required; view the formula for calculating the projected costs of property charges; and view the formulas for calculating the Fully- and Partially-Funded LESA amounts.

(3) *Annual analysis of LESA.* Mortgagees shall perform an annual analysis of the LESA to determine whether the funds are sufficient to make required distributions for the next year. If funds are exhausted or there is an insufficient balance determination, the mortgagee shall notify the borrower, in writing and within 15 calendar days of the annual analysis of the determination, that LESA funds are exhausted or insufficient and the borrower will be responsible for the payment of property charges.

(4) *Non-payment of property charges—* (i) *Fully-Funded LESA for an adjustable interest rate HECM with no remaining funds.* (A) If the LESA is exhausted and the borrower fails to make property charge payments, the mortgagee shall use any available principal limit to pay the outstanding property charge amount in full and charge the borrower's account.

(B) The mortgagee shall provide the borrower with a written notification within 30 days of the mortgagee receiving notification that a property charge payment is outstanding. The borrower shall have 30 days to respond to the mortgagee to explain the circumstances which resulted in the nonpayment. (C) If there is no available principal limit from which the mortgagee can pay the property charge amount in full, and the borrower fails to pay the property charges, the mortgage will become due and payable under § 206.27(c)(2).

(ii) *Fully-Funded LESA for a fixed interest rate HECM with no remaining funds.* If the LESA is exhausted and the borrower fails to make property charge payments, the mortgage will become due and payable under § 206.27(c)(2).—

(iii) *Partially-Funded LESA with remaining funds.* If funds remain in the LESA and the borrower fails to make property charge payments, the mortgagee shall:

(A) Immediately suspend future semi-annual payments to the borrower from the Partially-Funded LESA, although scheduled and unscheduled payments from the borrower's payment option may continue;

(B) Disburse funds from the Partially-Funded LESA to pay the full amount owed for the past due property charge; and

(C) Provide written notification to the borrower, within 30 days of the mortgagee receiving notification that a property charge payment is outstanding, that funds were advanced from the Partially-Funded LESA to pay the outstanding property charge. The borrower shall have 30 days to respond to the mortgagee to explain the circumstances which resulted in the non-payment.

(iv) *Partially-Funded LESA with no remaining funds.* (A) If the LESA is exhausted and the borrower fails to make property charge payments when due, the mortgagee shall use any funds available in the principal limit to pay the outstanding property charge amount in full and charge the borrower's account.

(B) The mortgagee shall provide written notification to the borrower within

30 days of the mortgagee receiving notification that a property charge payment is outstanding. The borrower shall have 30 days to respond to the mortgagee to explain the circumstances which resulted in the nonpayment.

(C) If there is no available principal limit from which the mortgagee can pay the property charge amount in full, and the borrower fails to pay the property charges, the mortgage will become due and payable under §206.27(c)(2).

(5) *Unused LESA funds.* During a Deferral Period or when one of the events listed in §206.27(c)(1) or (c)(2) have occurred, no unused funds from the LESA shall be disbursed.

(6) *Assignment of mortgage to the Commissioner.* If the insured first mortgage is assigned to the Commissioner, or if payments are made through the second mortgage under the Demand Assignment process, the Commissioner is not required to assume the responsibility for property charge payments, but may continue to administer payments for property charges for a borrower with a Fully-Funded LESA or semi-annual disbursements to a borrower with a Partially-Funded LESA to the extent that there are any funds available in the LESA. For adjustable interest rate HECMs, if the LESA has a positive remaining balance but funds are insufficient to pay all property charges due or semi-annual disbursements to the borrower, the Commissioner may provide the remaining funds to the borrower as a line of credit.

(d) *Borrower elects to have mortgagee pay property charges.* If, based on the results of the Financial Assessment, the mortgagee does not require the borrower to have a LESA, for adjustable interest rate HECMs, the borrower may elect at closing to require the mortgagee to pay property charges identified in paragraph (a)(2) of this section by withholding funds from monthly payments due to the borrower or by charging such funds to a line of credit. This voluntary election to have funds withheld by the mortgagee to pay property charges cannot be canceled by the borrower at any time. If the sum of the outstanding loan balance and any unused set aside for repairs and servicing charges has reached the principal limit or the HECM proceeds are otherwise insufficient to pay the property charges, the borrower shall pay such property charges, even though the borrower elected payment to be made by the mortgagee. Through FEDERAL REGISTER notice, the Commissioner may expand the borrower's options for property charge payment by the mortgagee.

(1) *Assignment of mortgage to the Commissioner.* If the insured first mortgage is assigned to the Commissioner under §206.107(a)(1) or §206.121(b), or if payments are made through the second mortgage under §206.121(c), the Commissioner is not required to assume the mortgagee's responsibility under paragraph (d) of this section, despite the election by the borrower.

(2) *Mortgagee's responsibilities.* (i) Funds withheld from payments due to the borrower for property charges under paragraph (d) of this section shall not be paid into an escrow account. When property charges are actually paid, the mortgagee may add the amount paid to the outstanding loan balance.

(ii) It is the mortgagee's responsibility to make disbursements for property charges before bills become delinquent. Mortgagees shall establish controls to ensure that the information needed to pay such bills is obtained on a timely basis. Penalties for late payments for property charges must not be charged to the borrower unless it can be shown that the penalty was the direct result of the borrower's error or omission. Early payment of a bill to take advantage of a discount should be made whenever it is to the borrower's benefit.

(iii) Not later than the end of the second loan year the mortgagee shall establish a system for the periodic analysis of the amounts withheld from monthly payments. The analysis shall be performed at least once a year thereafter. The amount shall be adjusted, after analysis, to provide sufficient available funds to make anticipated disbursements during the ensuing year. The borrower shall be given at least ten days' notice of adjustment in the amount of withholding and an adequate explanation of the reasons for any change. When the amount withheld is analyzed in accordance with this paragraph, any surplus shall be paid to the borrower and added to the outstanding loan balance. Any shortage shall be corrected through increasing the monthly withholding as provided in paragraph (d)(2)(iv) of this section. If amounts withheld are insufficient to pay a property charge before it is delinquent, and the borrower could request a payment equal to the shortage under § 206.26(b), then the mortgagee shall pay the full property charge and treat payment of the shortage as a payment requested by the borrower under § 206.26(b).

(iv) The mortgagee's estimate of withholding amount shall be based on the best information available as to probable payments which will be required to be made for property charges in the coming year. If actual disbursements during the preceding year are used as the basis, the resulting estimate may deviate from those disbursements by as much as ten percent. The mortgagee may not require withholding in excess of the current estimated total annual requirement, unless expressly requested by the borrower. Each monthly withholding for property charges shall equal one-twelfth of the annual amounts as reasonably estimated by the mortgagee.

(e) *Borrower elects to pay property charges.* (1) If, based on the results of the Financial Assessment, the mortgagee does not require the borrower to have a LESA, the borrower may elect to be responsible for the independent payment of all property charges and shall pay all property charges in a timely manner and shall provide evidence of payment to the mortgagee as required in the mortgage.

(2) *Failure to pay property charges.* If the borrower fails to pay the property charges in a timely manner, and has not elected to have the mortgagee make the payments in accordance with paragraph (d) of this section:

(i) The mortgagee may make the payment for the borrower and charge the borrower's account if there are available funds from which the mortgagee may make payment. If a pattern of missed payments occurs, the mortgagee may establish procedures to pay the property charges from the borrower's funds as if the borrower elected to have the mortgagee pay the property charges under this section.

(ii) The mortgagee shall provide a written notification to the borrower and notify the Commissioner that an obligation of the mortgage has not been performed within 30 days of the mortgagee receiving notification of a missed payment when there are no available HECM funds from which the mortgagee may make payment. The borrower shall have 30 days to respond to the mortgagee to explain the circumstances which resulted in the nonpayment. The mortgagee may provide any permissible loss mitigation made available by the Commissioner through notice. If the borrower is unable or unwilling to repay the mortgagee for any funds advanced by the mortgagee to pay property charges outside of a LESA, the mortgagee shall submit a due and payable request under the provisions of § 206.27(c)(2).

§ 206.207 **Allowable charges and fees after endorsement.**

(a) *Reasonable and customary charges.* The mortgagee may collect reasonable and customary charges and fees from the borrower after insurance endorsement, only to the extent that the mortgagee is not reimbursed for such fees by FHA, by adding them to the outstanding loan balance, but only for: items listed in paragraph (a)(1) of this section; items authorized by the Commissioner under paragraph (a)(2) of this section, or as provided at § 206.26(b)(1)(iii); or charges and fees related to additional documents described in § 206.27(b)(10) and related title search costs.

(1)(i) Charges for substitution of a hazard insurance policy at other than the expiration of term of the existing hazard insurance policy;

(ii) Attorney's and trustee's fees and expenses actually incurred (including the cost of appraisals and cost of advertising) when a case has been referred for foreclosure in accordance with the provisions of this part after a firm decision to foreclose if foreclosure is not completed because of a reinstatement of the account (no attorney's fee may be charged for the services of the mortgagee's or servicer's staff attorney or for the services of a collection attorney other than the attorney handling the foreclosure);

(iii) A trustee's fee if the security instrument in deed-of-trust states provides for payment of such a fee for execution of a satisfactory, release, or trustee's deed when the deed of trust is paid in full;

(iv) Where permitted by the security instrument, attorney's fees and expenses actually incurred in the defense of any suit or legal proceeding wherein the mortgagee shall be made a party thereto by reason of the mortgage (no attorney's fee may be charged for the services of the mortgagee's or servicer's staff attorney); and

(v) Property preservation expenses incurred pursuant to §206.140.

(2) Such other reasonable and customary charges as may be authorized by the Commissioner, but which shall not include:

(i) Charges for servicing activities of the mortgagee or servicer;

(ii) Fees charged by independent tax service organizations which contract to furnish data and information necessary for the payment of property taxes;

(iii) *Satisfaction, termination,* or *reconveyance* fees when a mortgage is paid in full (other than as provided in paragraph (a)(1)(iii) of this section); or

(iv) The fee for recordation of a satisfaction of the mortgage in states where recordation is the responsibility of the mortgagee.

(b) *Servicing charges.* (1) If the following conditions are met, the mortgagee may include a servicing charge in the mortgage Note rate, starting with the month of loan closing and continuing through the life of the loan, including any applicable Deferral Period:

(i) The charge is authorized by the Commissioner;

(ii) The charge is selected by the mortgagee;

(iii) The charge is within the range established by the Commissioner, which shall be set, through notice, in an amount which shall be between 36 and 150 basis points. The Commissioner may, through a FEDERAL REGISTER notice for comment, extend the range of permissible charges below 36 basis points and above 150 basis points; and

(iv) The charge is disclosed as required by §206.43 to the borrower in a manner acceptable to the Commissioner at the time the mortgagee provides the borrower with a loan application; or

(2) If the following conditions are met, the mortgagee may collect a fixed monthly charge for servicing activities of the mortgagee or servicer, starting with the month of loan closing and continuing through the life of the loan, including any applicable Deferral Period.

(i) The charge is authorized by the Commissioner;

(ii) The charge is disclosed as required by §206.43 to the borrower in a manner acceptable to the Commissioner at the time the mortgagee provides the borrower with a loan application;

(iii) Amounts to pay the charge are set aside as a portion of the principal limit in accordance with §206.19(f)(3); and

(iv) The charge is payable only from the Servicing Fee Set Aside.

§206.209 Prepayment.

(a) *No charge or penalty.* The borrower may repay a mortgage in full or prepay a mortgage in part without charge or penalty at any time, regardless of any limitations on repayment or prepayment stated in a mortgage.

(b) *Insurance and condemnation proceeds.* If insurance or condemnation proceeds are paid to the mortgagee, the principal limit and the outstanding loan balance shall be reduced by the amount of the proceeds not applied to restoration or repair of the damaged property.

(c) Funds received from a partial prepayment shall be applied in accordance with the Note.

§206.211 Determination of principal residence and contact information.

(a) *Annual certification.* At least once during each calendar year, the mortgagee shall verify the contact information for the borrower(s) and determine whether or not the property is the principal residence of at least one borrower. The mortgagee shall require each borrower to make an annual certification of his or her contact information and principal residence. As part of the annual certification, the borrower may designate an alternate individual as specified in § 206.40 to receive copies of the notifications from the mortgagee, and who the mortgagee shall contact if the borrower is unwilling or unable to reply to requests from the mortgagee. The mortgagee may rely on the certification unless it has information indicating that the certification may be false.

(b) *Requirements when an Eligible Non-Borrowing Spouse exists.* Where an Eligible Non-Borrowing Spouse has been identified, the mortgagee shall obtain an additional annual certification from the borrower confirming the Eligible Non-Borrowing Spouse remains his or her spouse and the Eligible Non-Borrowing Spouse continues to reside in the property as his or her principal residence.

(1) *Death of borrower with Eligible Non-Borrowing Spouse.* If a borrower with an Eligible Non-Borrowing Spouse has died, the mortgagee shall obtain the annual certification in paragraph (a) of this section from the Eligible Non-Borrowing Spouse. For purposes of this paragraph, the term "Eligible Non-Borrowing Spouse" shall replace the term "borrower" in paragraph (a) of this section.

(2) *Failure of previously Eligible Non-Borrowing Spouse to reside in the property as his or her principal residence.* If a Non-Borrowing Spouse fails to reside in the property as his or her principal residence, the Non-Borrowing Spouse becomes an Ineligible Non-Borrowing Spouse and the deferral of due and payable status that would prevent the displacement of an Eligible Non-Borrowing Spouse will no longer be in effect. Once this occurs, the Eligible Non-Borrowing Spouse annual certifications are no longer required to be obtained.

Subpart E—HECM Counselor Roster

§ 206.300 General.

This subpart provides for the establishment of the HECM Counselor Roster (Roster) and sets forth the requirements for the operation of the HECM Counselor Roster.

§ 206.302 Establishment of the HECM Counselor Roster.

(a) *HECM Counselor Roster.* FHA maintains a Roster of HECM counselors. Only counselors listed on the Roster and employed by a participating agency are approved to provide HECM counseling. A prospective borrower applying for a HECM loan to be insured by FHA must receive the required HECM counseling from one of the counselors on the Roster.

(b) *Disclaimer.* The inclusion of a HECM counselor on the Roster does not create or imply a warranty or endorsement by FHA of the listed counselor to a prospective HECM borrower or to any other organization or individual, nor does it represent a warranty of any counseling provided by the listed HECM counselor. The inclusion of a counselor on the Roster means that a listed counselor has met the FHA-prescribed qualifications and conditions for inclusion on the Roster and that the counselor is approved to provide HECM counseling by telephone or face-to-face.

§ 206.304 Eligibility for placement on the HECM Counselor Roster.

(a) *Application.* To be considered for placement on the Roster, a housing counselor must apply to FHA in a form and in a manner prescribed by the Commissioner.

(b) *Eligibility.* FHA will approve an application for placement on the Roster if the application demonstrates that the housing counselor:

(1) Is employed by a HUD-approved housing counseling agency or an affiliate of a HUD-approved intermediary or State housing finance agency;

(2) Successfully passed a standardized HECM counseling exam administered by FHA, or a party selected by FHA, within the last 3 years. In order to maintain eligibility, a HECM counselor must successfully pass a standardized HECM counseling exam every 3 years;

(3) Received training and education related to HECMs within the prior 2 years;

(4) Has access to and is supported by technology that enables FHA to track

the results of the counseling offered to each loan applicant, *e.g.*, what action(s), if any, did the client take after receiving the HECM counseling; and

(5) Is not listed on:

(i) The General Services Administration's Suspension and Debarment List;

(ii) HUD's Limited Denial of Participation List; or

(iii) HUD's Credit Alert Interactive Response System.

§206.306 Removal from the HECM Counselor Roster.

(a) *General.* FHA reserves the right to remove a HECM counselor from the Roster, in accordance with this section.

(b) *Cause for removal.* Cause for removal of a HECM counselor from the Roster includes, but is not limited to:

(1) Failure to comply with the education and training requirements of §206.308;

(2) Failure to respond within a reasonable time to HUD inquiries or requests for documentation;

(3) Misrepresentation or fraudulent statements;

(4) Promotion, representation, or recommendation of any specific mortgagee;

(5) Failure to comply with applicable fair housing and civil rights requirements;

(6) Failure to comply with applicable statutes and regulations;

(7) Failure to comply with applicable statutory counseling requirements found at section 255(f) of the National Housing Act, which include, but are not limited to, providing information about: options other than a HECM, the financial implications of entering into a HECM, the tax consequences of a HECM, and any other information that HUD or the applicant may request;

(8) Failure to maintain any registration, license, or certification requirements of a State or local authority;

(9) Unsatisfactory performance in providing counseling to HECM loan applicants. FHA may determine that a HECM counselor's performance is unsatisfactory based on a review of counseling files or other monitoring activities, or if the counselor fails to employ the minimum competencies, as measured by the FHA-administered HECM counseling exam; or

(10) For any other reason HUD determines to be so serious as to justify an administrative sanction.

(c) *Automatic removal from HECM Counselor Roster for failure to maintain required State or local licensure.* A HECM counselor who is required to maintain a State or local registration, license, or certification and whose registration or certification is revoked, suspended, or surrendered will be automatically suspended from the Roster until FHA receives evidence demonstrating that the local- or State-imposed sanction has been lifted.

(d) *Removal procedure.* Except as provided in paragraph (c) of this section, the following procedures apply to removal of a HECM counselor from the Roster.

(1) FHA will give the HECM counselor written notice of the proposed removal. The notice will state the reasons for and the duration of the proposed removal.

(2) The HECM counselor will have 30 days from the date of receipt of the notice (or such time as described in the notice, but in no event less than a period of 30 days) to submit a written appeal of the proposed removal, along with a written request for a conference.

(3) An FHA official will review the appeal and render a response affirming, modifying, or canceling the removal. The FHA official will not be a person who was involved in FHA's initial removal decision. FHA will respond with a decision within 30 days after the date of receiving the appeal or, if the HECM counselor has requested a conference, within 30 days after the conference was held. FHA may extend the 30-day period by providing written notice to the counselor.

(4) If the HECM counselor does not submit a timely written response, the removal will be effective 31 days after the date of FHA's initial removal notice (or after the period provided in the notice, if longer than 30 days). If a written response is submitted, and the removal decision is affirmed or modified, the removal will be effective on the date of FHA's notice affirming or modifying the initial removal decision.

(e) *Maximum time period of removal.* The maximum time period for removal from the Roster is 12 months from the effective date of removal for all removed counselors. A counselor who has been removed must apply for reinstatement on the Roster.

(f) *Placement on the Roster after removal.* A counselor who has been removed from the Roster must apply for reinstatement on the Roster (in accordance with § 206.304) after the period of the counselor's removal from the Roster has expired. FHA may require the counselor to retake and pass the HECM exam for reinstatement when the reason for removal from the Roster was particularly egregious. Typically, the counselor will not be required to take and pass the HECM exam; however, FHA must be ensured by the counselor that the HECM counseling requirements are understood and will be followed. An application from a counselor for reinstatement on the Roster will be rejected if the period of the counselor's removal from the Roster has not expired.

(g) *Voluntary removal.* A HECM counselor will be removed from the Roster upon FHA's receipt of a written request from the counselor.

(h) *Other action.* Nothing in this section prohibits HUD from taking such other action against a HECM counselor or from seeking any other remedy against a counselor available to HUD by statute or other authority.

§ 206.308 Continuing education requirements of counselors listed on the HECM Counselor Roster.

A HECM counselor listed on the Roster must receive, on a continuing basis, training, education, and technical assistance related to HECMs. The HECM counselor must maintain evidence of the successful completion of such continuing education, and such evidence must be made available to FHA upon request. FHA will consider a HECM counselor's successful completion of a HECM course no less than once every 2 years as satisfying the requirements of this section.

PART 207—MULTIFAMILY HOUSING MORTGAGE INSURANCE

Subpart A—Eligibility Requirements

AUTHORITY: 12 U.S.C. 1701z–11(e), 1709(c)(1), 1713, 1715(b), and 1735d; 42 U.S.C. 3535(d).

SOURCE: 36 FR 24537, Dec. 22, 1971, unless otherwise noted.

Subpart A—Eligibility Requirements

§207.1 Eligibility requirements.

The eligibility requirements set forth in 24 CFR part 200, subpart A, apply to multifamily project mortgages insured under section 207 of the National Housing Act (12 U.S.C. 1713), as amended.

[61 FR 14405, Apr. 1, 1996]

Subpart B—Contract Rights and Obligations

§207.251 Definitions.

As used in this subpart:

(a) The term *Commissioner* means the Federal Housing Commissioner.

(b) The term *act* means the National Housing Act, as amended.

(c) The term *mortgage* means such a first lien upon real estate and other property as is commonly given to secure advances on, or the unpaid purchase price of, real estate under the laws of the State, district or territory in which the real estate is located, together with the credit instrument or instruments, if any, secured thereby. In any instance where an operating loss loan is involved, the term shall include both the original mortgage and the instrument securing the operating loss loan.

(d) The term *insured mortgage* means a mortgage which has been insured by the endorsement of the credit instrument by the Commissioner, or his duly authorized representative.

(e) The term *contract of insurance* means the agreement evidenced by such endorsement and includes the terms, conditions and provisions of this part and of the National Housing Act.

(f) The term *mortgagor* means the original borrower under a mortgage and its successors and such of its assigns as are approved by the Commissioner.

(g) The term *mortgagee* means the original lender under a mortgage its successors and such of its assigns as are approved by the Commissioner, and includes the holders of the credit instruments issued under a trust indenture, mortgage or deed of trust pursuant to which such holders act by and through a trustee therein named.

§207.252 First, second and third premiums.

The mortgagee, upon the initial endorsement of the mortgage for insurance, shall pay to the Commissioner a first mortgage insurance premium equal to not less than one-fourth of one percent nor more than one percent as the Secretary shall determine of the original face amount of the mortgage. The specific premium to be charged will be set forth in FEDERAL REGISTER notice.

(a) If the date of the first principal payment is more than one year following the date of such initial insurance endorsement, the mortgagee, upon the anniversary of such insurance date, shall pay a second premium equal to not less than one-fourth of one percent nor more than one percent as the Secretary shall determine of the original face amount of the mortgage. On the date of the first principal payment, the mortgagee shall pay a third premium equal to not less than one-fourth of one percent nor more than one percent of the average outstanding principal obligation of the mortgage for the following year which shall be adjusted so as to accord with such date and so that the aggregate of the said three premiums shall equal the sum of:

(1) One percent of the average outstanding principal obligation of the mortgage for the year following the date of initial insurance endorsement; and

(2) Not less than one-fourth of one percent nor more than one percent per annum as the Secretary shall determine of the average outstanding principal obligation of the mortgage for the period from the first anniversary of the date of initial insurance endorsement to one year following the date of the first principal payment.

(b) If the date of the first principal payment is one year, or less than one year following the date of such initial insurance endorsement, the mortgagee, upon such first principal payment date, shall pay a second premium equal to not less than one-fourth of one percent nor more than one percent as the Secretary shall determine of the average outstanding principal obligation of the mortgage for the following year which shall be adjusted so as to accord with such date and so that the aggregate of the said two premiums shall equal the sum of:

(1) One percent per annum of the average outstanding principal obligation of the mortgage for the period from the date of initial insurance endorsement to the date of first principal payment; and

(2) Not less than one-fourth of one percent nor more than one percent as the Secretary shall determine of the average outstanding principal obligation of the mortgage for the year following the date of the first principal payment.

(c) Where the credit instrument is initially and finally endorsed for insurance pursuant to a Commitment to Insure Upon Completion, the mortgagee on the date of the first principal payment shall pay a second premium equal to not less than one-fourth of one percent nor more than one percent as the Secretary shall determine of the average outstanding principal obligation of the mortgage for the year following such first principal payment date which shall be adjusted so as to accord with such date and so that the aggregate of the said two premiums shall equal the sum of not less than one-fourth of one percent nor more than one percent per annum as the Secretary shall determine of the average outstanding principal obligation of the mortgage for the period from the date of the insurance endorsement to one year following the date of the first principal payment.

(d) Until the mortgage is paid in full, or until receipt by the Commissioner of an application for insurance benefits, or until the contract of insurance is otherwise terminated with the consent of the Commissioner, the mortgagee, on each anniversary of the date of the first principal payment, shall pay an annual mortgage insurance premium equal to not less than one-fourth of one percent nor more than one percent as the Secretary shall determine of the average outstanding principal obligation of the mortgage for the year following the date on which such premium becomes payable.

(e) The premiums payable on and after the date of the first principal payment shall be calculated in accordance with the amortization provisions without taking into account delinquent payments or prepayments.

(f) Premiums shall be payable in cash or in debentures at par plus accrued interest. All premiums are payable in advance and no refund can he made of any portion thereof except as hereinafter provided in this subpart.

(g) Any change in mortgage insurance premiums pursuant to this section will apply to new commitments issued or reissued on or after August 1, 2001 and any notice setting mortgage insurance premiums issued pursuant to this section.

[66 FR 35072, July 2, 2001]

§ 207.252a Premiums—operating loss loans.

(a) The mortgagee, upon the insurance endorsement of the increase loan credit instrument covering the operating loss loan, shall pay to the Commissioner a first mortgage insurance premium of not less than one-fourth of one percent nor more than one percent as the Secretary shall determine of the original amount of the loan.

(b) The provisions of paragraphs (d), (e), (f) and (g) of Sec. 207.252 shall apply to operating loss loans.

[66 FR 35073, July 2, 2001]

§ 207.252b Premiums—mortgages insured pursuant to section 223(f) of the Act.

(a) The mortgagee, upon the initial-final endorsement of the mortgage for insurance pursuant to a Commitment to Insure Upon Completion issued in accordance with § 207.32a, shall pay to the Commissioner a first mortgage insurance premium equal to one percent of the original face amount of the mortgage.

(b) The mortgagee, on the date of the first principal payment, shall pay a second premium equal to one percent of the average outstanding principal obligation of the mortgage for the year following such first principal payment date which shall be adjusted as of that date so that the aggregate of the first and second premiums shall equal the sum of one percent per annum of the average outstanding principal obligation of the mortgage for the period from the date of the insurance endorsement to one year following the date of the first principal payment.

(c) The provisions of paragraphs (d), (e) and (f) of §207.252 shall apply to mortgages insured pursuant to section 223(f) of the Act.

[40 FR 10177, Mar. 5, 1975]

§207.252c Premiums—mortgages insured pursuant to section 238(c) of the Act.

All of the provisions of §§207.252 and 207.252a governing mortgage insurance premiums shall apply to mortgages insured under this subpart pursuant to section 238(c) of the Act except that all mortgage insurance premiums due on such mortgages in accordance with §§207.252 and 207.252a shall be calculated on the basis of one percent.

[42 FR 59674, Nov. 18, 1977]

§207.252d Mortgagee's late charge.

Mortgage insurance premiums which are paid to the Commissioner more than 15 days after the billing date or due date, whichever is later, shall include a late charge of 4 percent of the amount of the payment due, except that no late charge shall be required with respect to any case for which HUD fails to render a proper billing to the mortgagee.

[43 FR 60154, Dec. 26, 1978, as amended at 44 FR 23067, Apr. 18, 1979]

§207.252e Method of payment of mortgage insurance premiums.

In the cases that the Commissioner deems appropriate, the Commissioner may require, by means of instructions communicated to all affected mortgagees, that mortgage insurance premiums be remitted electronically.

[63 FR 1303, Jan. 8, 1998]

§207.253 Termination by prepayment and voluntary termination.

All rights under the insurance contract and all obligations to pay future insurance premiums shall terminate on the following conditions:

(a) *Termination by prepayment.* Notice of the prepayment in full of the mortgage or loan shall be given to the Commissioner, on a form prescribed by the Commissioner, within 30 days from the date of prepayment. The insurance contract shall terminate, effective as of the date of prepayment. No adjusted premium charge shall be due the Commissioner on account of such termination by prepayment.

(b) *Termination by voluntary agreement.* Receipt by the Commissioner of a written request, by the mortgagor and mortgagee or lender for termination of the insurance on the mortgage or loan, on a form prescribed by the Commissioner, accompanied by the original credit instrument for cancellation of the insurance endorsement and the remittance of all sums to which the Commissioner is entitled. The termination shall become effective as of the date these requirements are met. No voluntary termination charge shall be due the Commissioner on account of such termination by voluntary agreement.

(c) Upon termination of the mortgage or loan insurance contract by a payment in full or by a voluntary termination, the Commissioner shall refund to the mortgagee or lender for the account of the mortgagor or borrower an amount equal to the pro rata portion of the current annual mortgage insurance premium theretofore paid, which is applicable to the portion of the year subsequent to (1) the date of the prepayment or (2) the effective date of the voluntary termination of the contract of insurance.

(d) Notwithstanding any provision in the mortgage instrument, this section shall apply to all mortgage or loan insurance contracts terminated by either prepayment or voluntary termination where: (1) The mortgage is prepaid in full or (2) the Commissioner receives a request for voluntary termination, on or after May 1, 1972.

[37 FR 8662, Apr. 29, 1972]

§207.253a Termination of insurance contract.

(a) *Reason for termination.* The happening of any of the following events shall constitute an additional reason for terminating the contract of insurance in cases where the mortgagee has elected to convey the property to the Commissioner:

303

(1) The acquisition by the mortgagee of the mortgaged property without conveying it to the Commissioner.

(2) The acquisition of the property at the foreclosure sale by a party other than the mortgagee.

(3) The redemption of the property after foreclosure.

(4) Notice given by the mortgagee after the foreclosure and during the redemption period that it will not tender the property to the Commissioner.

(b) *Notice of termination.* No contract of insurance shall be terminated until the mortgagee has given written notice thereof to the Commissioner within 30 days from the happening of any one of the events set forth in paragraph (a) of this section.

(c) *Effective termination date.* The Commissioner shall notify the mortgagee that the contract of insurance has been terminated and the effective termination date. The termination shall be effective as of the date any one of the events set forth in paragraph (a) of this section occur.

(d) *Effect of termination.* Upon termination of the contract of insurance the obligation to pay any subsequent MIP shall cease and all rights of the mortgagor and mortgagee shall be terminated.

[36 FR 24537, Dec. 22, 1971, as amended at 37 FR 8662, Apr. 29, 1972]

§ 207.254 Changes in premiums; manner of publication.

Notice of future premium changes will be published in the FEDERAL REGISTER. The Department will propose MIP changes for multifamily mortgage insurance programs and provide a 30-day public comment period for the purpose of accepting comments on whether the proposed changes are appropriate. After the comments have been considered, the Department will publish a final notice announcing the premiums for each program and their effective date. The provisions of paragraph (g) of 24 CFR 207.252 shall apply to any notice of future premium changes published pursuant to this section.

[66 FR 35073, July 2, 2001]

RIGHTS AND DUTIES OF MORTGAGEE UNDER THE CONTRACT OF INSURANCE

§ 207.255 Defaults for purposes of insurance claim.

(a)(1) Except as provided in paragraph (b) of this section, the following shall be considered a default under the terms of a mortgage insured under this subpart:

(i) Failure of the mortgagor to make any payment due under the mortgage (also referred to as a "Monetary Event of Default" in certain mortgage security instruments); or

(ii) A material violation of any other covenant under the provisions of the mortgage, if because of such violation, the mortgagee has accelerated the debt, subject to any necessary HUD approval (also referred to as a "Covenant Event of Default" in certain mortgage security instruments).

(2) For purposes of a mortgagee filing an insurance claim with the Commissioner, the failure of the mortgagor to make any payment due under an operating loss loan or under the original mortgage shall be considered a default under both the operating loss loan and original mortgage.

(3) If a default as defined in paragraphs (a)(1) and (a)(2) of this section continues for a minimum period of 30 days, the mortgagee shall be entitled to receive the benefits of the insurance provided for the mortgage, subject to the procedures in this subpart.

(4) For the purposes of paragraph (a) of this section, the date of default shall be:

(i) The date of the first failure to make a monthly payment that subsequent payments by the mortgagor are insufficient to cover when those subsequent payments are applied by the mortgagee to the overdue monthly payments in the order in which they became due; or

(ii) The date of the first uncorrected violation of a covenant or obligation for which the mortgagee has accelerated the debt.

(5) For multifamily project mortgages for which HUD issued a firm commitment for mortgage insurance on or after September 1, 2011, the regulations of paragraph (a) of this section

shall apply, unless the mortgagor demonstrates to the satisfaction of the Commissioner that financial hardship to the mortgagor would result from application of the regulations in paragraph (a) of this section due to the reasonable expectations of the mortgagor that the transaction would close under the regulations in effect prior to September 1, 2011, in which case, the regulations of paragraph (b) shall apply.

(b)(1) For multifamily project mortgages for which HUD issued a firm commitment for mortgage insurance before September 1, 2011, and for multifamily project mortgages insured under section 232 of the Act (12 U.S.C. 1715w), and section 242 of the Act (12 U.S.C. 1715z–7), the following shall be considered a default under the terms of a mortgage insured under this subpart:

(i) Failure of the mortgagor to make any payment due under the mortgage; or

(ii) Failure to perform any other covenant under the provisions of the mortgage, if the mortgagee, because of such failure, has accelerated the debt.

(2) In the case of an operating loss loan, the failure of the mortgagor to make any payment due under such loan or under the original mortgage shall be considered a default under both the loan and original mortgage.

(3) If such defaults, as defined in paragraph (b) of this section, continue for a period of 30 days the mortgagee shall be entitled to receive the benefits of the insurance hereinafter provided.

(4) Except for mortgages insured under section 232 of the Act, for the purposes of paragraph (b) of this section, the date of default shall be considered as:

(i) The date of the first uncorrected failure to perform a covenant or obligation; or

(ii) The date of the first failure to make a monthly payment which subsequent payments by the mortgagor are insufficient to cover when applied to the overdue monthly payments in the order in which they became due.

(5) For mortgages insured under section 232 of the Act, for purposes of this section, the date of default shall be considered as:

(i) The first date on which the borrower has failed to pay the debt when due as a result of the lender's acceleration of the debt because of the borrower's uncorrected failure to perform a covenant or obligation under the regulatory agreement or security instrument; or

(ii) The date of the first failure to make a monthly payment that subsequent payments by the borrower are insufficient to cover when applied to the overdue monthly payments in the order in which they become due.

[76 FR 24370, May 2, 2011, as amended at 77 FR 55135, Sept. 7, 2012]

§ 207.256 Notice to the Commissioner of default.

(a) If a default as defined in § 207.255(a) or (b) is not cured within the grace period of 30 days provided under § 207.255(a)(3) or (b)(3), the mortgagee must, within 30 days after the date of the end of the grace period, notify the Commissioner of the default, in the manner prescribed in 24 CFR part 200, subpart B.

(b) The mortgagee must give notice to the Commissioner, in the manner prescribed in 24 CFR part 200, subpart B, of the mortgagor's violation of any covenant, whether or not the mortgagee has accelerated the debt.

[76 FR 24370, May 2, 2011]

§ 207.256a Reinstatement of defaulted mortgage.

If, after default and prior to the completion of foreclosure proceedings, the mortgagor cures the default, the insurance shall continue on the mortgage as if a default had not occurred, provided the mortgagee gives notice of reinstatement to the Commissioner, in the manner prescribed in 24 CFR part 200, subpart B.

[76 FR 24370, May 2, 2011]

§ 207.256b Modification of mortgage terms.

(a) The mortgagor and the mortgagee may, with the approval of the Commissioner, enter into an agreement that extends the time for curing a default under the mortgage or modifies the payment terms of the mortgage.

(b)(1) Except as provided in paragraph (b)(2), the Commissioner's approval of the type of agreement specified in paragraph (a) of this section shall not be given, unless the mortgagor agrees in writing that, during such period as the mortgage continues to be in default, and payments by the mortgagor to the mortgagee are less than the amounts required under the terms of the original mortgage, the mortgagor or mortgagee, as may be appropriate in the particular situation, will hold in trust for disposition, as directed by the Commissioner, all rents or other funds derived from the secured property that are not required to meet actual and necessary expenses arising in connection with the operation of such property, including amortization charges, under the mortgage.

(2) For multifamily project mortgages for which HUD issued a firm commitment for mortgage insurance before September 1, 2011, and for multifamily project mortgages insured under section 232 of the Act (12 U.S.C. 1715w), and section 242 (12 U.S.C. 1715z–7), the Commissioner's approval of the type of agreement specified in paragraph (a) of this section shall not be given unless the mortgagor agrees in writing that, during such period as payments to the mortgagee are less than the amounts required under the terms of the original mortgage, the mortgagor will hold in trust for disposition as directed by the Commissioner all rents or other funds derived from the property which are not required to meet actual and necessary expenses arising in connection with the operation of such property, including amortization charges, under the mortgage.

(3) For multifamily project mortgages for which HUD issued a firm commitment for mortgage insurance on or after September 1, 2011, the regulations of paragraph (b)(1) of this section shall apply, unless the mortgagor demonstrates to the satisfaction of the Commissioner that financial hardship to the mortgagor would result from application of the regulations in paragraph (b)(1) of this section due to the reasonable expectations of the mortgagor that the transaction would close under the regulations in effect prior to September 1, 2011, in which case, the regulations of paragraph (b)(2) shall apply.

(c) The Commissioner may exempt a mortgagor from the requirement of paragraph (b) of this section in any case where the Commissioner determines that such exemption does not jeopardize the interests of the United States.

[76 FR 24370, May 2, 2011]

§ 207.257 Commissioner's right to require acceleration.

Upon receipt of notice of violation of a covenant, as provided for in § 207.256(b), or otherwise being apprised of the violation of a covenant, the Commissioner reserves the right to require the mortgagee to accelerate payment of the outstanding principal balance due in order to protect the interests of the Commissioner.

[76 FR 24371, May 2, 2011]

§ 207.258 Insurance claim requirements.

(a) *Alternative election by mortgagee.* (1) When the mortgagee becomes eligible to receive mortgage insurance benefits pursuant to § 207.255(a)(3) or (b)(3), the mortgagee must, within 45 calendar days after the date of eligibility, such period is referred to as the "Eligibility Notice Period" for purposes of this section, give the Commissioner notice of its intention to file an insurance claim and of its election either to assign the mortgage to the Commissioner, as provided in paragraph (b) of this section, or to acquire and convey title to the Commissioner, as provided in paragraph (c) of this section. Notice of this election must be provided to the Commissioner in the manner prescribed in 24 CFR part 200, subpart B. HUD may extend the Eligibility Notice Period at the request of the mortgagee under the following conditions:

(i) The request must be made to and approved by HUD prior to the 45th day after the date of eligibility; and

(ii) The approval of an extension shall in no way prejudice the mortgagee's right to file its notice of its intention to file an insurance claim and of its election either to assign the mortgage to the Commissioner or to acquire and convey title to the Commissioner within the 45-day period or any extension prescribed by the Commissioner.

(2) For mortgages funded with the proceeds of state or local bonds, Ginnie Mae mortgage-backed securities, participation certificates, or other bond obligations specified by the Commissioner (such as an agreement under which the insured mortgagee has obtained the mortgage funds from third-party investors and has agreed in writing to repay such investors at a stated interest rate and in accordance with a fixed repayment schedule), any of which contains a lock-out or prepayment premium, in the event of a default during the term of the prepayment lock-out or prepayment premium, and for any mortgage insured under section 232 of the Act, the mortgagee must:

(i) Request a 90-day extension of the deadline for filing the notice of the mortgagee's intention to file an insurance claim and the mortgagee's election to assign the mortgage or acquire and convey title in accordance with the mortgagee certificate, which HUD may further extend at the written request of the mortgagee;

(ii) Assist the mortgagor in arranging refinancing to cure the default and avert an insurance claim, if the Commissioner grants the requested (or a shorter) extension of notice filing deadline;

(iii) Report to the Commissioner at least monthly on any progress in arranging refinancing;

(iv) Cooperate with the Commissioner in taking reasonable steps in accordance with prudent business practices to avoid an insurance claim;

(v) Require successors or assigns to certify in writing that they agree to be bound by these conditions for the remainder of the term of the prepayment lock-out or prepayment premium; and

(vi) After commencement of amortization of the refinanced mortgage, notify HUD of a delinquency when a payment is not received by the 10th day after the date the payment is due.

(3) For multifamily project mortgages for which HUD issued a firm commitment for mortgage insurance on or after September 1, 2011, the regulations of paragraph (a)(2) of this section shall apply, unless the mortgagor demonstrates to the satisfaction of the Commissioner that financial hardship to the mortgagor would result from application of the regulations in paragraph (a)(2) of this section due to the reasonable expectations of the mortgagor that the transaction would close under the regulations in effect prior to September 1, 2011, in which case, the regulations of paragraph (a)(2) shall not apply.

(4) *Acknowledgment of election.* For mortgages insured pursuant to section 232 of the Act, if the lender provides notice to the Commissioner of its election either to assign the mortgage to the Commissioner or to acquire and convey title to the Commissioner, the Commissioner shall, not later than 90 calendar days after the expiration of the Eligibility Notice Period, as defined in paragraph (a)(1) of this section, as the same may have been extended, acknowledge and accept, or reject for cause, pursuant to program requirements, the lender's election, provided that the Commissioner may, in the Commissioner's discretion, extend such 90-day period by no more than an additional 90 calendar days if the Commissioner determines that such an extension is in HUD's interest.

(b) *Assignment of mortgage to Commissioner— (1) Timeframe; request for extension.* (i) If the mortgagee elects to assign the mortgage to the Commissioner, the mortgagee shall, at any time within 30 calendar days after the date HUD acknowledges the notice of election, file its application for insurance benefits and assign to the Commissioner, in such manner as the Commissioner may require, any applicable credit instrument and the realty and chattel security instruments.

(ii) The Commissioner may extend this 30-day period by written notice that a partial payment of insurance claim under § 207.258b is being considered. A mortgagee may consider failure to receive a notice of an extension approval by the end of the 30-day time period a denial of the request for an extension.

(iii) The extension shall be for such term, not to exceed 60 days, as the Commissioner prescribes; however, the

Commissioner's consideration of a partial payment of claim, or the Commissioner's request that a mortgagee accept partial payment of a claim in accordance with § 207.258b, shall in no way prejudice the mortgagee's right to file its application for full insurance benefits within either the 30-day period or any extension prescribed by the Commissioner.

(iv) The requirements of paragraphs (b)(2) through (b)(6) of this section shall also be met by the mortgagee.

(2) *Notice of assignment.* On the date the assignment of the mortgage is filed for record, the mortgagee must notify the Commissioner, in the manner prescribed in 24 CFR part 200, subpart B, of such assignment, and must also notify the FHA Comptroller by telegram of such recordation.

(3) *Warranty of mortgagee.* The assignment shall be made without recourse or warranty, except that the mortgagee shall warrant that:

(i) No act or omission of the mortgagee has impaired the validity and priority of the mortgage.

(ii) The mortgage is prior to all mechanics' and materialmen's liens filed on record subsequent to the recording of the mortgage, regardless of whether such liens attached prior to the recording date.

(iii) The mortgage is prior to all liens and encumbrances which may have attached or defects which may have arisen subsequent to the recording of the mortgage, except such liens or other matters as may be approved by the Commissioner.

(iv) The amount stated in the instrument of assignment is actually due under the mortgage and there are no offsets or counterclaims against such amount.

(v) The mortgagee has a good right to assign the mortgage.

(4) *Chattel lien warranty.* In assigning its security interest in chattels, including materials, located on the premises covered by the mortgage, or its security interest in building components stored either on-site or off-site at the time of the assignment, the mortgagee shall warrant that:

(i) No act or omission of the mortgagee has impaired the validity or priority of the lien created by the chattel security instruments; and

(ii) The mortgagee has a good right to assign the security instruments; and

(iii) The chattel security instruments are a first lien on the items covered by the instruments except for such other liens or encumbrances as may be approved by the Commissioner.

(5) *Items delivered by mortgagee.* The mortgagee shall deliver to the Commissioner, within 45 days after the assignment is filed for record, the items enumerated below:

(i) An assignment of all claims of the mortgagee against the mortgagor or others arising out of the mortgage transaction.

(ii) All policies of title or other insurance or surety bonds or other guaranties, and any and all claims thereunder, including evidence satisfactory to the Commissioner that the effective date of the original title coverage has been extended to include the assignment of the mortgage to the Commissioner.

(iii) All records, ledger cards, documents, books, papers, and accounts relating to the mortgage transaction.

(iv) All property of the mortgagor held by the mortgagee or to which it is entitled (other than the cash items which are to be retained by the mortgagee) pursuant to paragraph (b)(5) of this section.

(v) Any additional information or data which the Commissioner may require.

(6) *Disposition of cash items.* The following cash items shall either be retained by the mortgagee or delivered to the Commissioner in accordance with instructions to be issued by the Commissioner at the time the insurance claim is filed:

(i) Any balance of the mortgage loan not advanced to the mortgagor.

(ii) Any cash held by the mortgagee or its agents or to which it is entitled, including deposits made for the account of the mortgagor, and which have not been applied in reduction of the principal of the mortgage indebtedness.

(iii) All funds held by the mortgagee for the account of the mortgagor received pursuant to any other agreement.

(iv) The amount of any undrawn balance under a letter of credit used in lieu of a cash deposit.

(c) *Conveyance of title to Commissioner.* If the mortgagee elects to acquire and convey title to the Commissioner, the following requirements shall be met:

(1) *Alternative actions by mortgagee.* At any time within a period of 30 days after the date of the notice of such election, the mortgagee shall take one of the alternative actions in paragraph (c) (2) or (3) of this section.

(2) *Foreclosure of mortgage.* The mortgagee may elect to commence foreclosure proceedings. If the laws of the State where the property is located do not permit institution of foreclosure within such 30-day period, foreclosure shall be commenced not less than 30 days after such action can be taken. Under such proceedings, the mortgagee shall take one of the following actions:

(i) Obtain possession of the mortgaged property and the income therefrom through the voluntary surrender thereof by the mortgagor.

(ii) Institute and prosecute with reasonable diligence, proceedings for the appointment of a receiver to manage the mortgaged property and collect income therefrom.

(iii) Proceed to exercise such other rights and remedies as may be available to it for the protection and preservation of the mortgaged property and to obtain the income therefrom under the mortgage and the law of the particular jurisdiction.

(iv) With the prior approval of the Commissioner, exercise the power of sale under a deed of trust.

(3) *Acquisition of title and possession.* The mortgagee, with the approval of the Commissioner, may elect to acquire possession of, and title to, the mortgaged property by means other than foreclosure. With the prior approval of the Commissioner, title may be transferred directly to the Commissioner.

(4) *Notice of foreclosure.* The mortgagee shall given written notice to the Commissioner within 30 days after the institution of foreclosure proceedings and shall exercise reasonable diligence in prosecuting such proceedings to completion. Any developments which might delay the consummation of such proceedings shall be promptly reported to the Commissioner.

(5) *Transfer by mortgagee.* After acquiring title to and possession of the property, the mortgagee shall (within 30 days of such acquisition) transfer title and possession of the property to the Commissioner. The transfer shall be made in such manner as the Commissioner may require. On the date the deed is filed for record, the mortgagee shall notify the Commissioner on a form prescribed by him of the filing of such conveyance, and shall also notify the FHA Assistant Commissioner-Comptroller by telegram of such recordation.

(6) *Filing of deed and application.* The mortgagee shall file its application for insurance benefits at the time of filing for record of the deed conveying the property to the Commissioner.

(7) *Deed covenants and documents.* The deed conveying the property to the Commissioner shall contain covenants satisfactory to the Commissioner. The original deed shall be forwarded to the Commissioner as soon as received from the recording authority. The following documents shall be forwarded with the deed:

(i) A bill of sale covering any personal property to which the mortgagee is entitled by reason of the mortgage transaction or by the acceptance of a deed in lieu of foreclosure.

(ii) An assignment of all claims of the mortgagee against the mortgagor or others arising out of the mortgage transaction and out of the foreclosure proceedings or other means by which the property was acquired.

(iii) An assignment of any claims on account of title insurance and fire or other hazard insurance, except claims which have been released with the prior approval of the Commissioner.

(8) *Title evidence.* Evidence of title, satisfactory to the Commissioner and meeting the requirements of §207.258a shall be furnished to the Commissioner (without expense to him) within 45 days of the filing for record of the deed conveying the property to him.

(9) *Disposition of cash items.* The provisions of paragraph (b)(4) of this section, relating to the retention or delivery of cash items, shall be applicable to cases

involving the conveyance of property to the Commissioner.

(Information collection requirements in paragraph (b) were approved by the Office of Management and Budget under control number 2535–0061)

[36 FR 24537, Dec. 22, 1971, as amended at 44 FR 8195, Feb. 8, 1979; 50 FR 38786, Sept. 25, 1985; 51 FR 27838, Aug. 4, 1986; 64 FR 4770, Jan. 29, 1999; 76 FR 24371, May 2, 2011; 77 FR 55135, Sept. 7, 2012]

§ 207.258a Title requirements.

(a) *Form of title evidence.* The title evidence submitted with a conveyance of the property to the Commissioner shall be in the form of an owner's policy of title insurance, except that, if an abstract and attorney's opinion were accepted by the Commissioner at the time of insurance, the title evidence may be in such form. The title evidence shall be effective on or after the date of the recording of the conveyance to the Commissioner.

(b) *Content of title evidence.* To be satisfactory to the Commissioner, the title evidence covering the property conveyed to him shall show the same title vested in the Commissioner as was vested in the mortgagor as of the date of the mortgage was filed for record, with the exception of such liens or other matters affecting the title as may be approved by the Commissioner.

§ 207.258b Partial payment of claim.

(a) Whenever the Commissioner receives notice under § 207.258 of a mortgagee's intention to file an insurance claim and to assign the mortgage to the Commissioner, the Commissioner may request the mortgagee, in lieu of assignment, to accept partial payment of the claim under the mortgage insurance contract and to recast the mortgage, under such terms and conditions as the Commissioner may determine.

(b) The Commissioner may request the mortgagee to participate in a partial payment of claim in lieu of assignment only after a determination that partial payment would be less costy to the Federal government than other reasonable alternatives for maintaining the low- and moderate-income character of the project. This determination shall be based upon the findings listed below and such other findings as the Commissioner deems appropriate:

(1) The mortgagee is entitled, under § 207.255, to assign the mortgage in exchange for the payment of insurance benefits;

(2) The relief resulting from partial payment, when considered with other resources available to the project, would be sufficient to restore the financial viability of the project;

(3) The project is, or can at reasonable cost be made, structurally sound;

(4) The management of the project is satisfactory to the Commissioner; and

(5) The default under the insured mortgage was beyond the control of the mortgagor.

(c) Partial payment of a claim under this section shall be made only when:

(1) The project is, or potentially could serve as, a low- and moderate-income housing resource;

(2) The property covered by the mortgage is free and clear of all liens other than the insured first mortgage and such other liens as the Commissioner may have approved;

(3) The mortgagee has voluntarily agreed to accept partial payment of the insurance claim under the mortgage insurance contract and to recast the remaining mortgage amount under terms and conditions prescribed by the Commissioner; and

(4) The mortgagor has agreed to repay to the Commissioner an amount equal to the partial payment, with the obligation secured by a second mortgage on the project containing terms and conditions prescribed by the Commissioner. The terms of the second mortgage will be determined on a case-by-case basis to assure that the estimated project income will be sufficient to cover estimated operating expenses and debt service on the recast insured mortgage. The Commissioner may provide for postponed amortization of the second mortgage.

(d) Payment of insurance benefits under this section shall be in cash. The Commissioner shall waive the deduction of one percent of the mortgage funds advanced to the mortgagor, provided for in § 207.259(b)(2)(iv), with respect to a partial payment of a claim under this section. The items referred to in § 207.258(b)(4) shall either be retained by the mortgagee or delivered to the Commissioner in accordance with instructions to be issued by the Commissioner with respect to a partial payment of claim under this section.

(e) Lenders receiving a partial payment of claim following the Commissioner's endorsement of the Mortgage for full insurance under parts 251, 252, or 255 of this chapter, will pay HUD a fee in an amount set forth through FEDERAL REGISTER notice. HUD, in its discretion, may collect this fee or deduct the fee from any payment it makes in the claim process.

[50 FR 38786, Sept. 25, 1985, as amended at 61 FR 49037, Sept. 17, 1996]

§ 207.259 Insurance benefits.

(a) *Method of payment.* (1) Upon either an assignment of the mortgage to the Commissioner or a conveyance of the property to the Commissioner in accordance with requirements in § 207.258, payment of an insurance claim shall be made in cash, in debentures, or in a combination of both, as determined by the Commissioner either at, or prior to, the time of payment.

(2) An insurance claim paid on a mortgage insured under section 223(e) of the National Housing Act shall be paid in cash from the Special Risk Insurance Fund.

(b) *Amount of payment; assignment of mortgage.* If the mortgage is assigned to the Commissioner, the insurance benefits shall be paid in an amount determined as follows:

(1) By adding to the unpaid principal amount of the mortgage, computed as of the date of default, the following items:

(i) The amount of all payments made by the mortgagee for taxes, special assessments and water rates which are liens prior to the mortgage; for insurance on the property; and for any mortgage insurance premiums paid after default.

(ii) An allowance for reasonable payments made by the mortgagee, with the approval of the Commissioner, for the completion and preservation of the property.

(iii) An amount equivalent to the debenture interest which would have been earned on the portion of the insurance benefits paid in cash, as of the date such cash payment is made, except that when the mortgagee fails to meet any one of the applicable requirements of §§ 207.256 and 207.258 within the specified time and in a manner satisfactory to the Commissioner (or within such further time as the Commissioner may approve in writing), the interest allowance in such cash payment shall be computed only to the date on which the particular required action should have been taken or to which it was extended.

(2) By deducting from the total of the items computed under paragraph (b)(1) of this section, the following items:

(i) Any amount received by the mortgagee on account of the mortgage after the date of default.

(ii) Any net income received by the mortgagee from the property covered by the mortgage after the date of default.

(iii) The sum of the cash items retained by the mortgagee pursuant to § 207.258(b)(6), except the balance of the mortgage loan not advanced to the mortgagor.

(iv) An amount equivalent to 1 percent of the mortgage funds advanced to the mortgagor and not repaid as of the date of default, except that all or part of the 1 percent may be waived by the Commissioner if, at his request and in lieu of foreclosure, the mortgage is assigned to the Secretary.

(v) In the case of a lender receiving insurance benefits for the full Mortgage amount upon the Commissioner's endorsement of the Mortgage for full insurance pursuant to 24 CFR parts 251, 252, or 255, the amount of the fee set forth through FEDERAL REGISTER notice. HUD may, in its discretion, collect this fee rather than deducting the fee from the total of the items computed under paragraph (b)(1) of this section.

(vi) Except for multifamily project mortgages for which HUD issued a firm commitment for mortgage insurance before September 1, 2011, and for multifamily project mortgages insured under section 232 of the Act (12 U.S.C. 1715w) and under section 242 of the Act (12 U.S.C. 1715z–7), when there is a covenant default as defined in

311

§ 207.255(a)(1)(ii) and a mortgagee refuses to comply promptly with the Commissioner's request to accelerate payment pursuant to § 207.257, an amount equal to the difference between the project's market value as of the date of the Commissioner's request and the project's market value as of the date the mortgagee makes an election to assign the mortgage, or convey title to the project, as determined by appraisal procedures established by the Commissioner.

(vii) For multifamily project mortgages for which HUD issued a firm commitment for mortgage insurance on or after September 1, 2011, the regulations of paragraph (b)(2)(vi) of this section shall apply, unless the mortgagor demonstrates to the satisfaction of the Commissioner that financial hardship to the mortgagor would result from application of the regulations in paragraph (b)(2)(vi) of this section due to the reasonable expectations of the mortgagor that the transaction would close under the regulations in effect prior to September 1, 2011, in which case, the regulations of paragraph (b)(2)(vi) shall not apply.

(c) *Amount of payment; conveyance of property.* If the property is conveyed to the Commissioner, the insurance benefits shall be paid in an amount determined in accordance with paragraph (b) of this section, except that the item set forth in paragraph (b)(2)(iv) of this section shall not be deducted.

(d) *Issuance of certificate of claim.* In addition to the insurance benefits paid under paragraph (b) or (c) of this section, a certificate of claim shall be issued to the mortgagee.

(1) In the case of an assignment of the mortgage, the certificate shall be for an amount which the Commissioner determines to be sufficient, when added to the amount of the insurance benefits to equal the amount the mortgagee would have received if, on the date of assignment to the Commissioner, the mortgagor had paid in full all obligations under the mortgage. Where a conveyance is involved, there shall also be included in the certificate an allowance in a reasonable amount for any necessary expenses incurred by the mortgagee in connection with the foreclosure proceedings or the acquisition of the mortgaged property otherwise and in connection with the conveyance of the property to the Commissioner.

(2) The certificate of claim shall provide for an uncompounded annual interest increment of 3 percent to begin as of the date of either assignment or conveyance.

(e) *Issuance of debentures.* Where debentures are issued, they shall meet the following requirements:

(1) Be issued as of the date of default.

(2) Be registered as to principal and interest.

(3) At the option of the Commissioner and with the approval of the Secretary of the Treasury, be redeemable at par plus accrued interest on any semiannual interest payment date on 3 months' notice of redemption given in such manner as the Commissioner shall prescribe. The debenture interest on the debentures called for redemption shall cease on the semiannual interest payment date designated in the call notice. The Commissioner may include with the notice of redemption an offer to purchase the debentures at par plus accrued interest at any time during the period between the notice of redemption and the redemption date. If the debentures are purchased by the Commissioner after such call and prior to the named redemption date, the debenture interest shall cease on the date of purchase.

(4) Mature 20 years from the date thereof.

(5) Be issued in such forms and amounts; and be subject to such terms and conditions; and include such provisions for redemption, if any, as may be prescribed by the Secretary, with the approval of the Secretary of the Treasury; and may be in book entry or certificated registered form, or such other form as the Secretary by regulation may prescribe.

(6) Bear interest from the date of issue, payable semiannually on the first day of January and the first day of July of each year at the rate in effect as of the date the commitment was issued, or as of the date of initial insurance endorsement of the mortgage, whichever rate is higher. The applicable rates of interest will be published twice each year as a notice in the FEDERAL REGISTER.

(7) Debentures representing the portion of the claim applicable to an operating loss loan shall bear interest at the rate in effect as of the date the commitment to insure such loan was issued, or as of the date of endorsement for insurance of such loan, whichever rate is the higher, although debentures representing the portion of the claim applicable to the original mortgage may bear interest at a different rate.

(f) *Mortgagee Time Limits for Supplemental Claims for Additional Insurance Benefits.* A mortgagee may not file for any additional payments of its mortgage insurance claim more than six months after the date of final settlement of the insurance claim by the Commissioner. For the purpose of this section, the term final settlement shall mean the payment of the insurance claim (in cash or debentures) or billing for any overpayment of a partial claim that is made by the Commissioner. Final settlement is based upon the submission by the mortgagee of all required documents and information pursuant to part 207 of this chapter.

[36 FR 24537, Dec. 22, 1971, as amended at 41 FR 45829, Oct. 18, 1976; 47 FR 26125, June 17, 1982; 49 FR 24654, June 14, 1984; 51 FR 13142, Apr. 17, 1986; 51 FR 27838, Aug. 4, 1986; 57 FR 55112, Nov. 24, 1992; 59 FR 49816, Sept. 30, 1994; 61 FR 49038, Sept. 17, 1996; 71 FR 18153, Apr. 10, 2006; 76 FR 24371, May 2, 2011; 80 FR 51468, Aug. 25, 2015]

§207.259a Waiver of title objection; mortgages formerly Commissioner-held.

If the Commissioner sells a mortgage and such mortgage is later reassigned to him in exchange for debentures or the property covered by such mortgage is later conveyed to him in exchange for debentures, the Commissioner will not object to title by reason of any lien or other adverse interest that was senior to the mortgage on the date of the original sale of such mortgage by the Commissioner.

§207.260 Maintenance and inspection of property.

As long as the mortgage is insured or held by the Commissioner, the mortgagor must maintain the insured project in accordance with the physical condition requirements in 24 CFR part 5, subpart G; and the mortgagee must inspect the project in accordance with the physical inspection requirements in 24 CFR part 5, subpart G.

[63 FR 46578, Sept. 1, 1998]

§207.261 Capturing excess bond proceeds.

(a) A mortgagee that finances multifamily housing or healthcare facilities insured under Title II of the National Housing Act through the issuance and sale of bonds or bond anticipation notes and uses a project-specific trust indenture agreement, that clearly outlines the project and identifies by project the trust funds established by and administered in accordance with the terms of the trust indenture, shall:

(1) Include the following clause in the trust indenture: In the event of an assignment or conveyance of the mortgage to the Commissioner, subsequent to the issuance of the bonds, all money remaining in all funds and accounts other than the rebate fund, and any other funds remaining under the trust indenture after payment or provision for payment of debt service on the bonds and the fees and expenses of the credit enhancer, issuer, trustee, and other such parties unrelated to the mortgagor (other than funds originally deposited by the mortgagor or related parties on or before the date of issuance of the bonds) shall be returned to the mortgagee.

(2) Upon the Commissioner's payment of an FHA mortgage insurance claim under §207.259, the mortgagee shall take all legally-entitled actions to enforce the clause required by paragraph (a)(1) of this section and pay the Commissioner any trust funds remaining after discharge by the trustee of all obligations of the trust indenture, no later than 6 months after the date of the Commissioner's final settlement of the FHA mortgage insurance claim.

(b) For purposes of paragraph (a) of this section, the term "rebate fund" means a separate fund established under a contract or agreement for tax-exempt bonds in which amounts (excess interest earnings from the tax-exempt bonds) must be deposited to make rebate payments to the federal government under the Internal Revenue Code.

[79 FR 43933, July 29, 2014]

RIGHTS IN HOUSING FUND

§ 207.263 Responsibility for servicing.

After January 10, 1994, servicing of insured mortgages must be performed by a mortgagee which is approved by HUD to service insured mortgages.

[57 FR 58350, Dec. 9, 1992]

AMENDMENTS

§ 207.499 Effect of amendments.

The regulations in this subpart may be amended by the Commissioner at any time and from time to time, in whole or in part, but such amendment shall not adversely affect the interests of a mortgagee or lender under the contract of insurance on any mortgage or loan already insured and shall not adversely affect the interests of a mortgagee or lender on any mortgage or loan to be insured on which the Commissioner has made a commitment to insure.

PART 208—ELECTRONIC TRANSMISSION OF REQUIRED DATA FOR CERTIFICATION AND RECERTIFICATION AND SUBSIDY BILLING PROCEDURES FOR MULTIFAMILY SUBSIDIZED PROJECTS

Sec.
208.101 Purpose.
208.104 Applicability.
208.108 Requirements.
208.112 Cost.

AUTHORITY: 12 U.S.C. 1701s, 1715l, 1715z–1; 42 U.S.C. 1437f and 3535(d).

SOURCE: 58 FR 61022, Nov. 19, 1993, unless otherwise noted.

§ 208.101 Purpose.

The purpose of this part is to require owners of subsidized multifamily projects to electronically submit certain data to HUD for the programs listed in § 208.104. This electronically submitted data is required by HUD Forms, Owner's Certification of Compliance with Tenant's Eligibility and Rent Procedure, Worksheets to Compute Tenant Payment/Rent (Form HUD–50059 and 50059 Worksheets), and the Monthly Subsidy Billing Forms, Housing Owner's Certification and Application for Housing Assistance Payments (HUD–

52670), Schedule of Tenant Assistance Payments Due (HUD–52670A, Part 1), Schedule of section 8 Special Claims (HUD–52670A, Part 2), and Special Claims Worksheets, HUD–52671 A through D), as applicable.

§ 208.104 Applicability.

(a) This part applies to HUD administered subsidized multifamily projects, either insured or non-insured, under:

(1) The section 236 Interest Reduction and Rental Assistance Payments program;

(2) The section 8 Housing Assistance Payments Programs, including, but not limited to, section 8 Housing Assistance Payments Programs for New Construction (24 CFR part 880), section 8 Housing Assistance Payments Program for Substantial Rehabilitation (24 CFR part 881), section 8 Housing Assistance Payments Program, New Construction Set-Aside for section 515 Rural Rental Housing Projects (24 CFR part 884); Loans for Housing for the Elderly or Handicapped (24 CFR part 885) and section 8 Loan Management and Property Disposition Set-aside program (24 CFR part 886);

(3) The section 221(d)(3) Below Market Interest Rate Housing for Low and Moderate Income Mortgage Insurance program (24 CFR part 221); and

(4) The section 101 Rent Supplement program (24 CFR part 215).

(b) This part applies to those multifamily projects having subsidy contracts, either insured or non-insured, where State housing finance and development agencies and other Public Housing Agencies are the subsidy contract administrator under:

(1) The section 236 Interest Reduction and Rental Assistance Payments program (24 CFR part 236);

(2) The section 8 Housing Assistance Payments Programs, including, but not limited to, section 8 Housing Assistance Payments Program for New Construction (24 CFR part 880), section 8 Housing Assistance Payments Program for Substantial Rehabilitation (24 CFR part 881), and section 8 Housing Assistance Payments Program, New Construction Set-Aside for section 515 Rural Rental Housing Projects (24 CFR part 884);

(3) The section 221(d)(3) Below Market Interest Rate Housing for Low and Moderate Income Mortgage Insurance Program (24 CFR part 221); and

(4) The section 101 Rent Supplement program (24 CFR part 215).

(c) This part applies to all other subsidized section 202 projects, which include: section 202 projects with rent supplement or loan management set aside, section 202 projects with section 162 assistance, and section 202 Supportive Housing for the Elderly. This part also applies to section 811 Supportive Housing for Persons With Disabilities.

(d) This part does not apply to the section 8 Existing Housing Program or the Moderate Rehabilitation program.

§ 208.108 Requirements.

(a) *Projects specified in § 208.104(a) that are automated.* Project owners of applicable projects under § 208.104(a) who currently use an automated software package to process certifications and recertifications and to provide subsidy billings to HUD must update their software packages and begin electronic transmission of that data in a HUD specified format by March 21, 1994. These project owners are required to transmit data collected for the 12 months preceding March 21, 1994, as well as data collected on or after this date. Data collected for the 12 months preceding March 21, 1994, is to include only the tenant's most recent "complete certification" (move-in, initial certification, interim recertification, or annual recertification). When the most recent certification for a tenant is a partial certification (gross rent change, unit transfer, or correction), both the complete and partial certifications must be transmitted.

(b) *Projects specified in § 208.104(a) that are not automated.* Nonautomated project owners and agents (those owners and agents that currently prepare the certification, recertification, and subsidy billing forms manually) of applicable projects under § 208.104(a) must:

(1) Complete the search and either obtain the necessary hardware or software, or sign service contracts;

(2) Complete their data loading; and

(3) Begin electronic transmission by May 20, 1994. These project owners are required to transmit data collected for the 12 months preceding May 20, 1994, as well as data collected on or after this date. Data collected for the 12 months preceding May 20, 1994, is to include only the tenant's most recent "complete certification" (move-in, initial certification, interim recertification, or annual recertification). When the most recent certification for a tenant is a partial certification (gross rent change, unit transfer, or correction), both the complete and partial certifications must be transmitted.

(c) *Projects specified in § 208.104(b)*—(1) *Project owners.* Project owners of applicable projects under § 208.104(b) must electronically transmit data for certification, recertification and subsidy billing procedures in a HUD specified format to the contract administrator. These project owners are required to transmit data collected for the 12 months preceding September 23, 1994, as well as data collected on or after that date. Data collected for the 12 months preceding September 23, 1994 is to include only the tenant's most recent "complete certification" (move-in, initial certification, interim recertification, or annual recertification). When the most recent certification for a tenant is a partial certification (gross rent change, unit transfer, or correction), both the complete and partial certifications must be transmitted.

(2) *Contract administrators.* State housing finance and development agencies and Public Housing Agencies that serve as the subsidy contract administrator must accept the electronic transmission of the HUD forms listed below in § 208.108(e) from the projects they administer, and electronically transmit that data to HUD in a HUD specified format after appropriate review and correction of the data.

(d) *Projects specified in § 208.104(c).* Project owners of applicable projects under § 208.104(c) must electronically transmit data for certification, recertification and subsidy billing procedures to HUD in a HUD specified format. In the case of partially assisted section 202 projects, owners are required to electronically transmit data only for subsidized units. These project owners are required to transmit data collected for the 12 months preceding the effective date of the rule, as well as data collected on or after the effective date of the rule. Data collected for the 12 months preceding September 23, 1994 is to include only the tenant's most recent "complete certification" (move-in, initial certification, interim recertification, or annual recertification). When the most recent certification for a tenant is a partial certification (gross rent change, unit transfer, or correction), both the complete and partial certifications must be transmitted.

(e) *Data to be transmitted.* Electronic transmission consists of data transmitted from the HUD–50059, 50059 worksheets, 52670 and 52670A, Parts 1 and 2 and 52671 A through D correctly formatted in accord with the HUD data requirements and in lieu of the hard copy forms.

[58 FR 61022, Nov. 19, 1993, as amended at 59 FR 43474, Aug. 24, 1994]

§ 208.112   Cost.

(a) The costs of the electronic transmission of the correctly formatted data, including either the purchase and maintenance of computer hardware or software, or both, the cost of contracting for those services, or the cost of centralizing the electronic transmission function, shall be considered project operating costs to be paid from project income, and considered project operating costs for the purpose of processing and approving requests for HUD approval of rent increases.

(b) At the owner's option, the cost of the computer software may include service contracts to provide maintenance or training, or both. Regardless of whether an owner obtains service contracts to provide maintenance or training or both, the software must be updated to incorporate changes or revisions in legislation, regulations, handbooks, notices or HUD electronic transmission data format requirements.

(c) The source of funds for the purchase of hardware or software, or contracting for services for electronic transmission, may include current project operating income; an expense item in processing rent increases; a loan from the Reserve for Replacement Account, or a release from the Residual Receipts Account.

(d) A loan from the Reserve for Replacements Account must be repaid within a five year period from the release date.

(e) Owners of smaller projects or partially assisted projects with few subsidized units and CAs that administer no more than one project that determine that the purchase of hardware and/or software is not cost effective may contract out the electronic data transmission function to organizations that provide such services, including, but not limited to the following organizations: local management agents, local management associations and management agents with centralized facilities. Owners of multiple projects may centralize the electronic transmission function. However, owners that contract out or centralize the electronic transmission function are required to retain the ability to monitor the day-to-day operations of the project at the project site and be able to demonstrate that ability to the relevant HUD field office.

[58 FR 61022, Nov. 19, 1993, as amended at 59 FR 43475, Aug. 24, 1994]

PART 213—COOPERATIVE HOUSING MORTGAGE INSURANCE

Subpart A—Eligibility Requirements— Projects

Subpart C—Individual Properties Released From Project Mortgage; Expiring Program

AUTHORITY: 12 U.S.C. 1715b, 1715e; 42 U.S.C. 3535(d).

SOURCE: 36 FR 24553, Dec. 22, 1971, unless otherwise noted.

Subpart A—Eligibility Requirements—Projects

§ 213.1 Eligibility requirements.

The eligibility requirements set forth in 24 CFR part 200, subpart A, apply to multifamily project mortgages insured under section 213 of the National Housing Act (12 U.S.C. 1715e), as amended.

[61 FR 14405, Apr. 1, 1996]

Subpart B—Contract Rights and Obligations—Projects

§ 213.251 Cross-reference.

(a) All of the provisions of subpart B, part 207 of this chapter covering mortgages insured under section 207 of the National Housing Act, apply with full force and effect to mortgages insured under section 213 of the National Housing Act, except the following provisions:

(b) For the purposes of this subpart, all references in part 207 of this chapter to section 207 of the National Housing Act shall be deemed to refer to section 213 of the Act, and all references in part 207 of this chapter to the General Insurance Fund shall be deemed to refer to the Cooperative Management Housing Insurance Fund in cases involving mortgages which are the obligation of the Cooperative Management Housing Insurance Fund.

(c) The provisions of §§ 207.255, 207.256, 207.257, 207.261, 207.262 and 207.263 of this chapter shall apply to supplementary loans insured under section 213(j) of the Act. In connection with the foregoing provisions the terms *mortgagor, mortgagee, mortgage* shall be construed to mean *borrower, lender,* and *supplementary loan, including required security instrument*.

(d) Where the provisions of this subpart are applicable to supplementary loans, the terms *mortgagor, mortgagee, mortgage,* shall be construed to mean *borrower, lender,* and *supplementary loan, including required security instrument*.

(e) Where the provisons of this subpart are applicable to operating loss loans, the terms *mortgagor, mortgagee* and *mortgage* shall be construed to mean *borrower, lender* and *operating loss loan, including required security instrument,* respectively.

[36 FR 24553, Dec. 22, 1971, as amended at 37 FR 8662, Apr. 29, 1972]

§ 213.252 Definitions.

The definitions contained in § 213.1 shall apply to this subpart and in addition the following terms shall have the meaning indicated.

(a) *Contract of Insurance* means the agreement evidenced by endorsement of the credit instrument by the Commissioner or his duly authorized representative and includes the terms, conditions and provisions of this subpart and of the National Housing Act.

(b) *Insured mortgage* means a mortgage which has been insured by the endorsement of the credit instrument by the Commissioner.

(c) *Mortgage* means such a first lien upon real estate and other property as is commonly given to secure advances on, or the unpaid purchase price of, real estate under the laws of the State, district or territory in which the real estate is located, together with the credit instrument or instruments, if any, secured thereby. In any instance where an operating loss loan is involved, the term shall include both the original mortgage and the instrument securing the operating loss loan.

(d) *Mortgagee* means the original lender under a mortgage, its successors and such of its assigns as are approved by the Commissioner, and includes the holders of the credit instruments issued under a trust indenture, mortgage or deed of trust pursuant to which such holders act by and through a trustee therein named.

(e) *Mortgagor* means the original borrower under a mortgage and its successors and such of its assigns as are approved by the Commissioner.

(f) *Project Mortgage* means a blanket mortgage insured under section 213 of the Act, covering a group of not less than five single-family dwellings.

§ 213.253 Premiums upon initial endorsement.

(a) *Management and Sales Types and Investor Sponsored Projects.* The mortgagee, upon the initial endorsement of the mortgage for insurance, shall pay to the Commissioner a first mortgage insurance premium equal to one-half of one percent of the original face amount of the mortgage.

(b) *Purchasing cooperatives.* The provisions of paragraph (a) of this section do not apply to the mortgage or a purchasing nonprofit cooperative housing corporation or trust where such mortgage is endorsed for insurance pursuant to the sale of an Investor Sponsored Project to such purchasing nonprofit cooperative housing corporation or trust.

(c) *Existing Construction.* The provisions of paragraph (a) of the section shall apply to a mortgage covering Existing Construction which involves insurance of advances for Commissioner approved or required repairs, improvements, alterations and additions.

(d) *Operating loss loans and supplementary loans.* The provisions of paragraph (a) of this section shall apply to any operating loss loan and to any supplementary loan, except a supplementary loan to finance the acquisition of an existing community facility.

§ 213.254 Premiums where first principal payment more than one year after initial endorsement.

(a) *Management and Sales Types and Investor Sponsored Projects.* (1) If the date of the first principal payment is more than one year following the date of such initial insurance endorsement, the mortgagee, upon the anniversary of such insurance date, shall pay a second premium equal to one-half of one percent of the original face amount of the mortgage. On the date of the first principal payment, the mortgagee shall pay a third premium equal to one-half of one percent of the average outstanding principal obligation of the mortgage for the following year which shall be adjusted so as to accord with such date and so that the aggregate of the first, second and third premiums shall equal the sum of:

(i) One percent of the average outstanding principal obligation of the mortgage for the year following the date of initial insurance endorsement, and

(ii) One-half of one percent per annum of the average outstanding principal obligation of the mortgage for the period from the first anniversary of the date of initial insurance endorsement to one year following the date of the first principal payment.

(2) If the date of the first principal payment of a mortgage is more than one year following the date of the initial insurance endorsement and the mortgage is paid in full prior to the date of such first principal payment, the first and second premiums collected shall be adjusted so that the aggregate of the two premiums shall equal the sum of:

(i) One percent of the average outstanding principal obligation of the mortgage for the year following the date of the initial insurance endorsement and

(ii) One-half of one percent per annum of the average outstanding principal obligation of the mortgage for the period from the first anniversary of the date of initial endorsement to the date the mortgage was paid in full.

(b) *Purchasing cooperatives.* The provisions of paragraph (a) of this section do not apply to the mortgage of a purchasing nonprofit cooperative housing corporation or trust where such mortgage is endorsed for insurance pursuant to the sale of an Investor Sponsored Project to such purchasing nonprofit cooperative housing corporation or trust.

(c) *Existing Construction.* The provisions of paragraph (a) of this section shall apply to a mortgage covering Existing Construction which involves insurance of advances for Commissioner approved or required repairs, improvements, alterations and additions.

(d) *Supplementary loan; insurance of advances.* The provisions of paragraph (a) shall apply to any supplementary loan involving insurance of advances.

§213.255 **Premiums where first principal payment one year or less after initial endorsement.**

(a) *Management and Sales Types and Investor Sponsored Projects.* (1) If the date of the first principal payment is one year, or less than one year following the date of such initial insurance endorsement, the mortgagee, upon such first principal payment date, shall pay a second premium equal to one-half of one percent of the average outstanding principal obligation of the mortgage for the following year which shall be adjusted so as to accord with such date and so that the aggregate of the first and second premiums shall equal the sum of

(i) One percent per annum of the average outstanding principal obligation of the mortgage for the period from the date of initial insurance endorsement to the date of first principal payment, and

(ii) One-half of one percent of the average outstanding principal obligation of the mortgage for the year following the date of the first principal payment.

(2) If the date of the first principal payment of a mortgage is one year or less than one year following the date of the initial insurance endorsement and

the mortgage is paid in full prior to the date of such first principal payment, the first and only premium collected shall be adjusted so that the total premium shall equal one percent per annum of the average outstanding principal obligation of the mortgage for the period from the date of initial insurance endorsement to the date the mortgage was paid in full.

(b) *Purchasing cooperatives.* The provisions of paragraph (a) of this section do not apply to the mortgage of a purchasing nonprofit cooperative housing corporation or trust where such mortgage is endorsed for insurance pursuant to the sale of an Investor Sponsored Project to such purchasing nonprofit cooperative housing corporation or trust.

(c) *Existing Construction.* The provisions of paragraph (a) of this section shall apply to a mortgage covering Existing Construction which involves insurance of advances for Commissioner approved or required repairs, improvements, alterations and additions.

(d) *Supplementary loan; insurance of advances.* The provisions of paragraph shall apply to a supplementary loan involving insurance of advances.

§213.256 **Premiums; insurance upon completion.**

(a) *Management and Sales Types and Investor Sponsored Projects.* (1) Where the mortgage is initially and finally endorsed for insurance pursuant to a Commitment to Insure Upon Completion, the mortgagee on the date of the first principal payment shall pay a second premium equal to one-half of one percent of the average outstanding principal obligation of the mortgage for the year following such first principal payment date which shall be adjusted so as to accord with such date and so that the aggregate of the first and second premiums shall equal the sum of one-half of one percent per annum of the average outstanding principal obligation of the mortgage for the period from the date of the insurance endorsement to one year following the date of the first principal payment.

(2) Where the mortgage is initially and finally endorsed for insurance pursuant to a Commitment to Insure Upon

Completion and is paid in full prior to the date of the first principal payment, the first and only premium collected shall be adjusted so that the total premium shall equal one-half of one percent per annum of the average outstanding principal obigation of the mortgage for the period from the date of the insurance endorsement to the date the mortgage was paid in full.

(b) *Purchasing cooperatives.* The provisions of paragraph (a) of this section do not apply to the mortgage of a purchasing nonprofit cooperative housing corporation or trust where such mortgage is endorsed for insurance pursuant to the sale of an Investor Sponsored Project to such purchasing nonprofit cooperative housing corporation or trust.

(c) *Existing Construction.* The provisions of paragraph (a) of this section shall apply to Existing Construction not involving insurance of advances but involved Commissioner approved or required repairs, improvements, alterations and additions.

(d) *Supplementary loans; Commitment to Insure Upon Completion.* The provisions of paragraphs (a) and (b) of this section shall apply to a supplementary loan endorsed for insurance pursuant to a Commitment to Insure Upon Completion.

§ 213.257 Premiums; purchasing cooperatives; Existing Construction; supplementary loans to purchase existing community facility.

(a) Where a mortgage is endorsed for insurance pursuant to the sale of an Investor Sponsor Project or covers Existing Construction not involving Commissioner approved or required repairs, improvements, alterations and additions, the mortgagee, on the date of the insurance endorsement, shall pay a first premium equal to one-half of one percent of the principal obligation of the mortgage for the period from the date of the insruance endorsement to one year following the date of the first principal payment. On the anniversary of the first principal payment, this first premium shall be adjusted to equal one-half of one percent of the average outstanding principal obligation of the mortgage for the period from the date of the insurance endorsement to

one year following the date of the first principal payment.

(b) The premium provisions of paragraph (a) of this section shall apply to a supplementary loan to purchase an existing community facility.

§ 213.258 Subsequent annual premiums.

(a) Until the mortgage is paid in full or until receipt by the Commissioner of an application for insurance benefits, or until the contract of insurance is otherwise terminated with the consent of the Commissioner, the mortgagee, on each anniversary of the date of the first principal payment, shall pay an annual mortgage insurance premium equal to one-half of one percent of the average outstanding principal obligation of the mortgage for the year following the date on which such premium becomes payable.

(b) The provisions of paragraph (a) of this section shall apply to operating loss loans and to supplementary loans.

§ 213.259 Computation of subsequent annual premiums.

The premiums payable on and after the date of the first principal payment shall be calculated in accordance with the amortization provisions without taking into account delinquent payments or prepayments.

§ 213.259a Premiums—mortgages insured pursuant to section 238(c) of the Act.

All of the provisions of §§ 213.253 through 213.259 governing mortgage insurance premiums shall apply to mortgages insured under this subpart pursuant to section 238(c) of the Act, except that all mortgage insurance premiums due on such mortgages in accordance with §§ 213.253 through 213.259 shall be calculated on the basis of one percent.

[42 FR 59675, Nov. 18, 1977]

§ 213.260 Allowable methods of premium payment.

Premiums shall be payable in cash or in debentures at par plus accrued interest. All premiums are payable in advance and no refund can be made of any portion thereof except as hereinafter provided in this part.

§213.265 Modifications and consolidations.

Where a mortgage covering an investor sponsored project is modified and consolidated with the mortgage of a purchasing nonprofit cooperative housing corporation or trust, it shall be deemed to be paid in full as of the date of such modification and consolidation.

[37 FR 8662, Apr. 29, 1972]

§213.266 Initial insurance endorsement.

The Commissioner shall indicate his insurance of the mortgage or supplementary loan by endorsing the original credit instrument and identifying the section of the Act and the regulations under which the mortgage or supplementary loan is insured and the date of insurance.

§213.266a Insurance fund obligations.

A mortgage endorsed for insurance under section 213 of the Act shall be the obligation either of the Cooperative Management Housing Insurance Fund or of the General Insurance Fund. The determination of the applicable fund shall be governed by the following:

(a) A mortgage insured under section 213(a)(1) of the Act or under section 213(a)(3) if the project has been acquired by a cooperative corporation or under section 213 (i) or (j) shall be the obligation of the Cooperative Management Housing Insurance Fund, where it has been insured pursuant to a commitment issued on or after August 10, 1965, or insured pursuant to a commitment issued prior to such date, and transferred to the Cooperative Management Housing Insurance Fund.

(b) A mortgage insured under section 213(a)(2) of the Act or under section 213(a)(3) where the project has not been acquired by a cooperative corporation shall be the obligation of the General Insurance Fund. A mortgage insured prior to August 10, 1965, or insured pursuant to a commitment issued prior to such date, where the project has not been transferred to the Cooperative Management Housing Insurance Fund, shall also be the obligation of the General Insurance Fund.

§213.267 Effect of insurance endorsement.

From the date of initial endorsement, the Commissioner and the mortgagee or lender shall be bound by the provisions of this subpart to the same extent as if they had executed a contract including the provisions of this subpart and the applicable sections of the Act.

§213.268 Final insurance endorsement.

When all advances of mortgage or loan proceeds have been made and all the terms and conditions of the commitment have been complied with to the satisfaction of the Commissioner, he shall indicate on the original credit instrument the total of all advances he has approved for insurance and again endorse such instrument.

§213.269 Endorsement of supplementary loans.

The provisions of §§213.266, 213.267, and 213.268 shall apply to supplementary loans.

§213.270 Supplementary loans; election of action; claims; debentures.

(a) *Election of action.* Where a real estate mortgage, deed of trust, conditional sales contract, chattel mortgage, lien, judgement, or any other security device has been used to secure the payment of a loan made under the provisions of this section, the lender may not, except with the approval of the Commissioner, both proceed against such security and also make claim under its contract of insurance, but shall elect which method it desires to pursue.

(b) *Maximum claim period.* Notice of intention to file claim on a form prescribed by the Commissioner shall be filed within 45 days after the lender becomes eligible for the benefits of the loan insurance, or within such later time as may be agreed upon by the Commissioner in writing.

(c) *Items to be filed on submitting claim.* Within 30 days after the filing of the notice of intention to file claim, or within such further period as may be agreed upon by the Commissioner in writing, the lender shall file with the Commissioner:

321

(1) The fiscal data pertaining to the loan transaction;

(2) Receipts covering all disbursements as required by the fiscal data form;

(3) The original note and any security instrument or instruments which shall be assigned to the Commissioner without recourse or warranty, except that the lender must warrant that no act or omission of the lender has impaired the validity and priority of such security instrument or instruments, that the security instrument or instruments, are prior to all mechanics' and materialmen's liens filed of record subsequent to the recording of such security instrument or instruments regardless of whether such liens attached prior to such recording date, and prior to all liens and encumbrances which may have attached or defects which may have arisen subsequent to the recording of such security instrument or instruments, except such liens or other matters as may be approved by the Commissioner, that the amount stated in the instrument of assignment is actually due and owing under the security instrument or instruments, that there are no offsets or counterclaims thereto, and that the lender has a good right to assign such note and security instrument or instruments;

(4) All hazard insurance policies held on property serving as security for the loan or other evidence of insurance coverage acceptable to the Commissioner, together with a copy of the lender's notification to the carrier authorizing the amendment of the loss payable clause substituting the Commissioner as the holder of the security instrument;

(5) The assignment to the Commissioner of all rights and interests arising under the note and security instrument or instruments so in default, and all claims of the lender against the borrower or others arising out of the loan transaction;

(6) All policies of title or other insurance or surety bonds, or other guarantees and any and all claims thereunder; including evidence satisfactory to the Commissioner that the original title coverage has been extended to include the assignment of the note and the security instrument or instruments to the Commissioner;

(7) Any balance of the loan not advanced to the borrower;

(8) Any cash or property held by the lender or its agents or to which it is entitled; including deposits made for the account of the borrower and which have not been applied in reduction of the principal obligation under the note and security instrument or instruments;

(9) All records, ledger cards, documents, books, papers and accounts relating to the loan transaction;

(10) Any additional information or data which the Commissioner may require.

(d) *Claim computation.* Upon an acceptable assignment of the note and security instrument, the Commissioner shall pay the claim of the lender in cash, in debentures or in a combination of both, as determined by the Commissioner at the time of payment. The payment shall be in an amount equal to the unpaid principal balance of the supplementary loan plus:

(1) Any accrued interest due on the supplementary loan as of the date of execution of its assignment to the Commissioner;

(2) Any advance made previously under the provisions of the loan instrument and approved by the Commissioner;

(3) Reimbursement for such reasonable collection costs, court costs, and attorney's fees as may be approved by the Commissioner;

(4) An amount equivalent to the debenture interest which would have been earned on the portion of the insurance benefits paid in cash, as of the date such cash payment is made, except that when the lender fails to meet any one of the applicable requirements of paragraphs (b) and (c) of this section within the specified time and in a manner satisfactory to the Commissioner (or within such further time as the Commissioner may approve in writing), the interest allowance in such cash payment shall be computed only to the date on which the particular required action should have been taken or to which it was extended.

(e) *Debenture interest.* The debentures shall bear interest as provided in §207.259(e)(6) of this chapter.

(f) *Maturity of debentures.* Debentures shall mature 20 years from the date of issue.

(g) *Registration of debentures.* Debentures shall be registered as to principal and interest.

(h) *Denomination of debentures.* Debentures shall be issued in multiples of $50 and any difference not in excess of $50 between the amount of debentures to which the lender is otherwise entitled hereunder and the aggregate face value of the debentures issued shall be paid in cash by the Commissioner to the lender.

(i) *Redemption of debentures.* Debentures shall, at the option of the Commissioner and with the approval of the Secretary of the Treasury, be redeemable at par plus accrued interest on any semiannual interest payment date on 3 months' notice of redemption given in such manner as the Commissioner shall prescribe. The debenture interest on the debentures called for redemption shall cease on the semiannual interest payment date designated in the call notice. The Commissioner may include with the notice of redemption an offer to purchase the debentures at par plus accrued interest at any time during the period between the notice of redemption and the redemption date. If the debentures are purchased by the Commissioner after such call and prior to the named redemption date, the debenture interest shall cease on the date of purchase.

(j) *Issue date of debentures.* The debentures shall be issued as of the date of the execution of the assignment of the supplementary loan in accordance with the requirements of paragraph (c)(3) of this section.

COOPERATIVE MANAGEMENT HOUSING INSURANCE AND DISTRIBUTIVE SHARES

§213.275 Nature of the Cooperative Management Housing Insurance Fund.

The Cooperative Management Housing Insurance Fund shall consist of the General Surplus Account and the Participating Reserve Account.

§213.276 Allocation of Cooperative Management Housing Insurance Fund income or losses.

For any semiannual period in which Cooperative Management Housing Insurance Fund operations shall result in a net income, or loss, the Commissioner shall allocate such net income or such loss to the General Surplus Account, to the Participating Reserve Account, or to both, as he may determine to be in accordance with sound actuarial and accounting practice. In determining net income or loss, the Commissioner shall take into consideration all income received from fees, premiums, and earnings on investments of the Fund, operating expenses, and provision for losses of the Fund.

§213.277 Right and liability under the Cooperative Management Housing Insurance Fund.

No mortgagor or mortgagee shall have any vested right in a credit balance in either the General Surplus Account or the Participating Reserve Account. No mortgagor or mortgagee shall be subject to any liability arising under the mutuality of the Cooperative Management Housing Insurance Fund.

§213.278 Distribution of distributive share.

When the contract of insurance is terminated by reason of payment in full of the mortgage or by voluntary termination approved by the Commissioner, and at such time or times prior to such termination as the Commissioner may approve, the Commissioner may distribute to a mortgagor under a mortgage that is the obligation of the Cooperative Management Housing Insurance Fund a share of the Participating Reserve Account in such manner and amount as he shall determine to be equitable and in accordance with sound actuarial and accounting practice.

§213.279 Maximum amount of distributive share.

In no event shall a distributive share of the Participating Reserve Account exceed the aggregate paid scheduled annual premiums of the mortgagor paid to the year of termination of the insurance or to the year of payment of the share, if paid prior to termination.

§ 213.280 Finality of determination.

The determination of the Commissioner as to the amount to be paid to any mortgagor from the Cooperative Management Housing Insurance Fund shall be final and conclusive.

Subpart C—Individual Properties Released From Project Mortgage; Expiring Program

§ 213.501 Savings clause.

No new loans are being insured under the Cooperative Housing Mortgage Insurance Program for individual properties released from a project mortgage. Any existing insured loans on individual properties released from a project mortgage under this program will continue to be governed by the regulations on eligibility requirements, contract rights and obligations, and servicing responsibilities in effect as they existed immediately before December 26, 1996.

[61 FR 60160, Nov. 26, 1996]

PART 214—HOUSING COUNSELING PROGRAM

Subpart A—General Program Requirements

AUTHORITY: 12 U.S.C. 1701x, 1701x-1; 42 U.S.C. 3535(d).

SOURCE: 72 FR 55648, Sept. 28, 2007, unless otherwise noted.

Subpart A—General Program Requirements

§ 214.1 Purpose.

This part implements the Housing Counseling Program authorized by section 106 of the Housing and Urban Development Act of 1968 (12 U.S.C. 1701x). Section 106 authorizes HUD to make grants to, or contract with, public or private organizations to provide a broad range of housing counseling services to homeowners and tenants to assist them in improving their housing conditions and in meeting the responsibilities of tenancy or homeownership. Section 106 also directs HUD to provide housing counseling services only through agencies or individuals that have been certified by HUD as competent to provide such services. The regulations contained in this part prescribe the procedures and requirements by which the Housing Counseling Program will be administered, including the process by which agencies are approved and individuals will be certified to provide the homeownership and rental counseling, as defined by section 106. These regulations apply to all agencies participating in HUD's Housing Counseling Program, and to all organizations or entities that deliver housing counseling, including homeownership counseling or rental housing counseling, required under or provided in connection with HUD programs.

[81 FR 90657, Dec. 14, 2016]

§ 214.3 Definitions.

The following definitions apply throughout this part:

Action plan. A plan that outlines what the housing counseling agency and the client will do in order to meet the client's housing goals and, when appropriate, addresses the client's housing problem(s).

Affiliate. A nonprofit organization participating in the HUD-related Housing Counseling program of a regional or national intermediary, or state housing finance agency. The affiliate organization is incorporated separately from the regional or national intermediary or state housing finance agency. An affiliate is:

(1) Duly organized and existing as a tax-exempt nonprofit organization;

(2) In good standing under the laws of the state of the organization; and

(3) Authorized to do business in the states where it proposes to provide housing counseling services.

Branch or branch office. An organizational and subordinate unit of a local housing counseling agency, multi-state organization, regional or national intermediary, or state housing finance agency not separately incorporated or organized, that participates in HUD's Housing Counseling program. A branch or branch office must be in good standing under the laws of the state where it proposes to provide housing counseling services. A branch or branch office cannot be a subgrantee or affiliate.

Clients. Individuals or households who seek the assistance of an agency participating in HUD's Housing Counseling program to meet a housing need or resolve a housing problem.

Counseling. Counselor to client assistance that addresses unique financial circumstances or housing issues and focuses on ways of overcoming specific obstacles to achieving a housing goal such as repairing credit, addressing a rental dispute, purchasing a home, locating cash for a down payment, being informed of fair housing and fair lending requirements of the Fair Housing Act, finding units accessible to persons with disabilities, avoiding foreclosure, or resolving a financial crisis. Except for reverse mortgage counseling, all counseling shall involve the creation of an action plan.

Education. Formal classes, with established curriculum and instructional goals provided in a group or classroom setting, covering topics applicable to groups of people such as, but not limited to:

(1) Renter rights;

(2) The homebuying process;

(3) How to maintain a home;

(4) Budgeting;

(5) Fair housing;

(6) Identifying and reporting predatory lending practices;

(7) Rights for persons with disabilities; and

(8) The importance of good credit.

Homeownership counseling. See definition at 24 CFR 5.100.

Housing counseling. See definition at 24 CFR 5.100.

Housing counseling grant funds. Grants awarded to participating agencies under section 106 of the Housing and Urban Development Act of 1968 (12 U.S.C. 1701x).

Housing counseling work plan. A participating agency's plan to provide housing counseling activities and services in a specified geographic area to resolve or mitigate identified community needs and problems. The plan will also describe the objectives of the agency and the resources available to meet those objectives. An intermediary's state housing finance agency's (SHFA) or multistate organization's (MSO) plan includes similar information regarding the services they propose to provide to the network of affiliated agencies or branches participating in their HUD-related Housing Counseling program.

Housing goal. A realistic, short- or long-term objective set by the client, with advice from a housing counselor.

HUD-approved housing counseling agency. Private and public nonprofit organizations that are exempt from taxation under section 501(a), pursuant to section 501(c) of the Internal Revenue Code of 1996, 26 U.S.C. 501(a) and 501(c) and approved by HUD, in accordance with this part and 106(e) of the Housing and Urban Development Act of 1968 (12 U.S.C. 1701x(e)), to provide housing counseling services to clients directly, or through their affiliates or branches, and which meet the requirements set forth in this part.

HUD certified housing counselor. A housing counselor who has passed the HUD Certification examination, works for a participating agency, and is certified by HUD as competent to provide housing counseling services pursuant to this part.

Intermediary. A HUD-approved organization that provides housing counseling services indirectly through its branches or affiliates, for whom it exercises control over the quality and type of housing counseling services rendered. The Housing Counseling program recognizes two types of intermediaries, which include:

(1) *National intermediary.* A national intermediary provides, in multiple regions of the United States:

(i) Housing counseling services through its branches or affiliates or both; and

(ii) Administrative and supportive services to its network of affiliates or branches, including, but not limited to, pass-through funding, training, and technical assistance.

(2) *Regional intermediary.* A regional intermediary provides in a generally recognized region within the United States, such as the Southwest, Mid-Atlantic, New England:

(i) Housing counseling services through its branches or affiliates or both; and

(ii) Administrative and supportive services to its network of affiliates, or branches, including, but not limited to, pass-through funding, training, and technical assistance.

Local housing counseling agency (LHCA). A housing counseling agency that directly provides housing counseling services. An LHCA may have a main office, and one or more branch offices, in no more than two contiguous states.

Multi-state organization (MSO). A multi-state organization provides housing counseling services through a main office and branches in two or more states.

Nonprofit organization. Shall have the meaning given in section 104(5) of the Cranston-Gonzalez National Affordable Housing Act (42 U.S.C. 12704(5)), except that subparagraph (D) of such section shall not apply.

Participating agency. Participating agencies are all housing counseling and intermediary organizations participating in HUD's Housing Counseling program, including HUD-approved agencies, and affiliates and branches of HUD-approved intermediaries, HUD-approved MSOs, and state housing finance agencies.

Rental housing counseling. See definition at 24 CFR 5.100.

Reverse mortgage. A mortgage that pays a homeowner loan proceeds drawn from accumulated home equity and that requires no repayment until a future time.

State. Each of the several States, the Commonwealth of Puerto Rico, the District of Columbia, the Commonwealth of the Northern Mariana Islands, Guam, the Virgin Islands, American Samoa, or any other possession of the United States.

State housing finance agency (SHFA). Any public body, agency, or instrumentality created by a specific act of a state legislature empowered to finance activities designed to provide housing and related facilities through land acquisition, construction, or rehabilitation throughout an entire state. SHFAs may provide direct counseling services or subgrant housing counseling funds, or both, to affiliated housing counseling agencies within the SHFA's state. "State" includes the several states, Puerto Rico, the District of Columbia, Guam, the Commonwealth of the Northern Mariana Islands, American Samoa, and the U.S. Virgin Islands.

Subgrantee. An affiliate of a HUD-approved intermediary or SHFA that receives a subgrant of housing counseling funds provided under a HUD grant.

Unit of general local government. Any city, county, parish, town, township, borough, village, or any other general purpose political subdivision of a State.

[72 FR 55648, Sept. 28, 2007, as amended at 81 FR 90658, Dec. 14, 2016]

Subpart B—Approval and Disapproval of Housing Counseling Agencies

§214.100 General.

An organization may be approved by HUD as a HUD-approved housing counseling agency upon meeting the requirements of §214.103 and upon completing the application procedures set forth in this subpart B.

(a) *Approval.* The approval of a housing counseling agency and the certification of a HUD certified housing counselor does not create or imply a warranty or endorsement by HUD of the approved agency, or its employees, including counselors, to a prospective client or to any other organization or individual, nor does it represent a warranty of any housing counseling provided by the agency or a HUD certified housing counselor working for an agency. Approval means only that the agency has met the qualifications and conditions prescribed by HUD, and a HUD certified housing counselor only means the housing counselor has successfully passed an examination pursuant to these regulations and works for a participating agency.

(b) *Effective date.* Agencies approved by HUD on or before October 29, 2007 and agencies that have submitted applications to HUD on or before September 28, 2007 and that are subsequently approved, are required to be in full compliance with the requirements in this part on October 1, 2007. Agencies approved after October 29, 2007 must comply with this part.

[72 FR 55648, Sept. 28, 2007, as amended at 81 FR 90658, Dec. 14, 2016]

§214.103 Approval criteria.

The following criteria for approval apply to all agencies, MSOs, and intermediaries, including all local housing counseling agencies, branches, and affiliates that are included in one application:

(a) *Nonprofit and tax-exempt status.* A housing counseling agency must function as a private or public nonprofit organization, or be a unit of local, county, or state government. The agency must submit evidence of nonprofit status and tax-exempt status under section 501(a), pursuant to section 501(c) of the Internal Revenue Code of 1996 (26 U.S.C. 501(a) and (c)). Units of local, county, or state government must submit proof of their authorization to provide housing counseling services.

(b) *Experience.* An agency must have successfully administered a Housing Counseling program for at least one year. An intermediary must have operated in an intermediary capacity for at least one year. To be considered part of an LHCA's, MSO's, or intermediary's approval application, and to participate in the HUD-approved portion of the intermediary's, SHFA's, or MSO's Housing Counseling program, affiliates and branches must have successfully administered a Housing Counseling program for at least one year.

(c) *Ineligible participants.* An agency, including any of the agency's directors, partners, officers, principals, or employees, must not be:

(1) Suspended, debarred, or otherwise restricted under the Department's, or any other federal regulations;

(2) Indicted for, or convicted of, a criminal offense that reflects upon the responsibility, integrity, or ability of the agency to participate in housing counseling activities. These offenses include criminal offenses that can be prosecuted at a local, state, or federal level;

(3) Subject to unresolved findings as a result of HUD or other government audit or investigations.

(d) *Community base.* A housing counseling agency and its HUD Program branches and affiliates must have functioned for at least one year in the geographical area(s) the agency set forth in its housing counseling work plan.

(e) *Recordkeeping and reporting.* The agency must have an established system of recordkeeping so that client files, electronic and paper, can be reviewed and annual activity data for the agency can be verified, reported, and analyzed. Client files, both electronic and paper, must be kept confidential, in accordance with §214.315. This system must meet the requirements of 2 CFR part 200, subpart D, 24 CFR 1.6, and 24 CFR part 121 and can be easily accessible to HUD for all monitoring and audit purposes.

(f) *Client management system.* All participating agencies shall utilize an automated housing counseling client management system for the collection and reporting of client-level information, including, but not limited to, financial and demographic data, counseling services provided, and outcomes data. The system used must provide the counseling agency with the tools necessary to track and manage all counseling and educational activities associated with each client. Agencies must utilize a Client Management System that satisfies HUD's requirements and interfaces with HUD's databases.

(g) *Housing counseling resources.* The agency must have the following resources sufficient to implement the proposed housing counseling work plan no later than the date of HUD approval:

(1) *Funding.* The application for approval must provide evidence of funds immediately available, or written commitment for funds to cover the cost of operating the housing counseling work plan during the initial 12-month period of HUD approval.

(2) *Staff.* The agency must employ staff trained in housing counseling. All staff providing housing counseling, including homeownership counseling or rental housing counseling, must be HUD certified housing counselors, and at least half the agency's counselors must have at least 6 months of experience in the job they will perform in the agency's housing counseling program.

(3) *Language skills.* The agency must have housing counselor(s) who are fluent in the language of the clients they serve, or the housing counseling agency must use the services of an interpreter, or the agency must refer the client to another agency that can meet the client's needs.

(h) *Knowledge of HUD programs and local housing market.* The agency's housing counseling staff must possess a working knowledge of HUD's housing and single-family mortgage insurance programs, other state and local housing programs available in the community, consolidated plans, and the local housing market. The staff should be familiar with housing programs offered by conventional mortgage lenders and other housing or related programs that may assist their clients.

(i) *Contracts or agreements to provide eligible housing counseling services.* An agency and its branches or subgrantees or affiliates must deliver all of the housing counseling activities set forth in the agency's housing counseling work plan. It is not permissible to contract out housing counseling services, except:

(1) In geographic areas where a need for housing counseling services is demonstrated and no HUD-approved housing counseling agency or its branches, affiliates, or subgrantees exists. Under this exception, the contract must delineate the respective Housing Counseling program responsibilities of the contracting parties, the agency providing services (contractor) must meet the HUD approval eligibility standards, and the contracting agency must receive prior written approval from HUD.

(2) Intermediaries and SHFAs may enter into agreements with affiliates to provide housing counseling services. The agreements with affiliates may be in the form of an exchange of letters that delineate the respective Housing Counseling program responsibilities of the parties. Agreements must be sufficiently detailed to establish accountability and allow for adequate monitoring in accordance with 2 CFR part 200.

(3) With prior approval from HUD, and at HUD's discretion, intermediary organizations may operate a Housing Counseling program with a network of affiliated counselors, rather than affiliated counseling agencies, if the structure is designed to meet a special housing counseling need identified by HUD.

(j) *Community resources.* The housing counseling agency must have established working relationships with private and public community resources to which it can refer clients who need help the agency cannot offer, including agencies offering similar or related services to non-English speaking clients.

(k) *State and local requirements.* An agency and its branches and affiliates must meet all state and local requirements for its operation.

(l) *Facilities.* All housing counseling facilities of the agency and its branches, affiliates, and subgrantees must meet the following criteria:

(1) Have a clearly identified office, with space available for the provision of housing counseling services. The office should operate during normal business hours and offer extended hours when necessary;

(2) Provide privacy for in-person counseling and confidentiality of client records;

(3) Provide accessibility features or make alternate accommodations for persons with disabilities, in accordance with section 504 of the Rehabilitation Act of 1973 (29 U.S.C. 794), 24 CFR parts 8 and 9, and the Americans with Disabilities Act (42 U.S.C. 12101 et seq.).

(m) *Housing counseling work plan.* (1) The agency must submit a detailed yet concise housing counseling plan that explains: The needs and problems of the target population; how the agency will address one or more of these needs and problems with its available resources; the type of housing counseling services offered; fee structure, if applicable; the geographic service area to be served; and the anticipated results (outcomes) to be achieved within the period of approval.

(2) The plan must be periodically reviewed and, when changed or amended, the agency must notify and provide a copy to HUD.

(3) The plan must meet the basic requirements described in §214.300.

(4) An agency's housing counseling work plan must also address, if appropriate, alternative settings and formats for the provision of housing counseling services.

(n) *Certification of housing counselors.* (1) In order for an agency to participate in HUD's Housing Counseling Program, all individuals who provide counseling, including homeownership and rental housing counseling, must be HUD certified according to requirements in this section.

(2) For an individual to become a HUD certified counselor, an individual must pass a standardized written examination to demonstrate competency in each of the following areas:

(i) Financial management;

(ii) Property maintenance;

(iii) Responsibilities of homeownership and tenancy;

(iv) Fair housing laws and requirements;

(v) Housing affordability; and

(vi) Avoidance of, and response to, rental or mortgage delinquency and avoidance of eviction or mortgage default.

(3) HUD will certify an individual housing counselor who has met the requirements of paragraph (n)(1) of this section upon verification that the individual works for a participating agency.

(4) Participating agencies and housing counselors must be in compliance with requirements of paragraph (n) of this section by 36 months after HUD commences the administration of the certification examination by publication in the FEDERAL REGISTER.

[72 FR 55648, Sept. 28, 2007, as amended at 80 FR 75936, Dec. 7, 2015; 81 FR 90658, Dec. 14, 2016]

§214.105 Preliminary application process.

(a) *Submission.* All agencies must complete the forms prescribed by HUD and submit the application and all supporting documentation to HUD. Agencies with branches or affiliates for which the parent entity exercises control over the quality and type of housing counseling services rendered must submit a single application for approval.

(b) Notwithstanding paragraph (a), SHFAs are not required to submit an application for HUD approval. However, to participate in HUD's Housing Counseling program, SHFAs must either submit a request and provide HUD with a list of affiliates, if applicable, and assure that they meet all program requirements, or submit a request through such other application procedure as HUD may periodically announce in the FEDERAL REGISTER or other informational sources.

§214.107 Approval by HUD.

(a) *Notice of approval.* If an application package meets all requirements outlined in §214.103, HUD will approve an agency for a period of up to 3 years. HUD will advise the agency of its approval in the form of an approval letter to the agency's main office.

329

(b) *Certificate of Approval.* HUD will issue a "Certificate of Approval" to the approved agency. The certificate will show the period of approval.

(c) *Appearance on list of HUD-approved and participating housing counseling agencies.* For purposes of client referrals, participating agencies that provide housing counseling services directly to clients must provide HUD with the agency name and contact information, which may appear on HUD's Web site. In addition, names and addresses of all participating agencies that provide housing counseling services directly may be made available to the public through HUD's toll-free housing counseling hotline.

§ 214.109 Disapproval by HUD.

If an application package does not meet all requirements in § 214.103, HUD will provide the agency with the reasons for the denial in writing. Within 30 calendar days of the written notice of denial, the agency may submit a revised application, or appeal HUD's decision in writing to HUD, as provided in § 214.205. If an agency decides to submit a revised application, the agency may consult HUD, to determine the specific actions needed to resolve the deficiencies.

Subpart C—Inactive Status, Termination, and Appeals

§ 214.200 Inactive status.

(a) HUD may change a participating agency's status to inactive, in lieu of terminations of HUD-approved status or removals from the list of HUD-approved agencies, under certain circumstances that may temporarily impair an agency from complying with its housing counseling plan. An agency's status may be changed to inactive on a case-by-case basis for a period not to exceed 6 months, unless an extension is provided by HUD under paragraph (d) of this section. HUD may change an agency's status through either a request submitted to HUD or as a result of information obtained by the Department. Some of the conditions under which inactive status may be considered include, but are not limited to:

(1) Loss of counselor(s);

(2) Damage to facilities by natural disasters that renders the agency unable to function properly;

(3) Loss of funds;

(4) Relocation;

(5) Other circumstances caused by reasons beyond the agency's control; or

(6) Results of performance review.

(b) Agencies that seek temporary inactive status must submit a request to HUD in writing. Documentation or evidence of the condition(s) that rendered the agency incapable of carrying out its housing counseling plan must be submitted along with the request, if possible. Upon receipt of the request, HUD will review and notify the agency of approval or rejection, in writing. If approved, the agency's name and contact information will be temporarily removed from the HUD-approved Web list of agencies and the telephone referral system.

(c) The agency must notify HUD in writing and provide supporting documentation or evidence when it is ready to resume operation, or no later than the end of the inactive period. After review and acceptance by HUD, the agency's contact information may be restored to the Web list of HUD-approved and participating agencies and the telephone referral system.

(d) At HUD's discretion, if the condition(s) still exists, an extension of the inactive period may be considered or the agency may be terminated or removed from the Housing Counseling program. HUD will notify the agency in writing of its decision.

§ 214.201 Termination of HUD-approved status and grant agreements.

(a) *Cause for termination by HUD.* HUD may terminate an agency's approval; remove an SHFA; remove one or more branches or affiliates from the HUD portion of an intermediary's, MSO's, or SHFA's counseling program; and terminate any grant agreements (if applicable) upon confirmation of any of the following reasons:

(1) Noncompliance with program requirements;

(2) Failure to implement in whole or in part the agency's approved housing

counseling work plan or failure to notify HUD of changes in the agency's housing counseling work plan;

(3) Lack of the capacity to deliver the housing counseling activities described in its approved housing counseling work plan;

(4) Failure to achieve outcomes described in the work plan;

(5) Misuse of grant funds; or

(6) HUD determines that there is good cause.

(b) *Agency withdrawal.* The participating agency may withdraw from the Housing Counseling program at any time.

(c) *Post-termination, post-withdrawal requirements.* All terminations by HUD, or an agency's withdrawal, must be in writing. When a termination or withdrawal occurs, the agency must return to HUD any unexpired "Certificate of Approval." A terminated or inactive agency cannot continue to display the certificate. If HUD has determined that an agency will be terminated from participating in the Housing Counseling program, and an agency does not voluntarily withdraw, then HUD may follow the provisions found in 24 CFR part 24.

§214.203 Re-approval or removal as a result of a performance review.

HUD may conduct a periodic performance review for all agencies participating in the Housing Counseling program. The performance review and the terms of re-approval or removal of a participating agency are described in §214.307 and §214.309. At the end of the approval period, and upon completion of a successful performance review, if conducted, HUD will reapprove agencies.

§214.205 Appeals.

An agency making an application for approval, or an approved agency seeking reapproval, shall have the right to appeal any adverse decisions rendered by HUD under this part:

(a) *Appeal must be in writing.* An agency may make a formal written appeal to HUD.

(b) *Timeliness.* HUD must receive an appeal within 30 days of the date of the HUD decision letter to the applicant agency. HUD is not bound to review appeals received after this 30-calendar day period.

(c) *Other action.* Nothing in this section prohibits HUD from taking such other action against an agency as provided in 24 CFR part 24, or from seeking any other remedy against an agency available to HUD by statute or otherwise.

Subpart D—Program Administration

§214.300 Counseling services.

(a) *Basic requirements.* (1) Agencies must provide counseling to current and potential homeowners and tenants to assist them in improving their housing conditions and in meeting the responsibilities of homeownership or tenancy.

(2) Except for reverse mortgage counseling, housing counselors and clients must establish an action plan for each counseling client.

(3) Counseling may take place in the office of the housing counseling agency, at an alternate location, or by telephone, as long as mutually acceptable to the housing counselor and client. All agencies participating in HUD's Housing Counseling program that provide services directly to clients must provide in-person counseling to clients that prefer this format.

(4) Regardless of setting or format, counseling activities must be limited to the geographic area specified in the agency's approved housing counseling work plan.

(5) With prior approval from HUD, a network of affiliated counselors or a HUD roster of counselors, designed to meet a special housing counseling need, may be permitted to provide specified types of counseling nationally.

(6) All participating agencies that offer group educational sessions must also offer individual counseling on the same topics covered in the group educational sessions.

(7) All participating agencies that provide homeownership counseling, shall address the entire process of homeownership, including, but not limited to, the decision to purchase a home, the selection and purchase of a home, the home inspection process, issues arising during or affecting the

period of ownership of a home (including, but not limited to, financing, refinancing, default, and foreclosure, and other financial decisions), and the sale or other disposition of a home.

(8) All participating agencies that provide rental housing counseling shall address issues related to the rental of residential property, which may include counseling regarding future homeownership opportunities, the decision to rent, responsibilities of tenancy, affordability of renting, and eviction prevention.

(9) As part of the homeownership counseling process, participating agencies shall provide clients with such materials as HUD may require regarding the availability and importance of obtaining an independent home inspection.

(b) *Counseling services.* For each client, all agencies participating in HUD's Housing Counseling program shall offer the following basic services:

(1) Housing counseling, on at least one of the topics described in paragraph (d) of this section, that enables a client to make informed and reasonable decisions to achieve his or her housing goal.

(2) Referrals to local, state, and federal resources.

(c) *Follow-up.* Make a reasonable effort to have follow-up communication with the client, when possible, to assure that the client is progressing toward his or her housing goal, to modify or terminate housing counseling, and to learn and report outcomes.

(d) *Agency's housing counseling work plan.* (1) A participating agency shall deliver housing counseling services consistent with the agency's housing counseling work plan. The work plan should identify housing counseling services to be provided in response to one or more of the needs in targeted communities and geographic areas where the agency and its branches and affiliates provide their housing counseling services.

(2) Participating agencies may also conduct marketing and outreach, including, but not limited to, providing general information about housing opportunities, conducting information campaigns, and raising awareness about critical housing topics such as predatory lending and fair housing topics.

(e) *Approved housing counseling, education, and outreach topics.* The following are examples of approved housing counseling, education, and outreach topics that participating agencies may provide to and discuss with clients:

(1) Prepurchase/homebuying, including, but not limited to: Advice regarding readiness and preparation, Federal Housing Administration-insured financing, housing selection and mobility, search assistance, fair housing and predatory lending, budgeting and credit, loan product comparison, purchase procedures, and closing costs;

(2) Resolving or preventing mortgage delinquency, including, but not limited to: Default and foreclosure, loss mitigation, budgeting, and credit;

(3) Home maintenance and financial management for homeowners, including, but not limited to: Escrow funds, budgeting, refinancing, home equity, home improvement, utility costs, energy efficiency, rights and responsibilities of home owners, and reverse mortgages;

(4) Rental topics, including, but not limited to: HUD rental and rent subsidy programs; other federal, state or local assistance; fair housing; housing search assistance; landlord tenant laws; lease terms; rent delinquency; and

(5) Homeless assistance, including, but not limited to: Information regarding emergency shelter, other emergency services, and transitional housing.

[72 FR 55648, Sept. 28, 2007, as amended at 81 FR 90658, Dec. 14, 2016]

§ 214.303 Performance criteria.

To maintain HUD-approved status, a participating agency must meet the following requirements:

(a) *Approval status.* Agencies must continue to comply with approval requirements in § 214.103.

(b) *Workload.* During each 12-month period, the participating agency must provide housing counseling to at least 30 clients. Agencies that offer only housing counseling services limited to reverse mortgages, including home equity conversion mortgages (HECMs), are exempt from this requirement.

(c) *Reporting.* The agency must submit to HUD complete, accurate, and timely activity reports, as described in §214.317.

(d) *Agency's housing counseling work plan.* The agency must implement the housing counseling work plan and demonstrate reasonable achievement of the outcome objectives approved by HUD, as described in §214.103(k).

(e) *Client referrals from HUD and other participating agencies.* Except as described in this paragraph, all clients who contact the agency as a result of these referrals must be served. In cases where the agency does not offer the unique services requested by the client or does not have sufficient resources, the agency must refer the client to another participating agency, preferably in the area, or, failing the availability of a participating agency, must make a reasonable effort to refer the client to another agency, that can help the client meet his or her needs.

(f) *Conflicts of interest.* (1) A director, employee, officer, contractor, or agent of a participating agency shall not engage in activities that create a real or apparent conflict of interest. Such a conflict would arise if the director, employee, officer, contractor, agent, his or her spouse, child, general partner, or organization in which he or she serves as employee (other than with the participating counseling agency), or with whom he or she is negotiating future employment, has a direct interest in the client as a landlord, broker, or creditor, or originates, has a financial interest in, services, or underwrites a mortgage on the client's property, owns or purchases a property that the client seeks to rent or purchase, or serves as a collection agent for the client's mortgage lender, landlord, or creditor.

(2) A director, employee, officer, contractor, or agent of a participating agency shall not refer clients to mortgage lenders, brokers, builders, or real estate sales agents or brokers in which the officer, employee, director, his or her spouse, child, or general partner has a financial interest, neither may they acquire the client's property from the trustee in bankruptcy or accept a fee or any other consideration for referring a client to mortgage lenders, brokers, builders, or real estate sales agents or brokers.

(3) A director, employee, officer, contractor, or agent of a participating agency or any member of his or her immediate family shall avoid any action that might result in, or create the appearance of, administering the housing counseling operation for personal or private gain; providing preferential treatment to any organization or person; or undertaking any action that might compromise the agency's ability to ensure compliance with the requirements of this part and to serve the best interests of its clients.

(4) HUD may investigate agency practices and may take action to inactivate or terminate the agency's approval or participation in the Housing Counseling program.

(5) Participating agencies must notify HUD of conflicts of interest not later than 15 calendar days after the conflict occurred and report to HUD on the corrective action taken to cure the immediate, and avoid future, conflicts.

(g) *Disclosure requirements.* A participating agency must provide to all clients a disclosure statement that explicitly describes the various types of services provided by the agency and any financial relationships between this agency and any other industry partners. The disclosure must clearly state that the client is not obligated to receive any other services offered by the organization or its exclusive partners. Furthermore, the agency must provide information on alternative services, programs, and products.

(h) *Staff and supervision.* The agency must employ staff trained in housing counseling, and at least half the counselors must have at least 6 months of experience in the job they will perform in the agency's Housing Counseling program. Supervisors of the housing counselors must periodically monitor the work of the housing counselors by reviewing client files with the housing counselor to determine the adequacy and effectiveness of the housing counseling. The agency must document these monitoring activities and make the documentation available to HUD upon request.

(i) *Funding.* The agency must maintain a level of funds that enables it to provide housing counseling to at least the required workload of clients every year, whether or not the agency receives HUD funding.

§ 214.305 Agency profile changes.

Participating agencies must notify HUD within 15 days when any of the following occurs:

(a) The agency loses or changes its tax-exempt, nonprofit status.

(b) The agency no longer complies with local and state requirements.

(c) Changes occur in any of the items below:

(1) Address(es) of the agency's main office and the address(es) of its branches and affiliates;

(2) Staff personnel responsible for the Housing Counseling program, such as the housing counselors and management staff;

(3) Telephone numbers of the main office, affiliates, and branches; or

(4) Any other aspect of the agency's purpose or functions that may impair its ability to comply with these regulations or the applicable grant agreement (e.g., lack of qualified housing counselors).

§ 214.307 Performance review.

(a) HUD may conduct periodic on-site or desk performance reviews of all participating agencies.

(b) The performance review will consist of a review of the participating agency's compliance with all program requirements, including applicable civil rights requirements, and the agency's level of success in delivering counseling services.

§ 214.309 Reapproval and disapproval based on performance review.

Based on the performance review, HUD may determine whether to renew the approval unconditionally or conditionally, temporarily change status to inactive, or terminate approval or participation of the agency.

(a) *Unconditional Reapproval.* If the agency is in full compliance with the performance criteria of this part, HUD may reapprove the agency unconditionally for up to 3 years.

(b) *Conditional Reapproval.* If the agency fails to meet the performance criteria, but the failure does not seriously impair the agency's counseling capability as required in this part, HUD may extend the agency's approval or participation for up to 120 calendar days.

(c) *Inactive status.* HUD may temporarily change an agency's status to inactive, as provided in § 214.200.

(d) *Follow-up Review.* HUD may conduct a follow-up review to determine if the deficiencies have been corrected.

(e) *Termination of HUD Approval.* When HUD determines that the agency's program deficiencies seriously impair the agency's ability to comply with this part, HUD may terminate approval or participation of the agency immediately.

(f) *Appeal.* If HUD does not reinstate the approval, or terminates participation, the agency may file an appeal, as prescribed under § 214.205.

§ 214.311 Housing counseling grant funds.

(a) *HUD housing counseling grant funds.* HUD approval or program participation does not guarantee housing counseling grant funding. Funding for the Housing Counseling Program depends on appropriations from Congress, and are awarded competitively under Federal and HUD regulations and policies governing assistance programs, including the Department of Housing and Urban Development Reform Act of 1989 (42 U.S.C. 3545 *et seq.*). If housing counseling grant funds become available that are to be competitively awarded, HUD will notify the public through a Notice of Funding Availability (NOFA) in the FEDERAL REGISTER and by the Internet or other electronic media.

(b) *Local funding sources.* HUD recommends that approved agencies seek and secure funding from funding sources that may include local and state governments, private foundations, and lending or real estate organizations. Agencies must assure that such arrangements do not violate the provisions regarding conflicts of interest described in § 214.303(e).

(c) *Limitation on distribution of funds.* No housing counseling funds made available under the Housing Counseling Program shall be distributed to:

(1)(i) Any organization that has been convicted for a violation under Federal law relating to an election for Federal office or any organization that employs applicable individuals. For the purposes of this section, applicable individual means an individual who is:

(A) Employed by the organization in a permanent or temporary capacity;

(B) Contracted or retained by the organization; or

(C) Acting on behalf of, or with the express or apparent authority of, the organization; and

(D) Has been convicted for a violation under Federal law relating to an election for Federal office.

(ii) For the purposes of this paragraph (c)(1), a violation under Federal law relating to an election for Federal office includes, but is not limited to, a violation of one or more of the following statutory provisions related to Federal election fraud, voter intimidation, and voter suppression: 18 U.S.C. 241–242, 245(b)(1)(A), 592–611, and 42 U.S.C. 1973.

(2) A participating agency that provides housing counseling through housing counselors who are not HUD certified housing counselors in accordance with §214.103(n).

(d) *Misuse of housing counseling grant funds.* If any participating agency that receives housing counseling grant funds under the Housing Counseling Program is determined by HUD to have used those housing counseling grant funds in a manner that constitutes a material violation of applicable statutes and regulations, or any requirements or conditions under which such funds were provided:

(1) HUD shall require that, within 12 months after the date of the determination of such misuse, the agency shall reimburse HUD for such misused amounts and return to HUD any such amounts that remain unused or unobligated for use; and

(2) Such agency shall be ineligible, at any time after the date of such determination of material misuse, to apply for or receive further funds under the Housing Counseling Program.

(3) The remedies under paragraph (d) of this section are in addition to any other remedies that may be available under law.

[72 FR 55648, Sept. 28, 2007, as amended at 81 FR 90658, Dec. 14, 2016]

§214.313 **Housing counseling fees.**

(a) Participating agencies may charge reasonable and customary fees for housing education and counseling services, as long as the cost does not create a financial hardship for the client. An agency's fee schedule must be posted in a prominent place that is easily viewed by clients, and be available to HUD for review.

(b) Agencies must inform clients of the fee structure in advance of providing services. Clients cannot be charged for client intake.

(c) If any agency chooses to charge fees, the agency must conform to the following guidelines:

(1) Provide counseling without charge to persons who cannot afford the fees;

(2) Fees must be commensurate with the level of services provided;

(3) Agencies may not impose fees upon clients for the same portion of or for an entire service that is already funded with HUD grant funds.

(d) The agency may also be reimbursed from clients for the direct cost of obtaining copies of clients' credit reports from credit reporting bureaus if this does not cause a hardship for the client. In cases where the participating agency receives a discount for the cost of credit reports, this discount must be passed on to the client.

(e) Lenders may pay agencies for counseling services, through a lump sum or on a case-by-case basis, provided the level of payment does not exceed a level that is commensurate with the services provided, and is reasonable and customary for the area, and does not violate requirements under the Real Estate Settlement Procedures Act (12 U.S.C. 2601 *et seq.*). These transactions and relationships must be disclosed to the client as required in §214.303(g).

§214.315 **Recordkeeping.**

(a) *Recordkeeping system.* Each participating housing counseling agency

335

must maintain a recordkeeping system. The system must permit HUD to easily access all information needed for a performance review. This system must meet the requirements of 2 CFR part 200, subpart D, 24 CFR 1.6, and 24 CFR part 121.

(b) *File retention requirements.* Financial records, supporting documents, statistical records and all other pertinent records, both electronic and on paper, shall be retained for a period of 3 years from the date the case file was terminated for housing counseling. If the housing counseling agency is a recipient of a HUD housing counseling grant, then the client files for the housing counseling grant year must be retained for 3 years from the date the final grant invoice was paid by HUD.

(c) *Grant activities.* Recipients of HUD housing counseling grants are required to report activities under the grant in a format acceptable to HUD and within the designated time frames required by the applicable grant agreement.

(d) *Race, ethnicity, and income data.* Participating agencies must maintain current and accurate data on the race, ethnicity, and income of their counseling clients and education participants.

(e) *Client file.* The housing counseling agency must maintain a separate confidential file for each counseling client to document the action plan and the services provided to the client, as described in § 214.300. For all counseling, except for HECM counseling, the client file must include an action plan. The client file may be for an individual or household or for a group of clients with the same housing need.

(f) *Group education file.* The housing counseling agency must maintain a separate confidential file for each course provided. This file must contain a list of all participants, their race, ethnicity and income data, course title, course outline, instructors, and date of each course.

(g) *Confidentiality.* Participating agencies must ensure the confidentiality of each client's personal and financial information, including credit reports, whether the information is received from the client or from another source. Failure to maintain the confidentiality of, or improper use of,

credit reports may subject the agency to penalties under the Fair Credit Reporting Act (14 U.S.C. 1681 *et seq.*).

(h) *Termination of services.* The housing counseling agency must document in the client's file termination of housing counseling. Termination occurs or may occur under any of these conditions:

(1) The client meets his or her housing need or resolves the housing problem;

(2) The agency determines that further housing counseling will not meet the client's housing need or resolve the client's housing problem;

(3) The agency attempts to, but is unable to, locate the client;

(4) The client does not follow the agreed-upon action plan;

(5) The client otherwise terminates housing counseling; or

(6) The client fails to appear for housing counseling appointments.

[72 FR 55648, Sept. 28, 2007, as amended at 80 FR 75936, Dec. 7, 2015]

§ 214.317 Reporting.

All participating agencies shall submit to HUD activity reports, which may be required up to quarterly. The reports must be submitted in the format, by the deadline, and in the manner prescribed by HUD. Participating agencies that are also recipients of HUD grants or subgrants may be required to submit additional reports, as described in their grant agreements and prescribed by HUD.

Subpart E—Other Federal Requirements

§ 214.500 Audit.

Housing counseling grant recipients and subrecipients shall be subject to the audit requirements contained in 2 CFR part 200, subpart F. HUD must be provided a copy of the audit report within 30 days of completion.

[72 FR 55648, Sept. 28, 2007, as amended at 80 FR 75936, Dec. 7, 2015]

§ 214.503 Other requirements.

In addition to the requirements of this part, the Housing Counseling program is subject to applicable federal requirements in 24 CFR 5.105.

PART 219—FLEXIBLE SUBSIDY PROGRAM FOR TROUBLED PROJECTS

AUTHORITY: 12 U.S.C. 1715z-1a; 42 U.S.C. 3535(d).

SOURCE: 61 FR 14405, Apr. 1, 1996, unless otherwise noted.

§ 219.1 Program operations.

Effective May 1, 1996, the Flexible Subsidy Program for Troubled Projects will be governed and operate under the statutory provisions codified at 12 U.S.C. 1715z–1a, under the administrative policies and procedures contained in any applicable HUD Handbooks, and other administrative bulletins and notices as the Department may issue from time to time.

§ 219.2 Savings provision.

Part 219, as it existed immediately before May 1, 1996, (contained in the April 1, 1995 edition of 24 CFR, parts 200 to 219) will continue to govern the rights and obligations of housing owners, tenants, and the Department of Housing and Urban Development with respect to units and projects assisted under the Flexible Subsidy Program for Troubled Projects prior to May 1, 1996. A list of any amendments to this part published after the CFR revision date is available from the Office of the Rules Docket Clerk, Department of Housing and Urban Development, 451 Seventh Street, SW., Washington, DC 20410.

PART 220—MORTGAGE INSURANCE AND INSURED IMPROVEMENT LOANS FOR URBAN RENEWAL AND CONCENTRATED DEVELOPMENT AREAS

Subpart A [Reserved]

Subpart B—Contract Rights and Obligations—Homes

Subpart C—Eligibility Requirements—Projects

Subpart D—Contract Rights and Obligations—Projects

Subpart E—Servicing Responsibilites—Homes

AUTHORITY: 12 U.S.C. 1713, 1715b, 1715k, and 1735d; 42 U.S.C. 3535(d).

SOURCE: 36 FR 24573, Dec. 22, 1971, unless otherwise noted.

Subpart A [Reserved]

Subpart B—Contract Rights and Obligations—Homes

§ 220.251   Cross-reference.

(a) All of the provisions of subpart B, part 203 of this chapter covering mortgages insured under section 203 of the National Housing Act apply to mortgages covering 1- to 11-family dwellings insured under section 220 of the National Housing Act, except the following:

Sec.
203.258   Substitute mortgagors.
203.259   Scope.
203.280   One-time MIP.
203.281   Calculation of one-time MIP.
203.282   Mortgagee's late charge and interest.
203.283   Refund of one-time MIP.
203.340   Conditions of special forbearance relief.
203.342   Recasting of mortgage.
203.343   Partial release, addition or substitution of security.
203.350   Assignment of defaulted mortgage—ingeneral.
203.350a   Assignment of defaulted mortgage.
203.351   Application for insurance benefits and fiscal data.
203.353   Certification by mortgagee.
203.400   Method of payment.
203.402a   Reimbursement for uncollected interest.
203.420   Nature of Mutual Mortgage Insurance Fund.
203.421   Allocation of Mutual Mortgage Insurance Fund income or loss.
203.422   Right and liability under Mutual Mortgage Insurance Fund.
203.423   Distribution of distributive shares
203.424   Maximum amount of distributive shares.
203.425   Finality of determination.
203.438   Mortgages on Indian land insured pursuant to section 248 of the National Housing Act.
203.439   Mortgages on Hawaiian home lands insured pursuant to section 247 of the National Housing Act.
203.439a   Mortgages on property in Allegany Reservation of Seneca Nation of Indians authorized by section 203(q) of the National Housing Act.

(b) For the purposes of this subpart, all references in part 203 of this chapter to section 203 of the act shall be construed to refer to section 220 of the act, and all references to the Mutual Mort-gage Insurance Fund shall be construed to refer to the General Insurance Fund.

[36 FR 24573, Dec. 22, 1971, as amended at 42 FR 29304, June 8, 1977; 48 FR 28807, June 23, 1983; 51 FR 21874, June 16, 1986; 52 FR 8069, Mar. 16, 1987; 52 FR 28470, July 30, 1987; 52 FR 48203, Dec. 21, 1987; 53 FR 9869, Mar. 28, 1988; 55 FR 34808, Aug. 24, 1990]

§ 220.252   Forbearance of foreclosure and assignment of mortgage.

All of the provisions of §§ 203.340 through 203.342, 203.350, 203.352 and 203.353 of this chapter shall apply to mortgages insured under this subpart, except that the provisions relating to forbearance of foreclosure, recasting of the mortgage and assignment of a defaulted mortgage, shall be applicable only to a mortgage covering a property having not more than four dwelling units.

§ 220.253   Substitute mortgagors.

(a) *Selling mortgagor.* The mortgagee may effect the release of a mortgagor from personal liability on the mortgage note only if it obtains the Commissioner's approval of a substitute mortgagor, as provided by this section.

(b) *Purchasing mortgagor.* (1) The Commissioner may approve a substitute mortgagor with respect to any mortgage insured under subpart A of this part, if the substitute mortgagor is to occupy the dwelling as a principal residence or a secondary residence (as these terms are defined in § 220.30(d)).

(2) The Commissioner may approve as a substitute mortgagor an eligible non-occupant mortgagor (as defined in § 220.30(d)) with respect to any mortgage insured under this part, only if the outstanding balance of the mortgage does not exceed the Commissioner's estimate of:

(i) The replacement cost of the property as of the date the mortgage was originally accepted for insurance, or the date the substitute mortgagor is approved by the Commissioner, which ever is greater, in the case of a dwelling described in § 220.30(a) (1) or (2); or

(ii) The cost of repair or rehabilitation, plus the Commissioner's estimate of the replacement cost of the property as of either the date the mortgage was originally accepted for insurance, or the date the substitute mortgagor is approved by the Commissioner, whichever is greater, in the case of a dwelling described in §220.30(a) (3) or (4).

(c) *Applicability—current mortgagor.* Paragraph (b) of this section applies to the Commissioner's approval of a substitute mortgagor, only if the mortgage executed by the original mortgagor met the conditions of §203.258(c) of this chapter.

(d) *Applicability—earlier mortgagor.* The occupancy and similar requirements set forth in §203.258(d) of this chapter apply to mortgages insured under subpart A of this part.

(e) Mortgagees approved for participation in the Direct Endorsement program under §203.3 may, subject to limitations established by the Commissioner, themselves approve an appropriate substitute mortgagor under this section for mortgages which they own or service, and need not obtain further specific approval from the Commissioner.

(f) *Definition.* As used in this section, the term *substitute mortgagor* includes: (1) Persons who, upon the release by a mortgagee of a previous mortgagor from personal liability on the mortgage note, assume this liability and agree to pay the mortgage debts; and (2) persons who purchase without assuming liability on the mortgage note, or purchase where no release is given by the mortgagee to the previous mortgagor.

[55 FR 34808, Aug. 24, 1990, as amended at 57 FR 58351, Dec. 9, 1992]

§220.275 Method of paying insurance benefits.

If the application for insurance benefits is acceptable to the Commissioner, all of the insurance claim shall be paid in cash unless the mortgagee files a written request with the application for payment in debentures. If such a request is made, all of the claim shall be paid by issuing debentures and by making a cash payment adjusting any differences between the total amount of the claim and the amount of the debentures issued.

INSURED HOME IMPROVEMENT LOANS

§220.350 Cross-reference.

(a) All of the provisions of §§203.440 through 203.495 of this chapter covering insured home improvement loans under section 203(k) of the Act shall apply to home improvement loans on one-to-four family dwellings under section 220(h) of the Act, except as set out in paragraph (b).

(b) The provisions of §§203.473(a) shall not be applicable to home improvement loans on one-to-four family dwellings under section 220(h) of the Act.

[52 FR 1330, Jan. 13, 1987]

Subpart C—Eligibility Requirements—Projects

§220.501 Eligibility requirements.

The requirements set forth in 24 CFR part 200, subpart A, apply to multifamily project mortgages insured under section 220 of the National Housing Act (12 U.S.C. 1715k), as amended.

[61 FR 14405, Apr. 1, 1996]

Subpart D—Contract Rights and Obligations—Projects

PROJECT MORTGAGE INSURANCE

§220.751 Cross-reference.

(a) All of the provisions of subpart B, part 207, of this chapter, covering mortgages insured under section 207 of the National Housing Act, apply with full force and effect to multifamily project mortgages insured under section 220 of the National Housing Act, except §207.256b Modification of mortgage terms.

(b) For the purposes of the portion of this subpart, covering multifamily project mortgages, all references in part 207 of this chapter to section 207 of the National Housing Act shall be deemed to refer to section 220 of the National Housing Act.

[36 FR 24573, Dec. 22, 1971, as amended at 80 FR 51468, Aug. 25, 2015]

§ 220.753 Forbearance relief.

(a) In a case where the mortgage is in default, the mortgagor and the mortgagee may enter into a forbearance agreement for the reduction or suspension of regular mortgage payments for a specified period of time, if the following requirements are met:

(1) The mortgage was endorsed for insurance on or after July 7, 1961.

(2) The Commissioner determines that the default was due to circumstances beyond the mortgagor's control and that the mortgage probably will be restored to good standing within a reasonable period of time and evidences such determination by written approval of the forbearance agreement.

(b) The time specified in § 207.258(a) of this chapter, within which a mortgagee shall give the Commissioner written notice of its intention to file an insurance claim, shall be suspended for the period of time specified in the forbearance agreement as long as the mortgagor complies with the requirements of such agreement.

(c) If the mortgagor fails to meet the requirements of a forbearance agreement or to cure the default under the mortgage at the expiration of the forbearance period, and such failure continues for a period of 30 days, the mortgagee shall notify the Commissioner of such failure. Within 45 days thereafter, unless a modification or extension of the forbearance agreement has been approved by the Commissioner, the mortgagee shall notify the Commissioner of its election to file an insurance claim and of its decision to either assign the mortgage to the Commissioner or acquire and convey title to the property to the Commissioner. If the mortgage is assigned to the Commissioner, the special insurance benefits prescribed in § 220.765 shall be applicable.

§ 220.765 Special insurance benefits—forbearance relief cases.

(a) Upon a failure of the mortgagor to meet the requirements of a forbearance agreement or to cure the default under the mortgage at the expiration of the forbearance period, the mortgagee shall be entitled to obtain a special insurance payment in cash, in lieu of the insurance benefits otherwise provided under this subpart. To receive the special insurance payment, the mortgagee shall assign the mortgage to the Commissioner in compliance with the requirements of § 207.258(b) of this chapter.

(b) The special insurance benefits to the mortgagee shall be a cash payment computed in accordance with § 207.259(b) of this chapter, except that in lieu of the allowance for debenture interest in § 207.259(b)(1)(iii) of this chapter, the payment shall include the amount of the unpaid accrued mortgage interest computed to the date the assignment of the mortgage to the Commissioner is filed for record. In addition, there shall be included in the cash payment an amount equivalent to the debenture interest which would have been earned from the date the mortgage assignment was filed for record to the date the payment is made; except that when the mortgagee fails to meet any of the applicable requirements of § 207.258(b) of this chapter and § 220.753(c) within the specified times and in a manner satisfactory to the Commissioner (or within such further time as the Commissioner may approve in writing), such debenture interest allowance shall be computed only to the date on which the particular required action should have been taken.

INSURED PROJECT IMPROVEMENT LOANS

§ 220.800 Definitions.

All of the definitions contained in § 220.550 shall apply to §§ 220.800 *et seq.* In addition the following terms shall have the meaning indicated:

(a) *Contract of insurance* means the agreement evidenced by the endorsement of the Commissioner upon the note given in connection with an insured loan, incorporating by reference the regulations in §§ 220.800 *et seq.* and the applicable provisions of the Act.

(b) *Maturity* means the date on which the loan indebtedness would be extinguished if paid in accordance with periodic payments provided for in the loan.

§ 220.801 Initial insurance endorsement.

The Commissioner shall indicate his insurance of the loan by endorsing the original credit instrument and identifying the section of the Act and the regulations under which the loan is insured and the date of insurance.

§ 220.802 Final insurance endorsement.

When all advances of loan proceeds have been made, and all the terms and conditions of the commitment have been complied with to the satisfaction of the Commissioner, he shall indicate on the original credit instrument the total of advances he has approved for insurance and again endorse such instrument.

§ 220.803 Effect of insurance endorsement.

From the date of initial endorsement, the Commissioner and the lender shall be bound by the provisions of this subpart to the same extent as if they had executed a contract including the provisions of this subpart and the applicable sections of the Act.

§ 220.804 Insurance premiums.

(a) *First premium.* The lender, upon the initial endorsement of the loan for insurance, shall pay to the Commissioner a first loan insurance premium equal to one-half of one percent of the original face amount of the note.

(b) *Second premium; first payment more than one year following initial endorsement.* If the date of the first principal payment is more than one year following the date of initial insurance endorsement, the lender, upon the anniversary of such insurance date, shall pay a second premium equal to one-half of one percent of the original face amount of the loan.

(c) *Third premium.* On the date of the first principal payment, the lender shall pay a third premium equal to one-half of one percent of the average outstanding principal obligation of the note for the following year which shall be adjusted so as to accord with such date and so that the aggregate of the three premiums shall equal the sum of (1) one percent of the average outstanding principal obligation of the note for the year following the date of initial insurance endorsement and (2) one-half of one percent per annum of the average outstanding principal obli-

gation of the note for the period from the first anniversary of the date of initial insurance endorsement to one year following the date of the first principal payment.

(d) *Second premium; first payment one year or less following initial endorsement.* If the date of the first principal payment is one year, or less than one year following the date of initial insurance endorsement, the lender upon such first principal payment date, shall pay a second premium equal to one-half of one percent of the average outstanding principal obligation of the note for the following year which shall be adjusted so as to accord with such date and so that the aggregate of the said two premiums shall equal the sum of (1) one percent per annum of the average outstanding principal obligation of the note for the period from the date of initial insurance endorsement to the date of first principal payment and (2) one-half of one percent of the average outstanding principal obligation of the note for the year following the date of the first principal payment.

(e) *Second premium; commitment to insure upon completion.* Where the note is initially and finally endorsed for insurance pursuant to a Commitment to Insure Upon Completion, the lender on the date of the first principal payment shall pay a second premium equal to one-half of one percent of the average outstanding principal obligation of the note for the year following such first principal payment date which shall be adjusted so as to accord with such date and so that the aggregate of the said two premiums shall equal the sum of one-half of one percent per annum of the average outstanding principal obligation of the note for the period from the date of the insurance endorsement to one year following the date of the first principal payment.

(f) *Annual insurance premium.* Until the note is paid in full, or until the loan is assigned to the Commissioner, or until the contract of insurance is otherwise terminated with the consent of the Commissioner, the lender, on each anniversary of the date of the first principal payment shall pay an annual loan insurance premium equal to one-half of one percent of the average outstanding principal obligation of the loan for the year following the date on which such premium becomes payable.

(g) *Method of premium payment.* Premiums shall be payable in cash or in debentures at par plus accrued interest. All premiums are payable in advance and no refund can be made of any portion thereof except as hereinafter provided in §§ 220.800 *et seq.*

(h) *Calculation of premiums.* The premiums payable on and after the date of the first principal payment shall be calculated in accordance with the amortization provisions without taking into account delinquent payments or prepayments.

§ 220.804a Mortgagee's late charge.

Mortgage insurance premiums which are paid to the Commissioner more than 15 days after the billing date or due date, whichever is later, shall include a late charge of 4 percent of the amount of the payment due, except that no late charge shall be required with respect to any case for which HUD fails to render a proper billing to the mortgagee.

[43 FR 60154, Dec. 26, 1978]

§ 220.805 Termination of insurance.

(a) *Prepayment in full.* The contract of insurance shall be terminated if the loan is paid in full prior to its maturity. Notice of the prepayment shall be given to the Commissioner, on a form prescribed by the Commissioner, within 30 days from the date of the prepayment. The insurance termination shall become effective as of the date of the prepayment.

(b) *Voluntary termination.* The contract of insurance shall be voluntarily terminated upon receipt by the Commissioner of a written request, on a form prescribed by the Commissioner, by the borrower and the lender for such termination, accompanied by a submission of the original credit instrument for cancellation of the insurance endorsement and the remittance of all sums to which the Commissioner is entitled. The termination shall become effective as of the date these requirements are met.

§ 220.806 Pro rata refund of insurance premium.

Upon termination of loan insurance contract by a payment in full or by a voluntary termination, the Commissioner shall refund to the lender for the account of the borrower an amount equal to the pro rata portion of the current annual loan insurance premium theretofore paid which is applicable to the portion of the year subsequent to the date of the prepayment or the effective date of the voluntary termination of the contract of insurance.

§ 220.810 Definition of default.

(a) If the borrower fails to make any payments due under or provided to be paid by the terms of the note or security instrument and such default continues for a period of 30 days, the note or security instrument shall be considered in default for the purposes of §§ 220.800 *et seq.*

(b) The failure to perform any other covenant under the note or security instrument shall be considered a default, provided the lender because of such default, has exercised its right under the note or security instrument and accelerated the debt.

(c) If such defaults as defined in paragraphs (a) and (b) of this section continue for a period of 30 days, the lender shall be entitled to receive the benefits of insurance hereinafter provided.

§ 220.811 Date of default.

For the purposes of §§ 220.800 *et seq.,* the date of default shall be considered as:

(a) The date of the first uncorrected failure to perform a covenant or obligation under the note or security instrument; or

(b) The date of the first failure to make a monthly payment which subsequent payments by the borrower are insufficient to cover when applied to the overdue monthly payments in the order in which they became due.

§ 220.812 Notice of default.

(a) If the default as defined in § 220.810 is not cured within the 30 day grace period, the lender shall, within 30 days thereafter, notify the Commissioner in writing of such default.

(b) The lender shall give notice in writing to the Commissioner of the failure of the borrower to comply with any covenant or obligation under the security instrument or note regardless of the fact the lender may not have elected to accelerate the debt.

§220.813 Commissioner's right to require acceleration.

Upon receipt of notice of the failure of the borrower to comply with any covenant or obligation under the security instrument or note, or otherwise being apprised thereof, the Commissioner reserves the right to require the lender to accelerate payment of the outstanding principal balance due in order to protect the interests of the Federal Housing Commissioner.

§220.814 Election of action.

Where a real estate mortgage, deed of trust, conditional sales contract, chattel mortgage, lien, judgment, or any other security device has been used to secure the payment of a loan made under the provisions of this section, the lender may not, except with the approval of the Commissioner, both proceed against such security and also make claim under its contract of insurance, but shall elect which method it desires to pursue.

§220.820 Maximum claim period.

Notice of intention to file claim on a form prescribed by the Commissioner shall be filed within 45 days after the lender becomes eligible for the benefits of the loan insurance, or within such later time as may be agreed upon by the Commissioner in writing.

§220.821 Items to be filed on submitting claim.

Within 30 days after the filing of the notice of intention to file claim, or within such further period as may be agreed upon by the Commissioner in writing, the lender shall file with the Commissioner:

(a) The fiscal data pertaining to the loan transaction;

(b) Receipts covering all disbursements as required by the fiscal data form;

(c) The original note and any security instrument or instruments which shall be assigned to the Commissioner without recourse or warranty, except that the lender must warrant that no act or omission of the lender has impaired the validity and priority of such security instrument or instruments, that the security instrument or instruments are prior to all mechanics' and materialmen's liens filed of record subsequent to the recording of such security instrument or instruments regardless of whether such liens attached prior to such recording date, and prior to all liens and encumbrances which may have attached or defects which may have arisen subsequent to the recording of such security instrument or instruments, except such liens or other matters as may be approved by the Commissioner, that the amount stated in the instrument of assignment is actually due and owing under the security instrument or instruments, that there are no offsets or counter claims thereto, and that the lender has a good right to assign such note and security instrument or instruments;

(d) All hazard insurance policies held on property serving as security for the loan, together with a copy of the lender's notification to the carrier authorizing the amendment of the loss payable clause substituting the Commissioner as the holder of the security instrument;

(e) The assignment to the Commissioner of all rights and interests arising under the note and security instrument or instruments so in default, and all claims of the lender against the borrower or others arising out of the loan transaction;

(f) All policies of title or other insurance or surety bonds, or other guarantees and any and all claims thereunder; including evidence satisfactory to the Commissioner that the original title coverage has been extended to include the assignment of the note and security instrument or instruments to the Commissioner.

(g) Any property held by the lender or its agents or to which it is entitled and, if payment is requested in debentures, any cash held by the lender or its agents or to which it is entitled, including deposits made for the account of the borrower, and which have not been applied in reduction of the principal of the mortgage indebtedness;

(h) All records, ledger cards, documents, books, papers and accounts relating to the loan transaction;

(i) Any additional information or data which the Commissioner may require.

§ 220.822 Claim computation; items included.

(a) *Assignment of loan.* Upon an acceptable assignment of the note and security instrument, the Commissioner shall pay the claim of the lender in an amount equal to the unpaid principal balance of the loan plus:

(1) Any accrued interest due as of the date of execution of the assignment of the loan to the Commissioner.

(2) Any advances approved by the Commissioner made previously by the lender under the provisions of the note of security instrument or instruments.

(3) Reimbursement for such reasonable collection costs, court costs, and attorney's fees as may be approved by the Commissioner.

(4) Reimbursement for premiums paid on any hazard insurance policies held on the property.

(5) If payment is made in cash, an amount equivalent to the debenture interest which would have been earned as of the date insurance settlement occurs, except that when the lender fails to meet any one of the applicable requirements of §§ 220.812, 220.820, and 220.821 within the specified time (or within such further time as the Commissioner may approve in writing), the debenture interest shall be computed only to the date to which the particular action should have been taken or to which it was extended.

(b) [Reserved]

[36 FR 24573, Dec. 22, 1971, as amended at 80 FR 51468, Aug. 25, 2015]

§ 220.823 Claim computation; items deducted.

If the lender is to receive payment in cash, there shall be deducted from the total of the added items in § 220.822 the following:

(a) Any balance of the loan not advanced to the borrower;

(b) Any cash held by the lender or its agents or to which it is entitled; including deposits made for the account of the borrower and which have not been applied in reduction of the principal obligation under the note and security instrument or instruments.

§ 220.830 Debenture interest rate.

Debentures shall bear interest from the date of issue, payable semiannually on the first day of January and the first day of July of each year at the rate in effect as of the date the commitment was issued or as of the date the loan was endorsed for insurance, whichever rate is higher. The applicable rates of interest will be published twice each year as a notice in the FEDERAL REGISTER.

[47 FR 26125, June 17, 1982]

§ 220.832 Maturity of debentures.

Debentures shall mature 10 years from the date of issue.

§ 220.834 Registration of debentures.

Debentures shall be registered as to principal and interest.

§ 220.836 Form and amounts of debentures.

Debentures issued under subpart D of this part shall be in such form and amounts; and shall be subject to such terms and conditions; and shall include such provisions for redemption, if any, as may be prescribed by the Secretary, with the approval of the Secretary of the Treasury; and may be in book entry or certificated registered form, or such other form as the Secretary by regulation may prescribe.

[59 FR 49816, Sept. 30, 1994]

§ 220.838 Redemption of debentures.

Debentures shall, at the option of the Commissioner and with the approval of the Secretary of the Treasury, be redeemable at par plus accrued interest on any semiannual interest payment date on three months' notice of redemption given in such manner as the Commissioner shall prescribe. The debenture interest on the debentures called for redemption shall cease on the semiannual interest date designated in the call notice. The Commissioner may include with the notice of redemption an offer to purchase the debentures at par plus accrued interest at any time during the period between the notice of redemption and the redemption date. If the debentures are purchased by the Commissioner after such call and prior to the named redemption date, the debenture interest shall cease on the date of purchase.

§220.840 Issue date of debentures.

The debentures shall be issued as of the date of the execution of the assignment of the loan to the Commissioner.

§220.842 Cash adjustment.

Any difference of less than $50 between the amount of debentures to be issued to the lender and the total amount of the lender's claim, as approved by the Commissioner, may be adjusted by the issuance of a check in payment thereof.

[59 FR 49816, Sept. 30, 1994]

§220.850 Assignment of insured loans.

(a) An insured loan may not be transferred or pledged prior to the full disbursement of the loan, except with the prior written approval of the Commissioner which approval may be subject to such conditions and qualifications as the Commissioner may prescribe. Subsequent to full disbursement such loan may be transferred only to a transferee who is a lender approved by the Commissioner. Upon such transfer and the assumption by the transferee of all obligations under the contract of insurance the transferor shall be released from its obligations under the contract of insurance.

(b) The contract of insurance shall terminate with respect to loans described in paragraph (a) of this section upon the happening of either of the following events:

(1) The transfer or pledge of the insured loan to any person, firm, or corporation, public or private, other than an approved lender.

(2) The disposal by a lender of any partial interest in the insured loan by means of a declaration of trust or by a participation or trust certificate or by any other device, unless with the prior written approval of the Commissioner, which approval may be subject to such conditions and qualifications as the

Commissioner in his discretion may prescribe: *Provided,* That this paragraph shall not be applicable to any loan so long as it is held in a common trust fund maintained by a bank or trust company exclusively for the collective investment and reinvestment of moneys contributed thereto by the bank or trust company in its capacity as a trustee, executor or administrator; and in conformity with the rules and regulations prevailing from time to time of the Board of Governors of the Federal Reserve System, pertaining to the collective investment of trust funds: *Provided further,* That this paragraph shall not be applicable to any loan so long as it is held in a common trust estate administered by a bank or trust company which is subject to the inspection and supervision of a governmental agency, exclusively for the benefit of other banking institutions which are subject to the inspection and supervision of a governmental agency, and which are authorized by law to acquire beneficial intersts in such common trust estate, nor to any loan transferred to such a bank or trust company as trustee exclusively for the benefit of outstanding owners of undivided interest in the trust estate, under the terms of certificates issued and sold more than three years prior to said transfer, by a corporation which is subject to the inspection and supervision of a governmental agency.

Subpart E—Servicing Responsibilities—Homes

§220.900 Cross-reference.

All of the provisions of subpart C, part 203 of the chapter concerning the responsibilities of servicers of mortgages insured under section 203 of the National Housing Act apply to mortgages covering 1- to 11-family dwellings insured under section 220 of the National Housing Act, except §§203.664 through 203.666.

[52 FR 48203, Dec. 21, 1987, and 53 FR 9869, Mar. 28, 1988]

PART 221—LOW COST AND MODERATE INCOME MORTGAGE INSURANCE—SAVINGS CLAUSE

SOURCE: 36 FR 24587, Dec. 22, 1971, unless otherwise noted.

Subpart A—Eligibility Requirements—Low Cost Homes—Savings Clause

§ 221.1   Savings clause.

(a) Effective February 20, 2001, the authority to insure mortgages under section 221(d)(2) of the National Housing Act (12 U.S.C. 1715l(d)(2)) for low cost and moderate income mortgage insurance is terminated, except that HUD will endorse for insurance validly processed mortgages under direct endorsement where the credit worksheet was signed by the mortgagee's underwriter before February 20, 2001.

(b) Subpart A of this part, as it existed immediately before February 20, 2001, will continue to govern the rights and obligations of insured mortgage lenders, mortgagors, and HUD with respect to section 221(d)(2) single family loans insured before February 20, 2001, or in accordance with paragraph (a) of this section, pursuant to the applicable provisions of this subpart.

[66 FR 5913, Jan. 19, 2001]

Subpart B—Contract Rights and Obligations—Low Cost Homes

§ 221.251   Cross-reference.

(a) All of the provisions of subpart B, part 203 of this chapter covering mortgages insured under section 203 of the National Housing Act apply to mortgages covering one- to four-family dwellings insured under section 221 of the National Housing Act, except the following provisions:

(b) For the purposes of this subpart, all references in part 203 of this chapter to section 203 of the Act shall be construed to refer to section 221 of the Act, and all references to the Mutual Mortgage Insurance Fund shall be construed to refer to the General Insurance Fund.

[36 FR 24587, Dec. 22, 1971, as amended at 37 FR 8663, Apr. 29, 1972; 41 FR 42949, Sept. 29, 1976; 42 FR 29304, June 8, 1977; 47 FR 30754, July 15, 1982; 48 FR 28807, June 23, 1983; 51 FR 21874, June 16, 1986; 52 FR 8069, Mar. 16, 1987; 52 FR 28470, July 30, 1987; 52 FR 48204, Dec. 21, 1987; 53 FR 9869, Mar. 28, 1988; 55 FR 34810, Aug. 24, 1990; 61 FR 37801, July 19, 1996]

§221.252 Substitute mortgagors.

(a) *Selling mortgagor.* The mortgagee may effect the release of a mortgagor from personal liability on the mortgage note only if it obtains the Commissioner's approval of a substitute mortgagor, as provided by this section.

(b) *Purchasing mortgagor.* The Commissioner may approve a substitute mortgagor with respect to any mortgage insured under subpart A of this part, if the substitute mortgagor is to occupy the dwelling as a principal residence or a secondary residence (as these terms are defined in §221.20(c)) or is a private nonprofit or public entity as provided in section 221(h) of the National Housing Act.

(c) *Applicability—current mortgagor.* Paragraph (b) of this section applies to the Commissioner's approval of a substitute mortgagor, only if the mortgage executed by the original mortgagor met the conditions of §203.258(c) of this chapter.

(d) *Applicability—earlier mortgagor.* The occupancy and similar requirements set forth in §203.258(d) of this chapter apply to mortgages insured under subpart A of this part.

(e) Mortgagees approved for participation in the Direct Endorsement program under §203.3 of this chapter may, subject to limitations established by the Commissioner, themselves approve an appropriate substitute mortgagor under the section and need not obtain further specific approval from the Commissioner.

(f) *Definition.* As used in this section, the term *substitute mortgagor* includes:

(1) Persons who, upon the release by a mortgagee of a previous mortgagor from personal liability on the mortgage note, assume this liability and agree to pay the mortgage debts and

(2) Persons who purchase without assuming liability on the mortgage note or purchase where no release is given by the mortgagee to the previous mortgagor.

[55 FR 34810, Aug. 24, 1990, as amended at 57 FR 58351, Dec. 9, 1992]

§221.254 Mortgage insurance premiums.

(a) All of the provisions of §§203.260 through 203.295 of this chapter relating to mortgage insurance premiums shall apply to mortgages insured under this subpart, except that as to mortgages meeting the special requirements of §221.60 or §221.65, such provisions shall only be applicable under the circumstances prescribed in paragraph (b) of this section. Notwithstanding any provision in the mortgage instrument, there shall be no adjusted mortgage insurance premium or voluntary termination charge due the Commissioner on account of the prepayment of any mortgage or the voluntary termination of any mortgage insurance contract where (1) The mortgage is prepaid in full, or (2) the Commissioner receives a request for voluntary termination on or after May 1, 1972.

(b) Whenever the interest rate on a mortgage insured under this part as having met the special requirement of § 221.60 or § 221.65 shall have been increased to the maximum rate in accordance with § 221.60(j), § 221.65(d)(4), or § 221.65(d)(5), the provisions of §§ 203.260 through 203.295 of this chapter relating to mortgage insurance premiums shall apply except that:

(1) References to the original principal amount shall be construed as the scheduled unpaid principal balance, without taking into account delinquent payments or prepayments, on the date of the change in interest rate required under the mortgage.

(2) References to the date of the issuance of a Mortgage Insurance Certificate or the date of the endorsement of the credit instrument or the date the insurance becomes effective shall be construed as the date of the change in interest required under the mortgage.

(3) References to the first year of amortization under the mortgage shall be construed as the period beginning on the date of the change in interest rate required under the mortgage and ending on the next anniversary of the beginning of amortization.

[36 FR 24587, Dec. 22, 1971, as amended at 37 FR 8663, Apr. 29, 1972]

§ 221.255 Assignment option.

(a) A mortgagee holding a mortgage insured pursuant to a conditional or firm commitment issued on or before November 30, 1983 has the option to assign, transfer and deliver to the Commissioner the original credit instrument and the mortgage securing it, provided the mortgage is not in default at the expiration of 20 years from the date of final endorsement of the credit instrument. In processing a mortgagee's claim for insurance benefits under this section, the Commissioner may direct the mortgagee to assign, transfer and deliver the original credit instrument, and the mortgage securing it, directly to the Government National Mortgage Association (GNMA). Upon such assignment, transfer and delivery, either to the Commissioner or to GNMA, as directed, the mortgage insurance contract shall terminate and the mortgagee shall be entitled to receive insurance benefits in accordance with this section.

(b) The mortgagee may exercise its assignment option within 1 year following the twentieth anniversary of the date the mortgage was endorsed for insurance.

(c) Upon the exercise of the assignment option the Commissioner shall issue to the assignor mortgagee debentures having a total face value equal to the amount of the original principal obligation of the mortgage which was unpaid on the date of the assignment, plus accrued interest to such date.

(d) The debentures issued pursuant to the exercise of an assignment option shall be dated as of the date the mortgage is assigned to the Commissioner and shall mature 10 years after such date.

(e) The debentures issued pursuant to the exercise of an assignment option shall bear interest at the *going Federal rate* at date of issuance. The *going Federal rate* means the annual rate of interest specified by the Secretary of the Treasury as applicable to the 6-month period which includes the issuance date of the debentures. The Secretary of the Treasury shall determine this applicable rate by estimating the average yield to maturity, on the basis of daily closing market bid quotations or prices during the month of May or the month of November, as the case may be, next preceding such 6-month period, on all outstanding marketable obligations of the United States having a maturity date of 8 to 12 years from the first day of May or November, as the case may be. If there should be no outstanding marketable obligations of the United States having the 8 to 12 year maturity at the time the Secretary of the Treasury is required to determine the debenture rate involved, the obligation next shorter than 8 years and the obligation next longer than 12 years respectively, shall be used.

(f) Debentures shall bear interest from the date of issue, payable semiannually on the first day of January and the first day of July of each year at the rate in effect on the issue date, a date which shall be established as provided in § 203.410 of this chapter. The interest rate shall be established by the Commissioner in an amount not in excess of the annual rate of interest which the Secretary of the Treasury shall specify as applicable to the 6-month period (consisting of January through June, or July through December) which includes the issuance date of such debentures, which applicable rate for each 6-month period shall be determined by the Secretary of the Treasury, at the request of the Commissioner, by estimating the average yield to maturity, on the basis of daily closing market bid quotations or prices during the calendar month next preceding the establishment of such rate of interest, on all outstanding marketable obligations of the United States having a maturity date of 15 years or more from the first day of such next preceding month, and by adjusting such estimated average annual yield to the nearest one-eighth of 1 per centum.

[36 FR 24587, Dec. 22, 1971, as amended at 49 FR 12697, Mar. 30, 1984]

§221.256 Interest rate increase and payment of mortgage insurance premiums on mortgages under §221.60 and §221.65.

(a) Where a mortgage meets the special requirements of §221.60 or §221.65, the following procedures are applicable:

(1) The mortgagee shall determine, at least biennially, whether the mortgagor has continued to occupy the property securing the mortgage. If the mortgagee determines that the mortgagor is not occupying the property or that the mortgagor has sold the property subject to the mortgage to a purchaser not qualifying under the provisions of §221.60(h) or §221.65(d)(4) (as appropriate) for the continuation of a below market interest rate, interest on such mortgage shall be computed by the mortgagee at the highest rate permissible under the mortgage. The computation at the higher rate shall be effective from the first day of the month following the month in which the right to collect interest at the increased rate first accrued, as determined by the mortgagee.

(2) The mortgagee shall determine the mortgagor's family income, at least biennially, and shall increase the mortgage interest pursuant to the requirements of §§221.60(g) and

221.65(d)(5), as appropriate, to comply with the requirements of such sections. The computation at the higher rate shall be effective from the first day of the month following the month in which the mortgagee determines that the mortgagor's family income was increased.

(b) The mortgagee shall notify the Commissioner, on a form prescribed by the Commissioner, within 30 days of making the determination of the right to compute interest at the higher rate, as provided in paragraph (a) of this section, of:

(1) The date on which such right first accrued, and

(2) The outstanding principal balance of the mortgage on the first day of the month following the date on which such right first accrued.

(c) The liability for payment of mortgage insurance premiums shall begin on and be computed from the first day of the month following the date on which the right to compute interest at the higher rate shall have first accrued.

[36 FR 24587, Dec. 22, 1971, as amended at 37 FR 8663, Apr. 29, 1972]

§221.275 Method of paying insurance benefits.

If the application for insurance benefits is acceptable to the Commissioner, all of the insurance claim shall be paid in cash unless the mortgagee files a written request with the application for payment in debentures. If such a request is made, all of the claim shall be paid by issuing debentures and by making a cash payment adjusting any differences between the total amount of the claim and the amount of the debentures issued.

§221.280 Waived title objections.

(a) *General provisions.* All of the provisions of §203.389 of this chapter (relating to the waiver by the Commissioner of objections to title) shall apply to mortgages insured under this subpart, with the exception of mortgages involving condominium units.

(b) *Provisions applicable to condominium units.* Where the mortgage involves a condominium unit, the Commissioner shall not object to title by reason of the following matters:

(1) Violations of a restriction based on race, color, or creed, even where such restriction provides for a penalty of reversion or forfeiture of title or a lien for liquidated damage.

(2) Easements for public utilities along one or more of the property lines, provided the exercise of the rights thereunder do not interfere with any of the buildings or improvements located on the subject property.

(3) Encroachments on the subject property by improvements on adjoining property, provided such encroachments do not interfere with the use of any improvements on the subject property.

(4) Variations between the length of the subject property lines as shown on the application for insurance and as shown by the record or possession lines, provided such variations do not interfere with the use of any of the improvements on the subject property.

(5) Customary buildings or use restrictions for breach of which there is no reversion and which have not been violated to a material extent.

SPECIAL PROVISIONS APPLICABLE ONLY TO MORTGAGES INVOLVING CONDOMINIUM UNITS

§ 221.300 Changes in the plan of apartment ownership.

The mortgagee shall notify the Commissioner of any changes in the plan of apartment ownership and in the administration of the property. Such notification shall be given either at the time of the conveyance of the property or at the time of the assignment of the mortgage. Any changes in such plan shall require approval by the Commissioner.

§ 221.305 Condition of the multifamily structure.

(a) When a family unit is conveyed or a mortgage is assigned to the Commissioner, the family unit and the common areas and facilities (including restricted common areas and facilities) designated for the particular unit shall be undamaged by fire, earthquake, tornado, or boiler explosion, except if the property has been damaged, either of the following actions shall be taken:

(1) The property may be repaired prior to its conveyance or prior to the assignment of the mortgage to the Commissioner.

(2) With the prior approval of the Commissioner, the property may be conveyed or the mortgage assigned to the Commissioner without repairing the damage. In such instances, the Commissioner shall deduct from the insurance benefits either his estimate of the decrease in value of the family unit or the amount of any insurance recovery received by the mortgagee, whichever is the greater.

(b) If the property has been damaged by fire and such property was not covered by fire insurance at the time of the damage, the mortgagee may convey the property or assign the mortgage to the Commissioner without deduction from the insurance benefits for any loss occasioned by such fire if the following conditions are met:

(1) The property shall have been covered by fire insurance at the time the mortgage was insured.

(2) The fire insurance shall have been later cancelled or renewal shall have been refused by the insuring company.

(3) The mortgagee shall have notified the Commissioner within 30 days (or within such further time as the Commissioner may approve) of the cancellation of the fire insurance or of the refusal of the insuring company to renew the fire insurance. This notification shall have been accompanied by a certification of the mortgagee that diligent efforts were made, but it was unable to obtain fire insurance coverage at reasonably competitive rates and that it will continue its efforts to obtain adequate fire insurance coverage at competitive rates.

§ 221.310 Assessment of taxes.

When a family unit is conveyed to the Commissioner or a mortgage is assigned to the Commissioner, the unit shall be assessed and subject to assessment for taxes pertaining only to that unit.

§ 221.315 Certificate of tax assessment.

The mortgagee shall certify, as of the date of filing for record of the deed or assignment of the mortgage to the Commissioner, that the family unit is assessed and subject to assessment for taxes pertaining to that unit.

§ 221.320 Certificate or statement of condition.

(a) At the time of the assignment of the mortgage or conveyance of the property to the Commissioner, the mortgagee shall, as of the date of the filing for record of the deed or assignment,

(1) Certify that the conditions of § 221.305(a) have been met; or

(2) Submit a statement describing any such damage that may still exist.

(b) In the absence of evidence to the contrary, the mortgagee's certificate or its statement as to damage shall be accepted by the Commissioner as establishing the condition of the family unit and the common areas and facilities including restricted common areas and facilities designated for the particular unit.

§ 221.325 Cancellation of hazard insurance.

The provisions of § 203.382 of this chapter are incorporated by reference and shall apply to hazard insurance policies carried solely for the family unit.

Subpart C—Eligibility Requirements—Moderate Income Projects

§ 221.501 Eligibility requirements.

The requirements set forth in 24 CFR part 200, subpart A, apply to multifamily project mortgages insured under section 221 of the National Housing Act (12 U.S.C. 17151), as amended.

[61 FR 14405, Apr. 1, 1996]

Subpart D—Contract Rights and Obligations—Moderate Income Projects

§ 221.751 Cross-reference.

(a) All of the provisions of subpart B, part 207 of this chapter, covering mortgages insured under section 207 of the National Housing Act, apply with full force and effect to multifamily project mortgages insured under section 221 of the National Housing Act, except the following provisions:

Sec.
207.252 First, second, and third premium.

207.252a Premiums—operating loss loans.
207.259 Insurance benefits.

(b) For the purposes of this subpart, all references in part 207 of this chapter to section 207 of the act shall be construed to refer to section 221 of the Act, and all references to part 207 shall be construed to refer to this subpart.

[36 FR 24587, Dec. 22, 1971, as amended at 37 FR 8663, Apr. 29, 1972; 42 FR 59675, Nov. 18, 1977]

§ 221.753 Termination of mortgage insurance.

In addition to the provisions of § 207.253a, the following requirements apply to certain multifamily mortgages insured under section 221 of the National Housing Act:

(a) For those projects qualifying as eligible low income housing under § 248.201, the contract of insurance may be terminated only as provided in part 248.

(b) For those projects subject to section 250(a) of the National Housing Act, the contract of insurance may be terminated only if the Commissioner determines that the requirements of section 250(a) are met.

[55 FR 38958, Sept. 21, 1990]

§ 221.755 Premiums first, second, third and operating loss loans.

All of the provisions of §§ 207.252 and 207.252a of this chapter, relating to mortgage insurance premiums, apply to mortgages insured under this subpart that provide for interest at the market rate prescribed in § 221.518(a) except that as to mortgages insured under this subpart pursuant to section 238(c) of the Act all mortgage insurance premiums due in accordance with §§ 207.252 and 207.252a shall be calculated on the basis of one percent. The provisions of § 207.252 shall not apply to:

(a) Mortgages that provide for interest during the construction period at the market rate and for interest subsequent to final endorsement at the below market rate prescribed in § 221.518(b); or

(b) Mortgages encumbering a project in which all units are covered by an annual contributions contract issued pursuant to section 10(c) of the Housing Act of 1937.

[36 FR 24587, Dec. 22, 1971, as amended at 42 FR 59675, Nov. 18, 1977]

§ 221.761 Forbearance relief.

(a) In a case where the mortgage is in default, the mortgagor and the mortgagee may enter into a forbearance agreement for the reduction or suspension of regular mortgage payments for a specified period of time, if the following requirements are met:

(1) The mortgage was endorsed for insurance on or after July 7, 1961.

(2) The Commissioner determines that the default was due to circumstances beyond the mortgagor's control and that the mortgage probably will be restored to good standing within a reasonable period of time and evidences such determination by written approval of the forbearance agreement.

(b) The time specified in § 207.258(a) of this chapter, within which a mortgagee shall give the Commissioner written notice of its intention to file an insurance claim, shall be suspended for the period of time specified in the forbearance agreement as long as the mortgagor complies with the requirements of such agreement.

(c) If the mortgagor fails to meet the requirements of a forbearance agreement or to cure the default under the mortgage at the expiration of the forbearance period, and such failure continues for a period of 30 days, the mortgagee shall notify the Commissioner of such failure. Within 45 days thereafter, unless a modification or extension of the forbearance agreement has been approved by the Commissioner, the mortgagee shall notify the Commissioner of its election to file an insurance claim and of its decision to either assign the mortgage to the Commissioner or to acquire and convey title to the property to the Commissioner. If the mortgage is assigned to the Commissioner, the special insurance benefits prescribed in § 221.763 shall be applicable.

[36 FR 24587, Dec. 22, 1971, as amended at 51 FR 27838, Aug. 4, 1986]

§ 221.762 Payment of insurance benefits.

All of the provisions of § 207.259 of this chapter relating to insurance benefits apply to multifamily project mortgages insured under this subpart, except as provided in this section:

(a) [Reserved]

(b) *Below market interest rate mortgages.* Where the mortgage has been finally endorsed and the special below market interest rate provided in § 221.518(b) is applicable as of the date of default, the 1 percent deduction from insurance benefits prescribed in § 207.259(b)(2)(iv) of this chapter shall not be applicable.

(c) *Mortgages financed with section 11(b) obligations.* Where the funds for a mortgage loan are provided by obligations that are tax-exempt under section 11(b) of the United States Housing Act of 1937 (24 CFR part 811), the one percent deduction from insurance benefits prescribed in § 207.259(b)(2)(iv) of this chapter shall not be applicable to claims with respect to multifamily rental housing projects for which a firm commitment for mortgage insurance was issued on or after March 12, 1979.

[36 FR 24587, Dec. 22, 1971, as amended at 44 FR 40890, July 13, 1979; 80 FR 51468, Aug. 25, 2015]

§ 221.763 Special insurance benefits—forbearance relief cases.

(a) In the case of a mortgage that provides for payment of interest at the market rate prescribed in § 221.518(a), if the mortgagor fails to meet the requirements of a forbearance agreement or to cure the default under the mortgage at the expiration of the forbearance agreement, the mortgagee shall be entitled to obtain a special insurance payment in cash, in lieu of the insurance benefits otherwise provided under this subpart. To receive the special insurance payment, the mortgagee shall assign the mortgage to the Commissioner in compliance with the requirements of § 207.258(b) of this chapter.

(b) The special insurance benefit to the mortgagee shall be a cash payment computed in accordance with § 207.259(b) of this chapter, except that in lieu of the allowance for debenture interest in §207.259(b)(1)(iii) of this chapter, the payment shall include the amount of the unpaid accrued mortgage interest computed to the date the assignment of the mortgage to the Commissioner is filed for record. In addition, there shall be included in the cash payment an amount equivalent to the debenture interest which would have been earned from the date the mortgage assignment was filed for record to the date the payment is made; except that when the mortgagee fails to meet any of the applicable requirements of §207.258(b) of this chapter and §221.761(c) within the specified times and in a manner satisfactory to the Commissioner (or within such further time as the Commissioner may approve in writing), such debenture interest allowance shall be computed only to the date on which the particular required action should have been taken.

§221.770   Assignment option.

A mortgagee holding a conditional or firm commitment issued on or before November 30, 1983 (or, in the Direct Endorsement program, a property appraisal report signed by the mortgagee's approved underwriter on or before November 30, 1983) has the option to assign, transfer and deliver to the Commissioner the original credit instrument and the mortgage securing it, provided that the mortgage is not in default at the expiration of 20 years from the date of final endorsement of the credit instrument. In processing a mortgagee's claim for insurance benefits under this section, the Commissioner may direct the mortgagee to assign, transfer and deliver the original credit instrument, and the mortgage securing it, directly to the Government National Mortgage Association (GNMA). Upon such assignment, transfer and delivery either to the Commissioner or to GNMA, as directed, the mortgage insurance contract shall terminate and the mortgagee shall be entitled to receive insurance benefits in accordance with §221.780.

[49 FR 12698, Mar. 30, 1984, as amended at 57 FR 58351, Dec. 9, 1992]

§221.775   Option period.

The mortgagee may exercise its option to assign within one year following the twentieth anniversary of the date the mortgage was finally endorsed for insurance.

§221.780   Issuance of debentures.

Upon the exercise of the assignment option and the satisfactory performance of the requirements as to assignment set out in §207.258 of this chapter, the Commissioner shall issue the assignor mortgagee debentures having a total par value equal to the amount of the original principal obligation of the mortgage which was unpaid on the date of the assignment, plus accrued interest to such date.

[59 FR 49816, Sept. 30, 1994]

§221.785   Date of maturity of debentures.

The debentures issues pursuant to the exercise of an assignment option shall be dated as of the date the mortgage is assigned to the Commissioner and shall mature 10 years after such date.

§221.790   Debenture interest rate.

The debentures issued pursuant to the exercise of an assignment option shall bear interest at the *going Federal rate* at date of issuance. The *going Federal rate* means the annual rate of interest specified by the Secretary of the Treasury as applicable to the 6-month period which includes the issuance date of the debentures. The Secretary of the Treasury shall determine this applicable rate by estimating the average yield to maturity, on the basis of daily closing market bid quotations or prices during the month of May or the month of November, as the case may be, next preceding such 6-month period, on all outstanding marketable obligations of the United States having a maturity date of 8 to 12 years from the first day of May or November, as the case may be. If there should be no outstanding marketable obligations of the United States having the 8 to 12 year maturity at the time the Secretary of the Treasury is required to determine the debenture rate involved, the obligation next shorter than 8 years and the obligation next longer than 12 years respectively shall be used.

§ 221.795 Displacement—below market interest rate mortgages.

(a) *Minimizing displacement.* Consistent with the other goals and objectives of this part, Owners shall assure that they have taken all reasonable steps to minimize the displacement of persons (households, businesses, nonprofit organizations, and farms) as a result of a project assisted under this part.

(b) *Temporary relocation.* The following policies cover residential tenants who will not be required to move permanently but who must relocate temporarily to permit rehabilitation or other work for the project. Such tenants must be provided:

(1) Reimbursement for all reasonable out-of-pocket expenses incurred in connection with the temporary relocation, including the cost of moving to and from the temporarily occupied housing, any increase in monthly rent/utility costs and any incidental expenses.

(2) Appropriate advisory services, including reasonable advance written notice of:

(i) The date and approximate duration of the temporary relocation;

(ii) The location of the suitable, decent, safe, and sanitary dwelling to be made available for the temporary period;

(iii) The terms and conditions under which the tenant may lease and occupy a suitable, decent, safe, and sanitary dwelling in the building/complex following completion of the rehabilitation; and

(iv) The provisions of paragraph (b)(1) of this section.

(c) *Relocation assistance for displaced persons.* A "displaced person" (defined in paragraph (g) of this section) must be provided relocation assistance at the levels described in, and in accordance with the requirements of, the Uniform Relocation Assistance and Real Property Acquisition Policies Act of 1970, as amended (URA) (42 U.S.C. 4201–4655) and implementing regulations at 49 CFR part 24. A "displaced person" shall be advised of his or her rights under the Fair Housing Act (42 U.S.C. 3601–19), and, if the representative comparable replacement dwelling used to establish the amount of the replacement housing payment to be provided to a minority person is located in an area of minority concentration, such person also shall be given, if possible, referrals to comparable and suitable, decent, safe and sanitary replacement dwellings not located in such areas.

(d) *Real property acquisition requirements.* The acquisition of real property for a project is subject to the URA and the requirements described in 49 CFR part 24, subpart B.

(e) *Appeals.* A person who disagrees with the Owner's determination concerning whether the person qualifies as a "displaced person," or with the amount of relocation assistance for which the person is eligible, may file a written appeal of that determination with the Owner. A person who is dissatisfied with the Owner's determination on his or her appeal may submit a written request for review of that determination to the HUD Field Office.

(f) *Responsibility of Owner.* (1) The Owner shall certify (i.e., provide assurance of compliance as required by 49 CFR part 24) that the Owner will comply with the URA, the regulations at 49 CFR part 24, and the requirements of this section. The Owner shall ensure such compliance notwithstanding any third party's contractual obligation to the Owner to comply with these provisions.

(2) The cost of required relocation assistance is an eligible project cost in the same manner and to the same extent as other project costs. Such costs also may be paid with funds available from other sources.

(3) The Owner shall maintain records in sufficient detail to demonstrate compliance with these provisions. The Owner shall maintain data on the race, ethnic, gender, and disability status of displaced persons.

(g) *Definition of displaced person.* (1) For purposes of this section, the term *displaced person* means a person (household, business, nonprofit organization, or farm) that moves from real property, or moves personal property from real property, permanently, as a direct result of acquisition, rehabilitation, or demolition for a project assisted under this part. The term "displaced person" includes, but may not be limited to:

(i) A tenant-occupant of a dwelling unit who moves from the building/complex, permanently, after the Owner executes the agreement covering the rehabilitation, demolition or acquisition, if the move occurs before the tenant is provided written notice offering him or her the opportunity to lease and occupy a suitable, decent, safe, and sanitary dwelling in the same building/complex, under reasonable terms and conditions, upon completion of the project. Such reasonable terms and conditions include a monthly rent and estimated average monthly utility costs that do not exceed the amount approved by HUD;

(ii) A tenant-occupant of a dwelling who is required to relocate temporarily, but does not return to the building/complex, if either:

(A) The tenant is not offered payment for all reasonable out-of-pocket expenses incurred in connection with the temporary relocation, including the cost of moving to and from the temporarily occupied unit, any increased housing costs and incidental expenses; or

(B) Other conditions of the temporary relocation are not reasonable; or

(iii) A tenant-occupant of a dwelling who moves from the building/complex, permanently, after he or she has been required to move to another dwelling unit in the same building/complex in order to carry out the project, if either:

(A) The tenant is not offered reimbursement for all reasonable out-of-pocket expenses incurred in connection with the move; or

(B) Other conditions of the move are not reasonable; or

(iv) Any person, including a person who moves before the Owner's execution of the agreement covering the rehabilitation, demolition, or acquisition, if the Owner or HUD determines that the displacement resulted directly from rehabilitation, demolition or acquisition for the assisted project.

(2) Notwithstanding the provisions of paragraph (g)(1) of this section, a person does not qualify as a "displaced person" (and is not eligible for relocation assistance under the URA or this section), if:

(i) The person has been evicted for serious or repeated violation of the terms and conditions of the lease or occupancy agreement, violation of applicable Federal, State or local law, or other good cause, and HUD determines that the eviction was not undertaken for the purpose of evading the obligation to provide relocation assistance;

(ii) The person moved into the property after the execution of the agreement covering the rehabilitation, demolition or acquisition and, before signing a lease and commencing occupancy, received written notice of the project, its possible impact on the person (e.g., the person may be displaced, temporarily relocated or suffer a rent increase) and the fact that he or she would not qualify as a "displaced person" (or for any assistance provided under this section) as a result of the project;

(iii) The person is ineligible under 49 CFR 24.2(g)(2); or

(iv) HUD determines that the person was not displaced as a direct result of acquisition, rehabilitation, or demolition for the project.

(3) The Owner may ask HUD, at any time, to determine whether a displacement is or would be covered by this section.

(h) *Definition of initiation of negotiations.* For purposes of determining the formula for computing the replacement housing assistance to be provided to a residential tenant displaced as a direct result of privately undertaken rehabilitation, demolition, or acquisition of the real property, the term *initiation of negotiations* means the Owner's execution of the agreement covering the rehabilitation, demolition, or acquisition.

(Approved by Office of Management and Budget under OMB Control Number 2506–0121)

[59 FR 29330, June 6, 1994]

Subpart E—Servicing Responsibilities—Low Cost Homes

§221.800 Cross-reference.

All of the provisions of subpart C, part 203 of the chapter concerning the responsibilities of servicers of mortgages insured under section 203 of the

National Housing Act apply to mortgages covering one- to four-family dwellings to be insured under section 221 of the National Housing Act, except §§ 203.664 through 203.666.

[52 FR 48204, Dec. 21, 1987, and 53 FR 9869, Mar. 28, 1988]

PART 231—HOUSING MORTGAGE INSURANCE FOR THE ELDERLY

Subpart A—Eligibility Requirements

AUTHORITY: 12 U.S.C. 1715b, 1715v; 42 U.S.C. 3535(d).

SOURCE: 36 FR 24615, Dec. 22, 1971, unless otherwise noted.

Subpart A—Eligibility Requirements

§ 231.1   Eligibility requirements.

The requirements set forth in 24 CFR part 200, subpart A, apply to multifamily project mortgages insured under section 231 of the National Housing Act (12 U.S.C. 1715v), as amended.

[61 FR 14406, Apr. 1, 1996]

Subpart B—Contract Rights and Obligations

§ 231.251   Cross-reference.

(a) All of the provisions of part 207, subpart B of this chapter covering mortgages insured under section 207 of the National Housing Act apply to mortgages insured under section 231 of such Act.

(b) For the purposes of this subpart all references in part 207 of this chapter to section 207 of the Act shall be construed to refer to section 231 of the Act.

PART 232—MORTGAGE INSURANCE FOR NURSING HOMES, INTERMEDIATE CARE FACILITIES, BOARD AND CARE HOMES, AND ASSISTED LIVING FACILITIES

Subpart A—Eligibility Requirements

AUTHORITY: 12 U.S.C. 1715b, 1715w, 1735d, and 1735f–19; 42 U.S.C. 3535(d).

SOURCE: 36 FR 24618, Dec. 22, 1971, unless otherwise noted.

Subpart A—Eligibility Requirements

SOURCE: 61 FR 14406, Apr. 1, 1996, unless otherwise noted.

§232.1 Eligibility requirements, generally; applicability of certain requirements.

(a) *Eligibility, generally.* All of the requirements set forth in 24 CFR part 200, subpart A, except for the requirements for "eligible mortgagor" in 24 CFR 200.5, apply to mortgages insured under section 232 of the National Housing Act (12 U.S.C. 1715w), as amended.

(b) *Applicability of certain requirements.* As of October 9, 2012 the provisions in 24 CFR 207.255(b)(5), 207.258, 232.3, 232.11, 232.254, 232.903(c) and (d), and subpart F of part 232, excluding §§232.1007, 232.1009, and 232.1015 of subpart F are applicable only to transactions for which a firm commitment has been issued under this part on or after July 12, 2013.

[77 FR 55136, Sept. 7, 2012, as amended at 78 FR 25185, Apr. 30, 2013]

§232.2 License.

The Commissioner shall not insure any mortgage under this part unless the facility is regulated by the State, municipality or other political subdivision in which the facility is or is to be located, and the appropriate agency for such jurisdiction provides a license, certificate or other assurances the Commissioner considers necessary, that the facility complies with any applicable State or local standards and requirements for such facility.

§ 232.3 Eligible borrower.

The borrower shall be a single asset entity acceptable to the Commissioner, as may be limited by the applicable section of the Act, and shall possess the powers necessary and incidental to owning the project, except that the Commissioner may approve a non-single asset borrower entity under such circumstances, terms, and conditions determined and specified as acceptable to the Commissioner.

[77 FR 55136, Sept. 7, 2012]

§ 232.7 Bathroom.

Not less than one full bathroom must be provided for every four residents of a board and care home or assisted living facility, and bathroom access from any bedroom or sleeping area must not pass through a public corridor or area.

[61 FR 14406, Apr. 1, 1996. Redesignated at 77 FR 55136, Sept. 7, 2012]

§ 232.11 Establishment and maintenance of long-term debt service reserve account.

(a) To be eligible for insurance under this part, and except with respect to Supplemental Loans to Finance Purchase and Installation of Fire Safety Equipment (subpart C of this part), if HUD determines the mortgage presents an atypical long-term risk, HUD may require that the borrower establish, at final closing and maintain throughout the term of the mortgage, a long-term debt service reserve account.

(b) The long-term debt service reserve account, if required, may be financed as part of the initial mortgage amount, provided that the maximum mortgage amount as otherwise calculated is not thereby exceeded.

(c) The amount required to be initially placed in the long-term debt service reserve account and the minimum long-term balance to be maintained in that account will be determined during underwriting and separately identified in the firm commitment. Although HUD may, when appropriate to avert a mortgage insurance claim, permit the balance to fall below

the required minimum long-term balance, the borrower may not take any distribution of mortgaged property except when both the long-term debt service reserve account is funded at the minimal long-term level and such distribution is otherwise permissible.

[77 FR 55136, Sept. 7, 2012]

Subpart B—Contract Rights and Obligations

§ 232.251 Cross-reference.

(a) All of the provisions, except § 207.258b, of part 207, subpart B of this chapter relating to mortgages insured under section 207 of the National Housing Act, apply to mortgages insured under section 232 of the Act.

(b) For the purposes of this subpart all references in part 207 of this chapter to section 207 of the Act shall be construed to refer to section 232 of the Act.

[36 FR 24618, Dec. 22, 1971, as amended at 50 FR 38787, Sept. 25, 1985]

§ 232.252 Definitions.

All of the definitions contained in § 232.1 shall apply to this subpart. In addition, as used in this part, the following term shall have the meaning indicated:

(a) *Contract of insurance* means the agreement evidenced by the Commissioner's insurance endorsement and includes the provisions of this subpart and of the Act.

§ 232.254 Withdrawal of project funds, including for repayments of advances from the borrower, operator, or management agent.

Borrower may make and take distributions of mortgaged property, as set forth in the mortgage loan transactional documents, to the extent and as permitted by the law of the applicable jurisdiction, provided that, upon each calculation of borrower surplus cash (as defined by HUD), which calculation shall be made no less frequently than semi-annually, borrower must demonstrate positive surplus cash, or to the extent surplus cash is negative, repay any distributions taken during such calculation period within 30 calendar days unless a longer time period is approved by HUD. Borrower shall be deemed to have taken distributions to the extent that surplus cash is negative unless, in conjunction with the calculation of surplus cash, borrower provides to HUD documentation evidencing, to HUD's reasonable satisfaction, a lesser amount of total distributions. To the extent that the provisions of this section are inconsistent with the provisions in a borrower's existing transactional loan documents, including without limitation any HUD-required regulatory agreement, the provisions of the transactional loan documents shall apply.

[77 FR 55136, Sept. 7, 2012]

§232.256 Partial payment of claims.

(a) When a lender for a loan on a healthcare project becomes eligible to file an insurance claim and to assign the mortgage to the Commissioner pursuant to §207.258, the Commissioner may request the lender, in lieu of assignment, to accept a partial payment of the claim under the mortgage insurance contract and recast the mortgage, under such terms and conditions as the Commissioner may determine.

(b) The Commissioner may request the lender to participate in a partial payment of claim in lieu of assignment only after a determination that partial payment would be less costly to the Federal Government than other reasonable alternatives for maintaining the project and that would keep the healthcare facility operational to serve community needs. In addition to any findings that may be provided in other guidance, the Commissioner shall base the determination on the findings listed below:

(1) The lender is entitled, after a default as defined in §207.255, to assign the mortgage in exchange for the payment of insurance benefits;

(2) The relief resulting from partial payment, when considered with other resources available to the project, would be sufficient to restore the financial viability of the project;

(3) The project is or can (at reasonable cost) be made physically sound;

(4) The current or proposed operator of the facility is satisfactory to the Commissioner, as demonstrated by past experience in operating similar types of healthcare facilities and by state regulatory performance;

(5) The default under the insured mortgage was beyond the control of the borrower and/or operator, or in the case of a transfer of physical assets (TPA), the proposed borrower or operator, unless the Commissioner determines that any borrower/operator deficiencies giving rise to the default have clearly been addressed; and

(6) The project is serving as, or potentially could serve as, a needed nursing home, intermediate care facility, board and care home, or assisted living facility.

(c) Partial payment of a claim under this section shall be made only when:

(1) The property covered by the mortgage is free and clear of all liens other than the insured first mortgage and such other liens as the Commissioner may have approved;

(2) The lender has voluntarily agreed to accept a PPC under the mortgage insurance contract and to recast the remaining mortgage amount under terms and conditions prescribed by the Commissioner; and

(3) The borrower has agreed to repay to the Commissioner an amount equal to the partial payment, with the obligation secured by a second mortgage on the project containing terms and conditions prescribed by the Commissioner. The terms of the second mortgage will be determined on a case-by-case basis to ensure that the estimated project income will be sufficient to cover estimated operating expenses and debt service on the recast insured mortgage. The Commissioner may provide for postponed amortization of the second mortgage.

(d) Payment of insurance benefits under this section shall be in cash.

(e) A lender receiving a partial payment of claim, following the Commissioner's endorsement of the mortgage for full insurance under 24 CFR part 252, will pay HUD a fee in an amount set forth through FEDERAL REGISTER notice. HUD, in its discretion, may collect this fee or deduct the fee from any payment it makes in the claim process.

[77 FR 72922, Dec. 7, 2012]

Subpart C—Eligibility Requirements—Supplemental Loans To Finance Purchase and Installation of Fire Safety Equipment

SOURCE: 39 FR 28966, Aug. 12, 1974, unless otherwise noted.

§ 232.500 Definitions.

In addition to the definitions contained in subpart A, incorporated herein by reference, the following terms, as used in §§ 232.500 et seq., shall have the meaning indicated:

(a) *Insured loan* means a loan insured by the endorsement of the credit instrument by the Commissioner.

(b) *Insurance premium* means the loan insurance premium paid by the financial institution to the Commissioner in consideration of the contract of insurance.

(c)(1) *Fire safety equipment* means equipment that is purchased, installed, and maintained in a nursing home, intermediate care facility, assisted living facility, or board and care home and that meets the following standards for the applicable occupancy:

(i) The edition of The Life Safety Code of the National Fire Protection Association as accepted by the Department of Health and Human Services in 42 CFR 483.70; or

(ii) A standard mandated by a State under the provisions of section 1616(e) of the Social Security Act.

(iii) Any appropriate requirement approved by the Secretary of Health and Human Services for providers of services under title XVIII or title XIX of the Social Security Act.

(2) In addition to those requirements approved by the Secretary of Health and Human Services as necessary for the appropriate level of occupancy, *fire safety equipment* may also include fire safety-related improvements that are not mandatory under the requirements of the Secretary of Health and Human Services, but which the Secretary of Health and Human Services considers acceptable and reasonable for protection against the hazards of fire and which the borrower agrees to install.

(3) For the purposes of this definition, the terms *nursing home* and *inter-* *mediate care facility* shall include those facilities designated as skilled nursing facilities or intermediate care facilities by the Department of Health and Human Services.

(d) *Fire safety loan* means any form of secured or unsecured obligation determined by the Commissioner to be eligible for insurance under this subpart and, in the case of an assisted living facility or a board and care home, made with respect to such a home located in a State which the Secretary has determined is in compliance with the provisions of section 1616(e) of the Social Security Act.

(e) *Equipment cost* means the reasonable cost of fire safety equipment fully installed as determined by the Commissioner.

(f) *Insured loan maturity* means the date on which the loan indebtedness would be extinguished if paid in accordance with periodic payments provided for in the loan instrument or instruments.

(g) *Approved lender* means a financial institution or other mortgagee approved by the Commissioner as eligible for insurance under section 2 of the National Housing Act, or a mortgagee approved under section 203(b)(1) of the National Housing Act.

[39 FR 28966, Aug. 12, 1974, as amended at 50 FR 37522, Sept. 16, 1985; 59 FR 61228, Nov. 29, 1994; 80 FR 48027, Aug. 11, 2015]

FEES AND CHARGES

§ 232.505 Application and application fee.

(a) *Filing of application.* An application for insurance of a fire safety loan for a nursing home, intermediate care facility, assisted living facility or board and care home shall be submitted on an approved HUD form by an approved lender and by the owners of the project to the HUD office.

(b) *Application fee.* See 24 CFR 200.40(d)(2).

[80 FR 48027, Aug. 11, 2015]

§ 232.510 Commitment and commitment fee.

(a) *Issuance of commitment.* Upon approval of an application for insurance, a commitment shall be issued by the Commissioner setting forth the terms and conditions upon which the fire safety loan will be insured.

(b) *Type of commitment.* The commitment will provide for the insurance of the loan after satisfactory completion of installation of the fire safety equipment, as determined by the Commissioner.

(c) *Term of commitment.* A commitment shall have a term as the Commissioner deems necessary for satisfactory completion of installation.

(d) *Commitment fee.* See 24 CFR 200.40(d)(2).

(e) *Increase in commitment prior to endorsement.* An application, filed prior to endorsement, for an increase in the amount of an outstanding firm commitment shall be accompanied by an additional application fee. The additional application fee shall be in an amount determined by the Secretary as equal to the amount determined under 24 CFR 200.40(d)(2), which shall not exceed $5.00 per thousand dollars of the amount of the requested increase. If an inspection fee was required in the original commitment, an additional inspection fee shall be paid in an amount computed at the same dollar rate per thousand dollars of the amount of increase in commitment as was used for the inspection fee required in the original commitment. The additional inspection fee shall be paid prior to the date installation of fire safety equipment is begun, or, if installation has begun, it shall be paid with the application for increase.

[39 FR 28966, Aug. 12, 1974, as amended at 80 FR 48027, Aug. 11, 2015]

§232.515 Refund of fees.

If the amount of the commitment issued or an increase in the loan amount prior to endorsement is less than the amount applied for, the Commissioner shall refund the excess amount of the application fee submitted by the applicant. If an application is rejected before it is assigned for processing, or in such other instances as the Commissioner may determine, the entire application fee or any portion thereof may be returned to the applicant.

[80 FR 48027, Aug. 11, 2015]

§232.520 Maximum fees and charges by lender.

See 24 CFR 200.40 titled "HUD fees" and 200.41 titled "Maximum mortgage fees and charges" for maximum fees and charges applicable to mortgages insured under 24 CFR part 232.

[80 FR 48027, Aug. 11, 2015]

§232.522 Inspection fee.

See 24 CFR 200.40 titled "HUD fees" and 200.41 titled "Maximum mortgage fees and charges" for maximum fees and charges applicable to mortgages insured under 24 CFR part 232.

[80 FR 48027, Aug. 11, 2015]

ELIGIBLE SECURITY INSTRUMENTS

§232.525 Note and security form.

The lender shall present for insurance a note and security instrument, if required, on forms approved by the Commissioner for use in the jurisdiction in which the property to be improved is located.

§232.530 Disbursement of proceeds.

At the time of endorsement for insurance of the note by the Commissioner, the entire principal amount of the note shall have been disbursed to the borrower or to his creditors for his account and with his consent.

§232.535 Loan multiples—minimum principal.

The loan shall involve a principal obligation in multiples of $100, and the minimum principal obligation shall be $10,000.

[40 FR 4908, Feb. 3, 1975]

§232.540 Method of loan payment and amortization period.

See 24 CFR 200.82 titled "Maturity" for loan payment and amortization period requirements applicable to mortgages insured under 24 CFR part 232.

[80 FR 48027, Aug. 11, 2015]

§232.545 Covenant against liens.

(a) The security instrument shall contain a covenant against the creation by the borrower of additional liens against the property superior or inferior to the lien of such instrument, except with the prior approval of the Commissioner.

(b) The covenant required under paragraph (a) of this section shall not apply where a lien inferior to the lien of the insured mortgage is given in favor of a Federal, State or local governmental agency or instrumentality under such circumstances as may be approved by the Commissioner, provided the source of funds for repayment of the inferior lien is limited to surplus cash or residual receipts.

[36 FR 24641, Dec. 22, 1971, as amended at 48 FR 35393, Aug. 4, 1983; 49 FR 12215, Mar. 29, 1984]

§ 232.550 Accumulation of next premium.

The security instrument shall provide for payments by the borrower to the lender on each interest payment date of an amount sufficient to accumulate in the hands of the lender one payment period prior to its due date the next annual insurance premium payable by the lender to the Commissioner.

§ 232.555 Security instrument and lien.

The security instrument shall cover the entire property included in the project, shall be a lien on the real property of the project under the laws of the jurisdiction in which the project is located, and may be junior to such prior liens or mortgages indebtedness as the Commissioner may approve. The Commissioner may from time to time require such other security, in lieu of, or in addition to, a lien on real property as he may prescribe.

§ 232.560 Interest rate.

(a) The loan shall bear interest at the rate agreed upon by the lender and the borrower.

(b) Interest shall be payable in monthly installments on the principal amount of the loan outstanding on the due date of each installment.

[39 FR 28966, Aug. 12, 1974, as amended at 53 FR 3366, Feb. 5, 1988; 53 FR 8885, Mar. 18, 1988]

§ 232.565 Maximum loan amount.

The principal amount of the loan shall not exceed the lower of the Commissioner's estimate of the cost of the fire safety equipment, including the cost of installation and eligible fees, or the amount supported by ninety percent (90%) of the residual income, which is ninety percent (90%) of the amount of net income remaining after payment of all existing debt service requirements, as determined by the Commissioner. The cost of installation may include the cost of such other work to be performed on the project necessary to meet the requirements of the Secretary of Health and Human Services and the Commissioner to enhance the fire safety of the project, and such costs incidental to installation as may be approved by the Commissioner.

[40 FR 4908, Feb. 3, 1975, as amended at 80 FR 48028, Aug. 11, 2015]

§ 232.570 Endorsement of credit instrument.

The Commissioner shall indicate his insurance of the loan by endorsing the credit instrument and identifying the section of the Act and regulations under which the loan is insured and the date of insurance, subject to the presentation and approval by him of the following:

(a) Certification of full disbursement of loan proceeds as provided for in § 232.530.

(b) Certification of costs as required by § 232.610.

(c) Certification that fire safety equipment was installed as required by § 232.500(c).

[39 FR 28966, Aug. 12, 1974, as amended at 80 FR 48028, Aug. 11, 2015]

§ 232.580 Application of payments.

(a) The security instrument shall provide that all monthly payments to be made by the borrower shall be added together and this aggregate amount shall be paid by the borrower upon each monthly payment date in a single payment. The lender shall apply the payment to the following items in the order set forth:

(1) Premium charges under the contract of insurance;

(2) Interest on the loan;

(3) Amortization of the principal of the loan;

(b) Any deficiency in the amount of any monthly payments required under paragraph (a) of this section shall constitute an event of default and the loan shall further provide for a grace period of 30 days within which time the default must be cured.

§232.585 Prepayment privilege and prepayment charge.

The security instrument shall contain a provision permitting prepayment of the loan in whole or in part upon any interest payment date after giving to the lender 30 days' advance written notice and it may contain a provision, with the approval of the Commissioner, for a reasonable charge in the event of prepayment.

§232.586 Minimum principal loan amount.

A mortgagee may not require, as a condition of providing a loan secured by a mortgage insured under this subpart, that the principal amount of the mortgage exceed a minimum amount established by the mortgagee.

[53 FR 8885, Mar. 18, 1988]

PROPERTY REQUIREMENTS

§232.590 Eligibility of property.

(a) A loan to be eligible for insurance shall be on real estate held:

(1) In fee simple; or

(2) On the interest of the lessee under a lease for not less than ninety-nine years which is renewable; or

(3) Under a lease having a period of not less than "twenty-five" years to run from the date the loan is executed.

(b) The property constituting security for the loan transaction must be held by an eligible borrower as herein defined and must at the time the loan is insured be free and clear of all liens other than those specifically approved by the Commissioner.

[39 FR 28966, Aug. 12, 1974; 39 FR 30349, Aug. 22, 1974]

§232.591 Smoke detectors.

After October 30, 1992, each occupied room must include at least one battery-operated or hard-wired smoke detector in proper working condition. If the room is occupied by hearing-impaired persons, the smoke detector must have an alarm system designed for hearing-impaired persons, unless the smoke alarm is connected to a central alarm system that is monitored on a 24-hour basis, or otherwise meets industry standards.

[57 FR 33850, July 30, 1992]

TITLE

§232.595 Eligibility of title.

In order for the property which is to be the security for a loan to be insured under this subpart to be eligible for insurance, the Commissioner shall determine that the title to the property is vested in the borrower as of the date the security instrument is filed for record. The title evidence will be examined by the Commissioner and the endorsement of the credit instrument for insurance shall be evidence of its acceptability.

§232.600 Title evidence.

The lender, without expense to the Commissioner, shall furnish to the Commissioner a policy of title insurance, or if the lender is unable to furnish a policy for reasons satisfactory to the Commissioner, the lender, without expense to the Commissioner, shall furnish an abstract of title. The following are the requirements covering the title insurance and abstract of title:

(a) The policy of title insurance shall be issued by a company, and in a form, satisfactory to the Commissioner. The policy shall name as the insureds the lender and the Secretary of Housing and Urban Development, as their respective interests may appear. The policy shall provide that upon acquisition of title by the lender or the Secretary, the policy of title insurance will continue to provide the same coverage as the original policy, and will run to the lender or the Secretary, as the case may be.

(b) The abstract of title shall be satisfactory to the Commissioner, prepared by an abstract title company or an individual engaged in the business of preparing abstracts of title, accompanied by a legal opinion satisfactory to the Commissioner, as to the quality of such title, signed by an attorney at law experienced in the examination of titles.

[39 FR 28966, Aug. 12, 1974, as amended at 58 FR 34216, June 24, 1993]

FORM OF CONTRACT

§ 232.605　Contract requirements.

The contract between the mortgagor and the general contractor may be in the form of a lump sum contract, a cost plus contract, or different or alternative forms of contract specified by the Commissioner.

[80 FR 48028, Aug. 11, 2015]

COST CERTIFICATION REQUIREMENTS

§ 232.610　Certification of cost requirements.

(a) *Certificate and adjustment.* No loan shall be insured unless a certification of actual cost is made by the contractor.

(b) *Cost computation.* The term *actual cost of the improvements* shall mean the cost to the borrower of the improvements, after deducting the amount of any kickbacks, rebates, or trade discount received in connection with the improvements, and including the amounts paid under any contract for the improvements, labor, materials, and for any other items of expense approved by the Commissioner.

(c) *Statement of facts.* Any agreement, undertaking, statement or certification required in connection with cost certification shall specifically state that it has been made, presented and delivered for the purpose of influencing an official action of the Commissioner and may be relied upon as a true statement of the facts contained therein.

(d) *Incontestability.* Upon the Commissioner's approval of the cost certification, such certification shall be final and incontestable except for fraud or material misrepresentation on the part of the borrower.

(e) *Records.* The borrower shall keep and maintain adequate records of all costs of any construction improvements or other cost items not representing work under the general contract and shall require the builder to keep similar records and, upon request by the Commissioner, shall make

available for examination such records, including any collateral agreements.

[39 FR 28966, Aug. 12, 1974, as amended at 80 FR 48028, Aug. 11, 2015]

ELIGIBLE BORROWERS

§ 232.615　Eligible borrowers.

(a) In order to be eligible as a borrower under this subpart the applicant shall be a profit or non-profit entity, which owns a nursing home or intermediate care facility for which the Secretary of Health and Human Services has determined that the installation of fire safety equipment in such facility is necessary to meet the applicable requirements of the Secretary of Health and Human Services for providers of services under Title XVIII and Title XIX of the Social Security Act and that upon completion of the installation of such equipment the nursing home or intermediate care facility will meet the applicable fire safety requirements of HHS. Until the termination of all obligations of the Commissioner under an insurance contract under this subpart and during such further period of time as the Commissioner shall be the owner, holder, or reinsurer of the loan, the borrower shall be regulated or restricted by the Commissioner as to methods of operation including requirements for maintenance of fire safety equipment.

(b) Also eligible as a borrower shall be a profit or nonprofit entity which owns an assisted living facility or board and care home for which HUD has determined that the installation of fire safety equipment is approvable under the definition contained in § 232.500(c).

[39 FR 28966, Aug. 12, 1974; 39 FR 30349, Aug. 22, 1974, as amended at 50 FR 37523, Sept. 16, 1985; 59 FR 61228, Nov. 29, 1994; 80 FR 48028, Aug. 11, 2015]

§ 232.616　Disclosure and verification of Social Security and Employer Identification Numbers.

To be eligible for mortgage insurance under this subpart, the borrower must meet the requirements for the disclosure and verification of Social Security and Employer Identification Numbers, as provided by part 200, subpart U, of this chapter.

(Approved by the Office of Management and Budget under control number 2502–0118)

[54 FR 39695, Sept. 27, 1989]

SPECIAL REQUIREMENTS

§232.620 Determination of compliance with fire safety equipment requirements.

Prior to Endorsement, applicant must provide certification that the installed improvements will meet HHS, as well as all other Federal, state and local requirements for fire safety equipment, if applicable.

[80 FR 48028, Aug. 11, 2015]

§232.625 Discrimination prohibited.

Any contract or subcontract executed for the installation of equipment, or construction of improvements to the project shall provide that there shall be no discrimination against any employee or applicant for employment because of sex, religion, race, color, creed or national origin.

§232.630 Assurance of completion.

If the property upon which the fire safety equipment is to be installed is subject to a mortgage insured or held by the Commissioner pursuant to subpart B of this part, the Commissioner may require such assurance of completion of the contract for installation as he may from time to time prescribe.

Subpart D—Contract Rights and Obligations

SOURCE: 39 FR 28970, Aug. 12, 1974, unless otherwise noted.

§232.800 Definitions.

All of the definitions contained in §232.500 shall apply to this subpart. In addition, as used in this subpart, the following term shall have the meaning indicated:

(a) *Contract of insurance* means the agreement evidenced by the endorsement of the Commissioner upon the note given in connection with an insured loan and includes the provisions of this subpart and the applicable provisions of the Act.

(b) *Maturity* means the date on which the loan indebtedness would be extinguished if paid in accordance with periodic payments provided for in the loan.

PREMIUMS

§232.805 Insurance premiums.

(a) *First premium.* The lender, upon the endorsement of the loan for insurance, shall pay to the Commissioner a first loan insurance premium equal to one percent of the original face amount of the note.

(b) *Second premium.* The lender, on the date of the first principal payment, shall pay a second premium equal to one percent of the average outstanding principal obligation of the loan for the year following such first principal payment date which shall be adjusted as of that date so that the aggregate of the first and second premiums shall equal the sum of one percent per annum of the average outstanding principal obligation of the loan for the period from the date of the insurance endorsement to one year following the date of the first principal payment.

(c) *Annual insurance premium.* Until the note is paid in full, or until the loan is assigned to the Commissioner, or until the contract of insurance is otherwise terminated with the consent of the Commissioner, the lender, on each anniversary of the date of the first principal payment shall pay an annual loan insurance premium equal to one percent of the average outstanding principal obligation of the loan for the year following the date on which such premium becomes payable.

(d) *Method of premium payment.* Premiums shall be payable in cash or in debentures of the General Insurance Fund at par plus accrued interest. All premiums are payable in advance and no refund can be made of any portion thereof except as provided in §232.800 *et seq.*

(e) *Calculation of premiums.* The premiums payable on and after the date of the first principal payment shall be calculated in accordance with the amortization provisions without taking into account delinquent payments or prepayments.

365

§ 232.805a   Mortgagee's late charge.

Mortgage insurance premiums which are paid to the Commissioner more than 15 days after the billing date or due date, whichever is later, shall include a late charge of 4 percent of the amount of the payment due, except that no late charge shall be required with respect to any case for which HUD fails to render a proper billing to the mortgagee.

[43 FR 60154, Dec. 26, 1978]

§ 232.815   Termination of insurance.

(a) *Prepayment in full.* The contract of insurance shall be terminated if the loan is paid in full prior to its maturity. Notice of the prepayment shall be given to the Commissioner, on a form prescribed by the Commissioner, within 30 days from the date of the prepayment. The insurance termination shall become effective as of the date of the prepayment, or 30 days prior to the Commissioner's receipt of the prepayment notice, whichever is later.

(b) *Voluntary termination.* The contract of insurance shall be voluntarily terminated upon receipt by the Commissioner of a written request, on a form prescribed by the Commissioner, by the borrower and the lender for such termination, accompanied by a submission of the original credit instrument for cancellation of the insurance endorsement and the remittance of all sums to which the Commissioner is entitled. The termination shall become effective as of the date these requirements are met.

§ 232.825   Pro rata refund of insurance premium.

Upon termination of a loan insurance contract by a payment in full or by a voluntary termination, the Commissioner shall refund to the lender for the account of the borrower an amount equal to the pro rata portion of the current annual loan insurance premium theretofore paid which is applicable to the portion of the year subsequent to the effective date of the termination.

RIGHTS AND DUTIES OF LENDER UNDER THE CONTRACT OF INSURANCE

§ 232.830   Definition of default.

(a) If the borrower fails to make any payments due under or provided to be paid by the terms of the note or security instrument, the note shall be considered in default for the purposes of this subpart.

(b) The failure to perform any other covenant under the note or security instrument shall be considered a default, provided the lender, because of such default, has exercised its rights under the note or security instrument and accelerated the debt.

(c) If such defaults as defined in paragraphs (a) and (b) of this section continue for a period of 30 days, the lender shall be entitled to receive the benefits of insurance hereinafter provided.

§ 232.840   Date of default.

In computing loan insurance benefits, the date of default shall be considered as:

(a) The date of the lender's acceleration of the debt because of the borrower's uncorrected failure to perform a covenant or obligation under the note or security instrument; or

(b) The date of the first failure to make a monthly payment which subsequent payments by the borrower are insufficient to cover when applied to the overdue monthly payments in the order in which they become due.

§ 232.850   Notice of default.

(a) If the default is not cured within the 30 day grace period, as defined in § 232.830(c), the lender shall, within 30 days thereafter, notify the Commissioner in writing of such default.

(b) The lender shall give notice in writing to the Commissioner of the failure of the borrower to comply with any covenant or obligation under the security instrument or note regardless of the fact that the lender may not have elected to accelerate the debt.

§ 232.860   Commissioner's right to require acceleration.

Upon receipt of notice of the failure of the borrower to comply with any covenant or obligation under the security instrument or note, or otherwise being apprised thereof, the Commissioner may require the lender to accelerate payment of the outstanding principal balance due.

§232.865 Election by lender.

Where a real estate mortgage, or other security instrument has been used to secure the payment of a loan made under the provisions of this subpart and subpart C of this part, the lender may either elect to assign the loan to the Commissioner in exchange for the payment of insurance benefits or may exercise its rights under the note and security instrument in lieu of making a claim for insurance benefits. If the lender elects the latter course, the Commissioner shall be so notified and the contract of insurance shall be deemed terminated upon the date of receipt of such notification.

§232.875 Maximum claim period.

Notice of intention to file claim on a form prescribed by the Commissioner shall be filed within 45 days after the lender becomes eligible for the benefits of the loan insurance, or within such later time as may be agreed upon by the Commissioner in writing.

§232.880 Items to be delivered on submitting claim.

Within 30 days after the filing of the notice of intention to file claim, or within such further period as may be agreed upon by the Commission in writing, the lender shall deliver to the Commissioner:

(a) The fiscal data pertaining to the loan transactions;

(b) Receipts covering all disbursements as required by the fiscal data form;

(c) The original note and any security instrument or instruments which shall be assigned to the Commissioner without recourse or warranty, except that the lender must warrant that no act or omission of the lender has impaired the validity and priority of such security instrument or instruments, that the security instrument or instruments are prior to all mechanics' and material-men's liens filed of record subsequent to the recording of such security instrument or instruments regardless of whether such liens attached prior to such recording date, and prior to all liens and encumbrances which may have attached or defects which which may have arisen subsequent to the recording of such security instrument or instruments, except such liens or other matters as may be approved by the Commissioner, that the amount stated in the instrument of assignment is actually due and owing under the security instrument or instruments, that there are no offsets or counterclaims thereto, and that the lender has a good right to assign such note and security instrument or instruments;

(d) The assignment to the Commissioner of all rights and interests arising under the note and security instrument or instruments so in default and all claims of the lender against the borrower or others arising out of the loan transaction;

(e) All policies of title or other insurance or surety bonds, or other guarantees and any and all claims thereunder; including evidence satisfactory to the Commissioner that the original title coverage has been extended to include the assignment of the note and security instrument or instruments to the Commissioner;

(f) All records, ledger cards, documents, books, papers and accounts relating to the loan transaction;

(g) Any additional information or data which the Commissioner may require;

(h) The following cash items, held in connection with the loan insured under this subpart, shall either be retained by the lender or delivered to the Commissioner in accordance with instructions to be issued by the Commissioner at the time the insurance claim is filed.

(1) Any cash held by the lender or its agents or to which it is entitled including deposits made for the account of the borrower and which have not been applied in reduction of the principal of the loan indebtedness.

(2) All funds held by the lender for the account of the borrower received pursuant to any other agreement.

§232.885 Insurance benefits.

(a) *Method of payment.* Payment of an insurance claim shall be made in cash, in debentures, or in a combination of both, as determined by the Commissioner either at, or prior to, the time of payment.

(b) *Amount of payment.* Upon an acceptable assignment of the note and security instrument, the Commissioner shall pay the claim of the lender in an amount equal to the unpaid principal balance of the loan as of the date of default determined as follows:

(1) By adding the following items:

(i) Any accrued interest due as of the date of execution of the assignment of the loan to the Commissioner.

(ii) Any advances approved by the Commissioner made previously by the lender under the provisions of the note or security instrument or instruments.

(iii) Reimbursement for such reasonable collection costs, court costs, and attorney's fees as may be approved by the Commissioner.

(iv) Any loan insurance premiums paid after default.

(v) If payment is made in cash, an amount equivalent to the debenture interest which would have been earned thereon, as of the date such cash payment is made, except when the lender fails to meet any one of the applicable requirements of §§ 232.850, 232.875, and 232.880, within the specified time and in a manner satisfactory to the Commissioner (or within such further time as the Commissioner may approve in writing), the interest allowance in such cash payment shall be computed only to the date on which the particular required action should have been taken or to which it was extended.

(2) By deducting from the total of the items computed under paragraph (b)(1) of this section the following items:

(i) Any amount received by the lender on account of the loan after the date of default.

(ii) Any net income received by the lender from the property covered by the note or security instrument and not applied to prior debts held by that lender.

(iii) The sum of the cash items retained by the lender pursuant to § 232.880(h)(i)(ii).

[39 FR 28970, Aug. 12, 1974, as amended at 80 FR 51468, Aug. 25, 2015]

§ 232.890   Characteristics of debentures.

Debentures issued in settlement of insurance claims under this subpart shall have the same characteristics and the same requirements for registration and redemption as those issued pursuant to subpart B of this part except that debentures shall bear interest at the rate in effect as of the date the commitment was issued, or as of the date the loan was first endorsed for insurance, whichever rate is higher and shall mature 10 years from the date of issue which date shall be the date of execution of the assignment of the loan to the Commissioner.

§ 232.893   Cash adjustment.

Any difference of less than $50 between the amount of debentures to be issued to the lender and the total amount of the lender's claim, as approved by the Commissioner, may be adjusted by the issuance of a check in payment thereof.

[59 FR 49816, Sept. 30, 1994]

ASSIGNMENTS

§ 232.895   Assignment of insured loans.

(a) An insured loan may be transferred only to a transferee who is a lender approved by the Commissioner. Upon such transfer and the assumption by the transferee of all obligations under the contract of insurance the transferor shall be released from its obligations under the contract of insurance.

(b) The contract of insurance shall terminate with respect to loans described in paragraph (a) of this section upon the happening of either of the following events:

(1) The transfer or pledge of the insured loan to any person, firm, or corporation, public or private, other than an approved lender.

(2) The disposal by a lender of any partial interest in the insured loan to other than an approved lender.

EXTENSION OF TIME

§ 232.897   Actions to be taken by lender.

With respect to any action required of the lender within a period of time prescribed by this subpart, the Commissioner may extend such period.

Subpart E—Insurance of Mortgages Covering Existing Projects

SOURCE: 53 FR 33735, Aug. 31, 1988, unless otherwise noted.

§ 232.901 Mortgages covering existing projects are eligible for insurance.

A mortgage executed in connection with the purchase or refinancing of an existing project without substantial rehabilitation may be insured under this subpart pursuant to section 223(f) of the Act. A mortgage insured pursuant to this subpart shall meet all other requirements of this part except as expressly modified by this subpart.

[59 FR 61228, Nov. 29, 1994]

§ 232.902 Eligible project.

Existing projects (with such repairs and improvements as are determined by the Commissioner to be necessary) are eligible for insurance under this subpart. The project must not require substantial rehabilitation and three years must have elapsed from the date of completion of construction or substantial rehabilitation of the project, or from the beginning of occupancy, whichever is later, to the date of application for insurance. In addition, the project must have attained sustaining occupancy (occupancy that produces income sufficient to pay operating expenses, annual debt service and reserve fund for replacement requirements) as determined by the Commissioner, before endorsement of the project for insurance; alternatively, the borrower must provide an operating deficit fund at the time of endorsement for insurance, in an amount, and under an agreement, approved by the Commissioner.

[59 FR 61228, Nov. 29, 1994]

§ 232.903 Maximum mortgage limitations.

Notwithstanding the maximum mortgage limitations set forth in 24 CFR 200.15, a mortgage within the limits set forth in this section shall be eligible for insurance under this subpart.

(a) *Value limit.* The mortgage shall involve a principal obligation of not in excess of eighty-five percent (85%) for a profit motivated borrower (ninety percent (90%) for a private nonprofit borrower) of the Commissioner's estimate of the value of the project, including major movable equipment to be used in its operation and any repairs and improvements. The Commissioner's estimate of value shall result from consideration of:

(1) Estimated market value of the Project by capitalization,

(2) Estimated market value of the Project by direct sales comparison, and

(3) Total estimated replacement cost of the Project.

In the event the mortgage is secured by a leasehold estate rather than a fee simple estate, the value of the property described in the mortgage shall be the value of the leasehold estate (as determined by the Commissioner) which shall in all cases be less than the value of the property in fee simple.

(b) *Debt service limit.* The insured mortgage shall involve a principal obligation not in excess of the amount that could be amortized by eighty-five percent (85%) for a profit motivated borrower (ninety percent (90%) for a private nonprofit borrower) of the net projected project income available for payment of debt service. Net projected Project income available for debt service shall be determined by reducing the Commissioner's estimated gross income for the Project by a vacancy and collection loss factor and by the cost of all estimated operating expenses, including deposits to the reserve for replacements and taxes.

(c) *Project to be refinanced—additional limit.* (1) In addition to meeting the requirements of paragraphs (a) and (b) of this section, if the Project is to be refinanced by the insured mortgage, the maximum mortgage amount must not exceed the cost to refinance the existing indebtedness. For the purposes of this requirement:

(i) The Project shall not have changed ownership subsequent to the date of application, or

(ii) The Project shall have been sold to a purchaser who has an identity of interest with the seller (as defined by the Commissioner).

(2) The cost to refinance the existing indebtedness will consist of the following items, the eligibility and amounts of which must be determined by the Commissioner:

(i) The amount required to pay off the existing indebtedness;

(ii) The amount of the initial deposit for the reserve fund for replacements;

(iii) Reasonable and customary legal, organization, title, and recording expenses, including mortgagee fees under § 200.41;

(iv) The estimated repair costs, if any;

(v) Architect's and engineer's fees, municipal inspection fees, and any other required professional or inspection fees; and

(vi) The amount of any long-term debt service reserve account required by the Commissioner pursuant to § 232.11.

(d) *Project to be acquired—additional limit.* In addition to meeting the requirements of paragraphs (a) and (b) of this section, if the project is to be acquired by the borrower and the purchase price is to be financed with the insured mortgage, the maximum amount must not exceed 85 percent for a profit-motivated borrower and 90 percent for a private nonprofit borrower of the cost of acquisition as determined by the Commissioner. The cost of acquisition shall consist of the following items, to the extent that each item (except for paragraph (d)(1) of this section) is paid by the purchaser separately from the purchase price. The eligibility and amounts of these items must be determined in accordance with standards established by the Commissioner.

(1) Purchase price is indicated in the purchase agreement;

(2) An amount for the initial deposit to the reserve fund for replacements;

(3) Reasonable and customary legal, organizational, title, and recording expenses, including mortgagee fees under § 200.41;

(4) The estimated repair cost, if any;

(5) Architect's and engineer's fees, municipal inspection fees, and any other required professional or inspection fees; and

(6) The amount of any long-term debt service reserve account required by the Commissioner pursuant to § 232.11.

[53 FR 33735, Aug. 31, 1988, as amended at 59 FR 61228, Nov. 29, 1994; 77 FR 55136, Sept. 7, 2012]

§ 232.904 Term of the mortgage.

Notwithstanding the provisions of § 232.27, a mortgage insured under this subpart must have a maturity satisfactory to the Commissioner which is not less than 10 years, nor more than the lesser of 35 years or 75 percent of the estimated remaining economic life of the physical improvements. The term of the mortgage will begin on the first day of the second month following the date of endorsement of the mortgage for insurance.

§ 232.905 Labor standards and prevailing wage requirements.

The provisions of §§ 232.70–232.74 of this part shall not apply to mortgages insured under commitments issued in accordance with this subpart.

§ 232.906 Processing of applications and required fees.

(a) *Processing of applications.* The local HUD Office will determine whether participation in a preapplication conference is required as a condition to submission of an initial application for either a conditional or firm commitment. After the preapplication conference an application for a conditional or firm commitment for insurance of a mortgage on a project shall be submitted by the sponsor and an approved mortgagee. Such application shall be submitted to the local HUD Office on a HUD approved form. An application may, at the option of the applicant, be submitted for a firm commitment omitting the conditional commitment stage. No application shall be considered unless accompanied by all exhibits required by the form and program handbooks. An application may be made for a commitment which provides for the insurance of the mortgage upon completion of any improvements or for a commitment which provides, in accordance with standards established by the Commissioner, for the completing of specified repairs and improvements after endorsement.

(b) *Application fee—conditional commitment.* An application-commitment fee of $3 per thousand dollars of the requested mortgage amount shall accompany an application for conditional commitment.

(c) *Application fee—firm commitment.* An application for firm commitment shall be accompanied by an application-commitment fee of $5 per thousand dollars of the requested mortgage amount to be insured less any amount previously received for a conditional commitment.

(d) *Inspection fee.* Where an application provides for the completion of repairs, replacements and/or improvements (repairs), the Commissioner will charge an inspection fee equal to one percent (1%) of the cost of the repairs. However, where the Commissioner determines the cost of repairs is minimal, the Commissioner may establish a minimum inspection fee that exceeds one percent of the cost of repairs and can periodically increase or decrease this minimum fee.

(e) *Cross-reference.* The provisions of paragraphs (f)(1) (Fee on increases), (g) (Reopening of expired commitments), (h) (Transfer fee), (i) (Refund of fees), and (j) (Fees not required) of §200.40 of this chapter apply to applications submitted under subpart E of this part.

[61 FR 14416, Apr. 1, 1996]

Subpart F—Eligible Operators and Facilities and Restrictions on Fund Distributions

SOURCE: 77 FR 55137, Sept. 7, 2012, unless otherwise noted.

§232.1001 Scope.

This subpart establishes requirements applicable to the operators of healthcare facilities and the facilities under this part.

§232.1003 Eligible operator.

Operator shall be a single asset entity acceptable to the Commissioner, and shall possess the powers necessary and incidental to operating the healthcare facility, except that the Commissioner may approve a non-single asset entity under such circumstances, terms, and conditions determined and specified as acceptable to the Commissioner. A master tenant under a master lease approved by the Commissioner who has subleased the healthcare facility to an operator is not an Operator.

§232.1005 Treatment of project operating accounts.

All accounts deriving from the operation of the property, including operator accounts and including all funds received from any source or derived from the operation of the facility, are project assets subject to control under the insured mortgage loan's transactional documents, including, without limitation, the operator's regulatory agreement. Except as otherwise permitted or approved by HUD, funds generated by the operation of the healthcare facility shall be deposited into a federally insured bank account, provided that an account held in an institution acceptable to Ginnie Mae may have a balance that exceeds the amount to which such insurance is limited. Any of the owner's project-related funds shall be deposited into a federally insured bank account in the name of the borrower provided that an account held in an institution acceptable to Ginnie Mae may have a balance that exceeds the amount to which such insurance is limited.

§232.1007 Operating expenses.

Goods and services purchased or acquired in connection with the project shall be reasonable and necessary for the operation or maintenance of the project, and the costs of such goods and services incurred by the borrower or operator shall not exceed amounts normally paid for such goods or services in the area where the services are rendered or the goods are furnished, except as otherwise permitted or approved by HUD.

§232.1009 Financial reports.

(a) The borrower must provide HUD and lender an audited annual financial report based on an examination of its books and records, in such form and substance required by HUD in accordance with 24 CFR 5.801 and 24 CFR 200.36.

(b) Operators must submit financial statements quarterly within 60 calendar days of the date of the end of each fiscal quarter, setting forth both quarterly and fiscal year-to-date information, except that the final fiscal year end quarter must be submitted to HUD within 90 calendar days of the end of the quarter, in accordance with 24 CFR 5.801(c)(4), or within such additional time as may be provided by the Commissioner for good cause shown. HUD may direct that such forms be submitted to the lender or another third party in addition to or in lieu of submission to HUD.

[79 FR 55362, Sept. 16, 2014]

§ 232.1011   Management agents.

(a) An operator or borrower may, with the prior written approval of HUD, execute a management agent agreement setting forth the duties and procedures for matters related to the management of the project. The management agent, each initial management agent agreement with that agent, and any amendments to such management agent agreements deemed material by the Commissioner must be acceptable to HUD and approved in writing by HUD.

(b) An operator or borrower may not enter into any agreement that provides for a management agent to have rights to or claims on funds owed to the operator.

§ 232.1013   Restrictions on deposit, withdrawal, and distribution of funds, and repayment of advances.

(a) *Deposit of funds.* An operator must deposit all revenue the operator receives directly or indirectly in connection with the operation of the healthcare facility in an account with a financial institution whose deposits are insured by an agency of the Federal Government, *provided* that an account held in an institution acceptable to Ginnie Mae may have a balance that exceeds the amount to which such insurance is limited.

(b) *Withdrawal of funds.* If a quarterly/year-to-date financial statement demonstrates negative working capital as defined by HUD, or if the operator fails to timely submit such statement, then until a current quarterly/year-to-date financial statement demonstrates positive working capital or until otherwise authorized by HUD, the operator may not distribute, advance, or otherwise use funds attributable to that facility for any purpose other than operating that facility.

§ 232.1015   Prompt notification to HUD and mortgagee of circumstances placing the value of the security at risk.

(a) HUD and the mortgagee shall be informed of any notification of any failure to comply with governmental requirements including the following:

(1) The licensed operator of a project shall promptly provide HUD and the mortgagee with a copy of any notification that has placed the licensure, a provider funding source, and/or the ability to admit new residents at risk, and any responses to those notices, provided that HUD may determine certain information to be exempt from this requirement based upon severity level. With respect to the requirements of this section:

(i) The operator shall deliver to HUD and the mortgagee electronically, within 2 business days after the date of receipt, unless a longer time period is approved by HUD, copies of any and all notices, reports, surveys, and other correspondence (regardless of form) received by the operator from any governmental authority that includes any statement, finding, or assertion that:

(A) The operator or the project is or may be in violation of (or default under) any of the permits and approvals or any governmental requirements applicable to the operation of the facility;

(B) Any of the permits and approvals is to be terminated, limited in any way, or not renewed;

(C) Any civil money penalty (other than a de minimis amount) is being imposed with respect to the facility; or

(D) The operator or the project is subject to any governmental investigation or inquiry involving fraud.

(ii) The operator shall also deliver to HUD and the mortgagee, simultaneously with delivery to any governmental authority, any and all responses given by or on behalf of the operator to any of the foregoing and shall provide to HUD and the mortgagee, promptly upon request, such additional information relating to any of the foregoing as HUD or the mortgagee may request. The receipt by HUD and/or the mortgagee of notices, reports, surveys, correspondence, and other information shall not in any way impose any obligation or liability on HUD, the mortgagee, or their respective agents, representatives, or designees to take (or refrain from taking) any action; and HUD, the mortgagee, and their respective agents, representatives, and designees shall have no liability for any failure to act thereon or as a result thereof.

(2) The operator shall provide additional and ongoing information as requested by the borrower, mortgagee, or HUD pertaining to matters related to that risk. Controlling documents between or among any of the parties may provide further requirements with respect to such notification and communication.

(b) This section is applicable to all operators as of October 9, 2012.

PART 234—CONDOMINIUM OWNERSHIP MORTGAGE INSURANCE

Subpart A—Eligibility Requirements— Individually Owned Units

Subpart B—Contract Rights and Obligations—Individually Owned Units

Subpart C—Eligibility Requirements— Projects—Conversion Individual Sales Units

Subpart D—Contract Rights and Obligations—Projects

Subpart E—Servicing Responsibilities— Individually Owned Units

AUTHORITY: 12 U.S.C. 1715b and 1715y; 42 U.S.C. 3535(d).

SOURCE: 36 FR 24628, Dec. 22, 1971, unless otherwise noted.

Subpart A—Eligibility Requirements—Individually Owned Units

SOURCE: 61 FR 60161, Nov. 26, 1996, unless otherwise noted.

§ 234.1 Cross-reference.

(a) All of the provisions of subpart A of part 203 of this chapter concerning eligibility requirements of mortgages covering one- to four-family dwellings under section 203 of the National Housing Act (12 U.S.C. 1709) apply to mortgages on individually owned units insured under section 234 of the National Housing Act (12 U.S.C. 1715y), except the following provisions:

Sec.
203.12   Mortgage insurance on proposed or new construction.
203.14   Builders' warranty.
203.18a Solar energy system.
203.18c One-time or up-front mortgage insurance premium excluded from limitations on maximum mortgage amounts.
203.38   Location of dwelling.
203.42   Rental properties.
203.43c Eligibility of mortgages involving a dwelling unit in a cooperative housing development.
203.43d Eligibility of mortgages in certain communities.

203.43f Eligibility of mortgages covering manufactured homes.

203.43g Eligibility of mortgages in certain communities.

203.43h Eligibility of mortgages on Indian land insured pursuant to section 248 of the National Housing Act.

203.43i Eligibility of mortgages on Hawaiian Home Lands insured pursuant to section 247 of the National Housing Act.

203.43j Eligibility of mortgages on Allegany Reservation of Seneca Nation of Indians.

203.50 Eligibility of rehabilitation loans.

(b) For the purposes of this subpart, all references in part 203 of this chapter to section 203 of the Act shall be construed to refer to section 234 of the Act.

[61 FR 60161, Nov. 26, 1996, as amended at 64 FR 56111, Oct. 15, 1999]

§ 234.3 Definitions.

The terms *Act, Beginning of amortization, Commissioner, FHA, Insured Mortgage, Mortgage, Mortgagee, Mortgagor,* and *State,* as used in this part, are defined in § 203.251 of this chapter. The following terms, as used in this part, are defined as follows:

Bona fide tenants' organization means an association of tenants formed by the tenants to promote their interests in a particular project, with membership in the association open to each tenant, and all requirements of the association applying equally to every tenant.

Common areas and facilities means those areas of the project and of the property upon which it is located that are for the use and enjoyment of the owners of family units located in the project. The areas may include the land, roofs, main walls, elevators, staircases, lobbies, halls, parking space and community and commercial facilities.

Conversion means the date on which all documents necessary to create a condominium under state law (and under local law, where applicable) have been recorded, except that in the case of the Commonwealth of Puerto Rico, *conversion* is defined as the date on which the legal documents (which must be in compliance with applicable law) to create a condominium are presented for inscription (*i.e.*, recordation) to the Commonwealth Office of the Property Registry.

Family unit means a one-family unit including the undivided interest in the common areas and facilities, and such restricted common areas and facilities as may be designated.

Project means a structure or structures containing four or more family units.

Project mortgage means a mortgage which is or has been insured under any of the FHA multifamily housing programs, other than sections 213(a)(1) and 213(a)(2) of the Act (12 U.S.C. 1715e).

Restricted common areas and facilities means those areas and facilities restricted to a particular family unit or number of family units.

Tenant means the occupant(s) named in the lease or rental agreement of a housing unit in a project as of the date the condominium conversion documents are properly filed for the project, or as of the date on which the occupants are notified by management of intent to convert the project to a condominium, whichever is earlier.

[61 FR 60161, Nov. 26, 1996, as amended at 68 FR 6597, Feb. 7, 2003]

§ 234.17 Mortgagor and mortgagee requirements for maintaining flood insurance coverage.

The maintenance of flood insurance coverage on the project by the condominium association will satisfy the requirements of § 203.16a of this chapter if such coverage protects the interest of the mortgagor in the family unit. For this purpose, "the interest of the mortgagor" is defined as insurance coverage equal to the replacement cost of the project less land costs.

§ 234.26 Project requirements.

No mortgage shall be eligible for insurance unless the following requirements are met:

(a) *Location of family unit.* The family unit shall be located in a project that the Commissioner determines to be acceptable.

(b) *Plan of condominium ownership.* The project in which the unit is located shall have been committed to a plan of condominium ownership by a deed, or other recorded instrument, that is acceptable to the Commissioner. In the case of condominium documents in the Commonwealth of Puerto Rico, the

Commissioner will accept documents presented for inscription (recordation) to the Commonwealth Office of the Property Registry so long as the mortgagor obtains a title insurance policy that reflects the condominium regime.

(c) *Releases.* The family unit shall have been released from any mortgage covering the project or any part of the project.

(d) *Certificate by mortgagee.* The mortgagee shall certify that:

(1) The deed of the family unit and the deed or other recorded instrument committing the project to a plan of condominium ownership must comply with legal requirements of the jurisdiction. In the case of condominium documents in the Commonwealth of Puerto Rico, the Department will accept documents presented for inscription (recordation) to the Commonwealth Office of Property Registry for certification purposes so long as the mortgagor obtains a title insurance policy that reflects the condominium regime.

(2) The mortgagor has good marketable title to the family unit, subject only to a mortgage that is a valid first lien on the family unit.

(3) The family unit is assessed and subject to assessment for taxes pertaining only to that unit.

(e) *Conditions and provisions.* (1) The Commissioner may require such conditions and provisions as the Commissioner determines are necessary for the protection of consumers and the public interest.

(2) An application for mortgage insurance of a unit will not be approved if approval would result in less than 80 percent of the FHA-insured mortgages covering units in the project being occupied by mortgagors or co-mortgagors as a principal residence or a secondary residence (as these terms are defined in §203.18 of this chapter).

(3) In addition to the other requirements of this section, in order for a project to be acceptable to the Secretary, at least 51 percent of all family units (including units not covered by FHA-insured mortgages) must be occupied by the owners as a principal residence or a secondary residence (as these terms are defined in §203.18 of this chapter), or must have been sold

to owners who intend to meet this occupancy requirement.

(f) *Limitations on conversion of rental housing to condominium use.* With respect to a family unit in any project that was converted from rental housing, no insurance will be provided under this section unless:

(1) The conversion occurred more than one year before the application for insurance; or

(2) The mortgagor or comortgagor was a tenant of a unit in the rental housing project converted to condominium use; or

(3) The conversion of the property is sponsored by a bona fide tenants' organization representing a majority of the households in the project.

(g) *Projects covered by an insured or Secretary-held mortgage.* In addition to the requirements contained in paragraphs (a) through (f) of this section, projects which are covered by an FHA-insured project mortgage, or by a mortgage held by the Secretary, must be in compliance with a conversion plan approved by the Commissioner. The conversion plan shall provide for:

(1) The termination by payment in full of the mortgage or by voluntary termination of the insurance contract covering any HUD/FHA-insured or Secretary-held mortgage on the project, unless the Commissioner determines that the Commissioner's interests, and those of the individuals purchasing the family units, are best served by not requiring the termination of the insurance or payment in full of the mortgage.

(2) On release of a family unit from the project mortgage, payment shall be made on the outstanding balance of the project mortgage in an amount equal to the share of the balance determined by HUD to be attributable to the family unit.

(3) The project mortgagee shall certify that, notwithstanding any provisions of the mortgage covering prepayment, no charge is contemplated or has been collected for prepayment in full of the project mortgage.

(h) *Projects not covered by an insured or Secretary-held mortgage.* In addition to the requirements contained in paragraphs (a) through (f) of this section, projects which are not covered by an insured project mortgage or by a Secretary-held mortgage and which have not been approved by the Department of Veterans Affairs for its guaranty, insurance, or direct loan programs shall meet the requirements of this paragraph. Except with the approval of the Commissioner for the purpose of constructing or converting the project in phases or stages, any special right of the declarant (as declarant and not as a unit owner) to do any or all of the following must have expired or must have been waived in a recorded instrument:

(1) Add land or units to the condominium;

(2) Convert common elements into additional units or limited common elements;

(3) Withdraw land from the condominium;

(4) Use easements through the common elements for the purpose of making improvements within the condominium or within any adjacent land; or

(5) Convert a unit into two or more units, common elements, or into two or more units and common elements.

(i) Notwithstanding the requirements of paragraphs (a) through (h) of this section, a loan on a single unit in an unapproved condominium project (spot loan) may qualify for mortgage insurance under this part.

(1) The project must meet the following criteria:

(i) All units, common elements, and facilities—including those that are part of any master association—must have been completed, and the project cannot be subject to additional phasing or annexation. The project must provide for undivided ownership of common areas by unit owners;

(ii) Control of the owners' association must have been turned over to the unit purchasers, and the unit purchasers must have been in control for at least one year;

(iii) At least 90 percent of the total units in the project must have been conveyed to the unit purchasers, and at least 51 percent of the total units in the project must have been conveyed to purchasers who are occupying the units as their principal residences or second homes. No single entity (the same individual, investor group, partnership, or corporation) may own more than 10 percent of the total units in the project;

(iv) The units in the project must be owned in fee simple or be an eligible leasehold interest, as described in § 234.65, and the unit owners must have sole ownership interest in, and right to the use of, the project's facilities, common elements, and limited common elements including parking, recreational facilities, etc.;

(v) The project must be covered by hazard, flood, and liability insurance acceptable to the Commissioner;

(vi) For projects with more than 30 units, no more than 10 percent of the total units in the project may be encumbered by FHA-insured mortgages. (If endorsement would result in more than 10 percent of the units in such a project being encumbered by FHA-insured mortgages, the condominium project must be approved under paragraphs (a) through (h) of this section.) For projects with between 5 and 30 units inclusive, no more than 20 percent of the total units may be encumbered by FHA-insured mortgages. For projects with four units, only one unit may be encumbered by an FHA-insured mortgage under the spot loan procedure of this paragraph (i); and

(vii) The assumability provisions of § 234.66 must be satisfied.

(2) Lenders must perform an underwriting analysis and certify that a project satisfies the eligibility criteria for a spot loan in a condominium project that has not been approved by FHA. Lenders may use information from the appraiser, the owners' association, the management company, the real estate broker, and the project developer, but the lender must ensure the accuracy of the information obtained from these sources.

(Approved by the Office of Management and Budget under control number 2502–0513)

[61 FR 60161, Nov. 26, 1996, as amended at 72 FR 16689, Apr. 4, 2007]

§ 234.54 Eligibility of assigned mortgages and mortgages covering acquired property.

The Commissioner may insure under this part, without regard to any limitation upon eligibility contained in this subpart (except that the property must be located in a condominium project approved under §234.26), any mortgage assigned to the Commissioner in connection with payment under a contract of mortgage insurance, or executed in connection with a sale by the Commissioner of any property acquired in the settlement of an insurance claim under any section or title of the Act.

§234.63 Location of property.

The mortgage, to be eligible for insurance, shall be on property located in a State, as defined in §203.251 of this chapter, and not located on "Hawaiian home lands," as that term is defined in section 247(d)(2) of the Act.

§234.65 Nature of title.

A mortgage, to be eligible for insurance, shall be on a fee interest in, or on a leasehold interest in, a one-family unit in a project including an undivided interest in the common areas and facilities, and such restricted common areas and facilities as may be designated. To be eligible, a leasehold interest shall be under a lease for not less than 99 years which is renewable, or under a lease having a period of not less than 10 years to run beyond the maturity date of the mortgage.

§234.66 Free assumability; exceptions.

For purposes of HUD's policy of free assumability with no restrictions, as provided in §203.41 of this chapter, the definition of *Legal restrictions on conveyance* in §203.41(a)(3) of this chapter does not include rights of first refusal held by a condominium association for a project approved by the Secretary under this subpart prior to September 10, 1993.

Subpart B—Contract Rights and Obligations—Individually Owned Units

§234.251 Definitions.

The definitions in §203.251 of this chapter apply to this subpart.

[61 FR 60163, Nov. 26, 1996]

§234.255 Cross-reference.

(a) *Provisions.* All of the provisions of §§203.251 through 203.436 of this chapter (part 203, subpart B) covering mortgages insured under section 203 of the National Housing Act shall apply to mortgages insured under section 234(c) of the National Housing Act except the following provisions:

Sec.
203.258 Substitute mortgagors.
203.259a Scope.
203.280 One-time MIP.
203.281 Calculation of one-time MIP.
203.282 Mortgagee's late charge and interest.
203.283 Refund of one-time MIP.
203.357 Deed in lieu of foreclosure.
203.378 Property condition.
203.379 Adjustment for damage or neglect.
203.380 Certificate of property condition.
203.389 Waived title objections.
203.420 Nature of Mutual Mortgage Insurance Fund.
203.421 Allocation of Mutual Mortgage Insurance Fund income or loss.
203.422 Right and liability under Mutual Mortgage Insurance Fund.
203.423 Distribution of distributive shares.
203.424 Maximum amount of distributive shares.
203.425 Finality of determination.
203.440 *et seq.* Insured home improvement loans.

(b) *References.* For the purposes of this subpart, all references in §§203.251 through 203.436 of this chapter (part 203, subpart B) to section 203 of the Act, one- to four-family, and the Mutual Mortgage Insurance Fund, shall be construed to refer to section 234 of the act, one-family unit, and the General Insurance Fund. The term *property* or *each family dwelling unit* as used in §§203.251 through 203.436 of this chapter (part 203, subpart B) shall be construed to include "the one-family unit and the undivided interest in the common areas and facilities as may be designated".

[36 FR 24628, Dec. 22, 1971, as amended at 41 FR 42949, Sept. 29, 1976; 42 FR 29305, June 8, 1977; 48 FR 28807, June 23, 1983; 55 FR 34814, Aug. 24, 1990]

§234.256 Substitute mortgagors.

(a) *Selling mortgagor.* The requirements for the selling mortgagor are set forth in §203.258(a) of this chapter.

(b) *Purchasing mortgagor.* (1) If the dwelling is a principal or secondary place of residence, the requirements for the purchasing mortgagor are set forth in §203.258(b)(1) of this chapter.

(2) [Reserved]

(c) *Applicability—current mortgagor.* Paragraph (b) of this section applies to the Commissioner's approval of a substitute mortgagor only if the mortgage executed by the original mortgagor met the conditions of § 203.258(c) of this chapter.

(d) *Applicability—earlier mortgagor.* The occupancy and similar requirements set forth in § 203.258(d) of this chapter apply to mortgages insured under subpart A of this part.

(e) *Direct endorsement.* Requirements for the direct endorsement program are set forth in § 203.258(f) of this chapter.

(f) *Substitute mortgagor* is defined in § 203.258(f) of this chapter.

[55 FR 34814, Aug. 24, 1990, as amended at 57 FR 38352, Dec. 9, 1992; 61 FR 60163, Nov. 26, 1996]

§ 234.259 Claim procedure—graduated payment mortgages.

Section 203.436 of this chapter applies to mortgages under this subpart.

[61 FR 60163, Nov. 26, 1996]

§ 234.260 Assignment of mortgage and certificate by mortgagee.

In addition to the requirements of §§ 203.350 through 203.353 incorporated by reference, the mortgagee shall certify as to any changes in the plan of apartment ownership including the administration of the property. Any changes shall require FHA approval.

[36 FR 24628, Dec. 21, 1971, as amended at 42 FR 29305, June 8, 1977]

§ 234.262 Exception to deed in lieu of foreclosure.

All of the provisions of § 203.357 of this chapter relating to acceptance of a deed in lieu of foreclosure shall apply to mortgages insured under this part only if the mortgagee establishes to the satisfaction of the Commissioner that there are no unpaid assessments owed the Association or Cooperative of Owners.

§ 234.265 Contents of deed and supporting documents.

In addition to the requirements of § 203.367, incorporated by reference, the deed shall comply with the plan of apartment ownership. Any changes therein, including the administration

of the property, shall require FHA approval.

§ 234.270 Condition of the multifamily structure.

(a) When a family unit is conveyed or a mortgage is assigned to the Commissioner, the family unit and the common areas and facilities designated for the particular unit shall be undamaged by fire, flood, earthquake, tornado, or boiler explosion, or, as to mortgages insured on or after January 1, 1977, due to failure of the mortgagee to take action as required by § 203.377. If the property has been damaged, either of the following actions shall be taken:

(1) The property may be repaired prior to its conveyance or prior to the assignment of the mortgage to the Commissioner.

(2) If the prior approval of the Commissioner is obtained, the damaged property may be conveyed or the mortgage assigned to the Secretary without repairing the damage. In such instances, the Commissioner shall deduct from the insurance benefits either his estimate of the decrease in value of the family unit or the amount of any insurance recovery received by the mortgagee, whichever is the greater.

(b) If the property has been damaged by fire and such property was not covered by fire insurance at the time of the damage, the mortgagee may convey the property or assign the mortgage to the Commissioner without deduction from the insurance benefits for any loss occasioned by such fire if the following conditions are met:

(1) The property shall have been covered by fire insurance at the time the mortgage was insured.

(2) The fire insurance shall have been later cancelled or renewal shall have been refused by the insuring company.

(3) The mortgagee shall have notified the Commissioner within 30 days (or within such further time as the Commissioner may approve) of the cancellation of the fire insurance or of the refusal of the insuring company to renew the fire insurance. This notification shall have been accompanied by a certification of the mortgagee that diligent efforts were made, but it was unable to obtain fire insurance coverage at reasonably competitive rates

and that it will continue its efforts to obtain adequate fire insurance coverage at competitive rates, including coverage under the FAIR Plan. A *reasonable rate* is a rate not more than 25 percent in excess of the rate or the advisory rate filed or used by the principal rating organization doing business in the state. If the property is located in a state which has no rate or advisory rate as provided in the preceding sentence, the mortgagee shall consult the Director of the local HUD office as to a reasonable rate. When hazard insurance coverage cannot be obtained in an amount equal to the unpaid principal balance of the loan but insurance can be obtained in a reduced amount from a FAIR Plan or another insurance carrier, the Secretary will accept the reduced coverage without reduction of mortgage, insurance benefits, if the rates do not exceed the guidelines stated herein. If coverage in any amount is only available at rates in excess of a reasonable rate as defined herein, the mortgagor may but shall not be required to purchase such coverage. If coverage is purchased, the amount of any claim for insurance benefits under this part shall be reduced by the amount of any recovery of hazard insurance benefits by the mortgagee.

(c) The provisions in paragraph (b) of this section shall be applicable with respect to the insurance of all mortgages whether insured prior to May 8, 1968, or insured on or after such date.

(d) The mortgagee shall not be liable for damage to the property by waste in connection with mortgage insurance claims paid on or after July 2, 1968. However, the mortgagee shall be responsible for damage to or destruction of security properties on which the loans are in default and which properties are vacant or abandoned due to the mortgagee's failure to take reasonable action to inspect, protect and preserve such properties as required by §203.377, as to all mortgages insured on or after June 8, 1977, but such responsibility shall not exceed the amount of its insurance claim as to a particular property.

[36 FR 24628, Dec. 22, 1971, as amended at 42 FR 29305, June 8, 1977]

§234.273 Assessment of taxes.

When a family unit is conveyed to the Commissioner or a mortgage is assigned to the Commissioner, the unit shall be assessed and subject to assessment for taxes pertaining only to that unit.

§234.274 Certificate of tax assessment.

The mortgagee shall certify, as of the date of filing for record of the deed or assignment of the mortgage to the Commissioner, that the family unit is assessed and subject to assessment for taxes pertaining only to that unit.

§234.275 Certificate or statement of condition.

The mortgagee shall either certify that as of the date of the filing of deed for record, or assignment of the mortgage to the Secretary, the property was (a) undamaged by fire, flood, earthquake, tornado or boiler explosion, and (b) as to mortgages insured or for which commitments to insure are issued on or after June 8, 1977, undamaged due to failure of the mortgagee to take action as required by §203.377, or its claim shall be accompanied by a statement describing any such damage that may still exist together with a copy of the Secretary's authorization to convey the property in damaged condition. In the absence of evidence to the contrary, the mortgagee's certificate or its statement as to damage shall be accepted by the Secretary as establishing the condition of the family unit and the common areas and facilities designated for the particular unit.

[42 FR 29305, June 8, 1977]

§234.280 Cancellation of hazard insurance.

The provisions of §203.382 incorporated by reference shall apply to hazard insurance policies carried solely for the family unit.

§234.285 Waived title objections.

The Commissioner shall not object to title by reason of the following matters:

(a) Violations of a restriction based on race, color or creed, even where such restriction provides for a penalty of reversion or forfeiture of title or a lien for liquidated damage.

(b) Easements for public utilities along one or more of the property lines, provided the exercise of the rights thereunder do not interfere with any of the buildings or improvements located on the subject property.

(c) Encroachment on the subject property by improvements on adjoining property, provided such encroachments do not interfere with the use of any improvements on the subject property.

(d) Variations between the length of the subject property lines as shown on the application for insurance and as shown by the record or possession lines, provided such variations do not interfere with the use of any of the improvements on the subject property.

(e) Customary building or use restrictions for breach of which there is no reversion and which have not been violated to a material extent.

(f) Federal tax liens and rights of redemption arising therefrom if the following conditions are observed. If the mortgagee acquires the property by foreclosure the mortgagee shall give notice to the Internal Revenue Service (IRS) of the foreclosure action. The Commissioner will not object to an outstanding right of redemption in IRS if: (1) The Federal tax lien was perfected subsequent to the date of the mortgage lien, and (2) the mortgagee has bid an amount sufficient to make the mortgagee whole if the property is in fact redeemed by the IRS.

[36 FR 24628, Dec. 22, 1971, as amended at 42 FR 29305, June 8, 1977]

Subpart C—Eligibility Requirements—Projects—Conversion Individual Sales Units

§ 234.501 Eligibility requirements.

The requirements set forth in 24 CFR part 200, subpart A, apply to blanket mortgages on condominium projects insured under section 234 of the National Housing Act (12 U.S.C. 1715y), as amended.

[61 FR 14406, Apr. 1, 1996]

Subpart D—Contract Rights and Obligations—Projects

§ 234.751 Cross-reference.

(a) All of the provisions, except § 207.258(b) of subpart B of this chapter, covering mortgages insured under section 207 of the National Housing Act shall apply to mortgages insured under section 234(d) of such Act.

(b) For the purposes of this subpart, all references in part 207 of this chapter to section 207 of the National Housing Act shall be construed to refer to section 234(d) of the act.

[36 FR 24628, Dec. 22, 1971, as amended at 50 FR 38787, Sept. 25, 1985]

Subpart E—Servicing Responsibilities—Individually Owned Units

§ 234.800 Cross-reference.

All of the provisions of subpart C, part 203 of this chapter covering mortgages insured under section 203 of the National Housing Act apply to mortgages insured under section 234(c) of the National Housing Act.

[42 FR 29306, June 8, 1977]

PART 236—MORTGAGE INSURANCE AND INTEREST REDUCTION PAYMENT FOR RENTAL PROJECTS

Subpart A—Eligibility Requirements for Mortgage Insurance

AUTHORITY: 12 U.S.C. 1715b, 1715z–1, and 1735d; 42 U.S.C. 3535(d).

SOURCE: 36 FR 24643, Dec. 22, 1971, unless otherwise noted.

Subpart A—Eligibility Requirements for Mortgage Insurance

§236.1 Applicability, cross-reference, and savings clause.

(a) *Applicability.* This section implements the eligibility requirements for mortgage insurance under the Rental and Cooperative Housing For Lower Income Families Program contained in section 236 of the National Housing Act (12 U.S.C. 1701), as amended. The program authorized the Secretary to insure mortgages to support new construction or rehabilitation of real property to be used primarily for residential rental purposes. A moratorium against issuance of commitments to insure new mortgages under section 236 was imposed January 5, 1973. Section 236(n) prohibits the insurance of mortgages under section 236 after November 30, 1983, except to permit the refinance of a mortgage insured under section 236, or to finance pursuant to section 236(j)(3), the purchase, by a cooperative or nonprofit corporation or association, of a project assisted under section 236. The definition of "family" in 24 CFR 200.3(a) applies to any refinancing of a mortgage insured under section 236, or to financing pursuant to section 236(j)(3) of the purchase, by a cooperative or nonprofit corporation or association of a project assisted under section 236.

(b) The mortgagor must comply with the financial reporting requirements in 24 CFR part 5, subpart H.

(c) *Savings provision.* Any mortgage approved by the Commissioner for insurance pursuant to sections 236(j) or 236(n) of the National Housing Act is governed by subpart A of this part as in effect immediately before May 1, 1996, contained in the April 1, 1995 edition of 24 CFR, parts 220 to 499, and by subparts B through E of this part, except as otherwise provided in this subpart.

[61 FR 14407, Apr. 1, 1996, as amended at 63 FR 46592, Sept. 1, 1998; 65 FR 61074, Oct. 13, 2000; 77 FR 5675, Feb. 3, 2012]

§236.2 Increased distributions to certain limited distribution mortgagors.

(a) *Increased distributions.* The Commissioner may permit increased distributions of surplus cash in excess of the amounts otherwise permitted by subpart A of this part to limited distribution mortgagors who participate in a HUD-approved initiative or program to preserve below-market housing stock. The increased distributions will be limited to a maximum amount based on market rents and calculated according to HUD instructions. Funds that the mortgagor is authorized to retain under section 236(g)(2) of the National Housing Act are not considered distributions to the mortgagor.

(b) *Pre-emption.* Any State or local law or regulation that restricts distributions to an amount lower than permitted by subpart A of this part as in effect immediately before May 1, 1996, contained in the April 1, 1995 edition of 24 CFR, parts 220 to 499, or permitted by the Commissioner under this section is preempted to the extent provided by section 524(f) of the Multifamily Assisted Housing Reform and Affordability Act of 1997.

[65 FR 61074, Oct. 13, 2000]

§ 236.3 Annual income exclusions.

The exclusions to annual income described in 24 CFR 5.609(c) apply to those program participants governed by the regulations at subpart A of 24 CFR part 236 in effect immediately before May 1, 1996 (contained in the April 1, 1995 edition of 24 CFR, parts 220 to 499), in lieu of the annual income exclusions described in 236.3(c) (contained in the April 1, 1995 edition of 24 CFR, parts 220 to 499).

[61 FR 54503, Oct. 18, 1996]

§ 236.60 Excess income.

(a) *Definition.* Excess Income consists of cash collected as rent from the residents by the mortgagor, on a unit-by-unit basis, that is in excess of the HUD-approved unassisted Basic Rent. The unit-by-unit requirement necessitates that, if a unit has Excess Income, the Excess Income must be returned to HUD. It is not permissible to do an aggregate calculation of the Excess Income for all occupied rent-paying units, and then to offset or subtract from that figure any unpaid rent from occupied or vacant units, before remitting Excess Income to HUD.

(b) *General requirement to return Excess Income.* Except as otherwise provided in this section, or as agreed to by HUD pursuant to a plan of action approved under 24 CFR part 248 or in connection with an adjustment of contract rents under section 8 of the United States Housing Act of 1937 Act (1937 Act) (42 U.S.C. 1437f), the mortgagor shall agree to pay monthly to HUD the total of all Excess Income in accordance with procedures prescribed by HUD.

(c) *Retention of Excess Income for project use*—(1) *Eligible mortgagors.* Any mortgagor of a project receiving Section 236 interest reduction payments may apply to retain Excess Income for project use unless the mortgagor owes prior Excess Income and is not current in payments under a HUD-approved Workout or Repayment Agreement.

(2) *Eligible uses.* Excess Income retained by a mortgagor for project use may be used for any necessary and reasonable operating expense of the project. Examples of necessary and reasonable operating expenses are:

(i) Project operating shortfalls, including repair costs;

(ii) Repair costs identified in the Comprehensive Needs Assessment, including increasing deposits to the Reserve Fund for Replacements to a limit necessary to adequately fund the reserve;

(iii) Service coordinators;

(iv) Neighborhood networks located at the project for project residents; and

(v) Enhanced supportive services for the residents.

(3) *Request for approval to retain Excess Income.* A mortgagor must submit a written request to retain Excess Income for project use to the local HUD Field Office. The request must describe:

(i) The amount or percentage of Excess Income requested;

(ii) The period from which Excess Income is being requested; and

(iii) The proposed use of the requested Excess Income.

(d) *Retention of Excess Income for non-project use*—(1) *Eligible mortgagors.* Any mortgagor of a project receiving Section 236 interest reduction payments may apply to retain Excess Income for non-project use unless the mortgagor owes prior Excess Income and is not current in payments under a HUD-approved Workout or Repayment Agreement or the mortgagor falls within any of the following categories:

(i) The mortgagor's Reserve for Replacement is not fully funded;

(ii) The mortgagor's project is not well maintained housing in good condition, as evidenced by:

(A) Failure to maintain the project in decent, safe, and sanitary condition and in good repair in accordance with

HUD's Uniform Physical Condition Standards and Inspection Requirements in 24 CFR part 5, subpart G;

(B) A score below 60 on the physical inspection conducted by HUD's Real Estate Assessment Center (REAC);

(C) The existence of uncorrected Exigent Health and Safety (EHS) deficiencies identified by REAC; or

(D) A Comprehensive Needs Assessment that finds there are significant repair or maintenance needs, and those repair or maintenance needs are still outstanding;

(iii) The mortgagor has engaged in any one of the following material adverse financial or managerial actions or omissions:

(A) Materially violating any federal, state, or local law or regulation with regard to the project or any other federally assisted project, including any applicable civil rights law or regulation, after receipt of notice and an opportunity to cure;

(B) Materially breaching a contract for assistance under section 8 of the 1937 Act, after receipt of notice and an opportunity to cure;

(C) Materially violating any applicable regulatory or other agreement with HUD or a participating administrative entity, after receipt of notice and an opportunity to cure;

(D) Repeatedly and materially violating any federal, state, or local law or regulation, including any applicable civil rights law or regulation, with regard to the project or any other federally assisted project;

(E) Repeatedly and materially breaching a contract for assistance under section 8 of the 1937 Act;

(F) Repeatedly and materially violating any applicable regulatory or other agreement with HUD or a participating administrative entity, including failure to submit audited financial statements or required tenant data;

(G) Repeatedly failing to make mortgage payments at times when project income was sufficient to maintain and operate the project;

(H) Materially failing to maintain the project in decent, safe, and sanitary condition and in good repair after receipt of notice and a reasonable opportunity to cure; or

(I) Committing any actions or omissions that would warrant suspension or debarment by HUD.

(2) *Eligible uses.* Excess Income retained by a mortgagor for non-project use may be used for any purpose, except that the non-project use of Excess Income by a nonprofit entity mortgagor is limited to activities that carry out the entity's nonprofit purpose.

(3) *Request for approval to retain Excess Income.* A mortgagor must submit a written request to retain Excess Income for non-project use to the local HUD Field Office. The request must describe:

(i) The amount or percentage of Excess Income requested; and

(ii) The period from which Excess Income is being requested.

(e) *Timing of request to retain Excess Income*—(1) *In general.* Except as provided in paragraph (e)(2) of this section, a mortgagor must submit a request to retain Excess Income at least 90 days before the beginning of each fiscal year before any other date during a fiscal year that the mortgagor plans to begin retaining Excess Income for that fiscal year.

(2) *Specific ongoing purpose.* A mortgagor requesting approval to retain Excess Income for a specific, ongoing purpose where the purpose extends beyond the current fiscal year may submit a request that describes the proposed use of Excess Income and advises that the intended use will extend beyond the current fiscal year. If HUD approves the request, following review of the request in accordance with paragraph (f) of this section, the mortgagor will not be required to submit a new request each fiscal year provided the use of Excess Income remains the same. The mortgagor will still be required to submit the Monthly Report of Excess Income and the end of year narrative under paragraph (g) of this section. If the use of Excess Income changes, the mortgagor must notify HUD of the change and submit a new request to retain Excess Income 90 days prior to the date the mortgagor intends to begin retaining Excess Income for the new purpose.

(f) *HUD review and response procedure.* HUD will review a mortgagor's request to retain Excess Income and issue a letter of approval or denial as follows:

(1) *Approval letter.* The approval letter from HUD permitting the mortgagor to retain Excess Income must, at a minimum, assert:

(i) Retention rights are for the time specified in the approval letter, but cannot extend beyond the current fiscal year except as provided in paragraph (e)(2) of this section;

(ii) Failure of the mortgagor to maintain the Reserve for Replacement account in a fully funded amount at all times is grounds for HUD to rescind the approval;

(iii) Failure of the mortgagor to maintain the project in a decent, safe, and sanitary condition and in good repair at all times is grounds for HUD to rescind the approval;

(iv) If the Excess Income requested for project use is not used for the proposed purpose described in the mortgagor's request, the income must be returned to HUD, unless the mortgagor has obtained prior HUD approval for the alternate use; and

(v) The failure of a mortgagor to return retained Excess Income to HUD for not complying with applicable requirements is a violation of the Regulatory Agreement for which there are enforcement remedies that HUD may take.

(2) *Denial letter.* A letter from HUD denying a mortgagor's request to retain Excess Income must cite the specific reasons for denial and state what requirements the mortgagor must meet to receive HUD's approval to retain Excess Income.

(3) *Environmental review.* Before approving a request to retain Excess Income for project use, HUD will perform an environmental review to the extent required under 24 CFR part 50 for activities that are not excluded under 24 CFR 50.19(b).

(g) *Post-approval requirements*—(1) *Monthly report.* A mortgagor approved to retain Excess Income must continue to prepare and submit to HUD a revised Form HUD–93104, Monthly Report of Excess Income, or successor form.

(2) *Other reporting requirements.* A mortgagor that retains Excess Income for project use must provide HUD, on an annual basis, two copies of a narrative description of the amount and the uses made of Excess Income during the prior fiscal year of the project. The calendar year or HUD's fiscal year is not relevant to this requirement unless the fiscal year of the project coincides with the calendar year or HUD's fiscal year. HUD may request additional follow-up information on a case-by-case basis. The report must contain the following certification: "I certify that (1) the amount of Excess Income retained and used was for the purposes approved by HUD; (2) all eligibility requirements for retaining Excess Income were satisfied for the entire reporting period; and (3) all the facts and data on which this report is based are true and accurate. Warning: HUD will prosecute false claims and statements. Conviction may result in criminal or civil penalties, or both (18 U.S.C. 1001, 1010, 1012; and 31 U.S.C. 3729 and 3802)."

(h) *Return of remitted Excess Income*—(1) *For project use.* A mortgagor that is eligible to retain Excess Income for project use under paragraph (c)(1) of this section may apply for the return of Excess Income remitted to HUD since October 21, 1998, in accordance with the procedures of paragraph (c)(3) of this section. A mortgagor that is eligible to retain Excess Income for project use may not apply for the return of Excess Income that was:

(i) Repaid in accordance with a Workout or Repayment Agreement with HUD; or

(ii) Generated between October 1, 2000, and October 27, 2000, by projects with state agency non-insured Section 236-assisted mortgages or HUD-held Section 236 mortgages

(2) *For non-project use.* A mortgagor that is eligible to retain Excess Income for non-project use under paragraph (d)(1) of this section may apply for the return of Excess Income remitted to HUD since October 21, 1998, in accordance with paragraph (d)(3) of this section. A mortgagor that is eligible to retain Excess Income for non-project use under paragraph (d)(1) of this section may not apply to retain Excess Income that was:

(i) Repaid in accordance with a Workout or Repayment Agreement with HUD; or

(ii) Generated between October 1, 2000, and October 27, 2000, by projects with state agency non-insured Section 236-assisted mortgages or HUD-held Section 236 mortgages.

(3) *Reporting requirement.* A mortgagor that receives returned Excess Income requested for project use is subject to the reporting requirements of paragraph (g)(2) of this section with respect to the returned Excess Income.

(4) *Time limit.* After September 1, 2005, a mortgagor may no longer apply for the return of any Excess Income remitted to HUD.

(i) *HUD withdrawal of approval to retain Excess Income*—(1) *Bases for withdrawal of approval.* HUD may withdraw approval for any of the following reasons:

(i) If, at any time after approval, a mortgagor fails to meet the eligibility requirements of paragraph (c)(1) or (d)(1) of this section, as applicable;

(ii) If the mortgagor does not use the Excess Income requested for project use for purposes and activities as approved by HUD; or

(iii) If at any time during the fiscal year that such approval is in effect, mortgagor, approved to retain Excess Income for non-project use, fails to maintain the project in decent, safe, and sanitary condition and in good repair, or maintain the Reserve for Replacement account in a fully funded amount.

(2) *Notification of withdrawal of approval.* HUD will notify the mortgagor by certified mail that the authorization to retain Excess Income is withdrawn. The notification will state:

(i) Specific reasons for HUD's withdrawal of approval;

(ii) The effective termination date, which may be the date of the violation resulting in the withdrawal or the date of HUD's determination that the mortgagor was out of compliance;

(iii) The amount of retained Excess Income improperly retained that must be returned to HUD; and

(iv) The actions that the mortgagor must take to restore the authorization to retain Excess Income.

(3) *Mortgagor's request for reconsideration*—(i) *Letter of reconsideration.* A mortgagor may request that HUD reconsider its decision by submitting, to the Hub/Field Office Director or other party identified by HUD in the notification, within 30 days of receipt of the notification of withdrawal, a letter stating the basis for reconsideration. The letter must include documentation supporting a review of the withdrawal.

(ii) *HUD response.* Within 30 days of HUD's receipt of the mortgagor's request for reconsideration, HUD will make a final determination and respond in writing to the mortgagor. HUD's response may:

(A) Affirm the withdrawal of authority to retain Excess Income;

(B) Reverse the withdrawal of authority to retain Excess Income; or

(C) Request additional information from the mortgagor before affirming or reversing the withdrawal of authority to retain Excess Income.

[69 FR 53560, Sept. 1, 2004]

Subpart B—Contract Rights and Obligations for Mortgage Insurance

§ 236.251 Cross-reference.

All of the provisions of subpart B, part 207 of this chapter covering mortgages insured under section 207 of the National Housing Act, apply with full force and effect to mortgages insured under section 236 of the National Housing Act except the following provisions:

Sec.
207.252 First, second, and third premiums.
207.252a Premiums—operating loss loans.
207.259 Insurance benefits.
207.262 No vested right in fund.

[37 FR 8664, Apr. 29, 1972, as amended at 42 FR 59675, Nov. 18, 1977]

§ 236.252 First, second, and third mortgage insurance premiums.

All of the provisions of § 207.252 of this chapter governing the first, second, and third mortgage insurance premiums shall apply to mortgages insured under this subpart, except:

(a) Where an application for a loan under section 202 of the Housing Act of 1959 has been filed previously in connection with the project, but it is being financed with a mortgage insured under this part because funds are not available to make the section 202 loan, the mortgage insurance premium due and payable between the dates of initial and final insurance endorsement shall be at the rate of one-fourth of one percent per annum of the average outstanding principal obligation of the mortgage and such premiums shall be prorated for any fractional part of a year. Following final endorsement, the mortgage insurance premium shall be increased to one-half of one percent and shall be paid as provided in § 207.252.

(b) Where a mortgage has been insured under this subpart pursuant to section 238(c) of the Act, the mortgage insurance premiums due in accordance with § 207.252 shall be calculated on the basis of one percent.

[42 FR 59675, Nov. 18, 1977]

§ 236.253 Premiums—operating loss loans.

All of the provisions of § 207.252a of this chapter relating to mortgage insurance premiums on operating loss loans shall apply to mortgages insured under this subpart, except that for mortgages insured pursuant to Section 238(c) of the Act the mortgage insurance premiums due in accordance with § 207.252a shall be calculated on the basis of one percent.

[42 FR 59675, Nov. 18, 1977]

§ 236.254 Termination of mortgage insurance.

In addition to the provisions of § 207.253a, the following requirements apply to multifamily mortgages insured under section 236 of the National Housing Act:

(a) For those projects qualifying as eligible low income housing under § 248.201, the contract of insurance may be terminated only as provided in part 248.

(b) For those projects subject to section 250(a) of the National Housing Act, the contract of insurance may be terminated only if the Commissioner determines that the requirements of section 250(a) are met.

[55 FR 38958, Sept. 21, 1990]

§ 236.255 Forbearance relief.

(a) In a case where the mortgage is in default, the mortgagor and the mort-

gagee may enter into a forbearance agreement for the reduction or suspension of the mortgagor's regular mortgage payments for a specified period of time, if the Commissioner determines that the default was due to circumstances beyond the mortgagor's control and that the mortgage probably will be restored to good standing within a reasonable period of time. Such determination shall be evidenced by the Commissioner's written approval of the forbearance agreement.

(b) The time specified in § 207.258(a) of this chapter, within which a mortgagee shall give the Commissioner written notice of its intention to file an insurance claim, shall be suspended for the period of time specified in the forbearance agreement as long as the mortgagor complies with the requirements of such agreement.

(c) If the mortgagor fails to meet the requirements of a forbearance agreement or to cure the default under the mortgage at the expiration of the forbearance period, and such failure continues for a period of 30 days, the mortgagee shall notify the Commissioner of such failure. Within 45 days thereafter, unless a modification or extension of the forbearance agreement has been approved by the Commissioner, the mortgagee shall notify the Commissioner of its election to file an insurance claim and of its election to either assign the mortgage to the Commissioner or acquire and convey title to the property to the Commissioner. If the mortgage is assigned to the Commissioner, the special insurance benefits prescribed in § 236.265(b) shall be applicable.

§ 236.260 Request by Commissioner for assignment of mortgage.

The mortgagee shall, when requested by the Commissioner, assign to the Commissioner a mortgage on which interest reduction payments are being made pursuant to the provisions of § 236.501 et seq. If the mortgage is not in default when the Commissioner requests its assignment, the first day of the month following the Commissioner's request shall be considered the date of default.

§236.265 Payment of insurance benefits.

All of the provisions of §207.259 of this chapter relating to insurance benefits apply to multifamily project mortgages insured under this subpart, except as follows:

(a) [Reserved]

(b) When the mortgage is assigned to the Commissioner pursuant to §236.260 or is assigned in a case where the mortgagor fails to comply with the requirements of a forbearance agreement approved by the Commissioner in accordance with the requirements of §236.255 or is assigned in a case where the mortgagor fails to cure the default at the expiration of the forbearance period, the insurance benefits shall be paid in cash and shall be computed in accordance with §207.259(b) of this chapter, except that in lieu of the allowance for debenture interest in §207.259(b)(1)(iii) of this chapter, the payment shall include the amount of the unpaid accrued mortgage interest computed to the date the assignment of the mortgage to the Commissioner is filed for record. In addition, an amount shall be included equivalent to the debenture interest which would have been earned from the date the mortgage assignment was filed for record to the date the cash payment is made, except that when the mortgagee fails to meet any one of the applicable requirements of §§207.256, 207.258(b), and 236.255(c) of this chapter within the specified time and in a manner satisfactory to the Commissioner (or within such further time as the Commissioner may approve in writing), such amount shall be computed only to the date on which the particular required action should have been taken or to which it was extended.

(c) Where the assignment of the mortgage is made pursuant to §236.260 and the mortgage is not in default at the time of such assignment, the one percent deduction prescribed in §207.259(b)(2)(iv) of this chapter shall not be applicable.

[36 FR 24643, Dec. 22, 1971, as amended at 59 FR 49817, Sept. 30, 1994; 80 FR 51468, Aug. 25, 2015]

Subpart C—Interest Reduction Payments

§236.501 Interest reduction payments contract.

This subpart shall constitute the interest reduction payment contract between the mortgagee and the Commissioner with respect to a mortgage insured under section 236 of the National Housing Act. The endorsement of the mortgage for insurance shall constitute the execution of the interest reduction payment contract with respect to the mortgage being insured.

§236.505 Eligible mortgages.

Interest reduction payments pursuant to this subpart shall be made only in connection with a mortgage which is insured under subparts A and B of this part.

§236.510 Term of payments.

(a) The term for which interest reduction payments shall be made shall begin on the following dates:

(1) With respect to a mortgage involving insurance of advances, on the date the Commissioner finally endorses the mortgage not for insurance or such earlier date as may be established by the Commissioner.

(2) With respect to a mortgage insured upon completion, the date on which the Commissioner endorses the mortgage note for insurance.

(b) The term of the interest reduction payments shall end upon the occurrence of one of the following events:

(1) The termination of the contract of insurance, except where the mortgage has been assigned to the Commissioner.

(2) The Commissioner's receipt of the mortgagee's notice of intention to file an insurance claim and to acquire and convey title to the Commissioner pursuant to §207.258(c) of this chapter. In the event the mortgagee fails to provide the Commissioner with such notice of intention within the time specified in §207.258(a) of this chapter, the last day on which the Commissioner should have received the mortgagor's notice shall be deemed the date the Commissioner receives such notice.

(3) At the discretion of the Commissioner, the mortgagor's failure to meet its obligations under the regulatory

agreement it has entered into with the Commissioner.

(c) Upon termination of the interest reduction payments contract, the payment due on the first of the month in which the termination occurs shall be the last payment to which the mortgagee shall be entitled.

(d) Where the term of interest reduction payments is ended pursuant to paragraph (b) (2) or (3) of this section, such interest reduction payment contract may be reinstated by the Commissioner, in his discretion and on such conditions as he may prescribe. In the event of such reinstatement, interest reduction payments will be made to the mortgagee for those months during which such payments were suspended.

§ 236.515 Time of payments.

The interest reduction payments shall be due on the first day of each month following the beginning of the term, and shall be paid upon the receipt of a billing (on a form prescribed by the Commissioner) from the mortgagee or its authorized agent.

§ 236.520 Amount of payments.

(a) The interest reduction payment to the mortgagee shall be in an amount not exceeding the difference between the following:

(1) The monthly installment for principal, interest, and mortgage insurance premium which the mortgagor is obligated to pay under the mortgage; and

(2) The monthly payment for principal and interest the mortgagor would be obligated to pay if the mortgage were to bear interest at the rate of 1 percent per annum.

(b) Where individual family units in the project are sold, subject to a plan approved by the Commissioner, and as the principal amount of the mortgage is reduced by payment of the portion of the mortgage attributable to the sold units and as the amount of the mortgage payments which the mortgagor is obligated to pay is reduced, proportionate reductions will be made in the interest reduction payments.

(c) In addition to the interest reduction payment referred to in paragraph (a) of this section, the mortgagee shall be entitled to the monthly payment of an amount the Commissioner deems sufficient to reimburse the mortgagee for its expenses in servicing the mortgage.

§ 236.525 Application of payments.

The mortgagee shall apply each monthly interest reduction payment, together with the mortgagor's monthly payment, to the items and in the order set out in the mortgage.

§ 236.530 Mortgagee records.

The mortgagee shall maintain such records as the Commissioner may require with respect to the mortgagor's payments and the interest reduction payments received from the Commissioner. Such records shall be kept on file for a period of time and in a manner prescribed by the Commissioner and shall be made available, when requested, for review and inspection by the Commissioner or the Comptroller General of the United States.

§ 236.535 Effect of assignment of mortgage.

In the event a mortgage subject to interest reduction payments is assigned to another approved mortgagee, the assignee shall thereupon succeed to all the rights and obligations of the assignor under the interest reduction contract.

§ 236.599 Effect of amendments.

The regulations in this subpart may be amended by the Commissioner at any time and from time to time, in whole or in part, but no such amendment shall adversely affect the interests of a mortgagee under a contract for interest reduction payments already in effect or to be put into effect pursuant to the Commissioner's commitment to enter into such contract.

Subpart D—Rental Assistance Payments

SOURCE: 40 FR 31872, July 29, 1975, unless otherwise noted.

§ 236.701 Scope of rental assistance.

The Secretary shall enter into Rental Assistance Contracts with the owners of section 236 projects which:

(a) Had received a commitment for mortgage insurance under this part on or before August 22, 1974, but are reprocessed before final endorsement with rental assistance pursuant to an agreement between the sponsor and the Secretary;

(b) Had not received a commitment for mortgage insurance under this part on or before August 22, 1974, but did so subsequently;

(c) Had received a reservation of section 236 contract authority (in the case of projects processed without HUD mortgage insurance and to be financed under a State or local government aided program pursuant to section 236(b) of the National Housing Act) on or before August 22, 1974, but are reprocessed with rental assistance pursuant to an Agreement between the sponsor, the State or local agency providing additional aid to the project, and the Secretary. Projects in this category which are converted from Rent Supplement shall have Rental Assistance Contracts with terms which do not exceed the unexpired terms of the Rent Supplement Contracts. Projects in this category which have no Rent Supplement Contract shall have Rental Assistance Contracts with terms which do not exceed the unexpired terms of Agreement for Interest Reduction Payments or equivalent documents or 40 years whichever is less; or

(d) Had not received a reservation of section 236 contract authority (in the case of projects processed without HUD mortgage insurance) on or before August 22, 1974, but did so subsequently.

Projects may not receive the benefit of rent supplement payments under part 215 of this Title and rental assistance payments at the same time. (Notwithstanding the provisions of this subpart, it shall be a matter of the Secretary's discretion whether he enters into contracts for such benefits in connection with the sale of HUD-owned projects.) The conditions of eligibility for a Rental Assistance Contract and its terms are specified in this subpart D.

[40 FR 31872, July 29, 1975, as amended at 45 FR 50734, July 31, 1980]

§236.705 Projects eligible for benefits.

(a) Rental assistance payments may be made with respect to section 236 projects with Rental Assistance Contracts pursuant to this subpart.

(b) Rental assistance payments to owners of projects pursuant to paragraph (a) of this section will normally be made available to 20 percent of the dwelling units, except that the Secretary may:

(1) Reduce that percentage in the case of any project if he determines that such action is necessary to assure the economic viability of the project; or

(2) Increase that percentage in the case of any project if he determines: (i) That such action is necessary and feasible, after taking into account the objective of assuring, insofar as is practicable, that there is in the project a reasonable range in the income levels of tenants, or (ii) that such action is to be taken to meet the housing needs of elderly or handicapped families.

§236.710 Qualified tenant.

(a) The benefits of rental assistance payments are available only to an individual or a family who is renting a dwelling unit in a project that is subject to a contract entered into under the requirements of this subpart or who is occupying such a dwelling unit as a cooperative member. To qualify for the benefits of rental assistance payments, the individual or family must satisfy the definition of Qualified Tenant found in §236.2 of subpart A (contained in the April 1, 1995 edition of 24 CFR, parts 220 to 499; see the Savings clause at §236.1(c)).

(b) To receive rental assistance under this subpart, the income of the individual or family must be determined to be too low to permit the individual or family to pay the approved Gross Rent with 30 percent of the individual's or family's Adjusted Monthly Income, as defined in §236.2 of subpart A (contained in the April 1, 1995 edition of 24 CFR, parts 220 to 499). Determination of the Adjusted Monthly Income must include the deductions required for adjusted income in 24 CFR 5.611(a) in lieu of the deductions provided in the definition of "adjusted income" in 24 CFR 236.2 (contained in the April 1, 1995 edition of 24 CFR, parts 220 to 499; see the Savings clause at §236.1(c)).

(c) For requirements concerning the disclosure and certification of Social Security Numbers, see 24 CFR part 5, subpart B. For requirements regarding the signing and submitting of consent forms for the obtaining of wage and claim information from State Wage Information Collection Agencies, see 24 CFR part 5, subpart B. For restrictions on financial assistance to noncitizens with ineligible immigration status, see 24 CFR part 5, subpart E.

(d) The definition of "persons with disabilities" in paragraph (d) of this section replaces the terms "disabled person" and "handicapped person" used in the regulations in 24 CFR part 236, subpart A (contained in the April 1, 1995 edition of 24 CFR, parts 220 to 499; see the Savings clause at § 236.1(c)). *Person with disabilities*, as used in this part, has the same meaning as provided in 24 CFR 891.305.

[66 FR 6224, Jan. 19, 2001]

§ 236.715 Determination of eligibility.

(a) The housing owner shall determine eligibility following procedures prescribed by the Commissioner when processing applications for admission and tenant applications for assistance. The requirements of 24 CFR part 5 govern the submission and verification of information related to citizenship and eligible immigration status for applicants, and the procedures for denial of assistance based upon a failure to establish eligible immigration status.

(b) The owner must use good faith efforts to admit tenants according to the following list, provided that the number of units authorized for a particular category would not be exceeded and provided that there is sufficient funding for the category:

(1) First: Applicants eligible for Rental Assistance Payments;

(2) Second: Applicants eligible to pay a below market rent under section 236;

(3) Third: Applicants who can pay the Market Rent.

(c) Before admitting an applicant who can pay the Market Rent, the owner must obtain written approval from HUD if at least 10 percent of the number of units authorized under the section 236 program are already occupied by tenants paying Market Rent.

(d) Before admitting an applicant who will not receive the benefit of Rental Assistance Payments, the owner must obtain written approval from HUD if fewer than 90 percent of the number of units authorized under the Rental Assistance Payments contract are already occupied by tenants receiving such assistance.

(e) Upon written request of the owner, the Commissioner may issue a written waiver of the requirements of paragraphs (b) through (d) of this section based on a finding of sufficient justification. Each such waiver shall be supported by a statement of the pertinent facts and grounds.

(Approved by the Office of Management and Budget under control numbers 2502–0352 and 2502–0354)

[51 FR 21862, June 16, 1986, as amended at 60 FR 14833, Mar. 20, 1995; 61 FR 13624, Mar. 27, 1996]

§ 236.720 Provisions applicable to co-operative members.

(a) A member of a cooperative who obtains a certificate of eligibility shall be required, as a condition of receiving the certificate, to agree that upon a sale of his membership, any equity increment accumulated through rental assistance payments will not be made available to the member, but will be turned over to the cooperative housing owner. Funds received by a cooperative representing an equity increment accumulated through rental assistance payments shall be deposited by the cooperative in a special account to be disbursed as directed by the Secretary.

(b) The term *tenant* as used in this subpart shall include a member of a cooperative, and the term *rental payment* shall include the carrying charges under the occupancy agreement between the members of the cooperative and the cooperative housing owner.

§ 236.725 Term of contract.

The rental assistance contract shall be limited to the term of the mortgage or 40 years from the date of the first payment made under the contract, whichever is the lesser.

§ 236.730 Maximum annual rental assistance contract amount.

The rental assistance contract shall specify the maximum amount of the rental assistance payments for the project for the rent-up period, or for any such other period of time as the Secretary may prescribe, based upon the Secretary's estimate of probable demand and tenant income, including a 10 percent contingency allowance. At the end of such period of time, and annually thereafter, appropriate adjustments, as the Secretary may prescribe, shall be made in the maximum annual rental assistance contract amount, to reflect the actual requirements of the eligible tenants and a 10 percent contingency allowance.

§ 236.735 Rental assistance payments and rental charges.

(a) *Amount of rental assistance payments.* The rental assistance contract shall provide that the payment on behalf of a Qualified Tenant shall not exceed the difference between the Gross Rent and the Total Tenant Payment.

(b) *Total tenant payment for qualified tenants who first receive rental assistance on or after May 1, 1983.* Notwithstanding § 236.55(b), the Total Tenant Payment payable for these Qualified Tenants shall be the highest of the following amounts, rounded to the nearest dollar:

(1) 30 percent of Adjusted Monthly Income as defined in subpart A;

(2) 10 percent of one-twelfth of Annual Income as defined in subpart A;

(3) If the family receives Welfare Assistance from a public agency and a part of such payments, adjusted in accordance with the family's actual housing costs, is specifically designated by such agency to meet the family's housing costs, the monthly portion of such payments which is so designated. If the family's Welfare Assistance is ratably reduced from the standard of need by applying a percentage, the amount calculated under this paragraph (b)(3) shall be the amount resulting from one application of the percentage.

(c) *Total tenant payment for qualified tenants who were receiving rental assistance on April 30, 1983 and whose assistance has been continuous thereafter.* Notwithstanding § 236.55(b), the Total Ten-

ant Payment for these Qualified Tenants shall be calculated in accordance with paragraph (b) of this section, except that instead of 30 percent, the percentage applied to Adjusted Monthly Income shall be as follows:

Effective date of recertification	Percentage
May 1, 1983 to Sept. 30, 1983	27
Oct. 1, 1983 to Sept. 30, 1984	28
Oct. 1, 1984 to Sept. 30, 1985	29
Oct. 1, 1985 and after	30

(d) *Special conditions.* (1) For the purposes of this section, a Qualified Tenant whose initial lease was effective before May 1, 1983 includes the following: A Qualified Tenant that resided in a unit assisted under the Rental Assistance Programs or Rent Supplement Program on April 30, 1983, and whose assistance under those programs has been continuous thereafter; and a family that resided in a unit with the benefit of section 8 Housing Assistance Payments on July 31, 1982 and whose participation in the section 8, Rent Supplement or the Rental Assistance Payment Program has been continuous thereafter. A Qualified Tenant or family shall not be disqualified if, after that date, it moved from one unit to another unit in the same project. For these purposes, units in buildings located on adjacent sites and managed as one project will be considered part of the same project even if they have separate project numbers and separate mortgages.

(2) Notwithstanding paragraphs (b) and (c) of this section, the Total Tenant Payment payable by a Qualified Tenant who continues to receive assistance in the same project shall not be increased by more than 10 percent during any 12-month period as a result of application of the percentages in paragraph (c) of this section, and application of the revised definitions in §§ 236.2 and 236.3. However, this 10 percent limit does not apply to Families subject to paragraph (b)(3) of this section, provided that the welfare agency includes as the housing component of the Family's grant an amount equal to their entire rent payment, without reduction. The Total Tenant Payment may be increased by more than 10 percent during any 12-month period to the

extent that the portion of such increase above 10 percent is attributable to increases in income or changes in family composition or family circumstances that are unrelated to the factors set out in this paragraph (d)(2).

(e) *Utility reimbursement.* Where applicable, the Utility Reimbursement shall be paid to the Qualified Tenant. If the tenant and the utility company consent, the owner may pay the Utility Reimbursement jointly to the Qualified Tenant and the utility company, or directly to the utility company.

[51 FR 21862, June 16, 1986]

§ 236.740 Time of payment under contract.

The rental assistance contract shall provide for payments to be made monthly to the housing owner on behalf of qualified tenants in the amounts set forth in the certificates of eligibility.

§ 236.745 Tenant occupancy limitations.

Eligible tenants shall not be permitted to occupy units larger than the Secretary determines necessary for their family needs, except on a temporary basis with the approval of the Secretary.

§ 236.750 Form of lease.

(a) *Lease form.* Eligible tenants shall be required to execute a lease in a form approved by the Commissioner.

(b) *Prohibited lease provisions.* Lease clauses of the nature described below shall not be included in new leases or occupancy agreements covered by paragraphs (a) and (b) of this section and shall be deleted from existing leases and agreements either by amendment thereto or by execution of a new lease or agreement.

(1) *Confession of judgment.* Prior consent by the tenant:

(i) To any lawsuit the landlord may bring against the tenant in connection with the lease; and

(ii) To a judgment in favor of the landlord.

(2) *Distraint for rent or other charges.* Agreement by the tenant that the landlord is authorized to take property of the tenant and hold it as a pledge until the tenant performs an obligation which the landlord has determined that tenant has failed to perform.

(3) *Exculpatory clauses.* Agreement by the tenant not to hold the landlord or the landlord's agents liable for any acts or omissions, whether intentional or negligent, on the part of the landlord or the landlord's authorized representatives or agents.

(4) *Waiver of legal notice by tenant before actions for eviction or money judgment.* Agreement by the tenant that the landlord may institute suit without notice to the tenant that the suit has been filed.

(5) *Waiver of legal proceedings.* Authorization to the landlord to evict the tenant or hold or sell the tenant's possessions whenever the landlord determines that a breach or default has occurred, without notice to the tenant or determination by a court of the rights and liabilities of the parties.

(6) *Waiver of jury trial.* Authorization to the landlord's lawyer to appear in court on behalf of the tenant and waive the right to a trial by jury.

(7) *Waiver of right to appeal judicial error in legal proceeding.* Authorization to the landlord's lawyer to waive the tenant's right:

(i) To appeal for judicial error in any suit brought against the tenant by the landlord or the landlord's agents; or

(ii) To file suit to prevent the execution of a judgment.

(8) *Tenant chargeable with cost of legal actions regardless of outcome.* Provision that the tenant agrees to pay attorney's fees or other legal costs if the landlord brings legal action against the tenant even if the tenant prevails in the action. Prohibition of this type of provision does not mean that the tenant, as a party to lawsuit, may not be obligated to pay attorney's fees or other costs if the tenant loses the suit.

[51 FR 21863, June 16, 1986]

§ 236.755 Housing owner's obligation under contract to report tenant income increase.

The rental assistance contract shall contain a provision obligating the housing owner to notify the Secretary upon receiving a report from a tenant of an increase in the tenant's income resulting in the tenant's ability to pay the approved basic monthly rental (plus, where applicable, the utility allowance established for utility charges paid by the tenant) with the amount the tenant is required to pay for rent in accordance with §236.735. The contract shall also obligate the housing owner, upon failing to notify the Secretary when a report of such increases in income is received from a tenant, to reimburse the Secretary for any rental assistance payments made during the period following receipt of such report when the tenant is receiving the increased income.

[48 FR 13982, Apr. 1, 1983]

§236.760 Change in tenant income status.

Appropriate adjustments will be made in rental assistance payments to reflect changes in income or other circumstances which are reported by a tenant and verified or are shown by the annual tenant income recertification, as required by §236.80. Rental assistance payments will be discontinued when it is determined by the Secretary that the amount the tenant is required to pay for rent, in accordance with §236.735, is sufficient to pay the approved basic monthly rental (plus, where applicable, the established utility allowance) for the unit occupied by the tenant. Where a tenant is no longer entitled to rental assistance payments, he/she may continue to occupy the unit. The rents charged for the unit shall not exceed those specified in subpart A.

[48 FR 13982, Apr. 1, 1983]

§236.765 Determination of eligible immigration status of applicants and tenants; protection from liability.

(a) *Housing owner's obligation to make determination.* A housing owner shall obtain and verify information regarding the citizenship or immigration status of applicants and tenants in accordance with the procedures of 24 CFR part 5.

(b) *Protection from liability.* HUD will not take any compliance, disallowance, penalty or other regulatory action against a housing owner with respect to any error in its determination to make an individual eligible for financial assistance based upon citizenship or eligible immigration status, as provided in 24 CFR part 5.

[61 FR 13624, Mar. 27, 1996]

Subpart E—Audits

§236.901 Audit.

Where a State or local government receives interest reduction payments under section 236(b) of the National Housing Act or is the mortgagor of a mortgage insured or held by the Commissioner under this part, it shall conduct audits in accordance with HUD audit requirements at 2 CFR part 200, subpart F.

[58 FR 37813, July 13, 1993, as amended at 80 FR 75936]

Subpart F—Uniform Relocation Assistance

§236.1001 Displacement, relocation, and acquisition.

(a) *Minimizing displacement.* Consistent with the other goals and objectives of this part, mortgagors shall assure that they have taken all reasonable steps to minimize the displacement of persons (households, businesses, nonprofit organizations, and farms) as a result of a project assisted under this part.

(b) *Temporary relocation.* The following policies cover residential tenants who will not be required to move permanently but who must relocate temporarily to permit rehabilitation or other work for the assisted project. Such tenants must be provided:

(1) Reimbursement for all reasonable out-of-pocket expenses incurred in connection with the temporary relocation, including the cost of moving to and from the temporary housing, any increase in monthly rent/utility costs, and any incidental expenses.

(2) Appropriate advisory services, including reasonable advance written notice of:

(i) The date and approximate duration of the temporary relocation;

(ii) The location of the suitable, decent, safe, and sanitary dwelling to be made available for the temporary period;

(iii) The terms and conditions under which the tenant may lease and occupy a suitable, decent, safe, and sanitary dwelling in the building/complex following completion of the repairs; and

(iv) The provisions of paragraph (b)(1) of this section.

(c) *Relocation assistance for displaced persons.* A "displaced person" (defined in paragraph (g) of this section) must be provided relocation assistance at the levels described in, and in accordance with the requirements of, the Uniform Relocation Assistance and Real Property Acquisition Policies Act of 1970, as amended (URA) (42 U.S.C. 4201–4655) and implementing regulations at 49 CFR part 24. A "displaced person" shall be advised of his or her rights under the Fair Housing Act (42 U.S.C. 3601–19), and, if the representative comparable replacement dwelling used to establish the amount of the replacement housing payment to be provided to a minority person is located in an area of minority concentration, such person also shall be given, if possible, referrals to comparable and suitable, decent, safe and sanitary replacement dwellings not located in such areas.

(d) *Real property acquisition requirements.* The acquisition of real property for a project is subject to the URA and the requirements of 49 CFR part 24, subpart B.

(e) *Appeals.* A person who disagrees with the mortgagor's determination concerning whether the person qualifies as a "displaced person," or with the amount of relocation assistance for which the person is eligible, may file a written appeal of that determination with the mortgagor. A person who is dissatisfied with the mortgagor's determination on his or her appeal may submit a written request for review of the determination to the HUD Field Office.

(f) *Responsibility of mortgagor.* (1) The mortgagor shall certify (i.e., provide assurance of compliance as required by 49 CFR part 24) that it will comply with the URA, the regulations at 49 CFR part 24, and the requirements of this section. The mortgagor shall ensure such compliance notwithstanding any third party's contractual obligation to the mortgagor to comply with these provisions.

(2) The cost of required relocation assistance is an eligible project cost in the same manner and to the same extent as other project costs. Such costs may also be paid for with funds available from other sources.

(3) The mortgagor shall maintain records in sufficient detail to demonstrate compliance with the provisions of this section. The mortgagor shall maintain data on the race, ethnic, gender, and disability status of displaced persons.

(g) *Definition of displaced person.* (1) For purposes of this section, the term *displaced person* means any person (household, business, nonprofit organization, or farm) that moves from real property, or moves personal property from real property, permanently, as a direct result of acquisition, rehabilitation, or demolition for a project assisted under this part. The term "displaced person" includes, but may not be limited to:

(i) A tenant-occupant of a dwelling unit who moves from the building/complex, permanently, after the mortgagor executes the agreement covering the rehabilitation, demolition or acquisition, if the move occurs before the tenant is provided written notice offering him or her the opportunity to lease and occupy a suitable, decent, safe, and sanitary dwelling in the same building/complex, under reasonable terms and conditions, upon completion of the project. Such reasonable terms and conditions include a monthly rent and estimated average monthly utility costs that do not exceed the amount approved by HUD;

(ii) A tenant-occupant of a dwelling who is required to relocate temporarily, but does not return to the building/complex, if either:

(A) The tenant is not offered payment for all reasonable out-of-pocket expenses incurred in connection with the temporary relocation, including the cost of moving to and from the temporarily occupied unit, any increased housing costs and incidental expenses; or

(B) Other conditions of the temporary relocation are not reasonable; or

(iii) A tenant-occupant of a dwelling who moves from the building/complex permanently after he or she has been required to move to another dwelling unit in the same building/complex in order to carry out the project, if either:

(A) The tenant is not offered reimbursement for all reasonable out-of-pocket expenses incurred in connection with the move; or

(B) Other conditions of the move are not reasonable; or

(iv) Any person, including a person who moves before the mortgagor's execution of the agreement covering the rehabilitation, demolition, or acquisition, if the mortgagor or HUD determines that the displacement resulted directly from rehabilitation, demolition or acquisition for the assisted project.

(2) Notwithstanding the provisions of paragraph (g)(1) of this section, a person does not qualify as a "displaced person" (and is not eligible for relocation assistance under the URA or this section), if:

(i) The person has been evicted for serious or repeated violation of the terms and conditions of the lease or occupancy agreement, violation of applicable Federal, State or local law, or other good cause, and HUD determines that the eviction was not undertaken for the purpose of evading the obligation to provide relocation assistance;

(ii) The person moved into the property after the execution of the agreement covering the rehabilitation, demolition or acquisition and, before signing a lease or commencing occupancy, was provided written notice of the project, its possible impact on the person (e.g., the person may be displaced, temporarily relocated or suffer a rent increase) and the fact that the person would not qualify as a "displaced person" (or for any assistance provided under this section) as a result of the project;

(iii) The person is ineligible under 49 CFR 24.2(g)(2); or

(iv) HUD determines that the person was not displaced as a direct result of acquisition, rehabilitation, or demolition for the project;

(3) The mortgagor may request, at any time, HUD's determination of whether a displacement is or would be covered by this section.

(h) *Definition of initiation of negotiations.* For purposes of determining the formula for computing the replacement housing assistance to be provided to a residential tenant displaced as a direct result of privately undertaken rehabilitation, demolition or acquisition of the real property, the term *initiation of negotiations* means the mortgagor's execution of the agreement covering the rehabilitation, demolition or acquisition.

(Approved by Office of Management and Budget under OMB Control Number 2506-0121)

[59 FR 29331, June 6, 1994]

PART 241—SUPPLEMENTARY FINANCING FOR INSURED PROJECT MORTGAGES

Subpart A—Eligibility Requirements

AUTHORITY: 12 U.S.C. 1715b, 1715z–6, and 1735d; 42 U.S.C. 3535(d).

SOURCE: 36 FR 24653, Dec. 22, 1971, unless otherwise noted.

Subpart A—Eligibility Requirements

§241.1 Eligibility requirements.

The requirements set forth in 24 CFR part 200, subpart A, apply to multifamily project mortgages insured under section 241 of the National Housing Act (12 U.S.C. 1715z–6), as amended.

[61 FR 14407, Apr. 1, 1996]

Subpart B—Contract Rights and Obligations

§241.251 Cross-reference.

(a) *Projects with a HUD-insured or HUD-held mortgage.* All of the provisions of subpart B, part 207 of this chapter, covering mortgages insured under section 207 of the National Housing Act, apply with full force and effect to multifamily project and group practice facility mortgages insured under section 241 of the National Housing Act, except the following provisions:

Sec.
207.251 Definitions.
207.253a Termination of insurance contract.
207.259 Insurance benefits.
207.260 Protection of mortgage security.
207.262 No vested right in fund.

(b) For the purposes of this subpart, the terms *mortgagor, mortgagee* and *mortgage,* as used in subpart B, part 207 of this chapter shall be construed to mean *borrower, lender* and *supplementary loan (including the security instrument),* respectively.

(c) *Projects without a HUD-insured or HUD-held mortgage.* The provisions of subpart D of this part shall be applicable to a project without a HUD-insured or HUD-held mortgage that is receiving a loan insured under subpart A of this part in connection with a plan of action approved by the Commissioner under part 248 of this chapter.

[36 FR 24653, Dec. 22, 1971, as amended at 37 FR 8664, Apr. 29, 1972; 48 FR 57129, Dec. 28, 1983; 57 FR 12037, Apr. 8, 1992]

§241.260 Definitions.

All of the definitions contained in §241.1 shall apply to this subpart. In addition, the term *contract of insurance,* as used in this subpart, means the agreement evidenced by endorsement of the credit instrument by the Commissioner or his duly authorized representative, and includes the provisions of this subpart and of the National Housing Act.

§241.261 Payment of insurance benefits.

All of the provisions of §207.259 of this chapter relating to insurance benefits shall apply to multifamily loans insured under this subpart.

[80 FR 51469, Aug. 25, 2015]

§241.265 Insurance of property against flood.

The mortgaged property shall be insured against flood as stipulated by the Federal Housing Commissioner. The mortgagee shall obtain such coverage in the event the mortgagor fails to do so. If the mortgagee fails to pay any premiums necessary to keep the mortgaged premises so insured, the contract of mortgage insurance may be terminated at the election of the Commissioner.

[39 FR 26023, July 16, 1974]

§241.270 Refund upon termination of insurance.

Upon termination of the insurance contract by payment in full or by voluntary termination, the Commissioner shall refund to the lender for the account of the borrower an amount equal to the pro rata portion of the current annual loan insurance premium theretofore paid, which is applicable to the portion of the year subsequent to (a) the date of the prepayment or (b) the effective date of the voluntary termination of the contract of insurance.

§241.275 No vested right in fund.

Neither the lender nor the borrower shall have any vested or other right in the insurance fund under which the loan is insured.

Subpart C—Eligibility Requirements—Supplemental Loans To Finance Purchase and Installation of Energy Conserving Improvements, Solar Energy Systems, and Individual Utility Meters in Multifamily Projects Without a HUD-Insured or HUD-Held Mortgage

SOURCE: 45 FR 57983, Aug. 29, 1980, unless otherwise noted.

§ 241.500 Definitions.

In addition to the definitions contained in subpart A of this part, incorporated herein by reference, except § 241.1(f), (h) and (i), the following terms, as used in § 241.500 *et seq.*, shall have the meaning indicated:

(a) *Approved lender* means a financial institution or other mortgagee approved by the Commissioner as eligible for insurance under section 2 of the National Housing Act, or a mortgagee approved under section 203(b)(1) of the National Housing Act, or a state housing agency approved pursuant to 24 CFR 883.102.

(b) *Borrower* means the owner of a project held in fee simple or of a leasehold interest which is not now covered by a mortgage insured or held by the Secretary.

(c) *Energy saving loan* means any form of secured obligation used in connection with the purchase and installation of energy conserving improvements.

(d) *Multifamily project* means a project which consists of not less than five dwelling units on one site, each such unit providing complete living facilities including provisions for cooking, eating, and sanitation within the unit and which is not now covered by a mortgage insured or held by the Secretary.

FEES AND CHARGES

§ 241.505 Processing of applications and required fees.

(a) *Preapplication conference.* The local HUD Office will determine whether participation in a preapplication conference is required as a condition to submission of an initial application for a firm commitment for insurance of an energy savings improvement loan on a project. An application for a firm commitment for insurance must be submitted by both the project sponsor and an approved lender. Applications shall be submitted to the local HUD Office on HUD-approved forms. No application will be considered unless accompanied by all exhibits required by the form and program handbooks.

(b) *Application for firm commitment.* An application for a firm commitment shall be accompanied by the payment of an application fee of $5 per thousand dollars of the requested loan amount to be insured.

(c) *Cross-reference.* The provisions of paragraphs (e) (Inspection fee), (f)(1) (Fee on increases), (g) (Reopening of expired commitments), (i) (Refund of fees), and (j) (Fees not required) of § 200.40 of this chapter apply to applications submitted under subpart E of this part.

[61 FR 14416, Apr. 1, 1996]

§ 241.510 Commitments.

(a) *Firm commitment.* The issuance of a firm commitment indicates the Commissioner's approval of the application for insurance and sets forth the terms and conditions upon which the loan will be insured.

(b) *Types of firm commitment.* (1) Where the amount of the loan is $250,000 or more, the firm commitment may provide for the insurance of advances of loan money made during construction or may provide for the insurance of the loan after completion of the improvements.

(2) Where the amount of the loan is less than $250,000, the firm commitment shall provide for insurance of the loan after completion of the improvements.

(c) *Term of commitment.* (1) A firm commitment to insure advances shall be effective for a period of not more than 60 days from the day of issuance.

(2) A firm commitment to insure upon completion shall be effective for a

designated term within which the borrower is required to begin construction, and if construction is begun as required, the commitment shall be effective for such additional period, estimated by the Commissioner, as will allow for completion of construction.

(3) The term of a firm commitment may be extended in such a manner as the Commissioner may prescribe.

[61 FR 14417, Apr. 1, 1996]

§241.515 Inspection fee.

The firm commitment may provide for the payment of an inspection fee in an amount not to exceed $5 per thousand dollars of the commitment. If an inspection fee is required, it shall be paid as follows:

(a) If the case involves the insurance of advances, it shall be paid at the time of initial endorsement.

(b) If the case involves insurance upon completion, it shall be paid prior to the date construction is begun.

§241.520 Fees on increases.

(a) *Increase in firm commitment prior to endorsement.* An application filed prior to initial endorsement (or prior to endorsement in a case involving insurance upon completion), for an increase in the amount of an outstanding firm commitment shall be accompanied by a combined additional application and commitment fee. This combined additional fee shall be in an amount which will aggregate $3 per thousand dollars of the amount of the requested increase. if an inspection fee was required in the original commitment, an additional inspection fee shall be paid in an amount computed at the same dollar rate per thousand dollars of the amount of increase in commitment as was used for the ispection fee required in the original commitment. When insurance of advances is involved, the additional inspection fee shall be paid at time of initial endorsement. When insurance upon completion is involved, the additional inspection fee shall be paid prior to the date construction is begun or if construction has begun, it shall be paid with the application for increase.

(b) *Increase in loan between initial and final endorsement.* Upon an application, filed between initial and final endorsement, for an increase in the amount of the loan, either by amendment or by substitution of a new loan, a combined additional application and commitment fee shall accompany the application. This combined additional fee shall be in an amount which will aggregate $3 per thousand dollars of the amount of the increase requested. If an inspection fee was required in the original commitment, an additional inspection fee shall accompany the application in an amount not to exceed $5 per thousand dollars of the amount of the increase requested.

§241.525 Refund of fees.

If the amount of the commitment issued or an increase in loan prior to endorsement is less than the amount applied for, the Commissioner shall refund the excess amount of the application and commitment fees submitted by the applicant. If an application is rejected before it is assigned for processing, or in such other instances as the Commissioner may determine, the entire application and commitment fees or any portion thereof may be returned to the applicant. Commitment, inspection, and reopening fees may be refunded, in whole or in part if it is determined by the Commissioner that the installation of energy conserving improvements for the project has been prevented because of condemnation proceedings or other legal action taken by a governmental body or public agency, or in such other instances as the Commissioner may determine.

§241.530 Maximum fees and charges by lender.

The lender may collect from the borrower the amount of the fees provided for in this subpart. The lender may also collect from the borrower an initial service charge in an amount not to exceed 2 percent of the original principal amount of the loan to reimburse the lender for the cost of originating and closing the transaction. Any additional charges shall be subject to the prior approval of the Commissioner.

ELIGIBLE SECURITY INSTRUMENTS

§ 241.530a Note and security form.

The lender shall present for insurance a note and security instrument, on forms approved by the Commissioner for use in the jurisdiction in which the property to be improved is located.

[45 FR 57983, Aug. 29, 1980, as amended at 45 FR 80276, Dec. 4, 1980]

§ 241.535 Loan multiples—minimum principal.

The loan shall involve a principal obligation in multiples of $100, and the minimum principal obligation shall be $10,000.

§ 241.540 Method of loan payment and amortization period.

(a) *Monthly payments.* The loan shall provide for monthly payments on the first day of each month on account of interest and principal and shall provide for payment in accordance with the amortization plan as agreed upon by the borrower, the lender and the Commissioner.

(b) *Amortization period.* (1) The loan shall have an amortization of either 5, 10, or 15 years by providing for either 60, 120, or 180 monthly amortization payments. No energy saving loan shall have an amortization period in excess of 15 years unless the amount of the loan exceeds $50,000.00, in which event the amortization period may be increased to 20 years, with a provision for 240 monthly amortization payments.

(2) In any event, the loan shall have a maturity satisfactory to the Commissioner of not less than 2 or more than 20 years from the date of the beginning of amortization, or the Commissioner's estimate of the remaining economic life of the structure, whichever is the lesser.

(3) The Commissioner shall establish the date of the first payment to principal, which shall be no later than the first day of the second month following the date of final endorsement (for projects involving insurance of advances) or endorsement (for projects involving insurance upon completion) of the loan for insurance.

§ 241.545 Covenant against liens.

The security instrument shall contain a covenant against the creation by the borrower of additional liens against the property superior or inferior to the lien of such instrument, except with the prior approval of the Commissioner.

§ 241.550 Accumulation of next premium.

The security instrument shall provide for payments by the borrower to the lender on each interest payment date of an amount sufficient to accumulate in the hands of the lender one payment period prior to its due date, the next annual insurance premium payable by the lender to the Commissioner.

§ 241.555 Security instrument and lien.

(a) The security instrument shall cover the entire property included in the project, shall be a lien on the real property of the project under the laws of the jurisdiction in which the project is located, and may be junior to such prior liens or mortgage indebtedness as the Commissioner may approve. The security instrument shall contain a provision that a default under the first mortgage is a default under the supplementary loan security instrument.

(b) For bond-financed projects where the bond resolution contains a provision prohibiting the creation of additional liens, the Commissioner may accept at his/her option:

(1) A first lien on another property whose fair market value as determined by the Commissioner equals or exceeds the amount of the loan insured under this part;

(2) A Collateral Account in an amount not less than the amount of the loan insured under this part funded with cash or negotiable bonds or securities backed by the full faith and credit of the United States Government; or

(3) Other security acceptable to the Commissioner.

§ 241.560 Agreed interest rate.

(a) The mortgage shall bear interest at the rate agreed upon by the lender and the borrower.

(b) Interest shall be payable in monthly installments on the principal amount of the loan outstanding on the due date of each installment.

[45 FR 57983, Aug. 29, 1980, as amended at 49 FR 19459, May 8, 1984]

§ 241.565 Maximum loan amount.

The principal amount of the loan shall in no event exceed the cost of the energy conserving improvements including the purchase thereof, cost of installation, architect's fees, interest during construction and such other miscellaneous fees and charges incident to construction as determined by the Commissioner. Nor shall the principal amount of the loan exceed the lesser of the following:

(a) An amount which can be supported by residual income, which is the amount of net income remaining after payment of all existing debt service requirements and deduction of proprietary earnings, as determined by the Commissioner. The computation of net income shall take into account the amount which will be saved in operating costs over the period of repayment of the loan as a result of the installation of the energy conserving improvements.

(b) An amount which, when added to the existing outstanding indebtedness, does not exceed the Commissioner's estimate of the value of the project after the energy conserving improvements are installed.

§ 241.570 Insurance endorsement.

(a) *Initial endorsement.* The Commissioner shall indicate his/her insurance of the mortgage by endorsing the original credit instrument and identifying the section of the Act and the regulations under which the mortgage is insured and the date of insurance.

(b) *Final endorsement.* When all advances of mortgage proceeds have been made and all the terms and conditions of the commitment have been complied with to the satisfaction of the Commissioner, he/she shall indicate on the original credit instrument the total approved for insurance and again endorse such instrument.

(c) *Effect of endorsement.* From the date of initial endorsement, the Commissioner and the mortgagee or lender shall be bound by the provisions of this subpart to the same extent as if they had executed a contract including the provisions of this subpart and the applicable sections of the Act.

(d) *Insurance upon completion.* When all advances of mortgage proceeds have been made and all the terms and conditions of the commitment have been complied with to the satisfaction of the Commissioner, he/she shall indicate the total approved for insurance and endorse the credit instrument, identifying the date of insurance.

§ 241.580 Application of payments.

(a) The security instrument shall provide that all monthly payments to be made by the borrower shall be added together and this aggregate amount shall be paid by the borrower upon each monthly payment date in a single payment. The lender shall apply the payment to the following items in the order set forth:

(1) Premium charges under the contract of insurance;

(2) Interest on the loan;

(3) Amortization of the principal of the loan.

(b) Any deficiency in the amount of any monthly payments required under paragraph (a) of this section shall constitute an event of default and the loan shall further provide for a grace period of 30 days within which time the default must be cured.

§ 241.585 Prepayment privileges and prepayment charge.

The security instrument shall contain a provision permitting prepayment of the loan in whole or in part upon any interest payment date after giving to the lender 30 days advance written notice and it may contain a provision, with the approval of the Commissioner, for a reasonable charge in the event of prepayment. The borrower shall be permitted to prepay up to 15 percent of the original principal amount of the loan in any one calendar year without an additional charge. A provision for a charge in the event of prepayment may not be included in a loan of $200,000 or less.

§ 241.586 Minimum principal loan amount.

A mortgagee may not require, as a condition of providing a loan insured under this subpart, that the principal amount of the mortgage exceed a minimum amount established by the mortgagee.

[53 FR 8886, Mar. 18, 1988]

PROPERTY REQUIREMENTS

§ 241.590 Eligibility of property.

(a) A loan to be eligible for insurance shall be on real estate held:

(1) In fee simple; or

(2) On the interest of the lessee under a lease for not less than seventy-five years which is renewable; or

(3) Under a lease having a period of not less than twenty-five years to run from the date the loan is executed.

(b) The property constituting security for the loan transaction must be held by an eligible borrower as herein defined and must at the time the loan is insured be free and clear of all liens other than those specifically approved by the Commissioner.

TITLE

§ 241.595 Eligibility of title.

In order for the property which is to be the security for a loan to be insured under this subpart to be eligible for insurance, the Commissioner shall determine that the title to the property is vested in the borrower as of the date the security instrument is filed for record. The title evidence will be examined by the Commissioner and the endorsement of the credit instrument for insurance shall be evidence of its acceptability.

§ 241.600 Title evidence.

(a) Upon insurance of the loan, the lender shall furnish to the Commissioner a survey, satisfactory to the Commissioner, and a policy of title insurance as provided in paragraph (a)(1) of this section. If the lender is unable to furnish such policy for reasons satisfactory to the Commissioner, the lender shall furnish such evidence of title as provided in paragraph (a) (2), (3), or (4) of this section as the Commissioner may require. Any survey, policy of title insurance, or evidence of title required under this section shall be furnished without expense to the Commis-

sioner. The acceptable types of title evidence are:

(1) A policy of title insurance issued by a company and in a form satisfactory to the Commissioner. The policy shall name the lender and the Secretary of Housing and Urban Development, as their respective interests may appear, as the insured. The policy shall provide that upon acquisition of title by the lender or the Secretary, it will continue to provide the same coverage as the original policy, and will run to the lender upon its acquisition of the property in extinguishment of the debt, and to the Secretary upon acquisition of the property pursuant to the loan insurance contract.

(2) An abstract of title satisfactory to the Commissioner, prepared by an abstract company or individual engaged in the business of preparing abstracts of title, accompanied by a legal opinion satisfactory to the Commissioner, as to the quality of such title, signed by an attorney at law experienced in the examination of titles.

(3) A Torrens or similar title certificate.

(4) Evidence of title conforming to the standards of a supervising branch of the Government of the United States of America, or of any State or territory thereof.

(b) The survey required by paragraph (a) of this section need not be furnished in connection with a project where the loan does not exceed $200,000.

[45 FR 57983, Aug. 29, 1980, as amended at 58 FR 34217, June 24, 1993]

FORM OF CONTRACT

§ 241.605 Contract requirements.

(a) When the principal amount of the loan is $100,000 or less, the form of contract between the borrower and the contractor shall be in accordance with the following:

(1) The contract between the borrower and the general contractor may be in the form of either a lump sum contract or a cost plus contract. Either form of contract shall include the cost of the energy conserving improvements, their installation, and such other work to be performed by the contractor as necessary to meet the requirements of the Secretary. A lump

sum contract shall provide for the payment of a specified amount. A cost plus contract shall provide for the payment of the contractor's actual cost of compliance with the requirements of the contract, plus such allowances for overhead and profit as may be approved by the Commissioner and shall provide that the total cost under the contract shall not exceed the upset price as approved by the Commissioner.

(2) If agreed to by the general contractor and borrower, a lump sum form of contract between the borrower and the general contractor may be used unless the Commissioner determines that a cost plus contract with a maximum upset price is necessary to protect the interest of the borrower or the Commissioner.

(b) When the principal amount of the loan is over $100,000, the form of contract between the borrower and the contractor shall be in accordance with the following:

(1) *Lump sum contract.* If the Commissioner determines that there is no identity of interest between the borrower or any of the officers, directors or stockholders of the borrower and the contractor, there may be used a lump sum contract providing for payment of the specified amount.

(2) *Cost plus fixed fee contract.* (i) If the Commissioner determines that there is any identity of interest (financial or otherwise) between the borrower, its officers, directors or stockholders and the contractor, the form of contract shall provide for payment of the actual cost of construction not to exceed an upset price and may provide for payment of a fixed fee not exceeding a reasonable allowance as established by the Commissioner in accordance with customary practices in the area.

(ii) In any case where the borrower is a nonprofit entity, a cost plus fixed fee contract shall be used unless it is established to the Commissioner's satisfaction that such form of contract is not required to protect his/her interests and the interests of the borrower, in which case, a lump sum form of contract may be used.

§241.610 **Assurance of completion.**

(a) The borrower shall furnish assurance of completion of the project in the following minimum forms and amounts:

(1) Where the estimated cost of construction of the improvements is $500,000 or less, the borrower shall furnish assurance of completion of the project in the form of a personal indemnity agreement executed by the principal officers, directors, stockholders, or partners of the entity acting as general contractor.

(2) Where the estimated cost of construction of the improvements is more than $500,000 or where such cost is less than $500,000 and a personal indemnity agreement is not executed, the assurance shall be in the form of corporate surety bonds for payment and performance, each in the minimum amount of 25 percent of the construction contract, or a completion assurance agreement secured by a cash deposit in the minimum amount of 15 percent of the amount of the construction contract.

(3) All types of assurance of completion shall be on forms approved by the Commissioner. Any surety company executing a bond and any party executing a personal indemnity agreement must be satisfactory to the Commissioner.

(4) A mortgagee may prescribe more stringent requirements for assurance of completion than the minimum requirements of this section.

(b) The lender may accept, in lieu of a cash deposit required by paragraph (a) of this section, an unconditional irrevocable letter of credit issued to the lender by a banking institution. In the event a demand under the letter of credit is not immediately met, the lender shall forthwith provide cash equivalent to the undrawn balance thereunder.

§241.615 **Certification of cost requirements.**

(a) *Certification agreement.* The lender shall submit with the application an agreement on a form prescribed by the Commissioner and executed by the borrower and the lender.

(b) *Certificate and adjustment.* No loan shall be insured unless:

403

(1) A certification of actual cost is made by the contractor in cases in which a cost plus form of contract is used; and

(2) The amount of the loan is adjusted to reflect the actual cost to the borrower of the improvements when either a cost plus or lump sum form or contract is used.

(c) *Cost computation.* The term *actual cost of the improvements* shall mean the cost to the borrower of the improvements, after deducting the amount of any kickbacks, rebates or trade discount received in connection with the improvements, and including the amounts paid under any contract for the improvements, labor, materials, and for any other items of expenses approved by the Commissioner.

(d) *Statement of facts.* Any agreement, undertaking, statement or certification required in connection with cost certification shall specifically state that it has been made, presented and delivered for the purpose of influencing an official action of the Commissioner and may be relied upon as a true statement of the facts contained therein.

(e) *Incontestability.* Upon the Commissioner's approval of the cost certification, such certification shall be final and incontestable except for fraud or material misrepresentation on the part of the borrower.

(f) *Records.* The borrower shall keep and maintain adequate records of all costs of any construction improvements or other cost items not representing work under the general contract and shall require the contractor to keep similar records and, upon request by the Commissioner, both shall make available for examination such records, including any collateral agreements.

(g) *Certificate of public accountant.* Where required by the Commissioner, each certificate of actual cost shall be supported by a certificate as to accuracy by an independent Certified Public Accountant or independent public accountant licensed by a regulatory authority of a State or other political subdivision of the United States on or prior to December 31, 1970, which shall include a statement that the accounts, records and supporting documents have been examined in accordance with gen-

erally accepted auditing standards to the extent deemed necessary to verify the actual costs.

ELIGIBLE BORROWERS

§ 241.625   Eligible borrowers.

In order to be eligible as a borrower under this subpart, the applicant shall be a profit, limited distribution, nonprofit, or cooperative owner of a multifamily housing project which is not covered by a mortgage insured or held by the Secretary and which the Commissioner has determined to be an acceptable risk in that energy conservation or solar energy benefits to be derived outweigh the risks of possible loss of the Federal Government.

§ 241.626   Disclosure and verification of Social Security and Employer Identification Numbers.

To be eligible for loan insurance under this subpart, the borrower must meet the requirements for the disclosure and verification of Social Security and Employer Identification Numbers, as provided by part 200, subpart U, of this chapter.

(Approved by the Office of Management and Budget under control number 2502–0118)

[54 FR 39696, Sept. 27, 1989]

SPECIAL REQUIREMENTS

§ 241.630   Maximum insurance against loss.

A loan insured under this subpart shall be insured for 90 percent of any loss incurred by the person holding the note for the loan.

§ 241.635   Regulatory agreement.

Any borrower obligated on the note for any loan insured under this subpart shall be regulated or restricted in a manner and on a form prescribed by the Secretary as to rents or sales, charges, capital structure, rate of return and methods of operation of the multifamily project to such an extent and in such manner as to provide reasonable rental to tenants and a reasonable return on the investment until the termination of all obligations of the Secretary under the contract of insurance.

§241.640 Employment discrimination prohibited.

Any contract or subcontract executed for the performance of constructing the improvements to the project shall provide that there shall be no discrimination against any employee or applicant for employment because of race, color, religion, sex, familial status, disability, age, or national origin.

[61 FR 14417, Apr. 1, 1996]

§241.645 Labor standards and prevailing wage requirements.

(a) Any contract, subcontract, or building loan agreement executed for the performance of construction of the project shall comply with all applicable labor standards and provisions of the regulations of the Secretary of Labor set forth in §§5.1 through 5.12 of title 29.

(b) No construction contract shall be entered into with a general contractor or any subcontractor if such contractor or any such subcontractor or any firm, corporation, partnership or association in which such contractor or subcontractor has a substantial interest is included on the ineligible list of contractors or subcontractors established and maintained by the Comptroller General, pursuant to §5.6(b) of title 29.

(c) No advance under the mortgage shall be eligible for insurance after notification from the Commissioner that the general contractor or any subcontractor or any firm, corporation, partnership or association in which such contractor or subcontractor has a substantial interest, was on the date the contract or subcontract was executed, on the ineligible list established by the Comptroller General, pursuant to the provision of the Secretary of Labor set forth in §§5.1 through 5.12 of title 29.

(d) No advance under any mortgage shall be eligible for insurance unless there is filed with the application of such advance a certificate or certificates in the form required by the Commissioner, supported by such other information as the Commissioner may prescribe, certifying that the laborers and mechanics employed in the construction of the dwelling or dwellings, or housing project involved, have been paid not less than the wage prevailing in the locality in which the work was performed for the corresponding classes of laborers and mechanics employed on construction of a similar character, as determined by the Secretary of Labor prior to beginning of construction and after the date of filing of the application for insurance.

(e) Compliance with the provisions of this subsection shall be evidenced at such time and in such manner as the Commissioner may prescribe.

Subpart D—Contract Rights and Obligations—Multifamily Projects Without a HUD-Insured or HUD-Held Mortgage

Source: 45 FR 57987, Aug. 29, 1980, unless otherwise noted.

§241.800 Definitions.

All of the definitions contained in §241.500 shall apply to this subpart. In addition, as used in this subpart, the following terms shall have the meaning indicated:

(a) *Contract of insurance* means the agreement evidenced by the endorsement of the Commissioner upon the note given in connection with an insured loan and includes the provisions of this subpart and the applicable provisions of the Act.

(b) *Maturity* means the date on which the loan indebtedness would be extinguished if paid in accordance with periodic payments provided for in the loan.

Premiums

§241.805 Insurance premiums.

(a) *First premium.* The lender, upon the endorsement of the loan for insurance, shall pay to the Commissioner a first loan insurance premium equal to one percent of the original face amount of the note.

(b) *Second premium.* The lender, on the date of the first principal payment, shall pay a second premium equal to one percent of the average outstanding principal obligation of the loan for the year following such first principal payment date which shall be adjusted as of that date so that the aggregate of the first and second premiums shall equal the sum of one percent per annum of the average outstanding principal obligation of the loan for the period from the date of the insurance endorsement to one year following the date of the first principal payment.

(c) *Annual insurance premium.* Until the note is paid in full, or until the loan is assigned to the Commissioner, or until the contract of insurance is otherwise terminated with the consent of the Commissioner, the lender, on each anniversary of the date of the first principal payment shall pay an annual loan insurance premium equal to one percent of the average outstanding principal obligation of the loan for the year following the date on which such premium becomes payable.

(d) *Method of premium payment.* Premiums shall be payable in cash or in debentures of the General Insurance Fund at par plus accrued interest. All premiums are payable in advance and no refund can be made of any portion thereof except as provided in this part.

(e) *Calculation of premiums.* The premiums payable on and after the date of the first principal payment shall be calculated in accordance with the amortization provisions without taking into account delinquent payments or prepayments.

§ 241.805a Mortgagee's late charge.

Mortgage insurance premiums which are paid to the Commissioner more than 15 days after the billing date or due date, whichever is later, shall include a late charge of 4 percent of the amount of the payment due, except that no late charge shall be required with respect to any case for which HUD fails to render a proper billing to the mortgagee.

§ 241.815 Termination of insurance.

(a) *Prepayment in full.* The contract of insurance shall be terminated if the loan is paid in full prior to its maturity. Notice of the prepayment shall be given to the Commissioner, on a form prescribed by the Commissioner, within 30 days from the date of the prepayment. The insurance termination shall become effective as of the date of the prepayment, or 30 days prior to the Commissioner's receipt of the prepayment notice, whichever is later.

(b) *Voluntary termination.* The contract of insurance shall be voluntarily terminated upon receipt by the Commissioner of a written request, on a form prescribed by the Commissioner, by the borrower and the lender for such termination, accompanied by a submission of the original credit instrument for cancellation of the insurance endorsement and the remittance of all sums to which the Commissioner is entitled. The termination shall become effective as of the date these requirements are met.

§ 241.825 Pro rata refund of insurance premium.

Upon termination of a loan insurance contract by a payment in full or by a voluntary termination, the Commissioner shall refund to the lender for the account of the borrower an amount equal to the pro rata portion of the current annual loan insurance premium theretofore paid which is applicable to the portion of the year subsequent to the effective date of the termination.

RIGHTS AND DUTIES OF LENDER UNDER THE CONTRACT OF INSURANCE

§ 241.830 Definition of default.

(a) If the borrower fails to make any payments due under or provided to be paid by the terms of the note or security instrument, the note shall be considered in default for the purposes of this subpart.

(b) The failure to perform any other covenant under the note or security instrument shall be considered a default: *Provided,* The lender, because of such default, has exercised its rights under the note or security instrument and accelerated the debt.

(c) The failure to make any payment or to perform any covenant under the first conventional note and mortgage by reason of which the holder thereof declares a default as evidenced by formal written declaration of said default to the Commissioner and the lender by the holder of the first note and mortgage, shall be considered a default under the insured loan.

(d) If such defaults as defined in paragraphs (a), (b), and (c) of this section continue for a period of 30 days, the lender shall be entitled to receive the benefits of insurance hereinafter provided.

§241.840   Date of default.

In computing loan insurance benefits, the date of default shall be considered as:

(a) The date of the lender's acceleration of the debt because of the borrower's uncorrected failure to perform a covenant or obligation under the note or security instrument; or

(b) The date of the first failure to make a monthly payment which subsequent payments by the borrower are insufficient to cover when applied to the overdue monthly payments in the order in which they become due.

(c) The date of the lender's acceleration of the debt because of the borrower's default under the first conventional note and mortgage.

§241.850   Notice of default.

(a) If the default is not cured within the 30 day grace period, as defined in §241.530(d), the lender shall, within 30 days thereafter, notify the Commissioner in writing of such default.

(b) The lender shall give notice in writing to the Commissioner of the failure of the borrower to comply with any covenant or obligation under the security instrument or note regardless of the fact that the lender may not have elected to accelerate the debt.

§241.860   Commissioner's right to require acceleration.

Upon receipt of notice of the failure of the borrower to comply with any covenant or obligation under the security instrument or note, or under the conventional note and mortgage, the Commissioner may require the lender to accelerate payment of the outstanding principal balance due.

§241.865   Election by the lender.

Where a real estate mortgage, or other security instrument has been used to secure the payment of a loan made under the provisions of this subpart and subpart C of this part, the lender may either elect to assign the loan to the Commissioner in exchange for the payment of insurance benefits or may exercise its rights under the note and security instrument in lieu of making a claim for insurance benefits. If the lender elects the latter course, the Commissioner shall be so notified and the contract of insurance shall be deemed terminated upon the date of receipt of such notification.

§241.875   Maximum claim period.

Notice of intention to file claim on a form prescribed by the Commissioner shall be filed within 45 days after the lender becomes eligible for the benefits of the loan insurance, or within such later time as may be agreed upon by the Commissioner in writing.

§241.880   Items to be delivered on submitting claim.

Within 30 days after the filing of the notice of intention to assign the loan to the Commissioner, or within such further period as may be agreed upon by the Commissioner in writing, the lender shall deliver to the Commissioner:

(a) The fiscal data pertaining to the loan transactions;

(b) Receipts covering all disbursements as required by the fiscal data form;

(c) The original note and any security instrument or instruments which shall be assigned to the Commissioner without recourse or warranty, except that the lender must warrant that no act or omission of the lender has impaired the validity and priority of such security instrument or instruments that the security instrument or instruments are prior to all mechanics' and materialmen's liens filed of record subsequent to the recording of such security instrument or instruments regardless of whether such liens attached prior to such recording date, and prior to all liens and encumbrances which may have attached or defects which may have arisen subsequent to the recording of such security instrument or instruments, except such liens or other matters as may be approved by the Commissioner, that the amount stated in the instrument of assignment is actually due and owing under the security instrument or instruments, that there are no offsets or counterclaims thereto, and that the lender has a good right to assign such note and security instrument or instruments;

(d) The assignment to the Commissioner of all rights and interests arising under the note and security instrument or instruments so in default and all claims of the lender against the borrower or others arising out of the loan transaction;

(e) All policies of title or other insurance or surety bonds, or other guarantees and any and all claims thereunder; including evidence satisfactory to the Commissioner that the original title coverage has been extended to include the assignment of the note and security instrument or instruments to the Commissioner;

(f) All records, ledger cards, documents, books, papers and accounts relating to the loan transaction;

(g) Any additional information or data which the Commissioner may require;

(h) The following cash items, held in connection with the loan insured under this subpart, shall either be retained by the lender or delivered to the Commissioner at the time the insurance claim is filed.

(1) Any cash held by the lender or its agents or to which it is entitled including deposits made for the account of the borrower and which have not been applied in reduction of the principal the loan indebtedness.

(2) All funds held by the lender for the account of the borrower received pursuant to any other agreement.

(i) On the date the assignment of the note and security instrument or instruments are filed for record, the lender shall notify the Commissioner and the Office of Finance and Accounting by telegram of such recordation.

§ 241.885 Insurance benefits.

(a) *Method of payment.* Payment of insurance claims shall be made in cash, in debentures, or in a combination of both, as determined by the Commissioner either at, or prior to, the time of payment.

(b) *Amount of payment.* Upon acceptable assignment of the note and security instrument to the Commissioner, the insurance benefits shall be paid in an amount equal to 90 percent of the amount determined as follows:

(1) By adding to the unpaid principal amount of the loan, computed as of the date of default, the following items:

(i) Any accrued interest due as of the date of execution of the assignment of the loan to the Commissioner.

(ii) Any advances approved by the Commissioner made previously by the lender under the provisions of the note or security instrument or instruments.

(iii) Reimbursements for such reasonable collection costs, court costs, and attorney's fees as may be approved by the Commissioner.

(iv) Any loan insurance premiums paid after default.

(v) If payment is made in cash, an amount equivalent to the debenture interest which would have been earned thereon, as of the date such cash payment is made, except when the lender fails to meet any one of the applicable requirements of §§ 241.850, 241.875, and 241.880, within the specified time and in a manner satisfactory to the Commissioner (or within such further time as the Commissioner may approve in writing), the interest allowance in such cash payment shall be computed only to the date on which the particular required action should have been taken or to which it was extended.

(2) By deducting from the total of the items computed under paragraph (b)(1) of this section the following items:

(i) Any amount received by the lender on account of the loan after the date of default.

(ii) Any net income received by the lender from the property covered by the note or security instrument and not applied to prior debts held by the lender.

(iii) The sum of the cash items retained by the lender pursuant to § 241.880(h) (1) and (2).

[45 FR 57987, Aug. 29, 1980, as amended at 80 FR 51469, Aug. 25, 2015]

§ 241.890 Characteristics of debentures.

Debentures issued in settlement of insurance claims under this subpart shall have the same characteristics and the same requirements for registration and redemption as those issued pursuant to subpart B of this part except that debentures shall bear interest at the rate in effect as of the date the commitment was issued, or as of the date the loan was first endorsed for insurance, whichever rate is higher, and shall mature 10 years from the date of issue which date shall be the date of execution of the assignment of the loan to the Commissioner.

§241.893 Cash adjustment.

Any difference of less than $50 between the amount of debentures to be issued to the lender and the total amount of the lender's claim, as approved by the Commissioner, may be adjusted by the issuance of a check in payment thereof.

[59 FR 49817, Sept. 30, 1994]

ASSIGNMENTS

§241.895 Assignment of insured loans.

(a) An insured loan may be transferred only to a transferee who is a lender approved by the Commissioner. Upon such transfer and the assumption by the transferee of all obligations under the contract of insurance the transferor shall be released from its obligations under the contract of insurance.

(b) The contract of insurance shall terminate with respect to loans described in paragraph (a) of this section upon the happening of either of the following events:

(1) The transfer or pledge of the insured loan to any person, firm or corporation, public or private, other than an approved lender.

(2) The disposal by a lender of any partial interest in the insured loan to other than an approved lender.

EXTENSION OF TIME

§241.897 Actions to be taken by lender.

With respect to any action required of the lender within a period of time prescribed by this subpart, the Commissioner may extend such period.

RIGHTS IN HOUSING FUND

§241.900 No vested right in fund.

Neither the lender nor the borrower shall have any vested or other right in the General Insurance Fund.

§241.905 Effect of amendments.

The regulations in this subpart may be amended by the Commissioner at any time and from time to time in whole or in part, but such amendment shall not adversely affect the interests of a lender under the contract of insurance on any loan already insured and shall not adversely affect the interests of a lender on any loan to be insured on which the Commissioner has made a commitment to insure.

Subpart E—Insurance for Equity Loans and Acquisition Loans—Eligibility Requirements

SOURCE: 57 FR 12037, Apr. 8, 1992, unless otherwise noted.

§241.1000 Purpose and scope.

(a) Section 231 of the Emergency Low Income Housing Preservation Act of 1989 ("ELIHPA") amended the National Housing Act by adding a new subsection (f) to section 241. This section authorizes the Secretary to provide insurance for an equity loan as a vehicle for the owner of an eligible multifamily project to capture a portion of the project's equity, in connection with a plan of action approved by the Commissioner under ELIHPA.

(b) Section 602 of the Low-Income Housing Preservation and Resident Homeownership Act of 1990 ("LIHPRHA") amended section 241 by expanding its scope to include both equity loans for owners, and acquisition loans for purchasers, under a plan of action approved under the provisions of the 1990 Act, and by making other changes. The provisions of section 241(f) as amended by LIHPRHA are applicable to owners with plans of action being processed under part 248, subpart B of this chapter, which implements LIHPRHA.

(c) The provisions of section 241(f) of the Act as they were in effect prior to LIHPRHA remain in effect for owners with plans of action being processed under part 248, subpart C of this chapter, which implements ELIHPA.

(d) The insurance of an equity loan or acquisition loan under subpart E of this part may be provided only as a

409

specific element of a plan of action approved by the Commissioner under part 248 of this chapter and is not available under any other departmental program.

(e) Unless otherwise indicated, the provisions of subparts E and F of this part are applicable to loans insured in connection with plans of action being processed under either subpart B or C of part 248 of this chapter.

(f) An owner or purchaser may obtain both a rehabilitation loan under subpart A of this part and an equity loan or acquisition loan under subpart E of this part.

§ 241.1005 Definitions.

(a) All of the definitions of § 241.1 apply to equity and acquisition loans insured under subpart E of this part except the following definitions:

§ 241.1(i)—Borrower;
§ 241.1(k)—Energy conserving improvements;
§ 241.1(1)—Solar energy system.

(b) As used in subpart E of this part, the following terms have the meaning indicated:

Acquisition loan means a loan or advance of credit made to a purchaser of eligible low income housing which is made for the purpose of implementing a plan of action approved in accordance with part 248 of this chapter.

Borrower means the owner or qualified purchaser of an eligible low income housing project, which owner receives and becomes primarily obligated for the repayment of an equity loan. With respect to loans insured in connection with a plan of action under part 248, subpart C of this chapter, the term includes a public entity, a nonprofit organization or a limited equity cooperative, which entity is purchasing an eligible low income housing project by means of an equity loan and is obligated for the payment of the equity loan.

Eligible low income housing has the same meaning as provided at § 248.101 or § 248.201 of this chapter, with respect to loans insured in connection with plans of action under subparts B or C of part 248 of this chapter.

Equity means, for purpose of subparts E and F of this part only, the difference between the fair market value

of the project as determined by the Commissioner and the outstanding indebtedness relating to the property.

Equity Loan means a loan or advance of credit to the owner of an eligible low income housing project which is made for the purpose of implementing a plan of action approved in accordance with part 248 of this chapter.

Extension preservation equity has the same meaning as provided at § 248.101 of this chapter.

Limited equity cooperative means a tenant cooperative corporation which, in a manner acceptable to the Commissioner, restricts the initial and resale price of the shares of stock in the cooperative corporation so that the shares remain affordable to low-income families and moderate income families.

Low-income families has the same meaning as provided at § 248.101 of this chapter.

Moderate income families has the same meaning as provided at § 248.101 of this chapter.

Plan of action has the same meaning as provided at § 248.101 or § 248.201 of this chapter.

Preservation equity has the same meaning as provided at § 248.101 of this chapter.

Priority purchaser has the same meaning as provided at § 248.101 of this chapter.

Qualified Purchaser has the same meaning as provided at § 248.101 of this chapter.

§ 241.1010 Feasibility letter.

(a) *Request for study.* The owner may request the Commissioner to undertake a feasibility analysis of an equity or acquisition loan, and issue a feasibility letter. At the discretion of the Commissioner the feasibility analysis may be undertaken or denied.

(b) *Findings.* The issuance of a feasibility letter indicates completion of the Commissioner's preliminary analysis for the insurance of an equity or acquisition loan. The feasibility letter shall contain the Commissioner's estimate of the supportable loan amount, based upon the project's equity in the case of an equity loan and based on the project's purchase price in the case of an acquisition loan, but such feasibility letter shall neither constitute a commitment to insure nor bind the Commissioner in any other manner.

(c) *Fee.* The Commissioner shall not charge a fee for undertaking a feasibility analysis or for the issuance of a feasibility letter.

§241.1015 Processing of applications and required fees.

(a) *Application.* An application for the issuance of a firm commitment for insurance of an equity or acquisition loan on a project shall be submitted by an approved lender and by the owner or purchaser of the project to the Commissioner on a form prescribed by the Commissioner. No application shall be considered unless the exhibits called for by such forms are furnished.

(b) *Commitment fees.* An application for a firm commitment shall be accompanied by the payment of an application-commitment fee of $5.00 per thousand dollars of the requested loan amount to be insured.

[61 FR 14417, Apr. 1, 1996]

§241.1020 Commitments.

(a) *Firm commitment.* The issuance of a firm commitment indicates the Commissioner's approval of the application for insurance and sets forth the terms and conditions upon which the equity or acquisition loan will be insured. The firm commitment may provide for the insurance of advances of the equity or acquisition loan immediately upon endorsement of the note.

(b) *Term of commitment.* (1) A firm commitment is effective for whatever term is specified in the text of the commitment.

(2) The term of a firm commitment may be extended in such manner as the Commissioner may prescribe.

(c) *Reopening of expired commitments.* An expired firm commitment may be reopened if a request for reopening is received by the Commissioner within 90 days of the expiration of the commitment. The reopening request shall be accompanied by a fee of 50 cents per thousand dollars of the amount of the expired commitment. If the reopening request is not received by the Commissioner within the required 90-day period, a new application, accompanied

by the required application and commitment fee, must be submitted.

[61 FR 14417, Apr. 1, 1996]

§241.1025 Refund of fees.

If the amount of the commitment issued is less than the amount applied for, the Commissioner shall refund the excess amount of the application and commitment fees submitted by the applicant. If an application is rejected before it is assigned for processing, or in such other instances as the Commissioner may determine, the entire application and commitment fees or any portion thereof may be returned to the applicant. Commitment and reopening fees may also be refunded to the applicant, in whole or in part, in such other instances as the Commissioner may determine.

§241.1030 Mortgage insurance premiums.

The lender, upon endorsement of the note, shall pay the Commissioner a first mortgage insurance premium equal to 0.5 percent of the original face amount of the equity or acquisition loan.

(a) If the date of the first principal payment is more than one year following the date of endorsement, the lender upon each anniversary of such endorsement date, shall pay a premium equal to 0.5 percent of the original face amount of the loan. On the date of the first principal payment, the lender shall pay another premium equal to 0.5 percent of the average outstanding principal obligation of the loan for the following year which shall be adjusted so as to accord with such date and so that the aggregate of said premiums shall equal the sum of:

(1) 0.5 percent of the average outstanding principal obligation of the loan for the year following the date of endorsement; and

(2) 0.5 percent per annum of the average outstanding principal obligation of the loan for the period from the first anniversary of the date of endorsement to one year following the date of the first principal payment.

(b) If the date of the first principal payment is one year or less than one year following the date of endorsement, the lender, upon such first principal payment date, shall pay a second premium equal to 0.5 percent of the average outstanding principal obligation of the loan for the following year which shall be adjusted so as to accord with such date and so that the aggregate of the said two premiums shall equal the sum of:

(1) 0.5 percent per annum of the average outstanding principal obligation of the loan for the period from the date of endorsement to the date of the first principal payment; and

(2) 0.5 percent of the average outstanding principal obligation of the loan for the year following the date of the first payment following the date of the first principal payment.

(c) Until the equity or acquisition loan is paid in full or until receipt by the Commissioner of an application for insurance benefits, or until the contract of insurance is otherwise terminated with the consent of the Commissioner, the lender on each anniversary date of the first principal payment, shall pay an annual insurance premium equal to 0.5 percent of the average outstanding principal obligation of the loan for the year following the date on which such premium becomes payable.

(d) The premiums payable on or after the date of the first principal payment shall be calculated in accordance with the amortizing provisions without taking into account delinquent payments or prepayments.

(e) Premiums shall be payable in cash or in debentures at par plus accrued interest. All premiums are payable in advance and no refund can be made of any portion thereof except as hereinafter provided in subpart E of this part.

§ 241.1035 Charges by lender.

(a) The lender may collect from the borrower the amount of the fees provided for by subpart E of this part.

(b) The lender may also collect from the borrower an initial service charge, as reimbursement for the cost of closing the transaction, in an amount not to exceed 2 percent of the original principal amount of the loan.

(c) Any charges to be collected by the lender in addition to those prescribed in paragraphs (a) and (b) of this section, shall be subject to the prior approval of the Commissioner.

§ 241.1040 Eligible lenders.

Lenders approved as mortgagees under §§ 202.6, 202.7 or 202.9 of this chapter are eligible for insurance of equity loans under this subpart.

[62 FR 20088, Apr. 24, 1997]

§ 241.1045 Note and security form.

The lender shall present for insurance a note and security instrument on forms approved by the Commissioner for use in the jurisdiction in which the property is located, which shall not be changed without the prior approval of the Commissioner. The security instrument shall provide for accelerated repayment at the request of the Commissioner pursuant to § 241.1046(b).

§ 241.1046 Rental assistance.

(a) When underwriting an equity or acquisition loan under subpart E of this part, the Commissioner may assume that the rental assistance provided in accordance with a plan of action approved under subparts B or C of part 248 of this chapter will be extended for the full term of the contract entered into under the plan of action.

(b) In the event that rental assistance is not extended under part 248 of this chapter, or the Commissioner is unable to develop a revised package of incentives to the owner comparable to those received under the original approved plan of action, the Commissioner may require the mortgagee to accelerate the debt of the equity or acquisition loan.

(c) If the Commissioner is unable to extend the term of rental assistance for the full term of the contract entered into under part 248 of this chapter, the Commissioner is authorized to take such actions as the Commissioner deems appropriate to avoid default, avoid disruption of the sound ownership and management of the property or otherwise minimize the cost to the Federal Government.

§ 241.1050 Method of loan payment.

The loan shall provide for monthly payments on the first day of each month on account of interest and principal and shall provide for payments in accordance with the amortization plan as agreed upon by the borrower, the lender, and the Commissioner.

§241.1055 Date of first payment to principal.

The date for first payment to principal shall be established by the Commissioner.

§241.1060 Maturity.

(a) Equity loans shall have a term not to exceed 40 years; and

(b) Acquisition loans shall have a term of 40 years.

[58 FR 37814, July 13, 1993]

§241.1065 Maximum loan amount—loans insured in connection with a plan of action under subpart C of part 248 of this chapter.

The amount of the equity loan shall not exceed ninety percent of the owner's equity in the project, as determined by the Commissioner. Notwithstanding the above, the equity loan shall not exceed an amount which, when added to the existing indebtedness on the property, can be supported by 90 percent of the projected net operating income of the project, as determined by the Commissioner. The Commissioner, in making a determination regarding the amount of an equity loan and sums available to service said loan, shall take into account the fact that the project's income may increase within the limits established by §248.233(d) of this chapter.

§241.1067 Maximum loan amount—loans insured in connection with a plan of action under subpart B of part 248 of this chapter.

(a) The amount of the equity loan shall not exceed:

(1) The amount of rehabilitation costs as determined under an approved plan of action and related charges; plus

(2) The lesser of 70 percent of the extension preservation equity of the project; or

(3) The amount the Commissioner determines can be supported by the project on the basis of an 8 percent return on extension preservation equity, assuming normal debt service coverage. To the extent practicable, equity loans shall have amortization provisions which will support the maximum loan amount authorized under this section.

(b) The amount of the acquisition loan shall not exceed:

(1) The amount of rehabilitation costs as determined under an approved plan of action and related charges; plus

(2) Ninety-five percent of the transfer preservation equity of the project; and

(3) If the purchaser is a priority purchaser, the loan may include any expenses associated with the acquisition, loan closing, and implementation of the plan of action, subject to the approval of the Commissioner.

[58 FR 37814, July 13, 1993]

§241.1068 Renegotiation of an equity loan.

The Commissioner shall renegotiate and modify the terms of an equity loan insured under this subpart at the request of the owner of the project for which a loan closing occurred if—

(a) The loan closing occurred between September 28, 1992 and January 26, 1993;

(b) The loan was made pursuant to a plan of action submitted under subpart C of part 248 of this chapter; and

(c) The plan of action was accepted by the Commissioner for processing in December 1991.

[58 FR 37814, July 13, 1993]

§241.1069 Escrow requirements.

(a) An equity loan provided in connection with a plan of action under subpart B of part 248 of this chapter shall provide for the lender to deposit, on behalf of the borrower, 10 percent of the loan amount in an escrow account, controlled by the Commissioner or a State housing finance agency approved by the Commissioner, which shall be made available to the borrower upon the expiration of the 5-year period beginning on the date the loan is made, subject to compliance with §248.147 of this chapter.

(b) An equity loan provided in connection with a plan of action under either subpart B or subpart C of part 248 of this chapter shall provide for the lender to phase in advances to reflect project rent levels.

§ 241.1070 Agreed interest rate.

The equity or acquisition loan shall bear interest at the rate agreed upon by the borrower and the lender.

§ 241.1080 Eligibility of title.

In order for the project to be eligible for insurance, the Commissioner shall determine that the title to the property is vested in the borrower as of the date the security instrument is filed for record. The title evidence will be examined by the Commissioner and the endorsement of the credit instrument for insurance shall be evidence of its acceptability.

§ 241.1085 Title evidence.

(a) Upon insurance of the loan, the lender shall furnish to the Commissioner a policy of title insurance as provided in paragraph (a)(1) of this section. If the lender is unable to furnish such policy for reasons satisfactory to the Commissioner, the lender shall furnish such evidence of title as provided in paragraphs (a)(2), (3) or (4) of this section as the Commissioner may require. Any policy of title insurance, or evidence of title required under this section shall be furnished without expense to the Commissioner. The acceptable types of title evidence are:

(1) A policy of title insurance issued by a company and in a form satisfactory to the Commissioner. The policy shall name the lender and the Secretary of Housing and Urban Development, as their respective interests may appear, as the insured. The policy shall provide that upon acquisition of title by the lender or the Secretary, it will continue to provide the same coverage as the original policy, and will run to the lender upon its acquisition of the property in extinguishment of the debt, and to the Secretary upon acquisition of the property pursuant to the loan insurance contract.

(2) An abstract of title satisfactory to the Commissioner, prepared by an abstract company or individual engaged in the business of preparing abstracts of title, accompanied by a legal opinion satisfactory to the Commissioner, as to the quality of such title, signed by an attorney at law experienced in the examination of titles;

(3) A Torrens or similar title certification; or

(4) Evidence of title conforming to the standards of a supervising branch of the Government of the United States of America, or of any State or territory thereof.

[57 FR 12037, Apr. 8, 1992, as amended at 58 FR 34217, June 24, 1993]

§ 241.1090 Accumulation of next premium.

The security instrument shall provide for payments by the borrower to the lender on each interest payment date of an amount sufficient to accumulate in the hands of the lender one payment period prior to its due date the next annual insurance premium payable by the lender to the Commissioner. These payments shall continue only as long as the contract of insurance remains in effect.

§ 241.1095 Application of payments.

(a) The security instrument shall provide that all monthly payments to be made by the borrower shall be added together and the aggregate amount shall be paid by the borrower upon each monthly payment date in a single payment. The lender shall apply the payment in the following order:

(1) Premium charges under the contact of insurance;

(2) Interest on the loan; and

(3) Amortization of the principal of the loan.

(b) Any deficiency in the amount of any monthly payments required under paragraph (a) of this section shall constitute a default. The security instrument shall provide for a grace period of 30 days within which time the default must be cured.

§ 241.1100 Prepayment privilege and charges.

(a) *Prepayment privilege.* (1) Except as otherwise provided in paragraph (b) of this section, the security instrument shall contain a provision permitting the borrower to prepay the loan, in whole or in part, upon any interest payment date after giving to the lender 30 days advance notice of its intention to prepay.

(2) If the loan exceeds $200,000, the security instrument may contain a provision for an additional charge in the event of prepayment of principal as may be agreed upon between the borrower and lender. These charges shall not be imposed if the loan is accelerated at the request of the Commissioner, pursuant to §241.1046(b). The borrower shall be permitted to prepay up to 15 percent of the original principal amount of the loan in any one calendar year without any additional charge. A provision for an additional charge in the event of prepayment may not be included in a loan of $200,000 or less.

(b) *Prepayment of bond-financed loan.* Where the lender has obtained the funds for the loan by the issuance and sale of bonds or bond anticipation notes, or both, the loan may contain a prepayment restriction and prepayment penalty charges acceptable to the Commissioner as to term, amount, and conditions.

§241.1105 Late charges.

The note and security instrument may provide for the lender's collection of a late charge, not to exceed 2 cents for each dollar of each payment to interest or principal more than 15 days in arrears, to cover the expense involved in handling delinquent payments. Late charges shall be separately charged to and collected from the borrower and shall not be deducted from any aggregate monthly payment.

§241.1120 Mortgagee's consent.

The holder of an insured mortgage which is recorded prior to the equity or acquisition loan shall not withhold its consent to the equity or acquisition loan (whether or not such equity or acquisition loan is insured by the Commissioner) or the security instrument executed in connection therewith, and may not charge a fee as a condition to its consent to such loan or security instrument.

Subpart F—Insurance for Equity Loans and Acquisition Loans—Contract Rights and Obligations

SOURCE: 57 FR 12040, Apr. 8, 1992, unless otherwise noted.

§241.1200 Cross-references.

(a) *Projects with a HUD-insured or HUD-held mortgage.* (1) All the provisions of part 207, subpart B of this chapter, covering mortgages insured under section 207 of the Act, apply to equity loans or acquisition loans on a project insured under section 241(f) of the Act, except the following provisions:

Sec.
207.251 Definitions.
207.252 First, second and third premium.
207.252a Premiums—operating loss loans.
207.252b Premiums—mortgages insured pursuant to section 223(f) of the Act.
207.252c Premiums—mortgages insured pursuant to section 238(c) of the Act.
207.254 Insurance endorsement.

(2) For the purposes of subpart F of this part, all references in part 207 of this chapter to section 207 of the Act and to the term "mortgage" shall be construed to refer to section 241(f) of the Act and "equity or acquisition loan," respectively.

(b) *Projects without a HUD-insured or HUD-held mortgage.* The provisions of subpart D of this part shall be applicable to a project without a HUD-insured or HUD-held mortgage that is receiving an equity loan or acquisition loan under subpart E of this part in connection with a plan of action approved by the Commissioner under part 248 of this chapter.

(c) All of the definitions in §241.1005 apply to subpart F of this part. In addition, as used in subpart F of this part, the term "contract of insurance" means the agreement evidenced by the Commissioner's insurance endorsement and includes the provisions of subpart F of this part and of the Act.

§241.1205 Payment of insurance benefits.

All the provisions of §207.259 of this chapter relating to insurance benefits shall apply to an equity or acquisition loan insured under subpart F of this part.

[80 FR 51469, Aug. 25, 2015]

§ 241.1210   Condition for payment of insurance benefits.

(a) All of the provisions of § 207.258 of this chapter apply to subpart F of this part, except that, if the holder of the senior insured mortgage institutes a foreclosure action, the lender shall notify the Commissioner in a timely manner of such action. The Commissioner, at its option, may then direct the lender to assign the equity or acquisition loan to the Commissioner, or bid an amount necessary to acquire the project and convey the project to the Commissioner.

(b) If the equity loan or acquisition loan is assigned in accordance with this section, the Commissioner at a foreclosure sale may bid, in addition to amounts otherwise authorized, any sum not in excess of the aggregate unpaid indebtedness secured by the senior insured mortgage and equity or acquisition loan, plus taxes, insurance, foreclosure costs, fees and other expenses.

§ 241.1215   Calculation of insurance benefits.

All of the provisions of § 207.259 of this chapter apply to subpart F of this part, except that if the lender, at the direction of the Commissioner, acquires title to the project at a foreclosure sale instituted by the holder of the senior insured mortgage, the amount of the claim determined under § 207.259(c) of this chapter shall also include an amount bid by the lender to satisfy the senior insured mortgage at the foreclosure sale.

§ 241.1220   Termination of insurance benefits.

All of the provisions of § 207.253a of this chapter apply to subpart F of this part, except that the following shall also constitute grounds for terminating the contract of insurance:

(a) The failure of the lender to notify the Commissioner in a timely manner of a foreclosure action initiated by the holder of the senior insured mortgage; and

(b) The failure of the lender when directed by the Commissioner to assign the equity or acquisition loan or bid an amount necessary to acquire title to the project and convey the project to the Commissioner, in accordance with § 241.1210.

§ 241.1230   No vested right in fund.

Neither the lender nor the borrower shall have any vested or other right in the insurance fund under which the loan is insured.

§ 241.1235   Cross default.

In the event the borrower commits a default under a prior recorded insured mortgage and the holder thereof initiates a foreclosure proceeding, said default under the prior recorded insured mortgage shall constitute a default under the equity or acquisition loan.

§ 241.1245   Insurance endorsement.

(a) *Endorsement.* The Commissioner shall indicate his insurance of the equity loan or acquisition loan by endorsing the original credit instrument and identifying the section of the Act and the regulations under which the loan is insured and the date of insurance.

(b) *Endorsement of phased loan.* In the event the loan is phased, the Commissioner shall indicate his insurance of each amount by endorsing the original credit instrument and identifying the section of the Act and the regulations under which such amount is insured and the date of the insurance.

(c) *Final advance of phased loan.* When all advances of a phased loan have been made and the terms and conditions of the commitment have been complied with to the satisfaction of the Commissioner, the Commissioner shall indicate on the original credit instrument the total of all advances the Commissioner has approved for insurance and again endorse such instrument.

§ 241.1250   Effect of endorsement.

From the date that the equity or acquisition loan is endorsed, the Commissioner and the lender shall be bound by the provisions of subpart F of this part to the same extent as if they had executed a contract including the provisions of subpart F of this part and the applicable sections of the Act.

PART 242—MORTGAGE INSURANCE FOR HOSPITALS

AUTHORITY: 12 U.S.C. 1709, 1710, 1715b, 1715n(f), and 1715u; 42 U.S.C. 3535(d).

SOURCE: 72 FR 67546, Nov. 28, 2007, unless otherwise noted.

Subpart A—General Eligibility Requirements

§ 242.1 Definitions.

As used in this subpart, the following terms shall have the meaning indicated:

Acquisition means the purchase by an eligible mortgagor of an existing hospital facility and ancillary property associated therewith.

Act means the National Housing Act (12 U.S.C. 1701 *et seq.*).

Affiliate means a person or entity which, directly orindirectly, either controls or has the power to control or exert significant influence on the other, or a person and entity both controlled by a third person or entity, which may be a parent entity. Indicia of control include, but are not limited to: Interlocking management or ownership, identity of interests among family members, shared facilities and equipment, common use of employees, or a business entity organized following the suspension or debarment of a person or entity that has the same or similar management, ownership, or principal employees as the suspended, debarred, ineligible, or voluntarily excluded person or entity or as defined in the Medicare reimbursement regulations.

AMPO (Allowance for Making Project Operational) relates to nonprofit projects and means a fund that is primarily for accruals during the course of construction for mortgage insurance premiums (MIPs), taxes, ground rents, property insurance premiums, and assessments, when funds available for these purposes under the Building Loan Agreement have been exhausted; and also for allocation to such accruals after completion of construction, if the income from the hospital at that time is insufficient to meet such accruals. AMPO may also be used for such other purposes as approved by HUD. Any balance remaining unused in the fund at final endorsement will be treated in accordance with § 242.43.

Applicant means a HUD multifamily-approved lender that would be the mortgagee of record.

Capital debt means the outstanding indebtedness used for the construction, rehabilitation, or acquisition of the physical property and equipment of a hospital, including those financing costs approved by HUD.

Chronic convalescent and rest means skilled nursing services, intermediate care services, respite care services, hospice services, and other services of a similar nature.

Construction means the creation of a new or replacement hospital facility, the substantial rehabilitation of an existing facility, or the limited rehabilitation of an existing facility. The cost of acquiring new or replacement equipment may be included in the cost of construction.

Days of cash on hand means the number of days of operating cash available to the hospital, calculated pursuant to standards determined by HUD.

Debt service coverage ratio is a measure of a hospital's ability to pay interest and principal with cash generated from current operations. Debt service ratio is calculated as follows: Debt Service Coverage Ratio (total debt service coverage on all long-term capital debt) equals the excess of revenues over expenses (not-for-profit) or net income (for-profit) plus interest expense plus depreciation expense plus amortization expense, all divided by current portion of long-term debt (including capital leases) from the previous year's audited financial statement plus interest expense. The calculation can be expressed as:

$$\frac{\text{(Excess of revenues over expenses OR net income)} + \text{interest expense} + \text{depreciation expense} + \text{amortization expense}}{\text{Current portion of long-term debt [prior year, including capital leases]} + \text{interest expense}}$$

Hard costs means the costs of the construction and equipment, including construction-related fees such as architect and construction manager fees.

Hospital means a facility that has been proposed for approval or has been approved by HUD under the provisions of this subpart, and:

(1) That provides community services for inpatient medical care of the sick or injured (including obstetrical care);

(2) Where not more than 50 percent of the total patient days during any year are customarily assignable to the categories of chronic convalescent and rest, drug and alcoholic, epileptic, mentally deficient, mental, nervous and mental, and tuberculosis, except that the 50 percent patient day restriction does not apply to Critical Access Hospitals (hospitals designated as such under the Medicare Rural Hospital Flexibility Program) between January 28, 2008 and July 31, 2011.

(3) That is a facility licensed or regulated by the state (or, if there is no such state law providing for such licensing or regulation by the state, by the municipality or other political subdivision in which the facility is located) and is:

(i) A public facility owned by a state or unit of local government or by an instrumentality thereof, or owned by a public benefit corporation established by a state or unit of local government or by an instrumentality thereof;

(ii) A proprietary facility; or

(iii) A facility of a private nonprofit corporation or association.

Identity of interest means a relationship that must be disclosed and may be prohibited pursuant to the requirements of the Regulatory Agreement. Examples of a prohibited Identity of Interest relationship are, but are not limited to, a financial or family relationship between the mortgagor (which includes but is not limited to an officer, director, or partner of the mortgagor) and general contractor, subcontractor, seller of the land or property, any consultants, or other parties to the transaction.

Limited rehabilitation means additions, expansion, remodeling, renovation, modernization, repair, and alteration of existing buildings, including acquisition of new or replacement equipment, in cases where the hard costs of construction and equipment are less than 20 percent of the mortgage amount.

Mortgage means such classes of first liens as are commonly given to secure advances on, or the unpaid purchase price of, real estate under the laws of the state in which the real estate is located, together with any mortgage note secured thereby. The mortgage may be in the form of one or more trust mortgages or mortgage indentures or deeds of trust securing notes, bonds, or other mortgage notes; and, by the same instrument or by a separate instrument, it may create a security interest in the personalty, including, but not limited to, the equipment, whether or not the equipment is attached to the realty, and in the revenues and receivables of the hospital.

Mortgagee or lender means the applicant for insurance or the original lender under a mortgage.

Mortgagor means the original borrower under a mortgage and its successors and assigns.

Mortgage Reserve Fund means a trust account, or an account held by the mortgagee, for and on behalf of the mortgagor, to which the mortgagor contributes and from which withdrawals must be approved by HUD. The purpose of the fund is to provide HUD a means to assist the hospital to avoid mortgage defaults and to preserve the value of the mortgaged property and the hospital's business.

Most recent audited financial statement means the audited financial statement required under the regulatory agreement for the prior fiscal year.

Net income means the net income of a for-profit entity, or, in the case of a nonprofit entity, the excess of revenues less expenses.

419

Non-operating revenues and expenses are those revenues and expenses not directly related to patient care, hospital-related patient services, or the sale of hospital-related goods. Examples of items classified as non-operating are state and federal income tax, general contributions, gains and losses from investments, unrestricted income from endowment funds, and income from related entities.

Classification of items as operating or non-operating shall follow written guidance by HUD.

Operating margin is operating income divided by operating revenue, where:

(1) *Operating revenue* is the revenue from the core patient care operations of the hospital. It includes revenues from the provision of such items as patient care (including, but not limited to, hospital-based nursing home and physicians' clinics); transfers from temporarily restricted accounts that are used for current operating expenses; and patient-related activities such as the operation of the cafeteria, parking facilities, television services to patients, sale of medical scrap or waste, etc. (Additional sources of revenue, which are classified as non-operating, are excluded from this measure, provided, however, at HUD's discretion, that revenue that has historically been received reliably and is expected to continue to be received may be considered operating revenue for underwriting purposes); and

(2) *Operating income* is operating revenue minus operating expenses, where operating expenses are the expenses incurred in providing patient care, including such items as salaries, supplies, and the cost of capital.

Parent means an organization or entity that controls or has a controlling interest in another organization or entity.

Personalty means all furniture, furnishings, equipment, machinery, building materials, appliances, goods, supplies, tools, books, records (whether in written or electronic form), computer equipment (hardware and software) and other tangible or electronically stored personal property (other than fixtures) that are owned or leased by the borrower or the lessee now or in the future in connection with the ownership, management, or operation of the land or the improvements or are located on the land or in the improvements, and any operating agreements relating to the land or the improvements, and any surveys, plans, specifications, and contracts for architectural, engineering, and construction services relating to the land or the improvements, chooses in action and all other intangible property and rights relating to the operation of, or used in connection with, the land or the improvements, including all governmental permits relating to any activities on the land. Personalty also includes all tangible and intangible personal property used for health care (such as major movable equipment and systems), accounts, licenses, bed authorities, certificates of need required to operate the hospital and to receive benefits and reimbursements under provider agreements with Medicaid, Medicare, state and local programs, payments from health care insurers and any other assistance providers ("Receivables"); all permits, instruments, rents, lease and contract rights, and equipment leases relating to the use, operation, maintenance, repair, and improvement of the hospital. Generally, intangibles shall also include all cash and cash escrow funds, such as but not limited to: Depreciation reserve fund or mortgage reserve fund accounts, bank accounts, residual receipt accounts, all contributions, donations, gifts, grants, bequests, and endowment funds by donors, and all other revenues and accounts receivable from whatever source paid or payable. All personalty shall be securitized with appropriate UCC filings and any excluded personalty shall be indicated in the Regulatory Agreement.

Preapplication meeting means a meeting among HUD, a potential mortgagee (applicant), and a potential mortgagor for mortgage insurance where there has been a positive Preliminary Review of the proposed project. The preapplication meeting is an opportunity for the potential mortgagee and mortgagor to summarize the proposed project, for HUD to summarize the application process, and for issues that could affect the eligibility or underwriting of the proposed loan to be identified and discussed.

Preliminary Review Letter means a letter from HUD to a potential applicant communicating the result of the Preliminary Review. The letter may state that an application for mortgage insurance would probably not be successful and provide the reasons for this determination, or state that no factors that would cause an application to be rejected have been identified, and therefore there appears to be no bar to the applicant proceeding to a preapplication meeting.

Project means the construction (which may include replacement of an existing hospital facility), or the substantial or limited rehabilitation of an eligible hospital, including equipment, which has been proposed for approval or has been approved by HUD under the provisions of this subpart, including the financing and refinancing, if any, plus all related activities involved in completing the improvements to the property. However, in particular closing documents, "project" may be used to mean the mortgagor entity, the operation of the mortgagor, the facility, or all of the mortgaged property, depending on the context in which the term "project" is used.

Refinancing means the discharging of the existing capital debt of a hospital through entering into new debt.

Regulatory Agreement means the agreement under which all mortgagors shall be regulated by HUD, as long as HUD is the insurer or holder of the mortgage, in a published format determined by HUD, and such additional covenants and restrictions as may be determined necessary by HUD on a case-by-case basis.

Secretary means the Secretary of Housing and Urban Development or his or her authorized representatives.

Section 242/223(f) refers to a loan insured under Section 242 of the Act pursuant to Section 223(f) of the Act.

Security instrument means a mortgage, deed of trust, and any other security for the indebtedness, and shall be deemed to be the mortgage as defined by the National Housing Act, as amended, implementing regulations, and HUD directives.

Service area means that geographical area, identified by zip codes, from which a substantial majority of a hospital's patients derive.

Soft costs means reasonable and customary legal, organizational, consulting, and such other costs associated with effecting the proposed project and its financing or refinancing, including, but not limited to, interest capitalized during construction; permanent financing fees; initial service charge; tax; title and recording expenses; special tax assessments; AMPO; insurance costs during construction; FHA fees and charges, including application, commitment, and inspection fees; mortgage insurance premium for advances during construction; prepayment penalties associated with retiring the hospital's existing bonds; and termination costs for interest rate protection facilities that are integrated into the original financing, as applicable.

State includes the several states, Puerto Rico, the District of Columbia, Guam, the Trust Territory of the Pacific Islands, American Samoa, and the United States Virgin Islands.

Substantial rehabilitation means additions, expansion, remodeling, renovation, modernization, repair, and alteration of existing buildings, including acquisition of new or replacement equipment, in cases where the hard costs of construction and equipment are equal to or greater than 20 percent of the mortgage amount.

Surplus Cash means any cash remaining after all of the following conditions have been met:

(1) Final endorsement of the HUD-insured note has occurred;

(2) Mortgage payments for the preceding 12 months have been made when due, including any grace period;

(3) The Debt Service Coverage Ratio is greater than or equal to 1.50 in the most recent audited financial statements and as of the date of distribution;

(4) Days in Accounts Receivable are less than or equal to 80 in the most recent audited financial statements and as of the date of distribution;

(5) The average payment period is less than or equal to 80 in the most recent audited financial statements and as of the date of distribution;

(6) The Mortgage Reserve Fund (MRF) is fully funded as of the date of the distribution in conformity with the MRF schedule;

(7) All income, property, and statutory employer payroll taxes and employee payroll withholding contributions (including penalties and interest, if applicable) have been deposited as of the date of the distribution, as required;

(8) The Current Ratio is greater than or equal to 1.50 in the most recent audited financial statements and immediately after the distribution;

(9) Days of cash on hand are greater than or equal to 21 days in the most recent audited financial statements and immediately after the distribution;

(10) The distribution may not be more than 50 percent of Net Income as reflected in the most recent audited financial statements, unless the Mortgagor has an equity financing ratio equal to or greater than 20 percent in the most recent audited financial statements and immediately after the distribution; and

(11) The Equity less any assets excluded from the mortgaged property is greater than 0.00 in the most recent audited financial statements and immediately after the distribution is made. As used in this definition:

"Most recent audited financial statements" refers to the audited financial statement required under section 242.58 for the prior fiscal year;

"Net Income" means Net Income for for-profit entities; Excess of Revenues over Expenses for not-for-profit entities; and Excess of Revenues over Expenses before Capital Grants, Contributions, and Additions to Permanent Endowment for governmental entities; and

"Equity financing ratio" means (Equity less any assets excluded from the mortgaged property)/(total assets less any assets excluded from the mortgaged property). Equity is defined as Equity for a for-profit entity, Total Net Assets for not-for-profit entities, and Total Net Assets for governmental entities.

[72 FR 67546, Nov. 28, 2007, as amended at 73 FR 35922, June 25, 2008; 78 FR 8341, Feb. 5, 2013]

§ 242.2 Program financial self-sufficiency.

The Commissioner shall administer the Section 242 program in such a way as to encourage financial self-sufficiency and actuarial soundness; i.e., to avoid mortgage defaults and claims for insurance benefits in order to protect the mortgage insurance fund.

§ 242.3 Encouragement of certain programs.

The activities and functions provided for in this part shall be carried out so as to encourage provision of comprehensive health care, including outpatient and preventive care as well as hospitalization, to a defined population, and in the case of public and certain not-for-profit hospitals, to encourage programs that are undertaken to provide essential health care services to all residents of a community regardless of ability to pay.

§ 242.4 Eligible hospitals.

(a) The hospital to be financed with a mortgage insured under this part shall involve the construction of a new hospital, the substantial rehabilitation (or replacement) of an existing hospital, the limited rehabilitation of an existing hospital, the acquisition of an existing hospital, or the refinancing of the capital debt of an existing hospital pursuant to Section 223(a)(7) or Section 223(f).

(b) This part applies only to applications for FHA mortgage insurance submitted after a pre-application meeting (as defined in § 242.1) with HUD that occurred on and after January 28, 2008. HUD's regulations and practices prior to January 28, 2008 apply to applications for FHA mortgage insurance submitted after a pre-application meeting that occurred before January 28, 2008.

[72 FR 67546, Nov. 28, 2007, as amended at 78 FR 8341, Feb. 5, 2013]

§ 242.5 Eligible mortgagees/lenders.

The lender requirements set forth in 24 CFR part 202 regarding approval, recertification, withdrawal of approval, approval for servicing, report requirements, and conditions for supervised mortgagees, nonsupervised mortgagees, investing mortgagees, and governmental and similar institutions, apply to these programs.

§ 242.6 Property requirements.

The mortgage, to be eligible for insurance, shall be on property located in a state, as defined in § 242.1. The mortgage shall cover real estate in which the mortgagor has one of the following interests:

(a) A fee simple title;

(b) A lease for not less than 99 years that is renewable; or

(c) A lease having a term of not less than 50 years to run from the date the mortgage is executed.

§ 242.7 Maximum mortgage amounts.

The mortgage shall involve a principal obligation not in excess of 90 percent of HUD's estimate of the replacement cost of the hospital, including the equipment to be used in its operation when the proposed improvements are completed and the equipment is installed.

§ 242.8 Standards for licensure and methods of operation.

The Secretary shall require satisfactory evidence that the hospital will be located in a state or political subdivision of a state with reasonable minimum standards of licensure and methods of operation for hospitals, and satisfactory assurance that such standards will be applied and enforced with respect to the hospital.

§ 242.9 Physician ownership.

Ownership of an interest in the mortgagor by physicians or other professionals practicing in the hospital is permitted within limits determined by HUD to avoid insurance risks that may be associated with such ownership. The Commissioner shall determine if the proposed mortgagor will be at low risk for violation of regulations of the U.S. Department of Health and Human Services, other federal regulations, and state regulations governing kickbacks, self-referrals, and other issues that could increase the risk of eventual default. The Commissioner's determination shall be based on an unqualified legal opinion as to compliance with applicable federal law, among other considerations.

§ 242.10 Eligible mortgagors.

The mortgagor shall be a public mortgagor (i.e., an owner of a public facility), a private nonprofit corporation or association, or a profit-motivated mortgagor meeting the definition of "hospital" in § 242.1. The mortgagor shall be approved by HUD and, except in those cases where the hospital is leased as permitted in § 242.72, shall possess the powers necessary and incidental to operating a hospital. Eligible proprietary or profit-motivated mortgagors may include for-profit corporations, limited partnerships, and limited liability corporations and companies, but may not include natural persons, joint ventures, and general partnerships. Any proposed mortgagor must demonstrate that it has a continuity of organization commensurate with the term of the mortgage loan being insured. For new organizations, or those whose continuity is necessarily dependent upon an individual or individuals, broad community participation is required.

[72 FR 67546, Nov. 28, 2007, as amended at 73 FR 35922, June 25, 2008]

§ 242.11 Regulatory compliance required.

An application for insurance of a mortgage under this part shall be considered only in connection with a hospital that is in substantial compliance with regulations of the Department of Health and Human Services and the regulations of the applicable state governing the operation and reimbursement of hospitals. A hospital that is under investigation by any state or federal agency for statutory or regulatory violations is not eligible so long as the investigation is unresolved, unless HUD determines that the investigation is minor in nature; that is, the investigation is unlikely to result in substantial liabilities or to otherwise substantially harm the creditworthiness of the hospital.

§ 242.13 Parents and affiliates.

As a condition of issuing a commitment, HUD may require corporate parents, affiliates, or principals of the proposed mortgagor to provide assurances, guarantees, or collateral to protect HUD's interests. The Commissioner may also require financial and operational information on the parent, other businesses owned by the parent, or affiliates of the proposed mortgagor and may also require a parent or affiliate to be regulated by HUD as to certain actions that could impact on the insurance of a mortgage loan for the benefit of the hospital.

§ 242.14 Mortgage reserve fund.

As a condition of issuing a commitment, HUD shall require establishment of a Mortgage Reserve Fund (MRF). The mortgagor shall be required to make contributions to the MRF such that, with fund earnings, the MRF will build to one year of debt service at 5 years following commencement of amortization, increasing thereafter to 2 years of debt service on and after 10 years following commencement of amortization according to a schedule established by HUD, unless HUD determines that a different schedule of contributions is appropriate based on the mortgagor's risk profile, reimbursement structure, or other characteristics. In particular, hospitals that receive cost-based reimbursement may be required to have MRFs that build to more than 2 years of debt service. Expenditures from the fund are made at HUD's sole discretion or in accordance with the mortgagor's MRF Schedule. Upon termination of insurance, the balance of the MRF shall be returned to the mortgagor, provided that all obligations to HUD have been met.

§ 242.15 Limitation on refinancing existing indebtedness.

(a) Some existing capital debt may be refinanced with the proceeds of a section 242-insured loan; however, the hard costs of construction and equipment must represent at least 20 percent of the total mortgage amount.

(b) In the case of a loan insured under Section 242/223(f), there is no requirement for hard costs. However, if there are hard costs, such costs must total less than 20 percent of the total mortgage amount.

[78 FR 8341, Feb. 5, 2013]

Subpart B—Application Procedures and Commitments

§ 242.16 Applications.

(a) *Application process*—(1) *Market need.* The approval process entails a determination of the market need of the proposal and stresses, on a market-wide basis, the impact of the proposed facility on, and its relationship to, other health care facilities and services (particularly other hospitals with mortgages insured under this part and hospitals that have a disproportionate share of Medicaid and uninsured patients or provide a substantial amount of charity care); the number and percentage of any excess beds; and demographic projections. Generally, Section 242 insurance may support start-up hospitals or major expansions of existing hospitals only if existing hospital capacity or services are clearly not adequate to meet the needs of the population in the service area.

(i) If the state has an official procedure for determining need for hospitals, HUD shall require that such procedure be followed before the application for insurance is submitted, and that the application document that need has also been established under that procedure.

(ii) The following factors are relevant in evaluating market need for the project and should be addressed, as applicable, in the study of market need and feasibility submitted with the application. Because each hospital presents a unique situation, there is no formula or cutoff level that applies to all applications:

(A) Service area definition;

(B) Existing or proposed hospital;

(C) Designation as sole community provider, Critical Access Hospital, or rural referral center;

(D) Community-wide use rates (discharges and days/1000);

(E) Statewide use rates (for benchmarking purposes);

(F) Current population and 5-year projection by age cohort;

(G) Staffed versus licensed beds;

(H) Applicant hospital's occupancy rate;

(I) Competitors' occupancy rates;

(J) Outpatient volume;

(K) Availability of emergency services;

(L) Teaching hospital status;

(M) Services offered by hospitals in the service area;

(N) Migration of patients out of the service area;

(O) Planned construction at other facilities in the region;

(P) Historical market share by major service category;

(Q) Disproportionate Share Hospital designation; and

(R) Distance to other hospitals.

(2) *Operating margin and debt service coverage ratio.* (i) Hospitals with an aggregate operating margin of less than 0.00 when calculated from the three most recent annual audited financial statements are not eligible for Section 242 insurance, unless HUD determines, based on the financial data in those statements, that the hospital has achieved a financial turnaround resulting in a positive operating margin in the most recent year, calculated using classifications of items as operating or non-operating in accordance with guidance that shall be provided in written directives by HUD. In any event, HUD shall not issue an insurance commitment for any hospital in a turnaround situation that has not achieved 2 consecutive years of positive operating margin immediately prior to issuance of the commitment.

(ii) Hospitals with an average debt service coverage ratio of less than 1.25 in the 3 most recent audited years are not eligible for Section 242 insurance, unless HUD determines, based on the audited financial data, that the hospital has achieved a financial turnaround resulting in a debt service coverage ratio of at least 1.4 in the most recent year. In cases of refinancing at a lower interest rate, HUD may authorize the use of the projected debt service requirement in lieu of the historical debt service in calculating the debt service coverage ratios for each of the prior 3 years. In cases where HUD authorizes the use of the projected debt service requirement in lieu of the historical debt service to determine the

debt service coverage ratio, hospitals must have an average debt service coverage ratio of 1.4 or greater.

(3) *Threshold requirements—refinancing candidates.* For an application to be considered for refinancing pursuant to Section 223(f), a hospital must meet the following requirements in lieu of those described in paragraph (a)(2) of this section:

(i) The hospital must have an aggregate operating margin and average debt service coverage ratio as follows:

(A) The hospital must have an aggregate operating margin of at least zero percent, when calculated from the three most recent annual audited financial statements.

(B) The hospital must have an average debt service coverage ratio of at least 1.4 when calculated from the three most recent annual audited financial statements; or

(ii) If the requirements of paragraphs (a)(3)(i)(A) and/or (B) of this section are not satisfied, HUD will recast the operating margin and debt service coverage ratio for prior periods by applying its estimate of the projected interest rate at the time the mortgage is expected to close in lieu of the historical interest rate(s).

(iii) In performing the calculations called for in paragraphs (a)(3)(i)(A) and (B) of this section, if HUD finds that performance in one of the three years was affected by exceptional, one-time events that substantially altered financial performance, HUD may calculate the three-year performance based on the four most recent years with the unusual year omitted.

(iv) The hospital must document that it provides an essential healthcare service to the community in which it operates and that its financial performance would be materially improved by refinancing its existing capital debt.

(v) The hospital may show that it provides an essential healthcare service to the community in which it operates by submitting an analysis quantifying how the community in which it presently operates would suffer from inadequate access to an essential healthcare service that the hospital presently provides if the hospital were no longer in operation.

425

(vi) The hospital may show that its financial performance would be materially improved by providing documentation of the following:

(A) There are limited comparable affordable refinancing vehicles available to the hospital; and,

(B) The hospital meets three of the following seven criteria:

(1) The proposed refinancing would reduce the hospital's total operating expenses by at least 0.25 percent;

(2) The interest rate of the proposed refinancing would be at least 0.5 percentage points less than the interest rate on the debt to be refinanced;

(3) The interest rate on the debt that the hospital proposes to refinance has increased by at least one percentage point at any time since January 1, 2008, or is very likely to increase by at least one percentage within one year of the date of application;

(4) The hospital's annual total debt service is in excess of 3.4 percent of total operating revenues, based on its most recent audited financial statement;

(5) The hospital has experienced a withdrawal or expiration of its credit enhancement facility, or the lender providing its credit enhancement facility has been downgraded, or the hospital can demonstrate that one of these events is imminent;

(6) The hospital is party to bond covenants that are substantially more restrictive than the Section 242 mortgage covenants; and

(7) There are other circumstances that demonstrate that the hospital's financial performance would be materially improved by refinancing its existing capital debt.

(4) *Financial feasibility.* The approval process entails a determination of the financial feasibility of the proposal, i.e., a determination that it is probable that the proposed mortgagor will be able to meet its debt service requirements during the period projected. It includes analysis of the reimbursement structure of the proposed hospital (including patient/payer mix); actions of competitors; and the probable projected impact on the proposed hospital of general health care system trends, such as the development of alternative health care delivery systems and new reimbursement methods. In addition to historical operating margin, determination of financial feasibility includes, but is not limited to, evaluation of the following factors, which the application must address and which HUD will review:

(i) Current and projected gains from operations and a manageable debt load using reasonable assumptions;

(ii) Current debt service coverage ratio of 1.25 or higher and projected debt service coverage ratio of 1.40 or higher;

(iii) Cushion in the balance sheet sufficient to demonstrate the ability to withstand short periods of net operating losses without jeopardizing financial viability;

(iv) Patient utilization forecasts (including average length of stay, case intensity, discharges, area-wide use rates) that are consistent with the hospital's historical trends, future service mix, market trends, population forecasts, and business climate;

(v) The hospital's demonstrated ability to position itself to compete in its marketplace;

(vi) Organizational affiliations or relationships that help optimize financial, clinical, and operational performance;

(vii) Management's demonstrated ability to operate effectively and efficiently, and to develop effective strategies for addressing problem areas;

(viii) Systems in place to monitor hospital operations, revenues, and costs accurately and in a timely manner;

(ix) A Board that is appropriately constituted and provides effective oversight;

(x) Required licensures and approvals; and

(xi) Favorable ratings from the Joint Commission on Accreditation of Healthcare Organizations or other organizations acceptable to HUD.

(5) *Preliminary Review.* A Preliminary Review is a general overview of the acceptability of a potential mortgagor performed at the request of a hospital, a financial consultant representing a hospital, or a lender, to identify any factors that would likely cause an application to be rejected, should an application be submitted.

(i) The purpose of the preliminary review is for HUD to identify any obvious factors that would cause an application to be rejected, before the potential mortgagor or mortgagee expends resources to prepare one. The hospital, financial consultant, or lender shall submit a preliminary information package to HUD that provides evidence of statutory eligibility, market need, financial strength, and such other documentation as HUD may require. The scope of the preliminary review does not include approval of any specific site in the community.

(ii) If HUD identifies factors that would cause an application to be rejected, HUD shall issue a Preliminary Review Letter notifying the potential applicant that an application for mortgage insurance would probably not be successful and providing the reasons for this decision. Also, no further request from the proposed applicant for a Preliminary Review shall be entertained for a period of one year from the date of HUD's notification. HUD may grant an exception to this one-year limitation if, during the year, there is a major change in the circumstances that caused HUD to determine that the project would be rejected. For example, if the sole reason for HUD's determination was the hospital's failure to meet the historical operating margin test, and a new audited annual financial statement contains results that would cause the hospital to meet the test, then the lender may request a new Preliminary Review within one year of HUD's notification.

(iii) If HUD does not identify any factors that would cause an application to be rejected, HUD shall issue a Preliminary Review Letter advising the potential applicant that there appears to be no bar to the applicant's proceeding to the next step in the application process, provided that if a complete application is not received by HUD within one year following the date of HUD's letter, another Preliminary Review may be required, at HUD's discretion, before the application process may proceed.

(iv) The Commissioner's determination in the preliminary review phase that no factors have been identified that would cause an application to be rejected shall in no way be construed as an indication that a subsequent application will be approved.

(6) *Preapplication meeting.* The next step in the application process is the preapplication meeting (this step is optional, at HUD's discretion, in Section 242/223(f) cases). At HUD's discretion, this meeting may be held at HUD Headquarters in Washington, DC, or at another site agreeable to HUD and the potential applicant. The preapplication meeting is an opportunity for the potential mortgagor to summarize the proposed project and refinancing, if any; for HUD to summarize the application process; and for issues that could affect the eligibility or underwriting of the project to be identified and discussed to the extent possible. Following the meeting, HUD may:

(i) Advise the potential applicant that there appears to be no bar to submitting an application for mortgage insurance; or

(ii) Identify issues that must be resolved before a full application should be submitted for processing.

(b) *Application contents.* The application for mortgage insurance shall include exhibits that follow such guidance as to content and format that HUD shall provide from time to time. The application shall include:

(1) A description of the proposed sources and uses of funds;

(2) A description of the mortgagor entity, its ownership structure, and its directors and managers;

(3) A description of the project, the business plan of the hospital, and how the project will further that plan, or, for applications pursuant to Section 223(f), a description of any limited rehabilitation to be financed with mortgage proceeds and how that limited rehabilitation will affect the hospital;

(4) Historical audited financial statements and interim year-to-date financial results (for existing hospitals);

(5) A study of market need and financial feasibility, addressing the factors listed in paragraphs (a)(1)(ii) and (a)(2), or (a)(3) of this section, (whichever applies), with assumptions and financial forecast clearly presented. The study should be prepared by a certified public accounting firm acceptable to HUD. In the case of an application for Section

242/223(f) mortgage insurance, the study may not be required to address market need and there may be no requirement for involvement of a certified public accounting firm;

(6) Architectural plans and specifications in sufficient detail to enable a reasonable estimate of cost (not applicable to a Section 242/223(f) application, except when architectural plans and specifications are requested by HUD);

(7) Evidence that the hospital will be located in a state or political subdivision of a state with reasonable minimum standards of licensure and methods of operation for hospitals and satisfactory assurance that such standards will be applied and enforced with respect to the hospital;

(8) If the state has an official procedure for determining need for hospitals, evidence that such procedure has been followed and that need has been established under that procedure;

(9) A Phase I environmental report; and

(10) Such other exhibits as HUD shall require based upon the facts pertaining to the particular case.

(c) *Fee.* An application fee of $1.50 per thousand dollars of the amount of the loan to be insured shall be paid to HUD at the time the application is submitted to HUD for approval.

(d) *Filing of application.* An application for insurance of a mortgage on a project shall be submitted on an approved FHA form, by an approved mortgagee and by the sponsors of such project, to FHA.

(e) *Complete application.* Only technically complete applications will be processed. Partial applications cannot be processed. Upon determination that an application is complete, HUD shall issue a Completeness Letter to the applicant stating that the application is complete.

(f) *Application review.* Upon receipt of a complete application, HUD shall evaluate the application to determine if eligibility, market need, financial feasibility, and compliance with applicable regulations (including but not limited to federal environmental regulations, wage rate regulations, and health care regulations) have been demonstrated, and to evaluate any other factors, including but not limited

to risk to the Insurance Fund, that should be considered in determining if the application for mortgage insurance should be approved. As a part of this review, HUD may solicit the advice of private consultants and expert staff in the Department of Health and Human Services and other federal agencies. Based on review of the complete application, HUD may request additional information from the applicant. The timeliness of the applicant's submission of the additional information may affect the approval or disapproval of the application. The Commissioner's decision shall be communicated in the form of a Commitment Letter or a Rejection Letter. HUD will not issue a Commitment Letter until HUD completes the environmental review under 24 CFR 242.79.

[72 FR 67546, Nov. 28, 2007, as amended at 78 FR 8341, Feb. 5, 2013]

§ 242.17 Commitments.

(a) *Issuance of commitment.* Upon approval of an application for insurance, a commitment shall be issued by HUD setting forth the terms and conditions under which an insurance endorsement shall be issued for the hospital. The commitment shall include the following:

(1) A commitment for insurance of advances reflecting the mortgage amount, interest rate, mortgage term, date of commencement of amortization, and other requirements pertaining to the mortgage and construction project;

(2) In the case of an application for Section 242/223(f) insurance where advances are not needed for funding any limited rehabilitation: a commitment for insurance upon completion, reflecting the mortgage amount, interest rate, mortgage term, date of commencement of amortization, and other requirements pertaining to the mortgage and to any limited rehabilitation;

(3) HUD's computation of the replacement cost and maximum insurable mortgage amount;

(4) Financial requirements for closing;

(5) Approval covenants, including any special conditions that must be satisfied prior to initial endorsement;

(6) Mortgage Reserve Fund Agreement.

(b) *Type of commitment.* The commitment will provide for the insurance of advances of mortgage funds during construction. In the case of a commitment for Section 242/223(f) insured refinancing or acquisition financing of an existing hospital, the commitment shall provide for insurance upon completion unless insured advances are needed for funding any limited rehabilitation approved by HUD, in which case the commitment shall provide for insurance of advances.

(c) *Term of commitment.* (1) The initial commitment shall be issued for a period of 90 days.

(2) The term of a commitment may be extended in such manner as HUD may prescribe, provided, however, that the combined term of the original commitment and any extensions do not exceed 180 days.

(d) *Commitment fee.* A commitment fee that, when added to the application fee, will aggregate $3 per thousand dollars of the amount of the loan set forth in the commitment, shall be paid within 30 days of the date of issuance of commitment. If such fee is not paid within this 30-day period, the commitment shall automatically terminate.

[72 FR 67546, Nov. 28, 2007, as amended at 78 FR 8342, Feb. 5, 2013]

§242.18 Inspection fee.

(a) The commitment may provide for the payment of an inspection fee in an amount not to exceed $5 per thousand dollars of the commitment. The inspection fee shall be paid no later than the time of initial endorsement.

(b) In the case of mortgages where the applicant is seeking only refinancing or acquisition, the inspection fee will not exceed 10 basis points on the loan. For applicants seeking a loan for refinancing or acquisition that also involves limited rehabilitation, the commitment shall provide for an inspection fee according to the following schedule:

Hard cost % of mortgage amount	Inspection fee limit (basis points)
Less than 5%	10
5% or greater but less than 10%	20
10% or greater but less than 15%	30
15% or greater but less than 20%	40
20% or greater	50

[78 FR 8343, Feb. 5, 2013]

§242.19 Fees on increases.

(a) *Increase in commitment prior to endorsement.* An application, filed prior to initial endorsement, for an increase in the amount of an outstanding commitment, shall be accompanied by an additional application fee of $1.50 per thousand dollars computed on the amount of the increase requested. Any increase in the amount of a commitment shall be subject to the payment of an additional commitment fee which, when added to the additional application fee, will aggregate $3 per thousand dollars of the amount of the increase. The additional commitment fee shall be paid within 30 days after the date of the amended commitment. If the additional commitment fee is not paid within 30 days, the commitment novation providing for the increased amount will automatically terminate and the previous commitment will be reinstated. If an inspection fee was required in the original commitment, an additional inspection fee shall be paid in an amount not to exceed $5 per thousand dollars of the amount of increase in commitment. The additional inspection fee shall be paid at the time of initial endorsement.

(b) *Increase in mortgage between initial and final endorsement.* Upon an application, filed between initial and final endorsement, for an increase in the amount of the mortgage, either by amendment, consolidation agreement, or by substitution of a new mortgage, an additional application fee of $1.50 per thousand dollars computed on the amount of the increase requested shall accompany the application. The approval of any increase in the amount of the mortgage shall be subject to the payment of an additional commitment fee which, when added to the additional application fee, will aggregate $3 per thousand dollars of the amount of the increase granted. If an inspection fee was required in the original commitment, an additional inspection fee shall be paid in an amount not to exceed $5 per thousand dollars of the amount of the increase granted. The additional commitment and inspection fees shall be paid within 30 days after the date that the increase is granted.

§ 242.20 Reopening of expired commitments.

An expired commitment may be reopened if a request for reopening is received by HUD no later than 90 days after the date of expiration of the commitment. The reopening request shall be accompanied by a fee of 50 cents per thousand dollars of the amount of the expired commitment. A commitment that has expired because of failure to pay the commitment fee may be reopened only upon payment of the commitment fee and the reopening fee. If the reopening request is not received by HUD within the required 90-day period, a new application accompanied by an application fee must be submitted. If a commitment for an increased amount has expired because of failure to pay an additional commitment fee based on the amount of the increase, the reopening fee shall be computed on the basis of the amount of the commitment increase rather than on the amount of the original commitment.

§ 242.21 Refund of fees.

Commitment, inspection, and reopening fees (but not application fees) may be refunded, in whole or in part, if HUD determines that the construction or financing of the project has been prevented because of condemnation proceedings or other legal action taken by a government body or public agency, or in such other instances as HUD may determine as being beyond the control of the applicant and resulting from no fault of the applicant. A transfer fee may be refunded only in such instances as HUD may determine. However, the portion of the inspection fee paid in connection with early commencement of work is not refundable.

§ 242.22 Maximum fees and charges by mortgagee.

The mortgagee may collect from the mortgagor the amount of the fees provided for in this subpart. The mortgagee may also collect from the mortgagor an initial service charge not to exceed 2 percent of the original principal amount of the mortgage to reimburse the mortgagee for the cost of closing the transaction. A permanent financing fee not to exceed 3.5 percent may be collected from the mortgagor; however, the combined initial service charge and permanent financing fee may not exceed 5.5 percent in bond transactions and 3.5 percent in all other transactions. Any additional charges or fees collected from the mortgagor shall be subject to prior approval of HUD and shall be clearly disclosed in the Mortgagee's Certificate.

§ 242.23 Maximum mortgage amounts and cash equity requirements.

(a) *Adjusted mortgage amount-rehabilitation projects.* A mortgage financing the substantial rehabilitation of an existing hospital shall be subject to the following limitations, in addition to those set forth in § 242.7:

(1) *Property held unencumbered.* If the mortgagor is the fee simple owner of the property and the property is not encumbered by an outstanding indebtedness, the mortgage shall not exceed 100 percent of HUD's estimate of the cost of the proposed substantial rehabilitation.

(2) *Property subject to existing mortgage.* If the mortgagor owns the property subject to an outstanding indebtedness, which is to be refinanced with part of the insured mortgage, the mortgage shall not exceed the total of the following:

(i) The Commissioner's estimate of the cost of substantial rehabilitation, plus

(ii) Such portion of the capital debt as does not exceed 90 percent of HUD's estimate of the fair market value of such land and improvements prior to substantial rehabilitation.

(3) *Property to be acquired.* If the property is to be acquired by the mortgagor and the purchase price is to be financed with a part of the insured mortgage,

the mortgage shall not exceed 90 percent of the total of the following:

(i) The Commissioner's estimate of the cost of substantial rehabilitation, plus

(ii) The actual purchase price of the land and improvements or HUD's estimate (prior to substantial rehabilitation) of the fair market value of such land and improvements, whichever is the lesser.

(b) *Section 242/223(f) refinancing and acquisition—additional limits.* (1) In addition to meeting the requirements of §242.7, if the hospital's existing capital debt is to be refinanced by the insured mortgage (i.e., without a change in ownership or with the hospital sold to a purchaser who has an identity of interest as defined by the Commissioner with the seller), the maximum mortgage amount must not exceed the cost to refinance the existing indebtedness, which will consist of the following items, the eligibility and amounts of which must be determined by the Commissioner:

(i) The amount required to pay off the existing capital debt;

(ii) The estimated hard costs, if any, totaling less than 20 percent of the mortgage amount; and

(iii) Soft costs that would normally be allowable in a Section 242 insured loan.

(2) In addition to meeting the requirements of §242.7, if mortgage proceeds are to be used for an acquisition, the maximum mortgage amount must not exceed the cost to acquire the hospital, which will consist of the following items, the eligibility and amounts of which must be determined by the Commissioner:

(i) The actual purchase price of the land and improvements or HUD's estimate (prior to repairs, renovation, and/or equipment replacement) of the fair market value of such land plus the replacement cost of improvements, whichever is the lesser;

(ii) The estimated hard costs, if any, totaling less than 20 percent of the mortgage amount; and

(iii) Soft costs that would normally be allowable in a Section 242 insured loan.

(c) *Reduced mortgage amount—leaseholds.* In the event the mortgage is secured by a leasehold estate rather than a fee simple estate, the value or replacement cost of the property described in the mortgage shall be the value or replacement cost of the leasehold estate (as determined by HUD), which shall in all cases be less than the value or replacement cost of the property in fee simple.

(d) *Cash equity.* Depending on the financial circumstances of each hospital facility, HUD shall have the discretion to evaluate, on a case-by-case basis, the amount of equity that a mortgagor must supply in addition to the value of plant, property, and equipment and other values recognized as loan security in the commitment process. Exercise of this discretion shall never cause a loan to exceed 90 percent of estimated replacement cost, although it may cause it to be less than 90 percent. The equity contribution may not be made from borrowed funds. A private nonprofit or public mortgagor, but not a proprietary mortgagor, at the mortgagee's option and subject to 24 CFR 242.49, may provide any such required equity in the form of a letter of credit.

[72 FR 67546, Nov. 28, 2007, as amended at 73 FR 35922, June 25, 2008; 78 FR 8343, Feb. 5, 2013]

§242.24 Initial operating costs.

In the case of a new hospital or a hospital expansion, HUD shall establish, on a case-by-case basis, the amount of initial operating capital, if any, that must be deposited in cash or a letter of credit (or combination) to be available to the new hospital upon commencement of operations. Generally, the initial operating capital other than AMPO shall not be borrowed funds unless HUD determines that there are offsetting financial strengths to compensate for the risk associated with borrowing.

Subpart C—Mortgage Requirements

§242.25 Mortgage form and disbursement of mortgage proceeds.

(a) *Mortgage form.* The mortgage shall be:

(1) Executed on a form approved by HUD for use in the jurisdiction in which the property covered by the

mortgage is situated; the form shall not be changed without the prior written approval of HUD.

(2) Executed by an eligible mortgagor.

(b) *Disbursement of mortgage proceeds.* The mortgagee shall be obligated, as a part of the mortgage transaction, to disburse the principal amount of the mortgage to (or for the account of) the mortgagor or to his or her creditors for his or her account and with his or her consent.

§ 242.26   Agreed interest rate.

(a) The mortgage shall bear interest at the rate or rates agreed upon by the mortgagee and the mortgagor.

(b) The amount of any increase approved by HUD in the mortgage amount between initial and final endorsement in excess of the amount that HUD had committed to insure at initial endorsement shall bear interest at the rate agreed upon by the mortgagee and the mortgagor.

§ 242.27   Maturity.

The mortgage shall have a maturity not to exceed 25 years from the date amortization begins.

§ 242.28   Allowable costs for consultants.

Consulting fees for work essential to the development of the project may be included in the insured mortgage. Allowable consulting fees include those for analysis of market demand, expected revenues, and costs; site analysis; architectural and engineering design; and such other fees as HUD may determine to be essential to project development. Fees for work performed more than 2 years prior to application are not allowable. Fees for work performed by any party with an identity of interest with the proposed mortgagor or mortgagee are not allowable.

§ 242.29   Payment requirements.

The mortgage shall provide for payments on the first day of each month in accordance with an amortization plan agreed upon by the mortgagor, the mortgagee, and HUD.

§ 242.30   Application of payments.

All payments to be made by the mortgagor to the mortgagee shall be added together and the aggregate amount thereof shall be paid by the mortgagor each month in a single payment. The mortgagee shall apply each payment received to the following items in the following order:

(a) Premium charges under the contract of mortgage insurance;

(b) Ground rents, taxes, special assessments, and fire and other hazard insurance premiums;

(c) Interest on the mortgage; and

(d) Amortization of the principal of the mortgage.

§ 242.31   Accumulation of accruals.

(a) The mortgage shall provide for payments by the mortgagor to the mortgagee on each interest payment date of an amount sufficient to accumulate, in the hands of the mortgagee one payment period prior to its due date, the next annual MIP payable by the mortgagee to HUD. Such payments shall continue only so long as the contract of insurance shall remain in effect.

(b) The mortgage shall provide for such equal monthly payments by the mortgagor to the mortgagee as will amortize the ground rents, if any, and the estimated amount of all taxes, water charges, special assessments, and fire and other hazard insurance premiums, within a period ending one month prior to the dates on which the same become delinquent. The mortgage shall further provide that such payments shall be held by the mortgagee, for the purpose of paying such items before they become delinquent. The mortgage shall also make provision for adjustments in case such estimated amounts shall prove to be more, or less, than the actual amounts so paid therefore by the mortgagor. Notwithstanding the foregoing, in particular circumstances, a mortgagor may purchase required fire and hazard insurance through a consortium of affiliated institutions or related organizations or, in the case of public institutions, through required state purchasing arrangements. In such circumstances, the mortgage accrual requirement may be modified to reflect circumstances in which it is inappropriate for the mortgagee to collect monthly payments and to make payments on behalf of the mortgagor.

§242.32 Covenant against liens.

The mortgage shall contain a covenant against the creation by the mortgagor of any liens against the property, except for such liens as may be approved by HUD.

§242.33 Covenant for malpractice, fire, and other hazard insurance.

The mortgage shall contain a covenant binding the mortgagor to maintain adequate liability, fire, and extended coverage insurance on the property. The mortgage shall also contain a covenant binding the mortgagor to maintain adequate malpractice coverage. All coverage shall be acceptable to the mortgagee or HUD.

[73 FR 35923, June 25, 2008]

§242.35 Mortgage lien certifications.

At initial and/or final endorsement of the mortgage note, each of the following requirements must be met:

(a) The mortgage is the first lien upon and covers all of the property used in the operation of the entire hospital;

(b) The property upon which the improvements have been made or constructed and the equipment financed with mortgage proceeds are free and clear of all liens other than the insured mortgage and such other secondary liens as may be approved by HUD;

(c) The Security Agreement and Uniform Commercial Code filings establish a first lien on the personalty of the mortgagor, including but not limited to equipment acquired with mortgage proceeds or otherwise not subject to a prior lien;

(d) The mortgagor has notified HUD in writing of all unpaid obligations in connection with the mortgage transaction, the purchase of the mortgaged property, the construction, limited rehabilitation, or substantial rehabilitation of the project, or the purchase of

the equipment financed with mortgage proceeds.

[72 FR 67546, Nov. 28, 2007, as amended at 73 FR 35923, June 25, 2008; 78 FR 8343, Feb. 5, 2013]

§242.37 Mortgage prepayment.

(a) *Prepayment privilege.* Except as provided in paragraph (c) of this section or otherwise established by HUD, the mortgage shall contain a provision permitting the mortgagor to prepay the mortgage in whole or in part upon any interest payment date, after giving the mortgagee a 30-day notice in writing in advance of its intention to so prepay. The 30-day notice may be extended with the prior written approval of HUD.

(b) *Prepayment charge.* The mortgage may contain a provision for such charge, in the event of prepayment of principal, as may be agreed upon between the mortgagor and the mortgagee, subject to the following:

(1) The mortgagor shall be permitted to prepay up to 15 percent of the original principal amount of the mortgage in any one calendar year without any such charge.

(2) Any reduction in the original principal amount of the mortgage resulting from the certification of cost, which HUD may require, shall not be construed as a prepayment of the mortgage.

(c) *Prepayment of bond-financed or GNMA-securitized mortgages.* Where the mortgage is given to secure GNMA mortgage-backed securities or a loan made by a lender that has obtained the funds for the loan by the issuance and sale of bonds or bond anticipation notes, or both, the mortgage may contain a prepayment restriction and prepayment penalty charge acceptable to HUD as to term, amount, and conditions.

(d) *HUD override of prepayment restrictions.* In the event of a default, HUD may override any lockout, prepayment penalty, or combination of penalties in order to facilitate a partial or full refinancing of the mortgaged property and avoid a claim.

§242.38 Late charge.

The mortgage may provide for the collection by the mortgagee of a late charge in accordance with terms, conditions, and standards of HUD for each dollar of each payment to interest or principal more than 15 days in arrears, to cover the expense involved in handling delinquent payments. Late charges shall be separately charged to and collected from the mortgagor and shall not be deducted from any aggregate monthly payment.

Subpart D—Endorsement for Insurance

§ 242.39 Insurance endorsement.

(a) *New construction/substantial rehabilitation.* Initial endorsement of the mortgage note shall occur before any mortgage proceeds are insured, and the time of final endorsement shall be as set forth in paragraph (a)(2) of this section.

(1) *Initial endorsement.* The Commissioner shall indicate the insurance of the mortgage by endorsing the original mortgage note and identifying the section of the Act and the regulations under which the mortgage is insured and the date of insurance.

(2) *Final endorsement.* When all advances of mortgage proceeds have been made and all the terms and conditions of the commitment have been met to HUD's satisfaction, HUD shall indicate on the original mortgage note the total of all advances approved for insurance and again endorse such instrument.

(b) *Section 242/223(f) refinancing/acquisition.* (1) In cases that do not involve advances of mortgage proceeds, endorsement shall occur after all relevant terms and conditions have been satisfied, including, if applicable, completion of any limited rehabilitation, or upon assurance acceptable to the Commissioner that all limited rehabilitation will be completed by a date certain following endorsement.

(2) In cases where advances of mortgage proceeds are used to fund limited rehabilitation, endorsement shall occur as described in paragraph (a) of this section immediately above, for new construction/substantial rehabilitation.

(c) *Contract rights and obligations.* The Commissioner and the mortgagee or lender shall be bound from the date of initial endorsement by the provisions of the Contract of Mortgage Insurance stated in subpart B of part 207, which is hereby incorporated by reference into this part.

[78 FR 8343, Feb. 5, 2013]

§ 242.40 Mortgagee certificate.

At initial endorsement, the mortgagee shall execute a Mortgagee Certificate in a form prescribed by HUD.

§ 242.41 Certification of cost requirements.

Before initial endorsement of the mortgage for insurance, the mortgagor, the mortgagee, and HUD shall enter into an agreement in form and content satisfactory to HUD for the purpose of precluding any excess of mortgage proceeds over statutory limitations. Under this agreement, the mortgagor shall disclose its relationship with the builder, including any collateral agreement, and shall agree:

(a) To execute a Certificate of Actual Costs, upon completion of all physical improvements on the mortgaged property.

(b) To apply any cost savings in accordance with the provisions below.

§ 242.42 Certificates of actual cost.

(a) The mortgagor's certificate of actual cost, in a form prescribed by HUD, shall be submitted upon completion of the physical improvements to the satisfaction of HUD and before final endorsement, except that in the case of an existing hospital that does not require substantial rehabilitation and where the commitment provides for completion of specified repairs after endorsement, a supplemental certificate of actual cost will be submitted covering the completed costs of any such repairs. The certificate shall show the actual cost to the mortgagor, after deduction of any kickbacks, rebates, trade discounts, or other similar payments to the mortgagor, any of its officers, directors, stockholders, partners, or other entity member ownership, of construction and other costs, as prescribed by HUD.

(b) The Certificate of Actual Cost shall be verified by an independent certified public accountant or independent public accountant in a manner acceptable to HUD.

434

(c) Upon HUD's approval of the mortgagor's certification of actual cost, such certification shall be final and incontestable except for fraud or material misrepresentation on the part of the mortgagor.

§242.43 Application of cost savings.

At the sole discretion of HUD, any cost savings shall be used to:

(a) Reduce the principal amount of the mortgage and the mortgagor's cash equity contribution proportionally, unless the mortgagor elects to have a greater portion of the savings used to reduce the mortgage; and/or

(b) Fund any additional construction or substantial rehabilitation approved by HUD.

Subpart E—Construction

§242.44 Construction standards.

Work designed and performed under this section shall conform to the standards adopted by HUD, which, at a minimum, shall include the "Guidelines for Construction and Equipment of Hospital and Medical Facilities," which is regularly updated and published by the American Institute of Architects.

§242.45 Early commencement of work.

(a) *Site preparation.* Prior to or following the submission of an application, the mortgagor may request for good cause the commencement of certain limited site preparation for the project within legal guidelines and state law. Such work can commence only after the review of the work and concurrence by HUD, including the environmental review under 24 CFR 242.79, previous participation review, and the agreement to certain conditions by the applicant. HUD will not approve such request until it has completed the environmental review under 24 CFR 242.79. The work must meet all requirements and guidelines as if it were approved for mortgage insurance and is to be accomplished at the sole risk of the mortgagor.

(b) *Construction completed prior to application.* Structures completed more than 2 years prior to application are eligible to be refinanced with insured mortgage proceeds.

(c) *Pre-commitment work.* Subsequent to submission of an application but prior to the issuance of a commitment or denial by HUD, the hospital and lender may request for good cause the commencement of certain necessary early site work and limited construction activity in connection with the improvements, within legal guidelines and state law. This work must be requested by both the hospital and the lender to be approved. Such work may be eligible to be financed with insured mortgage proceeds if the application is approved and the work complies with all specified conditions of HUD as set forth in a written agreement between the hospital and HUD. It is understood that in some cases the application submitted in order for pre-commitment work to begin may not be complete in all respects. However, at a minimum, the application shall include the approved FHA application form, the application fee (based on the amount of the total proposed insured loan), the inspection fee (based on the cost of the pre-commitment work), a project description of the pre-commitment work and its relation to the total project, and plans and specifications for the proposed pre-commitment work in sufficient detail to allow HUD to conduct its architectural and engineering review and obtain the necessary previous participation information and evidence of compliance with federal and state environmental regulations. Such work can commence only after the review of the work and concurrence by the lender and HUD, including previous participation review. HUD will not approve such request until it has completed the environmental review under 24 CFR 242.79. The work must meet all requirements and guidelines as if it were approved for mortgage insurance and is to be accomplished at the sole risk of the hospital. A request shall be accompanied by documentation required by HUD. That documentation shall include:

(1) A justification explaining the urgent and compelling circumstances that make it necessary to begin construction without waiting for the application process to run its course. The justification must specify the harm the hospital would suffer from waiting.

435

(2) A plan detailing how the hospital will finance the limited construction if the application for mortgage insurance is denied.

(3) A statement that financing the limited construction by means other than a HUD-insured mortgage in the event the application is denied will impose no significant financial hardship on the hospital. The statement shall be accompanied by supporting historical and projected financial data.

(4) A statement that HUD's agreement to include the cost of the limited construction in a subsequently approved application does not in any way indicate that the application will be approved.

(5) A resolution of the governing body (or, at HUD's discretion, the executive committee of the governing body) of the mortgagor attesting to paragraphs (c)(1) through (4).

(d) *Early Start.* Subsequent to the issuance of a commitment, if the hospital and lender request the commencement of the project, the work may commence after the review and approval of the request by HUD, including the agreement by the hospital and the lender to any conditions that HUD may require. Any work undertaken prior to the initial endorsement shall be at the sole risk of the hospital.

(e) *Prepayment of inspection fee.* The hospital shall pay a non-refundable inspection fee to HUD before the work described in paragraph (c) or (d) of this section commences. The fee shall be based on the amount of the pre-commitment and/or early start work requested to be included in the insured mortgage loan.

(f) *No expressed or implied intent.* Approval to proceed under paragraphs (c) or (d) of this section shall in no way be construed as indicating any intent, expressed or implied, on the part of HUD to approve, disapprove, or make any undertaking or promise whatsoever with respect to the application or with respect to any commitment for mortgage insurance. Any work under paragraphs (c) or (d) of this section shall be undertaken at the sole risk and responsibility of the hospital.

§ 242.46 Insured advances—building loan agreement.

Prior to the initial endorsement of the mortgage for insurance, the mortgagor and mortgagee shall execute a building loan agreement, approved by HUD, setting forth the terms and conditions under which progress payments may be advanced during construction. To be covered by mortgage insurance, or to be included as an eligible cost, each progress payment involving mortgage proceeds and the owner's equity requirement shall be approved by HUD.

§ 242.47 Insured advances for building components stored off-site.

(a) Building components. In insured advances for building components stored off-site, the term building component shall mean any manufactured or pre-assembled part of a structure that HUD has specifically identified for incorporation into the property and has designated for off-site storage because it is of such size or weight that:

(1) Storage of the number of components required for timely construction progress at the construction site is impractical, or

(2) Weather damage or other adverse conditions prevailing at the construction site would make storage at the site impractical or unduly costly.

(b) *Storage.* (1) An insured advance may be made for up to 90 percent of the invoice value (to exclude costs of transportation and storage) of the building components stored off-site, if the components are stored at a location approved by the mortgagee and HUD.

(2) Each building component shall be adequately marked so as to be readily identifiable in the inventory of the off-site location. Each component shall be kept together with all other building components of the same manufacturer intended for use in the same project for which insured advances have been made and separate and apart from similar units not for use in the project.

(3) Storage costs, if any, shall be borne by the contractor.

(c) *Responsibility for transportation, storage, and insurance of off-site building components.* The general contractor of the insured mortgaged property shall have the responsibility for:

(1) Insuring the components in the name of the mortgagor while in transit and storage; and

(2) Delivering or contracting for the delivery of the components to the storage area and to the construction site, including payment of freight.

(d) *Advances.* (1) Before an advance for a building component stored off-site is insured:

(i) The mortgagor shall:

(A) Obtain a bill of sale for the component;

(B) Give the mortgagee a security agreement; and

(C) File a financing statement in accordance with the Uniform Commercial Code; and

(ii) The mortgagee shall warrant to HUD that the security instruments are a first lien on the building components covered by the instruments except for such other liens or encumbrances as may be approved by HUD.

(2) Before each advance for building components stored off-site is insured, the mortgagor's architect shall certify to HUD that the components, in their intended use, comply with HUD-approved contract plans and specifications. Under those circumstances permitted by HUD in which there is no architect, compliance with the HUD-approved contract plans and specifications shall be determined by HUD.

(3) Advances may be made only for components stored off-site in a quantity required to permit uninterrupted installation at the site.

(4) At no time shall the invoice value of building components being stored off-site, for which advances have been HUD insured, represent more than 50 percent of the total estimated construction costs for the insured mortgaged project as specified in the construction contract. Notwithstanding the preceding sentence and other regulatory requirements that set bonding requirements, the percentage of total estimated construction costs insured by advances under this section may exceed 25 percent but not 50 percent if the mortgagor furnishes assurance of completion in the form of a corporate surety bond for the payment and performance each in the amount of 100 percent of the amount of the construction contract. In no event will insurance of advances for components stored off-site be made in the absence of a payment and a performance bond.

(5) No single advance that is to be insured shall be in an amount less than $10,000.

§242.48 Insured advances for certain equipment and long lead items.

The Commissioner may allow advances for certain pieces of equipment or other construction materials for which a manufacturer, fabricator, or other source requires an interim payment(s) in order to assure the timely manufacture or fabrication and delivery to the project site. Such advances can be made only if a bill of sale or an invoice describes the material or equipment and its completion and delivery dates in no uncertain terms, and that such displayed timetable is necessary to meet the requirements of the overall construction schedule cited in the construction contract.

§242.49 Funds and finances: deposits and letters of credit.

(a) *Deposits.* Where HUD requires the mortgagor to make a deposit of cash or securities, such deposit shall be with the mortgagee or a depository acceptable to the mortgagee and HUD. Any such deposit shall be held in a separate account for and on behalf of the mortgagor, and shall be the responsibility of that mortgagee or depository.

(b) *Letter of credit.* Where the use of a letter of credit is acceptable to HUD in lieu of a deposit of cash or securities, the letter of credit shall be issued to the mortgagee by a banking institution acceptable to the lender. The mortgagee shall be responsible to HUD for collection under the letter of credit. In the event a demand for payment thereunder is not immediately met, the mortgagee shall forthwith provide a cash deposit equivalent to the undrawn balance of the letter of credit.

(c) *Mortgagee not issuer.* The mortgagee of record may not be the issuer of the letter of credit without the prior written consent of HUD.

[72 FR 67546, Nov. 28, 2007, as amended at 78 FR 8343, Feb. 5, 2013]

§ 242.50 Funds and finances: off-site utilities and streets.

The Commissioner shall require assurance of completion of off-site public utilities and streets in all cases, except where a municipality or other public body has by agreement acceptable to HUD agreed to install such utilities and streets without cost to the mortgagor. Where such assurance is required, it shall be in the form of a cash escrow deposit, a letter of credit, the retention of a specified amount of mortgage proceeds by the mortgagee, or a combination thereof. In any case, the amount of deposit or retained cash (or both) must be sufficient to cover the cost of off-site utilities and streets. If a cash escrow is used, it shall be deposited with the mortgagee or with an acceptable trustee or escrow agent designated by the mortgagee. If mortgage proceeds are used, the mortgagee shall retain under terms approved by HUD, rather than disburse at the initial closing of the mortgage, a sufficient portion of the mortgage proceeds allocated to land in the project analysis. As additional assurance, HUD may also require a surety company bond or bonds.

[72 FR 67546, Nov. 28, 2007, as amended at 73 FR 35923, June 25, 2008]

§ 242.51 Funds and finances: Insured advances and assurance of completion.

(a) Where the estimated cost of construction or substantial rehabilitation is more than $500,000, the mortgagor shall furnish assurance of completion in the form of corporate surety bonds for payment and performance, each in the minimum amount of 100 percent of the construction contract (or Guaranteed Maximum Price, in the case of construction management) and each satisfactory to HUD.

(b) All types of assurance of completion shall be on forms approved by HUD. All surety companies executing a bond and all parties executing a personal indemnity agreement must be satisfactory to HUD.

(c) A mortgagee may prescribe more stringent requirements for assurance of completion than the minimum requirements provided for in this section.

§ 242.52 Construction contracts.

(a) *Awarding of contract.* A contract for the construction or substantial rehabilitation of a hospital shall be entered into by a mortgagor, with a builder selected by a competitive bidding procedure acceptable to HUD.

(b) *Form of contract.* The construction contract shall be: A lump sum form providing for payment of a specified amount; a construction management contract with a guaranteed maximum price, the final costs of which are subject to a certification acceptable to HUD; a design-build contract with terms and certification requirements acceptable to HUD; or such other form of contract as may be acceptable to HUD.

(c) *Competitive bidding.* A competitive bidding procedure acceptable to HUD must be used in the selection of bidders to perform work or otherwise provide service to the project, the costs of which are included in any form of construction contract cited in paragraph (b) of this section. Fixed equipment not included in the construction contract, and movable equipment, may be purchased by securing quotations or by using competitive bidding procedures.

[72 FR 67546, Nov. 28, 2007, as amended at 73 FR 35923, June 25, 2008]

§ 242.53 Excluded contractors.

(a) Contracts relating to the construction of the project shall not be made with any person or entity that has been excluded from participation in federal programs, including but not limited to: A general contractor, a subcontractor, or construction manager (or any firm, corporation, partnership, or association in which such contractor, subcontractor, or construction manager has a substantial interest). Before entering into contracts with any such person or entity, owners must consult the government-wide list of excluded parties, and any list of excluded parties maintained by HUD.

(b) Contracts relating to the construction of the project shall not be made with a general contractor that has an identity of interest, as defined by HUD, with the mortgagor or mortgagee.

(c) If HUD determines that a contract has been made contrary to the requirements of paragraphs (a) or (b) of this section and so notifies the mortgagee, HUD will require the contractor or construction manager to cost-certify and may require other remedial action in addition to taking enforcement action, as HUD deems appropriate.

Subpart F—Nondiscrimination and Wage Rates

§ 242.54 Nondiscrimination.

Hospital facilities financed with mortgages insured under this part must be made available without discrimination as to race, color, religion, sex, age, disability, or national origin. Hospitals must be operated in compliance with all applicable civil rights laws and regulations, including 24 CFR part 200, subpart J (Equal Employment Opportunity), and the Americans with Disabilities Act (42 U.S.C. 12101 *et seq.*). Racially restrictive covenants are per se illegal and their use is prohibited. The aforesaid provisions regarding age and sex discrimination do not affect the eligibility of hospitals for women and children.

§ 242.55 Labor standards.

(a) Projects financed under this part (except under 24 CFR 242.91) must comply with the prevailing wage rates determined under the Davis-Bacon Act (40 U.S.C. 3141 *et seq.*), and U.S. Department of Labor regulations in 29 CFR parts 1, 3, and 5 for compliance with labor standards laws, in accordance with section 212 of the Act, provided that supplemental loans under section 241 of the Act made in connection with loans insured under this part are subject to labor standards requirements in the same manner and to the same extent as mortgages insured under section 242 of the National Housing Act.

(b) The requirements stated in 24 CFR part 70 governing HUD waiver of Davis-Bacon prevailing wage rates for volunteers apply to hospitals with mortgages insured under this part.

(c) Each laborer or mechanic employed on any facility covered by a mortgage insured under this part (except under 24 CFR 242.91), but including a supplemental loan under section 241 of the Act made in connection with a loan insured under this part) shall receive compensation at a rate not less than one and one-half times the basic rate of pay for all hours worked in any workweek in excess of 8 hours in any workday or 40 hours in the workweek.

(d) Project commitments, contracts, and agreements, as determined by HUD, and construction contracts and subcontracts, shall include terms, conditions, and standards for compliance with applicable requirements set forth in 29 CFR parts 1, 3, and 5 and section 212 of the Act.

(e) No advance under a loan or mortgage that is subject to the requirements of section 212 shall be eligible for insurance unless there is filed with the application for the advance a certificate as required by HUD certifying that the laborers and mechanics employed in construction of the project have been paid not less than the wage rates required under section 212.

[72 FR 67546, Nov. 28, 2007, as amended at 78 FR 8344, Feb. 5, 2013]

Subpart G—Regulatory Agreement, Accounting and Reporting, and Financial Requirements

§ 242.56 Form of regulation.

As long as HUD is the insurer or holder of the mortgage, all mortgagors shall be regulated by HUD through the use of a regulatory agreement in a published format determined by HUD and such additional covenants and restrictions as may be determined necessary by HUD on a case-by-case basis. In addition, all mortgagors shall be subject to the provisions of 24 CFR part 24 and such other enforcement provisions as may be applicable. The mortgagor shall be subject to monitoring by HUD and its agents and contractors, on an ongoing basis for the life of the insured mortgage to ensure against the risk of default, and the mortgagor must make its financial records available to HUD and its agents and contractors upon request. In those cases in which the hospital facility is leased as permitted by

§ 242.72, the provisions of this section also shall apply to the lessee.

[72 FR 67546, Nov. 28, 2007, as amended at 73 FR 35923, June 25, 2008]

§ 242.57 Maintenance of hospital facility.

The mortgagor shall maintain the hospital's grounds, buildings, and the equipment financed with mortgage proceeds in good repair, and shall promptly complete such repairs and maintenance as HUD considers necessary.

§ 242.58 Books, accounts, and financial statements.

(a) *Books and accounts.* The mortgagor's books and accounts relating to the operation of the physical facilities of the hospital shall be established in a manner satisfactory to HUD, and shall be kept in accordance with the requirements of HUD as long as the mortgage is insured or held by HUD.

(b) *Financial reports.* The mortgagor shall file with HUD:

(i) Annual audited financial statements in accordance with the guidance below;

(ii) Quarterly unaudited financial reports, within 40 days following the end of each quarter of the mortgagor's fiscal year;

(iii) If requested by HUD, monthly financial reports within 40 days following the end of each month;

(iv) Board-certified annual financial results within 120 days following the close of the fiscal year (if the annual audited financial statement has not yet been filed with HUD) and at such other times as HUD may designate on a case-by-case basis; and

(v) Such other financial and utilization reports as HUD may require.

(c) *Audits.* (1) Not-for-profit and state and local governments shall conduct audits in accordance with the Consolidated Audit Guide for Audits of HUD Programs (Handbook 2000.04) and 2 CFR part 200, subpart F.

(2) For-profit organizations shall conduct audits in accordance with the Consolidated Audit Guide for Audits of HUD Programs (Handbook 2000.04).

(d) *Changes in accounting policies.* The annual audited financial statements shall identify any changes in accounting policies and their financial effect on the balance sheet and on the income statement.

(e) *Compliance reporting.* The mortgagor shall instruct the auditor of the annual financial statement to include in its report an evaluation of the mortgagor's compliance with the Regulatory Agreement.

(f) *Books of management agents.* The books and records of management agents, lessees, operators, managers, and affiliates, as they pertain to the operations of the hospital, shall be maintained in accordance with Generally Accepted Accounting Principles (GAAP) or Governmental Accounting Standards and shall be open and available to inspection by HUD, after reasonable prior notice, during normal office hours, at the hospital or other mutually agreeable location. Every contract executed on behalf of the hospital with any of the aforesaid parties shall include the provision that the books and records of such entities shall be properly maintained and open to inspection during normal business hours by HUD at the hospital or other mutually agreeable location.

(g) *Medicare cost reports.* Upon request, the mortgagor shall provide to HUD a copy of the Medicare Cost Report most recently submitted to the Centers for Medicare and Medicaid Services (an agency of the Department of Health and Human Services), along with related financial documents.

(h) In those cases in which the hospital facility is leased as permitted by § 242.72, the requirements pertaining to the mortgagor in § 242.58 (a) through (g) also shall pertain to the lessee.

[72 FR 67546, Nov. 28, 2007, as amended at 73 FR 35923, June 25, 2008; 80 FR 75936, Dec. 7, 2015]

§ 242.59 Inspection of facilities by Commissioner.

The mortgaged property (including buildings and equipment) and the books, records, and documents relating to the operation of the physical facilities of the hospital shall be subject to inspection and examination by HUD or its authorized representative at all reasonable times.

§242.61 Management.

The mortgagor shall provide for management of the hospital in a manner satisfactory to HUD.

(a) *Contract Management of Hospital.* The mortgagor shall not execute a management agreement or any other contract for management of the hospital without HUD's prior written approval. (Management of the hospital, which requires HUD's prior written approval, refers to management of the hospital not management of components within the hospital such as the hospital cafeteria or hospital pharmacy.) Any management agreement or contract for management of the hospital shall contain a provision that it shall be subject to termination without penalty and with or without cause, upon written request by HUD addressed to the mortgagor and management agent.

(b) *Principals.* HUD shall have the authority to require that any principals of the mortgagor, including but not limited to board members of a corporate entity, be removed, substituted, or terminated for cause upon written request by HUD addressed to the mortgagor.

(c) *Employees.* HUD shall have the authority to require that any key management employees of the mortgagor (as defined and determined solely by HUD) be terminated for cause upon written request by HUD addressed to the mortgagor.

(d) *Procedures upon receipt of request under paragraphs (a) through (c) of this section.* Upon receipt of such requests under paragraphs (a) through (c) of this section, the mortgagor shall immediately terminate said management agreement, principals, or employees within the shortest applicable period HUD determines appropriate and shall make arrangements satisfactory to HUD for ongoing proper management of the hospital.

[72 FR 67546, Nov. 28, 2007, as amended at 73 FR 35923, June 25, 2008]

§242.62 Releases of lien.

The mortgagor shall not sell, dispose of, transfer, or permit to be encumbered any security property without the prior approval of the lender and Commissioner, subject to thresholds or such other standards as HUD may establish for the approval requirement. Where there is a partial release of lien, the lender must make a determination, subject to prior review and approval by HUD, that the remaining or replacement property subject to the first lien provides adequate security for the remaining principal indebtedness.

§242.63 Additional indebtedness and leasing.

The mortgagor shall not enter into any long-term debt, short-term debt (including receivables or line of credit financing), equipment leases, or derivative-type transactions, except in conformance with policies and procedures established by HUD.

§242.64 Current and future property.

All current or future property (including personalty) of the mortgagor on or off mortgaged real estate (except that specifically restricted by donors or specifically excluded by HUD) will be considered as part of the HUD-insured hospital and subject to all provisions of the HUD regulatory agreement. All equipment acquired by the hospital following initial endorsement and at any time during the term of the loan shall become subject to the lien of the security agreement and any Uniform Commercial Code Financing Statements filed pursuant to the security agreement, unless the mortgagor specifically requests and HUD, for good cause, approves subordination of the lien of the insured mortgagee on specific personalty for specific periods of time. The first lien on the realty (as defined in the regulatory agreement and as identified in the security instrument) cannot be subordinated in whole or in part.

§242.65 Distribution of assets.

The Commissioner shall establish financial thresholds and procedures for the distribution of surplus cash and other assets. Surplus cash that meets the definition in 24 CFR 242.1, or cash that has been expressly approved for distribution by HUD, may be distributed to other organizations formally affiliated with the mortgagor, a parent organization with which the mortgagor is also affiliated, partners, or stock-holders, in accordance with those financial thresholds and procedures set forth in the regulatory agreement. Other assets may be distributed to other organizations formally affiliated with the mortgagor, a parent organization with which the mortgagor is also affiliated, partners, or stockholders, in accordance with those financial thresholds and procedures set forth in the regulatory agreement, and in accordance with the release of lien conditions in 24 CFR 242.62, if applicable.

§ 242.66   Affiliate transactions.

Transactions with affiliates that are arms-length are permitted as specified in the Regulatory Agreement. Transactions with affiliates that are not arms-length are not permitted except with the prior written approval of HUD.

§ 242.67   New corporations, subsidiaries, affiliations, and mergers.

The mortgagor shall not establish, develop, organize, acquire, become the sole member of, or acquire an interest sufficient to require disclosure on the audited financial statements of the mortgagor, in any corporation, subsidiary, or affiliate organization other than those with which the mortgagor was affiliated as of date of application, without the prior approval of HUD. The mortgagor shall obtain HUD's written approval for all future mergers.

Subpart H—Miscellaneous Requirements

§ 242.68   Disclosure and verification of Social Security and Employer Identification Numbers.

The requirements set forth in 24 CFR part 5, regarding the disclosure and verification of Social Security Numbers and Employer Identification Numbers, and Employer Identification Numbers by "applicants for and participants in" assisted mortgage and loan insurance and related programs, apply to this program.

§ 242.69   Transfer fee.

Upon application for review of a transfer of physical assets or the substitution of mortgagors, a transfer fee of 50 cents per thousand dollars of the outstanding principal balance of the mortgage shall be paid to HUD. A transfer fee is not required if both parties to the transfer transaction are not-for-profit or public organizations.

§ 242.70   Fees not required.

The payment of an application, commitment, inspection, or reopening fee shall not be required in connection with the insurance of a mortgage involving the sale by the Secretary of any property acquired under any section or title of the Act.

§ 242.72   Leasing of hospital.

Leasing of a hospital in its entirety is prohibited. Notwithstanding this prohibition, any proposal in which leasing of the entire facility is a factor due to state law prohibitions against the mortgaging of health care facilities by state entities shall be considered on a case-by-case basis. Also, leasing of a hospital that has an existing Section 242-insured loan is permitted if HUD determines that leasing is necessary to reduce the risk of default by a financially troubled hospital.

§ 242.73   Waiver of eligibility requirements for mortgage insurance.

The Secretary may insure under this part, without regard to any limitation upon eligibility contained in this subpart, any mortgage assigned to him or her in connection with payment under a contract of mortgage insurance, or executed in connection with a sale by him or her of any property previously insured under this part and acquired subsequent to a claim.

§ 242.74   Smoke detectors.

Each occupied room must include such smoke detectors as are required by law.

§ 242.75   Title requirements.

In order for the mortgaged property to be eligible for insurance, HUD shall determine that marketable title thereto is vested in the mortgagor as of the date the mortgage is filed for record. The title evidence shall be examined by HUD and the endorsement of the mortgage note for insurance shall be evidence of its acceptability.

§242.76 Title evidence.

Upon insurance of the mortgage, the mortgagee shall furnish to HUD a survey of the mortgage property, satisfactory to HUD, and a policy of title insurance covering the property, as provided in paragraph (a) of this section. If, for reasons HUD considers to be satisfactory, title insurance cannot be furnished, the mortgagee shall furnish such evidence of title in accordance with paragraph (b) or (c) of this section as HUD may require. Any survey, policy of title insurance, or evidence of title required under this section shall be furnished without expense to HUD. The types of title evidence are:

(a) A policy of title insurance issued by a company and in a form satisfactory to HUD. The policy shall name as the insureds the mortgagee and the Secretary of Housing and Urban Development, and their successors and assigns, as their respective interests may appear. The policy shall provide that upon acquisition of title by the mortgagee or the Secretary, it will continue to provide the same coverage as the original policy, and will run to the mortgagee or the Secretary, as the case may be.

(b) An abstract of title satisfactory to HUD, prepared by an abstract company or individual engaged in the business of preparing abstracts of title, accompanied by a legal opinion satisfactory to HUD as to the quality of such title, signed by an attorney-at-law experienced in the examination of titles.

(c) A Torrens or similar title certificate.

§242.77 Liens.

The hospital must be free and clear of all liens other than the insured mortgage, except that the property may be subject to a lien as provided by terms and conditions established by HUD, as follows:

(a) An inferior lien made or held by a federal, state, or local government instrumentality;

(b) An inferior lien required in connection with a supplemental loan insured pursuant to section 241 of the Act;

(c) An inferior or superior lien on equipment as may be approved in connection with an equipment leasing program approved by HUD;

(d) An inferior or superior lien on accounts receivable as approved by HUD as collateral for a line of credit or other borrowing by a hospital insured under this part that has extraordinary needs such as cash flow difficulties; or

(e) Similar liens otherwise approved by HUD.

§242.78 Zoning, deed, and building restrictions.

The project when completed shall not violate any material zoning or deed restrictions applicable to the project site, and shall comply with all applicable building and other governmental codes, ordinances, regulations, and requirements.

§242.79 Environmental quality determinations and standards.

Requirements set forth in 24 CFR part 50, "Protection and Enhancement of Environmental Quality," 24 CFR part 51, "Environmental Criteria and Standards," and 24 CFR part 55, "Floodplain Management," governing environmental review responsibilities (as applicable) and any additional environmental standards, reviews, or determinations required by HUD apply to this program.

§242.81 Lead-based paint poisoning prevention.

Requirements set forth in 24 CFR part 35 apply to this program.

§242.82 Energy conservation.

Construction, mechanical equipment, and energy and metering selections shall provide cost-effective energy conservation in accordance with standards established by HUD.

§242.83 Debarment and suspension.

The requirements set forth in 24 CFR part 24 apply to this program.

§242.84 Previous participation and compliance requirements.

The requirements set forth in 24 CFR part 200, subpart H, apply to this program.

§ 242.86 Property and mortgage assessment.

The requirements set forth in 24 CFR part 200, subpart E, regarding the mortgagor's responsibility for making those investigations, analysis, and inspections it deems necessary for protecting its interests in the property apply to these programs.

§ 242.87 Certifications.

Any agreement, undertaking, statement, or certification required by HUD shall specifically state that it has been made, presented, and delivered for the purpose of influencing an official action of the FHA, and of HUD, and may be relied upon by HUD as a true statement of the facts contained therein.

§ 242.89 Supplemental loans.

A loan, advance of credit, or purchase of an obligation representing a loan or advance of credit made for the purpose of financing improvements or additions (including the refinancing of any indebtedness incurred in connection with the early commencement of work on such improvements or additions, subject to the requirements of §§ 242.15 and 242.45) to a hospital covered by a mortgage insured under this section of the Act or for a Commissioner-held mortgage, or equipment for a hospital, may be insured pursuant to the provisions of section 241 of the Act and under the provisions of this part as applicable and such additional terms and conditions as established by HUD. See subpart B of 24 CFR part 241 with respect to the contract of mortgage insurance for all loans insured under section 241 of the Act. See 24 CFR part 241, subpart C, for energy improvements.

§ 242.90 Eligibility of mortgages covering hospitals in certain neighborhoods.

(a) A mortgage financing the repair, substantial rehabilitation, or construction of a hospital located in an older declining urban area shall be eligible for insurance under this subpart, subject to compliance with the additional requirements of this section.

(b) The mortgage shall meet all of the requirements of this subpart, except such requirements (other than those relating to labor standards and prevailing wages or environmental review) as are judged to be not applicable on the basis of the following determinations to be made by HUD.

(1) That the conditions of the area in which the property is located prevent the application of certain eligibility requirements of this subpart.

(2) That the area is reasonably viable, and there is a need in the area for an adequate hospital to serve low and moderate income families.

(3) That the mortgage to be insured is an acceptable risk.

(c) Mortgages complying with the requirements of this section shall be insured under this subpart pursuant to section 223(e) of the National Housing Act. Such mortgages shall be insured under and be the obligation of the Special Risk Insurance Fund.

[72 FR 67546, Nov. 28, 2007, as amended at 73 FR 35923, June 25, 2008]

§ 242.91 Eligibility of refinancing transactions.

(a) *Refinancing an FHA-insured mortgage.* A mortgage given to refinance an existing insured mortgage under Section 241 or Section 242 of the Act covering a hospital may be insured under this subpart pursuant to Section 223(a)(7) of the Act. Insurance of the new, refinancing mortgage shall be subject to the following limitations:

(1) *Principal amount.* The principal amount of the refinancing mortgage shall not exceed the lesser of:

(i) The original principal amount of the existing insured mortgage; or

(ii) The unpaid principal amount of the existing insured mortgage, to which may be added loan closing charges associated with the refinancing mortgage, and costs, as determined by HUD, of improvements, upgrading, or additions required to be made to the property.

(2) *Debt service rate.* The monthly debt service payment for the refinancing mortgage may not exceed the debt service payment charged for the existing mortgage.

(3) *Mortgage term.* The term of the new mortgage shall not exceed the unexpired term of the existing mortgage, except that the new mortgage may have a term of not more than 12 years in excess of the unexpired term of the

existing mortgage in any case in which HUD determines that the insurance of the mortgage for an additional term will inure to the benefit of the FHA Insurance Fund, taking into consideration the outstanding insurance liability under the existing insured mortgage, and the remaining economic life of the property.

(4) *Minimum loan amount.* The mortgagee may not require a minimum principal amount to be outstanding on the loan secured by the existing mortgage.

(b) *Refinancing capital debt not insured by FHA.* A mortgage given to refinance the capital debt of an existing hospital that is not insured under section 241 or section 242 of the Act may be insured under this subpart pursuant to Section 223(f) of the National Housing Act. The mortgage may be executed in connection with the purchase or refinancing of an existing hospital without substantial rehabilitation. A mortgage insured pursuant to this subpart shall meet all other requirements of this part. The FHA Commissioner shall prescribe such terms and conditions as the FHA Commissioner deems necessary to assure that:

(1) The refinancing is employed to lower the monthly debt service costs (taking into account any fees or charges connected with such refinancing) of such existing hospital;

(2) The proceeds of any refinancing will be employed only to retire the existing capital debt; pay for limited rehabilitation totaling less than 20 percent of the mortgage amount; and pay the necessary cost of refinancing on such existing hospital;

(3) Such existing hospital is economically viable; and

(4) The applicable requirements of Section 242 for certificates, studies, and statements have been met.

[78 FR 8344, Feb. 5, 2013]

§ 242.92 Minimum principal loan amount.

A mortgagee may not require, as a condition of providing a loan secured by a mortgage insured under this part, that the principal amount of the mortgage exceed a minimum amount established by the mortgagee.

§ 242.93 Amendment of regulations.

The regulations in this subpart may be amended by HUD at any time and from time to time, in whole or in part, but such amendment shall not adversely affect the interests of a mortgagee or lender under the insurance on any mortgage or loan already insured, and shall not adversely affect the interests of a mortgagee or lender on any mortgage or loan to be insured on which HUD has issued a commitment to insure.

PART 244—MORTGAGE INSURANCE FOR GROUP PRACTICE FACILITIES [TITLE XI]

Subpart A—Eligibility Requirements

Sec.
244.1 Eligibility requirements.
244.2 License.

Subpart B—Contract Rights and Obligations

244.251 Cross-reference.

AUTHORITY: 12 U.S.C. 1715b, 1749aaa–5); 42 U.S.C. 3535(d).

SOURCE: 36 FR 24663, Dec. 22, 1971, unless otherwise noted.

Subpart A—Eligibility Requirements

SOURCE: 61 FR 14407, Apr. 1, 1996, unless otherwise noted.

§ 244.1 Eligibility requirements.

The requirements set forth in 24 CFR part 200, subpart A, apply to group practice facilities (title XI) of the National Housing Act (12 U.S.C. 1749aaa), as amended.

§ 244.2 License.

The Commissioner shall not insure any mortgage under this part unless the appropriate licensing agency for the State, municipality or other political subdivision in which a project is or is to be located provides such assurances as the Commissioner considers necessary that the facility will comply with any applicable State or local standards and requirements for such facilities.

Subpart B—Contract Rights and Obligations

§ 244.251 Cross-reference.

(a) All of the provisions, except § 207.258b, of part 207, subpart B of this chapter relating to mortgages insured under section 207 of the National Housing Act apply to a mortgage covering a group practice facility insured under title XI of the National Housing Act.

(b) For the purposes of this subpart all references in part 207 of this chapter to section 207 of the Act shall be construed to refer to title XI of the Act.

(c) All of the definitions in § 244.1 shall apply to this subpart. In addition as used in this part, the term *contract of insurance* means the agreement evidenced by the Commissioner's insurance endorsement and includes the provisions of this subpart and of the Act.

[36 FR 24663, Dec. 22, 1971, as amended at 50 FR 38787, Sept. 25, 1985]

PART 245—TENANT PARTICIPATION IN MULTIFAMILY HOUSING PROJECTS

Subpart A—General Provisions

AUTHORITY: 12 U.S.C. 1715z–1b; 42 U.S.C. 3535(d).

Subpart A—General Provisions

§ 245.5 Purpose.

The purpose of this part is to recognize the importance and benefits of cooperation and participation of tenants in creating a suitable living environment in multifamily housing projects and in contributing to the successful operation of such projects, including their good physical condition, proper maintenance, security, energy efficiency, and control of operating costs.

[50 FR 32402, Aug. 12, 1985]

§ 245.10 Applicability of part.

(a) Except as otherwise expressly limited in this section, this part applies in its entirety to a mortgagor of any multifamily housing project that meets the following—

(1) *Project subject to HUD insured or held mortgage under the National Housing Act.* The project has a mortgage that—

(i) Has received final endorsement on behalf of the Secretary and is insured or held by the Secretary under the National Housing Act (12 U.S.C. 1701—1715z–20); and

(ii) Is assisted under:

(A) Section 236 of the National Housing Act (12 U.S.C. 1715z–1);

(B) The Section 221(d)(3) BMIR Program;

(C) The Rent Supplement Program;

(D) The Section 8 Loan Management Set-Aside Program following conversion to such assistance from the Rent Supplement Program assistance;

(2) *Formerly HUD-owned project.* The project—

(i) Before being acquired by the Secretary, was assisted under:

(A) Section 236 of the National Housing Act (12 U.S.C. 1715z–1);

(B) The Section 221(d)(3) BMIR Program;

(C) The Rent Supplement Program; or

(D) The Section 8 LMSA Program following conversion to such assistance from assistance under the Rent Supplement Program; and

(ii) Was sold by the Secretary subject to a mortgage insured or held by the Secretary and an agreement to maintain the low- and moderate-income character of the project;

(3) *State or local housing finance agency project.* The project receives assistance under section 236 of the National Housing Act (12 U.S.C. 1715z–1) or the Rent Supplement Program (12 U.S.C. 1701s) administered through a state or local housing finance agency, but does not have a mortgage insured under the National Housing Act or held by the Secretary. Subject to the further limitation in paragraph (b) of this section, only the provisions of subparts A, B and C of this part, and of subpart E of this part for requests for approval of a conversion of a project from project-paid utilities to tenant-paid utilities or of a reduction in tenant utility allowances, apply to a mortgagor of such a project;

(4) The project receives project-based assistance under section 8 of the United States Housing Act of 1937 (this regulation does not cover tenant participation in PHAs that administer such project-based assistance);

(5) The project receives enhanced vouchers under the Low-Income Housing Preservation and Resident Homeownership Act of 1990, the provisions of the Emergency Low Income Housing Preservation Act of 1987, or the Multifamily Assisted Housing Reform and Affordability Act of 1997, as amended;

(6) The project receives assistance under the Section 202 Direct Loan program or the Section 202 Supportive Housing for the Elderly program; or

(7) The project receives assistance under the Section 811 Supportive Housing for Persons with Disabilities program.

(b) *Limitation for cooperative mortgagor.* Only the provisions of subparts A and C of this part apply to a mortgagor of any multifamily housing project described in paragraph (a) of this section if the mortgagor is a cooperative housing corporation or association.

(c) *Definitions. Rent Supplement Program* means the assistance program authorized by section 101 of the Housing and Urban Development Act of 1965 (12 U.S.C. 1701s).

Section 8 LMSA Program means the Section 8 Loan Management Set-Aside Program implemented under 24 CFR part 886, subpart A.

Section 221(d)(3) BMIR Program means the below-market interest rate mortgage insurance program under section 221(d)(3) and the proviso of section 221(d)(5) of the National Housing Act (12 U.S.C. 1715l(d)(3) and 1715l(d)(5)).

[61 FR 57961, Nov. 8, 1996, as amended at 65 FR 36280, June 7, 2000; 68 FR 20325, Apr. 24, 2003]

§245.15 Notice to tenants.

(a) Whenever a mortgagor is required under subparts D or E of this part to serve notice on the tenants of a project, the notice must be served by delivery, except, for a high-rise project, the notice may be served either by delivery or by posting. If service is made by delivery, a copy of the notice must be delivered directly to each unit in the project or mailed to each tenant. If service is made by posting, the notice must be posted in at least three conspicuous places within each building in which the affected dwelling units are located and, during any prescribed tenant period, in a conspicuous place at the address stated in the notice where the materials in support of the mortgagor's proposed action are to be made available for inspection and copying. Posted notices must be maintained intact and in legible form during any prescribed notice period.

(b) For purposes of computing time periods following service of notice, service is effected, in the case of service by delivery, when all notices have been delivered or mailed and, in the case of service by posting, when all notices have been initially posted.

[50 FR 32402, Aug. 12, 1985, as amended at 61 FR 57961, Nov. 8, 1996]

Subpart B—Tenant Organizations

SOURCE: 65 FR 36281, June 7, 2000, unless otherwise noted.

§ 245.100   Right of tenants to organize.

The tenants of a multifamily housing project covered under § 245.10 have the right to establish and operate a tenant organization for the purpose of addressing issues related to their living environment, which includes the terms and conditions of their tenancy as well as activities related to housing and community development.

§ 245.105   Recognition of tenant organizations.

Owners of multifamily housing projects covered under § 245.10, and their agents, must:

(a) Recognize legitimate tenant organizations; and (b) Give reasonable consideration to concerns raised by legitimate tenant organizations.

§ 245.110   Legitimate tenant organizations.

A tenant organization is legitimate if it has been established by the tenants of a multifamily housing project covered under § 245.10 for the purpose described in § 245.100, and meets regularly, operates democratically, is representative of all residents in the development, and is completely independent of owners, management, and their representatives.

§ 245.115   Protected activities.

(a) Owners of multifamily housing projects covered under § 245.10, and their agents, must allow tenants and tenant organizers to conduct the following activities related to the establishment or operation of a tenant organization:

(1) Distributing leaflets in lobby areas;

(2) Placing leaflets at or under tenants' doors;

(3) Distributing leaflets in common areas;

(4) Initiating contact with tenants;

(5) Conducting door-to-door surveys of tenants to ascertain interest in establishing a tenant organization and to offer information about tenant organizations;

(6) Posting information on bulletin boards;

(7) Assisting tenants to participate in tenant organization activities;

(8) Convening regularly scheduled tenant organization meetings in a space on site and accessible to tenants, in a manner that is fully independent of management representatives. In order to preserve the independence of tenant organizations, management representatives may not attend such meetings unless invited by the tenant organization to specific meetings to discuss a specific issue or issues; and

(9) Formulating responses to owner's requests for:

(i) Rent increases;

(ii) Partial payment of claims;

(iii) The conversion from project-based paid utilities to tenant-paid utilities;

(iv) A reduction in tenant utility allowances;

(v) Converting residential units to non-residential use, cooperative housing, or condominiums;

(vi) Major capital additions; and

(vii) Prepayment of loans.

(b) In addition to the activities listed in paragraph (a) of this section, owners of multifamily housing projects covered under § 245.10, and their agents, must allow tenants and tenant organizers to conduct other reasonable activities related to the establishment or operation of a tenant organization.

(c) Owners of multifamily housing projects and their agents shall not require tenants and tenant organizers to

Office of Assistant Secretary for Housing, HUD

§ 245.135

obtain prior permission before engaging in the activities permitted under paragraphs (a) and (b) of this section.

§ 245.120 Meeting space.

(a) Owners of multifamily housing projects covered under § 245.10, and their agents, must reasonably make available the use of any community room or other available space appropriate for meetings that is part of the multifamily housing project when requested by:

(1) Tenants or a tenant organization and used for activities related to the operation of the tenant organization; or

(2) Tenants seeking to establish a tenant organization or collectively address issues related to their living environment.

(b) Tenant and tenant organization meetings must be accessible to persons with disabilities, unless this is impractical for reasons beyond the organization's control. If the complex has an accessible common area or areas, it will not be impractical to make organizational meetings accessible to persons with disabilities.

(c) *Fees.* An owner of a multifamily housing project covered under § 245.10 may charge a reasonable, customary and usual fee, approved by the Secretary as may normally be imposed for the use of such facilities in accordance with procedures prescribed by the Secretary, for the use of meeting space. An owner may waive this fee.

§ 245.125 Tenant organizers.

(a) A tenant organizer is a tenant or non-tenant who assists tenants in establishing and operating a tenant organization, and who is not an employee or representative of current or prospective owners, managers, or their agents.

(b) Owners of multifamily housing projects covered under § 245.10, and their agents, must allow tenant organizers to assist tenants in establishing and operating tenant organizations.

(c) *Non-tenant tenant organizers.* (1) If a multifamily housing project covered under § 245.10 has a consistently enforced, written policy against canvassing, then a non-tenant tenant organizer must be accompanied by a tenant while on the property of the multi-

family housing project, except in the case of recipients of HUD Outreach and Assistance Training Grants ("OTAG") or other direct HUD grants designed to enable recipients to provide education and outreach to tenants concerning HUD's mark-to-market program (see 24 CFR parts 401 and 402), who are conducting eligible activities as defined in the applicable Notice of Funding Availability for the grant or other effective grant document.

(2) If a multifamily housing project covered under § 245.10 has a written policy favoring canvassing, any non-tenant tenant organizer must be afforded the same privileges and rights of access as other uninvited outside parties in the normal course of operations. If the project does not have a consistently enforced, written policy against canvassing, the project shall be treated as if it has a policy favoring canvassing.

§ 245.130 Tenants' rights not to be recanvassed.

A tenant has the right not to be recanvassed against his or her wishes regarding participation in a tenant organization.

§ 245.135 Enforcement.

(a) Owners of housing identified in § 245.10, and their agents, as well as any principals thereof (as defined in 2 CFR part 2424), who violate any provision of this subpart so as to interfere with the organizational and participatory rights of tenants, may be liable for sanctions under 2 CFR part 2424. Such sanctions may include:

(1) *Debarment.* A person who is debarred is prohibited from future participation in federal programs for a period of time. The specific rules and regulations relating to debarment are found at 2 CFR part 2424.

(2) *Suspension.* Suspension is a temporary action with the same effect as debarment, to be taken when there is adequate evidence that a cause for debarment may exist and immediate action is needed to protect the public interest. The specific rules and regulations relating to suspension are found at 2 CFR part 2424.

(3) *Limited Denial of Participation.* An LDP generally excludes a person from

449

future participation in the federal program under which the cause arose. The duration of an LDP is generally up to 12 months. The specific rules and regulations relating to LDPs are found at 2 CFR part 2424, subpart J.

(b) These sanctions may also apply to affiliates (as defined in 2 CFR part 2424) of these persons or entities.

(c) The procedures in 2 CFR part 2424 shall apply to actions under this subpart.

[72 FR 73495, Dec. 27, 2007]

Subpart C—Efforts To Obtain Assistance

§ 245.205 Efforts to obtain assistance.

(a) Mortgagors subject to the requirements of this subpart shall not interfere with the efforts of tenants to obtain rent subsidies or other public assistance.

(b) A mortgagor subject to the requirements of this subpart who is a party to a rent supplement contract under section 101 of the Housing and Urban Development Act of 1965 (12 U.S.C. 1701s), a rental assistance payments contract under part 236, subpart D, of this chapter, or a Housing Assistance Payments Contract under 24 CFR part 886 shall not refuse to make assistance under such contract available to an existing tenant who is eligible therefor, provided that sufficient contract and budget authority and contract units are available under the contract. However, this provision shall not be deemed to require the mortgagor to give priority in the allocation of any such available assistance to an existing tenant instead of an eligible applicant on the mortgagor's waiting list or otherwise to supersede tenant selection procedures which are not otherwise inconsistent with applicable program regulation or instructions.

(c) Subject to the provisions of any contract made in connection with the purchase of a multifamily housing project owned by the Secretary, this section shall not be deemed to require a mortgagor subject to the requirement of this subpart to enter into a Housing Assistance Payments Contract pursuant to 24 CFR part 982 for the benefit of an existing tenant who ob-

tains a Certificate of Family Participation.

[48 FR 28437, June 22, 1983. Redesignated at 50 FR 32403, Aug. 12, 1985, as amended at 61 FR 57961, Nov. 8, 1996]

§ 245.210 Availability of information.

A mortgagor subject to the requirements of this subpart shall make available to tenants any information concerning rent subsidies or other public assistance that is prepared and distributed by HUD to the project for the purpose of distribution to tenants.

[48 FR 28437, June 22, 1983. Redesignated at 50 FR 32403, Aug. 12, 1985]

Subpart D—Procedures for Requesting Approval of an Increase in Maximum Permissible Rents

Source: 50 FR 32403, Aug. 12, 1985, unless otherwise noted.

§ 245.305 Applicability of subpart.

(a) The requirements of this subpart apply to any request by a mortgagor, as provided by § 245.10, for HUD approval of an increase in maximum permissible rents.

(b) For purposes of this subpart, an increase in utility charges paid directly by the tenant does not constitute an increase in rents.

§ 245.310 Notice to tenants.

(a) At least 30 days before submitting a request to HUD for approval of an increase in maximum permissible rents, the mortgagor must notify the tenants of the proposed rent increase. Copies of the notice must be served on the tenants as provided in § 245.15. The notice must contain the following information in the following format or an equivalent format:

NOTICE TO TENANTS OF INTENTION TO SUBMIT A REQUEST TO HUD FOR APPROVAL OF AN INCREASE IN MAXIMUM PERMISSIBLE RENTS

Date of Notice

Take notice that on [date] we plan to submit a request for approval of an increase in the maximum permissible rents for [name of apartment complex] to the United States Department of Housing and Urban Development

(HUD). The proposed increase is needed for the following reasons:

1.
2.
3.

The rent increases for which we have requested approval are:

Bedrooms	Present rent [1]		Proposed increase [1]		Proposed rent [1]	
	Basic	Market	Basic	Market	Basic	Market
5	$	$	$	$	$	....	$
0	....	....	....	....	....	
1	....	....	....	....	....	
2	....	....	....	....	....	
3	....	....	....	....	....	
4	....	....	....	....	....	

[1] Separate columns for basic and market rent should be used only for projects assisted under sec. 236 of the National Housing Act. In addition, in projects with more than 1 type of apartment having the same number of bedroom but different rents, each type should be listed separately.

A copy of the materials that we are submitting to HUD in support of our request will be available during normal business hours at [address] for a period of 30 days from the date of service of this notice for inspection and copying by tenants of [name of apartment complex] and, if the tenants wish, by legal or other representatives acting for them individually or as a group.

During a period of 30 days from the date of service of this notice, tenants of [name of apartment complex] may submit written comments on the proposed rent increase to us at [address]. Tenant representatives may assist tenants in preparing those comments. (If, at HUD's request or otherwise , we make any material change during the comment period in the materials available for inspection and copying, we will notify the tenants of the change or changes, and the tenants will have a period of 15 days from the date of service of this additional notice (or the remainder of any applicable comment period, if longer) in which to inspect and copy the materials as changed and to submit comments on the proposed rent increase). These comments will be transmitted to HUD, along with our evaluation of them and our request for the increase. You may also send a copy of your comments directly to HUD at the following address: United States Department of Housing and Urban Development [address of local HUD field office with jurisdiction over rent increases for the project], Attention: Director, Housing Management Division, Re: Project No. [Name of Apartment Complex].

HUD will approve, adjust upward or downward, or disapprove the proposed rent increase upon reviewing the request and comments. When HUD advises us in writing of its decision on our request, you will be notified. If the request is approved, any allowable increase will be put into effect only after a period of at least 30 days from the date you are served with that notice and in accordance with the terms of existing leases.

[Name of mortgagor or managing agent]

(b) The mortgagor must comply with all representations made in the notice. The materials to be made available to tenants for inspection and copying are those specified in §245.315.

§245.315 Materials to be submitted to HUD.

When the notice referred to in §245.310 is served on the tenants, the mortgagor must send to the local HUD office copies of the following documents described in either paragraph (a) or (b) of this section, as specified by the local HUD office:

(a) Documents to be submitted under profit and loss approach:

(1) A copy of the notice to tenants;

(2) An annual Statement of Profit and Loss, Form HUD–92410, covering the project's most recently ended accounting year (this statement must have been audited by an independent public accountant if the project is required by HUD to prepare audited financial statements), and Form HUD–92410 for the intervening period since the date of the last annual statement if more than four months have elapsed since that date;

(3) A narrative statement of the reasons for the requested increase in maximum permissible rents; and

(4) An estimate of the reasonably anticipated increases in project operating costs that will occur within twelve months of the date of submission of materials under this section.

(5) A status report on the project's implementation of its current Energy Conservation Plan.

(b) Documents to be submitted under the forward-budget approach:

(1) A cover letter summarizing the reasons a rent increase is needed;

(2) A copy of the notice to tenants;

(3) A rent increase worksheet providing an income and expense budget for the 12 months following the anticipated effective date of the proposed rent increase;

(4) A brief statement explaining the basis for the expense lines on the rent increase worksheet;

451

(5) A partially completed Rent Schedule, Form HUD-92458;

(6) If the tenants receive utility allowances, the mortgagor's recommended utility allowance for each unit type and brief statement explaining the basis for the recommended increase; and

(7) A status report on the project's implementation of its current Energy Conservation Plan.

(The information collection requirements in paragraph (a) of this section were approved by the Office of Management and Budget under control number 2502-0310 and the information collection requirements in paragraph (b) were approved under control number 2502-0324)

§ 245.320 Request for increase.

Upon expiration of the period for tenant comments required in the notice format in § 245.310 and after review of the comments submitted to the mortgagor, the mortgagor must submit to the local HUD office, in addition to the materials enumerated in § 245.315 and any revisions thereto, the request for an increase in the maximum permissible rents, together with the following:

(a) Copies of all written comments submitted by the tenants to the mortgagor;

(b) The mortgagor's evaluation of the tenants' comments with respect to the request;

(c) A certification by the mortgagor that:

(1) It has complied with all of the requirements of this subpart;

(2) The copies of the materials submitted in support of the proposed increase were located in a place reasonably convenient to tenants in the project during normal business hours and that requests by tenants to inspect the materials, as provided for in the notice, were honored;

(3) All comments received from tenants were considered by the mortgagor in making its evaluation; and

(4) Under the penalties and provisions of title 18 U.S.C., section 1001, the statements contained in this request and its attachments have been examined by me and, to the best of my knowledge and belief, are true, correct, and complete.

§ 245.325 Notification of action on request for increase.

(a) When processing a request for an increase in maximum permissible rents, HUD shall take into consideration reasonably anticipated increases in project operating costs that will occur (1) within 12 months of the date of submission of materials to HUD under § 245.315(a) (profit and loss approach) or (2) within 12 months of the anticipated effective date of the proposed rent increase for submissions under § 245.315(b) (forward-budget approach).

(b) After HUD has considered the request for an increase in rents, has found that it meets the requirements of § 245.320, and has made its determination to approve, adjust upward or downward, or disapprove the request, it will furnish the mortgagor with a written statement of the reasons for approval, adjustment upward or downward, or disapproval. The mortgagor must make the reasons for approval, adjustment, or disapproval known to the tenants, by service of notice on them as provided in § 245.15.

§ 245.330 Non-insured projects.

(a) In the case of a proposed rent increase for a project assisted under section 236 of the National Housing Act or section 101 of the Housing and Urban Development Act of 1965, but which does not have a mortgage insured by HUD or held by the Secretary, the provisions of this section and of §§ 245.305 through 245.320 shall apply to the mortgagor (project owner), except that—

(1) The notice format prescribed in § 245.310 must be modified to reflect the procedural changes made by this section;

(2) The material (including tenant comments) required to be submitted to HUD under §§ 245.315 and 245.320 must be submitted to the State or local agency administering the section 236 assistance or rent supplement assistance contracts, rather than to HUD. An equivalent State or local agency form or standard accounting form may be substituted for the Statement of Profit and Loss, Form HUD-92410 required under § 245.315(a)(2), if approved by the local HUD office; and

(3) The State or local agency must certify that the mortgagor has complied with the requirements of §§245.310, 245.315, 245.320, and 245.325.

(b) After the State or local agency has considered the request for an increase in maximum permissible rents that meets the requirements of §245.320 (including consideration of anticipated cost increases, as provided in §245.325(a)), it must make a determination to approve, adjust upward or downward, or disapprove the request. If the agency determines to approve or adjust the request, it must submit to the appropriate local HUD office the mortgagor's requests for approval of an increase in maximum permissible rents, along with the comments of the tenants and the mortgagor's evaluation of the comments, and must certify to HUD that the mortgagor is in compliance with the requirements of this subpart. HUD shall review the agency's determination and certification and, within 30 days, of their submission to HUD, notify the agency of its approval, adjustment upward or downward, or disapproval of the proposed rent increase. HUD will not unreasonably withhold approval of a rent increase approved by the State or local agency.

(c) If the agency determines to disapprove the request, there is no HUD review of the agency's determination.

(d) The agency must notify the mortgagor of the final disposition of the request, and it must furnish the mortgagor with a written statement of the reasons for its approval, adjustment, or disapproval. The mortgagor must make the reasons for approval, adjustment or disapproval known to the tenants, by service of notice on them as provided in §245.15.

Subpart E—Procedures for Requesting Approval of a Covered Action

SOURCE: 61 FR 57962, Nov. 8, 1996, unless otherwise noted.

§245.405 Applicability of subpart.

The requirements of this subpart apply to any request by a mortgagor, as provided by §245.10, for HUD approval of one or more of the following covered actions:

(a) Conversion of a project from project-paid utilities to tenant-paid utilities, or a reduction in tenant utility allowances.

(b) Conversion of residential units in a multifamily housing project to a nonresidential use or to condominiums, or the transfer of the project to a cooperative housing mortgagor corporation or association. Conversion of a project to a cooperative or of a portion of a project to nonresidential use does not constitute a change of use requiring mortgagee approval.

(c) A partial release of mortgage security. The requirements of this subpart, however, do not apply to any release of property from a mortgage lien with respect to a utility easement or a public taking of such property by condemnation or eminent domain.

(d) Making major capital additions to the project. For the purposes of this subpart, the term "major capital additions" includes only those capital improvements that represent a substantial addition to the project. Upgrading or replacing existing capital components of the project does not constitute a major capital addition to the project.

§245.410 Notice to tenants.

At least 30 days before submitting a request to HUD for approval of an action described in §245.405, the mortgagor must serve notice of the proposed covered action on the project tenants, as provided in §245.15. The notice shall state that—

(a) The mortgagor intends to submit a request to HUD for approval of the covered action or actions specified in the notice;

(b) The tenants have the right to participate as provided in §245.420, and what those rights are, including the address at which the materials required to be made available for inspection and copying under that section are to be kept;

(c) Tenant comments on the proposed covered action may be sent to the mortgagor at a specified address or directly to the local HUD office, and comments sent to the mortgagor will be transmitted to HUD, along with the mortgagor's evaluation of them, when the request for HUD's approval is submitted;

(d) HUD will approve or disapprove the proposed action, based upon its review of the information submitted and all tenant comments received. In the case of a proposed reduction in tenant-paid utilities, the notice must also state that HUD may adjust the proposed reduction upward or downward;

(e) In the case of a proposed conversion of residential units, partial release of mortgage security, or major capital additions to the project, the proposed action may require the owner to request HUD approval of a rent increase; and

(f) The mortgagor will notify the tenants of HUD's decision and it will not begin to effect any approved action (in accordance with the terms of existing leases) until at least 30 days from the date of service of the notification.

§ 245.415 Submission of materials to HUD: Timing of submission.

(a) *Initial submission.* The mortgagor must submit the materials applicable to the covered action, as specified in §§ 245.416 through 245.419, to the local HUD office when the notice required under § 245.410 is served on the tenants.

(b) *Subsequent submission.* If additional notice under § 245.420(c) is required, the mortgagor must submit to HUD any changes to the materials required under §§ 245.416 through 245.419 when the notice required under § 245.420(c) is served on the tenants.

§ 245.416 Initial submission of materials to HUD: Conversion from project-paid utilities to tenant-paid utilities or a reduction in tenant utility allowances.

In the case of a conversion from project-paid utilities to tenant-paid utilities or a reduction in tenant utility allowances, the mortgagor must submit the following materials to the local HUD office:

(a) A copy of the notice to tenants;

(b) In the case of a proposed conversion from project-paid utilities to tenant-paid utilities—

(1) A statement indicating:

(i) The type of utility or utilities involved;

(ii) The number of units in the project by type and size;

(iii) The average utility consumption data by unit type and size for comparable projects, and utility rate information, as obtained from the utility supplier;

(iv) The estimated monthly cost of the utilities to be paid by the tenants by unit type and size, based upon the consumption data and rate information described in paragraph (b)(1)(iii) of this section;

(v) The monthly cost for the past year of paying for the utility or utilities involved on a project basis (actual cost) and by unit type and size (estimated breakdown);

(vi) An estimate of the cost of conversion, as obtained from the utility supplier or from bids from contractors;

(vii) The source and terms of financing for the conversion (to the extent known); and

(viii) The estimated effect of the conversion on the total housing costs of the tenants by unit type and size, taking into account the estimated cost of conversion (including the cost of its financing), the estimated monthly cost of utilities to be paid by the tenants by unit type and size, the proposed utility allowances, and the estimated change in the rents paid to the mortgagor resulting from the conversion; and

(2) A copy of the portion of the project's Energy Conservation Plan which addresses the cost-effectiveness determination associated with converting the project to tenant-paid utilities; and

(c) In the case of a proposed reduction in tenant utility allowances, a statement indicating the information described in paragraphs (b)(1)(i), (b)(1)(ii), (b)(1)(iii) and (b)(1)(iv) of this section, the utility allowances proposed for reduction, and a justification of the proposed reduction.

(Approved by the Office of Management and Budget under control number 2502–0310)

§ 245.417 Initial submission of materials to HUD: Conversion of residential units to a nonresidential use, or to cooperative housing or condominiums.

In the case of a conversion of residential units to a nonresidential use, or to cooperative housing or condominiums, the mortgagor must submit the following materials to the local HUD office in accordance with §§245.415 and 245.419:

(a) In the case of a proposed conversion of residential rental units to nonresidential use:

(1) A statement describing the proposed conversion;

(2) A statement describing the estimated effect of the proposed conversion on the value of the project, the project rent schedule, the number of dwelling units in the project, a list of the units to be converted and their occupancy, the amount of subsidy available to the project, and the project income and expenses (including property taxes);

(3) A statement assessing the compatibility of the proposed nonresidential use with the residential character of the project;

(4) Written approval of the mortgagee if required;

(5) An undertaking by the mortgagor to pay all relocation costs that may be required by HUD for tenants required to vacate the project because of the conversion; and

(6) A copy of the notice to tenants.

(b) In the case of a proposed transfer of the project to a cooperative housing mortgagor corporation or association (conversion of residential rental units to residential cooperative housing), the materials specified in paragraphs (a)(1), (a)(2) and (a)(3) of this section and the following additional materials:

(1) An estimate of the demand for cooperative housing, including an estimate of the number of present tenants interested in purchasing cooperative housing;

(2) Estimates of downpayments and monthly carrying charges that will be required; and

(3) Copies of proposed organizational documents, including By-Laws, Articles of Incorporation, Subscription Agreement, Occupancy Agreement, and Sale Document.

(c) In the case of a proposed conversion of residential rental units to condominium units, the materials specified in paragraphs (a)(1), (a)(4), and (a)(6) of this section and the following additional materials:

(1) An estimate of the demand for condominium housing, including an estimate of the number of present tenants interested in purchasing units;

(2) Estimates of downpayments, monthly mortgage payments and condominium association fees that will be required; and

(3) A list of the units to be converted and their occupancy.

(Approved by the Office of Management and Budget under control number 2502–0310)

§245.418 **Initial submission of materials to HUD: Partial release of mortgage security.**

In the case of a partial release of mortgage security, the mortgagor must submit the following materials to the local HUD office:

(a) A statement describing the portion of the property that is proposed to be released and the transaction requiring the release;

(b) A statement describing the estimated effect of the proposed release on the value of the project, the number of dwelling units in the project, the project income and expenses (including property taxes), the amount of subsidy available to the project, and the project rent schedule;

(c) A statement describing the proposed use of the property to be released and the persons who will have responsibility for the operation and maintenance of that property, and assessing the compatibility of that use with the residential character of the project;

(d) A statement describing the proposed use of any proceeds to be received by the mortgagor as a result of the release; and

(e) A copy of the notice to tenants.

(Approved by the Office of Management and Budget under control number 2502–0310)

§245.419 **Initial submission of materials to HUD: Major capital additions.**

In the case of major capital additions, the mortgagor must submit the following materials to the local HUD office:

(a) The general plans and sketches of the proposed capital additions;

(b) A statement describing the estimated effect of the proposed capital additions on the value of the project, the project income and expenses (including property taxes), and the project rent schedule;

(c) A statement describing how the proposed capital additions will be financed and the effect, if any, of that financing on the tenants;

(d) A statement assessing the compatibility of the proposed capital additions with the residential character of the project; and

(e) A copy of the notice to tenants.

(Approved by the Office of Management and Budget under control number 2502–0310)

§ 245.420   Rights of tenants to participate.

(a) The tenants (including any legal or other representatives acting for tenants individually or as a group) must have the right to inspect and copy the materials that the mortgagor is required to submit to HUD pursuant to § 245.415, for a period of 30 days from the date on which the notice required under § 245.410 is served on the tenants. During this period, the mortgagor must provide a place (as specified in the notice) reasonably convenient to tenants in the project where tenants and their representatives can inspect and copy these materials during normal business hours.

(b) The tenants have the right during this period to submit written comments on the proposed conversion to the mortgagor and to the local HUD office. Tenant representatives may assist tenants in preparing these comments.

(c) If the mortgagor, whether at HUD's request or otherwise, makes any material change during a tenant comment period in the materials submitted to HUD pursuant to § 245.415, the mortgagor must notify the tenants of the change, in the manner provided in § 245.15, and make the materials as changed available for inspection and copying at the address specified in the notice for this purpose. The tenants have a period of 15 days from the date of service of this additional notice (or the remainder of any applicable comment period, if longer) in which to inspect and copy the materials as changed and to submit comments on the proposed covered action, before the mortgagor may submit its request to

HUD for approval of the covered action.

§ 245.425   Submission of request for approval to HUD.

Upon completion of the tenant comment period, the mortgagor must review the comments submitted by tenants and their representatives and prepare a written evaluation of the comments. The mortgagor must then submit the following materials to the local HUD office:

(a) The mortgagor's written request for HUD approval of the covered action;

(b) Copies of all written tenant comments;

(c) The mortgagor's evaluation of the tenant comments on the proposed conversion or reduction;

(d) A certification by the mortgagor that it has complied with all of the requirements of § 245.410, § 245.415, §§ 245.416 through 245.419, as applicable, § 245.420, and this section; and

(e) Such additional materials as HUD may have specified in writing.

(Approved by the Office of Management and Budget under control number 2502–0310)

§ 245.430   Decision on request for approval.

(a) After considering the mortgagor's request for approval and the materials submitted in connection with the request, HUD must notify the mortgagor in writing of its approval or disapproval of the proposed covered action, including, if applicable, its adjustment upward or downward of the proposed reduction in tenant-paid utilities. HUD must provide its reasons for its determination.

(b) The mortgagor must notify the tenants of HUD's decision in the manner provided in § 245.15. If HUD has approved the proposed covered action, the notice must state:

(1) The effective date of the covered action (which must be at least 30 days from the date of service of the notice and in accordance with the terms of existing leases);

(2) In the case of HUD's approval of a conversion from project-paid utilities to tenant-paid utilities or a reduction in tenant utility allowances, the amount of the rent to be paid to the

mortgagor and the utility allowance for each unit; and

(3) In the case of HUD's approval of a conversion of residential units in a multifamily housing project to a non-residential use or the transfer of the project to a cooperative housing mortgagor corporation or association, which residential rental units are to be converted and whether the conversion is to nonresidential use or to cooperative or condominium units.

§ 245.435 Non-insured projects: Conversion from project-paid utilities to tenant-paid utilities or a reduction in tenant utility allowances.

(a) In the case of a proposed conversion from project-paid utilities to tenant-paid utilities or a reduction in tenant utility allowances involving a project that is assisted under section 236 of the National Housing Act (12 U.S.C. 1715z–1) or section 101 of the Housing and Urban Development Act of 1965 (12 U.S.C. 1701s) but that does not have a mortgage insured by HUD or held by the Secretary, the provisions of this section and of §§ 245.405 through 245.425 apply to the mortgagor (project owner), except that—

(1) The notice to tenants required under § 245.410 must be modified to reflect the procedural changes made by this section;

(2) The materials (including tenant comments) required to be submitted to HUD under §§ 245.415 and 245.425 must be submitted to the State or local agency administering the Section 236 assistance or rent supplement assistance contracts, rather than to HUD; and

(3) The State or local agency must certify that the mortgagor has complied with the requirements of §§ 245.410, 245.415, 245.416, 245.420, and 245.425.

(b) After the State or local agency has considered the request for approval of a conversion or reduction that meets the requirements of § 245.425, it must make a determination to approve or disapprove the conversion, or to approve, adjust upward or downward, or disapprove the reduction. If the agency determines to approve the conversion or reduction (as originally proposed or as adjusted), it must submit to the appropriate local HUD office the mortgagor's request for approval of the conversion or reduction, along with the comments of the tenants and the mortgagor's evaluation of the comments, and must certify to HUD that the mortgagor is in compliance with the requirements of this subpart. HUD must review the agency's determination and certification and notify the agency of its approval or disapproval of the proposed conversion or of its approval, adjustment upward or downward, or disapproval of the proposed reduction. HUD will not unreasonably withhold approval of a conversion or reduction approved by the State or local agency.

(c) If the agency determines to disapprove the conversion or reduction, there is no HUD review of the agency's determination.

(d) The agency must notify the mortgagor of the final disposition of the request, and it must furnish the mortgagor with a written statement of the reasons for its approval or disapproval. The mortgagor must make the reasons for approval or disapproval known to the tenants, by service of notice on them as provided in § 245.15. If the agency has approved the proposed conversion or a reduction, the notice must set forth the information prescribed in § 245.430(b) (1) and (2).

PART 246—LOCAL RENT CONTROL

Subpart A—General Provisions

Subpart B—Unsubsidized Insured Projects

Subpart C—Subsidized Insured Projects

AUTHORITY: 12 U.S.C. 1715b; 42 U.S.C. 3535(d).

Subpart A—General Provisions

§ 246.1   Scope and effect of regulations.

(a) The regulation of rents for a project coming within the scope of "Subpart B—Unsubsidized Insured Projects" is preempted under these regulations only when the Department determines that the delay or decision of the local rent control board, or other authority regulating rents pursuant to state or local law (hereinafter referred to as board) jeopardizes the Department's economic interest in a project covered by that subpart. The regulation of rents for projects coming within the scope of "Subpart C—Subsidized Insured Projects" is preempted in its entirety by the promulgation of these regulations. The regulation of rents for projects coming within the scope of "Subpart D—HUD-Owned Projects" rests within the exclusive jurisdiction of the Department.

(b) Any state or local law, ordinance, or regulation is without force and effect insofar as it purports to regulate rents of: (1) Projects for which a determination of preemption has been made pursuant to subpart B, or (2) projects coming within the scope of subpart C or D. Compliance with such law, ordinance, or regulation shall not be required as a condition of, or prerequisite to, the remedy of eviction, and any law, ordinance, or regulation which purports to require such compliance is similarly without force and effect.

(c) It is the purpose of the Department that these regulations shall bar all actions of a board that would in any way frustrate the purpose or effect of these regulations or that would in any way delay, prevent or interfere with the implementation of any increase in rental charges approved by HUD.

(d) These regulations may be offered as a defense to a proceeding by whomever initiated, which may be brought or threatened to be brought against any owner, mortgagor or managing agent of a project subject to these reg-ulations who demands, receives or retains, or seeks to demand, receive or retain, rental charges approved by HUD, or as a basis for declaratory, injunctive or other relief against any person or agency, public or private, who attempts to enforce, or threatens to enforce, any state or local law, ordinance, or regulation which is without force and effect by reason of this regulation.

(e) This part applies to mortgages insured under the National Housing Act. It does not apply to mortgages insured under section 542(c) of the Housing and Community Development Act of 1992 (12 U.S.C. 1707).

[40 FR 49318, Oct. 22, 1975. Redesignated at 49 FR 6713, Feb. 23, 1984, and amended at 58 FR 64038, Dec. 3, 1993; 59 FR 62524, Dec. 5, 1994]

Subpart B—Unsubsidized Insured Projects

SOURCE: 44 FR 58504, Oct. 10, 1979, unless otherwise noted. Redesignated at 49 FR 6713, Feb. 23, 1984.

§ 246.4   Applicability.

This subpart applies to all projects with mortgages insured or held by HUD, except those to which subpart C applies.

[40 FR 49318, Oct. 22, 1975. Redesignated at 49 FR 6713, Feb. 23, 1984]

§ 246.5   Rental charges.

The Department will generally not interfere in the regulation of rents by a rent control board or agency constituted under State or local laws (hereinafter referred to as board) for unsubsidized projects with mortgages insured or held by HUD. However, HUD will preempt the regulation of rents, together with any board regulations which require the mortgagor to offer a lease for a term in excess of one year, under certain conditions. This preemption may occur for such a project when the Department determines that the delay or decision of a board prevents the mortgagor from achieving a level of residential income necessary to maintain and operate adequately the project, which includes sufficient funds to meet the financial obligations under the mortgage."

§246.6 Initiation.

When a mortgagor determines that the permitted increase in rents as prescribed by the board will not provide a rent level necessary to maintain and operate adequately the project, and the mortgagor elects to request preemption under this subpart, it shall:

(a) File an application for whatever relief or redetermination is permitted under the State or local law and;

(b) Notify: (1) The tenants in accordance with §246.7 of this subpart, (2) the appropriate HUD office pursuant to §246.8, and (3) the board of the mortgagor's intention to file a request for preemption of local rent control regulation pursuant to the provisions of regulations in this subpart. This action may be taken if either the board's written decision is unacceptable to the mortgagor or no written decision is received from the board within 30 days of the mortgagor's request under paragraph (a) of this section.

§246.7 Notice to tenants.

At least 30 days before filing a formal request to HUD for preemption of local rent control regulations, the mortgagor shall notify the tenants of its intention to so file. Copies of the Notice shall be:

(a) Delivered directly or by mail to each tenant; and

(b) Posted in at least 3 conspicuous places within each structure or building in which the affected dwelling units are located.

The Notice shall contain the addresses where the materials, which constitute a complete submission as required by §246.8 in support of the proposed preemption request, are to be made available to tenants as well as the required information in the following equivalent format:

NOTICE TO TENANTS OF INTENTION TO FILE A REQUEST TO HUD FOR PREEMPTION OF LOCAL RENT CONTROL REGULATIONS

Date of Notice _____

Take notice that on (Date) we requested the (Name) board to review our application for redetermination of permitted rents.

Take further notice that on (Date), if the (Name) board fails to approve an income level necessary to maintain and operate adequately the project, or to act upon our request, we plan to file a request for preemp-

tion of local rent control regulations for (Name of Apartment Complex) with the United States Department of Housing and Urban Development (HUD) which will result in an increase in your rental rate as provided within the terms of your lease. The requested preemption action is supported by the following:

(1) HUD approved Gross Potential Income: Year approved, ____, $_____.

(2) Current Total Residential Rents Allowed by Local Rent Control Board, $_____.

(3) Projected Total Annual Residential Rents Allowable Under Local Board Regulations 6 Months After Date of this Notice, $_____.

(4) Income Required to Operate Project as Supported by Profit and Loss Statement Being Submitted to HUD, $_____.

Copies of the materials that we intend to submit to HUD in support of our request will be available during normal business hours as well as one evening a week after business hours which will be (Day) at (Address) for a period of 30 days from the date of this Notice. The materials may be inspected and copied by tenants of (Name of Apartment Complex and HUD Project No.) and if the tenants wish, by legal or other representatives duly authorized in writing to act for one or more of the tenants.

During a period of 30 days from the date of this notice, tenants of (Name of Apartment Complex and HUD Project No.) may submit written comments on the proposed preemption request to us at (Address). Tenant representatives may assist tenants in preparing those comments. The inspection and comment period will be extended as necessary to (a) assure a 30-day comment period on a complete mortgagor's submission and (b) to allow at least 5 days to comment on any written decision made by the board, if the decision is received by the mortgagor on or before the expiration of the thirty-day period and it was not available to the tenants during the first 25 days of the 30-day period. These comments will be transmitted to HUD, along with our evaluation of them and our preemption request. You may also send a copy of your comments directly to HUD at the following address: United States Department of Housing and Urban Development, (address of local HUD field office with jurisdiction over preemption of rents for the project) Attention: Director, Housing Re: (Project No.) and (Name of Apartment Complex). HUD will approve or diapprove the preemption request in whole or in part upon reviewing the materials and comments. When HUD advises us in writing of its decision on our request, you will be notified at least 30 days before any change in the rental structure is put into effect, in accordance with the terms of existing leases.

(Name of mortgagor or managing agent)

The mortgagor shall comply with all representations made in this Notice.

§ 246.8 Materials to be submitted to HUD in support of preemption request.

(a) After posting or delivery of the Notice as required by § 246.7, the mortgagor shall immediately send HUD notification of its intention to file a preemption request, to include:

(1) The written Notice to the tenants, which will state the date of its posting and distribution.

(2) An annual Statement of Profit and Loss, on a form prescribed by the Commissioner, audited by an independent public accountant and covering the most recently ended accounting year, and if more than four months have elapsed since the date of the Profit and Loss Statement, an unaudited accrual Profit and Loss Statement on a form prescribed by the Commissioner for the intervening period since the date of the annual statement, with the mortgagor's certification as to its accuracy.

(3) A certified statement which provides a separate breakdown for the percentage of vacancies for the present and previous year.

(4) A certified statement which provides a separate breakdown of the actual rent loss due to nonpayment of rent for the past 2 years.

(5) A certified statement which provides a separate breakdown of rent loss due to tenant turnover for the past 2 years.

(6) A certified statement covering known approved rate or cost increases not yet experienced by the project which can be documented by the following:

(i) Tax rates or appraisals,

(ii) Utility rates,

(iii) Contracts for employees or services,

(iv) Insurance, and

(7) A certified statement covering known decreases of rates or costs not yet experienced by the project which have been approved and can be documented as follows:

(i) Tax rates or appraisals,

(ii) Utility rates,

(iii) Contracts for employees or services,

(iv) Insurance.

If there are none, the mortgagor must so certify.

(8) A copy of the full application to the board with supporting documentation.

(b) The local HUD office shall review the mortgagor's submission promptly upon receipt, to ascertain that it is complete as required by paragraph (a) of this section. Should the submission be found to be incomplete, the local HUD office shall notify the mortgagor within 48 hours of the review of its determination that further material is necessary to constitute a complete submission as defined in paragraph (a) of this section.

(c) When the submission is complete, the HUD office shall hold the mortgagor's submission as specified in paragraph (a) of this section in abeyance until a preemption request is received pursuant to § 246.9.

(d) If the mortgagor subsequently resubmits any change to the submission as described in paragraphs (a) (1) through (7) of this section, it will be required to provide the tenants with an additional 30 days to comment.

§ 246.9 Request for preemption.

(a) Upon expiration of the period for tenant comments required by this rule and after review of the comments submitted to it, the mortgagor may submit its request for preemption. That request must include the following:

(1) A certification by the mortgagor following the requirements specified in paragraph (b) of this section;

(2) Copies of all written comments submitted by the tenants to the mortgagor;

(3) The mortgagor's evaluation of the tenant's comments with respect to the request; and

(4) The board's decision or a statement from the mortgagor certifying that a decision from the board has not been received.

(b) The certification of the mortgagor as required by paragraph (a)(1) of this section shall include the following:

(1) That the Notice required by § 246.7 was given pursuant to the provisions of that section;

(2) That the mortgagor has taken reasonable steps to assure that the substance of the Notice has been conveyed to each resident household, and that the mortgagor exercised its best efforts to assure that the posted Notices were maintained intact and in legible form for the specified thirty (30) days;

(3) That: (i) The copies of the materials submitted in support of the preemption request were located in a place reasonably convenient to tenants in the project during normal business hours and at least one evening a week after business hours, and (ii) that requests by tenants to inspect such materials, as provided for in the Notice, were honored;

(4) That copies of all comments received from the tenants were considered and are being transmitted to HUD together with the certifications; and

(5) A statement that "under the penalties and provisions of title 18 U.S.C., section 1001, the statements contained in this application and its attachments have been examined by me and, to the best of my knowledge and belief, are true, correct, and complete."

(c) Should the mortgagor receive a delayed decision from the board after filing its preemption request, HUD shall be informed immediately and furnished with a copy of the board's decision.

§246.10 HUD procedures.

(a) The local HUD office will review the information submitted by the mortgagor together with the decision of the board, if any. The local HUD office will, if it finds that the delay or decision of the board fails to provide adequate residential income to protect the Department's economic interest in the projects and the board will not modify its position to the satisfaction of the local HUD office, make a report with appropriate recommendations concerning the actions that should be taken by HUD to the Office of Multifamily Housing Management and Occupancy, Headquarters. The report shall be sent to the Office of Multifamily Housing Management and Occupancy, Headquarters, and shall include appropriate recommendations concerning the action that should be taken by HUD.

(b) The Office of Multifamily Housing Management and Occupancy will review the report and will consider whether to preempt the board's regulation. If it finds that the income level permitted by the board is inadequate to maintain the project as described in §246.5, it shall issue a formal certification to the board that its authority has been preempted as to such rents. Copies of the certification shall be transmitted to the mortgagor, the local HUD office, and the board.

§246.11 Notification of action on preemption request.

(a) After HUD has considered the preemption request which meets the requirements of §246.9 and has made its determination to approve or disapprove the request, it will furnish the mortgagor with a written statement of the reasons for approval or disapproval. The mortgagor shall make known to tenants, by posting or delivery in the manner outlined in §246.7, the reasons for approval or disapproval.

(b) The mortgagor may effect collection of the HUD-approved income level which is set at the time of the preemption determination after the expiration of 30-days notice to the tenants, subject to the terms and rights a tenant may have under the existing lease.

(c) Once the project reaches the income level approved under these procedures, the project will be returned to the control of the local rent control board covering both the rents and the terms of prospective leases.

§246.12 Preemption of prospective term of lease.

(a) In those instances where it will take more than 60 days (2 months) for the project to reach the new income levels, HUD preemption of prospective lease terms shall be effective for those new or renewed leases which by regulation of a local rent control board would require the mortgagor to offer a lease for a term in excess of one year.

(b) As a condition for HUD preemption, the mortgagor must give only one-year leases to tenants whose leases expire during the preemption period.

Subpart C—Subsidized Insured Projects

§ 246.20 Applicability.

This subpart applies to all projects with mortgages insured or held by HUD that receive a subsidy in the form of:

(a) Interest reduction payments under section 236 of the National Housing Act;

(b) Below-market interest rates under section 221(d)(3) and (5) of the National Housing Act;

(c) Direct loans at below-market interest rates under section 202 of the Housing Act of 1959 (as in effect immediately before October 1, 1991);

(d) Rent supplement payments under section 101 of the Housing and Urban Development Act of 1965;

(e) Housing assistance payments under 24 CFR part 886, subpart A (Section 8 Loan Management Set Aside), for projects that converted their rent supplement contracts under section 101 of the Housing and Urban Development Act of 1965 to such assistance for the term of the HAP contract; or

(f) Housing assistance payments pursuant to a contract under section 8 of the United States Housing Act of 1937 or section 23 of that Act (as in effect immediately before January 1, 1975), except that this subpart will only apply with respect to units occupied by tenants receiving housing assistance thereunder if the contract covers fewer than all units in the project.

[63 FR 64803, Nov. 23, 1998]

§ 246.21 Rental charges.

The Department finds that it is necessary and desirable to minimize defaults by the mortgagor in its financial obligations with regard to projects covered by this subpart, and to assist mortgagors to preserve the continued viability of those projects as a housing resource for low-income families. The Department also finds that it is necessary and desirable to protect the substantial economic interest of the Federal Government in those projects. Therefore, the Department concludes that it is in the national interest to preempt, and it does hereby preempt, the entire field of rent regulation by local rent control boards, (hereinafter referred to as board), or other authority, acting pursuant to state or local law as it affects projects covered by this subpart.

[40 FR 49318, Oct. 22, 1975. Redesignated at 44 FR 58506, Oct. 10, 1979, and at 49 FR 6713, Feb. 23, 1984]

§ 246.22 Procedures.

(a) The mortgagor shall file its application for approval of increases in rental charges with the appropriate local office of HUD.

(b) The local HUD office will process the application for increases in rental charges in accordance with HUD's regulations, including part 245 of this chapter, and instructions and procedures, all adopted pursuant to the statutory authority described in § 246.8, and shall notify in writing any board in the area in which the project is located that it is processing the application and, that, pursuant to this subpart, HUD has preempted the entire field of rent regulation by a board acting pursuant to state or local law as it affects the project.

(c) The mortgagor may effect collection of the new rents in accordance with the procedures described in part 245, subpart D of this chapter. The mortgagor shall furnish the board a schedule of any new rents approved by HUD within ten (10) days after the approved rents have become effective. Notice to the board of the approved increases in rents does not confer upon the board a right to approve or disapprove the Department's action or to exercise jurisdiction over the implementation of the rent increases by the mortgagor. The sole purpose of the notice is to inform the board of the lawful rents that may be charged for projects covered by this subpart.

[40 FR 49318, Oct. 22, 1975. Redesignated at 44 FR 58506, Oct. 10, 1979, and at 49 FR 6713, Feb. 23, 1984]

Subpart D—HUD-Owned Projects

§ 246.30 Rental charges.

The Department has exclusive jurisdiction over the rents of all projects which it owns, irrespective of the existence, or the provisions, of any State or local rent control law or ordinance.

[40 FR 49318, Oct. 22, 1975. Redesignated at 44 FR 58506, Oct. 10, 1979, and at 49 FR 6713, Feb. 23, 1984]

§ 246.31 Procedures.

(a) The local HUD office will notify in writing any local rent control board (hereinafter referred to as board) in the area in which the project is located that it is considering increasing the rents for a project within the scope of this subpart, and that the increases are expected to become effective after the expiration of thirty (30) days' notice to the tenants, subject to whatever rights a tenant may have under a lease. The local HUD office will also notify the board that, pursuant to this subpart, the Department has exclusive jurisdiction over the rents for the project.

(b) After the increases have become effective, the local HUD office will furnish the board a schedule of the new rents that are being charged by HUD. Notice to the board of the increased rents does not confer upon the board a right to approve or disapprove of the Department's action, or to exercise jurisdiction over the implementation of the rent increases by the Department. The sole purpose of the notice is to inform the board of the lawful rents that may be charged for projects covered by this subpart.

[40 FR 49318, Oct. 22, 1975. Redesignated at 44 FR 58506, Oct. 10, 1979, and at 49 FR 6713, Feb. 23, 1984]

PART 247—EVICTIONS FROM CERTAIN SUBSIDIZED AND HUD-OWNED PROJECTS

Subpart A—Subsidized Projects

AUTHORITY: 12 U.S.C. 1701q, 1701s, 1715b, 1715*l*, and 1715z–1; 42 U.S.C. 1437a, 1437c, 1437f, and 3535(d).

SOURCE: 41 FR 43330, Sept. 30, 1976, unless otherwise noted. Redesignated at 49 FR 6713, Feb. 23, 1984.

Subpart A—Subsidized Projects

§ 247.1 Applicability.

(a) Except as provided in §§ 247.5 and 247.6(c), the provisions of this subpart shall apply to all decisions by a landlord to terminate the occupancy of a tenant in a subsidized project as defined in § 247.2(e). (Termination of tenancy of a family assisted with tenant-based assistance under the Section 8 Existing Housing Certificate or Housing Voucher Program is not subject to this part.)

(b) Landlords of subsidized projects that have been assisted under a covered housing program listed in 24 CFR 5.2003 must comply with 24 CFR part 5, subpart L (Protection for Victims of Domestic Violence, Dating Violence, Sexual Assault, or Stalking), as described in § 200.38.

[54 FR 236, Jan. 4, 1989, as amended at 81 FR 80806, Nov. 16, 2016]

§ 247.2 Definitions.

Drug-related criminal activity means the illegal manufacture, sale, distribution, use or possession with the intent to manufacture, sell, distribute, or use, of a controlled substance as defined in section 102 of the Controlled Substances Act, 21 U.S.C. 802.

Eviction means the dispossession of the tenant from the leased unit as a result of the termination of the tenancy, including a termination prior to the end of a term or at the end of a term.

Landlord means either the owner of the property or his representative, or the managing agent or his representative, as shall be designated by the owner.

Rental agreement means all agreements, written or oral, between the landlord and tenant (and valid rules and regulations adopted by the landlord pursuant to a written agreement) relating to the use and occupancy of a dwelling unit and surrounding premises.

State landlord and tenant act means any state statute or local ordinance which imposes obligations on a landlord and tenant in connection with the occupancy of a dwelling unit and surrounding premises and which provides that violations of such obligations by the tenant constitute grounds for eviction.

Subsidized project means a multifamily housing project (with the exception of a project owned by a cooperative housing mortgagor corporation or association) that receives the benefit of subsidy in the form of: below-market interest rates under section 221(d) (3) and (5), interest reduction payments under section 236 of the National Housing Act, or below market interest rate direct loans under section 202 of the Housing Act of 1959. For purposes of this part, *subsidized project* also includes those units in a housing project that receive the benefit of:

(1) Rental subsidy in the form of rent supplement payments under section 101 of the Housing and Urban Development Act of 1965 (12 U.S.C. 1701s); or

(2) Housing assistance payments for project-based assistance under Section 8 of the 1937 Act (42 U.S.C. 1437f). However, this part is not applicable to Section 8 project-based assistance under parts 880, 881, 883 and 884 of this title (except as specifically provided in those parts).

[41 FR 43330, Sept. 30, 1976. Redesignated at 49 FR 6713, Feb. 23, 1984, and amended at 53 FR 3368, Feb. 5, 1988; 54 FR 236, Jan. 4, 1989; 61 FR 47381, Sept. 6, 1996; 66 FR 28797, May 24, 2001]

§ 247.3 Entitlement of tenants to occupancy.

(a) *General.* The landlord may not terminate any tenancy in a subsidized project except upon the following grounds:

(1) Material noncompliance with the rental agreement,

(2) Material failure to carry out obligations under any state landlord and tenant act,

(3) Criminal activity by a covered person in accordance with sections 5.858 and 5.859, or alcohol abuse by a covered person in accordance with section 5.860. If necessary, criminal records can be obtained for lease enforcement purposes under section 5.903(d)(3).

(4) Other good cause.

No termination by a landlord under paragraph (a)(1) or (2) of this section shall be valid to the extent it is based upon a rental agreement or a provision of state law permitting termination of a tenancy without good cause. No termination shall be valid unless it is in accordance with the provisions of § 247.4.

(b) *Notice of good cause.* The conduct of a tenant cannot be deemed other good cause under § 247.3(a)(4) unless the landlord has given the tenant prior notice that said conduct shall henceforth constitute a basis for termination of occupancy. Said notice shall be served on the tenant in the same manner as that provided for termination notices in § 247.4(b).

(c) *Material noncompliance.* The term *material noncompliance with the rental agreement* includes:

(1) One or more substantial violations of the rental agreement;

(2) Repeated minor violations of the rental agreement that:

(i) Disrupt the livability of the project,

(ii) Adversely affect the health or safety of any person or the right of any tenant to the quiet enjoyment of the leased premises and related project facilities,

(iii) Interfere with the management of the project, or

(iv) Have an adverse financial effect on the project;

(3) If the tenant:

(i) Fails to supply on time all required information on the income and composition, or eligibility factors, of the tenant household, as provided in 24 CFR part 5; or

(ii) Knowingly provides incomplete or inaccurate information as required under these provisions; and

(4) Non-payment of rent or any other financial obligation due under the rental agreement (including any portion thereof) beyond any grace period permitted under State law, except that the payment of rent or any other financial obligation due under the rental

464

agreement after the due date, but within the grace period permitted under State law, constitutes a minor violation.

(Approved by the Office of Management and Budget under control number 2502-0204)

[41 FR 43330, Sept. 30, 1976. Redesignated at 49 FR 6713, Feb. 23, 1984, and amended at 54 FR 39697, Sept. 27, 1989; 56 FR 7531, Feb. 22, 1991; 61 FR 13624, Mar. 27, 1996; 61 FR 47382, Sept. 6, 1996; 66 FR 28797, May 24, 2001]

§ 247.4 Termination notice.

(a) *Requisites of Termination Notice.* The landlord's determination to terminate the tenancy shall be in writing and shall: (1) State that the tenancy is terminated on a date specified therein; (2) state the reasons for the landlord's action with enough specificity so as to enable the tenant to prepare a defense; (3) advise the tenant that if he or she remains in the leased unit on the date specified for termination, the landlord may seek to enforce the termination only by bringing a judicial action, at which time the tenant may present a defense; and (4) be served on the tenant in the manner prescribed by paragraph (b) of this section.

(b) *Manner of service.* The notice provided for in paragraph (a) of this section shall be accomplished by: (1) Sending a letter by first class mail, properly stamped and addressed, to the tenant at his or her address at the project, with a proper return address, and (2) serving a copy of the notice on any adult person answering the door at the leased dwelling unit, or if no adult responds, by placing the notice under or through the door, if possible, or else by affixing the notice to the door. Service shall not be deemed effective until both notices provided for herein have been accomplished. The date on which the notice shall be deemed to be received by the tenant shall be the date on which the first class letter provided for in this paragraph is mailed, or the date on which the notice provided for in this paragraph is properly given, whichever is later.

(c) *Time of service.* When the termination of the tenancy is based on other good cause pursuant to § 247.3(a)(4), the termination notice shall be effective, and the termination notice shall so state, at the end of a term and in ac-

cordance with the termination provisions of the rental agreement, but in no case earlier than 30 days after receipt of the tenant of the notice. Where the termination notice is based on material noncompliance with the rental agreement or material failure to carry out obligations under a state landlord and tenant act pursuant to § 247.3(a)(1) or (2), the time of service shall be in accord with the rental agreement and state law.

(d) *Modification of rental agreement.* Notwithstanding any other provision of this subpart, the landlord may with the prior approval of HUD modify the terms and conditions of the rental agreement, effective at the end of the initial term or a successive term, by serving an appropriate notice on the tenant, together with the tender of a revised rental agreement or an addendum revising the existing rental agreement: Any increase in rent shall in all cases be governed by 24 CFR parts 245, 246 and other applicable HUD regulations. This notice and tender shall be served on the tenant in the same manner as provided for in § 247.4(b) and must be received by the tenant at least 30 days prior to the last date on which the tenant has the right to terminate the tenancy without being bound by the codified terms and conditions. The tenant may accept the modified terms and conditions by executing the tendered revised rental agreement or addendum, or may reject the modified terms and conditions by giving the landlord written notice in accordance with the rental agreement that he intends to terminate the tenancy.

(e) *Specificity of notice in rent nonpayment cases.* In any case in which a tenancy is terminated because of the tenant's failure to pay rent, a notice stating the dollar amount of the balance due on the rent account and the date of such computation shall satisfy the requirement of specificity set forth in paragraph (a)(2) of this section.

(f) *Failure of tenant to object.* The failure of the tenant to object to the termination notice shall not constitute a waiver of his rights to thereafter contest the landlord's action in any judicial proceeding.

[41 FR 43330, Sept. 30, 1976, as amended at 48 FR 22915, May, 23, 1983. Redesignated at 49 FR 6713, Feb. 23, 1984, as amended at 61 FR 47382, Sept. 6, 1996]

§ 247.5 Inapplicability to substantial rehabilitation or demolition.

This subpart shall not apply in any case in which the landlord terminates the occupancy of a tenant as a direct result of a determination, concurred in by HUD, to substantially rehabilitate or demolish the project or to dispose of the project to a purchaser who purchases for the purpose of substantial rehabilitation or demolition.

§ 247.6 Eviction.

(a) *General.* The landlord shall not evict any tenant except by judicial action pursuant to State or local law and in accordance with the requirements of this subpart.

(b) *Limitations on allegations of new grounds.* In any judicial action instituted to evict the tenant, the landlord must rely on grounds which were set forth in the termination notice served on the tenant under this subpart. The landlord shall not, however, be precluded from relying on grounds about which he or she had no knowledge at the time the termination notice was sent.

(c) *State and local law.* A tenant may rely on State or local law governing eviction procedures where such law provides the tenant procedural rights which are in addition to those provided by this subpart, except where such State or local law has been preempted under part 246 of this chapter or by other action of the United States.

[48 FR 22915, May, 23, 1983. Redesignated and amended at 49 FR 6713, 6715, Feb. 23, 1984]

§ 247.7 Implementation.

Every rental agreement entered into or renewed on and after the date on which this subpart is applicable to such tenant shall contain appropriate provisions implementing this subpart.

Subpart B—HUD-Owned Projects

§ 247.8 Incorporation by reference.

All of the provisions of subpart A of this part covering certain multifamily projects (excepting § 247.5) apply with full force to the property described in § 247.9 and they are hereby incorporated by reference.

§ 247.9 Applicability of procedures.

The procedures outlined in this subpart apply to all decisions to terminate the occupancy of a tenant by the termination of a lease prior to the end of its term or at the end of a term where the tenant resides in any multifamily project which is presently owned by HUD, regardless of whether said project was a subsidized project prior to the acquisition of title by HUD.

§ 247.10 Inapplicability to substantial rehabilitation or demolition; right of disposition unimpaired.

This subpart shall not apply in any case in which HUD terminates the occupancy of a tenant as a direct result of a determination by HUD to substantially rehabilitate or demolish the project or to dispose of the project to a purchaser who purchases for the purpose of substantial rehabilitation or demolition. Nothing in this subpart should be construed to affect in any way the right of HUD to exercise its full statutory authority and discretion to dispose of property acquired pursuant to the National Housing Act.

PART 248—PREPAYMENT OF LOW INCOME HOUSING MORTGAGES

Subpart A—General

Subpart B—Prepayments and Plans of Action Under the Low Income Housing Preservation and Resident Homeownership Act of 1990

AUTHORITY: 12 U.S.C. 17151 note, 4101 note, and 4101–4124; 42 U.S.C. 3535(d).

Subpart A—General

SOURCE: 57 FR 12041, Apr. 8, 1992, unless otherwise noted.

§ 248.1 Purpose.

The purpose of this part is to—

(a) Preserve and retain to the maximum extent practicable as housing affordable to low income families or persons those privately owned dwelling units that were produced for such purpose with Federal assistance, without unduly restricting the owners' prepayment rights;

(b) Minimize the involuntary displacement of tenants currently residing in such housing;

(c) Work in partnership with State and local government and the private sector in the provision and operation of housing that is affordable to very low, low and moderate income families; and

(d) Facilitate the sale of housing to residents under a resident homeownership program.

§ 248.3 Applicability.

The requirements of subparts B and C of this part apply to any project that is eligible low income housing, as defined in subparts B and C of this part respectively, on or after November 1, 1987, except that such requirements shall not apply to a project which receives assistance under title IV, subtitle B of the Cranston-Gonzalez National Affordable Housing Act in connection with a homeownership program approved by the Commissioner thereunder.

§ 248.5 Election to proceed under subpart B or subpart C of this part.

(a) Any owner who has not submitted a notice of intent prior to January 1, 1991, pursuant to either § 248.211 or § 248.105, shall proceed under subpart B of this part.

(b) Any owner who has filed a plan of action with the Commissioner on or before October 11, 1990 pursuant to subpart C of this part, regardless of whether or not the Commissioner has approved such plan of action or whether the owner has received incentives thereunder, may proceed under subpart B of this part by submitting a notice of intent to the Commissioner in accordance with § 248.105 within 30 days after publication of revised Appraisal Guidelines or within thirty days after the Commissioner notifies the owner of HUD's final approval of the plan of action, whichever is later. The notice of intent shall state that the owner is exercising its conversion right pursuant to this section. If the owner fails to file a notice of intent within that period, the owner forfeits its right of conversion. In awarding incentives to an owner who elects to proceed under subpart B of this part in accordance with this section, the Commissioner shall take into consideration any incentives which the owner has already received under subpart C of this part.

(c) Any owner of housing that becomes eligible low income housing, as defined in subpart B of this part, before January 1, 1991, and who before such date, filed a notice of intent under § 248.211 of subpart C of this part, may, unless a plan of action was submitted after October 11, 1990, elect to proceed under subpart B or under subpart C of this part. An owner must indicate its election by submitting to the Commissioner, within 30 days of the effective date of this part, a notice of election to proceed indicating whether it wishes to proceed under subpart B or subpart C of this part, or proceed under subpart B of this part until completion of the appraisals and then elect either subpart B or subpart C of this part. An owner who chooses to retain its option until after the completion of the appraisals under § 248.111 must submit a new notice of intent to the Commissioner within 30 days after receipt of the information provided by the Commissioner under § 248.131. The notice of intent shall be submitted in accordance with either § 248.105 (for owners electing to proceed under subpart B of this part) or § 248.211 (for owners electing to proceed under subpart C of this part). Any owner who fails to file a notice of intent within the 30-day period may not proceed under subpart C of this part, but may proceed under subpart B of this part by filing a new notice of intent thereafter. If an owner who has filed a notice of intent before January 1, 1991 elects under this paragraph to proceed under subpart C of this part, it may change its election within 30 days after receipt of the information provided by the Commissioner under § 248.131 by filing a new notice of intent under § 248.211. For purposes of calculating any time periods or deadlines under this part for actions following the filing of the notice of intent, the date on which the owner submits the new notice of intent under this paragraph shall be deemed the date of the filing of the notice of intent. Any owner who, exercising its option under paragraph (c) of this section, submits a notice of intent under § 248.211 after the Commissioner has incurred the cost of having an appraisal, or appraisals, performed pursuant to § 248.111 of subpart A of this part, shall reimburse the Commissioner for these expenses within 30 days of receipt of a bill covering these expenses.

(d) For an owner who has elected under paragraph (c) of this section to proceed under subpart C of this part, the Commissioner shall provide sufficient assistance to enable a nonprofit organization that has purchased, or will purchase, eligible low income housing to meet project oversight costs, as that term is defined in § 248.201.

(e) The Commissioner shall not refuse to offer incentives under § 248.231

to any owner who filed a notice of intent under §248.211 before October 15, 1991, based solely on the date of filing of the plan action.

(f) An owner who has filed a plan of action after October 11, 1990, pursuant to §248.213, may not elect to proceed under subpart B of this part.

[57 FR 12041, Apr. 8, 1992, as amended at 58 FR 37814, July 13, 1993]

Subpart B—Prepayments and Plans of Action Under the Low Income Housing Preservation and Resident Homeownership Act of 1990

SOURCE: 57 FR 12041, Apr. 8, 1992, unless otherwise noted.

§248.101 Definitions.

Acquisition Loan. A loan or advance of credit made to a qualified purchaser of eligible low income housing and insured by the Commissioner under part 241, subpart E of this chapter.

Adjusted Income. Annual income, as specified in part 5 of this title, less allowances specified in the definition of "Adjusted Income" in part 5 of this title.

Aggregate Preservation Rent. The extension preservation rent or transfer preservation rent, as defined under this section.

Annual Authorized Return. That amount an owner of an eligible low income housing project may receive in distributions from the project each year, plus debt service payments payable each year attributable to the equity take-out portion of any loan approved under the plan of action, expressed as a percentage of the project's extension preservation equity.

Bona Fide Offer. A certain and unambiguous offer to purchase an eligible low income housing project pursuant to subpart B of this part made in good faith by a qualified purchaser with the intent that such offer result in the execution of an enforceable, valid and binding contract. A bona fide offer shall include, for purposes of subpart B of this part, a contract of sale and an earnest money deposit, as set forth in §248.157(g). For mandatory sales under §248.161, the offer must include a con-

tract of sale, an earnest money deposit and also be for a purchase price which equals the transfer preservation value.

Capital Improvement Loan. A direct loan originated by the Commissioner under part 219, subpart C of this chapter.

Community-Based Nonprofit Organization. A private nonprofit organization that—

(1) Is organized under State or local laws;

(2) Has no part of its net earnings inuring to the benefit of any member, founder, contributor, or individual;

(3) Is neither controlled by, nor under the direction of, individuals or entities seeking to derive profit or gain from the organization.

(4) Has applied for, or has a tax exemption ruling from the Internal Revenue Service under section 501(c) of the Internal Revenue Code of 1986;

(5) Does not include a public body (including the participating jurisdiction) or an instrumentality of a public body. An organization that is State or locally chartered may qualify as a community-based nonprofit organization; however, the State or local government may not have the right to appoint more than one-third of the membership of the organization's governing body and no more than one-third of the board members can be public officials;

(6) Has standards of financial accountability that conform to 2 CFR 200.302 and 200.303;

(7) Has among its purposes the provision of decent housing that is affordable to low-income and moderate-income persons, as evidenced in its charter, articles of incorporation, resolutions or by-laws;

(8) Maintains accountability to low income community residents by—

(i) Maintaining at least one-third of its governing board's membership for low-income neighborhood residents, other low-income community residents, or elected representatives of low-income neighborhood organizations. For urban areas, "community" may be a neighborhood or neighborhoods, city, county, or metropolitan area; for rural areas, "community" may be a neighborhood or neighborhoods, town, village, county, or multi-county area (but not the entire State); and

(ii) Providing a formal process for low-income, program beneficiaries to advise the organization on its decisions regarding the acquisition, rehabilitation and management of affordable housing.

Default. For purposes of § 248.105(a), the failure of the owner to make any payment due under the mortgage (including the full amount of the debt if the mortgagee has accelerated the debt on the basis of a non-monetary default) within 30 days after such payment becomes due.

Eligible Low Income Housing. Any project that is not subject to a use restriction imposed by the Commissioner that restricts the project to low and moderate income use for a period at least equal to the remaining term of the mortgage, and that is financed by a loan or mortgage—

(1) That is—

(i) Insured or held by the Commissioner under section 221(d)(3) of the National Housing Act and assisted under part 886, subpart A of this title because of a conversion from assistance under 215 of this chapter;

(ii) Insured or held by the Commissioner under part 221 of this chapter and bearing a below market interest rate as provided under § 221.518(b) of this chapter;

(iii) Insured, assisted, or held by the Commissioner or a State or State agency under part 236 of this chapter; or

(iv) A purchase money mortgage held by the Commissioner with respect to a project which, immediately prior to HUD's acquisition, would have been classified under paragraphs (1)(i), (ii), or (iii) of this definition; and

(2) That, under regulation or contract in effect before February 5, 1988, is or will within 24 months become eligible for prepayment without prior approval of the Commissioner.

Equity Loan. A loan or advance of credit to the owner of eligible low income housing and insured by the Commissioner under part 241, subpart E of this chapter.

Extension Preservation Equity. The extension preservation equity of a project is:

(1) The extension preservation value of the project determined under § 248.111; less

(2) The outstanding balance of any debt secured by the property.

Extension Preservation Rent. The extension preservation rent is the gross potential income for the project that would be required to support:

(1) The annual authorized return;

(2) Debt service on any rehabilitation loan for the project;

(3) Debt service on the federally-assisted mortgage(s) for the project;

(4) Project operating expenses; and

(5) Adequate reserves.

Extension Preservation Value. The fair market value of the project based on the highest and best use of the project as multifamily market-rate rental housing.

Fair market rent. The section 8 existing fair market rent published for effect and as defined under § 982.4 of this title, applicable to the jurisdiction in which the project is located, with adjustments, where appropriate, for projects in which tenants pay their own utilities. (No utility adjustments will be made to the fair market rent for purposes of determining the Federal cost limit.)

Federal Cost Limit. The greater of 120 percent of the section 8 existing fair market rent for the market area in which the project is located or 120 percent of the prevailing rents in the relevant local market area in which the project is located.

Federally-assisted Mortgage. Any mortgage as defined in this section, any insured operating loss loan secured by the project and any loan insured by the Commissioner under part 241 of this chapter.

Good Cause. With respect to displacement, the temporary or permanent uninhabitability of the project justifying relocation of all or some of the project's tenants (except where such uninhabitability is caused by the actions or inaction of the owner), or actions of the tenant that, under the terms of the tenant's lease and applicable regulations, constitute a basis for eviction.

HOME Investment Trust Fund. A public fund established in the general local or State government in which a project is located pursuant to title II of the Cranston-Gonzalez National Affordable Housing Act.

Homeownership Program. A program developed by a resident council for the sale of an eligible low income housing project to the tenants in accordance with the standards in § 248.173 or § 248.175.

Interest Reduction Payments. Payments made by the Commissioner pursuant to a contract to reduce the interest costs on a mortgage insured under part 236 of this chapter, as provided under subpart C of part 236 of this chapter.

Limited Equity Cooperative. A tenant cooperative corporation which, in a manner acceptable to the Secretary, restricts the initial and resale price of the shares of stock in the cooperative corporation so that the shares remain affordable to low income families and moderate income families.

Low Income Affordability Restrictions. Limits imposed by regulation or regulatory agreement on tenant rents, rent contributions, or income eligibility with respect to eligible low income housing.

Low Income Families. Families or persons whose incomes do not exceed the levels established for low income families under part 5 of this title.

Low Vacancy Area. A market area in which the current supply of decent, safe and sanitary, vacant, available rental units, as a proportion of the total overall rental inventory in the area is not sufficient to allow for normal growth and mobility, taking into account the need for vacancies resulting from turnover and to meet growth in renter households. The determination of a low vacancy area, as set forth in § 248.165(h), will be made by the Commissioner, utilizing the most recent available data for the market area on the rental inventory, renter households, rental vacancy rates and other factors as appropriate.

Moderate Income Families. Families or persons whose incomes are between 80 percent and 95 percent of median area income, as determined by the Commissioner, with adjustments for smaller and larger families.

Mortgage. The mortgage or deed of trust insured or held by the Commis-

sioner or a State or State agency under parts 221 or 236 of this title or the purchase money mortgage taken back by the Commissioner in connection with the sale of a HUD-owned project and held by the Commissioner, where such mortgage, deed or trust or purchase money mortgage is secured by eligible low income housing.

Nonprofit Organization. Any private, nonprofit organization or association that—

(1) Is incorporated under State or local law;

(2) Has no part of its net earnings inuring to the benefit of any member, founder, contributor, or individual;

(3) Complies with standards of financial accountability acceptable to the Commissioner; and

(4) Has among its principal purposes significant activities related to the provision of decent housing that is affordable to very low, low, and moderate income families.

Notice of Intent. An owner's notification to the Commissioner of its intention to terminate the low income affordability restrictions on the project through prepayment of the mortgage or voluntary termination of the insurance contract, to extend the low income affordability restrictions on the project, or to transfer the project to a qualified purchaser.

Owner. The mortgagor or trustor under the mortgage secured by eligible low income housing.

Participating Jurisdiction. For purposes of the resident homeownership program established in § 248.173, any State or unit of general local government that has been so designated in accordance with section 216 of the Cranston-Gonzalez National Affordable Housing Act of 1990 (42 U.S.C. 12746).

Plan of Action. A plan providing for the termination of the low income affordability restrictions on the project through prepayment of the mortgage or voluntary termination of the insurance contract, for extension of the low income affordability restrictions on the project, or for the transfer of the project to a qualified purchaser. A homeownership program constitutes a plan of action for purposes of subpart B of this part.

Prepayment. Prepayment in full of a mortgage, or a partial prepayment or series of partial prepayments that reduces the mortgage term by a least six months, except where the prepayment in full or partial prepayment results from the application of condemnation proceeds.

Preservation Equity. The extension preservation equity or transfer preservation equity, as defined under this section.

Preservation Value. The extension preservation value or transfer preservation value, as defined under this section.

Priority Purchaser. Any entity that is not a related party to the owner and that is either—

(1) A resident council organized to acquire the project in accordance with a resident homeownership program that meets the requirements of subpart B of this part; or

(2) Any nonprofit organization or State or local agency that agrees to maintain low income affordability restrictions for the remaining useful life of the project. A nonprofit organization or State or local agency that is affiliated with a for-profit entity for purposes of purchasing a project under subpart B of this part shall not be considered a priority purchaser.

Project oversight costs. Reasonable expenses incurred by a priority purchaser in carrying out its ongoing ownership responsibilities under an approved plan of action. Project oversight costs must be directly related to educating the priority purchaser's board of directors or otherwise supporting the board in its decision making. Project oversight costs may include staff, overhead, or third-party contract costs for:

(1) Ensuring adequate and responsible participation by the board of directors and the membership of the priority purchaser in ownership decisions, including ensuring resident input in these decisions;

(2) Facilitating long-range planning by the board of directors to ensure the physical, financial and social viability of the project for the entire time the project is maintained as low income housing; and

(3) Assisting the ownership in complying with regulatory, use, loan and grant agreements.

Proprietary information. That information which cannot be released to the public because it consists of trade secrets, confidential financial information, audits, personal financial information about partners in the ownership entity, or income data on project tenants. Where proprietary information cannot be separated from the rest of a document, the entire document shall be deemed "proprietary information" and shall not be releasable to the public. Where proprietary information can be reasonably segregated from the rest of the document, the proprietary information shall be deleted and the remainder of the document shall be releasable to the public.

Public Housing Agency. A public housing agency, as defined in section 3(b) of the United States Housing Act of 1937 (42 U.S.C. 1437a(b)).

Qualified Purchaser. Any entity that is not a related party to the owner and that agrees to maintain low income affordability restrictions for the remaining useful life of the project, and includes for-profit entities and priority purchasers.

Regulatory Agreement. The agreement executed by the owner and the Commissioner or a State agency providing for the regulation of the operation of the project.

Related Party. An entity that, either directly or indirectly, is wholly or partially owned or controlled by the owner of the project being transferred under subpart B of this part, is under whole or partial common control with such owner, or has any financial interest in such owner or in which such owner has any financial interest. However, this shall not prohibit a nonprofit organization from buying out the interest of its limited dividend or for-profit partners in connection with the sale of eligible low income housing under subpart B of this part, as long as the sale is made on an arm's length basis and the partners who sell their interest completely divest themselves of any input in the continued operation of the project. The purchaser and the owner shall not be deemed related parties on the basis

472

that financing is provided to the purchaser by the seller, or a management company affiliated with the seller, as long as:

(1) Only a loan, and not a grant, is provided;

(2) The financing is provided for the acquisition of the project, the rehabilitation of the project, or both;

(3) In the case of financing for the acquisition of the project, the sum of the principal amount of the loan, plus the amount of the acquisition loan under section 241(f) of the National Housing Act (12 U.S.C. 1715z–6(f)), and any Federal grant to cover acquisition of the project, does not exceed the sum of the sales price and the expenses associated with the acquisition, loan closing and implementation of the plan of action; and in the case of financing for the rehabilitation of the project, the principal amount of the loan does not exceed the equity requirements applicable to the rehabilitation loan or capital improvement loan obtained by the purchaser under part 241 or part 219 of this chapter;

(4) The loan is not a condition of accepting a bona fide offer or entering into a sales contract;

(5) The seller has no input in the continued operation of the project as a result of the loan; and

(6) In the case of a loan provided by a management company that is affiliated with the seller, the execution of a management contract between the purchaser and the management company is not a condition of the loan. This rule does not bar an owner, or former owner, from membership on a nonprofit organization's board of directors, as long as the owner, or former owner, participates only in his or her personal capacity, without compensation, and holds a nonvoting membership. The purchaser and the owner shall not be deemed related parties solely by reason of the purchaser's retention of a property management entity of a company that is owned or controlled by the owner or a principal thereof, if retention of the management company is neither a condition of sale nor part of consideration paid for the project and the property management contract is negotiated by the qualified purchaser on an arm's length basis.

Relevant Local Market. An area geographically smaller than the market area established by the Commissioner for purposes of determining the section 8 existing fair market rent, that is identifiable as a distinct rental market area in which similar projects and units would effectively compete with the subject project, for potential tenants.

Relocation Expenses. Relocation expenses shall consist of payment for—

(1) Advisory services, including timely information, counseling (including the provision of information on a resident's rights under the Fair Housing Act (42 U.S.C. 3601–3619)), and referrals to suitable, affordable, decent, safe and sanitary alternative housing; and

(2) Payment for actual, reasonable moving expenses.

Remaining Useful Life. With respect to eligible low income housing, the period during which the physical characteristics of the project remain in a condition suitable for occupancy, assuming normal maintenance and repairs are made and major systems and capital components are replaced as becomes necessary.

Reserve for Replacements. The escrow fund established under the regulatory agreement for the purpose of ensuring the availability of funds for needed repair and replacement costs.

Resident Council. Any incorporated nonprofit organization or association in which membership is available to all the tenants, and only the tenants, of a particular project and—

(1) Is representative of the residents of the project;

(2) Adopts written procedures providing for the election of officers on a regular basis; and

(3) Has a democratically elected governing board, elected by the residents of the project.

Residual Receipt Fund. The fund established under the regulatory agreement for holding cash remaining after deducting from the surplus cash, as defined by the regulatory agreement, the amount of all allowable distributions.

Return on Investment. The amount of allowable distributions that a purchaser of a project may receive under a plan of action under §248.157 or §248.161.

Section 8 Assistance. Assistance provided under parts 880 through 887 and 982 and 983 of this title.

Special Needs Tenants. Those "elderly persons," 62 years of age or older, "elderly families," or families that include "disabled persons," as such terms are defined in part 5 of this title, or large families of five or more persons and requiring units with three or more bedrooms.

State assisted or subsidized mortgage. A mortgage which is assisted or subsidized by an agency of a State government without any Federal mortgage subsidy.

Tenant Representative. A designated officer of an organization of the project's tenants, a tenant who has been elected to represent the tenants of the project with respect to subpart B of this part, or a person or organization that has been formally designated or retained by an organization of the project's tenants to represent the tenants with respect to subpart B of this part.

Termination of Low Income Affordability Restrictions. The elimination of low income affordability restrictions under the regulatory agreement through termination of mortgage insurance or prepayment of the mortgage.

Transfer Preservation Equity. The transfer preservation equity of a project is:

(1) The transfer preservation value of the project determined under § 248.111; less

(2) The outstanding balance of the federally-assisted mortgage(s) for the project.

Transfer Preservation Rent. For purposes of receiving incentives pursuant to a sale of the project, transfer preservation rent shall be the gross income for the project that would be required to support:

(1) Debt service on the loan for acquisition of the project;

(2) Debt service on any rehabilitation loan for the project;

(3) Debt service on the federally-assisted mortgage(s) for the housing;

(4) Project operating expenses; and

(5) Adequate reserves.

Transfer Preservation Value. The fair market value of the project based on its highest and best use.

Very Low Income Families. Families or persons whose incomes do not exceed the level established for very low income families under part 5 of this title.

Voluntary Termination of Mortgage Insurance. The termination of all rights under the mortgage insurance contract and of all obligations to pay future insurance premiums.

[57 FR 12041, Apr. 8, 1992, as amended at 57 FR 57314, Dec. 3, 1992; 58 FR 37814, July 13, 1993; 59 FR 14369, Mar. 28, 1994; 64 FR 26639, May 14, 1999; 80 FR 75936, Dec. 7, 2015]

§ 248.103 General prepayment limitation.

(a) *Prepayment.* An owner of eligible low income housing may prepay, and a mortgagee may accept prepayment of, a mortgage on such project only in accordance with a plan of action approved by the Commissioner.

(b) *Termination.* A mortgage insurance contract with respect to eligible low income housing may be terminated pursuant to § 207.253 of this chapter only in accordance with a plan of action approved by the Commissioner.

(c) *Foreclosure.* A mortgagee of a mortgage insured by the Commissioner may foreclose the mortgage on, or acquire by deed in lieu of foreclosure, any eligible low income housing only if the mortgagee also conveys title to the project to the Commissioner in connection with a claim for insurance benefits.

(d) *Effect of unauthorized prepayment.* A mortgagee's acceptance of a prepayment in violation of paragraph (a) of this section, or the voluntary termination of a mortgage insurance contract in violation of paragraph (b) of this section, shall be null and void and any low income affordability restrictions on the project shall continue to apply to the project.

(e) *Remedies for unauthorized prepayment.* A mortgagee's acceptance of a prepayment in violation of paragraph (a) of this section, or attempt to obtain voluntary termination of a mortgage insurance contract in violation of paragraph (b) of this section, is grounds for administrative action under parts 24 and 25 of this title, in addition to any other remedies available by law, including rescission of the prepayment or reinstatement of the insurance contract.

§248.105 Notice of intent.

(a) *Eligibility for filing.* An owner of eligible low income housing intending to prepay the mortgage or voluntarily terminate the mortgage insurance contract pursuant to §248.141, extend the low income affordability restrictions of the housing in accordance with §248.153, or transfer the housing to a qualified purchaser under §248.157, may file a notice of intent unless the mortgage covering the project—

(1) Continued in default or fell into default on or after the November 28, 1990, and the mortgage has been assigned to the Commissioner as a result of such default;

(2) Continued in default or fell into default on or after November 28, 1990, while the mortgage was held by the Commissioner;

(3) Fell into default prior to November 28, 1990, if the owner entered into a workout agreement prior to that date, and on or after that date, the owner has defaulted under the workout agreement (and, if the agreement was with an insured mortgagee, the mortgage has been assigned to the Commissioner as a result of the default under the workout agreement); or

(4) Fell into default prior to November 28, 1990, but has been current since that date and the owner has not agreed to recompense the appropriate insurance fund for losses sustained by the fund as a result of any work-out or other arrangement agreed to by the Commissioner and the owner with respect to the defaulted mortgage.

(b) *Filing with the Commissioner.* The notice of intent shall be filed with the HUD Field Office in whose jurisdiction the project is located. The notice of intent shall identify the project by name, project number and location. It shall contain a statement indicating whether the owner intends to extend the affordability restrictions on the project by retaining ownership of the project or transferring it to a qualified purchaser, or whether the owner intends to terminate the affordability restrictions on the project through prepayment of the mortgage or termination of the mortgage insurance contract. The notice of intent shall also request the tenants to notify the owner, the Commissioner, and the State or local officer identified in the notice of intent of any individual or organization that has been designated or retained by the tenants to represent the tenants with respect to the actions to be taken under subpart B of this part.

(c) *Filing with the State or local government and tenants.* The owner simultaneously shall file the notice of intent with the chief executive officer of the appropriate State or local government in which the project is located, or any officer designated by executive order or State or local law to receive such information, and with the mortgagee. In addition, the owner shall deliver a copy of the notice of intent to each occupied unit in the project and to any tenant representative, if any, known to the owner, and shall post a copy of the notice of intent in readily accessible locations within each affected building of the project. The copies of the notice of intent delivered to the tenants and the tenant representative shall include a summary of possible outcomes of the filing which shall be furnished by the Commissioner. Upon the request of any non-English speaking tenants residing in the affected project, the owner shall tabulate the number and type of translations needed by the tenants and request the local HUD field office to provide the appropriate translations. The owner shall deliver a copy of the translated notice of intent to all of the tenants who requested such translation. The failure of an owner to comply with any non-federal notice requirements shall not invalidate the notice of intent.

§248.111 Appraisal and preservation value of eligible low income housing.

(a) *Appraisal.* Upon receiving a notice of intent indicating an intent to extend the low income affordability restrictions under §248.153 or transfer the project under §248.157, the Commissioner shall provide for determination of the preservation values of the project pursuant to this section.

(b) *Notice.* Within 30 days after the filing of a notice of intent to extend the income restrictions or to transfer the project, the Commissioner shall provide the owner with written notice of—

(1) The need for, and the rules and guidelines governing, an appraisal of the project;

(2) The filing deadline for submission of the appraisal;

(3) The need for an appraiser retained by the Commissioner to inspect the project and the project's financial records; and

(4) Any delegation to an appropriate State agency, if any, by the Commissioner of responsibilities regarding the performance of an appraisal pursuant to this section.

(c) *Appraisers.* The Commissioner and the owner shall each select and compensate an appraiser who shall:

(1) Neither be an employee of the Federal Government nor an employee or officer of any entity that is affiliated with the owner or the mortgagee of record;

(2) Be certified by the appropriate State agency under the standards established by the Federal Financial Institutions Reform, Recovery and Enforcement Act of 1989 (12 U.S.C. 1451–1459); and

(3) Have six years of experience in the appraisal profession and at least three years experience in the practice of appraising multifamily residential properties;

(4) Is not the subject of a charge issued following a reasonable cause determination under the Fair Housing Act (42 U.S.C. 3601–3619).

(d) *Guidelines.* The Commissioner shall provide to the owner and the appraiser retained by the Commissioner guidelines for conducting the appraisal. The guidelines established by the Commissioner shall be consistent with customary appraisal standards. The guidelines shall assume repayment of the existing federally-assisted mortgage(s), termination of the existing Federal low income affordability restrictions, simultaneous termination of any Federal rental assistance, and costs of compliance with any State or local laws of general applicability. The guidelines may permit reliance upon assessments of rehabilitation needs and other conversion costs determined by an appropriate State agency, as determined by the Commissioner.

(e) *Operating expenses.* For the purpose of determining preservation values, the guidelines shall instruct the appraiser to use the greater of actual project operating expenses at the time of the appraisal, based on the average of the actual project operating expenses during the preceding three years, or projected operating expenses after conversion, as determined by the Commissioner. However, if the current year operating expenses are higher than those of the preceding three years and the Commissioner has made a determination that these costs are unlikely to decrease in the future, the appraiser shall use current year operating expenses rather than operating expenses for the preceding three years for purposes of comparison with projected operating expenses after conversion. Likewise, if the current year operating expenses are lower than those of the preceding years and the Commissioner has made a determination that these costs are unlikely to increase in the future, the appraiser shall use current year operating expenses rather than operating expenses for the preceding three years for purposes of comparison with projected expenses after conversion. Where the highest and best use of a project is not as rental housing, the appraiser shall use projected operating expenses assuming conversion of the project to its highest and best use.

(f) *Preservation values.* The preservation values will be determined on the basis of the appraisals conducted by the owner's and the Commissioner's independent appraisers. Each appraiser will determine both the extension preservation value and the transfer preservation value, regardless of the owner's intentions as indicated in the notice of intent.

(g) *Highest and best use as residential property.* In determining the extension preservation value of the project, the appraiser shall assume conversion of the project to market-rate rental housing. The appraiser shall, in accordance with the guidelines established by the Commissioner, determine the amount of rehabilitation expenditures, if any, that would be necessary to bring the project up to quality standards required to attract and sustain a market-rate tenancy upon conversion and assess other costs that the owner could reasonably be expected to incur if the owner converted the property to market-rate multifamily rental housing.

(h) *Highest and best use.* In determining the transfer preservation value for the project, the appraiser shall assume conversion of the project to highest and best use for the property, and shall, in accordance with the guidelines established by the Commissioner, determine the amount of any rehabilitation expenditures, including demolition, that would be necessary to convert the project to such use and assess other costs that the owner could reasonably be expected to incur if the owner converted the property to its highest and best use.

(i) *Submission of appraisal.* Within four months after the filing of the notice of intent:

(1) The owner shall submit to the HUD Field Office in whose jurisdiction the project is located, the appraisal made by the owner's selected appraiser; and

(2) The Commissioner's selected appraiser shall conduct and submit an appraisal to the Commissioner.

(j) *Joint determination of preservation values.* No later than one month after the owner and the Commissioner exchange appraisals, the owner and the Commissioner shall, on the basis of the appraisals delivered to them, agree on the preservation values of the project. If no agreement as to preservation values can be reached, the owner and the Commissioner shall jointly select a third appraiser meeting the qualifications set forth in paragraph (c) of this section by the end of six months from the date that the notice of intent was filed. The cost of this third appraisal shall be borne equally by both parties. The third appraiser must comply with the guidelines set forth in paragraph (d) of this section and must conduct the appraisal and submit an appraisal within two months after accepting the assignment. The determination by the third appraiser of the project's preser-

vation values shall be binding on both the owner and the Commissioner.

(k) *Timeliness of appraisals.* The Commissioner may approve a plan of action to receive incentives under §§248.153, 248.157 or 248.161 only based upon an appraisal conducted in accordance with this section that is not more than 30 months old, unless the failure of the Commissioner to approve the plan of action within the 30-month period was due to circumstances beyond the control of the owner.

[57 FR 12041, Apr. 8, 1992, as amended at 58 FR 4871, Jan. 15, 1993]

§248.121 Annual authorized return and aggregate preservation rents.

(a) *Annual authorized return.* For each eligible low income housing project appraised under §248.111, the Commissioner shall set an annual authorized return on the project equal to 8 percent of the extension preservation equity.

(b) *Aggregate preservation rents.* For each eligible low income housing project appraised under §248.111, the Commissioner shall also determine the aggregate preservation rents. The aggregate preservation rents shall be used solely for the purposes of comparison with the Federal cost limit under §248.123. Actual rents received by the owner (or a qualified purchaser) shall be determined pursuant to §§248.153, 248.157, and 248.161.

(c) *Extension preservation rent.* The extension preservation rent shall be the gross potential income for the project, as determined by the Commissioner, that would be required to support—

(1) The annual authorized return determined under paragraph (a) of this section;

(2) Debt service on any rehabilitation loan for the project, assuming a market rate of interest and customary terms;

(3) Debt service on the federally-assisted mortgage(s) for the project;

(4) Project operating expenses as determined by the Commissioner; and

(5) Adequate reserves.

(d) *Transfer preservation rent.* The transfer preservation rent shall be the gross potential income for the project, as determined by the Commissioner, that would be required to support—

(1) Debt service on the loan for acquisition of the project;

(2) Debt service on any rehabilitation loan for the project, assuming a market rate of interest and customary terms;

(3) Debt service on the federally-assisted mortgage(s) for the project;

(4) Project operating expenses as determined by the Commissioner; and

(5) Adequate reserves.

(e) *Adequate reserves and operating expenses.* For purposes of this section—

(1) Adequate reserves are the amount of funds which, when added to existing reserves, are sufficient to maintain the project, including needed deferred maintenance, at a level that meets the standards set forth in § 248.147; and

(2) Project operating expenses shall be based on operating expenses for the preceding 3 years, adjusted for reasonable reductions in operating costs due to rehabilitation and energy improvements. For purposes of comparison to the gross rents used in determining the Federal cost limit, project operating expenses shall include the cost of utilities paid by the residents.

(f) *Debt service.* For purposes of this section, the amount of debt service for an acquisition loan will be estimated based on the maximum loan to which the purchaser is entitled under § 241.1067 of this chapter. The debt service on any rehabilitation loan will be estimated using costs derived from the appraisals conducted under § 248.111, taking into account any funds provided for rehabilitation by State or local governments and assuming market rate interest rates.

§ 248.123 Determination of Federal cost limit.

(a) *Initial determination.* For each eligible low income housing project appraised under § 248.111, the Commissioner shall determine whether the aggregate preservation rents for the project exceed the amount determined by multiplying the number of dwelling units in the project, according to appropriate unit sizes, by 120 percent of the section 8 existing fair market rent for the appropriate unit sizes.

(b) *Relevant local markets.* If either the extension or transfer preservation rent for a project exceeds the amount

determined under paragraph (a) of this section, the Commissioner shall determine whether such extension or transfer preservation rent exceeds the amount determined by multiplying the number of units in the project, according to the appropriate unit sizes, by 120 percent of the prevailing rents in the local market area. The relevant local market, and the prevailing rents in such relevant local market, shall be determined on the basis of the appraisal conducted by the appraiser selected by the Commissioner pursuant to § 248.111 and any other information that the Commissioner determines is appropriate. If there are no comparables in the relevant local market and it is not otherwise possible to determine prevailing rents in that area, the section 8 existing fair market rent shall be the sole measure for determining the Federal cost limit.

(c) *Effect.* The extension or transfer preservation rent for an eligible low income housing project appraised under § 248.111 shall be considered to exceed the Federal cost limit only if the extension or transfer preservation rent exceeds the amount determined under paragraphs (a) and (b) of this section.

§ 248.127 Limitations on action pursuant to Federal cost limit.

(a) *Retention of the project.* With respect to owners who seek to retain the project, the owner may file a plan of action to receive incentives under § 248.153, except that if the extension preservation rent exceeds the Federal cost limit, the amount of the incentives may not exceed an amount that can be supported by a projected income stream equal to the Federal cost limit.

(b) *Transfer of the project.* With respect to owners who seek to transfer the project—

(1) If the transfer preservation rent does not exceed the Federal cost limit, or if the transfer preservation rent exceeds the Federal cost limit and the owner is willing to transfer the project at a price which will result in project rents that, on an aggregate level, do not exceed the Federal cost limit, the owner may file a second notice of intent indicating an intention to transfer the project under § 248.157; or

(2) If the transfer preservation rent exceeds the Federal cost limit, the owner may file a second notice of intent to transfer the project under §248.161 or, if no bona fide offers are received, to prepay the mortgage or terminate the mortgage insurance.

§248.131 Information from the Commissioner.

(a) *Information to owners terminating affordability restrictions.* Within six months after receipt of a notice of intent to terminate the low income affordability restrictions under §248.141, the Commissioner shall provide the owner with a description of the criteria for such termination and with information that the owner needs to prepare a plan of action. This shall include information concerning the standards under §248.141 regarding the approval of a plan of action and a list of the Federal incentives authorized under §248.153 and available to those projects for which a plan of action involving termination of low income affordability restrictions, through prepayment of the mortgage or termination of the mortgage insurance contract, would not be approvable. The Commissioner shall also provide the owner with any other relevant information which the Commissioner may possess.

(b) *Information to owners extending affordability restrictions.* Within nine months of receipt of a notice of intent to extend the low income affordability restrictions under §248.153 or to transfer the project under §248.157, the Commissioner shall provide the owner who submitted the notice with—

(1) A statement of the preservation values of the project as determined under §248.111;

(2) A statement of the aggregate preservation rents for the project as calculated under §248.121;

(3) A statement of the applicable Federal cost limit for the market area (or relevant local market, if applicable) in which the project is located, and an explanation of the limitations under §248.127 on the amount of assistance the Commissioner may provide based on such cost limits;

(4) A statement of whether either of the aggregate preservation rents exceeds the Federal cost limit; and

(5) A direction to file a plan of action and the information necessary to file a plan of action; or

(6) A direction to submit a second notice of intent under §248.133.

(c) *Information to tenants and State or local governments.* The Commissioner shall provide any information provided to the owner under paragraphs (a) and (b) of this section to the tenant representative, if any, known to the Commissioner, and shall post a notice in each affected building informing tenants of the name(s), address(es), and telephone number(s) of the tenant representative(s) and appropriate personnel in the local HUD field office, from whom they may obtain this information. The Commissioner shall also provide this information to that officer of State or local government to whom the owner submitted a notice of intent pursuant to §248.105(c). The Commissioner shall include in the information packet made available to the tenants any other information relating to their rights and opportunities, including—

(1) The potential opportunity of the tenants to become priority purchasers under §§248.157 and 248.161; and

(2) The potential opportunity of resident homeownership under §§248.173 or 248.175.

§248.133 Second notice of intent.

(a) *Filing.* A second notice of intent must be filed by all owners who, after receiving the information provided by the Commissioner in §248.131, elect to transfer the project under §§248.157 or 248.161.

(b) *Timeliness.* A second notice of intent must be submitted not later than 30 days after receipt of the information provided by the Commissioner under §248.131. If an owner who is required to submit a second notice of intent fails to do so within this time period, the original notice of intent submitted under §248.105 shall be void and ineffective for purposes of subpart B of this part.

(c) *Filing with the State or local government and tenants.* The owner simultaneously shall file the second notice of intent with that officer of State and local government to whom the owner submitted a notice of intent under §248.105(c) and with the mortgagee. In addition, the owner shall deliver a copy of the second notice of intent to each tenant representative known to the owner, and if none is known, then to each occupied unit in the project.

§248.135   Plans of action.

(a) *Submission.* An owner seeking to terminate the low income affordability restrictions through prepayment of the mortgage or voluntary termination under §248.141, or to extend the low income affordability restrictions on the project under §248.153, shall submit a plan of action to the Commissioner in the form and manner prescribed in paragraph (d) or (e) of this section respectively, within 6 months after receipt of the information from the Commissioner under §248.131.

(b) *Joint Submission.* An owner and purchaser seeking a transfer of the project under §§248.157 or 248.161 shall jointly submit a plan of action to the Commissioner in the form and manner prescribed in paragraph (e) of this section within six months after the owner's acceptance of a bona fide offer under §248.157 or the purchaser's making of a bona fide offer under §248.161.

(c) *Filing with the State or local government and tenants.* The owner shall notify the tenants of the plan of action by posting in each occupied building a summary of the plan of action and by delivery of a copy of the plan of action to the tenant representative, if any. In addition, the summary must indicate that a copy of the plan of action shall be available from the tenant representatives, whose names, addresses and telephone numbers are indicated on the summary, the local HUD field office, and the on-site office for the project, or if one is not available, in the location where rents are collected, for inspection and copying, at a reasonable cost, during normal business hours. Simultaneously with the submission to the Commissioner, the owner shall submit the plan of action to that officer of State or local government to whom the owner submitted a notice of intent under §248.105(c). The Commissioner shall submit a copy of the plan of action to the chief executive officer of the appropriate agency of such State or local government which shall review the plan of action and advise the ten-

ants of the project of any programs that are available to assist the tenants in carrying out the purposes of this subpart. The summary of the plan of action posted by the owner and the copies of the plan of action submitted to the tenant representative, the officer of State or local government to whom the owner submitted a notice of intent under §248.105(c) and the chief executive officer of the appropriate State or local government, shall all state that, upon request, the tenants and the State or local government, may obtain from the owner or from the local HUD field office a copy of all documentation supporting the plan of action except for that documentation deemed "proprietary information" under §248.101.

(d) *Termination of affordability restrictions.* If the plan of action proposes to terminate the low income affordability restrictions through prepayment or voluntary termination in accordance with §248.141, it shall include:

(1) A description of any proposed changes in the status or terms of the mortgage or regulatory agreement;

(2) A description of any proposed changes in the low income affordability restrictions;

(3) A description of any change in ownership that is related to prepayment or voluntary termination;

(4) An assessment of the effect of the proposed changes on existing tenants;

(5) An analysis of the effect of the proposed changes on the supply of housing affordable to low and very low income families or persons in the community within which the project is located and in the area that the housing could reasonably be expected to serve;

(6) A list of any waivers requested by the owner pursuant to §248.7; and

(7) Any other information that the Commissioner determines is necessary to achieve the purposes of subpart B of this part.

(e) *Extension of affordability restrictions.* If the plan of action proposes to extend the low income affordability restrictions of the project in accordance with §248.153 or transfer the project to a qualified purchaser in accordance with §§248.157 or 248.161, the plan of action shall include:

(1) A description of any proposed changes in the status or terms of the mortgage or regulatory agreement;

(2) A description of the Federal incentives requested, including cash flow projections and analyses of how the owner will address any physical or financial deficiencies and maintain the low income affordability restrictions of the project;

(3) A description of any assistance from State or local government agencies, including low income housing tax credits that have been offered to the owner or purchaser or for which the owner or purchaser has applied or intends to apply;

(4) A description of any transfer of the property, including the identity of the transferee and a copy of any documents of sale;

(5) An income profile of the tenants as of the date of submission of the plan of action and as of January 1, 1987 (based on the area median income limits established by the Commissioner in February 1987), or if the January 1, 1987 profile is unavailable, a certification from the owner stating its unavailability and a profile as of January 1, 1988, or, if that is also unavailable, a profile as of January 1, 1989;

(6) A transfer of physical assets package, if a transfer is proposed;

(7) A list of any waivers requested by the owner pursuant to §248.7; and

(8) Any other information that the Commissioner determines is necessary to achieve the purposes of subpart B of this part.

(f) *Revisions.* The owner or owner and purchaser may from time to time revise and amend the plan of action as may be necessary to obtain approval under subpart B of this part and must amend the plan of action no later than 30 days after a change in any of the information required in paragraphs (d) or (e) of this section. The owner shall submit any revision to the Commissioner, and provide a copy of the revision and all documentation supporting the revision except for that documentation deemed "proprietary information" under §248.101, to the parties, and in the manner, specified in paragraph (c) of this section.

(g) *Failure to Submit.* If the owner fails to submit a plan of action to the Commissioner, when prepayment or termination is sought, within the 6 month period set forth in paragraph (a) of this section or, when a transfer is sought, if the owner and purchaser fail to submit a plan of action within the 6 month time period set forth in paragraph (b) of this section, the notice of intent filed by the owner under §248.105 shall be ineffective for the purposes of subpart B of this part and the owner shall be barred from submitting another notice of intent under §248.105 until 6 months after expiration of such period.

(h) *Comment Period for tenants and State or local governments.* Upon submission of the plan of action by the owner, the tenants of the affected project and the State or local government shall have 60 days in which to provide comments on the plan of action to the Commissioner or to the owner, who will then submit the comments to the Commissioner. The Commissioner shall not approve a plan of action under subpart B of this part before the end of this 60-day period and all comments received during this period will be considered by the Commissioner in making its determination to approve or disapprove a plan of action.

(i) *Notification to tenants and the State or local government of plan of action approval.* Upon the Commissioner's approval of the plan of action, the owner shall notify tenants of the terms thereof by posting in each occupied building a summary of the plan of action and by delivery of a copy of the plan of action to the tenant representative, if any. In addition, the summary must indicate that a copy of the plan of action shall be available for inspection and copying during reasonable hours in a location convenient to the tenants.

[57 FR 12041, Apr. 8, 1992, as amended at 58 FR 37814, July 13, 1993]

§248.141 **Criteria for approval of a plan of action involving prepayment and voluntary termination.**

(a) *Approval.* The Commissioner may approve a plan of action that provides for the termination of the low income affordability restrictions through prepayment of the mortgage or voluntary termination of the mortgage insurance contract only upon a written finding that—

(1) Implementation of the plan of action will not—

(i) Materially increase economic hardship for current tenants, and will not in any event result in a monthly rental payment by any current tenant that exceeds 30 percent of the monthly adjusted income of the tenant or an increase in the monthly rental payment in any year that exceeds 10 percent (whichever is lower); or in the case of a current tenant who already pays more than such percentage, an increase in the monthly rental payment in any year that exceeds the increase in the Consumer Price Index or 10 percent (whichever is lower); or

(ii) Involuntarily displace current tenants (except for good cause) where comparable and affordable housing is not readily available, determined without regard to the availability of Federal housing assistance that would address any such hardship or involuntary displacement; and

(2) The supply of vacant, comparable housing is sufficient to ensure that such prepayment will not materially affect—

(i) The availability of decent, safe, and sanitary housing affordable to low income and very low income families or persons in the area that the housing could reasonably be expected to serve;

(ii) The ability of low income and very low income families or persons to find affordable, decent, safe, and sanitary housing near employment opportunities; or

(iii) The housing opportunities of minorities in the community within which the housing is located.

(3) There are no open audit findings, open findings of noncompliance with title VI of the Civil Rights Act of 1964 (42 U.S.C. 2000d); the Fair Housing Act (42 U.S.C. 3601–3619); Executive Order 11063 (3 CFR 1959–1963 comp., p. 652); the Age Discrimination Act of 1975 (42 U.S.C. 6101–6107); section 504 of the Rehabilitation Act of 1973 (29 U.S.C. 794); and all regulations promulgated under such statutes and authorities (including, but not limited to 24 CFR part 100), or outstanding violations of the regulatory agreement.

(b) For purposes of approving a plan of action under this section, the Commissioner shall find that the requirements of paragraph (a)(1) of this section have been met if the owner agrees to execute a use agreement which provides that rents for all tenants residing at the project at the time of plan of action approval will not exceed the limit established in paragraph (a)(1)(i) of this section and that no tenant residing in the project at the time of plan of action approval will be involuntarily displaced without good cause.

(c) For purposes of approving a plan of action under this section, the Commissioner shall find that the requirements of paragraph (a)(2) of this section have been met if the project is located in a housing market area which has been determined to have an adequate supply of decent, safe and sanitary rental housing; and it has been determined, based on the specific characteristics of the project, that the prepayment would not materially affect the housing opportunities of low and very-low income families.

(1) For purposes of this section, a "housing market area" is defined as an area where rental housing units of similar characteristics are in relative competition with each other. If a project is in a non-metropolitan area, the housing market area is the county in which the project is located. If the project is located in a metropolitan area the housing market area is the primary metropolitan statistical area (PMSA), or in the case of very large metropolitan areas, the housing market area may be a portion of the PMSA.

(2) For purposes of this section, a housing market area may be determined to have an adequate supply of decent, safe, and sanitary rental housing if the housing market area has a soft rental market. A soft rental market is a housing market area in which the supply of vacant available rental housing significantly exceeds the demand. A soft rental market exists if:

(i) There is currently a surplus of rental housing such that the current excess supply of vacant available housing, plus units currently under construction, is expected to exceed demand for at lest the next 24 months; or

(ii) Within the next 12 months, based on the housing production (units currently under construction or with firm planning commitments), in combination with the current supply of available vacant units, supply is expected to exceed demand for at least 24 months.

(3) In order to determine whether the housing market area has a soft rental market, the Commissioner shall consider data from the 1990 Decennial Census and the most recent available local data concerning changes in population, households, employment, the housing inventory, residential construction activity, and the current and anticipated supply/demand conditions within the overall rental market, as well as the occupancy and vacancy situation in assisted housing projects in the area, including information on waiting lists and the experience of voucher holders in finding units.

(4) A determination must also be made on whether the prepayment would materially affect the housing opportunities of low and very-low income families in the area, based on the specific characteristics of the project including unit sizes, the type of tenants, e.g., elderly, handicapped, large families, minorities, the location of the project with respect to its proximity to employment opportunities; and the availability of other assisted housing within the immediate area. The prepayment would be determined to materially affect housing opportunities if:

(i) The project is needed to assist in preserving low income housing in a neighborhood which is being revitalized;

(ii) The project represents a rare source or the only source of low-and moderate-income rental housing in the immediate area;

(iii) There is a shortage of the particular type of rental housing provided by the project such as units suitable for the disabled, single room occupancy, or units for large families;

(iv) The preservation of the housing would be necessary to avoid adversely affecting the housing opportunities of low and very-low income families to find housing near employment opportunities; or

(v) The preservation of the housing would be necessary to avoid adversely affecting the housing opportunities of minorities in the community within which the housing is located.

(d) Once the Commissioner has compiled the necessary data and conducted the analysis under paragraph (c) of this section the Commissioner shall issue a written finding to the owner stating whether the plan of action to terminate the low income affordability restrictions is approved or disapproved. The written finding shall contain a specific determination of whether the market area is a soft rental market and prepayment would materially affect housing opportunities. The written finding shall include:

(1) A statement as to whether the owner has agreed to execute a use agreement to protect current tenants, in accordance with paragraph (b) of this section;

(2) A description of the geographic boundaries of the housing market area in which the project is located;

(3) An analysis of current and anticipated supply/demand conditions in both the overall rental market and the assisted housing inventory; and

(4) A discussion of whether the prepayment would materially affect the housing opportunities, given the specific characteristics of the project.

(e) *Disapproval.* If the Commissioner determines a plan of action to prepay a mortgage or terminate an insurance contract fails to meet the requirements of paragraph (a) of this section, the Commissioner shall disapprove the plan and within a reasonable time, shall inform the owner of the reasons for disapproval and suggest alternatives. In the case of disapproval of the plan of action, except for the failure to meet the requirement of paragraph (a)(3) of this section, the notice of intent filed under §248.105 shall be rendered ineffective for the purposes of this subtitle, and the owner, in order to receive incentives, must file a new notice of intent under such section. If the plan of action is disapproved because of an outstanding civil rights or audit finding, the finding must be closed before the Commissioner will approve a plan of action under this section.

[57 FR 12041, Apr. 8, 1992, as amended at 58 FR 37815, July 13, 1993; 64 FR 26639, May 14, 1999]

483

§ 248.145 Criteria for approval of a plan of action involving incentives.

(a) *Approval.* The Commissioner may approve a plan of action for extension of the low income affordability restrictions on an eligible low income housing project or for transfer of the housing to a qualified purchaser, other than a resident council acquiring the project under a resident homeownership plan, only upon a finding that—

(1) Due diligence has been given to ensuring that the package of incentives set forth in the plan of action is, for the Federal Government, the least costly alternative that is consistent with the full achievement of the purposes of this subpart;

(2) The project will be retained as housing affordable for very low, low and moderate income families and persons, as determined under paragraph (a)(8) of this section, for the remaining useful life of the project;

(3) Throughout the remaining useful life of the project, adequate expenditures will be made for maintenance and operation of the project and the project meets the housing standards established in § 248.147 as determined by inspections conducted by the Commissioner;

(4) Current tenants will not be involuntarily displaced, except for good cause;

(5) Any increase in rent contributions for current tenants will be to a level that does not exceed 30 percent of the adjusted income of the tenant or the fair market rent, whichever is lower. However, the rent contributions of any tenants occupying the project at the time of any increase may not be reduced by reason of this paragraph, except with respect to tenants receiving section 8 assistance in accordance with paragraph (a)(7) of this section;

(6) Any resulting increase in rents for current tenants (except for increases made necessary by increased operating costs) shall be phased in as follows:

(i) If such increase is 30 percent or more, the increase shall be phased in equally over a period of not less than three years, with the first increase occurring upon the effective date of the plan of action, and the subsequent two increases occurring annually thereafter;

(ii) If such increase is more than 10 percent but less than 30 percent, it shall be limited to not more than 10 percent per year;

(7) Section 8 assistance shall be provided, to the extent appropriations are available, if necessary to mitigate any adverse effect on current very low and low income tenants;

(8) Rents for units becoming available to new tenants shall be at levels approved by the Commissioner, taking into account any incentives provided under subpart B of this part, that will ensure, to the extent practicable, that the units will be available and affordable to the same proportions of very low, low and moderate income families and persons, including families and persons whose incomes are 95 percent or more of area median income, as based on the area median income limits established by the Commissioner in February 1987, as resided in the project as of the date of the tenant income profile submitted under § 248.135(e)(5), or the date the plan of action is approved, whichever date results in the highest proportion of very low income families. This limitation shall not prohibit a higher proportion of very low income families and persons from occupying the project;

(9) Future rent adjustments shall be—

(i) Made by applying an annual factor, to be determined by the Commissioner, to the portion of rent attributable to operating expenses for the project, and, where the owner is a priority purchaser, to the portion of rent attributable to project oversight costs, as that term is defined in § 248.101; and

(ii) Subject to a procedure, established by the Commissioner, for owners to apply for rent increases not adequately compensated by annual adjustment under paragraph (a)(9)(i) of this section, under which the Commissioner may increase rents in excess of the amount determined under paragraph (a)(9)(i) of this section only if the Commissioner determines such increases are necessary to reflect extraordinary necessary expenses of owning and maintaining the project;

(10) Any savings from reductions in operating expenses due to management efficiencies shall be deposited in

project reserves for replacement and the owner shall have periodic access to such reserves, to the extent the Commissioner determines that the level of the reserves is adequate and that the project is maintained in accordance with the standards established in § 248.147;

(11) The mortgage on the project is current; and

(12) There are no open audit findings, open findings of noncompliance with title VI of the Civil Rights Act of 1964 (42 U.S.C. 2000d); the Fair Housing Act (42 U.S.C. 3601–3619); Executive Order 11063 (3 CFR 1959–1963 comp., p. 652); the Age Discrimination Act of 1975 (42 U.S.C. 6101–6107); section 504 of the Rehabilitation Act of 1973 (29 U.S.C. 794); and all regulations promulgated under such statutes and authorities (including, but not limited to, 24 CFR part 100), or outstanding violations of the regulatory agreement.

(b) *Compliance with housing standards.* No incentives under § 248.153 may be provided, other than to qualified purchasers under §§ 248.157 and 245.161, and no distributions may be taken by the owner or purchaser, until the Commissioner determines that the project meets the housing standards set forth in § 248.147, except that incentives designed to correct deficiencies in the project may be provided.

(c) *Implementation.* Any agreement to maintain the low income affordability restrictions for the remaining useful life of the project may be made through execution of a new regulatory agreement, modifications to the existing regulatory agreement or mortgage, or in the case of prepayment of a mortgage or voluntary termination of mortgage insurance, a recorded instrument.

(d) *Determination of remaining useful life.* The Commissioner shall make determinations, on the record and after opportunity for a hearing, as to when the useful life of an eligible low income housing project has expired. Under procedures and standards to be established by the Commissioner, owners of eligible low income housing may petition the Commissioner for a determination that the useful life of such project has expired. Such petition may not be filed before the expiration of the 50-year period beginning upon the approval of a

plan of action under subpart B of this part with respect to such project. In making a determination pursuant to a petition under paragraph (d) of this section, the Commissioner shall presume that the useful life of the project has not expired, and the owner shall have the burden of proof in establishing such expiration. The Commissioner may not determine that the useful life of any project has expired if such determination results primarily from failure to make regular and reasonable repairs and replacement, as became necessary. In making a determination regarding the useful life of any project pursuant to a petition submitted under paragraph (d) of this section, the Commissioner shall provide for comment by tenants of the project and interested persons and organizations with respect to the petition. The Commissioner shall also provide the tenants and interested persons and organizations with an opportunity to appeal a determination under paragraph (d) of this section.

(e) In the case of any plans of action involving incentives the owner must agree to comply with title VI of the Civil Rights Act of 1964 (42 U.S.C. 2000d); the Fair Housing Act (42 U.S.C. 3601–3619); Executive Order 11063 (3 CFR 1959–1963 comp., p. 652); the Age Discrimination Act of 1975 (42 U.S.C. 6101–6107); section 504 of the Rehabilitiation Act of 1973 (29 U.S.C. 794) (including the Department's Accessibility Guidelines (24 CFR chapter I, subchapter A, appendix II) and all regulations issued pursuant to these authorities.

[57 FR 12041, Apr. 8, 1992, as amended at 57 FR 57314, Dec. 3, 1992; 58 FR 37815, July 13, 1993]

§ 248.147 Housing standards.

(a) *Standards.* As a condition to receiving incentives under subpart B of this part, the owner shall agree to maintain the project in accordance with local housing codes and the housing quality standards set forth in § 886.307 of this title. Where a housing quality standard conflicts with local housing codes, the owner shall maintain the project in compliance with the standard that is stricter.

(b) *Annual inspections.* The Commissioner shall inspect each project at

485

least annually in order to determine compliance with the housing quality standards. At least 30 days prior to the inspection, the Commissioner shall notify any tenant representatives, or if none exist, the Commissioner shall provide the owner with a notice to be posted in each affected building, stating the time and date of the inspection and advising any interested tenants that they may accompany HUD personnel on the inspection and/or submit any comments they may have on the physical condition of the project. The Commissioner shall notify the owner of any deficiencies within 30 days following the inspection. The owner shall have 90 days from the date of such notification to correct any deficiencies cited by the Commissioner and shall promptly notify the Commissioner when such deficiencies have been corrected. The Commissioner shall reinspect the project upon such notification or, if the owner does not notify the Commissioner, upon the expiration of the 90-day period.

(c) *Sanctions for noncompliance.* If the Commissioner determines, upon reinspection of the project, that the project is still not in compliance with the standards set forth in paragraph (a) of this section, the Commissioner shall take any action appropriate to bring the project into compliance, including—

(1) Directing the mortgagee, with respect to an equity take-out loan provided under part 241 of this chapter, to withhold the disbursement to the owner of any escrowed loan proceeds and requiring that such proceeds be used for repair of the project; and

(2) Reduce the amount of the allowable distributions to 4 percent of extension preservation equity or (in the case of a purchaser 4 percent of cash invested, as appropriate, for the period ending upon a determination by the Commissioner that the project is in compliance with the standards and requiring that such amounts be used for repair.

(d) *Continued compliance.* To ensure continued compliance with the standards set forth in paragraph (a) of this section for a project subject to any action under paragraph (c) of this section, the Commissioner may limit access of and use by the owner of such amounts set forth in paragraph (c) of this section, for not more than the 2-year period beginning upon the determination that the project is in compliance with the housing standards.

(e) *Sanctions for continuous noncompliance.* If, upon inspection, the Commissioner determines that any eligible low income housing project has failed to comply with the standards established under this section for two consecutive years, the Commissioner may, upon notification to the owner of the noncompliance, take one or more of the following actions;

(1) Subject to the availability of appropriations, provide assistance, other than project-based assistance attached to the project, under part 982 of this title for any tenant eligible for such assistance who desires to terminate occupancy in the project. For each unit in the project vacated pursuant to the provision of assistance under this paragraph, the Commissioner may, notwithstanding any other law or contract for assistance, cancel the provision of project-based assistance attached to the project for one dwelling unit, if the project is receiving such assistance, or convert the project-based assistance allocation for that unit to assistance under part 982 of this title;

(2) In the case of projects for which an equity take-out loan has been made under part 241 of this chapter, direct the mortgagee to declare such a loan to be in default and accelerate the maturity date of the loan;

(3) Declare, or direct the insured mortgagee to declare, any rehabilitation loan insured or provided by the Commissioner with respect to the project, including loans provided under part 219 of this chapter, to be in default and accelerate the maturity date of the loan; and

(4) Suspend payments under or terminate any contract for project-based rental assistance under section 8 of the United States Housing Act of 1937 (42 U.S.C. 1437f).

(f) *Sanctions not exclusive.* The Commissioner may take any other action authorized by law or the project regulatory agreement to ensure that the project will be brought into compliance with the standards established under this section or with other requirements pertaining to the condition of the project.

[57 FR 12041, Apr. 8, 1992, as amended at 64 FR 26639, May 14, 1999]

§ 248.149 Timetable for approval of a plan of action.

(a) *Notification of deficiencies.* Not later than 60 days after receipt of a plan of action, the Commissioner shall notify the owner in writing of any deficiencies that prevent the plan of action from being approved. Such notice shall describe alternative ways in which the plan may be revised to meet the criteria for approval set forth in § 248.145.

(b) *Notification of approval.* Not later than 180 days after receipt of a plan of action, or such longer period as the owner requests, but not more than 365 days, the Commissioner shall notify the owner in writing whether the plan of action, including any revisions, is approved. If approval is withheld, the notice shall describe—

(1) The reasons for withholding approval; and

(2) Suggestions to the owner for meeting the criteria for approval.

(c) *Opportunity to revise.* The Commissioner shall give the owner a reasonable opportunity of not more than 60 days to revise the plan of action when approval is denied. If the owner fails to comply with this time period, it shall not be eligible for relief under paragraph (d) of this section.

(d) *Delayed approval.* If the Commissioner fails to approve a plan of action within the time set forth in paragraph (b) of this section, the Commissioner shall provide incentives and assistance under subpart B of this part, to an owner who is entitled to receive such incentives and assistance, in the amount that the owner would have received if the Commissioner had complied with such time limitations. Paragraph (d) of this section does not apply to plans of action that are not approved because of deficiencies.

§ 248.153 Incentives to extend low income use.

(a) *Agreements by the Commissioner.* After approving a plan of action filed pursuant to § 248.145, from an owner of eligible low income housing that includes the owner's plan to extend the low income affordability restrictions of the project, the Commissioner shall, subject to the availability of appropriations for such purpose, enter into such agreements as are necessary to enable the owner to—

(1) Receive the annual authorized return for the project as determined under § 248.121 for each year after the approval of the plan of action;

(2) Pay debt service on the federally-assisted mortgage(s) covering the project;

(3) Pay debt service on any loan for rehabilitation of the project;

(4) Meet project operating expenses; and

(5) Establish adequate reserves.

(b) *Permissible incentives.* Such agreements may include one or more of the following incentives, as determined necessary by the Commissioner:

(1) Increased access to residual receipts accounts as necessary to enable the owner to realize the annual authorized return;

(2) An increase in the rents permitted under an existing project-based section 8 contract;

(3) Additional project-based section 8 assistance or an extension of any project-based assistance attached to the housing;

(4) An increase in the rents on non-section 8 units occupied by current tenants up to the maximum allowable rents;

(5) Financing of capital improvements under part 219 of this chapter;

(6) Financing of rehabilitation through provision of insurance for a second mortgage under part 241 of this chapter;

(7) Redirection of the Interest Reduction Payment subsidies to a second mortgage for projects which are insured, assisted, or held by the Commissioner or a State or State agency under part 236 of this chapter;

(8) Access by the owner to a portion of the preservation equity in the project through provision of insurance for an acquisition or equity loan insured under part 241, subpart E of this chapter or through a non-insured mortgage loan approved by the Commissioner and the mortgagee;

(9) An increase in the amount of allowable distributions up to the annual authorized return; and

(10) Other incentives authorized in law.

(c) *Limitation on the provision of permissible incentives.* (1) The total amount of incentives provided to a project under paragraphs (b)(2), (3), and (4) of this section shall not result in a projected rental income stream which exceeds the Federal cost limit.

(2) The debt service on the loan obtained by the owner under paragraph (b)(8) of this section, when added to the allowable distributions under paragraph (b)(9) of this section, shall not exceed the annual authorized return.

(d) *Rent phase-in period.* To the extent necessary to ensure that owners receive the annual authorized return during the tenant rent phase-in period established in § 248.145(a)(6), the Commissioner shall permit owners to receive the following additional incentives:

(1) Access to residual receipts accounts;

(2) Deferred remittance of excess rent payments; and

(3) Increases in rents, as permitted under an existing Section 8 contract.

These incentives shall be provided to owners in the order listed. An owner will not be eligible to receive these additional incentives unless it can demonstrate that it is not receiving the annual authorized return. Once an owner has adequately demonstrated that it is not receiving the annual authorized return, the Commissioner will provide the owner with each incentive in turn during the rent phase-in period, until it has been determined that the owner is receiving the annual authorized return.

(e) *Interest reduction subsidies.* Where Interest Reduction Payment subsidies are sought to be redirected, pursuant to paragraph (b)(7) of this section, the lender may not unreasonably withhold its consent to such redirection.

(f) *Recalculation of section 236 basic rent and market rent.* With respect to any project with a mortgage insured or otherwise assisted pursuant to part 236 of this chapter, the basic rent and market rent, as defined in § 236.2 of this chapter, for each unit in such project may be increased to take into account the allowable distributions permitted

under this section and the debt service on any equity loan, rehabilitation loan or acquisition loan approved under a plan of action under subpart B of this part.

[57 FR 12041, Apr. 8, 1992, as amended at 58 FR 37815, July 13, 1993]

§ 248.157 Voluntary sale of housing not in excess of Federal cost limit.

(a) *Offer to sell.* Where an owner has submitted a second notice of intent under § 248.133 for the purpose of transferring the project to a qualified purchaser, and the transfer preservation rent does not exceed the Federal cost limit, the owner shall offer the housing for transfer as provided in this section. The owner shall not be obligated to accept any offer made under this section, but may instead elect to retain the project and receive incentives under § 248.145.

(b) *Notification of qualified purchasers.* Upon receipt of a second notice of intent to transfer the project to a qualified purchaser, the Commissioner shall notify potential qualified purchasers of the availability of the project for sale, and of the names and addresses of the owner, or of a person representing the owner in the sale of the project, by—

(1) Mailing notices to non-profit organizations;

(2) Placing notices in the major local newspaper(s) in the jurisdiction in which the project is located;

(3) Mailing notices to clearinghouse networks; and

(4) Using any other means of notification which the Commissioner determines would be effective to notify potential qualified purchasers of the sale of the project.

(c) *Right of first offer to priority purchasers.* (1) For the 6-month period beginning on the date of receipt by the Commissioner of a second notice of intent under § 248.133, the owner may accept a bona fide offer only from:

(i) A resident council intending to purchase the project under §§ 248.173 or 248.175, which has met the requirements for tenant support, pursuant to those sections;

(ii) A resident council intending to purchase the project and retain it as rental housing, which has the support of a majority of the tenants; or

(iii) A community-based nonprofit organization which has the support of a majority of the tenants.

(2) If no bona fide offer to purchase the project is made and accepted during or at the end of the 6-month period specified in paragraph (c)(1) of this section, the owner may offer to sell the project during the next 6 months to any priority purchasers.

(3) If no bona fide offer to purchase the project is made and accepted during or at the end of the 6-month period specified in paragraph (c)(2) of this section, the owner may offer to sell the project during the 3 months immediately following that period only to qualified purchasers.

(d) *Purchase price.* The sale price, including assumption of the debt on the federally-assisted mortgage(s), or the amount of the debt on the federally-assisted mortgage(s) that the project is taken subject to, may not exceed the transfer preservation value of the project.

(e) *Expression of interest.* Any priority purchaser seeking to make an offer during the 6-month periods specified in paragraph (c) of this section shall, and other qualified purchasers may, submit written notice thereof to the Commissioner. Such notice, if made by a priority purchaser seeking to make an offer during either 6-month priority purchaser marketing period, shall contain the following:

(1) A statement identifying the priority purchaser as a State or local government agency, a nonprofit organization, or a resident council;

(2) A copy of its articles of incorporation, charter and list of officers and directors, if the purchaser is a nonprofit organization or a resident council and in the case of a nonprofit organization, proof that the organization is, or has applied to be, a tax exempt organization in accordance with 26 U.S.C. 501(c); and

(3) A statement as to whether the purchaser is affiliated with any other entity for purposes of purchasing the project and whether any Low Income Housing Tax Credits may be awarded in connection with the purchase of the project.

(f) *Information from the Commissioner.* Within 30 days of receipt of an expression of interest by a priority purchaser, the Commissioner shall determine the status of the priority purchaser with respect to the categories listed in paragraph (h) of this section, and provide such purchaser with:

(1) A list of all possible assistance available from the Federal Government to facilitate a transfer of the project;

(2) The appraisal reports for the project as submitted under §248.111;

(3) The Commissioner's determination as to the priority status of the purchaser and as to whether the purchaser qualifies as a resident council, community-based nonprofit organization or State or local government entity;

(4) A worksheet indicating the level of the earnest money deposit required upon the submission of a bona fide offer;

(5) An acknowledgment of the purchaser's right to inspect the project; and

(6) Any other relevant financial information that the Commissioner possesses concerning the project, including the information determined under §248.121.

Within the same 30-day period, the Commissioner shall also notify the owner of the purchaser's expression of interest and instruct the owner to provide to the purchaser any information concerning the project that the Commissioner deems relevant to the transfer of the project.

(g) *Bona fide offer.* A bona fide offer is an offer to purchase eligible low-income housing at a sales price which does not exceed the transfer preservation value of the project.

(1) A bona fide offer must include the following:

(i) A contract of sale signed by the purchaser, which states that acceptance of the contract is contingent upon approval by the Commissioner;

(ii) An earnest money deposit from every qualified purchaser equal to the lesser of one percent of the transfer preservation value, $50,000 or $500 per unit, unless the purchaser is a resident council purchasing the project under a resident homeownership plan under §248.173 or §248.175, in which case the earnest money deposit shall be equal to

$200 per unit from 75% of the occupied units; and

(iii) If the purchaser is a resident council intending to purchase the project pursuant to a resident home-ownership plan, the information required under § 248.173(b); or

(iv) If the purchaser is a resident council intending to retain the project as rental housing, or a community-based nonprofit and the offer is submitted within the marketing period established in paragraph (c)(1) of this section, a resolution of the resident council, or a petition signed by tenants representing a majority of the units indicating their support of the offer.

(2) An owner may waive the requirement of an earnest money deposit or agree to accept a smaller deposit for all qualified purchasers, except resident councils who intend to purchase the project pursuant to a resident homeownership plan under § 248.173 or § 248.175. In order to be effective:

(i) The waiver must be indicated in the second notice of intent submitted under § 248.133 and the waiver must apply equally to all qualified purchasers, except resident councils who intend to purchase the project pursuant to a resident homeownership plan under § 248.173 or § 248.175; or

(ii) If the second notice of intent has already been submitted, the owner must submit to the Commissioner, in writing, its decision to waive the earnest money deposit. The Commissioner shall notify all qualified purchasers who have submitted an expression of interest under paragraph (e) of this section that the owner has waived the earnest money deposit requirement.

(h) *Retention and acceptance of offers.* The owner shall accept or reject any bona fide offer within 30 days of receipt of such offer. For an offer to be bona fide, it must meet the requirements of paragraph (g) of this section, as well as be submitted to the owner within the appropriate marketing period under paragraph (c) of this section. If an owner rejects any offer, it must return the earnest money deposit to the offeror at the time of rejection. A bona fide offer which is rejected by the owner will still be considered a bona fide offer for purposes of this section, even after the earnest money deposit has been re-

turned. If an owner decides to accept the offer at a later date, the purchaser may renew the offer by resubmitting the earnest money deposit, if a deposit had originally been required, within 30 days of notification of the owner's acceptance of the offer.

(i) *Submission of offer to HUD.* The purchaser shall submit the offer to the Commissioner. The Commissioner shall review the offer which is preliminarily accepted by the owner to determine whether it meets the requirements of a bona fide offer. The Commissioner shall notify the owner and purchaser, within 30 days after acceptance, whether the offer meets such requirements. The owner's preliminary acceptance of any offer pursuant to this section shall be conditional upon the Commissioner's certification that the offer is bona fide. If the Commissioner determines that the offer is not a bona fide offer, the offer will be considered invalid for the purposes of subpart B of this part.

(j) *Submission of plan of action.* Upon a determination by the Commissioner that the offer is bona fide and final acceptance of such an offer, the owner and purchaser shall jointly submit a plan of action to the Commissioner pursuant to § 248.135. The plan of action shall include any request for assistance from the Commissioner for purposes of transferring the project.

(k) *Requirements for plan of action approval.* If the qualified purchaser of the project is a resident council seeking to purchase the project under a resident homeownership program, the Commissioner may approve a plan of action only if the resident council's proposed resident homeownership program meets the requirements under § 248.173 or § 248.175. For all other qualified purchasers, the Commissioner may approve a plan of action submitted pursuant to this section only if the plan of action meets the criteria listed in § 248.145.

(l) *Failure to consummate sales transaction.* (1) If the owner accepts an offer from a priority purchaser during either of the two 6-month periods specified in paragraph (c) of this section, and before the expiration of the period specified in paragraph (c) of this section, the sales transaction either falls through or does not close within 90 days after the Commissioner's approval of the plan of action, the owner shall:

(i) Immediately notify the Commissioner that the sale has fallen through;

(ii) Notify any other purchaser that had submitted an offer to purchase the project; and

(iii) Resume holding the project open for sale for the remainder of the time periods specified in paragraph (c) of this section.

(2) If the owner accepts an offer from a purchaser, and during the 3-month period specified in paragraph (c) of this section, or thereafter, the sales transaction either falls through or does not close within 90 days after the Commissioner's approval of the plan of action, the owner shall take the following steps:

(i) Immediately notify the Commissioner that the sale has fallen through;

(ii) Contact any other purchaser that had submitted an offer to purchase the project and give such purchaser and any other qualified purchaser 60 days from the date of notification to the Commissioner in which to resubmit an offer to purchase the project.

(3) At any time during the 60-day period the owner may accept an offer submitted under paragraph (1)(2) of this section.

(4) If an offer submitted during the 60-day period specified in paragraph (1)(2) of this section is made and accepted, but the sale is not consummated within 90 days after the Commissioner's approval of the plan of action for reasons not attributable in whole or in part to the owner, the owner may terminate the low-income affordability restrictions through prepayment or voluntary termination, subject to compliance with the provisions of §248.165.

(m) *Assistance.* Subject to the availability of amounts approved in appropriation acts, the Commissioner shall, for approvable plans of action, provide assistance sufficient to enable qualified purchasers to:

(1) Acquire the eligible low income housing project from the current owner for a purchase price not greater than the transfer preservation value of the project;

(2) Pay the debt service on the federally-assisted mortgage(s) covering the project;

(3) Pay the debt service on any loan for the rehabilitation of the project;

(4) Meet project operating expenses and establish adequate reserves for the housing, and in the case of a priority purchaser, meet project oversight costs;

(5) Receive a distribution equal to an 8 percent annual return on any actual cash investment made to acquire or rehabilitate the project;

(6) In the case of a priority purchaser, receive reimbursement for all reasonable transaction expenses associated with the acquisition, loan closing and implementation of an approved plan of action; and

(7) In the case of an approved resident homeownership program, cover the costs of training for the resident council, homeownership counseling and training, the fees for the nonprofit entity or public agency working with the resident council, if such entity or agency is approved by the Commissioner, and costs related to relocation of tenants who elect to move. Assistance for such costs, exclusive of relocation expenses, shall not exceed $500 per unit or $200,000 for the project, whichever is less.

(n) *Incentives.* The Commissioner may provide assistance for all qualified purchasers under this subpart in the form of one or more of the incentives authorized under §248.153. The incentives provided by the Commissioner to any qualified purchaser may include an acquisition loan under subpart E of part 241 of this chapter.

(o) *Grants to priority purchasers.* The Commissioner may provide assistance for priority purchasers under subpart B of this part in the form of a grant for each unit in the project in an amount, as determined by the Commissioner, that does not exceed the present value of the total of the projected fair market rent for the next ten years, or such longer period if additional assistance is necessary to cover the costs set forth in paragraph (m) of this section.

(p) *Reimbursement of assistance.* The Commissioner reserves the right to seek reimbursement from a priority purchaser who, within ten years of approval of a plan of action, becomes affiliated with or transfers the project to any non-priority purchaser. The Commissioner shall be entitled to receive reimbursement for the difference between the assistance provided to the priority purchaser and the assistance that would have been provided in the same circumstances to a non-priority purchaser.

(q) *Seller financing.* In order to finance the acquisition or rehabilitation of a project under this section, a qualified purchaser may receive take-back financing from the owner of the project. If the purpose of the seller financing is to aid acquisition of the project, the principal amount of such financing, together with an acquisition loan provided under part 241 of this chapter, may not exceed the transfer preservation equity of the project, plus, in the case of priority purchasers, any expenses associated with the acquisition, loan closing, and implementation of the plan of action. If the purpose of the seller financing is to fund rehabilitation of the project, the principal amount of such financing may not exceed the equity requirements for a rehabilitation loan under § 241.70 or § 219.305 of this chapter. The seller may not charge interest on any seller financing at a rate in excess of that of the Federal acquisition or rehabilitation loan.

[57 FR 12041, Apr. 8, 1992, as amended at 58 FR 37816, July 13, 1993]

§ 248.161 Mandatory sale of housing in excess of the Federal cost limit.

(a) *In general.* With respect to any eligible low income housing for which the transfer preservation rent determined under § 248.121 exceeds the Federal cost limit, the owner shall offer the housing for transfer to qualified purchasers as provided in this section.

(b) *Applicability of voluntary sale provisions.* The provisions of § 248.157, other than paragraphs (a) and (p) of this section thereof, shall be applicable to any sale conducted under this section. If the owner receives an offer to purchase the project for a sale price equal to the transfer preservation value of the project, as determined under § 248.111, the owner shall be obligated to accept the offer upon its receipt and sell the project to the purchaser. If the owner receives an offer to purchase the project for a sale price less than the transfer preservation value of the project, the owner may accept the offer, but is not obligated to do so. Any offer to purchase a project under this section for less than the transfer preservation value must comply with the requirements of a bona fide offer in § 248.101, except for the requirement that the sale price equal the transfer preservation value. At the time of submission of the offer, the potential purchaser must also submit the documentation required in § 248.157(g).

(c) *Section 8 assistance.* Subject to the availability of amounts approved in appropriation acts, the Commissioner shall, for approvable plans of action, provide assistance to qualified purchasers under part 886, subpart A of this title sufficient to produce a gross potential income equal to the amount determined by multiplying 120 percent of the prevailing rents in the relevant local market in which the project is located by the number of units in the project, according to appropriate unit size, and any other incentives authorized under § 248.153 that would have been provided to a qualified purchaser under § 248.157.

(d) *Grants to qualified purchasers.* From amounts made available by Congress, the Commissioner may make grants to assist in the completion of transfers under this section to any qualified purchasers. Any grant made pursuant to paragraph (d) of this section shall be in an amount not exceeding the difference between the amount of assistance provided under paragraph (c) of this section and the amount of assistance specified in § 248.157(m).

(e) *Securing State and local funding.* The Commissioner shall assist any qualified purchaser of a project pursuant to this section in securing funding and other assistance, including tax and assessment reductions from State and local governments to facilitate a transfer under this section.

492

§248.165 Assistance for displaced tenants.

(a) *Section 8 assistance.* Each low income family that is displaced as a result of the prepayment of the mortgage, or voluntary termination of an insurance contract, on eligible low income housing shall, subject to the availability of funds, be offered the opportunity to receive tenant-based assistance under the Housing Choice Voucher Program in accordance with part 982 of this title.

(b) *Notification of Commissioner.* The owner of any eligible low income housing project who prepays the mortgage or voluntarily terminates the mortgage insurance contract pursuant to subpart B of this part, shall notify the Commissioner of:

(1) The names and addresses of all of the tenants in the project who will be displaced;

(2) The size of the unit in which each of the displaced tenants is currently dwelling; and

(3) The names of all of the displaced tenants who are special needs tenants, as that term is defined in §248.101, as well as a statement as to the nature of their special need.

The owner shall provide the Commissioner with this information within 30 days of identifying such tenants for displacement, but in no event less than 30 days prior to the date when the tenants must vacate the premises.

(c) *Relocation of displaced tenants.* The Commissioner shall coordinate with public housing agencies to ensure that any very low or low income family displaced from eligible low income housing as the result of prepayment of the mortgage or termination of the mortgage insurance contract on such project is able to acquire a suitable, affordable dwelling unit in the area where the project from which the displaced family is located. The Commissioner, upon receiving information from the owner under paragraph (b) of this section stating that certain tenants will be displaced, shall request from the public housing agencies located in the same area as the affected project, notices of vacancies in other affordable projects which would be suitable for the displaced tenants. The Commissioner shall convey the notices of vacancies to the tenants who will be displaced along with the addresses of the local public housing agencies.

(d) *Relocation expenses.* The Commissioner shall require the owner of eligible low income housing who prepays or terminates the insurance contract resulting in the displacement of tenants to pay 50 percent of the relocation expenses of each family which is relocated, except that the Commissioner shall increase such percentage to the extent that State or local law of general applicability requires a higher payment by the owner.

(e) *Continued occupancy.* Each owner who prepays the mortgage or terminates the mortgage insurance contract on eligible low income housing shall, as provided in paragraph (g) of this section, allow the tenants occupying units in such project on the date of submission of a notice of intent under §248.105 to remain in the project for a period of three years, commencing on the date of prepayment or contract termination, at rent levels existing at the time of prepayment or termination, except for rent increases made necessary due to increased operating costs.

(f) *Replacement unit.* In any case in which the Commissioner requires an owner to allow tenants to occupy units under paragraph (e) of this section, an owner may fulfill the requirements of such paragraph by providing such assistance necessary for the tenant to rent a decent, safe, and sanitary unit in another project for the same 3-year period and at a rental cost to the tenant not in excess of the rental amount the tenant would have been required to pay to the owner in the owner's project, except that the tenant must freely agree to waive the right to occupy the unit in the owner's project. The provisions of paragraph (d) of this section requiring an owner who prepays or terminates an insurance contract to pay a portion of the relocation expenses incurred by displaced tenants shall also be applicable to tenants who relocate pursuant to this paragraph.

(g) *Applicability.* The provisions of paragraphs (e) and (f) of this section shall apply only to:

(1) All tenants in eligible low income housing projects located in a low-vacancy area; and

493

(2) Special needs tenants.

(h) *Low Vacancy Areas.* The Commissioner shall notify the owner, within 30 days of the owner's request to prepay under § 248.169, whether the project is located in a low vacancy area for purposes of paragraph (g) of this section.

(i) *Required acceptance of section 8 assistance.* Any owner who prepays the mortgage or terminates the mortgage insurance contract on eligible low income housing and maintains the project for residential rental occupancy may not refuse to rent, refuse to negotiate for the rental of, or otherwise make unavailable or deny the rental of a dwelling unit in such project to any person, or discriminate against any person in the terms, conditions, or privileges or rental of a unit, or in the provision of services or facilities in connection therewith, because the person receives tenant-based assistance under the Housing Choice Voucher Program.

(j) *Regional pools.* In providing assistance under this section, the Commissioner shall allocate the assistance on a regional basis through the regional offices of the Department of Housing and Urban Development. The Commissioner shall allocate assistance under this section in a manner so that the total number of assisted units in each such region available for occupancy by, and affordable to, low income families and persons does not decrease because of the prepayment of a mortgage on eligible low income housing or the termination of an insurance contract on such project.

(k) This section shall only apply to prepayments and terminations occurring pursuant to §§ 248.157(l) and 248.169.

[57 FR 12041, Apr. 8, 1992, as amended at 64 FR 26639, May 14, 1999]

§ 248.169 Permissible prepayment or voluntary termination and modification of commitments.

(a) *In general.* Notwithstanding any limitations on prepayment or voluntary termination under subpart B of this part, an owner may terminate the low income affordability restrictions through prepayment or voluntary termination, subject to compliance with the provisions of § 248.165, under one of the following circumstances:

(1) The Commissioner approves a plan of action under § 248.153(a), but does not provide the assistance approved in such plan and contained in an executed use agreement between the Commissioner and the owner, including section 8 assistance or a loan provided under part 219 of this chapter, but not including insurance of a rehabilitation or equity take-out loan under part 241 of this chapter, during the 15-month period beginning on the date of final approval of the plan of action;

(2) After the date that the project would have been eligible for prepayment pursuant to the terms of the mortgage, notwithstanding this part, the Commissioner approves a plan of action under § 248.157 or § 248.161, but does not provide the assistance approved in such plan, including section 8 assistance, a loan provided under part 219 of this chapter, a grant provided under § 248.157(o), or a grant under § 248.161(d), before the earlier of:

(i) The expiration of the 2-month period beginning on the commencement of the first fiscal year beginning after such final approval; or

(ii) The expiration of the 6-month period beginning on the date of final approval.

(3) The Commissioner approves a plan of action under §§ 248.157 or 248.161 for any eligible low income housing not covered by paragraph (a)(2) of this section, but does not provide the assistance approved in such plan before the earlier of:

(i) The expiration of the 2-month period beginning on the commencement of the first fiscal year beginning after such final approval; or

(ii) The expiration of the 9-month period beginning on the date of final approval.

(4) An owner who intended to transfer the project to a qualified purchaser under § 248.157 or § 248.161, and fully complied with the provisions of such section,

(i) Did not receive any bona fide offers from any qualified purchasers within the applicable time periods; or

(ii) Received and accepted a bona fide offer from a qualified purchaser, but the sales transaction fell through for reasons not attributable in whole or in part to the owner, and the owner then complied with the requirements of §248.157(1) and did not receive another bona fide offer from any qualified purchasers.

(b) *Section 8 assistance.* When providing section 8 assistance, the Commissioner may enter into a contract with an owner, contingent upon the future availability of appropriations, for the purpose of renewing expiring contracts for rental assistance as provided in appropriations acts, to extend the term of such rental assistance for such additional period or periods necessary to carry out an approved plan of action. The contract and approved plan of action shall provide that, if the Commissioner is unable to extend the term of such rental assistance or is unable to develop a revised package of incentives providing benefits to the owner comparable to those received under the original approved plan of action, the Commissioner, upon the request of the owner, shall take the following actions, subject to the limitations under the following paragraphs:

(1) Modify the binding commitments made pursuant to §248.145(a)(2)–(10) that are dependent upon such rental assistance; or

(2) If the Commissioner determines that such modification is infeasible, permit the owner to prepay the mortgage and terminate the plan of action and any implementing use agreements or restrictions, but only if the owner agrees in writing to comply with the provisions of §248.165.

(c) *Failure to provide section 8 assistance.* With regard to paragraph (b) of this section, the Commissioner shall notify the owner of an inability to either extend the term of section 8 rental assistance or to develop a revised package of incentives providing benefits comparable to those received under the original plan of action as soon as practicable upon discovering that fact. The owner shall inform the Commissioner in writing, within 30 days of receipt of the notice that, since the Commissioner is unable to fulfill the terms of the original plan of action, the owner intends to request that the Commissioner take action under paragraphs (b)(1) or (2) of this section. The Commissioner shall, no later than 90 days from receiving the owner's notice, take action to extend the rental assistance contract and to continue the binding commitments under §248.145(a)(2)–(10).

§248.173 Resident homeownership program.

(a) *Formation of resident council.* Tenants seeking to purchase eligible low income housing in accordance with §§248.157 and 248.161 shall organize a resident council for the purpose of developing a resident homeownership program in accordance with standards established by the Commissioner. In order to fulfill the purposes of this section, the resident council shall work with a public or private nonprofit organization or a public body, including an agency or instrumentality thereof. Such organization shall have sufficient experience to enable it to help the tenants to consider their options and to develop the capacity necessary to own and manage the project, where appropriate, and shall be approved by the Commissioner.

(b) *Submission of expression of interest.* A resident council shall identify itself as such in an expression of interest submitted pursuant to §248.157 or §248.161 and shall state that, it is interested in purchasing the project pursuant to a homeownership program.

(c) *Bona fide offer.* When submitting an offer to purchase the project pursuant to this section, the resident council must simultaneously submit a certified list of project tenants representing at least 75 percent of the occupied units in the project, and representing at least 50 percent of all of the units in the project, who have expressed an interest in participating in the homeownership program developed by the resident council. An offer made without this certified list will not be considered a bona fide offer for the purposes of subpart B of this part.

(d) *Submission of a homeownership program.* (1) The resident council shall prepare a homeownership program acceptable to the Commissioner for giving all residents of the project an opportunity to become homeowners. The plan shall describe the major elements of, and schedules for, the homeownership program and demonstrate how the program complies with all applicable requirements of this section. The plan shall also describe the resident council's current abilities and proposed capacity-building activities to successfully carry out the homeownership program in compliance with this section. The homeownership program shall include, at a minimum, the following information:

(i) The amount of grant funds requested from the Commissioner, and the expected amounts and sources of other funding;

(ii) The proposed use of the grant funds to be received from HUD and of all other funds, including proceeds from the sale of units to initial purchasers, consistent with paragraph (h) of this section;

(iii) A summary of major rehabilitation activities to be carried out, including repairs, replacements and improvements;

(iv) The price at which the resident council intends to transfer ownership interests in, or shares representing, units in the project, broken down by unit size and/or type; the factors that will influence the establishment of such price, including, but not limited to, the resident council's acquisition cost, estimated rehabilitation costs, capitalization of reserves and organizational costs; how the price arrived at by the resident council compares to the estimated appraised value of the ownership interests or shares; and the underwriting standard that the resident council plans to use, or reasonably expects a public or private lender to use, for potential tenant purchasers, consistent with paragraph (g)(2) of this section;

(v) The expected number of very low, low and moderate income tenants that will be initial owners under the program, consistent with paragraph (g)(1) of this section;

(vi) A pro forma analysis which demonstrates the financial feasibility and viability of the homeownership program, based on the required conditions specified in paragraph (g) of this section;

(vii) The financing arrangements that the tenants are expected to pursue or to be provided, including financing available through the resident council or a State or local governmental enti-ty, and criteria for acceptability of conventional financing;

(viii) A description of the estimated costs expected to be paid by the homeowner at closing;

(ix) The type of homeownership contemplated, consistent with paragraph (f) of this section;

(x) How the marketing of currently vacant units and units occupied by nonpurchasing tenants that become vacant will affect the sales price and occupancy charges to purchasers;

(xi) A workable schedule of sale, subject to the limitations of paragraph (o) of this section, based on estimated tenant incomes;

(xii) Any restrictions on resale by homeowners over and above those specified in paragraph (i) of this section, and any restrictions on homeowners' equity, over and above those specified in paragraph (k) of this section;

(xiii) The qualifications of the resident council or the proposed management entity to manage the project, in compliance with paragraph (n) of this section;

(xiv) The expected number of nonpurchasing tenants and their eligibility for section 8 rental assistance under paragraph (m)(2) of this section;

(xv) Expected scope and expenses of relocation activities, both for any temporary relocation due to rehabilitation as well as relocation assistance for nonpurchasing tenants, consistent with paragraph (m)(4) of this section;

(xvi) Expected scope and costs of technical assistance, training and counseling for the resident council, purchasers and non-purchasing tenants; and

(xvii) A certification that the resident council shall comply with the provisions of the Fair Housing Act (42 U.S.C. 3601–3619); title VI of the Civil Rights Act of 1964 (42 U.S.C. 2000d); Executive Order 11063 (3 CFR 1959–1963 comp., p. 652); section 504 of the Rehabilitation Act of 1973 (29 U.S.C. 794); the Age Discrimination Act of 1975 (42 U.S.C. 6101–6107); and all regulations issued pursuant to these statutes and authorities.

(2) The Commissioner shall give the resident council a reasonable opportunity to revise the homeownership program if approval is denied.

(e) *Approval of a homeownership program; assistance provided.* (1) When the Commissioner determines that the homeownership program submitted by the resident council meets the requirements of this section, is financially feasible, and is the least costly alternative that is consistent with establishing a viable homeownership program, the Commissioner shall approve the program.

(2) In connection with an approved homeownership program the Commissioner shall provide assistance sufficient to pay the following costs:

(i) The debt service on the federally-assisted mortgage(s) covering the project, when such mortgage is assumed by the resident council;

(ii) The purchase price, which shall not exceed the transfer preservation value;

(iii) Transaction costs, as provided in §248.157(m)(6);

(iv) Other costs, as provided in §248.157(m)(7);

(v) The costs of rehabilitation;

(vi) The establishment of an adequate reserve for replacements; and

(vii) If necessary, the establishment of operating reserve escrows including contingencies against unexpected increases in expenses or shortfalls in homeowners' payments.

(3) Upon approval of the homeownership program, the Commissioner and the resident council shall enter into an agreement, which shall include, among other matters, procedures governing the drawdown of funds and remedies for noncompliance with the requirements of this section.

(f) *Method of conversion.* The Commissioner shall approve the method for converting the project to homeownership, which may involve acquisition of ownership interests in, or shares representing, the units in a project under any arrangement determined by the Commissioner to be appropriate, such as cooperative ownership, and fee simple ownership, including condominium ownership.

(g) *Required conditions.* The Commissioner shall require that the form of homeownership impose appropriate conditions, including conditions to assure that:

(1) To the extent practicable, the number of initial owners that are very low, low, and moderate income persons at initial occupancy are of the same proportion of very low, low, and moderate income tenants (including families and persons whose incomes are 95 percent or more of area median income) as resided in the project on January 1, 1987 (or if the January 1, 1987 profile is unavailable, a certification from the owner stating its unavailability and a profile as of January 1, 1988, or, if that is also unavailable, a profile as of January 1, 1989) or as of the date of approval of the plan of action, whichever date results in the higher proportion of very low income families, except that the resident council may, at its option, increase the proportions of very low income and low income initial owners, however, no current tenant may be denied homeownership as a result of this paragraph;

(2) Projected debt service payments, occupancy charges and utilities payable by the owners shall not exceed 35 percent of the monthly adjusted gross income of the owners;

(3) The aggregate incomes of initial owners and other sources of funds for the project are sufficient to permit occupancy charges to cover the full operating costs of the project and any debt service; and

(4) Each initial owner occupies the unit it acquires for at least the initial 15 years of ownership, unless the resident council determines that the initial owner is required to move outside the market area due to a change in employment or an emergency situation.

(5) All units which remain as rental units, from the date of approval of the resident homeownership program, until they are purchased by an initial owner under the resident homeownership program, shall be maintained in accordance with §248.145 (a)(5), (a)(6), (a)(7), (a)(8), and (a)(9).

(h) *Use of proceeds from sales to eligible families.* The entity that transfers ownership interests in, or shares representing, units to eligible families, or another entity specified in the approved application, may use 50 percent of the proceeds, if any, from the initial sale for costs of the homeownership program, including improvements to the project, operating and replacement reserves for the project, additional homeownership opportunities in the project, and other project-related activities approved by the Commissioner. The remaining 50 percent of such proceeds shall be returned to the Commissioner for use under §§ 248.157 and 248.161, subject to the availability of appropriations. Such entity shall keep, and make available to the Commissioner, all records necessary to calculate accurately payments due the Commissioner under paragraph (h) of this section.

(i) *Restrictions on resale by homeowners.* Resale of a homeowner's interest in a project with an approved homeownership program may occur subject to any reasonable restrictions placed on such a transfer by the resident council and approved by the Commissioner.

(1) *Transfer permitted.* A homeowner may transfer the homeowner's ownership interest in the unit, subject to the right to purchase under paragraph (i)(2) of this section, the requirement for the purchaser to execute a promissory note, if required under paragraph (i)(3) of this section and the restrictions on retention of sales proceeds in paragraph (k) of this section. An applicant may propose in its application, and HUD may approve, reasonable restrictions on the resale of units under the program.

(2) *Right to purchase.* Where a resident management corporation, resident council, or cooperative has jurisdiction over the unit, it shall have the right to purchase the ownership interest in the unit from the initial homeowner for the amount specified in a firm contract between the homeowner and a prospective buyer. Where a resident management corporation, resident council, or a cooperative exercises a right to purchase, it shall resell the unit to an eligible family within a reasonable period of time.

(3) *Promissory note required.* At closing, the initial homeowner shall execute a nonrecourse promissory note for a term of twenty years, in a form acceptable to HUD, equal to the difference between the fair market value of the unit and the purchase price, payable to the Commissioner, together with a mortgage securing the obligation of the note.

(i) With respect to a sale by an initial homeowner, the note shall require payment upon sale by the initial homeowner, to the extent proceeds of the sale remain after paying off other outstanding debt incurred in connection with the purchase of the property, paying any other amounts due in connection with the sale, including closing costs and transfer taxes, and paying the family the amount of its equity in the property, computed in accordance with paragraph (k) of this section.

(ii) With respect to a sale by an initial homeowner during the first six years after acquisition, the family may retain only the amount computed under paragraph (k) of this section. Any excess is distributed as provided in paragraph (1) of this section.

(iii) With respect to a sale by an initial homeowner six to twenty years after acquisition, the amount payable under the note shall be reduced by 1/168th of the original principal amount of the note for each full month of ownership by the family after the end of the sixth year. The homeowner may retain all other proceeds of the sale.

(j) *Execution of promissory note by subsequent purchaser.* Where a subsequent purchaser during the 20-year period, measured by the term of the initial promissory note, purchases the property for less than the then current fair market value, the purchaser shall also execute at closing such a promissory note and mortgage, for the amount of the discount. The term of the promissory note shall be the period remaining of the original 20-year period. The note shall require payment upon sale by the subsequent homeowner, to the extent proceeds of the sale remain after paying off other outstanding debt incurred in connection with the purchase of the property, and paying any other amounts due in connection with the sale (such as closing costs and transfer taxes). The amount payable on the note shall be reduced by a percentage of the original principal amount of the note for each full month of ownership by the subsequent homeowner. The percentage shall be computed by determining the percentage of the term of the promissory note that the homeowner has owned the property. The remainder may be retained by the subsequent homeowner selling the property.

(k) *Homeowners' equity.* The amount of equity an initial homeowner has in the property is determined by computing the sum of the following:

(1) The contribution to equity paid by the family, if any, including any down payment and any amount paid towards principal on a mortgage loan during the period of ownership;

(2) The value of any improvements installed at the expense of the family during the family's tenure as owner, as determined by the resident council based on evidence of amounts spent on the improvements, including the cost of material and labor; and

(3) The appreciated value, determined by applying the Consumer Price Index (urban consumers) against the contribution to equity under paragraphs (k) (1) and (2) of this section, excluding the value of any sweat equity or volunteer labor used to make improvements to the unit. The resident council may, at the time of initial sale, enter into an agreement with the family to set a maximum amount which this appreciation may not exceed.

(1) *Use of recaptured funds.* Any net sales proceeds that may not be retained by the homeowner under the homeownership program approved under this section shall be paid to the HOME Investment Trust Fund for the unit of general local government in which the project is located. If the project is located in a unit of general local government that is not a participating jurisdiction, as such term is defined in §248.101, any such net sales proceeds shall be paid to the HOME Investment Trust Fund for the State in which the project is located. With respect to any proceeds transferred to a HOME Investment Trust Fund under paragraph (1) of this section, the Commissioner shall take such actions as are necessary to ensure that the proceeds shall be immediately available for eligible activities to expand the supply of affordable housing under section 212 of the Cranston-Gonzalez National Affordable Housing Act of 1990 (42 U.S.C. 12742). The Commissioner shall monitor the HOME Investment Trust Fund for each State and unit of local government and shall require maintenance of any records necessary to calculate accurately payments due under this paragraph (1) of this section.

(m) *Protection of nonpurchasing families.* Nonpurchasing families who continue to reside in a project subject to a homeownership program approved under this section shall be protected as follows:

(1) *Eviction.* No tenant residing in an eligible property on the date the Commissioner approves a plan of action may be evicted by reason of a homeownership program approved under this section. This does not preclude evictions for material violation of the terms of occupancy of the unit.

(2) *Section 8 assistance.* If a tenant decides not to purchase a unit, or is not qualified to do so, the Commissioner shall ensure that tenant-based assistance under the Housing Choice Voucher Program in accordance with part 982 of this title is available for use in that or another property by each tenant that meets the eligibility requirements thereunder.

(3) *Rent increases for ineligible tenants.* Rents for tenants who do not purchase a unit but are ineligible for assistance under paragraph (m)(2) of this section may be increased to a level that does not exceed 30 percent of the tenant's adjusted income or the section 8 existing fair market rent, whichever is lower. Rent increases shall be phased in in accordance with §248.145(a)(6).

(4) *Relocation assistance.* The resident council shall also inform each tenant that if the tenant chooses to move, the resident council, as owner of the project, will pay relocation expenses in accordance with the approved homeownership program. The provisions of §248.165 shall not apply to resident councils who are project owners pursuant to an approved homeownership program under this section.

(n) *Qualified management.* As a condition of approval of a homeownership program under subpart B of this section, the resident council shall have demonstrated its abilities to manage eligible properties by having done so effectively and efficiently for a period of not less than three years or by entering into a contract with a qualified management entity that meets such standards as the Commissioner may prescribe to ensure that the project will be maintained in a decent, safe and sanitary condition.

(o) *Timely homeownership.* The resident council shall acquire ownership of the project no later than 90 days after final approval of a plan of action pursuant to this section. The resident council shall transfer ownership of units in the project (other than units occupied by nonpurchasing tenants) to the tenants within a reasonable time thereafter, but in no event more than 4 years from the date of transfer of the project to the resident council. The Commissioner may seek contractual remedies against any resident council which fails to transfer ownership of all units within the 4-year period. During the interim period when the project continues to be operated and managed as rental housing, the resident council shall utilize written tenant selection policies and criteria that are approved by the Commissioner as consistent with the purpose of providing housing for very low income families. The resident council shall promptly notify in writing any rejected applicant of the grounds for any rejection.

(p) *Housing standards; inspections.* (1) Until the resident council has transferred all units in the project (other than those occupied by nonpurchasing tenants) to the initial purchasers, the project shall be maintained in accordance with the housing standards set forth in § 248.147.

(2) The Commissioner shall inspect the project at least annually in order to determine compliance with paragraph (p)(1) of this section.

(q) *Audits.* Each resident council shall be subject to the audit requirements in 2 CFR part 200, subpart F, and shall submit an annual audit to the Commissioner in such form as the Commissioner may prescribe. The resident council shall keep such records as may be reasonably necessary to fully disclose the amount and the disposition by such resident council of the proceeds of assistance received under subpart B of this part, including any proceeds from sales under paragraphs (h) and (l) of this section, the total cost of the homeownership program in connection with which such assistance is given or used, and the amount and nature of that portion of the program supplied by other sources, and such other sources as will facilitate an effective audit.

The Commissioner or his or her duly authorized representative shall have access for the purpose of audit and examination to any books, documents, papers, and records of the resident council that are pertinent to assistance received under subpart B of this part. The Comptroller General of the United States, or any of the duly authorized representatives of the Comptroller General, shall also have access, for the purpose of audit and examination, to any books, documents, papers, and records of the resident council that are pertinent to assistance received under subpart B of this part.

(r) *Reports.* The resident council shall submit reports, as required by the Commissioner, in order to demonstrate continued compliance with the requirements of this section.

(s) *Assumption of the federally assisted mortgage(s).* In connection with a resident homeownership plan, the resident council may assume a mortgage insured, held or assisted by the Commissioner under part 236 of this chapter or under part 221 of this chapter and bearing a below market interest rate as provided under § 221.518(b) of this chapter or may choose to pay off the mortgage. If the resident council decides to assume the mortgage, the project must be sold pursuant to § 248.175 and the project must be operated as a limited equity cooperative.

[57 FR 12041, Apr. 8, 1992, as amended at 58 FR 37816, July 13, 1993; 64 FR 26639, May 14, 1999; 80 FR 75936, Dec. 7, 2015]

§ 248.175 Resident homeownership program—limited equity cooperative.

(a) Tenants may carry out a resident homeownership program through the purchase of eligible low income housing by a limited equity cooperative and the operation of the project as a limited equity cooperative.

(b) The purchase of a project by a limited equity cooperative and the operation of the project by the limited equity cooperative shall be carried out in accordance with the provisions of §248.173 (a), (b), (c), (d), (except that paragraph (d)(1)(i) of this section shall include a statement of the amount and type of incentives requested, rather than only the amount of grant funds requested), (e), (g)(3), (i) (except paragraphs (i)(1) and (3)), (m) and (n).

(c) The purchase and operation of eligible low income housing by a limited equity cooperative under this section shall be carried out in accordance with all provisions of subpart B of this part otherwise, applicable to the transfer and operation of a project with continued low income affordability restrictions, except as provided in this section.

[57 FR 12041, Apr. 8, 1992, as amended at 58 FR 37816, July 13, 1993]

§248.177 Delegated responsibility to State agencies.

(a) *In general.* The Commissioner shall delegate some or all responsibility for implementing subpart B of this part to a State housing agency if such agency submits a preservation plan acceptable to the Commissioner.

(b) *Approval.* State preservation plans shall be submitted in such a form and in accordance with such procedures as the Commissioner shall establish. The Commissioner may approve plans that contain:

(1) An inventory of low income housing located within the State that is or will be eligible low income housing under subpart B of this part within five years;

(2) A description of the agency's experience in the area of multifamily financing and restructuring;

(3) A description of the administrative resources that the agency will commit to the processing of plans of action in accordance with subpart B of this part;

(4) A description of the administrative resources that the agency will commit to the monitoring of approved plans of action in accordance with subpart B of this part;

(5) An independent analysis of the performance of the multifamily housing inventory financed or otherwise monitored by the agency;

(6) A certification by the public official responsible for submitting the con-

solidated plan under 24 CFR part 91 that the proposed activities are consistent with the approved consolidated plan of the State within which the eligible low income housing is located; and

(7) Such other certifications or information that the Commissioner determines to be necessary to implement an approved State preservation plan, which may include incentives that are authorized under other provisions of subpart B of this part.

(c) *Implementation agreements.* The Commissioner may enter into any agreements necessary to implement an approved State preservation plan, which may include incentives that are authorized under other provisions of subpart B of this part.

(d) *Fees.* Any State agency with responsibility so delegated under subpart B of this part may not charge any owner of eligible low income housing any fee for accepting notices of intent, processing plans of action or any other process pursuant to approval of a plan of action under subpart B of this part. This prohibition shall not preclude:

(1) An owner paying for its appraisal or share of a joint appraisal under the provisions of §248.111; or

(2) A State agency from collecting fees normally associated with providing and processing financing insured under part 241 of this chapter.

[57 FR 12041, Apr. 8, 1994, as amended at 60 FR 16379, Mar. 30, 1995]

§248.179 Consultation with other interested parties.

The Commissioner shall confer with any appropriate State or local government agency to confirm any State or local assistance that is available to achieve the purposes of subpart B of this part and shall give consideration to the views of any such agency when making determinations under subpart B of this part. The Commissioner shall also confer with appropriate interested parties that the Commissioner believes could assist in the development of a plan of action that best achieves the purposes of subpart B of this part.

§248.181 Notice to tenants.

Except as provided in §§248.105 and 248.133, with respect to the first and second notices of intent, with regard to all provisions of subpart B of this part which mandate that information or material be given to the tenants, by the Commissioner, the owner, or a qualified purchaser, or other party, this requirement shall be satisfied where the notifying entity:

(a) Posts a copy of the information or material in readily accessible locations within each affected building, or posts notices in each location describing the information or material and specifying a location, as convenient to the tenants as is reasonably practical, where a copy may be examined and copied during reasonable hours; and

(b) Supplies a copy of the information or material to a tenant representative, if any.

§ 248.183 Preemption of State and local laws.

(a) *In general.* No State or political subdivision of a State may establish, continue in effect, or enforce any law or regulation that:

(1) Restricts or inhibits the prepayment of any mortgage described in § 248.101 or the voluntary termination of any insurance contract pursuant to § 207.253 of this chapter on eligible low income projects;

(2) Restricts or inhibits an owner of such projects from receiving the authorized annual return provided under § 248.121;

(3) Is inconsistent with any provision of subpart B of this part, including any law, regulation, or other restriction that limits or impairs the ability of any owner of eligible low income housing to receive incentives authorized under subpart B of this part, including authorization to increase rental rates, transfer the project, obtain secondary financing, or use the proceeds of any such incentives; or

(4) In its applicability to low income housing is limited only to eligible low income housing for which the owner has prepaid the mortgage or terminated the insurance contract.

(b) *Effect.* Any law, regulation or restriction described in paragraph (a) of this section shall be ineffective and any eligible low income housing exempt from the law, regulation, or re-striction, only to the extent that it violates the provisions of this section.

(c) *Laws of general applicability: contractual restrictions.* This section shall not prevent the establishment, continuing in effect, or enforcement of any law or regulation of any State or political subdivision of a State not inconsistent with the provision of this subpart, such as any law or regulation relating to building standards, zoning limitations, health, safety, or habitability standards for housing, rent control, or conversion of rental housing to condominium or cooperative ownership, to the extent such law or regulation is of general applicability to both projects receiving Federal assistance and nonassisted projects. This section shall not preempt, annul or alter any contractual restrictions or obligations existing before November 28, 1990 or voluntarily entered into by an owner of eligible low income housing on or after that date, and that limit or prevent that owner from prepaying the mortgage on the project or terminating the mortgage insurance contract.

[57 FR 12041, Apr. 8, 1992, as amended at 57 FR 57314, Dec. 3, 1992]

Subpart C—Prepayment and Plans of Action Under the Emergency Low Income Preservation Act of 1987

SOURCE: 55 FR 38952, Sept. 21, 1990, unless otherwise noted. Redesignated at 57 FR 12041, Apr. 8, 1992.

§ 248.201 Definitions.

The terms *Fair Market Rent (FMR)* and *Section 8* are defined in 24 CFR part 5.

Adjusted Income. Annual income, as specified in § 251.21 of this chapter, less allowances specified in the definition of *Adjusted Income* in § 215.1 of this chapter.

Allowable Distributions. The amount of cash or other assets that the owner may withdraw from the project under the terms of the regulatory agreement, applicable regulations, and administrative instructions, including the segregation of cash or assets for subsequent withdrawal, and excluding repayment of advances made for reasonable and necessary expenses incident to the operation and maintenance of the project.

Capital Improvement Loan. A direct loan originated by the Commissioner under part 219, subpart C of this chapter.

Eligible Low Income Housing. Any housing financed by a mortgage—

(a) That is—

(1) Insured or held by the Commissioner under section 221(d)(3) of the National Housing Act and assisted under part 886, subpart A of this title because of a conversion from assistance under part 215 of this chapter;

(2) Insured or held by the Commissioner under part 221 of this chapter and bearing a below market interest rate as provided under §221.518(b) of this chapter;

(3) Insured, assisted, or held by the Commissioner or a State or State agency under part 236 of this chapter; or

(4) A purchase money mortgage held by the Commissioner with respect to a project which, immediately prior to HUD's acquisition, would have been classified under paragraph (a) (1), (2), or (3) of this definition; and

(b) That, under regulation or contract in effect before November 1, 1987, is, or within one year from the date of the notice of intent would become, eligible for prepayment without the prior approval of the Commissioner.

Equity. The Owner's investment in the housing project, as approved or determined by the Commissioner.

Equity Loan. A loan insured by the Commissioner under part 241, subpart E of this chapter.

Flexible Subsidy Assistance. Assistance provided by the Commissioner under part 219 of this chapter, other than a capital improvement loan.

Good Cause. Temporary or permanent uninhabitability of the project justifying relocation of all or some of the project's tenants (except where such uninhabitability is caused by the actions or inaction of the owner), or actions of the tenant that, under the terms of the tenant's lease and applicable regulations, constitute a basis for eviction.

Limited Equity Cooperative. A cooperative housing corporation in which income eligibility of purchasers or appreciation upon resale of membership shares, or both, are restricted in order to maintain the housing as available to and affordable by low and moderate income families and persons.

Low Income Affordability Restrictions. Limits imposed by regulation or regulatory agreement on tenant rents, rent contributions, or income eligibility with respect to eligible low income housing.

Low-Income Families. Families or persons whose incomes do not exceed the levels established for low-income families under part 5 of this title.

Moderate Income Families. Families or persons whose incomes are between 80 percent and 95 percent of median area income, as determined by the Commissioner with adjustments for smaller and larger families.

Mortgage. The mortgage or deed of trust insured or held by the Commissioner or a State or State agency under parts 221 or 236 of this chapter, or the purchase money mortgage taken back by the Commissioner in connection with the sale of a HUD-owned project and held by the Commissioner, where such mortgage, deed of trust or purchase money mortgage is secured by eligible low income housing.

Notice of Intent. An owner's notification of its intent to seek prepayment of its mortgage, termination of the mortgage insurance contract or amendment of the mortgage or regulatory agreement pursuant to this part.

Owner. The mortgagor or trustor under the mortgage secured by eligible low income housing.

Plan of Action. A plan providing for prepayment of the mortgage, termination of the mortgage insurance contract, or continuation of the mortgage in place, and providing for either the termination of low income affordability restrictions, or the continuation of the project's use as low-income housing under modified terms and conditions.

Prepayment. Prepayment in full of a mortgage, or a partial prepayment or series of partial prepayments that reduce the mortgage term by at least six months, except where the prepayment in full or partial prepayment results from the application of condemnation proceeds.

503

Project oversight costs. Reasonable expenses incurred by a nonprofit purchaser in carrying out its ongoing ownership responsibilities under an approved plan of action. Project oversight costs must be directly related to educating the nonprofit purchaser's board of directors or otherwise supporting the board in its decision making. Project oversight costs may include staff, overhead, or third-party contract costs for:

(1) Ensuring adequate and responsible participation by the board of directors and the membership of the nonprofit purchaser in ownership decisions, including ensuring resident input in these decisions;

(2) Facilitating long-range planning by the board of directors to ensure the physical, financial and social viability of the project for the entire time the project is maintained as low income housing; and

(3) Assisting the ownership in complying with regulatory, use, loan and grant agreements.

Regulatory Agreement. The agreement executed by the owner and the Commissioner or a State agency providing for the Commissioner's regulation of the operation of the project.

Reserve for Replacements. The escrow fund established under the regulatory agreement for the purpose of ensuring the availability of funds for needed repair and replacement costs.

Residual Receipt Fund. The fund established under the regulatory agreement for holding cash remaining after deducting from the surplus cash, as defined by the regulatory agreement, the amount of all allowable distributions.

Return on Investment. The amount of allowable distributions, tax benefits, and other income or benefits received by the owner, as a percentage of the equity.

Termination of Low Income Affordability Restrictions. The elimination of low income affordability restrictions under the regulatory agreement through termination of mortgage insurance or prepayment of the mortgage.

Use Agreement. An agreement or covenant which is executed and recorded in the appropriate land records in connection with an approved plan of action, has lien priority over other mortgages and liens, is binding upon the owner and its successors and assigns, is enforceable by the Commissioner and by tenants, contains appropriate reporting requirements, and restricts or governs the use and operation of the project with respect to rent levels and increases, relocation, and, where appropriate, tenant eligibility, civil rights and other requirements. All tenants in occupancy at the time that the plan of action is approved will receive a copy of the use agreement.

Very Low Income Families. Families or persons whose incomes do not exceed the level established for very low income families under section 3(b) of the 1937 Act (42 U.S.C. 1437a(b)).

[55 FR 38952, Sept. 21, 1990. Redesignated at 57 FR 12041, Apr. 8, 1992, and amended at 57 FR 57314, Dec. 3, 1992; 58 FR 37816, July 13, 1993; 61 FR 5207, Feb. 9, 1996; 64 FR 26639, May 14, 1999]

§ 248.203 General prepayment limitation.

(a) An owner of eligible low income housing may prepay, and a mortgagee may accept prepayment of, a mortgage on such housing only in accordance with a plan of action approved by the Commissioner.

(b) A mortgage insurance contract with respect to eligible low income housing may be terminated pursuant to section 229 of the National Housing Act only in accordance with a plan of action approved by the Commissioner.

(c) A mortgagee's acceptance of a prepayment in violation of paragraph (a) or termination of a mortgage insurance contract in violation of paragraph (b) of this section is grounds for administrative action under parts 24 and 25 of this title, in addition to any other remedies available by law, including rescision of the prepayment or reinstatement on the insurance contract.

§ 248.211 Notice of intent to prepay.

(a) An owner of eligible low-income housing seeking to prepay its mortgage or to negotiate changes in the terms of the mortgage or regulatory agreement in accordance with this part, including termination of the insurance contract pursuant to section 229 of the National

Housing Act, shall file a notice of intent with the HUD field office in whose jurisdiction the project is located, and shall file a duplicate copy with the HUD Headquarters Office of Multifamily Housing Management, 451–7th Street, SW., Washington, DC 20410. The notice of intent shall identify the project by name, project number and location, briefly describe the owner's plans for the project, including any timetables or deadlines for actions to be taken, and the reason the owner seeks to prepay the mortgage or change the terms of the mortgage or regulatory agreement, and briefly describe any contacts that the owner has made or is making with other governmental agencies or other interested parties in connection with the notice of intent.

(b) An owner simultaneously shall file the notice of intent with:

(1) The chief executive officer of the appropriate State or local government in which the project is located, or any officer designated by executive order or State or local law to receive such information;

(2) Each tenant in the project; and

(3) The mortgagee.

In addition, the owner shall post a copy of the notice of intent in each occupied building in the project.

(c) Upon receipt of a notice of intent, the Commissioner will provide the owner with information that the owner needs to prepare a plan of action. This information shall include information regarding the Commissioner's standards under §248.221 of this part regarding the approval of a plan of action involving termination of low income affordability restrictions, and any relevant market area and demographic information that the Secretary has custody of and that the owner may use in preparing the plan of action; in addition, it shall include at a minimum a list of the Federal incentives authorized under §248.231 of this part for those projects for which a plan of action involving termination of low income affordability restrictions would not be approvable.

(d) Filing a notice of intent with the Commissioner will lead to one of the following results:

(1) Where the project meets the requirements of §248.221 of this part—

(i) The Commissioner will approve the prepayment or the termination of mortgage insurance pursuant to §248.221 of this part, and all low income affordability restrictions will be terminated with respect to some or all of the units; however, the owner would be responsible for ensuring that displaced current tenants are relocated to affordable housing, if necessary.

(ii) The Commissioner will approve the prepayment or termination of mortgage insurance pursuant to §248.221 of this part, and all low income affordability restrictions will be terminated, except (where necessary because the project is located in a housing market where there is insufficient comparable, decent, safe and sanitary affordable housing to meet the needs of all current tenants) with regard to protection of current very low income, low income and moderate income tenants;

(2) Where the plan of action would not be approvable under §248.221 of this part—

(i) The Commissioner will approve prepayment or the termination of mortgage insurance, but the owner will receive assistance under a State, local or other Federal government housing program, and will receive incentives pursuant to §248.231 of this part from the Federal government in return for agreeing to conditions related to the continued use of the project as low income housing in accordance with §248.233 of this part.

(ii) The Commissioner will not approve prepayment or the termination of mortgage insurance, but will provide incentives to the owner pursuant to §248.231 of this part in accordance with a plan of action meeting the standards of §248.233 of this part;

(iii) The Commissioner will not approve prepayment or the termination of mortgage insurance, but, after failing to reach agreement on a negotiated plan of action, the owner and the Commissioner will agree to a package of incentives and restrictions prescribed by §248.241 of this part; or

(iv) The Commissioner will not approve prepayment or the termination of mortgage insurance, and will not offer incentives of any kind.

(Approved by the Office of Management and Budget under control number 2502–0378)

[55 FR 38952, Sept. 21, 1990. Redesignated at 57 FR 12041, Apr. 8, 1992, and amended at 58 FR 37816, July 13, 1993]

§ 248.213 Plan of action.

(a) *Preparation and submission.* The owner shall submit the plan of action to the Commissioner in such form and manner as the Commissioner shall prescribe. The owner may submit the plan of action simultaneously to any appropriate State or local government agency, which shall, in reviewing the plan, consult with representatives of the tenants of the housing. An owner shall submit the plan of action to the Commissioner in such form and manner as the Commissioner shall prescribe. The owner shall notify the tenants of the plan of action by posting in each occupied building a summary of the plan of action and by delivery of a copy of the plan of action to the tenant representative, if any. In addition, the summary must indicate that a copy of the plan of action shall be available from the tenant representatives, whose names, addresses and telephone numbers are indicated on the summary, the local HUD field office, and the on-site office for the project, or if one is not available, in the location where rents are collected, for inspection and copying, at a reasonable cost, during normal business hours. Simultaneously with the submission to the Commissioner, the owner shall submit the plan of action to that officer of State or local government to whom the owner submitted a notice of intent under § 248.211(b). The summary of the plan of action posted by the owner and the copies of the plan of action submitted to the tenant representative and the officer of State or local government shall all state that, upon request, the tenants and the State or local government, may obtain from the owner or from the local HUD field office a copy of all documentation supporting the plan of action except for that documentation deemed "proprietary information" under § 248.101.

(b) *Contents.* The plan of action shall include:

(1) A description of any proposed changes in the status or terms of the mortgage or regulatory agreement, which may include a request for incentives to extend the low income use of the housing, as authorized under § 248.231 of this part; or may include a request to terminate the insurance contract.

(2) A description of any assistance that could be provided by State or local government agencies, as determined by prior consultation between the owner and the agencies;

(3) A description of any proposed changes in the low income affordability restrictions;

(4) A description of any proposed changes in ownership related to the plan of action, prepayment or termination of mortgage insurance;

(5) An assessment of the effect of the proposed changes on existing tenants.

(6) In the case of a plan of action involving incentives, an appraisal using the residential income approach;

(7) In the case of a plan of action involving the termination of low income affordability restrictions, a statement of the effect, if any, of the proposed changes on the supply of housing affordable to low and very low income families in the community within which the housing is located and in the area that the housing could reasonably be expected to serve; and

(8) A market study which demonstrates that the project is located in a market area that would enable the Commissioner to make the findings set forth at § 248.221(b)(1); and

(9) A list of any waivers requested by the owner pursuant to § 248.7 of this part; and

(10) Any other information which the owner may choose to submit which would enable the owner to meet the criteria for approval of the proposed plan of action.

(Approved by the Office of Management and Budget under control number 2502–0378)

[55 FR 38952, Sept. 21, 1990. Redesignated and amended at 57 FR 12041, 12060, Apr. 8, 1992; 58 FR 37816, July 13, 1993]

§ 248.215 Notification of deficiencies.

Not later than 60 days after receipt of a plan of action, the Commissioner will notify the owner in writing of any deficiencies that prevent the plan of action from being approved. If deficiencies are found, the notice shall describe ways, if any, in which the plan of action could be revised to meet the criteria for approval.

§248.217 Revisions to plan of action.

The owner may from time to time revise the plan of action before its approval as may be necessary to obtain the commissioner's approval thereof. An owner shall submit any revision to the Commissioner, and provide a copy of the revision and all documentation supporting the revision except for that documentation deemed "proprietary information" under §248.101, to the parties, and in the manner, specified in §248.213(a).

[58 FR 37817, July 13, 1993]

§248.218 Tenant notice and opportunity to comment.

When the owner and the Commissioner have reached preliminary agreement on the terms of a plan of action, the Commissioner shall prepare a summary of such terms and the anticipated impact of the plan of action on the current tenants. The owner shall send a copy of the summary to each tenant in the project, and shall post a copy of the summary in each occupied building in the project. The summary shall notify tenants that they have sixty calendar days in which to submit any comments to the Commissioner, who shall take any such comments into account before giving final approval to the plan of action.

(Approved by the Office of Management and Budget under control number 2502–0378)

§248.219 Notification of approval.

(a) Not later than 180 days after initial receipt of a plan of action, or within such longer period as the owner requests, the Commissioner shall notify the owner in writing whether the plan of action, including any revisions, is approved.

(b) If approval is withheld, the notice will—

(1) Describe the reasons for withholding approval, including prolonged delay by the owner in submitting a revised plan of action;

(2) Describe the actions that could be taken to meet the criteria for approval; and

(3) Afford the owner a reasonable opportunity to revise the plan of action and seek approval.

§248.221 Approval of a plan of action that involves termination of low income affordability restrictions.

The Commissioner may approve a plan of action that involves termination of the low income affordability restrictions only upon a written finding that—

(a) Implementation of the plan of action will not materially increase economic hardship for current tenants (and will not in any event result in: (1) A monthly rental payment by a current tenant that exceeds 30 percent of the monthly adjusted income of the tenant or an increase in the monthly rental payment in any year that exceeds 10 percent, whichever is lower, or (2) in the case of a current tenant who already pays more than such percentage, an increase in the monthly rental payment in any year that exceeds the increase in the Consumer Price Index or 10 percent, whichever is lower) or involuntarily displace current tenants (except for good cause) where comparable and affordable housing is not readily available, determined without regard to the availability of Federal housing assistance that would address any such hardship or involuntary displacement. Notwithstanding this limitation, the Commissioner may provide housing assistance to tenants if such assistance is not essential to the Commissioner's determination that the requirements of this paragraph have been met. The owner will agree to execute and allow the recordation of use agreements, where such agreements are necessary to safeguard current tenants against such adverse effects. Such use agreements will include a requirement that the owner comply with those provisions of part 247 of this chapter which relate to evictions; and

(b)(1) The supply of vacant, comparable housing is sufficient to ensure that the prepayment will not materially affect—

(i) The availability of decent, safe and sanitary housing affordable to low-income and very low income families in the area that the housing could reasonably be expected to serve;

(ii) The ability of low-income and very low income families to find decent, safe and sanitary housing near employment opportunities; or

(iii) The housing opportunities of minorities in the community within which the housing is located; or

(2) The plan of action has been approved by the appropriate State agency and any appropriate local government agency for the jurisdiction in which the housing is located as being in accordance with a State strategy approved by the Commissioner under § 248.223 of this part.

(c) There are no open audit findings, open findings of noncompliance with title VI of the Civil Rights Act of 1964 (42 U.S.C. 2000d); the Fair Housing Act (42 U.S.C. 3601–3619); Executive Order 11063 (3 CFR 1959–1963 comp., p. 652); the Age Discrimination Act of 1975 (42 U.S.C. 6101–6107); section 504 of the Rehabilitation Act of 1973 (29 U.S.C. 794); and all regulations promulgated under such statutes and authorities (including, but not limited to, 24 CFR part 100), or outstanding violations of the regulatory agreement.

(d) Any plan of action approved under this section shall specify actions that the Commissioner and the owner shall take to ensure that tenants displaced as a result of the termination of low-income affordability restrictions are relocated to affordable housing.

[55 FR 38952, Sept. 21, 1990. Redesignated and amended at 57 FR 12041, 12060, Apr. 8, 1992]

§ 248.223 Alternative State strategy.

(a) The Commissioner may approve a State strategy providing for State approval of plans of action that involve termination of low income affordability restrictions only upon finding that it is a practicable statewide strategy that ensures at a minimum that—

(1) Current tenants will not be involuntarily displaced (except for good cause);

(2) Housing opportunities for minorities will not be adversely affected in the communities in which the housing is located;

(3) Any increase in rent for current tenants will be to a level that does not exceed 30 percent of the adjusted income of the tenants or fair market rent, whichever is lower, and any increase not necessitated by increased operating costs shall be phased in equally over not less than 3 years if the increase exceeds 10 percent;

(4) Housing approved under the State strategy will remain affordable to very low income, low income and moderate income families for not less than the remaining term of the mortgage, if the housing is to be made available for rental use, or for not less than 40 years, if the housing is to be made available for homeownership;

(5)(i) Not less than 80 percent of all units in eligible low income housing approved under the State strategy will be retained as affordable to families or persons meeting the income eligibility standards for initial occupancy that applied to housing on January 1, 1987; and

(ii) Not less than 60 percent of the units in any one project will remain available to and affordable by such families or persons, within which not less than 20 percent of the units will remain available to and affordable by very low income families;

(6) Expenditures for rehabilitation, maintenance and operation will be at a level necessary to maintain the housing as decent, safe and sanitary and for the period specified in paragraph (a)(4) of this section;

(7) Not less than 25 percent of new assistance required to maintain the housing as available to and affordable by low income families in accordance with this section shall be provided through State and local actions, such as tax exempt financing, low income tax credits, State or local tax concessions, the provision of funds from housing finance agency reserves or housing trust funds, taxable bonds, and other incentives provided by the State or local governments; and

(8) For each unit of eligible low income housing approved under the State strategy that is not retained as affordable housing to families or persons meeting the income eligibility standards for initial occupancy on January 1, 1987, the State will provide, with

State funds, one additional unit of comparable housing in the same market area that is available to and affordable by such families and persons. Such units will be provided by conversion of existing units or construction of new units. These units or funds will be made available before the Commissioner approves the State strategy.

(b) *Additional requirements.* (1) The State must enter into all agreements necessary to carry out the State strategy before receiving the Commissioner's approval.

(2) Each State strategy shall include any other provision that the Commissioner determines to be necessary to implement the approved State strategy.

§248.231 Incentives to extend low income use.

The Commissioner may agree to provide one or more of the following incentives to induce the project owner to extend the low income use of the project, if the Commissioner determines that such incentives are warranted under the standards in §248.233 of this part:

(a) An increase in the allowable distribution, or other measures to increase the rate of return;

(b) Revisions to the method of calculating equity;

(c) Increased access to residual receipts funds or excess reserve for replacements funds;

(d) Provision of insurance for an equity loan;

(e) An increase in the rents permitted under an existing section 8 contract, within statutory and regulatory limits otherwise applicable, or (subject to the availability of amounts provided in appropriations Acts) additional assistance under section 8 or an extension of any project-based assistance attached to the housing;

(f) Provision of a capital improvement loan;

(g) Other actions to facilitate a transfer or sale of the housing to a qualified nonprofit organization, limited equity tenant cooperative, public agency, or other entity acceptable to the Commissioner, such as expedited review of a request for approval of a transfer of physical assets;

(h) Provision of flexible subsidy assistance;

(i) Termination of HUD's limitations on distributions, and release of residual receipts and reserve for replacements funds, through prepayment of the mortgage; and

(j) Any other incentives for which the owner is eligible.

§248.233 Approval of a plan of action that includes incentives.

The Commissioner may approve a plan of action that includes incentives, whether or not the plan of action allows for the prepayment of the mortgage, only upon a finding that—

(a) After taking into account local market conditions, the incentives are necessary to achieve the purposes of this part;

(b) The incentives are necessary to provide a fair rate of return to the owner. Incentives will only be provided in cases where the project's current use does not represent its highest and best use;

(c) The incentives are the least costly alternative for the Federal government to achieve the purposes of this part with respect to the housing;

(d) Binding commitments have been made to ensure that—

(1) The housing will be retained as housing affordable for very low income families, low-income families, and moderate income families for the remaining term of the mortgage;

(2) Throughout the remaining term of the mortgage, adequate expenditures will be made for the proper maintenance and operation of the housing;

(3) Current tenants will not be involuntarily displaced (except for good cause);

(4) Any increase in rent contributions for current tenants will be to a level that does not exceed 30 percent of the adjusted income of the tenant or the fair market rent, whichever is lower;

(5) Any resulting increase in rents for current tenants (except for increases made necessary by increased operating costs) will be phased in equally over a period of not less than 3 years, if the increase is 30 percent or more, and will be limited to not more than 10 percent per year, if the increase is more than 10 percent but less than 30 percent;

(6) Subject to the availability of funds, the Commissioner shall provide, and the owner shall accept, assistance under section 8 if the Commissioner determines that such assistance is necessary to mitigate any adverse effect of the rent increases on current tenants eligible for section 8 assistance; and

(7) Rents for units becoming available to new tenants will be at levels approved by the Commissioner that will ensure, to the extent practicable, that the units will be available to and affordable, with 30 percent of adjusted income, by the same proportion of very low income families, low-income families, and moderate income families as resided in the housing as of January 1, 1987 (based on the area median income limits established by the Commissioner in February 1987), or the date the plan of action is approved, whichever date results in the highest proportion of very low income families.

(i) For purposes of paragraph (d)(7) of this section—

(A) The percentage of moderate income families in occupancy as of January 1, 1987 shall include families who were admitted to the project as very low income, low income, or moderate income families but whose incomes had increased beyond the limit for moderate income families by January 1, 1987; and

(B) The proportions established shall not prohibit a higher proportion of very low income families from occupying the housing.

(ii) In approving rents under paragraph (d)(7) of this section, the Commissioner will take into account any additional incentives provided under this part and will make provision for annual rent adjustments necessary as a result of future reasonable increases in operating costs.

(e) In cases where the owner agrees to maintain only a portion of the project as low income housing, the incentives provided under § 248.231 of this part and the standards imposed under this section shall be adjusted accordingly.

(f) The Commissioner shall not approve a plan of action under this section if there are open findings of noncompliance with title VI of the Civil Rights Act of 1964 (42 U.S.C. 2000d); the

Fair Housing Act (42 U.S.C. 3601–3619); Executive Order 11063 (3 CFR 1959–1963 comp., p. 652); the Age Discrimination Act of 1975 (42 U.S.C. 6101–6107); section 504 of the Rehabilitation Act of 1973 (29 U.S.C. 794); and all regulations promulgated under such statutes and authorities, or if there are open audit findings with respect to violations of the regulatory agreement.

[55 FR 38952, Sept. 21, 1990. Redesignated and amended at 57 FR 12041, 12060, Apr. 8, 1992]

§ 248.234 Section 8 rental assistance.

(a) When providing rental assistance under section 8, the Commissioner may enter into a contract with an owner, contingent upon the future availability of appropriations for the purpose of renewing expiring contracts for rental assistance as provided in appropriations Acts, to extend the term of such rental assistance for such additional period or periods as is necessary to carry out an approved plan of action.

(b) The contract and the approved plan of action shall provide that, if the Commissioner is unable to develop a revised package of incentives providing benefits to the owner comparable to those received under the original approved plan of action, the Commissioner, upon the request of the owner, shall take the following actions (subject to the limitations under the following paragraphs):

(1) Modification of the binding commitments made pursuant to § 248.233(d) that are dependent on such rental assistance.

(2) If action under paragraph (b)(1) is not feasible, release of an owner from the binding commitments made pursuant to § 248.233(d) that are dependent on such rental assistance.

(3) If actions under paragraphs (b)(1) and (2) would, in the determination of the Commissioner, result in the default of the insured loan, approveal of the revised plan of action, notwithstanding § 248.221, that involves the termination of low-income affordability restrictions.

(c) The approved plan of action shall specify actions that the Commissioner and the owner shall take to ensure that any tenants displaced as a result of actions taken under paragraph (b) of this section are relocated to affordable housing.

(d) At least 30 days prior to making a request under the preceding sentence, an owner shall notify the Commissioner of the owner's intention to submit the request. The Commissioner shall have a period of 90 days following receipt of such notice to take action to extend the rental assistance contract and to continue the binding commitments under paragraph (b).

[55 FR 38952, Sept. 21, 1990. Redesignated and amended at 57 FR 12041, 12060, Apr. 8, 1992]

§248.241 Modification of existing regulatory agreements.

(a) If a plan of action is not approved within 300 days after initial submission, the Commissioner may, upon request of the owner and upon making a determination that the project's current use does not represent its highest and best use, modify existing regulatory agreements to—

(1) Prevent involuntary displacement of current tenants (except for good cause);

(2) Ensure that adequate expenditures will be made for maintenance and operation of the housing;

(3) Extend (subject to the availability of funds) any expiring project-based assistance on the housing for the term of the agreement;

(4) Permit an increase in the allowable distribution that could be accommodated by an increase in the rents on occupied units to a level no higher than 30 percent of the adjusted income of the tenants, as determined by the Commissioner, except that rents shall not exceed the fair market rent, and any resulting increase in rents for current tenants shall be phased in equally over a period of no less than 3 years, unless such increase is less than 10 percent; and

(5) Ensure that units becoming vacant during the term of the agreement are made available in accordance with §248.233(d)(7) of this part.

(b) *Expiration.* Agreements entered into under this section shall expire on February 5, 1992, unless earlier superseded by an agreement implementing a HUD-approved plan of action. Upon such expiration of the agreement on February 5, 1992, the housing covered

by the agreement shall be subject to any law then affecting low income affordability restrictions.

§248.251 Consultation with other interested parties.

The Commissioner will confer with any appropriate State or local government agency to confirm any State or local assistance that is available to achieve the purposes of this part and will give consideration to the views of the State or local agency when making the determinations under §§248.221 and 248.233 of this part. The Commissioner also will confer with other interested parties that the Commissioner believes could assist in the development of a plan of action that best achieves the purposes of this part.

§248.261 Agreements implementing plans of action and State strategies.

The Commissioner is authorized to enter into agreements, including those for the provision of incentives, necessary to implement any plan of action or State strategy approved by the Commissioner under this part.

Subpart D—State Preservation Project Assistance

SOURCE: 57 FR 12060, Apr. 8, 1992, unless otherwise noted.

§248.300 General.

Upon application by a State agency or a local public housing agency, the Commissioner may make available assistance for use in preventing the loss of housing affordable for low and moderate income families that is assisted under a State program under the terms of which the owner may prepay a State assisted or subsidized mortgage on such housing.

§248.301 Initial application.

A State agency shall make an initial application to the Commissioner which:

(a) Describes the manner by which the State housing program provides mortgage assistance or subsidy to private mortgagors to provide housing opportunities for low and moderate income families;

(b) Includes copies of the authorizing legislation, any implementing regulations and any administrative guidance provided to owners;

(c) Includes a comprehensive description of the terms and conditions under which a private owner may prepay the assisted or subsidized mortgage without the prior consent of the State agency;

(d) Includes a complete set of pro forma mortgage and/or regulatory documents which evidence an owner's ability to prepay the assisted or subsidized mortgage without the consent of the State agency;

(e) Includes a list of all properties assisted under the State or local housing program whose owners are eligible to prepay the assisted or subsidized mortgages without the consent of the State agency.

§ 248.303 Approval of a State agency's initial application.

(a) The Commissioner will evaluate the State agency's application and will notify the State agency within 90 days of receipt that the program and properties qualify under subpart D of this part or that the program and properties do not qualify under subpart D of this part.

(b) If the Commissioner determines that the program and projects do not qualify under subpart D of this part, it will state the reasons why the program and properties do not qualify and will give the State agency an opportunity to provide additional information, as the Commissioner determines, which would assist the Commissioner in qualifying the program and properties.

§ 248.305 Applicability of subpart B of this part.

The provisions of subpart B of this part shall be applicable to any application of a State agency or local housing authority for assistance under subpart D of this part, except the following provisions:

Sec.
248.103   General prepayment limitation.
248.105   Notice of intent.
248.131   Information from the Commissioner: Only paragraph (a).

248.141   Criteria for approval of a plan of action involving prepayment and voluntary termination.
248.153   Incentives to extend low income use: Only paragraphs (a)(7), (d) and (e).
248.165   Assistance for displaced tenants.
248.169   Permissible prepayment or voluntary termination and modification of commitments.
248.173   Resident homeownership program: Only paragraph (s).
248.177   Delegated responsibility to State agencies.

§ 248.307 Authority to process and approve notices of intent and plans of action.

(a) *Delegation of authority.* State agencies which regulate or otherwise supervise owners of projects with State assisted or subsidized mortgages shall have the authority, reserved to the Commissioner under subpart B of this part, to process and approve all notices of intent and plans of action submitted to the State agency or local housing authority under subpart D of this part. State agencies may redelegate such authority to local housing authorities at their discretion.

(b) *Designation of processing agency.* The Executive Director of the State agency whose State assisted or subsidized mortgage program has been approved under § 248.303 shall inform all owners of projects with State assisted or subsidized mortgages that the State agency or a designated local housing authority shall accept and process notices of intent and plans of action.

§ 248.311 Notice of intent.

(a) *Eligibility for filing.* An owner of a project with a State assisted or subsidized mortgage intending to extend the low income affordability restrictions of the housing in accordance with § 248.153 or transfer the housing to a qualified purchaser under § 248.157 may file a notice of intent.

(b) *Filing with the State agency.* The notice of intent shall be filed with the agency specified in § 248.307(b) or the agency which regulates or otherwise supervises the State assisted or subsidized mortgage. The notice of intent shall also request the tenants to notify the owner and the State agency of any individual or organization that has been designated or retained by the tenants to represent the tenants with respect to the actions to be taken under subpart B and subpart D of this part.

(c) *Filing with HUD, mortgagee and tenants.* The owner simultaneously shall file the notice of intent with the local HUD field office having jurisdiction over the area in which the project is located and with the mortgagee, if any. In addition, the owner shall deliver a copy of the notice of intent to each tenant in the project and to any tenant representative, if any, known to the owner, and shall post a copy of the notice of intent in readily accessible locations within each affected building of the project. The copies of the notice of intent delivered to the tenants and the tenant representative shall include a summary of possible outcomes of the filing which shall be furnished by the State agency. Upon the request of any non-English speaking tenants residing in the affected project, the owner shall tabulate the number and type of translations needed by the tenants and request the State agency to provide the appropriate translations. The owner shall deliver a copy of the translated notice of intent to all of the tenants who requested such a translation. The failure of an owner to comply with any non-federal notice requirements shall not invalidate the notice of intent.

§248.315 Preservation agreements.

(a) *Agreements required.* Owners of projects with State assisted or subsidized mortgages whose plans of action have been approved under §248.307 shall enter into agreements, contracts and/or mortgage modifications with the State agency or local housing authority to maintain the housing as affordable to tenants in accordance with §248.145. Such agreements may provide for the renewal of any assistance made available under §248.319(c).

(b) *Term of agreement.* Preservation agreements shall be coterminous with the expiration of any assistance provided under §248.153 and made available in accordance with §248.319(c).

§248.319 Application for assistance.

(a) *Application for assistance.* State agencies or local housing authorities shall submit an application for assistance in a form prescribed by the Commissioner with the local HUD field office having jurisdiction over the project. The application shall include:

(1) A copy of the approved plan of action, including all applicable notices of intent;

(2) A copy of any worksheet or other document which demonstrates the extension and transfer preservation values of the project, the Federal cost limits (including the determination of relevant local market rents if applicable), and the preservation rents;

(3) A request for each incentive required as part of the approved plan of action and the amount thereof;

(4) A demonstration and certification by the Executive Director of the State agency or local housing authority that the assistance and incentives requested as part of the approved plan of action do not exceed the level of incentives required for a similarly situated project which is eligible low income housing as defined in subpart B of this part;

(5) Copies of proposed agreements, contracts and mortgage modifications proposed pursuant to §248.315.

(b) *Notification of approval.* Not later than 90 days after receipt of the application for assistance, the local HUD field office shall notify the Executive Director of the State agency or local housing authority of the approval or disapproval of the application. If the application is disapproved, the notification shall state the reasons therefor and afford the State agency or local housing authority the opportunity to revise the application to make it approvable.

(c) *Funding.* After approving the State agency's or local housing authority's application for assistance, the HUD field office shall make the assistance in the approved application available to the State agency or local housing authority within the time frames specified in §248.169.

(d) *Agreements.* The State agency or local housing authority shall provide the local HUD field office with a copy of all agreements entered into with the owner pursuant to §248.315.

(e) *Section 8 contract administration.* Any contract for Section 8 assistance made pursuant to the approved plan of action, the State agency's or local housing authority's application for assistance and the regulations at 24 CFR 886, subpart A shall be administered by the State agency or local housing authority pursuant to § 886.120 of this title.

Subpart E—Technical Assistance and Capacity Building

SOURCE: 58 FR 37817, July 13, 1993, unless otherwise noted.

§ 248.401 Purposes.

The purposes of this subpart are:

(a) To promote the ability of residents of eligible low income housing to participate meaningfully in the preservation process established by this part and affect decisions about the future of their housing;

(b) To promote the ability of community-based nonprofit organizations and resident councils to acquire, rehabilitate, and competently own and manage eligible housing as rental or cooperative housing for low and moderate income people; and

(c) To assist the Commissioner in discharging the obligation under § 248.157(b) to notify potential qualified purchasers of the availability of projects for sale and to otherwise facilitate the coordination and oversight of the preservation program established under this part.

§ 248.405 Grants for building resident capacity and funding predevelopment costs.

(a) *General.* Assistance made available under this subpart shall be used for direct assistance grants to resident organizations and community-based nonprofit housing developers and resident councils to assist the acquisition of specific projects (including payment of reasonable administrative expense to participating intermediaries.) Assistance made available under subpart E of this part will be distributed on a noncompetitive basis. HUD will publish a Notice in the FEDERAL REGISTER announcing the availability of assistance, as well as the application requirements and procedures and selection criteria that HUD will use in making the assistance available.

(b) *Allocation.* Thirty percent of the assistance made available under this subpart shall be used for resident capacity grants in accordance with paragraph (d) of this section. The remainder shall be used for predevelopment grants in connection with specific projects in accordance with paragraph (e) of this section.

(c) *Limitation on grant amounts.* A resident capacity grant under paragraph (d) of this section may not exceed $30,000 per project and a grant under paragraph (e) of this section for predevelopment costs may not exceed $200,000 per project, exclusive of any fees paid to a participating intermediary by the Commissioner for administering grants under this subpart.

(d) *Resident Capacity grants—*(1) *Use.* Resident capacity grants under paragraph (d) of this section shall be available to eligible applicants to cover expenses for resident outreach, incorporation of a resident organization or council, conducting democratic elections, training, leadership development, legal and other technical assistance to the board of directors, staff and members of the resident organization or council.

(2) *Eligible housing.* Grants under this paragraph (d) of this section may be provided with respect to eligible low income housing for which the owner has filed a notice of intent under subpart B or subpart C of this part.

(e) *Predevelopment grants—*(1) *Use.* Predevelopment grants under paragraph (e) of this section shall be made available to community-based nonprofit housing developers and resident councils to cover the cost of organizing a purchasing entity and pursuing an acquisition, including third party costs for training, development consulting, legal, appraisal, accounting, environmental, architectural and engineering, application fees, and sponsor's staff and overhead costs.

(2) *Eligible housing.* These grants may only be made available with respect to any eligible low income housing project for which the owner has filed a notice of intent to transfer the housing to a qualified purchaser in accordance with § 248.105 or § 248.211, or has filed a notice of intent and entered into a binding agreement to sell the housing

to a resident organization or nonprofit organization.

(3) *Phase-in of grant payments.* Grant payments under paragraph (e) of this section shall be made in phases, based on performance benchmarks established by the Commissioner in consultation with intermediaries selected under §248,415.

(f) *Grant applications.* Grant applications for assistance under paragraphs (d) and (e) of this section shall be received monthly on a rolling basis and approved or rejected on at least a quarterly basis by intermediaries selected under §248.415(b).

(g) *Appeal.* If an application for assistance under paragraphs (d) or (e) of this section is denied, the applicant shall have the right to appeal the denial to the Commissioner and receive a binding determination within 30 days of the appeal.

§248.410   Grants for other purposes.

The Commissioner may provide grants under this subpart E:

(a) To resident-controlled or community-based nonprofit organizations with experience in resident education and organizing for the purpose of conducting community, city or county-wide outreach and training programs to identify and organize residents of eligible low income housing; and

(b) To State and local government agencies and nonprofit intermediaries for the purpose of carrying out such activities as the Commissioner deems appropriate to further the purposes of this part.

§248.415   Delivery   of   assistance through intermediaries.

(a) *General.* The Commissioner shall approve and disburse assistance under §248.405 and §248.410 through eligible intermediaries selected by the Commissioner under paragraph (b) of this section. If the Commissioner does not receive an acceptable proposal from an intermediary offering to administer assistance under this section in a given State, the Commissioner shall administer the program in such State directly.

(b) *Selection of eligible intermediaries—*
(1) *In General.* The Commission shall invite applications from and shall select eligible intermediaries to administer assistance under subpart E of this part through Notices of Funding Availability published in the FEDERAL REGISTER. The process shall include provision for a reasonable administrative fee.

(2) *Priority.* With respect to all forms of grants available under §248.405, the criteria for selecting eligible intermediaries shall give priority to applications from eligible intermediaries with demonstrated expertise under subpart B or subpart C of this part.

(3) *Criteria.* The criteria developed under this section shall:

(i) Not assign any preference or priority to applications from eligible intermediaries based on their previous participation in administering or receiving Federal grants or loans (but may exclude applicants who have failed to perform under prior contracts of a similar nature);

(ii) Require an applicant to prepare a proposal that demonstrates adequate staffing, qualifications, prior experience, and a plan for participation; and

(iii) Permit an applicant to serve as the administrator of assistance made available under §248.405(d) and (e), based on the applicant's suitability and interest.

(4) *Geographic coverage.* The Commissioner may select more than one State or regional intermediary for a single State or region. The number of intermediaries chosen for each State or region may be based on the number of eligible low income housing projects in the State or region, provided there is no duplication of geographic coverage by intermediaries in the administration of the direct assistance grant program.

(5) *National nonprofit intermediaries.* National nonprofit intermediaries shall be selected to administer the assistance made available under §248.405 only with respect to State or regions for which no other eligible intermediary, acceptable to the Commissioner, has submitted a proposal to participate.

(6) *Preference.* With respect to assistance made available under §248.410, preference shall be given to eligible regional, State and local intermediaries, over national nonprofit organizations.

515

(c) *Conflicts of interest.* Eligible intermediaries selected under paragraph (b) of this section to disburse assistance under § 248.405 shall certify that they will serve only as delegated program administrators, charged with the resposibility for reviewing and approving grant applications on behalf of the Commissioner. Selected intermediaries shall:

(1) Establish appropriate procedures for grant administration and fiscal management, pursuant to standards established by the Commissioner; and

(2) Receive a reasonable administrative fee, except that they may not provide other services to grant recipients with respect to projects that are the subject of the grant application and may not receive payment, directly or indirectly, from the proceeds of grants they have approved.

§ 248.420 Definitions.

Community-based nonprofit housing developer means a nonprofit community development corporation that:

(1) Has been classified by the Internal Revenue Service as an exempt organization under section 501(c)(3) of the Internal Revenue Code of 1986;

(2) Has been in existence for at least two years prior to the date of the grant application;

(3) Has a record of service to low and moderate income people in the community in which the project is located;

(4) Is organized at the neighborhood, city, county, or multi-county level; and

(5) In the case of a corporation acquiring eligible low income housing under subpart B of this part, agrees to form a purchaser entity that conforms to the definition of a community-based nonprofit organization under such subpart and agrees to use its best efforts to secure majority tenant consent to the acquisition of the project for which grant assistance is requested.

Eligible intermediaries. For purposes of this subpart, the term "eligible intermediary" means a State, regional, or national nonprofit organization (including a quasi-public organization) or a State or local housing agency that:

(1) Has as a central purpose the preservation of existing affordable housing and the prevention of displacement;

(2) Does not receive direct Federal appropriations for operating support;

(3) In the case of a national nonprofit organization, has been in existence for at least five years prior to the date of application and has been classified by the Internal Revenue Service as an exempt organization under section 501(c)(3) of the Internal Revenue Code of 1986;

(4) In the case of a regional or State nonprofit organization, has been in existence for at least three years prior to the date of application and has been classified by the Internal Revenue Service as an exempt organization under section 501(c)(3) of the Internal Revenue Code of 1986 or is otherwise a tax-exempt entity;

(5) Has a record of service to low income individuals or community-based nonprofit housing development in multiple communities and, with respect to intermediaries administering assistance under § 248.405, has experience with the allocation or administration of grant or loan funds; and

(6) Meets standards of fiscal responsibility established by the Commissioner.

PART 251—COINSURANCE FOR THE CONSTRUCTION OR SUBSTANTIAL REHABILITATION OF MULTIFAMILY HOUSING PROJECTS

Sec.
251.1 Termination of program.
251.2 GNMA right to assignment.
251.3 Case-by-case conversion to full insurance.
251.6 Method of payment of mortgage insurance premiums.

AUTHORITY: 12 U.S.C. 1715b, 1715z–9; 42 U.S.C. 3535(d).

§ 251.1 Termination of program.

(a) Effective on November 12, 1990, the authority to coinsure mortgages under this part is terminated, except that the Department

(1) Will honor legally binding and validly issued commitments issued before November 12, 1990 and

(2) Will accept for review the coinsurance applications described in paragraph (b) of this section.

Part 251, as it existed immediately before November 12, 1990, will continue to govern the rights and obligations of co-insured lenders, mortgagors, and the Department of Housing and Urban Development with respect to loans coinsured under this part.

(b) A precommitment review procedure applies to any application for mortgage coinsurance for which a lender has accepted a non-refundable application fee before November 12, 1990 under this part and for which a legally binding Conditional or Firm Commitment is proposed to be issued. This procedure applies to lenders with preliminary as well as full approval to process coinsurance applications and without regard to whether the lender is under probation. For any coinsurance application for which the lender has accepted an application and a non-refundable application fee before November 12, 1990, the lender shall, prior to commitment, submit to HUD headquarters and to the HUD field office with jurisdiction for the proposed project such exhibits and other information as has been specified in administrative instructions of the Commissioner. The lender shall not issue a commitment without written approval from the Commissioner. Field Offices shall not endorse any case covered by this precommitment review requirement unless the lender submits with the endorsement package evidence of the Commissioner's approval of the processing and evidence of compliance with any conditions imposed by the Commissioner.

(c) Extensions of commitments for projects which had outstanding legally binding commitments as of November 12, 1990 are limited as follows:

(1) Firm commitments for insurance of advances may be granted two 60-day extensions;

(2) Conditional commitments may be granted one 60-day extension;

(3) Firm commitments for insurance upon completion may not be extended.

However, should any underwriting conclusions be altered and reflected in the extension, the project must be submitted for precommitment review in accordance with paragraph (b) of this section. In the event an extension is required beyond those provided for in this paragraph, the case will be subject to the precommitment review process

described in paragraph (b) of this section.

(d) Reopened expired commitments are subject to precommitment review under paragraph (b) of this section.

(e) HUD considers a commitment to be *legally binding* if:

(1) It conforms to the format prescribed in the appropriate HUD Handbook and contains only such modifications as have been approved by HUD in writing;

(2) All required underwriting, analyses, reviews and approvals have been accomplished prior to issuance of the commitment;

(3) It conforms to HUD requirements pertaining to initial term and extension;

(4) It obligates the lender and HUD to proceed to the next stage (*i.e.*, firm commitment in the case of a conditional commitment, or endorsement in the case of a firm commitment) if the applicant mortgagor complies with all conditions of such commitment;

(5) It does not permit the lender to change unilaterally the conditions or terms of the commitment; and

(6) It is signed by an official of the coinsuring lender who has been designated and authorized in accordance with HUD requirements.

(Information collection requirements in paragraph (b) were approved by the Office of Management and Budget under control number 2502–0437)

[55 FR 41318, Oct. 10, 1990]

§251.2 GNMA right to assignment.

If the lender-issuer defaults on its obligations under the GNMA Mortgage-Backed Securities Program, GNMA will have the right to cause all Coinsured Mortgages held in GNMA pools by the defaulting coinsuring lender-issuer to be assigned to another GNMA-approved coinsuring lender-issuer, or to GNMA itself.

(a) For any Coinsured Mortgage that is not in default and is held by a defaulting lender-issuer, GNMA will have the right to perfect an assignment of the mortgage to itself. However, before exercising this right, GNMA will attempt to have the Mortgage assigned to another eligible coinsuring lender (unless GNMA determines, with the agreement of the Commissioner, that the attempt would prove ineffectual because of market conditions or other factors). This attempt will be undertaken by soliciting offers to assume the defaulting lender-issuer's rights and obligations under the Mortgage from those eligible coinsuring lenders that are also GNMA issuers and that are indicated on a periodically updated listing furnished to GNMA by the Commissioner.

(b) For any Coinsured Mortgage that is in default and held by a defaulting lender-issuer, GNMA will have the right to perfect an assignment of the Coinsured Mortgage directly to itself before extinguishing the Mortgage by completion of foreclosure action or acquisition of title by deed-in-lieu of foreclosure.

(c) GNMA, as assignee, will give the Commissioner written notice, within 30 days after taking a Mortgage by assignment in accordance with this section, in order to allow an appropriate endorsement and necessary changes in the Commissioner's records.

(d) The Commissioner will endorse any Mortgage assigned to GNMA as provided by this section for full insurance, effective as of the date of assignment in accordance with the appropriate provisions of 24 CFR part 221. Any future claim by GNMA, or any assignment of the fully insured Mortgage, will be governed by the appropriate provisions of 24 CFR part 221, except that any payment will be made in cash instead of debentures.

[59 FR 1475, Jan. 11, 1994]

§ 251.3 Case-by-case conversion to full insurance.

Upon the request of a coinsuring lender, the Commissioner may endorse a coinsured Mortgage for full insurance, effective as of the date of such endorsement, if the Commissioner is satisfied that:

(a) Continuing the Mortgage under coinsurance could jeopardize the lender's viability and ability to service its remaining portfolio of coinsured Mortgages;

(b) The lender has made reasonable efforts to work out any Mortgage default consistent under 24 CFR 251.811 (1990), but the remedies available to the

lender have not been adequate to reinstate the Mortgage;

(c) The conversion would be less costly to HUD than if the Mortgage remained coinsured;

(d) The lender has paid HUD the fee set forth through FEDERAL REGISTER notice; and

(e) The lender agrees to give the Commissioner written notice under 24 CFR 207.258 of its intent to file an insurance claim upon the Commissioner's endorsement of the Mortgage for full insurance.

[61 FR 49038, Sept. 17, 1996]

§ 251.6 Method of payment of mortgage insurance premiums.

In the cases that the Commissioner deems appropriate, the Commissioner may require, by means of instructions communicated to all affected lenders, that mortgage insurance premiums be remitted electronically.

[63 FR 1303, Jan. 8, 1998]

PART 252—COINSURANCE OF MORTGAGES COVERING NURSING HOMES, INTERMEDIATE CARE FACILITIES, AND BOARD AND CARE HOMES

Sec.
252.1 Termination of program.
252.2 GNMA right to assignment.
252.3 Case-by-case conversion to full insurance.
252.6 Method of payment of mortgage insurance premiums.

AUTHORITY: 12 U.S.C. 1715b, 1715z–9; 42 U.S.C. 3535(d).

§ 252.1 Termination of program.

(a) Effective on November 12, 1990, the authority to coinsure mortgages under this part is terminated, except that the Department

(1) Will honor legally binding and validly issued commitments issued before November 12, 1990, and

(2) Will accept for review the coinsurance applications described in paragraph (b) of this section.

Part 252, as it existed immediately before November 12, 1990, will continue to govern the rights and obligations of coinsured lenders, mortgagors, and the

Department of Housing and Urban Development with respect to loans coinsured under this part.

(b) A precommitment review procedure applies to any application for mortgage coinsurance for which a lender has accepted a non-refundable application fee before November 12, 1990 under this part and for which a legally binding Conditional or Firm Commitment is proposed to be issued. This procedure applies to lenders with preliminary as well as full approval to process coinsurance applications and without regard to whether the lender is under probation. For any coinsurance application for which the lender has accepted an application and a non-refundable application fee before November 12, 1990, the lender shall, prior to commitment, submit to HUD headquarters and to the HUD field office with jurisdiction for the proposed project such exhibits and other information as has been specified in administrative instructions of the Commissioner. The lender shall not issue a commitment without written approval from the Commissioner. Field Offices shall not endorse any case covered by this precommitment review requirement unless the lender submits with the endorsement package evidence of the Commissioner's approval of the processing and evidence of compliance with any conditions imposed by the Commissioner.

(c) Extensions of commitments for projects which had outstanding legally binding commitments as of November 12, 1990 are limited as follows:

(1) Firm commitments for insurance of advances may be granted two 60-day extensions;

(2) Conditional commitments may be granted one 60-day extension;

(3) Firm commitments for insurance upon completion may not be extended. However, should any underwriting conclusions be altered and reflected in the extension, the project must be submitted for precommitment review in accordance with paragraph (b) of this section. In the event an extension is required beyond those provided for in this paragraph, the case will be subject to the precommitment review process described in paragraph (b) of this section.

(d) Reopened expired commitments are subject to precommitment review under paragraph (b) of this section.

(e) HUD considers a commitment to be *legally binding* if:

(1) It conforms to the format prescribed in the appropriate HUD Handbook and contains only such modifications as have been approved by HUD in writing;

(2) All required underwriting, analyses, reviews and approvals have been accomplished prior to issuance of the commitment;

(3) It conforms to HUD requirements pertaining to initial term and extensions;

(4) It obligates the lender and HUD to proceed to the next stage (*i.e.*, firm commitment in the case of a conditional commitment, or endorsement in the case of a firm commitment) if the applicant mortgagor complies with all conditions of such commitment;

(5) It does not permit the lender to change unilaterally the conditions or terms of the commitment; and

(6) It is signed by an official of the coinsuring lender who has been designated and authorized in accordance with HUD requirements.

(Information collection requirements in paragraph (b) were approved by the Office of Management and Budget under control number 2502–0437)

[55 FR 41319, Oct. 10, 1990]

§252.2 GNMA right to assignment.

If the lender-issuer defaults on its obligations under the GNMA Mortgage-Backed Securities Program, GNMA will have the right to cause all Coinsured Mortgages held in GNMA pools by the defaulting coinsuring lender-issuer to be assigned to another GNMA-approved coinsuring lender-issuer, or to GNMA itself.

(a) For any Coinsured Mortgage that is not in default and is held by a defaulting lender-issuer, GNMA will have the right to perfect an assignment of the mortgage to itself. However, before exercising this right, GNMA will attempt to have the Mortgage assigned to another eligible coinsuring lender (unless GNMA determines, with the agreement of the Commissioner, that the attempt would prove ineffectual because of market conditions or other factors). This attempt will be undertaken by soliciting offers to assume the defaulting lender-issuer's rights and obligations under the Mortgage from those eligible coinsuring lenders that are also GNMA issuers and that are indicated on a periodically updated listing furnished to GNMA by the Commissioner.

(b) For any Coinsured Mortgage that is in default and held by a defaulting lender-issuer, GNMA will have the right to perfect an assignment of the Coinsured Mortgage directly to itself before extinguishing the Mortgage by completion of foreclosure action or acquisition of title by deed-in-lieu of foreclosure.

(c) GNMA, as assignee, will give the Commissioner written notice, within 30 days after taking a Mortgage by assignment in accordance with this section, in order to allow an appropriate endorsement and necessary changes in the Commissioner's records.

(d) The Commissioner will endorse any Mortgage assigned to GNMA as provided by this section for full insurance, effective as of the date of assignment in accordance with the appropriate provisions of 24 CFR part 232. Any future claim by GNMA, or any assignment of the fully insured Mortgage, will be governed by the appropriate provisions of 24 CFR part 232, except that any payment will be made in cash instead of debentures.

[59 FR 1475, Jan. 11, 1994]

§ 252.3 Case-by-case conversion to full insurance.

CROSS REFERENCE: The provisions of 24 CFR 251.3 apply to this part.

[61 FR 49038, Sept. 17, 1996]

§ 252.6 Method of payment of mortgage insurance premiums.

The provisions of 24 CFR 251.6 shall apply to this part.

[63 FR 1303, Jan. 8, 1998]

PART 255—COINSURANCE FOR THE PURCHASE OR REFINANCING OF EXISTING MULTIFAMILY HOUSING PROJECTS

Sec.
255.1 Termination of program.
255.2 GNMA right to assignment.
255.3 Case-by-case conversion to full insurance.
255.6 Method of payment of mortgage insurance premiums.

AUTHORITY: 12 U.S.C. 1515b, 1715z-9; 42 U.S.C. 3535(d).

§ 255.1 Termination of program.

(a) Effective on November 12, 1990, the authority to coinsure mortgages under this part is terminated, except that the Department:

(1) Will honor legally binding and validly issued commitments issued before November 12, 1990 and

(2) Will accept for review the coinsurance applications described in paragraph (b) of this section.

Part 255, as it existed immediately before November 12, 1990, will continue to govern the rights and obligations of coinsured lenders, mortgagors, and the Department of Housing and Urban Development with respect to loans coinsured under this part.

(b) A precommitment review procedure applies to any application for mortgage coinsurance for which a lender has accepted a non-refundable application fee before November 12, 1990 under this part and for which a legally binding Conditional or Firm Commitment is proposed to be issued. This procedure applies to lenders with preliminary as well as full approval to process coinsurance applications and without regard to whether the lender is under probation. For any coinsurance application for which the lender has accepted an application and a non-refundable application fee before November 12, 1990, the lender shall, prior to commitment, submit to HUD headquarters and to the HUD field office with jurisdiction for the proposed project such exhibits and other information as has been specified in administrative instructions of the Commissioner. The lender shall not issue a commitment without written approval from the Commissioner. Field Offices shall not endorse any case covered by this precommitment review requirement unless the lender submits with the endorsement package evidence of the Commissioner's approval of the processing and evidence of compliance with any conditions imposed by the Commissioner.

(c) Extensions of commitments for projects which had outstanding legally binding commitments as of November 12, 1990 are limited as follows:

(1) Conditional commitments may be extended not to exceed 180 days from the date of original issuance;

(2) Firm commitments may be granted two 60-day extensions.

However, should any underwriting conclusions be altered and reflected in the extension, the project must be submitted for precommitment review in accordance with paragraph (b) of this section. In the event an extension is required beyond those provided for in this paragraph, the case will be subject to the precommitment review process described in paragraph (b) of this section.

(d) Reopened expired commitments are subject to precommitment review under paragraph (b) of this section.

(e) HUD considers a commitment to be *legally binding* if:

(1) It conforms to the format prescribed in the appropriate HUD Handbook and contains only such modifications as have been approved by HUD in writing;

(2) All required underwriting, analyses, reviews and approvals have been accomplished prior to issuance of the commitment;

(3) It conforms to HUD requirements pertaining to initial term and extension;

(4) It obligates the lender and HUD to proceed to the next stage (*i.e.*, firm commitment in the case of a conditional commitment, or endorsement in the case of a firm commitment) if the applicant mortgagor complies with all conditions of such commitment;

(5) It does not permit the lender to change unilaterally the conditions or terms of the commitment; and

(6) It is signed by an official of the coinsuring lender who has been des-

ignated and authorized in accordance with HUD requirements.

(Information collection requirements in paragraph (b) were approved by the Office of Management and Budget under control number 2502–0437)

[55 FR 41320, Oct. 10, 1990, as amended at 56 FR 14642, Apr. 11, 1991]

§ 255.2 GNMA right to assignment.

If the lender-issuer defaults on its obligations under the GNMA Mortgage-Backed Securities Program, GNMA will have the right to cause all Coinsured Mortgages held in GNMA pools by the defaulting coinsuring lender-issuer to be assigned to another GNMA-approved coinsuring lender-issuer, or to GNMA itself.

(a) For any Coinsured Mortgage that is not in default and is held by a defaulting lender-issuer, GNMA will have the right to perfect an assignment of the mortgage to itself. However, before exercising this right, GNMA will attempt to have the Mortgage assigned to another eligible coinsuring lender (unless GNMA determines, with the agreement of the Commissioner, that the attempt would prove ineffectual because of market conditions or other factors). This attempt will be undertaken by soliciting offers to assume the defaulting lender-issuer's rights and obligations under the Mortgage from those eligible coinsuring lenders that are also GNMA issuers and that are indicated on a periodically updated listing furnished to GNMA by the Commissioner.

(b) For any Coinsured Mortgage that is in default and held by a defaulting lender-issuer, GNMA will have the right to perfect an assignment of the Coinsured Mortgage directly to itself before extinguishing the Mortgage by completion of foreclosure action or acquisition of title by deed-in-lieu of foreclosure.

(c) GNMA, as assignee, will give the Commissioner written notice, within 30 days after taking a Mortgage by assignment in accordance with this section, in order to allow an appropriate endorsement and necessary changes in the Commissioner's records.

(d) The Commissioner will endorse any Mortgage assigned to GNMA as provided by this section for full insurance, effective as of the date of assignment in accordance with the appropriate provisions of 24 CFR part 207. Any future claim by GNMA, or any assignment of the fully insured Mortgage, will be governed by the appropriate provisions of 24 CFR part 207, except that any payment will be made in cash instead of debentures.

[59 FR 1475, Jan. 11, 1994]

§ 255.3 Case-by-case conversion to full insurance.

CROSS REFERENCE: The provisions of 24 CFR 251.3 apply to this part.

[61 FR 49038, Sept. 17, 1996]

§ 255.6 Method of payment of mortgage insurance premiums.

The provisions of 24 CFR 251.6 shall apply to this part.

[63 FR 1303, Jan. 8, 1998]

PART 266—HOUSING FINANCE AGENCY RISK-SHARING PROGRAM FOR INSURED AFFORDABLE MULTIFAMILY PROJECT LOANS

AUTHORITY: 12 U.S.C. 1707; 42 U.S.C. 3535(d).

SOURCE: 59 FR 62524, Dec. 5, 1994, unless otherwise noted.

Subpart A—General Provisions

§266.1 Purpose and scope.

(a) *Authority and scope.* (1) Section 542 of the Housing and Community Development Act of 1992 directs the Secretary of the Department of Housing and Urban Development, acting through the Federal Housing Administration, to carry out programs that will demonstrate the effectiveness of providing new forms of Federal credit enhancement for multifamily loans. Section 542, entitled, "Multifamily Mortgage Credit Demonstrations," provides new independent insurance authority that is not under the National Housing Act.

(2) Section 542(c) of the Housing and Community Development Act of 1992 specifically directs the Secretary to carry out a pilot program of risk-sharing with qualified State and local housing finance agencies (HFAs). The qualified HFAs are authorized to underwrite and process loans. HUD will provide full mortgage insurance on affordable multifamily housing projects processed by such HFAs under this program. Through risk-sharing agreements with HUD, HFAs contract to reimburse HUD for a portion of the loss from any defaults that occur while HUD insurance is in force.

(3) The extent to which HUD will direct qualified HFAs regarding their underwriting standards and loan terms and conditions is related to the proportion of the risk taken by an HFA.

(b) *Purpose.* The primary purpose of this pilot program is to test the effectiveness of providing new forms of credit enhancement for multifamily loans, *i.e.*, utilization of full insurance by HUD, pursuant to risk-sharing agreements with qualified housing finance agencies, for the development of affordable housing. The utilization of Federal credit enhancements should increase access to capital markets and, thereby, increase the supply of affordable multifamily housing. By permitting HFAs to underwrite, process, and service loans and to manage and dispose of properties that fall into default, HUD expects affordable housing to be made available to eligible families and individuals in a timely manner.

§266.5 Definitions.

Act means the Housing and Community Development Act of 1992, as amended.

Affordable housing means a project in which 20 percent or more of the units are both rent-restricted and occupied by families whose income is 50 percent or less of the area median income as determined by HUD, with adjustments for household size, or in which 40 percent (25 percent in New York City) or more of the units are both rent-restricted and occupied by families whose income is 60 percent or less of the area median income as determined by HUD, with adjustments for household size. A residential unit is rent-restricted if the gross rent with respect to such unit does not exceed 30 percent of the imputed income limitation applicable to such unit.

Board and Care/Assisted Living Facility means a residential facility for independent living that is regulated by

523

State or local government that provides continuous protective oversight and assistance with the activities of daily living to frail elderly persons or other persons needing such assistance. Continuous protective oversight may range from as little as awareness on the part of management staff of residents' whereabouts (and the ability to intervene in the event of crisis) to a higher level of services and assistance. Assistance with the activities of daily living may include, but is not limited to, bathing, dressing, eating, getting in and out of bed or chairs, walking, going outdoors, using the toilet, laundry, home management, meal preparation, shopping, supervision of medication, and housework.

Commissioner means the Federal Housing Commissioner or his or her authorized representative.

Contract of insurance means the agreement evidenced by the endorsement of the Commissioner upon the credit instrument given in connection with an insured mortgage, incorporating by reference the regulations in this part and the applicable provisions of the Act.

Credit subsidy means the cost of a direct loan or loan guarantee under the Federal Credit Reform Act of 1990 as defined in subpart B of title 13 of the Omnibus Budget Reconciliation Act of 1990 (Pub.L. 101-508, approved Nov. 5, 1990).

Debenture means the instrument issued by the HFA to HUD upon payment of an insurance claim by HUD. The instrument must be in the standard form of a State or Municipal Debenture issued under the Uniform Commercial Code, where applicable, and must be supported by the full faith and credit of the HFA. The instrument must define the terms and conditions and the risk-sharing portion which the HFA will pay at the end of the term of the Debenture, and must be for the full amount of the claim payment. The term *Debenture* may include similar instruments, such as promissory notes and bonds, as mutually agreed upon by the Commissioner and the HFA.

Designated offices means the HUD Field Offices that are assigned the responsibility for program monitoring, imposing or recommending sanctions for program violations, and conducting informal hearings.

Firm approval letter means a letter issued by HUD to an HFA upon the positive completion of the HUD-retained reviews described in § 266.210. The letter will apportion units to the project and provide that, so long as the HFA is in good standing and absent fraud or misrepresentation by the HFA, HUD will endorse the project mortgage for insurance upon presentation by the HFA of the required Closing Docket and certifications required by this part and the Commissioner's administrative requirements.

Gross rent includes any utility allowance (including charges for the occupancy of a cooperative unit) determined by the Secretary after taking into account such determination under section 8 of the U.S. Housing Act of 1937 (42 U.S.C. 1437f). It does not include any payment under section 8 or any comparable rental assistance program (with respect to such unit or occupants thereof), nor does it include any fee for a supportive service that is paid to the owner of the unit (on the basis of the low-income status of the tenant of the unit) by any governmental program of assistance (or by an organization described in section 501(c)(3) of the Internal Revenue Code (26 U.S.C. 501(c)(3)) and exempt from tax under section 501(a) of the Code (26 U.S.C. 501(a)) if such program (or organization) provides assistance for rent and the amount of assistance provided for rent is not separable from the amount of assistance provided for supportive services. It also does not include any rental payment to the owner of the unit to the extent such owner pays an equivalent amount to the Farmers Home Administration under section 515 of the Housing Act of 1949 (42 U.S.C. 1485).

Housing finance agency or *HFA* means any public body, agency, or instrumentality created by a specific act of a State legislature or local municipality empowered to finance activities designed to provide housing and related facilities, through land acquisition, construction or rehabilitation. The term State includes the several States, Puerto Rico, the District of Columbia,

Guam, the Trust Territory of the Pacific Islands, American Samoa and the Virgin Islands.

Insured mortgage means a valid single first lien given to secure advances on, or the unpaid purchase price of, real estate, under the laws of the State in which the real estate is located, together with the credit instrument, if any, secured thereby. Any other financing permitting on property insured under this part must be expressly subordinate to the insured mortgage.

Level I participants means HFAs that elect to take 50 percent or more of the risk of loss in 10 percent increments on mortgages issued under this program.

Level II participants means HFAs that elect to take 10 or 25 percent of the risk of loss on mortgages issued under this program, dependent on the loan-to-replacement cost or loan-to-value ratio of the project to be insured.

Mortgage means such a single first lien upon the real estate as is commonly given to secure advances on, or the unpaid purchase price of, real estate under the laws of the jurisdiction where the real estate is situated, together with the credit instruments, if any, secured thereby.

Mortgagee means the original lender under a mortgage and its successors and assigns approved by the Commissioner.

Mortgagor means the original borrower under a mortgage and its successor and assigns.

Multifamily housing means housing accommodations on the mortgaged property that are designed principally for residential use, conform to standards satisfactory to the Secretary, and consist of not less than 5 rental units (including cooperative units) on 1 site. These units may be detached, semidetached, row house, or multifamily structures.

Qualified HFA means an HFA that meets the requirements described in §266.100(a).

Risk-Sharing Agreement means a contract between an HFA and the Commissioner that incorporates the terms, obligations, and conditions specified in this part.

Secondary financing means any grant, loan, inferior lien, or other form of indebtedness used during loan origination prior to HUD endorsement to finance a multifamily property insured under this part which is inferior to the insured mortgage as defined above and does not have first priority for payment.

Single Room Occupancy, or SRO, projects means multifamily projects consisting of units that are not required to contain food preparation or sanitary facilities for occupancy by single individuals capable of independent living.

Supportive services means any service provided under a planned program of services designed to enable residents of a residential rental property to remain independent and avoid placement in a hospital, nursing home, or intermediate care facility for the mentally or physically handicapped. In the case of a single room occupancy unit, the term includes any service provided to assist tenants in locating and retaining permanent housing. This definition is to be used in conjunction with the "gross rent" calculation.

§266.10 Allocations of assistance and credit subsidy.

(a) *Notice of availability of assistance.* HUD will announce the availability of assistance under this program through publication of a Notice in the FEDERAL REGISTER. Such Notice will invite qualified HFAs to submit an application for approval and/or for additional units under this part. The Notice will indicate the deadline date for submission of applications, required documentation, the address to which the applications must be submitted and other relevant information.

(b) Credit subsidy will be obligated and allocated in accordance with outstanding Department instructions.

§266.15 Risk-Sharing Agreement.

Execution of a Risk-Sharing Agreement is a prerequisite to participation in this program. The Risk-Sharing Agreement shall be in a form acceptable to the Commissioner.

[61 FR 7947, Feb. 29, 1996]

§266.20 Effect of amendments.

The Commissioner may amend the regulations in this part from time to time. Amendments to the regulations

525

will not adversely affect the interest of a lender under a Contract of Insurance on any mortgage already insured or on any mortgage to be insured on which HUD has already issued its firm approval letter.

§ 266.25 Limitation on HUD insurance liability.

The Commissioner shall have no obligation to recognize or deal with anyone other than the HFA in its role as mortgagee of record and as party to a risk-sharing agreement with HUD with respect to the rights, benefits, and obligations of the HFA under the contract of insurance.

§ 266.30 Nonapplicability of 24 CFR part 246.

The provisions of 24 CFR part 246 do not apply to projects that are security for mortgages insured under this part.

Subpart B—Housing Finance Agency Requirements

§ 266.100 Qualified housing finance agency (HFA).

(a) *Qualifications.* To participate in the program, an HFA must apply and be specifically approved for the pilot program described in this part, in addition to being approved as a mortgagee under § 202.10. The HFA must maintain eligibility by continuing to comply with the requirements set forth in the Risk-Sharing Agreement and this part. To qualify for participation in the program described in this part, an HFA must:

(1) Carry the designation of "top tier" or its equivalent as evaluated by Standard and Poor's or any other nationally recognized rating Agency; or

(2) Receive an overall rating of "A" for the HFA for its general obligation bonds from a nationally recognized rating agency; or

(3) Otherwise demonstrate its capacity as a sound and experienced HFA based on, but not limited to, experience in financing multifamily housing, fund balances, administrative capabilities, investment policy, internal controls, financial management, portfolio quality, and State or local support; and

(4) Be a HUD-approved multifamily mortgagee in good standing; and

(5) Have at least five years experience in multifamily underwriting; and

(6) Certify that:

(i) The Department of Justice has not brought a civil rights suit against the Agency, and no suit is pending;

(ii) There has not been an adjudication of a civil rights violation in a civil action brought against the HFA by a private individual, unless the HFA is operating in compliance with a court order, or implementing a HUD-approved compliance agreement designed to correct the areas of noncompliance;

(iii) There are no outstanding findings of noncompliance with civil rights statutes, Executive Orders, or regulations as a result of formal administrative proceedings, or the Secretary has not issued a charge against the HFA under the Fair Housing Act, unless the HFA is operating under a compliance agreement designed to correct the areas of noncompliance.

(b) *Approval levels.* Approval levels consist of the following:

(1) Level I approval to originate, service, and dispose of multifamily mortgages where the HFA uses its own underwriting standards and loan terms and conditions, and assumes 50 to 90 percent of the risk of loss (increments of 10 percent).

(2) Level II approval to originate, service, and dispose of multifamily mortgages where the HFA uses underwriting standards and loan terms and conditions approved by HUD, and:

(i) When the loan-to-replacement cost ratio for new construction and substantial rehabilitation projects or the loan-to-value ratio for existing projects is greater than or equal to 75 percent, the HFA shall assume 25 percent of the risk of loss.

(ii) When the loan-to-replacement cost ratio for new construction and substantial rehabilitation or the loan-to-value ratio for existing projects is less than 75 percent, the HFA shall assume 10 percent, or 25 percent at the HFA's option, of the risk of loss.

(3) For HFAs who plan to use Level I and Level II processing, the underwriting standards and loan terms and conditions to be used on Level II loans must be approved by HUD.

[59 FR 62524, Dec. 5, 1994, as amended at 62 FR 20088, Apr. 24, 1997]

§266.105 Application requirements.

(a) *Applications for approval as a HUD-approved multifamily mortgagee.* HFAs that are not HUD-approved mortgagees at the time of their application to participate in the program under this part must submit, concurrently, separate applications for approval to participate in the program and for approval to operate as a HUD-approved mortgagee. Application for approval as a HUD-approved mortgagee must be submitted to HUD in accordance with the applicable HUD requirements.

(b) *Applications for participation in program.* Applications from HFAs for approval to participate in the program under this part will be submitted in response to a notice published in the FEDERAL REGISTER. The notice will include the required application exhibits and any other information or documentation necessary for approval for participation in the Risk-Sharing Program.

[61 FR 7947, Feb. 29, 1996]

§266.110 Reserve requirements.

(a) *HFAs with top-tier designation or overall rating of "A" on general obligation bonds.* An HFA with a top tier or equivalent designation or an HFA with an overall rating of "A" on its general obligation bonds is not required to have additional reserves so long as the HFA maintains that designation or rating, unless the Commissioner determines that a prescribed level of reserves is necessary. If the designation or rating is lost, the HFA must immediately establish a reserve account funded in accordance with the requirements set forth in paragraph (b) of this section. The reserve account must reflect all loans in the HFA's portfolio endorsed under this part.

(b) *Other HFAs.* (1) For other HFAs, a specifically identified dedicated account consisting entirely of liquid assets (*i.e.*, cash or cash equivalents or readily marketable securities) must be established and maintained in a financial institution acceptable to HUD. This account may be drawn upon by HUD and may be used by the HFA only with the prior written approval of HUD for the purpose of meeting the HFA's risk-sharing obligations under this part. The account must be established prior to the execution of any Risk Sharing Agreement under this part in an initial amount of not less than $500,000. Thereafter, the HFA must deposit at each loan closing and thereafter maintain the following additional amounts in the dedicated account:

(i) $10.00 per $1,000 of the unpaid principal balance that is equal to or less than $50 million; plus

(ii) $7.50 per $1,000 of the unpaid principal balance that is greater than $50 million and less than $150 million; plus

(iii) $5.00 per $1,000 of the unpaid principal balance that is greater than $150 million.

(2) The Commissioner may determine that higher levels of reserves may be necessary.

§266.115 Program monitoring and evaluation.

(a) *HFA certifications.* HUD will rely heavily on the certifications required of an HFA under this part and such additional certifications as the Commissioner may require in his or her administrative procedures. An HFA's continued participation in the program is predicated upon compliance with these certifications and its recommending for endorsement only those mortgages that comply with requirements of the program, including the HFA's origination, underwriting and closing procedures incorporated by reference into the Risk-Sharing Agreement.

(b) *Monitoring and evaluation.* Monitoring and evaluation activities will focus on compliance with program requirements and performance of the HFA in meeting program objectives of providing affordable housing. They will enable HUD to evaluate the effectiveness of the program as required by section 542(d)(3) of the Act.

(c) *Responsibility for monitoring and evaluation.* The Commissioner or his or her designee will be responsible for overall program monitoring and evaluation.

(d) *HFA submissions.* (1) For each loan insured under this part, basic underwriting and closing information must be submitted in a format specified by HUD and must accompany the closing docket submitted in accordance with §266.420(b). Information relative to

527

project management and servicing (including disposition) will be required after endorsement.

(2) The HFA must submit semi-annual reports setting forth the original mortgage amounts and outstanding principal balances on mortgages the HFA has underwritten, and the status of all projects insured under this part (e.g., current, in default, acquired, under workout agreement, in bankruptcy). For projects where the mortgagor has declared bankruptcy, the HFA must submit information containing the date the bankruptcy was filed and the date the HFA requested the Court to dismiss the bankruptcy proceedings.

§ 266.120 Actions for which sanctions may be imposed.

Results of monitoring or other reviews may serve as the basis for the Commissioner's imposing sanctions on the HFA. Violations for which sanctions may be imposed include, but are not limited to:

(a) Commission of fraud or making a material misrepresentation by the HFA with respect to any mortgage insured or to any other matter under this part.

(b) Assignment or transfer of interest in any insured mortgage not in accord with the requirements of this part.

(c) Engagement in business practices that do not conform to generally accepted practices of prudent lenders or that demonstrate irresponsibility.

(d) Actions or conduct for which sanctions may be imposed against the HFA by HUD's Mortgagee Review Board under 24 CFR 25.9.

(e) Failure to:

(1) Reveal in its application for participation in the program all the information required by this part;

(2) Notify HUD in a timely manner of any pending or actual changes that would adversely affect HFA operations or financial status;

(3) Comply with all eligibility requirements for participation in the program;

(4) Issue debentures in the event of an initial claim payment by HUD, or to reimburse HUD for payment of a claim;

(5) Maintain its top tier designation or overall rating of "A" on general ob-

ligation bonds (or if such designation or rating is lost, comply with paragraph (e)(6) of this section);

(6) Establish and maintain a dedicated account, if required, or meet other financial obligations under this program;

(7) Perform underwriting, insurance of advances, cost certification, management, servicing or property disposition functions in a prudent and acceptable manner based on the standards incorporated by reference into the Risk-sharing Agreement;

(8) Submit financial and other reports required by this part;

(9) Comply with any regulatory requirement or with the Risk-Sharing Agreement;

(10) Maintain any other standards HUD may establish for participation in this program;

(11) Enforce the regulatory agreement provisions with respect to individual projects;

(12) Maintain a default ratio acceptable to HUD relative to the HFA's own portfolio and the defaults experienced under this part by other program participants;

(13) Consider adequately special risk circumstances without compensating for the higher risks of such transactions (e.g., high loan-to-value ratios in areas with high vacancy or default rates); or

(14) Remit mortgage insurance premiums on a timely basis or failure to refund or credit mortgagor's accounts with overpaid mortgage insurance premiums.

§ 266.125 Scope and nature of sanctions.

(a) *Actions by Designated Office.* Depending on the nature and extent of the noncompliance with the requirements of this part, the Designated Office may take any of the following actions:

(1) Require that the HFA execute a trust agreement, establish a trust account in accordance with such agreement, and fund such account which may be drawn upon by HUD for purposes of meeting the HFA's risk-sharing obligations;

(2) Require the HFA to assume a higher portion of risk for the subject and future mortgages;

(3) Recommend to the Commissioner that the HFA be required to contract its loan servicing or property disposition functions to a third party;

(4) Recommend to the Commissioner that the mortgage insurance be terminated in cases of fraud or material misrepresentation by the HFA, or transfer of interest in an insured mortgage or assignment of the mortgage not in accord with the requirements of this part;

(5) Recommend to the Commissioner that approval for the HFA to participate in the program be suspended or withdrawn;

(6) Recommend to the Commissioner that the HFA's mortgagee approval be withdrawn pursuant to 24 CFR part 25 and/or that penalties be imposed pursuant to 24 CFR part 30;

(7) Require additional financial or other reports as may be necessary to monitor the activities of the HFA more closely.

(b) *Actions by Headquarters.* HUD Headquarters may impose any of the sanctions set forth or recommended in paragraph (a) of this section based upon its responsibilities for monitoring and overall program oversight.

(c) *Effect of suspension or withdrawal.* A suspension or withdrawal action will not affect any mortgage insurance endorsement in effect on the date of the suspension or withdrawal action.

(d) *HFA right to informal hearing.* (1) Any sanction imposed by a Designated Office in writing will be immediately effective, will state the grounds for the action, and provide for the HFA's right to an informal hearing before the Designated Office Representative or his or her designee in the Designated Office. The HFA may request an informal hearing within 10 working days of receipt of the suspension or withdrawal action and the Designated Office shall give the HFA an opportunity to be heard within 10 working days of receipt of the HFA's request. The HFA may be represented by counsel. The Designated Office Representative, or his or her designee, will advise the HFA in writing of the decision within 10 working days of

the informal hearing, which decision will constitute final HUD action.

(2) Sanctions imposed by Headquarters will be handled in a similar manner, except that the informal hearing shall be before the Commissioner or his or her designee.

§266.130 **Reinsurance.**

Reinsurance will be permitted for the portion of the HFA risk, subject to the following requirements:

(a) Neither HUD's nor the HFA's position shall be subordinated;

(b) The reinsurance may not be used to reduce any reserve or fund balance requirements; and

(c) Such reinsurance does not incur an obligation to the Federal Government.

Subpart C—Program Requirements

§266.200 **Eligible projects.**

(a) *Minimum project size.* Projects insured under this part must consist of five or more rental dwelling units (including cooperative dwelling units) on one site. The site may consist of two or more non-contiguous parcels of land situated so as to comprise a readily marketable real estate entity within an area small enough to allow convenient and efficient management. The units may be detached, semi-detached, row houses, multifamily structures, or mobile home parks (exclusive of the mobile homes).

(b) *New construction or substantial rehabilitation.* Insurance under this part shall be for the purpose of financing the new construction or substantial rehabilitation of projects meeting the other requirements of this part as follows:

(1) *New construction* occurs when all project and construction elements are installed as part of the work.

(2) *Substantial rehabilitation* is any combination of the following work to the existing facilities of a project that aggregates to at least 15 percent of project's value after the rehabilitation and that results in material improvement of the project's economic life, liveability, marketability, and profitability: Replacement, alteration and/or modernization of building spaces, long-

lived building or mechanical system components, or project facilities. Substantial rehabilitation may include but not consist solely of any combination of: minor repairs, replacement of short-lived building or mechanical system components, cosmetic work, or new project additions.

(c) *Existing projects.* Financing of existing properties without substantial rehabilitation is allowed.

(1) If an existing multifamily project is being acquired and HUD insurance under this part will be used to facilitate the acquisition of projects to increase the supply of affordable housing, such acquisitions are permissible if the HUD insured mortgage does not exceed the sum of the total cost of acquisition, cost of financing, cost of repairs, and reasonable transaction costs as determined by the Commissioner.

(2) If the property is subject to an HFA-financed loan to be refinanced and such refinancing will result in the preservation of affordable housing, refinancing of these properties is permissible if project occupancy is not less than 93 percent (to include consideration of rent in arrears), based on the average occupancy in the project over the most recent 12 months, and the mortgage does not exceed an amount supportable by the lower of the unit rents being collected under the rental assistance agreement or the unit rents being collected at unassisted projects in the market area that are similar in amenities and location to the project for which insurance is being requested. The HUD-insured mortgage may not exceed the sum of the existing indebtedness, cost of refinancing, the cost of repairs and reasonable transaction costs as determined by the Commissioner. If a loan to be refinanced has been in default within the 12 months prior to application for refinancing, the HFA must assume not less than 50 percent of the risk.

(d) *Projects receiving Section 8 rental subsidies or other rental subsidies.* Projects receiving project-based housing assistance payments under section 8 of the U.S. Housing Act of 1937 or other rental subsidies and meeting the requirements of this part may be insured under this part only if the mortgage does not exceed an amount sup-portable by the lower of the unit rents being or to be collected under the rental assistance agreement or the unit rents being collected at unassisted projects in the market that are similar in amenities and location to the project for which insurance is being requested.

(e) *SRO projects.* Single room occupancy (SRO) projects, as defined in § 266.5, are eligible for insurance under this part. Units in SRO projects must be subject to 30-day or longer leases; however, rent payments may be made on a weekly basis in SRO projects.

(f) *Board and care/assisted living facilities.* Board and care projects and assisted living facilities may be insured if the facilities meet the definition of those terms in § 266.5.

(g) *Elderly projects.* Projects or parts of projects specifically designed for the use and occupancy by elderly families. An elderly family means any household where the head or spouse is 62 years of age or older, and also any single person who is 62 years of age or older.

(h) *Zoning requirements.* Projects insured under this part must meet applicable zoning and other State/local government requirements.

§ 266.205 Ineligible projects.

The following projects and facilities are not eligible for insurance under this part:

(a) *Transient housing or hotels.* Rental for transient or hotel purposes. For purposes of this part, rental for transient or hotel purposes means:

(1) Rental for any period less than 30 days, or

(2) Any rental, if the occupants of the housing accommodations are provided customary hotel services such as room service for food and beverages, maid service, furnishing and laundering of linens, or valet service.

(b) *Projects in military impact areas.* A project located in a military impact area, as determined by HUD. A military impact area is generally a small or medium size metropolitan housing market area or a remote or isolated nonmetropolitan area where:

(1) Military-connected households comprise 25 percent or more of the total households in the market area. Military-connected households include

active duty military personnel, civilian employees of the military service (Department of Defense) or other Federal agency at or in support of the installation, and employees of contractors and sub-contractors directly associated with the military installation, and their dependents. Unaccompanied active duty military personnel housed in military-controlled group quarters housing (barracks, BOQ's) are excluded; and

(2) There is concern about the continued stability of the current level of military strength and mission at the installation based on public announcements from the Department of Defense or the military service of impending changes; and

(3) The complete reduction of military-connected households living in nonmilitary rental housing over a 5 year period, at an annual average decline of 20 percent, would, taking into account growth in the civilian economy and normal changes in the housing inventory, cause an adverse impact on the private rental market resulting in an increase in the rental vacancy rate in the housing market of 10 percent or more at the end of that period.

(c) *Retirement service centers.* Projects designed for the elderly with extensive services and luxury accommodations that provide for central kitchens and dining rooms with food service or mandatory services.

(d) *Nursing homes or intermediate care facilities.* Nursing homes and intermediate care facilities licensed and regulated by State or local government and providing nursing and medical care.

§266.210 HUD-retained review functions.

Certain functions are retained by the Commissioner. The HFA must submit any information or certification required by the Commissioner to permit determination of compliance with requirements concerning:

(a) *Previous participation of principals.* Previous participation of the principals of the mortgagor, general contractor, consultant or management agent in accordance with the Previous Participation and Clearance Review Procedures of 24 CFR 200.210 through 200.218.

(b) *Environmental review requirements.* To determine compliance with the requirements of the National Environmental Policy Act of 1969 and related laws and authorities, the HUD Field Office (or other responsible entity through such delegation as may be in effect by regulation hereafter) will visit each project site proposed for insurance under this part and prepare the applicable environmental reviews as set forth in 24 CFR part 50 (or as set forth in 24 CFR part 58 for the other responsible entity). These requirements must be completed before HUD may issue the firm approval letter.

(c) *Intergovernmental review.* Intergovernmental review of Federal programs under Executive Order 12372, as implemented in 24 CFR part 52.

(d) *Subsidy layering.* The Commissioner, or Housing Credit Agencies through such delegation as may be in effect by regulation hereafter, shall review all projects receiving tax credits and some form of HUD assistance for any excess subsidy provided to individual projects and reduce subsidy sources in accordance with outstanding guidelines.

(e) *Davis-Bacon Act.* The Commissioner shall obtain and provide to the HFA the appropriate Department of Labor wage rate determinations under the Davis-Bacon Act, where they apply under this part.

[59 FR 62524, Dec. 5, 1994, as amended at 60 FR 16573, Mar. 31, 1995]

§266.215 Functions delegated by HUD to HFAs.

The following functions are delegated by HUD to the HFAs:

(a) *Affirmative Fair Housing Marketing Plan (AFHMP).* The HFA will perform information collection, reviews and ministerial activities associated with the review and approval of the AFHMP for all projects. (Enforcement of fair housing and equal opportunity laws is the responsibility of HUD.)

(b) *Labor standards and prevailing wage requirements.* The HFA will perform information collection (e.g., payroll review and routine interviews) and other routine administration and enforcement functions regarding labor standards, in accordance with §266.225(e). (Enforcement of Davis-

Bacon prevailing wage requirements and labor standards is the responsibility of HUD.)

(c) *Insurance of advances.* In cases involving insured advances, the HFA will approve periodic advances of mortgage insurance proceeds during construction of the project subject to terms specified by the Commissioner.

(d) *Cost certification.* The HFA will perform cost certification functions on each insured loan subject to terms specified by the Commissioner.

(e) *Lead-Based Paint.* The HFA will perform functions related to Lead-Based Paint requirements subject to terms specified by the Commissioner.

§ 266.220 Nondiscrimination in housing and employment.

The mortgagor must certify to the HFA that, so long as the mortgage is insured under this part, it will:

(a) Not use tenant selection procedures that discriminate against families with children, except in the case of a project that constitutes "housing for older persons" as defined in section 807(b)(2) of the Fair Housing Act (42 U.S.C. 3607(b)(2));

(b) Not discriminate against any family because of the sex of the head of household;

(c) Comply with the Fair Housing Act (42 U.S.C. 3601-3619), as implemented by 24 CFR part 100; titles II and III of the Americans with Disabilities Act of 1990 (42 U.S.C. 12101-12213), as implemented by 28 CFR part 35; section 3 of the Housing and Urban Development Act of 1968 (12 U.S.C. 1701u), as implemented by 24 CFR part 135; the Equal Credit Opportunity Act (15 U.S C. 1691-1691f), as implemented by 12 CFR part 202; Executive Order 11063, as amended by Executive Order 12259 (3 CFR 1958-1963 Comp., p. 652 and 3 CFR 1980 Comp., p. 307), and implemented by 24 CFR part 107; Executive Order 11246 (3 CFR 1964-1965 Comp., p. 339), as implemented by 41 CFR part 60; other applicable Federal laws and regulations issued pursuant to these authorities; and applicable State and local fair housing and equal opportunity laws. In addition, a mortgagor that receives Federal financial assistance must also certify to the HFA that, so long as the mortgage is insured under this part, it will comply with title VI of the Civil Rights Act of 1964 (42 U.S.C. 2000d), as implemented by 24 CFR part 1; the Age Discrimination Act of 1975 (42 U.S.C. 6101-6107), as implemented by 24 CFR part 146; and section 504 of the Rehabilitation Act of 1973 (29 U.S.C. 794), as implemented by 24 CFR part 8.

§ 266.225 Labor standards.

(a) *Applicability of Davis-Bacon.* (1) All laborers and mechanics employed by contractors or subcontractors on a project insured under this part shall be paid not less than the wages prevailing in the locality in which the work was performed for the corresponding classes of laborers and mechanics employed in construction of a similar character, as determined by the Secretary of Labor in accordance with the Davis-Bacon Act, as amended (40 U.S.C. 276a-276a-5), where the project meets all of the following conditions:

(i) Advances for the project are insured under this part;

(ii) The project involves new construction or substantial rehabilitation; and

(iii) The project will contain 12 or more dwelling units.

(2) Projects that do not meet these conditions are not subject to Davis-Bacon wage rates except to the extent required as a condition of other Federal assistance to the project.

(b) *Volunteers.* The provisions of this section shall not apply to volunteers under the conditions set out in 24 CFR part 70. In applying part 70, insurance under this part shall be treated as a program for which there is a statutory exemption for volunteers.

(c) *Labor standards.* Any contract, subcontract, or building loan agreement executed for a project subject to Davis-Bacon wage rates under paragraph (a) of this section shall comply with all labor standards and provisions of 29 CFR parts 1, 3 and 5 that would be applicable to a mortgage insurance program to which Davis-Bacon wage rates are made applicable by statute.

(d) *Advances.* (1) No advance under a mortgage on a project subject to Davis-Bacon wage rates under paragraph (a) of this section shall be eligible for insurance under this part unless the HFA determines (in accordance with the

Commissioner's administrative procedures) that the general contractor or any subcontractor or any firm, corporation, partnership or association in which the contractor or subcontractor has a substantial interest was not, on the date the contract or subcontract was executed, on the ineligible list established by the Comptroller General, pursuant 29 CFR 5.12, issued by the Secretary of Labor.

(2) No advance under any mortgage on a project subject to Davis-Bacon wage rates under paragraph (a) of this section shall be insured under this part unless there is filed with the application for the advance, and no such mortgage shall be insured under this part unless there is filed with the HFA after completion of the construction or substantial rehabilitation, a certificate or certificates in the form required by the Commissioner, supported by such other information as the Commissioner may prescribe, certifying that the laborers and mechanics employed in the construction of the project involved have been paid not less than the wages determined by the Secretary of Labor to be prevailing in accordance with paragraph (a) of this section.

(e) *Responsibility for enforcement and administration.* The Commissioner retains responsibility for enforcement of labor standards under this section, but the Commissioner may delegate to the HFA information collection (*e.g.*, payroll review and routine interviews) and other routine administration and enforcement functions, subject to monitoring by the Commissioner. Where routine administration and enforcement functions are delegated to the HFA, the HFA shall bear financial responsibility for any deficiency in payment of prevailing wages or, where applicable under 29 CFR part 1, any increase in compensation to a contractor, that is attributable to any failure properly to carry out its delegated functions. For example, failure of an HFA to supply or ensure inclusion of the proper contract clauses or wage determination in a contract or building loan agreement may require the HFA to fund increased compensation to a contractor as the result of increased wages attributable to incorpo-ration of the proper clauses and wage determination.

Subpart D—Processing, Development, and Approval

§266.300 HFAs accepting 50 percent or more of risk.

(a) *Underwriting standards.* An HFA electing to take 50 percent or more of the risk on loans may use its own underwriting standards and loan terms and conditions (as disclosed and submitted with its application) to underwrite and approve loans without further review by HUD.

(b) *HFA responsibilities.* The HFA is responsible for the performance of all functions except those HUD-retained functions specified in §§266.210 and 266.225(e). After acceptance of an application for a loan to be insured under this part, the HFA must:

(1) Determine that a market for the project exists, taking into consideration any comments from the HUD Field Office relative to the potential adverse impact the project will have on existing or proposed Federally insured and assisted projects in the area.

(2) Establish the maximum insurable mortgage and review plans and specifications for compliance with HFA standards;

(3) Determine the acceptability of the proposed mortgagor and management agent;

(4) Approve the Affirmative Fair Housing Marketing Plan; and

(5) Make any other determinations necessary to ensure acceptability of the proposed project.

(c) *HUD-retained reviews.* After positive completion of the HUD-retained reviews specified in §266.210(a), (b), and (c), the HUD Field Office will issue a firm approval letter.

(d) *Inspections and other reviews.* The HFA is responsible for inspections during construction, processing and approving advances of mortgage proceeds during construction, review and approval of cost certification, and closing of the loan.

(e) *Endorsement of mortgage note for insurance.* So long as the HFA is in good standing, and absent fraud or material misrepresentation on the part of the HFA, the Commissioner or designee will endorse the mortgage note for insurance upon presentation by the HFA of the Closing Docket and certifications required in § 266.420(b), subject to HUD's right to adjust under § 266.417.

§ 266.305 HFAs accepting less than 50 percent of risk.

(a) *Underwriting standards.* The underwriting standards and loan terms and conditions of any HFA electing to take less than 50 percent of the risk on certain projects are subject to review, modification, and approval by HUD in accordance with § 266.100(b)(2). These HFAs may assume 25 percent or 10 percent of the risk depending upon the loan-to-replacement-cost or loan-to-value ratios of the projects to be insured as specified in § 266.100(b)(2)(i) and (ii).

(b) *HFA responsibilities.* The HFA is responsible for the performance of all functions except those HUD-retained functions specified in § 266.210 and 266.225(e). After acceptance of an application for a loan to be insured under this part, the HFA must:

(1) Determine that a market for the project exists, taking into consideration any comments from the HUD Field Office relative to the potential adverse impact the project will have on existing or proposed Federally insured and assisted projects in the area;

(2) Establish the maximum insurable mortgage, and review plans and specifications for compliance with HFA standards as approved by HUD;

(3) Determine the acceptability of the proposed mortgagor and management agent;

(4) Approve the Affirmative Fair Housing Marketing Plan; and

(5) Make any other determinations necessary to ensure acceptability of the proposed project.

(c) *HUD-retained reviews.* After positive completion of the HUD-retained reviews specified in § 266.210 (a), (b), and (c), the HUD Field Office will issue a firm approval letter which, among other things, will apportion units and obligate credit subsidy to the project.

(d) *Inspections and other reviews.* The HFA is responsible for inspections during construction, processing and approving advances of mortgage proceeds during construction, review and ap-

proval of cost certification, and closing of the loan.

(e) *Endorsement of mortgage note for insurance.* So long as the HFA is in good standing, and absent fraud or material misrepresentation on the part of the HFA, the Commissioner or designee will endorse the mortgage note for insurance upon presentation by the HFA of the Closing Docket and certifications required in § 266.420(b), subject to HUD's right to adjust under § 266.417.

§ 266.310 Insurance of advances or insurance upon completion; applicability of requirements.

(a) *General.* HUD will agree to insure periodic advances of mortgage proceeds or to insure the entire mortgage upon completion of construction for projects involving new construction or substantial rehabilitation. Existing projects without the need for substantial rehabilitation will be considered insurance upon completion cases. In insurance upon completion cases, only the permanent loan is insured and a single endorsement is required after satisfactory completion of construction, substantial rehabilitation or repairs. In periodic advances cases, progress payments approved by the HFA and both an initial and final endorsement on the mortgage are required.

(b) *Insurance of advances.* Periodic advances will be authorized by the HFA subject to terms specified by the Commissioner.

(c) *Insurance upon completion*—(1) *New construction and substantial rehabilitation.* An HFA may approve a loan that will be insured upon completion of construction of the project. The HFA approval must prescribe a designated period during which the mortgagor must start construction or substantial rehabilitation. If construction or rehabilitation is started as required, the approval will be valid for the period estimated by the HFA for construction and loan closing, including any extension approved by the HFA.

(2) *Existing projects with no substantial rehabilitation.* Existing projects with or without repairs are only insured upon completion, although HFAs may permit noncritical repairs to be completed after endorsement upon establishment of escrows acceptable to the HFA.

534

(d) *Requirements applicable to both periodic advances and insurance upon completion cases*—(1) *Inspections.* The HFA must inspect projects under this part at such times during construction, substantial rehabilitation, or repairs as the HFA determines. The inspections must be conducted to assure compliance with plans and specifications, work write-ups, and other contract documents.

(2) *Approval of advances.* At all times, the loan must be kept in balance, and advances approved only if warranted by construction progress evidenced through HFA inspection, as well as in accord with plans, specifications, work write-ups and other contract documents. In approving advances, HFAs must make certain that other mortgageable items are supported with proper bills and/or receipts before funds can be approved and advanced for insurance.

(3) *Cost certification.* In order to ensure that the final amount for insurance is supported by certified costs:

(i) The mortgagor (and general contractor, if there is an identity of interest with the mortgagor) must execute a certificate of actual costs, in a form acceptable to the HFA, when all physical improvements are completed to the satisfaction of the HFA and before final endorsement; and

(ii) The cost certification provided by the mortgagor must be audited by an independent public accountant.

(4) *Contestability.* Although the HFA has authority to approve the mortgagor's (and general contractor's) certification of cost, the certification will be contestable by the Commissioner during the period up to and including final endorsement of the mortgage. After final endorsement, the certification will be final and incontestable except for fraud or material misrepresentation on the part of the mortgagor (and/or general contractor).

(5) *Assurance of completion.* The mortgagor must furnish assurance of completion of the project in accordance with any requirements of the HFA as to form and amount.

(6) *Latent defects escrow.* The mortgagor must furnish an escrow or other form of assurance required by the HFA to ensure that latent defects can be remedied within the time period required by the HFA.

(e) *Mortgagee of record.* The HFA must remain the mortgagee of record as long as mortgage insurance is in force.

§266.315 Recordkeeping requirements.

The mortgagor and the builder, if there is an identity of interest with the mortgagor, shall keep and maintain records of all costs of any construction or other cost items not representing work under the general contract and to make available such records for review by the HFA or HUD, if requested.

Subpart E—Mortgage and Closing Requirements; HUD Endorsement

§266.400 Property requirements—real estate.

The mortgage must be on real estate held:

(a) In fee simple;

(b) Under a renewable lease of not less than 99 years; or

(c) Under a lease executed by a governmental agency, or other lessor approved by the HFA, that has a term at least 10 years beyond the end of the mortgage term.

§266.402 Recordation.

At the time of initial endorsement in the case of insurance of advances or at the time of final endorsement in the case of insurance upon completion, the HFA shall make certain that the mortgage and the regulatory agreement are recorded.

§266.405 Title.

(a) *Eligibility of title.* Marketable title to the mortgaged property must be vested in the mortgagor on the date the mortgage is filed for record.

(b) *Title evidence.* The HFA must receive a title insurance policy that ensures that marketable title is vested in the mortgagor, that a survey acceptable to the HFA has been performed, and that no existing impediments to title concern, or exist on, the property.

§266.410 Mortgage provisions.

(a) *Form.* The mortgage and note must be executed on a form approved by the HFA for use in the jurisdiction in which the property is located.

(b) *Mortgagor.* The mortgage must be executed by a mortgagor determined eligible by the HFA.

(c) *First lien.* The mortgage must be a single first lien on property that has first priority for payment and that conforms with property standards prescribed by the HFA.

(d) *Single asset mortgagor.* The mortgage must require that the mortgagor is a single asset mortgagor.

(e) *Amortization.* The mortgage must provide for complete amortization (*i.e.*, regularly amortizing) over the term of the mortgage.

(f) *Use restrictions.* The mortgage must contain a covenant prohibiting the use of the property for any purpose other than the purpose intended on the day the mortgage was executed. The conversion of a project from rental to cooperative is not a "change in use" as that term is employed in the mortgage since the property will continue to have a residential use both before and after conversion.

(g) *Hazard insurance.* The mortgage must contain a covenant, acceptable to the HFA, that binds the mortgagor to keep the property insured by one or more standard policies for fire and other hazards stipulated by the HFA. A standard mortgagee clause making loss payable to the HFA must be included in the mortgage. The HFA is responsible for assuring that insurance is maintained in force and in the amount required by this paragraph and the mortgage. The HFA must ensure that the insurance coverage is in an amount that will comply with the coinsurance clause applicable to the location and character of the property, but not less than 80 percent of the actual cash value of the insurable improvements and equipment. If the mortgagor does not obtain the required insurance, the HFA must do so and assess the mortgagor for such costs. These insurance requirements apply as long as the HFA retains an interest in the project and final claim settlement has not been completed or the contract of insurance has not been otherwise terminated.

(h) *Modification of terms.* The mortgage must contain a covenant requiring that, in the event that the HFA and owner agree to a modification of the terms of the mortgage (*e.g.*, to reflect a reduction of the interest rate if reductions are realized in the underlying bond rates for the project), Section 8 rents would be reduced in accordance with HUD guidelines.

(i) *Regulatory Agreement.* The mortgage must contain a provision incorporating the Regulatory Agreement by reference.

§ 266.415 Mortgage lien and other obligations.

(a) *Liens.* At the initial and final closing of the loan, the mortgagor and the HFA must certify, and the HFA must determine, that the property covered by the mortgage is free from all liens other than the lien of the insured mortgage, except that the property may be subject to such inferior lien or liens as approved by the HFA as long as the insured mortgage has first priority for payment.

(b) *Contractual obligations.* At the final closing of the loan, the mortgagor and the HFA must certify, and the HFA must determine, that all contractual obligations in connection with the mortgage transaction, including the purchase of the property and the improvements to the property, are paid. An exception is made for obligations that are approved by the HFA and determined by the HFA to be of a lesser priority for payment than the obligation of the insured mortgage.

§ 266.417 Authority to adjust mortgage insurance amount.

In order to protect the mortgage insurance funds, the Commissioner has authority in his or her sole discretion, at any time prior to and including final endorsement, to adjust the amount of the mortgage insurance.

§ 266.420 Closing and endorsement by the Commissioner.

(a) *Closing.* Before disbursement of loan advances in periodic advances cases, and in all cases after completion of construction, repair or substantial rehabilitation, the HFA must hold a closing and submit a closing docket with required documentation to the Commissioner or the Commissioner's authorized Departmental representative for insurance of the mortgage by endorsement of the mortgage note. The note must provide that the mortgage is insured under section 542(c) of the Housing and Community Development Act of 1992 and the regulations set forth at 24 CFR part 266 in effect on the date of endorsement. The note must also specify the date of endorsement, *i.e.*, the date of HUD endorsement of the project mortgage, and the risk of loss assumed by the HFA and by HUD.

(b) *Closing docket.* The HFA's submission must include a certification that it has obtained written HUD approval of compliance with the requirements referred to in §266.210, and certifications and information as follows:

(1) Information concerning the mortgage amount and term, location, number and type of units, income and expenses, rents, projects and market occupancy percentages, value/replacement cost, interest rate, and similar statistical information in accordance with the Commissioner's administrative procedures.

(2) Copies of the amortization schedule, Note and Risk-Sharing Agreement.

(3) Certification that the loan has been processed, prudently underwritten (including a determination that a market exists for the project), cost certified (if the project is being submitted for final endorsement) and closed in full compliance with the HFA's standards and requirements (or where the mortgage is insured under Level II, in full compliance with the underwriting standards and loan terms and conditions as approved by HUD).

(4) At the time of final endorsement, a certification for periodic advances cases, if submitted for final endorsement, that advances were made proportionate to construction progress.

(5) A copy of the HFA-approved cost certification if the project is submitted for final endorsement.

(6) A certification that equal employment requirements are followed.

(7) A certification that the HFA has reviewed and approved the Affirmative Fair Housing Marketing Plan and found it acceptable.

(8) A certification that a dedicated account, if required, has been increased in accordance with §266.110(b).

(9) Certifications required under §266.415 concerning liens and contractual obligations.

(10) Copies of the Hazard Insurance Policy with a clause making the loss payable to the HFA.

(11) For projects subject to Davis-Bacon prevailing requirements under §266.225, the certification and information concerning payment of prevailing wage rates required by §266.225(d).

(12) Certified copies of mortgage (deed of trust) with attached regulatory agreement, and note for HUD files.

Subpart F—Project Management and Servicing

§266.500 General.

The HFA will have full responsibility for the administration of the provisions of this subpart and for managing and servicing projects insured under this part. The HFA is responsible for monitoring and determining the compliance of the project owner in accordance with the provisions of this subpart. HUD will monitor the performance of the HFA, not the project owner, to determine its compliance with the provisions covered under this subpart.

§266.505 Regulatory agreement requirements.

(a) *General.* (1) The HFA must execute a Regulatory Agreement, in recordable form, between the mortgagor and the HFA to be in force for the duration of the insured mortgage and note or bond. The Regulatory Agreement must include a description of the property. The Regulatory Agreement must be incorporated by reference into the mortgage and recorded with the mortgage.

(2) The Regulatory Agreement executed between the HFA and the mortgagor must be binding upon the mortgagor and any of its successors and assigns and upon the HFA and any of its successors for so long as the mortgage is insured by HUD or HUD holds an HFA debenture issued in connection with a claim arising from the insured mortgage. The HFA may not assign the Regulatory Agreement.

(3) The HFA will enforce the Regulatory Agreement and take actions against any mortgagors who violate its provisions. Such actions may involve a declaration of default and application to any court for specific performance of the agreement.

(b) *Requirements.* The Regulatory Agreement must require the mortgagor to comply with the provisions of this part and obligate the mortgagor, among other things, to:

(1) Make all payments due under the mortgage and note/bond.

(2) Where necessary, establish a sinking fund for future capital needs.

(3) Maintain the project as affordable housing, as defined in § 266.5.

(4) Continue to use dwelling units for their original purposes.

(5) Comply with such other requirements as may be established by the HFA and set forth in the Regulatory Agreement.

(6) [Reserved]

(7) Maintain complete books and records established solely for the project.

(8) Comply with the Affirmative Fair Housing Marketing Plan and all other fair housing and equal opportunity requirements.

(9) Operate as a single asset mortgagor.

(10) Make books and records available for HUD or General Accounting Office (GAO) review with appropriate notification.

(11) Permit HUD officials or employees to inspect the project upon request by the Commissioner.

(c) *Enforcement.* The Regulatory Agreement shall be enforced by the HFA.

[59 FR 62524, Dec. 5, 1994, as amended at 63 FR 46578, 46593, Sept. 1, 1998; 65 FR 16296, Mar. 27, 2000]

§ 266.507   Maintenance requirements.

The mortgagor must maintain the project in accordance with the physical condition standards in 24 CFR part 5, subpart G.

[63 FR 46578, Sept. 1, 1998]

§ 266.510   HFA responsibilities.

(a) *Inspections.* The HFA must perform inspections in accordance with the physical inspection procedures in 24 CFR part 5, subpart G.

(b) *Annual audits of projects.* The HFA must analyze projects' annual audits and provide a copy to HUD along with a summary of unresolved findings and actions planned, with target dates, to correct unresolved findings.

(c) *HFA's annual financial statement.* The HFA must provide HUD with annual audited financial statement in accordance with the requirements of 2 CFR part 200, subpart F.

[59 FR 62524, Dec. 5, 1994, as amended at 63 FR 46578, Sept. 1, 1998; 65 FR 16296, Mar. 27, 2000; 80 FR 75936, Dec. 7, 2015]

§ 266.515   Record retention.

(a) *Loan origination and servicing.* Records pertaining to the mortgage loan origination and servicing of the loan must be maintained for as long as the insurance remains in force.

(b) *Defaults and claims.* Records pertaining to a mortgage default and claim must be retained from the date of default through final settlement of the claim for a period of no less than three years after final settlement.

§ 266.520   Program monitoring and compliance.

HUD will monitor the performance of the HFA in accordance with the provisions covered under this subpart.

Subpart G—Contract Rights and Obligations

MORTGAGE INSURANCE PREMIUMS

§ 266.600   Mortgage insurance premium: Insurance upon completion.

(a) *Initial premium.* For projects insured upon completion, on the date of the final closing, the HFA shall pay to the Commissioner an initial premium equal to the prescribed percentage, in the sliding scale chart that is shown in § 266.604(b), of the face amount of the mortgage.

(b) *Premium payable with first payment of principal.* On the date of the first payment of principal the HFA shall pay a second premium (calculated on a per annum basis) equal to the prescribed percentage of the average outstanding principal obligation of the mortgage from the final closing date to the year following the date of the first principal payment, less the amount paid on the date of the final closing.

(c) *Subsequent premiums.* Until one of the conditions is met under §266.606(a), the HFA on each anniversary of the date of the first principal payment shall pay to the Commissioner an annual mortgage insurance premium equal to the prescribed percentage of the average outstanding principal obligation of the mortgage, without taking into account delinquent payments, or partial claim payment under §266.630, or prepayments, for the year following the date on which the premium becomes payable.

§266.602 **Mortgage insurance premium: Insured advances.**

(a) *Initial premium.* For projects involving insured advances, on the date of the initial closing, the HFA shall pay to the Commissioner an initial premium equal to the prescribed percentage, in the sliding scale chart that is shown in §266.604(b), of the face amount of the mortgage.

(b) *Interim premium.* On each anniversary of the initial closing, the HFA shall pay an interim mortgage insurance premium equal to the prescribed percentage of the face amount of the mortgage. The HFA shall continue to pay the interim mortgage insurance premiums until the date of the first principal payment.

(c) *Premium payable with first payment of principal.* On the date of the first principal payment, the HFA shall pay a mortgage insurance premium equal to the prescribed percentage of the average outstanding principal obligation of the mortgage for the year following the date of the first principal payment. The HFA shall adjust this payment by deducting an amount equal to the portion of the last premium paid that is attributable to the months after the date of the first payment to principal. Any partial month is to be counted as a whole month. The HFA shall remit the net adjusted mortgage premium to the Commissioner and refund the amount of the adjustment (overpayment) to the mortgagor.

(d) *Subsequent premiums.* Until one of the conditions is met under §266.606(a), the HFA on each anniversary of the

date of the first principal payment shall pay to the Commissioner an annual mortgage insurance premium equal to the prescribed percentage of the average outstanding principal obligation of the mortgage, without taking into account delinquent payments, prepayments, or a partial claim payment under §266.630, for the year following the date on which the premium becomes payable.

§266.604 **Mortgage insurance premium: Other requirements.**

(a) *Premium calculations on or after first principal payment.* The premiums payable to the Commissioner on and after the first principal payment shall be calculated in accordance with the amortization schedule prepared by the HFA for final closing and the prescribed percentage as set forth in the sliding scale chart in paragraph (b) of this section without taking into account delinquent payments or prepayments.

(b) *Prescribed percentages.* The following sliding scale chart provides the prescribed percentage, based upon the respective share of risk, that is to be used in calculating mortgage insurance premiums under this section:

Percentage share of risk		Prescribed percentage for calculating HFA's annual MIP
HUD	HFA	
90	10	.45
75	25	.375
50	50	.25
40	60	.2
30	70	.15
20	80	.1
10	90	.05

(c) *Closing information.* The HFA shall provide final closing information to the Commissioner within 15 days of the final closing in a format prescribed by the Commissioner. In addition, the HFA shall submit a copy of the amortization schedule. This amortization shall be used to compute and collect all future mortgage insurance premiums subject to §266.600(c) or §266.602(d). If the mortgage is modified, the HFA shall submit to the Commissioner a copy of the revised amortization schedule, which shall be used to compute and collect all future mortgage insurance premiums subject to §266.600(c) or §266.602(d).

(d) *Due date for premium payments.* Mortgage insurance premiums are due on the first day of the month of the anniversary of the first payment to principal. Any premium received by the Commissioner more than 15 days after the due date shall be assessed a late charge of 4 percent of the amount of the premium payment due. Mortgage insurance premiums that are paid to the Commissioner more than 30 days after the due date shall begin to accrue interest at the rate prescribed by the Treasury Fiscal Requirements Manual.

§ 266.606 Mortgage insurance premium: Duration and method of paying.

(a) *Duration of payments.* Mortgage insurance premium payments must continue annually until one of the following occurs:

(1) The mortgage is paid in full;

(2) A deed to the HFA is filed for record;

(3) An application for initial claim payment is received by the Commissioner; or

(4) The Contract of Insurance is otherwise terminated.

(b) *Method of payment.* The HFA shall pay any mortgage insurance premium required by this part in cash.

§ 266.608 Mortgage insurance premium: Pro rata refund.

If the Contract of Insurance is terminated by payment in full or is terminated by the HFA on a form prescribed by the Commissioner, after the date of the first payment to principal, the Commissioner shall refund any mortgage insurance premium for the period after the effective date of the termination of insurance. The refund shall be mailed to the HFA for credit to the mortgagor's account. In computing the pro rata portion of the annual mortgage insurance premium, the date of termination of insurance shall be the last day of the month in which the mortgage is prepaid or the Commissioner receives a notification of termination, whichever is later. No refund shall be made if the insurance was terminated because of the submission of an application for initial claim payment or if the termination occurs before the date of the first payment to principal.

§ 266.610 Method of payment of mortgage insurance premiums.

In the cases that the Commissioner deems appropriate, the Commissioner may require, by means of instructions communicated to all affected mortgagees, that mortgage insurance premiums be remitted electronically.

[63 FR 1303, Jan. 8, 1998]

INSURANCE ENDORSEMENT

§ 266.612 Insurance endorsement.

(a) *Initial endorsement.* The Commissioner shall indicate his or her insurance of the mortgage by endorsing the original credit instrument.

(b) *Final endorsement.* When all advances of mortgage proceeds have been made and all other applicable terms and conditions have been complied with to the satisfaction of the Commissioner, the Commissioner shall indicate on the original credit instrument the total of all advances that have been approved for insurance and again endorse such instrument.

(c) *Effect of endorsement.* From the date of initial endorsement, the Commissioner and the HFA shall be bound by the provisions of this subpart to the same extent as if they had executed a contract including the provisions of this subpart and the applicable sections of the Act.

ASSIGNMENTS

§ 266.616 Transfer of partial interest under participation agreement.

The HFA may not assign the mortgage. However, a partial interest in an insured mortgage or pool of insured mortgages may be transferred under a participation agreement or arrangement (such as a declaration of trust or the issuance of pass-through certificates), without obtaining the approval of the Commissioner, if the following conditions are met:

(a) Legal title to the insured mortgage or mortgages shall be held by the HFA; and

(b) The participation agreement, declaration of trust or other instrument under which the partial interest is transferred shall provide that:

(1) The HFA shall remain mortgagee of record under the contract of mortgage insurance;

(2) The Commissioner shall have no obligation to recognize or deal with anyone other than the HFA with respect to the rights, benefits, and obligations of the mortgagee under the contract of insurance; and

(3) The mortgagor shall have no obligation to recognize or do business with any one other than the HFA or, if applicable, its servicing agent with respect to rights, benefits, and obligations of the mortgagor or the mortgagee under the mortgage.

TERMINATION

§ 266.620 Termination of Contract of Insurance.

The Contract of Insurance shall terminate if any of the following occurs:

(a) The mortgage is paid in full;

(b) The HFA acquires the mortgaged property and notifies the Commissioner that it will not file an insurance claim;

(c) A party other than HFA acquires the property at a foreclosure sale;

(d) The HFA notifies the Commissioner of Termination of Insurance (voluntary termination);

(e) The HFA or its successors commit fraud or make a material misrepresentation to the Commissioner with respect to information culminating in the Contract of Insurance on the mortgage or while the Contract of Insurance is in existence;

(f) The receipt by the Commissioner of an Application for Final Claims Settlement;

(g) If the HFA acquires the mortgaged property and fails to make an initial claim.

§ 266.622 Notice and date of termination by the Commissioner.

The Commissioner shall notify the HFA that the Contract of Insurance has been terminated and shall establish the effective date of termination. The termination shall be the last day of the month in which one of the events specified in § 266.620 occurs.

CLAIM PROCEDURES

§ 266.626 Notice of default and filing an insurance claim.

(a) *Definition of default.* (1) A monetary default exists when the mortgagor fails to make any payment due under the mortgage.

(2) A covenant default exists when the mortgagor fails to perform any other covenant under the provision of the mortgage or the regulatory agreement, which is incorporated by reference in the mortgage. An HFA becomes eligible for insurance benefits on the basis of a covenant default only after the HFA has accelerated the debt and the owner has failed to pay the full amount due, thus converting a covenant default into a monetary default.

(b) *Date of default.* For purposes of this subpart, the date of default is:

(1) The date of the first uncorrected failure to perform a mortgage covenant or obligation; or

(2) The date of the first failure to make a monthly payment that is not covered by subsequent payments, when such subsequent payments are applied to the overdue monthly payments in the order in which they were due.

(c) *Notice of default.* If a default (as defined in paragraph (a) of this section) continues for a period of 30 days, the HFA must notify the Commissioner within 10 days thereafter, unless the default is cured within the 30-day period. Unless waived by the Commissioner, the HFA must submit this notice monthly, on a form prescribed by the Commissioner, until the default has been cured or the HFA has filed an application for an initial claim payment. In cases of mortgage acceleration, the mortgagee must first give notice of the default.

(d) *Timing of claim filing.* Unless a written extension is granted by HUD, the HFA must file an application for initial claim payment (or, if appropriate, for partial claim payment) within 75 days from the date of default and may do so as early as the first day of the month following the month for which a payment was missed. Upon request of the HFA, HUD may extend, up to 180 days from the date of default, the deadline for filing a claim. In those cases where the HFA certifies that the project owner is in the process of transacting a bond refunder, refinancing the mortgage, or changing the ownership for the purpose of curing the default and bringing the mortgage current, HUD may extend the deadline for filing a claim beyond 180 days, not to exceed 360 days from the date of default.

§ 266.628 Initial claim payments.

(a) *Determination of initial claim amount.* (1) The initial claim amount is based on the unpaid principal balance of the mortgage note as of the date of default, plus interest at the mortgage note rate from date of default to date of initial claim payment. The mortgage note interest component of the initial claim amount is subject to curtailment as provided in paragraph (b) of this section.

(2) HUD shall make an initial claim payment to the HFA that is equal to the initial claim amount, less any delinquent mortgage insurance premiums, late charges and interest, assessed under § 266.604(d).

(3) The HFA must use the proceeds of the initial claim payment to retire any bonds or any other financing mechanisms securing the mortgage within 30 days of the initial claim payment. Any excess funds resulting from such retirement or repayment shall be returned to HUD within 30 days of the retirement.

(b) *Curtailment of interest for late filings.* In determining the mortgage note interest component of the initial claim amount, if the HFA fails to meet any of the requirements of this section within the specified time (including any granted extension of time), HUD shall curtail the accrual of mortgage note interest by the number of days by which the required action was late.

(c) *Method of payment.* HUD shall pay the claim in cash.

§ 266.630 Partial payment of claims.

(a) *General.* When the Commissioner receives a claim for a partial payment under § 266.626(d), the Commissioner may make a partial payment of claim in accordance with the requirements of this section. If the HFA has not previously received a partial claim payment, the HFA may file a claim for a partial claim payment under § 266.630.

Otherwise, the HFA must file for an initial claim payment under § 266.628.

(b) *HFA submission.* In addition to any other requirements set forth in administration instructions, the HFA must provide the following information with its application for a partial claim payment:

(1) The amount by which the HFA will reduce the principal on the insured mortgage and the amount of delinquent interest on the insured mortgage that the HFA will defer based on the anticipated closing date; and

(2) A certification that:

(i) The amount of the principal reduction of the insured first mortgage does not exceed 50 percent of the unpaid principal balance;

(ii) The relief resulting from the partial claim payment when considered with other resources available to the project are sufficient to restore the financial viability of the project;

(iii) The project is or can (at reasonable cost) be made structurally sound;

(iv) The management of the project is satisfactory;

(v) The default under the insured mortgage was beyond the control of the mortgagor.

(c) *Claim processing—*(1) *Acceptable application.* If the HFA's application is acceptable, the Commissioner shall notify the HFA to process the partial payment, which will include the modification of the existing mortgage and the execution by the mortgagor of a second mortgage payable to the HFA. When the second mortgage is closed, the HFA shall notify the Commissioner, in a form and manner prescribed in administrative instructions. Upon receipt of notice from the HFA, the Commissioner shall make the partial claim payment.

(2) *Unacceptable application.* If the application is unacceptable, the Commissioner shall either advise the HFA of the information needed to make the application acceptable or return the application for further action. The HFA is granted an extension of 30 days from the date of any notification for further action.

(d) *Requirements—*(1) *One partial claim payment.* Only one partial claim payment may be made under a contract of insurance.

(2) *Partial claim payment amount.* The amount of the partial claim payment is equal to the amount of relief provided by the HFA in the form of a reduction in principal and a reduction of delinquent interest due on the insured mortgage times the lesser of HUD's percentage of the risk of loss or 50 percent.

(3) *HFA second mortgage.* Repayment of the relief provided by the HFA must be secured by a second mortgage to the HFA. This second mortgage may provide for postponed amortization and may not be assigned by the HFA. This second mortgage is not insured under this part and may not be insured under any other HUD-related insurance program.

(4) *Partial claim repayment by HFA.* The HFA must remit to HUD a percentage of all amounts collected on the HFA's second mortgage within 15 days of receipt by the HFA. The applicable percentage is equal to the percentage used in paragraph (d)(2) of this section to determine the partial claim payment amount. Payments made after the 15th day must include a 5 percent late charge plus accrued interest at the debenture rate.

(5) *Certified statements of amounts collected.* As long as the second mortgage remains of record, the HFA must submit to the Commissioner an annual certified statement of the amounts collected by the HFA. The HFA must submit a final certified statement within 30 days after the second mortgage is paid in full, foreclosed, or otherwise terminated.

§266.632 Withdrawal of claim.

In case of a default and subsequent filing of claim, the HFA shall determine the form of workout or modification and will inform HUD of the type of mortgage relief determined to be appropriate. If the default is cured after the claim is made but before the initial claim payment is paid by HUD, the HFA may, in writing, withdraw the claim, and insurance will continue as if the default had not occurred.

§266.634 Reinstatement of the contract of insurance.

(a) *Conditions for reinstatement.* After the initial claim payment, HUD may reinstate the contract of insurance on the following conditions:

(1) The HFA has not acquired the project;

(2) The mortgagor has cured the default; and

(3) The HFA requests that HUD reinstate the contract of insurance.

(b) *Notification of reinstatement.* If reinstatement is acceptable to HUD, HUD shall notify the HFA of the date the contract of insurance will be reinstated and shall advise the HFA of the payment needed to reinstate the contract of insurance.

(c) *Payment.* Within 30 days of the date of the notice under paragraph (b) of this section, the HFA shall pay HUD an amount equal to the initial claim amount, as determined under §266.628(a)(1), plus an amount equal to the accrued and unpaid interest on the HFA Debenture through the reinstatement date, plus an amount equal to the mortgage insurance premium for the period from the date of reinstatement of the contract of insurance to the next anniversary date for payment of the mortgage insurance premium.

(d) *Cancellation of debenture.* Upon receipt from the HFA of the amount specified in paragraph (c) of this section, HUD shall return the HFA debenture for cancellation.

(e) *Continuation of contract of insurance.* Upon reinstatement, the contract of insurance shall continue as if the default had not occurred.

§266.636 Insuring new loans for defaulted projects.

The HFA may not make another loan that is insured under this part to the same owner in the same project if HUD has paid a claim under this part.

§266.638 Issuance of HFA Debenture.

(a) *Condition to initial claim payment.* The HFA must issue an instrument in the form of a debenture to HUD within 30 days of receiving the initial claim payment. The HFA Debenture shall meet the following requirements and shall be in a form that has been approved by HUD as part of the application approval process.

(b) *Term of HFA Debenture.* The HFA Debenture shall be dated the same date that the initial claim payment is issued. The HFA Debenture shall have a term of five years in order to afford the mortgagor ample time to cure the default or the HFA time to foreclose and/or resell the project. HUD may provide a written extension of the five year term if the HFA certifies and provides documentation that the project owner has filed bankruptcy and the HFA is taking action to have the project discharged from the bankruptcy. The HFA Debenture shall, during this extended period, continue to bear interest as described below at HUD's published debenture rate at the earlier of initial endorsement or final endorsement. Interest shall be due and payable annually on the anniversary date of the initial claim payment. Interest is due on the full face amount of the HFA Debenture through the term of the HFA Debenture or through the date an application for final claim payment is received by the Commissioner.

(c) *HFA Debenture amount.* (1) The HFA Debenture shall be for the full initial claim amount as determined under § 266.628(a)(1) (minus any excess funds returned to HUD under § 266.628(a)(3)).

(2) The full amount of the HFA Debenture shall be payable to HUD upon maturity, unless the HFA Debenture is canceled because of:

(i) A reinstatement of the contract of insurance under § 266.634; or

(ii) Final claim settlement under § 266.654.

(d) *HFA Debenture interest rate.* The HFA Debenture shall bear interest at HUD's published debenture rate at the earlier of initial endorsement or final endorsement. Interest shall be due and payable annually on the anniversary date of the initial claim payment and on the date of redemption when redeemed or canceled before an anniversary date. Interest shall be computed on the full face amount of the HFA Debenture through the term of the HFA Debenture.

(e) *Form of HFA Debenture.* The HFA Debenture should follow the standard form of a State/Municipal Debenture issued under the Uniform Commercial Code, where applicable, and shall be supported by the full faith and credit of the HFA. For HFAs that operate as departments or divisions of States or units of local government and where

such HFAs cannot pledge the full faith and credit of the HFA, such HFAs may collateralize their obligation through a letter of credit, reinsurance, or other forms of credit acceptable to the Commissioner.

(f) *Debenture registration.* Unless otherwise required by law, including State or local laws, or other governing bodies, HUD will not require the HFA Debenture to be "Registered" (with the Securities and Exchange Commission) as it is a direct, or private, placement, and not a public offering, that is supported by the full faith and credit of the HFA.

§ 266.640 Foreclosure and acquisition.

The HFA is not required to foreclose the insured mortgage. It may accept a deed-in-lieu of foreclosure.

§ 266.642 Appraisals.

Where actions taken or caused to be taken by the HFA have the effect of the recovery of less than the face amount of the HFA Debenture held by HUD, an appraisal should be made to determine the value of the project. The appraisal should assume a willing buyer and a willing seller. The appraisal must be done within the 45-day period immediately preceding the date when the HFA files an application for final claim settlement. If at the time of final claim settlement the HFA has not sold the project, an appraisal should be made to determine the value of the project at its highest and best use.

§ 266.644 Application for final claim settlement.

The HFA shall file an application for final settlement in accordance with the Commissioner's administrative procedures not later than 30 days after any of the following:

(a) Sale of the property after foreclosure or after acquisition by deed-in-lieu of foreclosure; or

(b) Expiration of the term of the HFA debenture.

§ 266.646 Determining the amount of loss.

The amount of the total loss to be shared by HUD and the HFA is equal to:

(a) The amount of the initial claim payment;

(b) Plus all items set forth in §266.648; and

(c) Less all items set forth in §266.650.

§266.648 Items included in total loss.

In computing the total loss, the following items are added to the amount described in §266.646(a):

(a) The amount of all payments that the HFA made from its own funds and not from project income for:

(1) Taxes, special assessments, and water bills that are liens before the Mortgage; and

(2) Fire and hazard insurance on the property.

(b) A reasonable amount of acquisition costs actually paid by the HFA. These costs may not include loss or damage resulting from the invalidity or unenforceability of the Mortgage lien or the unmarketability of the Mortgagor's title.

(c) Reasonable payments that the HFA made from its own funds and not from project income for:

(1) Preservation, operation and maintenance of the property;

(2) Repairs necessary to meet the requirements of local laws;

(3) Expenses in connection with the sale of property; and

(4) Bankruptcy expenses approved by the Office of General Counsel.

(d) The amount of HFA Debenture interest paid by the HFA to HUD.

§266.650 Items deducted from total loss.

In computing insurance benefits, the following items are deducted from the amounts described in §266.646(a) and (b):

(a) All amounts received by the HFA on account of the mortgage after the date of default;

(b) All cash, and/or funds related to the mortgaged property, including deposits and escrows made for the account of the mortgagor that the HFA holds (or to which it is entitled);

(c) The amount of any undrawn balance under a letter of credit that the HFA accepted in lieu of a cash deposit for an escrow agreement;

(d) Any net income from the mortgaged property/project that the HFA received after the date of default.

(e) The proceeds from the sale of the project or the appraised value of the project as provided in §266.642 as follows:

(1) If the HFA disposes of the project through a negotiated sale, the amount deducted shall be the higher of the sales price or the appraised value.

(2) If the HFA disposes of the project through a competitive bid procedure approved by the Commissioner, the amount deducted shall be the sales price, even if it is lower than the appraised value.

(3) If the HFA has not disposed of the project within 5 years from the date of issuance of the HFA Debentures (unless an extension has been granted pursuant to §266.638), the amount deducted shall be the appraised value.

(f) Any and all claims that the HFA has acquired in connection with the acquisition and sale of the property. Claims include but are not limited to returned premiums from canceled insurance policies, interest on investments of reserve for replacement funds, tax refunds, refunds of deposits left with utility companies, and amounts received as proceeds of a receivership.

(g) The amount of daily HFA Debenture interest accrued but not paid from the anniversary date of the last HFA Debenture interest payment to the date an application for final claim payment is received by the Commissioner.

§266.652 Determining share of loss.

The total loss computed in §266.646 shall be shared by HUD and the HFA in accordance with their respective percentage of risk as specified in the note and the addendum to the Risk-Sharing Agreement between HUD and the HFA.

§266.654 Final claim settlement and HFA Debenture redemption.

(a) *Final claim payment.* If the initial claim amount, as determined under §266.628(a)(1), is less than HUD's share of the loss, HUD shall make a final claim payment to the HFA that is equal to the difference between HUD's share of the loss and the initial claim amount and shall return the HFA Debenture to the HFA for cancellation.

(b) *HFA reimbursement payment.* If the initial claim amount, as determined under § 266.628(a)(1), is more than HUD's share of the loss, the HFA shall, within 30 days of notification by HUD of the amount due, remit to HUD an amount that is equal to the difference between the initial claim amount and HUD's share of the loss. The funds must be remitted in a manner prescribed in the Commissioner's administrative procedures. The HFA Debenture will be considered redeemed upon receipt of the cash payment. A 5 percent penalty will be charged and interest at the debenture rate will begin to accrue if the cash payment is not received within the prescribed period. If an HFA is in default under an existing debenture and files a claim on another project under this part, HUD will charge the HFA's Dedicated Account for the amount owed the Department. In cases of top-tier or A-rated HFA's which are not required to maintain a Dedicated Account, HUD will inform the rating agencies of the HFA's failure to pay on their debt obligation and of its violation of the Risk-Sharing Agreement.

(c) *Losses.* Losses sustained as a consequence of the (sole) negligence of an HFA (*e.g.,* failure to acquire adequate hazard insurance where such insurance is available) shall be the sole obligation of the HFA, notwithstanding the risk apportionment otherwise agreed to by HUD and the HFA.

(d) *Supplemental claim.* Any supplemental claim must be filed within one year from date of final claim settlement.

§ 266.656 Recovery of costs after final claim settlement.

If, after final claim settlement, the HFA recovers additional sums as the result of the sale of the project or otherwise, the total amount of such recovery shall be shared by HUD and the HFA in accordance with the prescribed percentage of shared risk.

§ 266.658 Program monitoring and compliance.

HUD will monitor the performance of the HFA for compliance with the provisions of this subpart.

PART 267—CREDIT RISK RETENTION

Subpart A—Authority, Purpose, Scope and Definitions

Sec.
267.1 Credit risk retention exceptions and exemptions for HUD programs.
267.2 Definitions.

Subpart B—Credit Risk Retention

267.3 Base risk retention requirement.
267.4 Standard risk retention.
267.5 Revolving pool securitizations.
267.6 Eligible ABCP conduits.
267.7 Commercial mortgage-backed securities.
267.8 Federal National Mortgage Association and Federal Home Loan Mortgage Corporation ABS.
267.9 Open market CLOs.
267.10 Qualified tender option bonds.

Subpart C—Transfer of Risk Retention

267.11 Allocation of risk retention to an originator.
267.12 Hedging, transfer and financing prohibitions.

Subpart D—Exceptions and Exemptions

267.13 Exemption for qualified residential mortgages.
267.14 Definitions applicable to qualifying commercial loans, commercial real estate loans, and automobile loans.
267.15 Qualifying commercial loans, commercial real estate loans, and automobile loans.
267.16 Underwriting standards for qualifying commercial loans.
267.17 Underwriting standards for qualifying CRE loans.
267.18 Underwriting standards for qualifying automobile loans.
267.19 General exemptions.
267.20 Safe harbor for certain foreign-related transactions.
267.21 Additional exemptions.
267.22 Periodic review of the QRM definition, exempted three-to-four unit residential mortgage loans, and community-focused residential mortgage exemption.

AUTHORITY: 15 U.S.C. 78-o-11; 42 U.S.C. 3535(d).

SOURCE: 79 FR 77740, Dec. 24, 2014, unless otherwise noted.

Subpart A—Authority, Purpose, Scope and Definitions

§267.1 Credit risk retention exceptions and exemptions for HUD programs.

The credit risk retention regulations codified at 12 CFR part 43 (Office of the Comptroller of the Currency); 12 CFR part 244 (Federal Reserve System); 12 CFR part 373 (Federal Deposit Insurance Corporation); 17 CFR part 246 (Securities and Exchange Commission); and 12 CFR part 1234 (Federal Housing Finance Agency) include exceptions and exemptions in subpart D of each of these codified regulations for certain transactions involving programs and entities under the jurisdiction of the Department of Housing and Urban Development.

[79 FR 77766, Dec. 24, 2014]

§267.2 Definitions.

For purposes of this part, the following definitions apply:

ABS interest means:

(1) Any type of interest or obligation issued by an issuing entity, whether or not in certificated form, including a security, obligation, beneficial interest or residual interest (other than an uncertificated regular interest in a REMIC that is held by another REMIC, where both REMICs are part of the same structure and a single REMIC in that structure issues ABS interests to investors, or a non-economic residual interest issued by a REMIC), payments on which are primarily dependent on the cash flows of the collateral owned or held by the issuing entity; and

(2) Does not include common or preferred stock, limited liability interests, partnership interests, trust certificates, or similar interests that:

(i) Are issued primarily to evidence ownership of the issuing entity; and

(ii) The payments, if any, on which are not primarily dependent on the cash flows of the collateral held by the issuing entity; and

(3) Does not include the right to receive payments for services provided by the holder of such right, including servicing, trustee services and custodial services.

Affiliate of, or a person *affiliated* with, a specified person means a person that directly, or indirectly through one or more intermediaries, controls, or is controlled by, or is under common control with, the person specified.

Appropriate Federal banking agency has the same meaning as in section 3 of the Federal Deposit Insurance Act (12 U.S.C. 1813).

Asset means a self-liquidating financial asset (including but not limited to a loan, lease, mortgage, or receivable).

Asset-backed security has the same meaning as in section 3(a)(79) of the Securities Exchange Act of 1934 (15 U.S.C. 78c(a)(79)).

Collateral means, with respect to any issuance of ABS interests, the assets that provide the cash flow and the servicing assets that support such cash flow for the ABS interests irrespective of the legal structure of issuance, including security interests in assets or other property of the issuing entity, fractional undivided property interests in the assets or other property of the issuing entity, or any other property interest in or rights to cash flow from such assets and related servicing assets. Assets or other property *collateralize* an issuance of ABS interests if the assets or property serve as collateral for such issuance.

Commercial real estate loan has the same meaning as in §267.14.

Commission means the Securities and Exchange Commission.

Control including the terms "controlling," "controlled by" and "under common control with":

(1) Means the possession, direct or indirect, of the power to direct or cause the direction of the management and policies of a person, whether through the ownership of voting securities, by contract, or otherwise.

(2) Without limiting the foregoing, a person shall be considered to control another person if the first person:

(i) Owns, controls or holds with power to vote 25 percent or more of any class of voting securities of the other person; or

(ii) Controls in any manner the election of a majority of the directors, trustees or persons performing similar functions of the other person.

Credit risk means:

(1) The risk of loss that could result from the failure of the borrower in the case of a securitized asset, or the issuing entity in the case of an ABS interest in the issuing entity, to make required payments of principal or interest on the asset or ABS interest on a timely basis;

(2) The risk of loss that could result from bankruptcy, insolvency, or a similar proceeding with respect to the borrower or issuing entity, as appropriate; or

(3) The effect that significant changes in the underlying credit quality of the asset or ABS interest may have on the market value of the asset or ABS interest.

Creditor has the same meaning as in 15 U.S.C. 1602(g).

Depositor means:

(1) The person that receives or purchases and transfers or sells the securitized assets to the issuing entity;

(2) The sponsor, in the case of a securitization transaction where there is not an intermediate transfer of the assets from the sponsor to the issuing entity; or

(3) The person that receives or purchases and transfers or sells the securitized assets to the issuing entity in the case of a securitization transaction where the person transferring or selling the securitized assets directly to the issuing entity is itself a trust.

Eligible horizontal residual interest means, with respect to any securitization transaction, an ABS interest in the issuing entity:

(1) That is an interest in a single class or multiple classes in the issuing entity, provided that each interest meets, individually or in the aggregate, all of the requirements of this definition;

(2) With respect to which, on any payment date or allocation date on which the issuing entity has insufficient funds to satisfy its obligation to pay all contractual interest or principal due, any resulting shortfall will reduce amounts payable to the eligible horizontal residual interest prior to any reduction in the amounts payable to any other ABS interest, whether through loss allocation, operation of the priority of payments, or any other governing contractual provision (until

the amount of such ABS interest is reduced to zero); and

(3) That, with the exception of any non-economic REMIC residual interest, has the most subordinated claim to payments of both principal and interest by the issuing entity.

Eligible horizontal cash reserve account means an account meeting the requirements of § 267.4(b).

Eligible vertical interest means, with respect to any securitization transaction, a single vertical security or an interest in each class of ABS interests in the issuing entity issued as part of the securitization transaction that constitutes the same proportion of each such class.

Federal banking agencies means the Office of the Comptroller of the Currency, the Board of Governors of the Federal Reserve System, and the Federal Deposit Insurance Corporation.

GAAP means generally accepted accounting principles as used in the United States.

Issuing entity means, with respect to a securitization transaction, the trust or other entity:

(1) That owns or holds the pool of assets to be securitized; and

(2) In whose name the asset-backed securities are issued.

Majority-owned affiliate of a person means an entity (other than the issuing entity) that, directly or indirectly, majority controls, is majority controlled by or is under common majority control with, such person. For purposes of this definition, majority control means ownership of more than 50 percent of the equity of an entity, or ownership of any other controlling financial interest in the entity, as determined under GAAP.

Originator means a person who:

(1) Through an extension of credit or otherwise, creates an asset that collateralizes an asset-backed security; and

(2) Sells the asset directly or indirectly to a securitizer or issuing entity.

REMIC has the same meaning as in 26 U.S.C. 860D.

Residential mortgage means:

(1) A transaction that is a covered transaction as defined in § 1026.43(b) of Regulation Z (12 CFR 1026.43(b)(1));

(2) Any transaction that is exempt from the definition of "covered transaction" under § 1026.43(a) of Regulation Z (12 CFR 1026.43(a)); and

(3) Any other loan secured by a residential structure that contains one to four units, whether or not that structure is attached to real property, including an individual condominium or cooperative unit and, if used as a residence, a mobile home or trailer.

Retaining sponsor means, with respect to a securitization transaction, the sponsor that has retained or caused to be retained an economic interest in the credit risk of the securitized assets pursuant to subpart B of this part.

Securitization transaction means a transaction involving the offer and sale of asset-backed securities by an issuing entity.

Securitized asset means an asset that:

(1) Is transferred, sold, or conveyed to an issuing entity; and

(2) Collateralizes the ABS interests issued by the issuing entity.

Securitizer means, with respect to a securitization transaction, either:

(1) The depositor of the asset-backed securities (if the depositor is not the sponsor); or

(2) The sponsor of the asset-backed securities.

Servicer means any person responsible for the management or collection of the securitized assets or making allocations or distributions to holders of the ABS interests, but does not include a trustee for the issuing entity or the asset-backed securities that makes allocations or distributions to holders of the ABS interests if the trustee receives such allocations or distributions from a servicer and the trustee does not otherwise perform the functions of a servicer.

Servicing assets means rights or other assets designed to assure the servicing or timely distribution of proceeds to ABS interest holders and rights or other assets that are related or incidental to purchasing or otherwise acquiring and holding the issuing entity's securitized assets. Servicing assets include amounts received by the issuing entity as proceeds of securitized assets, including proceeds of rights or other assets, whether as remittances by obligors or as other recoveries.

Single vertical security means, with respect to any securitization transaction, an ABS interest entitling the sponsor to a specified percentage of the amounts paid on each class of ABS interests in the issuing entity (other than such single vertical security).

Sponsor means a person who organizes and initiates a securitization transaction by selling or transferring assets, either directly or indirectly, including through an affiliate, to the issuing entity.

State has the same meaning as in Section 3(a)(16) of the Securities Exchange Act of 1934 (15 U.S.C. 78c(a)(16)).

United States or U.S. means the United States of America, including its territories and possessions, any State of the United States, and the District of Columbia.

Wholly-owned affiliate means a person (other than an issuing entity) that, directly or indirectly, wholly controls, is wholly controlled by, or is wholly under common control with, another person. For purposes of this definition, "wholly controls" means ownership of 100 percent of the equity of an entity.

Subpart B—Credit Risk Retention

§ 267.3 Base risk retention requirement.

(a) *Base risk retention requirement.* Except as otherwise provided in this part, the sponsor of a securitization transaction (or majority-owned affiliate of the sponsor) shall retain an economic interest in the credit risk of the securitized assets in accordance with any one of §§ 267.4 through 267.10. Credit risk in securitized assets required to be retained and held by any person for purposes of compliance with this part, whether a sponsor, an originator, an originator-seller, or a third-party purchaser, except as otherwise provided in this part, may be acquired and held by any of such person's majority-owned affiliates (other than an issuing entity).

(b) *Multiple sponsors.* If there is more than one sponsor of a securitization transaction, it shall be the responsibility of each sponsor to ensure that at least one of the sponsors of the securitization transaction (or at least one of their majority-owned or wholly-owned affiliates, as applicable) retains an economic interest in the credit risk of the securitized assets in accordance with any one of §§ 267.4, 267.5, 267.8, 267.9, or 267.10.

§ 267.4   Standard risk retention.

(a) *General requirement.* Except as provided in §§ 267.5 through 267.10, the sponsor of a securitization transaction must retain an eligible vertical interest or eligible horizontal residual interest, or any combination thereof, in accordance with the requirements of this section.

(1) If the sponsor retains only an eligible vertical interest as its required risk retention, the sponsor must retain an eligible vertical interest in a percentage of not less than 5 percent.

(2) If the sponsor retains only an eligible horizontal residual interest as its required risk retention, the amount of the interest must equal at least 5 percent of the fair value of all ABS interests in the issuing entity issued as a part of the securitization transaction, determined using a fair value measurement framework under GAAP.

(3) If the sponsor retains both an eligible vertical interest and an eligible horizontal residual interest as its required risk retention, the percentage of the fair value of the eligible horizontal residual interest and the percentage of the eligible vertical interest must equal at least five.

(4) The percentage of the eligible vertical interest, eligible horizontal residual interest, or combination thereof retained by the sponsor must be determined as of the closing date of the securitization transaction.

(b) *Option to hold base amount in eligible horizontal cash reserve account.* In lieu of retaining all or any part of an eligible horizontal residual interest under paragraph (a) of this section, the sponsor may, at closing of the securitization transaction, cause to be established and funded, in cash, an eligible horizontal cash reserve account in the amount equal to the fair value of such eligible horizontal residual interest or part thereof, provided that the account meets all of the following conditions:

(1) The account is held by the trustee (or person performing similar func-

tions) in the name and for the benefit of the issuing entity;

(2) Amounts in the account are invested only in cash and cash equivalents; and

(3) Until all ABS interests in the issuing entity are paid in full, or the issuing entity is dissolved:

(i) Amounts in the account shall be released only to:

(A) Satisfy payments on ABS interests in the issuing entity on any payment date on which the issuing entity has insufficient funds from any source to satisfy an amount due on any ABS interest; or

(B) Pay critical expenses of the trust unrelated to credit risk on any payment date on which the issuing entity has insufficient funds from any source to pay such expenses and:

(*1*) Such expenses, in the absence of available funds in the eligible horizontal cash reserve account, would be paid prior to any payments to holders of ABS interests; and

(*2*) Such payments are made to parties that are not affiliated with the sponsor; and

(ii) Interest (or other earnings) on investments made in accordance with paragraph (b)(2) of this section may be released once received by the account.

(c) *Disclosures.* A sponsor relying on this section shall provide, or cause to be provided, to potential investors, under the caption "Credit Risk Retention", a reasonable period of time prior to the sale of the asset-backed securities in the securitization transaction the following disclosures in written form and within the time frames set forth in this paragraph (c):

(1) *Horizontal interest.* With respect to any eligible horizontal residual interest held under paragraph (a) of this section, a sponsor must disclose:

(i) A reasonable period of time prior to the sale of an asset-backed security issued in the same offering of ABS interests,

(A) The fair value (expressed as a percentage of the fair value of all of the ABS interests issued in the securitization transaction and dollar amount (or corresponding amount in the foreign currency in which the ABS interests are issued, as applicable)) of the eligible horizontal residual interest that the sponsor expects to retain at the closing of the securitization transaction. If the specific prices, sizes, or rates of interest of each tranche of the securitization are not available, the sponsor must disclose a range of fair values (expressed as a percentage of the fair value of all of the ABS interests issued in the securitization transaction and dollar amount (or corresponding amount in the foreign currency in which the ABS interests are issued, as applicable)) of the eligible horizontal residual interest that the sponsor expects to retain at the close of the securitization transaction based on a range of bona fide estimates or specified prices, sizes, or rates of interest of each tranche of the securitization. A sponsor disclosing a range of fair values based on a range of bona fide estimates or specified prices, sizes or rates of interest of each tranche of the securitization must also disclose the method by which it determined any range of prices, tranche sizes, or rates of interest.

(B) A description of the material terms of the eligible horizontal residual interest to be retained by the sponsor;

(C) A description of the valuation methodology used to calculate the fair values or range of fair values of all classes of ABS interests, including any portion of the eligible horizontal residual interest retained by the sponsor;

(D) All key inputs and assumptions or a comprehensive description of such key inputs and assumptions that were used in measuring the estimated total fair value or range of fair values of all classes of ABS interests, including the eligible horizontal residual interest to be retained by the sponsor.

(E) To the extent applicable to the valuation methodology used, the disclosure required in paragraph (c)(1)(i)(D) of this section shall include, but should not be limited to, quantitative information about each of the following:

(1) Discount rates;

(2) Loss given default (recovery);

(3) Prepayment rates;

(4) Default rates;

(5) Lag time between default and recovery; and

(6) The basis of forward interest rates used.

(F) The disclosure required in paragraphs (c)(1)(i)(C) and (D) of this section shall include, at a minimum, descriptions of all inputs and assumptions that either could have a material impact on the fair value calculation or would be material to a prospective investor's ability to evaluate the sponsor's fair value calculations. To the extent the disclosure required in this paragraph (c)(1) includes a description of a curve or curves, the description shall include a description of the methodology that was used to derive each curve and a description of any aspects or features of each curve that could materially impact the fair value calculation or the ability of a prospective investor to evaluate the sponsor's fair value calculation. To the extent a sponsor uses information about the securitized assets in its calculation of fair value, such information shall not be as of a date more than 60 days prior to the date of first use with investors; provided that for a subsequent issuance of ABS interests by the same issuing entity with the same sponsor for which the securitization transaction distributes amounts to investors on a quarterly or less frequent basis, such information shall not be as of a date more than 135 days prior to the date of first use with investors; provided further, that the balance or value (in accordance with the transaction documents) of the securitized assets may be increased or decreased to reflect anticipated additions or removals of assets the sponsor makes or expects to make between the cut-off date or similar date for establishing the composition of the asset pool collateralizing such asset-backed security and the closing date of the securitization.

(G) A summary description of the reference data set or other historical information used to develop the key inputs and assumptions referenced in paragraph (c)(1)(i)(D) of this section, including loss given default and default rates;

(ii) A reasonable time after the closing of the securitization transaction:

(A) The fair value (expressed as a percentage of the fair value of all of the ABS interests issued in the

551

securitization transaction and dollar amount (or corresponding amount in the foreign currency in which the ABS are issued, as applicable)) of the eligible horizontal residual interest the sponsor retained at the closing of the securitization transaction, based on actual sale prices and finalized tranche sizes;

(B) The fair value (expressed as a percentage of the fair value of all of the ABS interests issued in the securitization transaction and dollar amount (or corresponding amount in the foreign currency in which the ABS are issued, as applicable)) of the eligible horizontal residual interest that the sponsor is required to retain under this section; and

(C) To the extent the valuation methodology or any of the key inputs and assumptions that were used in calculating the fair value or range of fair values disclosed prior to sale and required under paragraph (c)(1)(i) of this section materially differs from the methodology or key inputs and assumptions used to calculate the fair value at the time of closing, descriptions of those material differences.

(iii) If the sponsor retains risk through the funding of an eligible horizontal cash reserve account:

(A) The amount to be placed (or that is placed) by the sponsor in the eligible horizontal cash reserve account at closing, and the fair value (expressed as a percentage of the fair value of all of the ABS interests issued in the securitization transaction and dollar amount (or corresponding amount in the foreign currency in which the ABS interests are issued, as applicable)) of the eligible horizontal residual interest that the sponsor is required to fund through the eligible horizontal cash reserve account in order for such account, together with other retained interests, to satisfy the sponsor's risk retention requirement;

(B) A description of the material terms of the eligible horizontal cash reserve account; and

(C) The disclosures required in paragraphs (c)(1)(i) and (ii) of this section.

(2) *Vertical interest.* With respect to any eligible vertical interest retained under paragraph (a) of this section, the sponsor must disclose:

(i) A reasonable period of time prior to the sale of an asset-backed security issued in the same offering of ABS interests,

(A) The form of the eligible vertical interest;

(B) The percentage that the sponsor is required to retain as a vertical interest under this section; and

(C) A description of the material terms of the vertical interest and the amount that the sponsor expects to retain at the closing of the securitization transaction.

(ii) A reasonable time after the closing of the securitization transaction, the amount of the vertical interest the sponsor retained at closing, if that amount is materially different from the amount disclosed under paragraph (c)(2)(i) of this section.

(d) *Record maintenance.* A sponsor must retain the certifications and disclosures required in paragraphs (a) and (c) of this section in its records and must provide the disclosure upon request to the Commission and its appropriate Federal banking agency, if any, until three years after all ABS interests are no longer outstanding.

§ 267.5 Revolving pool securitizations.

(a) *Definitions.* For purposes of this section, the following definitions apply:

Revolving pool securitization means an issuing entity that is established to issue on multiple issuance dates more than one series, class, subclass, or tranche of asset-backed securities that are collateralized by a common pool of securitized assets that will change in composition over time, and that does not monetize excess interest and fees from its securitized assets.

Seller's interest means an ABS interest or ABS interests:

(1) Collateralized by the securitized assets and servicing assets owned or held by the issuing entity, other than the following that are not considered a component of seller's interest:

(i) Servicing assets that have been allocated as collateral only for a specific series in connection with administering the revolving pool securitization, such as a principal accumulation or interest reserve account; and

(ii) Assets that are not eligible under the terms of the securitization transaction to be included when determining whether the revolving pool securitization holds aggregate securitized assets in specified proportions to aggregate outstanding investor ABS interests issued; and

(2) That is *pari passu* with each series of investor ABS interests issued, or partially or fully subordinated to one or more series in identical or varying amounts, with respect to the allocation of all distributions and losses with respect to the securitized assets prior to early amortization of the revolving securitization (as specified in the securitization transaction documents); and

(3) That adjusts for fluctuations in the outstanding principal balance of the securitized assets in the pool.

(b) *General requirement.* A sponsor satisfies the risk retention requirements of §267.3 with respect to a securitization transaction for which the issuing entity is a revolving pool securitization if the sponsor maintains a seller's interest of not less than 5 percent of the aggregate unpaid principal balance of all outstanding investor ABS interests in the issuing entity.

(c) *Measuring the seller's interest.* In measuring the seller's interest for purposes of meeting the requirements of paragraph (b) of this section:

(1) The unpaid principal balance of the securitized assets for the numerator of the 5 percent ratio shall not include assets of the types excluded from the definition of seller's interest in paragraph (a) of this section;

(2) The aggregate unpaid principal balance of outstanding investor ABS interests in the denominator of the 5 percent ratio may be reduced by the amount of funds held in a segregated principal accumulation account for the repayment of outstanding investor ABS interests, if:

(i) The terms of the securitization transaction documents prevent funds in the principal accumulation account from being applied for any purpose other than the repayment of the unpaid principal of outstanding investor ABS interests; and

(ii) Funds in that account are invested only in the types of assets in which funds held in an eligible horizontal cash reserve account pursuant to §267.4 are permitted to be invested;

(3) If the terms of the securitization transaction documents set minimum required seller's interest as a proportion of the unpaid principal balance of outstanding investor ABS interests for one or more series issued, rather than as a proportion of the aggregate outstanding investor ABS interests in all outstanding series combined, the percentage of the seller's interest for each such series must, when combined with the percentage of any minimum seller's interest set by reference to the aggregate outstanding investor ABS interests, equal at least 5 percent;

(4) The 5 percent test must be determined and satisfied at the closing of each issuance of ABS interests to investors by the issuing entity, and

(i) At least monthly at a seller's interest measurement date specified under the securitization transaction documents, until no ABS interest in the issuing entity is held by any person not a wholly-owned affiliate of the sponsor; or

(ii) If the revolving pool securitization fails to meet the 5 percent test as of any date described in paragraph (c)(4)(i) of this section, and the securitization transaction documents specify a cure period, the 5 percent test must be determined and satisfied within the earlier of the cure period, or one month after the date described in paragraph (c)(4)(i).

(d) *Measuring outstanding investor ABS interests.* In measuring the amount of outstanding investor ABS interests for purposes of this section, ABS interests held for the life of such ABS interests by the sponsor or its wholly-owned affiliates may be excluded.

(e) *Holding and retention of the seller's interest; legacy trusts.* (1) Notwithstanding §267.12(a), the seller's interest, and any offsetting horizontal retention interest retained pursuant to paragraph (g) of this section, must be retained by the sponsor or by one or more wholly-owned affiliates of the sponsor, including one or more depositors of the revolving pool securitization.

(2) If one revolving pool securitization issues collateral certificates representing a beneficial interest in all or a portion of the securitized assets held by that securitization to another revolving pool securitization, which in turn issues ABS interests for which the collateral certificates are all or a portion of the securitized assets, a sponsor may satisfy the requirements of paragraphs (b) and (c) of this section by retaining the seller's interest for the assets represented by the collateral certificates through either of the revolving pool securitizations, so long as both revolving pool securitizations are retained at the direction of the same sponsor or its wholly-owned affiliates.

(3) If the sponsor retains the seller's interest associated with the collateral certificates at the level of the revolving pool securitization that issues those collateral certificates, the proportion of the seller's interest required by paragraph (b) of this section retained at that level must equal the proportion that the principal balance of the securitized assets represented by the collateral certificates bears to the principal balance of the securitized assets in the revolving pool securitization that issues the ABS interests, as of each measurement date required by paragraph (c) of this section.

(f) *Offset for pool-level excess funding account.* The 5 percent seller's interest required on each measurement date by paragraph (c) of this section may be reduced on a dollar-for-dollar basis by the balance, as of such date, of an excess funding account in the form of a segregated account that:

(1) Is funded in the event of a failure to meet the minimum seller's interest requirements or other requirement to maintain a minimum balance of securitized assets under the securitization transaction documents by distributions otherwise payable to the holder of the seller's interest;

(2) Is invested only in the types of assets in which funds held in a horizontal cash reserve account pursuant to § 267.4 are permitted to be invested; and

(3) In the event of an early amortization, makes payments of amounts held in the account to holders of investor ABS interests in the same manner as payments to holders of investor ABS interests of amounts received on securitized assets.

(g) *Combined seller's interests and horizontal interest retention.* The 5 percent seller's interest required on each measurement date by paragraph (c) of this section may be reduced to a percentage lower than 5 percent to the extent that, for all series of investor ABS interests issued after the applicable effective date of this § 267.5, the sponsor, or notwithstanding § 267.12(a) a wholly-owned affiliate of the sponsor, retains, at a minimum, a corresponding percentage of the fair value of ABS interests issued in each series, in the form of one or more of the horizontal residual interests meeting the requirements of paragraphs (h) or (i).

(h) *Residual ABS interests in excess interest and fees.* The sponsor may take the offset described in paragraph (g) of this section for a residual ABS interest in excess interest and fees, whether certificated or uncertificated, in a single or multiple classes, subclasses, or tranches, that meets, individually or in the aggregate, the requirements of this paragraph (h);

(1) Each series of the revolving pool securitization distinguishes between the series' share of the interest and fee cash flows and the series' share of the principal repayment cash flows from the securitized assets collateralizing the revolving pool securitization, which may according to the terms of the securitization transaction documents, include not only the series' ratable share of such cash flows but also excess cash flows available from other series;

(2) The residual ABS interest's claim to any part of the series' share of the interest and fee cash flows for any interest payment period is subordinated to all accrued and payable interest due on the payment date to more senior ABS interests in the series for that period, and further reduced by the series' share of losses, including defaults on principal of the securitized assets collateralizing the revolving pool securitization (whether incurred in that period or carried over from prior periods) to the extent that such payments would have been included in

amounts payable to more senior interests in the series;

(3) The revolving pool securitization continues to revolve, with one or more series, classes, subclasses, or tranches of asset-backed securities that are collateralized by a common pool of assets that change in composition over time; and

(4) For purposes of taking the offset described in paragraph (g) of this section, the sponsor determines the fair value of the residual ABS interest in excess interest and fees, and the fair value of the series of outstanding investor ABS interests to which it is subordinated and supports using the fair value measurement framework under GAAP, as of:

(i) The closing of the securitization transaction issuing the supported ABS interests; and

(ii) The seller's interest measurement dates described in paragraph (c)(4) of this section, except that for these periodic determinations the sponsor must update the fair value of the residual ABS interest in excess interest and fees for the numerator of the percentage ratio, but may at the sponsor's option continue to use the fair values determined in (h)(4)(i) for the outstanding investor ABS interests in the denominator.

(i) *Offsetting eligible horizontal residual interest.* The sponsor may take the offset described in paragraph (g) of this section for ABS interests that would meet the definition of eligible horizontal residual interests in §267.2 but for the sponsor's simultaneous holding of subordinated seller's interests, residual ABS interests in excess interests and fees, or a combination of the two, if:

(1) The sponsor complies with all requirements of paragraphs (b) through (e) of this section for its holdings of subordinated seller's interest, and paragraph (h) for its holdings of residual ABS interests in excess interests and fees, as applicable;

(2) For purposes of taking the offset described in paragraph (g) of this section, the sponsor determines the fair value of the eligible horizontal residual interest as a percentage of the fair value of the outstanding investor ABS interests in the series supported by the

eligible horizontal residual interest, determined using the fair value measurement framework under GAAP:

(i) As of the closing of the securitization transaction issuing the supported ABS interests; and

(ii) Without including in the numerator of the percentage ratio any fair value based on:

(A) The subordinated seller's interest or residual ABS interest in excess interest and fees;

(B) the interest payable to the sponsor on the eligible horizontal residual interest, if the sponsor is including the value of residual ABS interest in excess interest and fees pursuant to paragraph (h) of this section in taking the offset in paragraph (g) of this section; and,

(C) the principal payable to the sponsor on the eligible horizontal residual interest, if the sponsor is including the value of the seller's interest pursuant to paragraphs (b) through (f) of this section and distributions on that seller's interest are available to reduce charge-offs that would otherwise be allocated to reduce principal payable to the offset eligible horizontal residual interest.

(j) *Specified dates.* A sponsor using data about the revolving pool securitization's collateral, or ABS interests previously issued, to determine the closing-date percentage of a seller's interest, residual ABS interest in excess interest and fees, or eligible horizontal residual interest pursuant to this §267.5 may use such data prepared as of specified dates if:

(1) The sponsor describes the specified dates in the disclosures required by paragraph (k) of this section; and

(2) The dates are no more than 60 days prior to the date of first use with investors of disclosures required for the interest by paragraph (k) of this section, or for revolving pool securitizations that make distributions to investors on a quarterly or less frequent basis, no more than 135 days prior to the date of first use with investors of such disclosures.

(k) *Disclosure and record maintenance.* (1) *Disclosure.* A sponsor relying on this section shall provide, or cause to be provided, to potential investors, under the caption "Credit Risk Retention" the following disclosure in written form and within the time frames set forth in this paragraph (k):

(i) A reasonable period of time prior to the sale of an asset-backed security, a description of the material terms of the seller's interest, and the percentage of the seller's interest that the sponsor expects to retain at the closing of the securitization transaction, measured in accordance with the requirements of this § 267.5, as a percentage of the aggregate unpaid principal balance of all outstanding investor ABS interests issued, or as a percentage of the aggregate unpaid principal balance of outstanding investor ABS interests for one or more series issued, as required by the terms of the securitization transaction;

(ii) A reasonable time after the closing of the securitization transaction, the amount of seller's interest the sponsor retained at closing, if that amount is materially different from the amount disclosed under paragraph (k)(1)(i) of this section; and

(iii) A description of the material terms of any horizontal residual interests offsetting the seller's interest in accordance with paragraphs (g), (h), and (i) of this section; and

(iv) Disclosure of the fair value of those horizontal residual interests retained by the sponsor for the series being offered to investors and described in the disclosures, as a percentage of the fair value of the outstanding investor ABS interests issued, described in the same manner and within the same timeframes required for disclosure of the fair values of eligible horizontal residual interests specified in § 267.4(c).

(2) *Adjusted data.* Disclosures required by this paragraph (k) to be made a reasonable period of time prior to the sale of an asset-backed security of the amount of seller's interest, residual ABS interest in excess interest and fees, or eligible horizontal residual interest may include adjustments to the amount of securitized assets for additions or removals the sponsor expects to make before the closing date and adjustments to the amount of outstanding investor ABS interests for expected increases and decreases of those interests under the control of the sponsor.

(3) *Record maintenance.* A sponsor must retain the disclosures required in paragraph (k)(1) of this section in its records and must provide the disclosure upon request to the Commission and its appropriate Federal banking agency, if any, until three years after all ABS interests are no longer outstanding.

(l) *Early amortization of all outstanding series.* A sponsor that organizes a revolving pool securitization that relies on this § 267.5 to satisfy the risk retention requirements of § 267.3, does not violate the requirements of this part if its seller's interest falls below the level required by § 267. 5 after the revolving pool securitization commences early amortization, pursuant to the terms of the securitization transaction documents, of all series of outstanding investor ABS interests, if:

(1) The sponsor was in full compliance with the requirements of this section on all measurement dates specified in paragraph (c) of this section prior to the commencement of early amortization;

(2) The terms of the seller's interest continue to make it *pari passu* with or subordinate in identical or varying amounts to each series of outstanding investor ABS interests issued with respect to the allocation of all distributions and losses with respect to the securitized assets;

(3) The terms of any horizontal interest relied upon by the sponsor pursuant to paragraph (g) to offset the minimum seller's interest amount continue to require the interests to absorb losses in accordance with the terms of paragraph (h) or (i) of this section, as applicable; and

(4) The revolving pool securitization issues no additional ABS interests after early amortization is initiated to any person not a wholly-owned affiliate of the sponsor, either at the time of issuance or during the amortization period.

§ 267.6 Eligible ABCP conduits.

(a) *Definitions.* For purposes of this section, the following additional definitions apply:

100 percent liquidity coverage means an amount equal to the outstanding balance of all ABCP issued by the conduit plus any accrued and unpaid interest without regard to the performance of the ABS interests held by the ABCP conduit and without regard to any credit enhancement.

ABCP means asset-backed commercial paper that has a maturity at the time of issuance not exceeding 397 days, exclusive of days of grace, or any renewal thereof the maturity of which is likewise limited.

ABCP conduit means an issuing entity with respect to ABCP.

Eligible ABCP conduit means an ABCP conduit, *provided that:*

(1) The ABCP conduit is bankruptcy remote or otherwise isolated for insolvency purposes from the sponsor of the ABCP conduit and from any intermediate SPV;

(2) The ABS interests acquired by the ABCP conduit are:

(i) ABS interests collateralized solely by assets originated by an originator-seller and by servicing assets;

(ii) Special units of beneficial interest (or similar ABS interests) in a trust or special purpose vehicle that retains legal title to leased property underlying leases originated by an originator-seller that were transferred to an intermediate SPV in connection with a securitization collateralized solely by such leases and by servicing assets;

(iii) ABS interests in a revolving pool securitization collateralized solely by assets originated by an originator-seller and by servicing assets; or

(iv) ABS interests described in paragraph (2)(i), (ii), or (iii) of this definition that are collateralized, in whole or in part, by assets acquired by an originator-seller in a business combination that qualifies for business combination accounting under GAAP, and, if collateralized in part, the remainder of such assets are assets described in paragraph (2)(i), (ii), or (iii) of this definition; and

(v) Acquired by the ABCP conduit in an initial issuance by or on behalf of an intermediate SPV:

(A) Directly from the intermediate SPV,

(B) From an underwriter of the ABS interests issued by the intermediate SPV, or

(C) From another person who acquired the ABS interests directly from the intermediate SPV;

(3) The ABCP conduit is collateralized solely by ABS interests acquired from intermediate SPVs as described in paragraph (2) of this definition and servicing assets; and

(4) A regulated liquidity provider has entered into a legally binding commitment to provide 100 percent liquidity coverage (in the form of a lending facility, an asset purchase agreement, a repurchase agreement, or other similar arrangement) to all the ABCP issued by the ABCP conduit by lending to, purchasing ABCP issued by, or purchasing assets from, the ABCP conduit in the event that funds are required to repay maturing ABCP issued by the ABCP conduit. With respect to the 100 percent liquidity coverage, in the event that the ABCP conduit is unable for any reason to repay maturing ABCP issued by the issuing entity, the liquidity provider shall be obligated to pay an amount equal to any shortfall, and the total amount that may be due pursuant to the 100 percent liquidity coverage shall be equal to 100 percent of the amount of the ABCP outstanding at any time plus accrued and unpaid interest (amounts due pursuant to the required liquidity coverage may not be subject to credit performance of the ABS interests held by the ABCP conduit or reduced by the amount of credit support provided to the ABCP conduit and liquidity support that only funds performing loans or receivables or performing ABS interests does not meet the requirements of this section).

Intermediate SPV means a special purpose vehicle that:

(1) (i) Is a direct or indirect wholly-owned affiliate of the originator-seller; or

(ii) Has nominal equity owned by a trust or corporate service provider that specializes in providing independent ownership of special purpose vehicles, and such trust or corporate service provider is not affiliated with any other transaction parties;

(2) Is bankruptcy remote or otherwise isolated for insolvency purposes from the eligible ABCP conduit and from each originator-seller and each majority-owned affiliate in each case

557

that, directly or indirectly, sells or transfers assets to such intermediate SPV;

(3) Acquires assets from the originator-seller that are originated by the originator-seller or acquired by the originator-seller in the acquisition of a business that qualifies for business combination accounting under GAAP or acquires ABS interests issued by another intermediate SPV of the originator-seller that are collateralized solely by such assets; and

(4) Issues ABS interests collateralized solely by such assets, as applicable.

Originator-seller means an entity that originates assets and sells or transfers those assets, directly or through a majority-owned affiliate, to an intermediate SPV, and includes (except for the purposes of identifying the sponsorship and affiliation of an intermediate SPV pursuant to this § 267.6) any affiliate of the originator-seller that, directly or indirectly, majority controls, is majority controlled by or is under common majority control with, the originator-seller. For purposes of this definition, majority control means ownership of more than 50 percent of the equity of an entity, or ownership of any other controlling financial interest in the entity, as determined under GAAP.

Regulated liquidity provider means:

(1) A depository institution (as defined in section 3 of the Federal Deposit Insurance Act (12 U.S.C. 1813));

(2) A bank holding company (as defined in 12 U.S.C. 1841), or a subsidiary thereof;

(3) A savings and loan holding company (as defined in 12 U.S.C. 1467a), provided all or substantially all of the holding company's activities are permissible for a financial holding company under 12 U.S.C. 1843(k), or a subsidiary thereof; or

(4) A foreign bank whose home country supervisor (as defined in § 211.21 of the Federal Reserve Board's Regulation K (12 CFR 211.21)) has adopted capital standards consistent with the Capital Accord of the Basel Committee on Banking Supervision, as amended, and that is subject to such standards, or a subsidiary thereof.

(b) *In general.* An ABCP conduit sponsor satisfies the risk retention requirement of § 267.3 with respect to the issuance of ABCP by an eligible ABCP conduit in a securitization transaction if, for each ABS interest the ABCP conduit acquires from an intermediate SPV:

(1) An originator-seller of the intermediate SPV retains an economic interest in the credit risk of the assets collateralizing the ABS interest acquired by the eligible ABCP conduit in the amount and manner required under § 267.4 or § 267.5; and

(2) The ABCP conduit sponsor:

(i) Approves each originator-seller permitted to sell or transfer assets, directly or indirectly, to an intermediate SPV from which an eligible ABCP conduit acquires ABS interests;

(ii) Approves each intermediate SPV from which an eligible ABCP conduit is permitted to acquire ABS interests;

(iii) Establishes criteria governing the ABS interests, and the securitized assets underlying the ABS interests, acquired by the ABCP conduit;

(iv) Administers the ABCP conduit by monitoring the ABS interests acquired by the ABCP conduit and the assets supporting those ABS interests, arranging for debt placement, compiling monthly reports, and ensuring compliance with the ABCP conduit documents and with the ABCP conduit's credit and investment policy; and

(v) Maintains and adheres to policies and procedures for ensuring that the requirements in this paragraph (b) of this section have been met.

(c) *Originator-seller compliance with risk retention.* The use of the risk retention option provided in this section by an ABCP conduit sponsor does not relieve the originator-seller that sponsors ABS interests acquired by an eligible ABCP conduit from such originator-seller's obligation to comply with its own risk retention obligations under this part.

(d) *Disclosures*—(1) *Periodic disclosures to investors.* An ABCP conduit sponsor relying upon this section shall provide, or cause to be provided, to each purchaser of ABCP, before or contemporaneously with the first sale of ABCP to such purchaser and at least monthly thereafter, to each holder of commercial paper issued by the ABCP conduit, in writing, each of the following items of information, which shall be as of a date not more than 60 days prior to date of first use with investors:

(i) The name and form of organization of the regulated liquidity provider that provides liquidity coverage to the eligible ABCP conduit, including a description of the material terms of such liquidity coverage, and notice of any failure to fund.

(ii) With respect to each ABS interest held by the ABCP conduit:

(A) The asset class or brief description of the underlying securitized assets;

(B) The standard industrial category code (SIC Code) for the originator-seller that will retain (or has retained) pursuant to this section an interest in the securitization transaction; and

(C) A description of the percentage amount of risk retention pursuant to the rule by the originator-seller, and whether it is in the form of an eligible horizontal residual interest, vertical interest, or revolving pool securitization seller's interest, as applicable.

(2) *Disclosures to regulators regarding originator-sellers.* An ABCP conduit sponsor relying upon this section shall provide, or cause to be provided, upon request, to the Commission and its appropriate Federal banking agency, if any, in writing, all of the information required to be provided to investors in paragraph (d)(1) of this section, and the name and form of organization of each originator-seller that will retain (or has retained) pursuant to this section an interest in the securitization transaction.

(e) *Sale or transfer of ABS interests between eligible ABCP conduits.* At any time, an eligible ABCP conduit that acquired an ABS interest in accordance with the requirements set forth in this section may transfer, and another eligible ABCP conduit may acquire, such ABS interest, if the following conditions are satisfied:

(1) The sponsors of both eligible ABCP conduits are in compliance with this section; and

(2) The same regulated liquidity provider has entered into one or more legally binding commitments to provide 100 percent liquidity coverage to all the ABCP issued by both eligible ABCP conduits.

(f) *Duty to comply.* (1) The ABCP conduit sponsor shall be responsible for compliance with this section.

(2) An ABCP conduit sponsor relying on this section:

(i) Shall maintain and adhere to policies and procedures that are reasonably designed to monitor compliance by each originator-seller which is satisfying a risk retention obligation in respect of ABS interests acquired by an eligible ABCP conduit with the requirements of paragraph (b)(1) of this section; and

(ii) In the event that the ABCP conduit sponsor determines that an originator-seller no longer complies with the requirements of paragraph (b)(1) of this section, shall:

(A) Promptly notify the holders of the ABCP, and upon request, the Commission and its appropriate Federal banking agency, if any, in writing of:

(1) The name and form of organization of any originator-seller that fails to retain risk in accordance with paragraph (b)(1) of this section and the amount of ABS interests issued by an intermediate SPV of such originator-seller and held by the ABCP conduit;

(2) The name and form of organization of any originator-seller that hedges, directly or indirectly through an intermediate SPV, its risk retention in violation of paragraph (b)(1) of this section and the amount of ABS interests issued by an intermediate SPV of such originator-seller and held by the ABCP conduit; and

(3) Any remedial actions taken by the ABCP conduit sponsor or other party with respect to such ABS interests; and

(B) Take other appropriate steps pursuant to the requirements of paragraphs (b)(2)(iv) and (v) of this section which may include, as appropriate, curing any breach of the requirements in this section, or removing from the eligible ABCP conduit any ABS interest that does not comply with the requirements in this section.

§ 267.7 Commercial mortgage-backed securities.

(a) *Definitions.* For purposes of this section, the following definition shall apply:

Special servicer means, with respect to any securitization of commercial real estate loans, any servicer that, upon the occurrence of one or more specified conditions in the servicing agreement, has the right to service one or more assets in the transaction.

(b) *Third-party purchaser.* A sponsor may satisfy some or all of its risk retention requirements under § 267.3 with respect to a securitization transaction if a third party (or any majority-owned affiliate thereof) purchases and holds for its own account an eligible horizontal residual interest in the issuing entity in the same form, amount, and manner as would be held by the sponsor under § 267.4 and all of the following conditions are met:

(1) *Number of third-party purchasers.* At any time, there are no more than two third-party purchasers of an eligible horizontal residual interest. If there are two third-party purchasers, each third-party purchaser's interest must be *pari passu* with the other third-party purchaser's interest.

(2) *Composition of collateral.* The securitization transaction is collateralized solely by commercial real estate loans and servicing assets.

(3) *Source of funds.* (i) Each third-party purchaser pays for the eligible horizontal residual interest in cash at the closing of the securitization transaction.

(ii) No third-party purchaser obtains financing, directly or indirectly, for the purchase of such interest from any other person that is a party to, or an affiliate of a party to, the securitization transaction (including, but not limited to, the sponsor, depositor, or servicer other than a special servicer affiliated with the third-party purchaser), other than a person that is a party to the transaction solely by reason of being an investor.

(4) *Third-party review.* Each third-party purchaser conducts an independent review of the credit risk of each securitized asset prior to the sale of the asset-backed securities in the securitization transaction that includes, at a minimum, a review of the underwriting standards, collateral, and expected cash flows of each commercial real estate loan that is collateral for the asset-backed securities.

(5) *Affiliation and control rights.* (i) Except as provided in paragraph (b)(5)(ii) of this section, no third-party purchaser is affiliated with any party to the securitization transaction (including, but not limited to, the sponsor, depositor, or servicer) other than investors in the securitization transaction.

(ii) Notwithstanding paragraph (b)(5)(i) of this section, a third-party purchaser may be affiliated with:

(A) The special servicer for the securitization transaction; or

(B) One or more originators of the securitized assets, as long as the assets originated by the affiliated originator or originators collectively comprise less than 10 percent of the unpaid principal balance of the securitized assets included in the securitization transaction at the cut-off date or similar date for establishing the composition of the securitized assets collateralizing the asset-backed securities issued pursuant to the securitization transaction.

(6) *Operating Advisor.* The underlying securitization transaction documents shall provide for the following:

(i) The appointment of an operating advisor (the Operating Advisor) that:

(A) Is not affiliated with other parties to the securitization transaction;

(B) Does not directly or indirectly have any financial interest in the securitization transaction other than in fees from its role as Operating Advisor; and

(C) Is required to act in the best interest of, and for the benefit of, investors as a collective whole;

(ii) Standards with respect to the Operating Advisor's experience, expertise and financial strength to fulfill its duties and responsibilities under the applicable transaction documents over the life of the securitization transaction;

(iii) The terms of the Operating Advisor's compensation with respect to the securitization transaction;

(iv) When the eligible horizontal residual interest has been reduced by principal payments, realized losses, and appraisal reduction amounts (which reduction amounts are determined in accordance with the applicable transaction documents) to a principal balance of 25 percent or less of its initial principal balance, the special servicer for the securitized assets must consult with the Operating Advisor in connection with, and prior to, any material decision in connection with its servicing of the securitized assets, including, without limitation:

(A) Any material modification of, or waiver with respect to, any provision of a loan agreement (including a mortgage, deed of trust, or other security agreement);

(B) Foreclosure upon or comparable conversion of the ownership of a property; or

(C) Any acquisition of a property.

(v) The Operating Advisor shall have adequate and timely access to information and reports necessary to fulfill its duties under the transaction documents, including all reports made available to holders of ABS interests and third-party purchasers, and shall be responsible for:

(A) Reviewing the actions of the special servicer;

(B) Reviewing all reports provided by the special servicer to the issuing entity or any holder of ABS interests;

(C) Reviewing for accuracy and consistency with the transaction documents calculations made by the special servicer; and

(D) Issuing a report to investors (including any third-party purchasers) and the issuing entity on a periodic basis concerning:

(1) Whether the Operating Advisor believes, in its sole discretion exercised in good faith, that the special servicer is operating in compliance with any standard required of the special servicer in the applicable transaction documents; and

(2) Which, if any, standards the Operating Advisor believes, in its sole discretion exercised in good faith, the special servicer has failed to comply.

(vi)(A) The Operating Advisor shall have the authority to recommend that the special servicer be replaced by a successor special servicer if the Operating Advisor determines, in its sole discretion exercised in good faith, that:

(1) The special servicer has failed to comply with a standard required of the special servicer in the applicable transaction documents; and

(2) Such replacement would be in the best interest of the investors as a collective whole; and

(B) If a recommendation described in paragraph (b)(6)(vi)(A) of this section is made, the special servicer shall be replaced upon the affirmative vote of a majority of the outstanding principal balance of all ABS interests voting on the matter, with a minimum of a quorum of ABS interests voting on the matter. For purposes of such vote, the applicable transaction documents shall specify the quorum and may not specify a quorum of more than the holders of 20 percent of the outstanding principal balance of all ABS interests in the issuing entity, with such quorum including at least three ABS interest holders that are not affiliated with each other.

(7) *Disclosures.* The sponsor provides, or causes to be provided, to potential investors a reasonable period of time prior to the sale of the asset-backed securities as part of the securitization transaction and, upon request, to the Commission and its appropriate Federal banking agency, if any, the following disclosure in written form under the caption "Credit Risk Retention":

(i) The name and form of organization of each initial third-party purchaser that acquired an eligible horizontal residual interest at the closing of a securitization transaction;

(ii) A description of each initial third-party purchaser's experience in investing in commercial mortgage-backed securities;

(iii) Any other information regarding each initial third-party purchaser or each initial third-party purchaser's retention of the eligible horizontal residual interest that is material to investors in light of the circumstances of the particular securitization transaction;

(iv) The fair value (expressed as a percentage of the fair value of all of the ABS interests issued in the securitization transaction and dollar amount (or corresponding amount in the foreign currency in which the ABS interests are issued, as applicable)) of the eligible horizontal residual interest that will be retained (or was retained) by each initial third-party purchaser, as well as the amount of the purchase price paid by each initial third-party purchaser for such interest;

(v) The fair value (expressed as a percentage of the fair value of all of the ABS interests issued in the securitization transaction and dollar amount (or corresponding amount in the foreign currency in which the ABS interests are issued, as applicable)) of the eligible horizontal residual interest in the securitization transaction that the sponsor would have retained pursuant to § 267.4 if the sponsor had relied on retaining an eligible horizontal residual interest in that section to meet the requirements of § 267.3 with respect to the transaction;

(vi) A description of the material terms of the eligible horizontal residual interest retained by each initial third-party purchaser, including the same information as is required to be disclosed by sponsors retaining horizontal interests pursuant to § 267.4;

(vii) The material terms of the applicable transaction documents with respect to the Operating Advisor, including without limitation:

(A) The name and form of organization of the Operating Advisor;

(B) A description of any material conflict of interest or material potential conflict of interest between the Operating Advisor and any other party to the transaction;

(C) The standards required by paragraph (b)(6)(ii) of this section and a description of how the Operating Advisor satisfies each of the standards; and

(D) The terms of the Operating Advisor's compensation under paragraph (b)(6)(iii) of this section; and

(viii) The representations and warranties concerning the securitized assets, a schedule of any securitized assets that are determined not to comply with such representations and warranties, and what factors were used to make the determination that such securitized assets should be included in the pool notwithstanding that the securitized assets did not comply with such representations and warranties, such as compensating factors or a de-

termination that the exceptions were not material.

(8) *Hedging, transfer and pledging*—(i) *General rule.* Except as set forth in paragraph (b)(8)(ii) of this section, each third-party purchaser and its affiliates must comply with the hedging and other restrictions in § 267.12 as if it were the retaining sponsor with respect to the securitization transaction and had acquired the eligible horizontal residual interest pursuant to § 267.4; provided that, the hedging and other restrictions in § 267.12 shall not apply on or after the date that each CRE loan (as defined in § 267.14) that serves as collateral for outstanding ABS interests has been defeased. For purposes of this section, a loan is deemed to be defeased if:

(A) cash or cash equivalents of the types permitted for an eligible horizontal cash reserve account pursuant to § 267.4 whose maturity corresponds to the remaining debt service obligations, have been pledged to the issuing entity as collateral for the loan and are in such amounts and payable at such times as necessary to timely generate cash sufficient to make all remaining debt service payments due on such loan; and

(B) the issuing entity has an obligation to release its lien on the loan.

(ii) *Exceptions*—(A) *Transfer by initial third-party purchaser or sponsor.* An initial third-party purchaser that acquired an eligible horizontal residual interest at the closing of a securitization transaction in accordance with this section, or a sponsor that acquired an eligible horizontal residual interest at the closing of a securitization transaction in accordance with this section, may, on or after the date that is five years after the date of the closing of the securitization transaction, transfer that interest to a subsequent third-party purchaser that complies with paragraph (b)(8)(ii)(C) of this section. The initial third-party purchaser shall provide the sponsor with complete identifying information for the subsequent third-party purchaser.

(B) *Transfer by subsequent third-party purchaser.* At any time, a subsequent third-party purchaser that acquired an eligible horizontal residual interest pursuant to this section may transfer its interest to a different third-party purchaser that complies with paragraph (b)(8)(ii)(C) of this section. The transferring third-party purchaser shall provide the sponsor with complete identifying information for the acquiring third-party purchaser.

(C) *Requirements applicable to subsequent third-party purchasers.* A subsequent third-party purchaser is subject to all of the requirements of paragraphs (b)(1), (b)(3) through (5), and (b)(8) of this section applicable to third-party purchasers, provided that obligations under paragraphs (b)(1), (b)(3) through (5), and (b)(8) of this section that apply to initial third-party purchasers at or before the time of closing of the securitization transaction shall apply to successor third-party purchasers at or before the time of the transfer of the eligible horizontal residual interest to the successor third-party purchaser.

(c) *Duty to comply.* (1) The retaining sponsor shall be responsible for compliance with this section by itself and for compliance by each initial or subsequent third-party purchaser that acquired an eligible horizontal residual interest in the securitization transaction.

(2) A sponsor relying on this section:

(i) Shall maintain and adhere to policies and procedures to monitor each third-party purchaser's compliance with the requirements of paragraphs (b)(1), (b)(3) through (5), and (b)(8) of this section; and

(ii) In the event that the sponsor determines that a third-party purchaser no longer complies with one or more of the requirements of paragraphs (b)(1), (b)(3) through (5), or (b)(8) of this section, shall promptly notify, or cause to be notified, the holders of the ABS interests issued in the securitization transaction of such noncompliance by such third-party purchaser.

§ 267.8 Federal National Mortgage Association and Federal Home Loan Mortgage Corporation ABS.

(a) *In general.* A sponsor satisfies its risk retention requirement under this part if the sponsor fully guarantees the timely payment of principal and interest on all ABS interests issued by the issuing entity in the securitization transaction and is:

(1) The Federal National Mortgage Association or the Federal Home Loan Mortgage Corporation operating under the conservatorship or receivership of the Federal Housing Finance Agency pursuant to section 1367 of the Federal Housing Enterprises Financial Safety and Soundness Act of 1992 (12 U.S.C. 4617) with capital support from the United States; or

(2) Any limited-life regulated entity succeeding to the charter of either the Federal National Mortgage Association or the Federal Home Loan Mortgage Corporation pursuant to section 1367(i) of the Federal Housing Enterprises Financial Safety and Soundness Act of 1992 (12 U.S.C. 4617(i)), provided that the entity is operating with capital support from the United States.

(b) *Certain provisions not applicable.* The provisions of § 267.12(b), (c), and (d) shall not apply to a sponsor described in paragraph (a)(1) or (2) of this section, its affiliates, or the issuing entity with respect to a securitization transaction for which the sponsor has retained credit risk in accordance with the requirements of this section.

(c) *Disclosure.* A sponsor relying on this section shall provide to investors, in written form under the caption "Credit Risk Retention" and, upon request, to the Federal Housing Finance Agency and the Commission, a description of the manner in which it has met the credit risk retention requirements of this part.

§ 267.9 Open market CLOs.

(a) *Definitions.* For purposes of this section, the following definitions shall apply:

CLO means a special purpose entity that:

(i) Issues debt and equity interests, and

(ii) Whose assets consist primarily of loans that are securitized assets and servicing assets.

CLO-eligible loan tranche means a term loan of a syndicated facility that meets the criteria set forth in paragraph (c) of this section.

CLO manager means an entity that manages a CLO, which entity is registered as an investment adviser under

563

the Investment Advisers Act of 1940, as amended (15 U.S.C. 80b-1 *et seq.*), or is an affiliate of such a registered investment adviser and itself is managed by such registered investment adviser.

Commercial borrower means an obligor under a corporate credit obligation (including a loan).

Initial loan syndication transaction means a transaction in which a loan is syndicated to a group of lenders.

Lead arranger means, with respect to a CLO-eligible loan tranche, an institution that:

(i) Is active in the origination, structuring and syndication of commercial loan transactions (as defined in § 267.14) and has played a primary role in the structuring, underwriting and distribution on the primary market of the CLO-eligible loan tranche.

(ii) Has taken an allocation of the funded portion of the syndicated credit facility under the terms of the transaction that includes the CLO-eligible loan tranche of at least 20 percent of the aggregate principal balance at origination, and no other member (or members affiliated with each other) of the syndication group that funded at origination has taken a greater allocation; and

(iii) Is identified in the applicable agreement governing the CLO-eligible loan tranche; represents therein to the holders of the CLO-eligible loan tranche and to any holders of participation interests in such CLO-eligible loan tranche that such lead arranger satisfies the requirements of paragraph (i) of this definition and, at the time of initial funding of the CLO-eligible tranche, will satisfy the requirements of paragraph (ii) of this definition; further represents therein (solely for the purpose of assisting such holders to determine the eligibility of such CLO-eligible loan tranche to be held by an open market CLO) that in the reasonable judgment of such lead arranger, the terms of such CLO-eligible loan tranche are consistent with the requirements of paragraphs (c)(2) and (3) of this section; and covenants therein to such holders that such lead arranger will fulfill the requirements of paragraph (c)(1) of this section.

Open market CLO means a CLO:

(i) Whose assets consist of senior, secured syndicated loans acquired by such CLO directly from the sellers thereof in open market transactions and of servicing assets,

(ii) That is managed by a CLO manager, and

(iii) That holds less than 50 percent of its assets, by aggregate outstanding principal amount, in loans syndicated by lead arrangers that are affiliates of the CLO or the CLO manager or originated by originators that are affiliates of the CLO or the CLO manager.

Open market transaction means:

(i) Either an initial loan syndication transaction or a secondary market transaction in which a seller offers senior, secured syndicated loans to prospective purchasers in the loan market on market terms on an arm's length basis, which prospective purchasers include, but are not limited to, entities that are not affiliated with the seller, or

(ii) A reverse inquiry from a prospective purchaser of a senior, secured syndicated loan through a dealer in the loan market to purchase a senior, secured syndicated loan to be sourced by the dealer in the loan market.

Secondary market transaction means a purchase of a senior, secured syndicated loan not in connection with an initial loan syndication transaction but in the secondary market.

Senior, secured syndicated loan means a loan made to a commercial borrower that:

(i) Is not subordinate in right of payment to any other obligation for borrowed money of the commercial borrower,

(ii) Is secured by a valid first priority security interest or lien in or on specified collateral securing the commercial borrower's obligations under the loan, and

(iii) The value of the collateral subject to such first priority security interest or lien, together with other attributes of the obligor (including, without limitation, its general financial condition, ability to generate cash flow available for debt service and other demands for that cash flow), is adequate (in the commercially reasonable judgment of the CLO manager exercised at the time of investment) to repay the loan and to repay all other indebtedness of equal seniority secured by such first priority security interest or lien in or on the same collateral, and the CLO manager certifies, on or prior to each date that it acquires a loan constituting part of a new CLO-eligible tranche, that it has policies and procedures to evaluate the likelihood of repayment of loans acquired by the CLO and it has followed such policies and procedures in evaluating each CLO-eligible loan tranche.

(b) *In general.* A sponsor satisfies the risk retention requirements of §267.3 with respect to an open market CLO transaction if:

(1) The open market CLO does not acquire or hold any assets other than CLO-eligible loan tranches that meet the requirements of paragraph (c) of this section and servicing assets;

(2) The governing documents of such open market CLO require that, at all times, the assets of the open market CLO consist of senior, secured syndicated loans that are CLO-eligible loan tranches and servicing assets;

(3) The open market CLO does not invest in ABS interests or in credit derivatives other than hedging transactions that are servicing assets to hedge risks of the open market CLO;

(4) All purchases of CLO-eligible loan tranches and other assets by the open market CLO issuing entity or through a warehouse facility used to accumulate the loans prior to the issuance of the CLO's ABS interests are made in open market transactions on an arms-length basis;

(5) The CLO manager of the open market CLO is not entitled to receive any management fee or gain on sale at the time the open market CLO issues its ABS interests.

(c) *CLO-eligible loan tranche.* To qualify as a CLO-eligible loan tranche, a term loan of a syndicated credit facility to a commercial borrower must have the following features:

(1) A minimum of 5 percent of the face amount of the CLO-eligible loan tranche is retained by the lead arranger thereof until the earliest of the repayment, maturity, involuntary and unscheduled acceleration, payment default, or bankruptcy default of such CLO-eligible loan tranche, provided

that such lead arranger complies with limitations on hedging, transferring and pledging in §267.12 with respect to the interest retained by the lead arranger.

(2) Lender voting rights within the credit agreement and any intercreditor or other applicable agreements governing such CLO-eligible loan tranche are defined so as to give holders of the CLO-eligible loan tranche consent rights with respect to, at minimum, any material waivers and amendments of such applicable documents, including but not limited to, adverse changes to the calculation or payments of amounts due to the holders of the CLO-eligible tranche, alterations to *pro rata* provisions, changes to voting provisions, and waivers of conditions precedent; and

(3) The pro rata provisions, voting provisions, and similar provisions applicable to the security associated with such CLO-eligible loan tranches under the CLO credit agreement and any intercreditor or other applicable agreements governing such CLO-eligible loan tranches are not materially less advantageous to the holder(s) of such CLO-eligible tranche than the terms of other tranches of comparable seniority in the broader syndicated credit facility.

(d) *Disclosures.* A sponsor relying on this section shall provide, or cause to be provided, to potential investors a reasonable period of time prior to the sale of the asset-backed securities in the securitization transaction and at least annually with respect to the information required by paragraph (d)(1) of this section and, upon request, to the Commission and its appropriate Federal banking agency, if any, the following disclosure in written form under the caption "Credit Risk Retention":

(1) *Open market CLOs.* A complete list of every asset held by an open market CLO (or before the CLO's closing, in a warehouse facility in anticipation of transfer into the CLO at closing), including the following information:

(i) The full legal name, Standard Industrial Classification (SIC) category code, and legal entity identifier (LEI)

565

issued by a utility endorsed or otherwise governed by the Global LEI Regulatory Oversight Committee or the Global LEI Foundation (if an LEI has been obtained by the obligor) of the obligor of the loan or asset;

(ii) The full name of the specific loan tranche held by the CLO;

(iii) The face amount of the entire loan tranche held by the CLO, and the face amount of the portion thereof held by the CLO;

(iv) The price at which the loan tranche was acquired by the CLO; and

(v) For each loan tranche, the full legal name of the lead arranger subject to the sales and hedging restrictions of § 267.12; and

(2) *CLO manager.* The full legal name and form of organization of the CLO manager.

§ 267.10   Qualified tender option bonds.

(a) *Definitions.* For purposes of this section, the following definitions shall apply:

Municipal security or *municipal securities* shall have the same meaning as the term "municipal securities" in Section 3(a)(29) of the Securities Exchange Act of 1934 (15 U.S.C. 78c(a)(29)) and any rules promulgated pursuant to such section.

Qualified tender option bond entity means an issuing entity with respect to tender option bonds for which each of the following applies:

(i) Such entity is collateralized solely by servicing assets and by municipal securities that have the same municipal issuer and the same underlying obligor or source of payment (determined without regard to any third-party credit enhancement), and such municipal securities are not subject to substitution.

(ii) Such entity issues no securities other than:

(A) A single class of tender option bonds with a preferred variable return payable out of capital that meets the requirements of paragraph (b) of this section, and

(B) One or more residual equity interests that, in the aggregate, are entitled to all remaining income of the issuing entity.

(C) The types of securities referred to in paragraphs (ii)(A) and (B) of this definition must constitute asset-backed securities.

(iii) The municipal securities held as assets by such entity are issued in compliance with Section 103 of the Internal Revenue Code of 1986, as amended (the "IRS Code", 26 U.S.C. 103), such that the interest payments made on those securities are excludable from the gross income of the owners under Section 103 of the IRS Code.

(iv) The terms of all of the securities issued by the entity are structured so that all holders of such securities who are eligible to exclude interest received on such securities will be able to exclude that interest from gross income pursuant to Section 103 of the IRS Code or as "exempt-interest dividends" pursuant to Section 852(b)(5) of the IRS Code (26 U.S.C. 852(b)(5)) in the case of regulated investment companies under the Investment Company Act of 1940, as amended.

(v) Such entity has a legally binding commitment from a regulated liquidity provider as defined in § 267.6(a), to provide a 100 percent guarantee or liquidity coverage with respect to all of the issuing entity's outstanding tender option bonds.

(vi) Such entity qualifies for monthly closing elections pursuant to IRS Revenue Procedure 2003–84, as amended or supplemented from time to time.

Tender option bond means a security which has features which entitle the holders to tender such bonds to the issuing entity for purchase at any time upon no more than 397 days' notice, for a purchase price equal to the approximate amortized cost of the security, plus accrued interest, if any, at the time of tender.

(b) *Risk retention options.* Notwithstanding anything in this section, the sponsor with respect to an issuance of tender option bonds may retain an eligible vertical interest or eligible horizontal residual interest, or any combination thereof, in accordance with the requirements of § 267.4. In order to satisfy its risk retention requirements under this section, the sponsor with respect to an issuance of tender option bonds by a qualified tender option bond entity may retain:

(1) An eligible vertical interest or an eligible horizontal residual interest, or

any combination thereof, in accordance with the requirements of §267.4; or

(2) An interest that meets the requirements set forth in paragraph (c) of this section; or

(3) A municipal security that meets the requirements set forth in paragraph (d) of this section; or

(4) Any combination of interests and securities described in paragraphs (b)(1) through (b)(3) of this section such that the sum of the percentages held in each form equals at least five.

(c) *Tender option termination event.* The sponsor with respect to an issuance of tender option bonds by a qualified tender option bond entity may retain an interest that upon issuance meets the requirements of an eligible horizontal residual interest but that upon the occurrence of a "tender option termination event" as defined in Section 4.01(5) of IRS Revenue Procedure 2003–84, as amended or supplemented from time to time will meet the requirements of an eligible vertical interest.

(d) *Retention of a municipal security outside of the qualified tender option bond entity.* The sponsor with respect to an issuance of tender option bonds by a qualified tender option bond entity may satisfy its risk retention requirements under this Section by holding municipal securities from the same issuance of municipal securities deposited in the qualified tender option bond entity, the face value of which retained municipal securities is equal to 5 percent of the face value of the municipal securities deposited in the qualified tender option bond entity.

(e) *Disclosures.* The sponsor shall provide, or cause to be provided, to potential investors a reasonable period of time prior to the sale of the asset-backed securities as part of the securitization transaction and, upon request, to the Commission and its appropriate Federal banking agency, if any, the following disclosure in written form under the caption "Credit Risk Retention":

(1) The name and form of organization of the qualified tender option bond entity;

(2) A description of the form and subordination features of such retained interest in accordance with the disclosure obligations in §267.4(c);

(3) To the extent any portion of the retained interest is claimed by the sponsor as an eligible horizontal residual interest (including any interest held in compliance with §267.10(c)), the fair value of that interest (expressed as a percentage of the fair value of all of the ABS interests issued in the securitization transaction and as a dollar amount);

(4) To the extent any portion of the retained interest is claimed by the sponsor as an eligible vertical interest (including any interest held in compliance with §267.10(c)), the percentage of ABS interests issued represented by the eligible vertical interest; and

(5) To the extent any portion of the retained interest claimed by the sponsor is a municipal security held outside of the qualified tender option bond entity, the name and form of organization of the qualified tender option bond entity, the identity of the issuer of the municipal securities, the face value of the municipal securities deposited into the qualified tender option bond entity, and the face value of the municipal securities retained by the sponsor or its majority-owned affiliates and subject to the transfer and hedging prohibition.

(f) *Prohibitions on Hedging and Transfer.* The prohibitions on transfer and hedging set forth in §267.12, apply to any interests or municipal securities retained by the sponsor with respect to an issuance of tender option bonds by a qualified tender option bond entity pursuant to of this section.

Subpart C—Transfer of Risk Retention

§267.11 Allocation of risk retention to an originator.

(a) *In general.* A sponsor choosing to retain an eligible vertical interest or an eligible horizontal residual interest (including an eligible horizontal cash reserve account), or combination thereof under §267.4, with respect to a securitization transaction may offset the amount of its risk retention requirements under §267.4 by the amount of the eligible interests, respectively, acquired by an originator of one or more of the securitized assets if:

(1) At the closing of the securitization transaction:

(i) The originator acquires the eligible interest from the sponsor and retains such interest in the same manner and proportion (as between horizontal and vertical interests) as the sponsor under § 267.4, as such interest was held prior to the acquisition by the originator;

(ii) The ratio of the percentage of eligible interests acquired and retained by the originator to the percentage of eligible interests otherwise required to be retained by the sponsor pursuant to § 267.4, does not exceed the ratio of:

(A) The unpaid principal balance of all the securitized assets originated by the originator; to

(B) The unpaid principal balance of all the securitized assets in the securitization transaction;

(iii) The originator acquires and retains at least 20 percent of the aggregate risk retention amount otherwise required to be retained by the sponsor pursuant to § 267.4; and

(iv) The originator purchases the eligible interests from the sponsor at a price that is equal, on a dollar-for-dollar basis, to the amount by which the sponsor's required risk retention is reduced in accordance with this section, by payment to the sponsor in the form of:

(A) Cash; or

(B) A reduction in the price received by the originator from the sponsor or depositor for the assets sold by the originator to the sponsor or depositor for inclusion in the pool of securitized assets.

(2) *Disclosures.* In addition to the disclosures required pursuant to § 267.4(c), the sponsor provides, or causes to be provided, to potential investors a reasonable period of time prior to the sale of the asset-backed securities as part of the securitization transaction and, upon request, to the Commission and its appropriate Federal banking agency, if any, in written form under the caption "Credit Risk Retention", the name and form of organization of any originator that will acquire and retain (or has acquired and retained) an interest in the transaction pursuant to this section, including a description of the form and amount (expressed as a percentage and dollar amount (or corresponding amount in the foreign currency in which the ABS interests are issued, as applicable)) and nature (*e.g.*, senior or subordinated) of the interest, as well as the method of payment for such interest under paragraph (a)(1)(iv) of this section.

(3) *Hedging, transferring and pledging.* The originator and each of its affiliates complies with the hedging and other restrictions in § 267.12 with respect to the interests retained by the originator pursuant to this section as if it were the retaining sponsor and was required to retain the interest under subpart B of this part.

(b) *Duty to comply.* (1) The retaining sponsor shall be responsible for compliance with this section.

(2) A retaining sponsor relying on this section:

(i) Shall maintain and adhere to policies and procedures that are reasonably designed to monitor the compliance by each originator that is allocated a portion of the sponsor's risk retention obligations with the requirements in paragraphs (a)(1) and (3) of this section; and

(ii) In the event the sponsor determines that any such originator no longer complies with any of the requirements in paragraphs (a)(1) and (3) of this section, shall promptly notify, or cause to be notified, the holders of the ABS interests issued in the securitization transaction of such noncompliance by such originator.

§ 267.12 Hedging, transfer and financing prohibitions.

(a) *Transfer.* Except as permitted by § 267.7(b)(8), and subject to § 267.5, a retaining sponsor may not sell or otherwise transfer any interest or assets that the sponsor is required to retain pursuant to subpart B of this part to any person other than an entity that is and remains a majority-owned affiliate of the sponsor and each such majority-owned affiliate shall be subject to the same restrictions.

(b) *Prohibited hedging by sponsor and affiliates.* A retaining sponsor and its affiliates may not purchase or sell a security, or other financial instrument, or enter into an agreement, derivative or other position, with any other person if:

(1) Payments on the security or other financial instrument or under the agreement, derivative, or position are materially related to the credit risk of one or more particular ABS interests that the retaining sponsor (or any of its majority-owned affiliates) is required to retain with respect to a securitization transaction pursuant to subpart B of this part or one or more of the particular securitized assets that collateralize the asset-backed securities issued in the securitization transaction; and

(2) The security, instrument, agreement, derivative, or position in any way reduces or limits the financial exposure of the sponsor (or any of its majority-owned affiliates) to the credit risk of one or more of the particular ABS interests that the retaining sponsor (or any of its majority-owned affiliates) is required to retain with respect to a securitization transaction pursuant to subpart B of this part or one or more of the particular securitized assets that collateralize the asset-backed securities issued in the securitization transaction.

(c) *Prohibited hedging by issuing entity.* The issuing entity in a securitization transaction may not purchase or sell a security or other financial instrument, or enter into an agreement, derivative or position, with any other person if:

(1) Payments on the security or other financial instrument or under the agreement, derivative or position are materially related to the credit risk of one or more particular ABS interests that the retaining sponsor for the transaction (or any of its majority-owned affiliates) is required to retain with respect to the securitization transaction pursuant to subpart B of this part; and

(2) The security, instrument, agreement, derivative, or position in any way reduces or limits the financial exposure of the retaining sponsor (or any of its majority-owned affiliates) to the credit risk of one or more of the particular ABS interests that the sponsor (or any of its majority-owned affiliates) is required to retain pursuant to subpart B of this part.

(d) *Permitted hedging activities.* The following activities shall not be considered prohibited hedging activities under paragraph (b) or (c) of this section:

(1) Hedging the interest rate risk (which does not include the specific interest rate risk, known as spread risk, associated with the ABS interest that is otherwise considered part of the credit risk) or foreign exchange risk arising from one or more of the particular ABS interests required to be retained by the sponsor (or any of its majority-owned affiliates) under subpart B of this part or one or more of the particular securitized assets that underlie the asset-backed securities issued in the securitization transaction; or

(2) Purchasing or selling a security or other financial instrument or entering into an agreement, derivative, or other position with any third party where payments on the security or other financial instrument or under the agreement, derivative, or position are based, directly or indirectly, on an index of instruments that includes asset-backed securities if:

(i) Any class of ABS interests in the issuing entity that were issued in connection with the securitization transaction and that are included in the index represents no more than 10 percent of the dollar-weighted average (or corresponding weighted average in the currency in which the ABS interests are issued, as applicable) of all instruments included in the index; and

(ii) All classes of ABS interests in all issuing entities that were issued in connection with any securitization transaction in which the sponsor (or any of its majority-owned affiliates) is required to retain an interest pursuant to subpart B of this part and that are included in the index represent, in the aggregate, no more than 20 percent of the dollar-weighted average (or corresponding weighted average in the currency in which the ABS interests are issued, as applicable) of all instruments included in the index.

(e) *Prohibited non-recourse financing.* Neither a retaining sponsor nor any of its affiliates may pledge as collateral for any obligation (including a loan, repurchase agreement, or other financing

569

transaction) any ABS interest that the sponsor is required to retain with respect to a securitization transaction pursuant to subpart B of this part unless such obligation is with full recourse to the sponsor or affiliate, respectively.

(f) *Duration of the hedging and transfer restrictions*—(1) *General rule.* Except as provided in paragraph (f)(2) of this section, the prohibitions on sale and hedging pursuant to paragraphs (a) and (b) of this section shall expire on or after the date that is the latest of:

(i) The date on which the total unpaid principal balance (if applicable) of the securitized assets that collateralize the securitization transaction has been reduced to 33 percent of the total unpaid principal balance of the securitized assets as of the cut-off date or similar date for establishing the composition of the securitized assets collateralizing the asset-backed securities issued pursuant to the securitization transaction;

(ii) The date on which the total unpaid principal obligations under the ABS interests issued in the securitization transaction has been reduced to 33 percent of the total unpaid principal obligations of the ABS interests at closing of the securitization transaction; or

(iii) Two years after the date of the closing of the securitization transaction.

(2) *Securitizations of residential mortgages.* (i) If all of the assets that collateralize a securitization transaction subject to risk retention under this part are residential mortgages, the prohibitions on sale and hedging pursuant to paragraphs (a) and (b) of this section shall expire on or after the date that is the later of:

(A) Five years after the date of the closing of the securitization transaction; or

(B) The date on which the total unpaid principal balance of the residential mortgages that collateralize the securitization transaction has been reduced to 25 percent of the total unpaid principal balance of such residential mortgages at the cut-off date or similar date for establishing the composition of the securitized assets collateralizing the asset-backed securi-

ties issued pursuant to the securitization transaction.

(ii) Notwithstanding paragraph (f)(2)(i) of this section, the prohibitions on sale and hedging pursuant to paragraphs (a) and (b) of this section shall expire with respect to the sponsor of a securitization transaction described in paragraph (f)(2)(i) of this section on or after the date that is seven years after the date of the closing of the securitization transaction.

(3) *Conservatorship or receivership of sponsor.* A conservator or receiver of the sponsor (or any other person holding risk retention pursuant to this part) of a securitization transaction is permitted to sell or hedge any economic interest in the securitization transaction if the conservator or receiver has been appointed pursuant to any provision of federal or State law (or regulation promulgated thereunder) that provides for the appointment of the Federal Deposit Insurance Corporation, or an agency or instrumentality of the United States or of a State as conservator or receiver, including without limitation any of the following authorities:

(i) 12 U.S.C. 1811;

(ii) 12 U.S.C. 1787;

(iii) 12 U.S.C. 4617; or

(iv) 12 U.S.C. 5382.

(4) *Revolving pool securitizations.* The provisions of paragraphs (f)(1) and (2) are not available to sponsors of revolving pool securitizations with respect to the forms of risk retention specified in § 267.5.

Subpart D—Exceptions and Exemptions

§ 267.13 Exemption for qualified residential mortgages.

(a) *Definitions.* For purposes of this section, the following definitions shall apply:

Currently performing means the borrower in the mortgage transaction is not currently thirty (30) days or more past due, in whole or in part, on the mortgage transaction.

Qualified residential mortgage means a "qualified mortgage" as defined in section 129C of the Truth in Lending Act (15 U.S.C.1639c) and regulations issued thereunder, as amended from time to time.

(b) *Exemption.* A sponsor shall be exempt from the risk retention requirements in subpart B of this part with respect to any securitization transaction, if:

(1) All of the assets that collateralize the asset-backed securities are qualified residential mortgages or servicing assets;

(2) None of the assets that collateralize the asset-backed securities are asset-backed securities;

(3) As of the cut-off date or similar date for establishing the composition of the securitized assets collateralizing the asset-backed securities issued pursuant to the securitization transaction, each qualified residential mortgage collateralizing the asset-backed securities is currently performing; and

(4)(i) The depositor with respect to the securitization transaction certifies that it has evaluated the effectiveness of its internal supervisory controls with respect to the process for ensuring that all assets that collateralize the asset-backed security are qualified residential mortgages or servicing assets and has concluded that its internal supervisory controls are effective; and

(ii) The evaluation of the effectiveness of the depositor's internal supervisory controls must be performed, for each issuance of an asset-backed security in reliance on this section, as of a date within 60 days of the cut-off date or similar date for establishing the composition of the asset pool collateralizing such asset-backed security; and

(iii) The sponsor provides, or causes to be provided, a copy of the certification described in paragraph (b)(4)(i) of this section to potential investors a reasonable period of time prior to the sale of asset-backed securities in the issuing entity, and, upon request, to the Commission and its appropriate Federal banking agency, if any.

(c) *Repurchase of loans subsequently determined to be non-qualified after closing.* A sponsor that has relied on the exemption provided in paragraph (b) of this section with respect to a securitization transaction shall not lose such exemption with respect to such transaction if, after closing of the securitization transaction, it is determined that one or more of the residential mortgage loans collateralizing the asset-backed securities does not meet all of the criteria to be a qualified residential mortgage *provided that:*

(1) The depositor complied with the certification requirement set forth in paragraph (b)(4) of this section;

(2) The sponsor repurchases the loan(s) from the issuing entity at a price at least equal to the remaining aggregate unpaid principal balance and accrued interest on the loan(s) no later than 90 days after the determination that the loans do not satisfy the requirements to be a qualified residential mortgage; and

(3) The sponsor promptly notifies, or causes to be notified, the holders of the asset-backed securities issued in the securitization transaction of any loan(s) included in such securitization transaction that is (or are) required to be repurchased by the sponsor pursuant to paragraph (c)(2) of this section, including the amount of such repurchased loan(s) and the cause for such repurchase.

§267.14 Definitions applicable to qualifying commercial loans, qualifying commercial real estate loans, and qualifying automobile loans.

The following definitions apply for purposes of §§267.15 through 267.18:

Appraisal Standards Board means the board of the Appraisal Foundation that develops, interprets, and amends the Uniform Standards of Professional Appraisal Practice (USPAP), establishing generally accepted standards for the appraisal profession.

Automobile loan:

(1) Means any loan to an individual to finance the purchase of, and that is secured by a first lien on, a passenger car or other passenger vehicle, such as a minivan, van, sport-utility vehicle, pickup truck, or similar light truck for personal, family, or household use; and

(2) Does not include any:

(i) Loan to finance fleet sales;

(ii) Personal cash loan secured by a previously purchased automobile;

(iii) Loan to finance the purchase of a commercial vehicle or farm equipment that is not used for personal, family, or household purposes;

(iv) Lease financing;

(v) Loan to finance the purchase of a vehicle with a salvage title; or

(vi) Loan to finance the purchase of a vehicle intended to be used for scrap or parts.

Combined loan-to-value (CLTV) ratio means, at the time of origination, the sum of the principal balance of a first-lien mortgage loan on the property, plus the principal balance of any junior-lien mortgage loan that, to the creditor's knowledge, would exist at the closing of the transaction and that is secured by the same property, divided by:

(1) For acquisition funding, the lesser of the purchase price or the estimated market value of the real property based on an appraisal that meets the requirements set forth in § 267.17(a)(2)(ii); or

(2) For refinancing, the estimated market value of the real property based on an appraisal that meets the requirements set forth in § 267.17(a)(2)(ii).

Commercial loan means a secured or unsecured loan to a company or an individual for business purposes, other than any:

(1) Loan to purchase or refinance a one-to-four family residential property;

(2) Commercial real estate loan.

Commercial real estate (CRE) loan means:

(1) A loan secured by a property with five or more single family units, or by nonfarm nonresidential real property, the primary source (50 percent or more) of repayment for which is expected to be:

(i) The proceeds of the sale, refinancing, or permanent financing of the property; or

(ii) Rental income associated with the property;

(2) Loans secured by improved land if the obligor owns the fee interest in the land and the land is leased to a third party who owns all improvements on the land, and the improvements are nonresidential or residential with five or more single family units; and

(3) Does not include:

(i) A land development and construction loan (including 1- to 4-family residential or commercial construction loans);

(ii) Any other land loan; or

(iii) An unsecured loan to a developer.

Debt service coverage (DSC) ratio means:

(1) For qualifying leased CRE loans, qualifying multi-family loans, and other CRE loans:

(i) The annual NOI less the annual replacement reserve of the CRE property at the time of origination of the CRE loan(s) divided by

(ii) The sum of the borrower's annual payments for principal and interest (calculated at the fully-indexed rate) on any debt obligation.

(2) For commercial loans:

(i) The borrower's EBITDA as of the most recently completed fiscal year divided by

(ii) The sum of the borrower's annual payments for principal and interest on all debt obligations.

Debt to income (DTI) ratio means the borrower's total debt, including the monthly amount due on the automobile loan, divided by the borrower's monthly income.

Earnings before interest, taxes, depreciation, and amortization (EBITDA) means the annual income of a business before expenses for interest, taxes, depreciation and amortization are deducted, as determined in accordance with GAAP.

Environmental risk assessment means a process for determining whether a property is contaminated or exposed to any condition or substance that could result in contamination that has an adverse effect on the market value of the property or the realization of the collateral value.

First lien means a lien or encumbrance on property that has priority over all other liens or encumbrances on the property.

Junior lien means a lien or encumbrance on property that is lower in priority relative to other liens or encumbrances on the property.

Leverage ratio means the borrower's total debt divided by the borrower's EBITDA.

Loan-to-value (LTV) ratio means, at the time of origination, the principal balance of a first-lien mortgage loan on the property divided by:

(1) For acquisition funding, the lesser of the purchase price or the estimated market value of the real property based on an appraisal that meets the requirements set forth in §267.17(a)(2)(ii); or

(2) For refinancing, the estimated market value of the real property based on an appraisal that meets the requirements set forth in §267.17(a)(2)(ii).

Model year means the year determined by the manufacturer and reflected on the vehicle's Motor Vehicle Title as part of the vehicle description.

Net operating income (NOI) refers to the income a CRE property generates for the owner after all expenses have been deducted for federal income tax purposes, except for depreciation, debt service expenses, and federal and state income taxes, and excluding any unusual and nonrecurring items of income.

Operating affiliate means an affiliate of a borrower that is a lessor or similar party with respect to the commercial real estate securing the loan.

Payments-in-kind means payments of accrued interest that are not paid in cash when due, and instead are paid by increasing the principal balance of the loan or by providing equity in the borrowing company.

Purchase money security interest means a security interest in property that secures the obligation of the obligor incurred as all or part of the price of the property.

Purchase price means the amount paid by the borrower for the vehicle net of any incentive payments or manufacturer cash rebates.

Qualified tenant means:

(1) A tenant with a lease who has satisfied all obligations with respect to the property in a timely manner; or

(2) A tenant who originally had a lease that subsequently expired and currently is leasing the property on a month-to-month basis, has occupied the property for at least three years prior to the date of origination, and has satisfied all obligations with respect to the property in a timely manner.

Qualifying leased CRE loan means a CRE loan secured by commercial non-farm real property, other than a multi-family property or a hotel, inn, or similar property:

(1) That is occupied by one or more qualified tenants pursuant to a lease agreement with a term of no less than one (1) month; and

(2) Where no more than 20 percent of the aggregate gross revenue of the property is payable from one or more tenants who:

(i) Are subject to a lease that will terminate within six months following the date of origination; or

(ii) Are not qualified tenants.

Qualifying multi-family loan means a CRE loan secured by any residential property (excluding a hotel, motel, inn, hospital, nursing home, or other similar facility where dwellings are not leased to residents):

(1) That consists of five or more dwelling units (including apartment buildings, condominiums, cooperatives and other similar structures) primarily for residential use; and

(2) Where at least 75 percent of the NOI is derived from residential rents and tenant amenities (including income from parking garages, health or swim clubs, and dry cleaning), and not from other commercial uses.

Rental income means:

(1) Income derived from a lease or other occupancy agreement between the borrower or an operating affiliate of the borrower and a party which is not an affiliate of the borrower for the use of real property or improvements serving as collateral for the applicable loan; and

(2) Other income derived from hotel, motel, dormitory, nursing home, assisted living, mini-storage warehouse or similar properties that are used primarily by parties that are not affiliates or employees of the borrower or its affiliates.

Replacement reserve means the monthly capital replacement or maintenance amount based on the property type, age, construction and condition of the property that is adequate to maintain the physical condition and NOI of the property.

Salvage title means a form of vehicle title branding, which notes that the vehicle has been severely damaged and/or deemed a total loss and uneconomical to repair by an insurance company that paid a claim on the vehicle.

Total debt, with respect to a borrower, means:

(1) In the case of an automobile loan, the sum of:

(i) All monthly housing payments (rent- or mortgage-related, including property taxes, insurance and home owners association fees); and

(ii) Any of the following that is dependent upon the borrower's income for payment:

(A) Monthly payments on other debt and lease obligations, such as credit card loans or installment loans, including the monthly amount due on the automobile loan;

(B) Estimated monthly amortizing payments for any term debt, debts with other than monthly payments and debts not in repayment (such as deferred student loans, interest-only loans); and

(C) Any required monthly alimony, child support or court-ordered payments; and

(2) In the case of a commercial loan, the outstanding balance of all long-term debt (obligations that have a remaining maturity of more than one year) and the current portion of all debt that matures in one year or less.

Total liabilities ratio means the borrower's total liabilities divided by the sum of the borrower's total liabilities and equity, less the borrower's intangible assets, with each component determined in accordance with GAAP.

Trade-in allowance means the amount a vehicle purchaser is given as a credit at the purchase of a vehicle for the fair exchange of the borrower's existing vehicle to compensate the dealer for some portion of the vehicle purchase price, not to exceed the highest trade-in value of the existing vehicle, as determined by a nationally recognized automobile pricing agency and based on the manufacturer, year, model, features, mileage, and condition of the vehicle, less the payoff balance of any outstanding debt collateralized by the existing vehicle.

Uniform Standards of Professional Appraisal Practice (USPAP) means generally accepted standards for professional appraisal practice issued by the Appraisal Standards Board of the Appraisal Foundation.

§ 267.15 Qualifying commercial loans, commercial real estate loans, and automobile loans.

(a) *General exception for qualifying assets.* Commercial loans, commercial real estate loans, and automobile loans that are securitized through a securitization transaction shall be subject to a 0 percent risk retention requirement under subpart B, provided that the following conditions are met:

(1) The assets meet the underwriting standards set forth in §§ 267.16 (qualifying commercial loans), 267.17 (qualifying CRE loans), or 267.18 (qualifying automobile loans) of this part, as applicable;

(2) The securitization transaction is collateralized solely by loans of the same asset class and by servicing assets;

(3) The securitization transaction does not permit reinvestment periods; and

(4) The sponsor provides, or causes to be provided, to potential investors a reasonable period of time prior to the sale of asset-backed securities of the issuing entity, and, upon request, to the Commission, and to its appropriate Federal banking agency, if any, in written form under the caption "Credit Risk Retention", a description of the manner in which the sponsor determined the aggregate risk retention requirement for the securitization transaction after including qualifying commercial loans, qualifying CRE loans, or qualifying automobile loans with 0 percent risk retention.

(b) *Risk retention requirement.* For any securitization transaction described in paragraph (a) of this section, the percentage of risk retention required under § 267.3(a) is reduced by the percentage evidenced by the ratio of the unpaid principal balance of the qualifying commercial loans, qualifying CRE loans, or qualifying automobile loans (as applicable) to the total unpaid principal balance of commercial loans, CRE loans, or automobile loans (as applicable) that are included in the pool of assets collateralizing the asset-backed securities issued pursuant to the securitization transaction (the qualifying asset ratio); provided that:

(1) The qualifying asset ratio is measured as of the cut-off date or similar date for establishing the composition of the securitized assets collateralizing the asset-backed securities issued pursuant to the securitization transaction;

(2) If the qualifying asset ratio would exceed 50 percent, the qualifying asset ratio shall be deemed to be 50 percent; and

(3) The disclosure required by paragraph (a)(4) of this section also includes descriptions of the qualifying commercial loans, qualifying CRE loans, and qualifying automobile loans (qualifying assets) and descriptions of the assets that are not qualifying assets, and the material differences between the group of qualifying assets and the group of assets that are not qualifying assets with respect to the composition of each group's loan balances, loan terms, interest rates, borrower credit information, and characteristics of any loan collateral.

(c) *Exception for securitizations of qualifying assets only.* Notwithstanding other provisions of this section, the risk retention requirements of subpart B of this part shall not apply to securitization transactions where the transaction is collateralized solely by servicing assets and either qualifying commercial loans, qualifying CRE loans, or qualifying automobile loans.

(d) *Record maintenance.* A sponsor must retain the disclosures required in paragraphs (a) and (b) of this section and the certifications required in §§ 267.16(a)(8), 267.17(a)(10), and 267.18(a)(8), as applicable, in its records until three years after all ABS interests issued in the securitization are no longer outstanding. The sponsor must provide the disclosures and certifications upon request to the Commission and the sponsor's appropriate Federal banking agency, if any.

§ 267.16 Underwriting standards for qualifying commercial loans.

(a) *Underwriting, product and other standards.* (1) Prior to origination of the commercial loan, the originator:

(i) Verified and documented the financial condition of the borrower:

(A) As of the end of the borrower's two most recently completed fiscal years; and

(B) During the period, if any, since the end of its most recently completed fiscal year;

(ii) Conducted an analysis of the borrower's ability to service its overall debt obligations during the next two years, based on reasonable projections;

(iii) Determined that, based on the previous two years' actual performance, the borrower had:

(A) A total liabilities ratio of 50 percent or less;

(B) A leverage ratio of 3.0 or less; and

(C) A DSC ratio of 1.5 or greater;

(iv) Determined that, based on the two years of projections, which include the new debt obligation, following the closing date of the loan, the borrower will have:

(A) A total liabilities ratio of 50 percent or less;

(B) A leverage ratio of 3.0 or less; and

(C) A DSC ratio of 1.5 or greater.

(2) Prior to, upon or promptly following the inception of the loan, the originator:

(i) If the loan is originated on a secured basis, obtains a perfected security interest (by filing, title notation or otherwise) or, in the case of real property, a recorded lien, on all of the property pledged to collateralize the loan; and

(ii) If the loan documents indicate the purpose of the loan is to finance the purchase of tangible or intangible property, or to refinance such a loan, obtains a first lien on the property.

(3) The loan documentation for the commercial loan includes covenants that:

(i) Require the borrower to provide to the servicer of the commercial loan the borrower's financial statements and supporting schedules on an ongoing basis, but not less frequently than quarterly;

(ii) Prohibit the borrower from retaining or entering into a debt arrangement that permits payments-in-kind;

(iii) Impose limits on:

(A) The creation or existence of any other security interest or lien with respect to any of the borrower's property that serves as collateral for the loan;

(B) The transfer of any of the borrower's assets that serve as collateral for the loan; and

(C) Any change to the name, location or organizational structure of the borrower, or any other party that pledges collateral for the loan;

(iv) Require the borrower and any other party that pledges collateral for the loan to:

(A) Maintain insurance that protects against loss on the collateral for the commercial loan at least up to the amount of the loan, and that names the originator or any subsequent holder of the loan as an additional insured or loss payee;

(B) Pay taxes, charges, fees, and claims, where non-payment might give rise to a lien on any collateral;

(C) Take any action required to perfect or protect the security interest and first lien (as applicable) of the originator or any subsequent holder of the loan in any collateral for the commercial loan or the priority thereof, and to defend any collateral against claims adverse to the lender's interest;

(D) Permit the originator or any subsequent holder of the loan, and the servicer of the loan, to inspect any collateral for the commercial loan and the books and records of the borrower; and

(E) Maintain the physical condition of any collateral for the commercial loan.

(4) Loan payments required under the loan agreement are:

(i) Based on level monthly payments of principal and interest (at the fully indexed rate) that fully amortize the debt over a term that does not exceed five years from the date of origination; and

(ii) To be made no less frequently than quarterly over a term that does not exceed five years.

(5) The primary source of repayment for the loan is revenue from the business operations of the borrower.

(6) The loan was funded within the six (6) months prior to the cut-off date or similar date for establishing the composition of the securitized assets collateralizing the asset-backed securities issued pursuant to the securitization transaction.

(7) At the cut-off date or similar date for establishing the composition of the securitized assets collateralizing the asset-backed securities issued pursuant to the securitization transaction, all payments due on the loan are contractually current.

(8)(i) The depositor of the asset-backed security certifies that it has evaluated the effectiveness of its internal supervisory controls with respect to the process for ensuring that all qualifying commercial loans that collateralize the asset-backed security and that reduce the sponsor's risk retention requirement under § 267.15 meet all of the requirements set forth in paragraphs (a)(1) through (7) of this section and has concluded that its internal supervisory controls are effective;

(ii) The evaluation of the effectiveness of the depositor's internal supervisory controls referenced in paragraph (a)(8)(i) of this section shall be performed, for each issuance of an asset-backed security, as of a date within 60 days of the cut-off date or similar date for establishing the composition of the asset pool collateralizing such asset-backed security; and

(iii) The sponsor provides, or causes to be provided, a copy of the certification described in paragraph (a)(8)(i) of this section to potential investors a reasonable period of time prior to the sale of asset-backed securities in the issuing entity, and, upon request, to its appropriate Federal banking agency, if any.

(b) *Cure or buy-back requirement.* If a sponsor has relied on the exception provided in § 267.15 with respect to a qualifying commercial loan and it is subsequently determined that the loan did not meet all of the requirements set forth in paragraphs (a)(1) through (7) of this section, the sponsor shall not lose the benefit of the exception with respect to the commercial loan if the depositor complied with the certification requirement set forth in paragraph (a)(8) of this section and:

(1) The failure of the loan to meet any of the requirements set forth in paragraphs (a)(1) through (7) of this section is not material; or

(2) No later than 90 days after the determination that the loan does not meet one or more of the requirements

of paragraphs (a)(1) through (7) of this section, the sponsor:

(i) Effectuates cure, establishing conformity of the loan to the unmet requirements as of the date of cure; or

(ii) Repurchases the loan(s) from the issuing entity at a price at least equal to the remaining principal balance and accrued interest on the loan(s) as of the date of repurchase.

(3) If the sponsor cures or repurchases pursuant to paragraph (b)(2) of this section, the sponsor must promptly notify, or cause to be notified, the holders of the asset-backed securities issued in the securitization transaction of any loan(s) included in such securitization transaction that is required to be cured or repurchased by the sponsor pursuant to paragraph (b)(2) of this section, including the principal amount of such loan(s) and the cause for such cure or repurchase.

§267.17 Underwriting standards for qualifying CRE loans.

(a) *Underwriting, product and other standards.* (1) The CRE loan must be secured by the following:

(i) An enforceable first lien, documented and recorded appropriately pursuant to applicable law, on the commercial real estate and improvements;

(ii)(A) An assignment of:

(*1*) Leases and rents and other occupancy agreements related to the commercial real estate or improvements or the operation thereof for which the borrower or an operating affiliate is a lessor or similar party and all payments under such leases and occupancy agreements; and

(*2*) All franchise, license and concession agreements related to the commercial real estate or improvements or the operation thereof for which the borrower or an operating affiliate is a lessor, licensor, concession granter or similar party and all payments under such other agreements, whether the assignments described in this paragraph (a)(1)(ii)(A)(*2*) are absolute or are stated to be made to the extent permitted by the agreements governing the applicable franchise, license or concession agreements;

(B) An assignment of all other payments due to the borrower or due to any operating affiliate in connection with the operation of the property described in paragraph (a)(1)(i) of this section; and

(C) The right to enforce the agreements described in paragraph (a)(1)(ii)(A) of this section and the agreements under which payments under paragraph (a)(1)(ii)(B) of this section are due against, and collect amounts due from, each lessee, occupant or other obligor whose payments were assigned pursuant to paragraphs (a)(1)(ii)(A) or (B) of this section upon a breach by the borrower of any of the terms of, or the occurrence of any other event of default (however denominated) under, the loan documents relating to such CRE loan; and

(iii) A security interest:

(A) In all interests of the borrower and any applicable operating affiliate in all tangible and intangible personal property of any kind, in or used in the operation of or in connection with, pertaining to, arising from, or constituting, any of the collateral described in paragraphs (a)(1)(i) or (ii) of this section; and

(B) In the form of a perfected security interest if the security interest in such property can be perfected by the filing of a financing statement, fixture filing, or similar document pursuant to the law governing the perfection of such security interest;

(2) Prior to origination of the CRE loan, the originator:

(i) Verified and documented the current financial condition of the borrower and each operating affiliate;

(ii) Obtained a written appraisal of the real property securing the loan that:

(A) Had an effective date not more than six months prior to the origination date of the loan by a competent and appropriately State-certified or State-licensed appraiser;

(B) Conforms to generally accepted appraisal standards as evidenced by the USPAP and the appraisal requirements[1] of the Federal banking agencies; and

---

[1] 12 CFR part 34, subpart C (OCC); 12 CFR part 208, subpart E, and 12 CFR part 225, subpart G (Board); and 12 CFR part 323 (FDIC).

(C) Provides an "as is" opinion of the market value of the real property, which includes an income approach;[2]

(iii) Qualified the borrower for the CRE loan based on a monthly payment amount derived from level monthly payments consisting of both principal and interest (at the fully-indexed rate) over the term of the loan, not exceeding 25 years, or 30 years for a qualifying multi-family property;

(iv) Conducted an environmental risk assessment to gain environmental information about the property securing the loan and took appropriate steps to mitigate any environmental liability determined to exist based on this assessment;

(v) Conducted an analysis of the borrower's ability to service its overall debt obligations during the next two years, based on reasonable projections (including operating income projections for the property);

(vi)(A) Determined that based on the two years' actual performance immediately preceding the origination of the loan, the borrower would have had:

(1) A DSC ratio of 1.5 or greater, if the loan is a qualifying leased CRE loan, net of any income derived from a tenant(s) who is not a qualified tenant(s);

(2) A DSC ratio of 1.25 or greater, if the loan is a qualifying multi-family property loan; or

(3) A DSC ratio of 1.7 or greater, if the loan is any other type of CRE loan;

(B) If the borrower did not own the property for any part of the last two years prior to origination, the calculation of the DSC ratio, for purposes of paragraph (a)(2)(vi)(A) of this section, shall include the property's operating income for any portion of the two-year period during which the borrower did not own the property;

(vii) Determined that, based on two years of projections, which include the new debt obligation, following the origination date of the loan, the borrower will have:

(A) A DSC ratio of 1.5 or greater, if the loan is a qualifying leased CRE loan, net of any income derived from a tenant(s) who is not a qualified tenant(s);

___
[2] See USPAP, Standard 1.

(B) A DSC ratio of 1.25 or greater, if the loan is a qualifying multi-family property loan; or

(C) A DSC ratio of 1.7 or greater, if the loan is any other type of CRE loan.

(3) The loan documentation for the CRE loan includes covenants that:

(i) Require the borrower to provide the borrower's financial statements and supporting schedules to the servicer on an ongoing basis, but not less frequently than quarterly, including information on existing, maturing and new leasing or rent-roll activity for the property securing the loan, as appropriate; and

(ii) Impose prohibitions on:

(A) The creation or existence of any other security interest with respect to the collateral for the CRE loan described in paragraphs (a)(1)(i) and (a)(1)(ii)(A) of this section, except as provided in paragraph (a)(4) of this section;

(B) The transfer of any collateral for the CRE loan described in paragraph (a)(1)(i) or (a)(1)(ii)(A) of this section or of any other collateral consisting of fixtures, furniture, furnishings, machinery or equipment other than any such fixture, furniture, furnishings, machinery or equipment that is obsolete or surplus; and

(C) Any change to the name, location or organizational structure of any borrower, operating affiliate or other pledgor unless such borrower, operating affiliate or other pledgor shall have given the holder of the loan at least 30 days advance notice and, pursuant to applicable law governing perfection and priority, the holder of the loan is able to take all steps necessary to continue its perfection and priority during such 30-day period.

(iii) Require each borrower and each operating affiliate to:

(A) Maintain insurance that protects against loss on collateral for the CRE loan described in paragraph (a)(1)(i) of this section for an amount no less than the replacement cost of the property improvements, and names the originator or any subsequent holder of the loan as an additional insured or lender loss payee;

(B) Pay taxes, charges, fees, and claims, where non-payment might give rise to a lien on collateral for the CRE loan described in paragraphs (a)(1)(i) and (ii) of this section;

(C) Take any action required to:

(1) Protect the security interest and the enforceability and priority thereof in the collateral described in paragraphs (a)(1)(i) and (a)(1)(ii)(A) of this section and defend such collateral against claims adverse to the originator's or any subsequent holder's interest; and

(2) Perfect the security interest of the originator or any subsequent holder of the loan in any other collateral for the CRE loan to the extent that such security interest is required by this section to be perfected;

(D) Permit the originator or any subsequent holder of the loan, and the servicer, to inspect any collateral for the CRE loan and the books and records of the borrower or other party relating to any collateral for the CRE loan;

(E) Maintain the physical condition of collateral for the CRE loan described in paragraph (a)(1)(i) of this section;

(F) Comply with all environmental, zoning, building code, licensing and other laws, regulations, agreements, covenants, use restrictions, and proffers applicable to collateral for the CRE loan described in paragraph (a)(1)(i) of this section;

(G) Comply with leases, franchise agreements, condominium declarations, and other documents and agreements relating to the operation of collateral for the CRE loan described in paragraph (a)(1)(i) of this section, and to not modify any material terms and conditions of such agreements over the term of the loan without the consent of the originator or any subsequent holder of the loan, or the servicer; and

(H) Not materially alter collateral for the CRE loan described in paragraph (a)(1)(i) of this section without the consent of the originator or any subsequent holder of the loan, or the servicer.

(4) The loan documentation for the CRE loan prohibits the borrower and each operating affiliate from obtaining a loan secured by a junior lien on collateral for the CRE loan described in paragraph (a)(1)(i) or (a)(1)(ii)(A) of this section, unless:

(i) The sum of the principal amount of such junior lien loan, plus the principal amount of all other loans secured by collateral described in paragraph (a)(1)(i) or (a)(1)(ii)(A) of this section, does not exceed the applicable CLTV ratio in paragraph (a)(5) of this section, based on the appraisal at origination of such junior lien loan; or

(ii) Such loan is a purchase money obligation that financed the acquisition of machinery or equipment and the borrower or operating affiliate (as applicable) pledges such machinery and equipment as additional collateral for the CRE loan.

(5) At origination, the applicable loan-to-value ratios for the loan are:

(i) LTV less than or equal to 65 percent and CLTV less than or equal to 70 percent; or

(ii) LTV less than or equal to 60 percent and CLTV less than or equal to 65 percent, if an appraisal used to meet the requirements set forth in paragraph (a)(2)(ii) of this section used a direct capitalization rate, and that rate is less than or equal to the sum of:

(A) The 10-year swap rate, as reported in the Federal Reserve's H.15 Report (or any successor report) as of the date concurrent with the effective date of such appraisal; and

(B) 300 basis points.

(iii) If the appraisal required under paragraph (a)(2)(ii) of this section included a direct capitalization method using an overall capitalization rate, that rate must be disclosed to potential investors in the securitization.

(6) All loan payments required to be made under the loan agreement are:

(i) Based on level monthly payments of principal and interest (at the fully indexed rate) to fully amortize the debt over a term that does not exceed 25 years, or 30 years for a qualifying multifamily loan; and

(ii) To be made no less frequently than monthly over a term of at least ten years.

(7) Under the terms of the loan agreement:

(i) Any maturity of the note occurs no earlier than ten years following the date of origination;

(ii) The borrower is not permitted to defer repayment of principal or payment of interest; and

579

(iii) The interest rate on the loan is:

(A) A fixed interest rate;

(B) An adjustable interest rate and the borrower, prior to or concurrently with origination of the CRE loan, obtained a derivative that effectively results in a fixed interest rate; or

(C) An adjustable interest rate and the borrower, prior to or concurrently with origination of the CRE loan, obtained a derivative that established a cap on the interest rate for the term of the loan, and the loan meets the underwriting criteria in paragraphs (a)(2)(vi) and (vii) of this section using the maximum interest rate allowable under the interest rate cap.

(8) The originator does not establish an interest reserve at origination to fund all or part of a payment on the loan.

(9) At the cut-off date or similar date for establishing the composition of the securitized assets collateralizing the asset-backed securities issued pursuant to the securitization transaction, all payments due on the loan are contractually current.

(10)(i) The depositor of the asset-backed security certifies that it has evaluated the effectiveness of its internal supervisory controls with respect to the process for ensuring that all qualifying CRE loans that collateralize the asset-backed security and that reduce the sponsor's risk retention requirement under § 267.15 meet all of the requirements set forth in paragraphs (a)(1) through (9) of this section and has concluded that its internal supervisory controls are effective;

(ii) The evaluation of the effectiveness of the depositor's internal supervisory controls referenced in paragraph (a)(10)(i) of this section shall be performed, for each issuance of an asset-backed security, as of a date within 60 days of the cut-off date or similar date for establishing the composition of the asset pool collateralizing such asset-backed security;

(iii) The sponsor provides, or causes to be provided, a copy of the certification described in paragraph (a)(10)(i) of this section to potential investors a reasonable period of time prior to the sale of asset-backed securities in the issuing entity, and, upon request, to its appropriate Federal banking agency, if any; and

(11) Within two weeks of the closing of the CRE loan by its originator or, if sooner, prior to the transfer of such CRE loan to the issuing entity, the originator shall have obtained a UCC lien search from the jurisdiction of organization of the borrower and each operating affiliate, that does not report, as of the time that the security interest of the originator in the property described in paragraph (a)(1)(iii) of this section was perfected, other higher priority liens of record on any property described in paragraph (a)(1)(iii) of this section, other than purchase money security interests.

(b) *Cure or buy-back requirement.* If a sponsor has relied on the exception provided in § 267.15 with respect to a qualifying CRE loan and it is subsequently determined that the CRE loan did not meet all of the requirements set forth in paragraphs (a)(1) through (9) and (a)(11) of this section, the sponsor shall not lose the benefit of the exception with respect to the CRE loan if the depositor complied with the certification requirement set forth in paragraph (a)(10) of this section, and:

(1) The failure of the loan to meet any of the requirements set forth in paragraphs (a)(1) through (9) and (a)(11) of this section is not material; or;

(2) No later than 90 days after the determination that the loan does not meet one or more of the requirements of paragraphs (a)(1) through (9) or (a)(11) of this section, the sponsor:

(i) Effectuates cure, restoring conformity of the loan to the unmet requirements as of the date of cure; or

(ii) Repurchases the loan(s) from the issuing entity at a price at least equal to the remaining principal balance and accrued interest on the loan(s) as of the date of repurchase.

(3) If the sponsor cures or repurchases pursuant to paragraph (b)(2) of this section, the sponsor must promptly notify, or cause to be notified, the holders of the asset-backed securities issued in the securitization transaction of any loan(s) included in such securitization transaction that is required to be cured or repurchased by the sponsor pursuant to paragraph (b)(2) of this section, including the

principal amount of such repurchased loan(s) and the cause for such cure or repurchase.

§267.18 Underwriting standards for qualifying automobile loans.

(a) *Underwriting, product and other standards.* (1) Prior to origination of the automobile loan, the originator:

(i) Verified and documented that within 30 days of the date of origination:

(A) The borrower was not currently 30 days or more past due, in whole or in part, on any debt obligation;

(B) Within the previous 24 months, the borrower has not been 60 days or more past due, in whole or in part, on any debt obligation;

(C) Within the previous 36 months, the borrower has not:

(*1*) Been a debtor in a proceeding commenced under Chapter 7 (Liquidation), Chapter 11 (Reorganization), Chapter 12 (Family Farmer or Family Fisherman plan), or Chapter 13 (Individual Debt Adjustment) of the U.S. Bankruptcy Code; or

(*2*) Been the subject of any federal or State judicial judgment for the collection of any unpaid debt;

(D) Within the previous 36 months, no one-to-four family property owned by the borrower has been the subject of any foreclosure, deed in lieu of foreclosure, or short sale; or

(E) Within the previous 36 months, the borrower has not had any personal property repossessed;

(ii) Determined and documented that the borrower has at least 24 months of credit history; and

(iii) Determined and documented that, upon the origination of the loan, the borrower's DTI ratio is less than or equal to 36 percent.

(A) For the purpose of making the determination under paragraph (a)(1)(iii) of this section, the originator must:

(*1*) Verify and document all income of the borrower that the originator includes in the borrower's effective monthly income (using payroll stubs, tax returns, profit and loss statements, or other similar documentation); and

(*2*) On or after the date of the borrower's written application and prior to origination, obtain a credit report regarding the borrower from a consumer reporting agency that compiles and maintain files on consumers on a nationwide basis (within the meaning of 15 U.S.C. 1681a(p)) and verify that all outstanding debts reported in the borrower's credit report are incorporated into the calculation of the borrower's DTI ratio under paragraph (a)(1)(iii) of this section;

(2) An originator will be deemed to have met the requirements of paragraph (a)(1)(i) of this section if:

(i) The originator, no more than 30 days before the closing of the loan, obtains a credit report regarding the borrower from a consumer reporting agency that compiles and maintains files on consumers on a nationwide basis (within the meaning of 15 U.S.C. 1681a(p));

(ii) Based on the information in such credit report, the borrower meets all of the requirements of paragraph (a)(1)(i) of this section, and no information in a credit report subsequently obtained by the originator before the closing of the loan contains contrary information; and

(iii) The originator obtains electronic or hard copies of the credit report.

(3) At closing of the automobile loan, the borrower makes a down payment from the borrower's personal funds and trade-in allowance, if any, that is at least equal to the sum of:

(i) The full cost of the vehicle title, tax, and registration fees;

(ii) Any dealer-imposed fees;

(iii) The full cost of any additional warranties, insurance or other products purchased in connection with the purchase of the vehicle; and

(iv) 10 percent of the vehicle purchase price.

(4) The originator records a first lien securing the loan on the purchased vehicle in accordance with State law.

(5) The terms of the loan agreement provide a maturity date for the loan that does not exceed the lesser of:

(i) Six years from the date of origination; or

(ii) 10 years minus the difference between the current model year and the vehicle's model year.

(6) The terms of the loan agreement:

(i) Specify a fixed rate of interest for the life of the loan;

(ii) Provide for a level monthly payment amount that fully amortizes the amount financed over the loan term;

(iii) Do not permit the borrower to defer repayment of principal or payment of interest; and

(iv) Require the borrower to make the first payment on the automobile loan within 45 days of the loan's contract date.

(7) At the cut-off date or similar date for establishing the composition of the securitized assets collateralizing the asset-backed securities issued pursuant to the securitization transaction, all payments due on the loan are contractually current; and

(8)(i) The depositor of the asset-backed security certifies that it has evaluated the effectiveness of its internal supervisory controls with respect to the process for ensuring that all qualifying automobile loans that collateralize the asset-backed security and that reduce the sponsor's risk retention requirement under § 267.15 meet all of the requirements set forth in paragraphs (a)(1) through (7) of this section and has concluded that its internal supervisory controls are effective;

(ii) The evaluation of the effectiveness of the depositor's internal supervisory controls referenced in paragraph (a)(8)(i) of this section shall be performed, for each issuance of an asset-backed security, as of a date within 60 days of the cut-off date or similar date for establishing the composition of the asset pool collateralizing such asset-backed security; and

(iii) The sponsor provides, or causes to be provided, a copy of the certification described in paragraph (a)(8)(i) of this section to potential investors a reasonable period of time prior to the sale of asset-backed securities in the issuing entity, and, upon request, to its appropriate Federal banking agency, if any.

(b) *Cure or buy-back requirement.* If a sponsor has relied on the exception provided in § 267.15 with respect to a qualifying automobile loan and it is subsequently determined that the loan did not meet all of the requirements set forth in paragraphs (a)(1) through (7) of this section, the sponsor shall not lose the benefit of the exception with respect to the automobile loan if the depositor complied with the certification requirement set forth in paragraph (a)(8) of this section, and:

(1) The failure of the loan to meet any of the requirements set forth in paragraphs (a)(1) through (7) of this section is not material; or

(2) No later than ninety (90) days after the determination that the loan does not meet one or more of the requirements of paragraphs (a)(1) through (7) of this section, the sponsor:

(i) Effectuates cure, establishing conformity of the loan to the unmet requirements as of the date of cure; or

(ii) Repurchases the loan(s) from the issuing entity at a price at least equal to the remaining principal balance and accrued interest on the loan(s) as of the date of repurchase.

(3) If the sponsor cures or repurchases pursuant to paragraph (b)(2) of this section, the sponsor must promptly notify, or cause to be notified, the holders of the asset-backed securities issued in the securitization transaction of any loan(s) included in such securitization transaction that is required to be cured or repurchased by the sponsor pursuant to paragraph (b)(2) of this section, including the principal amount of such loan(s) and the cause for such cure or repurchase.

§ 267.19 General exemptions.

(a) *Definitions.* For purposes of this section, the following definitions shall apply:

Community-focused residential mortgage means a residential mortgage exempt from the definition of "covered transaction" under § 1026.43(a)(3)(iv) and (v) of the CFPB's Regulation Z (12 CFR 1026.43(a)).

First pay class means a class of ABS interests for which all interests in the class are entitled to the same priority of payment and that, at the time of closing of the transaction, is entitled to repayments of principal and payments of interest prior to or pro-rata with all other classes of securities collateralized by the same pool of first-lien residential mortgages, until such class has no principal or notional balance remaining.

Inverse floater means an ABS interest issued as part of a securitization transaction for which interest or other income is payable to the holder based on a rate or formula that varies inversely to a reference rate of interest.

Qualifying three-to-four unit residential mortgage loan means a mortgage loan that is:

(i) Secured by a dwelling (as defined in 12 CFR 1026.2(a)(19)) that is owner occupied and contains three-to-four housing units;

(ii) Is deemed to be for business purposes for purposes of Regulation Z under 12 CFR part 1026, Supplement I, paragraph 3(a)(5)(i); and

(iii) Otherwise meets all of the requirements to qualify as a qualified mortgage under §1026.43(e) and (f) of Regulation Z (12 CFR 1026.43(e) and (f)) as if the loan were a covered transaction under that section.

(b) This part shall not apply to:

(1) *U.S. Government-backed securitizations.* Any securitization transaction that:

(i) Is collateralized solely by residential, multifamily, or health care facility mortgage loan assets that are insured or guaranteed (in whole or in part) as to the payment of principal and interest by the United States or an agency of the United States, and servicing assets; or

(ii) Involves the issuance of asset-backed securities that:

(A) Are insured or guaranteed as to the payment of principal and interest by the United States or an agency of the United States; and

(B) Are collateralized solely by residential, multifamily, or health care facility mortgage loan assets or interests in such assets, and servicing assets.

(2) *Certain agricultural loan securitizations.* Any securitization transaction that is collateralized solely by loans or other assets made, insured, guaranteed, or purchased by any institution that is subject to the supervision of the Farm Credit Administration, including the Federal Agricultural Mortgage Corporation, and servicing assets;

(3) *State and municipal securitizations.* Any asset-backed security that is a security issued or guaranteed by any State, or by any political subdivision of a State, or by any public instrumentality of a State that is exempt from the registration requirements of the Securities Act of 1933 by reason of section 3(a)(2) of that Act (15 U.S.C. 77c(a)(2)); and

(4) *Qualified scholarship funding bonds.* Any asset-backed security that meets the definition of a qualified scholarship funding bond, as set forth in section 150(d)(2) of the Internal Revenue Code of 1986 (26 U.S.C. 150(d)(2)).

(5) *Pass-through resecuritizations.* Any securitization transaction that:

(i) Is collateralized solely by servicing assets, and by asset-backed securities:

(A) For which credit risk was retained as required under subpart B of this part; or

(B) That were exempted from the credit risk retention requirements of this part pursuant to subpart D of this part;

(ii) Is structured so that it involves the issuance of only a single class of ABS interests; and

(iii) Provides for the pass-through of all principal and interest payments received on the underlying asset-backed securities (net of expenses of the issuing entity) to the holders of such class.

(6) *First-pay-class securitizations.* Any securitization transaction that:

(i) Is collateralized solely by servicing assets, and by first-pay classes of asset-backed securities collateralized by first-lien residential mortgages on properties located in any state:

(A) For which credit risk was retained as required under subpart B of this part; or

(B) That were exempted from the credit risk retention requirements of this part pursuant to subpart D of this part;

(ii) Does not provide for any ABS interest issued in the securitization transaction to share in realized principal losses other than pro rata with all other ABS interests issued in the securitization transaction based on the current unpaid principal balance of such ABS interests at the time the loss is realized;

(iii) Is structured to reallocate prepayment risk;

(iv) Does not reallocate credit risk (other than as a consequence of reallocation of prepayment risk); and

(v) Does not include any inverse floater or similarly structured ABS interest.

(7) *Seasoned loans.* (i) Any securitization transaction that is collateralized solely by servicing assets, and by seasoned loans that meet the following requirements:

(A) The loans have not been modified since origination; and

(B) None of the loans have been delinquent for 30 days or more.

(ii) For purposes of this paragraph, a *seasoned loan* means:

(A) With respect to asset-backed securities collateralized by residential mortgages, a loan that has been outstanding and performing for the longer of:

(*1*) A period of five years; or

(*2*) Until the outstanding principal balance of the loan has been reduced to 25 percent of the original principal balance.

(*3*) Notwithstanding paragraphs (b)(7)(ii)(A)(*1*) and (*2*) of this section, any residential mortgage loan that has been outstanding and performing for a period of at least seven years shall be deemed a seasoned loan.

(B) With respect to all other classes of asset-backed securities, a loan that has been outstanding and performing for the longer of:

(*1*) A period of at least two years; or

(*2*) Until the outstanding principal balance of the loan has been reduced to 33 percent of the original principal balance.

(8) *Certain public utility securitizations.* (i) Any securitization transaction where the asset-back securities issued in the transaction are secured by the intangible property right to collect charges for the recovery of specified costs and such other assets, if any, of an issuing entity that is wholly owned, directly or indirectly, by an investor owned utility company that is subject to the regulatory authority of a State public utility commission or other appropriate State agency.

(ii) For purposes of this paragraph:

(A) *Specified cost* means any cost identified by a State legislature as appropriate for recovery through securitization pursuant to specified cost recovery legislation; and

(B) *Specified cost recovery legislation* means legislation enacted by a State that:

(*1*) Authorizes the investor owned utility company to apply for, and authorizes the public utility commission or other appropriate State agency to issue, a financing order determining the amount of specified costs the utility will be allowed to recover;

(*2*) Provides that pursuant to a financing order, the utility acquires an intangible property right to charge, collect, and receive amounts necessary to provide for the full recovery of the specified costs determined to be recoverable, and assures that the charges are non-bypassable and will be paid by customers within the utility's historic service territory who receive utility goods or services through the utility's transmission and distribution system, even if those customers elect to purchase these goods or services from a third party; and

(*3*) Guarantees that neither the State nor any of its agencies has the authority to rescind or amend the financing order, to revise the amount of specified costs, or in any way to reduce or impair the value of the intangible property right, except as may be contemplated by periodic adjustments authorized by the specified cost recovery legislation.

(c) *Exemption for securitizations of assets issued, insured or guaranteed by the United States.* This part shall not apply to any securitization transaction if the asset-backed securities issued in the transaction are:

(1) Collateralized solely by obligations issued by the United States or an agency of the United States and servicing assets;

(2) Collateralized solely by assets that are fully insured or guaranteed as to the payment of principal and interest by the United States or an agency of the United States (other than those referred to in paragraph (b)(1)(i) of this section) and servicing assets; or

(3) Fully guaranteed as to the timely payment of principal and interest by the United States or any agency of the United States;

584

(d) *Federal Deposit Insurance Corporation securitizations.* This part shall not apply to any securitization transaction that is sponsored by the Federal Deposit Insurance Corporation acting as conservator or receiver under any provision of the Federal Deposit Insurance Act or of Title II of the Dodd-Frank Wall Street Reform and Consumer Protection Act.

(e) *Reduced requirement for certain student loan securitizations.* The 5 percent risk retention requirement set forth in §267.4 shall be modified as follows:

(1) With respect to a securitization transaction that is collateralized solely by student loans made under the Federal Family Education Loan Program ("FFELP loans") that are guaranteed as to 100 percent of defaulted principal and accrued interest, and servicing assets, the risk retention requirement shall be 0 percent;

(2) With respect to a securitization transaction that is collateralized solely by FFELP loans that are guaranteed as to at least 98 percent but less than 100 percent of defaulted principal and accrued interest, and servicing assets, the risk retention requirement shall be 2 percent; and

(3) With respect to any other securitization transaction that is collateralized solely by FFELP loans, and servicing assets, the risk retention requirement shall be 3 percent.

(f) *Community-focused lending securitizations.* (1) This part shall not apply to any securitization transaction if the asset-backed securities issued in the transaction are collateralized solely by community-focused residential mortgages and servicing assets.

(2) For any securitization transaction that includes both community-focused residential mortgages and residential mortgages that are not exempt from risk retention under this part, the percent of risk retention required under §267.4(a) is reduced by the ratio of the unpaid principal balance of the community-focused residential mortgages to the total unpaid principal balance of residential mortgages that are included in the pool of assets collateralizing the asset-backed securities issued pursuant to the securitization transaction (the community-focused residential mortgage asset ratio); provided that:

(i) The community-focused residential mortgage asset ratio is measured as of the cut-off date or similar date for establishing the composition of the pool assets collateralizing the asset-backed securities issued pursuant to the securitization transaction; and

(ii) If the community-focused residential mortgage asset ratio would exceed 50 percent, the community-focused residential mortgage asset ratio shall be deemed to be 50 percent.

(g) *Exemptions for securitizations of certain three-to-four unit mortgage loans.* A sponsor shall be exempt from the risk retention requirements in subpart B of this part with respect to any securitization transaction if:

(1)(i) The asset-backed securities issued in the transaction are collateralized solely by qualifying three-to-four unit residential mortgage loans and servicing assets; or

(ii) The asset-backed securities issued in the transaction are collateralized solely by qualifying three-to-four unit residential mortgage loans, qualified residential mortgages as defined in §267.13, and servicing assets.

(2) The depositor with respect to the securitization provides the certifications set forth in §267.13(b)(4) with respect to the process for ensuring that all assets that collateralize the asset-backed securities issued in the transaction are qualifying three-to-four unit residential mortgage loans, qualified residential mortgages, or servicing assets; and

(3) The sponsor of the securitization complies with the repurchase requirements in §267.13(c) with respect to a loan if, after closing, it is determined that the loan does not meet all of the criteria to be either a qualified residential mortgage or a qualifying three-to-four unit residential mortgage loan, as appropriate.

(h) *Rule of construction.* Securitization transactions involving the issuance of asset-backed securities that are either issued, insured, or guaranteed by, or are collateralized by obligations issued by, or loans that are issued, insured, or guaranteed by, the Federal National Mortgage Association, the Federal Home Loan Mortgage Corporation, or a Federal home loan bank shall not on that basis qualify for exemption under this part.

§ 267.20 Safe harbor for certain foreign-related transactions.

(a) *Definitions.* For purposes of this section, the following definition shall apply:

U.S. person means:

(i) Any of the following:

(A) Any natural person resident in the United States;

(B) Any partnership, corporation, limited liability company, or other organization or entity organized or incorporated under the laws of any State or of the United States;

(C) Any estate of which any executor or administrator is a U.S. person (as defined under any other clause of this definition);

(D) Any trust of which any trustee is a U.S. person (as defined under any other clause of this definition);

(E) Any agency or branch of a foreign entity located in the United States;

(F) Any non-discretionary account or similar account (other than an estate or trust) held by a dealer or other fiduciary for the benefit or account of a U.S. person (as defined under any other clause of this definition);

(G) Any discretionary account or similar account (other than an estate or trust) held by a dealer or other fiduciary organized, incorporated, or (if an individual) resident in the United States; and

(H) Any partnership, corporation, limited liability company, or other organization or entity if:

(1) Organized or incorporated under the laws of any foreign jurisdiction; and

(2) Formed by a U.S. person (as defined under any other clause of this definition) principally for the purpose of investing in securities not registered under the Act; and

(ii) "U.S. person(s)" does not include:

(A) Any discretionary account or similar account (other than an estate or trust) held for the benefit or account of a person not constituting a U.S. person (as defined in paragraph (i) of this section) by a dealer or other professional fiduciary organized, incorporated, or (if an individual) resident in the United States;

(B) Any estate of which any professional fiduciary acting as executor or administrator is a U.S. person (as defined in paragraph (i) of this section) if:

(1) An executor or administrator of the estate who is not a U.S. person (as defined in paragraph (i) of this section) has sole or shared investment discretion with respect to the assets of the estate; and

(2) The estate is governed by foreign law;

(C) Any trust of which any professional fiduciary acting as trustee is a U.S. person (as defined in paragraph (i) of this section), if a trustee who is not a U.S. person (as defined in paragraph (i) of this section) has sole or shared investment discretion with respect to the trust assets, and no beneficiary of the trust (and no settlor if the trust is revocable) is a U.S. person (as defined in paragraph (i) of this section);

(D) An employee benefit plan established and administered in accordance with the law of a country other than the United States and customary practices and documentation of such country;

(E) Any agency or branch of a U.S. person (as defined in paragraph (i) of this section) located outside the United States if:

(1) The agency or branch operates for valid business reasons; and

(2) The agency or branch is engaged in the business of insurance or banking and is subject to substantive insurance or banking regulation, respectively, in the jurisdiction where located;

(F) The International Monetary Fund, the International Bank for Reconstruction and Development, the Inter-American Development Bank, the Asian Development Bank, the African Development Bank, the United Nations, and their agencies, affiliates and pension plans, and any other similar international organizations, their agencies, affiliates and pension plans.

(b) *In general.* This part shall not apply to a securitization transaction if all the following conditions are met:

(1) The securitization transaction is not required to be and is not registered under the Securities Act of 1933 (15 U.S.C. 77a *et seq.*);

(2) No more than 10 percent of the dollar value (or equivalent amount in

the currency in which the ABS interests are issued, as applicable) of all classes of ABS interests in the securitization transaction are sold or transferred to U.S. persons or for the account or benefit of U.S. persons;

(3) Neither the sponsor of the securitization transaction nor the issuing entity is:

(i) Chartered, incorporated, or organized under the laws of the United States or any State;

(ii) An unincorporated branch or office (wherever located) of an entity chartered, incorporated, or organized under the laws of the United States or any State; or

(iii) An unincorporated branch or office located in the United States or any State of an entity that is chartered, incorporated, or organized under the laws of a jurisdiction other than the United States or any State; and

(4) If the sponsor or issuing entity is chartered, incorporated, or organized under the laws of a jurisdiction other than the United States or any State, no more than 25 percent (as determined based on unpaid principal balance) of the assets that collateralize the ABS interests sold in the securitization transaction were acquired by the sponsor or issuing entity, directly or indirectly, from:

(i) A majority-owned affiliate of the sponsor or issuing entity that is chartered, incorporated, or organized under the laws of the United States or any State; or

(ii) An unincorporated branch or office of the sponsor or issuing entity that is located in the United States or any State.

(c) *Evasions prohibited.* In view of the objective of these rules and the policies underlying Section 15G of the Exchange Act, the safe harbor described in paragraph (b) of this section is not available with respect to any transaction or series of transactions that, although in technical compliance with paragraphs (a) and (b) of this section, is part of a plan or scheme to evade the requirements of section 15G and this part. In such cases, compliance with section 15G and this part is required.

§267.21   **Additional exemptions.**

(a) *Securitization transactions.* The federal agencies with rulewriting authority under section 15G(b) of the Exchange Act (15 U.S.C. 78o-11(b)) with respect to the type of assets involved may jointly provide a total or partial exemption of any securitization transaction as such agencies determine may be appropriate in the public interest and for the protection of investors.

(b) *Exceptions, exemptions, and adjustments.* The Federal banking agencies and the Commission, in consultation with the Federal Housing Finance Agency and the Department of Housing and Urban Development, may jointly adopt or issue exemptions, exceptions or adjustments to the requirements of this part, including exemptions, exceptions or adjustments for classes of institutions or assets in accordance with section 15G(e) of the Exchange Act (15 U.S.C. 78o-11(e)).

§267.22   **Periodic review of the QRM definition, exempted three-to-four unit residential mortgage loans, and community-focused residential mortgage exemption**

(a) The Federal banking agencies and the Commission, in consultation with the Federal Housing Finance Agency and the Department of Housing and Urban Development, shall commence a review of the definition of qualified residential mortgage in §267.13, a review of the community-focused residential mortgage exemption in §267.19(f), and a review of the exemption for qualifying three-to-four unit residential mortgage loans in §267.19(g):

(1) No later than four years after the effective date of the rule (as it relates to securitizers and originators of asset-backed securities collateralized by residential mortgages), five years following the completion of such initial review, and every five years thereafter; and

(2) At any time, upon the request of any Federal banking agency, the Commission, the Federal Housing Finance Agency or the Department of Housing and Urban Development, specifying the reason for such request, including as a

result of any amendment to the definition of qualified mortgage or changes in the residential housing market.

(b) The Federal banking agencies, the Commission, the Federal Housing Finance Agency and the Department of Housing and Urban Development shall publish in the FEDERAL REGISTER notice of the commencement of a review and, in the case of a review commenced under paragraph (a)(2) of this section, the reason an agency is requesting such review. After completion of any review, but no later than six months after the publication of the notice announcing the review, unless extended by the agencies, the agencies shall jointly publish a notice disclosing the determination of their review. If the agencies determine to amend the definition of qualified residential mortgage, the agencies shall complete any required rulemaking within 12 months of publication in the FEDERAL REGISTER of such notice disclosing the determination of their review, unless extended by the agencies.

SUBCHAPTER C—PLANNING ASSISTANCE TO HOUSING SPONSORS [RESERVED]
SUBCHAPTER D—PUBLICLY FINANCED HOUSING PROGRAMS [RESERVED]
SUBCHAPTERS E–H [RESERVED]

SUBCHAPTER I—HUD-OWNED PROPERTIES

PART 290—DISPOSITION OF MULTI-FAMILY PROJECTS AND SALE OF HUD-HELD MULTIFAMILY MORTGAGES

Subpart A—Disposition of Multifamily Projects

Subpart B—Sale of HUD-Held Multifamily Mortgages

AUTHORITY: 12 U.S.C. 1701z–11, 1701z–12, 1713, 1715b, 1715z–1b, 1715z–11a; 42 U.S.C. 3535(d) and 3535(i).

SOURCE: 61 FR 11685, Mar. 21, 1996, unless otherwise noted.

Subpart A—Disposition of Multifamily Projects

§ 290.1 Applicability.

The requirements of this part supplement the requirements of 12 U.S.C. 1701z–11 for the management and disposition of multifamily housing projects and the sale of HUD-held multifamily mortgages. The goals and objectives of this part are the same as the goals and objectives of 12 U.S.C. 1701z–11, which shall be referred to in this part as "the Statute." With respect to the disposition of multifamily projects under subpart A, HUD may follow any other method of disposition, as determined by the Secretary.

[64 FR 72412, Dec. 27, 1999]

§ 290.3 Definitions.

The terms *Department* and *URA* are defined in 24 CFR part 5. The following definitions apply to this part:

Cooperative means a nonprofit, limited equity, or consumer cooperative as defined under 24 CFR part 213. It may include mutual housing associations.

HUD-owned project means a multifamily project that has been acquired by HUD.

Market area means the area from which a multifamily housing project may reasonably be expected to draw a substantial number of its tenants, as determined by HUD, taking into consideration the knowledge of the HUD office with jurisdiction over the project of the local real estate market and HUD's project underwriting experience. Submarkets may be used in large, complex metropolitan areas.

Multifamily housing project means a multifamily project that is or was insured under sections 207, 213, 220, 221(d)(3), 221(d)(4), 223(f), 231, 236, or 608 of the National Housing Act (12 U.S.C. 1713, 1715e, 1715k, 1715l, 1715n, 1715v, 1715z–1, or 1742–1746); or is or was subject to a loan under section 202 of the Housing Act of 1959 (12 U.S.C. 1701q); or was a Real Estate Owned (REO) multifamily project transferred by the Government National Mortgage Association to the Department. Multifamily housing project does not include projects consisting of one to eleven units insured under section 220(d)(3)(A) of the National Housing Act (12 U.S.C. 1715l); or mobile home parks under section 207(m) of that Act (12 U.S.C. 1713); or vacant land; or property covered by a homeownership program approved under the Homeownership and Opportunity for People Everywhere ("HOPE") program.

Multifamily project means a project consisting of five or more units that has or had a mortgage (even if subordinate to other mortgages) insured under the National Housing Act or is or was subject to a loan under section 202 of the Housing Act of 1959, or a hospital, intermediate care facility, nursing home, group practice facility, or board and care facility that has or had a mortgage insured, or is or was subject to a loan under, these authorities. Multifamily project does not include projects consisting of one to eleven units insured under section 220(d)(3)(A) of the National Housing Act (12 U.S.C. 1715k), which are classified as single family homes.

Nonprofit organization means a corporation or association organized for purposes other than making a profit or gain for itself. Stockholders or trustees do not share in profits or losses. Profits are used to accomplish the charitable, humanitarian, or educational purposes of the corporation.

Preexisting tenant means a family that resides in a unit in a multifamily housing project immediately before the project is acquired under this part by a purchaser other than the Department.

Subsidized project means a multifamily housing project that is receiving, or immediately before its mortgage was foreclosed by HUD or the project was acquired by HUD, pursuant to this regulation, was receiving any of the following types of assistance:

(1) Below market interest rate mortgage insurance under the proviso of section 221(d)(5) of the National Housing Act (12 U.S.C. 1715l) (hereinafter, a BMIR project);

(2) Interest reduction payments made in connection with mortgages insured under section 236 of the National Housing Act (hereinafter, a 236 project);

(3) Direct loans made under section 202 of the Housing Act of 1959 (hereinafter, a 202 project);

(4) Assistance, to more than 50 percent of the units in the project, in the form of:

(i) Rent supplement payments under section 101 of the Housing and Urban Development Act of 1965 (12 U.S.C. 1701s) (hereinafter, Rent Supp);

(ii) Additional assistance payments under section 236(f)(2) of the National Housing Act (hereinafter, RAP);

(iii) Housing assistance payments under section 23 of the United States Housing Act of 1937 (42 U.S.C. 1437 *note*) (as in effect before January 1, 1975) (hereinafter, Sec. 23); or

(iv) Housing assistance payments under Section 8 of the United States Housing Act of 1937 (42 U.S.C. 1437f) (excluding payments of tenant-based Section 8 assistance) (hereinafter, project-based Section 8 assistance).

Sufficient habitable, affordable, rental housing is available means that the HUD office with jurisdiction determines that there is an adequate supply of habitable, affordable housing for low- and very low-income families available in the market area. Submarkets, consisting of portions of units of general local government, may be used in large, complex metropolitan areas. Local housing markets having an adequate supply of standard-quality rental housing would include housing markets in which the supply of rental housing available and in production is adequate to meet the anticipated demand (*e.g.*, the housing market is balanced), as well as those in which there is an excess supply of rental housing (*e.g.*, the housing market is soft). Rental markets that do not have an adequate supply (*e.g.*, tight markets) are characterized by low rental vacancy rates, low levels of production and turnover of rental housing, and, usually, by high levels of rent inflation. HUD will make the determination of whether sufficient habitable, affordable, rental housing is available using established market analysis techniques, and will consider information that demonstrates:

(1) The rental housing vacancy rate is at a low level relative to the rate required for a balanced market, typically a four percent vacancy rate; except that a rate lower than four percent may be considered in unusual circumstances if it can be demonstrated that there is an adequate supply of affordable housing for low-income families;

(2) The number of rental housing units being produced on an annual

basis is not large enough to satisfy demand arising from the increase in households, or, in markets where there is little or no growth, evidence that the number of additional rental units being supplied is not sufficient to meet the demand arising from net losses to the available inventory and the inadequate supply of rental housing has inhibited growth;

(3) The shortage of housing is resulting in rent increases that exceed normal increases commensurate with the costs of operating rental housing;

(4) A significant number, or proportion, of the households holding Section 8 certificates or rental vouchers are unable to find adequate housing because of the shortage of rental housing, including PHA data showing a lower than average percentage of units under lease and a longer than average time required to find units.

Unsubsidized project means a multifamily housing project that is not a subsidized project.

Useful life means, generally, twenty years, but it may be more or less, as determined by the Department.

§290.7 Occupancy requirements.

(a) *Multifamily housing project that is HUD-owned or for which HUD is mortgagee-in-possession.* Occupancy in a multifamily housing project that is HUD-owned or for which HUD is mortgagee-in-possession shall be available on a basis that is comparable to the occupancy requirements that applied to the project immediately before HUD acquired the project or became mortgagee-in-possession, except that preference shall be given to tenants of other HUD-owned multifamily housing projects who are eligible for assistance in accordance with the displacement and relocation provisions at §290.17.

(b) *Evictions.* Eviction from a HUD-owned multifamily housing project is governed by 24 CFR part 247, subpart B.

(c) *Threat to health and safety.* Whenever HUD determines that there is an immediate threat to the health and safety of the tenants, HUD may require the tenants to vacate the premises and shall provide temporary relocation benefits as provided in §290.17 to tenants required to vacate the premises.

§290.9 Setting rental rates.

Because of the subsidies involved in making multifamily housing projects affordable, the setting of rents involves two steps: first, establishing the rent on a unit that will be paid to the owner, and second, determining the rent that the tenant pays (with the difference made up by a subsidy), using a number of procedures to obtain income verification and notify tenants of changes in rent. These procedures for a property owned by HUD or where HUD is mortgagee-in-possession are explained below.

(a) *Setting unit rents.* Except as modified by this section, for a property where HUD is mortgagee-in-possession (MIP), HUD will set unit rents in accordance with the rent setting requirements of the project's mortgage insurance or direct loan program; or for a property owned by HUD, rents will be set in accordance with the rent setting requirements of the project's mortgage insurance or direct loan program in effect immediately before HUD became the owner of the project.

(b) *Setting rents payable by tenants*—(1) *Tenant rent.* The rent the tenant pays will be based on the income certification and the rent payment requirements of the project's mortgage insurance or direct loan program in effect while HUD is MIP or immediately before HUD became the owner of the project, as affected by any of the factors in paragraphs (b)(2) through (b)(4) of this section. However, if a tenant does not certify income as required by this section, the tenant must pay the unit rent as determined under the rent setting requirements in paragraph (a) of this section.

(2) *Utility allowance.* For a tenant whose rent is based on a percentage of adjusted income (except for rental voucher or rental certificate holders), if the cost of utilities (except telephone) and other housing services for the unit is the responsibility of the tenant to pay directly to the provider of the utility or service, HUD will deduct from the rent to be paid by the tenant to HUD a utility allowance, which is an amount equal to HUD's estimate of the monthly costs of a reasonable consumption of the utilities and other services for the unit for an

energy-conservative household of modest circumstances consistent with the requirement of a safe, sanitary, and healthful living environment. If the utility allowance exceeds the percentage of the tenant's adjusted income payable as rent, HUD will pay the difference between the amount payable as rent and the utility allowance to the tenant or, with the consent of the tenant and the utility company, either jointly to the tenant and the utility company or directly to the utility company.

(3) *Rent adjustments for project viability.* For a HUD-owned project, HUD may adjust the rent provided for in paragraphs (b)(1) or (b)(2) of this section if necessary or desirable to maintain the existing economic mix in the project, prevent undesirable turnover, or increase occupancy.

(4) *Tenants who are rental voucher or rental certificate holders.* Tenants assisted with rental vouchers or certificates certify their income to the public housing agency (PHA) administering the assistance, and pay rent pursuant to the policies and procedures governing such assistance.

(c) *Income verification and rent notification procedures*—(1) *Income certification by tenants*—(i) *In subsidized projects.* (A) For families residing in subsidized projects, when HUD becomes MIP or owner, HUD will request an income certification from each family as soon as practicable after HUD initially assumes management, unless the family's income has been examined by the owner or by HUD not more than four months before HUD's assumption of management.

(B) For each family applying for admission to subsidized projects, HUD will request an income certification to determine the family's eligibility for a subsidized rent, and (if the rent is based on a percentage of adjusted income) the family's subsidized rent, in accordance with part 813 of this title.

(ii) *In unsubsidized projects.* (A) For tenants in occupancy when HUD becomes mortgagee-in-possession or owner of an unsubsidized project, HUD may request an income certification from families who are not paying a subsidized rent.

(B) For families applying for admission to such projects, HUD will request sufficient information for income verification to determine the family's ability to pay the unit rent.

(2) *Notice of increases in the amount of rent payable.* Whenever HUD proposes an increase in rents in a HUD-owned multifamily project or a project where HUD is mortgagee-in-possession, HUD will provide tenants 30 days notice of the proposed changes and an opportunity to review and comment on the new rent and supporting documentation. After HUD considers the tenants' comments and has made a decision with respect to its proposed rent change, HUD shall notify the tenants of its decision, with the reasons for the decision. A tenant in occupancy before the effective date of any revised rental rate must be given 30 days notice of the revised rate, and any change in the tenant's rent is subject to the terms of an existing lease. Notices to each tenant must be personally delivered or sent by first class mail. General notices of rent increases to all tenants must be posted in the project office and in appropriate conspicuous and accessible locations around the project.

(3) *Disclosure and verification of Social Security numbers.* Any certifications or reexaminations of the income of tenants or prospective tenants in connection with tenancy under this section are subject to the requirements for the disclosure and verification of Social Security Numbers, as provided by part 200, subpart T, of this title.

(4) *Signing of consent forms for income verification.* Any certifications or reexaminations of the income of tenants or prospective tenants in connection with tenancy under this section are subject to the requirements for the signing and submitting of consent forms for the obtaining of wage and claim information from State Wage Information Collection Agencies, as provided by part 200, subpart V, of this title.

(Approved by the Office of Management and Budget under control number 2502–0204)

§ 290.11   Notification requirements.

(a) *In general.* HUD may combine two or more of the required notifications, as appropriate, to simplify the disposition process.

(b) *Timing of notifications.* Disposition-related notifications (i.e., pre-foreclosure notification to tenants and units of general local government; pre-disposition community and tenant input notification; state and local government right of first refusal notification) will be made, as appropriate:

(1) 60 or more days before HUD forecloses on a project; or

(2) Before, or not more than 30 days after, HUD acquires a project.

(c) *Methods of notification*—(1) *To tenants.* Pre-disposition notification will be delivered to each unit in the project, or sent to each unit by first class mail. Where HUD is mortgagee-in-possession or owner of a project, the notice will also be posted in the project office and in appropriate conspicuous and accessible locations around the project.

(2) *To units of general local government.* Pre-disposition notification to a unit of general local government will be sent to the chief executive officer of the unit of general local government by first class mail. For purposes of receiving or sending any notices or information under this part, the unit of general local government is its chief executive officer, or the person designated by the chief executive officer to receive or send the notice or information.

(3) *To the community or any other party.* HUD will consult with tenants and their organizations, officials of units of general local government, and other entities as HUD determines to be appropriate, to identify community recipients of any required notification. Any notice required to be made to any party other than a tenant or a unit of general local government will be sent by first class mail.

(d) *Content of notifications.* Notifications will, as appropriate, identify the project acquired or to be foreclosed by HUD; provide the general terms and conditions concerning the sale, future use, and operation of the project as proposed by HUD; indicate the time by which any offers must be made or any comments must be submitted; and state that the full disposition recommendation and analysis and other supporting information will be available for inspection and copying at the HUD Field Office.

§290.13 Negotiated sales.

When HUD conducts a negotiated sale involving the disposition of a project to a person or entity without a public offering, the following provisions apply:

(a) HUD may negotiate the sale of any project to an agency of the federal, State, or local government.

(b) When HUD determines that a purchaser can demonstrate the capacity to own and operate a project in accordance with standards set by HUD, and/or a competitive offering will not generate offers of equal merit from qualified purchasers, HUD may approve a negotiated sale of a subsidized project to:

(1) A resident organization wishing to convert the project to a nonprofit or limited equity cooperative;

(2) A cooperative (*e.g.,* nonprofit limited equity, consumer cooperative, mutual housing organization) with demonstrated experience in the operation of nonprofit (and preferably low-income) housing;

(3) A nonprofit entity that will continue to operate the project as low-income housing and whose governing board is composed of project residents;

(4) A State or local governmental entity with the demonstrated capacity to acquire, manage, and maintain the project as housing available to and affordable by low-income residents;

(5) A State or local governmental or nonprofit entity with the demonstrated capacity to acquire, manage, and maintain the project as a shelter for the homeless or other public purpose, generally when the project is vacant or has minimal occupancy and is not needed in the area for continued use as rental housing for the elderly or families; or

(6) Other nonprofit organizations.

§290.15 Disposition plan.

(a) *In general.* Before disposing of a HUD-owned multifamily housing project, HUD will develop an initial and a final disposition plan for the project that specifies the minimum terms and conditions for the disposition of the project, the sales price that is acceptable to HUD, and the assistance that HUD plans to make available to a prospective purchaser.

(b) *Environmental requirements.* HUD will perform, and include in the final disposition plan, the environmental reviews required by 24 CFR part 50.

§ 290.17 Displacement of tenants and relocation assistance.

(a) *Scope of section.* This section applies to all HUD-owned multifamily housing projects and all multifamily housing projects subject to HUD-held mortgages. When HUD is not the mortgagee-in-possession or owner, the owner of the project shall comply with this section, if HUD has authorized the demolition of, repairs to, or conversion of the use of the multifamily housing project.

(b) *Minimizing displacement.* Consistent with the other goals and objectives of this part, all reasonable steps shall be taken to minimize the displacement of persons (families, individuals, businesses, and nonprofit organizations) from a project covered by this part. If displacement or temporary relocation will occur in connection with the disposition of a project, HUD may require the purchaser of the project to provide assistance in accordance with this section.

(c) *Relocation assistance at non-URA levels.* Whenever the displacement of a residential tenant (family or individual) occurs in connection with the management or disposition of a multifamily housing project, but is not subject to paragraph (d) of this section (*e.g.,* occurs as a direct result of HUD repair or demolition of all or a part of a HUD-owned multifamily housing project or as a direct result of the foreclosure of a HUD-held mortgage on a multifamily housing project or sale of a HUD-owned project without federal financial assistance), the displaced tenant shall be eligible for the following relocation assistance:

(1) Advance written notice of the expected displacement shall be provided at least 60 days before displacement, describe the assistance and the procedures for obtaining the assistance, and contain the name, address and phone number of an official responsible for providing the assistance;

(2) Other advisory services, as appropriate, including counseling, referrals to suitable (and where appropriate, accessible), decent, safe, and sanitary replacement housing, and fair housing-related advisory services;

(3) Payment for actual reasonable moving expenses, as determined by HUD; and

(4) Such other federal, State or local assistance as may be available.

(d) *Relocation assistance at URA levels*—(1) *General.* The requirements of this paragraph apply to any displacement that results whenever assistance under 24 CFR part 886, subpart C, (or other federal financial assistance, as defined in 49 CFR 24.2(j)) is provided in connection with the purchase, demolition, or rehabilitation of a multifamily property by a third party. A displaced person (defined in paragraph (d)(3) of this section) must be provided relocation assistance at the levels described in, and in accordance with the requirements of, the URA, implementing regulations at 49 CFR part 24, and this section.

(2) *Definition of "initiation of negotiations".* Under the URA, for purposes of determining the method for computing the replacement housing assistance to be provided to a residential tenant displaced as a direct result of privately undertaken rehabilitation, demolition, or acquisition of the real property, the term "initiation of negotiations" means the transfer of title to the purchaser.

(3) *Definition of displaced person.* The term "displaced person" means any person (family, individual, business, or nonprofit organization) that moves from the real property, or moves personal property from the real property, permanently, as a direct result of acquisition, rehabilitation or demolition for a federally assisted project. However, a person does not qualify as a "displaced person" if:

(i) The person is excluded under 49 CFR 24.2(g)(2);

(ii) The person has been evicted for a serious or repeated violation of the terms and conditions of the lease or occupancy agreement, violation of applicable federal, State, or local law, or other good cause, and HUD determines that the eviction was not undertaken for the purpose of evading the obligation to provide relocation assistance;

(iii) The person moves into the property after transfer of title to the purchaser; or

(iv) HUD determines that the person was not displaced as a direct result of acquisition, rehabilitation, or demolition for an assisted project.

(e) *Temporary relocation (URA and non-URA relocation assistance).* Residential tenants, who will not be required to move permanently, but who must relocate temporarily (*e.g.*, to permit property repairs), shall be provided:

(1) Reimbursement for all reasonable out-of-pocket expenses incurred in connection with the temporary relocation, including the cost of moving to and from the temporary housing and any increase in monthly rent or utility costs. The party responsible for this requirement may, at its option, perform the services involved in temporarily relocating the tenants or pay for such services directly; and

(2) Appropriate advisory services, including reasonable advance written notice of the date and approximate duration of the temporary relocation; the suitable (and where appropriate, accessible), decent, safe, and sanitary housing to be made available for the temporary period; the terms and conditions under which the tenant may lease and occupy a suitable, decent, safe, and sanitary dwelling in the building/complex following completion of the repairs; and the right to financial assistance provided under paragraph (e)(1) of this section.

(f) *Appeals.* If a person disagrees with the purchaser's determination concerning the person's eligibility for relocation assistance or the amount of the assistance for which the person is eligible, the person may file a written appeal of that determination with the owner or purchaser. A person who is dissatisfied with the purchaser's determination on his or her appeal may submit a written request for review of that decision to the HUD Field Office responsible for administering the URA in the area.

§290.18 Restrictions on sale to former mortgagors.

The defaulting mortgagor, or any principal, successor, affiliate, or assignee thereof, on the mortgage on the property at the time of the default resulting in acquisition of the property by HUD shall not be eligible to purchase the property. A "principal" and an "affiliate" are defined as provided at 24 CFR 24.105.

[66 FR 35847, July 9, 2001]

§290.19 Restrictions concerning non-discrimination against Section 8 certificate holders and voucher holders.

The purchaser of any multifamily housing project shall not refuse unreasonably to lease a dwelling unit offered for rent, offer to sell cooperative stock, or otherwise discriminate in the terms of tenancy or cooperative purchase and sale because any tenant or purchaser is the holder of a Certificate of Family Participation or a Voucher under Section 8 of the United States Housing Act of 1937 (42 U.S.C. 1437f), or any successor legislation. This provision is limited in its application, for tenants or applicants with Section 8 Certificates or their equivalent (other than Vouchers), to those units which rent for an amount not greater than the Section 8 Fair Market Rent, as determined by HUD. The purchaser's agreement to this condition must be contained in any contract of sale and also may be contained in any regulatory agreement, use agreement, or deed entered into in connection with the disposition.

§290.21 Computing annual number of units eligible for substitution of tenant-based assistance or alternative uses.

(a) *Substitution of tenant-based Section 8 assistance to low-income families instead of project-based assistance to units.* The number of units eligible, as permitted by the Statute, for this form of substitution within the 10 percent limit will be estimated at the beginning of each fiscal year, taking into consideration the aggregate number of subsidized project units disposed of by HUD in the immediately preceding fiscal year and the disposition activity planned for the current fiscal year.

(b) *Alternate uses.* The number of units eligible for alternate uses in any fiscal year, as permitted by the Statute, will be determined at the beginning of the fiscal year as the applicable percentages (*i.e.*, either 10 percent or 5 percent) of the estimated total number of units to be disposed of in the fiscal year, taking into consideration the total number of units in multifamily housing projects disposed of by the Department in the immediately preceding fiscal year, and the extent of the disposition activity planned in the current fiscal year.

§ 290.23 Rebuilding.

HUD may provide project-based assistance to support the rebuilding of a HUD-owned multifamily housing project only. The required determination that rebuilding the project would be less expensive than substantial rehabilitation means that the costs to HUD for rebuilding are such that the monthly debt service needed to amortize the cost of relocating tenants, demolition, site preparation, rebuilding, operating expenses, and a reasonable return to the purchaser cannot be provided with rents that are within 120 percent of the most recently published Section 8 Fair Market Rents for Existing Housing (24 CFR part 888, subpart A), and would be less expensive than rehabilitation.

§ 290.25 Determination not to preserve a project or a part of a project.

HUD may determine to demolish, or otherwise dispose of, a HUD-owned multifamily housing project, or any portion of such a project, or to foreclose a HUD-held mortgage on a multifamily housing project, without ensuring its continued availability as affordable rental or cooperative housing for low- and very low-income families under appropriate circumstances which may include one or more those listed in paragraphs (a) through (g) of this section. If HUD decides not to preserve an occupied multifamily housing project at a foreclosure sale or sale of a HUD-owned project, tenants must be provided relocation assistance as described in § 290.17.

(a) The costs to HUD of rehabilitation are such that the monthly debt service needed to amortize the cost of rehabilitation, operating expenses, and

a reasonable return to the purchaser cannot be provided with rents that are, for subsidized and formerly subsidized projects, within 120 percent of the most recently published Section 8 Fair Market Rents for Existing Housing (24 CFR part 888, subpart A) or, for unsubsidized and formerly unsubsidized projects, within rents obtainable in the market.

(b) Construction is substantially incomplete.

(c) Preservation is not feasible because of environmental factors that cannot be mitigated by HUD or the purchaser. For example, when the project is located on a site that cannot be made to comply with the Section 8 Site and Neighborhood standards in 24 CFR 886.307(k) because of factors that adversely affect the health, safety and general welfare of residents such as air pollution; smoke; mud slides; fire or explosion hazards. Preservation may also be infeasible because of significantly deteriorated surrounding neighborhood conditions with inadequate police or fire protection; high crime rates; drug infestation; or lack of public community services needed to support a safe and healthy living environment for residents.

(d) HUD determines the project is unfit for rehabilitation.

(e) Rehabilitation would cost more than constructing comparable new housing.

(f) A reduction in the number of units in the project will enhance long-term project viability, for example, demolition of a building to provide space for a playground, open space, or combining one-bedroom units to create larger units for families.

(g) Continued preservation of the project as rental or cooperative housing is not compatible with State or local land use plans for the area in which the project is located.

§ 290.27 Up-front grants and loans.

(a) *General.* HUD may provide up-front grants and loans for rehabilitation, demolition, rebuilding and other related development costs as part of the disposition of a multifamily housing project that is HUD-owned, upon making a determination that such a grant or loan, plus any additional project-based assistance made available, would be more cost-effective than the use of the maximum permissible project-based rental assistance alone.

(b) *Eligible projects.* An up-front grant or loan can be made available in the sale of a HUD-owned multifamily housing project that meets all of the following requirements:

(1) Has more than 50% of the units in the project occupied by very low-income residents at the time a disposition plan is approved by HUD, or that HUD determines is essential, as affordable housing, to the revitalization of its community;

(2) Is located in a housing market or submarket in which there is not sufficient habitable, affordable, rental housing, as defined in §290.3;

(3) Will generate, after rehabilitation or rebuilding, sufficient rental income in a competitive market to cover all operating expenses, meet after sale debt service requirements, fund required reserves and throw off positive cash flow;

(4) Will provide affordable housing for at least 20 years or the term of the loan, whichever is shorter, after the rehabilitation and/or rebuilding is completed; and

(5) Meets such other requirements, including deed restrictions, loan provisions, and monetary penalties for nonperformance, as HUD may determine are appropriate on a case-by-case basis.

(c) *Eligible sales and purchasers*—(1) *Negotiated sales to governmental entities.* A negotiated sale of a project with an up-front grant or loan can only be made to the unit of general local government, which includes public housing agencies, in the area in which the project is located; or a State agency designated by the chief executive officer of the State in which the project is located; or an agency of the Federal government. The governmental entity in such a sale must take title to the project.

(2) *Other sales and purchasers.* All sales which provide up-front grants or loans to entities other than those described in paragraph (c)(1) of this section must be conducted through a competitive selection process. All general and limited partnerships or their nominees, joint ventures or other entities

assembled for purposes of purchasing the project and which have a governmental entity as a partner or other participant are considered profit motivated purchasers and not governmental entities, whether or not there is a nonprofit, public, corporate or individual general partner.

(d) *Up-front grant or loan amount.* The maximum that HUD will fund per project in an up-front grant or loan is 50 percent of total development cost (TDC), or $40,000 per affordable, finished unit, whichever amount is less. TDC covers demolition, environmental hazard remediation, construction materials, artisan services, professional services, developers services, and overhead, relocation and operating losses that are incurred to plan, perform and complete repairs or rebuilding.

[64 FR 72412, Dec. 27, 1999]

Subpart B—Sale of HUD-Held Multifamily Mortgages

§290.30 General.

(a) Except as otherwise provided in §290.31(a)(2), HUD will sell HUD-held multifamily mortgages on a competitive basis. HUD retains full discretion to offer any qualifying mortgage for sale and to withhold or withdraw any offered mortgage from sale. However, when a qualifying mortgage is offered for sale, the procedures set out in this subpart will govern the sale.

(b) References in subpart B of this part to mortgages securing subsidized projects include HUD-held purchase money mortgages on subsidized projects.

[61 FR 11685, Mar. 21, 1996, as amended at 61 FR 32265, June 21, 1996]

§290.31 Sale of current mortgages securing subsidized projects.

HUD will sell current mortgages securing subsidized projects, as follows:

(a) *Current mortgages with FHA mortgage insurance* will be sold either:

(1) On a competitive basis to FHA-approved mortgagees; or

(2) On a negotiated basis, to State or local governments, or to a group of investors that includes an agency of a State or local government if, in addition to meeting the requirements of

the Statute, the sales price is the best price that HUD can obtain from an agency of a State or local government while maintaining occupancy for the tenant group originally intended to be served by the subsidized housing program.

(b) *Current mortgages without FHA mortgage insurance* will be sold if HUD can offer protections equivalent to those listed for an insured sale in paragraph (a) of this section.

§ 290.33 Sale of delinquent mortgages securing subsidized projects.

Delinquent mortgages securing subsidized projects will be sold only if, as part of the sales transaction:

(a) The mortgages are restructured; and

(b) Either FHA mortgage insurance or equivalent protections are provided.

§ 290.35 Sale of HUD-held mortgages securing unsubsidized projects.

HUD's policy for selling HUD-held mortgages securing unsubsidized projects is as follows:

(a) *Current mortgages* may be sold with or without FHA mortgage insurance.

(b) *Delinquent mortgages* may be sold without FHA mortgage insurance. However, delinquent mortgages will not be sold if:

(1) HUD believes that foreclosure is unavoidable; and

(2) The project securing the mortgage is occupied by very low-income tenants who are not receiving housing assistance and would be likely to pay rent in excess of 30 percent of their adjusted monthly income if HUD sold the mortgage.

§ 290.37 Requirements for continuing Federal rental subsidy contracts.

For any mortgage that, at the time HUD offers the mortgage for sale without FHA mortgage insurance, is delinquent and secures a subsidized project or unsubsidized project that receives any of the forms of assistance enumerated in paragraphs (4)(i) to (4)(iv) of the "subsidized project" definition in § 290.3:

(a) The mortgage purchaser and its successors and assigns shall require the mortgagor to record a covenant run-

ning with the land as part of any loan restructuring or of a final compromise of the mortgage debt and shall include a covenant in any foreclosure deed executed in connection with the mortgage. The covenant shall continue in effect until the last federal project-based rental assistance contract expires by its own terms. The covenant shall provide that, except where otherwise approved by HUD, a project purchaser shall agree to assume the obligations of any outstanding:

(1) Project-based federal rental subsidy contract; and

(2) Tenant-based Section 8 housing assistance payments contract with a public housing agency and the related lease.

(b) In the event of foreclosure of the mortgage sold by HUD, the mortgage purchaser and its successors and assigns:

(1) Shall foreclose in a manner that does not interfere with any lease related to federal project-based assistance or any lease related to tenant-based, Section 8 housing assistance payments; and

(2) Shall foreclose in manner that ensures that the right of possession of the purchaser at a foreclosure sale shall be subject to the terms of any residential lease not subject to paragraph (b)(1) of this section for the remaining term of the lease or for one year, whichever period is shorter.

[61 FR 11685, Mar. 21, 1996, as amended at 61 FR 32265, June 21, 1996]

§ 290.39 Nondiscrimination in admitting certificate and voucher holders.

(a) *Nondiscrimination requirement.* For any mortgage described in paragraphs (c) or (d) of this section that HUD sells without FHA mortgage insurance, the project owner shall not unreasonably refuse to lease a dwelling unit offered for rent, offer to sell cooperative stock, or otherwise discriminate in the terms of tenancy or cooperative purchase and sale because any tenant or purchaser is a certificate or voucher holder under 24 CFR part 982.

(b) *Inapplicability to current mortgages securing unsubsidized projects that receive no project based-assistance.* The nondiscrimination requirements of this section do not apply to any mortgage that is current under the terms of the mortgage at the time HUD offers it for sale, if the mortgage secures an unsubsidized project that does not receive any of the forms of project-based assistance enumerated in paragraphs (4)(i) to (4)(iv) of the "subsidized project" definition in § 290.3.

(c) *Applicability to mortgages securing unsubsidized projects receiving project-based assistance (partially-assisted projects) or securing subsidized projects.* (1) The nondiscrimination requirement in paragraph (a) of this section applies to the project owner upon the sale of a mortgage without FHA mortgage insurance if, at the time HUD offers it for sale, the mortgage secures:

(i) An unsubsidized project that receives any of the forms of assistance enumerated in paragraphs (4)(i) to (4)(iv) of the "subsidized project" definition in § 290.5; or

(ii) A subsidized project, as defined in § 290.3.

(2) This requirement shall continue in effect until the mortgage debt is satisfied.

(d) *Covenant requirement for all delinquent mortgages sold without FHA mortgage insurance.* This paragraph (d) applies to the sale of any mortgage that is delinquent at the time HUD offers it for sale without FHA mortgage insurance, without regard to the subsidy status of the project. The mortgage purchaser and its successors and assigns shall require the mortgagor to record a covenant running with the land as part of any loan restructuring or final compromise of the mortgage debt and shall include a covenant in any foreclosure deed executed in connection with the mortgage. The covenant shall set forth the nondiscrimination requirement in paragraph (a) of this section. The covenant shall continue in effect until a date that is the same as the maturity date of the mortgage sold by HUD.

[61 FR 11685, Mar. 21, 1996; 61 FR 19188, May 1, 1996, as amended at 61 FR 32265, June 21, 1996]

PART 291—DISPOSITION OF HUD-ACQUIRED AND -OWNED SINGLE FAMILY PROPERTY

AUTHORITY: 12 U.S.C. 1701 *et seq.;* 42 U.S.C. 1441, 1441a, 1551a, and 3535(d).

SOURCE: 56 FR 46956, Sept. 16, 1991, unless otherwise noted.

Subpart A—General Provisions

SOURCE: 64 FR 6479, Feb. 9, 1999, unless otherwise noted.

§ 291.1 Purpose and general requirements.

(a) *Purpose.* (1) This part governs the acquisition, possession, and disposition of one-to-four family properties acquired by the Federal Housing Administration (FHA) through foreclosure of an insured or Secretary-held mortgage or loan under the National Housing Act, or acquired by HUD under section 204(g) of the National Housing Act (12 U.S.C. 1710(g)). HUD will issue detailed policies and procedures that must be followed in specific areas.

(2) The purpose of the property disposition program is to dispose of properties in a manner that expands homeownership opportunities, strengthens neighborhoods and communities, and ensures a maximum return to the mortgage insurance funds.

(b) *Nondiscrimination policy.* The requirements set forth in 24 CFR parts 5 and 110 apply to the administration of any activity under this part. In addition, in accordance with 24 CFR 9.155(a), HUD must ensure that its policies and practices in conducting the single family property disposition program do not discriminate on the basis of disability.

[64 FR 6479, Feb. 9, 1999, as amended at 81 FR 53002, Aug. 11, 2016]

§ 291.5 Definitions.

Terms used in this part are defined as follows:

Competitive sale of individual property means a sale of an individual property to an individual bidder through a sealed bid process (or other bid process specifically authorized by the Secretary) in competition with other bidders in which properties have been publicly advertised to all prospective purchasers for bids.

Direct sale means a sale to a selected purchaser to the exclusion of all others without resorting to advertising for bids. Such a sale is available only to approved applicants.

Eligible properties means HUD-acquired properties designated by HUD for property disposition or other housing programs.

HUD means the Department of Housing and Urban Development or its contractor, as appropriate.

Insured mortgage means a mortgage insured under the National Housing Act (12 U.S.C. 1701 *et seq.*).

Investor purchaser means a purchaser who does not intend to use the property as his or her principal residence.

Owner-occupant purchaser means a purchaser who intends to use the property as his or her principal residence; a State, governmental entity, tribe, or agency thereof; or a private nonprofit organization as defined in this section. Governmental entities include those with general governmental powers (e.g., a city or county), as well as those with limited or special powers (e.g., public housing agencies).

Private nonprofit organization means a secular or religious organization, no part of the net earnings of which may inure to the benefit of any member, founder, contributor, or individual. The organization must:

(1) Have a voluntary board;

(2)(i) Have a functioning accounting system that is operated in accordance with generally accepted accounting principles; or

(ii) Designate an entity that will maintain a functioning accounting system for the organization in accordance with generally accepted accounting principles;

(3) Practice nondiscrimination in the provision of assistance in accordance with the authorities described in § 291.435(a); and

(4) Have nonprofit status as demonstrated by approval under section 501(c)(3) of the Internal Revenue Code (26 U.S.C. 501(c)(3)), or demonstrate that an application for such status is currently pending approval.

Secretary is defined in 24 CFR 5.100.

State means any of the several States, the District of Columbia, the Commonwealth of Puerto Rico, the Virgin Islands, Guam, American Samoa, the Northern Mariana Islands, the Trust Territory of the Pacific Islands, and any other territory or possession of the United States.

Tribe has the meaning provided for the term "Indian tribe" in section 102 of the Housing and Community Development Act of 1974 (42 U.S.C. 5302).

[64 FR 6479, Feb. 9, 1999, as amended at 81 FR 53002, Aug. 11, 2016]

§291.10 General policy regarding rental of acquired property.

HUD will lease acquired property to comply with other designated HUD programs, or when the Secretary determines that it is in the interest of HUD. Leases may include an option to purchase in appropriate circumstances.

Subpart B—Disposition by Sale

SOURCE: 64 FR 6480, Feb. 9, 1999, unless otherwise noted.

§291.90 Sales methods.

In accordance with section 204(g) of the National Housing Act (12 U.S.C. 1710(g)), HUD will prescribe the terms and conditions for all methods of sale. HUD may dispose of assets using any method that the Secretary deems appropriate, including, but not limited to the following:

(a) *Future REO acquisition method.* The Future Real Estate-Owned (REO) acquisition method consists of a property acquisition agreement (or agreements) between HUD and a transferor (or transferors), which shall provide for the right and obligation of the transferor(s) to acquire a future quantity of properties designated by HUD as they become available. HUD will select such transferor(s) through a competitive process, in accordance with all applicable laws and regulations, including the requirements in §291.200. The transferor(s) shall have the right and obligation to manage and dispose of the properties upon such terms and conditions as are approved by the Secretary;

(b) *Competitive sales of individual properties.* This method consists of competitive sales of individual properties to individual buyers, the procedures for which are described in §291.205;

(c) *Direct sales methods.* There are three types of direct sales methods:

(1) Direct sales of properties without insured mortgages to governmental entities and private nonprofit organizations, the procedures for which are described in §291.210(a);

(2) Direct sales to displaced persons, sales of razed lots, or auctions, the procedures for which are described in §291.210(b);

(3) Direct sales to other individuals or entities that do not meet any of the categories specified in paragraphs (a) through (d) of this section, under the circumstances and procedures described in §291.210(c);

(d) *Bulk sales,* the procedures for which are described in §291.210(d); or

(e) *Other sales methods.* HUD may select any other methods of sale, as determined by the Secretary.

[64 FR 6480, Feb. 9, 1999, as amended at 81 FR 53002, Aug. 11, 2016]

§291.100 General policy on HUD acquisition, ownership, and disposition of real estate assets.

For all sales, except as otherwise specifically indicated, those sales conducted in accordance with §§291.90(a) and 291.200 or with subpart D of this part, the following general policies apply:

(a) *Qualified purchaser.* (1) Anyone, including a purchaser from a transferor of a property pursuant to §§291.90(a) and 291.200, regardless of race, color, religion, sex, national origin, familial status, age, or disability may offer to buy a HUD-owned property, except that:

(i) No member of or delegate to Congress is eligible to buy or benefit from a purchase of a HUD-owned property; and

(ii) No nonoccupant mortgagor (whether an original mortgagor, assumptor, or a person who purchased "subject to") of an insured mortgage who has defaulted, thereby causing HUD to pay an insurance claim on the mortgage, is eligible to repurchase the same property.

(2) Neither HUD nor any transferor pursuant to §§ 291.90(a) or 291.200 will offer former mortgagors in occupancy who have defaulted on the mortgage the right of first refusal to repurchase the same property.

(3) HUD will offer tenants accepted under the occupied conveyance procedures outlined in 24 CFR 203.670 through 203.685 the right of first refusal to purchase the property only if:

(i) The tenant has a recognized ability to acquire financing and a good rent-paying history, and has made a request to HUD to be offered the right of first refusal; or

(ii) State or local law requires that tenants be offered the right of first refusal.

(b) *List price.* The list price, or "asking price," assigned to the property is based upon one or more evaluation tools (e.g., appraisal, Broker Price Opinion, Automated Valuation Model). An appraisal, when used, must be conducted by an independent real estate appraiser who meets all of the requirements of 24 CFR part 200, subpart G, and is in good standing on the appraiser roster established under that section. The appraiser must provide an opinion of the "as-is" market value using a valuation method that is commonly employed in the industry and that is consistent with FHA appraisal requirements.

(c) *Insurance.* When listing properties, HUD may elect to include information to indicate whether the property is eligible for FHA-insured financing under section 203(B) of the National Housing Act (12 U.S.C. 1709(b)).

(d) *Financing.* (1) Subject to underwriting requirements, REO properties that have not been identified as uninsurable in accordance with paragraph (c) of this section can be purchased and financed with a mortgage insured under section 203(b) or 203(k) of the National Housing Act (12 U.S.C. 1709(b), 1709(k)), if supported by an FHA appraisal, in one of the following ways:

(i) *Insured.* A property that meets the Minimum Property Standards (MPS), as defined in HUD Handbook 4905.1 or any successor handbook, as determined by the Secretary, for existing dwellings will be offered for sale in "as-is" condition with FHA mortgage insurance available as provided in part 203 of this chapter.

(ii) *Insured with repair escrow.* (A) A property that requires no more than $10,000 for repairs to meet the MPS, as defined in HUD Handbook 4905.1 or any successor handbook, as determined by the Secretary, will be offered for sale in "as-is" condition with FHA mortgage insurance available, as provided in part 203 of this chapter, provided the mortgagor establishes a cash escrow to ensure the completion of the required repairs.

(B) *Changes in repair escrow.* HUD may adjust the escrow balance required under this paragraph based on changes to the Consumer Price Index by publishing a FEDERAL REGISTER notice that provides for a public comment period of 30 calendar days for the purpose of accepting comments on the amount of the change. After comments have been considered, HUD will publish a final notice announcing the revised escrow amounts.

(iii) *Insured with rehabilitation loan* in accordance with section 203(k) of the National Housing Act and pursuant to § 203.50 of this chapter.

(2) REO properties that have been identified as uninsurable in accordance with paragraph (c) of this section can be purchased and financed with a mortgage insured under section 203(k) of the National Housing Act (12 U.S.C. 1709(k)), subject to underwriting requirements supported by an FHA-specified appraisal and in accordance with 24 CFR 203.50.

(3) HUD, in its sole discretion and subject to appropriations, may take back Purchase Money Mortgages (PMMs) on property purchased by governmental entities or private nonprofit organizations who buy property for ultimate resale to owner-occupant purchasers with incomes at or below 115 percent of the area median income. When offered by HUD, a PMM will be available in an amount determined by the Secretary to be appropriate, at market rate interest, for a period not to exceed 5 years. Mortgagors must meet FHA mortgage credit standards.

(i) For purposes of this section, the term "purchase money mortgage," or PMM means a note secured by a mortgage or trust deed given by a buyer, as mortgagor, to the seller, as mortgagee, as part of the purchase price of the real estate.

(ii) Except as provided in paragraph (d)(3) of this section, the purchaser is entirely responsible for obtaining financing for purchasing a property.

(e) *Environmental requirements and standards.* Sales under this part are subject to the environmental requirements and standards described in 24 CFR part 50, as applicable.

(f) [Reserved]

(g) *Lead-based paint poisoning prevention.* Properties constructed before 1978 are subject to the requirements of the Lead-Based Paint Poisoning Prevention Act (42 U.S.C. 4821–4846), the Residential Lead-Based Paint Hazard Reduction Act of 1992 (42 U.S.C. 4851–4856), and implementing regulations at part 35, subparts A, B, F, and R, of this title.

(h) Any real estate broker who has agreed to comply with HUD requirements may be eligible to participate in the sales program. Purchasers participating in the competitive sales program, except government entities and nonprofit organizations, must submit bids through a participating broker. In accordance with section 204(g) of the National Housing Act (12 U.S.C. 1710(g)), HUD will prescribe the terms and conditions for all methods of listing properties. HUD may dispose of properties using any method that the Secretary deems appropriate, including, but not limited to the following:

(1) *Open listings.* Properties may be sold on an open listing basis with participating real estate brokers.

(2) *Asset management and listing contracts.* (i) HUD may invite firms experienced in property management to compete for contracts that provide for an exclusive right to manage and list specified properties in a given area.

(ii) In areas where a broker has an exclusive right to list properties, a purchaser may use a broker of his or her choice. The purchaser's broker must submit the bid through HUD's designated electronic bid system.

(i) *Disciplinary actions against HUD-qualified real estate brokers.* (1) *In general.* Real estate brokers that are involved in Real Estate Owned (REO) sales will be removed from HUD's qualified selling broker list and will be prohibited from using HUD systems to participate in the sale of HUD-owned single family properties for good cause in accordance with the procedures of this paragraph. Nothing in this section prohibits HUD from taking such other action against a broker as provided in 24 CFR part 24 or from seeking any other available remedy.

(2) *Good cause.* Good cause includes, but is not limited to:

(i) Conviction under 18 U.S.C. 371 or 1010 of a broker or an agent supervised by that broker and acting within the scope of the agent's duties;

(ii) Any of the following actions by a broker or an agent supervised by that broker and acting within the scope of the agent's duties:

(A) Falsifying loan documents or aiding or abetting persons in the use of false or misleading information including, but not limited to, forged or fraudulent gift letters and owner occupant certifications;

(B) Acting in concert with an appraiser to arrive at an artificial appraised value;

(C) Engaging in fraudulent activities (with or without the assistance of an appraiser) that have led to default and payment of an insurance claim;

(D) Failing to comply with earnest money collection, management, and disbursement procedures as set forth in this part;

(E) Failing to maintain a current state license;

(F) Violating the Real Estate Settlement Procedures Act (RESPA) (12 U.S.C. 2601 *et seq.*);

(G) Non-compliance with civil rights requirements regarding the sale of HUD-owned single family properties;

(H) Involvement in, or knowledge of, any fraudulent activity by any person involved in the REO sales transaction; and

(I) Any other actions or omissions that evidence a lack of business integrity or non-compliance with the laws, regulations, and rules applicable to housing, lending, or real estate sales.

(3) *Written notice.* Once HUD makes an initial finding that there is good cause to remove a broker, HUD will provide the broker with written notice

of proposed removal from HUD's qualified selling broker list and deactivation of the broker's access to HUD systems to participate in the sale of HUD-owned properties. The notice will:

(i) State the reasons that HUD is taking the action;

(ii) Identify the violations or deficiencies involved;

(iii) Provide a citation to the relevant regulation, statute, or policy; and

(iv) State the effective date and duration of the removal and deactivation.

(4) *Effective date and duration of removal.* (i) The effective date of the broker's removal will be the 30th day after the date of the notice, unless the broker submits a written response or requests a conference in accordance with paragraph (i)(5) of this section;

(ii) HUD's determination of the duration of removal and deactivation will be based upon HUD's consideration of the number and seriousness of the broker's violations and deficiencies.

(5) *Response and conference.* Real estate brokers will be given 20 days after the date of the notice (or longer, if provided in the notice) to submit a written response to HUD opposing the proposed removal and to request a conference. A request for a conference must be in writing and must be submitted along with the written response. If a conference is requested, it will occur within 15 days after the date of receipt of the request. HUD may extend the 15-day period by providing written notice to the broker. HUD may request additional information at or following a conference and provide additional time to submit such information. If the information is not submitted by the time set by HUD, the conference is completed. If the information is timely submitted, the conference is not completed until HUD has considered the additional information.

(6) *Disposition.* (i) *No response from real estate broker.* If the real estate broker does not submit a written response within the time provided, the removal and deactivation take effect in accordance with the notice.

(ii) *Response from real estate broker.* If the real estate broker submits a written response within the time provided, the removal and deactivation are delayed until HUD considers the response and makes a final determination. HUD will consider the sufficiency of any corrective actions taken by a broker with respect to its procedures and, if relevant, its agents, in reaching its decision. Within 20 days after the date of receipt of the written response, or if a conference is requested, within 20 days after the date of completion of the conference, HUD will advise the real estate broker in writing of the decision to rescind, modify, or affirm the removal from HUD's qualified selling broker list and the deactivation of the broker's access to HUD systems to participate in the sale of HUD-owned properties. The written decision by HUD shall constitute final agency action.

(7) *Effect of removal proceeding on bids.* All bids submitted and commissions earned by the real estate broker prior to removal will be honored, unless HUD determines they were made under fraudulent circumstances.

[64 FR 6480, Feb. 9, 1999, as amended at 64 FR 50225, Sept. 15, 1999; 71 FR 65325, Nov. 7, 2006; 81 FR 53002, Aug. 11, 2016]

Subpart C—Sales Procedures

SOURCE: 64 FR 6481, Feb. 9, 1999, unless otherwise noted.

§ 291.200   Future   REO   acquisition method.

(a) Under this method of property disposition, HUD will enter into a property acquisition agreement (or agreements) with a transferor (or transferors), which shall provide for the right and obligation of the transferor(s) to acquire a future quantity of properties designated by HUD as they become available. The transferor(s) will be selected through a competitive process, conducted in accordance with applicable laws. HUD will negotiate the specific terms of the property acquisition agreement(s) with the selected transferor(s). The properties will be available on an "as-is" basis only, without repairs or warranties.

(b) *Eligible entities.* An individual, partnership, corporation, or other legal entity will not be eligible to participate in this process if at the time of the sale, that individual or entity is debarred, suspended, or otherwise precluded from doing business with HUD under 2 CFR part 2424.

[64 FR 6481, Feb. 9, 1999, as amended at 72 FR 73495, Dec. 27, 2007]

§291.205 Competitive sales of individual properties.

When HUD conducts competitive sales of individual properties to individual buyers, it will generally sell the properties on an "as-is" basis, without repairs or warranties, and it will follow the sales procedures provided in this section.

(a) *General.* (1) Properties that are sold on an individual competitive bid basis are sold through local real estate brokers, except as provided in §291.100(h).

(2) For properties being offered with insured mortgages, priority will be given to owner-occupant purchasers, as defined in §291.5, for a period of up to 30 days, as determined by HUD. For properties offered without insured mortgages, priority will be given to governmental entities and nonprofit organizations prior to other owner-occupant purchasers.

(b) *Net offer.* (1) The net offer is calculated by subtracting from the bid price the dollar amounts for the financing and loan closing costs and the broker's sales commission, as described in paragraph (b)(2) of this section.

(2) If an owner-occupant purchaser of the property requests in the bid, HUD may pay all or a portion of the financing and loan closing costs, not to exceed the percentage of the purchase price determined appropriate by the Secretary for the area. In no event will the total amount for broker's sales commission exceed 6 percent of the purchase price, except for cash bonuses offered to brokers by HUD for the sale of hard-to-sell properties. No assistance for financing and loan closing costs or for the broker's sales commission will be provided to investor purchasers.

(c) *Acceptable bid.* HUD will accept the bid producing the greatest net return to HUD and otherwise meeting the terms of HUD's offering of the property, with priority given to owner-occupant purchasers as described in paragraph (a)(2) of this section. The great-

est net return is calculated based on the net offer, as described in paragraph (b) of this section.

(d) *Bid period.* (1) HUD will establish a bid period for properties available for sale. Generally, the bid period will be 10 days, but may be lengthened or shortened by HUD. After properties are initially advertised, bids may be submitted by all potential purchasers. However, in the case of properties offered with insured mortgages, HUD may give priority to owner-occupant purchasers for a period of up to 30-days, as described in paragraph (a)(2) of this section.

(2) HUD may treat all bids received during a specified period of time during the bid period to have been received simultaneously. HUD may also choose to review bids on a daily basis, with all bids submitted during each day considered to have been received simultaneously. HUD may use either (or both) of these methods during the bid period, as described in the bid materials accompanying a particular sale.

(3) Offers received on a property before the bid period begins will be returned. Offers received after the bid period will not be considered at the bid opening, but will be considered during the extended listing period if no acceptable bid was received during the bid period (see paragraph (f) of this section).

(e) *Full price offers.* HUD local offices that operate under a "full price offer" program open offers at specified times during the bid period. If an offer for the full list price and otherwise meeting the terms of the offering is received, it will be accepted at the time of the opening and the bid period cancelled.

(f) *Extended listing period.* Properties not sold during the bid period will remain available for an extended listing period. All bids received on each day of the extended listing period will be considered as being received simultaneously, and will be opened together at the next scheduled daily bid opening. Properties that fail to sell within 45 days after being offered for competitive bidding will be reanalyzed and made available for sale. If a property's price or terms are changed, it may be subject to another competitive bid period as described in paragraph (d) of this section.

(g) *Bid requirements.* (1) All successful bids submitted, whether during the bid period or the extended listing period, must be in a form prescribed by HUD, and must be submitted in accordance with procedures established by HUD. If the purchase is to be an insured sale, a local HUD office may also require that supporting exhibits for mortgage credit analysis accompany the initial submission of the bid. All bids not indicating that the purchaser will occupy the property will be considered as offers from investor purchasers.

(2) Noncomplying bids will be returned to the broker with an explanation for the noncompliance decision and information about whether the property is still available.

(h) *Earnest money deposits.* (1) The amount of earnest money deposit required for a property with a sales price of $50,000 or less is $500, except that for vacant lots the amount is 50 percent of the list price. For a property with a sales price greater than $50,000, the amount of earnest money deposit required in the area is set by the local HUD office, in an amount not less than $500 or more than $2,000. Information on the amount of the required earnest money deposit is available from the local HUD office or participating real estate brokers.

(2) All bids must be accompanied by earnest money deposits in the form of a cash equivalent as prescribed by the Secretary, or a certification from the real estate broker that the earnest money has been deposited in the broker's escrow account. If a bid is accepted by HUD, the earnest money deposit will be credited to the purchaser at closing; if the bid is rejected, the earnest money deposit will be returned. Earnest money deposits are subject to total or partial forfeiture for failure to close a sale.

(i) *Multiple bids.* Real estate brokers may submit unlimited numbers of bids on an individual property provided each bid is from a different prospective purchaser. If a purchaser submits multiple bids on the same property, only the bid producing the highest net return to HUD will be considered. If a prospective owner-occupant purchaser

submits a bid on more than one property, the bid that produces the greatest net return to HUD will be accepted and all other bids from that purchaser will be eliminated from consideration. However, if the prospective owner-occupant purchaser has submitted the only acceptable bid on another property, then that bid must be accepted and all other bids from that purchaser on any other properties will be eliminated from consideration.

(j) *Identical bids.* In the case of identical bids submitted by an owner-occupant purchaser and an investor purchaser, HUD will select the bid submitted by the owner-occupant purchaser. If identical bids are submitted by two or more owner-occupant purchasers, or by two or more investor purchasers, award will be determined by drawing lots.

(k) *Opening the bids.* Unless the Secretary specifically authorizes another bid process:

(1) The Secretary will make all winning bids available publicly.

(2) Successful bidders will be notified through their real estate brokers by electronic mail, mail, telephone, or other means. Acceptance of a bid is final and effective only upon HUD's execution of the sales contract, signed by both the submitting real estate broker and the prospective purchaser, and sending a copy of the executed contract by electronic mail to the successful bidder or the bidder's agent.

(l) *Counteroffers.* HUD may present counteroffers during competitive bid periods, as it deems appropriate to minimize losses to its insurance fund. "Best and Final" offers requested by HUD are considered counteroffers.

[64 FR 6481, Feb. 9, 1999, as amended at 81 FR 53003, Aug. 11, 2016]

§ 291.210 Direct sales procedures.

When HUD conducts the sales listed in § 291.90(c), it will sell the properties on an "as-is" basis, without repairs or warranties, and it will follow the applicable sales procedures provided in this section.

(a) *Direct sales of properties without insured mortgages to governmental entities and private nonprofit organizations.* (1) State and local governments, public agencies, and qualified private nonprofit organizations that have been preapproved to participate by HUD, according to standards determined by the Secretary, may purchase properties directly from HUD at a discount off the list price determined by the Secretary to be appropriate, but not less than 10 percent, for use in HUD and local housing or homeless programs.

(2)(i) Purchasers under paragraph (a)(1) of this section must designate geographical areas of interest by ZIP code. Upon request, before those properties without insured mortgages are publicly listed, HUD will assure that governmental entities and nonprofit organizations are notified in writing when eligible properties become available in the areas designated by them. HUD will coordinate the dissemination of the information to ensure that if more than one purchaser designates a specific area, those purchasers receive the list of properties at the same time, based on intervals agreed upon between HUD and the purchasers. A property in this section will be sold to the first eligible purchaser submitting an acceptable contract. All bids received on the same business day will be considered to have been received simultaneously. In the case of identical bids submitted on the same business day, award will be determined by drawing lots.

(ii) Purchasers under paragraph (a)(1) of this section must notify HUD of preliminary interest in specific properties within 5 days of the notification of available properties (if notification is by mail, the 5 days will begin to run 5 days after mailing). HUD will provide a consideration and inspection period for these purchasers. The consideration and inspection period will usually be for ten days from the date of notification of interest, but may be lengthened or shortened by HUD, as appropriate. Those properties in which purchasers express an interest will be held off the market for the duration of the consideration and inspection period. Other properties on the list will continue to be processed for public sale. HUD may limit the number of properties held off the market for a purchaser at any one time, based upon the purchaser's financial capacity as determined by HUD and upon past performance in HUD programs. At the end of the consideration and inspection period, properties in which no governmental entity or nonprofit organization has expressed a specific intent to purchase will be offered for sale under the competitive bid process. Properties in which a governmental entity or nonprofit organization expressed an intent to purchase, during the consideration and inspection period, will continue to be held off the market pending receipt of the sales contract. If a sales contract is not received within a time period of up to 10 days, as determined by HUD, following expiration of the consideration and inspection period, and no other governmental entity or nonprofit organization has expressed an interest, then the property will be offered for sale under the competitive bid process.

(3) In order to ensure that properties purchased at a discount are being utilized for expanding affordable housing opportunities, HUD may require, as appropriate, periodic, limited information regarding the purchase and resale of such properties, and certain restrictions on the resale of such properties.

(b) *Direct sales to displaced persons; razed lots; auctions.* HUD may seek to dispose of individual properties to individual buyers through methods such as direct sales to displaced persons, sales of razed lots, or auctions. These sales will be upon such terms and conditions as the Secretary may prescribe.

(c) *Direct sales to individuals or entities.* HUD may also seek to dispose of properties through direct sales to other individuals or entities that do not meet any of the categories specified in this section, if the Assistant Secretary for Housing-Federal Housing Commissioner (or his or her designee) finds in writing that such sales would further the goals of the National Housing Act (12 U.S.C. 1701 *et seq.*) and would be in the best interests of the Secretary. These sales will be upon such terms and conditions as the Secretary may prescribe.

(d) *Bulk sales.* HUD may seek to dispose of properties through bulk sales. Such sales will be upon such terms and conditions as the Secretary may prescribe.

Subpart D—Sale of HUD-Held Single Family Mortgage Loans

SOURCE: 62 FR 3769, Jan. 24, 1997, unless otherwise noted.

§ 291.301 Definitions.

For purposes of this subpart, the following definitions apply:

Bid package means the documents prepared for bidders in a mortgage loan sale, and includes the following: An Executive Summary containing information on FHA single family mortgage loan sales and background on HUD programs; a description of post-sale servicing requirements; due diligence information and reports; mortgage loan information; a copy of the Loan Sale Agreement and its exhibits; bidding and closing information; and such other information and requirements as the Secretary may determine necessary.

Payment plan agreement, for purposes of § 291.307(c)(2), means an agreement between the purchaser and the mortgagor for payments after the 36-month period of statutorily authorized forbearance relief has expired.

Single family mortgage loan means a mortgage loan on a single family property assigned to HUD under section 230(b) of the National Housing Act (as that subsection existed prior to January 26, 1996) (12 U.S.C. 1715u), a mortgage loan on a single family property insured by HUD under section 221 of the National Housing Act (12 U.S.C. 1715l), a mortgage loan on a single family property issued in connection with the settlement of the *Ferrell* litigation, a purchase money mortgage loan issued by HUD on a single family property sold from HUD's inventory that was not connected with the settlement of the *Ferrell* litigation, or any other single family mortgage loan owned by HUD and representing an asset to HUD's Title II mortgage insurance funds.

Single family property means a residence with one to four dwelling units.

§ 291.302 Purpose and general policy.

This subpart sets forth HUD's policy and procedures for the sale of HUD-held single family mortgage loans. In general, HUD will sell both performing and nonperforming HUD-held single family mortgage loans. HUD will sell all mortgage loans without recourse and without FHA insurance. HUD will package pools of single family mortgage loans for sale to the general public on a competitive basis; however, HUD may sell mortgage loans to government-sponsored enterprises (GSEs) on a negotiated basis. Nothing in this subpart shall be construed to prevent HUD from packaging single family mortgage loans with other types of HUD assets for sale. The Secretary retains full discretion to offer any qualifying pool of mortgage loans for sale and to withhold or withdraw any offered pool of mortgage loans from sale. However, when HUD offers a qualifying mortgage loan for sale, the procedures set out in this subpart and in the bid package will govern the sale of HUD-held single family mortgage loans.

§ 291.303 Eligible bidders.

HUD will provide information on the eligibility of bidders in the bid package, a notice in the FEDERAL REGISTER, or other means, at the Secretary's full discretion. However, an individual, partnership, corporation, or other legal entity will not be eligible to bid for any loan pool, either as an individual or a participant, if, at the time of the sale, that individual or entity is debarred or suspended from doing business with HUD under 2 CFR part 2424.

[72 FR 73495, Dec. 27, 2007]

§ 291.304 Bidding process.

(a) *Submission of bids.* All bids must be submitted to HUD in accordance with instructions in the bid package for a particular sale.

(b) *Effect of bid.* By submitting a bid, the bidder is making an offer to purchase single family mortgage loans as presented in the bid package. Submission of a bid constitutes acceptance of the terms and conditions set forth in the bid package. Along with the bid, the bidder must submit an executed copy of the Loan Sale Agreement, which is included in the bid package.

(c) *Earnest money deposits.* The bidder must submit to HUD, along with its bid, an earnest money deposit in an amount to be determined by HUD. The earnest money deposit is nonrefundable to the winning bidder and will be credited toward the purchase price.

(d) *Termination of offering.* HUD reserves the right to terminate an offering in whole or in part at any time before the bid date.

(e) *Withdrawal of loans.* HUD reserves the right, in its sole discretion and for any reason whatsoever, to withdraw loan assets from a pool prior to the bid date. Any earnest money deposits relating to withdrawn loan assets will be retained by HUD and credited toward the total purchase price of the remaining loan assets in the pool, in accordance with the Loan Sale Agreement. After the bid date, HUD can withdraw mortgage loans in accordance with the Loan Sale Agreement.

(f) *Rejection of bids.* (1) HUD may, in its sole discretion, reject any bid under the following circumstances:

(i) If the bid does not conform with the instructions in the bid package; or

(ii) If, in HUD's sole discretion, it determines that such action would be in the best interests of the U.S. Government.

(2) HUD can also issue a conditional rejection that will become an acceptance upon fulfillment of HUD's requests.

(g) *Withdrawal of bids.* A bidder may withdraw a previously submitted bid in accordance with the instructions in the bid package for a particular sale.

(h) *Bids by brokers or agents.* Any bid by a broker or agent for a principal must be in the name of the principal and signed by the broker/agent as the attorney-in-fact for the principal. All such bid documents must be executed so as to bind the principal by the broker/agent as the attorney-in-fact. A power of attorney satisfactory to HUD as to form and content must be submitted with each bid.

§291.305 Selection of bids and execution of Loan Sale Agreement.

HUD will evaluate bids, select successful bids, and notify the successful bidder in a manner set forth in the bid package. HUD will complete the execution of the Loan Sale Agreement when it accepts the successful bid.

§291.306 Closing requirements.

(a) *Closing date payment.* On the closing date, the purchaser must pay to HUD the closing date payment, consisting of the balance of the amount due on the bid price, as adjusted in accordance with the Loan Sale Agreement.

(b) *Closing documents.* HUD will execute and deliver to the purchaser a bill of sale transferring title to the mortgage loans sold in the sale. The purchaser must deliver to HUD the documents required at closing, in addition to the closing date payment.

§291.307 Servicing requirements.

(a) *Use of HUD-approved servicing mortgagees.* All mortgage loans must be serviced by HUD-approved servicing mortgagees for the remaining life of the mortgage loans. A purchaser that is not a HUD-approved servicing mortgagee must retain a HUD-approved servicing mortgagee to service the mortgage loans.

(b) *Continuation of mortgagor rights.* The purchaser may take all lawful steps to collect the amounts due under the mortgage loans. These steps may include foreclosure, but only after the servicer has provided all required forms of relief for the mortgagor in accordance with paragraph (c) of this section. The purchaser and its servicer, and any subsequent transferee of or servicer for the mortgage loan, will be fully bound by the terms of the Loan Sale Agreement, including those terms that provide the mortgagor with any rights regarding forbearance, assistance, or reinstatement of the mortgage loan.

(c) *Purchaser's protection of mortgagor's rights*—(1) *Assigned mortgage loans during forbearance period.* This paragraph (c)(1) explains how a purchaser (or a servicer of a purchased mortgage loan) must service a mortgage loan that was assigned to HUD under section 230(b) of the National Housing Act (as that subsection existed prior to January 26, 1996), for which not more than 36 months has expired since the mortgage loan assignment was accepted by the Secretary. Such a purchaser must service these mortgage loans in essentially the same manner as HUD was required to service the loans while

HUD held them. Specific servicing requirements will be set forth in the Loan Sale Agreement for each sale.

(2) *Assigned mortgage loans after the initial 36-month forbearance period.* This paragraph (c)(2) explains how a purchaser (or a servicer of a purchased mortgage loan) must service a mortgage loan that was assigned to HUD under section 230(b) of the National Housing Act (as that subsection existed prior to January 26, 1996), for which more than 36 months has expired since the mortgage loan assignment was accepted by the Secretary.

(i) Such purchaser may require the mortgagor to pay at least the full monthly payment due under the mortgage loan. A purchaser may also require a mortgagor to pay increased monthly mortgage loan payments under a renewed payment plan agreement to reduce the amount in arrears if the mortgagor's available income (as calculated according to the Loan Sale Agreement) can support the increased payments. A purchaser must renew payment plan agreements at least through and including the expiration of the original term of the mortgage loan, so long as the mortgagor complies with the prior payment plan agreement.

(ii) If the mortgagor defaults under a payment plan agreement established by the purchaser, the mortgagor shall have the right to reinstate the most recent payment plan agreement if the mortgagor makes a lump sum payment in an amount necessary to cure the default. If the mortgagor defaults under the most recent payment plan agreement and does not reinstate, the purchaser may terminate the payment plan agreement and take such action as may be permitted under the terms of the mortgage.

(iii) The purchaser's right to demand payment of a reinstatement amount from the mortgagor may be limited by the terms of the Loan Sale Agreement.

(3) *Section 221 Mortgages.* This paragraph (c)(3) explains how a purchaser (or a servicer of a purchased mortgage) must service a mortgage assigned to HUD under section 221(g)(4) of the National Housing Act.

(i) *Current section 221(g)(4) mortgage loans.* Section 221(g)(4) mortgage loans that are current as of the closing date

are not subject to the servicing requirements set forth in paragraphs (c)(1) and (c)(2) of this section.

(ii) *Defaulted section 221(g)(4) mortgage loans.* With respect to any section 221(g)(4) mortgage loan as to which a payment default has occurred, and as to which HUD, as of the closing date, was providing or had agreed to provide forbearance relief, the purchaser must continue to provide forbearance relief and must service such mortgage loans as set forth in paragraphs (c)(1) and (c)(2) of this section.

(d) *Section 235 mortgage loans*—(1) *Assistance payments contract.* If, prior to the mortgage loan sale, the assistance payments contract has not been previously terminated under 24 CFR 235.375(a), the contract will terminate as to each mortgage loan upon the sale of the mortgage loan. The purchasing mortgagee will therefore not receive any assistance payments on behalf of the mortgagor for any Section 235 mortgage loan sold.

(2) *Reduction in interest rates.* For a Section 235 mortgage loan that was accompanied by an assistance payments contract that was still in effect on the date of the sale, the Secretary will reduce the interest rate on the mortgage loan to a rate to be determined by the Secretary.

Subpart E—Lease and Sale of HUD-Acquired Single Family Properties for the Homeless

§ 291.400 Purpose and scope.

(a) *Purpose.* HUD seeks to assist individuals and families who are homeless by providing them with transitional housing and appropriate supportive services with the goal of helping them move to independent living. Therefore, HUD will make available, to applicants approved by HUD, certain HUD-acquired single family properties for use by the homeless.

(b) *Applicant preapproval.* Before a field office may notify an applicant of eligible properties, the applicant must be preapproved by HUD, according to procedures available from the field office.

(c) *Property available for lease with option to purchase.* HUD will make available up to 10 percent of its total inventory of properties, before or after they are listed for sale to the public.

(d) *Property available under a McKinney Act Supportive Housing program lease-option agreement.* Eligible properties will be available under a lease-option to purchase agreement to Supportive Housing program applicants for acquisition grants under 24 CFR part 583.

(e) *Properties available for sale.* Eligible properties will be available for competitive sale or direct sale for fair market value, less a discount determined appropriate by the Secretary but not less than 10 percent.

(f) *Concentration of properties.* To the extent practicable and possible, HUD will avoid excessive concentration in a single neighborhood of properties leased or sold under this subpart.

(g) *Failure to comply with requirements.* Failure to comply with this subpart, or a lease issued under this subpart, may result in termination from the program.

(Approved by the Office of Management and Budget under OMB control number 2502–0412)

[61 FR 55714, Oct. 28, 1996]

§ 291.405 Definitions.

For purposes of this subpart E:

Applicant means a State, metropolitan city, urban county, governmental entity, tribe, or private nonprofit organization that submits a written expression of interest in eligible properties under this subpart E. Governmental entities include those that have general governmental powers (e.g., a city or county), as well as those with limited or special powers (e.g., public housing agencies or State housing finance agencies). In the case of applicants leasing properties while their applications for Supportive Housing assistance are pending, "applicant" is defined in 24 CFR part 583.

Homeless means:

(1) Individuals or families who lack the resources to obtain housing, whose annual income is not in excess of 50 percent of the median income for the area, as determined by HUD, and who:

(i) Have a primary nighttime residence that is a public or private place not designed for, or ordinarily used as, a regular sleeping accommodation for human beings;

(ii) Have a primary nighttime residence that is a supervised publicly or privately operated shelter designed to provide temporary living accommodations (including welfare hotels, congregate shelters, and transitional housing, but excluding prisons or other detention facilities); or

(iii) Are at imminent risk of homelessness because they face immediate eviction and have been unable to identify a subsequent residence, which would result in emergency shelter placement (except that persons facing eviction on the basis of criminal conduct such as drug trafficking and violations of handgun prohibitions shall not be considered homeless for purposes of this definition); or

(2) Persons with disabilities who are about to be released from an institution and are at risk of imminent homelessness because no subsequent residences have been identified and because they lack the resources and support networks necessary to obtain access to housing.

Lessee means the applicant, approved by HUD as financially responsible, that executes a lease agreement with HUD for an eligible property.

[64 FR 6482, Feb. 9, 1999]

§ 291.415 Lease with option to purchase properties for use by the homeless.

(a) *Certification.* Eligible properties are available for lease to applicants, approved by HUD, that certify that the property will be utilized only for the purpose of providing transitional housing for the homeless during the lease term, and that the intended use of the property will be consistent with all local laws and regulations. The lease agreement will be in a form prescribed by the Secretary. Lessees must execute a sublease with occupants in a form prescribed by the Secretary limiting an occupant's tenancy to no longer than two years.

(b) *Term of lease.* (1) A lease of an eligible property may be negotiated for such time as the lessee requires, not to exceed one year. Leases are renewable, at the option of the lessee and with the approval of HUD, at the end of the first lease term for up to four additional one-year terms, on a year-to-year basis, provided the lessee has met the requirements under this program.

(2) Approvals for lease renewals will be denied if HUD determines that the lessee has not complied with the requirements of this part of the lease.

(3) A property will not be leased to a lessee for a period longer than five years. At the end of the five-year period, if the lessee has not exercised the option to purchase, HUD will notify the lessee to vacate the property and, if necessary, will take appropriate action under the eviction laws of the jurisdiction in which the property is located. All property returned to HUD must be vacant, and will be placed on the market for sale to the general public.

(4) Within 30 days of leasing a property from HUD or within 30 days after a property is vacated, a lessee must sublease the property to the homeless, unless a longer period is approved by HUD.

(c) *Rent.* (1) The lessee must pay HUD a nominal rent of $1 for each one-year lease period.

(2) A lessee may charge rent, including utilities, to an occupant at a rate appropriate to the financial means of the occupant. Unless HUD approves after consideration of such factors as the cost of operating housing in the area and the amount of the lessee's contributions to the program, such rent may not exceed the highest of:

(i) Thirty percent of the family's monthly adjusted income (adjustment factors include the number of people in the family, age of family members, medical expenses, and child care expenses);

(ii) Ten percent of the family's monthly income; or

(iii) If the family is receiving payments for welfare assistance from a public agency and a part of the payments, adjusted in accordance with the family's actual housing costs, is specifically designated by the agency to meet the family's housing costs, the portion of the payments that is designated.

(3) In no event may the rent charged an occupant exceed the occupant's pro rata share of the lessee's costs of operating the property.

(d) *Damage to leased properties.* Any damage to leased property caused by the intentional or negligent acts of the lessee or occupants must be repaired by the lessee at its own expense. If the lessee does not make the necessary repairs within a reasonable time after the damage occurs, HUD may, at its option, make the repairs and charge the cost to the lessee. Failure by the lessee to make the necessary repairs or to reimburse HUD for the cost of repairs will constitute grounds for termination of the lease and may result in termination from the program.

(e) *Purchase of leased properties.* (1) Lessees that desire to purchase leased properties during the lease term will be offered the properties at the lower of the fair market value established at the time of the initiation of the lease or at the time of the sale, less a discount determined appropriate by the Secretary but not less than 10 percent, provided lessees agree to use the properties either to house low-income tenants for a period of not less than 10 years or to resell the properties to low-income buyers. If the lessee does not agree to such conditions, the lessee must purchase the properties at the higher of the fair market value at the time of the initiation of the lease or at the time of the sale, less 10 percent. Any repairs to or rehabilitation of a property done by a lessee during the lease term will not be reflected in the purchase price.

(2) Sales of leased properties will be on as-is, all-cash basis. HUD will not pay a fee for a selling broker. HUD will pay the closing agent's fee. The purchaser must pay all other closing costs.

[61 FR 55715, Oct. 28, 1996]

§ 291.430 Elimination of lead-based paint hazards.

The Lead-Based Paint Poisoning Prevention Act (42 U.S.C. 4821–4846), the Residential Lead-Based Paint Hazard Reduction Act of 1992 (42 U.S.C. 4851–4856), and implementing regulations at part 35, subparts A, B, F, and R of this title, apply to activities covered by this subpart.

[64 FR 50225, Sept. 15, 1999, as amended at 69 FR 34275, June 21, 2004]

§291.435 Applicability of other Federal requirements.

In addition to the requirements set forth in 24 CFR part 5, the following Federal requirements apply to lessees and purchasers under this subpart:

(a) *Nondiscrimination and equal opportunity.* (1) The nondiscrimination and equal opportunity requirements set forth in 24 CFR part 5 are modified as follows:

(i) As applicable, lessees and purchasers must also comply with the Americans With Disabilities Act (42 U.S.C. 12131) and implementing regulations in 28 CFR parts 35 and 36.

(ii) The requirements of section 3 of the Housing and Urban Development Act of 1968 (12 U.S.C. 1701u), and Executive Order 11246 (30 FR 12319, 12935, 3 CFR, 1946–1965 Comp., p. 339; Executive Order 11625 (36 FR 19967, 3 CFR, 1971–1975 Comp., p. 616); Executive Order 12432 (48 FR 32551, 3 CFR, 1983 Comp., p. 198; and Executive Order 12138 (44 FR 29637, 3 CFR, 1979 Comp., p. 393) do not apply to this subpart.

(2) Lessees or purchasers that intend to serve designated populations of the homeless must comply, within the designated population, with the requirements for nondiscrimination on the basis of race, color, religion, sex, national origin, age, familial status, and disability.

(3) If the procedures that the lessee or purchaser intends to use to make known the availability of housing are unlikely to reach persons of any particular race, color, religion, sex, age, national origin, familial status, or disability who may qualify for admission to the housing, the recipient must establish additional procedures that will ensure that interested persons can obtain information concerning the availability of the housing.

(4) The lessee or purchaser must adopt procedures to make available information on the existence and locations of facilities and services that are accessible to persons with a handicap and maintain evidence of implementation of the procedures.

(b) *Conflicts of interest.* No person who is an employee, agent, consultant, officer, or elected or appointed official of the lessee or purchaser of property under this subpart, or who is in a position to participate in a decisionmaking process or gain inside information with regard to the lease or purchase of the property, may obtain a personal or financial interest or benefit from the lease or purchase of the property, or have an interest in any contract, subcontract, or agreement with respect thereto, or the proceeds thereunder, either for himself or herself or for those with whom he or she has family or business ties, during his or her tenure or for one year thereafter.

[61 FR 55715, Oct. 28, 1996]

§291.440 Recordkeeping requirements.

Each lessee must establish and maintain sufficient records to enable the Secretary to determine whether the requirements of this subpart have been met. This includes, where available, racial, ethnic, gender, and disability status data on the applicants for, and beneficiaries of, this homeless initiative.

(Approved by the Office of Management and Budget under OMB control number 2502–0412)

[61 FR 55716, Oct. 28, 1996]

Subpart F—Good Neighbor Next Door Sales Program

SOURCE: 71 FR 64426, Nov. 1, 2006, unless otherwise noted.

§291.500 Purpose.

This subpart describes the policies and procedures governing the Good Neighbor Next Door (GNND) Sales Program. The purpose of the GNND Sales Program is to improve the quality of life in distressed urban communities. This is to be accomplished by encouraging law enforcement officers, teachers, and firefighters/emergency medical technicians to purchase and live in homes that are located in the same communities where they perform their daily responsibilities and duties.

[81 FR 53003, Aug. 11, 2016]

§ 291.505 Definitions.

For purposes of this subpart:

Locality means the community, neighborhood, or jurisdiction of the unit of general local government, or Indian tribal government;

Unit of general local government means a county or parish, city, town, township, or other political subdivision of a State.

[81 FR 53003, Aug. 11, 2016]

§ 291.510 Overview of the GNND Sales Program.

(a) *General.* The GNND Sales Program enables a full-time law enforcement officer, teacher, or firefighter/emergency medical technician to purchase a specifically designated HUD-acquired home located in a HUD-designated revitalization area:

(1) At a 50 percent discount from the list price; and

(2) With a downpayment of $100, but only if the law enforcement officer, teacher, or firefighter/emergency medical technician finances the home through a Federal Housing Administration (FHA) insured mortgage.

(b) *Eligible properties.* Under the GNND Sales Program, single-unit properties acquired by HUD located in HUD-designated revitalization areas (except occupied properties, those located in Asset Control Areas, or those that HUD has determined will be sold through an alternative sales method) will be made available to interested law enforcement officers, teachers, and firefighters/emergency medical technicians prior to listing the properties for sale to other purchasers.

(c) *Multiple bids.* In the event that several bids are received on a single property, HUD will randomly select a winning offer by lottery and will also randomly select two backup bids, to be utilized in the order selected, in the event the winning purchaser is unable to close on the property. If both of the backup purchasers are also unable to close on the property, the property will then be made available for sale to purchasers through other sales methods.

(d) *Real estate brokers.* Law enforcement officers, teachers, and firefighters/emergency medical technicians must submit bids through a participating real estate broker. Any real estate broker who has agreed to comply with HUD requirements may participate in the GNND Sales Program. Real estate brokers may submit unlimited numbers of bids on an individual property provided each bid is from a different prospective purchaser.

(e) *Cap on sales.* The number of HUD-acquired homes sold under the GNND Sales Program in a fiscal year shall not exceed 5 percent of the number of "Part A" mortgage insurance conveyance claims paid by HUD in the prior fiscal year. The cap shall apply on a national basis, but HUD reserves the right to geographically apportion the cap to address regional or local differences in the number of homes sold through the GNND Sales Program. Additionally, HUD may adjust the percentage of the cap for any fiscal year. Any HUD determination to geographically distribute the cap, change a current geographic distribution, or adjust the percentage of the cap will be announced by HUD through publication of a notice in the FEDERAL REGISTER at least 30 days before the revision takes effect.

[71 FR 64426, Nov. 1, 2006, as amended at 73 FR 1974, Jan. 11, 2008]

§ 291.515 Purchaser qualifications.

To qualify to purchase a home through the GNND Sales Program:

(a) The person must be employed as a law enforcement officer (as described in § 291.520), teacher (as described in § 291.525), or firefighter/emergency medical technician (as described in § 291.530) at the time he/she submits a bid to purchase a home through the program and at the time of closing on the purchase of the home;

(b) The person must certify to his/her good faith intention to continue employment as a law enforcement officer (as described in § 291.520), teacher (as described in § 291.525), or firefighter/emergency medical technician (as described in § 291.530) for at least one year following the date of closing;

(c) The person must make an earnest money deposit at the time of signing the contract for purchase of the home, as described in § 291.535;

(d) The person must agree to own, and live in as his/her sole residence, the home for the entire duration of the owner-occupancy term, as described in §291.540, and to certify to that occupancy, as described in §291.565;

(e) The person must agree to execute a second mortgage and note on the home, as described in §291.550, for the difference between the list price and the discounted selling price;

(f) Neither the person (nor his/her spouse) may have owned any residential real property during the year prior to the date of submitting a bid on the home being acquired through the GNND Sales Program;

(g) Neither the person (nor his/her spouse) must ever have purchased another home under the GNND Sales Program or under the predecessor Officer Next Door Sales and Teacher Next Door Sales Programs; and

(h) Although both spouses, if otherwise eligible, may submit a bid on a single home made available for sale under the GNND Sales Program, HUD will approve a bid from only one spouse.

§291.520 Eligible law enforcement officers.

A person qualifies as a law enforcement officer for the purposes of the GNND Sales Program if the person is:

(a) Employed full-time by a law enforcement agency of the federal government, a state, a unit of general local government, or an Indian tribal government;

(b) In carrying out such full-time employment, the person is sworn to uphold, and make arrests for violations of, federal, state, tribal, county, township, or municipal laws and

(c) The full-time employment in paragraph (a) of this section must, in the normal course of business, directly serve the locality in which the home is located.

[71 FR 64426, Nov. 1, 2006, as amended at 81 FR 53003, Aug. 11, 2016]

§291.525 Eligible teachers.

A person qualifies as a teacher for the purposes of the GNND Sales Program if the person is:

(a) Employed as a full-time teacher by a state-accredited public school or private school that provides direct services to students in grades pre-kindergarten through 12; and

(b) The full-time employment in paragraph (a) of this section must, in the normal course of business, serve students from the locality where the home is located.

[71 FR 64426, Nov. 1, 2006, as amended at 81 FR 53003, Aug. 11, 2016]

§291.530 Eligible firefighter/emergency medical technicians.

A person qualifies as a firefighter/ emergency medical technician for the purposes of the GNND Sales Program if the person is:

(a) Employed full-time as a firefighter or emergency medical technician by a fire department or emergency medical services responder unit of the Federal Government, a State, unit of general local government, or an Indian tribal government; and

(b) The full-time employment in paragraph (a) of this section must, in the normal course of business, directly serve the locality where the home is located.

[81 FR 53003, Aug. 11, 2016]

§291.535 Earnest money deposit.

(a) *General.* The earnest money deposit is the sum of money that must be paid by the law enforcement officer, teacher, or firefighter/emergency medical technician at the time of submitting a bid to purchase a property under the GNND Sales Program. Each bid must be accompanied by a certification from the real estate broker that the earnest money deposit has been deposited in the broker's escrow account.

(b) *Amount of earnest money deposit.* The amount of the earnest money deposit required is an amount equal to one percent of the list price, but no less than $500 and no more than $2,000.

(c) *Acceptance or rejection of offer.* If an offer is accepted, the earnest money deposit will be credited to the purchaser at closing. If the offer is rejected, the earnest money deposit will be returned. Earnest money deposits are subject to total forfeiture for failure of the participant to close a sale.

§ 291.540 Owner-occupancy term.

(a) *General.* The owner-occupancy term is the number of months a participant in the GNND Sales Program must agree to own, and live in as his/her sole residence, a home purchased through the GNND Sales Program.

(b) *Start of owner-occupancy term.* The owner-occupancy term is 36 months, commencing either:

(1) Thirty days following closing if HUD determines that the home requires no more than $10,000 in repairs prior to occupancy;

(2) Ninety days following closing if HUD determines that the home requires more than $10,000, but not more than $20,000 in repairs prior to occupancy; or

(3) One hundred and eighty days following closing if HUD determines that the home requires more than $20,000 in repairs prior to occupancy.

(c) *Interruptions to owner-occupancy term*—(1) *General.* HUD may, at its sole discretion, allow interruptions to the 36-month owner-occupancy term if it determines that the interruption is necessary to prevent hardship, but only if the law enforcement officer, teacher, or firefighter/emergency medical technician submits a written and signed request to HUD containing the following information:

(i) The reason(s) why the interruption is necessary;

(ii) The dates of the intended interruption; and

(iii) A certification from the law enforcement officer, teacher, or firefighter/emergency medical technician that:

(A) The law enforcement officer, teacher, or firefighter/emergency medical technician is not abandoning the home as his/her permanent residence; and

(B) The law enforcement officer, teacher, or firefighter/emergency medical technician will resume occupancy of the home upon the conclusion of the interruption and complete the remainder of the 36-month owner-occupancy term.

(2) *Timing of written request to HUD.* The written request for approval of an interruption to the owner-occupancy term must be submitted to HUD at least 30 calendar days before the antici-pated interruption. Military service members protected by the Servicemembers Civil Relief Act need not submit their written request to HUD 30 days in advance of an anticipated interruption, but should submit their written request as soon as practicable upon learning of a potential interruption, in order to ensure timely processing and approval of the request.

§ 291.545 Financing purchase of the home.

(a) *Purchase using conventional financing.* If the law enforcement officer, teacher, or firefighter/emergency medical technician uses conventional financing to purchase a home under the GNND Sales Program, the amount of the mortgage may not exceed the discounted sales price of the home.

(b) *Purchase with FHA-insured mortgage.* (1) A law enforcement officer, teacher, or firefighter/emergency medical technician using an FHA-insured mortgage to finance purchase of the home may finance reasonable and customary closing costs with the FHA-insured mortgage.

(2) The amount of the FHA-insured mortgage may not exceed the discounted sales price of the home plus:

(i) The closing costs; and

(ii) The costs of rehabilitating and/or improving the home, where purchase of the home is being financed with an FHA-insured 203(k) rehabilitation loan (see 24 CFR part 203).

(c) *Closing costs and selling broker's commissions.* In no event will HUD pay a buyer's closing costs on the purchase of a property or a selling broker's commission through the GNND Sales Program.

§ 291.550 Second mortgage.

(a) *General.* The second mortgage is a mortgage and note, payable to HUD, on the home purchased through the GNND Sales Program in the amount of the difference between the list price of the home and the discounted selling price.

(b) *Second mortgage term.* The term of the second mortgage is equal to the owner-occupancy term (36 months) plus 30, 90, or 180 days, as provided in § 291.540(b). The amount of the second mortgage will be reduced by 1/36th on the last day of each month of occupancy following the occupancy start date. At the end of the 36th month of occupancy, the amount of the second mortgage will be zero.

(c) *Sale or vacancy of home.* If the law enforcement officer, teacher, or firefighter/emergency medical technician sells his/her home or stops living in the home as his/her sole residence prior to the expiration of the owner-occupancy term, he/she will owe HUD the amount due on the second mortgage as of the date the property is either sold or vacated.

§291.555 Refinancing.

(a) *General.* A law enforcement officer, teacher, or firefighter/emergency medical technician may refinance the mortgage and note used to purchase the home. However, the total of the refinanced mortgage and the remaining principal balance of the second mortgage may not exceed 95 percent of the value of the property, as appraised at the time of the refinancing. Unless HUD permits subordination pursuant to paragraph (b) of this section, the second mortgage described in §291.550 must hold a superior lien position to the refinanced mortgage.

(b) *Subordination of second mortgage.* HUD may permit subordination of the second mortgage to the refinanced mortgage, but only if HUD, at its sole discretion, determines that the refinancing will satisfy one of the following:

(1) Will result in a lower annual percentage rate (APR) on the first mortgage;

(2) Will be undertaken pursuant to HUD's Section 203(k) Rehabilitation Loan Insurance Program in order to rehabilitate or repair the home; or

(3) Is necessary to prevent the law enforcement officer, teacher, or firefighter/emergency medical technician from defaulting on the first mortgage.

§291.560 Ineligibility of multiple-unit properties.

Only single-unit properties are eligible for the GNND Sales Program.

§291.565 Continuing obligations after purchase.

To remain in compliance with the GNND Sales Program, the law enforcement officer, teacher, or firefighter/emergency medical technician must, for the entire duration of the owner-occupancy term:

(a) Continue to own, and live in as his/her sole residence, the home purchased through the GNND Sales Program; and

(b) Certify initially and once annually thereafter during and at the conclusion of the owner-occupancy term that he/she was at all times fully in compliance with paragraph (a) of this section.

PARTS 292–299 [RESERVED]

CHAPTER III—GOVERNMENT NATIONAL MORTGAGE ASSOCIATION, DEPARTMENT OF HOUSING AND URBAN DEVELOPMENT

PART 300—GENERAL

AUTHORITY: 12 U.S.C. 1723a, unless otherwise noted, and 42 U.S.C. 3535(d).

SOURCE: 60 FR 42015, Aug. 14, 1995, unless otherwise noted.

§ 300.1   Scope of chapter.

This chapter consists of general information and does not purport to set forth all of the procedures and requirements that apply to the operations of the Association. Complete specific information as to any aspect of such operations may be obtained from the office listed in § 300.9.

§ 300.3   Description.

The Government National Mortgage Association (hereinafter in this chapter called the Association, GNMA or Ginnie Mae) furnishes fiduciary services to itself and other departments and agencies of the Government, and guarantees privately issued securities backed by trusts or pools of mortgages or loans which are insured or guaranteed by the Federal Housing Administration (FHA), the Department of Veterans Affairs (VA) or the Rural Housing Service (RHS) and certain other loans or mortgages guaranteed or insured by the Government. In the course of its business, the Association is referred to as GNMA or Ginnie Mae.

[66 FR 44265, Aug. 22, 2001]

§ 300.5   Creation and status.

The Association is a Government corporation in the Department of Housing and Urban Development. It is derived from the Federal National Mortgage Association, which was partitioned by the Congress into two corporations effective September 1, 1968, one of which is the Association. The operations of the Association are conducted under its statutory charter contained in title III of the National Housing Act, 12 U.S.C. 1716, *et seq.*

§ 300.7   Area of operations.

The Association is authorized to conduct its business in any State of the United States, the District of Columbia, the Commonwealth of Puerto Rico, the Commonwealth of the Northern Mariana Islands, and the territories and possessions of the United States.

§ 300.9   Office.

The Association directs its operations from its office located at 451 Seventh Street, SW., Washington DC 20410.

§ 300.11   Authority of officers.

The President, each Vice President, and each Assistant Vice President of the Association are severally expressly empowered in the name of the Association to sign all contracts and other documents, instruments, and writings which call for execution by the Association in the conduct of its business and affairs, and to encumber, mortgage, pledge, convey or otherwise alien any property which the Association may own or in which it may have an estate, right, title or interest. In addition, the President, each Vice President, each Assistant Vice President, the Secretary of the Association, each Assistant Secretary, the Treasurer and the Controller shall have the authority as may be provided in the Bylaws of the Association or as may be delegated to them in a manner not inconsistent with the Bylaws.

§ 300.13   Power of attorney.

In order to efficiently carry out the purposes of the Association, the Association may appoint any person its true and lawful attorney-in-fact by publication in the FEDERAL REGISTER or by appointment from the President of the Association in writing. Any such attorney-in-fact shall have the power outlined in the publication or appointment.

§ 300.15   Exceptions.

In the conduct of its affairs, in individual cases or classes of cases, the Association reserves the right, consistent with law, without prior notice and at any time, to alter or waive any of the requirements contained in this chapter or elsewhere or to impose other and additional requirements; it further reserves the right, without prior notice and at any time, to amend or rescind any or all of the material set forth herein.

§ 300.17 Audits and reports.

The Association and its designees may at any reasonable time audit the books and examine the records of any issuer, mortgage servicer, trustee, agent or other person bearing on compliance with the requirements of the Association's programs, and the Association may require reasonable and necessary reports from such persons.

PART 310—BYLAWS OF THE GOVERNMENT NATIONAL MORTGAGE ASSOCIATION

AUTHORITY: 12 U.S.C. 1723 and 42 U.S.C. 3535(d).

SOURCE: 60 FR 42015, Aug. 14, 1995, unless otherwise noted.

§ 310.1 Bylaws of the Association.

The bylaws of the Association shall be duly adopted by the Secretary of Housing and Urban Development pursuant to section 308 of the National Housing Act (12 U.S.C. 1723) and shall govern the performance of the powers and duties granted to or imposed upon the Association by law.

PART 320—GUARANTY OF MORTGAGE-BACKED SECURITIES

Subpart A—Pass-Through Type Securities

AUTHORITY: 12 U.S.C. 1721(g) and 1723a(a); and 42 U.S.C. 3535(d).

SOURCE: 60 FR 42015, Aug. 14, 1995, unless otherwise noted.

Subpart A—Pass-Through Type Securities

§ 320.1 General.

The Association is authorized by section 306(g) of the National Housing Act (12 U.S.C. 1721(g)) upon such terms and conditions as it may deem appropriate, to guarantee the timely payment of principal of and interest on securities that are based on and backed by a trust or pool composed of mortgages which are insured or guaranteed by FHA, FmHA or VA. The Association's guaranty of mortgage-backed securities is backed by the full faith and credit of the United States. This subpart is limited to "modified pass-through" securities, and does not purport to set forth all the procedures and requirements that apply to the issuance and guaranty of such securities. All such transactions are governed by the specific terms and provisions of the Association's Mortgage-Backed Securities Guides (MBS Guides) and contracts entered into by the parties.

§ 320.3 Eligible issuers of securities.

(a) *Eligibility requirements.* A mortgage lender, including an instrumentality of a State or local government, to be eligible to issue or service mortgage-backed securities guaranteed by the Association must satisfy all of the following standards:

(1) Be in good standing as a mortgagee approved by the FHA;

(2) Be in good standing as a mortgage seller or servicer approved by the Federal National Mortgage Association (FNMA), the Federal Home Loan Mortgage Corporation (FHLMC), or the Association. Loss of either FNMA approval or FHLMC approval may cause

the issuer to become ineligible to issue and service the Association's mortgage-backed securities and constitute a default under the applicable guaranty or contractual agreement whether or not the issuer qualified for new issuer approval on the basis of FNMA or FHLMC approval;

(3) Have management with adequate experience, and access to adequate facilities to issue or service mortgage-backed securities, as determined by the Association;

(4) Maintain the applicable minimum net worth discussed in paragraph (c) of this section; and

(5) Meet the requirements, conditions, and limitations prescribed by the Association in this part or the applicable MBS Guides.

(b) *Time of eligibility.* The Association shall not commit to guarantee, or guarantee any issue of mortgage-backed securities unless the mortgage lender requesting such commitment or guaranty qualifies as an eligible issuer both at the time of commitment approval and at the time of the issuance of the guaranty.

(c) *Net worth requirements.* Issuers shall maintain at all times a net worth acceptable to the Association of not less than the applicable minimum amount. The applicable minimum amount shall be published in the MBS Guides.

(d) *Disqualification.* A mortgage lender shall not qualify as an eligible issuer at any time in which:

(1) The lending policies of the issuer permit any discrimination based on race, religion, color, national origin, age, or sex of a borrower; or

(2) The issuer is not in compliance with any rules, regulations, or orders issued under title VI of the Civil Rights Act of 1964; Executive Order 11063, Equal Opportunity in Housing, November 20, 1962; Executive Order 11246, Equal Employment Opportunity, issued on September 24, 1965 and amended on October 13, 1967; title VII of the Civil Rights Act of 1968; title VIII of the Civil Rights Act of 1968 as amended by the Fair Housing Amendments Act of 1988; or by the FHA or VA.

(e) *Ethics and standards.* A mortgage lender shall qualify as an eligible issuer only so long as it conducts its business operations in accordance with accepted mortgage banking practices, ethics, and standards, as determined by the Association, and maintains its books and records in accordance with generally accepted accounting principles.

(f) *Change in control.* Issuers shall notify the Association of any change in issuer control. A change in control occurs whenever a new party obtains significant influence over an issuer, as defined by the Association. In a merger where the surviving party is not the approved issuer and in a consolidation, the surviving party must apply formally for approval as a new issuer prior to the merger or consolidation taking place. In other business combinations, such as a stock sale of an existing issuer, which result in a change in control of issuer, the issuer shall demonstrate that it continues to meet all issuer eligibility requirements prior to the business combination being finalized.

(g) *Cross-Default.* Related issuers, as defined by the Association, shall execute a cross-default agreement, in a form prescribed by the Association, that authorizes the default of one or more related issuers in the event of a default by any one of the related issuers. Issuers may be granted an exemption from this section, provided that they submit a legal opinion, acceptable to the Association, which demonstrates that the execution of a cross-default agreement would be prohibited by the issuer's Federal regulator.

(h) *Failure to comply.* In the event that an issuer subsequently fails to comply with any of the requirements prescribed in this part or the applicable MBS Guide, as determined by the Association, the Association may, among other things, withhold further commitments to guarantee securities until such time as the Association is satisfied that the issuer has resumed business operations in compliance with such requirements.

(Approved by the Office of Management and Budget under control numbers 2503–0003, 2503–0004, 2503–0006, 2503–0007, and 2503–0026)

§ 320.5 Securities.

(a) *Instruments.* Securities issued pursuant to the provisions of this subpart must be modified pass-through securities, that provide for payment, whether or not collected, of both specified principal installments and interest on the unpaid principal balance, with all prepayments and other unscheduled recoveries of principal being passed through to the holder. In the case of delinquent mortgages in a pool backing modified pass-through securities, the issuer is required to make advances if necessary to maintain the specified schedule of interest and principal payments to the holders, or at its option, at any time 90 days or more after default of any such mortgage, the issuer may repurchase such mortgage for an amount equal to the unpaid principal balance of the mortgage. The securities, if issued in certificated form, must specify the dates by which payments are to be made to the holders thereof, and must indicate the accounting period for collections on the pool's mortgages relating to each such payment, and the securities, if issued in certificated form, must also specify a date on which the entire principal will have been paid or will be payable.

(b) *Issue amount.* Each issue of guaranteed securities must be in a minimum face amount as specified in the applicable MBS Guide. The total face amount of any issue of securities cannot exceed the aggregate unpaid principal balances of the mortgages in the pool. The Association may provide for issuers to submit packages of mortgages that may be consolidated, with other packages of similar types of mortgages, into multiple issuer pools.

(c) [Reserved]

(d) *Transferability.* Securities are transferable, but the share of the proceeds collected on account of the pool of mortgages is payable only to the registered holder of a security according to the policies established by the Association.

(e) *Issue Date.* Securities backed by single-family mortgages with issue dates of October 1, 1998, or before, serial notes with issue dates of July 1, 2002, or before, and securities backed by multifamily mortgages with issue dates of February 1, 2002, or before, have been issued in certificated form. Securities issued after these dates will be issued in book-entry form. The Association may approve the issuance of certificated securities for good cause.

(f) *Delivery.* Delivery of uncertificated securities occurs when the book-entry depository's nominee is registered as the registered owner of the securities on Ginnie Mae's central registry.

(g) *Registered Ownership.* Ownership of mortgage-backed securities issued pursuant to this subpart registered in the name of a Depository shall be conclusively established by registration in the name of the Depository as owner on the Association's central registry and it shall be unnecessary for a Depository to maintain custody of any physical certificates evidencing such ownership.

(h) *Payments on Mortgage-Backed Securities.* Issuers must remit all payments due to holders of mortgage-backed securities such that holders will receive their installments as follows:

(1) *Payment to a Depository.* (i) For all securities registered in the name of a Depository or the designated nominee for a Depository, issuers are required to make payments in immediately available funds by ACH transaction, Fedwire, or by such other method as directed and/or authorized by the Association pursuant to the MBS Guide, including requiring that issuers maintain funds accounts in institutions that are accessible by debit ACH transactions originated by such Depository or its designee.

(ii) Payment must be made by the hour specified in the MBS Guide on the calendar day of the month specified in the MBS Guide for payment on such mortgage-backed securities (the "applicable Payment Date"), with adjustments to such time as may be specified in the MBS Guide for Payments Dates that do not fall on business days.

(2) *Payments to other holders.* An issuer of mortgage-backed securities that are not registered in the name of a Depository or its nominee may make payments to a security holder by ACH transaction or Fedwire, provided that it obtains the prior written approval of

the holder of such mortgage-backed securities. If an issuer begins to make such payments by electronic transfer, it must continue to do so while the securities are registered in the name of that security holder. If an issuer makes payments on mortgage-backed securities by check, the check must be received by the security holder not later than the applicable Payment Date each month.

(i) *Guaranty.* The Association's guaranty described in §320.13 is a guaranty that payment will be made to the registered owner of securities as reflected in the Association's central registry. The Association makes no other guaranty, including any guaranty that a Depository will appropriately credit payments to beneficial owners of such mortgage-backed securities. The Association's guarantee of securities payable to a Depository or its nominee becomes effective when the Depository or its nominee is registered as the registered owner of the securities on the Association's central registry.

(j) *Definition of Depository.* As used in this section, Depository means a clearing corporation within the meaning of Article 8 of the Uniform Commercial Code, including any Federal Reserve Bank, that maintains systems by which ownership and transfer of interests in mortgage-backed securities are made through the books of such clearing corporation.

(Approved by the Office of Management and Budget under control number 2503–0009)

[60 FR 42015, Aug. 14, 1995, as amended at 63 FR 51251, Sept. 24, 1998; 64 FR 34106, June 24, 1999; 66 FR 44265, Aug. 22, 2001; 70 FR 33652, June 8, 2005; 72 FR 49125, Aug. 27, 2007]

§320.7 Mortgages.

Each issue of guaranteed securities must be backed by a separate pool of mortgages which meet the requirements of the applicable MBS Guide.

§320.8 Excess Yield Securities.

(a) *Definition.* Excess Yield Securities are securities backed by the excess servicing income relating to mortgages underlying previously issued Ginnie Mae mortgage-backed securities.

(b) *GNMA guaranty.* The Association guarantees the timely payment of in-terest as provided by the terms of the security.

[71 FR 32389, June 5, 2006]

§320.9 Pool administration.

The Association will only guarantee securities if the issuer executes a guaranty agreement or contractual agreement in the form prescribed by the Association. Pool administration requirements are set forth in such agreements or the applicable MBS Guide.

(Approved by the Office of Management and Budget under control numbers 2503–0003, 2503–0004, 2503–0006, 2503–0007, and 2503–0026)

§320.10 Financial reporting.

Issuers shall submit to the Association audited annual financial statements within 90 days of their fiscal year end. All financial statements shall include a balance sheet and a statement of operations and cash flows. The audit shall be conducted in accordance with the standards for financial audits of the U.S. Government Accountability Office's *Government Auditing Standards,* issued by the Comptroller General of the United States.

[72 FR 49125, Aug. 27, 2007]

§320.11 Insurance coverage.

The issuer shall maintain, for the benefit of the Association, insurance, errors and omissions, fidelity bond and other coverage as required by the Association and set forth in the appropriate MBS Guide.

§320.12 Integrity.

(a) *Background.* Issuers shall disclose the background of all individuals serving on their Board of Directors and all individuals acting as authorized signatories. The disclosures shall include any prior convictions, fines or other adverse actions against these individuals by a Federal, state or local agency, or a government-related entity where the action is related to the responsibilities that are commensurate with those of the financial services industry. The term government-related entity includes, but is not limited to, FHA, VA, FmHA, FNMA, FHLMC, Office of Thrift Supervision, Federal Deposit Insurance Corporation, Office of the Comptroller of the Currency, Board of Governors of the Federal Reserve System, and National Credit Union Administration.

(b) *Change in status.* Issuers shall disclose material changes in their status with other government-related entities and regulatory agencies, or state or local agencies with similar authority, within 5 business days of their occurrence. The disclosures shall include, but not be limited to, voluntary and non-voluntary terminations, defaults, fines, and material non-compliance with agency rules and policies. Disclosures that are specifically prohibited by an agency are exempted from this section.

§ 320.13   Guaranty.

The Association guarantees the timely payment, whether or not collected, of the interest on the outstanding balance and the specified principal installments on securities that are registered on Ginnie Mae's central registry. The Association's guaranty is backed by the full faith and credit of the United States.

[64 FR 34107, June 24, 1999]

§ 320.15   Default.

(a) *Issuer default.* Any failure or inability of the issuer to make payments as due as well as such other events as may be identified by the Association and included in the applicable guaranty agreement, contractual agreement or MBS Guide, shall constitute a default of the issuer.

(b) *Action upon default.* Upon any default by the issuer, the Association may:

(1) Institute a claim against the issuer's insurance, bond or other coverage, as specified in § 320.11;

(2) Pursuant to section 306(g) of the National Housing Act (12 U.S.C. 1721(g)), extinguish all the right, title, or other interest of the issuer in the pooled mortgages; and

(3) Exercise such other rights and remedies as it may have.

§ 320.17   Fees.

The Association may impose application fees, guaranty fees, securities transfer fees and other fees.

Subpart B—Bond-Type Securities

§ 320.21   General.

In addition to the "pass-through" securities dealt with in subpart A of this part, the Association is authorized by section 306(g) of the National Housing Act, 12 U.S.C. 1721(g), upon such terms and conditions as it may deem appropriate, to guarantee the timely payment of principal of and interest on "bond-type" securities which are based on and backed by a trust or pool composed of mortgages which are insured or guaranteed by FHA, FmHA or the VA. The Association's guaranty of mortgage-backed securities is backed by the full faith and credit of the United States. This subpart deals with such "bond-type" securities and does not purport to set forth all the procedures and requirements that apply to the issuance and guaranty of such securities. All such transactions are governed by the specific terms and provisions of the contracts entered into by the parties and the Bond-Type Securities Guide (the "Bond Guide").

§ 320.23   Eligible issuers.

Any corporation, trust, partnership, or other entity with a net worth acceptable to the Association as set forth in the Bond Guide, which has the capability to assemble acceptable and eligible mortgages in sufficient quantity to support required minimum issuances of securities and which meets such other requirements as are set forth in the Bond Guide, may be approved to issue and service bond-type securities guaranteed by the Association. Further, the Association reserves the right to limit the number of issuers in the interest of conducting an orderly market of securities of this type.

§ 320.25   Securities.

(a) *Instruments.* Securities to be issued pursuant to the provisions of this subpart B may be in registered or bearer form. Each security shall have terms acceptable to the Association as provided in the Bond Guide.

(b) *Issue amount.* Each issue of guaranteed securities must be in a minimum face amount as specified in the Bond Guide. The total face amount of any issue of securities cannot exceed

626

the aggregate unpaid principal balances of the mortgages in the pool.

(c) *Face amount of securities.* The face amount of any security cannot be less than $25,000.

(d) *Transferability.* Bearer securities are freely transferrable. Registered securities are transferable only on the books of an agent, as shall be agreed upon by the Association and the issuer.

(e) *Treasury approval.* Issues of $100 million or larger will be subject to approval of the Secretary of the Treasury.

§ 320.27 Mortgages.

Guaranteed securities issued under these provisions must be based on and backed by mortgages pooled under trust arrangements satisfactory to the Association. Such mortgages must meet the requirements of the Bond Guide.

§ 320.29 Guaranty.

With respect to bond-type securities, the Association will guarantee the timely payment of principal of and interest on such securities, subject to the terms and conditions of the securities. The Association's guaranty is backed by the full faith and credit of the United States.

§ 320.31 Default.

Upon default of the issuer, the Association has the right, pursuant to section 306(g) of the National Housing Act (12 U.S.C. 1721(g)), to take title to the mortgages and other assets that are subject to the trust arrangements, and to proceed against other assets of the issuer to the extent necessary to satisfy its own claims and the rights of the holders of securities then outstanding. Such action by the Association shall be taken subject to an accounting to the issuer.

§ 320.33 Fees.

The Association may impose application and guaranty fees, which may vary with relation to the size or risk of the guaranty transaction undertaken.

PART 330—GUARANTY OF MULTICLASS SECURITIES

AUTHORITY: 12 U.S.C. 1721(g) and 1723a(a); and 42 U.S.C. 3535(d).

SOURCE: 60 FR 42018, Aug. 14, 1995, unless otherwise noted.

§ 330.1 Scope of part.

This part is limited to multiclass securities. It does not purport to set forth all the procedures and requirements that apply to the issuance and guaranty of such securities. All such transactions are governed by the specific terms and provisions of the contracts entered into by the parties and by the GNMA Multiclass Securities Guide (Multiclass Guide).

§ 330.5 Definitions.

As used in this part, the following terms shall have the meanings indicated:

Consolidated securities. A series of multiclass securities, each class of which provides for payments proportionate with payments on the underlying eligible collateral.

Depositor. The entity that deposits, or executes an agreement to deposit, as contained in the Multiclass Guide, eligible collateral into a trust in exchange for consolidated securities.

Depository. A clearing corporation within the meaning of Article 8 of the Uniform Commercial Code, including any Federal Reserve Bank, that maintains systems by which ownership and transfer of interests in Ginnie Mae multiclass securities are made through entries on the books of such clearing corporation.

GNMA electronic bulletin board. An information distribution system established by the Association for the Multiclass Securities program.

GNMA MBS certificates. The guaranteed mortgage-backed securities issued under part 320 of this chapter.

Government mortgages. Mortgages that are eligible under section 306(g) of the National Housing Act (12 U.S.C. 1721(g)) for inclusion in GNMA mortgage-backed securities pools.

Multiclass Registrar. The institution that is specified by the Association as the registrar of the related class and series of multiclass securities.

Participant. For structured securities, the sponsor, co-sponsor, trustee, trust counsel, and accounting firm. For consolidated securities, the depositor. Other entities may be designated as participants in the Multiclass Guide.

Sponsor. With respect to structured securities, the entity that establishes the required trust executing the trust agreement and depositing the eligible collateral in the trust in exchange for the structured securities.

Structured securities. Securities of a series at least one class of which provides for payments of principal or interest disproportionately from payments on the underlying eligible collateral.

[66 FR 44265, Aug. 22, 2001]

§ 330.10 Eligible collateral.

The Association, in its discretion, shall determine what collateral is eligible for inclusion in the Multiclass Securities program. Eligible collateral may include GNMA MBS certificates, government mortgages, consolidated securities, and other securities approved by the Association. Categories of these GNMA MBS certificates, government mortgages, consolidated securities, and other securities as approved by the Association become eligible collateral when they are published as eligible collateral in the Multiclass Guide or on the GNMA electronic bulletin board. Eligible collateral may differ for various Association guaranteed multiclass securities.

§ 330.15 Participation requirements.

To participate in the Multiclass Securities program, a participant must meet the following criteria:

(a) *Certification.* A participant must submit such certifications and other documents as are required by the Multiclass Guide.

(b) *Compliance with Multiclass Guide.* By completing a multiclass securities transaction, a participant is deemed to have represented and warranted to the Association that it has complied with, and that it agrees to comply with, the Multiclass Guide in effect as of the date that the Association's guaranty is placed on the securities.

(c) *Material changes in status.* A participant must report, as required in the Multiclass Guide, material adverse changes in status including voluntary and non-voluntary termination, defaults, fines and findings of material non-conformance with rules and policies of state and federal agencies and federal government sponsored enterprises.

(d) *Integrity.* The participant must conduct its business operations in accordance with industry practices, ethics and standards, and maintain its books and records in an appropriate manner, as determined by the Association.

(Approved by the Office of Management and Budget under control number 2503–0030)

§ 330.20 Eligible participants.

In addition to requirements set forth in this part, a participant must meet the following requirements.

(a) *Structured securities*—(1) *Description.* The Association guarantees the payment of principal and interest on structured securities issued by trusts organized by sponsors in accordance with procedures established and approved by the Association. The structured securities are backed by eligible collateral, as described in this part, held by the trustee.

(2) *Eligibility requirements for participants*—(i) *Sponsors.* A sponsor must:

(A) Apply and be approved by the Association;

(B) Demonstrate to the satisfaction of the Association its capacity to accumulate the eligible collateral, as described in this part, needed for a proposed structured securities issuance;

(C) Be in good standing with and either have been responsible for at least one structured securities transaction with FNMA or FHLMC, or have demonstrated to the Association's satisfaction its capability to act as sponsor of GNMA guaranteed structured securities;

(D) Have the minimum required amount, as set forth in the Multiclass Guide, in shareholders' equity or partners' capital, evidenced by the sponsor's audited financial statements, which must have been issued within the preceding 12-month period;

(E) Represent the structural integrity of the issuance under all cash flow scenarios and demonstrate to the Association's satisfaction its ability to indemnify the Association for a breach of this representation;

(F) Comply with the Association's policies regarding participation by minority and/or women-owned businesses and take appropriate measures to assure compliance by the other participants as specified in the Multiclass Guide; and

(G) Provide the Association with the opinions of trust counsel and accounting firms which are acceptable to the Association and on which the Association may rely.

(ii) *Co-sponsors.* A Co-sponsor must submit to the Association an application and a certification, as set forth in the Multiclass Guide, as to its status as a minority and/or women-owned business.

(iii) *Trustees.* A trustee is selected by the Sponsor from institutions approved by the Association using such procedures as the Association deems appropriate.

(b) *Consolidated securities*—(1) *Description.* A Depositor delivers, or executes an agreement to deliver, eligible collateral to a trust in exchange for a single Association guaranteed multiclass security, as set forth in the Multiclass Guide.

(2) *Eligibility requirements for participant.* A Depositor must certify that:

(i) It is an "accredited investor" within the meaning of 17 CFR 230.501(a)(1), (a)(3) or (a)(7);

(ii) It has authority to deliver, and will deliver, the collateral to the trustee and that the collateral is free and clear of all liens and encumbrances; and

(iii) The information set forth by the depositor regarding the eligible collateral is true and correct.

(c) *Other types of Association guaranteed multiclass securities.* The Association will set forth the requirements for the guaranty by the Association of other types of multiclass securities, and the eligibility requirements for the appropriate participants, in the Multiclass Guide or on the GNMA electronic bulletin board.

§330.25 Fees.

The Association, in its discretion, through publication in the Multiclass Guide or on the GNMA electronic bulletin board, may impose fees for application, guaranty, transfer, change from book entry to certificated form, or other related fees. Fees may vary, at the Association's discretion, depending upon, but not limited to, such factors as size, collateral characteristics, expense or risk of the guaranty transaction undertaken.

§330.30 GNMA Guaranty.

(a) *Securities held by Depositories.* Ownership of multiclass securities registered in the name of a Depository shall be conclusively established by registration in the name of the Depository as owner on the books and records of the Multiclass Registrar, and it shall be unnecessary for a Depository to maintain custody of any physical certificates evidencing such ownership.

(b) *Guaranty.* The Association's guaranty is a guaranty that payment will be made to the registered owner of securities as reflected on the books and records of the Multiclass Registrar.

(1) The Association makes no other guaranty, including any guaranty that a Depository will appropriately credit payments to beneficial owners of GNMA multiclass securities. The Association's guarantee of securities payable to a Depository or its nominee becomes effective when the Depository or

its nominee is registered as the registered owner of the securities on the books and records of the Multiclass Registrar.

(2) The Association guarantees the timely payment of principal and interest as provided by the terms of the multiclass security. The Association's guaranty is backed by the full faith and credit of the United States.

[66 FR 44266, Aug. 22, 2001]

§ 330.35 Investors.

Association guaranteed multiclass securities may not be suitable investments for all investors. No investor should purchase securities of any class unless the investor understands, and is able to bear, the prepayment, yield, liquidity and market risks associated with the class. The Association assumes no obligation or liability to any person with regard to determining the suitability of such securities for such investor.

§ 330.40 Consultation.

The Association may consult with persons or entities in such manner as the Association deems appropriate to ensure the efficient commencement and operation of the Multiclass Securities program.

§ 330.45 Limitation on GNMA liability.

Except for its guaranty, the Association undertakes no obligation and assumes no liability to any person with regard to or on account of the existence or operation of this part or the conduct of any participants in the Multiclass Securities program.

§ 330.50 Administration of multiclass securities.

The GNMA guaranteed multiclass securities will be administered in accordance with the Association's requirements described in the Multiclass Guide.

§ 330.55 Basis for removal from participation.

A participant may be removed from the Multiclass Securities program if the Association, in its discretion, determines that any of the following exists or has occurred:

(a) The participant, at any time, fails to meet any condition for eligibility;

(b) The participant fails to comply with any provision of the Multiclass Guide or this part;

(c) The participant is unable or fails to truthfully, correctly or fully submit such certifications as are required; and

(d) Such further reasons as the Association determines necessary to protect the safety and soundness of the Multiclass Securities program, as set out in the Multiclass Guide.

§ 330.60 Removal procedure.

(a) A participant may be suspended from participation in the Multiclass Securities program upon written notice from the Association, which shall include the reasons for the suspension. The participant shall have the opportunity to submit a written presentation to the President of the Association, or designee, in support of its reinstatement, subject to such limitations as the Association in its discretion may impose as to length, time for submission, or otherwise. A determination by the President of the Association, or designee, shall exhaust the participant's administrative remedies.

(b) If a participant is suspended from the Multiclass Securities program, the Association shall have no obligation to complete a pending transaction involving the participant.

(c) After a participant has been removed from the Multiclass Securities program, the participant may request reinstatement. Approval of the reinstatement is at the sole discretion of the Association.

PART 340—FIDUCIARY ACTIVITIES

Sec.
340.1 General.
340.3 Appropriations.

AUTHORITY: 12 U.S.C. 1723a and 42 U.S.C. 3535(d).

SOURCE: 60 FR 42019, Aug. 14, 1995, unless otherwise noted.

§ 340.1 General.

The Association is authorized by section 302(c) of the National Housing Act (12 U.S.C. 1717(c)) to create, accept, execute, and administer trusts and other fiduciary undertakings appropriate for financing purposes. Under this authority, the Association is authorized to acquire and otherwise deal in any mortgages or other types of obligations in which any department or agency of the United States listed in section 302(c)(2) of such Act may have a financial interest. Under its fiduciary powers, the Association may create, accept, and administer trusts consisting of interests in mortgages and obligations, sell to private investors certificates of beneficial interest, or participations, in the mortgages or obligations or in the interest and principal payments derived therefrom, and provide for payment of interest and principal and for retirement of the participations. The Association, in its ordinary corporate capacity as contrasted to its fiduciary capacity, is expressly authorized to guarantee the participations.

§ 340.3 Appropriations.

There is authority for Congress to appropriate such sums as may be necessary to enable the trustor of any trust (as described in § 340.1) to pay to the Association, as trustee, any insufficiency in aggregate receipts from the obligations subject to the trust to provide for the timely payment by the trustee of all interest or principal on the beneficial interests or participations related to such trust.

PARTS 341–349 [RESERVED]

PART 350—BOOK-ENTRY PROCEDURES

Sec.

AUTHORITY: 12 U.S.C. 1721(g) and 1723a(a); 42 U.S.C. 3535(d).

SOURCE: 66 FR 44266, Aug. 22, 2001, unless otherwise noted.

§ 350.1 Purpose.

The purpose of this part is to achieve the efficiencies and fungibility through use of a single system for transferring interests both in Ginnie Mae Securities and other United States Government securities and in mortgage-backed securities issued by the Federal National Mortgage Association and the Federal Home Loan Mortgage Corporation. The Association only guarantees that payments required to be made by issuers of Ginnie Mae Securities will be made to the registered owner of those Ginnie Mae Securities. The Association undertakes no other obligation. Under the Book-entry System, the Federal Reserve Banks will be the registered owner of Book-entry Ginnie Mae Securities, not the agent of the Association, and the Association makes no warranty or guaranty with respect to the maintenance of the Book-entry System by the Federal Reserve Banks.

§ 350.2 Definitions.

(a) *Specified Terms.* As used in this part, the following terms shall have the meanings indicated:

Book-entry Ginnie Mae Security. A Ginnie Mae Security issued or maintained in the Book-entry System. Book-entry Ginnie Mae Security also means the separate interest and principal components of a Book-entry Ginnie Mae Security if such security has been designated by Ginnie Mae as eligible for division into such components and the components are maintained separately on the books of one or more Federal Reserve Banks.

Book-entry System. The automated book-entry system operated by the Federal Reserve Banks acting as Depositories for Ginnie Mae, on which Book-entry Ginnie Mae Securities are

631

recorded, transferred and maintained in book-entry form.

Definitive Ginnie Mae Security. A Ginnie Mae Security in engraved or printed form, or that is otherwise represented by a certificate.

Depository. A clearing corporation within the meaning of Article 8 of the Uniform Commercial Code, including any Federal Reserve Bank, that maintains systems by which ownership and transfer of interests in Book-entry Ginnie Mae Securities are made through entries on the books of such clearing corporation.

Eligible Book-entry Ginnie Mae Security. A Book-entry Ginnie Mae Security issued or maintained in the Book-entry System which by the terms of its Security Documentation is eligible to be converted from book-entry form into definitive form.

Entitlement Holder. A Person to whose account an interest in a Book-entry Ginnie Mae Security is credited on the records of a Securities Intermediary.

Federal Reserve Bank Operating Circular. The publication issued by each Federal Reserve Bank that sets forth the terms and conditions under which the Reserve Bank maintains book-entry securities accounts (including Book-entry Ginnie Mae Securities accounts) and transfers book-entry Securities (including Book-entry Ginnie Mae Securities).

Ginnie Mae Security. Any security or obligation guaranteed as to payment of principal and/or interest by Ginnie Mae under its Charter Act and issued in the form of a Definitive Ginnie Mae Security or a Book-entry Ginnie Mae Security.

Participant. A Person that maintains a Participant's Securities Account with a Federal Reserve Bank.

Person. An individual, corporation, company, governmental entity, association, firm, partnership, trust, estate, representative, and any other similar organization, but such term does not mean or include the United States or a Federal Reserve Bank.

Revised Article 8. The same meaning as in 31 CFR 357.2.

Secretary. The Secretary of Housing and Urban Development and, where appropriate, any person designated by the Secretary to perform a particular function for the Secretary, including any HUD officer, employee, or agent.

Security. Any mortgage participation certificate, note, bond, debenture, evidence of indebtedness, collateral-trust certificate, transferable share, certificate of deposit for a security, or, in general, any interest or instrument commonly known as a security.

Securities Documentation. The applicable statement of terms, trust agreement, trust indenture, securities agreement or other documents establishing the terms of a Book-entry Ginnie Mae Security.

Transfer message. An instruction of a member of a Federal Reserve Bank to effect a transfer of a Book-entry Security (including a Book-entry Ginnie Mae Security) maintained in the Book-entry System, as set forth in Federal Reserve Bank Operating Circulars.

(b) *Other Terms.* Unless the context requires otherwise, terms used in this part that are not defined in this part, have the meanings as set forth in 31 CFR 357.2. Definitions and terms used in 31 CFR part 357 should read as though modified to effectuate their application to Ginnie Mae Securities.

§ 350.3 Maintenance of Ginnie Mae Securities.

A Ginnie Mae Security may be maintained in the form of a Definitive Ginnie Mae Security or a Book-entry Ginnie Mae Security. A Book-entry Ginnie Mae Security shall be maintained in the Book-entry System.

§ 350.4 Law governing rights and obligations of United States, and Federal Reserve Banks as Depositories; Rights of any Person against United States, and Federal Reserve Banks as Depositories; Law Governing Other Interests.

(a) Except as provided in paragraph (b) of this section, the following rights and obligations are governed solely by the book-entry regulations contained in this part, the Securities Documentation, and Federal Reserve Bank Operating Circulars (but not including any choice of law provisions in the Security Documentation to the extent such provisions conflict with the Book-entry regulations contained in this part):

(1) The rights and obligations of a Federal Reserve Bank as a Depository with respect to:

(i) A Book-entry Ginnie Mae Security or Security Entitlement; and

(ii) The operation of a book-entry system operated by a Depository as it applies to Ginnie Mae Securities; and

(2) The rights of any Person, including a Participant, against the Federal Reserve Banks as Depositories with respect to:

(i) A Book-entry Ginnie Mae Security or Security Entitlement; and

(ii) The operation of the book-entry system operated by the Federal Reserve Banks as Depositories as it applies to Ginnie Mae Securities.

(b) A security interest in a Security Entitlement that is in favor of a Federal Reserve Bank from a Participant and that is not recorded on the books of a Federal Reserve Bank pursuant to §350.5(c)(1), is governed by the law (not including the conflict-of-law rules) of the jurisdiction where the head office of the Federal Reserve Bank maintaining the Participant's Securities Account is located. A security interest in a Security Entitlement that is in favor of a Federal Reserve Bank from a Person that is not a Participant, and that is not recorded on the books of a Federal Reserve Bank pursuant to §350.5(c)(1), is governed by the law determined in the manner specified in paragraph (d) of this section.

(c) If the jurisdiction specified in the first sentence of paragraph (b) of this section is a State that has not adopted Revised Article 8, then the law specified in paragraph (b) of this section shall be the law of that State as though Revised Article 8 had been adopted by that State.

(d) To the extent not otherwise inconsistent with this part, and notwithstanding any provision in the Security Documentation setting forth a choice of law, the provision set forth in 31 CFR 357.11 regarding law governing other interests apply and shall be read as though modified to effectuate the application of 31 CFR 357.11 to Book-entry Ginnie Mae Securities.

§ 350.5 Creation of Participant's Security Entitlement; Security Interests.

(a) A Participant's Security Entitlement is created when a Federal Reserve Bank indicates by book-entry that a Book-entry Ginnie Mae Security has been credited to a Participant's Securities Account.

(b) A security interest in a Security Entitlement of a Participant in favor of the United States to secure deposits of public money, including without limitation deposits to the Treasury tax and loan accounts, or other security interests in favor of the United States that is required by Federal statute, regulation, or agreement, and that is marked on the books of a Federal Reserve Bank is thereby effected and perfected, and has priority over any other interest in the securities. Where a security interest in favor of the United States in a Security Entitlement of a Participant is marked on the books of a Federal Reserve Bank, such Reserve Bank may rely, and is protected in relying, exclusively on the order of an authorized representative of the United States directing the transfer of the security. For purposes of this paragraph, an "authorized representative of the United States" is the official designated in the applicable regulations or agreement to which a Federal Reserve Bank is a party, governing the security interest.

(c)(1) The Federal Reserve Banks as Depositories have no obligation to agree to act on behalf of any Person or to recognize the interest of any transferee of a security interest or other limited interest in favor of any Person except to the extent of any specific requirement of Federal law or regulation or to the extent set forth in any specific agreement with the Federal Reserve Bank on whose books the interest of the Participant is recorded. To the extent required by such law or regulation or set forth in an agreement with a Federal Reserve Bank, or the Federal Reserve Bank Operating Circular, a security interest in a Security Entitlement that is in favor of a Federal Reserve Bank or a Person may be created and perfected by a Federal Reserve Bank as Depository marking its books to record the security interest. Except as provided in paragraph (b) of this section, a security interest in a Security Entitlement marked on the books of a Federal Reserve Bank shall have priority over any other interest in the securities.

(2) In addition to the method provided in paragraph (c)(1) of this section, a security interest, including a security interest in favor of a Federal Reserve Bank, may be perfected by any method by which a security interest may be perfected under applicable law as described in § 350.4(b) or (d). The perfection, effect of perfection or non-perfection and priority of a security interest are governed by such applicable law. A security interest in favor of a Federal Reserve Bank shall be treated as a security interest in favor of a clearing corporation in all respects under such law, including with respect to the effect of perfection and priority of such security interest. A Federal Reserve Bank Operating Circular shall be treated as a rule adopted by a clearing corporation for such purposes.

§ 350.6 Obligations of the Reserve Banks as Depositories; No Adverse Claims.

Except in the case of a security interest in favor of the United States or a Federal Reserve Bank or otherwise as provided in § 350.5(c)(1), for the purposes of this part, the Federal Reserve Banks as Depositories shall treat the Participant to whose Securities Account an interest in a Book-entry Ginnie Mae Security has been credited as the person exclusively entitled to issue a Transfer Message, to receive interest and other payments with respect thereof and otherwise to exercise all the rights and powers with respect to such Security, notwithstanding any information or notice to the contrary. The Federal Reserve Banks as Depositories are not liable to a Person asserting or having an adverse claim to a Security Entitlement or to a Book-entry Ginnie Mae Security in a Participant's Securities Account, including any such claim arising as a result of the transfer or disposition of a Book-entry Ginnie Mae Security by a Federal Reserve Bank pursuant to a Transfer Message that the Federal Reserve Bank reasonably believes to be genuine.

§ 350.7 Authority of Federal Reserve Banks as Depositories.

(a) Each Federal Reserve Bank is hereby authorized as Depository for Book-entry Ginnie Mae Securities to perform the following functions with respect to Book-entry Ginnie Mae Securities to which this part applies, in accordance with the Securities Documentation, Federal Reserve Bank Operating Circulars, this part, and procedures established by the Secretary consistent with these authorities:

(1) To service and maintain Book-entry Ginnie Mae Securities in accounts established for such purposes;

(2) To make payments with respect to such securities;

(3) To effect transfer of Book-entry Ginnie Mae Securities between Participants' Securities Accounts as directed by the Participants;

(4) To effect conversions between Book-entry Ginnie Mae Securities and Definitive Ginnie Mae Securities pursuant to the applicable Securities Documentation; and

(5) To perform such other duties as the Federal Reserve Banks as Depositories may be requested by Ginnie Mae.

(b) Each Federal Reserve Bank as Depository may issue Operating Circulars, not inconsistent with this part, governing the details of its handling of Book-entry Ginnie Mae Securities, Security Entitlements, and the operation of the book-entry system under this part.

§ 350.8 Withdrawal of Eligible Book-entry Ginnie Mae Securities for Conversion to Definitive Form.

(a) Eligible book-entry Ginnie Mae securities may be withdrawn from the book-entry system after Ginnie Mae has approved a request for the delivery of definitive Ginnie Mae securities in the same amount.

(b) A Reserve Bank as Depository shall, upon receipt of appropriate instructions to withdraw Eligible Book-entry Ginnie Mae Securities from book-entry in the Book-entry System, facilitate the conversion of such securities into Definitive Ginnie Mae Securities and their delivery in accordance with such instructions. No such conversion shall affect existing interests in such Ginnie Mae Securities.

(c) All requests for withdrawal of Eligible Book-entry Ginnie Mae Securities must be made prior to the maturity or date of call of the securities.

(d) Definitive Ginnie Mae Securities that are to be delivered upon withdrawal may be issued in either registered or bearer form, to the extent permitted by the applicable Securities Documentation.

[66 FR 44266, Aug. 22, 2001, as amended at 72 FR 49125, Aug. 27, 2007]

§350.9 Waiver of Regulations.

Ginnie Mae reserves the right in its discretion, to waive any provision(s) of these regulations in any case or class of cases for the convenience of Ginnie Mae or the United States, or in order to relieve any Person(s) of unnecessary hardship, if such action is not inconsistent with law, does not adversely affect any substantial existing rights, and the Association is satisfied that such action will not subject the Association or the United States to any substantial expense or liability.

§350.10 Liability of Federal Reserve Banks as Depositories.

The Federal Reserve Banks as Depositories may rely on the information provided in a Transfer Message, and are not required to verify the information. The Federal Reserve Banks as Depositories shall not be liable for any action taken in accordance with the information set out in a Transfer Message, or evidence submitted in support thereof.

§350.11 Notice of Attachment for Ginnie Mae Securities in Book-entry System.

The interest of a debtor in a Security Entitlement may be reached by a creditor only by legal process upon the Securities Intermediary with whom the debtor's securities account is maintained, except where a Security Entitlement is maintained in the name of a secured party, in which case the debtor's interest may be reached by legal process upon the secured party. These regulations do not purport to establish whether a Federal Reserve Bank as Depository is required to honor an order or other notice of attachment in any particular case or class of cases.

PARTS 351–399 [RESERVED]

CHAPTER IV—OFFICE OF HOUSING AND OFFICE OF MULTIFAMILY HOUSING ASSISTANCE RESTRUCTURING, DEPARTMENT OF HOUSING AND URBAN DEVELOPMENT

Subpart F—Owner Dispute of Rejection and Administrative Appeal

401.645 Owner request to review HUD decision.
401.650 When may the owner request an administrative appeal?
401.651 Appeal procedures.
401.652 No judicial review.

AUTHORITY: 12 U.S.C. 1715z–1 and 1735f–19(b); 42 U.S.C. 1437(c)(8), 1437f(t), 1437f note, and 3535(d).

SOURCE: 65 FR 15485, Mar. 22, 2000, unless otherwise noted.

Subpart A—General Provisions; Eligibility

§ 401.1 What is the purpose of part 401?

This part contains the regulations implementing the authority in the Multifamily Assisted Housing Reform and Affordability Act of 1997 (MAHRA) for the Mark-to-Market Program. Section 511(b) of MAHRA details the purposes, and section 512(2) details the scope, of the Program.

§ 401.2 What special definitions apply to this part?

(a) *MAHRA* means the Multifamily Assisted Housing Reform and Affordability Act of 1997, title V of Pub. L. 105–65, 42 U.S.C. 1437f note.

(b) *Statutory terms.* Terms defined in section 512 of MAHRA are used in this part in accordance with their statutory meaning. These terms are: comparable properties, expiring contract, expiration date, fair market rent, mortgage restructuring and rental assistance sufficiency plan, nonprofit organization, qualified mortgagee, portfolio restructuring agreement, participating administrative entity, project-based assistance, renewal, State, tenant-based assistance, and unit of general local government.

(c) *Other terms.* As used in this part, the term—

Affiliate means an "affiliate of the owner" or an "affiliate of the purchaser", as such terms are defined in section 516(a) of MAHRA.

Applicable Federal rate has the meaning given in section 1274(d) of the Internal Revenue Code of 1986, 26 U.S.C. 1274(d).

Community-based nonprofit organization means a nonprofit organization that maintains at least one-third of its governing board's membership for low-income tenants from the local community, or for elected representatives of community organizations that represent low-income tenants.

Comparable market rents has the meaning given in § 401.410(b).

Disabled family has the meaning given in § 5.403(b) of this title.

Elderly family has the meaning given in § 5.403(b) of this title.

Eligible project means a project that meets the requirements for eligibility for a Restructuring Plan in § 401.100.

HUD means a HUD official authorized to act under the provisions of MAHRA, and otherwise has the meaning given in § 5.100 of this title.

NHA means the National Housing Act, 12 U.S.C. 1702 *et seq.*

OAHP means the Office of Affordable Housing Preservation, and any successor office.

Owner means the owner of a project and any purchaser of the project.

PAE means a participating administrative entity as defined in section 512(10) of MAHRA, or HUD when appropriate in accordance with section 513(b)(4) of MAHRA.

PCA means a physical condition assessment of a project prepared by a PAE under § 401.451.

PRA means a portfolio restructuring agreement as defined in section 512(9) of MAHRA.

Priority purchaser means a purchaser of a project, meeting qualifications established by HUD, that is:

(1) A tenant organization;

(2) A tenant-endorsed community-based nonprofit organization or public agency; or

(3) A limited partnership with a sole general partner that itself is a priority purchaser under this definition.

Rental Assistance Assessment Plan means the plan described in section 515(c)(2) of MAHRA.

Restructured rent means the rent determined at the time of restructuring in accordance with section 514(g) of MAHRA.

Restructuring Plan or *Plan* means the Mortgage Restructuring and Rental

Assistance Sufficiency Plan described in section 514 of MAHRA.

Section 8 means section 8 of the United States Housing Act of 1937, 42 U.S.C. 1437f.

Section 541(b) claim means a claim paid by HUD under an insurance contract under authority of section 541(b) of the National Housing Act, 12 U.S.C. 1735f–19(b).

Tenant organization of a project means an organization that meets regularly, whose officers are elected by a majority of heads of households of occupied units in the project, and whose membership is open to all tenants of the project.

Unit of local government means the smallest unit of general local government in which the project is located.

Voucher means any tenant-based assistance.

(d) *Conflicts of interest.* Additional definitions applicable to §§ 401.310 through 401.313 appear in § 401.310.

[65 FR 15485, Mar. 22, 2000, as amended at 65 FR 53900, Sept. 6, 2000; 71 FR 2120, Jan. 12, 2006; 72 FR 66038, Nov. 26, 2007]

§ 401.3 Who may waive provisions in this part?

The Assistant Secretary for Housing-Federal Housing Commissioner may waive any provision of this part, subject to § 5.110 of this title.

[68 FR 3363, Jan. 23, 2003]

§ 401.99 How does an owner request a section 8 contract renewal?

(a) *Requesting Restructuring Plan.* An owner may request a section 8 contract renewal as part of a Restructuring Plan by, at least 3 months before the expiration date of any project-based assistance, certifying to HUD that to the best of the owner's knowledge:

(1) Project rents are above comparable market rents; and

(2) The owner is not suspended or debarred or has been notified by HUD of any pending suspension or debarment or other enforcement action, or, if so, a voluntary sale or transfer of the property is proposed in accordance with § 401.480.

(b) *Eligible but not requesting Restructuring Plan.* If an owner is eligible for a Restructuring Plan but requests a renewal of project-based assistance without a Plan, in accordance with the applicable requirements in § 402.6 of this chapter, HUD will consider the request in accordance with § 402.4(a)(2) of this chapter.

(c) *Not eligible for Restructuring Plan.* Section 402.5 of this chapter addresses renewal of project-based assistance for a Restructuring Plan. An owner of such a project may also request renewal under § 402.4 of this chapter.

[65 FR 15485, Mar. 22, 2000, as amended at 65 FR 53900, Sept. 6, 2000]

§ 401.100 Which projects are eligible for a Restructuring Plan under this part?

(a) *What are the requirements for eligibility?* To be eligible for a Restructuring Plan under this part, a project must:

(1) Have a mortgage insured or held by HUD;

(2) Be covered in whole or in part by a contract for project-based assistance under—

(i) The new construction or substantial rehabilitation program under section 8(b)(2) of the U.S. Housing Act of 1937 as in effect before October 1, 1983;

(ii) The property disposition program under section 8(b) of the U.S. Housing Act of 1937;

(iii) The moderate rehabilitation program under section 8(e)(2) of the United States Housing Act of 1937;

(iv) The loan management assistance program under section 8 of the United States Housing Act of 1937;

(v) Section 23 of the United States Housing Act of 1937 as in effect before January 1, 1975;

(vi) The rent supplement program under section 101 of the Housing and Urban Development Act of 1965;

(vii) Section 8 of the United States Housing Act of 1937, following conversion from assistance under Section 101 of the Housing and Urban Development Act of 1965; or

(viii) Section 8 of the U.S. Housing Act of 1937 as renewed under section 524 of MAHRA;

(3) Have current gross potential rent for the project-based assisted units that exceeds the gross potential rent for the project-based assisted units using comparable market rents;

(4) Have a first mortgage that has not previously been restructured under this part or under HUD's Portfolio Re-engineering demonstration authority as defined in § 402.2(c) of this chapter;

(5) Not be a project that is described in section 514(h) of MAHRA; and

(6) Otherwise meet the definition of "eligible multifamily housing project" in section 512(2) of MAHRA or meet the following three criteria:

(i) The project is assisted pursuant to a contract for Section 8 assistance renewed under section 524 of MAHRA;

(ii) It has an owner that consents for the project to be treated as eligible; and

(iii) At the time of its initial renewal under section 524, it met the requirements of section 512(2)(A), (B), and (C) of MAHRA.

(b) *When is eligibility determined?* Eligibility for a Restructuring Plan under paragraph (a) of this section is determined by the status of a project on the earlier of the termination or expiration date of the project-based assistance contract, which includes a contract renewed under section 524 of MAHRA, or the date of the owner's request to HUD for a Restructuring Plan. Eligibility is not affected by a subsequent change in status, such as contract extension under § 401.600 or part 402 of this chapter.

[71 FR 2121, Jan. 12, 2006]

§ 401.101 Which owners are ineligible to request Restructuring Plans?

(a) *Mandatory rejection.* The request of an owner of an eligible project will not be considered for a Restructuring Plan if the owner is debarred or suspended under 2 CFR part 2424.

(b) *Discretion to reject.* HUD may also decide not to accept a request for a Restructuring Plan if:

(1) An affiliate is debarred or suspended under 2 CFR part 2424; or

(2) HUD notifies the owner that HUD is engaged in a pending suspension, debarment or other enforcement action against an owner or affiliate, and the grounds for the pending action are included in § 401.403(b)(2)(ii).

(c) *Exception for sale.* This section does not apply if a sale or transfer of the property is proposed in accordance with § 401.480.

(d) *Notice to tenants.* The PAE or HUD will give notice to tenants of a rejection in accordance with §§ 401.500(f)(2), 401.501, and 401.502.

[65 FR 15485, Mar. 22, 2000, as amended at 72 FR 66038, Nov. 26, 2007; 72 FR 73496, Dec. 27, 2007]

Subpart B—Participating Administrative Entity (PAE) and Portfolio Restructuring Agreement (PRA)

§ 401.200 Who may be a PAE?

A PAE must qualify under the definition in section 512(10) of MAHRA. It must not have any outstanding violations of civil rights laws, determined in accordance with criteria in use by HUD. If the PAE is a private entity, whether nonprofit or for-profit, it must enter into a partnership with a public purpose entity, which may include HUD. A PAE may delegate responsibilities only as agreed in the PRA.

§ 401.201 How does HUD select PAEs?

(a) *Selection of PAE.* HUD will select qualified PAEs in accordance with the criteria established in 513(b) of MAHRA and criteria established by HUD. The selection method is within HUD's discretion, including but not limited to a request for qualifications.

(b) *Priority for public agencies.* HUD will provide a one-time priority period for State housing finance agencies and local housing agencies to qualify as the PAEs for their jurisdictions. If more than one agency qualifies for the same jurisdiction, HUD will provide an opportunity for the agencies to allocate responsibility for projects in the jurisdiction. If the agencies are unable to agree, HUD will choose a PAE in accordance with section 513(b)(2) of MAHRA.

(c) *Qualification for PAE by nonprofit and for-profit entities.* After the priority period expires, HUD will consider other eligible entities as PAEs for jurisdictions in which no public agency has qualified as the PAE, or for projects that have not been assigned to a qualified public agency.

(d) *No PAE for project.* If HUD does not select a PAE for a project, HUD may perform the functions of the PAE, or contract with other qualified entities to perform those functions.

§ 401.300 What is a PRA?

A PRA is an agreement between HUD and a PAE that delineates rights and responsibilities in connection with development and implementation of a Restructuring Plan. The PRA must contain or incorporate by reference the matters required by section 513(a)(2) of MAHRA and §§ 401.301 through 401.314, as well as other terms and conditions required by HUD.

§ 401.301 Partnership arrangements.

If the PAE is in a partnership, the PRA must specify the following:

(a) The responsibilities of each partner regarding the Restructuring Plan;

(b) The resources each partner will provide to accomplish its designated responsibilities; and

(c) All compensation to each partner, whether direct or indirect.

§ 401.302 PRA administrative requirements.

(a) *Inapplicability of certain requirements.* Part 200 of 2 CFR and contract procurement requirements do not apply to a PRA.

(b) *Recordkeeping.* The PAE must keep complete and accurate records of all activities related to the PAE's performance under the PRA. The PAE must retain the records for at least 3 years after the PRA terminates.

(c) *Inspection of records and audit.* Upon reasonable notice, the PAE must permit the Comptroller General of the United States and HUD (including representatives of the HUD Office of Inspector General) to inspect, audit, and copy any records required to be retained under this section.

[65 FR 15485, Mar. 22, 2000, as amended at 80 FR 75936, Dec. 7, 2015]

§ 401.303 PRA indemnity provisions for SHFAs and HAs.

When a PRA requires HUD to indemnify a PAE in accordance with section 513(a)(2)(G) of MAHRA, any payment under this indemnity is contingent upon the availability of funds that are permitted by law to be used for this purpose.

§ 401.304 PRA provisions on PAE compensation.

(a) *Base fee.* (1) The PRA will provide for base fees to be paid by HUD.

(2) HUD will establish a substantially uniform baseline for base fees for public entities. The base fee for a PAE will be adjusted, if necessary, after the first term of the PRA.

(3) Private PAEs will be compensated based on the results of a competitive bid process which evaluates bidders' capability, timeliness, ability to work with tenant and community groups, and cost.

(b) *Incentives.* The PRA may provide for incentives to be paid by HUD. While individual components may vary between PAEs (both public and private), the total amount potentially payable under the incentive package will be uniform. Objectives may include maximizing savings to the Federal Government, timely performance, tenant satisfaction with the PAE's performance, the infusion of public funds from non-HUD sources, and other benchmarks that HUD considers appropriate.

(c) *Expenses.* The PRA will identify expenses incurred by the PAE that will qualify for reimbursement by HUD. Limits on these expenses will be established annually by HUD, but HUD may waive the limits for high-cost areas.

(d) *Other matters.* HUD will retain the right of final approval of any fee schedule. HUD will publish the standard form of PRA and the compensation package annually on its Internet Web site.

[65 FR 15485, Mar. 22, 2000, as amended at 72 FR 66038, Nov. 26, 2007]

§ 401.309 PRA term and termination provisions; other provisions.

(a) *1-year term with renewals.* The PRA will have a term of 1 year, to be renewed for successive terms of 1 year with the mutual agreement of both parties. The PRA will provide for HUD to pay final compensation to the PAE and to assign responsibility for continuing activities if the PRA is not renewed.

(b) *Termination for cause or convenience of Federal Government—*(1) *Termination for cause.* HUD may terminate a PRA at any time for cause, with payment required by HUD as provided in the PRA only for matters authorized by the PRA and performed by the PAE to the date of termination. HUD will retain the right of set-off against any payments due as well as such other rights afforded at law and in equity.

(2) *Termination for convenience of Federal Government.* HUD may terminate a PRA, and may remove an eligible property from a PRA, at any time in accordance with the PRA or applicable law, regardless of whether the PAE is in default of any of its obligations under the PRA, if such termination is in the best interests of the Federal Government. The PRA will provide for payment to the PAE of a specified percentage of the base fee authorized by § 401.304(a) and amounts for reimbursement of third-party vendors to the PAE authorized by § 401.304(c).

(3) *Transfer to another PAE; temporary waiver of rights.* If a PRA is terminated:

(i) HUD may order an immediate transfer of some or all of the PAE's duties to another PAE designated by HUD; and

(ii) HUD may temporarily waive its right of immediate termination in order to allow an orderly transfer of duties and responsibilities under a PRA, without waiving the right of termination after the transfer has been completed to HUD's satisfaction.

(c) *Liability for damages.* During the term of a PRA, and notwithstanding any termination of a PRA, HUD may seek its actual, direct, and consequential damages from any PAE for failure to comply with its obligations under PRA.

(d) *Cumulative remedies.* The remedies under this section are cumulative and in addition to any other remedies or rights HUD may have under the terms of the PRA, at law, or otherwise.

[65 FR 15485, Mar. 22, 2000, as amended at 72 FR 66038, Nov. 26, 2007]

§ 401.310 Conflicts of interest.

(a) *Definitions*—(1) *Conflict of interest* means a situation in which a PAE or other restricted person:

(i) Has a financial interest, direct or indirect, that prevents or may prevent the PAE or other restricted person from acting at all times in the best interests of HUD;

(ii) Has one or more personal, business, or financial interests or relationships that would cause a reasonable person with knowledge of the relevant facts to question the integrity or impartiality of those who are or will be acting under the PRA; or

(iii) Is taking an adverse position to HUD or to an owner whose project is covered by a PRA in a lawsuit, administrative proceeding, or other contested matter.

(2) *Control* means the power to vote, directly or indirectly, 25 percent or more of any class of the voting stock of a company; the ability to direct in any manner the election of a majority of a company (or other entity's) directors or trustees; or the ability to exercise a controlling influence over the company or entity's management and policies. For purposes of this definition, a general partner of a limited partnership is presumed to be in control of that partnership.

(3) *Restricted person* means a PAE; any management official of the PAE; any legal entity that is under the control of the PAE, is in control of the PAE, or is under common control with the PAE; or any employee, agent or contractor of the PAE, or employee of such agent or contractor, who will perform or has performed services under a PRA with HUD.

(b) *General prohibitions.* (1) The PAE may not permit conflicts of interest to exist without obtaining a waiver in accordance with this section.

(2) The PAE must establish procedures to identify conflicts of interest and to ensure that conflicts of interest do not arise or continue, subject to waiver under paragraph (c) of this section.

(3) HUD will not enter into PRAs with potential PAEs who have conflicts of interest associated with a particular project, or permit PAEs to continue performance under existing PRAs when such PAEs have conflicts of interest, unless such conflicts have been eliminated to HUD's satisfaction by the PAE or potential PAE or are waived by HUD.

(4) The PAE has a continuing obligation to take all action necessary to

identify whether it or any other restricted person has a conflict of interest.

(c) *Waivers.* HUD will waive conflicts of interest only when, in light of all relevant circumstances, the interests of HUD in the PAE's or another restricted persons's participation outweigh the concern that a reasonable person may question the integrity of HUD's operations.

(d) *Conflicts of interest arising prior to PAE selection*—(1) *Request for review of conflicts of interest.* (i) A potential PAE, with its request to HUD for consideration for selection as a PAE, must identify existing conflicts of interest and may make a written request for a determination as to the existence of a conflict of interest, may request that the conflict of interest, if any, be waived, or may propose how it could eliminate the conflict.

(ii) If, after submitting a request but prior to selection, a potential PAE discovers that it has a conflict, it must notify HUD in writing within 10 days of submitting the request or prior to selection, whichever is earlier. Such notification must contain a detailed description of the conflict. The potential PAE may, with its notification, request that the conflict be waived or may propose how it may eliminate the conflict. The potential PAE may also request a determination as to the existence of the conflict. The potential PAE may also request a determination as to the existence of the conflict.

(2) *Review by HUD.* Subject to the restrictions set forth in this section, HUD in its sole discretion may determine whether a conflict of interest exists, may waive the conflict of interest, or may approve in writing a PAE's proposal to eliminate a conflict of interest.

(e) *Conflicts of interest that arise or are discovered after PAE selection.* (1) A PAE must notify HUD in writing within 10 days after discovering that it or another restricted person has a conflict of interest. Such notification must contain a detailed description of the conflict of interest and state how the PAE intends to eliminate the conflict. The PAE may also request a determination as to the existence of a conflict.

(2) HUD will, after receipt of such notification or other discovery of the PAE's conflict or potential conflict of interest, take such action as it determines is in its best interests, which may involve proceeding under §401.313 or as provided in the following sentences. HUD may notify the PAE in writing of its findings as to whether a conflict of interest exists and the basis for such determination, whether or not a waiver will be granted, or whether corrective actions may be taken in order to eliminate the conflict of interest. Corrective action must be completed by the PAE not later than 30 days after notification is mailed by HUD unless HUD, at its sole discretion, determines that it is in its best interests to grant the PAE an extension in which to complete the corrective action.

(f) *Reconsideration of decisions.* Decisions issued pursuant to this section may be reconsidered by HUD upon application by the PAE. Such requests must be in writing and must contain the basis for the request. HUD may, at its discretion and after determining that it is in its best interests, stay any corrective or other actions previously ordered pending reconsideration of a decision.

[65 FR 15485, Mar. 22, 2000, as amended at 65 FR 53900, Sept. 6, 2000]

§401.311 Standards of conduct.

(a) *Minimum ethical standards for PAEs.* In connection with the performance of any PRA and during the term of such PRA, a PAE or other restricted person (as defined in §401.310) may not:

(1) Solicit for itself or others favors, gifts, or other items of monetary value from any person who is seeking official action from HUD or the PAE in connection with the PRA or has interests that may be substantially affected by the restricted person's performance or nonperformance of duties to HUD;

(2) Use improperly (or allow the improper use of) HUD property or property over which the restricted person has supervision or charge by reason of the PRA;

(3) Use its status as PAE for its own benefit, or the financial or business benefit of a third party, except as contemplated by the PRA; or

(4) Make any unauthorized promise or commitment on behalf of HUD.

(b) *18 U.S.C. 201.* Pursuant to 18 U.S.C. 201, whoever acts for or on behalf of HUD in connection with the matters covered by this part is deemed to be a public official. Public officials are prohibited from soliciting or accepting anything of value in return for being influenced in the performance of official actions. Violators are subject to criminal sanctions.

(c) *18 U.S.C. 1001.* Pursuant to 18 U.S.C. 1001, whoever knowingly and willingly falsifies a material fact, makes a false statement or utilizes a false writing in connection with a PRA is subject to criminal sanctions. Other Federal civil statutes also apply to making false statements to the United States.

(d) *18 U.S.C. 207.* Former Federal Government employees are subject to the prohibitions in 18 U.S.C. 207.

§ 401.312 Confidentiality of information.

A PAE and every other restricted person (as defined in § 401.310) has a duty to protect confidential information, except as provided in §§ 401.500 through 401.503, and to prevent its use to further a private interest other than as contemplated by the PRA. As used in this section, confidential information means information that a PAE or other restricted person obtains from or on behalf of HUD or a third party in connection with a PRA but does not include information generally available to the public unless the information becomes available to the public as a result of unauthorized disclosure by the PAE or another restricted person.

§ 401.313 Consequences of PAE violations; finality of HUD determination.

(a) *Effect on PRA.* If a PAE, potential PAE or other restricted person (as defined in § 401.310) violates §§ 401.310, 410.311, or 401.312, HUD may:

(1) Find the potential PAE unqualified to enter into a PRA;

(2) Find the PAE unqualified to receive additional projects for restructuring under an existing PRA;

(3) Find the PAE in default under an existing PRA with the right of termination for cause under § 401.309; or

(4) Seek from a PAE or other restricted person HUD's actual, direct, and consequential damages resulting from the violation.

(b) *Cumulative remedies.* The remedies under this section are cumulative and in addition to any other remedies or rights HUD may have under the terms of the PRA, at law, or otherwise.

(c) *Finality of determination.* Any determination made by HUD pursuant to this section is at HUD's sole discretion and is not subject to further administrative review.

§ 401.314 Environmental review responsibilities.

HUD will retain all responsibility for environmental review under part 50 of this title. Compliance with part 50 of this title will be completed before any HUD approval of the Restructuring Commitment under § 401.405.

Subpart C—Restructuring Plan

§ 401.400 Required elements of a Restructuring Plan.

(a) *General.* A PAE is responsible for the development of a Restructuring Plan for each project included in its PRA.

(b) *Required elements.* The Restructuring Plan must contain a narrative that fully describes the restructuring transaction. The Restructuring Plan must include the elements required by section 514(e) of MAHRA. The Restructuring Plan must describe the use of any restructuring tools listed at sections 517(a) and (b) of MAHRA, and must contain other requirements as determined by HUD.

§ 401.401 Consolidated Restructuring Plans.

A PAE may request HUD to approve a Consolidated Restructuring Plan that presents an overall strategy for more than one project included in the PRA. HUD will consider approval of a Consolidated Restructuring Plan for projects having common ownership, geographic proximity, common mortgagee or servicer, or other factors that contribute to more efficient use of the

PAE's resources. Notwithstanding the more efficient use of a PAE's resources, HUD will not approve any Consolidated Restructuring Plans that have a detrimental effect on tenants or the community, or a higher cost to the Federal Government. HUD's decision to approve or disapprove a Consolidated Restructuring Plan will be made on a case-by-case basis.

[65 FR 15485, Mar. 22, 2000, as amended at 72 FR 66038, Nov. 26, 2007]

§401.402 Cooperation with owner and qualified mortgagee in Restructuring Plan development.

A PAE must comply with section 514(a)(2) of MAHRA by using its best efforts to seek the cooperation of the owner and qualified mortgagee or its designee in the development of the Restructuring Plan. If the owner fails to cooperate (as demonstrated by reasonable progress in development of a Restructuring Plan) to the satisfaction of the PAE and HUD agrees, the PAE must notify the owner that the PAE will not develop a Restructuring Plan. This notice will be subject to dispute and administrative appeal under subpart F of this part. If the qualified mortgagee does not cooperate in modifying the mortgage, the PAE and owner may continue to develop a Restructuring Plan to restructure the loan using alternative financing.

§401.403 Rejection of a request for a Restructuring Plan because of actions or omissions of owner or affiliate or project condition.

(a) *Ongoing determination of owner and project eligibility.* Notwithstanding an initial determination to accept the owner's request for a Restructuring Plan, the PAE is responsible for a further more complete and ongoing assessment of the eligibility of the owner and project while the Restructuring Plan is developed. The PAE must advise HUD if at any time any of the grounds for rejection listed in paragraph (b) of this section exist.

(b) *Grounds for rejection*—(1) *Suspension or debarment.* Neither a PAE nor HUD will continue to develop or consider a Restructuring Plan if, at any time before a closing under §401.407,

the owner is debarred or suspended under 2 CFR part 2424.

(2) *Other grounds.* HUD may elect not to permit continued consideration of the Restructuring Plan at any time before closing under §401.407, if:

(i) An affiliate is debarred or suspended under 2 CFR part 2424;

(ii) HUD or the PAE determines that the owner or an affiliate has engaged in material adverse financial or managerial actions or omissions as described in section 516(a) of MAHRA, including any outstanding violations of civil rights laws in connection with any project of the owner or affiliate; or

(iii) HUD or the PAE determines (under §401.451(c) or otherwise) that the project does not meet the housing quality standards in §401.558 and that the poor condition of the project is not likely to be remedied in a cost-effective manner through the Restructuring Plan.

(3) *Exception for sale.* This paragraph does not apply (except (2)(iii)) if a sale or transfer is proposed under §401.480.

(c) *Dispute and appeal.* An owner may dispute a rejection under this section and seek administrative review under the procedures in subpart F of this part.

[65 FR 15485, Mar. 22, 2000, as amended at 72 FR 73496, Dec. 27, 2007]

§401.404 Proposed Restructuring Commitment.

A PAE must submit a Restructuring Plan and a proposed Restructuring Commitment to HUD for approval, prior to submitting the Commitment to the owner for execution. The submission may not occur earlier than 10 days after the public meeting required by §401.500(d). The proposed Restructuring Commitment must be in a form approved by HUD, incorporate the Restructuring Plan, and include the following:

(a) The lender, loan amount, interest rate, and term of any mortgages or unsecured financing for the mortgage restructuring and rehabilitation, and any credit enhancement;

(b) The amount of any payment of a section 541(b) claim;

(c) The type of section 8 assistance and the section 8 restructured rents;

(d) The rehabilitation required, the source of the owner contribution, and escrow arrangements;

(e) The uses for project accounts;

(f) The terms of any sale or transfer of the project;

(g) A schedule setting forth all sources and uses of funds to implement the Restructuring Plan, including setting forth the balances of project accounts before and after restructuring;

(h) All consideration, direct or indirect, received or to be received by the PAE or a related party, if known, in connection with any matter addressed in the Restructuring Commitment, except amounts paid or to be paid by HUD; and

(i) Other terms and conditions prescribed by HUD.

§ 401.405 Restructuring Commitment review and approval by HUD.

HUD will either approve the Restructuring Commitment as submitted, require changes as a condition for approval, or reject the Plan. If the Plan is rejected, HUD will inform the PAE of the reasons for rejection, and the PAE will inform the owner. HUD's rejection of the Plan is subject to the dispute and administrative appeal provisions of subpart F of this part.

§ 401.406 Execution of Restructuring Commitment.

When HUD approves the Restructuring Commitment, the PAE will deliver the Restructuring Commitment to the owner for execution. The Restructuring Commitment becomes binding upon execution by the owner. An owner who does not execute the Restructuring Commitment may appeal its terms and seek modification under subpart F of this part.

§ 401.407 Closing conducted by PAE.

After the owner has executed the Restructuring Commitment, the PAE must arrange for a closing to execute all documents necessary for implementation of the Restructuring Plan. The PAE must use standard documents approved by HUD, with modifications only as necessary to comply with applicable State or local laws, or such other modifications as are approved in writing by HUD.

§ 401.408 Affordability and use restrictions required.

(a) *General.* The Restructuring Plan must provide that the project will be subject to affordability and use restrictions in a Use Agreement acceptable to HUD. The Use Agreement must be recorded and in effect for at least 30 years. It must include at least the provisions required by paragraphs (b) through (j) of this section.

(b) *Use restriction.* The project must continue to be used for residential use with no reduction in the number of residential units without prior HUD approval.

(c) *Affordability restrictions.* Except during a period when at least 20 percent of the units in a project receive project-based assistance:

(1) At least 20 percent of the units in the project must be leased to families whose adjusted income does not exceed 50 percent of the area median income as determined by HUD, with adjustments for household size, at rents no greater than 30 percent of 50 percent of the area median income; or

(2) At least 40 percent of the units in the project must be leased to families whose adjusted income does not exceed 60 percent of the area median income as determined by HUD, with adjustments for household size, at rents no greater than 30 percent of 60 percent of the area median income.

(d) *Comparable configuration.* The type and size of the units that satisfy the affordability restrictions of paragraph (c) of this section must be comparable to the type and size of the units for the project as a whole.

(e) *Nondiscrimination against voucher holders.* An owner must comply with the nondiscrimination provisions of § 401.556.

(f) *Enforcement.* The Use Agreement must contain remedies for breach of the Use Agreement, including monetary damages for non-compliance with paragraphs (c) and (g) of this section.

(g) *Compliance with physical condition standards.* The Use Agreement must require that the property be maintained in compliance with the requirements of § 401.558.

(h) *Reporting.* The Use Agreement must contain appropriate financial and other reporting requirements for the

648

owner. These reports must comply with the Real Estate Assessment Center protocol or subsequent standards required by HUD.

(i) *Enforcement and amendment.* The Use Agreement will be enforceable by interested parties to be specified in the Agreement, which will include HUD, the PAE, project tenants, organizations representing project tenants, and the unit of local government. The Use Agreement must require the party bringing enforcement action to give the owner notice and a reasonable opportunity to cure any violations.

(j) *Modifications.* HUD will retain the right to approve modifications of the Use Agreement agreed to by the owner without the consent of any other party, including those having the right of enforcement. The owner must post prominently on project property notice of any modifications approved by HUD.

(k) *Owner obligation to accept project-based assistance.* Subject to the availability of appropriated funds, the owner of the project must accept any offer of renewal of project-based assistance if the offer is in accordance with the terms and conditions specified in the Restructuring Plan.

[65 FR 15485, Mar. 22, 2000, as amended at 65 FR 53900, Sept. 6, 2000]

§401.410 Standards for determining comparable market rents.

(a) *When are comparable market rents required?* The Restructuring Plan must establish restructured rents for project-based assistance at comparable market rents unless the PAE finds that exception rents are necessary under §401.411.

(b) *Comparable market rents defined.* Comparable market rents are the rents charged for properties that the PAE determines to be comparable properties (as defined in section 512(1) of MAHRA, but also excluding section 202 or section 811 projects assisted under part 891 of this title). For purposes of section 512(1), other relevant characteristics include any applicable rent control and other characteristics determined by the PAE. The PAE may make appropriate adjustments when needed to ensure comparability of properties.

(c) *Methodology for determining comparable market rents.* If the PAE is unable to identify at least three comparable properties within the local market, the PAE may:

(1) Use non-comparable housing stock within that market from which adjustments can be made; or

(2) If necessary to go outside the market, use comparable properties as far outside the local market as it finds reasonable, from which adjustments can be made.

(d) *Using FMR as last resort.* If the PAE is unable to identify enough properties under paragraph (c) of this section, comparable market rents must be set at 90 percent of the Fair Market Rents for the relevant market area.

§401.411 Guidelines for determining exception rents.

(a) *When do exception rents apply?* (1) The Restructuring Plan may provide for exception rents established under section 514(g)(2) of MAHRA for project-based assistance if the PAE determines that project income under the rent levels established under §401.410 would be inadequate to meet the costs of operating the project as described in paragraph (b) of this section and that the housing needs of the tenants and the community could not be adequately addressed.

(2) In any fiscal year, the PAE may not request HUD to approve Restructuring Plans with exception rents for more than 20 percent of all units covered by the PRA, except that HUD may approve a waiver of this 20 percent limitation based on the PAE's narrative explanation of special need.

(b) *How are exception rents calculated?* (1) Exception rents must be set at a level sufficient to support the costs of operating the project. The PAE must take into account the following cost items:

(i) Debt service on the second mortgage under §401.461(a) or a rehabilitation loan included in the Restructuring Plan;

(ii) The operating expenses of the project, as determined by the PAE, including:

(A) Contributions to adequate reserves for replacement;

(B) The costs of maintenance and necessary rehabilitation;

(C) Other eligible costs permitted under the section 8 program;

(iii) An adequate allowance for potential operating losses due to vacancies and failure to collect rents, as determined by the PAE;

(iv) A return to the owner to the extent permitted by § 401.461(b)(3)(ii)(A); and

(v) Other expenses determined by the PAE to be necessary for the operation of the project.

(2) The exception rent must not exceed 120 percent of the Fair Market Rent for the market area, except that HUD may approve an exception rent greater than 120 percent of Fair Market Rent, based on a narrative explanation of special need submitted by the PAE, subject to the 5 percent limitation in section 514(g)(2)(A) of MAHRA.

§ 401.412 Adjustment of rents based on operating cost adjustment factor (OCAF) or budget.

(a) *OCAF.* (1) The Restructuring Plan must provide for annual adjustment of the restructured rents for project-based assistance by an OCAF determined by HUD.

(2) *Application of OCAF.* HUD will apply the OCAF to the previous year's contract rent less the portion of that rent paid for debt service. This paragraph applies to renewals of contracts in subsequent years which receive restructured rents under either section 514(g)(1) or (2) of MAHRA.

(b) *Budget-based.* Rents will be adjusted on a budget basis instead of OCAF only upon owner request, subject to HUD approval.

§ 401.420 When must the Restructuring Plan require project-based assistance?

The Restructuring Plan must provide for the section 8 contract to be renewed as project-based assistance, subject to the availability of funds for this purpose, if:

(a) The PAE determines there is a market-wide vacancy rate of 6 percent or less;

(b) At least 50 percent of the units in the project are occupied by elderly families, disabled families, or elderly and disabled families; or

(c) The project is held by a nonprofit cooperative ownership housing corporation or nonprofit cooperative housing trust.

§ 401.421 Rental Assistance Assessment Plan.

(a) *Plan required.* For any project not subject to mandatory project-based assistance under § 401.420, the PAE must develop a Rental Assistance Assessment Plan in accordance with section 515(c)(2) of MAHRA to determine whether assistance should be renewed as project-based assistance or whether some or all of the assisted units should be converted to tenant-based assistance.

(b) *Matters to be assessed.* The PAE must include an assessment of the impact of converting to tenant-based assistance and the impact of renewing project-based assistance on:

(1) The ability of the tenants to find adequate, available, decent, comparable, and affordable housing in the local market;

(2) The types of tenants residing in the project (such as elderly families, disabled families, large families, and cooperative homeowners);

(3) The local housing needs identified in the applicable Consolidated Plan developed under part 91 of this title;

(4) The cost of providing assistance, comparing the applicable payment standard to the rent levels permitted by §§ 401.410 and 401.411;

(5) The long-term financial stability of the project;

(6) The ability of residents to make reasonable choices about their individual living situations;

(7) The quality of the neighborhood in which the tenants would reside; and

(8) The project's ability to compete in the marketplace.

(c) *Conversion may be phased in.* Any conversion from project-based assistance to tenant-based assistance may occur over a period of not more than 5 years if the PAE decides the transition period is needed for the financial viability of the project.

(d) *Reports to HUD.* The PAE must report to HUD on the matters specified in section 515(c)(2)(C) of MAHRA at least semi-annually.

[65 FR 15485, Mar. 22, 2000, as amended at 65 FR 53900, Sept. 6, 2000]

§401.450 Owner evaluation of physical condition.

(a) *Initial evaluation.* The owner must evaluate the physical condition of the project and provide the following information to the PAE in a form acceptable to the PAE:

(1) All work items required to bring the project to the standard in §401.452, including any work items needed to ensure compliance with applicable requirements of part 8 of this title concerning accessibility to persons with disabilities;

(2) The capital repair or replacement items that will be necessary to maintain the long-term physical integrity of the property;

(3) A plan for funding the rehabilitation work included in paragraph (a)(1) of this section, which work must be completed in a timely manner after closing the restructuring transaction, that identifies the source of the required owner contribution of non-project funds; and

(4) An estimate of the initial deposit, if any, and the estimated monthly deposit to the reserve for replacement account for the next 20 years.

(b) *Use of CNA.* An owner may comply with paragraph (a) of this section by submitting a comprehensive needs assessment in accordance with title IV of the Housing and Community Development Act of 1992 (12 U.S.C. 1715z–1a note) if the CNA:

(1) Was completed or updated within 1 year; and

(2) Contains all of the matters required by paragraph (a) of this section.

(c) *Reconsideration and modification of evaluation.* If the PAE, after its independent review under §401.451, determines that the owner's evaluation either fails to address specific necessary work items or fails to propose a cost-effective approach to rehabilitation, the owner may modify its evaluation to satisfy the concerns of the PAE.

[65 FR 15485, Mar. 22, 2000, as amended at 65 FR 53900, Sept. 6, 2000]

§401.451 PAE Physical Condition Analysis (PCA).

(a) *Review and certification of owner evaluation.* (1) The PAE must independently evaluate the physical condition of the project by means of a PCA. If the PAE finds any immediate threats to health and safety, the owner must complete those work items immediately, or the PAE must evaluate the project's eligibility in accordance with §401.403(b)(2)(iii).

(2) After consultation with the owner and an opportunity for the owner to modify its evaluation performed under §401.450, the PAE must either certify to the accuracy and completeness of the owner's evaluation performed under §401.450 for each project covered by the PRA, or state that the evaluation fails to address certain items or does not propose a cost effective approach.

(b) *Rejection due to inaccurate or incomplete owner evaluation.* If the PAE cannot certify to the accuracy and completeness of the owner's evaluation due to its failure to address specific work items or because it does not propose a cost effective approach, the PAE must notify HUD. If HUD agrees with the PAE's determination, the PAE must notify the owner that the request for a Restructuring Plan is rejected.

(c) *Rejection due to poor condition of the project.* Based on the completed PCA, the PAE must determine whether proceeding with a Restructuring Plan with necessary rehabilitation is more cost-effective in terms of Federal resources than rejecting the Request for a Restructuring Plan under §401.403(b)(2)(iii) and providing tenant-based assistance for displaced tenants under §401.602. HUD will provide guidance to PAEs for making the determination. If the PAE concludes that a request for a Restructuring Plan should be rejected because of lack of cost-effectiveness due to poor condition of the project, it must also consider the effect on tenants and the community and advise HUD of the effect. HUD will make the final decision after considering the PAE's recommendation.

(d) *Dispute and appeal of rejection.* The dispute and appeal provisions of subpart F of this part apply to rejections under paragraphs (b) and (c) of this section.

§401.452 Property standards for rehabilitation.

The restructuring plan must provide for the level of rehabilitation needed to restore the property to the non-luxury standard adequate for the rental market for which the project was originally approved. If the standard has changed over time, the rehabilitation may include improvements to meet the current standards. The rehabilitation also may include the addition of significant features, in accordance with § 401.472. The result of the rehabilitation should be a project that can attract non-subsidized tenants, but competes on rent rather than on amenities. When a range of options exists for satisfying the rehabilitation standard, the PAE must choose the least costly option considering both capital and operating costs and taking into account the marketability of the property and the remaining useful life of all building systems. Nothing in this part exempts rehabilitation from the requirements of part 8 of this title concerning accessibility to persons with disabilities.

[72 FR 66038, Nov. 26, 2007]

§ 401.453 Reserves.

The Restructuring Plan must provide for reserves for capital replacement sufficient to ensure the property's long-term structural integrity so that the property can be maintained as affordable housing in decent, safe, and sanitary condition meeting the standards of § 401.558.

§ 401.460 Modification or refinancing of first mortgage.

(a) *Principal amount.* As part of the Restructuring Plan, the PAE will determine the size of the restructured first mortgage that will result from the modification or refinancing of the existing FHA-insured or HUD-held first mortgage. The restructured first mortgage must be in the amount that can be supported by net operating income based on the lower of the restructured section 8 rents or the rents allowed by the Use Agreement under § 401.408. Neither the outstanding principal balance of the existing first mortgage, nor the monthly principal and interest payments on that debt, may be increased through modification under the Restructuring Plan. The debt service coverage used by the PAE must be adequate for purposes of the Restructuring Plan and for the requirements of any refinancing.

(b) *Fully amortizing.* The modified or refinanced first mortgage must be fully amortizing through level monthly payments.

(c) *Rates and other terms.* Interest rates and other terms of the modified or refinanced first mortgage must be competitive in the market.

(d) *Fees.* Any fees or costs associated with mortgage modification or refinancing determined by the PAE to be above normal processing fees must be paid by the owner from non-project funds and must not be included in the modified or refinanced first mortgage.

(e) *Refinancing.* (1) The owner must contact the mortgagee to determine the mortgagee's willingness to consider a modification and re-amortization of the existing first mortgage through a Restructuring Plan before considering any other source of first mortgage financing. If the mortgagee does not agree to modify and re-amortize in accordance with the Restructuring Plan, the loan must be refinanced.

(2) The refinancing may be either without credit enhancement or with credit enhancement under one of the following:

(i) *FHA mortgage insurance.* If the Restructuring Plan provides for FHA mortgage insurance for the refinanced first mortgage, the insurance will be provided in accordance with all usually applicable FHA legal requirements except that insurance will be documented as provided in section 517(b)(2) of MAHRA. HUD will issue the commitment for mortgage insurance but may adapt its procedures as necessary to facilitate development and implementation of a Restructuring Plan.

(ii) *Other FHA credit enhancement.* If FHA credit enhancement, including risk-sharing, is provided under part 266 of this title, the credit enhancement will be provided in accordance with all usually-applicable FHA legal requirements under part 266 of this title, except that special approval from HUD will be required before the PAE engages in risk-sharing with FHA under part 266 of this title. HUD will approve risk-sharing financing that complies with part 266 whenever required by section 517(b)(3) of MAHRA.

(iii) *Credit enhancement from non-FHA sources.* If credit enhancement is to be provided by a non-FHA source under section 517(b)(4) of MAHRA, HUD will consider waiver of any non-statutory provision in this part only if the waiver will not materially impair achievement of the purposes of MAHRA and if the waiver is essential to meet the legitimate business or legal requirements of the provider of credit enhancement.

§ 401.461   HUD-held second mortgage.

(a) *Amount.* (1) The Restructuring Plan must provide for a second mortgage to HUD whenever the Plan provides for either payment of a claim under section 541(b) of the National Housing Act (541(b) claim) or the modification or refinancing of a HUD-held first mortgage that results in a first mortgage with a lower principal amount. The term "second mortgage" in this section also includes a new HUD-held first mortgage (not a refinancing mortgage), if a full payment of claim is made under § 401.471 or if a full payment of claim is unnecessary because surplus project accounts are available to facilitate the Restructuring Plan, pursuant to section 517(b)(6) of MAHRA, or if § 401.460(a) does not permit a restructured first mortgage in any amount.

(2) The second mortgage must be in a principal amount that does not exceed the lesser of:

(i) The amount the PAE reasonably expects to be repaid based on objective criteria such as the amount of anticipated net cash flow, trending assumptions, amortization provisions, and expected residual value of the property; and

(ii) The greater of:

(A) The section 541(b) claim (or the difference between the unpaid principal balance on HUD-held mortgage debt immediately before and after the restructuring), plus surplus project accounts from residual receipts accumulated pursuant to 24 CFR 880.205(e), 881.205(e), or 883.306(e) and derived from an expiring Section 8 Housing Assistance Payments contract and not otherwise distributed to the owner and made available to facilitate the Restruc-

turing Plan pursuant to section 517(b)(6) of MAHRA, and

(B) The difference between the unpaid balance on the first mortgage immediately before and after the restructuring.

(b) *Terms and conditions.* (1) The second mortgage must have an interest rate of at least one percent, but not more than the applicable Federal rate.

(2) The second mortgage must have a term concurrent with the modified or refinanced first mortgage, if any. HUD may provide that if there is no first mortgage, the second mortgage may continue for a term established by HUD.

(3)(i) Principal and interest on the second mortgage is payable only out of net cash flow during its term. "Net cash flow" means that portion of project income that remains after the payment of all required debt service payments on the modified or refinanced first mortgage, if any, including payment of any past due principal or interest, and payment of all reasonable and necessary operating expenses (including deposits to the reserve for replacement account) and any other expenditure approved by HUD.

(ii) The priority and distribution of net cash flow is as follows:

(A) HUD or the PAE may approve the payment to the owner of up to 25 percent of net cash flow based on consideration of relevant conditions and circumstances including, but not limited to, compliance with the management standards prescribed in § 401.560 and the physical condition standards prescribed in § 401.558; and

(B) All remaining net cash flow will be applied to the principal and interest on the second mortgage, until paid in full, and then to any additional subordinate mortgage under § 401.461(c).

(4) HUD may cause the second mortgage to be immediately due and payable on the grounds provided in section 517(a)(4) of MAHRA, including an assumption of the mortgage in violation of HUD standards for approval of transfers of physical assets (if applicable), or if the owner materially fails to comply with other material HUD requirements after a reasonable opportunity for the owner to cure such failure. A decision by HUD in this regard is subject to the

administrative appeals procedure in subpart F of this part, unless HUD acts on the basis of the grounds specified in sections 517(a)(4)(A) or (B) of MAHRA.

(5) HUD will consider modification, assignment to the acquiring entity, or forgiveness of all or part of the second mortgage, if: The Secretary holds the second mortgage; and if the project has been sold or transferred to a tenant organization or tenant-endorsed community-based nonprofit or public agency that meets eligibility guidelines determined by HUD; accepts additional affordability requirements acceptable to HUD; and requests such modification, assignment, or forgiveness. A community-based nonprofit group or public agency demonstrates that it is tenant-endorsed in accordance with § 401.480(e).

(c) *Additional mortgage to HUD.* (1) A Restructuring Plan shall require the owner to give an additional mortgage on the project to HUD in an amount that:

(i) For the restructuring of a mortgage insured by HUD, does not exceed the difference between:

(A) The amount of a section 541(b) claim paid under § 401.471 increased by any residual receipts, pursuant to 24 CFR 880.205(e), 881.205(e), or 883.306(e); and

(B) The principal amount of the second mortgage; or

(ii) For the restructuring of a mortgage held by HUD, does not exceed the difference between:

(A) The principal amount of a restructured HUD-held mortgage and the sum of, as applicable, a restructured HUD-held first mortgage at reduced principal amount, new mortgage funds paid to HUD at closing, and surplus project accounts other than residual receipts, pursuant to 24 CFR 880.205(e), 881.205(e), or 883.306(e); and

(B) The principal amount of the second mortgage.

(2) HUD may approve a Plan that does not require an additional mortgage, or provides for less than the full difference to be payable under the additional mortgage, or allows for subsequent modification, assignment, or forgiveness of the additional mortgage under any of the following circumstances:

(i) The anticipated recovery on the additional mortgage is less than the servicing costs; or

(ii) HUD has approved modification, assignment, or forgiveness of the second mortgage, pursuant to paragraph (b)(5) of this section.

(3) With respect to the second mortgage required by paragraph (a) of this section, any additional mortgage must:

(i) Be junior in priority;

(ii) Bear interest at the same rate; and

(iii) Require no payment until the second mortgage is satisfied, at which time it will be payable upon demand of HUD or as otherwise agreed by HUD.

[65 FR 15485, Mar. 22, 2000, as amended at 72 FR 66038, Nov. 26, 2007]

§ 401.471 HUD payment of a section 541(b) claim.

HUD will pay a section 541(b) claim from the appropriate insurance fund to the insured mortgagee on behalf of the mortgagor. The mortgagee must use the claim payment to prepay the principal balance of the insured mortgage, in whole or in part, as provided in the Restructuring Plan. All section 541(b) claims will be paid in cash. Part 207 of this title and sections 207(g) and 541(a) of the NA do not apply to a section 541(b) claim.

§ 401.472 Rehabilitation funding.

(a) *Sources of funds*—(1) *Project accounts.* The Restructuring Plan for funding rehabilitation must include funds from the project's residual receipts account, surplus cash account, replacement reserve account, and other project accounts, to the extent the PAE determines that those accounts will not be needed for the initial deposit to the reserves.

(2) *Debt restructuring.* The Restructuring Plan may provide for funding of rehabilitation through a new first mortgage in conjunction with a payment of a section 541(b) claim. The payment of claim may be in an amount necessary to facilitate the funding of the rehabilitation, by reducing the existing first mortgage debt to make refinancing proceeds available to fund rehabilitation.

(3) *Section 236(s) rehabilitation grant.* The Restructuring Plan may include a

direct grant from HUD under section 236(s) of the NA made in accordance with § 401.473, to the extent that HUD has determined that funding is available for such a grant.

(4) *Section 8 budget authority increase.* The Restructuring Plan may include funding of rehabilitation from budget authority provided to HUD for increases in section 8 contracts, to the extent that HUD has determined that funding from this source is available.

(b) *Statutory restrictions.* Any rehabilitation funded from the sources described in paragraph (a) of this section is subject to the requirements in section 517(c) of MAHRA for an owner contribution.

(1) *Addition of significant features.* With respect to significant added features, the required owner contribution will be as proposed by the PAE and approved by HUD, and not to exceed 20 percent of the total cost. Significant added features include the addition of air conditioning (including conversions from window air conditioning to central air conditioning), an elevator, or additional community space.

(2) *Cap on owner contribution.* If a restructuring plan includes additions other than those specified, and the PAE considers the additions significant, the PAE may propose to make those additions subject to the cap on owner contribution. In general, the owner will contribute 3 percent toward the cost of each significant addition. The PAE may propose a lower or higher owner contribution, not to exceed 20 percent, with respect to significant additions.

(3) *Other rehabilitation.* With respect to other rehabilitation, the required owner contribution will be calculated as 20 percent of the total cost of rehabilitation, unless HUD or the PAE determines that a higher percentage is required. The owner contribution must include a reasonable proportion (as determined by HUD) of the total cost of rehabilitation from nongovernmental resources.

(4) *Cooperatives.* The PAE may exempt housing cooperatives from the owner contribution requirement.

(c) *Escrow agent.* The Restructuring Plan must provide for progress payments for rehabilitation, which must be disbursed by an acceptable escrow agent subject to PAE oversight or as otherwise provided by HUD.

[65 FR 15485, Mar. 22, 2000, as amended at 72 FR 66039, Nov. 26, 2007]

§ 401.473 HUD grants for rehabilitation under section 236(s) of NA.

HUD will consider a direct grant for rehabilitation under section 236(s) of the NA only if the owner provides an acceptable work schedule and cost-analysis that is consistent with the owner's evaluation of physical condition under § 401.450, as certified by the PAE. The owner must execute a grant agreement with terms and conditions acceptable to HUD. If the PAE is a State or local government, or an agency or instrumentality of such a government, the PAE and HUD may agree that the PAE will be delegated the responsibility for the administration of any grant made under this section. HUD may make grant funding available for the cost of administration if HUD has determined that such funding is available.

§ 401.474 Project accounts.

(a) *Accounts from other projects.* The accounts listed in § 401.472(a)(1) may be used for other eligible projects only if:

(1) The projects are included in a Consolidated Restructuring Plan under § 401.401; and

(2) The funds are used for rehabilitation or to reduce a section 541(b) claim paid by HUD under § 401.471.

(b) *Distribution to owner.* The Restructuring Plan may provide for a one-time distribution to the owner, not to exceed 10 percent of the excess funds in project accounts, to be released after completion of the rehabilitation required by the Restructuring Plan.

§ 401.480 Sale or transfer of project.

(a) *May the owner request a Restructuring Plan that includes a sale or transfer of the property?* The owner may request a Restructuring Plan that includes a condition that the property be sold or transferred to a purchaser acceptable to HUD in a reasonable period needed to consummate the transaction. The failure to consummate a sale or transfer of the property requested under paragraph (a) of this section will neither adversely affect an owner's eligibility for a Restructuring Plan nor exempt the owner from the requirements of § 401.600. There are no priority purchaser requirements for a voluntary sale or transfer by an owner that is eligible for a Restructuring Plan.

(b) *When must the restructuring plan include sale or transfer of the property?* If the owner is determined to be ineligible pursuant to § 401.101 or § 401.403, or if the property is subject to an approved plan of action under the Emergency Low Income Housing Preservation Act of 1987 or the Low Income Housing Preservation and Resident Homeownership Act of 1990, as described in section 524(e)(3) of MAHRA, the property must be sold or transferred as a condition of implementation of a restructuring plan, which must include a condition that the owner sell or transfer the property to a purchaser acceptable to HUD, in accordance with paragraph (c) of this section. Such sale or transfer shall be a condition to the implementation of the Restructuring Plan.

(c) *Owner's notice of intent to sell or transfer.* (1) The owner must provide notice to the PAE affirming the owner's intent to sell or transfer the property. This notice must be received by the PAE no later than 30 days after a notice of rejection under § 401.101 or § 401.403 has become a final determination under subpart F of this part.

(2) The owner must cooperate in selling or transferring the property. Failure to do so will result in the PAE's determination to reject the owner's request for a Restructuring Plan. The owner must distribute and publish, in an appropriate publication, a notice to potential purchasers that describes the property, proposed terms of sale, and procedures for submitting a purchase offer. The notice in form and substance must be acceptable to HUD, and must inform potential offerors of a preference for priority purchasers.

(3) During a period to be determined by HUD that begins when the owner gives notice of intent to sell or transfer, an owner may accept an offer only from a priority purchaser.

(4) No sale or transfer to a non-priority purchaser will be approved without evidence of tenant support.

(d) *Informing PAE; approval required.* The owner must inform the PAE of any offer to purchase the property and the owner must advise the PAE of the substance and on-going status of the owner's discussions with any prospective purchaser. The owner's acceptance of the offer must be subject to PAE approval, and HUD approval of the Restructuring Plan.

(e) *Tenant endorsement procedure for priority purchaser status.* (1) *Required meeting.* (i) A community-based nonprofit or public agency purchaser requesting tenant endorsement to obtain priority purchaser status must conduct an informational meeting with the tenants of the project to disseminate information about both the endorsement request and the purchaser's plans for the project.

(ii) If the purchaser is acting contemporaneously with the Restructuring Plan, the informational meeting must occur at the second meeting of tenants convened by the PAE to discuss the restructuring plan pursuant to § 401.500(d).

(iii) A representative of the purchasing entity must attend the informational meeting to present its plans for the acquisition and improvement of the project and to respond to questions about the purchaser's plans for the property.

(iv) Tenants shall have the opportunity, but are not to be required, to vote for or against the acquisition at the informational meeting.

(v) For the purpose of obtaining tenant endorsement, a purchaser may conduct additional meetings with tenants in accordance with the notice requirements of paragraphs (e)(2) and (e)(3) of this section.

(2) *Parties who must receive notice.* The purchaser must deliver notice of the informational meeting, and any subsequent meeting, to each tenant household in the project and any tenant organization for the project, and post notices of the meeting in the project.

(3) *Notice contents.* The notice must identify the place, date, and time of the informational meeting, and any subsequent meeting. Include a brief description of the purpose of the meeting and provide a narrative outlining the

purchaser's plans for the project, including any request made to HUD for debt relief under §401.461(b)(5) of the second and any additional mortgage.

(4) *Tenant endorsement.* (i) A purchaser may demonstrate that it is tenant endorsed by submitting documentation to HUD that a majority (51 percent) of the tenant heads of household have given their endorsement in writing. Such documentation may include, but is not limited to, ballots, letters of support, or petitions. The endorsement of tenants who did not attend, or vote at, the informational meeting, or any subsequent meeting, may be sought directly from each of these tenants subsequent to the meeting.

(ii)(A) If the purchaser has made a reasonable effort to obtain the endorsement of a majority (51 percent) of the tenants and the necessary percentage of votes was not obtained, the purchaser may seek HUD approval to obtain endorsement based on a lower percentage of endorsing tenants.

(B) The purchaser must deliver notice to each tenant household that the purchaser is seeking HUD approval of a tenant endorsement based on less than 51 percent of tenant approval and provide tenants with at least 10 days from the date of the notice to submit comments to the purchaser on the approval of endorsement.

(C) The purchaser and/or seller must submit, in writing, to HUD an account of the efforts taken to secure tenant endorsement, the number and percentage of tenants voting for and against endorsement, and any comments received from tenants regarding the approval of endorsement.

(D) HUD will determine whether or not to approve endorsement on the basis of all the information available to HUD and will promptly notify the purchaser of HUD's determination.

[65 FR 15485, Mar. 22, 2000, as amended at 72 FR 66039, Nov. 26, 2007]

§401.481 Subsidy layering limitations on HUD funds.

(a) *PAE subsidy layering certification required for Restructuring Plan.* The PAE must certify to HUD that any Restructuring Plan for which it submits a proposed Restructuring Commitment meets the requirements of either paragraph (d) or (e) of this section.

(b) *Purpose of subsidy layering certification.* The purpose of the subsidy layering certification is to ensure that any HUD assistance provided to the owner of a project pursuant to a Restructuring Plan is no more than is necessary to permit the project to continue to house tenants with an income mix comparable to the income mix of the project before the Restructuring Plan is implemented, after taking into account other Government assistance described in section 102(b)(1) of the Department of Housing and Urban Development Reform Act of 1989 (42 U.S.C. 3545(b)(1)). This section does not limit a PAE from presenting for approval a Restructuring Plan that includes project reconfiguration (*e.g.*, conversion of efficiency units to one-bedroom units) where necessary to meet the needs of the community, provided the conditions of §401.452 are also met.

(c) *Relationship to section 102(d) of HUD Reform Act.* HUD is not required to perform a separate subsidy layering analysis under section 102(d) of the Department of Housing and Urban Development Reform Act of 1989 (42 U.S.C. 3545(d)), section 911 of the Housing and Community Development Act of 1992 (42 U.S.C. 3545 note), or §4.13 of this title for any HUD assistance that is included in the Restructuring Plan. HUD will adopt the PAE certification under this section if a HUD certification otherwise would be required under section 102(d).

(d) *Certification under existing HUD guidelines.* If the PAE has delegated authority from HUD to make section 102(d) subsidy layering certifications in accordance with section 911 of the Housing and Community Development Act of 1992, the PAE may comply with this section by using a procedure substantially similar to the procedure described in the Administrative Guidelines published on December 15, 1994 (59 FR 64748), or any subsequent procedure adopted by HUD to implement section 911.

(e) *Other procedures.* If the PAE does not have the delegated authority described in paragraph (d) of this section, the PAE must submit to HUD for approval proposed procedures for making the subsidy layering certification under this section. Any procedures must conform to the procedures described in paragraph (d) of this section to the extent feasible and appropriate.

§ 401.500 Required notices to third parties and meeting with third parties.

(a) *General*. The PAE must solicit, and document the consideration of, tenant and local community comments. As a minimum, the notices described in paragraphs (b), (c) and (f) of this section, in form and substance acceptable to HUD, must be provided. The PAE may require the owner to give the notices if permitted by HUD.

(b) *Notice of intent to restructure and consultation meeting*. (1) This notice must include at a minimum:

(i) The project, including its name and FHA Project Number;

(ii) The responsible PAE and contact person, including the address and telephone number;

(iii) The owner's notice of intent to restructure through the Mark-to-Market Program; and

(iv) The date of expiration of the project-based assistance.

(2) This notice must state how comments may be provided to the PAE regarding any of the following: the physical condition of the property, whether the rental assistance should be tenant-based or project-based, any proposed sale or transfer of the property, and other matters regarding the property and its management. The notice must establish the date, time, and place for a public meeting to be held no sooner than 20 days and no later than 40 days following the date of this notice. The public may provide written comments up to the date of the meeting.

(c) *Access to Restructuring Plan*. (1) The PAE must make the Restructuring Plan available to the parties identified in § 401.501 at least 20 days before the PAE submits the Restructuring Plan to HUD (subject to any Federal, State, or local laws restricting access to any information in the Plan or related documents).

(2) As soon as the PAE determines that the Restructuring Plan is substantively complete and ready for submission to HUD, notice of the following must be provided:

(i) The location of the Plan for inspection and copying; and

(ii) The date, time, and place of a public meeting to be held at least 10 days before the PAE submits the Plan to HUD.

(3) When the PAE gives notice under this section, it must make the Plan available during normal business hours at the management office of the project, or if there is no such office, at another location specified by the PAE that is convenient to the tenants.

(d) *Meeting to discuss the Restructuring Plan*. After the PAE has given notice under this section and at least 10 days before the PAE submits the Plan to HUD, the PAE must conduct a public meeting to obtain comments on the substantively completed Plan. The PAE must accept written comments through the date of the meeting.

(e) *Disposition of comments*. The PAE must document and provide to HUD with the Restructuring Plan a summary of the disposition of all public comments.

(f) *Notice of completion of Restructuring Plan*. (1) Within 10 days after the owner executes the Restructuring Commitment, notice must be provided that describes the completed Restructuring Plan and Restructuring Commitment. The PAE must make the completed Restructuring Plan and Restructuring Commitment available during normal business hours to the public at a place described in paragraph (c)(3) of this section, subject to Federal, State, or local laws restricting access to any information in any of these documents.

(2) Within 10 days after a determination that the Restructuring Plan will not move forward for any reason, HUD or the PAE shall provide notice to affected tenants that describes the reasons for the failure of the Plan to move forward and the availability of tenant-based assistance under § 401.602(c).

[65 FR 15485, Mar. 22, 2000, as amended at 72 FR 66040, Nov. 26, 2007]

§ 401.501 Delivery of notices and recipients of notices.

(a) *Whom must the owner or PAE notify?* The PAE must notify, or ensure that the owner notifies, each tenant and any tenant organization for the project, and post a notice in the project, for all notices required by §§401.500 and 401.502.

(b) *Whom must the PAE notify?* The PAE must notify:

(1) The Chief Executive Officer of the unit of local government and the Executive Director of the Public Housing Authority with jurisdiction over the project location;

(2) The recipient of any Outreach and Training Grant (OTAG) or Intermediary Technical Assistance Grant (ITAG) for the project location; and

(3) Other appropriate neighborhood representatives and other affected parties.

[65 FR 15485, Mar. 22, 2000, as amended at 65 FR 53900, Sept. 6, 2000]

§401.502 Notice requirement when debt restructuring will not occur.

(a) *PAE responsibility.* If an owner of an eligible project requests a renewal of a section 8 contract without a Restructuring Plan under §402.4 of this chapter, HUD or the PAE must notify, or ensure that the owner notifies, all parties identified in §401.501 of the request and of:

(1) The availability (as provided in §401.500(c)(3)) of the following information:

(i) The owner evaluation of physical condition (OEPC), or a comprehensive needs assessment (CNA) if used instead of an OEPC, as required by §401.450 and §402.6(a)(3) of this chapter;

(ii) The market analysis required by §402.6(a)(2) of this chapter, but without addresses (or other specific information indicating location) for comparable properties; and

(iii) The items identified in §401.500(b)(1)(i), (ii), and (iv); and

(2) A procedure for submitting public comments regarding this information.

(b) *Expense and profit/loss information.* The PAE should remove project expense, property valuation, and profit and loss information before disclosing any information obtained by the PAE directly from an owner or project manager, unless the owner has given written consent to disclosure with that information included.

(c) *Consideration of comments.* The PAE must consider written public com-

ments on the information listed in paragraph (a) of this section, if the comments are submitted within 30 days after giving notice under paragraph (a), and document the consideration for HUD. No public meeting is required.

[65 FR 15485, Mar. 22, 2000, as amended at 65 FR 53900, Sept. 6, 2000]

§401.503 Access to information.

(a) *PAE responsibilities.* The PAE must provide to parties entitled to notice under §401.501 access to information obtained by the PAE about the project and its management if the PAE determines that such information is reasonably likely to contribute to effective participation by those parties in the restructuring process, or if HUD requires the PAE to provide access to the information. The PAE is not required to make public any information received from the owner or manager that the PAE reasonably characterizes as confidential or proprietary information that would not ordinarily be made public, except:

(1) Owner evaluation of physical condition (OEPC), or a comprehensive needs assessment (CA) if used instead of an OEPC, as required by §401.450;

(2) Owner-prepared 1-year project rent analysis; and

(3) As directed by HUD.

(b) *Information on expenses and profit/loss.* Before disclosing any information, the PAE must remove any information obtained by the PAE directly from the owner or project manager that is related to project expenses, property valuation, or profit and loss, unless the owner gives written consent to disclosure with that information.

Subpart D—Implementation of the Restructuring Plan After Closing

§401.550 Monitoring and compliance agreements.

(a) *Compliance agreements.* The PAE must ensure long-term compliance by the owner with MAHRA, this part, and the Restructuring Plan. As part of this responsibility, the PAE must require each owner with an approved Restructuring Plan to execute and record a Use Agreement that satisfies the requirements of §401.408. All provisions of this subpart apply as long as the Use Agreement is in effect.

(b) *Periodic monitoring and inspection.* At least once a year, a PAE must review the status of each project for which it developed an executed restructuring Plan. Monitoring must include on-site inspections. HUD will accept an inspection by a PAE that complies with subpart G of part 5 of this title in lieu of an inspection required by any other party under that subpart.

(c) *HUD acting instead of PAE.* HUD will perform, or contract with other parties to perform, the PAE's functions under this section if:

(1) The project is subject to a PRA with a PAE that is not qualified to be a section 8 contract administrator; or

(2) The project is not currently subject to a PRA.

(d) *Regulatory agreement.* As long as the Secretary is the holder of a second mortgage or an additional mortgage under § 401.461, HUD will regulate the operations of the mortgagor through a regulatory agreement providing terms, conditions, and standards established by HUD, which may be in addition to any regulatory agreement otherwise required in connection with mortgage insurance programs. The regulatory agreement must contain remedies for breach, including monetary damages in the event of non-compliance.

[65 FR 15485, Mar. 22, 2000, as amended at 65 FR 53901, Sept. 6, 2000]

§ 401.552 Servicing of second mortgage.

HUD or its designee will be responsible for servicing the second mortgage, including determining the amounts receivable by the owner under § 401.461(b)(3)(ii)(A). HUD may designate the PAE, with the PAE's consent, as servicer for the second mortgage.

§ 401.554 Contract renewal and administration.

HUD will offer to renew or extend section 8 contracts as provided in each Restructuring Plan, subject to the availability of appropriations and subject to the renewal authority available at the time of each contract expiration (§ 402.5 of this chapter or another appropriate renewal authority). The offer will be made by HUD directly or through a PAE that has contracted with HUD to be a contract administrator for such contracts. HUD will offer to any PAE that is qualified to be the section 8 contract administrator the opportunity to serve as the section 8 contract administrator for a project restructured under a Restructuring Plan developed by the PAE under the Mark-to-Market Program. Qualifications will be determined under both statutory requirements and requirements issued by the appropriate office within HUD, depending on the type of section 8 assistance that is provided.

[65 FR 15485, Mar. 22, 2000, as amended at 65 FR 53901, Sept. 6, 2000]

§ 401.556 Leasing units to voucher holders.

A Restructuring Plan must prohibit any refusal of the owner to lease a unit solely because of the status of the prospective tenant as a section 8 voucher holder.

§ 401.558 Physical condition standards.

The Restructuring Plan must require the owner to maintain the project in a decent and safe condition that meets the applicable standards under this section. As long as project-based assistance is provided, the applicable standards are the physical conditions standards for HUD housing in § 5.703 of this title. At any other time, the applicable standards are the local housing codes or codes adopted by the public housing agency if such codes meet or exceed the standards in § 5.703 of this title and do not severely restrict housing choice or, if there are no such local housing codes or codes adopted by the public housing agency, the standards in § 5.703 of this title will apply. In addition, any unit in which the tenant receives tenant-based assistance must comply with the housing quality standards of the section 8 tenant-based programs.

[65 FR 15485, Mar. 22, 2000, as amended at 65 FR 53901, Sept. 6, 2000]

§ 401.560 Property management standards.

(a) *General.* Each PAE is required by section 518 of MAHRA to establish management standards consistent with

660

industry standards and HUD guidelines. The management standards must be included or referenced in the Restructuring Plan.

(b) *HUD guidelines.* At a minimum, the PAE's management standards must require the project management to:

(1) Protect the physical integrity of the property over the long term through preventative maintenance, repair, or replacement;

(2) Ensure that the building and grounds are routinely cleaned;

(3) Maintain good relations with the tenants;

(4) Protect the financial integrity of the project by operating the property with competitive and reasonable costs and maintaining appropriate property and liability insurance at all times;

(5) Take all necessary measures to ensure the tenants' physical safety; and

(6) Comply with other provisions that are required by HUD, including termination of the management agent for cause.

(c) *Conflicts of interest.* The PAE management standards must also conform to any guidelines established by HUD, and industry standards, governing conflicts of interest between owners, managers, and contractors.

Subpart E—Section 8 Requirements for Restructured Projects

§401.595 Contract and regulatory provisions.

The provisions of chapter VIII of this title will apply to renewal of a section 8 project-based assistance contract under this part only to the extent, if any, provided in the contract. Part 983 of this title will not apply. The term of the contract renewals under this part will be determined by the appropriate HUD official.

[65 FR 53901, Sept. 6, 2000]

§401.600 Will a section 8 contract be extended if it would expire while an owner's request for a Restructuring Plan is pending?

(a) If a section 8 contract for an eligible project would expire before a Restructuring Plan is implemented, the contract may be extended at rents not exceeding current rents:

(1) For up to the earlier of one year or closing on the Restructuring Plan under §401.407; or

(2) For such period of time beyond one year as HUD may approve, up to the closing of the Restructuring Plan.

(b) Any extension of the contract beyond one year for a pending Restructuring Plan, other than an extension approved under this section, must be at comparable market rents or exception rents. An extension at comparable market rents will not affect a project's eligibility for the Mark-to-Market program once it has been established under this part.

(c) HUD may terminate the contract earlier if the PAE or HUD determines that an owner is not cooperative under §401.402 or if the owner's request is rejected under §401.403 or §401.405.

[71 FR 2121, Jan. 12, 2006]

§401.601 [Reserved]

§401.602 Tenant protections if an expiring contract is not renewed.

(a) *Required notices.* (1)(i) The owner of an eligible project who has requested a Restructuring Plan and contract renewal must provide a 12-month notice as provided in section 514(d) if MAHRA, if the owner later decides not to renew an expiring contract (except due to a rejection under §§401.101, 401.403, 401.405, or 401.451.) If the owner gives such 12-month notice, the owner is not required to give a separate notice under section 8(c)(8) of the United States Housing Act of 1937.

(ii) An owner who gives the 12-month notice required by paragraph (a)(1)(i) of this section and who determines not to renew a contract must give additional notice not less than 120 days before the contract expiration.

(2) The owner of an eligible project who has requested a Restructuring Plan but who has been rejected under §§401.101, 401.403, 401.405, or 401.451 must provide 12 months advance notice under section 8(c)(8)(A) of the United States Housing Act of 1937, unless project-based assistance is renewed under §402.4 of this chapter.

(3) Notices required by this paragraph must be provided to tenants and

to HUD or the contract administrator. HUD will prescribe the form of notices under this paragraph, to the extent that the form is not prescribed by section 8(c)(8) of the United States Housing Act of 1937.

(b) *If owner does not give notice.* If an owner described in paragraph (a)(1) or (a)(2) of this section does not give timely notice of non-renewal or termination, the owner must permit the tenants in assisted units to remain in their units for the required notice period with no increase in the tenant portion of their rent, and with no eviction due to inability to collect an increased tenant portion of rent.

(c) *Availability of tenant-based assistance.* (1) Subject to the availability of amounts provided in advance in appropriations and the eligibility requirements of the tenant-based assistance program regulations, HUD will make tenant-based assistance available under the following circumstances:

(i) If the owner of an eligible project does not renew the project-based assistance, any eligible tenant residing in a unit assisted under the expiring contract on the date of expiration will be eligible to receive assistance on the later of the date of expiration or the date the owner's obligations under paragraph (b) of this section expire; and

(ii) If a request for a Restructuring Plan is rejected under § 401.101, § 401.403, § 401.405, or 401.451, and project-based assistance is not otherwise renewed, any eligible tenant who is a low-income family or who resides in a project-based assisted unit on the date of Plan rejection will be eligible to receive assistance on the later of the date the Restructuring Plan is rejected, or the date the owner's obligations under paragraph (b) of this section expire.

(2) If the tenant was assisted under the expiring contract, assistance under this paragraph will be in the form of enhanced vouchers as provided in section 8(t) of the United States Housing Act of 1937.

[65 FR 15485, Mar. 22, 2000, as amended at 65 FR 53901, Sept. 6, 2000]

§ 401.605 Project-based assistance provisions.

The project-based assistance rents for a restructured project must be the restructured rents determined under the Restructuring Plan in accordance with §§ 401.410 or 401.411.

§ 401.606 Tenant-based assistance provisions.

If the Restructuring Plan provides for tenant-based assistance, each assisted family residing in a unit assisted under the expiring project-based assistance contract when the contract terminates will be offered tenant-based assistance if the family meets the eligibility requirements under part 982. Whenever permitted by section 515(c)(4) of MAHRA, the tenant-based assistance will be in the form of enhanced vouchers as provided in section 8(t) of the United States Housing Act of 1937.

Subpart F—Owner Dispute of Rejection and Administrative Appeal

§ 401.645 Owner request to review HUD decision.

(a) *HUD notice of decision.* (1) HUD will provide notice to the owner of:

(i) A decision that the owner or project is not eligible for the Mark-to-Market program;

(ii) A decision not to offer a proposed Restructuring Commitment to the owner; and

(iii) A decision to offer a proposed Restructuring Commitment. The proposed Restructuring Commitment provided to the owner constitutes the notice of decision for purposes of requesting a review of a HUD decision.

(2) The notice of decision will include the reasons for the decision.

(3) The notice of decision will also notify the owner of the right to request a review of the decision or to cure any deficiencies on which the decision was based; the date by which the review request must be submitted or the deficiencies must be cured, which will be at least 30 days after the date of the notice of decision; and the address to which the review request is to be submitted.

(b) *Review request by owner.* (1) *Written statement.* The review request must specify in writing:

(i) Each item of the decision to which the owner objects;

(ii) The reasons for the owner's objections; and

(iii) All information in support of the objections that the owner wants HUD to consider.

(2) *Scope of information submitted.* HUD will not consider information first submitted to HUD in conjunction with an owner's request for review except for:

(i) Information that could not have been submitted previously; and

(ii) New health and safety information.

(c) *HUD review and final decision.* (1) HUD may expand the scope of review beyond the issues raised by the owner and may review and modify any term within the Restructuring Commitment without regard to whether the owner has raised an objection to that term, including adjustments to rents or expenses as underwritten by the PAE. If HUD does expand the scope of review, HUD will notify the owner of such action and provide an additional 30 days for the owner to raise any additional objections and provide additional information.

(2) Within 30 days of HUD's receipt of the owner's review request and any additional objections and information, HUD will review the request and, using a standard of what is reasonable in light of all of the evidence presented, issue a final decision. The final decision will:

(i) Affirm the notice of decision; or

(ii) Modify the notice of decision and, if applicable, modify the Restructuring Commitment, in which event HUD will issue an amended or restated Restructuring Commitment that incorporates the final decision; or

(iii) Revoke the notice of decision and, if applicable, terminate the Restructuring Commitment and notify the owner that the owner is not eligible for participation in the Mark-to-Market program or that a restructuring of the property is not feasible.

[72 FR 66040, Nov. 26, 2007]

§401.650 When may the owner request an administrative appeal?

(a) *No review request by owner.* If the owner does not request a review of the notice of decision under §401.645 or does not execute the proposed Restructuring Commitment within the time provided in the notice of decision, HUD will send a written notice to the owner stating that the notice of decision is HUD's final decision and that the owner has 10 days after receipt of the letter to accept the decision, including a Restructuring Commitment, if applicable, or request an administrative appeal in accordance with §401.651.

(b) *Upon receipt of final decision.* HUD will send the owner a written notice of the final decision under §401.645 that will also provide the owner with 10 days to request an administrative appeal of the final decision.

(c) *HUD decision to accelerate the second mortgage.* Upon receipt of notice from HUD of a decision to accelerate the second mortgage under §401.461(b)(4), the owner may request an administrative appeal in accordance with §401.651.

[72 FR 66040, Nov. 26, 2007]

§401.651 Appeal procedures.

(a) *How to appeal.* An owner may submit a written appeal to HUD, within 10 days of receipt of written notice of the decision described in §401.650, contesting the decision and requesting a conference with HUD. At the conference, the owner may submit (in person, in writing, or through a representative) its reasons for appealing the decision. The HUD or PAE official who issued the decision under appeal may participate in the conference and submit (in person, in writing, or through a representative) the basis for the decision.

(b) *Written decision.* Within 20 days after the conference, or 20 days after any agreed-upon extension of time for submission of additional materials by or on behalf of the owner, HUD will review the evidence presented for the administrative appeal and, using the standard of whether the determination of the final decision was reasonable, will advise the owner in writing of the decision to terminate, modify, or affirm the original decision. HUD will act, as necessary, to implement the decision, for example, by offering a revised Restructuring Commitment to the owner.

(c) *Who is responsible for reviewing appeals?* HUD will designate an official to review any appeal, conduct the conference, and issue the written decision. The official designated must be one who was neither directly involved in, nor reports to another directly involved in, making the decision being appealed.

[65 FR 15485, Mar. 22, 2000, as amended at 72 FR 66040, Nov. 26, 2007]

§ 401.652 No judicial review.

The reviewing official's decision under § 401.651 is a final determination for purposes of section 516(c) of MAHRA and is not subject to judicial review.

PART 402—SECTION 8 PROJECT-BASED CONTRACT RENEWAL UNDER SECTION 524 OF MAHRA

AUTHORITY: 42 U.S.C. 1437(c)(8), 1437f note, and 3535(d).

SOURCE: 63 FR 48953, Sept. 11, 1998, unless otherwise noted.

§ 402.1 What is the purpose of part 402?

This part sets out the terms and conditions under which HUD will renew project-based assistance contracts

under the authority provided in section 524 of MAHRA.

[71 FR 2121, Jan. 12, 2006]

§ 402.2 Definitions.

(a) *Terms defined in part 401.* In this part, the following terms have the meanings given in § 401.2 of this chapter: affiliate, disabled family, elderly family, eligible project, HUD, MAHRA, owner, PAE, Restructuring Plan, and section 8.

(b) *Terms defined in MAHRA.* In this part, the following terms have the meanings given in section 512 of MAHRA: expiration date, fair market rent, renewal, and tenant-based assistance.

(c) *Other defined terms.* In this part, the term—

Comparable market rents means rents determined in accordance with section 524(a)(5) of MAHRA and HUD's instructions.

Large family means a family of five or more persons.

OCAF means an operating cost adjustment factor established by HUD, which may not be negative, that is applied to the existing contract rent (less the portion of that rent paid for debt service).

Portfolio Reengineering demonstration authority means the authority specified in section 524(e)(2)(B) of MAHRA.

Project-based assistance means the types of assistance listed in section 512(2)(B) of MAHRA, or a project-based assistance contract under the Section 8 program renewed under section 524 of MAHRA.

Project eligible for exception rents means a project described in section 524(b) of MAHRA.

SRO contract and *SRO project* mean, respectively, a project-based assistance contract for single-room occupancy dwellings under section 441 of the Stewart B. McKinney Homeless Assistance Act (42 U.S.C. 11401), and a project with units covered by such a contract.

[71 FR 2121, Jan. 12, 2006]

§ 402.3 Contract provisions.

The renewal HAP contract shall be construed and administered in accordance with all statutory requirements, and with all HUD regulations and other requirements, including changes in HUD regulations and other requirements during the term of the renewal HAP contract, unless the contract provides otherwise.

[71 FR 2121, Jan. 12, 2006]

§402.4 Contract renewals under section 524(a)(1) of MAHRA.

(a) *Initial renewal.* (1) HUD may renew any expiring section 8 project-based assistance contract at initial rents that do not exceed comparable market rents.

(2) *Procedure for projects eligible for Restructuring Plan.* (i) If an owner requests renewal of a contract under this section for a project that is eligible for a Restructuring Plan under the Mark-to-Market program under part 401 and that has not been rejected under that part, HUD or a PAE will determine whether renewal under this section, instead of through a Restructuring Plan under part 401 of this chapter, would be sufficient. Renewal without a Restructuring Plan will be considered sufficient if the rents after renewal would be sufficient to maintain both adequate debt service coverage on the HUD-insured or HUD-held mortgage and necessary replacement reserves to ensure the long-term physical integrity of the project, taking into account any comments received under §401.502(c) of this chapter.

(ii) If HUD or the PAE determines that renewal under this section would be sufficient, HUD will not require a Restructuring Plan.

(iii) If HUD or the PAE determines that renewal under this section would not be sufficient, HUD or the PAE may require a Restructuring Plan before the owner's request for contract renewal will be given further consideration. If the owner does not cooperate in the development of an acceptable Restructuring Plan, HUD will pursue whatever administrative actions it considers necessary.

(b) [Reserved]

[65 FR 15498, Mar. 22, 2000, as amended at 71 FR 2121, Jan. 12, 2006]

§402.5 Contract renewals under section 524(b) or (e) of MAHRA.

(a) *Renewal of projects eligible for exception rents at owner's request.* HUD will offer to renew project-based assistance for a project eligible for exception rents under section 524(b) of MAHRA at rent levels determined under this section instead of §402.4, except as provided in §402.7, but the owner of a project other than a project with assistance under the Section 8 moderate rehabilitation program may request renewal under §402.4.

(b) *Rent levels for projects eligible for exception rents.* HUD will renew the contract with rent levels at the least of:

(1) Existing rents adjusted by an OCAF;

(2) A budget-based rent determined in accordance with instructions issued by HUD, subject to a determination by HUD that such a rent level is appropriate; or

(3) In the case of a contract under the Section 8 moderate rehabilitation program (other than an SRO contract), the lesser of existing rents adjusted by an OCAF, fair market rents (less any amounts for tenant-purchased utilities), or comparable market rents, as provided in section 524(b)(3) of MAHRA.

(c) *Rent adjustments.* (1) After rents have been established under this section, rent adjustments will comply with section 524(c) of MAHRA except as otherwise required by paragraph (d)(1) of this section for preservation projects.

(2) Rent adjustments for projects assisted under the Section 8 moderate rehabilitation program, other than projects assisted under the moderate rehabilitation single-room occupancy program, shall be determined in accordance with section 524(b)(3) of MAHRA.

(d) *Preservation projects and demonstration projects.* (1) Notwithstanding any other provision of this part except §402.7, upon expiration of a section 8 contract for a project subject to an approved plan of action under the Emergency Low-Income Housing Preservation Act of 1987 (ELIHPA) or the Low-Income Housing Preservation and Resident Homeownership Act of 1990 (LIHPRHA), the Secretary will provide

665

benefits that are comparable to those provided under such plan of action. This paragraph (d)(1) applies only to the extent amounts are specifically made available in appropriations acts.

(2) Notwithstanding any other provision of this part except § 402.7, upon expiration of a Section 8 contract entered into pursuant to a Portfolio Reengineering demonstration authority for which HUD made a determination that debt restructuring is inappropriate, and the owner of the project executed a Portfolio Reengineering Demonstration Program Use Agreement, the Secretary will provide the owner, at the request of the owner, with benefits comparable to those provided under the contract that is expiring. This paragraph (d)(2) applies only to the extent amounts are made available in appropriations acts.

[71 FR 2122, Jan. 12, 2006]

§ 402.6 What actions must an owner take to request section 8 contract renewal under this part?

(a) *In general.* An owner requesting contract renewal under this part must submit to HUD or HUD's designee, at least 120 days before the termination or expiration date of any project-based assistance contract, all documents or information prescribed by HUD.

(b) *Subsequent renewals.* A contract that was initially renewed under MAHRA will be renewed at the owner's request under any renewal option for which the project is eligible. However, in the case of a project that is eligible for a Restructuring Plan under § 401.100, HUD or a PAE will determine whether renewal with a Restructuring Plan under part 401, or without a Restructuring Plan under this part, is necessary.

[71 FR 2122, Jan. 12, 2006]

§ 402.7 Refusal to consider an owner's request for a Section 8 contract renewal because of actions or omissions of owner or affiliate.

(a) *Determination of eligibility.* Notwithstanding 2 CFR part 2424, HUD may elect to not consider a request for renewal of project-based assistance, if at any time before contract renewal:

(1) The owner or an affiliate is debarred or suspended under part 2 CFR part 2424;

(2) HUD determines that the owner or an affiliate has engaged in material adverse financial or managerial actions or omissions as described in section 516 of MAHRA, including any outstanding violations of civil rights laws, or has failed to certify to compliance with the nondiscrimination requirements of 24 CFR 5.105(a), in connection with any project of the owner or an affiliate; or

(3) The project does not meet the physical condition standards in 24 CFR 5.703 of this title, unless HUD determines that the project will meet the standards within a reasonable time after renewal.

(b) *Dispute and appeal.* An owner may dispute a rejection under this section and seek administrative review under the procedures in subpart F of part 401 of this chapter.

[71 FR 2122, Jan. 12, 2006, as amended at 72 FR 73496, Dec. 27, 2007]

§ 402.8 Tenant protections if a contract is not renewed.

(a) *Notice of termination.* An owner who is not eligible for a Restructuring Plan under part 401 of this chapter, or who is eligible but does not request restructuring, and who does not renew a contract, must provide one year's notice to tenants, to HUD, and to the contract administrator as provided in section 8(c)(8)(A) of the United States Housing Act of 1937.

(b) *If an owner does not give timely notice.* If an owner does not give one year's notice of termination as described in paragraph (a) of this section, the owner must permit the tenants in assisted units to remain in their units at a rental rate no higher than the tenant rent payable for the tenants' last month of assisted occupancy under the terminated HAP contract until one year after notice is given, even if HUD does not continue to make housing assistance payments with respect to such units.

(c) *If an owner opts out or fails to renew.* In the case where a contract for Section 8 rental assistance for a project is terminated or expires, an assisted family may elect to remain in the project and, if eligible, receive tenant-based Section 8 assistance under Section 8(t) of the United States Housing Act of 1937.

[71 FR 2122, Jan. 12, 2006]

§402.9 Waivers and delegations of waiver authority.

All waivers of provisions of this part, and delegations of the authority to waive provisions of this part, are governed by §5.110 of this title.

[71 FR 2123, Jan. 12, 2006]

PARTS 403–499 [RESERVED]

FINDING AIDS

A list of CFR titles, subtitles, chapters, subchapters and parts and an alphabetical list of agencies publishing in the CFR are included in the CFR Index and Finding Aids volume to the Code of Federal Regulations which is published separately and revised annually.

Table of CFR Titles and Chapters

(Revised as of April 1, 2019)

Title 1—General Provisions

Title 2—Grants and Agreements

671

672

Title 6—Domestic Security

Title 7—Agriculture

675

Title 8—Aliens and Nationality

Title 9—Animals and Animal Products

Title 10—Energy

Title 11—Federal Elections

Title 12—Banks and Banking

677

Title 15—Commerce and Foreign Trade—Continued

Title 16—Commercial Practices

Title 17—Commodity and Securities Exchanges

Title 18—Conservation of Power and Water Resources

Title 19—Customs Duties

Title 20—Employees' Benefits

679

II National Highway Traffic Safety Administration and Federal Highway Administration, Department of Transportation (Parts 1200—1299)

III National Highway Traffic Safety Administration, Department of Transportation (Parts 1300—1399)

Title 24—Housing and Urban Development

SUBTITLE A—OFFICE OF THE SECRETARY, DEPARTMENT OF HOUSING AND URBAN DEVELOPMENT (PARTS 0—99)

SUBTITLE B—REGULATIONS RELATING TO HOUSING AND URBAN DEVELOPMENT

I Office of Assistant Secretary for Equal Opportunity, Department of Housing and Urban Development (Parts 100—199)

II Office of Assistant Secretary for Housing-Federal Housing Commissioner, Department of Housing and Urban Development (Parts 200—299)

III Government National Mortgage Association, Department of Housing and Urban Development (Parts 300—399)

IV Office of Housing and Office of Multifamily Housing Assistance Restructuring, Department of Housing and Urban Development (Parts 400—499)

V Office of Assistant Secretary for Community Planning and Development, Department of Housing and Urban Development (Parts 500—599)

VI Office of Assistant Secretary for Community Planning and Development, Department of Housing and Urban Development (Parts 600—699) [Reserved]

VII Office of the Secretary, Department of Housing and Urban Development (Housing Assistance Programs and Public and Indian Housing Programs) (Parts 700—799)

VIII Office of the Assistant Secretary for Housing—Federal Housing Commissioner, Department of Housing and Urban Development (Section 8 Housing Assistance Programs, Section 202 Direct Loan Program, Section 202 Supportive Housing for the Elderly Program and Section 811 Supportive Housing for Persons With Disabilities Program) (Parts 800—899)

IX Office of Assistant Secretary for Public and Indian Housing, Department of Housing and Urban Development (Parts 900—1699)

XII Office of Inspector General, Department of Housing and Urban Development (Parts 2000—2099)

XV Emergency Mortgage Insurance and Loan Programs, Department of Housing and Urban Development (Parts 2700—2799) [Reserved]

XX Office of Assistant Secretary for Housing—Federal Housing Commissioner, Department of Housing and Urban Development (Parts 3200—3899)

XXIV Board of Directors of the HOPE for Homeowners Program (Parts 4000—4099) [Reserved]

XXV Neighborhood Reinvestment Corporation (Parts 4100—4199)

Title 25—Indians

Title 26—Internal Revenue

Title 27—Alcohol, Tobacco Products and Firearms

Title 28—Judicial Administration

Title 29—Labor

Title 29—Labor—Continued

Title 30—Mineral Resources

Title 31—Money and Finance: Treasury

Title 31—Money and Finance: Treasury—Continued

Title 32—National Defense

Title 33—Navigation and Navigable Waters

Title 34—Education

Title 34—Education—Continued

Title 35 [Reserved]

Title 36—Parks, Forests, and Public Property

Title 37—Patents, Trademarks, and Copyrights

Title 38—Pensions, Bonuses, and Veterans' Relief

Title 42—Public Health

Title 43—Public Lands: Interior

Title 44—Emergency Management and Assistance

Title 45—Public Welfare

Title 45—Public Welfare—Continued

Title 46—Shipping

Title 47—Telecommunication

Title 49—Transportation

Title 50—Wildlife and Fisheries

Alphabetical List of Agencies Appearing in the CFR

(Revised as of April 1, 2019)

Agency	CFR Title, Subtitle or Chapter
Administrative Conference of the United States	1, III
Advisory Council on Historic Preservation	36, VIII
Advocacy and Outreach, Office of	7, XXV
Afghanistan Reconstruction, Special Inspector General for	5, LXXXIII
African Development Foundation	22, XV
Federal Acquisition Regulation	48, 57
Agency for International Development	2, VII; 22, II
Federal Acquisition Regulation	48, 7
Agricultural Marketing Service	7, I, IX, X, XI
Agricultural Research Service	7, V
Agriculture, Department of	2, IV; 5, LXXIII
Advocacy and Outreach, Office of	7, XXV
Agricultural Marketing Service	7, I, IX, X, XI
Agricultural Research Service	7, V
Animal and Plant Health Inspection Service	7, III; 9, I
Chief Financial Officer, Office of	7, XXX
Commodity Credit Corporation	7, XIV
Economic Research Service	7, XXXVII
Energy Policy and New Uses, Office of	2, IX; 7, XXIX
Environmental Quality, Office of	7, XXXI
Farm Service Agency	7, VII, XVIII
Federal Acquisition Regulation	48, 4
Federal Crop Insurance Corporation	7, IV
Food and Nutrition Service	7, II
Food Safety and Inspection Service	9, III
Foreign Agricultural Service	7, XV
Forest Service	36, II
Grain Inspection, Packers and Stockyards Administration	7, VIII; 9, II
Information Resources Management, Office of	7, XXVII
Inspector General, Office of	7, XXVI
National Agricultural Library	7, XLI
National Agricultural Statistics Service	7, XXXVI
National Institute of Food and Agriculture	7, XXXIV
Natural Resources Conservation Service	7, VI
Operations, Office of	7, XXVIII
Procurement and Property Management, Office of	7, XXXII
Rural Business-Cooperative Service	7, XVIII, XLII
Rural Development Administration	7, XLII
Rural Housing Service	7, XVIII, XXXV
Rural Telephone Bank	7, XVI
Rural Utilities Service	7, XVII, XVIII, XLII
Secretary of Agriculture, Office of	7, Subtitle A
Transportation, Office of	7, XXXIII
World Agricultural Outlook Board	7, XXXVIII
Air Force, Department of	32, VII
Federal Acquisition Regulation Supplement	48, 53
Air Transportation Stabilization Board	14, VI
Alcohol and Tobacco Tax and Trade Bureau	27, I
Alcohol, Tobacco, Firearms, and Explosives, Bureau of	27, II
AMTRAK	49, VII
American Battle Monuments Commission	36, IV
American Indians, Office of the Special Trustee	25, VII
Animal and Plant Health Inspection Service	7, III; 9, I

692

693

Agency	CFR Title, Subtitle or Chapter
Contract Appeals, Board of	48, 61
Federal Acquisition Regulation	48, 5
Federal Management Regulation	41, 102
Federal Property Management Regulations	41, 101
Federal Travel Regulation System	41, Subtitle F
General	41, 300
Payment From a Non-Federal Source for Travel Expenses	41, 304
Payment of Expenses Connected With the Death of Certain Employees	41, 303
Relocation Allowances	41, 302
Temporary Duty (TDY) Travel Allowances	41, 301
Geological Survey	30, IV
Government Accountability Office	4, I
Government Ethics, Office of	5, XVI
Government National Mortgage Association	24, III
Grain Inspection, Packers and Stockyards Administration	7, VIII; 9, II
Gulf Coast Ecosystem Restoration Council	2, LIX; 40, VIII
Harry S. Truman Scholarship Foundation	45, XVIII
Health and Human Services, Department of	2, III; 5, XLV; 45, Subtitle A
Centers for Medicare & Medicaid Services	42, IV
Child Support Enforcement, Office of	45, III
Children and Families, Administration for	45, II, III, IV, X, XIII
Community Services, Office of	45, X
Family Assistance, Office of	45, II
Federal Acquisition Regulation	48, 3
Food and Drug Administration	21, I
Indian Health Service	25, V
Inspector General (Health Care), Office of	42, V
Public Health Service	42, I
Refugee Resettlement, Office of	45, IV
Homeland Security, Department of	2, XXX; 5, XXXVI; 6, I; 8, I
Coast Guard	33, I; 46, I; 49, IV
Coast Guard (Great Lakes Pilotage)	46, III
Customs and Border Protection	19, I
Federal Emergency Management Agency	44, I
Human Resources Management and Labor Relations Systems	5, XCVII
Immigration and Customs Enforcement Bureau	19, IV
Transportation Security Administration	49, XII
HOPE for Homeowners Program, Board of Directors of	24, XXIV
Housing and Urban Development, Department of	2, XXIV; 5, LXV; 24, Subtitle B
Community Planning and Development, Office of Assistant Secretary for	24, V, VI
Equal Opportunity, Office of Assistant Secretary for	24, I
Federal Acquisition Regulation	48, 24
Federal Housing Enterprise Oversight, Office of	12, XVII
Government National Mortgage Association	24, III
Housing—Federal Housing Commissioner, Office of Assistant Secretary for	24, II, VIII, X, XX
Housing, Office of, and Multifamily Housing Assistance Restructuring, Office of	24, IV
Inspector General, Office of	24, XII
Public and Indian Housing, Office of Assistant Secretary for	24, IX
Secretary, Office of	24, Subtitle A, VII
Housing—Federal Housing Commissioner, Office of Assistant Secretary for	24, II, VIII, X, XX
Housing, Office of, and Multifamily Housing Assistance Restructuring, Office of	24, IV
Immigration and Customs Enforcement Bureau	19, IV
Immigration Review, Executive Office for	8, V
Independent Counsel, Office of	28, VII
Independent Counsel, Offices of	28, VI
Indian Affairs, Bureau of	25, I, V
Indian Affairs, Office of the Assistant Secretary	25, VI

697

List of CFR Sections Affected

All changes in this volume of the Code of Federal Regulations (CFR) that were made by documents published in the FEDERAL REGISTER since January 1, 2014 are enumerated in the following list. Entries indicate the nature of the changes effected. Page numbers refer to FEDERAL REGISTER pages. The user should consult the entries for chapters, parts and subparts as well as sections for revisions.

For changes to this volume of the CFR prior to this listing, consult the annual edition of the monthly List of CFR Sections Affected (LSA). The LSA is available at *www.govinfo.gov*. For changes to this volume of the CFR prior to 2001, see the "List of CFR Sections Affected, 1949–1963, 1964–1972, 1973–1985, and 1986–2000" published in 11 separate volumes. The "List of CFR Sections Affected 1986–2000" is available at *www.govinfo.gov*.

2019

(No regulations published from
January 1, 2019, through April 1, 2019)

○